VEDA-LAKṢAṆA

VEDIC ANCILLARY LITERATURE

A DESCRIPTIVE BIBLIOGRAPHY

VEDA-LAKṢAṆA
VEDIC ANCILLARY LITERATURE

A DESCRIPTIVE BIBLIOGRAPHY

Compiled by

K. PARAMESWARA AITHAL

MOTILAL BANARSIDASS PUBLISHERS
PRIVATE LIMITED • DELHI

First Indian Edition: Delhi, 1993

ISBN: 81-208-1120-8

First published by the South Asia Institute of
Heidelberg University as volume No. 143 of the series
Beitraege zur Suedasienforschung through Franz Steiner
Verlag Stuttgart, Germany, 1991

Also available at:

MOTILAL BANARSIDASS

41 U.A. Bungalow Road, Jawahar Nagar, Delhi 110 007
120 Royapettah High Road, Mylapore, Madras 600 004
16 St. Mark's Road, Bangalore 560 001
Ashok Rajpath, Patna 800 004
Chowk, Varanasi 221 001

PRINTED IN INDIA

BY JAINENDRA PRAKASH JAIN AT SHRI JAINENDRA PRESS,
A-45 NARAINA INDUSTRIAL AREA, PHASE I, NEW DELHI 110 028
AND PUBLISHED BY NARENDRA PRAKASH JAIN FOR MOTILAL
BANARSIDASS PUBLISHERS PVT. LTD., BUNGALOW ROAD,
JAWAHAR NAGAR, DELHI 110 007

FOREWORD

It is with great pleasure that I comply with Pandit K. Parameswara Aithal's wish to say a few words on his latest book. For I have not only seen it grow both in volume as also in substance and accuracy, over the last years, but I was also convinced right from the beginning when I came to know about it that his project is of extraordinary importance.

The group of ancillary 'Vedic'[1] texts, in (South) India traditionally referred to by the term Veda-Lakṣaṇa, was given the attention due to it both by scholars in India and the West from the middle of the 19th century until approximately the first half of our century. To be sure, the study of Vedic texts in the strict sense, i.e. of those of a non-ancillary character, can be said no longer to form the centre and main focus of Indology. But the situation is much worse in the case of the Veda-Lakṣaṇa part of Sanskrit literature: they have been virtually forgotten since about 40 years. This is hardly the occasion for analysing the reasons for this change, but rather for emphasizing its highly problematic, nay in fact deplorable character. In my view it is sufficient to just glance through the present "Catalogue", and read some of the entries more carefully, in order to immediately realize that these texts – and not only the better known class of Prātiśākhyas, Śikṣās and Anukramaṇīs, but also the works on accentuation, on different forms of modified recitation and the various kinds of lists of special Vedic words – are in spite of their apparently highly technical and scholastic nature of extraordinary general indological importance; I should even say: they are simply fascinating, for a number of reasons, most of which have already been pointed out by Pandit Aithal himself in his "Introduction".

Oral transmission has played an enormous role in India, and has deeply formed her culture until the present day; but it is in India, too, that in addition to and side by side with texts which have been transmitted in this manner (even after writing came into use) we find a great number of texts which allow us to look behind the curtain and to study the various mnemonics, the techniques and methods developed for the sake of preserving orally transmitted texts; again, this type of material is extremely valuable also as evidence for the process which led to the formation of certain sciences, e.g. phonetics, grammar and lexicography, on the basis of an already established, richly developed tradition of passing on orally fixed (religious and sacred) knowledge from one generation to another.

---

[1] The inverted commas are meant to indicate that most of these texts do not date back to the Vedic period itself though all of them do indeed deal with Vedic texts in the strict sense of the word.

It would, however, be wrong to believe that the Veda-Lakṣaṇa texts are of relevance only to the various aspects of the historical process of the transmission of the Veda through the ages and of the technique of this transmission; for they can certainly also render assistance in reaching a better understanding of the Veda itself – as has been shown most convincingly by G. Cardona in a recent article on the accentuation of the *Śatapathabrāhmaṇa* : with the help of the *Bhāṣikasūtra* (on which see below pp. 463-67) and similar texts he has, following F. Kielhorn, definitively solved the much discussed problem of the nature and marking of the accent in this Brāhmaṇa. I do not, of course, want to suggest that what is said in these texts can and should be blindly accepted by Vedic scholars; the critical attitude which Indologists have learned to adopt towards them is certainly not to be simply thrown overboard. But, to be sure, these texts are also not to be pushed aside as being by their very nature of, if at all, secondary importance only. They fully deserve the philologists', especially of course the Vedologists', attention, but equally as historical documents in their own right.

Pandit Aithal has to his credit not only that he has reminded us of the multifaceted importance of the Veda-Lakṣaṇa texts. He has done much more, viz. given us an excellent tool for research which proves to be a most reliable source of information on the available manuscripts, the existing editions and the published literature on them, and it is a tool which designedly and most efficiently paves the way for what may well lead to something like a renaissance in studies in this branch of Sanskrit literature. I for one join Pandit Aithal in hoping that his "Catalogue" will not remain a mere documentation of the work done by former generations, from Śaunaka down to e.g. Devasthali and from Pertsch down to e.g. Cardona, but that it will fulfil its true purpose as a mighty incentive to resume the editorial and similar scholarly activities in this highly interesting field of traditional Indian learning: after all there still are some pandits who have full command over this kind of texts, the tradition of oral transmission is not yet entirely extinct. It would, I feel, be a tragedy, if now that Indologists have finally realized the importance of the living oral tradition of Vedic literature – all editions are, as well known, based on written sources only – our last chance of profiting from what has survived of a once vast world of living learning and erudition were to pass unheeded; and, to be sure, the task of preparing critical editions of these texts, irrespective of whether they have already been published or not, and of studying their contents would be palpably facilitated by the cooperation of traditional specialists.

No one who has ever himself done similar exploratory work in a manuscript library needs to be told that Pandit Aithal has suffered quite some privations in the course of the last years – a fact which he himself does not mention, thus displaying that unassumingness which together with his other outstanding virtues is the mark of a true Brahmin. The thanks we, his fellow Indologists, owe him we should give to him by directly or indirectly supporting and furthering his noble aim which will ultimately enable us to comprehensively evaluate the Veda-Lakṣaṇa texts also in terms of their more general contribution to Indian culture and Indian History of ideas.

Reinbek, December 1990 A. Wezler

CONTENTS

INTRODUCTION

The aim of this bibliography is to compile a comprehensive list of all Vedic ancillary texts known so far through printed editions, manuscript catalogues of libraries and references in literature. These texts are known as "*Lakṣaṇa-grantha-s*".[1] Since they define the characteristics and describe the special features of Vedic texts, they are generally termed "*Veda-lakṣaṇa*".[2] These texts are of ancillary nature and generally classified under *Vedāṅga*, though only a few of them belong to the proper *Vedāṅga* known as the *Śikṣā-s*. They include *Prātiśākhya-s*, *Anukramaṇī-s*, works on accentuation (*svara*) and on different forms of modified recitation (*vikṛti*), and various kinds of indexes. It is generally not realised that these texts contain an abundance of valuable material for Vedic text-critical studies.

The idea of compiling this descriptive bibliography arose as a reaction to the difficulties one encounters in obtaining details on manuscripts of Sanskrit texts. Those who have attempted to edit a Sanskrit text from original manuscripts know how difficult it is to get reliable information about the existence of and access to manuscript material. Manuscript catalogues that contain relevant information are available only in specialized libraries, and not even in the catalogues can one find all the information one is looking for.

There are a large number of important *Veda-lakṣaṇa* texts. Very few of them, mostly published in the last century or in the beginning of this century by scholars such as Weber, Pertsch, Whitney, Max Müller, Macdonell, Thibaut, Satyavrata Samasrami and others, are available in print. Some of the texts that appeared in India in Grantha, Malayalam and Telugu scripts have almost been forgotten. Very few publications on them exist. The few exceptions are such articles as "Remarks on the Śikṣās" by

---

[1] Cf. Somayārya in his commentary called *Tribhāṣya-ratna* on the *Taittirīya-prātiśākhya*, I 1: *praṇamyāhaṃ . . . girāṃ devīm idaṃ lakṣaṇaṃ vakṣyāmi.*
See also Gārgya Gopāla-yajvan in his *Vaidikābharaṇa* on the same : *prātiśākhyaṃ nāma lakṣaṇaṃ praṇīyate.*

[2] This tradition, mainly prevalent in South India, can be noticed in most library registers and published manuscript catalogues, in which the term *Veda-lakṣaṇa* is used as one of the subject titles of Vedic literature. Accordingly, one of the earliest editions of the *Taittirīya-prātiśākhya* is printed under the title *Prātiśākhyaṃ nāma Vedalakṣaṇam.* Ed. by Lakshmanacharya Ghanapathi and Sundara Ghanapathi (in Grantha script). – Tiruvadi (Pañcanada), 1891. 40 pp.

Franz Kielhorn,[3] "La Forme et l'Arrangement interne des Prātiśākhya", by Louis Renou,[4] the extraordinary study on the *Vyāsa-śikṣā* by Heinrich Lüders,[5] and some incomplete references by Suryakanta.[6] The book *Critical Studies in the Phonetic Observations of Indian Grammarians* by Siddheshwar Varma contains some details on *Śikṣā-s*.[7]

Literary manuals generally tend to neglect the *Veda-lakṣaṇa* works. Histories of literature, even the most recent ones, make only passing remarks on *Veda-lakṣaṇa* works or confine themselves to dealing with well-known texts such as *Prātiśākhya-s* and *Śikṣā-s* in general.[8] It is indeed striking that these texts seem to have failed to attract the attention of scholars in modern Vedic research. Such texts are not only interesting from the point of view of the preservation of Vedic texts, but are also very instructive for an understanding of the various devices or methods of learning that were exclusively developed for this purpose. Moreover, they can help us to understand the various aspects of the history of the transmission of Vedic texts.

It is well known that most Vedic texts have been transmitted orally – from teacher to pupil – from early times to the present day. In spite of the fact that innumerable manuscripts of these sacred texts have existed for centuries and that printed books are available since the middle of the last century, only the oral tradition is recognized as authentic and authoritative. During Vedic rituals printed books, manuscripts or written notes are not allowed to be used. Even when one is reciting for ritual purposes, tradition generally does not permit the use of written material.[9] This would divert the attention from the ritual act. Usually entire texts are learnt by heart before they are recited for ritual application.

---

[3] Published in : *Indian Antiquary*, vol. V (1876), pp. 141-44; 193-200. Reprint in : Franz Kielhorn : *Kleine Schriften*, ed. by Wilhelm Rau. – Wiesbaden : Steiner, 1969. Vol. I, pp. 158-69. – (Glasenapp-Stiftung, Band 3,1).

[4] In : *Journal Asiatique*, vol. 248 (1960), pp. 1-40.

[5] *Die Vyāsa-śikṣā, besonders in ihrem Verhältnis zum Taittirīya-prātiśākhya.* – Göttingen, 1893.

[6] See *Laghu-ṛktantra-saṃgraha*, ed. by Suryakanta. – Lahore, 1940. Introduction, pp. 1-18. Reprint : New Delhi : Meharchand Lachhmandas, 1982.

[7] – London : Royal Asiatic Society, 1929. xiii, 190 pp. Reprint : Delhi : Munshiram Manohar Lal, 1961.

[8] Cf. Hartmut Scharfe: *Grammatical Literature.* – Wiesbaden : Harrassowitz, 1977, pp. 127-34, 176-77 – (A History of Indian Literature, vol. V, fasc. 2).
Cf. also Klaus Mylius: *Geschichte der Literatur im alten Indien.* – Leipzig : Reclam, 1983, p. 92.

[9] Cf. *Pāṇinīya-śikṣā*, 32; *Yājñavalkya-śikṣā*, 198; *Nārada-śikṣā*, II 8,9.

For the purpose of easy learning and memorization as well as preservation of the sacred texts, tradition has evolved some peculiar but very useful devices which have been applied from time immemorial, and even now practised in the traditional system of education. These devices help the students to learn and memorize entire texts – even large texts like the *Ṛgveda* – with utmost accuracy.[10] This methodological and didactic aspect of Vedic and ritual text tradition has not yet been thoroughly and systematically investigated in modern Vedic scholarship.

For the documentation of materials which constitute the theoretical basis of the method of traditional Vedic learning, my modest attempt has been first of all to prepare a consolidated list of all the works known so far, with a brief description of the contents of those works. I have also indicated the availability of the manuscript material in order to facilitate the editing and publishing of some of the important texts. The preliminary list, which I have prepared mainly on the basis of the *New Catalogus Catalogorum*, Aufrecht's *Catalogus Catalogorum*, and other manuscript catalogues, contains over 1600 titles. The titles pertaining to the Ṛgvedic school alone run up to three hundred.

During my visits to different manuscript libraries in India and Europe I have collected a number of manuscripts, or procured transcripts or microfilms of several minor works that are used by reciters. There are hundreds of such manuscripts in private possession, and hundreds more in various manuscript libraries in India and abroad. In the Adyar Library and Research Centre (Madras), where I worked from 1962 to 1970, there are over 500 such manuscripts.[11] In the Oriental Research Institute, Mysore, there are more than 600 manuscripts.[12] The case is similar with other manuscript libraries. As I have already noted, publications on these works are very rare and only a few texts are available in print.

1. Importance and Categories of Veda-lakṣaṇa works

Although traditional pandits do not use any written material during the actual recitation, there exist a large number of important texts which are used as an external aid to instruction. A few of them, such as *Prātiśākhya-s* and *Śikṣā-s*, are well known and, therefore, need not be elaborated upon here. But in this connection it would be interesting to note the remarks of Louis Renou, who wrote in 1960, regarding the post-

---

[10] See George Thibaut : *Das Jaṭāpaṭala : Lehrbuch des Jaṭāpāṭha für den Ṛgveda.* – Leipzig : F. A. Brockhaus, 1870. Introduction.

[11] *Descriptive Catalogue of Sanskrit Manuscripts* in the Adyar Library. Vol. I. Vedic, ed. by Madhava Krishna Sarma. – Madras, 1942, nos. 710-1103.

[12] *Descriptive Catalogue of Sanskrit Manuscripts* in the Oriental Research Institute. Vol. II. – Mysore, 1978, nos. 3036-4079.

Vedic literature on the Veda :

> This long period is not lacking in erudite works devoted to the Veda. Since the *pariśiṣṭa* of the Kalpa and Śikṣās, . . . an uninterrupted continuation of minor works encumbers the catalogues of manuscripts, . . . which, lacking any other merit, have the one merit of attesting to a certain productivity of schools of specialists. Literary manuals hardly notice them; before future manuals can record them, these abundant monographs must be set in order. . . . Let us take, at random, the catalogue of A. B. Keith for the India Office Library: . . . indices of strange names like – Rāvaṇabhaiṭ, No. 4248; Calākṣara, (or Chal.) (index of *gānas*), nos. 4296-99, 4317-20; a Chalaprakriyā, No. 4325; several Yajurvedic tracts like Aniṅgya, No. 4460-64, Nyāyapañcāśāt, 4459, Avarṇi, 4465-72, Āvarṇi, 4473-77, Uccodarki, 4478, Tapara, 4480-81, Napara 4482, Vilaṅghya 4491-96, Śamāna 4497-4508, etc. . . . In this field, contemporary Vedology is less active than that of earlier times, when critical works were devoted to the texts, such as the *Upalekha* or the *Jaṭāpaṭala*, and even an Indianist like G. Thibaut did not scorn to sit down to such work. Where is the time when all Indianists held it in their hearts to start their careers by editing some Vedic document, however, modest ?[13]

For the sake of convenience, the *Veda-lakṣaṇa* works can broadly be classified, on the basis of their essential features, into four categories:

1. Works on Vedic phonetics, phonology, and some elements of Vedic grammar. Examples are the *Prātiśākhya-s* and the *Śikṣā-s*, which deal with such topics as the alphabet (*varṇa-samāmnāya*), organs of articulation, etc. (*sthāna, karaṇa, prayatna*), correct pronunciation (*uccāraṇa*), euphonic combination (*saṃdhi*), proper accentuation (*svara*), etc.
2. *Anukramaṇī-s* – like the *Sarvānukramaṇī*, *Bṛhaddevatā* (indices of the Seers, Deities and metres), etc. To this category belongs also a large number of texts known as *Baiṭh-s*, which deal with the same topic as the *Anukramaṇī-s* but are composed in a code language and contain their own *paribhāṣā-s* and explanatory remarks. Some of these texts also make use of the *kaṭapayādi* system.
3. Works containing lists of words, sometimes alphabetically arranged, words having peculiar characteristics in the Vedic texts, e.g., the *Cāturjñāna*, the *Saptasaṃkhyā*, and the *Saptalakṣaṇa*, this last one comprising seven short tracts with the titles 1) *Aniṅgya*, 2) *Avarṇi*, 3) *Āvarṇi*, 4) *Tapara*, 5) *Napara*, 6) *Vilaṅghya* and 7) *Śamāna*.
4. Works mainly dealing with the modified forms of recitation. Some of them instruct in the formation of only one mode of recitation, like the *Upalekha-sūtra* on the *Krama-pāṭha* or the *Jaṭā-paṭala* on the *jaṭā-pāṭha*. But others, like the

---

[13] *The Destiny of the Veda in India* (English trans.). – Delhi : Motilal Banarsidass, 1965, p. 23 and 81 fn.

Aṣṭa-vikṛti-kārikā, or *Vikṛti-vallī*, describe eight varieties of recitation.

The importance of the works on Vedic recitation was recognized long ago, e.g. the *Upalekha-sūtra* was edited with a translation[14] in Latin by Pertsch as far back as 1854, and the *Jaṭā-paṭala* was published with a German translation by George Thibaut[15] in 1870. At the end of the last century Satyavrata Samasrami published some of these texts in Calcutta. There are a few booklets printed in South India in Grantha, Malayalam, or Telugu script. None of these editions can now be obtained.

Recently, an attempt to make some of the *Veda-lakṣaṇa* works available to the scholarly world has been made by K. V. Abhyankar through his publication of the *Veda-padapāṭha-carcā* along with a text on the *kramapāṭha*, called *Upalekhasūtra.*[16] G. V. Devasthali has continued the work of Abhyankar in publishing the *Veda-vikṛti-lakṣaṇa-saṃgraha* – a collection of twelve texts on *vedavikṛti-s* and allied topics.[17] In the introduction to that edition Devasthali has pointed out the importance of many of these works. Illustrating the three basic forms and eight modified forms of Vedic recitation, Devasthali has clearly shown the distinction between the different forms of recitation.[18]

Accordingly, the well-known modes of Vedic recitation fall into two classes: the *prakṛti* and the *vikṛti.* To the former class belong the *saṃhitā*, *padapāṭha* and *kramapāṭha*, which are quite ancient. These have been mentioned in the *Aitareya Āraṇyaka* under the designations *nirbhuja, pratṛṇṇa* and *ubhayam antareṇa.*[19] Of these three, the *saṃhitāpāṭha* and the *padapāṭha* are, no doubt, more ancient than the *kramapāṭha*. . . . *prakṛti* is the mode of recitation in which the original order of words is retained, while in *vikṛti* the word order is occasionally reversed. Tradition is unanimous

---

[14] *Upalekha : de Kramapāṭha libellus.* – Berolini (Berlin) : Dümmler, 1854.

[15] *Das Jaṭāpaṭala : Lehrbuch des Jaṭāpāṭha für den Ṛgveda.* – Leipzig : F. A. Brockhaus, 1870.

[16] Ed. by K[ashinath] V[asudev] Abhyankar with English exposition. – Poona : Bhandarkar Oriental Research Institute, 1974. viii, 82 pp. – (Postgraduate and Research Department Series No. 10). Reprint from the *Annals of the Bhandarkar Oriental Research Institute*, vol. 54 (1973), pp. 9-76.

[17] With an elaborate introduction by G[ovind] V[inayak] Devasthali. – Poona : Bhandarkar Oriental Research Institute, 1979. – (Research Unit Publication 5). For details of the texts included in this book, see below under *Veda-vikṛti-lakṣaṇa-saṃgraha* in the descriptive bibliography.

[18] Ibid., pp. xvii-xix.

[19] *Aitareya Āraṇyaka* (III 1.3): *yad dhi saṃdhiṃ vivartayati tan nirbhujasya rūpam, atha yac chuddhe akṣare abhivyāharati tat pratṛṇṇasya, agra u evobhayam antareṇa, ubhayaṃ vyāptaṃ bhavati* | – *annādyakāmo nirbhujaṃ brūyāt, svargakāmaḥ pratṛṇṇam, ubhayakāma ubhayam antareṇa* |

in declaring the three together as forming the three *saṃhitā-s* that lie at the root of the eight *vikṛti-s*. It may be noted that *saṃhitā*, *pada*, and *krama*, being *ārṣa-saṃhitā-s*, were considered as equal in authenticity. It is well known that the *jaṭā* is the first and the oldest of the *vikṛti-s* and was the first to introduce the element of *viloma* (the reverse order) in the recitation. And this element, thus introduced, has persisted through all the other modes of recitation. This element of *viloma* or *vyutkrama*, being just the reverse of the original order of words, was enough to acquire for it the name *vikṛti*, a name which then naturally came to describe all the modes of recitation containing that element. Even these *vikṛti-s* are quite ancient and some of them find occasional mention and even treatment in some of the *Prātiśākhya* works and also in the *Śikṣā-s*, for *jaṭā* is presupposed or mentioned in the *Taittirīya-prātiśākhya* and the *Atharva-prātiśākhya* while the *Caraṇavyuha* refers to *jaṭā* and *daṇḍa*, on which the remaining six *vikṛti-s* are based.

Further, in the same introduction Devasthali observes:[20]

> Some of these works – small handy tracts – were published by scholars interested in Vedic studies more than a century ago. But unfortunately these works seem to have failed to attract due attention, with the result that this branch of Vedic studies appears to have dwindled to the point of extinction. The importance of these and similar other works for Vedic text-critical studies can hardly be exaggerated – particularly today when the indigenous tradition of this branch of learning is fast becoming extinct. And if no serious efforts are made to retrieve this valuable heritage, it is feared that an invaluable treasure of source material for Vedic text-critical studies, comprising the quintessence of ancient Indian learning and thought would be lost – and lost for good.

2. Tradition of Vedic Recitation

As is well known, the traditional system of learning the Veda-s has two different aspects: the *svādhyāya* and the *prayoga*.[21] The *svādhyāya* comprises committing the Veda to memory, imparting it to pupils, and reciting the Veda of one's own *śākhā*, usually as part of the daily *brahmayajña*, one of the five great sacrifices (*pañca-mahāyajña*).[22] The five great sacrifices to be performed daily have been pre-

---

[20] Ibid., pp. xix-xx.

[21] Cf. J[ohan] F[rederik] (Frits) Staal, *Nambudiri Veda Recitation*. – The Hague : Mouton, 1961, pp. 11-12.

[22] For more on this see P[andurang] V[aman] Kane, *History of Dharmaśāstra*, vol. II. – Poona : Bhandarkar Oriental Research Institute, (second ed.) 1974, pp. 696 ff.

scribed and described in the *Śatapatha Brāhmaṇa* (XI 5.6.1),[23] in the *Taittirīya Āraṇyaka* (II 10),[24] in the *Āśvalāyana Gṛhyasūtra* (III 1.1-4)[25] and in many *dharmaśāstra* and *smṛti* texts. The sentence *svādhyāyo 'dhyetavyaḥ* (one should study one's own Veda) has often been repeated, and is discussed in several *mīmāṃsā* and *dharmaśāstra* works. In the *Taittirīya Saṃhitā* (VI 3.10.5)[26] there is a well-known passage referring to three kinds of obligations – to sages, gods and *pitṛ-s* – with which every Brāhmaṇa is born. In order to absolve oneself from the obligation to the sages, it is clearly stated that one has to study the Veda : *Brāhmaṇena niṣkāraṇaṃ dharmaḥ ṣaḍaṅgo vedo 'dhyetavyaḥ* (a Brāhmaṇa should study the Veda along with its six ancillary texts without any motive). This passage is quoted by Patañjali in his *Mahābhāṣya*[27] as an *āgama*. Accordingly, *adhyayana* and *adhyāpana* have been regarded as duties of a Brāhmaṇa, along with *yajana*, *yājana*, *dāna* and *pratigraha*.[28]

The second aspect of learning the Veda, i.e. *prayoga*, is the application of the Veda in the rituals, particularly in the *śrauta* sacrifices. According to the Pūrvamīmāṃsā the main purpose of the study of the Veda is the performance of sacrifices (*āmnāyasya kriyārthatvam*).[29] Although elaborate *śrauta* sacrifices rarely take place in these days, there are still quite a few people who have kept up the tradition of reciting the Veda.

From early times to the present day, oral instruction has been regarded as the accurate method of teaching Vedic texts. Since there has been great prejudice, as it were, against learning from books in general[30] and Vedic texts in particular, oral instruction and committing the Veda to memory have been the rule. In order to preserve the Veda in its pristine purity and transmit it with proper pronunciation and accentuation, various devices were evolved. The earliest and most important of these devices is the *padapāṭha*. As the *Atharva-prātiśākhya* (IV 107): remarks: "The study of word-isolates is

---

23 *pañcaiva mahāyajñāḥ. tāny eva mahāsatrāṇi . . . . atha brahmayajñaḥ. svādhyāyo vai brahmayajñaḥ.*

24 *pañcaiva vā ete mahāyajñāḥ . . . . yat svādhyāyam adhīyītaikām apy ṛcaṃ yajuḥ sāma vā tad brahmayajñaḥ.*

25 *athātaḥ pañcayajñāḥ . . . . yat svādhyāyam adhīte sa brahmayajñaḥ.* Commenting on this Nārāyaṇa, the Vṛttikāra, quotes the above passage of the *Taittirīya Āraṇyaka* as the source of the five great sacrifices: *pañcayajñānāṃ hi taittirīyāraṇyakaṃ mūlam.*

26 *jāyamāno ha vai brāhmaṇas tribhir ṛṇavān jāyate . . . .* Cf. Kane, *op. cit.*, p. 270.

27 *Mahābhāṣya* on Pāṇini, I 1.1.

28 Cf. *Gautama-dharmasūtra*, X 1-3: *dvijātīnām adhyayanam ijyā dānam; brāhmaṇasyādhikāḥ pravacana-yājana-prati-grahāḥ.* Cf. Kane, *op. cit.*, p. 105, *passim.*

29 See *Mīmāṃsāsūtra* I 2.1 and Śabara's *Bhāṣya* thereon, where it is argued that those portions of the Veda which do not directly concern the sacrificial injunction are meaningless and irrelevant.

30 See Kane, *op. cit.*, p. 348 ff.

designed to teach the beginnings and ends of words, and their correct form, tone, and meaning" (*padādhyayanam antādi-śabda-svarārtha-jñānārtham*). The commentator adds: "Without studying the word-isolates one might make errors in the *saṃhitā* text; it is for this reason that the study of the word-isolates is necessary" (*apadādhyāyī saṃhitāṃ vināśayet; tasmād ebhiḥ kāraṇair avaśyādheyayāni*). In modern Vedic research, although the importance of the *padapāṭha* has been recognized, it has not yet been systematically studied. Surprisingly there is no proper edition of the *padapāṭha* as it is recited by traditional pandits. The observance of *samaya* (the conventional omission or the non-recital of three or more words) in the *padapāṭha* after they have occurred thrice in the same order as a group in the *Saṃhitā*, e.g. *bṛhad vadema vidathe suvīrāḥ*, has been completely ignored in the available printed editions of the *Ṛgveda-saṃhitā* accompanied by the *padapāṭha*.[31] These words omitted in the *padapāṭha* to avoid further repetition after they have occurred thrice in the same order are also called *galita*, *galanta* or *galat-pada*.[32] They are not recited in the *padapāṭha*. This feature, although observed by the traditional reciters and carefully recorded in the manuscript copies of the *padapāṭha*, is not noticed by modern editors of the *padapāṭha*. C. Kunhan Raja drew the attention of scholars to this important aspect nearly 60 years ago, when he published the commentary of Mādhava on the *Ṛgveda*[33] and the *Anukramaṇī-s*[34] in which the necessity of the *galita-s* for the interpretation of the *Ṛgveda* is emphasized. Since then there have been only sporadic attempts by scholars such as G. V. Devasthali, K. P. Jog,[35] C. G. Kashikar,[36] Ganapati Sastri, Hebbar[37] and others, to study this problem. Reference has already been made to a more recent publication on the subject, an elaborate essay

---

[31] K. V. Abhyankar, *op. cit.*, pp. 28-29.

[32] A text on this topic called *Galita-pradīpa* of Lakṣmīdhara has been published with a commentary by Srikrishna Deva in the Sanskrit magazine *Sārasvatī Suṣamā* from the Sanskrit University, Varanasi, vol. 14, pt. 4, Saṃvat 2016 (A.D. 1960).

[33] – Madras : Adyar Library, 1939, 1947. – (Adyar Library Series 22 and 61).

[34] *Ṛgvedānukramaṇī*. – Madras : University of Madras, 1932.

[35] K[eshav] P[andurang] Jog, "On the Galitas in the Padapāṭha as a Means of Ṛgvedic Interpretation", in : *Indian Antiquary* (III Series), vol. III. – (Prof. R. N. Dandekar Felicitation Volume). – Bombay, 1969, pp. 56-82. "On the *Galitapradīpa* of Lakṣmīdharasūri", in : *Journal of the Ganganatha Jha Kendriya Sanskrit Vidyapeetha*, vol. 27.3-4 (1971), Allahabad, pp. 275-87.

[36] C[hintamani] G[anesh] Kashikar, "The Problem of the Galantas in the Ṛgveda Padapāṭha", in : *Proc. of the All-India Oriental Conference* (XIII) in Nagpur, Part 2, pp. 39-46.
"Repetitions in the Ṛgveda Padapāṭha", in : *Annals of the Bhandarkar Oriental Research Institute*, vol. 28 (1947), pp. 301-05.

[37] "Ekā svaramīmāṃsā" (in Sanskrit), in : *Annals of the Bhandarkar Oriental Research Institute*, vol. 51 (1970), pp. 210-12.

[38] – Poona : Bhandarkar Oriental Research Institute, 1974. Reprint of the "Prole-

called *Veda-padapāṭha-carcā*,[38] by K. V. Abhyankar[39] in which the author has dealt with the grammatical regulations and conventions governing the *padapāṭha*, especially those about the meaning of the word *pada* and about the splitting of the *pada-s* into their component parts. This essay is a very valuable contribution to the proper understanding of the meaning and importance of the *padapāṭha*. Still, a systematic edition and the critical study of the *padapāṭha* is a desideratum.

The next step in the preservation and the prevention from corruption of the Vedic texts is the *krama-pāṭha*.[40] This is based on the *saṃhitāpāṭha* and the *padapāṭha* and is in turn the basis for the other eight varieties of more difficult methods of recitations, called *vikṛti-s*. The eleven varieties of Vedic recitation, which require great patience and many years of strenuous study, are still practised by some pandits, though their number is very small and is dwindling at a rapid pace. In a few years this kind of recitation will be a matter of the past.

3. Present Position of Vedic Recitation

In recent years, there has been a growing interest in the study of the tradition of Vedic recitation. As the practice of reciting the Veda in the traditional manner is becoming fast extinct, it would be appropriate to focus attention on this aspect of Vedic learning. In an article I read at the International Congress of Human Sciences in Asia and Africa held in Tokyo in 1983 there is an account of my investigation of the subject,

---

gomena to the Veda-padapāṭha", in : *Annals of the Bhandarkar Oriental Research Institute*, vol. 54 (1973), pp. 9-44.

39 See also his article : "Methods of the Recital of Veda-texts", in : *Proc. of the First International Sanskrit Conference* in New Delhi 1972. General editor : R[am] K[aran] Sharma, vol. IV. – New Delhi : Rashtriya Sanskrit Samsthanam, 1972, pp. 1-10.

40 For a detailed exposition of the rules for *krama* formation with illustrations based on the *Krama-paṭala* of the *Ṛgveda-prātiśākhya* see G. V. Devasthali, *Annals of the Bhandarkar Oriental Research Institute* – (Diamond Jubilee Volume), vol. 50 (1969), pp. 573-82.
See also the article by the same : "Pre-fixation Fermentation of the (Ṛgveda) Krama-pāṭha", in : *Indologica Taurinensia* – (Sternbach Commemoration Volume), vols. 8-9, 1980-81 (Torino), pp. 123-35.
"The Krama-pāṭha Unit", in : *Amṛtadhārā* – Prof. R. N. Dandekar Felicitation Volume, ed. by S[hivram] D[attatrey] Joshi. – Delhi : Ajanta Publications, 1984, pp. 105-13.
"Importance of the Kramapāṭha", in : *Proc. of the Fifth World Sanskrit Conference* in Varanasi 1981. – New Delhi : Rashtriya Sanskrit Samsthanam, 1985, pp. 143-49.

which was carried out in Karnataka. I have not only observed and recorded some of the Vedic recitations but also gathered information on the method of instruction and the practice of different modes of recitation, particularly of the *Ṛgveda.* It is hardly necessary to emphasize the importance of collecting this kind of material for the proper understanding and the study of the tradition of Vedic recitation.

It may not be out of place to give a brief account of the present position of the practice of Vedic recitation in order to describe and explain the various devices of transmission of the Vedic texts and ritual practices. V. Raghavan of the University of Madras, who was uniquely qualified for an investigation on the present position of the practice of Vedic recitation, gathered extensive information and valuable materials on this subject. As a member of the Sanskrit Commission appointed by the Government of India in the years 1956-57 he had ample facilities and opportunities for this work. Some details of his findings have been published in the report of the Commission.[41] But this was done in the wider context of a general survey of Sanskrit studies in the whole of the country. He has also published a fairly elaborate report entitled "Present Position of Vedic Chanting and Its Future" in the *Bulletin of the Institute of Traditional Cultures*, Madras in 1957.[42] V. Raghavan has also brought out a booklet with the title "Present Position of Vedic Recitation and Vedic Śākhās – In Different Parts of India", in which he discussed among others the problems of the recitation of Vedic texts.[43]

Nambudiri Veda Recitation by J. F. Staal, published in 1961, is an important contribution to the subject. It contains interesting details on the tradition of Vedic recitation in Kerala, particularly that of the Nambudiri Brahmins. It represents the results of thorough investigation and documentation of information derived through painstaking field-work.[44]

The recent publication, *Sāmavedic Chant*, by Wayne Howard is a very elaborate and informative work. It deals with the chanting of the Sāmaveda of different schools in different parts of India. In his introduction Howard also discusses the general problems of Vedic recitation.[45]

"Kramapāṭha of Ṛgveda 2.1 Explained", in : *The Adyar Library Bulletin*, vol. 52 (1986), pp. 586-617.

41 *Report of the Sanskrit Commission 1956-1957.* – Delhi : The Manager of Publications, Govt. of India, 1958.

42 "Reports of Seminars", 10.7.1957, Institute of Traditional Cultures. – Madras : University of Madras, 1957, pp. 48-69.

43 Published by Veda Dharma Paripalana Sabha, Kumbakonam, 1959.

44 – The Hague : Mouton, 1961.

45 – New Haven : Yale University Press, 1977.

I have taken hints from these and other publications, some of which will be mentioned later on, and have made a modest attempt to investigate the present position of the tradition of Vedic recitation. During several trips to India since 1983 I have visited many different centers of traditional Vedic learning. I began gathering details in my own village, Kota-Saligrama (in the South Kanara District), where I made the *adhyayana*, learning the *Ṛgveda* in the traditional method in the 1940s. There is still a Veda-pāṭhaśālā in the village, with now only a handful of pupils concentrating on the chanting of the Vedas. Through my acquaintances in the village and in the neighbouring areas I made enquiries about the Veda-pāṭhaśālā-s. There are a few individual families of Veda-pāṭhin-s teaching a couple of pupils. In Udipi, the great Vaiṣṇava centre in the South, there is a Sanskrit College maintained by the religious heads of the Maṭha-s. Here the Veda-s are taught to young pupils only in the early stages. There is no provision for advanced studies of the Veda-s. The largest number of persons engaged in teaching and learning recitation of the Veda-s and also in performing the *śrauta* rituals may be found in Gokarna in the North Kanara District. Experts in the recitation of the Veda-s who are also well-versed in the practice of performing Vedic rituals go from here to far away places like Bangalore, Mysore, Madras and Poona. The next important places I visited in Karnataka were the Sanskrit Colleges in Bangalore and Mysore where there are regular courses up to *ghana-pāṭha*. There are public examinations in the Veda-s conducted by the Government of Karnataka.[46]

I have likewise gathered information in other parts of India : Tirupati, Rajamahendri (Andhra Pradesh), Madras, Kanchipuram, Kumbakonam, Thanjavur (Tamil Nadu), Trivandrum, Tripunittura (Kerala), Poona, Satara, Wadi (Maharashtra), and Varanasi. In all these places I have had extensive discussions both with the teachers and with the students. Altogether I have spoken with over a hundred persons, several of them Ghana-pāṭhin-s, i.e. persons well-versed in the various difficult modified methods of recitation, of which more will be stated later. During my survey I have particularly observed the methodological aspects of the learning of the Veda-s, for which the *Veda-lakṣaṇa* texts described in this bibliography constitute the theoretical authority. In this traditional system of learning and recitation greater importance is attached to the sound than to the meaning (as in music). A mere recitation of the Vedic hymns in the proper way is believed to produce a spiritual effect irrespective of understanding the meaning of the texts recited. Though the knowledge of meaning is regarded as useful in the performance of the rituals by enhancing their effects, this aspect is usually ignored.[47]

---

[46] Edwin Gerow, "Some Thoughts on Indian Government Policy as It Affects Sanskrit Education", in : *Studies in the Language and Culture of South Asia.* – Seattle and London : University of Washington Press, 1974, pp. 111-24.

[47] Here one is reminded of the well-known Kautsa controversy referred to by Yāska in the *Nirukta*, I 15: *anarthakā hi mantrāḥ*.

One of the important questions I discussed in all these places is the present day situation of traditional Vedic recitation. The general situation, as described by many of my informants, is rather hopeless. Everywhere there is a decline of interest in serious and complete study of the Veda with *pada, krama*, etc. On the other hand, one finds a marked increase in popular interest in the Veda. Paradoxically, a considerably large number of people, adults who are engaged in different professions, even elderly persons, seek a Ghana-pāṭhin and try to learn by heart certain specific portions or hymns of the Veda.

Where there is a regular and complete recitation of the Veda, with the modified forms of *pada, krama*, etc., the course extends to more than eight years, with ten to twelve hours of learning each day. The regular study is carried on from the second day after the full moon day (or the new moon day), until the twelfth day of the each fortnight of the month. The full moon and new moon days, along with the two days before and the day after each, are vacation days (*anadhyayana*). During these days, although *śruti* texts such as the Saṃhitā-s or Brāhmaṇa-s, are not recited, auxiliary texts like the *Prātiśākhya-s, Śikṣā-s* or other non-Vedic texts such as *prayoga-s* or *stotra-s* are studied.

The method of teaching is naturally still traditional. In the early stages the procedure is somewhat like this: The young boys who have had their initiation (*upanayana*), sit in front of the teacher after they have finished their purificatory baths and performed the daily rituals, etc. The teaching begins early in the morning, soon after sunrise, with the chanting of the sacred syllables HARIḤ OṂ, as prescribed by the *Veda-lakṣaṇa* texts. First the teacher recites each *mantra, pāda* by *pāda*, and the pupil recites it three times immediately after the teacher. This *pāda* by *pāda* recitation is repeated twelve times. The same method is followed for the recitation of the halves of the *mantra-s* and for the full *mantra-s*. Usually one session lasts until one *adhyāya* is completed. Altogether each *mantra* is repeated 108 times. The study of *pada, krama, jaṭā*, etc., is variously graded according to the ability of the individual student. The procedure is very strenuous and time-consuming and thus requires great patience. Since no material reward, nor any kind of professional prospect can be expected from such a study these days, firm faith in the spiritual efficacy and divinity of the Vedic Word is the essential prerequisite for such a rigorous course of study.

4. Vague and Inaccurate Catalogues

One of the reasons why the *Veda-lakṣaṇa* works have been so far neglected in modern Vedic research appears to be the fact that the subject matter of most of these works is useful mainly for *svādhyāya*. Only orthodox Brahmins well-versed in Vedic recitation seem to have been able to appreciate the value of these works. Otherwise, it would be difficult to explain the seeming disinterest of modern Vedic researchers concerning these works. However, for a proper study of the tradition of Vedic recitation in its different variations these works are indispensable. Though a large number of manuscripts is to be found in different manuscript libraries, they fail to attract the attention of research scholars. It would appear that the compilers of descriptive catalogues of Sanskrit manuscripts, through which one derives information on such works, did not show any great interest in them either. Thus one finds them catalogued rather indifferently under *Prātiśākhya-s* or *Śikṣā-s*, sometimes under *Vedāṅga* or under the sub-title *Vedalakṣaṇa* or even simply under *Miscellaneous*, without proper verification and identification. The descriptions of many of these works in the descriptive catalogues are either very vague or inaccurate. Sometimes one gets the impression that the compilers are only concerned with the better-known works and have little interest in these ancillary works.

Take, for example, the work called *Cāturjñāna*. It contains lists of words of the *Ṛgveda* in sixty-four sections for the sixty-four Adhyāya-s. Each section has four different groups of words :

1) words ending in a *visarga* that is lost in the *saṃhitāpāṭha* (called *śamāna*),
2) words ending in *n*,
3) words expanding into *ay, av, āy, āv* (technically called *vivṛtapada-s*) and
4) simple non-compound words (*ekapada-s*).

Theodor Aufrecht in his *Catalogus Catalogorum*[48] described this text as "a list of the Sūkta, Varga, Maṇḍala and Ashṭaka of the ṚV." This is obviously not correct. But this description is reproduced in some descriptive catalogues. On this manuscript A. B. Keith in the Catalogue of the India Office Library says:[49] "An index to the *Ṛig-Veda*, styled on the cover of the MS. *Ṛgveda-ciṭṭa*, the principle of whose construction is not given, but is shown by T. Aufrecht (*Munich Catal.*, pp. 13-14) to be the enumeration of words whose visarga after 'ā' is lost in *sandhi*. . . . It is called *Cāturgāna* in the left margin of fol. 71; this may be compared with *Cāturjñāna*, perhaps erroneously given as the title in the *Calcutta Sansk. Coll. Catal.*, I. 339 and *Cāṭrijñāna* in the *Deccan Coll. Catal.*, I. 37, 38. . . . For the term *Cāturjñāna* see Haraprasāda Śāstrī, *Notices* III.iii.57." Albrecht Weber also in the Berlin Catalogue, p. 15, says: "Eine Art *anukramaṇī* zu den 64 *adhyāya-s* der *Ṛksaṃhitā*: der Zweck der Zusammenstellung ist mir nicht klar." The purpose of the treatise is given in the introductory verses of the work in the Adyar manuscript (TR 112); and it also contains the title *Cāturjñānādilakṣaṇa*. In this manuscript the words *cātu* and *jñāna* are also written separately on the left and right hand side of the margin of each folio. The author's name is mentioned in one of the introductory verses as Paṅgu Nārāyaṇa.[50] The Munich Catalogue[51] describes the manuscript correctly, but further remarks: "Manchmal werden

---

48 Vol. I. – Leipzig, 1891, p. 184a.

49 *Catalogue of the Sanskrit and Prākrit Manuscripts in the Library of the India Office*, by Arthur Berriedale Keith. – London, 1935, vol. II, pt. 1, pp. 15-16, nos. 4250-51.

50 *Descriptive Catalogue of Sanskrit Manuscripts in the Adyar Library*, vol. I, Vedic. – Madras, 1942, pp. 247-48.

51 By Theodor Aufrecht, *Die Sanskrit-Handschriften der K. Hof- und Staatsbibliothek*

Ausnahmen von der Regel angegeben. *aiha deveti varjayitvā* (fol. 1b 8. RV. I.92.18). Hier steht *devā* vor *mayobhuvā*, ist aber ein Dual. *yuktā māteti* (fol. 2a 9. RV. I.164.9). Ein schlechtes Beispiel, weil jeder Leser sicht, daß *yuktā* ein Femininum ist. *iṣukṛteva devā nāsatyā* (fol. 2b 5. RV. I.184.3). *devā* steht im Dual. *yā mameti* (fol. 7b 4. RV. X.145.3). *yā* ist Femininum sg." Aufrecht points out the inconsistencies in the manuscript, but does not seem to be aware of the fact that this text is meant for young pupils who have no knowledge of grammar whatsoever and merely recite the *padapāṭha* to learn the Vedic texts by heart; this work provides such students valuable help in dividing the *saṃdhi* properly.

Some other examples of vague and partly inaccurate descriptions of this text may be added: *A Descriptive Catalogue of Sanskrit Manuscripts* in the Library of the Calcutta Sanskrit College:[52] " A book treating the passages of the Ṛigveda Saṃhitā called *Cāturjñāna*. Anonymous." The *Descriptive Catalogue of the Government Collections of Manuscripts* (now deposited in the Bhandarkar Oriental Research Institute, Poona), remarks:[53] " . . . Something bearing on the Pada text of Ṛigveda. Subject: – Vedic information of the nature of the Saptasaṃkhyā."

Yet another example for an indifferent but interesting description of a manuscript dealing with eight varieties of modified recitation called *Aṣṭavikṛti-vivṛti* may be found in vol. IV, no. 1492 of Rajendralal Mitra's *Notices of Sanskrit MSS:*[54]

> A set of memorial verses on the principles of reading in eight different arbitrary ways the Saṃhitā of the Rig Veda. By Madhusūdana, a muni or saint, son of Krishṇa-daipāyana [*sic*] which name would at first sight suggest Vyāsa, but it is not so. The commentary is anonymous. The colophon is incorrect and quite unreliable. From the introductory portion of the commentary it appears that Madhusūdana wrote the treatise in verse, borrowing his materials from Prātiśākhya treatises by Vyāḍi and Hayagrīva. The works of the latter have not yet been met with . . . .
>
> The real and original object of these artificial forms of writing the text of the Riksaṃhitā, was the prevention of corruptions, interpolations and accidental omissions of the words of the text, but the love of mystery soon attached to it a religious meaning. The practice of reading or keeping by heart these arbitrary forms is still held highly meritorious, and there are many pandits in the Marhatta, Karnāṭa and Drāviḍa countries, who go

---

in München. – München, vol. I, 1909, pp. 13-14.

52 Vol. I : Vedic Manuscripts / by Hṛṣīkeśa Śāstrī and Śiva Chandra Gui. – Calcutta, 1892, p. 339; no. 530.

53 – Bombay, 1916, vol. I, pt. 1, p. 37; no. 43.

54 – Calcutta, 1878, pp. 87-89.

through a part of the text every day before breakfast as a pious act. The practice is very similar to that of medieval monks of Europe who used to read the Bible backward.

Then Mitra illustrates what he says is the formation of the recitation of *jaṭā*, but what is rather the illustration of the *pañcakrama* also known as the *pañcasaṃdhi*, with certain omissions. Further, the description runs as follows: "The others are new forms and made up by different fanciful arrangements of the five-fold order. The rules, however, are exceedingly brief and obscure, and examples given are so manifestly incorrect that they do not help one to elucidate them."

In *A Descriptive Catalogue of the Saṃskṛta and Prākṛta Manuscripts* in the Library of the University of Bombay[55] a *Veda-lakṣaṇa* work called *Aṣṭākṣarī-baiṭh*, also known as the *Dakṣiṇāmūrti-padavarṇa-saṃkhyā*, is mistakenly described as "some Tantric work attributed to Śrīpāda", and is related to the *Dakṣiṇāmūrti-saṃhitā*.

5. Unsatisfactory Editions

The position of the printed editions of the *Veda-lakṣaṇa* texts is no better. There is a great deal of confusion regarding the authorship, exact titles, and even the extent of the texts. As already noted, histories of literature hardly deal with these works, except for some passing remarks on the well-known texts like the *Prātiśākhya-s*. And the printed editions, with only a few exceptions, have been edited in a very uncritical manner. The following examples should serve to illustrate this anomaly.

Mention has already been made of a recent edition of the *Veda-vikṛti-lakṣaṇa-saṃgraha* by Devasthali. In this collection one text called *Aṣṭavikṛtivivṛti* in 54 verses on the eight modes of recitation has been included. In this edition the text is ascribed to Madhusūdanamaskarin and a commentary named *Prakāśa*[56] has been attributed to Purogamācārya. The edition is based on six manuscripts and a printed edition by Dashagranthi K. S. Venkatarama Sastri of Tiruvanaikoil.[57] Its title and sub-title in this latter edition are : *Ṛgvedīya-jaṭāpaṭalam – śrī madhusūdanīya-śikṣāntargatam, śrī satyavratavyākhyā-sahitam*. It consists of only 45 verses with the commentary thereon and runs up to the section on *jaṭā*. The last eight verses (and the commentary thereon) dealing with the other varieties of recitation are omitted. The editor of the Srirangam edition says in his preface in Sanskrit that about the author Madhusūdana and the

---

55 (Bhagavatsinghji & H. M. Bhadkamkar Collection). – Bombay : University of Bombay, 1944. Book II, p. 592.

56 *Notices of Sanskrit MSS.* by Rajendralal Mitra, vol. IV. – Calcutta, 1878, p. 88.

57 K[rishnarajapuram] S[ubbaratna] Venkatarama Sastri. – Srirangam : Vani Vilas Press, 1964.

commentator Satyavrata nothing is known, as is the case with most Indian authors. The booklet contains two letters of blessings by two famous heads of religious Maṭha-s. and two more letters of appreciation by well-known Vedic scholars commending the editor's efforts to bring out the edition of a rare text. Obviously, no one seems to have realised that this edition is a reprint of the publication by Satyavrata Samasrami printed in Calcutta in the Sanskrit journal, *Uṣā*, in 1889 under the title: *Aṣṭavikṛtivivṛtiḥ* – (*vedāṅgam*) *Madhusūdanamunikṛtā*. It is accompanied by an introduction in Sanskrit, *atha luptakalpa-vedāṅgam*, which was also reprinted by Venkatarama Sastri in 1966 under the different title *Ṛgvedaghanasāra*.

Interestingly, the same text and the commentary published by Satyavrata Samasrami has been reprinted with some additional notes in Sanskrit in the Mysore Sanskrit College magazine *Śrīmanmahārāja Saṃskṛta Mahāpāṭhaśālā Patrikā*, (vol. 23-26) in the years 1947-50 under the title *Vyāḷiśikṣā*.[58] The editor, Kesavasiva Ghanapathi, says in the beginning that, although the work is also known as the *Madhusūdanaśikṣā*, Madhusūdana is only a compiler, the actual name of the original author is Vyāḍi. In the preface the editor acknowledges that the work was previously printed in Calcutta. Thus we have a single text printed under four different titles and varying sub-titles with all the confusion accompanying it.

The case is similar with respect to the text of the *Jaṭāpaṭala* ascribed to Hayagrīva. In Devasthali's collection (*Hayagrīvakṛtaṃ Jaṭāpaṭalam*) it is printed with the sub-title : *Hayagrīvīśikṣā*.[59] Here the text is based on a single manuscript and there are two commentaries, each based on three manuscripts. Both the text and one of the commentaries were published in Leipzig in 1870 with a German translation by George Thibaut. In the introduction Thibaut noted that in one of the three manuscripts he used from the Berlin Library the colophon read: *Hayagrīvaproktaṃ Jaṭāpaṭalam* and the last verse of the text has the word *acala* in a corrupted form. V. Raghavan, who recorded over 25 manuscripts of this text in the *New Catalogus Catalogorum*, comments under Acalācārya :

> In Thibaut's edn., in BBRAS. 490 and PUL. I., p.6, the ms. has a verse in the end ascribing the text to one Acala; in the other mss., without the last verse, this text on Jaṭā is ascribed to Hayagrīva and accompanied by an an. C. See BBRAS. 489. L. 1234. Weber 369.
> In the PUL. ms. however, the reference to Hayagrīva as the author is absent. (It reads instead:)
> *ayaṃ prakāra uttamo 'nādiś ceti sarveṣām ācāryāṇāṃ matam* |
> *idaṃ jaṭāpāṭha . . .* || *iti śrī acalācāryakṛtaṃ jaṭāpaṭalaṃ samāptam* |

---

58 Devasthali does not seem to know of this publication since he mentions only Samasrami's edition, though he could not utilise it.

59 Cf. *op. cit.*, p. 47.

> Cf. Dr. Thibaut's edn. and BBRAS. 490.
> In BBRAS. 490, the verse does not have a reading mentioning Acala : *mahattamānusmuratajvalena* | Thibaut and PUL. read – *-tācalena.*
> TCD. 34 J same text with C. and without the additional verse, is ascribed in the colophon to Vyāḍi; so also in Cs. I. 35 and 37, where, however, the name *Vikṛtivallī* is given to the text.

Raghavan further gives more details of manuscripts in which the variations of the titles and of the ascription occur. At the end he remarks: "The name of the a. Acala is entirely dependent on this verse which has so many confusing readings" (and in some manuscripts is completely missing).[60]

The unsatisfactory state of the printed editions is more evident from the recent publication of a work called *Kriyā-svara-lakṣaṇa* also known as the *Yohi-bhāṣya* of Sūru Bhaṭṭa.[61] This work in 23 verses deals with the changes in the accent of verbs caused by their being compounded with prepositions or being in conjunction with *yat*, etc., in the *Taittirīya Saṃhitā.* Over 40 manuscripts of this work are known to exist.[62] The editor of the text has made use of altogether nine manuscripts. The basic MS (K) of the edition is obviously mixed with extraneous material. But the editor did not realise this. On close perusal of the the text as printed here it becomes clear that folios of three different texts are mixed together in the basic MS. Thus only pp. 1-10, 17-27 and 86-128 are parts of the *Kriyā-svara-lakṣaṇa.* The rest is portions of *Avarṇi* (pp. 11-16, 28-56, 85) and *Āvarṇi* (pp. 57-84). Other manuscripts, including those of India Office, Madras and Mysore, collated for this edition do not contain these extraneous portions.

6. The Method Followed in the Bibliography

In view of the importance of this vast material for the study of Vedic texts and the unsatisfactory nature of the information about the *Veda-lakṣaṇa* texts, I have attempted to compile this annotated bibliography of *Veda-lakṣaṇa* literature. I have begun to prepare a consolidated list of all the works known so far, with brief descriptions of the contents of these works, recording the availability of manuscript material in different libraries. The preliminary list, mainly based on the *Catalogus Catalogorum*

---

60 *New Catalogus Catalogorum.* – Madras : University of Madras, vol. I, (revised ed.) 1969, p. 70.

61 *Kriyā Svara Lakṣaṇaṃ or Yohi Bhāṣyam*, ed. by Pullela Sri Ramachandrudu. – Hyderabad : Osmania University, 1983. xviii, 128, xxiv pp. – (Sanskrit Academy Series 30).

62 See below in the descriptive bibliography under *Kriyā-svara-lakṣaṇa* and *Yohi-prāpti(-śikṣā) or Yohi-bhāṣya.*

of Theodor Aufrecht, *New Catalogus Catalogorum* (which is yet to be completed), and other descriptive catalogues of manuscripts clearly indicates the usual phenomenon with respect to Indian manuscripts: one and the same text appearing with different titles attributed to different authors and vice versa. Moreover, several titles are obviously parts of, or extracts from larger works. There are also manuscripts in which a number of works are mixed up together and appear with the colophon of a single work (e.g. MD. 958; CD.34J). This could be due to the fact that these are very short tracts and the copyists or the reciters themselves copied together whatever they found useful. One of the most important but difficult tasks in preparing this bibliography is to verify and distinguish the similar or identical titles on the same topic. For example, the *New Catalogus Catalogorum* (vol. VII, pp. 145 ff.) records more than 300 manuscripts on the mode of recitation called *jaṭā*. These include six different entries of *Jaṭālakṣaṇa* and five of *Jaṭāpaṭala*, with their commentaries and sub-commentaries. There are also the *Jaṭādarpaṇa*, *Jaṭānyāya* (*-pañcāśat*), *Jaṭāmaṇi*, etc. These and many more similar entries do not necessarily represent so many different works. Only through a careful examination and differentiation can one get a clear picture. The number of titles collected up to now is about 1650; most of these texts remain so far unpublished.

The method of description in this bibliography is broadly as follows:

1. Each entry of the title of a text is numbered serially. Entries with asterisks, but without a serial number, refer to authors (about 225 entries). If manuscripts of one and the same work are found with different titles in different catalogues, they are brought together under one main title, one which is generally accepted and easily recognizable. The variant titles are given as they are found in the catalogues with a cross reference to the main title (e.g., Atharva-veda-śikṣā → Māṇḍūkī-śikṣā; Ṛkpādānukramaṇikā Śaunakīyā → Pāda-vidhāna of Śaunaka).

2. If the author of a work is known, his name is given immediately after the title. Most of the titles are followed by a brief description of the nature of the work and its contents. However, in many cases this was not possible as no manuscript was accessible.

3. The extracts of the beginning and end, particularly from the unpublished texts (often with unintelligible readings), are given as they are found in the catalogues, or in the printed edition in the case of a printed work. This should facilitate the identification of the text.

4. The details of available manuscripts from the respective descriptive catalogues or alphabetical lists of various public libraries have been given. Such details include the serial number in the catalogue, the accession number, shelf-marks, or call-number of the library, the material (e.g. PL = Palm-leaf), only if it is not paper; the script (Gr., Mal., Na., Tel., Śāradā, etc.), only if it is other than Devanāgarī; the extent of the manuscript, either in the number of pages (pp.) or folios (fol.) or in the number of Grantha-s (units of 32 sylla-

bles). Further details, such as the date of the manuscript, the copyist, the previous owner, etc., are given whenever they are found in the catalogue. In doubtful cases, every attempt has been made to verify the details of the original manuscripts wherever they are accessible. For this purpose I have visited over 35 manuscript libraries in India and in Europe. I was able to examine and record a number of uncatalogued manuscripts in the public libraries and also some in private possession.

5. References to the printed editions (Ptd.) include, besides the usual bibliographical details, particulars concerning the availability of a copy of the book, e.g. the accession number, shelf-marks or call-number of a public library (given in square brackets). Such references are thought to be helpful, particularly in the case of rare publications such as the *Lakṣaṇa-traya*, *Chalaprakriyā*, *Ṣaḍviṃśati-sūtra.*

6. References to the volume, pages and columns of the *New Catalogus Catalogorum* (NCC), or the *Catalogus Catalogorum* (CC) are given within square brackets at the end of each entry. They are aligned to the right-hand margin.

The Appendix at the end contains a Verse Index in Devanāgarī script of metrical passages in the extracts cited from the beginning and end of the works described. The illegible or seamingly unintelligible or corrupt readings of manuscripts have been left without any attempt of emendation since that is the task of text editing rather than the bibliography.[63] Abbreviations are generally as in the CC and NCC. Details thereof, with special reference to *An Annotated Bibliography of the Catalogues of Indian Manuscripts* by Klaus L. Janert, are given separately in "Abbreviations with Bibliographical Notes". This contains information also on additional catalogues not included in the CC or NCC, together with their abbreviations. In compiling this bibliography, I have been benefited from the knowledge of Vedic texts that I acquired while learning in the traditional manner. Moreover, the practical experience in handling Sanskrit manuscripts that I gained at the Adyar Library and Research Centre, Madras, has proven to be of immense help. Similarly, I have drawn upon my experience in preparing descriptive catalogues of Sanskrit manuscripts and editing Sanskrit texts, and upon my familiarity with the various scripts, e.g. Grantha, Kannada, Malayalam, Telugu, Nandināgarī, in which most of the South Indian manuscripts are written.

---

[63] The computer programme for the font face of this script has been especially developed in the Computer Centre of Heidelberg University. This has been possible only through the untiring and constant support of Mr. E. Dietrich, Mr. J. Wilhelm, and Mr. J. Walsdorf of the Universitätsrechenzentrum, and my collegues, Th. Malten and Th. Lehmann at the South Asia Institute. I wish to express my sincere thanks to them all.

I intend to take up the work of editing the following (mostly unpublished) *Śikṣā-s*:

Amoghānandinī-śikṣā
Ātreya-śikṣā
Āraṇya-(ka-)śikṣā Savyākhyā
Kālanirṇaya-śikṣā Savyākhyā
Kauśikī-śikṣā
Cārāyaṇīya-śikṣā
Pāriśikṣā Savyākhyā
Yohi-prāpti(-śikṣā)
Lakṣmīkānta-śikṣā
Laugākṣi-śikṣā
Varṇa-krama-śikṣā
Vāsiṣṭhī-śikṣā (1)
Vāsiṣṭhī-śikṣā (2)
Śambhu-śikṣā
Śikṣā-samuccaya
Sarva-sammata-śikṣā Savyākhyā
Siddhānta-śikṣā Savyākhyā
Svara-vyañjana-śikṣā

7. Acknowledgements

Thankful acknowledgements are due to the German Research Council (Deutsche Forschungsgemeinschaft) and the South Asia Institute of the University of Heidelberg for the generous travel grants that enabled me to visit various manuscript libraries in India as well in Europe in order to collect material for this bibliography. During these visits I was able to consult several specialists on the subject and to clarify many difficult problems of *Veda-lakṣaṇa* literature.

I am indebted to the authorities and staff members of the following Institutions for their willingness to help and co-operate : Adyar Library and Research Centre, Govt. Oriental Manuscripts Library, New Catalogus Catalogorum Office, the Kuppuswami Sastri Research Institute, Madras; Saraswati Mahal Library, Thanjavur; Oriental Research Institute and Manuscripts Library, Trivandrum; Oriental Research Institute, University of Mysore, Mysore; Oriental Research Institute of Sri Venkateswara University, Tirupati; Oriental Institute, M. S. University, Baroda; Asiatic Society of Bombay, Library of the University of Bombay, Bombay; Banaras Hindu University Library, Sarasvati Bhavana Library of Sampurnanand Sanskrit Vishvavidyalaya, Varanasi; Ganganatha Jha Kendriya Sanskrit Vidyapeetha, Allahabad; Calcutta Sanskrit College, the Asiatic Society, National Library, Sanskrit Sahitya Parishat, Calcutta; Anandashrama Pustakalaya, Bhandarkar Oriental Research Institute, Bharata Itihasa Samshodhaka Mandala, Deccan College Postgraduate and Research Institute, Vaidika Samshodhana Mandala, Poona; Prajna Pathashala Mandala, Wai (Satara Dist.); Staatsbibliothek Preußischer Kulturbesitz, Berlin; Staats- und Universitätsbibliothek, Göttingen; Staats- und Universitätsbibliothek, Hamburg; Bayerische Staatsbibliothek, München; Universitätsbibliothek, Tübingen; Indian Institute Library in the Bodleian Library, Oxford; India Office Library, Library of the School of Oriental and African Studies, Royal Asiatic Society, Wellcome Institute for the History of Medicine, London.

ABBREVIATIONS WITH BIBLIOGRAPHICAL NOTES

I. Catalogues of Manuscripts

Most of the abbreviations in this list are the same as in the CC and NCC. However, there are a few changes (e.g. Cs. = Calcutta Skt. Coll.) and the inclusion of some additional catalogues that the NCC has not taken into account (e.g. GJKSV, Hoshiarpur). Detailed bibliographical information, particularly on older catalogues, can be found in the ABC, reference to which is given (in parentheses) at the end of an entry, aligned with the right-hand margin. References in square brackets are to the identification marks (call numbers, shelf-marks, accession numbers or "Signatur") of the libraries where the particular item can be consulted. This information would be useful paricularly in the case of out of print catalogues and books.

ABC

An Annotated Bibliography of the Catalogue of Indian Manuscripts / by Klaus Ludwig Janert. Part I. – Wiesbaden : Steiner, 1965. 175 pp. – (Verzeichnis der Orientalischen Handschriften in Deutschland, Supplementband 1)
[Adyar (A080 VOH Sup); SAI (inf 25 I 10); UBHD (HS 4R 14); IIO (8 E 56/1); SOAS (Ref. KC. 016.091/187865)]

Adyar

Alphabetical Index of Sanskrit Manuscripts in the Adyar Library / by V. Krishnamacharya, under the Supervision of C[hittanjore] Kunhan Raja. – (Madras:) The Adyar Library, 1944. vi, 210 pp. – (The Adyar Library Series 45)
(Without reference to parts or pages, it refers to manuscripts in the Adyar Library that were added subsequent to the publication of Part II of the two-volume catalogue noted below.)
[Adyar (H080 ALS 45); SAI (ind S 1, 45); SKGI (Pa III 204); IIO (8 E 2c); SOAS (Ref. KC. 016.091/49947)]

(ABC 192)

Adyar I or II

A Catalogue of the Sanskrit Manuscripts in the Adyar Library / by the Pandits of the Library. – (Madras :) Adyar Library (Theosophical Society). – (The Adyar Library Series 11)

Part I. – 1926. xii, 252, v pp.

Part II. – 1928. xv, 242, xiii pp.

(Quoted by parts and pages. To facilitate easy verification, these entries together with the former shelf-marks of the library are identified with the corresponding serial numbers of the Descriptive Catalogue [Adyar D] and the new call numbers [accession numbers in six digits] of the library.)

[Adyar (H080 ALS 11); SAI (inf 25 I 29); IIO (8 E 2a); SOAS (Ref. KC. 016.091/52347)]

(ABC 190)

Adyar D

Descriptive Catalogue of Sanskrit Manuscripts in the Adyar Library. – (Madras :) The Adyar Library (and Research Centre).

Vol. I : Vedic / by K. Madhava Krishna Sarma, under the Supervision of C. Kunhan Raja. – 1942. xxxvi, 415 pp. (Mss. 1-1103). – (The Adyar Library Series 35)

(ABC 191)

Vol. XIII. : Viśvabhāratī Collection / compiled by E[lapully] R[amaswami] Sreekrishna Sarma. 1976. – (The Adyar Library Series 103)

Part 1 : xvi, 621 pp.

(Description, in tabular columns, of 2730 manuscripts)

Part 2 : 451 pp. Appendix.

(With extracts from rare and important works)

[Adyar (H080 ALS 35, 103); SAI (ind S 1, 35; 103); SKGI (Pa III 203); IIO (8 E 2/1; 13); SOAS (Ref. KC. 016.091/52365)]

Ahmedabad

A hand-list of 409 manuscripts in the Gujarat Vidyāpīṭh Granthālaya, Ahmedabad (as in the NCC).

AK

Report on the Search for Sanskrit Manuscripts in the Bombay Presidency during the years 1891-92, 1892-93, 1893-94 and 1894-95 / by Abaji Vishnu Kathavate. – Bombay : Govt. Central Press, 1901. 21, 121 pp. [= BORI . . . of 1891-95].

[Adyar (H020 BG R 1.2); UBTÜ (Ci XII 407a / SLS = Orient allg A 422); SKGI (Pa II 50); IIO (8 C 3c)]

(ABC 273.7)

Alph. List Beng. Govt.

"An Alphabetical Index of MSS. Purchased upto 1891", printed at the end of *Notices of Sanskrit Manuscripts* (cf. L. below), vol. XI. – (Calcutta : Baptist Mission Press, 1895.) 138, 3 pp. Many manuscripts in this Index are described in the volumes of *A Descriptive Catalogue of Sanskrit Manuscripts in the Government Collection*, by Haraprasad Shastri (cf. RASB below), and in tabular form in ASB.

(ABC 219.11)

Alwar

Catalogue of the Sanskrit Manuscripts in the Library of His Highness the Maharaja of Ulwar [Alwar] / by Peter Peterson. – Bombay : (Times of India Press), 1892. 2, 101, 261 pp.

[BUL (016.091 Sa U/W Pet – 5833); IIO (82 E 3)]

(ABC 323)

America

A Census of Indic Manuscripts in the United States and Canada / compiled by Horace I. Poleman. – New Haven, Connecticut : American Oriental Society, 1938. xxix, 542 pp. – (American Oriental Series 12)
Reprint: New York : Kraus Reprint Corporation, 1967.
[Adyar (A080 AOS 12); SAI (ind S 2, 12); IIO (8 D 17)]

(ABC 328)

Ānandāśrama

A hand-list of 8518 manuscripts in the Ānandāśrama, Poona. Numbering slightly irregular in places. Quoted by library numbers (as in the NCC).

ASB

A Catalogue of Sanskrit Manuscripts in the Library [Collections] of the Asiatic Society [the Indian Museum and the Asiatic Society Collection] / compiled by Narendra Chandra Vedantatirtha and [partially] revised by Pulinabihari Chakravarthy [with the Assistance of Amitabha Bhattacharya]. – Calcutta : Asiatic Society.

Vol. I : Vedic Texts (Manuscripts):

Part 1 : Vedic Texts. – 1978. 153 pp.

(Curiously, only a single incomplete copy of this part is found in the Manuscript Section of the Asiatic Society, Calcutta. No other copy has been found anywhere else.)

Part 2 : Vedic Manuscripts. – 1971. 423 pp.

[SKGI (Pa III 201)]

Part 3 : Vedic Manuscripts. – 1973. 217 pp. (Mss. 1-747).

[Adyar (H091C RAS Be); SAI (inf 25 I 38); SOAS (Ref. KC. 016/299879)]

AU

A hand-list of manuscripts in the Andhra University Library, Waltair (as in the NCC).

B

A Catalogue of Sanskrit Manuscripts contained in the Private Libraries of Gujarāt, Kāṭhiāvāḍ, Kachchh, Sindh and Khāndeś / compiled under the superintendence of Georg Bühler. – Bombay : "Indu-Prakaśa" Press.

Fasc. I : Vedic Literature. – 1871. ix, 245 pp.

[Adyar (H020 IG 1); IIO (8 B 21); SOAS (Ref. KC. 016.091/6400)]

(ABC 108.1)

BA

Report on Sanskrit Manuscripts, 1974-75 / by Georg Bühler. – [Girgaum : Indu-Prakash Press, 1875.] 21 pp. [= BORI . . . of 1874-75].

(ABC 268)

Baroda

An Alphabetical List of Manuscripts in the Oriental Institute, Baroda / compiled by Raghavan Nambiyar. – Baroda : Oriental Institute. – (Gaekwad's Oriental Series 97)

Vol. I. – 1942. viii, 741 pp.

(Classified alphabetical list of 7352 manuscripts in tabular form. Quoted by library numbers and combined with CLB. There are now over 26,000 manuscripts in the Library of which about 8000 are uncatalogued. Some of them are examined by me during a visit to the Library [August 5-10, 1988].)
[Adyar (H080 GOS 97); SAI (ind S 60, 97); SKGI (Pa III 209); SOAS (Ref. KC. 016.091/49774)]

(ABC 8)

BBRAS

A Descriptive Catalogue of Saṃskṛta and Prākṛta Manuscripts in the Library of the Bombay Branch of the Royal Asiatic Society [BBRAS] / compiled by H[ari] D[amodar] Velankar. – Bombay : BBRAS.; London : Arthur Probsthain.

Vol. I. – 1926. 147 pp. (Mss. 1-434).

Vol. II. – 1928. 4, 149-379 pp. (Mss. 435-1382).

[Adyar (H020 ASB D); SAI (inf 25 I 14); SKGI (Pa III 230); IIO (8 E 43); SOAS (Ref. KC. 016.091/21918)]

(ABC 33)

Bd.

Report on the Search for Sanskrit Manuscripts in the Bombay Presidency during the years 1887-88, 1888-89, 1889-90 and 1890-91 / by Ramkrishna Gopal Bhandarkar. – Bombay : Govt. Central Press, 1897. 114, xci pp. [= BORI . . . of 1887-91].
[UBTÜ (20 A 3400); SKGI (Pa II 50); IIO (8 C 3d); SOAS (Ref. KC. 016.091/1910)]

(ABC 273.6)

Ben.

Rājakīya vārāṇasī vidyāmandira sarasvatībhavana-vartti-pustakānāṃ Sūcī-patram (Catalogue of Manuscripts in the Sarasvatī Bhavana Library of the Benares Sanskrit College), in : *The Pandit* (Benares). Supplement to vols. 3-10 (1869-75). cclxi pp. [IIO (Per. 10 d. 42 / 56)]

(ABC 13)

Berlin StB-PrK
Staatsbibliothek Preußischer Kulturbesitz in Berlin.

Bh.

A Report on 122 Manuscripts by Ramkrishna Gopal Bhandarkar, dated Bombay, 7th July 1880. – Bombay : Govt. Central Press, 1880. 37 pp. [= BORI . . . of A 1879-80].
[Adyar (H020 BG R 3); IIO (82 F 11); SOAS (Ref. KC. 016.091/1910)]
(ABC 272)

Bhau Dāji

Catalogue of Manuscripts and Books belonging to the Bhau Dāji Memorial (Collection in the Bombay Branch of the Royal Asiatic Society), prepared under the superintendence of . . . Vishvanāth Nārāyan Mandlik and Ardaseer Framjee Moos. – Bombay : Education Society's Press, 1882. 147, clx pp.
(ABC 31)

Bhk.

A Report on the Search for Sanskrit Manuscripts in the Bombay Presidency during the year 1881-82 / by Ramkrishna Gopal Bhandarkar, dated Poona, 1st June 1882. – Bombay : Govt. Central Press, 1882. 39 pp. [= BORI . . . of A 1881-82].
[Adyar (H020 BG R 3)]
(ABC 273.2)

Bhr.

Report on the Search for Sanskrit MSS. in the Bombay Presidency during the year 1882-83 / by Ramkrishna Gopal Bhandarkar, dated 6th September 1883. – Bombay : Govt. Central Press, 1884. 229 pp. [= BORI . . . of 1882-83].
[SKGI (Pa II 50); IIO (8 F 11/ (8); 8 C 3a); SOAS (Ref. KC. 016.091/1910)]
(ABC 273.3)

BHU

Descriptive Catalogue of Sanskrit Manuscripts in Gaekwada Library, Bhārat Kalā Bhavana and Samskrit Mahāvidyālaya Library of Banaras Hindu University / by Ramā Śaṅkar Tripāṭhī. – Banaras : Hindu University, 1971. x, 1099 pp. – (Banaras Hindu University Sanskrit Series VI)
[BUL (016.191 Sa BHU/Tri – 292514); SAI (***)]

Bik.

A Catalogue of Sanskrit Manuscripts in the Library of His Highness the Mahārāja of Bikāner / compiled by Rajendralala Mitra. – Calcutta : Baptist Mission Press, 1880. x, 745 pp. (1547 Mss.).
[Adyar (H020 RG B1); UBTÜ (Ci XII 409 / SLS = Orient allg A 429); SKGI (Pa III 220); SOAS (Ref. KC. 016.091/4524 + 6414)]
(ABC 30)

Bikaner

Catalogue of the Anup Sanskrit Library (housed in the Bikaner Fort) / prepared by C. Kunhan Raja and K. Madhava Krishna Sarma. – Bikaner : (Govt. Press), 1944-48. iv, 500 pp. (6682 Mss.)

(Five fascicules, each in 100 pages, with continued pagination. Numbers not in the printed Catalogue refer to a hand-list prepared by C. Kunhan Raja.)

[UBTÜ (Ci XII 134 4'); IIO (8 F 36); SOAS (Ref. KC. 016.091/48860)]

(ABC 28)

BISM

Bhārata Itihāsa Saṃśodhaka Maṇḍalastha Hastalikhita-granthānukramaṇikā / prepared by Ganesh Hari Khare. – Poona : Aryabhushana Press, 1960. ka-ta, 348 pp.

(This catalogue is an one-line list of about 18,000 Mss. A few entries without page numbers are as given in the NCC based on two lists of Sanskrit manuscripts copied from the card-index of the library. Supplemented by means of the examination of some of the codices.)

[Adyar (H091C BIS A1960); SAI (inf 25 I 30); IIO (8 D 26); SOAS (Ref. KC. 016.091/144413)]

(ABC 266)

Bombay 1879-82

Lists of Sanskrit Manuscripts Collected for the Government of Bombay in 1879-80 and 1881-82 / (by Franz Kielhorn; no place, no date). 13 pp.

(Originally published in the Nāgarī characters and in the Sanskrit language).

[= BORI . . . of 1879-80 and BORI . . . of 1881-82].

[Adyar (H020 BG R 3)]

(ABC 271)

Bomb. Uni.

A Descriptive Catalogue of the Saṃskṛta and Prākṛta Manuscripts (Bhagavatsinghji & H. M. Bhadkamkar Collection) in the Library of the University of Bombay / compiled by G[ovind] V[inayak] Devasthali. – Bombay : University of Bombay, 1944.

Book I : (vols. I & II, pts. I-III). 9, 496 pp.

Book II : (vol. II. pts. IV-VII & vols. III and IV). Pp. 497-877.

[SAI (inf 25 I 33); IIO (8 F 3); SKGI (Pa III 480); SOAS (Ref. KC. 016.091/50256)]

(There are more than 7500 Sanskrit manuscripts in the library; for the nearly 3000 uncatalogued manuscripts only index cards are available. In addition, 181 palm-leaf manuscripts in Grantha script remain uncatalogued. I examined most of the Veda-lakṣaṇa titles from the uncatalogued manuscripts [August 10-15, 1988] and have included them in this bibliography with their accession numbers.)

(ABC 37)

Bomb. Uni. (Itcharam)

A Descriptive Catalogue of the Sanskrit Manuscripts in "the Itchāram Suryarām Desāi Collection" in the Library of the University of Bombay / compiled by H[ari] D[amodar] Velankar. – Bombay : University of Bombay, 1953. 340 pp.

[SAI (inf 25 I 33); SKGI (Pa III 228); SOAS (Ref. KC. 016.091/99285)]

(ABC 38)

Bomb. Uni. (Moropant)

A Descriptive Catalogue of the Sanskrit Manuscripts in the Moropant Collection in the Library of the University of Bombay / compiled by Usha R. Bhise (Centinary Publication). – Bombay : University of Bombay.

Vol. I. – 1981. xv, 307, xxiv pp.

[Adyar (H091C BUL MC)]

BORI

Bhandarkar Oriental Research Institute, Poona. Shelf-marks or call numbers of the manuscripts in the library indicate the year of collection (e.g. 5 of 1875-76, 56 of A 1881-82). Details of these collections, originally published at different times and in different catalogues (cf. AK, BA, Bd, Bh, Bhk, Bhr, BP, Kh, P, Peters. Rgb.), are included in the consolidated catalogues (cf. D, and BORI. List). Some of the Veda-lakṣaṇa manuscripts from these collections are described in BORI. D.I.i. The entries in the NCC are based on a copy (prepared in 1940) of the card index of the library. A number of manuscripts, particularly those which are not included in the BORI. D.I.i, have been consulted for verification.

BORI. D

Descriptive Catalogue of the Government Collections of Manuscripts, deposited at the Deccan College, Poona / compiled by the Assistant to the Professor of Sanskrit, Deccan College Poona. – Bombay : Govt. of Bombay.

Vol. I : Vedic Literature. Part 1: Saṃhitās and Brāhmaṇas / by Shripad Krishna Belvalkar. – 1916. xlv, 420 pp. (nos. 1-566).

(Supplemented by means of the examination of some of the codices. The manuscripts are now in the Bhandarkar Oriental Research Institute, Poona.)

[Adyar (H091C BORI D I.1); SAI (inf 25 I 37,1); IIO (8 E 36/1); SOAS (Ref. K. 016.091/59300)]

(ABC 264.1)

BORI. List

Lists of Manuscripts Collected for the Government Manuscripts Library by the Professors of Sanskrit at the Deccan and Elphinstone Colleges, since 1895 and 1899 / compiled by the Manuscripts Department of the Bhandarkar Oriental Research Institute. – Poona : BORI, 1925. v, 94 pp.

[Adyar (H020 BOR I); SAI (inf 25 I 68); UBTÜ (Ci XII 399a / SLS = Orient allg A 3720); SKGI (Pa III 362); IIO (82 C 8); SOAS (Ref. KC.

016.091/17916)]

(ABC 265)

BORI. TM

A hand-list of about 390 manuscripts of Sri Trymbaka Sastri (Manjul) collection, presented to and preserved in the BORI, Poona. There are more than 25 Veda-lakṣaṇa manuscripts in this collection. Most are related to the Kāṇva Śākhā of the VS.

BP

Report on the Search for Sanskrit Manuscripts in the Bombay Presidency during the year 1883-84 / by Ramkrishna Gopal Bhandarkar. – Bombay : Govt. Central Press, 1887. 479, viii pp. [= BORI . . . of 1883-84].
[Adyar (H020 BG R 1.1); SKGI (Pa II 50); IIO (8 C 3b); SOAS (Ref. KC. 016.091/1910)]

(ABC 273.4)

Brahmasva Maṭha

A hand-list of 168 manuscripts in the Brahmasva Maṭham, Trichur, Cochin, Kerala State (as in the NCC).

Brl.

Catalogue of a Collection of Sanskrit Manuscripts / by A[rthur] C[oke] Burnell. – London : Trübner.

Part I : Vedic Manuscripts. 1869 (1870 on the cover page). 65 pp.

(These manuscripts were presented to the India Office Library, London, and have been described in IO.)
[SAI (ind 50 D 85/1778); UBTÜ (Ci XII 508)]

(ABC 162)

Br. Mus.

A Catalogue of the Sanskrit Manuscripts in the British Museum / by Cecil Bendall. – London : (Gilbert and Rivington) 1902. vii, 261 pp. [IIO (8 E 6)]

(ABC 157)

Br. Mus. II

A Catalogue of Sanskrit and Prakrit Manuscripts in the British Museum, vol. II. / compiled by J[eremiah] P. Losty (typescript). – (London : 1972), vi, 70 ll. (A handlist of 763 items acquired 1898-1971, including all Jaina manuscripts of earlier collections).
[IIO (8 E 6/2); SOAS (Ref. KC. 016/51232 + 276225)]

Bühler

Two Lists of Sanskrit Manuscripts Together with Some Remarks on my Connection with the Search for Sanskrit Manuscripts / by Georg Bühler, in : *Zeitschrift der Deutschen Morgenländischen Gesellschaft*, vol. 42 (1888), pp.

530-559.

(321 manuscripts of this collection [list no. 1] were presented to the India Office Library, London. The second list containing details of 201 manuscripts was reprinted ["corrected and brought up to date"] in the BORI. List [pp. 87-92]. Most of the manuscripts of the latter list are now in the Bhandarkar Oriental Research Institute, Poona.)

(ABC 44)

Burnell

A Classified Index to the Sanskrit Manuscripts in the Palace at Tanjore / prepared for the Madras Government, by A[rthur] C[oke] Burnell. – London : Trübner, 1880. xii, 239 pp.

[Adyar (H020 TPL C1); UBHD (F 9428); SKGI (Pa III 450); IIO (8 F 31); SOAS (L. Ref. KC. 016.091/6401)]

(ABC 306)

Cabaton

Catalogue sommaire des manuscrits Sanscrits et Pālis, par A[ntoine] Cabaton. Bibliotheque nationale, Departement des Manuscrits. – Paris : Leroux.

Fasc. I : Manuscrits Sanscrits. 1907. 189 pp.

[SOAS (Ref. KC. 016.091/14504)]

(ABC 252)

Calcutta Skt. College

A Descriptive Catalogue of Sanskrit Manuscripts in the Library of the Calcutta Sanskrit College. – Calcutta : Baptist Mission Press.

Vol. I : Vedic Manuscripts / by Hṛṣīkeśa Śāstrī and Śiva Chandra Gui. – 1895. v, 392 pp. (Mss. 1-643).

[Adyar (H020 CSC D.1); SAI (inf 25 I 21,1); SKGI (Pa III 235); IIO (8 D 3); SOAS (Ref. KC. 016.091/1896)]

(ABC 55.1)

Cambr.

A Catalogue of Sanskrit Manuscripts in the Library of Trinity College, Cambridge / by Theodor Aufrecht. – Cambridge : Deighton, Bell (etc.), 1869. viii, 111 pp.

[Adyar (H020 CTC 1); SOAS (Ref. KC. 016.091/6397)]

(ABC 60)

CC

Catalogus Catalogorum : An Alphabetical Register of Sanskrit Works and Authors / by Theodor Aufrecht. Parts (1)-3. – Leipzig : Brockhaus (Part 3: Harrassowitz).

Part I. – 1891. VIII, 795 pp.

(Additions and Corrections : pp. 770-95).

Part II. – 1896. IV, 239 pp.

(Appendix and Corrections : pp. 185-239).

Part III. – 1903. IV, 161 pp.

(Additions and Corrections : 160-61).

Reprint: Wiesbaden : Steiner Verlag, 1962.

[Adyar (H020 Auf C 1-3); SAI (inf 63 P 2); IIO (8 E 17); SOAS (Ref. KC. 016.091/7747 + 164810)]

(ABC 6)

CLB

A Descriptive Catalogue of Manuscripts in the Central Library, Baroda. – Baroda : Central Library. – (Gaekwad's Oriental Series 27)

Vol. I : Vedic / compiled by Gajanan K. Shrigondekar and K. S. Ramaswamy Sastri. – 1925. xxvii, 264 pp.

(With an appendix of extracts from some manuscripts. Quoted by page numbers, identified with the manuscript numbers of the Alphabetical List [see above Baroda] and entered together.)

[Adyar (H080 GOS 27); SAI (ind S 60, 27); SKGI (Pa III 208); SOAS (Ref. KC. 016.091/18376)]

(ABC 7)

CPB

Catalogue of Sanskrit and Prakrit Manuscripts in the Central Provinces and Berar / by Rai Bahadur Hiralal. – Nagpur : Govt. Press, 1926. 2, 3, lv, 808, 8 pp.

[Adyar (H020 CP 1); UBHD (F 9426); SKGI (Pa II 630); IIO (82 C 101); SOAS (Ref. KC. 016.091/19598)]

(ABC 67)

CU. Add.

A section of Sanskrit manuscripts in the University Library, Cambridge (as in the NCC).

D

A Catalogue of the Collections of Manuscripts Deposited in the Deccan College, with an index / compiled by Shridhar R. Bhandarkar. – Bombay : Govt. Central Press, 1888. 3, 539 pp.

(This "consolidated catalogue" contains details of 19 collections originally published at different times and in different catalogues [cf. AK, BA, Bd, Bh, Bhk, Bhr, BP, Kh, P, Peters. Rgb]. Most of these manuscripts are now in the Bhandarkar Oriental Research Institute, Poona.)

[Adyar (H020 BG 1); SAI (inf 25 I 69); UBTÜ (Ci XII 399 / SLS = Orient allg A 428); SKGI (Pa III 360); SOAS (Ref. KC. 016.091/10489)]

(ABC 276)

Deccan College

Card-index in the Library of the Deccan College Postgraduate and Research Institute, Poona.

Deccan College (1964)

Catalogue of Sanskrit Manuscripts in the Deccan College Postgraduate and Research Institute, Poona. – Poona : Deccan College.

Vol. I : Veda Manuscripts / edited by Madhukar Anant Mehendale. – 1964. viii, 72 pp. – (Deccan College Monograph Series 28)

(Supplemented by means of the card catalogues in the library)

[Adyar (H080 DC); SAI (ind S 32, 28); IIO (8 A 1a)]

(ABC 278.1)

GB

Die Sanskrit-Handschriften (*der Universitäts-Bibliothek zu Göttingen*) [150 manuscripts] / beschrieben von Franz Kielhorn, in : Die Handschriften in Göttingen. Band 3. – Berlin : Bath, 1894. Pp. 416-62. Aus dem Verzeichnis der Handschriften im Preussischen Staate (Abteilung Hannover, Göttingen. Band 3). Reprinted in : Franz Kielhorn : *Kleine Schriften*, ed. by Wilhelm Rau. – Wiesbaden : Steiner Verlag, 1969, vol. II, pp. 936-82. – (Glasenapp Stiftung 3,2)

[SAI (ind 70 B 369); UBHD (HS 4R 5/ 1.3.3); SKGI (Pa III 40)]

(ABC 99)

GD

A Descriptive Catalogue of the Sanskrit Manuscripts in H. H. the Maharajah's Palace Library [Granthappura], Trivandrum / edited by K. Sambasiva Sastri. – Trivandrum : V. V. Press Branch.

Vol. I : Veda, Śrauta, Smṛti and Purāṇa. – 1937. xviii, 380 pp.

[Adyar (H020 TG PD 1); SAI (inf 25 I 76,1)]

(ABC 313.1)

GJKSV

Descriptive Catalogue of Sanskrit Manuscripts in Ganganatha Jha Research Institute (Kendriya Sanskrit Vidyapeetha), Allahabad. – Allahabad : GJKSV.

Vol. I, part 1 / edited by Umesha Mishra. – 1967. ix, 387 pp. (nos. 1-2098).

Vol. I, part 2 / edited by Umesha Mishra. – 1967. Pp. 388-929 (nos. 2099-4593).

Vol. II, part 1. – 1973. xi, 503 pp. (nos. 4594-7168).

Vol. II, part 2. – 1973. Pp. 504-1117 (nos. 7169-9591).

Vol. III / compiled by V[addagiri] Hanumanthacharya and Jeeveswara Jha. – 1975. xi, 528 pp. (nos. 9592-11778).

[Adyar (H091C GJR D 1-3); SAI (inf 25 I 63); SKGI (Pa III 222); IIO (8 D 41); SOAS (Ref. KC. 016.091/224403)]

(Of the more than 44,000 manuscripts only a few Veda-lakṣaṇa manuscripts have been included in these catalogues. A greater number of them are to be found in the four volumes of hand-lists [Accession Register of Manuscripts], meant for the internal use of the library, written as and when the manuscripts were acquired. They are yet to be verified and properly catalogued. The titles are only provisional. There are no classified catalogues or card indexes. There are about 250 manuscripts of Veda-lakṣaṇa in these Registers. I have verified several of them during my visits to the library in Allahabad [September 23-27, 1987 and August 29-30, 1988]. The four Registers contain):

Vol. I : Nos. 1 to 11,200 (most of them are included in the Descriptive Catalogues).

Vol. II : Nos. 11,201 to 23,884 (roughly classified and listed alphabetically, written 1974-82).

Vol. III : Nos. 23,885 (6.1.82) to 38,078 (27.8.84).

Vol. IV : Nos. 38,079 (27.8.84) to 44,238 (19.8.88).

Göttingen

Kielhorns Handschriften-Sammlung / von Richard Fick. – Berlin : Weidmannsche Buchhandlung, 1930. Pp. 65-94. – (Nachrichten von der Gesellschaft der Wissenschaften zu Göttingen, Philologisch-Historische Klasse, Fachgruppe 3. Nr. 1, 1930).
[SOAS (Ref. KC. 016.091/23811)]

(ABC 100)

Gough

Papers Relating to the Collection and Preservation of the Records of Ancient Sanskrit Literature in India / by Archibald Edward Gough. – Calcutta : Office of Superintendent of Govt. Printing, 1878. viii, 234 pp.
[Adyar (Rare 1878 Gou PR); UBTÜ (Ci XII 395); SOAS (Ref. KC. 091/6341)]

(ABC 104)

Govt. Or. Libr. Madras

Alphabetical Index of Manuscripts in the Government Oriental MSS. Library, Madras. – Madras : Govt. Press, 1893. Various paginations.
[Adyar (H020 MG A 1.1); SAI (inf 25 M 150); SKGI (Pa III 346)]

(ABC 197)

Govt. Or. Libr. Madras (1938-42)

An Alphabetical Index of Sanskrit Manuscripts in the Government Oriental Manuscripts Library, Madras / by S. Kuppuswami Sastri and P. P. Subrahmanya Sastri. 3 parts. – Madras : Govt. Press, 1938-42.
[Adyar (H020 MG A 1.1-3); SAI (inf 25 I 24)]

(ABC 208)

Granthappura

A Revised Catalogue of the Palace Granthappura (Library), Trivandrum / by K. Sambasiva Sastri. – Trivandrum : Govt. Press, 1929. 2, 226 pp.
(A list of manuscripts and printed books)
[Adyar (H020 TG P1); IIO (8 F 55)]

(ABC 315)

Hall

A Contribution Towards an Index to the Bibliography of the Indian Philosophical Systems / by Fitzedward Hall. – Calcutta : (Baptist Mission Press), 1859. ii, 236 pp.
[Adyar (H020 NWP 2); UBHD (F 8426); UBTÜ (Ci XII 112 / SLS = Orient allg A 410); IIO (8 B 18)]

(ABC 112)

Hamburg

A typed hand-list (called Raghavan 's List) of Indian manuscripts in the Staats- und Universitäts-Bibliothek, Hamburg.

1. A collection of Palm-leaf (Cod.Palmbl.) and a few paper manuscripts (altogether 77 codices), belonging to Gustav Oppert. List prepared by V. Raghavan, dated 04.10.54.
2. A list of 20 codices in a card board box (Sammlung Schrader). Also prepared by V. Raghavan, dated 04.10.54. (Only Purāṇa texts; no Veda-lakṣaṇa works).

The following three classified lists must also have been checked by V. Raghavan as there are remarks and corrections in his handwriting:

3. List I. : 200 Palm-leaf Mss. (nos. 1-200) and 11 paper Mss. (Cod. Orient).
4. List II. : 47 Palm-leaf Mss. (nos. 201-247).
5. List III. : 134 Palm-leaf Mss. (nos. 1-134).

A few Veda-lakṣaṇa manuscripts of these nearly 500 codices have been described in VOHD (II.1-9).

Harshe

A Descriptive Catalogue of Sanskrit Manuscripts of the Vinayak Mahadev Gorhe Collection / by R[amakrishna] G[anesh] Harshe. – Poona : Deccan College Postgraduate and Research Institute, 1942. 49 pp.
(With an appendix containing a consolidated list of manuscripts in possession of Messrs. Gaṅgādhara Rāmakṛṣṇa Dharmādhikārī, Śaṅkara Vināyaka Nidre and Śaṅkara Bālakṛṣṇa Lumpāṭhakī, of Puṇatāmbe, district Ahmednagar.)
[Adyar (H020 DC D1); IO (V 13502)]

(ABC 277)

Haug

Verzeichnis der Orientalischen Handschriften aus dem Nachlasse des Professor Dr. Martin Haug in München (/ von E. West u. Georg Orterer). – München : Ackermann, 1876. 47 [Nachtrag : + 6] pp.
(These manuscripts are now in the Bayerische Staatsbibliothek in München and described in its catalogue. See München below.)
[UBTÜ (Ci I 117 / SLS = Orient allg A 5460)]
(ABC 221)

Hoshiarpur

Catalogue of VVRI. Manuscript Collection in Two Parts, / by Vishva Bandhu with the assistance of Bhim Dev, Pitambar Datt, Padmanabh and other scholars. – Hoshiarpur : Vishveshvaranand Vedic Research Institute, 1959. – (Vishveshvaranand Indological Series 10, 11)

Part I : Classified Descriptive Tables. – xxviii, 436 pp.

Part II : Initial and Colophonal Extracts. – 2, 481 pp.

[Adyar (H080 VVRI I.10, 11); SAI (inf 25 I 64); SKGI (Pa III 214); SOAS (Ref. KC. 016.091/138885)]

Hoshiarpur (BRS)

Descriptive Catalogue of Manuscripts of the VVBISIS Collection, Panjab University / compiled by B. R. Sharma. – Hoshiarpur : Vishveshvaranand Vishva Bandhu Institute of Sanskrit and Indological Studies, 1975. xi, 130 pp. (Classified descriptive tables of 1736 manuscripts) [SAI (inf 25 I 65); IIO (8 D 37)]
(ABC 121)

Hpr.

Notices of Sanskrit MSS. (Deposited in Several Libraries), Second Series / by Haraprasad Shastri, published under orders of the Govt. of Bengal. – Calcutta : Baptist Mission Press.

1. – 1900. xl, 432 pp.
2. – 1904. xxii, 238 pp.
3. – 1907. xxiv, 258, 18 pp.
4. – 1911. 265 pp.

[SKGI (Pa I 20/2.1-3); IIO (8 D 2); SOAS (Ref. KC. 016.091/6424)]
(ABC 118)

Hz.

Reports on Sanskrit Manuscripts [*of private libraries*] in Southern India (published by order of the Govt. of Madras) / by E[ugen] Hultzsch. – Madras : Superintendent, Govt. Press (etc.).

1. – 1895. xi, 98 pp.
   (Classified list of Mss. nos. 1-663 and extracts).
2. – 1896. xviii, 161 pp.
   (Classified list of Mss. nos. 664-1563 and extracts).
3. – 1905. xii, 148 pp.

(Classified list of Mss. nos. 1564-2190 and extracts).
[Adyar (H020 MG Hul R 1-3); SAI (inf 25 I 46); UBTÜ (Ci XII 169a / SLS = Orient allg A 449); SKGI (Pa II 350); IIO (8 C 9a-c); SOAS (Ref. KC. 016.091/10492)]

(ABC 293)

IIO. Stein

Catalogue of the Stein Collection of Sanskrit MSS. from Kashmir (now deposited in the Indian Institute Library, Oxford), by Gerard L. M. Clauson (with an Introductory Note by Arthur A. Macdonell), in : *Journal of the Royal Asiatic Society of Great Britain and Ireland*, 1912. Pp. 587-627.
[Adyar (H020 OII 1)]

(ABC 244)

IM

A hand-list of the 11,286 Sanskrit manuscripts of the Indian Museum, Calcutta. These manuscripts, which originally belonged to the Archaeological Survey of India, are now in the possession of the Asiatic Society of Bengal, Calcutta. Some of these manuscripts are included in ASB. I.1-3. Most of the manuscripts of Veda-lakṣaṇa (numbering about 300), including the entries as given in the NCC, have been verified in the Library of the Asiatic Society, Calcutta (September 14-28, 1987).

IO

Catalogue of the Sanskrit [*vol. II. : and Prākṛt*] *Manuscripts* in the Library of the India Office. – London : Gilbert and Rivington [vol. II. : Oxford : Clarendon Press].

[Vol. I.] Part I: Vedic Manuscripts / by Julius Eggeling. – 1887. vi, 154 pp.

Vol. II : Brahmanical and Jaina Manuscripts / by Arthur Berriedale Keith. – 1935. Part 1. – x, 920 pp. Part 2. – Pp. 921-1851.

[Adyar (H091C IO); SAI (inf 25 I 5-6); UBHD (F 9017); SKGI (Pa III 65); IIO (8 E 18); SOAS (Ref. KC. 016.091/6406)]

(ABC 164)

Jammu RSRI

Descriptive Catalogue of [*vol. II : Sanskrit*] *Manuscripts* in the Shri Ranbir Sanskrit Research Institute, Jammu (Kashmir) / compiled by M[adhukar] M[angesh] Patkar. – Jammu : SRSR Institute.

Vol. I. – 1970. viii, 257 pp.

Vol. II. – 1973. iii, pp. 260-591.

[Adyar (H091C RSR D); SAI (inf 25 I 80); IIO (8 D 39)]

Jodhpur

A hand-list of 2046 manuscripts in the Archaeological Department of the Jodhpur State, Jodhpur (as in the NCC).

Jodhpur (R)

A Classified List of Manuscripts in the Rajasthan Oriental Research Institute / Jodhpur, by Gopala Narayana Bahura. – Jodhpur : Rajasthan Oriental Research Institute.

Vol. 1. – 1959. 2, 302, 19 pp.

Vol. 2. – 1960. 2, 391, 3 pp.

[SOAS 1: (Ref. K. 016/296068); 2: (Ref. KC. 016.091/253816)]

K

A Catalogue of Sanskrit MSS. Existing in the Central Provinces / edited by Franz Kielhorn. – Nagpur : Govt. Book Depot, 1874. 251 pp.

Title on the cover : *A Classified Alphabetical Catalogue of Sanskrit MSS. in the Central Provinces.*

[IIO (45 C 69); SOAS (Ref. KC. 016.091/6410)]

(ABC 65)

Kavīndrācārya

Kavīndrācārya-sūcīpatram : *Kavīndrācārya's List* / edited with an Introduction by R. Ananta Krishna Sastri. – Baroda : Central Library, 1921. xv, 3, 2, 34 pp. – (Gaekwad's Oriental Series 17)

(A list of the manuscripts that existed once in the Kavīndrācārya's Library [17th century] at Benares.)

[Adyar (H080 GOS 17); UBTÜ (Ci XII 627, Bd. 17 / SLS = Orient allg A 5555); SKGI (Pa I 60); SOAS (Ref. KC. 016.091/15096)]

(ABC 140)

Kh.

Report on the Search for Sanskrit MSS. in the Bombay Presidency during the year 1880-81 / by Franz Kielhorn. – Bombay : Govt. Central Book Depot, 1881. xiv, 103 pp. (Appendix, pp. 82-103 : Mss. collected in 1973-74). [= BORI . . . of 1880-81 and BORI . . . of 1873-74].

[UBHD (F 9427); IIO (82 C 12); SOAS (Ref. KC. 016.091/1910)]

(ABC 273.1)

Khn.

A Classified Alphabetical Catalogue of Sanskrit MSS. in the Southern Division of the Bombay Presidency / compiled by Franz Kielhorn. Fasc. 1. – Bombay : "Indu-Prakash" Press. 1869. 95 pp.

[Adyar (H020 BG 2); UBHD (F 9428); IIO (8 C 1); SOAS (Ref. KC. 016.091/6412)]

(ABC 39)

L

Notices of Sanskrit MSS. / by Rajendralala Mitra [volumes X and XI by Haraprasad Shastri], published under orders of the Government of Bengal. Vols. I - XI. – Calcutta : Baptist Mission Press, 1871-95.

(Many of the manuscripts listed in these volumes have again been described in RASB and also included in the tabular statement in ASB. Most of them are now in the library of the Asiatic Society, Calcutta.)
[Adyar (H020 BEG DN 1-11); SAI (inf 25 I 15); UBTÜ (Ci XII 392 / SLS = Orient allg A 425); SKGI (Pa I 20); IIO (8 D 1); SOAS (Ref. KC. 016.091/6424)]

(ABC 219)

Lahore

Catalogue of Newly Discovered, Rare and Old Manuscripts in the Lahore Division (for the year 1879/80) / by Kashi Nath Kunte. – Lahore : Punjab Govt. Press, 1881. 5, 23 pp.
[Adyar (H020 BG R 3); IO (P/W 182)]

(ABC 146-47)

Lucknow ABSP

A Catalogue of Manuscripts in the Akhila Bharatiya Sanskrit Parishad, Lucknow / edited by a Board of Directors and compiled by Daulat Ram Juyal. (Second Series). – Lucknow : ABSP, 1970. xiii, 274 pp.
[Adyar (H091C ABSP)]

Lucknow Mus.

Sanskrit manuscripts recently brought for the Lucknow Museum from Devakinandana Sharma, Satghata, Muttra. A printed list (as in the NCC).

Lz.

Katalog der Sanskrit-Handschriften der Universitäts-Bibliothek zu Leipzig / von Theodor Aufrecht. – Leipzig : Harrassowitz, 1901. vi, 493 pp. – (Katalog der Handschriften der Universitäts-Bibliothek zu Leipzig 1)
[Adyar (H020 Lei UI); UBHD (F 8740.9 = HS 5L 36); IIO (8 D 22)]

(ABC 149)

Mad. Uni. R.A.S.

A hand-list of a collection of 350 Sanskrit Manuscripts acquired for the Madras University by R. A. Sastri. In the Sanskrit Department, University of Madras (as in the NCC).

Mad. Uni. R.K.S.

A hand-list of 577 Sanskrit manuscripts of the late R. Krishnaswami Sastri, Sub-Registrar, Tanjore, acquired for the Madras University by R. A. Sastri. In the Sanskrit Department, University of Madras (as in the NCC).

Mandlik

A Catalogue of the Manuscripts in the Mandlik Library, Fergusson College, Poona (as in the NCC).

Mandlik Sup.

Supplementary list of the manuscripts in the Mandlik Library that were collected subsequent to the publication of the printed catalogue. A copy of the card-index in the library (as in the NCC).

Max Müller Mem.

A Catalogue of the Sanskrit Manuscripts, purchased for the Administraters of the Max Müller Memorial Fund / compiled by T. R. Gambier-Parry. – Oxford : Clarendon Press, 1922. iv, 62 pp. [IIO (8 C 20);

MD

A Descriptive Catalogue of the Sanskrit Manuscripts in the Government Oriental Manuscripts Library, Madras, prepared under the orders of the Govt. of Madras. – Madras : Superintendent, Govt. Press (etc.).

Vol. I : Vedic Literature:

Part 1 / by M. Seshagiri Sastri. – 1901. 110 pp. (nos. 1-46).

Part 2 / by M. Seshagiri Sastri and M[alur] Rangacharya. – 1904. Pp. i-iv, 106-278 (nos. 47-245).

Part 3 / by M. Seshagiri Sastri and M[alur] Rangacharya. – 1905. Pp. i-vii, 268-590, i-xvi (nos. 246-852).

Vol. II : Vedic Literature / by M[alur] Rangacharya. – 1905. Pp. i-viii, 592-906, i-xi (nos. 853-1245).

Vol. XXV-XXXV (Supplemental) / by S. Kuppuswami Sastri . . . [et al.]. – 1924-66.

[Adyar (H020 MG D 1-35); SAI (inf 25 I 24,1-35); UBTÜ (Ci XII 651 / SLS = Orient allg A 2820); IIO (82 C 1); SOAS (Ref. KC. 016.091/4979)]

(ABC 199)

Mithila

A Descriptive Catalogue of Manuscripts in Mithila. – Patna : The Bihar and Orissa Research Society.

Vol. IV : Vedic Mss. / by Ananta Prasad Banerji-Sastri. – 1940. 5, viii, 353, 7 pp.

[Adyar (H020 PBO D4); SAI (inf 25 I 27); IIO (8 C 7); SOAS (Ref. KC. 016.091/64771)]

(ABC 218.4)

MT

A Triennial Catalogue of Manuscripts Collected During the Triennium of . . . for the Government Oriental Manuscripts Library, Madras. – Madras : Superintendent, Govt. Press (etc.).

Vol. I / by M[alur] Rangacharya and S. Kuppuswami Sastri. – 1913 (3 parts).

Vol. II-V / by S. Kuppuswami Sastri. – 1917-1932 (each in 3 parts).

Vol. VI / by S. Kuppuswami Sastri. – 1935.

Vol. VII / by S. Kuppuswami Sastri and P. P. S[ubrahmanya] Sastri. – 1937.

Vol. VIII / by P. P. S. Sastri. – 1939.

Vol. IX / by P. P. S. Sastri and A[mbasamudram] Sankaran. – 1943.

Vol. X / by T[irukkalikundram] Chandrasekharan. – 1950, 1952, 1958 (3 parts).

Vol. XI / by T. Chandrasekharan. – 1958.

Vol. XII / by T. Chandrasekharan. – 1967.

Vol. XIII / by R. K. Parthasarathi – 1970.

[Adyar (H091C MGO T sk); SAI (inf 25 I 23); UBTÜ (Ci XII 651b); IIO (82 C 2); SOAS (Ref. KC. 016.091/2706)]

(ABC 201)

Müller

Catalogue of the late Prof. Fr. Max Müller's Sanskrit Manuscripts (82 codices used for the editing of the Ṛgveda) / compiled by Don M. de Z. Wickremasinghe, in : *Journal of the Royal Asiatic Society of Great Britain and Ireland* 1902. Pp. 611-651.

(These manuscripts were acquired for the University of Tokyo, but were reported to have been lost [burnt ?] during the war.)

(ABC 311)

München

Die Sanskrit-Handschriften der K. Hof- und Staatsbibliothek in München / von Theodor Aufrecht. – München : Palm [in Komm.], 1909. VII, 228 pp. – (Catalogus codicum manu scriptorum Bibliothecae regiae Monacensis I, 5)

[Adyar (H020 Mun D 1.5); SAI (inf 25 I 7); SKGI (Pa III 100); SOAS (Ref. KC. 016.091/2219)]

(ABC 222)

Mysore

A Supplementary Catalogue of Sanskrit Works in the Saraswati Bhandaram Library of His Highness the Maharaja of Mysore / (by Franz Kielhorn). – Bombay : "Indu-Prakash" Press. 1874. 9 pp.

(List of 607 manuscripts in tabular form)

[SAI (87/1687***); UBTÜ (Ci I 16 Fol. ang. 1874)]

(ABC 226)

Mysore (1898)

A Descriptive Catalogue of Sanskrit Manuscripts in the Sarasvati-Bhandara of H. H. the Maharaja of Mysore / by A[lladi] Mahada[e]vasastri, under the Authority of the Government of Mysore. – Mysore : Govt. Branch Press, 1898. iii, 175 pp.

(513 titles. Veda-lakṣaṇa Mss. on pp. 5-6. There is an extra note after the title page : "Since the catalogue was sent to the Press, Saraswatī-Bhandāra located in the Palace has been completely burnt . . .".)

[Adyar (H020 MyG SB1)]

Mysore (1900)

Catalogue of Sanskrit Manuscripts in the Government Oriental Library, Mysore (Maisūr Rājakīya Prācyakośāgārastha Likhita-saṃskṛta-pustaka-pradarśinī).
– Mysore : Govt. Branch Press, 1900. vi, 330 pp.
(Veda-lakṣaṇa Mss. : pp. 11-20 [nos. 28-35]; p. 39 [nos. 62-63]; p. 308 [nos. 762-63])
[Adyar (H020 MyG 1.1)]

Mysore (1910)

Catalogue of Sanskrit Manuscripts in the Government Oriental Library, Mysore. Part II. (Maisūr Rājakīya Prācyakośāgārastha Likhita Saṃskṛta Pustaka-pradarśinī, dvitīyo bhāgaḥ). – Mysore : Govt. Branch Press, 1910. 4, 212 pp.
(Veda-lakṣaṇa Mss. on pp. 7-13, 197-99)
[Adyar (H020 MyG 1.2)]

Mysore I

Catalogue of Sanskrit Manuscripts in the Govt. Oriental Library, Mysore (Maisūru Rājakīya Prācyakośāgārastha Likhita Saṃskṛta Pustaka-pradarśinī).
– Mysore : Govt. Branch Press, 1922. vi. 672 pp.
(Veda-lakṣaṇa Mss. : pp. 20-41, 611-14)

(ABC Appendix I. UC.26.1)

Mysore II

A Supplemental Catalogue of Sanskrit Manuscripts in the Government Oriental Library. – Mysore : Govt. Branch Press, 1928.

(ABC Appendix I. UC.26.2)

Mysore III

This refers to a hand-list of the latest additions to the Mysore Government Oriental Library. The list was secured for the Catalogus Catalogorum work from the library authorities. Quoted by manuscript numbers. A printed catalogue of these manuscripts was published later (1942), and page references to this catalogue have also been added (as in the NCC).

(ABC Appendix I. UC.26.3)

Mysore IV

A Supplemental Catalogue of Sanskrit Manuscripts secured for the Oriental Research Institute, Mysore, during 1941-1954. – Mysore : Govt. Branch Press, 1955. 29 pp.

Mysore ND

Descriptive Catalogue of Sanskrit Manuscripts in the Oriental Research Institute, University of Mysore. – Mysore : Oriental Research Institute.

Vol. II : (Vedāṅgam, etc.). – 1978. xvi, 391, 285 pp.

(Tabular statement of Mss. nos. 3036-5311 on pp. 1-391. Appendix with extracts from some Mss. on pp. 1-285). – (Oriental Research Institute Series 124)

[Adyar (H091C Mys DN); SAI (inf 25 I 66, 2); IIO (8 A 11); SOAS (Ref. KC. 011.31/521446)]

Mysore Skt. Coll.

Maisūru śrīmanmahārāja saṃskṛta-mahāpāṭhaśālāyāṃ sthāpite sarasvatībhaṇḍāranāmni rājāsthānīye pustakālaye vidyamānānāṃ (amudritānāṃ) hastalikhitānāṃ saṃskṛta-kannada-bhāṣāgranthānāṃ sūcikā (The List of the Unprinted Sanskrit and Kannada Manuscripts in the Palace Saraswati Bhandara [Maharaja's Sanskrit College], Mysore). – Mysore : Sanskrit College, 1942. 12 pp.

(A list of Sanskrit manuscripts including 23 works of Veda-lakṣaṇa. Reprint from the Maharaja's Sanskrit College Magazine, vol. 18 [1942])

[Adyar (H020 MyG 1)]

Some of the manuscripts from this list are described in:

Mysore Skt. Coll. (D)

Maisūru śrīmanmahārāja-saṃskṛta-mahāpāṭhaśālāyāṃ sthāpite sarasvatībhaṇḍāranāmni rājasthānīye pustakālaye vidyamānānām amudritānāṃ hastalikhitānāṃ pustakānāṃ savivaraṇasūcanī (A Descriptive Catalogue of the Unprinted Manuscripts in the Palace Saraswati Bhandara, Mysore), in : The *Maharaja's Sanskrit College Magazine* vol. 18 (1942). Pp. 1-18

(Description with extracts of 18 Veda-lakṣaṇa manuscripts).

[SAI (87/1686***)]

NCC

New Catalogus Catalogorum : An Alphabetical Register of Sanskrit and Allied Works and Authors. – Madras : University of Madras.

(Thus far 12 volumes):

Vol. I : (A) / by V[enkatarama] Raghavan. – 1949. xxxvi, 380 pp. – (Madras University Sanskrit Series [MUSS] 18)

(Catalogues, Lists, etc. used in the NCC, with the Abbreviations used for them : pp. viii-xxxvi. Additions and Corrections : pp. 358-80).

Vol. I : (A) (Revised Edition) / by V. Raghavan. – 1969. x, xliv, 505 pp. – (MUSS 30)

(Catalogues, Lists, etc. used in the NCC, with the Abbreviations used for them : pp. i-xliv. Additions and Corrections : pp. 491-505).

Vol. II : (Ā - Ū) / by V. Raghavan. – 1966. 13, xl, 415 pp. – (MUSS 26)

(Catalogues, Lists, etc. used in the NCC, with the Abbreviations used for them : pp. i-xl. Additions and Corrections : pp. 403-15).

Vol. III : (Ū - Kārtavīrya) / by V. Raghavan and K[umarapuram] Kunjunni Raja. – 1967. iv, 398 pp. – (MUSS 28)
(Additions and Corrections : pp. 391-98).

Vol. IV : (Kārtavīryārjuna - Kṛṣṇasarasvatī) / by V. Raghavan and K. Kunjunni Raja. – 1968. iv, 374 pp. – (MUSS 29)
(Additions and Corrections : pp. 367-74).

Vol. V : (Kṛṣṇasahasranāma - Gāyatrīkalpalatā) / by V. Raghavan and K. Kunjunni Raja. – 1969. 359 pp. – (MUSS 30)
(Additions and Corrections : pp. 353-59).

Vol. VI : (Gāyatrīkavaca - Cahāgītā) / by K. Kunjunni Raja. – 1971. ii, 412 pp. – (MUSS 31)
(Additions and Corrections : pp. 408-12).

Vol. VII : (CĀ - ÑA) / by K. Kunjunni Raja. – 1973. x, 389 pp. – (MUSS 32)
(Additions and Corrections : pp. 383-89).

Vol. VIII : (ṬA - DA) / by K. Kunjunni Raja. – 1974. 371 pp. – (MUSS 33)
(Additions and Corrections : pp. 367-71).

Vol. IX : (DĀ - NA) / by K. Kunjunni Raja. – 1977. viii, 419 pp. – (MUSS 34)
(Additions and Corrections : pp. 409-19).

Vol. X : (NĀ - NVĀ) / by K. Kunjunni Raja and C. S. Sundaram. – 1978. 317 pp. – (MUSS 35)
(Additions and Corrections : pp. 289-317).

Vol. XI : (PA) / by K. Kunjunni Raja, N[arayanaswami] Veezhinathan and C. S. Sundaram. – 1983. vi, lxiii, 280 pp. – (MUSS 37)
(Catalogues, Lists, etc. used in the NCC, with the Abbreviations used for them : pp. i-lxiii. Additions and Corrections : pp. 260-80).

Vol. XII : (Pāiyalacchināmamālā - Pradhyāna) / by N. Veezhinathan, C. S. Sundaram and N. Gangadharan. – 1988. ix, 308 pp. – (MUSS 38)
(Additions and Corrections : pp. 297-308).

[Adyar (H080 MUS sk NCC); SAI (inf 63 P 1, 1-12); SKGI (Pa I 31); IIO (8 E 41); SOAS (Ref. KC. 016/66270)]

(ABC 231)

NGMPP

Nepal-German Manuscript Preservation Project. The entries are based on the examination of some of the index cards and, parts of microfilm copies (of over 110,000 Mss. from Nepal and Tibet) deposited in the Staatsbibliothek Preußischer Kulturbesitz in Berlin. For a detailed report of the project, cf. Albrecht Wezler in : *Zeitschrift der Deutschen Morgenländischen Gesellschaft*, Band 136 - Heft 1 (1986), pp. *2* - *14*. See also *ibid*, Band 140 - Heft 1 (1990), pp. *13* - *14*.

N-W P

A Catalogue of Sanskrit Manuscripts in Private Libraries of the North-West (-Western) Provinces, parts I-X. – Benares : Medical Hall Press; Allahabad : N-W P. and Oudh Govt. Press, 1874-86.
[Adyar (H020 NWP 01.1-2); UBTÜ (Ci XII 396a / SLS = Orient allg A 450); IIO (82 D 5); SOAS (Ref. KC. 016.091/6403)]

(ABC 232)

Oppert

Lists of Sanskrit Manuscripts in Private Libraries of Southern India / by Gustav Oppert. – Madras : Keys, Govt. Press.
Vol. I. – 1880. vii, 620 pp.
Vol. II. – 1885. ix, 694 pp.
[Adyar (H020 MG 1); UBTÜ (Ci XII 394 / SLS = Orient allg A 5010); SKGI (Pa II 400); IIO (8 D 4-5); SOAS (Ref. KC. 016.091/6419)]

(ABC 292)

OU

A Catalogue of the Sanskrit Manuscripts in the Osmania University Library, Hyderabad / edited by Aryendra Sharma . . . [et al.]. – Hyderabad : The Sanskrit Academy, 1964. 328 pp.

Oudh

[*A*] *Catalogue of Sanskrit Manuscripts Existing in Oudh* [*Province*] [*List of Sanskrit Manuscripts Discovered* in Oudh during the year . . . .] / prepared by John C. Nesfield [Colin Browning], assisted by Pandit Deviprasada, edited by Rajendralala Mitra. – Calcutta : Central (Ganesh) Press; Allahabad : N-W P. and Oudh Govt. Press.
III-XII. – 1873-80.
XIII. – 1881 . . . for the year 1880.
XIV. – 1882 . . . for the year 1881.
XV. – 1883 . . . for the year 1882.
XVI. – 1884 . . . for the year 1883.
XVII. – 1885 . . . for the year 1884.
XVIII. – 1886 . . . for the year 1885.
XIX. – 1888 . . . for the year 1887.
XX. – 1890 . . . for the year 1888.
XXI. – 1893 . . . for the year 1889.
XXII. – 1893 . . . for the year 1890.
[Adyar (H020 NWP 01.3-4); IIO (82 D 5, 6, 7, 8 (1-4), 12-13); SOAS (Ref. KC. 016.091/6399)]

(ABC 235)

Oxf.

Catalogus codicum Sanscriticorum Bibliothecae Bodleianae / by Theodor Aufrecht. – Oxonii : Typograph acad., 1864. viii, 575 pp. – (Catalogi Cod-

icum Manuscriptorum Bibliothecae Bodleianae pars 8)
[Adyar (H020 BL 2); UBTÜ (Ka XXIII 6b 4'); SKGI (Pa III 149); IIO (8 E 14); SOAS (Ref. KC. 016.091/6398)]

(ABC 238.1,2)

Oxf. II

Catalogue of Sanskrit Manuscripts in the Bodleian Library. Vol. II / by Moriz Winternitz and Arthur Berriedale Keith. – Oxford : Clarendon Press. 1905. xxiv, 350 pp.
[Adyar (H020 BL 1.2); UBHD (F 9027 P. VIII); SAI (inf 25 I 74)] IIO (8 E 15); SOAS (Ref. KC. 016.091/6398)]

(ABC 238.2)

Oxf. CS

Manuscripts of Chandra Shum Shere Collection in the Indian Institute of the Bodleian Library, Oxford. Entries are based on the three volumes of Index Catalogue of Manuscripts, prepared by T. Gambier-Parry and the Card Catalogue in the Oriental Reading Room of the Library (only a few Mss. are checked : 24.03.88).

P

Lists of Sanskrit Manuscripts purchased for the Government during the years 1877-78 and 1879-80 and a list of the manuscripts purchased from May to November 1881 / by Franz Kielhorn, dated Poona, 30th November 1881. – Bombay : Govt. Central Press, 1881. 26 pp. [= BORI . . . of 1877-78 and BORI . . . of 1879-80].
[Adyar (H020 BG R 3)]

(ABC 270)

Peters.

Reports on the Search for Sanskrit Manuscripts / by Peter Peterson. – Bombay : BBRAS (Govt. Central Press); London : Trübner.

Vol. I : Detailed Report of Operations in Search of Sanskrit Manuscripts in the Bombay Circle, August 1882 - March 1883. – (Journal of the BBRAS, 16. Extra No. 41. 1883). [= BORI . . . of A 1882-83].

Vol. II : April 1883 - March 1884. – (Journal of the BBRAS, 17. Extra No. 44. 1884). [= BORI . . . of A 1883-84].

Vol. III : April 1884 - March 1886. – (Journal of the BBRAS, 17. Extra No. 45. 1887). [= BORI . . . of 1884-86].
[Adyar (H020 BG R 2.2); UBTÜ (Ci I 1b Extra Nr.1887); IIO (8 C 2a)]

Vol. IV : April 1886 - March 1892. – (Journal of the BBRAS, 18. Extra No. 49A. 1894). [= BORI . . . of 1886-92].
[Adyar (H020 BG R 2.2); UBTÜ (Ci I 1b Extra Nr. 1894); IIO (8 C 2b)]

Vol. V : April 1892 - March 1895. [= BORI . . . of 1892-95].

[Adyar (H020 BG R 2.3); UBTÜ (21 A 8756); IIO (8 C 2c)]
Vol. VI : April 1895 - March 1898. [= BORI . . . of A 1895-98].
[Adyar (H020 BG R 2.3); SKGI (Pa II 60); IIO (8 C 2d); SOAS (Ref. KC. 091/10757 + 185237)]

(ABC 274)

PUL

A Catalogue of the Sanskrit Manuscripts in the Punjab University Library. – Lahore : University of the Punjab.
Vol. I. – 1932. 138, 138 pp.
Vol. II. – 1941. xvi, 292, 65 pp.
[UBTÜ (19 A 12212 / SLS = Orient allg A 1923); SKGI (Pa III 233); IIO (8 D 21); SOAS (Ref. KC. 016.091/36569)]

(ABC 145)

Radh.

Pustakānām Sūcīpatram, no place and date, 48 pages. At the end: *likhitaṃ paṇḍiṭa-rājārāma-śāstriṇā kāśmīravāsinā.*
(This important collection of manuscripts belonged to the late Pandit Radhakrishna of Lahore [as in the NCC].)

Rajapur

A hand-list of 1038 manuscripts in the Saṃskṛta Pāṭhaśālā in Rajapur, Ratnagiri District, Bombay Presidency (as in the NCC).

R. A. Sastri

Four parts of the Diary of Pandit R. A. Sastri's tour in search of Sanskrit manuscripts handed over to the Catalogus Catalogorum work (as in the NCC).

RASB

A Descriptive Catalogue of Sanskrit Manuscripts in the Government Collection under the Care of the (Royal) Asiatic Society of Bengal / by Haraprasad Shastri. – Calcutta : Baptist Mission Press.
Vol. II : Vedic Manuscripts. – 1923. x, 222-1455 pp. (Nos. 120-1845).
[Adyar (H091C RAS Be D2); SAI (inf 25 I 70,2); UBTÜ (Ci XII 646, vol. 2 / SLS = Orient allg A 1810, vol. 2); SKGI (Pa III 490); IIO (8 B 10)]

(ABC 51.2)

Rep. Hpr.

Report on the Search of Sanskrit Manuscripts / by Haraprasad Shastri. – Calcutta : Asiatic Society of Bengal.
1. 1895 to 1900. – 1901. 25 pp.
2. 1901-1902 to 1905-1906. – 1902. 18 pp.
3. 1906-1907 to 1910-1911. – 1911. 10 pp.
[Adyar (H020 ASBE R); IIO (82 F 12)]

(ABC 115)

Rep. Raj. & C. I.

Report of a Second Tour in Search of Sanskrit Manuscripts made in Rajputana and Central India in 1904-05 and 1905-06 / by Shridhar R. Bhandarkar. – Bombay : Govt. Central Press, 1907. 100 pp.
[Adyar (H020 BG R 4); UBTÜ (10 A 9111, Nr. 6); SKGI (Pa II 600); IIO (8 C 16; 82 F 11/9)]

(ABC 283)

Report

Detailed Report of a Tour in Search of Sanskrit Manuscripts made in Kāsmīr, Rajputana, and Central India / by Georg Bühler. – Bombay : BBRAS; London : Trübner, 1877. 90, clxxi pp. – (Journal of the BBRAS, 12. Extra No. 34A. 1877).
[Adyar (H020 ASB 1); SKGI (Pa II 55 (7 = 24A)); IIO (8 C 19)]

(ABC 269)

Rgb.

Report on the Search for Sanskrit Manuscripts in the Bombay Presidency during the years 1884-85, 1885-86 and 1886-87 / by Ramkrishna Gopal Bhandarkar. – Bombay : Govt. Central Press, 1894. 138 pp. [= BORI . . . of 1884-87].
[SKGI (Pa II 50); IIO (8 C 3c); SOAS (Ref. KC. 016.091/1910)]

(ABC 273.5)

Rice

Catalogue of Sanskrit Manuscripts in Mysore and Coorg / compiled by Lewis Rice. – Bangalore : Mysore Govt. Press, 1884. 2, 2, 327 pp.
[Adyar (H020 My G 2); UBTÜ (Ci XII 400 / SLS = Orient allg A 447); IIO (82 C 13); SOAS (Ref. KC. 016.091/10490)]

(ABC 224)

SB

Catalogue of Sanskrit Manuscripts in the Sanskrit College Library, Benares. – Allahabad : Govt. Press, 1888. 75, 459 pp.
(This gives a more correct and more compiete account than that printed in : *The Pandit*. Cf. Ben. above.)
[Adyar (H020 BASC 1); SKGI (Pa III 210); SOAS (Ref. KC. 016.091/10488)]

(ABC 14)

SBD

A Descriptive Catalogue of the Sanskrit Manuscripts acquired for and deposited in the Government Sanskrit College [now Sampurnananda Samskrita Vishvavidyalaya] Library (Sarasvatī Bhavana) during the years 1791-1950

/ prepared under the guidance of T[ribhuvan] P[rasad] Upadhyaya and under the supervision of Subhadra Jha (compiled by the Staff of the Manuscript[e]s Section of the Sampurnananda Sanskrit University Library). – Banaras [Varanasi] : Gopaldas, Shri Vishweshwar [Vishvavidyalaya] Press.

Vol. I [.1] : Vedic Manuscripts. – 1953. 405 pp. (nos. 1-4443).

Vol. I.2 : Vedic Manuscripts. – 1953. Pp. 406-601, 56, 7 (nos. 4444-6627).

Vol. I.3. : Vedic Manuscripts, 345 pp. (nos. 52,176-55,948). Mss. acquired after 1950 and up to 1980.

(This volume, though printed, is yet to be released.)

Vol. XIII. 1987 : Veda Manuscripts, etc. 6, 436 (pp. 225-32 repeated), 71 pp. (nos. 46,912-52,175).

(It is stated that there are now 109,254 Mss. in the library. The number of Veda-lakṣaṇa Mss. is about 1090 representing circa 250 works.)

[Adyar (H091C SB); SAI (inf 25 I 11)]

(ABC 17)

Śg.

Report on a Search for Sanskrit and Tamil Manuscripts / by M. Seshagiri Sastri (as in the NCC). – Madras : Superintendent, Govt. Press.

No. 1: for the year 1896-97. – 1898.

No. 2: for the year 1893-94. – 1899.

[Adyar (H020 MG Ses R 1-2); SKGI (Pa II 410); IIO (82 C 5)]

(ABC 198)

SK. Ray

A hand-list of manuscripts with Saratkumar Ray, 1-4, European Asylum Lane, Calcutta (as in the NCC).

SK. Ray DC

Refers to an unfinished Descriptive Catalogue of the above Collection, unfortunately stopped in p. 196, manuscript numbers 277 (as in the NCC).

Skt. Coll. Ben.

List of Sanskrit (Jaina) and Hindi . . . Manuscripts [with varying titles], purchased by order of the Government and deposited in the Sanskrit College, Benares. 22 parts. – Allahabad : Govt. Press, 1902-1919.

[SKGI (Pa III 211a); SOAS (Ref. KC. 016.091/6555)]

(ABC 15)

Continued in : *A Catalogue of Sanskrit Manuscripts*, acquired [during the years 1918-30] for and deposited in the Govt. Sanskrit College Library, Sarasvati Bhavana, Benares, prepared under the supervision of Gopinath Kaviraj. – Allahabad : Superintendent, Printing and Stationery (U. P.), 1934. 132 pp. (circa 1020 Mss.).

[Adyar (H020 BASC 2); SOAS (Ref. KC. 016.091/6555)]

(ABC 9)

Stein

Catalogue of the Sanskrit Manuscripts in the Raghunātha Temple Library of His Highness the Maharaja of Jammu & Kashmir / prepared by M[arc] A[urel] Stein. – Bombay : Nirnaya-Sagara Press, 1894. XVI, L, 423 pp.
[Adyar (H020 KG 1); UBHD (F 9430); SKGI (Pa III 380); IIO (8 F 5); SOAS (Ref. KC. 016.091/9709)]

(ABC 130)

Sūcīpattra

Sūcīpustakam [Containing a list of the manuscripts of Fort William / compiled by Ramagovinda-tarkaratna]. – (Calcutta : Asiatic Society,) 1838. 149 pp.
[Adyar (H010 ASBE 1)]

(ABC 46)

Tb.

Verzeichniss der Indischen Handschriften der Königlichen Universitäts-Bibliothek. (Zuwachs der Jahre 1865-1899) / von Richard Garbe. – Tübingen : Laupp, 1899. 114 pp.
[Adyar (H020 Tub ge1); SAI (inf 25 I 42); SKGI (Pa III 170)]

(ABC 320)

TCD

A Descriptive Catalogue of Sanskrit Manuscripts in the Curator's Office Library, Trivandrum / edited by K. Sambasiva Sastri. – Trivandrum : V. V. Press Branch.

Vol. I : Veda, Śrauta, Smṛti and Purāṇa. – 1937. xvii, 396 pp.

[Adyar (H020 TG CD1); SAI (inf 25 I 75,1)]

(ABC 312.1)

TD

A Descriptive Catalogue of the Sanskrit Manuscripts in the Tanjore Mahārāja Serfoji's Saraswatī Mahāl Library, Tanjore. – Srirangam : Sri Vani Vilas Press.

Vol. III : Vedas (continued), Vedāṅgas / by P. P. S. Sastri, 1929. xl, 921-1470, 37 pp.

(The total number of Mss. in the library is said to exceed 40,000. Nearly 18,000 of them have been described in the early catalogues. For the remaining Mss. there are only the Accession Registers. Some of them I have examined [September 22-24, 1988] and included them in this Bibliography with their accession numbers.)

[Adyar (H091C TSM D); SAI (inf 25 I 22,3); SKGI (Pa III 460); IIO (82 C 19); SOAS (Ref. KC. 016.091/22521)]

(ABC 302.3)

Tirupati SVUORI

An Alphabetical Index of Sanskrit, Telugu and Tamil Manuscripts [Palm-leaf and Paper], in the Sri Venkateswara [University] Oriental Research Institute Library, Tirupati. – Tirupati : Sri Venkateswara Oriental Research Institute, 1956. iv, 369 pp.

(Supplemented by means of the examination of some of the codices)

[Adyar (H091C VOR A)]

(ABC 310)

Trav. Uni.

Alphabetical Index of the Sanskrit Manuscripts in the [Kerala] University [vol. III-IV : Oriental Research Institute and] Manuscripts Library, Trivandrum. – Trivandrum : Alliance Printing Works (III. Vijnana Bhavan Printers) (IV. Santosh Printers).

Vol. I : (A to Ṇa) / by Suranad Kunjan Pillai. – 1957 (M.E. 1133). 241 pp. (nos. 1 - 6079). – (Trivandrum Sanskrit Series 186)

Vol. II : (Ta to Ma) / by K. Raghavan Pillai. – 1965 (M.E. 1140), 324 pp. (nos. 6080 - 14059). – (Trivandrum Sanskrit Series 215)

Vol. III : (Ya to Ṣa) / by T. Bhaskaran. – 1984 (M.E. 1159). 258 pp. (nos. 14060 - 19312). – (Trivandrum Sanskrit Series 254)

Vol. IV : (Sa to Ha) / by T. Bhaskaran and K. Visweswari Amma. – 1986. 125 pp. (nos. 19313 - 21530). – (Trivandrum Sanskrit Series 256)

[Adyar (H080 TSS 186, 215); SAI (inf 25 I 1); IIO (Sansk ser. B 1/92 (186))]

(Alphabetical list of titles in tabular columns. A few entries are as given in the NCC which are based on a hand-list of the manuscripts supplied by the library to the NCC office. Supplemented by checking the Accession Registers and the supplementary volumes and examining several codices.)

(ABC 316)

Triv. Cur.

A Catalogue of Sanskrit Manuscripts, Collected . . . by the Curator of the Department for the Publication of Sanskrit Manuscripts, Trivandrum / by T[aruvagraharam] Ganapati Sastri. – Trivandrum : Travancore Govt. Press.

No. I. – 1912 (M.E.1087). 4, 32 pp. Classified list of 320 manuscripts.

No. II. – 1913 (M.E.1088). 18 pp. Classified list of 147 manuscripts.

No. III. – 1915 (M.E.1090). 13 pp. Classified list of 97 manuscripts.

No. IV. – 1916 (M.E 1091). 26 pp. Classified list of 187 manuscripts.

No. V. – 1918 (M.E.1093). 33 pp. Classified list of 241 manuscripts.

No. VI. – 1921 (M.E.1096). 15 pp. Classified list of 144 manuscripts.

No. VII. – 1923 (M.E.1098). 26 pp. Classified list of 193 manuscripts.

[Adyar (H091C Gan DE); SAI (87/1678***)]

(ABC Appendix I. UC.33)

Udaipur I

Two lists.

A. - a list of manuscripts in the Sajjan Vani Vilas Library, Udaipur, Mewar.

B. - a list of manuscripts in the Sarasvati Bhandar Library, Mewar.
These have appeared in print in :
A Catalogue of Manuscripts in the (Saraswati Bhandar) Library of H. H. the Maharana of Udaipur (Mewar) / compiled by M[oti] L[al] Menaria. – Udaipur : Itihās Kāryālaya, 1943. 5, 5, 287, 40, 9 pp. (as in the NCC).
(ABC 321)

Udaipur II
A hand-list of the manuscripts in the Library of Nathdwara, Udaipur, Mewar State (as in the NCC).

Vaṅgīya
A Descriptive Catalogue of the Sanskrit Manuscripts in the Vangiya Sahitya Parishat, Calcutta / by Chintaharan Chakravarti. – Calcutta : Vangiya Sahitya Parishat, 1935. 8, xlv, 277 pp. – (Sahitya Parishat Series 85)
[SAI (inf 25 I 43); SKGI (Pa III 485); SOAS (Ref. KC. 016.091/32787)]
(ABC 57)

Venkatesiah
A hand-list of 85 manuscripts in the possession of Venkatesiah, 451, Subbiah's Road, Chamarajpet, Mysore (as in the NCC).

VOHD
Verzeichnis der Orientalischen Handschriften in Deutschland. . . . herausgegeben von Wolfgang Voigt . . . [et al.]. – Stuttgart (Wiesbaden) : Franz Steiner Verlag, 1962– .
(In volume II of this series have thus far been published: six parts of descriptive catalogue, three parts of 'handlists, a cumulative index (Generalregister A) to parts 1-6 as part 10; and another cumulative index (Generalregister B) to parts 7-9 as part 11).

Part 1. – 1962 : Indische Handschriften / von Klaus L. Janert (ed. by Walther Schubring). (XXXVI), 293 pp. (Nos. 1-495).

Part 2. – 1970 : Indische und Nepalische Handschriften / von Klaus L. Janert und N. Narasimhan Poti. 359 pp. (Nos. 496-1000).

Part 3. – 1967 : Indische Handschriften / compiled by E[lapully] R[amaswami] Sreekrishna Sarma. (ed. by Klaus L. Janert). IX, 48 pp. (Nos. 1-113).

Part 4. – 1975 : Indische und Nepalische Handschriften / von Klaus L. Janert und N. Narasimhan Poti. 298 pp. (Nos. 1114-1500).

Part 5. – 1979 : Indische Handschriften / von Klaus L. Janert und N. Narasimhan Poti. Pp. 299-660. (Nos. 1501 2000).

Part 6. – 1980 : Indische Handschriften / von Klaus L. Janert und N. Narasimhan Poti. Pp. 661-838. (Nos. 2001-2250).

Part 7. – 1985 : Indische Handschriften / von N. Narasimhan Poti (ed. by Klaus L. Janert). Pp. 839-1000. (Nos. 2251-3000).

Part 8. – 1987 : Indische Handschriften / von N. Narasimhan Poti (ed. by Klaus L. Janert). Pp. 1001-168. (Nos. 3001-3750).
Part 9. – 1990 : Indische Handschriften / von N. Narasimhan Poti (ed. by Klaus L. Janert). Pp. 1169-358. (Nos. 3751-4381).
Part 10. – 1982 : Indische Handschriften – Generalregister A (cumulative index) to II, 1-6. / von Klaus L. Janert. 238 pp.
Part 11. – 1991 : Indische Handschriften – Generalregister B (cumulative index) to II, 7-9. / von Klaus L. Janert. Pp. 239-430.
[Adyar (A080 VOH); SAI (inf 26 I 4); SKGI (Pa II 710); IIO (8 E 55); SOAS (Ref. KC. 016.091/161882)]

VSM

Descriptive Catalogue of Sanskrit Manuscripts (in the Vaidika Saṃśodhana Maṇḍala, Poona) / edited by T[rivikram] N[arayan] Dharmadhikari. – Poona : Vaidika Saṃśodhana Maṇḍala.
Vol. I : Veda and Vedic. – 1974. ix, 388 pp.
(Description, in tabular form, of 1693 Mss. and a few extracts.)
Vol. III : Upādhye Collection. – 1985. 279 pp.
(Description, in tabular form, of 1000 Mss. and a few extracts.)
[Adyar (H091C VSM D); SAI (inf 25 I 56); SKGI (Pa III 216); IIO (8 D 40); SOAS (Ref. KC. 016/328204)]

Wai

Descriptive Catalogue of Sanskrit Manuscripts (Prājña Pāṭhaśālā Maṇḍala Collection) / edited by Laxman Shastri Joshi. – Wai (Satara dist.) : Prājña Pāṭhaśālā Maṇḍala, 1970.
Part I. – 2, 717 pp.
(Description, in tabular form; Mss. nos. 1-5674)
Part II. – 4, 720-1361 pp..
(Description, in tabular form; Mss. nos. 5675-10712)
[Adyar (H091C PPM DC.1); SAI (inf 25 I 9); SKGI (Pa III 219); IIO (8 E 53)]
(As this catalogue does not give extracts from the Mss. most of them have been examined by me for verification. A few entries are from a hand-list with extracts and notes of the Sanskrit manuscripts in the Prājña Pāṭhaśālā [Dharmakośa Kāryālaya], Wai, Satara district, Bombay Presidency, prepared by Pandit Lakshman Shastri Joshi. Quoted by bundle numbers [as in the NCC].)

Weber

Verzeichniss der Sanskṛit- [II, 1-3: und Prākṛt-] Handschriften [II, 1-3: der Königlichen Bibliothek zu Berlin]. von Albrecht Weber. – Berlin : Nicolai [Schade, Asher]. – (Die Handschriften-Verzeichnisse der Königlichen Bibliothek).
[Vol. I :] 1853. XXIV, 481 pp.
Vol. II.1 : 1886. VIII, 352 pp.

Vol. II.2 : 1888. X, pp. 355-827.
Vol. II.3 : 1891. XVII, pp. 829-1363.
[Adyar (H020 Ber 1-3); UBHD (HS 5B 35); SKGI (Pa III 30); IIO (8 F 6); SOAS (Ref. KC. 016.091/9157 + L. Ref. KC. 016.091/9557)]
(ABC 20)

Wellcome Inst. London
A typed list of circa 3000 manuscripts (out of ca. 7000), prepared by V. Raghavan (17.07 to 27.11.1954). This list has been alphabetically rearranged for the internal use of the library in : Alphabetical Shelflist of Sanskrit and Other Indian Languages Manuscripts on Medicine and Science in the Wellcome Institute for the History of Medicine, London, 1978 (based on the list of Raghavan). 1003 of the manuscripts are included in:
A Handlist of the Sanskrit and Prakrit Manuscripts in the Library of the Wellcome Institute for the History of Medicine, London. – London : Wellcome Institute.
Vol. I. – / by D[ominik] Wujastyk. – 1985. xvi, 317 pp.
[SAI (inf 25 I 77); IIO (8 F 67)]

Whish
A Catalogue of South Indian Sanskrit Manuscripts (especially those of the Whish Collection) belonging to the Royal Asiatic Society, London / compiled by Moriz Winternitz. – London : Royal Asiatic Society, 1902. xv, 340 pp.
[Adyar (A080 RAS M 2); UBTÜ (Ci I 1d, Bd. 2, / SLS = Orient allg A 2475); SKGI (Pa III 80); IIO (8 B 7); SOAS (Ref. KC. 016.091/1902)]
(ABC 176)

II. Catalogues of Printed Books

BM : Ptd. Bks. Cat. 1876
Catalogue of Sanskrit and Pali Books in the British Museum / by Ernst Haas, printed by Permission of the Trustees of the British Museum. – London : Trübner, 1876. viii, 188 pp.
[Adyar (H010 BM AA1); UBHD (F 8997/1)] IIO (8 E 4);

BM : Ptd. Bks. Cat. 1876-92
Catalogue of Sanskrit, Pali, and Prakrit Books in the British Museum acquired during the years 1876-92 (Supplement 1877-92), printed by order of the Trustees of British Museum / by Cecil Bendall. – London : Gilbert and Rivington, 1893. x pp. and 624 columns.
[Adyar (H010 BM 1); UBHD (F 8997/2); IIO (8 E 5)]

BM : Ptd. Bks. Cat. 1892-1906

A Supplementary Catalogue of Sanskrit, Pali, and Prakrit Books in the Library of the British Museum acquired during the years 1892-1906 / compiled by Lionel David Barnett, printed by order of the Trustees of British Museum. – London : William Clowes and Sons, 1908. viii pp. and 1096 columns.
[Adyar (H010 BM 2); SAI (inf 10 C 37,1); IIO (8 E 5)]

BM : Ptd. Bks. Cat. 1906-1928

A Supplementary Catalogue of Sanskrit, Pali, and Prakrit Books in the Library of the British Museum acquired during the years 1906-1928 / compiled by Lionel David Barnett, printed by order of the Trustees. – London : William Clowes and Sons, 1928. viii pp. and 1694 columns.
[Adyar (H010 BM 3); SAI (inf 10 C 37,2); IIO (8 E 5)]

Emeneau

A Union List of Printed Indic Texts and Translations in American Libraries / compiled by M[urray] B. Emeneau. – New Haven, Connecticut : American Oriental Society, 1935. xv, 540 pp. – (American Oriental Series 7)
Reprint: New York : Kraus Reprint Corporation, 1967.
[Adyar (A080 AOS 7); SAI (inf 40 I 20,7 and ind S 2,7); SKGI (Pa II 700); IIO (8 E 7); SOAS (Ref. K. 016/30919)]

IO : Ptd. Bks. Cat.

Catalogue of the Library of the India Office [Section II - IV : Catalogue of the India Office Library] – London : Stationery Office.

Vol. II, Part I : Sanskrit Books / by Prana Natha and Jitendra Bimala Chaudhuri [Section III - IV : revised and edited by C[harles] J[ames] Napier]. Revised Edition.
Section I (A - G). – 1938. xxiv, 990 pp.
Section II (H - Kṛṣṇa-līlāmṛta). – 1951. Pp. 991-1374.
Section III (Kṛṣṇa-līlāmṛta - R). – 1953. Pp. viii, 1375-2220.
Section IV (S - Z). – 1957. Pp. 2221-3149.

[Adyar (H010C IO 2.1-4); SAI (inf 10 C 7); IIO (8 C 11); SOAS (Ref. KC. 016/51953)]

III. Bibliographies and Other Works

Bibliographic Survey of Catalogues of Indic Manuscripts : Being a Union Catalogue of Indic Languages Manuscripts Catalogues Available in Delhi / compiled by Manibhai K. Prajapati. – New Delhi, 1986. 33, 307 ll. (type script).
An Indian National Trust for Art and Cultural Heritage Project. Document Project Coordinator : Subhas C Biswas.
Catalogues of Sanskrit, Pali and Prakrit Manuscripts : 221 titles.

Catalogues of Modern Indic Languages Manuscripts : 222-337 titles.
Appendix 1 : Manuscripts Catalogues not available locally : 338-632 titles.
Appendix 2 : Hand lists of Sanskrit Manuscripts : 224 titles.
Appendix 3 : List of Institutions (123) that received Grant-in-Aid by the Govt. of India 1980-86.
General Index : pp. 245-307.
[A copy with K. V[enkateswara] Sarma, Adyar Library and Research Centre, Madras]

Bibliographie Védique, par Louis Renou. – Paris : Librairie d'Amérique et d'Orient (Adrien-Maisonneuve), 1931. V, 340 pp.
Photo-lithographic reproduction of a typescript containing about 6500 entries under 201 headings with an index.
[Adyar (H210 Ren BV fr); SAI (inf 87 G 16); IIO (8 D 9); SOAS (Ref. KC. 016.2941/24779)]

Critical Studies in the Phonetic Observations of Indian Grammarians / by Siddheshwar Varma. – London : Royal Asiatic Society, 1929. xiii, 190 pp.
Reprint: Delhi : Munshi Ram Manohar Lal, 1961.
[SAI (nsp 49.6 C 4)]

A Critical Study of Sanskrit Phonetics / by Vidhata Mishra. – Varanasi : Chowkhamba Sanskrit Series Office, 1972. xvi, 258 pp. – (Chowkhamba Sanskrit Series Studies 83)
[SAI (ind S 21, 83)]

Pāṇini : A Survey of Research / by Georg Cardona. – The Hague : Mouton, 1976. xvi, 384 pp. First Indian reprint : Delhi : Motilal Banarsidas, 1980.
[SAI (ind 54 B 81/1594)]

Grammatical Literature / by Hartmut Scharfe. – Wiesbaden : Otto Harrassowitz,, 1977. Pp. 78-216. – (A History of Indian Literature, vol. V, fasc. 2).

Saṃskṛta Vyākaraṇa Śāstra kā Itihāsa / by Yudhisthira Mimamsaka. – Bahalgadh (Sonipath-Haryana) : Ramalal Kapur Trust, 1984.
Vol. I (revised 4th ed.). – 32, 724, 8 pp.
Vol. II (revised 3rd ed.). – 24, 495 pp.
Vol. III (revised 2nd ed.). – 299, 23 pp.
[SAI (ind 54 B 21a)]

Sanskrit Texts on Phonetics : A Collection of Śikṣā Texts from the papers of the late Prof. Raghu Vira / reproduced by Lokesh Chandra. – New Delhi, 1981. 696 pp. – (Satapitaka Series : Indo-Asian Literatures 282)
(It contains the texts of 27 Śikṣā works. Only 18 of them are listed in the table of contents of the volume. They are actually Devanāgarī copies of Mss. belonging to the Adyar Library or Govt. Oriental Manuscripts Library,

Madras, though nowhere mentioned in this volume.)
[SAI (ind S 180, 282); UBTÜ (22 A 14022); SOAS (KC 414/461805)]

The Śrautasūtras of Lāṭyāyana and Drāhyāyaṇa and Their Commentaries : An English translation and Study / by Asko Parpola. – Helsinki - Helsingfors. – (Commentationes Humanavum Litterarum - Societas Scientiarum Finnica 42,2)
vol. I.1 : (General Introduction). – 1968.
[SAI (ind 70 C 244,I.1)]

Vedāṅga : Vaidika V:aṅmaya kā Bṛhad Itihāsa (*A Critical and Comprehensive History of Vedic Literature*) / by Kundanalal Sarma. – Hoshiarpur : Vishveshvaranand Vedic Research Institute, 1983. 32, 792 pp. – (Vishveshvaranand Indological Series 72) [IIO (Sansk ser. E 12/72)]

Vedic Bibliography : An up-to-date, comprehensive, and analytically arranged register of all important work done since 1930 in the field of the Veda and allied antiquities including the Indus Valley Civilisation / by R[amachandra] N[arayan] Dandekar. – Bombay : Karnatak Publishing House; Poona : University (BORI).
[Vol. I.] – 1946. xx, 398 pp. – (New Indian Antiquary, Extra Series VII)
Second edition: Poona : BORI, 1986.
Vol. II. – 1961. xxiii, 760 pp. Reprint: Poona : BORI, 1978. – (Govt Oriental Series, Class B, No. 11)
Vol. III. – 1973. xxiv, 1082 pp. – (Govt Oriental Series, Class B, No. 10)
Vol. IV. – 1985. xxv, 1432 pp. – (Govt Oriental Series, Class B, No. 13)
[Adyar (H210.16 Dan VB); SAI (inf 63 G 5); IIO (8 C 4); SOAS (Ref. KC. 016.2941/55608)]

IV. Abbreviations of Libraries

In these Bibliographical Notes, at the end of an entry of a catalogue or book, references to the shelf-marks or call numbers of public libraries are given [in brackets]. The same is the case with regard to the printed editions of the texts described in the main Descriptive Bibliography. This is done, wherever possible, in addition to the usual bibliographical details. This list contains abbreviations as well as addresses of those libraries where one can find copies of the catalogues and printed editions. Most of the European libraries have special identifying codes that enable speedy lending service.

Adyar :

Adyar Library and Research Centre
The Theosophical Society, Adyar
Madras – 600 020 (India)

BORI :

Bhandarkar Oriental Research Institute
Poona – 411 004 (India)

BUL :

Library of the University of Bombay
Fort
Bombay – 400 032 (India)

IIO :

Indian Institute Library in the
Bodleian Library
Oxford OX1 3BG (England)

IO : (LO/N12)

The British Library
Oriental and India Office Collections
197, Blackfriars Road
London SE1 8NG (England)

MUL :

Madras University Library, Chepauk
Madras – 600 005 (India)

MyORI :

Oriental Research Institute
University of Mysore
Mysore – 570 005 (India)

NL :

National Library
Belvedere
Calcutta – 700 027 (India)

SAI : (16/77)

Zentralbibliothek
Südasien-Institut der Universität Heidelberg
Im Neuenheimer Feld 330
D-6900 Heidelberg
(Entries with asterisks indicate accession numbers;
final call-numbers are in the process of computerisation)

SKGI :

Seminar für Kultur und Geschichte Indiens
Grindelalle 53
D-2000 Hamburg 13

SOAS : (LO/U14)
Library of the School of Oriental and African Studies
University of London
Malet Street
London WC1E 7HP (England)

UBHD : (16)
Universitätsbibliothek Heidelberg
Plöck 2
D-6900 Heidelberg

UBTÜ : (21)
Universitätsbibliothek Tübingen
Orientabteilung
Wilhelmstraße 32, Postfach 2620
D-7400 Tübingen

VSM :
Vaidika Samshodhana Mandala
T. M. V. Nagar
Poona – 411 037 (India)

DESCRIPTIVE BIBLIOGRAPHY

1 AKĀRAVARJA-LAKṢAṆA (अकारवर्जलक्षण)

Enumeration of the verses of the *Ṛgveda* containing the verbal forms without the augment "a". It is actually a section of the work called *Pada-gāḍha*. (Cf. p. 53 of the *Pada-gāḍha*, Srirangam edition).

Beginning:

त्रिः सौभगत्वं मो षु णः परापरेन्द्र यथा विद् वा नरो मा त्वा तन।

End:

मो षु ण आरे अघा ग्राहिर्जग्राह गर्भं धेहि ··· इति पदकाले अकारवर्जम्॥

Mysore ND II 3036 (P 4906/11). PL. Na. 1 fol. (115). Extract no. 1.

2 AKṢARA-TANTRA (अक्षरतन्त्र)

of Āpiśali, according to Satyavrata Samasrami who published this text with his own gloss based on an earlier incomplete commentary. The work deals with Stobha-s, i.e. insertion of different sounds and syllables, or even complete sentences or verses in Sāmagāna. It consists of about 260 Sūtra-s divided into two Prapāṭhaka-s. In all available Mss. there are 12 sections (Daśaka) in the first Prapāṭhaka and 13 sections in the second. This is corroborated by the statement in the *Sāmaveda-sarvānukramaṇī* (p. 4). But Samasrami's edition, which is based on incomplete and defective manuscript material, has 13 sections in both the Prapāṭhaka-s. It has been assumed by him that a few Sūtra-s are missing and the first section has been divided into two parts. The text is also known as the *Saṃjñā-lakṣaṇa* or *Saṃjñā-(pra-)karaṇa*, being a supplement to the *Sāma-tantra*, of which it is regarded as the 14th and 15th Prapāṭhaka-s.

Beginning:

अथ सामतन्त्रे अक्षरतन्त्रप्रारम्भः । अनृगाद्यक्षरम् । औहौओहो-इ-भ्यो हो-इ । वाचि । औहो। हो-ई। औहोओहायौ। हा-इ-नि। हो। वा। उहुवा। इये। प्रथमो दशकः ।

End:

ध्वरात्सिबापूष्णध्र्या । वारा । आयवाचु । ओ । ता-इवसूमागाग्रा-इमृडा । होतोतत्वद । त्रयोदशदशकः । होहवे। हुवेसंचाभ्यः । इति सामतन्त्रे अक्षरतन्त्रस्य द्वितीयः प्रपाठकः । समाप्तमिदं सामतन्त्रव्याकरणमक्षरतन्त्रं च।

Adyar D I 1067 (33 E 12 = 75259). PL. Gr. 3 fol. (8b-10a). At the end of the *Sāmatantra* as a supplement to it.

Baroda 9805(g). PL. Gr. 3 fol. (13-15). 50 Grantha-s. = CLB I, p. 22.

Baroda 9916(b). PL. Gr. 21 fol. 1000 Grantha-s. = CLB I, p. 22 (with C. of Satyavrata Samasrami !) This reference in the Catalogues must be to the printed edition, since Samasrami's commentary in a palm-leaf Ms. in Grantha script is improbable. On verification it was found to be a fragment of the commentary (only 3 fol.) noted below. Samasrami's name is written on the title slip, probably by the cataloguer.

IM 1967. 1 fol. Incomplete. Col.: Saṃjñā-karaṇaṃ nāma pariśiṣṭam.

IO 4332 (Burnell 360b). Gr. 28 pp. (with Bhāṣya). (Saṃjñā-prakaraṇa). Written ca. A.D. 1867.

IO 4333 (Burnell 437c). Gr. 19 fol. (with Bhāṣya). (Saṃjñā-prakaraṇa). Written ca. A.D. 1875.

MD 894. PL. Gr. 13 pp. (68ff.). Catalogued as Gāyatrī-gāna-lakṣaṇa. But that work is, however, only on fol. 1a; fol. 1b-7a contain 2 Prapāṭhaka-s of the Saṃjñā-(pra-)karaṇa with C. Col.: Saṃjñā-prakaraṇa.

MD 895. Tel. 22 pp. (92ff.). Copy of MD 894 made in 1896.

Oxf. CS c.26(7). 3 fol. Col.: iti saṃjñā-parkaraṇaṃ nāma pariśiṣṭam. Paper dated 25.11.1903. Ascribed to Kātyāyana in the catalogue.

SBD 4354. 2 fol. (2-3). Incomplete. (Saṃjñā-karaṇa-pariśiṣṭa).

Ptd.: ed. by Satyavrata Samasrami with a commentary (Akṣaratantram – Vedāṅgam – mahāmuninā āpiśalinā proktam, sāmagācāryeṇa sāmaśramīti labdhopanāmakena satyavratabhaṭṭācāryeṇa vṛttipūraṇena bodhopayogitām ānīya prakāśitam), in the Sanskrit journal *Uṣā*. – Calcutta : Satya Press, Śakābda 1811 (1889), vol. I, pt. 2, pp. 1-56. 1891, vol. I, pts. 11-12, pp. 1-4. [Adyar (H 211.3 x Sat); NL (180 Qc 88 1); Emeneau (77); SAI (85/1963*); BM : Ptd. Bks. Cat. 1876-92 (503 : 14010.c.43)]

Also printed in the edition of the *Stobha-bhāṣya* of Bhaṭṭa Śobhākara, ed. by Mayuram Ramanatha Dikshita. – Madras : Sir C. P. Ramaswami Iyer Foundation, "the Grove", 1984, pp. 99-162. [BORI (49260); SAI (ind B 287/725)]

[NCC I 12b]

– C. Bhāṣya.

Baroda 9916(b). PL. Gr. 21 fol. 1000 Grantha-s (with text). = CLB I, p. 22. Contrary to the description in the Catalogues, there are only three fol. in the Ms. now.

IO 4332 (Burnell 360b). Gr. 28 pp. (with text). Written ca. A.D. 1867.

IO 4333 (Burnell 437c). Gr. 19 fol. (with text). Written ca. A.D. 1875.

MD 894. PL. Gr. 13 pp. (68ff.) (with text). Col.: Saṃjñā-prakaraṇa.

MD 895. Tel. 22 pp. (92ff.). Copy of MD 894 made in 1896.

– C. called Saṃjñā-(pra-)karaṇa-bhāṣya, of Tripāṭhī Kahnajī, son of Śivajī.

Beginning:

अथ संज्ञाकरणं वर्तिष्यते। अनृगाद्यक्षरम्। (अन्) न प्रतिषेधे न ऋगाद्यक्षरमनृगाद्यक्षरम्। ऋग्वर्जिताक्षरस्य स्तोभसंज्ञा भवति। उदाहरणानि -- आ उप्। मो-ई। ऊम्। एवं स्तोभाक्षरस्य एकमेकं संज्ञा उक्ता। १।

End:

हो हवौ हुवे सिंचाभ्यः । चत्वारि सूत्राणि गतानि । त्रिपाठीशिवजीसूनुना त्रिपाठीकान्हजीकृते संज्ञाकरणभाष्ये द्वितीयः प्रपाठकः समाप्तः ॥ इति संज्ञाकरणभाष्यं समाप्तम् ॥

RASB II 1329 (G 1006). 39 fol. 585 Grantha-s. Dated V.S. 1726.

3 AKṢARA-LAKṢAṆA-PARIBHĀṢĀ (अक्षरलक्षणपरिभाषा)

A work giving the details, such as the number of words, words analysed with Avagraha, requiring "iti" in the Pada-pāṭha, words ending with Visarga, "si", "se", "n", etc. for each Varga of the *Ṛgveda*. Similar to the printed *Ṛgveda-pada-ratna* (Srirangam edition), with 15 verses of paribhāṣā.

Beginning:

गणेशवाग्गुरून् नत्वा रामं चाक्षरलक्षणम् ।
करोति सुखबोधाय (वर्ग)स्यैकेन वर्णतः ॥
शिखामणिरिदं नाम्ना पदस्य दशनिर्णयम् ।
पदपद्येतिकाराश्च सितुसेन्तानि चात्र तु ॥

End:

प्रोक्ता तु परिभाषैषा लक्षणस्य यथामति ।
सम्यग् वाप्यन्यथा वेदं ग्राह्यं विद्वद्भिरादरात् ॥

Adyar D XIII 28 (VB 737h). PL. Gr. 3 fol. Incomplete. Full text of the paribhāṣā is printed. The last two fol. contain the list of code words which show a few variants to the printed edition of the *Ṛgveda-pada-ratna*. Up to the fifth Adhyāya of the third Aṣṭaka of the *Ṛgveda*.

4 AKṢARA-SAṂKHYĀ (अक्षरसंख्या)

Mentioned together with some other Veda-lakṣaṇa works, on a fly-leaf in Adyar D I 848 (25 L 2 = 71120), a Ms. of the commentary on the *Taittirīya-prātiśākhya* – *Taibhāṣya-ratna*.

[NCC I 14a]

5 AKṢARA-SAṂJÑĀ (अक्षरसंज्ञा)

This is identical with the *Iṅgya-ratna* attributed to Nemāni Bhairavāvadhānin.
Baroda 10333(a). PL. Tel. 6 fol. 150 Grantha-s. Incomplete.

[NCC I 14a]

6 AKṢARA-SVARA-SAṂDHI (अक्षरस्वरसंधि)

About 40 verses on general rules of Saṃdhis; the illustrations are from Vedic texts.

Beginning:

शषहेषु रलवर्णौ दृश्येते चेत् स्वरोदये ।

रेफो ऋवर्णतां याति लकारो लृत्वमेव च ॥

Trav. Uni. 10245. 250 Grantha-s (with C.). Incomplete.

[NCC I 14a]

7 AKHAṆḌA-MAÑJARĪ (अखण्डमञ्जरी)

Title of the *Aniṅgya-lakṣaṇa* (which see) of Śeṣa Nārāyaṇa.

*AGASTYA (अगस्त्य)

Quoted in the *Ṛgveda-prātiśākhya*, I 2.

[NCC I 21b]

8 AGASTYA-ŚIKṢĀ (अगस्त्यशिक्षा)

Referred to in the commentary on the Śikṣā-samuccaya, TCD 32-B.

9 AṄGA-KRAMA-LAKṢAṆA (अङ्गक्रमलक्षण)

Oppert I 1732. PL. Gr. 40 pp. Belonged to Sivasuri Sastri of Bhavani, Coimbatore Dist.

[NCC I 62a]

10 AṄGA-PRAKARAṆA (अङ्गप्रकरण)

Adyar I, p. 48a (8 E 34; 70 fol.). The Ms. of this entry in Adyar contains Vedāṅgāni (pp. 1-62) and *Sarva-sammata-śikṣā* (Adyar D I 1042) with the C. of Mañci-bhaṭṭa (pp. 64-143), in the middle of which there is a colophon on p. 96 : "ityaṅga-prakaraṇam".

[NCC I 63b]

*ACALĀCĀRYA (अचलाचार्य)

– Jaṭā-paṭala.

PUL I, p. 6 (no.88). See BBRAS 490. Ptd.: ed. by George Thibaut. – Leipzig : F. A. Brockhaus, 1870. See below under Jaṭā-paṭala.

[NCC I 70ab]

*AJĀTAŚATRU (अजातशत्रु)

Guru of Viṣṇuyaśas, for whom he wrote the *Phulla-(Puṣpa-)sūtra-bhāṣya*. He probably lived after A.D. 950, as he refers to Halāyudha. See below under the Cs. on the *Phulla-sūtra*.

– Phulla-(Puṣpa-)sūtra-bhāṣya. Ptd.: Benares : Chowkhamba, 1922-27. – (Chowkhamba Sanskrit Series 57). Also ed. by B. R. Sarma. – Kathmandu : Nepal Research Centre; Stuttgart : Steiner (Wiesbaden), 1979, 1985.

[NCC I 81b]

*ATRI-ṚṢI (अत्रि-ऋषि)

– Ātreya-śikṣā. MT 2188(a).

– Ātreya-sūtra-s(Śikṣā). Said to be the basis of the *Ātreya-śikṣā;* see MT 2188(a).

[NCC I 102a]

11 ATRI-SŪTRA (अत्रिसूत्र)

Oppert I 15. PL. Gr. 300 pp. Belonged to Ammanapakam Narasimhacharyar, Chingelpet Dist. Is this text the same as the *Ātreya-sūtra* (a Śikṣā) on which the *Ātreya-śikṣā* is said to be based ? (Cf. MT 2188).

[NCC I 102b]

12 ATHAKĀRI-LAKṢAṆA (अथकारिलक्षण)

A conjectural title. It is a list of Ṛk-s of the *Ṛgveda* containing the word "atha". It is identical to Khaṇḍa 14 of *Pada-gāḍha*. (Cf. pp. 55-56 of the *Pada-gāḍha*, Srirangam edition).

Beginning:

अथ गानप्रारम्भः । अग्निमीळे अथा ते अन्तमानां युक्ष्वा हि केशिनायं ते स्तोम उदुत्तमं वरुणाथा न उभयेषामश्विना मधुमत्तमम् ...

End:

प्र होता कुर्मस्त आयुरहरहर्जायत आ बाह्वोर्द्वे ते चक्रे सुमङ्गलीरियं दैवी पूर्ति (रा च गच्छाद्) एह गमन् वज्रेण हि यावया वृक्यमर्वाग् देवा अथा हि वामहमस्मि सहमाना बृहस्पतिर्नयत्विति पञ्चदश। अथकारिणः ।

Adyar D I 710 (22 H 6 = 69060). PL. Tel. 1 fol. The full text is printed.
L 786. Cf. Remarks at the end of the *Pada-gāḍha* – athaśabdavatīnāṃ saptāśītyṛcāṃ kathanam |
Mysore ND II 3864 (P 4906/21). PL. Na. 2 fol. (117-18). (Ṣaṇṇavati-athakāralakṣaṇa).
[NCC I 103b]

13 ATHARVA-KAUTSA-VYĀKARAṆA (अथर्वकौत्सव्याकरण)

→ Atharva-veda-prātiśākhyā – Caturadhyāyikā Śaunakīyā. The Ms. below contains an unpublished commentary. The name of the commentator is Kṛṣṇadāsa. According to the introduction in the commentary it consists of six chapters dealing with the following topics: 1) Śāstra-praśaṃśā, 2) Sthāna-prayatna-viveka, 3) Saṃjñā, 4) Paribhāṣā, 5) Saṃdhi-sādhana. The sixth chapter on Svarasādhana, according to description in the catalogue, is not available.

VSM I 808 (no.4179). 36 fol. (with C. of Kṛṣṇadāsa). Extract p. 360.

14 ATHARVAṆA-RAHASYA or ĀTHARVAṆA-RAHASYA (अथर्वणरहस्य / आथर्वणरहस्य)

53 verses with a commentary of Dhīra Govinda Śarman, compiled in the early 19th century for H. H. Wilson; a dissertation on the literature pertaining to the *Atharva-veda (Brahma-veda-dūṣaṇoddhāra)* including the Brāhmaṇa-s and Upaniṣad-s. The latest authority quoted here is the *Viśvaguṇādarśa-campū*.

Beginning:

प्रणवतुरीयार्णभवो नवशाखो ऽभीष्टफलदाता।
वल्लीत्रयरचिततनूरागमकल्पद्रुमो जयति॥ १॥
तुर्याम्नायरहस्यं चिकीर्षुरादौ गिरां देवीम्।
गोविन्दशास्त्रिसूरिर्ध्यायत्याद्येन पद्येन॥ २॥

वाचस्पत्यादीति --

वाचस्पत्यादिदिविषद्वन्द्यविग्रहवीरकाम्।

तारतूर्यां स्वसंवेद्यां भारतीं भावयेतराम्॥

End:

इत्थमनवद्यपद्यसंदोहैरथर्ववेदाभिव्यक्ति शाखाचार्यादि भेदतन्माहात्म्यतद्विषय दूषणोन्मूलनाद्यनेकपरामर्शपदवीं प्रदर्श्य संप्रति मङ्गलानुगतानि च शास्त्राणि प्रथन्त इति भगवत्पतञ्जलिस्मृत्यनुपूर्वाथर्वस्मरण रूपमङ्गलमाचरन् प्रस्थमप्युपसंहरति असाविति।

असावथर्वसंमोदो अथर्वनिगमानुगः।
अथर्वणरहस्याख्यो निबन्धः प्राप पूर्णताम्॥

इति गोविन्दशास्त्रिणः कृतावथर्वणरहस्यं संपूर्णम्॥

At the beginning of the Oxford Ms. the following two additional verses are given. The second mentions the name of Wilson:

वाचस्पत्यादिदिविषन्नुतनूतनविग्रहाम्।
नीरकुन्देन्दुधवलां शारदां समुपास्महे॥ १॥
विदितनिखिलविद्यः ख्यातलेखर्षभश्रीर्विलसिनिति खिलायं भाव्यते भूमिपालः।
तदुपचरितवृत्तिर्धीरगोविन्दशर्मा कमपि लघुनिबन्धं तुर्यवेदे तनोति॥ २॥

Hall p. 55.
Oxf. II 1059 (Ms. Mill 54). 30 fol. Dated A.D. 1830. = Oxf. 391a. According to the description in the catalogue this Ms. is an autograph.
RASB II 1417 (G 8151). 82 fol.
SK Ray DC. 1

[NCC I 104b and II 69b]

15 ATHARVAṆA-LAKṢAṆA-GRANTHA-SAṂGRAHA (अथर्वणलक्षणग्रन्थसंग्रह)
SBD 2074. 27 fol. Dated V.S. 1734. It includes among others the *Māṇḍūkī-śikṣā, Pañca-paṭalikā, Dantyoṣṭhya-vidhi, Caturadhyāyikā* and *Prātiśākhya.*

16 ATHARVA-PARIŚIṢṬA (or -VIDHĀNA) (अथर्वपरिशिष्ट /-विधान)
20 verses giving a list of works pertaining to the *Atharva-veda* and prescribing certain hymns and mantra-s for attaining specific gains, in the nature of the *Ṛgvidhāna.* Thus, it is called in the last verse *Atharva-vidhāna.*

Beginning:

अथातो ऽथर्ववेदस्य शौनकस्य महात्मनः।
स्वशाखीयं श्रौतसूत्रं वैतानाख्यमुदाहृतम्॥ १॥
गोपथब्राह्मणं तद्वत् कौशिकं गृह्यसूत्रकम्।
संहिता चार्कसाहस्री पिप्पलाद्यङ्गशाखिनः॥ २॥

End:

तुभ्यमेव जवीमन्नित्ययुतं तु हुतं भवेत्।
अग्ने गीर्भिर्न इत्येतन्मेधावृद्धिकरं परम्॥ १९॥
ये मे पाशास्तथाप्येतद् बन्धनान्मोक्षकारणम्।
एतदथर्वविधानाख्यं परिशिष्टं निरूपितम्॥ २०॥

Ptd.: in Śikṣā-saṃgraha. – Benares, 1889, pp. 479-80. – (Ben. S. S. 10).

17 ATHARVA-VEDA-KRAMA-PĀṬHA (अथर्ववेदक्रमपाठ)

Baroda 7597(b). 22 fol. 300 Grantha-s. = CLB I, p. 1. Incomplete (I-XII). A list of Pratīka-s (ādipadadvayamātram) of the Śaunaka Śākhā of the *Atharva-veda.*

Bombay 1879-82, p. 3. (Kāṇḍa XX).

BORI 133 of 1879-80. = BORI D I i.386. 88 fol. 1940 Grantha-s (XX. Kāṇḍa). Dated V.S. 1598.

PUL I, p. 1 (no.3). 13 fol. Incomplete (I 2 - III).

[NCC I 111a]

18 ATHARVA-VEDA-JAṬĀ-PĀṬHA (अथर्ववेदजटापाठ)

Baroda 9100. 11 fol. 200 Grantha-s (XVII. Kāṇḍa). = CLB I, p. 1.

BORI 128 of 1879-80. = BORI D I i.387. 58 fol. (XVI. Kāṇḍa).

BORI 83 of 1880-81. = BORI D I i.388. 12 fol. (XVII. Kāṇḍa). Dated V.S. 1727 / Śaka 1593. Copied by Govinda of Aṇahillapura.

VSM I 795 (no.4129). 11 fol. Incomplete (of 15.1-2.1; 16.1.1-2). Extract p. 359.

VSM I 796 (no.4130). 10 fol. Incomplete (of 15.14.7-15.18). Extract p. 360.

[NCC I 111a]

19 ATHARVA-VEDA-JAṬĀ-PĀṬHA (PAIPPALĀDA-ŚĀKHĀ)
(अथर्ववेदजटापाठ / पैप्पलादशाखा)

B I, p. 2 (no.10). 12 fol. Dated V.S. 1727. Kh. 55.

[NCC I 111b]

20 ATHARVA-VEDA-PRĀTIŚĀKHYA -- CATURADHYĀYIKĀ ŚAUNAKĪYĀ
(अथर्ववेदप्रातिशाख्य / चतुरध्यायिका शौनकीया)

Ascribed to Śaunaka. A Prātiśākhya for the *Atharva-veda* in four chapters. In some Mss. (e.g. SBD 2086, Ujjain II, p. 37, VSM I 808 and 811) it is attributed to Kautsa and is described as Kautsa-Vyākaraṇa. See L. Sadasiva Katre, *New Indian Antiquary,* I, 6 (September) 1938, pp. 383-96. It is also known as the *Caturadhyāyika-Vyākaraṇa.* For details of Mss. material and a proposed critical edition see Madhava M. Deshpande, "Announcing a Critical Edition of the *Śaunakīyā Caturadhyāyikā* [alias Whitney's *Atharva-veda Prātiśākhya]*" in : *The Adyar Library Bulletin,* vols. 44-45 (1980-81), pp. 241-52 where altogether 14 Mss. are described. Cf. also *Journal of Oriental Institute,* Baroda, vol. 26, no. 2 (1976), pp. 131-44.

Beginning:

चतुर्णां पदजातानां नामाख्यातोपसर्गनिपातानां संध्यपद्यौ गुणौ प्रातिज्ञम्। एवमिहेति च विभाषाप्राप्तं सामान्ये। पदान्त्यः पद्यः। अन्त्ऌकारः स्वरः पद्यः। ऌकारविसर्जनीयौ च। स्पर्शाः प्रथमोत्तमाः। न चवर्गः।

End:

द्वाभ्यामुकारः । अनुनासिकदीर्घत्वं प्रयोजनम्। प्लुतश्चाप्लुतवत्। अनुनासिकः पूर्वश्च शुद्धः । यथाशास्त्रं प्रसंधानम् । प्रगृह्यावगृह्यचर्चायां क्रमवदुत्तरमस्मिन्नवग्रहः । समापाद्यानाम्न्ते संहितावद् वचनम्। तस्य पुनरास्थापितं नाम। स एकपदः परिहार्यश्च॥

B I, p. 210 (no.77).

BORI 11 of 1870-71. = BORI D I i.403. 13 fol. 180 Grantha-s. Dated V.S. 1718. Copied by Bhavadeva, son of Nāgajit, a resident of Kaṇvālaya.

BORI 1(iv) of 1873-74. = BORI D I i.406. 10 fol. (12b-21b). From Bikaner.

BORI 87(ii) of 1880-81. = BORI D I i.407. 6 fol. (64-69). From III 2 to the end. Cf. above 178(vii) of 1880-81.

BORI 178(vii) of 1880-81. = BORI D I i.405. 6 fol. (58-63). Up to III 2. Cf. below 87(ii) of 1880-81.

BORI 179(vii) of 1880-81. = BORI D I i.408. 10 fol. (57-66). Dated V.S. 1717.

BORI 2 of 1884-86. = BORI D I i.404. 8 fol.

GJKSV 41855. 11 fol. (Śaunakīyātharvaṇa-prātiśākhya).

Haug p. 42 (no.167). Though it is described here as identical with the text edited by Whitney, it is the same as the *Atharva-prātiśākhya(mūlasūtra)* = München 173.

IM 3718. 12 fol. Incomplete. Up to the 3rd Pāda of the 4th Adhyāya. Title on the cover page : *Atharva-vedīya-catuḥsūtrī*. Kau. Sū. Bhā on the margin of each fol.

Kh. 56.

Kh. 82.

Müller 71a (MM 50). 11 fol. Sent by Bühler from India on 13.11.1871.

Peters. III 383 (no.2).

PUL I, p. 18 (no.3). 7 fol. Dated V.S. 1462.

PUL I, p. 18 (no.4). 9 fol. Dated V.S. 1961.

RASB II 1415(II) (G 7852). 36-43 fol. Dated V.S. 1671 = A.D. 1613.

RASB II 1416 (G 1272). 110 fol. (of which 62-63, 65-109 are missing; with C.). Dated V.S. 1689.

SBD 2074. 27 fol. Dated V.S. 1734. Title: Atharvaṇa-lakṣaṇa-grantha-saṃgraha.

SBD 2086. 10 fol. Col.: ityatharvavede kautsavyākaraṇe caturādhyāyikāyāṃ caturthādhyāyasya caturthaḥ pādaḥ iti.

SBD 2134. 12 fol. (Ātharvaṇa-prātiśākhya).

Tb. 210. Only the Sūtra-s and a few passages from the C. transcribed by Roth from the Ms. Weber 361. Dated 21 Nov. 1846.

Tb. 211. Roth's transcript of Whitney's copy of the Ms. Weber 361. Dated March 1853.

Tb. 213(H). A copy of the beginning portion only (up to I 31).

Ujjain II, p. 37 (no.3576). 12 fol. (Kautsa-vyākaraṇa).

VSM I 808 (no.4179). 36 fol. (with C. of Kṛṣṇadāsa). Extract p. 360. (Atharva-kautsa-vyākaraṇa).

VSM I 810 (no.4177). 12 fol. Dated V.S. 1877 ? Copied by Mārtaṇḍa Raghunātha.

VSM I 811 (no.4178). 22 fol. (with C. of Bhārgava Bhāskara). Extract p. 361. (Kautsa-vyākaraṇa).

Weber 361 (Chambers 143). 77 fol. (with an. C.; said to be by Ciratna). Dated V.S. 1714.

Ptd.:

Ed. by William D. Whitney, with an introduction, translation and notes in : *Journal of the American Oriental Society*, VII (1862), pp. 333-616. [NL (PP 1549); SKGI (Ri IX 91); Emeneau (376)]

Also issued separately: – New Haven : American Oriental Society, 1862. 285 pp. [Adyar (H 215 Sau Ca x=); BM : Ptd. Bks. Cat. 1876, p. 132)]

Reprint of the above : Benares : Chowkhamba, 1962 (2nd edition). – (Chowkhmba Sanskrit Studies 20) [Adyar (H080 CSS S 20); BORI (18442); NL (180 Pc 96 22); SAI (ind S 21, 20); SKGI (Ri IX 90)]

[NCC I 109ab]

– C.

RASB II 1416 (G 1272). 110 fol. (of which 62-63, 65-109 are missing; with text). Dated V.S. 1689.

Tb. 211. Roth's transcript of Whitney's copy of the Ms. Weber 361. Dated March 1853.

Weber 361 (Chambers 143). 77 fol. (with text). Dated V.S. 1714.

– C. of Bhārgava Bhāskara.

VSM I 811 (no.4178). 22 fol. Incomplete (I 1.1 to I 4.8). Extract p. 361.

– C. of Kṛṣṇadāsa.

VSM I 808 (no.4179). 36 fol. (with text). Extract p. 360.

21 ATHARVA-VEDA-PRĀTIŚĀKHYA(-MŪLA-SŪTRA) (अथर्ववेदप्रातिशाख्य / मूलसूत्र)

Another Prātiśākhya of the *Atharva-veda* in three Prapāṭhaka-s. The introduction in Suryakanta's edition discusses several problems connected with this Prātiśākhya and distinguishes two recensions of the text.

Beginning:

ओं नमस्कृत्य ब्रह्मणे शंकराय ऋषिभ्यः पूर्वेभ्यः शमु वाचास्तु मे गीः ।
प्रज्ञां ब्रह्म मेधां तपश्चादिश्याद् ब्रह्म यशसं मा कृणोतु ॥

अथातो न्यायाध्यनस्य पार्षदं वर्तयिष्यामः । १ । पदानां संहितां विद्यात् । २ । समर्थः पदविधिरिति । ३ । द्विरुदात्तं बृहस्पत्यादीनाम् । ४ ।

End:

स्वरलिङ्गस्वरविभक्तिवचनविशेषेष्विति यावद् वा । शास्त्रे पुराणे कविभिर्दृष्टमेतत् । वर्णलिङ्गस्वरविभक्तिवाक्यव्यत्ययश्छन्दसीति । वर्णलोपागमह्रस्वदीर्घप्लुतात्मनेभाषा परस्मैभाषा अपियन्त्यपियन्ति ।

(न तर्कबुद्ध्या न च शास्त्रदृष्ट्या यथाम्नातमन्यथा नैव कुर्यात् ।
आम्नातं परिषत् तस्य शास्त्रं दृष्टो विधिर्व्यत्ययः पूर्वशास्त्रे ॥
आम्नातव्यमनाम्नातं प्रपाठे ऽस्मिन् क्वचित् पदम् ।
छन्दसो ऽपरिमेयत्वात् परिषत् तस्य लक्षणम् ॥)

परिषत् तस्य लक्षणमिति। आथर्वणे संहितालक्षणग्रन्थे प्रातिशाख्यमूलसूत्रं समाप्तम्।
(इत्यथर्वप्रातिशाख्यं मूलसूत्रं समाप्तम्)

Alwar 327. Dated A.D. 1908. Col.: Laghu-prātiśākhya. Ms. Al. of Suryakanta's edition.

Baroda 7598. 4 fol. 60 Grantha-s. = CLB I, p. 22. Ms. Ṣa. of Suryakanta's edition.

Bikaner 664(6). Dated V.S. 1735 (A.D. 1678). Copied at Pattanapura.

Bikaner 665(6). Copy of the above.

BORI 12 of 1870-71. = BORI D I i.396. 6 fol. Dated V.S. 1718. Copied by Bhavadeva, a resident of Kaṇvālaya, son of Nāgajit, grandson of Rāmacandra. Ms. J. of Suryakanta's edition.

BORI 1(v) of 1873-74. = BORI D I i.399. 2 fol. (21b-23). Contains up to the end of the second Prapāṭhaka. From Bikaner. Ms. P. of Suryakanta's edition.

BORI 87(iii) of 1880-81. = BORI D I i.401. 4 fol. (70-74a). Dated V.S. 1753. Ms. Vr. of Suryakanta's edition.

BORI 175 of 1880-81. = BORI D I i.397. 4 fol. Dated V.S. 1676. Copied by Nṛsiṃha of Stambhatīrtha. Ms. N. of Suryakanta's edition.

BORI 179(viii) of 1880-81. = BORI D I i.400. 5 fol. (66-70). Dated V.S. 1717. Ms. B. of Suryakanta's edition.

BORI 6 of 1884-86. = BORI D I i.398. 8 fol. Copied by Mādhavajīka. Ms. M. of Suryakanta's edition.

BORI 7 of 1884-86. 84 fol. Dated V.S. 1908 (described as Bhāṣya). Ms. Vn. of Suryakanta's edition.

Göttingen 158(5). 3 fol. Copied in V.S. 1918 from a Ms. dated V.S. 1719.

Haug p. 42 (no.167). Described here as identical with the text edited by Whitney. = München 173.

IM 2035. 5 fol.

IM 2036. 5 fol.

Jammu RSRI p. 172 (no. 5209). Śāradā. 6 fol. (Stein 252).

Kh. 56.

Kh. 61 (2).

Kh. 82.

Müller 71b (MM 50). 5 fol. Sent by Bühler from India on 13.11.1871.

München 173. 63 fol. Dated A.D. 1865.

Peters. II, p. 182 (no.15). 4 fol.

Peters. III, p. 383.

PUL I, p. 18 (no.5). 54 fol. (with C.). 800 Grantha-s. Dated V.S. 1668. Ms. APrM. of Suryakanta's edition.

PUL I, p. 18 (no.6). 53 fol. (with C.). Ms. Ben. of Suryakanta's edition.

R. A. Sastri III, p. 256.

RASB II 1415(III) (G 7852). 4 fol. (43-46) Dated V.S. 1671 = A.D. 1615. Ms. V. of Suryakanta's edition.

SBD 2074. 27 fol. Dated V.S. 1734. Title: Atharvaṇa-lakṣaṇa-grantha-saṃgraha.

SBD 2085. 5 fol.

Tb. 36. 17 fol. (Only Sūtra-s). Copied in July 1875, obviously from the Ms. BORI 12 of 1870-71 and collated with the original by Kielhorn.

Tb. 213(I). Copy of the Bikaner Ms. made by Roth.
Udaipur I. B. 8, 13 (p. 2, no.13 of ptd. Cat.).
Ujjain II, p. 8 (no. 3521). 6 fol. Dated V.S. 1692.
VSM I 813 (no.3340). 18 fol. Dated Śaka 1718. Copied by Sāṭhe Mahādeva.
VSM I 814 (no.39). 59 fol. with C. Dated Śaka 1563. Copied by Deśapāṇḍe Sakho from Khṭāva ?
VSM I 815 (no.38). 10 fol. (Prātiśākhya-mūlasūtram). Copied by Daivajña Bālam-bhaṭṭa.

Ptd.: ed. by Vishva Bandhu Vidyarthi Shastri (the Phonetico-grammatical Aphorisms of the *Atharva-veda*, Critically Edited for the First Time from Original Mss. with an Introduction and Appendices). – Lahore : Punjab University, 1923. 5, 79, 1 pp. [BORI (2099); NL (180 Jc 92 141); UBTÜ (21 A 5777)]
Also ed. by Suryakanta, with an introduction, an English translation, notes and indices. – Lahore : Mehar Chand Lachhman Das, 1939. viii, 72, 21, 139, 65, 35 pp. [Adyar (H 216.1 Ath x= Sur); BORI (8734); NL (180 Ja 93 5)]
Reprinted : Delhi : Mehar Chand Lachhaman Das, 1968. [SAI (ind 51 D 702); SKGI (Ri IX 9.5); BORI (22061)]

– C. Some of the Mss. below are described as Bhāṣya; they are apparently identical with the longer version of Suryakanta's edition.
Alwar 328. Extract 97.
BORI 7 of 1884-86. = BORI D I i.402. 37 fol. Dated V.S. 1908.
Haug p. 42 (no.167) = München 173.
IM 2034. 29 fol. Title: Ātharvaṇa-prātiśākhya.
München 173. 63 fol. Dated A.D. 1865.
Peters. II, p. 182 (no.16). 4 fol.
Peters. II, p. 182 (no.17). 37 fol.
Peters. III, p. 383 (no.7).
PUL I, p. 18 (no.5). 54 fol. (with text). 800 Grantha-s. Dated V.S. 1668. Ms. APrM. of Suryakanta's edition.
PUL I, p. 18 (no.6). 53 fol. (with text). Ms. Ben. of Suryakanta's edition.

[NCC I 109b]

22 ATHARVA-VEDA-BṚHAT-SARVĀNUKRAMAṆIKĀ (अथर्ववेदबृहत्सर्वानुक्रमणिका)

Also known as the *Brahmaveda-mantrānukramaṇī* in eleven Paṭala-s. Paṭala-s I-X deal with the Kāṇḍa-s I-XIX and the Paṭala XI with the Kāṇḍa XX of the *Atharva-veda*. For the argument that the two units are by different authors, see the preface of the Hoshiarpur edition.

Beginning:

ब्रह्मवेदं नमस्कृत्य दुर्गां विश्वेश्वरं गुरुम्।
नृसिंहं दक्षिणामूर्तिमथर्वाणमभेदतः ॥ १॥
आविष्कुर्वे ब्रह्मवेदमन्त्रानुक्रमणीं यथा।
ऋषिदैवतच्छन्दोभिर्युक्तां पाठफलाप्तये॥ २॥

अथाथर्वण(गण)मन्त्राणामृषिदैवतच्छन्दांसि । यत्काम ऋषिर्मन्त्रद्रष्टा वा भवति । यस्यां देवतायामार्थपत्यमिच्छता स्तुतिः प्रयुज्यते सा देवता तस्य मन्त्रस्य भवति । छन्दोक्षरसंख्यावच्छेदकम् । उच्यते तावत् तत्र छन्दोनुक्रमण्याम् -- गायत्र्युष्णिगनुष्टुब्बृहती ...

End:

आद्याश्चतस्त्र अनुष्टुभः । अन्त्ये गायत्र्यौ । तं वां नव । पुरुमीळ्हाजमीळ्हौ । आश्विनम् । त्रैष्टुभम् । मधुमतीर्वामदेवः । क्षेत्रस्य-पतिः पनाय्यं मेध्यातिथिर्मेध्यातिथिरिति । इति श्रीब्रह्मवेदोक्तमन्त्राणां बृहत्सर्वानुक्रमणिकायामेकादशः पटलः समाप्तः ॥ समाप्ता चेयं बृहत्सर्वानुक्रमणिका ॥

AK 64. 67 fol. Dated V.S. 1811.

Alwar 322. Extract 96.

Ānandāśrama 7501. 60 fol. Up to 11th Paṭala. A modern copy entitled Sarvānukramaṇī or Bṛhat-sarvānukramaṇikā.

Bik. 271. 60 fol. Title: Brahma-veda-mantrānukramaṇī.

B I, p. 198 (no.2). 94 fol. Dated V.S. 1771.

Baroda 7595. 53 fol. (1-23, 53-82). 1500 Grantha-s. = CLB I, p. 22. Incomplete. Dated V.S. 1826.

Baroda 9704. 56 fol. 1500 Grantha-s. = CLB I, p. 22. Dated A.D. 1920 (both Mss. lack the portion from the middle of the 3rd Paṭala to the beginning of the 7th).

Bikaner 615. 57 fol.

Bikaner 616. 60 fol. Dated V.S. 1747 (A.D. 1690). Copied in Pattanapura.

Bikaner 617. 77 fol. Dated V.S. 1735 (A.D. 1678).

BORI 14 of 1870-71. = BORI D I i.390. 48 fol. (Paṭala-s I-V). Dated V.S. 1647(?). From Broach. Bhā3 of VVRI edition.

BORI 15 of 1870-71. = BORI D I i.391. 50 fol. (Paṭala-s VI-XI). Dated V.S. 1767. From Broach. Bhā4 of VVRI edition.

BORI 112 of 1880-81. = BORI D I i.394. 13 fol. (Paṭala I). Bhā6 of VVRI edition.

BORI 8 of 1884-86. = BORI D I i.392. 87 fol. (up to X 21). Bhā1 of VVRI edition.

BORI 9 of 1884-86. = BORI D I i.393. 33 fol. (Paṭala-s I-IV). Bhā2 of VVRI edition.

BORI 64 of 1891-95. = BORI D I i.389. 67 fol. Dated V.S. 1811. Contains tables of Gaṇa-s, etc. Bhā5 of VVRI edition.

Br. Mus. 548 (Add. 5355c). 33 fol. (40-72). Copied Written ca. A.D. 1783. for Col. Polier.

Hoshiarpur p. 56 (no.3201). 51 fol. 1500 Grantha-s. Bī of VVRI edition. (Transcript of a Bikaner Ms.).

IM 4895. 61 fol. (20-80). Incomplete.

IO 235 (2142a). 29 fol. La of VVRI edition.

Jodhpur 1508.

Kh. 57 (Paṭala I).

Mysore ND II 3659 (P 3333/ 1). PL. Gr. 47 fol. Extract no. 234. Title: Bṛhatsarvānukramaṇikā.

Peters. II, p. 183 (no.35). 64 fol.

Peters. III, p. 383 (no.8).
PUL I, p. 18 (no.7). 24 fol. 600 Grantha-s.
RASB II 1414 (G 4175). 40 fol. 1400 Grantha-s. Dated V.S. 1947.
Stein p. 3 (no. 27). 36 fol.
VSM I 809 (no.4170). 107 fol. (3-22; 26-67; 70-114). Dated Śaka 1743.
Weber 1487 (Ms. or. fol. 624d). 74 fol. Dated V.S. 1767.

Ptd.: ed. by Pandit Rama Gopala Sastri. – Lahore : D. A. V. College, 1922. 42, 204, 22 pp. – (Dayānanda Mahā-vidyālaya Saṃskṛta-granthamālā 6). [Adyar (H080 DAV 6); NL (180 Jc 92 50); Emeneau (397)]

Also ed. by Vishva Bandhu, in Collaboration with Bhim Dev and Pitambar Datt. – Hoshiarpur : Vishveshvaranand Vedic Research Institute, 1966. 21, 197 pp. – (Woolner Indological Series 11). [Adyar (H080 VVRI WI 11); BORI (23570); SAI (ind 51 D 70/4); SKGI (Ri IX 1 and Ri II 17)]

For both these editions, besides the Mss. from BORI, IO, and Bikaner a Ms. (134 fol.) in the Kangaḍi (Gurukul) Viśvavidyālaya, Haridwar, has been used.

[NCC I 109b]

23 ATHARVA-VEDA-ŚIKṢĀ (अथर्ववेदशिक्षा)
→ Māṇḍūkī Śikṣā.
IM 9221. 2 fol. Incomplete. Lacks end. Begins as : Atharva-vedīya-māṇḍūkī-śikṣā.

[NCC I 110a]

24 ATHARVA-VEDA-SAṂHITĀ-MANTRĀNUKRAMAṆIKĀ (अथर्ववेदसंहितामन्त्रानुक्रमणिका)
Beginning:

अथर्ववेदमन्त्राणामनुक्रमणिका स्फुटा।
ऋषिच्छन्दोदैवतानि निरूप्याथ निरूप्यते॥
तत्रादौ प्रथमकाण्डानुक्रमणिका -- प्रथमे ऽनुवाके सूक्तानि ६ ऋचः १९॥

End:

इत्यथर्ववेदसंहिताया विंशतिकाण्ड्या मन्त्रानुक्रमणिका समाप्ता

Bik. 271. 60 fol. (Title: Brahma-veda-mantrānukramaṇī → Atharvavedabṛhatsarvānukramaṇikā).
RASB II 1413 (G 4174). 27 fol. 200 Grantha-s.

[NCC I 111b]

25 ATHARVA-VEDĪYA-CATUḤSŪTRĪ (अथर्ववेदीयचतुःसूत्री)
→ Atharva-veda-prātiśākhya – Caturadhyāyikā Śaunakīyā.
IM 3718. 12 fol. Incomplete. Up to the 3rd Pāda of the 4th Adhyāya.

26 ATHARVA-VEDĪYA-PAÑCAPAṬALIKĀ (अथर्ववेदीयपञ्चपटलिका)
A Prātiśākhya (?) in five Paṭala-s; a metrical Anukramaṇī "throwing light on the arrangement, division and text of the Atharva-veda Saṃhitā".

Beginning:

(ओं) उक्तानुक्तस्य यं न्यायं प्रोवाच परिबभ्रवः ।
पर्यायाणामृचां वापि तद् वक्ष्यामो यथाक्रमम् ॥
बहूनामव्यवेतानां व्यनेकं सदृशं पदम् ।
आदिष्टं तेषु वा यत् स्यात् तदुक्तानुक्तमुच्यते ॥

End:

प्राजापत्यस्य सर्वस्य परमस्य पुनः शृणु ।
त्रयोदशाद्यं (वि)जानीयाद् द्वौ षट्कौ सप्तमः परः ॥
आद्यं दशकं ह्येकादशकं तस्माच्च परं व्यधिकं विहितम् ।
एकादश वै त्रिगुणान्यपरश्चत्वारि वै वचनानि
परश्चत्वारि वै वचनानि पर इति ॥ १९ ॥

इति पञ्चपटलिका समाप्ता

BORI 1(i) of 1873-74. = BORI D I i.399. 10 fol. (1-10). From Bikaner.
BORI 178 (iv) of 1880-81. = BORI D I i.405.
BORI 179(iv) of 1880-81. = BORI D I i.400. Dated V.S. 1717.
Kh. 61 (no.178).
RASB II 1415(IV) (G 7852). 7 fol. (47-53).
SBD 2074. 27 fol. Dated V.S. 1734. Title: Atharvaṇa-lakṣaṇa-grantha-saṃgraha.
Tb. 213(E). Copy of a Ms. from Bikaner made by Roth.
VSM I 812 (no.4176). 9 fol. (3-11).

Ptd.: ed. by Bhagavaddatta, with a Hindi translation and an index of the Pratīka-s. – Lahore : D. A. V. College, 1920. 14, 39 pp. – (Dayānanda Mahāvidyālaya Saṃskṛta-granthamālā 1). [Adyar (H080 DAV 1); BORI (830); NL (180 Jc 92 46); IO (San D 624,b); SOAS (III.1.f.7 – 7984); Emeneau (398)]
Reprinted : New Delhi : Meharchand Lachhmandas Publications, 1970. [SAI (ind 51 D 888/2322)]

[NCC I 112a]

27 ATHARVA(ṆA)-ŚIKṢĀ (अथर्व(ण)-शिक्षा)

Oppert I 7162. Belonged to Ivattur Nandikesvara Sastri of Vijayanagaram.
Oppert II 5153. Belonged to Pichchu Dikshitar of Akhilandapuram, Thanjavur Dist.
Taylor I 67.

[NCC I 112b]

28 ADHIKĀRI-NIRŪPAṆA (अधिकारिनिरूपण)

Dharmaśāstra ? A tract on the qualifications for the study of the Veda. It consists of an anonymous commentary on four mantra-s which are quoted by Yāska in the *Nirukta* II 4. These four mantra-s are also referred to by Sāyaṇa in his Bhāṣya on *Ṛgveda* I 1.1 as from *śāstrāntara* and commented on. The mantra-s are:

१) विद्या ह वै … २) य आ तृणत्यवितथेन … ३) अध्यापिता ये गुरुं नाद्रियन्ते … ४) यमेव विद्या शुचिमप्रमत्तम् …

Beginning:

अथाधिकारी निरूप्यते । इह खलूपवेदैरङ्गैरुपाङ्गैश्च सहितायाः भगवत्यास्त्रयीविद्यायाः ग्रहणाधिकारी निरूप्यते । तल्लक्षणेन ग्राहकलक्षणमर्थात् सिध्यति । तल्लक्षणं च चतुर्भिर्वैदिकैर्मन्त्रैर्निरूपितम् । तांश्च मन्त्रान् वेदानामर्थं निर्वक्ष्यन् यास्को नाम महामुनिः स्वप्रणीतग्रन्थादौ अधिकारिलक्षणं द्योतयितुकामः सन्निरूपयामास । तत्रायं प्रथमो मन्त्रः । विद्याभिमानिनी देवता ब्राह्मणमुपदेष्टारमाचार्यमाजगाम । आगत्य चैवं प्रार्थयामास ॥

End:

इत्थं विद्यादेवतया प्रार्थितत्वादाचार्येण मुख्यं शिष्याय वेदविद्योपदेष्टव्या । यस्मादित्थं मन्त्रचतुष्टयेन अधिकारिलक्षणं निरूपितं तस्मादध्येतृलक्षणपरीक्षापुरःसरमध्यापयिता अध्येतारमध्यापनीयमध्यापयेदिति तात्पर्यार्थः ।

Adyar D I 711 (35 B 117 = PM 100). 3 fol. (4-6). = Adyar I, p. 104a.

[NCC I 143b]

29 ADHYĀYA-NĀMĀDI-PADĀBHIDHĀNA-KAṆḌIKĀ-PĀṬHA
(अध्यायनामादिपदाभिधानकण्डिकापाठ)

→ Cāturjñāna. Contains two additional verses at the beginning. This title is apparently based on the wordings of the second verse which reads: *adhyāyanāmādipadābhidhānayā ekaikayā kaṇḍikayābhidhīyate.*

SBD 2324. 16 fol. Incomplete. Dated V.S. 1881.

*ANANTA **(अनन्त)**

– Svarāṣṭaka-śikṣā. IM 2483.

Ptd.: in Śikṣā-saṃgraha. – Benares, 1889, pp. 362-68. – (Ben. S. S. 10).

[NCC I 159a]

*ANANTA (son of Bhīma) **(अनन्त)**

– Naigeyārcikānukrama. Oxf. II 855(16). = Oxf. 378a (no.375).

[NCC I 160b]

*ANANTA-GOPĀLAKṚṢṆA **(अनन्तगोपालकृष्ण)**

Son and disciple of Ananta-Veṅkaṭeśa of Śrīvatsa-gotra. He offers reverence to Gopālakṛṣṇa, author of *Śābdika-cintāmaṇi* (Adyar D VI 138-39), and Guru of Vijaya-raghunātha, Toṇḍamān of Pudukottai (A.D. 1736-69).

– Veda-śabda-vibhūṣṇa, MT 1640.

*ANANTA-DEVA **(अनन्तदेव)**

– Avasāna-nirṇaya(-śikṣā). Catch words of the *Śukla Yajurveda.*

Ptd.: in Śikṣā-saṃgraha. – Benares, 1889, pp. 166-71. – (Ben. S. S. 10). [BM : Ptd. Bks. Cat. 1892-1906. 36 (14093.b.31)]

*ANANTA-DEVA (-BHAṬṬA) or ANANTĀCĀRYA **(अनन्तदेव (-भट्ट) / अनन्ताचार्य)**

of the Kāṇva Śākhā of the *Śukla-yajurveda*, son of Bhāgīrathī and Nāgadeva; a resident of Benares (fl. ca. A.D. 1626). For details of his works on Śrauta, etc. see NCC I 174b-176a.

– Kāṇva-pada-lakṣaṇa. Govt. Or. Libr. Madras, p. 16. In MD is not traceable.

– Jaṭā-paṭala-vyākhyā, C. on Vyāḍi's Jaṭā-paṭala. BBRAS 491. Bhk. 9. Mithila IV 73. RASB II 906. Ptd.: in *Veda-vikṛti-lakṣaṇa-saṃgraha.* – Poona : BORI, 1978, pp. 33-46.

– Bhāṣika-sūtra-bhāṣya, on the Bhāṣika-sūtra of Kātyāyana dealing with the svara-s of the *Śatapatha-brāhmaṇa.* MT 2504. Mithila IV 116. 116(A). Hpr. III 205.
Ptd.: at the end of Kātyāyana's *Śukla-yajuḥ-prātiśākhya.* – Benares, 1888. – (Ben. S. S. 4). See below under Vājasaneyi-prātiśākhya.
Also ed. by B. B. Chaubey. – Hoshiarpur, 1975. – (Panjab University Indological Series 4).

– Varṇa-krama-lakṣaṇa. Adyar D I 966.

– Vājasaneyi- or Śukla-yajurveda-prātiśākhya-bhāṣya – Padārtha-prakāśa. Adyar I, p. 53b. Adyar D I 970. BORI D I i.286 = BORI 518 of 1882-83. GB 17. L 4119. MD 935. RASB II 900-03. Weber 2060.
Ptd.: in *Vājasaneyi-prātiśākhya* with two commentaries. – Madras : University of Madras, 1934. – (Madras University Sanskrit Series 5) and – Varanasi : Jnanaprakasa Pratisthana, Chowkhamba, 1975.

[NCC I 174-6]

*ANANTA(-DEVA) YĀJÑIKA or DEVA-YĀJÑIKA or YĀJÑIKĀNANTA-DEVA
(अनन्तदेव-याज्ञिक / देवयाज्ञिक / याज्ञिकानन्त-देव)
Also called Yājñika-deva or Śrīdeva or simply Deva, son of Mahādeva (Prajāpati), elder brother of Lakṣmīdhara (Weber, p. 53).

– Pratijñā-sūtrabhāṣya. BORI 46 of A 1881-82. L 2578. Ptd.: See below under *Pratijñā-sūtra* of Kātyāyana.

– Śukla-yajurveda-(Vājasaneyi-saṃhitā-)sarvānukrama-bhāṣya. Ptd.: See below under *Śukla-yajurveda-sarvānukrama* of Kātyāyana.

*ANANTĀCĀRYA **(अनन्ताचार्य)**
According to an entry in PUL II. App. p. 11, he redacted the *Sarvānukramaṇī* of Kātyāyana (anantācārya-samīkṛtā ?).

[NCC I 186a]

30 ANAVAGRAHA **(अनवग्रह)**
A Pariśiṣṭa of the *Sāmaveda* → Sāmaveda-sapta-lakṣaṇa.

Adyar D I 1075 (Sāmaveda-sapta-lakṣaṇa).
Adyar D I 1076 (Sāmaveda-sapta-lakṣaṇa).
Oxf. II 855(9) (Ms. Wilson 375). 1 fol. (fragment). = Oxf. 377b (no.375, fol. 57a)

[NCC I 193b]

31 ANIṄGYA(-PRAKARAṆA) (अनिङ्ग्य-प्रकरण)

The expression "aniṅgya" means "not separable" and is used to denote those compoud or simple words, which are not to be separated by an Avagraha in the Pada-pāṭha (iṅgyate vibhāgena cālyate iti iṅgyam | iṅgyam it vibhāgapadasya saṃjñā | sāvagrahaṃ padam iṅgyam | ... *Tribhāṣya-ratna* on the *Taittirīya-prātiśākhya,* I 48). Also included in the Sapta-lakṣaṇa (which see).

Adyar D I 984 → Veda-lakṣaṇa (A 2).

MT 485(f). PL. Tel. 2 fol. (58-59) (with C.). Incomplete. This Ms. is a collection of Veda-lakṣaṇa topics without any system or order. Presented in 1910-11 by C. Visvanatha Shastrigal of Viziyanagaram.

MT 689(d). PL. Gr. 8 fol. (27a-34a). Purchased in 1912-13 through Seshasayi Ayyangar of Kottaiyur near Kumbakonam.

MT 1205(b). PL. Tel. 4 fol. (11-14). Copied by Sītārāma of Bharadvāja-gotra. Presented in 1913-14 by K. Ramakrishnayya of Musalipattanam.

MT 1964(b). PL. Tel. 17 fol. (4-20) (with C.). Copied by Rayaprolu Veṅkaṭaśiva Somayajulu. Presented in 1916-17 by Rayaprolu Ramabrahmangaru of Guruza, Gudivada Taluk, Krishna Dist.

Mysore I, p. 20.

Oppert I 949. Belonged to Viraraghava Tatacharyar, Head Master, Sanskrit School of Sathakopacharya, Kanchipuram, Chingelpet Dist.

Oppert II 728. Belonged to Ghanapathi Shingaracharyar of Alasur, Madurantakam Taluk.

Oppert II 1298. Belonged to Gopalacharyar of Pillapakkam, Kanchipuram Taluk.

Oppert II 8996. Belonged to Ganapati Lakshminarayana Sastri of Tiruvadi, Thanjavur Dist.

PUL I, p. 18 (no.8). PL. Gr. 4 fol.

PUL II. App. p. 10 (no.129). PL. Gr. 10 fol. (A. 1048 ?).

PUL II. App. p. 10 (no.130). PL. Gr. 8 fol. (with Varṇānukrama).

TD 1804 (6th work in the codex of Sapta-lakṣaṇa) → Sapta-lakṣaṇa.

Trav. Uni. 2346 L. PL. Gr. 400 Grantha-s (with C.). (M.E. 1013 = A.D. 1838).

Trav. Uni. 4369 E. PL. Gr. 6 fol. 100 Grantha-s.

Trav. Uni. 5778 G.

Ujjain I, p. 10 (Anīthya mūla ?).

– C.

Adyar D I 718 (22 C 49 = 68749). PL. Gr. 5 fol. (16-20). Incomplete. Breaks off in verse 13 of the paribhāṣā. = Adyar I, p. 48a.

Adyar D I 719 (29 I 28 = 73580). PL. Gr. 19 fol. (39ff.). Incomplete. = Adyar I, p. 54a. Title: Sapta-lakṣaṇa Savyākhya.

Adyar D I 984 → Veda-lakṣaṇa (A 2).

MT 1964(b). PL. Tel. 17 fol. (4-20) (with text). Copied by Rayaprolu Veṅkaṭaśiva Somayajulu. Presented in 1916-17 by Rayaprolu Ramabrahmangaru of Guruza, Gudivada Taluk, Krishna Dist.

Mysore (1898), p. 6 (no. 52). 32 fol. (65-96). Incomplete.

Mysore I, p. 20 (2 Mss.).

Oppert II 729. Belonged to Ghanapathi Shingaracharyar of Alasur, Madurantakam Taluk.

Oppert II 8997. Belonged to Ganapati Lakshminarayana Sastri of Tiruvadi, Thanjavur Dist.

PUL I, p. 18 (no.9). PL. Gr. 16 fol.

Trav. Uni. 2346 L. PL. Gr. 400 Grantha-s (with text). (M.E. 1013 = A.D. 1838).

Trav. Uni. 2593. 73 fol. 1850 Grantha-s. Title: Aniṅgya-vyākhyānādi. This is actually the Sapta-lakṣaṇa-vyākhyā.

[NCC I 196a]

32 ANIṄGYA(-PRAKARAṆA) (Taitt.) **(अनिङ्ग्य-प्रकरण)**

of Śrīvatsāṅka, son of Devamanīṣin. A work in 100 verses, on words which are not split up in the Pada-pāṭha of the *Taittirīya-saṃhitā,* though prima facie compounds.

Beginning:

मुनिमानसमन्थानमथितागमसागरात्।
उदिताय नमो भूयादमृताय मुरारये॥ १॥
गुणत्रयविहीनाय जगत्त्रयविधायिने।
श्रुतित्रयदृशे शश्वत् पुरत्रयमथे नमः ॥ २॥
नमस्कृत्य विनेतारं विघ्नानामनुशिष्यते।
अनिङ्ग्यमिङ्ग्यसादृश्याद्यत् संदेहास्पदं भवेत्॥ ३॥

End:

साहन्त्यसावित्रसपत्नसूनृताश्रुतो हविष्यं च हलीक्ष्णशब्दाः ।
हेमन्तहोत्रीयहिरण्मयश्रुतो हैमन्तिकश्च हिकं हिरण्मयम्॥ ९८॥
प्रपञ्चत्वादनिङ्ग्यानां दिङ्मात्रमिह दर्शितम्।
अतो ऽनुक्तं च यत् किंचिदुन्नेयं तन्मनीषिभिः॥ ९९॥
एषानिङ्ग्यपदानां पदवी संदर्शिता सुभगा सुधिया।
देवमनीषिसुतेन श्रीवत्साङ्केन तैत्तिरीयाणाम्॥ १००॥

Adyar D I 712 (22 B 38 = 68690). PL. Tel. 8 fol. = Adyar I, p. 48a.

Adyar D I 713 (25 H 6 = 70967). PL. Gr. 8 fol. (1-8). = Adyar I, p. 48a.

Adyar D I 983 → Veda-lakṣaṇa (A 1). The paribhāṣā section is here called Pūrvāniṅgya and the main text Aparāniṅgya.

Adyar D I 988 → Veda-lakṣaṇa (A 6).

Adyar D I 1030 → Sapta-lakṣaṇa.

Adyar D I 1031 → Sapta-lakṣaṇa.

Adyar D I 1033 → Sapta-lakṣaṇa.

Adyar D I 1034 → Sapta-lakṣaṇa.

Baroda 6131(d). PL. Gr. 7 fol. (11-17). 100 Grantha-s. = CLB I, p. 22.

Baroda 6255(g). PL. Tel. 7 fol. (141-47). 100 Grantha-s. = CLB I, p. 22.

Baroda 10034(f). PL. Gr. 4 fol. (6-9). 100 Grantha-s. = CLB I, p. 22.

Brl. p. 12 (no.XLVII) = IO 4462.

Brl. p. 12 (no.XLVIII) = IO 4460.
Brl. p. 12 (no.XLIX) = IO 4461.
Burnell 5b.
Hamburg StUB (Oppert 10f). PL. Gr.
Hoshiarpur p. 49 (no.4105). PL. Gr. 7 fol. 100 Grantha-s. Incomplete.
Hoshiarpur p. 49 (no.4118). PL. Gr. 5 fol. 70 Grantha-s.
Hz 1435. PL. Gr. 33 fol. (Aniṅgya-lakṣaṇa) (with 3 other Veda-lakṣaṇa works). Belonged to the late Raja Ghanapathi of Tiruvidaimarudur, Thanjavur Dist.
IO 4460 (Burnell 146f). PL. Gr. 6 fol. (10-15).
IO 4461 (Burnell 350c). Tel. 28 fol. (21-48) (with C.). Written ca. A.D. 1867.
IO 4462 (Burnell 49f). PL. Gr. 7 fol. (11-17).
IO 4463 (Mackenzie II 94h). PL. Na. 5 fol.
IO 4464 (Mackenzie II 94m). PL. Na. 22 fol.
MD 853. PL. Gr. 29 pp. (24ff.).
MD 854. PL. Tel. 10 pp. (34ff.). The first 3 verses are omitted.
MD 855. Gr. 58 pp. (42ff.) (with C.).
MD 856. PL. Tel. 50 pp. (29ff.) (with C.).
MD 16395. PL. Gr. 13 pp. 120 Grantha-s.
MD 16713. PL. Tel. 54 Grantha-s.
MD 16808. PL. Gr. 200 Grantha-s.
MD 16815. PL. Gr. 21 pp. 400 Grantha-s.
MD 17365. PL. Tel. 10 pp. 160 Grantha-s.
MD 17366. PL. Tel. 18 pp. 250 Grantha-s (with C. of the a.).
MD 17442. PL. Gr. 13 pp. 126 Grantha-s.
MT 95(c). PL. Gr. 4 fol. (8-11) (called here Aniṅgya-śataka). Purchased in 1910-11 from Gopalaswami Ayyangar of Mannargudi.
MT 1233(b). PL. Tel. 36 fol. (24-59) (with C.). Presented in 1913-14 by K. Rama-krishnayya of Musalipattanam.
MT 1240(f). PL. Tel. 19 fol. (26-44) (with C.). Presented in 1913-14 by K. Rama-krishnayya of Musalipattanam.
MT 1964(c). PL. Tel. 7 fol. Copied by Rayaprolu Veṅkaṭaśiva Somayajulu. Dated Sunday the 10th day of Māgha-śukla, Hevilambi year. Presented in 1916-17 by Rayaprolu Ramabrahmangaru of Guruza, Gudivada Taluk, Krishna Dist.
MT 2881(a). PL. Gr. 15 fol. (with C.). Presented in 1918-19 by Venkatagiri Appalacharyar of Triplicane.
MT 3887(j). PL. Gr. 4 fol. (80-83). Purchased in 1921-22 from Annasvami Sastrigal, Bhavani, Coimbatore Dist.
MT 4600(a). PL. Gr. 5 fol. (13-17). Title: Aniṅgya-śataka. Presented in 1924-25 by the Secretary to the Trustees of Sri Yogi Parthasarathi Ayyangar's Charities, Triplicane, Madras.
Mysore I, p. 20 (Aniṅgya-śataka, 2 Mss.); p. 613.
Mysore ND II 3038-58. Extract no. 3, 4.
PUL I, p. 18 (no.10). PL. Gr. 17 fol.
PUL II. App. p. 13 → Veda-lakṣaṇa.
RASB II 487-88(VII) (G 6063). 7 fol. (12-18). Dated V.S. 1913 / Śaka 1778.
TD 1793. PL. Gr. 12 fol. (19-30) → Sapta-lakṣaṇa.

Tirupati SVUORI 252 (1510b). PL. Gr.
Tirupati SVUORI 253 (4378c). PL. Gr. 6 fol. (17-22). Title: Aniṅgya-grantha.
Tirupati SVUORI 254 (3041a). PL. Gr. Title: Aniṅgya-prakaraṇa.
Tirupati SVUORI 255 (1746a). PL. Gr. (a. Nārāyaṇa in the catalogue).
Trav. Uni. 2630 O. PL. Gr. 100 Grantha-s.
Trav. Uni. 2938 F. PL. Gr. 100 Grantha-s.
Trav. Uni. 3040 F. PL. Gr. 100 Grantha-s.
Trav. Uni. 5778 O. PL. Tel. 100 Grantha-s.

Ptd.:

(1) Ed. by Lakshmanacharya, in : *Sapta-lakṣaṇa*, pub. by Sundaresvara Srauti (in Grantha script). – Kumbakonam : Jyotirvilasa Press, 1888. 3, 22 pp. (Title page: Sapta-lakṣaṇākhyaṃ kṛṣṇayajurvedalakṣaṇaratnaṃ kṛṣṇayajurvedapadādhyāyādhyetṛ-janānām atyantopakārāya pañcanadakṣetravāstvayaiḥ vicitraśatāvadhānividvanmaṇimahābhāgavataghanapāṭhibāḻegaḍḍekaṭṭe- lakṣmaṇācāryaiḥ samyak pariśodhya vicchedasūcakāṅkaiḥ saha śrīpañcanadakṣetravāstavyaiḥ jyotistantrasūkṣmadarśibhiḥ sundareśvaraśrautibhiḥ svīyajyotirvilāsamudrākṣaraśālāyāṃ mudrāpitam | sarvadhāri – vaiyyāci). [IO : Skt. 290]

Contents of this volume:

(2) Ed. by Mul̲languḍi A. Vaidyanatha Sastri with commentary, in *Sapta-lakṣaṇa* (in Grantha script). – Kumbakonam : Srividya Press, 1899, pp. 122. (Title page: śrīmattaittirīyayajuḥsaṃhitāpadaviṣayakavicikitsāndhatamasamihirāyamāṇaṃ saptalakṣaṇam idaṃ kila kumbhakoṇākhyamahākṣetrasamīpavartikolludam ityaparanāmakottarakāverīdakṣiṇatīravirājamānamul̲langaḍigrāmābhijanena śāṇḍilyānvayasaṃbhavena A. Vaidyanāthaśāstriṇā racitayā saṃgrahavyākhyayā sākaṃ tenaiva samyak pariśodhitaṃ kumbhakoṇasthaśrīvidyāmudrākṣaraśālāyāṃ mudritaṃ sad vijayatetarām) [Adyar (H 215.4 SLxy Vai); MyORI (B 1385); BM : Ptd. Bks. Cat. 1892-1906. 670-71, 805 (14092.b.43)]

Contents of this volume:

(3) Ed. by T. M. Narayana Sastri, in : *Sapta-lakṣaṇa* (in Grantha script), with the commentary of Vaidyanātha Sastri. (Title page : Sapta-lakṣaṇaṃ savyākhyānam | idaṃ kila T. M. Nārāyaṇaśāstriṇā yathāmati pariśoditam | R. sundareśāryeṇa kumbhaghoṇasthasvakīyaśāradāvilāsamudraṇālaye mudrāpitaṃ kumbhaghoṇe prakāśitañca vijayatetarām | kālayukti-vatsarasya siṃhamāsi) – Kumbakonam : Sarada Vilas Press, 1918. 158 pp. [IO (San C 181); MUL (P15:25A 1X8 15E8); SAI (89/2154*); UBTÜ (Ci XII 665)]

Contents of this volume:

(4) Ed. by Gomatham Srinivasa Jyosyar, in : *Lakṣaṇa-traya* (in Telugu script), together with the *Ṣaḍviṃśati-sūtra* and the *Jaṭāmaṇi*, under the sub-title: *Yajurāmnāya-lakṣaṇa-trayam.* – Mysore, 1919. 73 pp. (Title page: Sapta-lakṣaṇī Ṣaḍvig'ṃśatisūtram (savyākhyā) Jaṭāmaṇiḥ – iti Lakṣaṇatrayam | Taittirīya-yajussambandhi | maisūru gomaṭhaṃ śrīnivāsa jyotiṣikeṇa cittūru śrīśāradāmudrālaye siddhārthi-śrāvaṇāmāyāṃ samamudryata | [MyORI (B 4109/12669)]

Contents of this volume:

(5) Also ed. by V. Venkatarama Sharma, with a Ṭīkā based on the commentaries (in Roman script) in : *the Indian Historical Quarterly,* vol. 7, no. 4 (December 1931. Supplement). 43 pp. Based on three Mss. from Adyar : 20 G 21 (TR 20 = D I 714); 22 B 39 (68691 = D I 717); 22 C 49 (68749 = D I 712). [Adyar (H 215.4 Sri An); Emeneau (98); SAI (inf Zs 459.7)]

– C. Some of the Mss. mention Śrīvatsāṅka himself as the commentaṭor.

Beginning:

मुनिमानसमन्थानेत्यादिना श्लोकत्रयेण तावदादौ प्रारिप्सितस्य शास्त्रस्याविघ्नपरिसमाप्तये मङ्गलमादधानो ऽभीष्टदेवतां नमस्कृत्य विषयं दर्शयति -- अनिङ्ग्यमनुशिष्यत इति । अनिङ्ग्यमिति अविभागं पदमुच्यते । न त्वसमासपदम् । सत्यपि समासत्वे

शचीपतिर्बृहस्पतिरित्यादीनामनिङ्ग्यत्वात्।

End:

प्रपञ्चत्वात् ... तन्मनीषिभिः । इहाध्याये इङ्ग्यपदानामनन्तत्वात् प्रपञ्चत्वात् प्रकीर्णत्वादेकोपाधिना लक्षयितुमशक्यत्वात् प्रतिपदोपादाने तु ग्रन्थगौरवप्रसङ्गाद् दिङ्मात्रं संक्षिप्योक्तम्। अतो ऽनुक्तं च किंचित् संशयविषयमनिङ्ग्यपदं मनीषिभिरूहनीयं प्रयोगतो ऽवगन्तव्यम्। एषानिङ्ग्य ... तैत्तिरीयाणाम्। इत्यनिङ्ग्यव्याख्यानं समाप्तम्॥ (७१५: अनेन तैत्तिरिशाखामधिकृत्य शास्त्रं प्रवर्तितमिति दर्शितम्। शास्त्रकृतः जन्मनाम कीर्तितमविच्छेदायेति।)

Adyar D I 714 (10 G 21 = TR 20). 49 fol. (pp. 361-459). Complete with the text in 100 verses. = Adyar I, p. 54a. Title: Sapta-lakṣaṇa-vyākhyā.

Adyar D I 715 (19 D 63 = 66255). PL. Tel. 22 fol. (3-24; fol. 1 and 2 missing). = Adyar I, p. 54a. Title: Sapta-lakṣaṇa-vyākhyā. Incomplete; the C. on the first seven verses and part of the eighth is lost in the missing leaves.

Adyar D I 716 (19 N 32 = 66868). PL. Gr. 36 fol. (107ff.). The first verse as printed in the catalogue is that of Avarṇi.

Adyar D I 717 (22 B 39 = 68691). PL. Gr. 22 fol. = Adyar I, p. 48a.

Adyar D I 1037 (19 D 62) → Sapta-lakṣaṇa-vyākhyā.

Adyar D I 1039 (30 H 35) → Sapta-lakṣaṇa-vyākhyā.

AU 29710.

Baroda 6131(h). PL. Gr. 32 fol. (61-92). 600 Grantha-s. = CLB I, p. 22.

Baroda 6255(a). PL. Tel. 38 fol. 600 Grantha-s. = CLB I, p. 22.

Baroda 10032(f). PL. Gr. 29 fol. (83-111). 600 Grantha-s. = CLB I, p.

Baroda 10381(i). PL. Gr. 14 fol. (20-33). 250 Grantha-s. = CLB I, p. 22.

Burnell 6a.

Hoshiarpur p. 49 (no.5613). PL. Gr. 19 fol. 400 Grantha-s. Extract p. 405.

IO 4461 (Burnell 350c). Tel. 28 fol. (21-48) (with text). Written ca. A.D. 1867.

MD 855. Gr. 58 pp. (42ff.) (with text).

MD 856. PL. Tel. 50 pp. (29ff.) (with text).

MD 16741. PL. Tel. 46 pp. 414 Grantha-s (with slightly different beginning and end).

MD 17366. PL. Tel. 18 pp. 250 Grantha-s (with text).

MT 1233(b). PL. Tel. 36 fol. (24-59) (with text). Presented in 1913-14 by K. Rama-krishnayya of Musalipattanam.

MT 1240(f). PL. Tel. 19 fol. (26-44) (with text). Presented in 1913-14 by K. Rama-krishnayya of Musalipattanam.

MT 2881(a). PL. Gr. 15 fol. (with text). Presented in 1918-19 by Venkatagiri Appalacharyar of Triplicane.

Mysore ND II 3059-67. Extract no. 5, 6.

PUL I, p. 18 (no.10). 17 fol. 75 Grantha-s.

TD 1807 → Sapta-lakṣaṇa-vyākhyā.

Tirupati SVUORI 256 (4378k). PL. Gr. 25 fol. (64-88). Title: Aniṅgya-vṛtti.

Tirupati SVUORI 257 (6171b). PL. Gr. (ascribed to Śrīvatsāṅka in the catalogue.

Whish 25a (7). PL. Gr. 20 fol. (39-58). Title: Aniṅgya-vyākhyāna.

[NCC I 196ab]

33 ANIṄGYA-PADA (अनिङ्ग्यपद)

Mysore ND II 3070 (P 4906/52). PL. Na. 2 fol. (130-31). Extract no. 8. RV ?

34 ANIṄGYA-PADA-VYĀKHYĀNA (अनिङ्ग्यपदव्याख्यान)

Gough p. 163. Gr.

[NCC I 196b]

35 ANIṄGYA-PADĀNI (अनिङ्ग्यपदानि)

List of words that are not divisible in the Pada-pāṭha of the *Taittirīya-saṃhitā* (alphabetically arranged). Cf. Aveṣṭana-padāni, MD 873.

Beginning:

अवत्याय। अवत्याभ्यः। अवार्याय। अवार्येभ्यः। अवर्ष्याय। अदन्तकाय। अदन्तकः। अप्राय। अलोमकाय। अमेध्याय। अनस्थिकाय।

End:

हस्ताभ्याम्। हविष्मन्तः। हन्तवै। हारुकाः। हविष्मान्। हिरण्मयम्॥

MT 1964(a). PL. Tel. 3 fol. (written in columns). Presented in 1916-17 by Rayaprolu Ramabrahmangaru of Guruza, Gudivada Taluk, Krishna Dist.

[NCC I 196b]

36 ANIṄGYA-PARIBHĀṢĀ (अनिङ्ग्यपरिभाषा)

The same as the paribhāṣā portion of the Aniṅgya of Śrīvatsāṅka.

MD 17442. PL. Gr. 280 Grantha-s.

Mysore I, p. 20.

Mysore ND II 3068-69 (P 2265/14). PL. Gr. 6 fol. (107-12) (with C.). Extract no. 7.

– C.

Mysore ND II 3068-69 (P 2265/14). PL. Gr. 6 fol. (107-12) (with text). Extract no. 7 (same as the C. on the paribhāṣā portion of Aniṅgya).

[NCC I 196b]

37 ANIṄGYA-LAKṢAṆA (अनिङ्ग्यलक्षण)

→ Aniṅgya(-prakaraṇa) (Taitt).

[NCC I 196b]

38 ANIṄGYA-LAKṢAṆA (AKHAṆḌA-MAÑJARĪ) (अनिङ्ग्यलक्षण -- अखण्डमञ्जरी)

of Śeṣa Nārāyaṇa, composed in A.D. 1610-11.

Beginning:

सजलाम्बुदसंकाशं विमलाम्बुजलोचनम्।
सकलाभीष्टदं देवं कमलापतिमाश्रये॥ १॥
येष्विङ्ग्यपदसादृश्यात् संदेहो जायते भृशम्।
पदानि तान्यनिङ्ग्यानि ज्ञातुं वक्ष्यामि लक्षणम्॥ २॥

End:

हृणायन्तं हियानश्रुत् हृषीवन्तो हृषीवतः ।
हरिद्रवः शुद्धिरिमान् हरयाणे हरीमयः ॥
विकृताद्यान्यकारेण न तावदेवयोरिति ।
इत्येषा दर्शिताखण्डमञ्जरी नातिविस्तृता ॥
प्रियासभा च कल्यब्दे (श्री)षडमर्षणजन्मना ।
साङ्गत्रयीविदा शेषनारायणमनीषिणा ॥

Adyar D XIII 45 (VB 120a). PL. Gr. 62 fol. (59 fol. contain Aniṅgya words).
TCD 34-E. 10 pp. (24-33). 100 Grantha-s.
Trav. Uni. 4254 E. PL. Mal. 8 fol. 85 Grantha-s. Belonged to Vishnu Nambudiri of Ettikada Illam Ayankudi, Kaduttirutti, Kottayam.
Trav. Uni. 22209 F. PL. Mal. 85 Grantha-s.
Trav. Uni. 22749 M. PL. Mal. 85 Grantha-s.
Trav. Uni. T.223 E. = TCD 34-E. A transcript of the Ms. no. 4254.
Triv. Cur. III 1. Mal. 100 Grantha-s.

[NCC I 196b]

39 ANIṄGYA-ŚATAKA (अनिङ्ग्यशतक)

→ Aṅingya(-prakaraṇa) (Taitt.).
MT 4600(a). Presented in 1924-25 by the Secretary to the Trustees of Sri Yogi Parthasarathi Ayyangar's Charities, Triplicane, Madras.

[NCC I 196b]

40 ANIṄGYA-ŚIKṢĀ (अनिङ्ग्यशिक्षा)

Oppert I 7164. Belonged to Ivattur Nandikesvara Sastri of Vijayanagaram.

[NCC I 196b]

41 ANIṄGYĀDI (अनिङ्ग्यादि)

MD 16741. PL. Tel. 57 fol. Aniṅgya(-vyākhyā) is the first work of the codex. Other works therein are: *Avarṇi-vyākhyā, Āvarṇi-vyākhyā, Napara-vyākhyā, Yohi-prāpti, Lakṣmīkānta-śikṣā Savyākhyā* (in four stanzas).

[NCC I 196b]

42 ANIṄGYĀNTA (अनिङ्ग्यान्त)

Taitt. It is actually the *Vilaṅghya-vyākhyā* of which the last passage has the words: "iṅgyānto na bhavatīty aniṅgyāntaḥ".
MD 16709. PL. Tel. 60 Grantha-s.
MT 485(b). PL. Tel. 13 fol. (20-32) (with C. of Mallināthārya). Presented in 1910-11 by C. Visvanatha Shastrigal of Viziyanagaram.
MT 485(g). PL. Tel. 2 fol. (60-61). Presented in 1910-11 by C. Visvanatha Shastrigal of Viziyanagaram.
MT 2649(c). PL. Tel. 11 fol. (95-105). maharṣikṛtau padadarpaṇe vyaktiveluk.. (with C.). Presented in 1917-18 by Prava Surayya Shastrigaru of Penumanchilli, Narasapur Taluk, Krishna Dist.

– C. of Pogala Mallayārya (also called Mallinātha).

MT 485(b). PL. Tel. 13 fol. (20-32) (with text). Presented in 1910-11 by C. Visvanatha Shastrigal of Viziyanagaram.

MT 2649(c). PL. Tel. 11 fol. (95-105). maharṣikṛtau padadarpaṇe vyaktiveluk ... (with text). Presented in 1917-18 by Prava Surayya Shastrigaru of Penumanchilli, Narasapur Taluk, Krishna Dist.

[NCC I 196b]

43 ANĪTHYA(-MŪLA) (?) (अनीथ्यमूल)

Ujjain I, p. 10 (no.1417). This is probably Aniṅgya(-mūla) as it is listed together with Śamāna, etc.

44 ANUKRAMA (अनुक्रम)

GJKSV 29881. 15 fol. (49-63). Incomplete.

45 ANUKRAMAṆIKĀ (अनुक्रमणिका)

Ahmedabad 73(5).

Alph. List Beng. Govt. p. 4.

Ben. 3.

BHU B 946 (D 11/628). 96 fol. Dated V.S. 1810 → Ṛgveda-sarvānukramaṇī.

Brahmasva Maṭha 47. 98a.

Deccan College (1964). 278 (762 of Dikshit Collection). 72 fol. Arranged in two columnes, giving the names of the ṛṣi, deity, the beginning and the number of syllables of each verse of the *Ṛgveda.*

Gough p. 30.

Haug App. p. 2 (no.314) = München 21.

Hz 433. PL. Tel. 50 fol. Belonged to Gottimukkula Viraraghava Somayaji of Brahmanakraka (Agrahara), Nellur Dist.

IM 2315. 2 fol. Contains 12 verses of Chandaḥ-saṃkhyā and Anuvākānukramaṇī ending with the verse : śākalyadṛṣṭe ...

München 21. 2 fol. (ca. A.D. 1800). Of 12 Saura Sūkta-s of *Ṛgveda.*

Peters. II, p. 179 (no.34). 4 fol. SV.

Radh. 42.

SBD 2267. 44 fol. (ascribed to Āśvalāyana). Dated V.S. 1685 → Ṛgveda-sarvānukramaṇikā.

SBD 2309. 43 fol. (1-23, 26-45). Dated V.S. 1671. (Śākala-sūktānām; ascribed to Śaunaka) → Ṛgveda-sarvānukramaṇikā.

Sūcīpattra 111.

– C. of Vaijanātha-sūri (son of Divākara).

IM 9927. 3 fol. Though entered as Veda-lakṣaṇa in the NCC, on verification it was found to be an Anukramaṇī of a Dharmaśāstra work of his father.

[NCC I 199b]

46 ANUKRAMAṆIKĀ-ḌHUṆḌHŪ (अनुक्रमणिकाढुण्ढू)

A rearrangement in a tabulated form of Kātyāyana's *Ṛgveda-sarvānukramaṇī* in the order of the hymns, giving an identification of each hymn, such as its number, first pada, Ṛṣi, deity and metre. For a note on this work, see Ramkrishna Gopal Bhandarkar : *Proceedings of the International Congress of Orientalists,* IX (1892), London, vol. I, p. 411. For a detailed description of the work see Rgb. 39.

Beginning:

ऋषिदैवतच्छन्दांस्यनुक्रमिष्यामः । १ ओं अग्निमीळे पुरोहितं। वर्ग २ ऋच ९। मधुच्छन्दा ऋषिः । अग्निर्देवता। गायत्री छन्दः ।

End:

सं समिद्युवसे वृषन्। वर्ग १ ऋ· ४। संवनन ऋषिः । संज्ञानं दे·। अनुष्टुप्। तृतीया त्रिष्टुप्। आद्या १ आग्नेयी। इति अनुक्रमणीढुण्ढू समाप्तः ॥

Baroda 336. 56 fol. 1400 Grantha-s. Dated V.S. 1869. = CLB I, p. 25. Col.: Sūkta-pratīka.

Baroda 8248. 109 fol. 1400 Grantha-s. = CLB I, p. 25. Col.: Catuḥ-ṣaṣṭi-chanda-ṛṣidevatā.

Baroda 10587. 50 fol. 1400 Grantha-s. = CLB I, p. 25. Dated V.S. 1672. Col.: Anu-kramaṇikā.

Baroda 23412. 147 fol. 1820 Grantha-s. Dated V.S. 1894 / Śaka 1759. (Ṛkśākhāsūkta-pratīka).

BORI 39 of 1884-87. = BORI D I i.39. 53 fol. (Sarvānukramaṇikā-ḍhuṇḍhū). Copied on Sunday, 7th of the dark fortnight of Bhādrapada, V.S. 1796.

RASB II 238 (G 7882). 29 fol. (3-31). Dated Śaka 1587. Sūkta-s are listed numbering 1-1027.

Rgb. 39.

Cf. Ṛṣi-daivata-cchandonukrama.

[NCC I 199b]

47 ANUKRAMAṆIKĀ-BHĀṢYA (1) (अनुक्रमणिकाभाष्य)

→ Ṛgvedānukramaṇikā.

GJKSV 13720. 46 fol. Dated V.S. 1817. Title: Anukramaṇikā-bhāṣya.

48 ANUKRAMAṆIKĀ-BHĀṢYA (2) (अनुक्रमणिकाभाष्य)

Cf. Śukla-yajurveda-sarvānukrama-bhāṣya of Deva-yājñika.

49 ANUKRAMAṆIKĀ-VIVARAṆA (1) (अनुक्रमणिकाविवरण)

Unspecified:

Ben. 3.

Gough p. 30.

50 ANUKRAMAṆIKĀ-VIVARAṆA (2) (अनुक्रमणिकाविवरण)

of Jagannātha → Ṛgveda-sarvānukramaṇī-vivaraṇa.

GJKSV 16303. 25 fol. Dated Śaka 1835.

GJKSV 29833. 62 fol.

[NCC I 200a]

51 ANUKRAMAṆĪ (MĀDHYANDINĪYĀ) (अनुक्रमणी -- माध्यन्दिनीया)
→ Śukla-yajurveda-sarvānukrama.
SBD 48297. 9 fol. Incomplete.

52 ANUKRAMAṆĪ-VYĀKHYĀ (अनुक्रमणीव्याख्या)
of Devadatta, son of Prajāpati → Bhāṣya of Yājñika-deva on the *Śukla-yajur-veda-sarvānu-krama.*
SB p. 101 (no.31). 1, 3-194, 197-265 fol. 4719 Grantha-s. (1-5 Adhyāya-s). Dated V.S. 1591 (?). Cf. Śukla-yajurveda-sarvānukrama-bhāṣya, of Yājñika-deva. SB p. 47 (no.157).

[NCC I 200a]

53 ANUDĀTTA-GĀNA (अनुदात्तगान)
Mysore ND II 3072 (P 4906/13). PL. Na. 1 fol. (115). Extract no. 10. (Cf. pp. 41, 43 of the *Pada-gāḍha,* Srirangam edition).
Mysore ND II 3073 (P 4906/46). PL. Na. 1 fol. (127). Extract no. 11.

54 ANUDĀTTA-PRAKARAṆA (अनुदात्तप्रकरण)
Mysore ND II 3074-76 (P 4772/6/24/25). PL. Tel. Extract no. 12.

55 ANUDĀTTĀDĪNĀṂ VYĀKHYĀNA (अनुदात्तादीनां व्याख्यानम्)
America 2676. 1 fol.

[NCC I 203a]

56 ANUNĀSIKA-LAKṢAṆA (अनुनासिकलक्षण)
Appears to be an extract of some work on Veda-lakṣaṇa. The following is the complete text as given in the catalogue :

अनुनासिकलक्षणमाह --
स्पर्शानां यवलानां च मकारः पूर्वतः स्थितः ।
तेषामवाप्नुयाच्छिष्टः सवर्णमनुनासिकम्॥ १॥
अस्यार्थः -- स्पर्शे ऽन्त्यः परे अन्तस्थान्तगतिरेफराहित्ययवलानां परस्परसन्निकर्षत्वे सति सवर्णमनुनासिकसंज्ञं भवति। यथा -- इमं लोकम् -- इमँल्लोकम्। यं कामयेत -- यङ्कामयेत। तं देवाः -- तन्देवाः । कांडात् कांडात् -- काण्डात् काण्डात्। यं ब्रह्माणम् -- यम्ब्रह्माणम् । तं युञ्जाथाम् -- तँय्युञ्जाथाम् । तं वोदस्नम् -- तँवोदस्नम् । इत्युदाहरणानि। इत्यनुनासिकलक्षणं समाप्तम्॥

Mysore Skt. Coll. p. 1 = D. No.1 (846/13). PL. Na. 1 fol. (45).

[NCC I 203b]

57 ANUVĀKA (अनुवाक)
ASB I iii.26 (IM 7468). 9 fol. 128 Grantha-s.
IM 2637 → Anuvāka-pañcāśī.
IM 5346. 67 fol. This is actually the Pada-pāṭha of the VS.
IM 5536. 5 fol.
IM 7468. 9 fol. (1-7, 14-15). Incomplete.

Mithila.
Nasik II 388. 567.

– C. of Sāyaṇācārya. Sūcīpattra 54.

[NCC I 213a]

58 ANUVĀKA-PAÑCĀŚĪ (अनुवाकपञ्चाशी)
→ Anuvākānukrama.
Ānandāśrama 4975. 1 fol. Enumeration of the 85 Anuvāka-s, indicating the number of sūkta-s in each. Title: Anuvākānukramaṇī. Ends: śāsa itthā catvāriṃśat | pañcāśītir anuvākāḥ |
ASB I ii.660 (IM 2485/4). 5 fol. 150 Grantha-s (together with 3 other other works). Dated V.S. 1744 = A.D. 1687.
GJKSV 24407(B). 1 fol. (40).
IM 2485D. 1 fol. (5).
IM 2637B. 2 fol. (3-4). Dated V.S. 1860. Copied by Janārdana.
Oxf. CS c.26(10). 1 fol. Paper dated 25.11.1903.
Oxf. CS d.77(6). 2 fol. (5-6). Dated A.D. 1861.
RASB II 248 (G 2069). 1 fol. (7).
SBD 55270c. 2 fol. (2-3). Dated V.S. 1859. (Sarvānukramaṇikā).

[NCC I 213a]

59 ANUVĀKA-LAKṢAṆA (अनुवाकलक्षण)
Wai 136 (2 Mss. fragment). 139 (8).

[NCC I 213a]

60 ANUVĀKA-SAṂKHYĀ(-SŪTRA) or ANUVĀKĀDHYĀYA
(अनुवाकसंख्या /-सूत्र / अनुवाकाध्याय)
of Kātyāyana. Also called Anuvāka-pariśiṣṭa or Anuvākānukramaṇī. The fourth of the 18 Pariśiṣṭa-s of Kātyāyana. An index of the Ṛṣi-s, deities and metres of the verses of Vājasaneyi-saṃhitā in the Mādhyandina school, including the Khila (Adhyāya-s 26-35) and the Śukriya portions (Adhyāya-s 36-40). One Sūtra is quoted in ĀpDh. 1.3.26 (?) The division of Anuvāka-s is referred to in I 11.16.

Beginning:

(ब्रह्माणं संप्रणम्यादौ वेदानामेकपारगम्।)
अथानुवाकान् वक्ष्यामि ब्रह्मणा निर्मितान् पुरा।
शिष्याणामुपदेशाय यज्ञसंस्करणाय (-कार एव) च।
विप्राणां यज्ञकालेपु जपहोमार्चनादिपु॥

इषे त्वैका वसोः पवित्रं तिस्रो ऽग्ने व्रतपते सप्त पवित्रे स्थो द्वे शर्मासि तिस्रो धृष्टिरसि शर्मासि द्विकौ देवस्य त्वा तिस्रो देवस्य त्वा पञ्च प्रत्युष्टं रक्षस्तिस्रो दशैकत्रिंशत्। १०। ३१।

End:

स्वाहा प्राणेभ्यः षडुग्रश्च सप्त द्वौ त्रयोदश। २। १३। ३९। ईशावास्यमष्टौ अन्धं तमो नव द्वौ सप्तदश। २। १७। ४०।

दशाध्याये समाख्याता अनुवाकास्तु संख्यया।

शतं दशानुवाकाश्च नवान्ये (११९) च मनीषिभिः ॥
सप्तषष्टिश्चितौ (६७) ज्ञेयाः सौत्रे द्वाविंशतिस्तथा (२२)
अश्व एकोनपञ्चाशत् (४९) पञ्चत्रिंशत् (३५) खिले स्मृताः ॥
शुक्रियेषु तु विज्ञेया एकादश (११) मनीषिभिः ।
एकीकृत्य समाख्यातं त्रिशतं त्र्यधिकं (३०३) मतम् ॥
इत्यनुवाकसूत्राध्यायः संपूर्णः ॥

AK 54. Extract p. 106.
AK 68 (2).
Allahabad 161.
Alwar 202.
America 209. 5 fol.
Baroda 10568. 7 fol. 50 Grantha-s. CLB I, p. 33. Dated V.S. 1729.
Baroda 11960. 8 fol. 50 Grantha-s. CLB I, p. 33.
Bd. 53. 4 fol.
Bd. 54. 6 fol.
Berlin StB-PrK (NGMPP). D 77/15(a). 5 fol. (1-5). Title: Anuvāka-sūtra. Lithographic print dated V.S. 1941 / Śaka 1806 (Mādhyandina-saṃhitā Sarvānukramaṇikānuvākādhyāyayājñavalkyaśikṣopetā sasvarā ca mumbayyāṃ pure kālikādevīmārge Hariprasāda-Bhagīrathajī-śarmaṇaḥ pustakālaye ...) (microfilm dated 28.07.1976).
Berlin StB-PrK (NGMPP). E 315/11. 6 fol. Title: Anuvākādhyāya. (microfilm dated 11.10.1977).
Berlin StB-PrK (NGMPP). E 683/22. 2 fol. (5-6). (4th work in Veda-lakṣaṇa).
Berlin StB-PrK (NGMPP). E 1240/26. 5 fol. Title: Anuvākādhyāya. Dated V.S. 1874 (microfilm dated 11.08.1981).
Berlin StB-PrK (NGMPP). E 1657/50. PL. Newari. 4 fol. 20 verses. A different text (?). Title: Anuvākādhyāya. (Belonging to Dharmaraja Vajracharya of Kathmandu; microfilm dated 18.04.198).
Bombay Uni. 722 (BMC 50 13). 8 fol. Dated Śaka 1747.
Bombay Uni. 723 (BMC 55 8). 5 fol.
Bombay Uni. (Itchharam 5 12) 65. 6 fol. Dated V.S. 1935.
BORI 27 of 1884-86. = BORI D I i.264. 9 fol.
BORI 2 of 1886-92. = BORI D I i.268. 3 fol.
BORI 53 of 1887-91. = BORI D I i.255. 4 fol. (36b-39). Dated V.S. 1721.
BORI 54 of 1887-91. = BORI D I i.267. 6 fol. Dated V.S. 1888.
BORI 54 of 1891-95. = BORI D I i.265. 8 fol. (Anuvāka-kaṇḍikā). Dated V.S. 1747. Copied by Gaṇe-bhaṭṭa, son of Nārāyaṇa-bhaṭṭa.
BORI 3 of 1895-98. = BORI D I i.266. 10 fol. Dated V.S. 1874 / Śaka 1739.
BORI 38 of 1895-98. = BORI D I i.263. 6 fol. Dated V.S. 1734. Copied by Morabhaṭṭa, son of Sadāśiva at Mumbāpura.
BORI 50 of 1895-98. = BORI D I i.256. 49 fol. Dated V.S. 1728. Copied by Vāsudeva.
BORI TM 135. Title: Mādhyandinīya-anuvāka-sūtra.

Br. Mus. 49 (Add. 5349i). 3 fol. (289a-91). Copied for Col. Colier ca. A.D. 1783 at Jaipur, Rajaputana.
Bühler p. 553 (no. 14. Anuvākānukramaṇī).
CU Add. 2079. 2493.
GJKSV 1/1 (D I 1, no.1). 6 fol. Dated V.S. 1878.
GJKSV 26442. 7 fol.
GJKSV 28183. 27 fol. Identified as the *Ṛgveda-sarvānukramaṇī*.
GJKSV 33109. 5 fol. Dated V.S. 1874. Title: Mādhyandinīya-anuvāka.
GJKSV 36345. 8 fol.
GJKSV 37235. 13 fol.
GJKSV 42201. 17 fol. (120-36).
Hoshiarpur p. 49 (no.122). 7 fol. 84 Grantha-s.
IM 2495. 5 fol.
IM 2550. ? fol.
IM 9936. 4 fol. (2-5). Incomplete.
IO 191 (311b). 2 fol. (166-67).
Jodhpur (R). 273 (D I, p. 21; no.2). 6 fol. Dated V.S. 1839.
Jodhpur (R). 376 (D I, p. 21; no.3). 10 fol. 19th century.
Jodhpur (R). 1224 (D I, p. 21; no.4). 5 fol. Dated V.S. 1763.
Jodhpur (R). 1252 (D I, p. 21; no.5). 8 fol. Dated V.S. 1829.
Jodhpur (R). 1296 (D I, p. 21; no.6). 6 fol. Dated V.S. 1887.
L 1806. 6 fol. 40 Grantha-s. Dated V.S. 1933.
L 4135. Together with the Sarvānukrama.
Mithila IV 6. 5 fol.
Mithila IV 6(A). 5 fol.
Mithila IV 6(B). 26 fol.
N-W P V 64 (no.21). 6 fol. Belonged to Pt. Balamukunda of Benares.
N-W P V 64 (no.22). 3 fol. Belonged to Pt. Makhana Misra of Mathura.
N-W P V 146 (no.27). 3 fol.
Oudh III 8.
Oxf. CS c.26(11). 6 fol. Title: Anuvāka-pariśiṣṭa. Dated V.S. 1811.
Peters. III, p. 384 (no.27).
Peters. IV, p. 1 (no.2). Extract 2.
Peters. VI, p. 58 (no.3). 10 fol. Dated V.S. 1874.
PUL I, p. 18 (no.11). 7 fol. 43 Grantha-s. Dated V.S. 1825
PUL I, p. 18 (no.12). 5 fol. 43 Grantha-s. Title: Anuvākādhyāya.
RASB II 888 (G 1782). 6 fol. 80 Grantha-s.
RASB II 888A (G 9770). 4 fol. 100 Grantha-s.
RASB II 889 (G 932) = L 1806. Dated V.S. 1933.
RASB II 890 (G 6142). 6 fol. Dated V.S. 1861.
Rep. Hpr. 1901-06, p. 2.
SB p. 55 (no.58). 3 fol. 61 Grantha-s.
SBD 2277. 56 fol. (2-34, 37-59). Incomplete.
SBD 47943. 6 fol. (Anuvāka-saṃkhyā-pariśiṣṭa).
SBD 53552. 7 fol. Dated Śaka 1757. (Anuvāka-sūtrādhyāya).
SBD 53788. 8. fol. (Anuvākāḥ).

Skt. Coll. Ben. 1897- 1901, p. 131 (no.538).
Viśvabhāratī 1909.
VOHD II 8.3045 (Ms.or.quart 861. StaatsB-PrK, Berlin). Latin. 4 fol. (fol. 21-24).
Wai I 653. 21 fol. (with Sarvānukrama-sūtra).
Weber 165 (Weber 13,4). From E I H 309. 965. (With Śukla-yajurveda- sarvānukrama).
Weber 1459 (p. 41 ?). This is actually Śukla-yajurveda-sarvānukrama. Cf. CC I 794.

Ptd.: as an appendix to the edition of the *Vājasaneyi-saṃhitā*, with the Pratijñā-sūtra, Yājñavalkya-śikṣā and Sarvānukrama :

Ed. by Dvarakanathadeva Sarma, with commentary. *Vedārtha-pradīpākhya-giridhara-bhāṣya* (śrīśuklayajurvede mādhyandinīyavājasaneyīsaṃhitā śrīmatsomavaṃśodbhavapāṇḍavagiriprasādadevavarmaviracitaśrīvedārthapradīpākhyagiridhara-bhāṣyasahitā). – Mathura 1873 (vyomarāmāṅkabhū = V.S. 1930 / Śaka 1795), pp. 1173-80 (with Hindi commentary). [Adyar (H 211.21 Ms. xy Gir)]

Ed. by Hariprasad Bhagirathaji, Jagadisvara Press. – Bombay.: Jyestharam Mukundaji, 1884. 17, 2, 36, 40 pp. [Adyar (H 215.1 Yaj Har); Gö(4 / H E E 1062/53); Emeneau (104); IO : Ptd. Bks. Cat. 1953, p. 1968 (12 K 28)]

– Bombay : Venkatesvara Press, 1887. [Emeneau : 105]

– Bombay : Tattvaviveka Press, 1896. [Emeneau : 107]

– Bombay : Nirnaya Sagar Press, 1901. [Emeneau : 108]

– Bombay : Nirnaya Sagar Press, 1912. [Emeneau : 109] [BM : Ptd. Bks. Cat. 1906-1928. 1203 (14010.cc.13)]

4th volume of the *Vājasaneyi-saṃhitā* with commentaries of Uvaṭa and Mahīdhara. – Benares, 1915, pp. 41-43. – (Kashi Sanskrit Series 34). [NL (180 Jc 91 109; V 4 C 3)]

Ed. by Amritalal Sastri of Jamnagar, in : *Śukla-yajurveda-mādhyandina-saṃhitā* (prāstāvikasaṃhitāmantrāṇām akārādyanukramaṇikāvedapārāyaṇavidhyanuvāka-sūtrādhyāyāṣṭavikṛtiyājñavalkyaśikṣāpratijñāsūtrasarvānukramasūtra- ... samalaṃkṛtā). – Bombay : Nirnaya Sagar Press, Śaka 1872 (1950), pp. 36-38. [SKGI (Rh III 125)]

Ed. by Jagadisha Lal Shastri (with commentaries of Uvaṭa and Mahīdhara). – Delhi : Motilal Banarsidass, 1971. Appendix, pp. 17-18. [Adyar (H 212.21 VM xy Sha)]

With the Yājñavalkya-śikṣā and Sarvānukrama, lithographic print. – Bombay, Saṃ. 1946 (1889). 89 fol. [BM : Ptd. Bks. Cat. 1876-92. 490 (14010.c.15)]

Ed. by Yugalakishora (Vyasa) Pathaka, at the end of Kātyāyana's *Śukla-yajuḥ-prātiśākhya*. – Benares, 1888, pp. 501-06. – (Ben. S. S. 4).

Also in *Kātyāyanīya-pariśiṣṭa-daśakam*, with commentary, *Viṣama-padālaṃkriyā* of Sridhara Anna Sastri Ware of Nasik. – Poona (Yajnavalkya Ashrama, 121 Kasaba Peth) : Madhyandina Madhyavarti Mandala (V. T. Shete Vakil), 1958, pp. 11-59. [BORI (33438); SOAS (III.1.g.27 – 143871)]

Also ed. by Vasanta Sripada Satwalekar, with *Śukla-yajurveda-sarvānukrma-sūtra* (under the title *Vājasaneyi-mādhyandina-śukla-yajurveda-saṃhitāyāḥ Sarvānu-krama-sūtram)*. – Aundh, Pardi (Balsad Dist. Gujarat) : Svadhyaya Mandala, 1929, pp. 87-90. [SAI (ind 51 D 703)]

[NCC I 213ab]

61 ANUVĀKĀNUKRAMA (अनुवाकानुक्रम)

Also called Anuvāka-pañcāśī (see above). An enumeration of the 85 Anuvāka-s of the *Ṛgveda*. An abridgement, in prose, of the *Anuvākānukramaṇī* of Śaunaka, which is the other work contained in most of the Mss. Full text is printed in the Adyar catalogue.

Beginning:

> अथ अनुवाकानुक्रमः । अग्निमीळे सुरूपकृत्नुमेन्द्र सानसिमग्निं दूतं सोमानं कस्य नूनं त्वमग्ने प्रथमः प्र वो यह्वं अग्ने विवस्वदभित्यं मेषं नू चित् सहोजाः पश्यानतायुमुपप्रयन्तः प्र ये शुम्भन्ते …

End:

> प्र देवत्राच्छाम इन्द्रमिदमित्था भद्रा अग्नेः सत्येनोत्तभिता संजागृवद्भिरिन्द्र दृह्य तमस्य द्यावापृथिवी नासदासीच्छास इत्थेत्यनुवाकाः पञ्चाशीतिः । अनुवाकानुक्रमः समाप्तः ।

Adyar D I 720 (40 C 7 = PM 101). 1 fol. Dated V.S. 1686. Copied by Gopāla Dube of Sūrya-pura.
Baroda 21515. 2 fol. 15 Grantha-s. Dated V.S. 1945. (Ṛgvedānuvāka-sūkta-saṃkhyā).
Baroda 23666. 1 fol. (5). At the end of the Anuvākānukramaṇī. Dated V.S. 1728.
BHU B 1124c (D II/630). 2 fol. (5-6). Incomplete.
BHU C 1687c (D II/673). 1 fol. Col.: Sarvānukrama.
GJKSV 13624(B). 1 fol. (begins: athānuvāka-prārambhaḥ).
München 22(3). 2 fol. (33-34). Dated A.D. 1812. At the end of the Ṛgvedasarvānukramaṇī and Chandaḥ-saṃkhyā.
RASB II 242(C) (G 1990). 1 fol. Col.: Sarvānukrama.
SBD 2319. 1 fol. Dated V.S. 1740. At the end of the Ṛgveda-sarvānukramaṇī and Chandaḥ-saṃkhyā.
SBD 47916b. 2 fol. (5-6). At the end of Pādānukramaṇī.
Trav. Uni. 5001 B1. 2 fol. 40 Grantha-s.

Ptd.: In the Introduction to the *Ṛgveda-saṃhitā*, ed. by Vasanta Sripada (Damodar) Satwalekar (Anuvāka-sūtram). – Aundh, Pardi (Balsad Dist. Gujarat) : Svadhyaya Mandala, 1929 (several reprints), pp. 67-69.

Photographic reprint of the above with an additional preface in Sanskrit, edited by V. R. Laksmikanta Sarma. – Kumbakonam (612001, 14 Kamakshi Josier Street) : The Maharaja Saheb Sri Govinda Deekshitar Punya Smarana Samiti, 1979.

[NCC I 213b]

62 ANUVĀKĀNUKRAMAṆĪ (1) (अनुवाकानुक्रमणी)

Trav. Uni. 2318 A = Prakṛti-cchalākṣara.

[NCC I 213b]

63 ANUVĀKĀNUKRAMAṆĪ (2) (अनुवाकानुक्रमणी

RV.
B I, p. 198 (no.3). 3 fol.
CU Add. 1914-20.
PUL I, p. 18 (no.13). 4 fol. 41 Grantha-s (with Anuvākānukrama ?).

PUL I, p. 18 (no.14). 4 fol. Dated Śaka 1823 (with Anuvākānukrama ? and Chandaḥ-saṃkhyā)

PUL I, p. 18 (no.15). 3 fol. 22 Grantha-s.

PUL II. App. p. 10 (no.150) PL. Gr. 83 fol. (50-132). 1500 Grantha-s (is this Sarvānukramaṇī ?)

PUL II. App. p. 10 (no.151) PL. Gr. 57 fol. 900 Grantha-s (up to 7.5; is this Sarvānukramaṇī ?).

SBD 2275. 4 fol. (2-5). Incomplete. (Ṛganuvākānukrama).

SBD 2317. 28 fol. Incomplete. (Ṛganuvākānukramaṇī).

Vangiya p. 23.

64 ANUVĀKĀNUKRAMAṆĪ (3) **(अनुवाकानुक्रमणी)**

of Śaunaka. A short index containing about 40 verses. It states the initial words of each of the 85 Anuvāka-s of the *Ṛgveda* and the number of hymns contained in each Anuvāka. It also contains at the end some statistical details such as the total number of hymns (1017), verses (10,580 and a half), words (153,826), syllables (432,000).

Beginning:

पितृदेवर्षिसाध्येभ्यो ब्राह्मणेभ्यश्च सर्वशः ।
आचार्येभ्यो गुरुभ्यश्च प्रणम्य प्रयतः शुचिः ॥
मधुच्छन्दःप्रभृतिभिर्ऋषिभिर्हि तपोबलात् ।
दृष्टानामनुवाकानामृक्षु वक्ष्याम्यतन्द्रितः ॥
सूक्तादि परिमाणं तु संख्यां च क्रममेव च ।
मण्डले मण्डले चैव यावन्तो हि समीरिताः ॥

End:

अर्धर्चानां सहस्राणामेकविंशतिकं तथा ।
शतद्वयं तु द्वात्रिंशत् सपादं मुनिभिः पुरा ॥
शाकल्यदृष्टे पदलक्षमेकं सार्धं च वेदे त्रिसहस्रयुक्तम् ।
शतानि चाष्टौ दशकद्वयं च पदानि षट् चेति हि चर्चितानि ॥
एकं च शतसहस्रं दश च सहस्राणि सप्त शतानि ।
चर्चापदानि ज्ञेयानि पदानि चान्यानि चत्वारि ।
चत्वारि वाव शतसहस्राणि द्वात्रिंशच्चाक्षरसहस्राणि ।
द्वात्रिंशच्चाक्षरसहस्राणि । इत्यनुवाकनुक्रमणी समाप्ता ॥ ४३२००० ॥

Adyar D I 721 (28 G 53 = 72918). PL. Tel. 2 fol. It contains variants to Macdonell's edition.

Adyar D I 722 (40 C 7 = PM 101). 4 fol.

Ānandāśrama 46. 17 fol. Contains Anuvākānukramaṇī with Ṣaḍguru-śiṣya's C. (fol. 1-8); the introductory verses of the Vedārtha-dīpikā (fol. 8-12); The paribhāṣā section of the Ṛgveda-sarvānukramaṇī (Dvādaśa-khaṇḍī, fol. 12-15); Varṇakrama-lakṣaṇa (fol. 16) and the jaṭā for a few passages (śatacakraṃ : RV 10 144 4). Dated Śaka 1710.

Ānandāśrama 4975 → Anuvāka-pañcāśī.

Baroda 21514. 4 fol. 45 Grantha-s. Col.: Anuvākādyanukramaṇikā.

Baroda 23384. 3 fol. Dated Śaka 1812. (Sūktānuvākādyanukramaṇika).

Baroda 23666. 5 fol. 55 Grantha-s. Last fol. contains Anuvākānukrama. Dated V.S. 1728.

BHU B 959 (D 11/629). 3 fol. Dated V.S. 1699.

BHU B 1124b (D 11/630). 4 fol. (2-5). Incomplete.

BHU C 1687b (D 11/673). 3 fol. (2-4). Col.: Sarvānukrama-kārikā.

Bombay Uni. (BMC 155 3). 3 fol. (35-37). Dated Śaka 1738. Copied by Baccambhaṭṭa Upādhyāya, son of Lakṣmaṇa Paṭaṇakara.

Brl. p. 5 (no.111) = IO 4237.

Bühler p. 537. = IO 4238.

Calcutta Skt. Coll. I 26. 19 fol. (with C. of Ṣaḍguru-śiṣya).

GD I 6-C. PL. Mal. 2 1/2 fol. 50 Grantha-s. Title: Ṛganuvāka-pratīka-sūkta-saṃkhyā-parimāṇa-kramāḥ.

GJKSV 25096. 2 fol.

GJKSV 38309(B). 3 fol. (42-44). Dated V.S. 1853. (Caraṇa-vyūha on the title page).

IM 1806B. 2 fol. (39-40). Dated V.S. 1664. Begins with verse 15 of the printed edition.

IO 4237 (Burnell 205i). PL. Gr. 8 fol. (157-64).

IO 4238 (Bühler 9). 2 fol.

L 1219. 5 fol. 78 Grantha-s.

L 4243. 12 fol. 75 Grantha-s.

L 4252. 6 fol. 244 Grantha-s (with C. of Ṣaḍguru-śiṣya). Dated V.S. 1863.

Oxf. CS d.77(6). 6 fol. Dated A.D. 1861. Incomplete. 32 verses only. Contains Chandaḥ-saṃkhyā and Anuvāka-pañcāśī.

Oxf. CS d.78(4). 4 fol. Dated A.D. 1553. Title: Sarvānukrama.

Oxf. II 892(1a) (Ms. Wilson 379). 5 fol. (with C. of Ṣaḍguru-śiṣya).

Oxf. II 1077(3) (Ms. Wilson 502). 3 fol. (73-75). Incomplete. Begins with verse 15.

RASB II 239(4) (G 1896). 2 fol.

RASB II 242(B) (G 1990). 3 fol. Col.: Sarvānukramaṇī.

RASB II 245 (G 1676) = L 4252.

RASB II 246(4) (G 6022). 2 fol. (28-29).

SBD 2320. 3 fol. Incomplete. Dated V.S. 1715. (Anuvākānukramaṇikā).

SBD 2336. 3 fol. (Anuvākānukramaṇikā).

SBD 47198. 6 fol.

SBD 47199b. 6 fol. (a. Āśvalāyana).

SBD 55270b. 2 fol. (2-3). Dated V.S. 1859. (Sarvānukramaṇikā).

SBD 55290. 3 fol. (30-32). Dated V.S. 1748. (Ṛgvedasyānukramaṇikā).

Trav. Uni. 2405 C. PL. Gr. 50 Grantha-s.

Trav. Uni. 3694 B. PL. Gr. 50 Grantha-s.

Trav. Uni. 4907. 50 Grantha-s. Dated Śaka 1709.

Trav. Uni. 4913. 50 Grantha-s.

Trav. Uni. 4918. 50 Grantha-s. Dated V.S. 1801.

Trav. Uni. 4924. 50 Grantha-s.

Trav. Uni. 4929. 50 Grantha-s.
Trav. Uni. 5001 B2. 50 Grantha-s.
Trav. Uni. 5424. PL. Gr. 50 Grantha-s.
Trav. Uni. 17800 B. 50 Grantha-s.
Trav. Uni. 18019 C. 50 Grantha-s.
Trav. Uni. 19027 B. PL. Mal. 50 Grantha-s.
Trav. Uni. 22221 B. 50 Grantha-s.
VSM I 419 (no.7739). 3 fol. Remarks: "The manuscript also contains additional 35 verses related to Pada-pāṭha of ṚV." Actually it has the Anuvāka-pañcāśī and 35 sections of the *Pada-gāḍha*, partly identical to those in the printed edition. Title: Anuvākānukramaṇī.
Weber 48 (Chambers 209b, 3). 1 fol. (7 verses only).
Weber 53 (Chambers 192). 6 fol. (with C. of Ṣaḍguru-śiṣya).
Weber 1405 (Ms. or. fol. 816). 7 fol. (with C. of Ṣaḍguru-śiṣya). Transcript of a Ms. dated V.S. 1582.

Ptd.: Ed. by Arthur A. Macdonell, in the edition of the *Kātyāyana's Sarvānukramaṇī of the Rigveda.* – Oxford : Clarendon Press, 1886, pp. 47-53. – (Anecdota Oxoniensia, Aryan Series vol. I, pt. iv). [SAI (88/2122*)]
Ed. by Rajendralal Mitra, as an Appendix to the *Bṛhaddevatā.* – Calcutta : Asiatic Society, 1893, pp. 326-33. – (Bibliotheca Indica 127). [NL (180 Jc 89 40); Emeneau (389); BM : Ptd. Bks. Cat. 1892-1906. 626 (14002.a.; vol.127); IO : Ptd. Bks. Cat. 1938, p. 544 (Bibl. Ind. 127)]
Also printed as an appendix to the *Ṛgveda-saṃhitā,* ed. by Vasanta Sripada (Damodar) Satwalekar. – Aundh, Pardi (Balsad Dist. Gujarat) : Svadhyaya Mandala, 1929 (several reprints), pp. 826-28.
Photographic reprint of the above with an additional preface in Sanskrit, edited by V. R. Laksmikanta Sarma. – Kumbakonam (612001, 14 Kamakshi Josier Street) : The Maharaja Saheb Sri Govinda Deekshitar Punya Smarana Samiti, 1979.
Ed. by Umesh Chandra Sharma, together with the *Ṛgveda-sarvānukramaṇī.* – Aligarh : Viveka Publications, 1977, pp. 43-47. This is actually a reprint of Macdonell's edition without extracts from Ṣaḍguru-śiṣya's Bhāṣya.

For details see below under Ṛgveda-sarvānukramaṇī.

– C. Vivaraṇa of Jagannātha → Ṛgveda-sarvānukramaṇī-vivaraṇa.
Trav. Uni. 4920. 1100 Grantha-s. Dated V.S. 1818.
Vangiya p. 23.

– C. of Ṣaḍguru-śiṣya.

Beginning (Adyar):

सर्वं कर्म सफलं यत्र तुष्टे ऽतुष्टे (रुष्टे) न किंचित् तमहं नमामि।
विनायकं गिरिराजेन्द्रपुत्रीमहेश्वरप्रियसूनुं घृणाब्धिम्॥
बह्वृचानाम्भोजमानस्य(?) शौनकस्य प्रसादतः ।

अनुवाकानुक्रमणी त्वधि किंचित् प्रवर्ण्यते॥
पितृदेवर्षिसाध्येभ्यो ब्राह्मणेभ्यश्च सर्वशः।
आचार्येभ्यो गुरुभ्यश्च प्रणम्य प्रयतः शुचिः॥

तादर्थ्ये भ्यस्। प्रयतः जितेन्द्रियः। द्विविधं शौचं मृज्जलाभ्यां बाह्यमान्तरं मूर्द्धश्शुचिः प्रणम्य ततः किम्॥

मधुच्छन्दःप्रभृतिभिर्ऋषिभिर्हि तपोबलात्।
दृष्टानामनुवाकानामृजु वक्ष्याम्यतन्द्रितः॥

यावन्तो हि समीरिताः अनुवाकाः तावन्तः पदाक्षरसमाम्नायच्छन्दांस्येव प्रतिष्ठितम्। तत् सर्वं वक्ष्यामीत्यन्वयः। अनुवाकज्ञानस्य नित्याध्यने प्रयोजनमित्याह।

एकैकमनुवाकं तु खिलानि ब्राह्मणानि च।
संवत्सरे संवत्सरे पठेदहरहः शुचिः॥

End:

चेति खल्वित्यर्थः। वावेति पाठे ऽपि स एवार्थः। द्वात्रिंशत्सहस्राधिकचतुर्लक्षम् अक्षराणीत्यर्थः। द्विरुक्तिः समाप्तिवाचकार्था। एषा वा ऋक्। एष वा अर्धर्चः। एष वै पदम्। एष वा अक्षरमित्यादि सर्वेषामात्मरूपत्वोक्तेराराण्यके। अत्रापि सर्वं सम्यक् संख्यातं भगवता शौनकेन बह्वृचसिंहेनेति वेदितव्यम्॥

इति षड्गुरुशिष्यविरचितानुवाकानुक्रमणीवृत्तिः॥

Adyar D I 723 (28 G 53 = 72918). PL. Tel. 4 fol. (6-9). = Adyar I, p. 48a. Supplies a few variants to Macdonell's edition.

Calcutta Skt. Coll. I 26. 19 fol. (with text).

Hz 410(b). PL. Tel. 44 fol. (with Pada-varṇa-saṃkhyā). Belonged to Kesari Yajnayya of Brahmanakraka (Agrahara), Nellur Dist.

L 4252. 6 fol. 244 Grantha-s (with text). Dated V.S. 1863.

München 23. (ca. A.D. 1650).

Oxf. II 892(1a) (Ms. Wilson 379). 5 fol. (with text).

RASB II 245 (G 1976) = L 4252.

SBD 2317. 28 fol. Incomplete. (Ṛganuvākānukramaṇī). Also contains the C. on the Ṛgveda-sarvānikramaṇī-parbhāṣā with the long introduction.

VOHD II 8.3046 (Ms.or.quart 861. StaatsB-PrK, Berlin). Roman. 4 fol. (17-20).

Weber 53 (Chambers 192). 6 fol. (with text).

Weber 1405 (Ms. or. fol. 816). 7 fol. (with text). Transcript of a Ms. Dated V.S. 1582.

Ptd.: Ed. by Arthur A. Macdonell, in the edition of the *Kātyāyana's Sarvānukramaṇī* of the Rigveda. – Oxford : Clarendon Press, 1886, pp. 169-74. – (Anecdota Oxoniensia, Aryan Series vol. I, pt. iv). [SAI (88/2122*)]

For details see below under Ṛgveda-sarvānukramaṇī.

[NCC I 213b]

65 ANUSTOTRA-SŪTRA (**अनुस्तोत्रसूत्र**)

It is a Sāmavedic Śrauta text, not a Veda-lakṣaṇa. But in most of the catalogues it is listed under Veda-lakṣaṇa. It comprises eight sections. For details see Asko Parpola : *The Śrautasūtras of Lāṭyāyana and Drāhyāyaṇa and Their Commentaries.* – An English translation and Study. – Helsinki - Helsingfors, 1968, vol. I 1 (General Introduction), p. 66. (Commentationes Humanavum Litterarum – Societas Scientiarum Finnica, vol. 42, no. 2). [SAI (ind 70 C 244/I.1-2)]

Beginning:

> स्वरवर्णमात्राक्रममृङ्ङ्नियमाद् वर्णक्रमं वा प्रवचनशास्त्रानुवचनस्वराख्यत्वात् चतुर्विंशत्यक्षरेति चाक्षरतः कालः प्रसङ्गात् प्रवचने त्वपूर्वोत्पत्तिस्तत्र नियमस्तदङ्गत्वाद् वर्णवतिकः स्वरच्छन्दसो ऽक्षरपक्षतो ग्रहणमग्निष्टोमवन्न च स्वरनियमादक्षरप्रतिषेधः ॥

End:

> सामिहेतुत्वात् त्वाग्निवत् तत्प्रत्यक्षमृगाहवा इति चाविकारेण ताः संहितान्तरे रूपान्तरमकारस्य ताच्छन्द्याद्युक्तं प्रतिसंहितं संतनितस्तत् त्वशब्दः सहस्रे सहस्रे ॥

Alwar 253.
ASB I iii.15 (I D 28/1 and 4). Beng. 4 fol. (two copies). Dated V.S. 1717 = A.D. 1660.
Baroda 9911(a). PL. Gr. 5 fol. 150 Grantha-s. = CLB I, p. 23.
Ben. 18(2).
Bombay 1879-82.
BORI 90 of 1879-80. 9 fol. 90 Grantha-s. Dated V.S. 1723.
Hoshiarpur p. 49 (no.6357). 5 fol. 120 Grantha-s. Dated V.S. 1806. Extract p. 72.
IL. 212(1).
IM 2530. 6 fol. Dated V.S. 1598. Catalogued as Anustoma-sūtra.
IM 5337. 2 fol. Incomplete. Dated V.S. 1681.
Mysore I, p. 611 (2 Mss.).
Mysore ND II 3077 (C 2032). Na. 9 fol. Extract no. 13.
Oxf. CS c.21(14). 5 fol. The entire volume with 14 tracts were copied or belonged to Paṇḍita Bālamukunda Mālavīya.
Oxf. CS d.94(12). 12 fol. (with Pañca-vidha-sūtra).
P 6.
Peters. II, p. 180 (no.67). 3 fol.
PUL I, p. 18 (no.16). 8 fol. (8 Sūtra-s). Dated V.S. 1599.
RASB II 1332 (G 994A). 8 fol. 100 Grantha-s.
SB p. 33 (no. 30). 8 fol. 99 Grantha-s. = SBD 3936.
SB p. 33 (no. 31). 9 fol. 100 Grantha-s. = SBD 3937.
SBD 3936. 8 fol. Dated V.S. 1684.
SBD 3937. 9 fol.

[NCC I 215a]

66 ANUSTOMA-SŪTRA (**अनुस्तोमसूत्र**)

IM 2530. 6 fol. Dated V.S. 1598 → Anustotra-sūtra.

[NCC I 215a]

67 ANUSVĀRA-MĀTRĀ-LAKṢAṆA (अनुस्वारमात्रालक्षण)
18 verses on the nature of Anusvāra in the Taittirīya school.

Beginning:

अनुस्वारस्य या मात्रा संहिताकाल एव तु।
पदमध्ये द्विमात्रं स्यादेकमात्रा द्विरूपवत्॥
अनुस्वारो द्विमात्रः स्याद् रेफोष्मसु परासु च।
संयोगे परभूते च मात्रिकस्तु द्विरूपवत्॥

End:

स्वरिताग्राह्यनुस्वारस्तथा यरलवा अपि।
परस्वरेण संयुक्ताः स्वरिताग्राहिणो मताः ॥

Baroda 6255. PL. Tel. 2 fol. (39b-40b).

68 ANTAḤ-ŚAMĀNA (अन्तःशमान)
Trav. Uni. 16408 N. PL. Mal. 1 fol. 15 Grantha-s.

69 ANTA-NIRDEŚI-PARIBHĀṢĀ (अन्तनिर्देशिपरिभाषा)
MD 16820. PL. Gr. 1 p. (a fragment found at the end of the Pluta-vyākhyāna).
[NCC I 224b]

70 ANTA-NIRDEŚĪ (अन्तनिर्देशी)
→ Ardhāntika-sūtra (Mysore ND II 3087).

Beginning:

ओं धृष्टिर्भुवनमस्यंशुना ते अयं वां यावामुदायुषा ···

End:

समितं चत्वारिंशत्। प्रदेवमेकचत्वारिंशत्। हिरण्यगर्भो ऽष्टाचत्वारिंशत्। अग्निर्वृत्राणि चतुष्पञ्चाशत्। त्वमग्ने रुद्रः पञ्चपञ्चाशत्। अग्निना रयिं सप्तपञ्चाशत्। अग्निर्मूर्धैकान्नषष्टिः

Adyar D I 724 (30 D 29 = 73919). PL. Tel. 2 fol.
Adyar D I 983 → Veda-lakṣaṇa (A 1).
Adyar D I 984 → Veda-lakṣaṇa (A 2).
Hamburg StUB (cod.Palmbl. III 8/133) → Veda-lakṣaṇa (HB).
MT 485(o). Title in the margin : Kumbakarṇa-bheṭ. Presented in 1910-11 by C. Visvanatha Shastrigal of Viziyanagaram.
Mysore I, p. 21 (5 Mss.).
Mysore ND II 3078 (P 232/11). PL. Gr. 2 fol. Extract no. 14.
Mysore ND II 3079 (P 972/ 9). PL. Tel. 2 fol. (34-35).
Mysore ND II 3080 (P 2262/ 3). PL. Gr. 2 fol.
Mysore ND II 3081 (P 2265/30). PL. Gr. 2 fol. (142-43).

Mysore ND II 3088 (P 4468/ 5). PL. Na. 4 fol. (13-16). (Ardhāntika-sūtra). Extract no. 19.

Mysore ND II 3089 (P 8065). PL. Tel. 6 fol. (113-18). (Ardhāntika-sūtra).

Mysore ND II 3090 (B 600/ 6). Na. 2 fol. (28-29). (Ardhāntika-sūtra). Extract no. 20.

Trav. Uni. 16408 R. PL. Mal. 2 fol. 30 Grantha-s.

Trav. Uni. L.988 F. PL. Mal. 50 Grantha-s.

[NCC I 224b]

71 ANTA-PRADĪPA or ANTA-PRADĪPIKĀ **(अन्तप्रदीप / अन्तप्रदीपिका)**

Beginning:

अथावसानविसर्जनीयस्यान्तप्रदीपो नाम लक्षणमुच्यते --

दीर्घा विसर्जनीयान्ता विरामेषु तु संस्थिताः ।
ये शब्दाः संहितायां स्युस्ते ज्ञाप्यन्ते ऽधुना मया ॥
वर्णक्रमेण गृह्यन्त एते शब्दा यथाक्रमम् ।
व्यवहारो ऽत्र भेदेन समासपदभागयोः ॥
अन्तप्रदीपो नामेदं लक्षणं क्रियते मया ।
वेदात्मा भगवान् विष्णुरन्तेन प्रीयतां मम ॥ इति परिभाषा ॥
अना अर्का अगा अद्रेररातीरप्यरोचथाः ।
अप्रा अश्वा अनीका स्यादजिरा अप्रिया इति ॥
अन्तोदात्तकमग्ने(ग्रा) स्यादश्रमिष्ठा अजायथाः ।

End:

शर्रीरैरपि शुष्मा श्रीश्शंभुस्सपर एव च ।
सूनोस्साधोस्सुतास्साविस्सेनास्सत्यासनं परः ॥
सूराः प्रसुवरीस्साहा हिता होत्रा हिरण्ययोः ।
हिरण्यैर्हस्तयोरत्र नैभ्यः सन्त्वधिकाः खलु ॥

अन्तप्रदीपलक्षणं संपूर्णम् ॥

MD 857. PL. Gr. 3 pp. (41ff.).

MD 17444. PL. Gr. 3 pp. 50 Grantha-s.

MT 4818(d). PL. Gr. 1 fol. (97) (fragment). Presented in 1924-25 by the Secretary to the Trustees of Sri Yogi Parthasarathi Ayyangar's Charities, Triplicane, Madras.

Mysore I, p. 21 (2 Mss.).

Mysore ND II 3082 (P 541/ 1b). PL. Gr. 3 fol. (8-10). Extract no. 15.

Mysore ND II 3083 (P 972/ 8). PL. Tel. 2 fol. (33-34).

Mysore ND II 3084 (P 2262/33). PL. Gr. 2 fol. Extract no. 16.

Mysore ND II 3085 (P 2265/29). PL. Gr. 3 fol. (140-42).

[NCC I 224b]

72 ANTA-PRADĪPIKĀ **(अन्तप्रदीपिका)**

of Śrīraṅgārya. Mysore I, p. 21 (3 Mss.).

[NCC I 224b]

73 ANTODĀTTA (अन्तोदात्त)

→ Ucca-svara-nirṇaya. It appears that due to the word "antodādāttapadam" in the first verse the work is so called.

Mysore I, p. 21.

Mysore ND II 3086 (P 997/ 8). PL. Na. 3 fol. (Svara-lakṣaṇa). Extract no. 17.

[NCC I 227b]

*ANNAM-BHAṬṬA (अन्नम्भट्ट)

Son of Tirumalārya of Rāghava Somayāji family.

– Svara-viveka. MT 2175(a).

[NCC I 237a]

74 APARA-KHAṆḌA (अपरखण्ड)

Adyar D I 983 → Veda-lakṣaṇa (A 1).

[NCC I 244a]

75 APARA-DĪRGHĪ (अपरदीर्घी)

→ Uttara-dīrghī.

Adyar D I 986 → Veda-lakṣaṇa (A 1).

Adyar D I 986 → Veda-lakṣaṇa (A 4).

Trav. Uni. 1497 Z 6. PL. Mal. 8 Grantha-s.

[NCC I 244a]

76 APARĀNIṄGYA (अपरानिङ्ग्य)

The text of the Aniṅgya of Śrīvatsāṅka is called so in :

Adyar D I 983 → Veda-lakṣaṇa (A 1).

*APPAYĀCĀRYA (अप्पयाचार्य)

– (Taittirīya-)Prātiśākhya-vyākhyāna – Varṇakramadarpaṇa. MD 15503. But the same text is ascribed to Vemāna Bhairavāvadhānin in Adyar D XIII 192.

[NCC I 260a]

*APPĀJI-BHAṬṬA (अप्पाजिभट्ट)

– Ṛgveda-sarvānukramaṇī-ṭīkā, in Kannada. Mysore ND II 3288-90.

*AMAREŚA (अमरेश)

of Bharadvāja-gotra. See the next.

77 AMAREŚA-ŚIKṢĀ or VARṆA-RATNA-PRADĪPIKĀ (अमरेशशिक्षा / वर्णरत्नप्रदीपिका)

of Amareśa. An epitome of Kātyāyana's *Vājasaneyi-prātiśākhya* in 227 Kārikā-s, the topics being differently arranged.

Beginning:

श्रेयो दिशतु नः कृष्णः कंसमातङ्गकेसरी।
राधाकेलिकलाभिज्ञो गोपीवादकुतूहली ॥ १॥
उत्पन्नो यः स्तुते वंशे बुद्धिमान् कृतनिश्चयः।
अमरेश इति ख्यातो भारद्वाजकुलोद्भवः ॥ २॥
सो ऽहं शिक्षां प्रवक्ष्यामि प्रातिशाख्यानुसारिणीम्।
बालानां पाठशुद्ध्यर्थं वर्णज्ञानादिहेतवे ॥ ३॥

जपादिशुभकार्येषु पुमान्नाधिकृतो भवेत्।
सम्यक् पाठं विना यस्मात् तन्निमित्तं वदाम्यहम्॥ ४॥
स्वरसंस्कारयोर्वेदे नियमः कथितो यतः ।
ततो विचार्य वक्तव्यो वर्णसंघात उत्तमः ॥ ५॥

End:

रहस्यं यो न जानाति लक्षणं चार्षकादिकम्।
सो ऽध्यापने न योग्यः स्याज्जपहोमादिकर्मसु॥ २२६॥
अमरेशकृतामेतां शिक्षां यो धारयेत् सुधीः ।
विद्वज्जनसभामध्ये जयं स लभते सुधीः ॥ २२७॥
इत्यमरेशकृता वर्णप्रदीपिकाशिक्षा समाप्ता

BORI TM 275. (Varṇa-ratna-pradīpikā-śikṣā).
GJKSV 13072. 27 fol. (Varṇa-ratna-pradīpikā).
IM 3371. 10 fol.
Jodhpur (R). 1483 (D I, p. 25; no. 97). 22 fol. Dated V.S. 1920.
L 1932. 24 fol. 276 Grantha-s.
Mithila IV 168 (11 Mss.).
Oxf. CS d.177(2). 8 fol.
PUL I, p. 23 (no.127). 18 fol. 228 Grantha-s.
RASB II 1519 (G 3261). 11 fol. 260 Grantha-s. Dated V.S. 1941.
Rep. Raj. and C. I. p. 3.
SBD 2058. 11 fol. (Varṇa-ratna-pradīpikā-śikṣā).
SBD 53751. 21 fol. Dated V.S. 1925 / Śaka 1790. (Varṇa-ratna-pradīpikā-śikṣā).

Ptd.: in Śikṣā-saṃgraha. – Benares, 1889, pp. 117-37. – (Ben. S. S. 10).

[NCC I 341a]

78 AMṚTĀBHIṢEKA (अमृताभिषेक)

America 51. 3 fol.
BORI 83 of A 1882-83.
Peters. I, p. 116 (no.83).

[NCC I 356b]

79 AMOGHĀNANDINĪ-ŚIKṢĀ (1) (अमोघानन्दिनीशिक्षा)

130 verses enumerating words containing labials and dentals; letters which appear in their short and long forms in the Saṃhitā; the change of a short letter into a long one, if it occurs in the Pada-pāṭha; the three different pronunciation of "v" (guru, laghu and laghutara); the characteristics of Nāda and nasals; the five kinds of "raṅga"; the seven kinds of "pluta", etc. in the *Vājasaneyi-saṃhitā*. There appears to be another text of the Śikṣā containing about 57 verses. See F. Kielhorn : Remarks on the Śikṣās in : *Indian Antiquary*, vol. V, p. 193 (reprint in : *Kleine Schriften*, vol. I, pp. 158-69).

Beginning:

अथ शिक्षां प्रवक्ष्यामि ह्यमोघानन्दकारिणीम्।
यस्याः श्रवणमात्रेण सर्वत्र विजयी भवेत्॥ १॥
ओष्ठ्या दन्त्या लघुश्चैव पुनरेव लघूतरः ।
नादनासिक्यसहितांल्लक्षणानि पृथक् पृथक्॥ २॥
ब्रह्मबाहू बृहद् बद्धो बृहती द्यौर्बधानयोः ।
बर्हिर्बृहस्पते बिभ्राड् बिभितो बहु बोधय॥ ३॥
बर्हिषा च पिब ब्रूते त्र्यम्बकं बाध बुध्नयः ।
बन्धुस्तब्भ्नी च बध्नीताम्बिकया बभ्लुशाय च॥ ४॥
ब्रवीद् द्बबासि बम्भारे अम्बश्चैव बभुर्बहुः ।
क्षत्रस्योल्बं तथाब्दं च शतम्बस्त्यज्यते बुधैः ॥ ५॥

End:

लक्ष्यलक्षणयोर्ज्ञानी तद्धि पात्रं प्रचक्षते।
लक्षणेन विना वाणी निर्मलापि न शुध्यति (शोभते)॥ १२५॥
प्रमदा रूपसंपन्ना दरिद्रस्येव योपिता।
स्वरहीना यथा वाणी वस्त्रहीनास्तु योषितः ॥ १२६॥
एवं वर्णा न शोभन्ते प्राणहीनाः शरीरिणः ।
वेदपाठी सदा सम्यग् विचार्यैवं पुनः पठेत्॥ १२७॥
विश्वा रूपाण्यबोध्यग्निरेधो ऽसीति तथापरः ।
केतुं कृण्वन्निति च ते षकारा मूर्धजाः स्मृताः ॥ १२८॥
अग्नेरनीकं युक्ष्वा हि विश्वे देवा द्वितीयकम्।
उदग्ने चायमुत्तरान्नमो वन्याय हीत्ययम्॥ १२९॥
देवं बर्हिर्यदापो ऽस्ति त्वामद्य स्वस्तिनस्तथा।
मा नो मित्रो हि वक्ष्यन्ती क्षकारा ययुतास्तथा॥ १३०॥

इत्यमोघानन्दिनी शिक्षा समाप्ता

Bd. 55. 10 fol. Dated V.S. 1805.

Berlin StB-PrK (NGMPP). D 77/2. 9 fol. 96 verses. Lithographic print of V.S. 1940 / Śaka 1806 (microfilm dated 28.07.76).

Bhau Daji 121.

BORI 65 of 1884-87.

BORI 55 of 1887-91. 10 fol. Dated V.S. 1805.

BORI 1 of 1895-1902. 1 fol.

GJKSV 13069. 11 fol. Dated V.S. 1902. (End differs).

GJKSV 41854. 7 fol. (Keśavīyā Amoghānandinī-śikṣā).

Hoshiarpur p. 50 (no.4209). 4 fol. 100 Grantha-s.

IM 2024. 4 fol. Incomplete. 56 verses.

IM 2058. 10 fol.

IM 4957. 3 fol. 105 verses. Incomplete.
Jodiya II 13.
Kh. 82.
L 133. 3 fol. 120 Grantha-s. Dated V.S. 1926.
Mithila IV 169. 169(A)-(D). (5 Mss.).
Oudh IX 4 (no.1). 2 pp. 20 Grantha-s. Belonged to Pandit Ramanarayana of Lucknow.
Oxf. CS d.185(11). 7 fol. (2-4 missing).
PUL I, p. 18 (no.17). 8 fol. 100 Grantha-s.
PUL I, p. 18 (no.18). 6 fol. 106 Grantha-s. Dated V.S. 1924.
RASB II 1517 G 666). 2 fol. 17 Grantha-s. (= Laghvamoghānandinī-śikṣā).
RASB II 1518 (G 3258). 7 fol. 160 Grantha-s. Dated V.S. 1939.
SBD 2024. 1 fol. Dated V.S. 1934.
SBD 2063. 1 fol.
Rgb. 65.
Trav. Uni. 2057 B. 1 fol. 25 Grantha-s. Dated V.S. 1896. (a. given as Keśava).

Ptd.: in Śikṣā-saṃgraha. – Benares, 1889, pp. 93-106. – (Ben. S. S. 10). [BM : Ptd. Bks. Cat. 1892-1906. 28 (14093.b.31)]

[NCC I 358a]

80 AMOGHĀNANDINĪ-ŚIKṢĀ (2) (अमोघानन्दिनीशिक्षा)

57 verses. Different from the above. It includes twelve verses from the printed Laghvamoghānandinī-śikṣā and a few verses from the *Kauśika-śikṣā*.

Beginning:

प्रणम्य शिरसा स्थाणुं त्रिलोकेशं त्रिलोचनम्।
त्रिपुरघ्नं त्रयीमूर्तिं शिक्षेयं क्रियते मया॥ १॥
यथाबुद्ध्या यजुर्वेदे सोमेश्वरप्रसादतः ।
माध्यन्दिनस्य शाखायामुदाहरणसंयुता॥ २॥
पाणिनीयादिशिख्षाभ्यो यत् साक्षान्नोपलभ्यते।
शिष्याणामुपदेशाय तदशेषं मयोच्यते॥ ३॥
अनुस्वारो विसर्गश्च नासिक्याश्च यमास्तथा।
जिह्वामूलमुपध्मा च नवैते स्युः पराश्रयाः ॥ ४॥
अयोगवाहा विज्ञेया निजस्वरविवर्जिताः ।
पूर्वस्याङ्गं भवन्त्येते स्वर एतेषु पूर्ववत्॥ ५॥

End:

द्वैधे चैव समुत्पन्ने लक्षणान्निर्णयो भवेत्।
लक्षणं न विनाशि स्यात् संप्रदायो विनाशवान्॥ ५२॥
श्रुत्वा वेदं विधानात् तु सम्यग् ब्रूयात् स वै बुधः ।
प्राहूय तं विवक्रं तु तथा धर्मो न हीयते॥ ५३॥
एकः सर्वं न जानाति सर्वमेको न विन्दति।

इति मत्वा न मुह्यन्ति पण्डिताः शुद्धभाविनः ॥ ५४॥
प्रमाणानुगतं वाक्यं मोहाद्यो हन्तुमिच्छति।
प्रतिवातं स मूढात्मा पांशूनुत्क्षिपति स्वयम् ॥ ५५॥
मयात्र बाल्यबुद्धित्वाद्यत्किंचिद्ध्यन्यथाकृतम्
विद्वद्भिस्तत्तथा कार्यं कर्ता को न विमुह्यति ॥ ५६॥
लक्ष्यानुसारिणी ह्येषा कृता वाजसनेयिनाम्।
अमोघानन्दसंज्ञेयं पूजनीया मनीषिभिः ॥ ५७॥

Bik. 348. 17 fol. (57 verses).
Bikaner 618. 17 fol. Dated V.S. 1686.
Baroda 7346. 3 fol. 56 Grantha-s. = CLB I, p. 23.
BORI 2 of 1873-74. 3 fol. (12b-14b). Dated V.S. 1931. From Bikaner. (A xerox-copy of this Ms. is in SAI : 87/790*).

81 (LAGHV-)AMOGHĀNANDINĪ-ŚIKṢĀ (लघ्वमोघानन्दिनीशिक्षा)
17 Kārikā-s on the pronunciation of "y", "v" and "anusvāra" with illustrations from *Vājasaneyi-saṃhitā*.

Beginning:

पादादौ च पदादौ च संयोगावग्रहेषु च।
जः शब्द इति विज्ञेयो योऽन्यः स य इति स्मृतः ॥ १॥
युक्तेन मनसा तद्वत् तत् त्वायामि तथापरम्।
अनूकाशेन बाह्यं च तुरीयमनुया पदे ॥ २॥
पदादावप्यविच्छेदे संयोगान्ते च तिष्ठताम्।
वर्जयित्वा रहौ यानामीषत्स्पृष्टत्वमिष्यते ॥ ३॥
विदद्यदी न्यमित्रांश्च रोचनास्य यथा भवेत्।
तथा पार्याय सूर्यश्च मुह्यन्त्वन्ये समूह्यवत् ॥ ४॥
उपसर्गपरो यस्तु पदादिरपि दृश्यते।
ईषत्स्पृष्टो यथा विद्यात् पदच्छेदात् परो भवेत् ॥ ५॥

End:

ज्ञात्वा वेदविनाशं तु सम्यग् ब्रूयान्न वै बुधः ।
आहूय तं विवक्ते वै तस्य धर्मो न हीयते ॥ १७॥

Baroda 7345(b). 1 fol. (8). 17 Grantha-s. = CLB I, p. 23.
BBRAS I (B D 278). 1 fol. 17 Grantha-s. It contains variants from the printed edition.
IM 5152B. 1 fol. (4). Dated V.S. 1825.
Mithila IV 170. 2 fol. Dated V.S. 1936.
N-W P V 150 (no.45). 1 fol.

RASB II 1512 (G 3259). 2 fol. Dated V.S. 1939.
RASB II 1517 (G 666). 2 fol. 17 Grantha-s . (Amoghānandinī-śikṣā).
SB p. 54 (no.98). 1 fol. 17 Grantha-s. = SBD 47250.
SB p. 54 (no.269). 1 fol. 18 Grantha-s. = SBD 2015.
SB p. 54 (no.286). 1 fol. 23 Grantha-s. = SBD 2016.
SBD 2015. 1 fol. Dated V.S. 1934.
SBD 2016. 1 fol. Dated V.S. 1934.
SBD 47250. 1 fol.
SBD 48291. 1 fol. Dated V.S. 1930.

Ptd.: in Śikṣā-saṃgraha. – Benares, 1889, pp. 107-08. – (Ben. S. S. 10).

[NCC I 358a]

82 AYAḤPIṆḌĀDI-VARṆA-LAKṢAṆA (अयःपिण्डादिवर्णलक्षण)
MD 20101. PL. Gr. 2 fol. Cf. Yājñavalkya- (201ff.) and Śaunaka-śikṣā.

*AYYĀ-ŚĀSTRIN (अय्याशास्त्रिन्)
Son of Veṅkaṭārya of Aṣṭa-gotra family of Viṭṭhala-pura, on the banks of Tāmraparṇī.

– Sapta-svara-sindhu, written in A.D. 1750. TCD 33. Triv. Cur. IV 2.

83 ARAṆA-ŚIKṢĀ (अरणशिक्षा)
→ Āraṇya-(ka-)śikṣā.
Adyar I, p. 52a (1 A 19 = TR 19) (Aruṇa-śikṣā).
Tirupati SVUORI 692 (4446a). PL. Gr. 29 fol. (with C.).

[NCC I 368a]

84 ARUṆA-ŚIKṢĀ (अरुणशिक्षा)
→ Āraṇya-(ka-)śikṣā.
Hamburg StUB (cod.Palmbl. III 8/133) → Veda-lakṣaṇa (HB).

85 ARUṆA-SAMĀNA (अरुणसमान)
It may refer to a list of words dropping their Visarga, in the portion of *Taittirīya Āraṇyaka* known as Aruṇa. Cf. the previous entry and Āraṇya-(ka-)śikṣā.
Mysore p. 2 (no. 57). 2 fol.
Mysore (1898), p. 6 (no. 57). 2 fol. (105-06). (Āruṇa-samāna).

[NCC I 374]

86 ARDHĀNTĀḤ or ARDHĀNTIKA or ARDHĀNTYA or ARDHĀNTA-ṬĪKĀ
(अर्धान्ताः / अर्धान्तिक / अर्धान्त्य / अर्धान्तटीका)
Index of Anuvāka-s of the *Taittirīya-saṃhitā* that consist of more than one sentence and therefore require pauses in the middle.

Beginning:

उभा वाँ होतर्दोषागन्म सुवः संज्योतिषा सोमाय पितृमते सुवा नः सोमो वर्धन्तु त्वा ...

End:

य इमा वीरः शतमन्युः पयसा महीँ सुहिरण्ये सुशिल्पे शुक्रास्ताः पुष्टं पशुमन्यते त्रिंशत्॥

Adyar D I 725 (22 E 36 = 68884). PL. Tel. 1 fol. (24b) (printed here in extenso). The same Ms. as no.1024, Śiroveṣṭana (a double entry ?). The same text is called Śiroveṣṭana in MD 14743 also.

Adyar D I 986 → Veda-lakṣaṇa (A 4).

Adyar D I 989 → Veda-lakṣaṇa (A 7).

Baroda 10032(b). PL. Gr. 2nd fol. 12 Grantha-s.

MD 16737. PL. Tel. 3 pp. 40 Grantha-s. Title in the catalogue: Ardhāntika-ṭīkā. Col.: Ardhāntika-saṃkhyā.

MT 485(m). PL. Tel. 2 fol. (66-67) Presented in 1910-11 by C. Visvanatha Shastrigal of Viziyanagaram. (printed in extenso). ubhāvāṃ hotar ... triṃśat.

MT 485(u). PL. Tel. 7 fol. (80-86). Incomplete. Presented in 1910-11 by C. Visvanatha Shastrigal of Viziyanagaram. (Ardhāntikasaṃgrahādi).

MT 1240(g). PL. Tel. 4 fol. (45-48). (Ardhāntika-sūtrāṇi). Presented in 1913-14 by K. Ramakrishnayya of Musalipattanam. The same as the Kumbakarṇa-bheṭ. MT 485(o): dhṛṣṭir ... ekānna ....

Mysore I, p. 21 (2 Mss.).

Mysore ND II 3087 (P 2262/ 8). PL. Gr. 1 fol. Extract no. 18.

Ptd.: in the edition of Ṣaḍviṃśati-sūtra (in Grantha script), as *Vākyāntāḥ Pañcadaśa* ... p. 16.

Also printed in Lakṣaṇa-traya (in Telugu script), p. 40.

C.

MD 16737. PL. Tel. 3 pp. 40 Grantha-s. Though catalogued as Ardhāntika-ṭīkā the Ms. contains the text as above. Col.: Ardhāntika-saṃkhyā.

[NCC I 392a]

87 ALOPA-SAṂJÑĀ(-PRAKARAṆA) (अलोपसंज्ञा-प्रकरण)

Mysore ND II 3091 (B 601/ 3). Kan. 3 fol. (13-15). Extract no. 21.

88 AVAGRAHA-PARIŚIṢṬA or AVAGRAHA-SŪTRA (अवग्रहपरिशिष्ट / अवग्रहसूत्र)

A Pariśiṣṭa of the Kauthuma *Sāmaveda* on Avagraha, i.e. separation of the component parts of a compound word, or of the stem and certain suffixes and terminations. The original text consists of twelve (or fourteen) Sūtra-s and five additional passages. See also Ṛktantra-pariśiṣṭa. The following is the complete text of the Sūtra-s:

अथावगृह्यम्। अतिच्चतुरक्षरे पदे। १। विभागे च। २। अनीचमदन्त्यमशक्करीष्वेवयामरुत् । ३। अभ्यस्तश्चानेकाक्षरः । ४। एको नीचे। ५। कृद्धित्सातौपतिवसोरन्तं च। ६। वीर्दंहाः ऋतुबाहुम्। ७। उपसर्गादि। ८। चन्द्रशतसधहव्यम्। ९। सूर्यःसाकायां च। १०। समासो ऽतो ऽन्यत्र । ११ । नवं पुराणेन बहुपदश्चेत् । १२ । सर्वत्र मित्रपुत्रसखिशब्दा अद्रिशतक्रतोरवग्राह्याः । १। आदित्यविप्रजातवेदाश्च। २। सत्पतिगोपतिवृत्रहासमुद्राश्च। ३ । अद्य न इन्द्राग्नी स्वस्ति न आदिपु । ४ । स्वर्युवो देवयवश्चारतिं देवतातये । निकितिश्चुकुधश्चैवैता नावगृह्णन्ति पण्डिताः । ५। इति अवग्रहदशकपरिशिष्टम्॥

Alwar 264.
Baroda 9805(d). PL. Gr. 3 fol. 40 Grantha-s. = CLB I, p. 26 (no.36). (12 Sūtra-s, in the Ms. of the Gāyatra-vidhāna)
IL. 7.
IM 1969B. 2 fol. (2-3) (with C.). Title: Avagraha-daśaka-pariśiṣṭa.
IM 2421. 1 fol. Title: Avagraha-daśaka-pariśiṣṭa.
IO 4322 (Burnell 496g). 1 fol.
Oxf. II 855(6) (Ms. Wilson 375). 1 fol. Dated A.D. 1582. = Oxf. 377b (no.375).
Oxf. CS c.26(4). 2 fol. with Vivaraṇa. Paper dated 25.11.1903.
Peters. II, p. 181 (no.83).
PUL I, p. 131 (no.18). 1 fol. (no. 10).
SBD 2111c. 1 fol. (13a). At the end of the Sāma-tantra.
SBD 2303. 4 fol. (Avagraha-daśaka-pariśiṣṭa with C. and Granthānukramaṇī).

Ptd.: Ed. by Suryakanta, based on a single Ms. (c.26) of the Chandra Shum Shere Collection, Bodleian Library, Oxford, with commentary, notes and examples, in : Woolner Commemoration Volume. – Lahore : Mehar Chand Lachhman Das, 1940, pp. 321-28 (at the end). [Adyar (H080 MCL 8)]
Also printed with a Vivaraṇa in the collection of Sāmavedic tracts, ed. by Krishnaswami Srauti (in Grantha script). – Kumbakonam : Jyotirvilasa Press, pp. 39-43. See below under Chala-prakriyā. [SAI (87/783*)]
Reprinted with a Vivaraṇa in the *Sāmaprātiśākhya-saṃgraha*, part I, p. 10-13.

– C.
IM 1969B. 2 fol. (with text). Title: Avagraha-daśaka-pariśiṣṭa.
Mithila.
SBD 2303. 4 fol. (with text).
Cf. Burnell, Saṃhitopaniṣad-brāhmaṇa, p. xv. Caland, Jaiminīya-saṃhitā, p. 15(n).
[NCC I 411a]

89 AVAGRAHA-LAKṢAṆA (and PRAGṚHYA) **(अवग्रहलक्षण / प्रगृह्य)**
Divided into 18 sections. Some of them are identical with those of the *Pada-gāḍha* (cf. p. 58, 98 of the *Pada-gāḍha*, Srirangam edition).

Beginning:

जनित्वावगृह्यम् । सनित्वा यथासंहितम् । ... स्मभित्वीवर्जम् । बहुत्रावगृह्यम् । बहुधा यथासंहितम् । पुरुत्रावगृह्यम् । पुरुधा यथासंहितम् । विश्वथावगृह्यम् ... । विश्वधा यथासंहितम् ... ।

End:

उत्तिष्ठ ब्रह्मणस्पते आ नो भद्रा सं ते पयांसि ... प्रत्यञ्चो यन्त्विति त्रिंशद्यन्तु तुकारेण । इति बोन्तलु समासम् ।

Adyar I, p. 48a (25 C 8 = 70785). PL. Tel. 13 fol. Not described in Adyar D I
[NCC I 411a]

90 AVADHĀNA-SVARA (अवधानस्वर)

Mysore ND II 3092 (P 4772/ 5). PL. Tel. 8 fol. Extract no. 22.

91 AVARṆA-DĪPA (अवर्णदीप)

→ Avarṇi-dīpa, IO 4243.

92 AVARṆI(-PRAKARAṆA) (1) (अवर्णि-प्रकरण)

Avarṇi is the designation for tracts containing a list of Vedic words beginning with tha vowel "a" which elide with "e" or "o" of the previous words in saṃdhi. Also called Hrasva-saṃgraha in many Mss. Also included in the *Sapta-lakṣaṇa* (which see).

MD 1002 → Sapta-lakṣaṇa with C.

Oppert I 953. Belonged to Viraraghava Tatacharyar, Head Master, Sanskrit School of Sathakopacharya, Kanchipuram, Chingelpet Dist.

Oppert I 7827 (Avarṇi-śikṣā). Belonged to Paravastu Venkatarangacharyar of Vishakhapattanam.

Oppert II 730. Belonged to Ghanapathi Shingaracharyar of Alasur, Madurantakam Taluk.

Oppert II 1301. Belonged to Gopalacharyar of Pillapakkam, Kanchipuram Taluk.

Oppert II 9000. Belonged to Ganapati Lakshminarayana Sastri of Tiruvadi, Thanjavur Dist.

PUL I, p. 18 (no.19). PL. Gr. 3 fol.

PUL I, p. 19 (no.20). PL. Tel. 12 fol. 250 Grantha-s.

PUL II. App. p. 13 → Veda-lakṣaṇa.

Rice 12.

Trav. Uni. 2346 D. PL. Gr. 180 Grantha-s (with C.).

Trav. Uni. 2938 E. PL. Gr. 55 Grantha-s.

Trav. Uni. 3040 E. PL. Gr. 70 Grantha-s.

Trav. Uni. 4369 C. PL. Gr. 2 fol. 35 Grantha-s.

Trav. Uni. 5512 A. PL. Tel. 400 Grantha-s (with C.).

93 AVARṆI(-PRAKARAṆA) (2) (अवर्णि-प्रकरण)

Of the *Taittirīya-saṃhitā*. Also included in the *Sapta-lakṣaṇa* (which see).

Beginning:

अवर्णिन्यनुक्तं समोप्यातिरिक्तं परिष्कृत्य (-त्यज्य) दुष्कीर्तितं चाभिवीक्ष्य।
ककारादिवर्णक्रमेणाहमेतां सुवृत्तिं करिष्यामि विस्पष्टवाच्याम्॥ १॥
ओदेदवर्णसंछन्नं संहितायां पदादिगम्।
अवर्णं ज्ञातुमस्माभिरिदं शास्त्रं प्रणीयते॥ २॥
नोदात्तो यः पदाध्याय उदात्तः संहितागमे।
यश्चोदात्तः पदाध्याये स्वरितः संहितागमे॥ ३॥
अघोषाक्षरतः पूर्व ओकारः सांहितश्च यः।
तेभ्यः परः पदाध्याये त्वकारः स्यात् पदादिगः॥ ४॥

End:

अस्यन्त्यस्तुवतास्थे ऽङ्गये ऽस्थन्नस्मे चास्तमस्ति च।
अस्मै चास्थान्यसीदच्चास्मानस्यां निहतो न तु॥ ४०॥
अस्याहिरहभूनो ऽहन्नहुतादो ऽहरन्नहः।
अहरच्चाहरन्ताहा अहार्षं चाहुतादहम्।
अहास्थाहरतां चैवेत्युक्तो ह्रस्वस्य संग्रहः॥ ४१॥

Adyar D I 727 (22 D 2 = 68760). PL. Gr. 6 fol. (1-6) (with C.). = Adyar I, p. 48a.
Adyar D I 728 (28 A 35 = 72511). PL. Gr. 8 fol. (8-15) (with C.). = Adyar I, p. 48a.
Adyar D I 729 (30 C 3 = 73873). PL. Tel. 11 fol. (with C.) = Adyar I, p. 54a.
Adyar D I 1034 → Sapta-lakṣaṇa.
Adyar D I 1037 (with C.) → Sapta-lakṣaṇa-vyākhyā.
Adyar D I 1038 (with C.) → Sapta-lakṣaṇa-vyākhyā.
Brl. p. 11 (no.XLI) = IO 4471.
Brl. p. 11 (no.XLII) = IO 4470.
Burnell 5b.
Hoshiarpur p. 50 (no.4105). PL. Gr. 4 fol. 50 Grantha-s. Extract p. 406.
Hoshiarpur p. 50 (no.4118). PL. Gr. 1 fol.
Hoshiarpur p. 300 (no.5947). PL. Gr. 1 fol. 10 Grantha-s.
IO 4465 (Burnell 350c). Tel. 7 fol. (58-64) (with C.). Written ca. A.D. 1867.
IO 4466 (Mackenzie II 94d). PL. Na.7 fol. (49-55) (with C.). Written ca. A.D. 1770.
IO 4467 (Mackenzie III 234k). PL. Tel. 18 fol. (103-120) (with C.).
IO 4468 (Mackenzie III 59c). PL. Tel. 3 fol.
IO 4469 (Mackenzie III 186j). PL. Tel. 3 fol.
IO 4470 (Burnell 146d). PL. Gr. 2 fol. (8-9).
IO 4471 (Burnell 49d). PL. Gr. 3 fol. (8-10).
IO 4472 (Mackenzie III 234e). PL. Tel. 4 fol. (33-36).
MD 858. PL. Gr. 11 pp. (16ff.).
MD 860. Gr. 7 pp. (12ff.) (with C.).
MD 861. PL. Tel. 27 pp. (89ff.) (with C.).
MD 862. PL. Tel. 5 pp. (93ff.).
MD 16711. PL. Tel. 2 pp. 35 Grantha-s.
MD 16734. PL. Tel. 4 pp. 56 Grantha-s.
MT 485(d). PL. Tel. 9 fol. (43-51) (with C.). Presented in 1910-11 by C. Visvanatha Shastrigal of Viziyanagaram.
MT 689(d). PL. Gr. 3 fol. (8-10) (with Āvarṇi). Purchased in 1912-13 through Seshasayi Ayyangar of Kottaiyur near Kumbakonam.
MT 1240(a). PL. Tel. 12 fol. (with C.). Presented in 1913-14 by K. Rama-krishnayya of Musalipattanam.
MT 1240(b). PL. Tel. 3 fol. (13-15). Presented in 1913-14 by K. Rama-krishnayya of Musalipattanam.
MT 1964(g). PL. Tel. 10 fol. (67-76) (with C.). Presented in 1916-17 by Rayaprolu Ramabrahmangaru of Guruza, Gudivada Taluk, Krishna Dist.

MT 1976(d). Tel. 12 fol. (42-53) (with C.). Presented in 1916-17 by Nimmagadda Narasimhavadhanulugaru, Godavarru, Godavari Dist.

MT 2591(c). PL. Tel. 4 fol. (199-202). Presented in 1917-18 by Vasireddi Chandramaulisvaraprasada Bahadur, Zamindar of Muktyala, Krishna Dist.

MT 2881(d). PL. Gr. 5 fol. (26-30) (with C.). Presented in 1918-19 by Venkatagiri Appalacharyar of Triplicane.

MT 3887(h). PL. Gr. 2 fol. (78-79). Purchased in 1921-22 from Annasvami Sastrigal, Bhavani, Coimbatore Dist.

MT 4600(a). PL. Gr. 2 fol. (10-11). Presented in 1924-25 by the Secretary to the Trustees of Sri Yogi Parthasarathi Ayyangar's Charities, Triplicane, Madras.

Mysore ND II 3093-107. Extract no. 23. (Hrasva-saṃgraha).

RASB II 487-88(V) (G 6063). Dated V.S. 1913 / Śaka 1778.

TD 1794 → Sapta-lakṣaṇa.

TD 1804 (4) → Sapta-lakṣaṇa.

Tirupati SVUORI 477 (4411c). PL. Gr. (Avarṇi-grantha).

For Avarṇi see also Sapta-lakṣaṇa Mss.

Ptd.: There are five editions. See Sapta-lakṣaṇa.

94 AVARṆI(-PRAKARAṆA) (3) (अवर्णि-प्रकरण)

Taitt. Of Śaurisūri with C. Also included in the *Sapta-lakṣaṇa* (which see).

Baroda 6131(c) PL. Gr. 4 fol. (8-11). 40 Grantha-s. = CLB I, p. 23.

Baroda 6255(d). PL. Tel. 9 fol. (55-63) (with a.'s C.). = CLB I, p. 23. 120 Grantha-s.

Baroda 10032(d) PL. Gr. 16 fol. (60-75). 250 Grantha-s. = CLB I, p. 23 (with author's C.).

Baroda 10034(d). PL. Gr. 2 fol. (4b-5b). 40 Grantha-s. = CLB I, p. 23.

Baroda 10381(g). PL. Gr. 4 fol. (12-15). 40 Grantha-s. = CLB I, p. 23.

[NCC I 423a]

95 AVARṆI(-PRAKARAṆA) (4) (अवर्णि-प्रकरण)

SV. Also included in the *Sāmaveda-sapta-lakṣaṇa* (which see).

Adyar D I 1075 → Sāmaveda-sapta-lakṣaṇa.

Adyar D I 1076 → Sāmaveda-sapta-lakṣaṇa.

[NCC I 422b]

96 AVARṆI(-LAKṢAṆA) (अवर्णि-लक्षण)

Adyar D I 983 → Veda-lakṣaṇa (A 1).

Adyar D I 984 → Veda-lakṣaṇa (A 2).

Adyar D I 985 → Veda-lakṣaṇa (A 3).

Adyar D I 988 → Veda-lakṣaṇa (A 6).

Adyar D I 1030 → Sapta-lakṣaṇa.

Adyar D I 1031 → Sapta-lakṣaṇa.

Adyar D I 1032 → Sapta-lakṣaṇa.

Adyar D I 1033 → Sapta-lakṣaṇa.

– C.

Adyar D I 984 → Veda-lakṣaṇa (A 2).

Adyar D I 1035 → Sapta-lakṣaṇa.
Adyar D I 1039 → Sapta-lakṣaṇa-vyākhyā.
IO 4465 (Burnell 350c). Tel. 7 fol. (58-64) (with text). Written ca. A.D. 1867.
IO 4466 (Mackenzie II 94d). PL. Na. 7 fol. (49-55) (with. text). Written ca. A.D. 1770.
IO 4467 (Mackenzie III 234k). PL. Tel. 18 fol. (103-120) (with text).

– C. Bhāṣya.
Adyar D I 985 → Veda-lakṣaṇa (A 3).

– RV. Bh. p. 7.?

[NCC I 422b]

97 AVARṆI-(LAKṢAṆA-)VYĀKHYĀNA (अवर्णि-लक्षण-व्याख्यान)
AU 25A.
MD 1002 → Sapta-lakṣaṇa with C.
Oppert II 731. Belonged to Ghanapathi Shingaracharyar of Alasur, Madurantakam Taluk.
Oppert II 9001. Belonged to Ganapati Lakshminarayana Sastri of Tiruvadi, Thanjavur Dist.
PUL II. App. p. 10 (no.134). PL. Gr. 7 fol. 250 Grantha-s.
Trav. Uni. 2346 D. PL. Gr. 180 Grantha-s.

98 AVARṆI-GRANTHA (अवर्णिग्रन्थ)
Tirupati SVUORI 477 (4411c). PL. Gr. → Avarṇi.

[NCC I 423a]

99 AVARṆI-DĪPA or Avarṇi-lakṣaṇa (अवर्णिदीप / अवर्णिलक्षण)
of Dakṣiṇāmūrti of Śrīvatsagotra. A treatise on words beginning with the letter "a" in the *Ṛgveda.*

Beginning:

गुरुं गुणाब्धिं निखिलाप्तवाङ्मयं प्रणम्य संसारसमुद्रतारकम्।
पदाद्यवर्णावगमाय वच्म्यृचामवर्णिदीपाख्यमहं सुलक्षणम्॥
अत्रेष्टौ सौ वेदवर्णैस्संच्छन्नो थाकारादीन्येतदन्तात् पराणि।
उच्चो नोच्चस्वार उच्चो ऽपि सान्ध्ये पद्ये दीर्घो ह्रस्वभागः प्लुतश्चेत्॥

End:

अहन्यो ह्यन्नहिंसन्तीरहिन्वन्नप्यहेम च।
अहन्नयाद्यः पूर्वो ह चक्रे हिन्वन् यथामति॥
श्रीवत्सदक्षिणामूर्तिविदुषाकारसंग्रहः।
अकारादिपदानां तु कृतो विद्वद्भिरिष्यताम्॥

Adyar D I 726 (20 K 38 = 67500). PL. Tel. 2 fol. (7-8). = Adyar I, p. 48a. On the margin of fol. 1a the name of the work is given as Avarṇi-lakṣaṇa.
Adyar D XIII 29 (VB 266d). PL. Gr. 5 fol.

Brl. p. 7 (no.VI, title : Paribhāṣā) = IO 4243.

IO 4243 (Burnell 205g). PL. Gr. 2 fol. (154-55). Paribhāṣā only.

MD 859. Tel. 4 pp. (88ff.).

MT 3911(f). PL. Gr. 1 fol. (90). Incomplete. Purchased in 1921-22 from Narasimha Sastrigal, Bhavani, Coimbatore Dist.

Mysore ND II 3118 (P 4906/ 9). PL. Na. 2 fol. (113-14). Title in the catalogue : Avarṇi-vyākhyā.

Mysore ND II 3119 (C 3764/ 4). 3 fol. (23-25). Extract no. 26. Title in the catalogue : Avarṇi-vyākhyā.

Mysore ND II 3120 (C 3764/ 8). 15 fol. (60-74). Title in the catalogue : Avarṇi-vyākhyā.

TCD 34-C. 5 pp. (17-21). 50 Grantha-s.

Trav. Uni. 1116 C. PL. Mal. 50 Grantha-s.

Trav. Uni. 4254 C. PL. Mal. 4 fol. 50 Grantha-s. Belonged to Vishnu Nambudiri of Ettikada Illam Ayankudi, Kaduttirutti, Kottayam.

Trav. Uni. 22200 D. PL. Mal. 100 Grantha-s.

Trav. Uni. 22209 B. PL. Mal. 50 Grantha-s.

Trav. Uni. 22749 C. PL. Mal. 20 Grantha-s.

Trav. Uni. 22749 I. PL. Mal. 150 Grantha-s.

Trav. Uni. T.223 C. = TCD 34-C. A transcript of the Ms. no. 4254.

Triv. Cur. III 2. Mal. 50 Grantha-s.

Whish 73,2 (7). PL. Gr. 1 fol. (18).

Whish 73,3 (1). PL. Gr. 1 fol. Paribhāṣā only.

Whish 73,3 (2). PL. Gr. 3 fol. (1-3). Title: Avarṇi-lakṣaṇa.

Ptd. in the collection called *Tāṇḍaṅgaḻ* (in Malayalam script). – Kunnankulam (Kerala) : Panchangam Pustakashala, 1930 (M.E. 1105). 92 pp (pp. 24-28; 45 verses).

This booklet contains a number of useful short tracts of Veda-lakṣaṇa, including a few texts in Malayalam language. The following Sanskrit texts are found in Mss. of different libraries also:

1. Śamānam .... pp. 5-11 (in prose, with five paribhāṣā verses)
2. Vilaṅghyam .... pp. 12-18 (68 verses)
3. Naparam .... pp. 18-22 (33 verses)
4. Taparam .... pp. 22-23 (13 verses)
5. Avarṇi .... pp. 24-28 (45 verses)
6. Āvarṇi .... pp. 28-29 (17 verses)

[SAI (87/1683*)]

– C.

Beginning: (3911)

संध्याचन्द्रकलामनोज्ञनखरैः पादप्रभाभासुरैः
भूषावन्मणिनूपुरौ प्रणमतां संदर्शयन् पाणिना।
वामं पादतलं विमुक्तपदवीसोपानमासोहि(रोह)तां

मध्ये हेममयं महो ऽस्तु सततं प्रत्यूहविच्छित्तये ॥
अथ दक्षिणामूर्तिनामा कश्चिद् विपश्चिदवर्णदीपनामकं लक्षणं चिकीर्षुः तदनन्तरायपरिपूरणाय विशिष्टेष्टदेवतां नमस्कृत्य श्रोतृजनमनःसमाधानाय विषयप्रयोजने निर्दिशति -- गुरुमिति । सकलजगद्गुरुमीश्वरं गुणत्रयात्मकाविद्याश्रयं शब्दब्रह्मस्वरूपं स्वभक्तानां ज्ञानप्रदानेन संसारसमुद्रसंतारकं भक्तिपुरःसरं नत्वा ।... अथ सर्वपदाद्यवर्णानां ग्रहणे प्राप्ते पदाद्यवर्णं विशिनष्टि -- अत्रेष्ट इति ॥

End:

अकारसंग्रहः कृत इत्यर्थः । यथामतीति वचनं विदुषः महतः प्रति केवलं स्वविनयप्रदर्शनार्थमेव तन्न्यूनातिरिक्तादिदोषपरिजिहीर्षया ॥ ऋगवर्णिन्यकारसंग्रहः समाप्तः ।

MT 3911(d). PL. Gr. 11 fol. (72-82). Purchased in 1921-22 from Narasimha Sastrigal, Bhavani, Coimbatore Dist.
Whish 73,3 (4). PL. Gr. 22 fol. (3-24).

[NCC I 423a]

100 AVARṆI-VYĀKHYĀ (अवर्णिव्याख्या)
of Mahādhipati-yajvan of Tintriṇī family.
Mysore I, p. 22 (3 Mss.) =
Mysore ND II 3108 (P 588/ 2). PL. Tel. 1 fol. (109).
Mysore ND II 3109 (P 997/11). PL. Na. 10 fol. (20-29). Extract no. 24.
Mysore ND II 3110 (P 1540/ 5b). PL. Tel. 12 fol. (28-39). Extract no. 25.
Trav. Uni. 5512 A. PL. Tel. 400 Grantha-s (with text).

[NCC I 423a]

101 AVARṆI-VYĀKHYĀNA (अवर्णिव्याख्यान)
Taitt.
Brl. p. 12 (no.XLIII) = IO 4465.
Burnell 5b.
IO 4465 (Burnell 350e). Tel. 7 fol. (58-64) (with text). Written ca. A.D. 1867.
MD 860. Gr. 7 pp. (12ff.) (with text).
MD 861. PL. Tel. 27 pp. (89ff.) (with text).
MD 16742. PL. Tel. 22 pp. 250 Grantha-s.
MD 16814. PL. Gr. 8 pp. 144 Grantha-s.
MT 485(d). PL. Tel. 9 fol. (43-51) (with text). Presented in 1910-11 by C. Visvanatha Shastrigal of Viziyanagaram. asyāyam arthaḥ lakṣaṇārambham ... end: ityanena prakāreṇa hrasvasya saṃgraha uktaḥ |
MT 1976(d). Tel. 12 fol. (42-53) (with text). Presented in 1916-17 by Nimmagadda Narasimhavadhanulugaru, Godavarru, Godavari Dist.
MT 2188(b). Tel. 14 fol. (3-16). (Avarṇy-āvarṇi-vyākhyāna). Transcribed in 1916-17 from a Ms. of Vemparla Subrahmanya Sastrigaru of Tondavaramu, Godavari Dist. The scribe of the original Ms. is Ponnamalli Subrahmaṇya. Dated: nalanāma-saṃvatsaraśrāvaṇabahulaprathamā ādivāram |

MT 2591(g). PL. Tel. 17 fol. (205-21). Presented in 1917-18 by Vasireddi Chandramaulisvaraprasada Bahadur, Zamindar of Muktyala, Krishna Dist.

MT 2881(d). PL. Gr. 5 fol. (26-30) (with text). Presented in 1918-19 by Venkatagiri Appalacharyar of Triplicane.

Mysore (1898), p. 6 (no. 52). 10 fol. (46-65).

Mysore ND II 3108-17. Extract no. 24, 25.

Mysore ND II 3121 (P 2265/11). PL. Gr. 6 fol. (99-104). Extract no. 27.

Mysore ND II 3122 (P 2265/35). PL. Gr. 3 fol. (148-49).

TD 1807(1) → Sapta-lakṣaṇa-vyākhyā.

TD 1808. PL. Gr. 13 fol. (3-15). 200 Grantha-s. Col.: Hrasva-saṃgraha.

Whish 25a (5). PL. Gr. 8 fol. (28-35).

[NCC I 423a]

102 AVARṆYĀDI (अवर्ण्यादि)

MD 16807. Under this number Āvarṇi of Mahādhipati-yajvan is described; see below.

Mysore I, p. 612 (Avarṇyādi).

PUL II. App. p. 10 (no.133). PL. Gr. 7 fol. (6-12). 250 Grantha-s (Avarṇādi-lakṣaṇa).

[NCC I 423a]

103 AVARṆYĀDI-VARṆAMĀLĀ (अवर्ण्यादिवर्णमाला)

Two lists of phonetically fused words in the *Yajurveda*, alphabetically arranged, containing such words that begin with an elided "a" or "ā".

Beginning:

१) अपहतो ऽररुः । २) अग्ने ऽदब्धायो । ३) अदब्धायो ऽशीततनो । ४) अच्युतो ऽमात्यः । ५) अग्ने ऽयाशया । ६) अपावधीम् । ७) अतन्द्रासो ऽवृकाः । ८) अत्राह तनुत् । ९) अपानो अङ्गे अङ्गे । १०) अजराजरन्त ।

End:

स्वावेशो ऽसि । स्वाहासीनाय । स्वाहापलयिताय पर्वः । स्वाहासिताय । स्वाहाण्डाभ्याम् ।

MD 863. PL. Tel. 60 pp. (64ff.).

[NCC I 423a]

104 AVARṆY-ĀVARṆI-VYĀKHYĀNA (अवर्ण्यावर्णिव्याख्यान)

MT 2188(b). Tel. 14 fol. (3-16). (C. on Avarṇi and Āvarṇi = MD 860 and 870). Transcribed in 1916-17 from a Ms. of Vemparla Subrahmanya Sastrigaru of Tondavaramu, Godavari Dist. The scribe of the original Ms. is Ponnamalli Subrahmaṇya. Dated: nalanāmasaṃvatsara-śrāvaṇa-bahula-prathamā ādivāram |

Mysore Skt. Coll. p. 1 = D. No.2 (1123/4). PL. Tel. 6 fol. (46-51).

[NCC I 423a]

105 AVASĀNA-DĪPIKĀ (अवसानदीपिका)

IM 5556. 4 fol. (2-3, 5-6). Incomplete.

– of Govinda.

Ujjain Latest Additions 527.

[NCC I 426a]

106 AVASĀNA-NIYAMA (YAJURVEDA-SAṂHITĀYĀM)
(अवसाननियम / यजुर्वेदसंहितायाम्)
GJKSV 37945. 9 fol.

107 AVASĀNA-NIRṆAYA (-PARIŚIṢṬA) (or -ŚIKṢĀ) **(अवसाननिर्णयपरिशिष्ट /-शिक्षा)** of Ananta-deva. Altogether 1975 endings (avasāna) in the *Śukla Yajurveda*, classified into nine groups consisting of 2 to 9 words. These are regarded as helpful in the recitation of the Krama-pāṭha. Stated to have been written in V.S. 1946 (rasavedāṅkendumite). But this date, given at the end of the Benares edition, appears to be that of the printing.

Beginning:

अथातो ऽवसाननिर्णयं व्याख्यास्यामः --
नमस्कृत्य तु तं देवं शंकरस्य सुतं प्रभुम्।
यस्य प्रसादाद् देवस्य बुद्धिभेदो ऽत्यभून्मम ॥ १ ॥
अवसानं तु वक्ष्यामि यथा(दृष्टा यथाश्रुताः ।
मतेनैव च सर्वेषां यथा)वदनुपूर्वशः ॥ २ ॥
इषे त्वा भूताय कुक्कुटो ऽसि जनयत्त्यै त्वा मा भेः ...

End:

द्वे पञ्चावसाने द्वे षडवसाने द्वे नवावसाने भवतः । सर्वाण्यवसानान्येकीकृत्यैकानविंशतिः शतानि पञ्चसप्ततिः संख्या कण्डिकायाश्चत्वारिंशदध्याये १९७५ ॥ इत्यनन्तदेवविरचिता अवसाननिर्णयशिक्षा समाप्ता।
रसवेदाङ्केन्दुमिते (१९४६) फाल्गुने शुक्लपक्षके।
पूर्णिमायां गुरोर्वारे ऽवसानान्यङ्कितानि वै ॥
(This last verse is not found in the Mss.).

ASB I iii.98 (IM 2482). 4 fol. 60 Grantha-s. Title: Avasāna-nirṇaya-pariśiṣṭa.
Bhk. 9.
Bikaner 619. 20 fol. Dated V.S. 1686 (A.D. 1629).
Bikaner 677. ?
BISM p. 17 (2/66). 17 fol.
Bombay Uni. 1 (BMC 50 8). 4 fol. (14 Kaṇḍikā-s).
BORI 58 of A 1881-82. 2 fol.
IM 2482. 4 fol. Title: Avasāna-nirṇaya-pariśiṣṭa.
IM 3373. 4 fol. Title: Avasāna-nirṇaya-pariśiṣṭa.
SBD 4344. 5 fol.
Stein p. 11 (no. 178). 3 fol. Dated V.S. 1871.

Ptd.: in Śikṣā-saṃgraha. – Benares, 1889, pp. 166-71. – (Ben. S. S. 10).

[NCC I 426a]

108 AVASĀNA-NIRṆAYA-PARIŚIṢṬA (अवसाननिर्णयपरिशिष्ट)

ASB I iii.98 (IM 2482). 4 fol. 60 Grantha-s. The same as the above.

[NCC I 426b]

109 AVASĀNE HRASVĀKĀROCCĀRAṆA-VICĀRA (अवसाने ह्रस्वाकारोच्चारणविचार)

From the *Pārṣada-lāghava* of Viṭṭhala-panta.

Beginning:

अथ श्रीमत् चिदम्बरगुरुकृपाकटाक्षेण ज्ञातपार्षदमाटेत्युपनामकश्रीभास्करसूनु-केशवभट्टेन विरचिते ऋग्वेदकल्पद्रुमे अवसानस्थितह्रस्वाकारोच्चारणविषये विठलपन्तकृतपार्षदलाघवे ...

End:

तदपि आर्यादिषु मात्रासंख्याबोधकमेव न दीर्घवदुच्चारणबोधकम् । तच्छास्त्रस्य उच्चारणबोधनायाप्रवृत्तेः ॥ तद्भागस्य ऋक्प्रातिशाख्ये दोषश्रवणादिति दिक् । इत्यवसाने ह्रस्वाकारोच्चारणविचारः ॥

BISM p. 17 (35/304). 11 fol.

110 AVEṢṬANA-NĀMĀVALI (अवेष्टननामावलि)

About 90 verses containing a list of words not divisible in the Pada-pāṭha of the *Taittirīya-saṃhitā* (alphabetically arranged).

Beginning:

अनेकानिङ्ग्यशब्दानां परिज्ञानोपयोगिनी।
सर्वेषां सुखबोधार्थं क्रियते ऽक्षरमालिका॥
अंहतिश्चान्तरतो व्यधमानावसेन च।
अवसायाक्षीयमाणाश्नतश्चाजगरेण च॥

End:

शिक्षमाणश्च सिसृतं सालावृकि सचेमहि।
ननेमि सगरः शब्दः शीक्षते च सनिष्यवः ।
हवामहे हलिक्ष्णां च हरिमाणमनिङ्ग्यकाः ॥

MD 20081. PL. Tel. fol. 93ff. (See MD 856, last work in the codex).

111 AVEṢṬANA-PADĀNI (अवेष्टनपदानि)

List of words that are not divisible in Pada-pāṭha of the *Taittirīya-saṃhitā*, arranged alphabetically. Cf. Aniṅgya-padāni, MT 1964(a).

Beginning:

अजगरेण। अरोचथाः । अदन्दशूकाः । अनिष्टृतः । अंहतिः ।

End:

सालावृकेभ्यः । स्नावन्याभ्याम्। हवामहे। हरिमाणम्। हलीक्ष्णान्।

MD 873. PL. Tel. 6 pp. (78ff.).

112 AVEṢṬANA-SŪTRA (अवेष्टनसूत्र)

MT 485(p). PL. Tel. 1 fol. (70a). Lacks beginning and end. No extract. Presented in 1910-11 by C. Visvanatha Shastrigal of Viziyanagaram.

113 AṢṬAKA-ŚLOKA-VYĀKHYĀ (अष्टकश्लोकव्याख्या)

Trav. Uni. 18109 F. PL. Mal. 60 Grantha-s → Sūkta-ślokā-s.

114 AṢṬA-KHAṆḌA (अष्टखण्ड)

A collection of words and phrases from the *Ṛgveda* that show slight differences in their different occurences.

Beginning:

अग्निमीळे रत्नधातमम् (१·१·१) अयं देवाय रत्नधातमः (१·२·१) अस्मां ति (१·१·१८) प्रो ष्वस्मै त (८·७·२१) सुविवृतं सहस्रसातमां (१·१·२०) दूणाशं सहस्रसातमं (४·७·२६) तयोः कृतं (१·१·३३) मवानः कृधि (६·५·३६) सोमानं पते (१·१·३४) कृत्वा कवे (४·५·२६) अत्रैव हिनोति (१·१·३४) सं नः शिशी हिनोषि (५·७·३३)

Weber 44 (Chambers 791b). 12 fol. Dated V.S. 1714. Copied in Varanasi by Harirāma, son of Dīkṣita Rāmakṛṣṇa.

115 AṢṬA-LAKṢAṆA (अष्टलक्षण)

Mysore ND II 3123 (P 4906/30). PL. Na. 1 fol. (123). Extract no. 28. (Cf. p. 24 of the *Pada-gāḍha*, Srirangam edition).

116 AṢṬA-VIKṚTI (अष्टविकृति)

Rules for the krama-, jaṭā-pāṭha, etc.

Baroda 13804. 11 fol. 150 Grantha-s. Dated Śaka 1846.

BISM p. 19 (35/473). 2 fol. Illustrations of 8 Vikṛti-s of the verse : gāyanti tvā gāyatriṇaḥ. Title: Aṣṭa-vikṛti-dharmaḥ.

IM 2644A. Eight Vikṛti-s for the verse "trīṇi jānā paribhūṣanti" with introductory verses.

IM 9703. 3 fol. Incomplete.

PUL I, p. 19 (no.21). 2 fol. 8 Grantha-s.

PUL I, p. 19 (no.22). 3 fol. 50 Grantha-s (with C.).

SBD 1445. 4 fol. Dated V.S. 1893. Illustrations of the Vikṛti-s on the mantra "bṛhaspate paridīyā rathena ... " on fol. 1-3 and verses of definitions with examples of different verses on fol. 3-4.

SBD 1475. 3 fol. Incomplete. Dated V.S. 1893.

SBD 47894. 7 fol. Dated V.S. 1877. Copied by Moreśvara Gahvara.

Sūcīpattra 111 (Aṣṭa-vikṛti-śāstra).

[NCC I 454b]

117 AṢṬA-VIKṚTI-KĀRIKĀ (अष्टविकृतिकारिका)

→ Vikṛti-vallī of Vyāḍi.

SBD 47893. 8 fol. (with C.). Second part of the Vikṛti-kaumudī.

118 AṢṬA-VIKṚTI(-MANTRA) (अष्टविकृति-मन्त्र)

Definitions and illustrative verses from *Vājasaneyi-saṃhitā* for eight Vikṛti-s. It is largely based on the work described in the next entry.

Ptd.: in the edition of the *Vājasaneyi-saṃhitā*, ed. by Amritalal Sastri of Jamnagar, in : *Śukla-yajurveda-mādhyandina-saṃhitā* (prāstāvikasaṃhitāmantrāṇām akārādyanukramaṇikāvedapārāyaṇavidhyanuvākasūtrādhyāyāṣṭavikṛtiyājñavalkya-śikṣāpratijñāsūtrasarvānukramasūtra- ... samalaṃkṛtā) – Bombay : Nirnaya Sagar Press, Śaka 1872 (1950), pp. 148-76. [SKGI (Rh III 125)]

119 AṢṬA-VIKṚTI(-LAKṢAṆA) (अष्टविकृति-लक्षण)

Rules for krama-, jaṭā-pāṭha, etc. This is actually a part of the *Jyotsnā*, a commentary on the *Vājasaneyi-prātiśākhya* (cf. GB 18, fol. 47a-53b). This is also included in the *Prāti-śākhya-pradīpa-śikṣā* published in the Śikṣā-saṃgraha (on pp. 300-06) with some omissions (remark on p. 306 : śeṣaṃ jyotsnādiṣu jñeyam). There are also Mss. containing this text separately. But see Devasthali's introductory note (p. 23) to his edition.

Beginning:

अथ जटाद्यष्टविकृतीनां लक्षणानि लिख्यन्ते -- तत्र विकृतीनां पाठे फलं पङ्क्तिपावनत्वम्॥

जटादिविकृतीनां ये पारायणपरायणाः ।
महात्मानो द्विजश्रेष्ठास्ते ज्ञेयाः पङ्क्तिपावनाः॥

इत्यादिपुराणात्। अन्यान्यपि विष्णुलोकादिफलानि वराहपुराणपराशरस्मृत्यादिषु। तासां नामानि प्रदर्श्यन्ते --

जटा माला शिखा रेखा ध्वजो दण्डो रथो घनः ।
अष्टौ विकृतयः प्रोक्ताः क्रमपूर्वा मनीषिभिः॥ १॥

क्रमः पूर्वो यासां ताः । आसां क्रमः प्रकृतिरित्यर्थः । तत्र प्रथमत्वाज्जटालक्षणमाह --

क्रमं यथोक्तं प्रब्रूयाद् व्युत्क्रमेण क्रमेण च।
सलक्षणं सर्वसंधौ जटा सा प्रोच्यते बुधैः ॥ २॥

क्रमं यथोक्तं द्वित्रिचतुःक्रमात्मकं पुनश्च तमेव वैपरीत्येन पुनश्च क्रमेण। एवं त्रिवारं संधिषु लक्षणयुक्तं पठेत्। सा जटा इति तत्त्वज्ञैरुच्यते। वायवः स्थ स्थ वायवो वायवः स्थ॥

End:

शिखामुक्त्वा विपर्यस्य पुनस्त्रिपदमाहरेत्।
अयं घन इति प्रोक्त इत्यष्टौ विकृतीः पठेत्॥ १७॥

अस्यार्थः । शिखां पूर्वोक्तामुच्चार्य विपर्यासेन तानि पदान्युच्चार्य पुनः क्रमेण तानि पदानि उच्चारयेत्। अयं विकृतिविशेषो घन इति प्रोक्तः ऋषिभिः । दस्रा युवाकवो युवाकवो दस्रा दस्रा युवाकवः सुताः । .... आयातं यातमायातं रुद्रवर्तनी रुद्रवर्तनी यातमायातं रुद्रवर्तनी । यातं रुद्रवर्तनी रुद्रवर्तनी यातं यातं रुद्रवर्तनी । रुद्रवर्तनी इति रुद्रवर्तनी ॥ एवंप्रकारेण अष्टौ विकृतीः पठेत्॥

IM 2568. 12 fol. Dated V.S. 1905.
L 1931. 12 fol. 147 Grantha-s.
Mithila IV 9. 11 fol.
Mithila IV 9A. 12 fol.

Ptd.:
1) Ed. by G. Thibaut under the title: *Der Abschnitt der Prātiśākhyajyotsnā über die Vikṛti des Kramapāṭha*, together with the *Jaṭāpaṭala*. – Leipzig : F. A. Brockhaus, 1870, pp 36-53.
2) Ed. by Yugalakishora (Vyasa) Pathaka, under the title: *Jaṭādi-vikṛti-lakṣaṇam*, at the end of the *Śukla-yajuḥ-prātiśākhya*. – Benares, 1888, pp. 571-93. – (Ben. S. S. 4).
3) Ed. by K. V. Abhyankar and G. V. Devasthali, under the title: *Aṣṭa-vikṛti-lakṣaṇāni* in : *Veda-vikṛti-lakṣaṇa-saṃgraha*. – Poona : BORI, 1978, pp. 23-32.
4) Also included (with a few additional illustrations by the editor) in the edition of the *Jyotsnā-vṛtti* of Rāmaśarman on the *Vājasaneyi-prātiśākhya*, ed. by Yugal Kishore Misra. – Varanasi : Sampurnanand Sanskrit University, 1989, pp. 219-41.

[NCC I 454b]

120 AṢṬA-VIKṚTI-KĀRIKĀ-VYĀKHYĀ (अष्टविकृतिकारिकाव्याख्या)
of Rāmakṛṣṇa-bhaṭṭa → C. on Vikṛti-vallī (which see). It omits the first verse and is almost identical with the commentary, *Vikṛti-kaumudī* at the end.
IM 2521. 14 fol. (2-15). Incomplete.
IM 2572. 6 fol. 6 fol.
SBD 4302. 21 fol.

121 AṢṬA-VIKṚTI-LAKṢAṆA (अष्टविकृतिलक्षण)
Said to be from Śaunaka's *Vikalpa-kaumudī*.

Beginning:

शौनको ऽहं प्रवक्ष्यामि विकृतीनां च लक्षणम्।
अष्टधा विकृतिर्ज्ञेया जटामालादिभेदतः ॥
पर्यायेण च नामानि तेषां वक्ष्ये ऽहमत्र तु।
जटा माला शिखा रेखा ध्वजो दण्डो रथो घनः ।
अष्टौ विकृतयः प्रोक्ताः पूर्वं व्यालिमहर्षिणा ॥

End:

तस्य पारायणे बुद्धिर्यस्य लोके सदा भवेत्।

स एव परमे लोके त्रिमूर्त्यात्मक उच्यते ॥
जटादिविकृतीनां तु लक्षणं च मयोदितम् ।
शाकलीमनुसृत्यैव संहितां विदुषां मुदे ॥
इति विकल्पकौमुद्यां शौनकोक्तमष्टविकृतिलक्षणं समाप्तम् ॥

Trav. Uni. L.1372 B. PL. Mal. 30 Grantha-s. (Not available for consultation as the Ms. was returned to its owner and a transcript prepared for the Library has been misplaced).
Trav. Uni. L.1429 F. PL. Mal. 2 fol. 30 Grantha-s.
TSM Acc. No. 1079a. PL. Gr. 1 fol.

[NCC I 454b]

122 AṢṬA-VIKṚTI-LAKṢAṆA (MASKARĪYA) (अष्टविकृतिलक्षण / मस्करीय)
Mysore I, p. 22. → Aṣṭa-vikṛti-vivṛti of Madhusūdana-maskarin.

123 AṢṬA-VIKṚTI-VIVṚTI (-KĀRIKĀ) (अष्टविकृतिविवृति-कारिका)
of Madhusūdana-maskarin. Though in most of the catalogues this work is entered and described as a commentary on the *Aṣṭa-vikṛti* (also called *Vikṛti-vallī)* it is in fact a different work of Madhusūdana-maskarin. Presumably, the cataloguers are misled by the word Vivṛti in the title. It is also known as the *Madhusūdanī-śikṣā*. Several Mss. and the Srirangam edition have only the portion up to jaṭā (verse 45) and hence entitled *Jaṭā-paṭala* or *Jaṭā-lakṣaṇa*. It is ascribed to Vyāḍi in some Mss. See under Jaṭā-paṭala and Jaṭā-lakṣaṇa.

Beginning:

श्रीमन्तौ श्रीनृहरिचरणावात्मनो न्यस्य चेत-
स्यृग्वेदाष्टौविकृतिविवृतिं वैदिकश्लोकनीयाम् ।
व्याख्याचार्यानुमति मधुसंसूदनाख्यो गुरुश्री-
कृष्णद्वैपायनतनुभवो मस्करी चर्करीति ॥ १ ॥
महाकृतिरियं मम प्रकृतिनिर्मला हारिणी
सुधाविमतिकारिणी विशयहारिणी सेविनाम् ।
वचस्यमपहारिणी परविपश्चितामन्वहं
मनोभुवि विहारिणी भवतु वेदविद्याविदाम् ॥ २ ॥
जटा-माला-दण्ड-रेखा-रथ-ध्वज-शिखा-घनाः ।
क्रममाश्रित्य निर्वृत्ता विकारा अष्ट विश्रुताः ॥ ३ ॥
द्विपदादिक्रमाः पञ्च प्राक् क्रमाद् व्युत्क्रमात् ततः ।
पुनः क्रमादुच्चरिता जटात्वं प्रापिता बुधैः ॥ ४ ॥

End:

क्रममुक्त्वा विपर्यस्य पुनश्च क्रममुत्तरम् ।
अर्धर्चादेवमुक्तोक्तैः क्रमदण्डो ऽभिधीयते ।

पादशो ऽर्धर्चशो वापि सहोक्त्या दण्डवद् रथः ॥ ५२॥
शिखामुक्त्वा विपर्यस्य पुनस्त्रिपदमुच्चरेत्।
शिखा जटा घनः प्रोक्त इत्यष्टौ विकृतीः पठेत्॥ ५३॥
इत्यष्टौ विकृतीनां स्वरूपकथनं मया विरचितं यत्।
तेन विष्णुर्जिष्णुः प्रीतो भवतात् भवाटवीपरशुः ॥ ५४॥

Baroda 8292. 7 fol. (1-6 and 14). 100 Grantha-s. = CLB I, p. 23. (Jaṭā-paṭala only).

Baroda 8565. 27 fol. 500 Grantha-s. = CLB I, p. 23. (Jaṭā-paṭala only).

Baroda 26336. 42 fol. 1200 Grantha-s. Incomplete. (Aṣṭa-vikṛti-śikṣā-bhāṣya).

Bhk. 9.

BISM p. 282 (22/1016). 37 fol. (with C.). Copied by Tambe Raghunātha Dīkṣita. Title: Śikṣā-vivaraṇa. Col.: iti Madhusūdana-kṛta-śikṣā-vivaraṇaṃ samāptam ||

Bombay Uni. 710 (BMC 85 15). 36 fol. (with C. Prakāśa). (described as Jaṭā-paṭala of Vyāḍi with Vivṛti of Madhusūdana, with Prakāśa of Purogamācārya). (Used for the Poona edition).

Bombay Uni. Acc. no. 5221. 25 fol. Ascribed to Madusūdana-sarasvatī in the colophon.

BORI 64 of A 1881-82. 22 fol. (Aṣṭa-vikṛti-vivaraṇa). (Used for the Poona edition).

BORI 378 of 1883-84. 6 fol. Incomplete. (Used for the Poona edition).

BP p. 286.

Haug p. 30 (no.79b) = München 14.

IM 2192. 17 fol. Title: Madhusūdana-śikṣā.

IM 2425. 18 fol. (18-35). Incomplete. Title: Jaṭādyaṣṭa-vikṛti-vivaraṇa and Madhusūdana-śikṣā-bhāṣya.

K 78.

L 1492. 30 fol. 641 Grantha-s.

München 14. 15 fol. (Written ca. A.D. 1700).

Mysore I, p. 22.

Mysore ND II 3125 (A 264/ 2). 15 fol. (121-35). Extract no. 29.

Mysore ND II 3126 (C 476/ 7). 1 fol. (3). Incomplete. Extract no. 30.

N-W P V 142 (no.7). 17 fol. (Title: Jaṭādi-vikṛti-vivaraṇa). Remarks : "A commentary by Madhusūdanamuni, commonly called Madhusūdanī-śikṣā-bhāṣya."

RASB II 282 (G 603) = L 1492. (Used for the Poona edition).

RASB II 283 (G 2506). 32 fol. 600 Grantha-s. Dated Śaka 1712.

RASB II 284 (G 6180A). 19 fol.

SB p. 8 (no.7). 17 fol. 631 Grantha-s (Jaṭādi-vikṛti-vivaraṇaṃ sabhāṣyam). = SBD 47936.

SBD 47936. 17 fol. (Jaṭādy-aṣṭa-vikṛti-vivaraṇa).

Visvanatha Vamana Deva, Varanasi. 40 fol. (with C.). Dated Śaka 1733.

Wai I 346. 23 fol. (with Vivaraṇa).

Wai I 347. 16 fol. (with Vivaraṇa). Incomplete.

[NCC I 454b]

Ptd.: ed. by Satyavrata Samasrami – with a Sanskrit introduction entitled: *Luptakalpa-vedāṅgam* – with the title *Aṣṭa-vikṛti-vivṛtiḥ (Vedāṅgam)* Madhusūdanamunikṛtā (sāmagācāryeṇa sāmaśramīti labdhopanāmakena satyavratabhaṭṭācāryeṇa saprastārodāharaṇavyākhyayā samalaṃkṛtya prakāśitā, 1811 śakābdīyaśrāvaṇe kalikātāsatyayantre tadādeśenaiva bhārate 'tra prathamaṃ mudritā) in the Sanskrit journal *Uṣā*. – Calcutta : Satya Press, 1889, vol. I, pt. 1, 8. 38 pp. (The Sanskrit introduction alone is reprinted in the *Ṛgveda-ghanasāra;* see below). [Adyar (H 211.3 x Sat); Emeneau (61); BM : Ptd. Bks. Cat. 1876-92. 206 (14010.c.43)]

Also ed. by Kesavasiva Ghanapathi, with the title *Vyāḻi-śikṣā*, in the magazine of the Mysore Sanskrit College, *Śrīmanmahārāja Saṃskṛta Mahāpāṭhaśālā Patrikā*, vols. 23-26 (1948-50), Mysore, xxix, 1-76 pp. (note on p. 1: etadgranthasya kartṛnāmnā "Madhusūdana-śikṣā" iti vyavahartavye 'pi vyāḻyācāryābhimatalakṣaṇānām eva etadgranthakṛtā madhusūdanācāryeṇa atra viśadīkriyamāṇatvāt mūlācāryanāmnā "Vyāḻiśikṣā" iti bhūyo vyavahāraḥ samajanīti vijñāyate). The text is the same as of Madhusūdana-maskarin, published by Satyavrata Samasrami to whom the commentary is attributed here. The Sanskrit introduction of Samasrami called "Lupta(kalpa)vedāṅgam" is also reprinted in this edition on pp. 71-76. [Adyar (H05sk MSC 23-26); SAI (87/774*)]

Also ed. by K[rishnarajapuram] S[ubbaratna] Venkatarama Sastri, with the title *Ṛgvedīya-jaṭā-lakṣaṇam* (śrīmadhusūdanīya-śikṣāntargataṃ śrīsatyavratakṛtavyākhyāsahitam), only up to the end of the Jaṭā-lakṣaṇa. – Srirangam : Sri Vani Vilas Press, 1964. iv, vi, 36 pp. [Adyar (PH 215.1 Ms. sxy Sat); SAI (87/772*)] also see the *Ṛgveda-ghanasāra* (with Gānilakṣaṇa and Svaralakṣaṇa), ed. by the same, Srirangam 1966.

Also ed. by K. V. Abhyankar and G. V. Devasthali, in *Veda-vikṛti-lakṣaṇa-saṃgraha*. – Poona : BORI, 1978, pp. 75-112. In this edition, however, the text is entitled *Aṣṭa-vikṛti-vivṛti*, and ascribed to Madhusūdana-maskarin, and the commentary called Prakāśa is attributed to Purogamācārya. This edition is based on the following Mss:

1) RASB II 282 (p. 311).
2) Bombay Uni. 710.
3) BORI 378 of 1883-84. 4 fol. Incomplete. Up to the commentary on verse 5.
4) BORI 64 of A 1881-82. 22 fol. Dated Śaka 1712.
5) Transcript of a Ms. from Satara; text only; 55 verses. Dated V.S. 1888.
6) Transcript of a Ms. from Satara, copied by Raghunātha Dīkṣita Tambe, at Indore, dated V.S. 1888.
7) And also the printed edition of *Ṛgvedīya-jaṭā-lakṣaṇa*, prepared by K[rishnarajapuram] S. Venkatarama Sastri. – Srirangam : Sri Vani Vilas Press, 1964.

– C. Prakāśa (attributed to Purogamācārya).

Beginning:

मधुसूदनमुनीश्वररचिताष्टौविकृतिसंवरणस्य तत्पूर्वाश्च पुरोगमाचार्यः प्रकाशमारभते।
(the text printed in the *Uṣā* and Srirangam edition begins from here :)

अथ मधुसूदनमहामुनिः स्वचिकीर्षितस्य निष्प्रत्यूहपरिसमापनफलकमिष्टदेवताध्यानरूपं मङ्गलमाचरन् स्वगुरुस्वनामकथनपूर्वकं स्वचिकीर्षितं प्रतिजानीते... गुरुभूतो यः

कृष्णद्वैपायनः तस्य तनुभवः तत्करजातत्वेन तत्कुमार इति ...

End:

इममङ्ग्या इत्यादिजटाकम्पास्तत्र तत्र द्रष्टव्याः । ४६ ।
(The text printed in the Srirangam edition ends here)
मीळ्हुषे भरध्वम् । भरध्वमिति भर-ध्वम् । इत्यादि घनः ॥

Bombay Uni. 710 (BMC 85 15). 36 fol. (with text).
BORI 378 of 1883-84. 6 fol. Incomplete. (Used for the Poona edition).
BP p. 286.
L 1492. 30 fol. 641 Grantha-s (with text).
Mysore ND II 3127 (A 264/ 3). 15 fol. (121-35). Extract no. 31.
Mysore ND II 3128 (C 476/ 8). 1 fol. Incomplete. Extract no. 32.
PUL I, p. 19 (no.22). 3 fol. 50 Grantha-s (with text).
RASB II 282 (G 603) = L 1492.
RASB II 283 (G 2506). 32 fol. 600 Grantha-s. Dated Śaka 1712.
RASB II 284 (G 6180A). 19 fol.
SBD 47936. 17 fol. Col.: Madhusūdanī-śikṣā-bhāṣyam.
Visvanatha Vamana Deva, Varanasi. 40 fol. Dated Śaka 1733.

Ptd.: with the text in all four editions noted above.

124 AṢṬA-VIKṚTI-ŚIKṢĀ-BHĀṢYA (अष्टविकृतिशिक्षाभाष्य)
of Madhusūdana → Aṣṭa-vikṛti-vivṛti (-kārikā).
Baroda 26336. 42 fol. 1200 Grantha-s. Incomplete.

125 AṢṬA-SAṂKHYĀ (अष्टसंख्या)
It describes the RV Varga-s by enumerating the number of Ṛk-s, Pada-s, and details about the word-endings, etc. Written in columns.
VSM III 162 (no.11282). 50 fol. Dated Śaka 1652. Copied by Nigalye Ananta. → Ṛgveda-pada-ratna-samīkṣā.

126 AṢṬĀKṢARĪ-PARIBHĀṢĀ (अष्टाक्षरीपरिभाषा)
Dealing with the number of Pada-s, etc. in the several Varga-s of the *Ṛgveda*.

Beginning:

श्रीशं प्रणम्य वाक्यानि वक्ष्ये शाकल्यवर्त्मना ।
ऋग्वेदप्रतिवर्गस्थपदसंख्यादिसिद्धये ॥
एकैकस्य तु वर्गस्य भवेद् वाक्यचतुष्टयम् ।
आद्येन ह्यक्षरेष्वेषु परिसंख्यायते पदम् ॥
द्वितीयेन विसर्गान्तं तृतीयेन त्ववग्रहम् ।
ह्रस्वान्तं तु चतुर्थेन वर्गैः कटपयादिभिः ॥

पकारे परतो राधो रथो ग्नाजा ऋतो दिवः ।
इत्येतानि ज(ष)ळंजस्या दुष्प्रेति च पदद्वयम्॥
नावग्रहेषु पठ्यन्ते न विसर्गेषु चाप्युत।
अकाराद्याः स्वरा ओजाः सप्त ह्रस्वा इहोदिताः ॥
मान्तं यत् प्रथमं वाक्यं पदसंख्या शताधिका। ...
द्विपदं पदसंख्यायामेकमेव नयेत् पदम्।
यत्र मान्तः श्लोकपादस्तत्र सूक्तं समाप्यते॥
अध्यायादावृचां संख्या वाक्येन त्र्यक्षरेण तु।
प्रदर्श्यते ऽग्निमीळे ऽस्मिन्नृक्संख्यां वर्धयेदिति॥

राधस्पते। रथस्पतिः । ग्नास्पतिः । अजस्पतिः । ऋतस्पते। दिवस्पृथिव्याः। अञ्जस्याः । दुष्प्राव्यः । इत्येतान्यष्टावग्रहेषु न पठ्यन्ते । अतो न विसर्गः ।... पदसंख्याग्निरक्षस्वच्छतान् समीची । अमी बृहत् । इन्द्रावरुणवामे तव वायो । धवा लेख्यार्थनाद्वारः वायो चण्डभुग्नश्च न स्वयमश्विना।

End: (MT as the 2nd paragraphs of Srirangam edition)

च्योफ धतु सेचा बुखो तो खुडे चुवैची कुडी षाढा। झा बू पुतो शोब ध्यो स च्छिद् पीवा झसौ तैणीजुणषयाटे गीदैति च्लिति तुगि। ऋतं च नास्ति॥

राववणेन कृतं ह्येतत् पदरत्नं सतां हितम्।
पठन् पदानि निश्चित्य परिपूर्णाशयो भवेत्॥

इति पदरत्नं समाप्तम्॥ अष्टाक्षरी परिभाषा समाप्ता॥

Brl. p. 6 (no.VI) = IO 4244.
IO 4244 (Burnell 205f). PL. Gr. 4 fol. (151-54).
MT 5295. 34 fol. Title: Pada-ratna. Transcribed in 1926-27 from a Ms. of Paramesvara Nambudiri, Tiyanuru-mana, Vaniyankolam, Malabar Dist.
Mysore P.4723 fol. 169-70. Incomplete. A codex of 159 disarranged fol. ; contains Upalekha-sūtra with Kannada commentery among many other works.
Trav. Uni. 823 B. PL. Mal. 750 Grantha-s. Incomplete. (Ṛgveda-varga-pada-saṃkhyā-nirṇaya). Also known as the Ṛgveda-prativarga-pada-nirṇaya-vākyāni.

127 AṢṬĀKṢARĪ-BAIṬH(-PARIBHĀṢĀ) **(अष्टाक्षरीबैठ्-परिभाषा)** of Dakṣiṇāmūrti. Code words of eight letters for each Varga of the *Ṛgveda*. It is variously called Ṛgveda-pada-varṇa-saṃkhyā, Dakṣiṇāmūrti-pada-varṇa-saṃkhyā, Dakṣiṇāmūrti-baiṭh, Pada-varṇa-lakṣaṇa-paribhāṣā, Baiṭh-paribhāṣā. For an analysis, in Sanskrit, of a Ms. in SB see Nandinatha Misra, "Ṛkpada-varṇānukramaṇī-paricayaḥ" in the *Ṛṣikalpanyāsa* (Panditaraja Rajeswara Shastri Dravida Felicitation Volume) – Prayag (Allhabad) : Bharati Parishad, 1971, pp. 21-36 Ve.). [SAI (ind 50 B 86/449)] The same is also printed in the Sanskrit journal : *Sārasvatī Suṣamā,* vol. 23.3, Varanasi, Saṃ. 2025 (1969), pp. 237-58. [SAI (ind 51 D 887/1731)] Cf. Chandrabhanu Pandeya : "Varṇāṅka-saṃketa-paddhati", in : *Nāgarī-Pracāriṇī Patrikā* (Saṃpūrṇānada-smṛtiviśeṣāṅka), vol. 73. Varanasi, Saṃ. 2025 (1968), pp. 318-26. [SOAS (Per 19 – 18679)] Cf. Janardana Sastri Pandeya, "Vaidika-vāṅmaye Baiṭha-saṃpradāyaḥ" (Sanskrit) in : *Padmasmṛti-granthaḥ* (Nepālasthasaṃskṛtaviduṣāṃ sarvaprathamasmṛtigranthaḥ), pub. by Padmasmṛti-grantha-prakāśana-samiti, Madanamohan Dhavan, C. K. 34/39, Lahori Tola, Varanasi, 1984, pp. 7-10. In some Mss. (e.g. BISM, p. 19 (35/481), the various Aṣṭaka-s are named as : "śaktiśrī", "parāśrī", "mantraśrī", "ātmaśrī", "jagacchrī", "gokulaṃ", "devaśrī" "tattvaśrī". Significance of these names is, however, not known. See remarks by G. V. Devasthali, introduction (p. xii, footnote 1) to *Veda-vikṛti-lakṣaṇa-saṃgraha*. Cf. also Hz 410(a). Extract p. 79 where the expressions like "devaśrī" are also found.

Beginning: (857)

अथातो दक्षिणामूर्ति(कृत)पदवर्णलक्षणपरिभाषा व्याख्यास्यामः । आदौ पदसंख्या विसर्गनकारान्तावगृह्यप्रगृह्य मकारतकारसंख्या सितु-सेन्ताविषमसमान्यादिवर्गेण दशेनोत्तरपदस्वरेण द्वितीयवर्गैकाक्षरं ....

सो ऽहं स्फुरन्तीमनुभूय सौरीं परां कलां सप्तदशीं स्वतन्त्राम्।
समाहरिष्ये पदवर्णसंख्यां यो दक्षिणामूर्तिरनुत्तमात्मा ॥ १॥
संहितायामहं वेद संख्या या भवता कृता(म्)।
देवः को ऽपि न को ऽप्यन्यो गिरां यन्ता च सर्वशः ॥ २॥
पदतद्वर्णानुदात्तविसर्गेङ्ग्यन्वितितप्रमा।
कादिक्षान्ताक्षरैर्वक्ष्ये युक्तायुक्तैः स्वरैरपि॥ ३॥
दशविंशतिमुख्या स्यात् संख्या काद्यक्षरैः परे।
तत्रैकमुख्या दशभिः स्वरैरनृ-लभिः क्रमात्॥ ४॥
काद्यैस्त्रिभिः स्वरैस्त्रीणि पदान्येकाक्षरादितः ।
काद्या एकादिसंख्याका आकाराद्याः स्वरा नव॥ ५॥
सप्ताक्षरं त्वनुदात्तं हलश्चाष्टाक्षरादिषु।
सत्स्वत्र कल्प्या हलचो सभ्यन्तः षोडश स्वराः ॥ ६॥
विसर्गपद्यमातानां काद्यानान्तेतिताः स्वराः ।
स्वराधिक्ये दशाद्यस्य रेफे स्यात् सप्तविंशतिः ॥ ७॥
वैषम्यसितुसेन्तानां वाक्यान्तस्तु विसृज्यते।
पञ्चत्रिंशद्धलो ल्यस्यान्त्यस्य वस्य तु विंशतिः ॥ ८॥
अतसंकणङमनातया वर्णसंख्यया।
स्वरान्तपदसंख्या स्यात् पदसंख्याप्यपद्यया॥ ९॥
पृथक्कृतिर्नो यदि खण्डितानामखण्डितानामपि नास्ति भेदः ।
न च स्फुटं सर्वतरं नदिङ्ग्यमायत्सु गोपातम इत्यमुत्र॥

इति दक्षिणामूर्तिदेवश्रीपादोपदिष्टायां पदवर्णसंख्यायां संज्ञा समाप्ता ॥ तदूर्ध्वमिक-ईक-ऊकान्यत्ये त्र्यक्षरं विसर्गादिषड्के पूर्वोक्तवर्णस्वरेण ज्ञेयो विसर्जनीये

विषमस्वरान्ते समेतिसितुसेताश्च ज्ञायते। नमो दक्षिणामूर्तये। इति दक्षिणामूर्तिपरिभाषा समाप्ता । दक्षिणामूर्तिज्ञापकलक्षणम् । प्रथमाक्षरेण पदसंख्या ज्ञातव्या । द्वितीयेनैकाक्षरचतुरक्षरे । तृतीयेन द्व्यक्षरपञ्चाक्षरे । चतुर्थेन त्र्यक्षरषडक्षरे । पञ्चमेन सर्वानुदात्तसप्ताक्षरे । षष्ठेन विसर्गनकारान्ते । सप्तमेनावगृह्यप्रगृह्ये । अष्टमेन मकारान्ततकारान्ते । पञ्चमेभ्योत्तरेणाष्टभ्यो ऽधिकेनाष्टाक्षरादि ज्ञातव्यम् । रेफस्य दशसंख्या ज्ञातव्या। अ आ इ ई उ ऊ ए ऐ ओ औ। पदसंख्योत्तरस्य अकारवर्जमिति ज्ञातव्यम्। अग्निमीळे -- घेजाशतछताजडुः । यदङ्ग -- घदुनञजजघसी। वायवायाहि -- घोञूरगठाकडछेजा । वायविन्द्रः -- गूङीबुछढश्छचुट । अश्विना यज्वरी -- घोङषणेखागङुग। ओमासः -- ङछैभनडपछछ।

End:

अपश्यं त्वा -- ४१ -- घीञोपठठछाछिद । विष्णुर्योनिं कल्पयतु -- ४२ -- गेजुथाञाढघगिझः । ऋतं च -- ४८ -- ऋयक-अकु-हग । सं समित् -- ४९ -- चिफिभपपधाचदा । इति श्रीदक्षिणामूर्तौ श्रीपादोपदिष्टायां पदवर्ण-संख्यायामष्टमाष्टके अष्टमो ऽध्यायः ॥

तर्जन्यादौ कनिष्ठादौ तथैवानामिके ऽन्तिके।
मध्यमाङ्गुलिमध्ये च उदात्तादिस्वरांशयोः ॥ १॥
स्वरितश्चाप्यनुस्वारस्तथा यरलवा अपि।
परस्वरेण संयुक्तस्वरितग्राहिणो मताः ॥ २॥
नकारान्तं पदं पूर्वं यवरेषु परेषु च।
नकारयहमध्ये तत्र ... संयुतम्॥ ३॥
ह्रस्वपूर्वो नकारो यः पदान्तो वपरो यदि।
विशेषं तत्र जानीयाद् द्वित्वमित्यभिधीयते॥ ४॥
यच्छब्दे च कुविच्छब्दे निहिशब्दहिशब्दयोः ।
तिङन्तं नानुदात्तं स्यात् तच्छब्देनान्वयं विना॥ ५॥

वनेषु जायुरा सूर्यः प्रातरग्निरग्निर्देवेषु वेद यस्त्रीणि वपुर्नु तदयं कविरेषस्य मित्रावरुणा महानोशिक्पावक इति दशमर्तेषु यकारवर्जम्॥
(Cf. *Pada-gāḍha*, p. 26)

Adyar D I 857 (22 H 6 = 69060). PL. Tel. 2 fol. (11-12). (Dakṣiṇāmūrti-khaṇḍa). The text printed here includes some extraneous portions at the end. = Adyar I, p. 50a.

Baroda 8666. 1 fol. 20 Grantha-s. = CLB I, p. 32. (Baiṭha-paribhāṣā). Also called Dakṣiṇāmūrti-baiṭh or Pada-varṇa-saṃkhyā.

BISM p. 19 (35/481). Dated Śaka 1690. Copied by Appābhaṭṭa Śivaṇekara, son of Nīlakaṇṭha. Colophon at the end of the first Aṣṭaka : iti śrī-dakṣiṇāmūrtideva-śrīpādopadiṣṭāyāṃ padavarṇasaṃkhyāyāṃ śaktiśrīr nāma prathamāṣṭakam ||

BISM p. 152 (36/693). 52 fol. Title: Pada-varṇa-saṃkhyā. Aṣṭaka-s are named as above. An old Ms. On the top left margin : dakṣiṇā-.

BISM p. 179 (13/75). (Baiṭha-paribhāṣā).

Bombay Uni. 1736 (BMC 25 38). 17 fol. Incomplete. Up to 3.8.11. (Dakṣiṇāmūrtipadavarṇasaṃkhyā).

Bombay Uni. 1737 (BMC 6 14). 24 fol. Incomplete. From 5.1 to the end. (Dakṣiṇāmūrtipadavarṇasaṃkhyā).

Calcutta Skt. Coll. I 493C (313). 1 fol. (3). Title: Ṛgveda-paribhāṣā. Dated V.S. 1661.

Calcutta Skt. Coll. I 529 (264). 39 fol. Dated V.S. 1376 (?). Title: Dakṣiṇāmūrtipadavarṇasaṃkhyā. Adhyāya-s are named as above.

Deccan College (1964). 280 (3102 of Dikshit Collection). 14 fol. Incomplete.

Hz 410(a). PL. Tel. 44 fol. (with Anuvākānukramaṇikā-bhāṣya). (Dakṣiṇāmūrtibhaiṭ). Belonged to Kesari Yajnayya of Brahmanakraka (Agrahara), Nellur Dist. Extract p. 79: Col.: iti śrīdakṣiṇāmūrtidevaśrīpādopadiṣṭāyāṃ padavarṇa-saṃkhyāyāṃ devaśrīr nāma aṣṭamāṣṭakaṃ saṃpūrṇam ||

Müller 53 (MM 41). 56 fol. Dated Śaka 1653 (1731-32). (Dakṣiṇāmūrti-pada-varṇa-saṃkhyā). Begins as in Adyar Ms. but the end differs.

PUL I, p. 22 (no.100). 1 fol. (Pada-varṇa-saṃkhyā).

SBD 2101. 20 fol. (Pada-varṇa-lakṣaṇa-paribhāṣa). This is the first half of the original Ms. up to Adhyāya 5 of Aṣṭaka 5. The remaining portion is SBD 2102 catalogued as Pada-varṇa-saṃkhyā.

SBD 2102. 16 fol. (21-36). (Pada-varṇa-saṃkhyā). Ascribed to Dakṣiṇāmūrti-śiṣya in the catalogue and on the title slip but this ascription is not found in the Ms. This is the latter half of SBD 2101. It is evident that the original Ms. has been divided into two parts and catalogued separately. The two numbers together contain the work complete.

SBD 2106. 2 fol. Incomplete. Baiṭha-paribhāṣā. Verses only.

SBD 2371. 16 fol. (2, 5-18). Incomplete (up to 3.8 : tṛtīyāṣṭake aṣṭamo 'dhyāyaḥ). Title: Ṛgvedapadavarṇasaṃkhyā.

SBD 2372. 26 fol. (1-22, 25-26, 31-32). Incomplete (1.1.16 to 7.8). (Pada-varṇa-saṃkhyā).

SBD 53793. 10 fol. Incomplete. Up to Adhyāya 2 of Aṣṭaka 3. Catalogued as Dakṣiṇāmūrti-pada-varṇa-lakṣaṇa-paribhāṣā-vyākhyā.

Skt. Coll. Ben. 1918-30. p. 3 (no.24). 2 fol.

Trav. Uni. 5206 A. 600 Grantha-s. (Pada-varṇa-saṃkhyā). (Begins with Svarāṣṭaka).

Visvanatha Vamana Deva, Varanasi. 4 fol.

128 AṢṬĀ-CATVĀRIṂŚAL-LAKṢAṆA (**अष्टाचत्वारिंशल्लक्षण**)

Mysore ND II 3129 (P 4906/19). PL. Na. 2 fol. (116-17). Extract no. 33. (Cf. pp. 40-41 of the *Pada-gāḍha*, Srirangam edition).

129 AṢṬĀDAŚA-LAKṢAṆA (**अष्टादशलक्षण**)

Mysore ND II 3130 (P 4906/40). PL. Na. 2 fol. (125-26). Extract no. 34. (Cf. p. 44 of the *Pada-gāḍha*, Srirangam edition).

130 AṢṬĀDHYĀYĪ-ŚUKLA-YAJURVEDA-PRĀTIŚĀKHYAYOR MATAVIMARŚAḤ (अष्टाध्यायीशुक्लयजुर्वेदप्रातिशाख्ययोर्मतविमर्शः)
of Vijayapal.

Ptd.: Bahalgadh (Sonipath-Haryana) : Ramalal Kapur Trust, 1983. 14, 284 pp. [Adyar (H425.1 Pan AS z Vij); SAI (ind 54 B 386/446)]

131 ASAṂDHI-VYAKTĪYA (असंधिव्यक्तीय)
Mysore ND II 3131 (P 2265/25a). PL. Gr. 1 fol. (138). Extract no. 35.

132 ĀKĀRA-PADDHATI (आकारपद्धति)
Name of an anonymous commentary on the *Āvarṇi-lakṣaṇa*.
Whish 25a (6). PL. Gr. 5 fol. (35-39) → Āvarṇi-lakṣaṇa-vyākhyā.

[NCC II 2a]

133 ĀKHYĀTA-NĀMĀNUKRAMAṆĪ (आख्यातनामानुक्रमणी)
GD I 1-2 → Ākhyātānukramaṇī and Nāmānukramaṇī of Mādhava.

[NCC II 8a]

134 ĀKHYĀTA-VIVEKA (आख्यातविवेक)
Adyar I, p. 48a (35 C 139 = PM 3028). 10 pp. Incomplete. This is actually a Nyāya work, also known as the *Ākhyāta-vāda* of Raghunātha Śiromaṇi (described in Adyar D VIII 1282).

[NCC II 10b]

135 ĀKHYĀTĀNUKRAMAṆĪ (आख्यातानुक्रमणी)
of Mādhava. About 335 verses on the verbs in the *Ṛgveda*. The 66 verses at the beginning constitute a kind of introduction mentioning ten Anukramaṇī-s. Catalogued as Ākhyāta-nāmānukramaṇī in Adyar D I 939. See C. Kunhan Raja's introduction (p. 22) to his edition of the text. See also *Journal of Oriental Research*, Madras, vol. V (1931), pp. 316ff.; vol. X (1936), pp. 256ff. *Annals of Oriental Research*, University of Madras, vols. I, II (1937-38), Sanskrit Section and Introduction to the Adyar Library edition of the *Ṛgveda-vyākhyā Mādhavakṛtā*. – Madras : Adyar Library, 1939. – (Adyar Library Series 22).

Beginning: (of the introductory section)

लोकः पदं स्वरो वाक्यं समभिव्याहृतिः श्रुतिः ।
आर्षाण्यपि च शास्त्राणि पदार्थज्ञानहेतवः ॥
व्युत्पत्तिस्तत्र लोकः स्यात् पारंपर्यक्रमागता ।
अग्निवाय्वादयः शब्दास्तत्र सर्वे निदर्शनम् ॥

Beginning: (of the *Ākhyātānukramaṇī*)

ओं नमो वासुदेवाय धातवो नामयोनयः ।
आचक्षते च वाक्यार्थं तिङ्विभक्तिसमन्विताः ॥
यजुर्ब्राह्मणभाषासु यद् रूपमनुवर्तते ।
अन्वये व्यतिरेके च धात्वात्मा स इति श्रुतिः ॥

भूयानृक्ष्वस्य रूपस्य लोपागमविकारजः ।
विपर्ययाः सन्ति चान्य आर्चिका एव धातवः ॥

End:

मरै मर्मर्तु मुमुरत् तथा मम्रुर्मरामहै ।
रूपाणि मरणार्थानि पृच्छा प्राद् प्रश्नमाहतुः ॥
रणद् रणन्त ररण रणन्ते राणिषुस्तथा ।
ररन्धि रतिकर्माणो निर्वापय शमक्रियः ॥
अध्येयानुक्रमण्येषा कृतोपनयनैर्द्विजैः ।
दाशतय्यर्थमिच्छद्भिः केशवाय नमो नमः ॥

Adyar D I 939 (39 I 18 = TR 27). 46 fol. (pp. 1-92). Contains Nāmānukramaṇī also. A transcript from a Ms. in the Palace Library of H. H. the Mahārāja of Travancore.
GD I 1. PL. Mal. 33 fol. 750 Grantha-s.
GD I 19-B. PL. Mal. 53 fol. (36-88). 400 Grantha-s.
Granthappura p. 1 (no.1). Mal. 750 Grantha-s.
Granthappura p. 1 (no.2). Mal. 735 Grantha-s. Incomplete. Lacks end.
Trav. Uni. 19020. PL. Mal. 800 Grantha-s.
Trav. Uni. 19021 B. PL. Mal. 600 Grantha-s.

Ptd.: ed by C. Kunhan Raja, with the title *Mādhavānukramaṇi*, as appendix IV to the *Ṛgvedānukramaṇī* of Mādhava-bhaṭṭa. – Madras : University of Madras, 1932. xxviii, 93, clxiv pp. – (Madras University Sanskrit Series 2). [Adyar (H080 MUS sk2); BORI (6440); NL (180 Jb 93 178); UBTÜ (Ci XII 666,2)]

[NCC II 10b]

136 ĀKHYEYA-BHĀṢYA (आख्येयभाष्य)

of Vararuci. "Adyar D I 1022 (p. 356); mentioned in an anonymous index of Śikṣā and allied literature (Śikṣādi-vedāṅgasūcī)." This entry in the NCC is apparently based on the defective Ms. in Adyar. Another Ms. of the same text in Hamburg reads it clearly as Ātreya-bhāṣya. Cf. below under Śikṣādi-vedāṅgasūcī and Veda-lakṣaṇa (HB). It is an obvious reference to the tradition of a Bhāṣya of Ātreya recorded by the *Tribhāṣya-ratna* (introductory portion).

[NCC II 11b]

137 ĀGNEYA-SĀMĀNUKRAMAṆĪ (आग्नेयसामानुक्रमणी)

Mysore ND II 3132 (P 396/ 4). PL. Na. 9 fol.

138 ĀCĀRYA-ŚIKṢĀ (आचार्यशिक्षा)

Oppert I 7166. Belonged to Ivattur Nandikesvara Sastri of Vijayanagaram.

[NCC II 38a]

*ĀTREYA (आत्रेय)

Mentioned together with Śākalya as Padakāra of the *Ṛgveda* by Devarāja in the *Nighaṇṭu-bhāṣya*, p. 26. Also mentioned as tha Padakāra of the *Kṛṣṇa Yajurveda*, in the *Kāṇḍānukramaṇī* and *Baudhāyana-gṛhya-sūtra*, III ix.6.

[NCC II 66b]

*ĀTREYA (आत्रेय)

Quoted in the *Taittirīya-prātiśākhya* V 31, XVII 8. According to the *Tribhāṣya-ratna* (introductory portion) Ātreya is the author of a commentary on the *Prātiśākhya* and is quoted in the *Tribhāṣya-ratna*, V 1 (p. 162 of the Mysore edition) and in the *Śabdabrahma-vilāsa*, a Prātiśākhya-vyākhyā, MT 2450(a). Mentioned in the *Bhāradvāja-śikṣā* (PUL II. App. p. 12) and also in the Śikṣā-samuccaya-vyākhyā (TCD 32-B). See TCD I, p. 71.

[NCC II 66b]

139 ĀTREYA-ŚIKṢĀ (1) (आत्रेयशिक्षा)

A treatise in 27 verses explaining the compounds or simple words which should be divided in the Pada-pāṭha of the Veda-s. It is stated that the work is based on the Ātreya-sūtra-s. It is not clear if this text is the same as the one mentioned as one of the 9 Śikṣā-s in MD 998.

Beginning: (2188)

आत्रेयोक्तेषु सूत्रेषु स्थितानीङ्ग्यपदान्यहम्।
श्लोकरूपेण वक्ष्यामि सौकर्याय सुपाठिनाम्॥
निष्केवल्यं च निष्टक्र्यं निषादेभ्यो निषङ्गथिः।
महिमानं च निष्कावमाह्वध्यै मदिन्तमः॥

End:

अमीवामम्बरीषाद् वा अम्बरीषे च दुन्दुभिः।
त्रैधातवीयेनामर्त्यमश्रमिष्ठाश्च विश्वतः।
प्राणाय नो विश्वतीना चयमाना अयस्मयी॥
वैकङ्कती सर्दिगृदिमाशुमाचवि हन्तवै॥

IL. 213.

MT 2188(a). Tel. 2 fol. Transcribed in 1916-17 from a Ms. of Vemparla Subrahmanya Sastrigaru of Tondavaramu, Godavari Dist. The scribe of the original Ms. is Ponnamalli Subrahmaṇya.

Oppert I 7126. Belonged to Pola Lakshmanavadhani of Vijayanagaram.

Oppert I 7168. Belonged to Ivattur Nandikesvara Sastri of Vijayanagaram.

Oppert II 7344. Belonged to Venkatarama Sastri of Pillur, Mayavaram Taluk.

[NCC II 67b]

140 ĀTREYA-ŚIKṢĀ (2) (आत्रेयशिक्षा)

Beginning:

अथ क्रमव्युत्क्रमणो(त्क्र)माद्यतो जटा भवेदार्षजसंधिजस्वरात्।
विलोक्य शिक्षादिकमादरात् ततः प्रकाश्यते सा विदुषां मुदे मया॥
पदद्वयनिमित्तं या(स्या)देकाभावेति तत्र तु।
संहितावत् क्रमे (मो) ज्ञेयस्तद्वज्ज्ञेया जटा बुधैः॥

End:

प्रथमस्य द्वितीयत्वं पूर्वं कुर्वीत पण्डितः ।
धूद्वक्ष्णौ द्वन्द्वक्ष्णषमित्यत्र अनुस्वारो विधर्मतः ॥
इत्यात्रेयशिक्षा ॥
(The last verse is the same as that of *Śaṃbhu-śikṣā)*

Hoshiarpur p. 300 (no.4371). PL. Gr. 3 fol. 100 Grantha-s. Extract p. 406.
PUL II. App. p. 10 (no.135). Gr. 8 fol. (8-15). 60 Grantha-s.
Tirupati SVUORI 618 (3792c). PL. Gr.
Trav. Uni. 5503 B (Jaṭāvallī). PL. Tel. 45 Grantha-s. Incomplete.

141 ĀTREYA-ŚIKṢĀ (3) **(आत्रेयशिक्षा)**

Only one manuscript of this Śikṣā is available. It deals with the following topics as given in the margin of respective folios:

Paribhāṣā
Saṃhitā-viṣayaḥ
Veda-pārāyaṇa-phalam
Pārāyaṇa-kramaḥ
Vāgvṛttiḥ
Pada-lakṣaṇam
Krama-lakṣaṇam
Jaṭā-lakṣaṇam
Kevala-varṇa-krama-lakṣaṇam
Dvitva-prakaraṇam
Āgama-prakaraṇam
Abhinidhāna-prakaraṇam
Kevalāgama-prakaraṇam
Yama-prakaraṇam
Yama-niṣedha-prakaraṇam
Nāda-prakaraṇam
Dvitvāgama-niṣedha-prakaraṇam
Svarabhakti-viṣayaḥ
Svarabhakti-saṃjñā
Vivṛtti-lakṣaṇam
Vivṛtty-udāharaṇam
Vyakti-madhya-nāsikyam
Raṅga-pluta-prakaraṇam
Raṅga-dīrgha-prakaraṇam
Svaritodātta-kampa-viṣayaḥ
Vaikṛta-prākṛtādi
Nāsikyatvorasyatvādi
Jihvā-mūlīyādi
Sthiti-saṃdhiḥ (before "kṣ-")
Praṇava-viṣayaḥ
Svara-varṇa-krama-lakṣaṇam
Udāttādīnāṃ saṃjñā
Sapta-svarita-lakṣaṇam
Svaritānāṃ prayatna-bhedāḥ
Mātrā-kāla-varṇa-krama-lakṣaṇam
Aṅga-varṇa-krama-lakṣaṇam
Aṅga-lakṣaṇam
Parāṅga-pūrvāṅga-lakṣaṇam
Varṇa-sārabhūta-varṇa-krama-nirvacanam
Varṇa-dharma-kramaḥ
Anusvāra-bhakti-kampa-viṣayaḥ
Raṅga-pluta-viṣayaḥ
Śabdotpatti-prakaraṇam
Dhvani-nirūpaṇaṃ
Varṇānāṃ sthāna-karaṇa-prayatna-vivekaḥ
Varṇānāṃ svarāṇāṃ ca devatā-jāti-nirūpaṇam
Varṇa-saṃjñā
Udāttādīnāṃ devatā-jāti-guṇa-lakṣaṇam
Hasta-svara-vinyāsa-lakṣaṇam
Svara-vinyāsa-phalam
Aṅgādyavasthā
Ṣaḍjādi-svara-nirūpaṇam
Udāttādi-svarotpatti-sthānam
Vedādhyayana-phalam
Veda-mahimā
Adhyayana-rahita-doṣaḥ
Sāṅga-vedādhyayana-phalam

Beginning:

आम्नाया यस्य निःश्वासाश्चन्द्रसूर्यौ च चक्षुषी।
तत् प्रणम्य परंज्योतिः शिक्षां वक्ष्यामि निर्मलाम्॥ १॥
अचः स्वरा इति प्रोक्ता व्यञ्जनानि हलः स्मृताः
ह्रस्वदीर्घप्लुतावर्णेवर्णोवर्णा ऋ ॠ ऌ च॥ २॥
एदैदोदौदिति ज्ञेयाः षोडशेहोदिताः स्वराः ।
कखौ गघौ ङचछजा झञौ टठडढा णतौ॥ ३॥
थदौ धनौ पफबभा मः स्पर्शाः पञ्चविंशतिः ।
यरौ लवौ चतस्रो ऽन्तस्थाश्च ःकशषसःपहाः ॥ ४॥
षड्रूष्माणो विसर्गो ऽनुस्वारो ङो नास्यपञ्चकम्।
इत्येते याजुषा वर्णा एकोना षष्टिरीरिताः ॥ ५॥

End:

अनुदात्तो हृदि ज्ञेयो मूर्ध्न्युदात्त उदाहृतः ।
स्वरितः कण्ठमूलीयः सर्वाङ्गे प्रचयः स्मृतः ॥ २८१।
अङ्गमात्रादयो धर्माः पूर्वमेवोदिताश्च ये।
तान् सर्वान् वर्णसारे ऽस्मिन् तत्र तत्र प्रयोजयेत्॥
एवं सलक्षणं वेदं यो ऽधीते ऽध्यापयत्यपि …।
वेदांश्च श्रोत्रियं ब्रह्म ये के दुष्यन्ति मानवाः ।
ते घोरं नरकं प्राप्य जायन्ते भुवि सूकराः ।
वेदरूपविलसत् परात्परं ये पठन्ति विधिना द्विजोत्तमाः ।
ते त्रिवर्गमिह चानुभूय तच्छाश्वतं पदमवाप्नुयुः परम्॥
इत्यात्रेयशिक्षामूलं संपूर्णम्॥ श्लोकसंख्या २९४॥

Hamburg StUB (cod.Palmbl. III 8/133) → Veda-lakṣaṇa (HB). One additional fol. contains the list of contents in 16 verses. Written by Ūḍitiri Cakram Aiyaṅgār.

142 ĀTREYA-SŪTRA (आत्रेयसूत्र)
Allegedly basis of the *Ātreya-śikṣā*, MT 2188(a). Cf. Atri-sūtra, above.

[NCC II 68b]

143 ĀTHARVAṆA-PRĀTIŚĀKHYA (आथर्वणप्रातिशाख्य)
SBD 2134. 12 fol. → Atharva-veda-prātiśākhya.

144 ĀTHARVAṆA-RAHASYA see ATHARVAṆA-RAHASYA
(आथर्वणरहस्य / अथर्वणरहस्य)

145 ĀDYUDĀTTA-PADĀNI (आद्युदात्तपदानि)
A fragment of the *Ucca-svara-nirṇaya* (MD 874).
Adyar D XIII 207 (VB 1141c). PL. Na. 1 fol.

Ptd.: ed. Vaidyanatha Sastri, Kumbakonam 1899. (?)

146 ĀDYUDĀTTĀNI (**आद्युदात्तानि**)

15 verses on the Ādyudātta words in the Taittirīya school. It is a section of the *Ucca-svara-nirṇaya* (cf. Skt. Texts on Phonetics, pp. 302ff.).

Beginning:

इदानीमाद्युदात्तानि गृह्यन्ते ऽत्र पदानि तु।
विषयो लक्षणस्यास्य ह्यन्तोदात्ततया पदम्॥
नेङ्गितं यत् पदं तस्मादाद्युदात्ततयेष्यते।
एष चेङ्ग्येषु नोदात्तः स्यात् तदादिस्तु गृह्यते॥ इति परिभाषा।
अमापेन्द्रेत्यनूबन्धेत्येतानि त्रीणि वर्जयेत्।
यासां यो यद्धि येनाहैतेभ्य आ सप्तमात् पदात्॥
बहुस्वरमकारादि चाद्युदात्तं पदं भवेत्।

End:

ऋगृद्धिमृषयश्चैकामेक एकादशेष्यते।
एति तद्यद्धिरण्येन चैकैकस्मात् तथा भवेत्।
ओषधीष्वोषधीनां च तदौषधय औषधीः॥

Baroda 6255. PL. Tel. 2 fol. (44-45). 15 Grantha-s.

*ĀPIŚALI (**आपिशलि**)

– Akṣara-tantra. On the Stobha-s in Sāmagāna. Adyar D I 1067. Baroda 9805(g). Baroda 9916(b). Ptd.: ed. with a commentary by Satyavrata Samasrami in the Sanskrit journal *Uṣā*. – Calcutta : Satya Press, 1889, vol. I, pt. 2, pp. 1-56. 1891, vol. I, pts. 11-12, pp. 1-4. For details see above under Akṣara-tantra.
– Āpiśali-śikṣā. See below.

[NCC II 143a]

147 ĀPIŚALI-ŚIKṢĀ(-SŪTRA) (**आपिशलिशिक्षा-सूत्र**)

of Āpiśali. A work consisting of about 100 Sūtra-s divided in eight Prakaraṇa-s and three verses at the beginning as well as at the end. It deals with the classification and pronunciation (sthāna and prayatna) of the letters of the alphabet. A very large portion of this Śikṣā is quoted by Hemacandra and Jinendrabuddhi; its contents are given in the Śikṣādhyāya of the Bharata-bhāṣya. See F. Kielhorn : Remarks on the Śikṣās in : *Indian Antiquary*, vol. V, p. 193 (reprint in : *Kleine Schriften*, vol. I, pp. 158-69). There are at least five editions of the text. A work of this title is referred to in the *Śikṣā-samuccaya-vyākhyā* (TCD 32-B). For the procedure of speech production described in this Śikṣā, see George Cardona, "On the Āpiśaliśikṣā", in : *A Corpus of Indian Studies – Essays in Honour of Prof. Gaurinath Sastri*. – Calcutta : Sanskrit Pustak Bhandar, 1980, pp. 245-56. About 20 additional Anuṣṭubh verses are found at the beginning at Adyar D I 730 and MD 864.

Beginning: (730)

(अथ शिक्षां प्रवक्ष्यामि मतामापिशलेर्मुनेः ।
गुरुलघ्वादिविज्ञानं तस्यारम्भप्रयोजकम् ॥
उक्तं तत् सर्वमङ्गेषु शिक्षाव्याकरणेषु यत् ।
विकल्पभाजां शास्त्राणामपि दृष्टानुवर्तिनाम् ॥
तत्तच्छाखाविशेषेषु व्यवस्थार्थमिदं स्मृतम् ।
संहिता तत्पदाध्यायः क्रमाध्याय इति त्रिधा ॥ ...)
आकाशवायुप्रभवः शरीरात् समुच्चरन् वक्त्रमुपैति प्राणः ।
स्थानान्तरेषु प्रविभज्यमानो वर्णत्वमागच्छति यः स शब्दः ॥
तमक्षरं ब्रह्म परं पवित्रं गुहाशयं सम्यगुशन्ति विप्राः ।
स श्रेयसा चाभ्युदयेन चैव सम्यक् प्रयुक्तः पुरुषं युनक्ति ॥

तत्र स्थानकरणप्रयत्नेभ्यो वर्णास्त्रिषष्टिः । तत्र वर्णानां केषां किं स्थानं किं करणं प्रयत्नश्च कः केषामित्युच्यते ॥

End:

यदा तु मन्दः प्रयत्नो भवति तदा गात्रस्य स्रंसनं कण्ठबिलस्य महत्त्वं स्वरस्य च वायोर्मन्दगतित्वात् स्निग्धता भवति तमुदात्तमाचक्षते । उदात्तानुदात्तस्वरितसंनिपातात् स्वरितः । इत्येवं प्रयत्नो ऽभिनिर्वृत्तः कृत्स्नः प्रयत्नो भवति ॥

अष्टौ स्थानानि वर्णानामुरः कण्ठः शिरस्तथा ।
जिह्वामूलं च दन्ताश्च नासिकौष्ठौ च तालु च ॥
स्पृष्टत्वमीषत्स्पृष्टत्वं संवृतत्वं तथैव च ।
विवृतत्वं च वर्णानामन्तःकरणमुच्यते ॥
कालो विवारसंवारौ श्वासनादावघोषता ।
घोषो ऽल्पप्राणता चैव महाप्राणः स्वरास्त्रयः ॥
(बाह्यं करणमाहुस्तद् वर्णानां वर्णवेदिनः ॥)

Adyar D I 730 (I A 19 = TR 19). Gr. 7 fol. (pp. 119-32). = Adyar I, p. 52a. 20 additional verses in the beginning. .... (= Skt. Texts on Phonetics, pp. 401-06).

Adyar D I 731 (21 Q 10 = 68514). PL. Mal. 5 fol. (32ff.). = Adyar II, App. p. iib (40 C 10). The additional verses found at the beginning of the above Ms. are not found in this Ms. .... (= Skt. Texts on Phonetics, pp. 395-400).

BORI 2 of 1873-74. 3 fol. (6a-8a). From Bikaner. (A xerox-copy of this Ms. is in SAI : 87/790*).

Göttingen 158. Only the title in a list of Śikṣā-s prepared by Kielhorn.

Kh. 82.

MD 864. 9 pp. (178-86).

Oppert I 957. Belonged to Viraraghava Tatacharyar, Head Master, Sanskrit School of Sathakopacharya, Kanchipuram, Chingelpet Dist.

Oppert I 7127. Belonged to Pola Lakshmanavadhani of Vijayanagaram.
Oppert I 7169. Belonged to Ivattur Nandikesvara Sastri of Vijayanagaram.
Trav. Uni. 624 F. PL. Mal. 50 Grantha-s.
Trav. Uni. L.1330 D. PL. Mal. 50 Grantha-s.
Trav. Uni. 16408 Z. PL. Mal. 4 fol. 50 Grantha-s.

Ptd.:

1) Ed. by Raghu Vira, on the basis of the two Adyar Mss, in : *Journal of Vedic Studies*, vol. I, 2 (May 1934), pp. 225ff. (where quotations from Āpiśali-śikṣā in well-known grammatical works are also collected).

Reprinted in : *Vedic Studies* – A Collection of the Research Papers of Prof. Raghuvira, ed. by Mrs. Sharada Rani. – New Delhi -- 110016 (Hauzkhas Enclave), 1981, pp. 346-69. (Śata-Piṭaka Series – Indo-Asian Literatures, vol. 272). On this Śikṣā text see also Siddheshwar Varma, *Critical Studies in the Phonetic Observations* ... p. 44. [Adyar (H080 SVS SP 272); NL (180 Jb 98 37); SAI (ind S 180, 272); UBTÜ (22 A 6435)]

2) Ed. by Amulya Charana Vidyabhushana with a Bengali translation. – Calcutta : Sri Bharati Publishing House (Indian Research Institute), 1939 (referred to in the introduction, p. 9 of the edition of Yudhisthira Mimamsaka; cf. below).

3) Ed. by Yudhisthira Mimamsaka in : *Śikṣā-sūtrāṇi* – Āpiśali-pāṇini-candragomi-viracitāni. – Ajmer : Prachya Vidya Pratisthana, 1949. 5, 17 pp. Revised 2nd edition. 1967-68. It includes: Hindi introduction, pp. 1-12 (where arguments for differentiating it from the Śikṣā-sūtra-s of Pāṇini, said to have been discovered by Dayananda Sarasvati, are given), Āpiśali-śikṣā, pp. 1-8, Pāṇinīya-śikṣā, pp. 9-23, Cāndra-varṇa-sūtra, pp. 24-26. [BORI (28075); SAI (85/1961*); IO (San D 3753)]

4) Ed. by K. Raghavan Pillai, in : *Journal of the Kerala University Oriental Research Institute and Manuscripts Library*, vol. 18 (2-3), Trivandrum 1971, pp. 199-204 (based on two Mss. : 624-F and 16408-Z). [UBTÜ (Z A 2330); SAI (ind 51 D 587/1715)]

5) Also ed. by B. A. van Nooten, with an English translation and a study : "The Structure of Sanskrit Phonetic Treatise" in : *(Töid Orientalistika Alalt) Tartu Oriental Studies* II, 2, Tartu (Konks-Numerkund-Mäll) 1973, pp. 408-37.

[NCC II 143ab]

148 ĀMAHĪYĀDI-SĀMA-PARIGAṆANA (ŪHA-SĀMA-PARIGAṆANA)
(आमहीयादिसामपरिगणन / ऊहसामपरिगणन)
Adyar I, p. 11a. See Adyar D I 757. 758.

[NCC II 146b]

149 ĀRAṆA(KA)-ŚA(SA)MĀNA **(आरण(क)श(स)मान)**
→ Āraṇyaka-śa(sa)māna.

[NCC II 155b]

150 ĀRAṆA-PA(YA)RAGĀḌI **(आरणप(य)रगाडि)**
Adyar D I 983 → Veda-lakṣaṇa (A I).

[NCC II 155b]

151 ĀRAṆYAKA-ŚA(SA)MĀNA or ŚĀKHĀŚAMĀNA (आरण्यकश(स)मान / शाखाशमान)

Beginning:

दीर्घा विसर्जनीयान्ता वर्णा वाक्यान्त(दि)संस्थिताः ।
काठकारुणशाखासु तान् प्रवक्ष्याम्यशेषतः ।
अरोचथा अवरुद्धा असुरा अनूराधा अषाढा अर्धमासाः ...

End:

बाह्वोः सक्थ्योः पार्श्वयोस्तद्वयोरश्विनोर्मासयोर्मयुरन्तोदात्तः । मृत्योरपनयोर्हस्तयोः पादयोर्जन्तोरुभयोर्गौर्यौः ॥

Adyar D I 983 → Veda-lakṣaṇa (A 1).
Adyar D I 984 → Veda-lakṣaṇa (A 2).
Baroda 10381(j). PL. Gr. 7 fol. (34-40). 80 Grantha-s. = CLB I, p. 37. Title: Śākhā-śamāna.
Brl. p. 17 (no.LXVIII) = IO 4507.
Brl. p. 18 (no.LXIX) = IO 4508.
IO 4507 (Burnell 350h). Tel. 4 fol. (69-72). Written ca. A.D. 1867. (Śākhā-śamāna).
IO 4508 (Burnell 146i). PL. Gr. 1 fol.
MD 984. Gr. 8 pp. (71ff.). (Śākhā-śamāna)
MD 985. PL. Tel. 9 pp. (35ff.). (Śākhā-śamāna)
MD 16738. PL. Tel. 4 pp. (58ff.). 50 Grantha-s.
MD 16817. PL. Gr. 3 pp. (52ff.). 50 Grantha-s.
MD 986. PL. Tel. 3 pp. (23ff.). Title: Śākhā-ṣamāna (Āraṇyaka). Text differs from the above).
MD 16818. PL. Gr. 2 pp. (53ff.). 18 Grantha-s.
Mysore I, p. 22 (2 Mss.).
Mysore ND II 3133 (P 4468/ 8). PL. Na. 9 fol. Extract no. 36. Col.: Āraṇasamāna-saṃdhi.
Mysore ND II 3134 (B 861/ 7). Gr. 2 fol. (88-89). Title: Āraṇyaka-samāna.
Mysore ND II 3135 (P 660/ 1). PL. Gr. 2 fol. Extract no. 37. Āraṇyakasamānasaṃdhi.
Mysore ND II 3136 (P 7891/ 3). PL. Na. 2 fol. (62-63)
Mysore ND II 3137 (P 8056/ 1). PL. Tel. 1 fol. (93).
Mysore ND II 3138 (B 600/ 1a). Na. 7 fol.
Mysore ND II 3139 (B 600/ 4). Na. 2 fol. (24-25).
PUL I, p. 19 (no.24). PL. Gr. 9 fol. (Āraṇa-śamāna, etc.).

– C. (Āraṇyakasamāna-saṃdhi-vyākhyana)

Beginning:

आरण्यस्य पदानि आरण्यपदानि तेषु आरण्यपदेपु ये वर्णाः विसर्जनीयान्ताः स्युः अशेषतः सर्वं वक्ष्यामि ...

End:

या एव देवता हुतभागाः एता वै होत्राः अनु सप्तहोत्रः । एतान्यारण्यवाक्यानि अवर्णपूर्वविसर्जनीयान्तानि ॥

MD 987. PL. Tel. 9 pp. (24ff.).
Mysore I, p. 22.
Mysore ND II 3140 (P 144/ 9). PL. Tel. 4 fol. (50-53). Extract no. 38.
Mysore ND II 3141 (B 600/ 1b). Na. 7 fol.

[NCC II 156a]

152 ĀRAṆYA-(KA-)ŚIKṢĀ (आरण्य(क)शिक्षा)
on the accentuation of the *Taittirīya Āraṇyaka.* Sometimes found in (South Indian) Mss. as Āruṇa and Aruṇa Śikṣā. It professes to have been based on nine other Śikṣā-s and hence called also *Āraṇya-śikṣāmṛta.* See above Araṇa-śikṣā and Aruṇa-śamāna.

Beginning:

गणपतिमभिवन्द्यावद्यजालामयघ्नं स्वरपदमितवर्णोद्बोधनं शीलनेन।
क्षितिसुरगणहेतोरेतदारण्यशिक्षामृतमिह नवशिक्षावारिधेरुद्धरामि ॥ १ ॥
आद्युदात्तानि वाक्यानि चैकद्वित्र्यादिसंख्यया।
विविधानि तु वृन्दानि विस्पष्टान्यत्र कृत्स्नशः ॥ २ ॥
उदाह्रियन्ते ऽध्येतॄणां संदेहानां निवृत्तये।
आदिमध्यान्तग्रहणं क्रियते यत्र तत्र तु ॥ ३ ॥

End:

लक्षणेन विना विद्या विमलापि न शोभते।
अप्राणस्येव देहस्य भूषणैरप्यलंकृतम् ॥ १२८ ॥
इत्थं न्यरूपि सकलं स्वरवर्णजालं स्वाध्यायपञ्चसु मुदे निगमे पटूनाम्।
आरण्यके यदिह किंचन न न्यरूपि तद् बुद्धिमद्भिरखिलं स्वयमूहनीयम् ॥ १२९ ॥

Adyar D I 732 (1 A 19 = TR 19). Gr. 13 fol. (pp. 19-44). = Adyar I, p. 52a. Title: Aruṇa-śikṣā.
Adyar D I 733 (22 E 43 = 68892). PL. Tel. 7 fol. (1-7). = Adyar I, p. 52a (Āraṇya-śikṣāmṛtam).
Adyar D XIII 323 (VB 128c). PL. Tel. 26 fol. (with C. of Nṛsiṃha-sūri).
GB 22. 31 fol. (with C.). Copied for Kielhorn in Mysore in 1875.
Gough p. 162. Gr.
Hamburg StUB (cod.Palmbl. III 8/133) → Veda-lakṣaṇa (HB).
Hoshiarpur p. 50 (no.6867). 12 fol. 131 Grantha-s. retract p. 406. (A xerox-copy of a Devanāgarī transcript of this is in SAI : 87/794*).
IO 4941 (Mackenzie II 94a). PL. Na. 11 fol. (21-31) (with C.). Written ca. A.D. 1770.
IO 4942 (Mackenzie II 81d). PL. Na. 6 fol. (16-21). Written ca. A.D. 1800.
MD 865. 17 pp. (18-34).
MD 866. PL. Tel. 38 pp. (with C.). .... (= Skt. Texts on Phonetics, pp. 173-210).

MD 867. Tel. 49 pp. (266ff.) (with C.). .... (= Skt. Texts on Phonetics, pp. 216-50).
MD 15959. PL. Gr. 14 pp. (62ff.).
MT 1165(f). PL. Tel. 4 fol. (49-52). Purchased in 1913-14 from Kashibhatta Subrahmanya Sastri of Vekanur, Krishna Dist.
MT 2591(c). PL. Tel. 10 fol. (160-69). One additional stanza at the end which actually belongs to the C. of Nṛsiṃha-sūri. Presented in 1917-18 by Vasireddi Chandramaulisvaraprasada Bahadur, Zamindar of Muktyala, Krishna Dist.
MT 4818(b). PL. Gr. 5 fol. (2-6). Presented in 1924-25 by the Secretary to the Trustees of Sri Yogi Parthasarathi Ayyangar's Charities, Triplicane, Madras.
Mysore I, p. 22 (4 Mss.); p. 612.
Mysore ND II 3144 (P 144/ 4). PL. Tel. 19 fol. (6-24). Extract no. 39.
Mysore ND II 3145 (P 2748/ 1). PL. Gr. 8 fol. (13-20).
Mysore ND II 3146 (P 4453/ 5). PL. Na. 8 fol. (28-35).
Mysore ND II 3147 (P 4521/ 9). PL. Kan. 4 fol. (32-35).
Mysore ND II 3148 (P 9312/ 4). PL. Na. 10 fol. (88-97).
Mysore ND II 3149 (B 861/ 6). Gr. 14 fol.
Oppert I 958. Belonged to Viraraghava Tatacharyar, Head Master, Sanskrit School of Sathakopacharya, Kanchipuram, Chingelpet Dist.
Oppert I 7129. Belonged to Pola Lakshmanavadhani of Vijayanagaram.
Oppert I 7849. Belonged to Paravastu Venkatarangacharyar of Vishakhapattanam.
Oppert II 376. Belonged to Venkatarama Srauti of Mullandram, N. Arcot Dist.
Oppert II 734. Belonged to Ghanapathi Shingaracharyar of Alasur, Madurantakam Taluk.
Oppert II 4485. Belonged to Sri Sankaracharya Matha of Sringeri.
Oppert II 7350. Belonged to Venkatarama Sastri of Pillur, Mayavaram Taluk.
Oppert II 7938. Belonged to Venkatarama Dikshita of Sorakayur, Thanjavur Dist.
Oppert II 9003. Belonged to Ganapati Lakshminarayana Sastri of Tiruvadi, Thanjavur Dist.
Oppert II 9877. Belonged to M.Raja Ghanapathi of Mahadanapuram, Trichinapalli.
PUL I, p. 19 (no.25). PL. Gr. 4 fol.
PUL I, p. 19 (no.26). PL. Tel. 62 fol. 1500 Grantha-s !.
PUL II. App. p. 10 (no.136). PL. Tel. 15 fol. 180 Grantha-s.
PUL II. App. p. 10 (no.137). 21 fol. Copy from Mysore.
Tirupati SVUORI 692 (4446a). PL. Gr. 29 fol. (with C.).
Trav. Uni. 2088 B. PL. Gr. 125 Grantha-s.
Trav. Uni. 2630 K. PL. Gr. 125 Grantha-s.
Trav. Uni. 5503 C. PL. Tel. 625 Grantha-s (with C. of Nṛsiṃha-sūri).
Udaipur II 1, 3.
Wai I 1449. 19 fol. (with C.). Dated Śaka 1780.
Whish 216(b). PL. Gr. (fol. 184-210) (with C.). Not described in the catalogue.

– C. anon.
Hamburg StUB (Oppert 53). PL. Gr. 32 fol.
Hz 1270. PL. Gr. 9 fol. Belonged to Anna Vajapeyi of Tiruvidaimarudur, Thanjavur Dist.
Mysore p. 2 (no. 51). 27 fol.
Mysore I, pp. 22, 612.

Mysore ND II 3150 (P 144/ 5). PL. Tel. 19 fol. (6-24).
Mysore ND II 3151 (P 285/ 4). PL. Gr. 6 fol. (25-30). Incomplete.
Mysore ND II 3152 (P 4744). PL. Tel. 24 fol. (190-213).
Mysore ND II 3153 (P 9312/ 3). PL. Na. 11 fol. (87-97).
Mysore ND II 3154 (B 252/ 7). Gr. 25 pp. (33-57).
Oppert I 7531. Belonged to S. Kodanda Ramavadhana Pantulu of Vijayanagaram.
Oppert II 735. Belonged to Ghanapathi Shingaracharyar of Alasur, Madurantakam Taluk.
Oppert II 9004. Belonged to Ganapati Lakshminarayana Sastri of Tiruvadi, Thanjavur Dist.
PUL I, p. 19 (no.27). PL. Tel. 22 fol. 300 Grantha-s.
PUL II. App. p. 10 (no.138). 70 fol. Copy from Mysore.
Trav. Uni. 2088 B. PL. Gr. 125 Grantha-s.
VSM I 1219 (no.3834). 2 fol. Dated Śaka 1697. Copied by Hardīkar Bālam-bhaṭṭa. Extract p. 363.
Wai I 1449. 19 fol. (with text). Dated Śaka 1780.
Whish 216(b). PL. Gr. (with text). Not described in the catalogue.

– C. anon. The following Mss. appear to represent an identical commentary, though there are very divergent readings. While the first verse is the same as that in Nṛsiṃha's commentary, the beginning is different.

Beginning: (736):

विघ्नराजं प्रणम्यादौ वामदेवं च कामदम्।
आरण्यशिक्षाव्याख्यानमहं वक्ष्ये यथामति॥

प्रारिप्सितप्रतिबन्धविघ्नविघाताय कृतं मङ्गलं ग्रन्थतो निरूप्य स्वग्रन्थस्य प्रयोजनं च दर्शयन् चिकीर्षितं प्रतिजानीते --

गणपतिमभिवन्द्यावद्यजालामयघ्नं स्वरपदमिति वर्णोद्बोधनं शीलनेन।
क्षितिसुरगणहेतोरेतदारण्यशिक्षामृतमिह नवशिक्षावारिधेरुद्धरामि॥

अवद्यजालामयघ्नं व्याधिवत् ग्रन्थरचनाप्रतिबन्धकसमूहविनाशकम् इति गणपतिविशेषणम् । शीलनेन सम्यगभ्यसनेन । स्वरपदमितवर्णोद्बोधनमिति आरण्यशिक्षामृत्तविशेषणम् । आरण्यकप्रथमप्रश्ने उदात्तादिस्वरविषये अध्येतॄणां बहुधा विप्रतिपत्तिसत्त्वात् तन्निर्णयार्थं प्रतिजानीते --

आद्युदात्तानि वाक्यानि चैकद्वित्र्यादिसंख्यया।
विविधानि तु बृन्दानि विस्पष्टान्यत्र कृत्स्नशः॥
उदाह्रियन्ते ऽध्येतॄणां संदेहानां निवृत्तये।

आरण्यके प्रथमप्रश्ने आद्युदात्तानि वाक्यानि कानिचिदेकैकशः विद्यन्ते । कानिचिद् द्वित्रिकादि नानाविधबृन्दरूपाणि तानि सर्वाणि विस्पष्टं यथा भवति तथा उदाह्रियन्ते । अस्मिन् ग्रन्थे निरूपतया आदिमध्यान्तग्रहणं यत्र क्रियते तद्वाक्यानामेव श्रुतिग्रहणमपि वक्ष्यमाणलक्षणश्रुतिवाक्यस्येत्याह -- आदिमध्यान्तग्रहणं क्रियते यत्र तत्र तु ।

वाक्यानामिति मन्तव्यम् ॥

End:

एकश्रुत्यादिकं वाक्यं विना सत्यसमस्वरम्।
प्राप्नोत्यवोमिति परे ह्यवर्णान्तस्सदाशिवोम्।
सुब्रह्मण्यों परं रूपं नवोमित्यादि सर्वतः ॥

पदान्तादवर्णादोमित्यस्मिन् परे पूर्वपरयोस्स्थाने पररूपमेकादेशस्स्यात्। सुब्रह्मण्यौं सुब्रह्मण्यौं सुब्रह्मण्योम्। ब्रह्मा शिवो मे अस्तु सदाशिवोम्॥

Adyar D I 736 (29 K 20 = 73657). PL. Tel. 27 fol. (117ff.). = Adyar I, p. 52a. Title: Āraṇya-śikṣā.
Adyar D I 737 (33 H 19 = 75356). PL. Gr. 29 fol. (1-29).
GB 22. 31 fol. (with text). Copied for Kielhorn in Mysore in 1875.
Hoshiarpur p. 50 (no.4375). PL. Gr. 19 fol. 400 Grantha-s. Extract p. 407.
IO 4941 (Mackenzie II 94a). PL. Na. 11 fol. (with text). Written ca. A.D. 1770.
MD 866. PL. Tel. 38 pp. (1ff.) (with text).
End differs from other Mss. .... (= Skt. Texts on Phonetics, pp. 173-210).
MD 867. Tel. 49 pp. (266ff.) (with text). .... (= Skt. Texts on Phonetics, pp. 216-50).
Tirupati SVUORI 692 (4446a). PL. Gr. 29 fol. (with text).

– C. of Nṛsiṃha-sūri, son of Liṅgāvadhānin.

Beginning:

विघ्नराजं प्रणम्यादौ वासुदेवं च कामदम्।
आरण्यशिक्षाव्याख्यानमहं वक्ष्ये यथामति।

अत्र भगवान् शिक्षाकारः कर्तव्यग्रन्थस्याविघ्नपरिसमाप्तये गणपतिनमस्कारपूर्वकं मङ्गळं कुर्वन् प्रतिज्ञां करोति -- गणपतिम् ... उद्धरामि ॥ अवद्यजालामयघ्नं दोषसमूहरूपव्याधिहरम्। शीलनेन सेवया (अभ्यासेन) स्वरपदमितवर्णानां यद् बोधदं ज्ञानदं गणपतिमभिवन्द्य प्रणम्य ...

End:

आरण्यके ऽन्ध्रजनपाठवशेन शिक्षापीयूषमध्ययनतत्परविप्रतुष्ट्यै।
वर्णस्वरोच्चरितसंशयनिर्णयाय पातुं समर्प्यांथ कृतं महतामभेद्यम्॥

आरण्यके आन्ध्रजनपाठवशेन ... महान्त इति शेषः ।

लोकोपकारार्थमरण्यशिक्षा व्याख्यानमवधानिकुलोद्भवेन।
नृसिंहभट्टेन कृतं यदूनं क्षन्तुं समर्हन्तु महाजनास्तत्॥
अवधानिवंशतिलकनृसिंहेण विपश्चिता।
आरण्यशिक्षाव्याख्यानं कृतं लघु यथामति॥
सन्मार्गवर्तिनः सन्तो वेदाध्ययनतत्पराः ।

अमायासहिता दान्ताः शान्ता ब्रह्मपरायणाः ॥
अत्र न्यूनातिरिक्तं यत् तत् सर्वं क्षन्तुमर्हथ ॥
इत्यारण्यकशिक्षाभाष्यमवधानिवंशतिलक लिङ्गावधानितनयनृसिंहसूरिविरचितं संपूर्णम्

Adyar D I 734 (22 E 36 = 68884). PL. Tel. 23 fol. = Adyar I, p. 52a.
Adyar D I 735 (26 I 3 = 71569). PL. Tel. 29 fol. = Adyar I, p. 52a.
Adyar D XIII 323 (VB 128c). PL. Tel. 26 fol. (with text). (jayanāmasaṃvatsare kārttika-kṛṣṇa-dvitīyāyāṃ bhānuvāsare śrīnivāsācāryeṇa ...).
AU 29393 (Sūrāvadhānin).
Tirupati SVUORI (3526). PL. Gr. 21 fol. (26-46).
Trav. Uni. 5503 C. PL. Tel. 625 Grantha-s (with text).

[NCC II 156ab]

153 ĀRAṆYAKA-SĀMA-DĪPA (आरण्यकसामदीप)
of Nāga-bhaṭṭa → Sāma-dīpa.
Mysore I, p. 22.
Mysore ND II 3964-65. Extract no. 318.

[NCC II 156b]

154 ĀRAṆYAKĀBHIDHA (?) (आरण्यकाभिध)
Mentioned in a list of Sāmavedic works in Adyar D I p. 230. Apparently it is not a title, but only the beginning (āraṇakābhidhaḥ ṣaṣṭho 'dhyāyo vyākriyate mayā) of a work entitled *Caturthasvara-mandrasvara-nirṇaya*, described under Adyar D I 781. These five verses are found in Sāyaṇa's commentary on the 6th chapter of the *Āraṇya-gāna*. Cf. Alwar 230 (extract no. 66; p. 23), *Āraṇya-gāna-vivaraṇa* of Bhaṭṭa Śobhākara.

[NCC II 156b]

155 ĀRAṆYA-SĀMA-PRAKĀŚIKĀ (SĀMA-SVARA-NIRṆAYA)
(आरण्यसामप्रकाशिका / सामस्वरनिर्णय)

Beginning: (738):

द्वितीयस्वरमारभ्य ईडामन्द्रस्वरावधि।
त्रयोविंशतिसंख्याकास्तदुदाहरणमुच्यते॥
क्षये पिबासु द्वितीये रेवती प्रथमे त्रये।
विदा मघ विदा राय इन्द्र घेषु पृथक् पृथक्॥
ईडाचतुष्टयं प्रोक्तं हि ये वाक्ये तु पञ्च वै।
इडा त्रयोविंशतेश्च प्रोक्तोदाहृतिरत्र वै॥

End:

मन्द्रस्वरमेष्यति ओ वा।
गोमतैकं न तस्योपप्रेक्षे च द्युम्नमाभर।
अभि प्रियाणि षष्ठं स्याद् घृतस्यैकं तथैव च॥
नित्यमो वा तुरीयेषु चैव सामसु दृश्यते।
अग्ने जरितमेषस्थ हो वा नित्यं तुरीयके॥

इति चतुर्थमन्द्रस्वरनिर्णयं समाप्तम्॥

Adyar D I 738 (33 D 12 = 75239). PL. Gr. 3 fol. (50-52). The colophon and some verses at the end are the same as in D I 781 (Caturtha-svara-mandra-svara-nirṇaya).

Adyar D I 739 (33 E 7 = 75254). PL. Gr. 2 fol. (49-50). = Adyar I, p. 54a. Title: Sāmaprakāśaka. Pudukkottai Pañcāpakeśan and Rāmasvāmi are mentioned as former owners of the Ms. See also Adyar D I, p. 230, in the list of works given there.

[NCC II 156b]

156 ĀRUṆA-SAMĀNA (आरुणसमान)

→ Aruṇa-samāna.

Mysore (1898), p. 6 (no. 57). 2 fol. (105-06).

157 ĀRCIKA-LAKṢAṆA (आर्चिकलक्षण)

Ptd.: in the collection of Sāmavedic tracts, ed. by Krishnaswami Srauti (in Grantha script). – Kumbakonam : Jyotirvilasa Press, pp. 33-35. See below under Chalaprakriyā. [SAI (87/783*)] Reprinted in the *Sāmaprātiśākhya-saṃgraha*, part I, pp. 1-6.

158 ĀRBHĀVA (आर्भाव)

Mysore ND II 3155 (P 2476/ 7). PL. Na. 8 fol. (43-50). Extract no. 40.

159 ĀRṢĀNUKRAMAṆĪ (आर्षानुक्रमणी)

of Śaunaka. It is a list of the Ṛṣi-s of the *Ṛgveda*. Quoted 16 times in the *Vedārthadīpikā* of Ṣaḍguru-śiṣya on the *Sarvānukramaṇī*. Divided into ten chapters corresponding to the ten Maṇḍala-s of the *Ṛgveda* containing about 300 verses (30, 5, 10, 5, 32, 8, 4, 47, 48 and 103 verses respectively, according to Rajendralal Mitra's edition). For a different anonymous prose text, called Ṛṣyanukrama see L 4214 = RASB II 241.

Beginning:

ऋग्वेदमखिलं ये हि द्रष्टारो मुनिपुङ्गवाः ।
तदनुक्रमणायाहं नमामि परमेश्वरीम्॥ १॥
अत्राग्निमीळ इत्यादि प्रथमं मण्डलं प्रति।
शतर्चिनस्तु विज्ञेया ऋषयः सुखसिद्धये॥ २॥
तेषां पूर्वो मधुच्छन्दा मेधातिथिरनन्तरः ।
शुनःशेफस्तृतीयो ऽयं हिरण्यस्तूप उत्तरः ॥ ३॥
कण्वस्तु पञ्चमः षष्ठः प्रस्कण्वः सव्य उत्तरः ।
नोधाः पराशरश्चान्यो गोतमः कुत्स उत्तरः ॥ ४॥
कश्यपस्त्वथ कक्षीवान् परुच्छेपस्तदुत्तरः ।
दीर्घतमास्ततो ऽगस्त्यः षोडशैते शतर्चिनः ॥ ५॥
ऋचां शतानां दृष्टत्वादेत एव शतर्चिनः ।

जेतादीनां तु तन्नास्ति तस्मान्नैते शतर्चिनः ॥ ६॥

End:

आ यं गौरिति सूक्तस्य सार्पराज्ञी मुनिः स्मृतः॥ ९८॥
मधुच्छन्दःसुतः सूक्त ऋतमित्यघमर्षणः ।
संसंसूक्ते संवनन ऋषिराङ्गिरसः स्मृतः ॥ ९९॥
गोधा घोषा विश्ववारापालोपनिषन्निषत् ।
ब्रह्मजाया जुहूर्नामा अगस्त्यस्य स्वसादितिः ॥ १००॥
इन्द्राणी चेन्द्रमाता च सरमा रोमशोर्वशी ।
लोपामुद्रा च नद्यश्च यमी नारी च शश्वती॥ १०१॥
श्रीर्लाक्षा सार्पराज्ञी वाक् श्रद्धा मेधा च दक्षिणा॥
रात्री सूर्या च सावित्री ब्रह्मवादिन्य ईरिताः ॥
स गौतमो वामदेवो याः खिलास्ता ऋचो जगौ॥ १०२॥
यैर्वेदमन्त्राः सकलाः सुदृष्टा यैरेव चार्षानुक्रमणी प्रदिष्टा ।
नमो ऽस्तु तेभ्यो मुनिपुङ्गवेभ्यो भवन्तु ते चापि मयि प्रसन्नाः ॥ १०३॥

BHU B 2051 (D 11/631). 19 fol. Dated V.S. 1854.
GD I 7. PL. Mal. 114 fol. 1140 Grantha-s (with Chandonukramaṇī and Devatānukramaṇī). Title: Ṛksarvānukramaṇī.
Haug p. 32 (no.89) = München 25.
L 2112. 22 fol. 320 Grantha-s. Dated V.S. 1820.
München 25(1). 12 fol. Dated A.D. 1784.
Oxf. CS d.74(9). 18 fol. Title: Ārṣānukramaṇī-pariśiṣṭa.
RASB II 239(2) (G 1896). 11 fol. (37-47).
RASB II 239(B) (G 1896). 9 fol. Incomplete. Dated V.S. 1820.
RASB II 240 (G 2854). Beng. 29 fol. Title: Ṛṣyanukramaṇī Ṛgvedīyā.
RASB II 246(2) (G 6022). 6 fol. (18-23).
SBD 2348. 16 fol.
SBD 2362. 11 fol. (1-8,1, 12, 37). Incomplete. (Ṛgvedānukramaṇikā).
SBD 2366. 14 fol. (Ṛgvedānukramaṇikā).
Trav. Uni. 4848. 325 Grantha-s. Dated V.S. 1881.
Trav. Uni. L.1325 C. PL. Mal. 400 Grantha-s.
Triv. Cur. V 5. Mal. 300 Grantha-s. Obtained from Thiruparpu Svamiyar Matham.
Ujjain Latest Additions 415.
Wai I 330. 28 fol. 295 verses.
Wai I 331. 26 fol.
Wai I 332. 19 fol. Dated Śaka 1758.

Ptd.: ed. by Rajendralal Mitra, in the edition of *Bṛhaddevatā*. – Calcutta : Asiatic Society, 1893. pp. 241-78. – (Bibliotheca Indica 127). [NL (180 Jc 89 40); Emeneau (389); BM : Ptd. Bks. Cat. 1892-1906. 626 (14002.a.; vol.127); IO : Ptd. Bks.

Cat. 1938, p. 544 (Bibl. Ind. 127); SAI (87/784*)]

Ed. by Umesh Chandra Sharma, with Hindi commentary. – Aligarh : Viveka Publications, 1982, 8, 64 pp. [BORI (41683)]

[NCC II 180a]

160 ĀRṢEYA-CHANDO-DEVATĀ (आर्षेयछन्दोदेवता)

of some selected mantra-s of the *Sāmaveda* (oṃkārasya daivī gāyatrī chando 'gnir devatā brahmā ṛṣiḥ).

SBD 2306. 2 fol. Dated V.S. 1719.

161 ĀRṢEYA-DĪPA (आर्षेयदीप)

of Bhaṭṭa Bhāskara Yajvan (Adhvarīndra) of Kāśyapa-gotra. An Anukramaṇī of Ṛṣi-s, Devatā-s and Chandas of the *Sāmaveda,* based on the *Ārṣeya-brāhmaṇa.* The text is divided into three Parvan-s:

I. Āgneya (1 ch.; 12 Khaṇḍa-s)

II. Aindra (3 chs.; each with 12 Khaṇḍa-s or Anuvāka-s)

III. Pavamāna (1 ch.; 11 Khaṇḍa-s)

See also Sāmavedārṣeya-dīpa.

Baroda 9792(c). PL. Gr. 26 fol. 1000 Grantha-s. = CLB I, p. 23.

IO 4561 (Burnell 505a). Gr. 53 fol. Dated A.D. 1871. A transcript of an Olai Ms. (written ca. A.D. 1600) in the possession of V. R. Śāstrin of Kumbakonam.

Mysore I, p. 4.

Mysore D I 75.

Ptd.: ed. by Bellikoth Ramachandra Sharma. – Tirupati : Kendriya Samskrit Vidyapeetha, 1967. xx, 202 pp. The edition is based on the Baroda, IO, and Mysore (no.SA 312) Mss. besides a transcript of a Ms. supplied by R. Santanam Sastrigal, Ammal Agraharam, Tiruvayuru, Tanjore (only the Āraṇyaka). [BORI (20429; 28367); SAI (ind 72 C 422)]

[NCC II 180b]

162 ĀRṢEYA-PRAKṚTI-CCHALĀKṢARA (आर्षेयप्रकृतिच्छलाक्षर)

Adyar D I 745 (33 M 2 = 75487). PL. Gr. 22 fol. (marked 1-23; no .20 is omitted; it contains an index to the *Sāmaveda* on three leaves at the beginning). = Adyar I, p. 49a. Title: Chalākṣara.

[NCC II 180b]

163 ĀRṢEYA-BRĀHMAṆĀNUKRAMAṆĪ (आर्षेयब्राह्मणानुक्रमणी)

Mysore ND II 3156 (P 6645/ 4). PL. Na. 1 fol. (131). Extract no. 41.

164 ĀVARṆI(-PRAKARAṆA) (or -LAKṢAṆA) (आवर्णि-प्रकरण /-लक्षण)

A list of words in the *Ṛgveda* beginning with "ā" merging with the last vowel of the preceding word. Also included in the *Sapta-lakṣaṇa* (which see).

Beginning:

आकूतिश्चाकूतिश्चैवाक्षितमाङ्गूषमागहि ।
आग्नीध्रादागमिष्ठागा आगमन्नागतेन च ॥

आगत्य स्यादाचरन्त्याचरेदाचरदाजि च।
इङ्ग्याजुह्वानाजताजदाजत्वात्मादैङ्ग्यकः ॥

End:

आकारादिपदानां तु स्पष्टाय प्रतिपादितम्।
यथामति हृदि प्रीत्या धार्यं विद्वज्जनैः सदा॥

Adyar D I 740 (20 K 38 = 67500). PL. Tel. 1 fol. = Adyar I, p. 48a. Title: Avarṇi-lakṣaṇa.
MD 872. Tel. 2 pp. (90ff.)
Mysore ND II 3631 (P 4906/10). PL. Na. 2 fol. (114-15). Extract no. 219. Title: Punar-āvarṇi (!).
TCD 34-D. 2 pp. (22-23). 15 Grantha-s.
Trav. Uni. 4254 D. PL. Mal. 1 fol. 15 Grantha-s. Belonged to Vishnu Nambudiri of Ettikada Illam Ayankudi, Kaduttirutti, Kottayam.
Trav. Uni. T.223 D. = TCD 34-D. A transcript of the Ms. no. 4254.
Triv. Cur. III 3. Mal. 100 Grantha-s.
Whish 73,3 (3). PL. Gr. 1 fol. (3).

Ptd. in the collection called *Tāṇḍaṅgaḻ* (in Malayalam script). – Kunnankulam (Kerala) : Panchangam Pustakashala, 1930 (M.E. 1105), pp. 28-29 (17 verses). [SAI (87/1683*)]

– C. anon.

Beginning:

आकारसंग्रहव्याख्यां स्वयमेव करोति च। अस्मिन् लक्षणे ऽपि प्रातिपदिकग्रहणं सर्वार्थं सर्वत्र। आकूतिश्चाकृतिश्चैवाक्षितमाङ्गूषमागहि। मह्यं यजन्तु मम यानि हव्याकूतिः सत्या (१०·१२८·४)। श्रद्धां हृदय्यायाकूत्या (१०·१५१·४)। आदित्यासो अपाकृतिम्। स हि ष्मा धन्वाक्षितम् (५·७·७)। ब्रह्माङ्गूषम्। सदनं रोदस्यों एनाङ्गूषेण वयमिन्द्र वयन्तम्। जुषाण उपागहि।

End:

इमं नो यज्ञमागमन्। नाभिरिति किम्। आभिर्याहि आयमामद्रया दृक्। उक्तमिङ्ग्येन नात्वमाकारकृतेङ्ग्येषु प्रतिषेधयति एकमिति। दुःखण्डत्वेन भिन्नाकारपूर्वपदाकर्षितस्यैकत्वसिद्धेः स्वस्वतः ग्रहाय ग्रहणार्थम्। आकारेण कृतखण्डं पदखण्डमेव। न नाना। किमर्थम्। ग्रहणसिद्ध्यर्थम्। इङ्ग्येकत्वाकारानुक्तौ इङ्ग्यांशभूतकेवलाकारस्यापृथक्त्वम्। पृथक्त्वात् अविषयत्वादग्रहणत्वम्। तस्याग्रहणे आरुजास्यारुन्धानादीनां ग्रहणाभावः। तस्मात् अग्रहणार्थमित्यर्थः।

आकारादिपदानां तु स्पष्टाय प्रतिपादितम्।

यथामति हृदि प्रीत्या धार्यं विद्वज्जनैः सदा ॥
आवर्णिव्याख्यानं समाप्तम् ॥

Whish 73,3 (5). PL. Gr. 5 fol. (24-30).

165 ĀVARṆI(-PRAKARAṆA) (or -LAKṢAṆA) **(आवर्णि-प्रकरण /-लक्षण)**

List of words from the *Taittirīya-saṃhitā* beginning with "ā" merging with the last vowel of the preceding word. Most of the Mss. give the author as Mahādhipati Yajvan of Tintriṇī Kula (Āndhra) but have slight differences; the text in many of the Mss. is accompanied by a commentary of which again Mahādhipati is noted as the author in a few catalogues. It is also called *Dīrgha-saṃgraha* in a few Mss. Also included in the *Sapta-lakṣaṇa* (which see).

Beginning:

अथाकारादीनि सर्वविभक्त्यन्तानि पदान्याह --
आग्नीध्राग्रयणाज्योपा वर्ताम्रोत्यायुधश्रुतिः ।
आशीराहवनीयाग्नेयाग्नामुष्यायणश्रुतिः ॥ १ ॥
आत्मशब्दो नोरसादिरायुःशब्दो न घात् परः ।
अन्तोदात्तो निहतो वाप्यादित्यश्रुतिरिष्यते ॥ २ ॥

End:

कल्पेनाद्याहरन्ति स्यादाहनन्याय चाहलम् ।
ऋतुना स्मोपहत्य प्र पराश्राव्यानुवाक्यया ॥ २३ ॥
आहैतत्पूर्वमाहुश्चेदेषावर्णिः सुनिर्मिता ।
(तिन्त्रिणीकुलसंभूतमहाधिपतियज्वना) ॥ २४ ॥
(वेदाध्ययनशीलानामुपकाराय कल्पताम्)

Adyar D I 741 (22 D 2 = 68760). PL. Gr. 4 fol. (7-10) (with C.). = Adyar I, p. 48a. Title: Avarṇi-vyākhyāna.
Adyar D I 742 (22 E 54 = 68903). PL. Gr. 3 fol. (with C.). = Adyar I, p. 48a. Title: Avarṇi-lakṣaṇa.
Adyar D I 743 (29 I 28 = 73580). PL. Gr. 4 fol. (95ff.) (with C.).
Adyar D I 744 (30 C 3 = 73873). PL. Tel. 6 fol. (11ff.) (with C.). = Adyar I, p. 54a.
Adyar D I 983 → Veda-lakṣaṇa (A 1).
Adyar D I 984 → Veda-lakṣaṇa (A 2).
Adyar D I 1030 → Sapta-lakṣaṇa.
Adyar D I 1031 → Sapta-lakṣaṇa.
Adyar D I 1032 → Sapta-lakṣaṇa.
Adyar D I 1034 → Sapta-lakṣaṇa.
Adyar D I 1035 → Sapta-lakṣaṇa.
Adyar D XIII 30 (VB 266c). PL. Gr. 2 fol.
Baroda 10032(c). PL. Gr. 9 fol. (75-83). 100 Grantha-s (with C.). = CLB I, p. 23.

Baroda 10034(c). PL. Gr. 2 fol. (5-6). 40 Grantha-s. = CLB I, p. 23.
Baroda 10381(h). PL. Gr. 2 fol. (15-16). 40 Grantha-s. = CLB I, p. 23.
Brl. p. 12 (no.XLIV) = IO 4474.
Brl. p. 12 (no.XLV) = IO 4473.
Hoshiarpur p. 50 (no.4105). PL. Gr. 1 fol. 10 Grantha-s.
Hoshiarpur p. 50 (no.4118). PL. Gr. 3 fol. Extract p. 407.
Hoshiarpur p. 300 (no.5947). PL. Gr. 1 fol. 10 Grantha-s.
Hz 1434. PL. Gr. 33 fol. (with 3 other Veda-lakṣaṇa works). Belonged to the late Raja Ghanapathi of Tiruvidaimarudur, Thanjavur Dist.
IO 4473 (Burnell 146c). PL. Gr. 2 fol. (9-10).
IO 4474 (Burnell 49c). PL. Gr. 2 fol. (10-11).
IO 4475 (Mackenzie II 94g). PL. Na. 2 fol. (66-67). Written ca. A.D. 1770.
IO 4477 (Mackenzie II 94c). PL. Na. 5 fol. (55-59) (with C.). Written ca. A.D. 1770.
MD 868. PL. Tel. 3 pp. (95ff.).
MD 869. PL. Gr. 6 pp. (21ff.).
MD 870. PL. Tel. 26 pp. (103ff.) (with C.).
MD 16397. PL. Gr. 2 pp. 36 Grantha-s.
MD 16712. PL. Tel. 2 pp. 36 Grantha-s.
MD 16735. PL. Tel. 3 pp. 36 Grantha-s.
MD 16807. PL. Gr. 3 pp. 30 Grantha-s.
MT 485(c). PL. Tel. 6 fol. (52-57) (with C.). Presented in 1910-11 by C. Visvanatha Shastrigal of Viziyanagaram.
MT 689(d). PL. Gr. 3 fol. (8-10) (with Avarṇi). Purchased in 1912-13 through Seshasayi Ayyangar of Kottaiyur near Kumbakonam.
MT 1240(c). PL. Tel. 7 fol. (15-21) (with C.). Copied by Vedam Anantanārāyaṇa. Presented in 1913-14 by K. Ramakrishnayya of Musalipattanam.
MT 1240(d). PL. Tel. 3 fol. (21-23). Presented in 1913-14 by K. Ramakrishnayya of Musalipattanam.
MT 1964(h). PL. Tel. 6 fol. (76-81). Presented in 1916-17 by Rayaprolu Ramabrahmangaru of Guruza, Gudivada Taluk, Krishna Dist.
MT 1976(c). Tel. 6 fol. (54-59) (with C.). Presented in 1916-17 by Nimmagadda Narasimhavadhanulugaru, Godavarru, Godavari Dist.
MT 2591(f). PL. Tel. 3 fol. (202-04). Presented in 1917-18 by Vasireddi Chandramaulisvaraprasada Bahadur, Zamindar of Muktyala, Krishna Dist.
MT 2881(c). PL. Gr. 4 fol. (30-33) (with C.). Presented in 1918-19 by Venkatagiri Appalacharyar of Triplicane.
MT 3887(i). PL. Gr. 2 fol. (79-80). Purchased in 1921-22 from Annasvami Sastrigal, Bhavani, Coimbatore Dist.
MT 4600(a). PL. Gr. 2 fol. (12-13). (10th in the Ms. of Veda-lakṣaṇa). Presented in 1924-25 by the Secretary to the Trustees of Sri Yogi Parthasarathi Ayyangar's Charities, Triplicane, Madras.
Mysore I, p. 22 (2 Mss.); p. 612.
Mysore ND II 3157-72. Extract no. 42.
Mysore ND II 3173 (different from the above ?).
Oppert I 959. Belonged to Viraraghava Tatacharyar, Head Master, Sanskrit School of Sathakopacharya, Kanchipuram, Chingelpet Dist.

Oppert II 736. Belonged to Ghanapathi Shingaracharyar of Alasur, Madurantakam Taluk.

Oppert II 1307. Belonged to Gopalacharyar of Pillapakkam, Kanchipuram Taluk.

Oppert II 9005. Belonged to Ganapati Lakshminarayana Sastri of Tiruvadi, Thanjavur Dist.

PUL I, p. 19 (no.28). PL. Gr. 6 fol.

RASB II 487-88(VI) (G 6063). Dated V.S. 1913 / Śaka 1778.

TD 1795 → Sapta-lakṣaṇa.

TD 1804 (5th) → Sapta-lakṣaṇa.

Tirupati SVUORI 705 (4411f). PL. Gr.

Trav. Uni. 1116 D. PL. Mal. 15 Grantha-s.

Trav. Uni. 2346 E. PL. Gr. 90 Grantha-s (with C.).

Trav. Uni. 4369 D. PL. Gr. 2 fol. 20 Grantha-s.

Ptd.: There are five editions. See Sapta-lakṣaṇa.

– C. In most Mss. the author is given as Mahādhipati-yajvan.

Beginning: (741)

आवर्णिव्याख्यानम् । आकारादीनि पदानि सर्वविभक्त्यन्तानि पदान्याह -- आग्नीध्रेति त्रिभिः श्लोकैः -- आग्नीद्ध्राग्रयणाज्योपा वर्त्ताप्नोत्यायुधश्रुतिः । नमो वृक्तिवत्त्यर्चाग्नीध्रे जुहुयात् । अन्तरिक्षमिवाग्नीध्रमाग्नीध्रे । इध्रेति किम् । दक्षिणाग्नीषोमीयम् । साग्रयणं प्रत्यागच्छत् । जगतैवर्त्तन्याग्रयणस्य । तं मा जिन्वाज्यस्याज्यमसि । पशव उपावर्तन्त । इयमुपावर्त्स्यति । उपेति किम् । सा दक्षिणावर्तत । तेन नाप्नुवन् । न परां प्राप्नोति । शतायुधाय । यज्ञायुधानि ।

End:

आहैतत्पूर्वमाहश्चेत्येषो ऽवर्णिः सुनिर्मितः -- अस्यायमर्थः । ऋतुना स्म । उपहत्य । प्रा । परा । आश्राव्य । अनुवाक्यया । इत्येतेषामन्यतमे पदे पूर्वे स्थिते सति आहेति पदं भवति । यथा -- द्विः पुनर्ऋतुनाह । अरुणो ह स्मा हौपवेशिः । पृषदाज्यस्योपहत्याह । आहृत्य प्राह । एतत् ते प्राह । आत्मानं पराह । आश्राव्याह देवान् । प्रैवनं पुरोनुवाक्ययाह । एतत्पूर्वमिति किम् । एतावता हैनसा भवति । यस्य समुद्रं रसया सह । एवमाकारादीनि पदानि उक्तानि । एषो ऽवर्णिः सुनिर्म्मितः । इत्यावर्णिव्याख्यानं समाप्तम् ।

Adyar D I 741 (22 D 2 = 68760). PL. Gr. 4 fol. (7-10) (with text). = Adyar I, p. 48a. Title: Avarṇi-vyākhyāna.

Adyar D I 742 (22 E 54 = 68903). PL. Gr. 3 fol. (with text). = Adyar I, p. 48a. Title: Avarṇi-lakṣaṇa.

Adyar D I 743 (29 I 28 = 73580). PL. Gr. 4 fol. (95ff.) (with text).

Adyar D I 744 (30 C 3 = 73873). PL. Tel. 6 fol. (11ff.) (with text). = Adyar I, p. 54a. Title: Sapta-lakṣaṇa-vyākhyā.

Adyar D I 984 (fol. 71a- 74a) → Veda-lakṣaṇa (A 2).

Adyar D I 1037 (fol. 18b-23b) → Sapta-lakṣaṇa-vyākhyā.
Adyar D I 1039 (fol. 71-75) → Sapta-lakṣaṇa-vyākhyā.
Adyar D I 1093. (fol. 75a). (All these Mss. have slight differences in their readings).
Baroda 10032(c). PL. Gr. 9 fol. (75-83). 100 Grantha-s. = CLB I, p. 23.
Brl. p. 12 (no.XLVI) = IO 4476.
IO 4476 (Burnell 350f). Tel. 4 fol. (65-68). Written ca. A.D. 1867.
IO 4477 (Mackenzie II 94c). PL. Na. 5 fol. (55-59) (with text). Written ca. A.D. 1770.
MD 870. PL. Tel. 26 pp. (103ff.) (with text).
MD 871. Gr. 8 pp. (20ff.).
MD 16743. PL. Tel. 14 pp. 315 Grantha-s.
MT 485(c). PL. Tel. 6 fol. (52-57) (with text). Presented in 1910-11 by C. Visvanatha Shastrigal of Viziyanagaram.
MT 1240(c). PL. Tel. 7 fol. (15-21). Copied by Vedam Anantanārāyaṇa. Presented in 1913-14 by K. Ramakrishnayya of Musalipattanam.
MT 1964(h). PL. Tel. 6 fol. (76-81) = Adyar D I 741. Presented in 1916-17 by Rayaprolu Ramabrahmangaru of Guruza, Gudivada Taluk, Krishna Dist.
MT 1976(c). Tel. 6 fol. (54-59) (with text). Dated Thursday, the 4th Vaiśākha-śukla, Sādhāraṇa year. Presented in 1916-17 by Nimmagadda Narasimhavadhanulugaru, Godavarru, Godavari Dist.
MT 2188(b). Tel. 14 fol. (3-16). (Avarṇyāvarṇi-vyākhyāna). Transcribed in 1916-17 from a Ms. of Vemparla Subrahmanya Sastrigaru of Tondavaramu, Godavari Dist. The scribe of the original Ms. is Ponnamalli Subrahmaṇya. Dated: nalanāmasaṃvatsara-śrāvaṇa-bahula-prathamā ādivāram |
MT 2591(h). PL. Tel. 10 fol. (222-31). Presented in 1917-18 by Vasireddi Chandramaulisvaraprasada Bahadur, Zamindar of Muktyala, Krishna Dist.
MT 2881(c). PL. Gr. 4 fol. (30-33) (with text). Presented in 1918-19 by Venkatagiri Appalacharyar of Triplicane.
Mysore I, p. 23 (2 Mss.); p. 612
Mysore ND II 3174-83 (no.3178, 3183 are different). Extract no. 43, 44.
Oppert II 737. Belonged to Ghanapaṭhi Shingaracharyar of Alasur, Madurantakam Taluk.
Oppert II 9006. Belonged to Ganapati Lakshminarayana Sastri of Tiruvadi, Thanjavur Dist.
TD 1807 (2nd).
TD 1809.
Trav. Uni. 2346 E. PL. Gr. 90 Grantha-s (with text).

– C.

Whish 25a (6). PL. Gr. 5 fol. (35-39). Title: Ākāra-paddhati.

[NCC II 185b-186b]

166 ĀVEṢṬANA-SŪTRA (**आवेष्टनसूत्र**)
Govt. Or. Libr. Madras, p. 10.

[NCC II 192b]

167 ĀŚVALĀYANA-PARIBHĀṢĀ (**आश्वलायनपरिभाषा**)
SBD 55360. 15 fol. = Ṛgveda-sarvānukramaṇī.

168 IṄGYA-RATNA or IṄGYĀNIṄGYA-PARIGAṆANA (इङ्ग्यरत्न / इङ्ग्यानिङ्ग्यपरिगणन)

An account of "iṅgya" and "aniṅgya" words in the *Kṛṣṇa-yajurveda* in verses. The texts in the Mss. vary from one another considerably.

Beginning:

वाणीं नत्वेङ्ग्यसंख्यानां वक्ष्याम्यक्षरसंख्यया।
इषे त्वाद्यनुवाकानामेकैकं पदशः क्रमात्॥
तत्र द्वे द्वे अक्षरे तु पदसंज्ञकमुच्यते।
पूर्वमेकं द्वयं वृद्धिर्दशादिपदमक्षरम्॥
कादयो नव वर्णाः स्युष्टादयो ऽपि तथैव च।
पादयः पञ्च याद्यष्टौ वर्णास्तत्र यथाक्रमम्॥
बिन्दुस्थाने नकारः स्यादभावे नहिनाप्युभौ।
मङ्गलार्थो ऽथशब्दः स्यात् पूरणार्थाः स्वरा अपि॥

(ओम्) अथ नानिसयो नाको लोके रेखाधनं सटः।
पयोपरतरनारीकापीसरनगा इति॥ १॥
लोकदूकजपं नाकसानुनीकधनं नयम्।
नेयं जयं साटी नारीमयाभावि द्वितीयके॥ २॥
भेकनागचयं देयं सानुवायुधनीकसः।
नळं धियो तनुं तेन धनु चापिस्तृतीयके॥ ३॥
मयि तनुर्सयुनीकमसौ वनं पनितनुः शनिभौन वने वनम्।
मनुगनं पनखानिविनागसौ गनवनीनयुतेन वने वने॥

End:

फणनवमतरेफनदं नभं शुभशुभं धर धीरधीयारिपुः।
हनरिपुं वनभानुकनं वहि चानदेनुत तदुत्तरके मतम्॥
नवल्यं सुखनाकफलं च यो जपकरं नगरामशरं गनम्।
धनरनं धनजायजयं तनुः रवननयं प्रजवन्त्विति पाठके॥
भगतुषा भुजितं पनिमं तनुं जलसुगं तनु भारखं मनः।
स्वनततनुं गन दान चयं च नः नटभनं धननीकमितीरितम्॥
सासोरायशकजराखलोलता मं मानि तं चलसनिपररिसा .. यः।
कूलजनसनो मुनिं च नौका यो धीनं नखधनहनिकायसंज्ञा॥
इतीङ्ग्यानि यजुर्वेदे संख्यातान्युक्तसंख्यया।
ततो ऽन्यानि त्वनिङ्ग्यानि बोद्धव्यानि सुधीमता॥

इति इङ्ग्यरत्नं समाप्तम्॥

Adyar D I 746 (19 D 63 = 66255). PL. Tel. 2 fol. (23-24) (complete text is printed here).

MT 95(d). PL. Gr. 2 fol. (11-12). Purchased in 1910-11 from Gopalaswami Ayyangar of Mannargudi.

Mysore I, p. 23 (4 Mss.).

Oppert I 7170. Belonged to Ivattur Nandikesvara Sastri of Vijayanagaram.

Oppert I 7855. Belonged to Paravastu Venkatarangacharyar of Vishakhapattanam.

Tirupati SVUORI 800 (4378d). PL. Tel. 3 fol. (22-24).

169 INGYA-RATNA (2) (इङ्ग्यरत्न)

of Nemāni Bhairavāvadhānin (in prose). In MT 485(t) the name is given as Setūni.

Beginning:

अथ यजुःसंहितायामिङ्ग्यपदान्यनुवाकमध्यावसानानि च विविच्य प्रत्यनुवाकमेकैकाक्षरं प्रतिप्रश्नमेकैकं वाक्यमिङ्ग्यरत्नं प्रवक्ष्यामः । अत्रेङ्ग्यप्रवर्तका वर्णा अकाराद्यौकारपर्यन्ता ऋकार-लृकारप्लुतवर्जिता दश । ते व्यञ्जनोपरि स्थिता इङ्ग्यानां यथाक्रमम् एकत्वद्वित्वादिसंख्याज्ञापनार्थाः ।... अथावसानप्रवर्तकव्यञ्जनानि -- कटतपेति पञ्च समावसानज्ञापकानि ।

End:

विसूङ्शूषौनूवै वेघूनि शाबुधाभूदिदैम्यूगूम्ये दीभोमौ हेममुनुवासीप्रुसौ क्काघेनैमेघेमैचचेते भूधूमदैनाभैतोम । इति श्रीसेतूनिभैरवावधानिविरचितमिङ्ग्यरत्नं समाप्तम् ।

Baroda 10333(a). PL. Tel. 6 fol. 150 Grantha-s. Incomplete. Catalogued as Akṣara-saṃjñā.

MD 17443. PL. Gr. 5 pp. 43 Grantha-s.

MT 485(t). PL. Tel. 2 fol. (78-79). Presented in 1910-11 by C. Visvanatha Shastrigal of Viziyanagaram.

MT 1240(g). PL. Tel. 1 fol. (no.49; fragment). Presented in 1913-14 by K. Ramakrishnayya of Musalipattanam.

Mysore ND II 3189 (P 232/ 3a). PL. Gr. 3 fol. (15-17). Extract no. 45.

Mysore ND II 3190 (P 4453/15). PL. Na. 3 fol. (23-24).

Mysore ND II 3191 (P 8061). PL. Tel. 1 fol. (100).

[NCC II 244b]

170 INGYA-RATNA (3) (इङ्ग्यरत्न)

– Different from the above ? by Śrīvatsāṅka ?

Mysore ND II 3184 (P 142/ 3). PL. Tel. 4 fol. (87-90). (a. Śrīvatsāṅka !).

Mysore ND II 3185 (P 977/ 7). PL. Tel. 2 fol. (53-54).

Mysore ND II 3186 (P 997/ 9). PL. Na. 5 fol. (8-12).

Mysore ND II 3187 (P 8066/ 2). PL. Tel. 3 fol.

Mysore ND II 3188 (B 600/ 7). Na. 3 fol. (30-32).

171 IṄGYA-LAKṢAṆA (इङ्ग्यलक्षण)
Adyar D I 988 → Veda-lakṣaṇa (A 6).

172 IṄGYA-ŚIKṢĀ (इङ्ग्यशिक्षा)
Oppert I 7130. Belonged to Pola Lakshmanavadhani of Vijayanagaram.
[NCC II 244b]

173 ITIHĀSĀNUKRAMAṆĪ (इतिहासानुक्रमणी)
of Mādhava; mentioned in his commentary on the *Ṛgveda*. See *Journal of Oriental Research*, Madras, V, pp. 317, 319, 324. [Adyar (H05R JOR 5)]
[NCC II 247a]

*INDRADATTOPĀDHYĀYA (इन्द्रदत्तोपाध्याय)
– Svara-vivṛti. BORI D I ii.4.

174 ĪKĀRĀNTA-LAKṢAṆA (ईकारान्तलक्षण)

Beginning:

ईकारान्ताः प्रकथ्यन्ते स्वरादौ च पदे परे।
आचरन्ती मधुमती द्युम्नी वाजी प्रवेपनी॥
उदीरयन्ती भ्राजन्ती प्रणीती सूनृतावती।
अपतिघ्नी चोदयन्ती मनीषी सीलमावती॥

End:

मीढुष्मती वेत्यर्धर्चे मदन्तीति समीरितम्।
एषां संख्यास्तथाश्चैव नवतिश्च यथाक्रमम्॥
इति पदकाल ईकारान्तलक्षणम्॥

Mysore Skt. Coll. p. 1 = D. No.3 (846/12). PL. Na. 2 fol. (44-45).

175 ĪKĀRĀNTĀḤ (ईकारान्ताः)
Ī-ending words in the Pada-pāṭha of the *Taittirīya-saṃhitā*.
MT 485(n). PL. Tel. 1 fol. (67). Presented in 1910-11 by C. Visvanatha Shastrigal of Viziyanagaram.
MT 3887(j). PL. Gr. 2 fol. (83-84). See remarks. Purchased in 1921-22 from Annasvami Sastrigal, Bhavani, Coimbatore Dist.

*ĪŚVARA or Parameśvara (ईश्वर / परमेश्वर)
– C. Vākya-pradīpikā on Pārṣada.
Trav. Uni. L.479.
Trav. Uni. L.1346 A. PL. Mal. 3500 Grantha-s.

176 UGUPARĪKṢĀ (उगुपरीक्षा)
Listed together with other works on Veda-lakṣaṇa.
Adyar D I 983 → Veda-lakṣaṇa (A 1).

Adyar D I 985 → Veda-lakṣaṇa (A 3).

[NCC II 282b]

177 UCCA-NĪCA-LAKṢAṆA (**उच्चनीचलक्षण**)

Mysore I, p. 23.

Mysore ND II 3193 (P 1978/ 7). PL. Na. 5 fol. (17-21). Extract no. 46. (SV)

Mysore ND II 3194 (P 2476/ 3). PL. Na. 9 fol. (21-29). (SV)

[NCC II 284b]

178 UCCA-SVARA-NIRṆAYA (**उच्चस्वरनिर्णय**)

of Sūri-bhaṭṭa Yajvan according to the Mysore Skt. Coll. catalogue. The title of the work varies in different Mss: *Antodātta* (or *Svara-lakṣaṇa)* (Mysore ND II 3086); *Ucca-svara* (Mysore ND II 3195-98); *Udātta-gaṇana* (Trav. Uni. 2364); *Udātta-svara-nirṇaya* (the commentary, Mysore Skt. Coll. no. 1530 and Trav. Uni. 5479 A); *Udāttādi-svara-prakaraṇa* (Mysore I, p. 24); *Svara-śikṣā* (Adyar D I 1096 and MD 1022). Strangely enough in MD 955 the same text with C. is entitled *Lakṣmīkānta-śikṣā* (col.: *Ucca-lakṣmīkānta-śikṣā)* Savyākhyā. The work consists of about 55 verses divided into two Prakaraṇa-s, the first containing 40 verses enumerates the words of Antodātta and the second those of Ādyudātta in the *Taittirīya-saṃhitā*. The commentary refers to *Svarāṣṭaka* and *Svara-samuccaya*.

Beginning: (with C.)

प्रणम्य नारायणपादपङ्कजे समस्तलोकत्रितयार्तिहारिणे।
करिष्यते वेदपदानि पाठतो निरूप्य चोच्चस्वरनिर्णयो मया॥

प्रारिप्सितस्य ग्रन्थस्य स्वरलक्षणस्याविच्छेदपरिसमाप्तये लोकत्रितयार्तिहारिणे नारायणपादपङ्कजे प्रणम्य तैत्तिरीयवेदपदानि लोकप्रसिद्धपाठानुसारेण तत्त्वतः प्रतीक्ष्य उदात्तस्वरनिर्णयो नाम लक्षणं क्रियत इति। ननु किमनेन लक्षणकरणेन। स्वत एव वेदपदानि इदमीदृशमिति प्रसिद्धाध्ययनादेव सर्वं तत्त्वतो निश्चिनुयुः (मुः)। तथापि तु प्रतिलक्षणं प्रतिपदं किमिदं किमेवमिति सर्वदा सर्वत्र संदेहिनां विस्मारिणामस्मादृशां निश्चायकं लक्षणमपेक्षणीयमेवेति। तथा स्वराष्टकस्वरसमुच्चयप्रातिशाख्यादीनि स्वरनिश्चायकानि पूर्वोक्तानि लक्षणानि सन्ति उदात्तस्वरनिर्णयनाम्ना किमनेन लक्षणकरणेनेत्याकाङ्क्षायामाह --

अन्तोदात्तपदं चेदमाद्योच्चमिदमीदृशम्॥
नियमो न कृतः कैश्चित् कस्मिंश्चित् स्वरलक्षणे॥

पदाध्ययन इदं पदमन्तोदात्तमिदमाद्युदात्तमेवेति ईदृशनियमः कस्मिंश्चित् स्वरलक्षणे कैश्चित् स्वरलक्षणकारैर्नाकारि। अत एवेदृशं लक्षणमारम्भणीयम्॥

End:

यजमानमभ्येति यदग्निः। तस्मिन्नेका। उत्तमैकस्मादक्षतात्।
ओषधीष्वोषधीनां च तदौषधय औषधीः।
एवमुच्चस्वरो ऽस्माभिर्निर्णीतो वर्णितः क्रमात्॥
सौषधीः। महीमोषधयः। एतान्याद्युदात्तानि पदानि व्याख्यातानि।

Adyar D I 1096 (29 K 20 = 73653). PL. Tel. 13 fol. (145ff.). (Svara-śikṣā). = Adyar I, p. 53b. Col.: Ucca-svara-nirṇaya. Copied by Kālakūri Devaṇṇa for Vedamūrti Maddūri Narasimulu and dated Sunday, the 5th day of the first half of Puṣya, Bharaṇī (year Khara is mentioned on another fol.).

MD 874. PL. Gr. 5 pp. (39ff.). About 50 verses. Incomplete.

MD 955. Tel. 19 pp. (300ff.).
(Lakṣmī-kānta-śikṣā Savyākhyā). .... (= Skt. Texts on Phonetics, pp. 290-307).

MD 1022. Tel. 25 pp. (253ff.) (with C.). Title: Svara-śikṣā. Col.: Ucca-svara-samuccaya.

Mysore I, p. 23.

Mysore ND II 3086 (P 997/ 8). PL. Na. 3 fol. (Antodātta / Svara-lakṣaṇa). Extract no. 17.

Mysore ND II 3195 (P 232/ 1). PL. Gr. 12 fol. (Ucca-svara). Extract no. 47.

Mysore ND II 3196 (P 285/ 5). PL. Gr. 4 fol. (31-34). (Ucca-svara).

Mysore ND II 3197 (P 972/ 4). PL. Tel. 7 fol. (22-28). (Ucca-svara).

Mysore ND II 3198 (P 4772/ 9). PL. Tel. 3 fol. (Ucca-svara).

Mysore ND II 3199 (P 972/ 5). PL. Tel. 10 fol. (22-31). (Ucca-svara-nirṇaya-vyākhyā). Extract no. 48.

Mysore Skt. Coll. p. 1 = D. No.4 (1536/1). PL. Gr. 10 fol. (Udātta-svara-nirṇaya).

RASB II 489(III) (G 6175). 2 fol. (9-10). Incomplete. Up to 36th Kārikā.

Tirupati SVUORI (1143g). PL. Gr. 7 fol.

Trav. Uni. 2346 I. PL. Gr. 125 Grantha-s. (Udātta-gaṇana).

Trav. Uni. 5479 A. PL. Tel. 155 Grantha-s. (Udātta-svara-nirṇaya).

– C.

Adyar D I 1096 (29 K 20 = 73653). PL. Tel. 13 fol. (145ff.).

MD 955. Tel. 19 pp. (300ff.).
(Lakṣmī-kānta-śikṣā Savyākhyā). .... (= Skt. Texts on Phonetics, pp. 290-307).

MD 1022. Tel. 25 pp. (253ff.) (with text). Title: Svara-śikṣā. Col.: Ucca-svara-samuccaya.

Mysore ND II 3199 (P 972/ 5). PL. Tel. 10 fol. (22-31).

Trav. Uni. 2346 I. PL. Gr. 125 Grantha-s. (Udātta-gaṇana).

Trav. Uni. 5479 A. PL. Tel. 155 Grantha-s. (Udātta-svara-nirṇaya).

[NCC II 284b]

179 UCCODARKI(-KĪYA) (उच्चोदर्कि) (-कीय)

Probably the same as the next.

Gough p. 162. Gr.

Mysore p. 2 (no. 52). 5 fol. (with C.).

Mysore p. 2 (no. 57). 5 fol. (with C.). (Svarāvadhānam).

Mysore (1898), p. 6 (no. 52). 5 fol. (97-101) (with C.).

Mysore (1898), p. 6 (no. 57). 15 fol. (45-59) (with C.).

Mysore I, p. 23 (2 Mss.).

Mysore ND II 3204 (P 4772/12). PL. Tel. 6 fol.

Oppert I 2282. PL. Gr. 15 pp. Sri Sarasvati Bhandaram Committee of Tiruvallikkeni, Madras.

Oppert I 7131. Belonged to Pola Lakshmanavadhani of Vijayanagaram.

Oppert I 7172. Belonged to Ivattur Nandikesvara Sastri of Vijayanagaram.

Oppert I 7534. Belonged to S. Kodanda Ramavadhana Pantulu of Vijayanagaram.

Oppert II 738. Belonged to Ghanapathi Shingaracharyar of Alasur, Madurantakam Taluk.

Oppert II 1308. Belonged to Gopalacharyar of Pillapakkam, Kanchipuram Taluk.

Oppert II 7940. Belonged to Venkatarama Dikshita of Sorakayur, Thanjavur Dist.

Trav. Uni. 2346 F. PL. Gr. 95 Grantha-s (with C.).

Trav. Uni. 2346 H. PL. Gr. 10 Grantha-s.

Trav. Uni. 3679 C. PL. Gr. 95 Grantha-s (with C.).

Trav. Uni. 5778 J. PL. Tel. 10 Grantha-s.

Trav. Uni. 5778 K. PL. Tel. 95 Grantha-s (with C.).

Triv. Cur. VII 1. Gr. 125 Grantha-s. Obtained from Seshu Ghanapathial, Vaikom.

– C.

Mysore (1898), p. 6 (no. 52). 5 fol. (97-101) (with text).

Mysore (1898), p. 6 (no. 57). 15 fol. (45-59) (with text).

Mysore I, p. 612.

Mysore ND II 3205 (P 977/ 4). PL. Na. 7 fol. (38-44). Extract no. 50.

Mysore ND II 3206 (P 4772/ 2). PL. Tel. 6 fol. Incomplete.

Mysore ND II 3207 (P 4772/ 4). PL. Tel. 6 fol.

Mysore ND II 3208 (P 9312/ 5). PL. Na. 7 fol. (93-99).

Oppert II 739. Belonged to Ghanapathi Shingaracharyar of Alasur, Madurantakam Taluk.

Taylor II 326.

Trav. Uni. 2346 F. PL. Gr. 95 Grantha-s (with text).

Trav. Uni. 3679 C. PL. Gr. 95 Grantha-s (with text).

Trav. Uni. 5778 K. Tel. 95 Grantha-s (with text).

[NCC II 284b]

180 UCCODARKĪ (उच्चोदर्की)

of Keśavācārya. A treatise in ten verses on the Udātta and Pracaya accents which are indicated by the movements of the fingers of the reciter.

Beginning:

नित्याभिनिहितक्षैप्रपूर्वोदात्तस्य संग्रहः ।
क्रियते हस्तविन्यासभेदोच्चारणसिद्धये ॥ १ ॥
यदेकस्मिन् पदे स्वारपूर्वोदात्तो न विद्यते ।
संहितालक्षणं तस्मादिदमित्यवगच्छत ॥ २ ॥
उदात्तप्रचयौ भिन्नौ स्थानवाक्स्थानभेदतः ।
अस्मिन् तावेव गोष्ठे ते राष्ट्रे लोके क्षये परः ॥ ३ ॥

End:

अस्येश्वरोन्नमासन् स्युर्वर्ष्माजो जामजा नहि ।
अस्माकमक्ष्योरस्मद् वा प्राणो ऽश्नात्यूर्जमश्विना ॥ ९ ॥
ज्योतिरन्नाद्यमन्वाग्मन् वै बृहस्पतये जया ।

स्वारपूर्वोच्चविज्ञार्थमुच्चोदर्कीत्युदीरितम् ॥ १० ॥

Adyar D I 747 (19 G 12 = 66413). PL. Tel. 2 fol. (5-6). = Adyar I, p. 48a.

Adyar D I 748 (23 E 25 = 69758). PL. Gr. 5 fol. (25-29). Incomplete.

Adyar D I 749 (29 K 20 = 73653). PL. Tel. 18 fol. (167-84) (with C.).

Baroda 6255. PL. Tel. 1 fol. (44). 12 Grantha-s. (Daśa-ślokī).

Baroda 6255(c). PL. Tel. 8 fol. (47-54). 120 Grantha-s (with C.). = CLB I, p. 34. (See remarks col.).

Hamburg StUB (cod.Palmbl. III 8/133) → Veda-lakṣaṇa (HB).

IO 4478 (Mackenzie II 81c). PL. Na. 1 fol. (no. 21).

MD 875. PL. Tel. 2 pp. (34ff.).

MD 876. PL. Tel. 9 pp. (28ff.) (with C.).

MD 877. PL. Gr. 10 pp. (17ff.) (with C.).

MD 14400. PL. Tel. 2 fol. (213-14).

MD 17436. PL. Gr. 2 pp. 11 Grantha-s.

MT 95(g). PL. Gr. 1 fol. (15). 3 verses of the C. at the end. Purchased in 1910-11 from Gopalaswami Ayyangar of Mannargudi.

MT 1964(m). PL. Tel. 4 fol. (106-09) with C. Laghuvṛtti. Presented in 1916-17 by Rayaprolu Ramabrahmangaru of Guruza, Gudivada Taluk, Krishna Dist.

MT 1964(n). PL. Tel. 1 fol. (no.109). Presented in 1916-17 by Rayaprolu Ramabrahmangaru of Guruza, Gudivada Taluk, Krishna Dist.

MT 2591(i). PL. Tel. 5 fol. (232-36) (with C.). Presented in 1917-18 by Vasireddi Chandramaulisvaraprasada Bahadur, Zamindar of Muktyala, Krishna Dist.

MT 2591(j). PL. Tel. 1 fol. (no.238). One additional stanza at the end. Presented in 1917-18 by Vasireddi Chandramaulisvaraprasada Bahadur, Zamindar of Muktyala, Krishna Dist.

Mysore ND II 3200 (P 997/14). PL. Na. 5 fol. (26-30). Extract no. 49.

Mysore ND II 3201 (P 4468/ 3). PL. Na. 1 fol. (12).

Mysore ND II 3202 (P 4772/ 1). PL. Tel. 6 fol.

Mysore ND II 3203 (P 4772/ 3). PL. Tel. 6 fol.

Mysore ND II 3311 (P 7074/ 1). PL. Tel. 1 fol. Extract no. 92. Title: Ecodarki (!).

Mysore ND II 3386 (P 4772/16). PL. Tel. 4 fol. Extract no. 148. Title: Jaṭāvallī. But begins as Uccodarkī.

Mysore ND II 3529 (P 144/ 1). PL. Tel. 3 Extract no. 177. Title: Daśaślokī of Vidyāmaṇi. Cf. the expression "vidvanmaṇīnām" in the introductory verse of the C. is read here as "vidyāmaṇi-" and taken as the author.

Mysore ND II 3530 (P 4521/ 5). PL. Kan. 1 fol. Title: Daśaślokī.

RASB II 489(I) (G 6175). 6 fol. (with C.). Col.: Hasta-svara-saṃgraha.

TCD 1-A. 10 Grantha-s. (Complete text is printed.)

Tirupati SVUORI (3516c). PL. Gr. 1 fol.

Tirupati SVUORI 835 (3280c). PL. Gr. Incomplete.

Tirupati SVUORI 836 (4378g). PL. Gr. 1 fol. (29).

Tirupati SVUORI 837 (1687). PL. Gr. (with C.).

Trav. Uni. T.628 A. = TCD 1-A

– C. anon.

RASB II 489(I) (G 6175). 6 fol. (with text).

– C.

IO 4479 (Mackenzie II 81f). PL. Na. 2 fol. (21-22).

MD 876. PL. Tel. 9 pp. (28ff.) (with text).

MD 877. PL. Gr. 10 pp. (17ff.) (with text).

MT 2591(i). PL. Tel. 5 fol. (232-36) (with text). Presented in 1917-18 by Vasireddi Chandramaulisvaraprasada Bahadur, Zamindar of Muktyala, Krishna Dist.

TCD 1-B. 8 pp. 95 Grantha-s.

Tirupati SVUORI 837 (1687). PL. Gr. (with text).

Trav. Uni. T.628 B. = TCD 1-B.

– C. Laghuvṛtti.

Beginning: (749; after a few verses of the text)

स्वरात् परो ऽनुदात्तस्य संग्रहो य ईरितः ।
नित्याभिनिहितक्षैप्रपूर्वोदात्तस्य संग्रहः ॥
सर्वान् देवान् गुरून्नत्वा लघुवृत्तिः प्रवक्ष्यते।
उच्चोदर्किदशश्लोक्या बालव्युत्पत्तिसिद्धये॥
श्रीकेशवार्यमार्याणां पादपङ्कजमञ्जसा।
विद्वन्मणीनां यज्जिह्वा कोशवेश्माय ते नमः ॥

टीका। नित्याभिनिहितक्षैप्र इति। अस्यायमर्थः -- नित्याभिनिहितक्षैप्रपूर्वोदत्तस्य संग्रह इति । अनेकदेशेषु आश्रयभेदाद् विप्रकीर्णानामेकत्र संगृह्य पठनं संग्रहः । तत्र नित्यलक्षणम् । यकारसहितो वकारसहितो वानुदात्तपूर्वो वा पूर्वरहितो वा अक्षरं यत्र स्वर्यते स नित्यः । यथा -- स धन्यस्त्वोताः (४·४·१४) । ततो बिल्वः । क्व तर्हि ऽभिनिहितलक्षणम् । अकारलोपः स्वर्यते साभिनिहितः । यथा -- सो ऽब्रवीत् । क्षैप्रलक्षणम्। उदात्तयोरिवर्णाकारयोः स्थाने यथाक्रमं यकारपकाराभावे सति यः स्वर्यते स क्षैप्रः ॥

End:

नेङ्ग्यांशः । वीर्यं वा अग्निः । पयस्या बृहस्पतये । चतुरक्षरा सत्यजया । इङ्ग्यांशपदेष्वेषूदात्तस्वारात् पराक्षरम्। उदात्तेष्वेतेषु पदेषु नित्यादिस्वाराक्षरमुदात्तं स्यात् । कथंभूतेषु । इङ्ग्यैकदेशेष्वित्यर्थः । न त्विङ्ग्यपदस्य । उदात्तप्रचयनिर्णयलघुवृत्तिः समाप्ता॥

Adyar D I 749 (29 K 20 = 73653). PL. Tel. 18 fol. (167-84) (with text). = Adyar I, p. 48a.

Baroda 6255(c). PL. Tel. 8 fol. (47-54). 120 Grantha-s. = CLB I, p. 34. (See remarks col.).

MD 878. Tel. 13 pp. (107ff.) (with text).

MT 1964(m). PL. Tel. 4 fol. (106-09) (with text). Presented in 1916-17 by Rayaprolu Ramabrahmangaru of Guruza, Gudivada Taluk, Krishna Dist.

MT 2591(k). PL. Tel. 13 fol. (238-50). A few additional verses at the end. Presented in 1917-18 by Vasireddi Chandramaulisvaraprasada Bahadur, Zamindar of Muktyala, Krishna Dist.

Mysore ND II 3531 (P 144/ 2). PL. Tel. 3 fol. Title: Daśaślokī-vivṛti.

Mysore ND II 3532 (P 4521/ 6). PL. Kan. 4 fol. (27-30). Title: Daśaślokī-vyākhyā. Extract no. 178.

[NCC II 284b]

181 UTTARA-ṚKKĀRIKĀ (**उत्तर-ऋक्कारिका**)

of the Jaiminīya Śākhā of the *Sāmaveda* in 75 Kārikā-s.

PUL II. App. p. 10 (no.140). PL. Gr. 7 fol. (5-11).

[NCC II 299b]

182 UTTARA-ṚKSVARITAMĀLĀ (**उत्तर-ऋक्स्वरितमाला**)

SV.

Beginning:

अथोत्तर-ऋक्स्वरितमाला प्रकाश्यते -- यथ नार्वाज्यं ताप्यूक्षम ल चामण्डरिश्वासानिधधुज्यद्रजन्दुनार।

End:

स्वाथाषक्तनाकैसनुमि । २ । यो विसुरी वेंन्तन्त त्र इधोर्णोंगैर्वयुः ॥ एकविंशः ॥ इत्युत्तर-ऋक्स्वरितमाला ॥

MT 4101(d). PL. Gr. 2 fol. (29-30). Presented in 1921-22 by Krishnasvami Ayyangar, Pulyur, Karur Taluk, Trichinapalli Dist.

[NCC II 299b]

183 UTTARA-ṚGUDĀTTAMĀLĀ (**उत्तर-ऋगुदात्तमाला**)

SV.

Beginning:

अथोत्तर-ऋगुदात्तमाला प्रकाश्यते -- उपास्मा एकम् । शङ्गवो दविद्युतानुदात्तम् । पवमानस्यैकम्। द्रमिन्द्र १। अग्न आयानुदात्तम्। आ नो मित्रानुदात्तम्।

End:

अमीषां द्वे अभिप्रेहि मामीषां कं का अनुदात्तम्। विरक्षो द्वे विरक्षो मौ योग मर्माणि तेऽनुदात्तं मृगोनैकं गोनही॥ एकविंशः ॥ इत्युत्तर-ऋगुदात्तमाला॥

MT 4101(c). PL. Gr. 5 fol. (25-29). Presented in 1921-22 by Krishnasvami Ayyangar, Pulyur, Karur Taluk, Trichinapalli Dist.

[NCC II 299b]

184 UTTARA-ṚGDHĀRIMĀLĀ (**उत्तर-ऋग्धारिमाला**)

SV.

Beginning:

उत्तर-ऋग्धारिणां दीर्घस्थानीयत्वादादौ धारिमाला प्रकाश्यते -- स्तै गायत नमा इ योदे पवङ्गजम। १४। द्युतत्याज्याङ्गत्वा आवान्तो म ... । १२। मानस्य ते कर्मवशन्तसमि हि गृहो सत्तिरङ्गिरो ऽग्ने। ९। ... इन्द्रसाधन्द्रगिर्वसानन्ति शूवृञ्चिदद्रिवो इरगेन्द्र। १७। प्रथमः ॥

End:

प्रयोरमणिणाच्छादयार्वं वस्ते कृणोमित्राभवताशीवो ऽन्वाहस्तं सलूपमामा । २५ । नगन्द्रविशन्ताम्र अभिशृणुयाम देवाश्येरंस्तु शेमहिदावारिष्टनेमि । १६ । एकविंशः ॥ इत्युत्तर-ऋग्धारिमाला।

MT 4101(b). PL. Gr. 9 fol. (16-24). Presented in 1921-22 by Krishnasvami Ayyangar, Pulyur, Karur Taluk, Trichinapalli Dist.

[NCC II 299b]

185 UTTARA-ṚGLAKṢAṆA (**उत्तर-ऋग्लक्षण**)

SV.

Beginning: (750)

अथोत्तर-ऋग्लक्षणम्। उलोकं धर्मवेदम्। दराशिनगम्। पैकादशकनम्। आनधिनयम्। आदित्यनलेः । आपङ्क्तिनेत्रनुम् इधेकाक्षि । उच्चा हस्तद्दष्टयुगम् । पुनिधिनभूतम् । प्रेयनबाणम्। अररेनयुगम्। कायत्परं नयनम्। तं रुद्रनवेदम्। तये सलिङ्गप्राणम्। स्वातिथिचन्द्रनेः ।

End:

हुजेयुगं लजम्। भिधवर्णगयम्। स्नोकरिबाणं भवेः । द्यशरन्नकले। यजकरं लयम्। रतवाह्निरोगम्। स्नोरधर्मरानम्। तायकं लोहमरम्। विसब्रह्मराकम्। मथयुगं रवम्। ते च लिङ्गारधम्। धीसचद्ररोमम्। एकोनविंशतिश्चतुर्थः ॥

Adyar D I 750 (33 D 12 = 75239). PL. Gr. 6 fol. (87-92). = Adyar I, p. 48b.

Hoshiarpur p. 50 (no.5948). PL. Gr. 24 fol. 1000 Grantha-s. Extract p. 407 (the beginning and end are different from the above).

[NCC II 299b]

186 UTTARA-GĀNA (**उत्तरगान**)

SV. On its relation to the *Ārṣeyakalpa* and *Puṣpa-sūtra,* see R. Simon, "Bemerkungen zum Ārṣeyakalpa und Puṣpa-sūtra", in : ZDMG. 63 (1909), pp. 730-38.

[NCC II 300b]

187 UTTARA-DĪRGHĪ (**उत्तरदीर्घी**)

Beginning: (751)

उपायवो विश्वायुरदब्धायो तिमायुधा वृद्धायुं शतायुः स्त्यायुः सर्वायुश्चि- त्रायुर्यज्ञायुधानि ...

End:

उपावर्त्स्यत्युपावेक्ष्यतो ऽप्रतीक्षं वीक्षिस्यते वीक्षमाणाय वीक्षिताय मृगाखर इत्येते उत्तरदीर्घिणः ॥

Adyar D I 902 → Pūrvottarobhaya-dīrghī.
Adyar D I 903 → Pūrvottarobhaya-dīrghī.
Adyar D I 904 → Pūrvottarobhaya-dīrghī.
Mysore I, p. 23. (Uttara-dīrghyādi).
Trav. Uni. 5778 E. PL. Tel. 20 Grantha-s. (Uttara-dīrghyādi).
Trav. Uni. 17346 E. PL. Tel. 10 Grantha-s.

Ptd.: in the edition of the Ṣaḍviṃśati-sūtra (in Grantha script), pp. 17-18.
Also printed in the Lakṣaṇa-traya (in Telugu script), pp. 41-42.

[NCC II 304b]

188 UTTHĀPANĀ (उत्थापना)

Name of an anonymous commentary on the *Ekākṣarī-baiṭh.* RASB II 257.

[NCC II 315b]

189 UDĀTTA-GAṆANA (उदात्तगणन)

Trav. Uni. 2364. PL. Gr. 6 fol. 125 Grantha-s → Ucca-svara-nirṇaya.

[NCC II 332a]

190 UDĀTTA-GĀNA (उदात्तगान)

Mysore ND II 3209 (P 4906/ 5). PL. Na. 1 fol. (108).
Mysore ND II 3210 (P 4906/12). PL. Na. 1 fol. (115).

191 UDĀTTA-PRACAYA-NIRṆAYA (उदात्तप्रचयनिर्णय)

Mysore ND II 3211 (P 4521/ 7). PL. Kan. 1 fol. (30).

192 UDĀTTA-PRACAYA-VṚTTI (उदात्तप्रचयवृत्ति)

Tirupati SVUORI 915 (4411b). PL. Gr.

193 UDĀTTA-SVARA-NIRṆAYA (उदात्तस्वरनिर्णय)

Title of the *Ucca-svara-nirṇaya* according to the commentary thereon. MD 874 → Ucca-svara-nirṇaya.

194 UDĀTTA-SVARA-NIRṆAYA (उदात्तस्वरनिर्णय)

of Sūri-bhaṭṭa Yajvan → Ucca-svara-nirṇaya.
Mysore Skt. Coll. p. 1 = D. No.4 (1536/1). PL. Gr. 10 fol.
Trav. Uni. 5479 A. PL. Tel. 155 Grantha-s.

[NCC II 332a]

195 UDĀTTĀDI-SVARA-PRAKARAṆA (**उदात्तादिस्वरप्रकरण**)
Mysore I, p. 24 → Ucca-svara-nirṇaya.

[NCC II 332a]

196 UDĀTTĀDI-SVARA-LAKṢAṆA (**उदात्तादिस्वरलक्षण**)
on the determination and notation of the accents, i.e. Udātta, etc. of the *Sāmaveda*.
Beginning: (751)

अग्न आयानुदात्तम्। नमस्ते द्वे। आदित्परो यदि -- अग्निं वो द्वेष्टुत्वमा -- शं यो र -- यज्ञा त्रीणि -- त्यावसोयो विश्वा -- त्वामित् -- एना षद्। आदित् दे -- तन्नरो -- व इन्द्रो -- राममाज -- नात्वंयंम -- रे सन्ति-देवो द्वेप्रयोरायंसमीदद्ध -- आ जुहोताष्टौ -- त्र इच्छिशोः -- न योमा -- मं स्तोमं -- द्राहीनः --

End:

इत्थं चतुर्दशशतमृचामाग्नेयपर्वणि।
शतानि त्रीण्यृचामैन्द्रं द्विपञ्चाशदृचो ऽधिकाः ॥
एकोनविंशतिशतं पावमान्य इतीरिताः ।
शतानि पञ्चाशीतिश्च पञ्च चाप्यखिला ऋचः ॥
इत्यारण्यकसामर्चि षद्पञ्चाशद् बहुश्रुताः ।
तृचे ऽस्मिन् शाक्करे तिस्रो द्विपदाः पञ्चकानि षद्॥
आग्नेयमाद्यं पर्वैन्द्रीपावमाने ततः परे।
त्रिपर्वा सामवेदस्य संहितैव विधीयते॥
आदिमध्यान्तवर्णानामुदात्तानां पदे पदे।
लक्षणं मूर्ध्नि बिन्दुः स्यात् तृचैकोदात्तवर्णकम्॥

उदात्तरनुदात्तस्य स्वरित । स्वरितसंज्ञायां स्वरितानुदात्तानामेकश्रुतिः । नोदात्तस्वरितपरस्य । उदात्तो ऽङ्गुष्ठोत्कर्षे प्रदृश्यः । अनुदात्तपरः तर्जनीमध्ययोगेन कम्प्यः । विरामयोर्द्वयाश्च एकश्रुतिः । स्वरितप्रकृतेस्तु प्रादेशिनीमध्यपार्श्वप्रदेशेन उदात्तस्वरितोदयः । तस्यादावर्धमुदात्तवत् । शेषमनुदात्तवत् । अनुदात्तो मध्यस्पर्शेन तत्पराद्यादयः । उक्तश्चिबकेन । तत्रोदात्तः । द्वाद्युदात्तम् । पूर्वे स्वरिते प्राकृते … स्वारप्रकृतिः ॥ इति लक्षणं समासम्॥

Adyar D I 751 (19 M 53 = 66821). PL. Gr. 9 fol. (1-3; 1-6). = Adyar I, p. 48b.

[NCC II 332a]

197 UDĀTTĀDI-SVARA-VICĀRA or VEDĀDHYAYANA-KRAMA
(**उदात्तादिस्वरविचार / वेदाध्ययनक्रम**)
IM 2509. 8 fol. Dated Śaka 1634. Title: Svara-vicāra. This is actually Saṃhitā-sūtra.

[NCC II 332a]

198 UDĀHARAṆA-MAṆḌITĀ (**उदाहरणमण्डिता**)
Name of the commentary of Viṣṇumitra on Pārṣada (-vṛtti ?) of Śaunaka.

[NCC II 334a]

199 UDIG -(D-)BHĀṢYA (उदिग(द्)भाष्य)

See col. of IO 4480 and MT 1964 (f). Napara-tapara-bhāṣya.

200 UDGĪTHA-SŪTRA (उद्गीथसूत्र)

This is found as part of Prastāva-sūtra or Pradhāna-sūtra.

Adyar D I 752 (26 L 3 = 71674). PL. Gr. 1 fol. (no. 13).

MT 641(c). PL. Gr. 1 fol. Purchased in 1912-13 through Seshasayi Ayyangar of Kottaiyur near Kumbakonam.

[NCC II 336a]

*UDDHAVA-BHAṬṬA (उद्धवभट्ट)

– Yajurveda-prātiśākhya (Veda-paṭhana-vidhi).

B I, p. 129, 2.

Udaipur.

[NCC II 339a]

201 UPANIDĀNA-SŪTRA (उपनिदानसूत्र)

of Kātyāyana. An Anukramaṇī of the metres of the *Sāmaveda;* in two Paṭala-s of 5 and 3 sections called chapters in the printed edition. Chs. 1-3 of general characters; chs. 4-5 Anukramaṇī of metres of the Pūrvārcika; ch. 6 metres of the Āraṇya-kāṇḍa; ch. 7 metres of the Uttarārcika; ch. 8 deals with the colours and deities of the various metres and describes the sources of the work in 4 verses.

Adyar D I 753 (33 E 7 = 75254). PL. Gr. 4 fol. (70-73). The last fol. (4b) at the end gives the contents of the codex which include 21 mainly Sāmavedic texts.

Adyar D I 754 (35 C 28 = PM 102). 6 fol. 8 sections numbered consecutively.

Adyar D I 755 (35 C 72 = PM 103). 8 fol. Dated V.S. 1681.

Adyar D I 756 (35 C 131 = PM 104). 6 fol. Dated V.S. 1923.

IM 1973. 9 fol. Title on the cover page : Gārgya-Chandas.

IM 1974. 9 fol. Title on the cover page : Gārgya-Chandas.

SB p. 29 (no.70). 8 fol. 144 Grantha-s. Dated V.S. 1675. = SBD 3928.

SBD 3927. 7 fol. Dated V.S. 1714.

SBD 3928. 8 fol. Dated V.S. 1675.

Ptd.: ed. with introduction by Mangal Deva Shastri. – Benares, 1931. (Princess of Wales Sarasvati Bhavan Texts 37). [Adyar (H080 SBT 37)]

[NCC II 360b]

*UPAMANYU Agnihotrin (उपमन्यु अग्निहोत्रिन्)

Title of Malla-śarman, author of the Mallaśarma-śikṣā also known as the *Hasta-svara-prakriyā.*

RASB II 1520 ("written in A.D. 1325 / V.S. 1381" ? in the catalogue. But see under Malla-śarma-śikṣā).

[NCC II 369a]

202 UPALEKHA(-SŪTRA) (उपलेख-सूत्र)

Variously ascribed to Śaunaka, Kātyāyana or Bhāradvāja. 136 Sūtra-s, divided into eight Varga-s (ca. 150 Sūtra-s, nine Varga-s in the edition of Pertsch), on the Krama-pāṭha of the *Ṛgveda.*

Beginning:

अकारादयो द्वादश स्वराः । शिष्टं व्यञ्जनम् । ककारादयः पञ्च वर्गाः स्पर्शाः । यकारादयश्चतस्रो ऽन्तस्थाः । शकारादयो ऽष्टा ऊष्माणः । प्रथमद्वितीया वर्गानाम् ऊष्माणश्च हकारवर्जमघोषवन्तः । शिष्टं घोषवत्। ह्रस्वमेकमात्रम्। दीर्घं द्विमात्रम्। प्लुतं त्रिमात्रम्। व्यञ्जनमर्धमात्रम्। स्वरभक्तिश्चाक्रमे। क्रमे त्वर्धोना।

End:

समयान्ते द्वैपदमवस्येन्न च तं समयं क्रामयेत्। संधाय समयं परे द्वैपदे ऽवस्येत्। एकं समयमध्ये चेदतिक्रम्य परेण तु। त्र्यम्बकं भद्रं नः प्रजापते ऋतं च सत्यं चेत्यपदक्रमम्।

क्रममिममुपयान्ति ये विशेषाः पदपाठात् समयेन संहिताभ्यः ।
लिखति परिगणय्य शौनकाद्यैः कथितांस्तानुपलेखशास्त्रमेतत्॥

(This verse, with corrupt readings, is found only in a few Mss.).

Adyar D I 765 (20 K 38 = 67500). PL. Tel. 3 fol. (3-5). (Described as Ṛgveda-lakṣaṇa)
Alwar 19.
Baroda 542. PL. Gr. 19 fol. 400 Grantha-s (with C.). = CLB I, p. 23 (a. Bharadvāja).
Baroda 23568. 5 fol. 80 Grantha-s. Dated V.S. 1737. (Upalekha-pariśiṣṭa).
BHU B 1963 (D 2A/712). 8 fol. Dated V.S. 1558.
BORI 13 of 1879-80. 12 fol. 110 Grantha-s. Dated V.S. 1740.
BORI 69 of 1884-87. 17 fol. (with Kannada explanations).
Burnell 2a (with C.).
Deccan College 932. 6 fol. (not noted in the catalogue).
IM 2520. 5 fol. (2-6). Dated V.S. 1577. Title: Leṣa(-kha)-grantha ?
IM 2599. 4 fol.
IM 4874. 4 fol. Incomplete. Breaks off in the 6th Varga.
IM 4979. 3 fol. (2-4). Incomplete. Dated V.S. 1756.
L 3207. 6 fol. 127 Grantha-s. Dated V.S. 1863.
Mysore I, p. 615 (entered under Śrauta).
Mysore ND II 3213 (P 4635/ 1). PL. Na. 9 fol. (with Kannada Ṭīkā). Extract no. 52.
Mysore ND II 3214 (P 4906/53). PL. Na. 3 fol. (131-33).
Mysore ND II 3215 (P 6694). PL. Na. 4 fol.
Mysore ND II 3216 (C 475/ 1). 4 fol. (Āśvalāyana is given as the author in the catalogue; but his name is not found in the Ms.).
Mysore ND II 3217 (C 3805/ 1). 3 fol.
Mysore ND II 3218 (C 2537/12). 7 fol. Extract no. 53.
P 4.
Peters. II, p. 169 (no.14). 6 fol.
PUL I, p. 19 (no.29). 18 fol. 350 Grantha-s (a. Śaunaka; with C.).
RASB II 262 (G 2129). 6 fol. 110 Grantha-s. Dated V.S. 1863.
RASB II 263 (G 1067). 5 fol. 110 Grantha-s. Dated V.S. 1614.
RASB II 264 (G 7942). 13 fol. (1 and 3 missing).
SB p. 21 (no.83). 7 fol. 70 Grantha-s. = SBD 2013.
SBD 2013. 7 fol. Dated V.S. 1825.

SBD 3962. 12 fol. (with C.). Dated V.S. 1755.
SBD 4145. 18 fol. (with C.).
SBD 4233. 7 fol. Dated V.S. 1966. Catalogued as Upalekha-grantha, with the remark : Sāmavedīya. But the text is the same as the above.
SBD 4338. 2 fol. Dated V.S. 1767.
SBD 47572. 4 fol.
SBD 47895. 6 fol. Incomplete. Dated V.S. 1871.
SBD 55287. 5 fol. Dated V.S. 1604.
SBD 55417. 5 fol.
Skt. Coll. Ben. 1909, p. 6 (no.1799) (with C.). Incomplete.
TD 1724. 8 fol. 100 Grantha-s.
TD 1725. 4 fol. (27-32; fol. 28 missing). 80 Grantha-s.
TD 1726. 26 fol. 300 Grantha-s (with C.).
VSM I 484 (no.5440). 5 fol. (a. Bhāradvāja). Śaka 1755. Copied by Ghaḻasāśī Ananta Mahādeva.
VSM I 485 (no.5441). 5 fol. (a. Bhāradvāja). Śaka 1755. Copied by Ghaḻasāśī Ananta Mahādeva.
Wai I 343. 14 fol. (with Bhāṣya). Dated Śaka 1702.
Wai I 344. 14 fol. (with Bhāṣya). Dated Śaka 1751.
Weber 38 (Chambers 666). 8 fol.
Weber 39 (Chambers 692). 7 fol. Dated V.S. 1709. Copied by Rāmacandra in Varanasi (Upalekha-pariśiṣṭa on the title page).
Weber 40 (Chambers 745). 5 fol. Dated V.S. 1513.

Ptd.:

Ed. by Guil. Pertsch, *Upalekha – de Kramapāṭha libellus. Textum sanscriticum recensuit ...*, with an introduction, Latin translation, notes and index. – Berolini (Berlin) : Dümmler, 1854. xxiii, 63 pp. [BORI (34568); NL (180 Jc 85 22); UBTÜ (Ci XII 73); Emeneau (56, 57); SAI (ind 54 B 585/1776); SKGI (Rf IX 180)]

Ed. by Satyavrata Samasrami with commemtary: *Upalekhasūtram – Ṛgvedasya – Śaunakācārya-śiṣyeṇa kenacin mahāmuninā proktam, sabhāṣyam)*, in the Sanskrit journal *Uṣā*. – Calcutta : Satya Press, 1895, vol. II, pt. 12. 2, 32 pp. [Emeneau (58)]

Ed. by K. S. Venkatarama Sastri, in : *Ṛgvedīyaṃ Śamāna-lakṣaṇam Upalekha-sūtraṃ ca.* – Srirangam : Sri Vani Vilas Press, 1967. 11, 2, 72 pp. [Adyar (H 215.4 Ven SA); SAI (87/770*)]

Also ed. by Kashinatha Vasudeva Abhyankar, with explanatioin in English, in the *Veda-padapāṭha-carcā*. – Poona : BORI, 1974. – (Post-Graduate and Research Department Series no. 10). Reprint from the *Annals of the Bhandarkar Oriental Research Institute*, vol. 54 (1973), pp. 9-76. Here the text is ascribed to Bhāradvāja-Bṛhaspati. This edition is based on three Mss, namely
1) of Bhalachandra Bhatta Karambelkar of Poona (with Bhāṣya),
2) of Marutibowa Bapat of Satara (also with Bhāṣya), and
3) from the Ghalashasi (Vighasāśi) family of Karad, now in Vaidika Samshodhana Mandala, Poona (the printed edition by Venkatarama Shastri has also been used).

– C. Most probably the same as the next.

B I, p. 198 (no.39). 359 Grantha-s. Dated V.S. 1679 (ascribed to Śaunaka).

Baroda 542. PL. Gr. 19 fol. 400 Grantha-s (with text). = CLB I, p. 23.

BORI 17 of 1871-72. 21 fol. (ascribed to Kātyāyana only in the title slip; not found in the Ms.). Copied in Kāśī in V.S. 1588.

BORI 69 of 1884-87. 17 fol. (7 chs. with short explanations in Kannada). In the left margin on fol. 1b: Rāmakṛṣṇaḥ and on each fol. Rāma in the right margin. Col.: Kholakāru Rāmakṛṣṇaḥ.

GJKSV 29666. 16 fol. (4-19). Incomplete. Dated V.S. 1886.

Gough p. 85 (no.17: Upalekha-vṛtti). 20 pp. Dated V.S. 1598.

IM 4989. 10 fol. (3-12). Incomplete. Dated V.S. 1602. Different from others. Title: Upalekha-vṛtti.

Mysore I, p. 24 (3 Mss.).

Mysore ND II 3219 (A 264/ 4). Tel. 11 fol. (135-45).

Mysore ND II 3220 (C 475/ 2). 8 fol. (5-12).

Mysore ND II 3221 (P 4635/ 2). PL. Na. 9 fol. (in Kannada ?).

SBD 3962. 12 fol. (with text). Dated V.S. 1755.

SBD 4145. 18 fol. (with text).

SBD 4373. 10 fol. (Sāmaveda-pariśiṣṭa ?).

Tirupati SVUORI 942 (427). PL. Na.

Wai I 343. 14 fol. (with text). Dated Śaka 1702.

Wai I 344. 14 fol. (with text). Dated Śaka 1751.

– C. Bhāṣya.

Beginning:

अकारादयो द्वादश स्वरा इति । अकार आदिः प्रथमो येषां ते अकारादयः (इति बहुव्रीहिः) । द्वौ च दश चेति द्वन्द्वः । स्वरा इति संज्ञा अभिधीयते । ननु यथा चित्रगुमानयेत्युक्ते विशेषणीभूतानां गवामानयने संबन्धो नास्ति एवमकारादयः स्वरा इत्युक्ते विशेषणीभूतस्याकारस्य स्वरसंज्ञा न प्राप्नोतीति चोद्यम् । नैतदस्ति । यथा लम्बकर्णमानयेत्युक्ते विशेषणीभूतयोरपि कर्णयोरानयने संबन्धः (अध्यवसीयते) तथेहापि विशेषणभूतस्याकारस्य स्वरसंज्ञा भवति । एवं प्रतिसूत्रं वेदितव्यम् । इदानीं सूत्रार्थः संक्षिप्यते। अकारादयो द्वादशसंख्येया वर्णाः स्वरसंज्ञका भवन्ति। के पुनस्ते। उच्यन्ते।

End:

इदानीं क्रमं तस्योक्तप्रवृत्या काच्छम् (?) आह। क्रममिममुमयाभिगीतमुप समीपे सदृशो विशेषाः सन्निहिता इत्यर्थः । ते लेख्यन्ते गण्यन्ते यस्मिन् । ऋतालेखयेति गण्यति कृत्स्नशो निरूपयति। इत्युपलेखभाष्ये ऽष्टमो वर्गः । इत्युपलेखशास्त्रम्। तथा च राज्ञा(?) विशेषाः स्वरादयः पूर्वमुक्ताः । ततस्त्रिक्रमचतुष्क्रमे विशेषाः । ततः एकपदाद्विपदाद्याः । ततः परिगृह्याद्याः । ततः षत्वणत्वाद्याः । ततो विसर्गान्तपदानां विशेषाः । ततः

पदान्तस्येति आद्यन्तयोः संधिविशेषाः । ततः स्वरविधयः । ततः कम्पविशेषाः । इत्येवं सदृशाः सदृशविधयः । तस्मादिदमुपलेखशास्त्रमिति । शास्त्रान्ते वृद्धाचार्यं नमस्करोति । नमः शौनकाय नमः शौनकाय ॥

B I, p. 198 (no.4). 15 fol. (a. Bharadvājācārya) (Pañjikā ?).

B I, p. 198 (no.5). 38 fol. (a. Bharadvājācārya).

Bombay Uni. Acc. no. 3176. 16 fol. Dated Śaka 1680.

Bombay Uni. (BMC 161 15). 11 fol. Dated Śaka 1723. Copied by Nārāyaṇa, son of Dinakarapādhye Goḻavalakara.

Cabaton I 546.

IM 2050. Dated Śaka 1542. (The text is attributed to Bharadvāja : bharadvājākhyo granthakṛd ācāryaḥ lakṣaṇaṃ saṃpradāyena jñeyam iti darśayan vṛddhācāryaṃ namaskaroti).

L 3236. 19 fol. 294 Grantha-s. Dated V.S. 1701.

RASB II 265 (G 1068). 9 fol. 230 Grantha-s. Dated V.S. 1680.

RASB II 266 (G 2140). 3-19 fol. Dated V.S. 1701.

Skt. Coll. Ben. 1906. p. 6 (no.1799).

TD 1726. 26 fol. 300 Grantha-s.

Weber 41 (Chambers 587). 19 fol. Dated V.S. 1669.

Weber 42 (Chambers 785b). 25 fol. (3-27) (ascribed to Bharadvāja). Dated V.S. 1669. Copied in Kāśī by Lakṣmīdhara, son of Govardhana.

Ptd.: in the Sanskrit journal *Uṣā* and in Srirangam edition, together with text. See above.

– C. Upalekha-ṭīkā.

Ānandāśrama 7791. 12 fol. with Kannada gloss.

– C. Upalekha-bhāṣya.

Beginning:

अकारादयो द्वादश स्वराः । अकार आदिर्येषां वर्णानां ते अकारादयः द्वादश वर्णाः स्वरसंज्ञा वेदितव्याः । के ते । अ आ इ ई उ ऊ ऋ ॠ ए ऐ ओ औ इति । तत्र चतुर्दश स्वरा इति केचित् । तेषाम् ऌ ॡ इति । षोडश स्वरा इत्येषाम् अं अः ॥

End:

कम्पस्य कालमाह । शौनकादय इति । उदात्तो यत्र न दृश्यते कम्पं तत्र न कुर्वन्ति । कम्पदो नीचस्वरितमित्यस्य सामान्यस्यापवादः । न चोदात्तेन संयुतम् । अथ ...

Ānandāśrama 5852. 26 fol. The different sections are called "adhikāra-s".

[NCC II 371ab]

203 UBHAYA-DĪRGHĪ (उभयदीर्घी)

The following is the complete text.

पराहदक्षिणावृतो दक्षिणावृतं यथायतनं यथायतनादित्येत उभयदीर्घिणः ॥

Adyar D I 902 → Pūrvottarobhaya-dīrghī.
Adyar D I 903 → Pūrvottarobhaya-dīrghī.
Adyar D I 983 → Veda-lakṣaṇa (A 1).
Adyar D I 984 → Veda-lakṣaṇa (A 2).
Adyar D I 986 → Veda-lakṣaṇa (A 4).
Baroda 10032(a). PL. Gr. 1 fol. 14 Grantha-s.
Trav. Uni. 16408 J. PL. Mal. 2 Grantha-s.

Ptd.: in the edition of Ṣaḍviṃśati-sūtra (in Grantha script), p. 18.
Also printed in Lakṣaṇa-traya (in Telugu script), p. 42.

→ Ubhaya-pūrvottara-dīrghī and Pūrvottarobhaya-dīrghī.

[NCC II 389a]

204 UBHAYA-PŪRVOTTARA-DĪRGHĪ (उभयपूर्वोत्तरदीर्घी)

→ Ubhaya-dīrghī and Pūrvottarobhaya-dīrghī, MD 926-27.
Mysore I, p. 24 (2 Mss.).
Mysore ND II 3222 (P 2265/28). PL. Gr. 2 fol. (139-40). Extract no. 55. (Ubhaya-dīrgha-padam).

[NCC II 389a]

205 UBHAYA-HRASVĪ (उभयह्रस्वी)

The following passage is the complete text.

उक्षान्नायोपावहरन्नुपावहरेदनवानं पराधर्येत्येते उभयह्रस्विणः ॥

MT 485(j). PL. Tel. 1 fol. (66a). Presented in 1910-11 by C. Visvanatha Shastrigal of Viziyanagaram.

Ptd.: in the edition of the Ṣaḍviṃśati-sūtra (in Grantha script), p. 18.
Also printed in the Lakṣaṇa-traya (in Telugu script), p. 42.

*UVAṬA or UVVAṬA or ŪVAṬA or ŪAṬA (उवट / उव्वट / ऊवट / ऊअट)
son of Vajraṭa; of Ānandapura; ca. 12th century A.D. , wrote under king Bhoja. On Uvaṭa and Mahīdhara, see Lakshman Sarup, *Indian Linguistics*, Grierson Commemoration Volume, Lahore, 1933.

– Ṛgveda-prātiśākhya-vyākhyā.

Ptd.: See below under the Cs. on the *Ṛgveda-prātiśākhya*. The designation "Pārṣada-vṛtti" with which name it is also printed is due to confusion with Viṣṇumitra's commentary. Mangal Deva Shastri (Oxford edition, 1922, introduction) discusses the relation between the *Ṛgveda-prātiśākhya-vyākhyā* of Uvaṭa and *Pārṣada-vṛtti* of Viṣṇumitra which correspond in certain portions and differ in others. The commentary on the first ten introductory verses is presumed as spurious.

– Vājasaneyi-prātiśākhya-bhāṣya.

Ptd.: Ben. S. S. 4, 1888. – Madras University Sanskrit Series 5, 1934.

– Sarvānukrama-bhāṣya. BORI D I i.38. (= Viśrāmabagh 9).

[NCC II 399ab]

206 ŪHA-KĀRIKĀ (ऊहकारिका)

The beginning is the same as that of the *Ūhasāma-pariganana.*

Mysore ND II 3223 (P 1970/ 9). PL. Na. 8 fol. (87-96). Extract no. 56. = Sāmakārikā.

207 ŪHA-CCHALĀKṢARA (ऊहच्छलाक्षर)

L 1415. 18 fol. 238 Grantha-s.

MD 14095. PL. Gr. 12 pp. Incomplete. The beginning is the same as in Adyar 802.

PUL I, p. 2 (no.23). 15 fol.

RASB II 1317 (G 259) = L 1415.

SBD 4188. 12 fol.

208 ŪHA-DĪPA (ऊहदीप)

of Nāga-bhaṭṭa or Nāgappa.

Mysore I, p. 24.

Mysore ND II 3224 (P 2485/ 5). PL. Na. 75 fol. (125-99). Extract no.57.

– C.

Mysore I, p. 612.

Mysore ND II 3225 (P 4768). PL. Na. 240 fol. Extract no. 58.

209 ŪHA-PRAKĀŚIKĀ (ऊहप्रकाशिका)

Tirupati SVUORI 8160 (6850). 64 pp. A transcript of a Ms. belonging to Dakshinamurti Shastrigal of Kanchipuram, copied in November 1941.

210 ŪHA-PRADĪPIKĀ (ऊहप्रदीपिका)

Tirupati SVUORI 8161 (6703). PL. Gr.

211 ŪHA-LAKṢAṆA-KĀRIKĀ (ऊहलक्षणकारिका)

PUL I, p. 10 (no.142). PL. Gr. 11 fol. 100 Grantha-s.

212 ŪHASĀMA-PARIGAṆANA or ĀMAHĪYĀDI-SĀMA-PARIGAṆANA
(ऊहसामपरिगणन / आमहीयादिसामपरिगणन)

Beginning: (757)

ऊहसामानि षट्त्रिंशच्छतानि नव संख्यया।
तेषु द्वे द्वे भवन्त्याश्वनार्मेधाक्षारनानदम्॥
वैतहव्योत्तरकौञ्चसोमसामाद्यदंष्ट्रकम्।
कक्षमौक्षप्लवक्रोशशौक्तव्यावनशैशवम्॥
पौरुमद्गोभयस्तोभगौतमे वा शशाकले।
वसिष्ठस्य प्रियं वात्सप्रोत्तरंत्रैतवाजजित्॥
सै .... वैखानसाजिगम्।

स्वः पृष्ठाङ्गरसं त्रियन्तं त्वाष्टी सामैध्मवाहके ॥

End:

जसेष्वाथमवैराजपिबा सोम तवा पुरः ।
अरिष्टे तु सुता सोम पवित्रं पार्थरश्मके ॥
स्वादोरिन्द्रामदाभान्ते स पुरो मूर्धाथ सप्तहे ।
त्वामित्तृचे पुनैकस्यां जम्भे तोषि पुरोजिति ॥
अष्टे सेतुजसा धर्ता सिमा उष्वाज सास्वरे ।
प्रथमे तु सुता प्रत्य द्वितीये पितृचेयेके ॥
पूषा मत्स्या चतुर्थे तु प्रसुयज्जायथेति च ।
पुनास्वेकाधिका षष्टिः साम्नां षष्टि पुरो तृचे ॥
ऊहसामानि समाप्तम् ॥

Adyar D I 757 (21 C 24 = 67836). PL. Gr. 5 fol. (38ff.). = Adyar I, p. 11a.
Adyar D I 758 (25 C 11 = 70788). PL. Gr. 5 fol. = Adyar I, p. 11a.
Adyar D I 759 (34 G 4 = 75668). PL. Gr. 6 fol. (10ff.). = Adyar I, p. 49a.
Mysore ND II 3223 (P 1970/ 9). PL. Na. 8 fol. (87-96). Extract no. 56. = Sāmakārikā
See Āmahīyādi-sāma-pariganana, NCC II 146b.

[NCC III 4b]

213 ṚKĀRA-VYAKTI-LAKṢAṆA (ऋकारव्यक्तिलक्षण)

Enumeration of verses of the *Ṛgveda,* in which a word with an initial "ṛ" is not elided with the previous word. Described under Rakāra-vyakti-lakṣaṇa in the catalogue.
Mysore ND II 3705 (P 4906/20). PL. Na. 1 fol. (117). Extract no. 255.

214 ṚKCHANDONUKRAMAṆĪ (ऋक्छन्दोनुक्रमणी)

of Śaunaka.
Trav. Uni. 4847. 4925 → Ṛgveda-chandonukramaṇī, Ṛṣicchandonukramaṇī, and Chandonukramaṇī.

[III.4b]

215 ṚKCHANDO-BHEDA (ऋक्छन्दोभेद)

MD 14778. PL. Na. 2 fol. (75a-76a) (with illustrations; written together with the *Sarvānukramaṇikā).*

[NCC III 5a]

216 ṚKCHALĀKṢARA (ऋक्छलाक्षर)

Trav. Uni. 18661 B. PL. Gr. 1250 Grantha-s.

217 ṚKTANTRA or ṚKTANTRA-VYĀKARAṆA or CHANDOGA-VYĀKARAṆA (ऋक्तन्त्र / ऋक्तन्त्रव्याकरण / छन्दोगव्याकरण)

Ascribed to Śākaṭāyana and by a few others to Audavraji. A Prātiśākhya of *Sāmaveda* (Kauthuma-Śākhā), in five Prapāṭhaka-s. There is a Bhāṣya for the second Prapāṭhaka onwards. For the first Prapāṭhaka Mss. give only the Sūtra-s.

Beginning:

अथ वाचो वृत्तिं व्याख्यास्यामः । वायुं प्रकृतिमाचार्याः । वायुर्मूर्च्छञ् छ्वासो भवति । श्वासो नाद इति शाकटायनः । वायुरयमस्मिन् काये मूर्छत्यटतीत्येषो ऽर्थः । स खलु खविशेषं प्रतिपन्नः कण्ठं प्रतिपन्नः श्वसितिर्भवति। स श्वसितिः शिरःप्रतिपन्न आकाशम्।

End:

उद आद्ये। क्षाज्जागते। सन्ध्यः । दन्त्ये स्पर्शे। द्विवैति परे। पाद् दन्त्यः । ११। सप्तमो दशकः । इति पञ्चमः प्रपाठकः । स्वरो ऽनन्त्यः
(*Sāma-tantra*, I 1.1) ||

Adyar D I 760 (33 E 12 = 75259). PL. Gr. 5 fol. = Adyar I, p. 48b. Ms. C. of Suryakanta's edition.

Alwar 285.

Baroda 9805(c). PL. Gr. 6 fol. 70 Grantha-s. = CLB I, p. 23.

Baroda 12912(a). 4 fol. 70 Grantha-s. = CLB I, p. 24. Dated V.S. 1682. Ms. A. of Suryakanta's edition.

Baroda 12917. 19 fol. 500 Grantha-s (with C.). = CLB I, p. 24. Ms. B. of Suryakanta's edition.

BBRAS 483 (B D 182). 14 fol.

BC. 437.

Bhau Daji 62.

Bikaner 620. 13 fol.

BISM p. 315 (22/982). Dated Śaka 1681.

BORI 10 of 1879-80. = BORI D II i.2. 14 fol.

BORI 92 of 1879-80. = BORI D II i.1. 7 fol. 50 Grantha-s. Dated V.S. 1723.

GJKSV 43778. 5 fol.

Gough p. 64 (no.10). 14 fol. 78 Grantha-s.

IM 2592. 8 fol. Title: Chandoga-vyākaraṇa-sūtra. Dated V.S. 1677.

Hpr. III 43. 5 fol. 105 Grantha-s. Col.: Chandoga-vyākaraṇa-sūtra.

Mad. Uni. R. A. S. 173(a).

Max Müller Mem. XVI. 27 fol. Dated ca. A.D. 1908.

Mysore I, p. 24.

Mysore ND II 3226 (A 404). Gr. 20 fol. Extract no. 59.

Oxf. CS d.80(6). 5 fol. Dated A.D. 1909. Col.: Chandoga-vyākaraṇa-sūtra.

Oxf. II 855(12) (Ms. Wilson 375). 4 fol. Dated A.D. 1582. = Oxf. 378a (no.375).

P 6.

Peters. II, p. 180 (no.56). 3 fol.

SB p. 9 (no.175). 21 fol. 335 Grantha-s. (1-4 Prapāṭhaka-s). Dated V.S. 1693.

SBD 2111a. 5 fol. (1-5). Dated V.S. 1768. The first Prapāṭhaka is called Brahma-rāśi and written separately.

SBD 47622. 21 fol.

Trav. Uni. 1733 A. 3 fol. 55 Grantha-s.

Trav. Uni. 2952 A. PL. Gr. 325 Grantha-s (with C.).

Trav. Uni. 5980 A. PL. Gr. 600 Grantha-s (with C.).

Trav. Uni. 11824 B. PL. Gr. 250 Grantha-s (with C.).
Trav. Uni. 11824 C. PL. Gr. ~~600~~ Grantha-s (with C.).

Ptd.:

1) Ed. by Arthur Coke Burnell, *A Prātiśākhya of the Sāmaveda* with an introduction, translation of the Sūtra-s, and indexes, part 1 (contains introduction and text in Roman script. Apparently part 2 did not appear). – Mangalore : Basel Mission Press, 1879. 1, lviii, 84 pp. [NL (180 Jd 87 5); BM : Ptd. Bks. Cat. 1876-92. 458 (14090.b.18); Emeneau (368)]
2) Ed. by Krishnasvami Srauti in the edition of the *Veyagāna* (in Grantha script). – Tiruvadi : Jyotirvilasa Press, 1889. [IO : Ptd. Bks. Cat. 1957, p. 2969 (16 D 39)]
3) Ed. by Suryakanta, with Introduction, Appendices, Exhaustive Notes and a Commentary called *Ṛktantra-vivṛti* (13 pp.) and *Sāmaveda-sarvānukramaṇi* (8 pp.). – Lahore : Meharchand Lachhmandas, 1933. viii, 3, vi, 101, 61, 15, 69, 13, 8 pp. [Adyar (H080 MCL 3); BORI (7382); NL (180 Jb 93 73); Emeneau (369)]

Reprinted : Delhi : Meharchand Lachhmandas, 1970. [BORI (24781; 26774); SAI (ind 74 B 554)]

Also printed with the Vivaraṇa and *Ṛktantra-vivṛti* in the *Sāmaprātiśākhya-saṃgraha*, part II, pp. 22-96.

– C. Bhāṣya.
Trav. Uni. 5980 A. PL. Gr. 600 Grantha-s (with text).
Trav. Uni. 11824 C.

– C. Vivṛti. Only a fragmentary portion, divided into three Prapāṭhaka-s.

Beginning:

अथ गायत्रगानप्रकारो निरूप्यते । यथासावित्रीगेयं यत्रागीतमिति देवताध्यायब्राह्मणेन यत्र गायत्रं न गीतं यत्र यत्र वा गायत्रं गेयं तत्र तत्र सावित्री तत् सवितुर्वरेण्यमित्यस्यां येन प्रकारेण गीयते गायत्रं तत् सावित्रीगानप्रकारमनतिक्रम्य गेयम् ॥

End:

एकोदात्तात् परस्वारप्रचयश्चोच्चवद् भवेत् ।
सर्वे ऽवशिष्टाः स्वरिताः स्वर्यन्ते सामशाखिनाम् ॥

इति ··· ऋक्तन्त्रकारादिवचनस्य सर्वे ऽपि स्वरिता आद्यार्धमात्रा एवोदात्ता भवन्तीत्यर्थ एव विवेकः ॥

Adyar D I 761 (26 G 34 = 71518). PL. Gr. 12 fol. = Adyar I, p. 48b.
Baroda 12917. 19 fol. 500 Grantha-s. = CLB I, p. 24.
IO 4323 (Burnell 437a). Gr. 16 fol. the text is cited in extenso. Written ca. A.D. 1875.
Mysore ND II 3333 (P 4591/ 1). PL. Na. 13 fol. Title: Gāyatra-gāna-lakṣaṇa. Extract no. 109.
Trav. Uni. 11824 B. PL. Gr. 250 Grantha-s (with text).

Trav. Uni. 2952 A. PL. Gr. 325 Grantha-s (with Text).

Ptd.: See the editions of the text above; IO notes that its Ms. differs partly; for Suryakanta's edition Adyar Ms. has also been used.

[NCC III 5a]

218 ṚKTANTRA-PARIBHĀṢĀ-ŚEṢA (ऋक्तन्त्रपरिभाषाशेष)

Ed. by Suryakanta, at the beginning of his edition of the *Laghu-ṛktantra-saṃgraha*. – Lahore, 1940. Based on a single Ms. in the Chandra Shumsher Collection, Bodleian Library, Oxford.

[NCC III 5a]

219 ṚKTANTRA-PARIŚIṢṬA (ऋक्तन्त्रपरिशिष्ट)
The Avagraha portion of the *Ṛktantra*. See Avagraha-pariśiṣṭa.

Ptd.: Ed. Suryakanta, *Woolner Commemoration Volume*. – Lahore, 1940, at the end, pp. 321-28.

[NCC III 5a]

220 ṚKTANTRA-SAṂGRAHA (ऋक्तन्त्रसंग्रह)
Adyar I, p. 48b → Laghu-ṛktantra-saṃgraha, Adyar D I 959.

[NCC III 5b]

221 ṚKPADA-CCHEDA (ऋक्पदच्छेद)
Trav. Uni. 15806 C. PL. Mal. 250 Grantha-s (similar to *Ṛgveda-prātiśākhya-pariśiṣṭa*; Whish 78).

222 ṚKPĀṬHA-DŪṢAṆODDHĀRA (ऋक्पाठदूषणोद्धार)
of Bālakṛṣṇa Nārāyaṇa Sāmaka. A tract on a few objections in the tradtional practice of the recitation of the *Ṛgveda*. Includes following topics: para-savarṇa, dvitva, kṣakāra-jñakāroccāraṇa, avasāne anusvāroccāraṇa and anusvāra vicāra.

Beginning:

विश्वाद्यं निगमैर्वेद्यं प्रणिपत्य हरिं परम्।
ऋक्पाठदूषणोद्धारं करिष्यामि यथामति ॥

यत् तु केचन ऋक्संहितापाठं चिरंतनशास्त्रसंमतमपि दूषणाभासैर्दूषयन्तः परसवर्णलब्धङकारादीनां स्पष्टमुच्चारणमाहुस्तदयुक्तम् ॥ ननु पञ्च अङ्गुलम् इत्यादावनुस्वारस्य ययीति पाणिनीयः परसवर्णः । यं कुमारवनं अहं च त्वं चेत्यादौ विस्थाने स्पर्शे उदये मकारः सर्वेषामेवोदयस्योत्तमं स्वमिति ऋक्प्रातिशाख्यचतुर्थपटलोक्तश्च भवति ॥

End:

तत् सिद्धमवसानगतह्रस्वस्यैकमात्राधिककालेनोच्चारणम् ॥
अहं पञ्चभिरेवात्र दूषणैरुद्धृतैर्ऋचि ।
स्थालीपुलाकन्यायेन कृत्स्नं जानन्ति पण्डिताः ॥

सदसद् वेह विज्ञाय तत्र पूर्वं तु गृह्यताम्।
यत् सूरयो ऽपि गृह्णन्ति बालादपि सुभाषितम्॥
इति श्रीमत्कृष्णातटनिकटवर्ति वैराजक्षेत्रनिवास्यत्रिगोत्रोद्भव सामकोपनामक नारायणाचार्यसूनु बालकृष्णाचार्यविरचित ऋक्पाठदूषणोद्धारः ॥

VSM I 436 (no.5439). 14 fol. (A xerox-copy of this in SAI).

223 ṚKPĀDA-KḶPTI (ऋक्पादक्लृप्ति)
Trav. Uni. 22125 C. PL. Mal. 90 Grantha-s.

224 ṚKPĀDA-MAÑJARĪ (ऋक्पादमञ्जरी)
Rajapur 322.

[NCC III 5b]

225 ṚKPĀDA-LAKṢAṆA or ṚGVEDA-PĀDA-LAKṢAṆA (ऋक्पादलक्षण / ऋग्वेदपादलक्षण)
→ Pāda-vidhāna of Śaunaka.
GD I 6-B.
Trav. Uni. 19026 B. PL. Mal. 30 Grantha-s = GD I 6-B.

[NCC III 5b]

226 ṚKPĀDĀNUKRAMAṆIKĀ ŚAUNAKĪYĀ (ऋक्पादानुक्रमणिका शौनकीया)
→ Pāda-vidhāna of Śaunaka.
Mysore I, p. 24.

[NCC III 5b]

227 ṚKPĀDĀVADHĀNA-VYĀKHYĀ (ऋक्पादावधानव्याख्या)
Trav. Uni. 22738. PL. Mal. 850 Grantha-s. Incomplete.

228 ṚKPRATĪKĀNUKRAMAṆĪ (ऋक्प्रतीकानुक्रमणी)
Trav. Uni. 509. PL. Mal. 1300 Grantha-s. Incomplete → Ṛṅmantra-pratīkānukramaṇī. See also under Ṛgvedānukramaṇī.

[NCC III 5b]

229 ṚKPRĀTIŚĀKHYA (ऋक्प्रातिशाख्य)
→ Ṛgveda-prātiśākhya. See also under Pārṣada.

[NCC III 5b]

230 ṚKPRĀTIŚĀKHYA-KĀRIKĀ (ऋक्प्रातिशाख्यकारिका)
GJKSV 38251. 7 fol. Incomplete (breaks off in verse 5 of Paṭala 3). Catalogued as Śukla-yajurveda-prātiśākhya-kārikā.

231 ṚKŚĀKHĀ-SŪKTA-PRATĪKA (ऋक्शाखासूक्तप्रतीक)
→ Anukramaṇikā-ḍhuṇḍhū.
Baroda 23412. 147 fol. 1820 Grantha-s. Dated V.S. 1894 / Śaka 1759.

232 ṚKSAṂHITĀ-KRAMA-PĀṬHA (ऋक्संहिताक्रमपाठ)
SBD 52480. 8 fol. It is actually Vājasaneyi-saṃhitā-krama-pāṭha of chs. 24 and 31.

233 ṚKSAṂHITĀNUKRAMAṆIKĀ (ऋक्संहितानुक्रमणिका)
Rajapur 324.

[NCC III 5b]

234 ṚKSAṂHITĀ-SARVĀNUKRAMA (ऋक्संहितासर्वानुक्रम)
Rajapur 326.

[NCC III 5b]

235 ṚKSAṂHITĀ-SŪKTA-PRATĪKA (ऋक्संहितासूक्तप्रतीक)
→ Ṛgveda-sūkta-pratīka or Sūkta-pratīka. But begins differently:

अथ ऋग्वेदाम्नाये शाकलके सूक्तप्रतीक- ऋक्संख्यर्षिदैवतच्छन्दांस्यनुक्रमिष्यामो यथोपदेशम्। सूक्तप्रतीक। शौनकीयार्षानुक्रमणिकाकारिका

अग्निमीळ इत्यारभ्य सूक्तानां दशकं प्रति।
वैश्वामित्रो मधुच्छन्दा ऋषिरित्यवगम्यताम्॥
(अविदित्वा ऋषिं छन्दो दैवतं योगमेव च।
यो ऽध्यापयेज्जपेद् वापि पापीयान् जायते तु सः ॥

अपि चोक्तम् --

ऋषिच्छन्दोदैवतानि ब्राह्मणार्थं स्वराद्यपि॥
अविदित्वा प्रयुञ्जानो मन्त्रकण्टक उच्यते॥)

अग्निमीळ इति नवर्चस्य सूक्तस्य वैश्वामित्रो मधुच्छन्दा ऋषिः । अग्निर्देवता । गायत्री छन्दः । १। वायविति ...

End:

इति शाकलसंहितायाः सूक्तप्रतीक-ऋषिदैवतच्छन्दोनुक्रमः समाप्तः

VSM I 480 (no.7503). 57 fol. Dated Śaka 1744. 7 verses at the end.
GJKSV 13612. 67 fol. Dated V.S. 1908.

236 ṚKSAṂKHYĀ (ऋक्संख्या)
Enumeration of the Ṛk-s of the *Ṛgveda* that have one or two Pāda-s or three half-verses (ardharca-s), instead of the normal four Pāda-s. The figures in the parentheses are added for easy reference. They refer to the Aṣṭaka, Adhyāya and Varga division, and not to Maṇḍala, Sūkta and Ṛk division. Cf. Dvipada or Dvipadaikapadau. The following is the full text as found in Whish 73,2 (6):

ऋगेकार्धद्वयं प्रायो विशेषो ऽत्र प्रदर्श्यते।
पश्वा न तायुम् (१.५.९) आरभ्य षड्वर्गे द्विपदाखिला॥
अग्निं होतारम् (२.१.१२) आरभ्यानुवाकद्वितये पुनः ।
अर्धर्चत्रितयेनैका मध्ये भेदो ऽत्र पठ्यते॥
स नो नव्येभि (२.१.१९) रित्येकोभे पुनामीति (२.१.२२) पञ्च च।
अति वायविति (२.१.२५) द्वे चोती देवानां (२.१.२६) तथा पुनः ॥
शचीभिर्नः शची (२.२.३) ये देवासो (२.२.४) ऽर्धद्वयात्मिका।

तव त्यन्नर्यम् (२·६·२८) इत्यृक् स्यादर्धर्चत्रितयात्मिका॥
सखे सखायम् (३·४·१२) इत्यृक् चासिक्न्याम् (३·५·२३) एकपदा भवेत्।
अग्ने त्वं नो अन्तमश्च (४·१·१६) चतस्रो द्विपदा ऋचः॥
सिषक्तु न (४·२·१६) उरौ देवा (४·२·१९) एते एकपदे स्मृते।
विद्वेषांसि (४·५·१२) ह्यया वाजं (४·६·३) महि राध (४·७·३४) इमा ऋचः
आ वां सुम्ने (५·१·४) चैकपदाग्ने भवाद्याश्च (५·२·२३) सप्त वै।
रायस्कामस्तथा (५·३·१७) चैका प्र शुक्रैत्वेकविंशतिः (५·३·२५)॥
क ईं व्येकादश (५·४·२३) तथा पितुर्नैका (६·१·३४) तथैव च।
बभ्रुरेको (६·२·३६) दश तथा स नो वाजेष्वितीयमृक् (६·४·३)॥
गावो न यूथम् (६·४·६) इत्येका ह्येतास्तु द्विपदाः स्मृताः।
पवस्व सोमेति (७·२·१६) नित्यद्विपदास्तिस्र एव हि॥
एका परि सुवानो (७·५·१२) ऽथ नृभिर्येमान (७·५·१५) एकिका।
परि प्र धन्वेति (७·५·२०) वर्गद्वितये द्विपदाखिला॥
अया रुचा हरिण्येति (७·५·२४) वर्गे ऽर्धर्चत्रयात्मिकाः।
इमा नु कं (८·८·१५) पञ्च तथैवा याहि वनसा सह (८·८·३०)॥
चतस्रो द्विपदा ऋक्शो ऽध्ययने द्विपदे पठेत्।
अर्धर्क्षु द्विपदामन्त्यां शौनकाय नमो नमः॥

इति ऋक्संख्या समाप्ता॥

Whish 73,2 (6). PL. Gr. 2 fol. (17-18). Cf. Ekapadādi-ṛksaṃkhyā (explained with tables). VSM I 421.

237 ṚKSAṂKHYĀ-PARIŚIṢṬA (ऋक्संख्यापरिशिष्ट)

12 verses giving the number of Ṛk-s from which Sāman-s have been derived in the Kauthumi Śākhā of the *Sāmaveda*.

Beginning:

शतद्वयं तथैकोनं गायत्रं परिकीर्तितम्।
आनुष्टुप्यं च पञ्चाशत् पञ्चषष्टिस्तथोष्णिहम्॥ १॥

End:

नवं शतं सहस्रैकं त्रिंशत् सप्ताधिकं तथा।
कौथुमानामृचां सम्यक् संख्यामाहुर्मनीषिणः॥ १२॥

Alwar 269.
L 1588. 1 fol. 14 Grantha-s.
PUL I, p. 131 (no.18). 10 fol. Title: Kauthuma-pariśiṣṭa.
RASB II 1319 (G 746A) = L 1588.

RASB II 1321a (G 746). 1 fol.
SBD 2378. 1 fol.

[NCC III 5b]

238 ṚKSAṂGRAHA (ऋक्संग्रह)
Index of the first words of the Ṛk-s of the *Ṛgveda*.
TCD 2-A. PL. Mal. 15 fol. 375 Grantha-s.
Trav. Uni. C.405 A. = TCD 2-A.

[NCC III 6a]

239 ṚKSARVA-ŚAMĀNA (-SAMĀNA) (ऋक्सर्वशमान) (-समान)
of Nāgadeva, son of Yajñanārāyaṇa. A treatise giving the list of such words in the *Ṛgveda* as have their final Visarga-s dropped by the operation of saṃdhi. Variously called *Ṛksarva-samāna, Laghu-samāna, Samāna-saṃdhi* and *Sarva-samāna.* It is regarded as the first Prakaraṇa of the *Ṛgveda-sapta-lakṣaṇa.* The text consists of five introductory verses and a list of words divided in 32 sections, arranged in alphabetical order.

Beginning:

प्रणम्य प्रणताभीष्टप्रदातारं पतिं श्रियः ।
बह्वृचानां सुबोधाय शमानं क्रियते लघु ॥
विसर्जनीय आकारपूर्वको घोषवत्परः ।
व्यञ्जनस्पृक् शसपरो लुप्यते संहितागमे (-क्षणे) ॥
एषु वर्णक्रमात् तानि प्रवक्ष्यामि पदान्यहम् ।
इङ्ग्यं पृथक्पदं चात्र निमित्तत्वं पदस्य च ॥
नानापदत्वमिङ्ग्यानां पूर्वभागस्त्ववग्रहः ।
निमित्तं गृह्यते यत् तत् पदमेवात्र लक्षणे ॥
प्रथमांश्च द्वितीयांश्च हित्वा वर्गास्त्रयस्त्रयः ।
अन्तस्थाश्च हकारश्च घोषवन्तः प्रकीर्तिताः ॥
परिभाषा शमानस्य संग्रहेणैवमीरितम् ।
(गजडाद्यास्त्रयो वर्णा दादयश्चैव बादयः ।
यादिवान्तो हकारश्च शसौ तावन्यसंयुतौ ॥)

अजोषा अवा अस्या अश्रधा अवाता अप्रा अप्या अमित्रा अपश्या अदृष्टा अयना अस्तभ्ना अन्यस्या अभ्रिया अस्मेरा अपा अपृणा अगा अदधा अर्का ...

End:

हिमा हवमाना हूयमाना हिन्वाना हर्या हुवाना ह्वृता हाया हेत्या वीरहव्याश्चहा दीयद्रश्मानो हिरण्यया विहोत्रा हिता अनिङ्ग्यान्तो वृष्णो नमसा वातापर्जन्यापरो हस्ताः पञ्चदश ॥

यज्ञनारायणाख्यस्य यज्वनः प्रियसूनुना ।
समानं साधु सव्याख्यं नागदेवेन निर्मितम् ॥

इति ऋक्सर्वसमानं (शमानशिक्षामूलं) समासम् ॥

(In the printed Malayalam script edition: *Śamānalakṣaṇam).*

Adyar D I 961 (20 K 23 = 67485). PL. Tel. 15 fol. (40ff.) (with C.) = Adyar I, p. 51b, 52a. An additional leaf at the end contains a note in Telugu, which mentions Vellāla Yajñāvadhānulu as the copyist, and the Vilaṅghya-lakṣaṇamūla, Sarvasamāna, Rāvaṇa-bhaiṭ, Anukramaṇikā and Anuvākānukramaṇikābhāṣya as the contents of the Ms.

Adyar D I 962 (20 K 38 = 67500). PL. Tel. 2 fol. (1-2). Incomplete; ends with words beginning with "m". = Adyar I, p. 51b.

Adyar D I 1011 (22 H 6 = 69060). PL. Tel. 5 fol. (1b-5a). = Adyar I, p. 48b.

IM 2497. 6 fol. Dated V.S. 1825. Col.: Samāna-saṃdhi.

MD 977. Tel. 5 pp. (85ff.)................................. (= Skt. Texts on Phonetics, pp. 280-86).

MD 978. PL. Kan. 7 pp. (10ff.). (Śamāna-śikṣā). The last passage is missing.

Mysore ND II 3243 (P 4906/ 6). PL. Na. 1 fol. (108).

Mysore ND II 3244 (P 4906/ 7). PL. Na. 3 fol. (108-10). (with Vṛtti).

Mysore ND II 3245 (P 5379/ 3). PL. Tel. 10 fol.

Mysore ND II 3246 (P 6997/ 3). PL. Na. 9 fol.

Mysore ND II 3247 (C 486/ 1). Tel. 6 fol.

Mysore ND II 3248 (C 3425/ 4). Na. 12 fol. (16-27).

Mysore ND II 3249 (C 3764/ 2). 2 fol. (17-18).

Mysore ND II 3250 (C 3764/ 6). 22 fol. (26-47).

Mysore ND II 3896 (P 966/ 9). PL. Tel. 2 fol. (28-29). Title: Saṃhitā-śamāna.

Mysore ND II 3897 (P 4906/50). PL. Na. 2 fol. (128-29). Title: Saṃhitā-śamāna.

PUL I, p. 24 (no.134). PL. Tel. 6 fol. (94-99)

PUL II. App. p. 13 (no.215). PL. Gr. 13 fol. 500 Grantha-s (with C. ?).

SBD 55664. 7 fol. Dated V.S. 1667. (Samāna-sūtra).

TCD 34-A. 8 pp. 75 Grantha-s. (Samāna-padādi).

Trav. Uni. 1116 A. PL. Mal. 75 Grantha-s.

Trav. Uni. 2510 D. PL. Tel. 75 Grantha-s. Damaged.

Trav. Uni. 4254 A. PL. Mal. 8 fol. 75 Grantha-s. Belonged to Vishnu Nambudiri of Ettikada Illam Ayankudi, Kaduttirutti, Kottayam.

Trav. Uni. T.223 A. = TCD 34-A. A transcript of the Ms. no. 4254.

Trav. Uni. 22209 A. PL. Mal. 150 Grantha-s (with C.).

Trav. Uni. 22749 A. PL. Mal. 150 Grantha-s (with C.).

Triv. Cur. III 12. Mal. 100 Grantha-s.

VSM III 168 (no.11345). 2 fol. Inc. (Aṣṭaka-s 5-7). Title : Samāna-pada.

Whish 73,2 (1). PL. Gr. 5 fol. (1-5).

Ptd.:

1) Ed. by Ramabhadra Dikshita (only Śamāna section), with commentary called *Bālabodhinī* of Śeṣa Nārāyaṇa (in Grantha script). – Palghat, Kalpatti : Srividya Kalpataru Press, 1915. 48 pp. Title page : brahmaśrī vedaśāstrasampannaiḥ śrīyajñanārāyaṇayajva-sūnubhiḥ brahmaśrī nāgadevapaṇḍitottamaiḥ praṇīte ṛgvedasaptalakṣaṇe prāthamikaṃ śamānaprakaraṇam, śrīśeṣanārāyaṇīyabālabodhinyākhyavyākhyayā saṃbhūṣitam | idaṃ kila pāṇḍyadeśamaṇḍanāyamānadakṣiṇakailāsakalpaśrījyotirvanādyanekānvarthanāmnā jagatprasiddhaśrīdakṣiṇa-

kāḻīpuragrāmavāstvyena ṛgvedapāṭhaśālādhyāpakena śrīrāmabhadradīkṣitena sutarāṃ pariṣkṛtya tenaiva kalpāttigrāmavāsinaḥ veṅkaṭācalaśāstriṇaḥ śrīvidyā-kalpataruyantrālaye mudrayitvā prakāśtaṃ ca – rākṣasanāma saṃvatsaram | 1915. [Adyar (PH 215 SLxy Nag); BM : Ptd. Bks. Cat. 1906-1928. (14092.b.49,4)]

2) Also printed in the collection called *Tāṇḍaṅgaḻ* (in Malayalam script). – Kunnankulam (Kerala) : Panchangam Pustakashala, 1930 (M.E. 1105), pp. 5-15. [SAI (87/1683*)]

3) Ed. by K. S. Venkatarama Sastri, in : *Ṛgvedīyaṃ Śamāna-lakṣaṇam Upalekha-sūtraṃ ca.* – Srirangam : Sri Vani Vilas Press, 1967. 11, 2, 72 pp. [Adyar (H 215.4 Ven SA); SAI (87/770*)]

– C. called *Bālabodhinī* and ascribed to Śeṣa Nārāyaṇa in the printed editions.

Beginning:

शमानमिति । यद्यपि संहिताकाले लुप्तविसर्जनीयानां पदानामेव पूर्वाचार्यकृता संज्ञा तथापि य एषः तत्प्रतिपादकग्रन्थो ऽपि लक्षणया उपचाराच्च शमानम् इत्युच्यते । पूर्वलक्षणानामतिविस्तृतत्वादसंगतत्वाच्च संग्रहरूपम् अकारादिवर्णक्रमेण सुबोधकत्वात् संगतमिदमेव लक्षणं ग्राह्यमिति दर्शयितुं लघ्वित्युक्तम्॥

End:

वृष्णोनमसावातापर्जन्याःपरो हस्ताः । एवंपरो हस्ता इति विसर्गान्तो भवति । उदा -- उत्तानहस्ता नमसोपसद्यः (वातापर्जन्या) धर्तारो दिव ऋभवः सुहस्ता वाता पर्जन्या । एवंपर इति किम्। एषामिळा घृतहस्ता दुरोण आ इत्यत्र न।

Adyar D I 961 (20 K 23 = 67485). PL. Tel. 15 fol. (40ff.) (with text). = Adyar I, p. 51b, 52a.
Trav. Uni. 22200 C. PL. Mal. 125 Grantha-s.
Trav. Uni. 22749 G. PL. Mal. 125 Grantha-s.

Ptd.: with text the in Grantha script edition and also in the Srirangam edition noted above.

[NCC III 6a]

240 ṚKSARVĀNUKRAMAṆĪ or ṚGVEDĀNUKRAMAṆĪ
(ऋक्सर्वानुक्रमणी / ऋग्वेदानुक्रमणी)

Unspecified:
Allahabad 161.
CU Add. 879. 1914. 1920(and C.).
Gough p. 30.
MD 14083. PL. Tel. 136 pp. Col.: Ṛgvedānukramaṇikā → Cāturjñāna.
MD 14776. PL. Na. 34 pp. Col.: Ṛgvedānukramanikā → Cāturjñāna.
Mim. Vid. 664.
Nasik II 107.
RASB II 233.

RASB II 237.
Rgb. 80.
Skt. Coll. Ben. 1910-11, p. 8 (no.2016). Incomplete.
Trav. Uni. 509. PL. Mal. 1300 Grantha-s Title: Ṛkpratīkānukramaṇī. The beginning and end of each verse of the *Ṛgveda.* Incomplete. Up to the end of the 3rd Aṣṭaka.
Trav. Uni. 4839. 215 fol. 5750 Grantha-s (with C. of Gaṇeśa Ḍokhale). Dated V.S. 1878 / Śaka 1743.
Trav. Uni. 4919. 45 fol. 800 Grantha-s (with C. of Gaṇeśa Ḍokhale). Incomplete.
Trav. Uni. 7521. 75 Grantha-s (with Udāharaṇa ?). Incomplete. Dated V.S. 1878 / Śaka 1743.

See Ṛgvedānukramaṇikā and Ṛgveda-sarvānukramaṇī.

[NCC III 6a]

241 ṚKSARVĀNUKRAMAṆĪ (ऋक्सर्वानुक्रमणी)
A common title for the *Ārṣānukramaṇī, Chandonukramaṇī* and *Devatānukramaṇī*.
GD I 7. PL. Mal. 114 fol. 1140 Grantha-s

242 ṚKSARVĀNUKRAMODĀHARAṆA-SAṂGRAHA (ऋक्सर्वानुक्रमोदाहरणसंग्रह)
Trav. Uni. 7521. 75 Grantha-s. Incomplete. Dated V.S. 1878 / Śaka 1743.

[NCC III 6a]

243 ṚKSŪKTA-VARGĀNUKRAMAṆĪ (ऋक्सूक्तवर्गानुक्रमणी)
Title of the *Sūkta-śloka* also called *Ṛgveda-sūkta-varga-saṃkhyā.*
Trav. Uni. 4254 P. PL. Mal. 5 fol. 25 Grantha-s. (Sūkta-ślokāḥ). Belonged to Vishnu Nambudiri of Ettikada Illam Ayankudi, Kaduttirutti, Kottayam.

[NCC III 6a]

244 ṚKSŪKTA-SAṂKHYĀ (ऋक्सूक्तसंख्या)
→ Ṛgveda-sarvānukramaṇī.
SBD 2352. 27 fol. (9-35). Incomplete.

245 ṚKSŪKTĀDY-ANUKRAMAṆĪ (ऋक्सूक्ताद्यनुक्रमणी)
Tra. Ad. Rep. 1104. 2, 3 (both incomplete).

[NCC III 6a]

246 ṚGANUKRAMAṆĪ (ऋगनुक्रमणी)
SBD 2338. 16 fol. (2-17). Incomplete.

247 ṚGANUKRAMAṆIKĀ (ऋगनुक्रमणिका)
Mysore I, p. 612 (2 Mss.; one with Kannada gloss). II, p. 2. III, p. 1 (with Kannada gloss). See below the Ṛgveda-sarvānukramaṇī with Kannada Vṛtti.

[NCC III 6b]

248 ṚGANUKRAMAṆIKĀ-VIVARAṆA (ऋगनुक्रमणिकाविवरण)
→ Ṛgveda-sarvānukramaṇī-vivaraṇa.
GJKSV 12945. 40 fol. Dated Śaka 1719.

249 ṚGANUVĀKA-PRATĪKA-SŪKTA-SAṂKHYĀ-PARIMĀṆA-KRAMA
(ऋगनुवाकप्रतीकसूक्तसंख्यापरिमाणक्रम)

GD I 6-C. PL. Mal. 3 fol. 50 Grantha-s.
Granthappura p. 1 (no.7c). Mal. 75 Grantha-s. Incomplete. Lacks end.
Granthappura p. 1 (no.8c). Mal. 100 Grantha-s.
Trav. Uni. 19026 C. PL. Mal. 30 Grantha-s. Incomplete.
Trav. Uni. 19027 C. PL. Mal. 200 Grantha-s. Incomplete. Damaged.
See NCC I rev. ed. p. 312b (? 213b), Anuvākānukramaṇī of Śaunaka.

[NCC III 6b]

250 ṚGANUVĀKA-SAṂKHYĀ (ऋगनुवाकसंख्या)
Trav. Uni. 5001 B. 40 Grantha-s. Incomplete. Dated V.S. 1816 / Śaka 1681 → Anuvākānukramaṇī of Śaunaka.

[NCC III 6b]

251 ṚGANUVĀKĀDI-VYĀKHYĀ (ऋगनुवाकादिव्याख्या)
Granthappura p. 1 (no.8b). Mal. 125 Grantha-s.

[NCC III 6b]

252 ṚGANUVĀKĀNUKRAMA (ऋगनुवाकानुक्रम)

Beginning:

अथानुवाकान् सूक्तसंख्याकाननुक्रमिष्यामः । अग्निमीळे त्रीणि। सुरूपकृत्नुमिति चत्वारि। एन्द्रसानसिमिति च। अग्निं दूतमिति षट्।

End:

नासदासीत् त्रयोविंशतिः । शास इत्था चत्वारिंशत्। इति पञ्चाशीतिसंख्याका अनुवाकाः शकलसंहितायाः समाप्ताः ॥

SBD 53400. 2 fol.

253 ṚGYAJUḤ-PARIŚIṢṬA or ṚGYAJŪṂṢI (ऋग्यजुःपरिशिष्ट / ऋग्यजूंषि)
of Kātyāyana. The ninth (or 8th ? Cf. the edition of Ware) of his 18 Pariśiṣṭa-s.

Beginning:

अथादित्ये यजुर्वेदे भेदे माध्यन्दिनीयके।
वक्ष्याम्यृग्यजुषां सम्यग् विभागं तु यथाश्रुतम्॥ १॥
ऋगादेशे यजुर्ज्ञेयमनादेशे तु केवलम्।
ऋतौ यजुरुदाहारे शेषा विद्यादृचः कविः ॥ २॥
उपयामः सयोनिश्च स्वाहाकारश्च यो ऽन्त्यभाक्।
ऋक्संबन्धं यजुर्ज्ञेयं यच्च वक्ष्याम्यतो ऽब्रुवन्॥ ३॥

End:

द्वे सहस्रे शते न्यूने मन्त्रे वाजसनेयके।
ऋग्गणः परिसंख्यातः शेषमन्यद्दचो यजुः ॥ १२॥
अष्टौ सहस्राणि शतानि चाष्टावशीत्यन्यान्यधिकानि यजूंषि।

एतत् प्रमाणं यजुषां तु केवलं सशुक्रियं सखिलं याज्ञवल्क्यम् ॥ १३ ॥
हारीतमाद्यं परमं पवित्रं विद्यात् प्रमाणं यजुषामृचां यः ।
स ब्रह्मसंतानमिहाब्रवीच्च सालोक्यतामृग्यजुषां च गच्छति ॥

ASB I iii.29 (IM 3377). 5 fol. 78 Grantha-s. Dated V.S. 1939 = A.D. 1882.
ASB I iii.30 (IM 2645). 4 fol. 78 Grantha-s.
ASB I iii.31 (IM 3372). 11 fol. 78 Grantha-s.
B I, p. 160.
Baroda 12011(g). 3 fol. 50 Grantha-s. Incomplete.
Bd. 74 (2nd work).
Bik. 332.
BORI 74 (ii) of 1887-91. = BORI D I i.200. 6 fol. (2nd work). Dated V.S. 1553.
GJKSV 43774. 12 fol. (1-7, 9-13). Incomplete.
IM 2645. 4 fol. (1-3, 5). Incomplete. Dated V.S. 1516.
IM 3372. 11 fol.
IM 3377. 5 fol.
IM 3381. 7 fol. Col.: Vasiṣṭha-śikṣā.
N-W P V 62 (no.15). 5 fol. Belonged to Pt. Balamukunda of Benares.
N-W P V 62 (no.26). 6 fol. Belonged to Pt. Makhana Misra of Mathura.
N-W P V 148 (no.30). 6 fol.
Oxf. CS c.21(14). Former owner: Mālavīya Paṇḍita Bālamukunda.
P 4.
P 5(?).
Peters. II, p. 174 (no.93). 8 fol.
RASB II 974(B) (G ?). 5 fol. (11-15).
Rep. Hpr. 1901-06, p. 2.
SB p. 55 (no.60). 6 fol. 100 Grantha-s. = SBD 47948.
SBD 47948. 6 fol. Dated V.S. 1936.
Stein p. 3 (no. 30). 6 fol.

Ptd.: at the end of the *Śukla-yajurveda-prātiśākhya*, with commentary of Uvaṭa. – Benares, 1888, pp. 494-501. – (Ben. S. S. 4).

Also in *Kātyāyanīya-pariśiṣṭa-daśakam*, with commentary *Viṣama-padālaṃkriyā* of Sridhara Anna Sastri Ware of Nasik. – Poona (Yajnavalkya Ashrama, 121 Kasaba Peth) : Madhyandina Madhyavarti Mandala (V. T. Shete Vakil), 1958, pp. 77-95. [BORI (33438); SOAS (III.1.g.27 – 143871)]

[NCC III 7a]

254 ṚGYAJUḤ-SĀMĀTHARVA-VIDHĀNĀNI (**ऋग्यजुःसामाथर्वविधानानि**)

SBD 4015. 7 fol. Incomplete. From *Āgneya-purāṇa*. Includes the Yajur-vidhāna (84 verses), Sāma-vidhāna (25 verses) and Atharva-vidhāna (inc.; 22 verses). See below under Ṛgvidhāna.

255 ṚGYAJUR-VIBHĀGA (**ऋग्यजुर्विभाग**)

ASB I iii.28 (IM 3381). 7 fol. 124 Grantha-s → Vāsiṣṭha-śikṣā.

256 ṚGYAJUṢA-LEṢA (?) (ऋग्यजुषलेष ?)
IM 2517. 7 fol. (2-8). Incomplete. *Actually Krama-kārikā(-śikṣā)* of Śaṃbhu-miśra.

257 ṚGLAKṢAṆA (ऋग्लक्षण)
Adyar D I 395 (the full text is printed). After the colophon to the Pūrvārcika five Anuṣṭubh verses and a prose passage giving a numerical count of the Ṛk-s of the *Sāmaveda* and their Svara characteristics. A few of the verses are identical with those in the *Udāttādi-svara-lakṣaṇa.*

Beginning:

उक्तं चतुर्दशशतमृचामाग्नेयपर्वणि ।
शतानि त्रीण्यृचामैन्द्रं द्विपञ्चाशदृचो ऽधिकाः ॥
एकोनविंशतिशतं पावमान्य इतीरिताः ।
शतानि पञ्चाशीतिश्च पञ्च चापि खिला ऋचः ॥

End:

उदात्तश्चिबुकेन । तत्रोदात्तः । द्वाद्युदात्तम् । पूर्वस्वरिते प्राकृतेपस्वारः प्रकृतिः ॥ इति ऋग्लक्षणं समासम् ॥

[NCC III 7a]

258 ṚGVARṆA-KRAMA-LAKṢAṆA (1) (ऋग्वर्णक्रमलक्षण)
of Jagannātha. Adyar D XIII 37 (VB.737d) → Ṛgveda-varṇa-krama-(jñāna-)lakṣaṇa.

259 ṚGVARṆA-KRAMA-LAKṢAṆA (2) (ऋग्वर्णक्रमलक्षण)
of Narasiṃha-sūri. 45 verses and a commentary thereon by the author himself. The work gives the rules of pronunciation of the Ṛgvedic mantra-s with illustrations of duplication, augmentation, elision, etc., of syllables. Edited from the Viśvabhāratī Ms. now in Adyar Library. See below Varṇa-krama-lakṣaṇa.

Beginning:

केशरूपधरं विष्णुं नरसिंहो नमन् सुधीः ।
तनोति पूर्वशास्त्रोक्तमृग्वर्णक्रमलक्षणम् ॥ १ ॥
पदक्रमविभागज्ञो वर्णक्रमविचक्षणः ।
स्वरमात्राविशेषज्ञो गच्छेदाचार्यसंसदम् ॥ २ ॥
तल्लक्षणं प्रातिशाख्याज्ज्ञेयं व्याकरणात् क्वचित् ।
द्वित्वं चाभिनिधानं च प्रतिषेधस्तयोः क्रमात् ॥ ३ ॥
सोष्मणः पूर्वरूपं च सोष्मा पूर्वस्य चागमः ।
यमायमनिषेधश्च विवृत्तिः स्वरभक्तयः ॥ ४ ॥

End:

पुरोहितिः सुप्रतीकं शवसा क्षत्रं दाशति ।

या निकृष्टं पदेष्वेवमृकारे दीर्घकण्ठजः ॥ ४३॥
प्रायेण स्वरमात्रादिस्थानवर्णगुणा अपि।
वर्णक्रमज्ञैर्वक्तव्याः संक्षिप्येदं प्रकाशितम्॥ ४४॥
वेदपारगपादाब्जनतेन विदुषां मुदे॥
नरसिंहेन रचिता वर्णशिक्षा ऋगाश्रया॥ ४५॥

Adyar D XIII 35 (VB 737b). PL. Gr. 4 fol.
Mysore ND II 3291 (C 476/ 6). 3 fol. Extract no. 77.
Mysore ND II 3740 (C 4237/ 3). 3 fol. Extract no. 267. Title: Varṇa-krama-lakṣaṇa.
Mysore ND II 3741 (C 4237/ 5). 19 fol. (3-21). Title: Varṇa-krama-lakṣaṇa. Dated V.S. 1734.

Ptd.: ed. by V. Krishnamacharya, with the commentary, in : *The Adyar Library Bulletin*, vol. 23 (1959), pp. 73-111. [BORI (22868)]
Also included in the *Ṛgvedīya-bonda-lakṣaṇa*, ed. by K. S. Venkatarama Sastri. – Srirangam : Sri Vani Vilas Press, 1968. [Adyar (PH 216.2 Ven RB); BORI (21936); SAI (85/1958*); UBTÜ (3 E 1286)]

– C. of the author himself.

Beginning:

मन्त्रराजं नमस्कृत्य नरसिंहेन सूरिणा।
ऋचां वर्णक्रमव्याख्या सम्यक् संतन्यते ऽधुना॥
मङ्गलं कुर्वन् चिकीर्षितं प्रतिजानीते -- केशेति। केशः कः अः ईशः ब्रह्मविष्णुरुद्राः। तद्रूपं विष्णुं विराट्पुरुषम्। यद् वा --
आ नाभेर्ब्रह्मणो रूपमा गलाद् वैष्णवं वपुः।
आ केशाद् रौद्रियं रूपं नृसिंहस्त्रिगुणात्मकः॥
इत्युक्तेः नरसिंहं वा नमन्नित्यर्थः। पूर्वशास्त्राणि शिक्षाप्रातिशाख्यादीनि। १। वर्णक्रमज्ञाने फलमाह -- पदक्रम ...

End:

महाप्राणादिवर्णगुणाः। अपिशब्दात् स्पर्शान्तःस्था ऊष्मसोष्मघोषाघोषादयः ब्राह्मण क्षत्रवैश्यशूद्रवर्णादयश्च ज्ञेयाः। तथापि तेषां बाहुल्यादुक्तमात्रमवश्यं ज्ञेयमिति संक्षिप्य लक्षणमुक्तम्। उपसंहरति -- वेदेति॥

Adyar D XIII 36 (VB 737c). PL. Gr. 15 fol.
Mysore ND II 3747 (C 4237/ 6). 19 fol. (3-21). Extract no. 268. Title: Varṇa-krama-lakṣaṇa. Dated V.S. 1734.

[NCC III 7b]

260 ṚGVIDHĀNA (1) (ऋग्विधान)
of Śaunaka. Also ascribed to Baudhāyana in a few Mss. On the use of various mantra-s of the *Ṛgveda* for Japa, Homa, etc. for attaining diverse ends. There are at least three texts, two qualified as Bṛhad- or Jyeṣṭha- and Laghu- or Saṃkṣipta- and the third in 4 chapters, with a short fifth added in a few Mss. There is a text called *Ṛgvidhāna-kārikā*, which appears to carry the former text with additional verses on Ṛṣi, Chandas, and Devatā of Ṛk-s dealt with in the *Ṛgvidhāna*. Sometimes a Ms. simply called Ṛgvidhāna has these verses. Cf. MD 884. MD 14782, called *Ṛṣidevatāchandovivaraṇa*, is really Ṛgvidhāna with these indications. Calcutta Skt. Coll. I 34, though agreeing with Jyeṣṭha- or Bṛhad- is called Laghu-. In these texts mantra-pratīka-s and phala or uses are generally common, but truly identical verses are only a few. A few Mss. give the indications of ṚV Aṣṭaka and Adhyāya (e.g. GD I 11. MD 884). MD 884, some verses of which agree with one version, some others with another (that in 4 or 5 chs.), has a unique supplement called Uttara-kalpa giving mantra-s and their prescriptions for various ailments and finishes with a Stotra on Devī in ten verses. A few Mss. give a small number of verses, i.e. about a hundred. But the numbering here, which is irregular, does not indicate a short text.

– Unspecified:
Ahmedabad 1650 (4).
Alwar 36.
Ānandāśrama 404. 34 fol. Dated Śaka 1679.
Ānandāśrama 7928.
B I, p. 160 (with C.).
BC. 390.
Ben. 5. Incomplete.
BHU B 272 (D 8/4273). 37 fol. Incomplete.
BHU S 61 (D 8/4274). 24 fol. Incomplete.
BISM p. 40 (10 Mss.; one is ascribed to Baudhāyana).
BORI 9 of 1899-1915. 100 fol.
Br. Mus. (Losty). 10. Nan. C 18/19 PL. or. 6861(3).
CPB 559-562.
CU Add. 907.
Deccan College 6828. 5 fol. Dated V.S.1847. Catalogued as Ṛgvidhāna, but it is Śrīsūktavidhāna.
GJKSV 24796. 22 fol.
GJKSV 39131. 32 fol. Dated Śaka 1669.
Hoshiarpur p. 50 (no.22). 29 fol. 964 Grantha-s. Dated Śaka 1538.
IM 1813. 50 fol. (1-3, 6-52). Incomplete (5 chs.). Dated V.S. 1551 and 1608.
IM 1866. 43 fol. (5 chs.)
IM 2045. 25 fol. (1-16, 33-41). Incomplete. Dated V.S. 1613.
IM 5542. 10 fol. (2-11). Incomplete.
IM 9693. 27 fol. (5-31). Incomplete.
Jammu RSRI p. 22 (no. 5060). 47 fol. Dated V.S. 1726 (Stein 32).
Jammu RSRI p. 22 (no. 5083). 5 fol. Incomplete. (Stein 31).
Jammu RSRI p. 22 (no. 19 ga-1). 53 fol. Dated V.S. 1984. A modern copy of Stein 32.

K 6.

Khn. p. 8 (no.16). 54 fol. ; from Nargund; Nānā Dīkshit Maṇerkar. (a. Nārāyaṇa ?).

Mysore I, p. 25 (5 Mss.; 2 Incomplete).

Mysore ND II 3300 (P 6825/ 2). PL. Na. 23 fol. (25-57). Extract no. 83.

Mysore ND II 3301 (P 7745/ 1). PL. Tel. 10 fol. Extract no. 84.

Mysore ND II 3302 (P 7843/ 1). PL. Na. 10 fol.

Mysore ND II 3303 (P 8858). PL. Na. 41 fol. Extract no. 85.

Mysore ND II 3304 (C 485). Tel. 60 fol. Extract no. 86.

N. S. Press 90.

N-W P VII 2 (no.2). 55 fol. Belonged to Raghupati Shastri, Bhinda.

N-W P VII 2 (no.10). 53 fol. Belonged to Pt. Narayana Shastri, Bhinda.

N-W P X 6 (no.39). 170 fol. 2300 (!) Grantha-s. Belonged to Balabhau Sapre, Benares.

Oppert I 1663. PL. Gr. 172 pp. Belonged to Krishna-bhatta Srauti of Bhavani, Coimbatore Dist.

Oppert II 6745. Belonged to Sri Sankaracharya Matham of Kumbakonam.

Oppert II 8013. Belonged to Raghu-bhatta of Sri Bhattugosvami Vattara, Thanjavur Dist.

OU 2 Vm (277/a). PL. Tel. 57 fol. Incomplete. (Paṭala-s 1-8). 16th century.

OU 3 Vm (840). PL. Tel. 51 fol. Incomplete. (Paṭala 8). 17th century.

Oxf. II 896 (Wilson 449). 54 fol. Dated A.D. 1707. = Oxf. 382a (no.449).

Peters. II, p. 168 (no.42). 48 fol.

Peters. VI, p. 63 (no.64). 31 fol.

PUL I, p. 19 (no.30). 48 fol. (4 Adhyāya-s).

PUL I, p. 19 (no.31). PL. Na. 104 fol.

PUL II. App. p. 10 (no.147). 75 fol. Copy of Calcutta Ms.

Rajapur 323. 535.

Rgb. 70.

SBD 3980. 39 fol. (a few fol. missing). Dated V.S. 1646.

SBD 4014. 6 fol. (11-16). Incomplete.

SBD 4018. 9 fol. Incomplete.

SBD 4021. 22 fol.

SBD 4022. 16 fol. Dated V.S. 1738.

SBD 4134. 41 fol. Dated V.S. 1526.

SBD 4143. 41 fol.

SBD 4167. 32 fol. Dated V.S. 1683.

SBD 4175. 23 fol.

SBD 4185. 34 fol. Dated V.S. 1705.

SBD 4186. 16 fol. Dated V.S. 1871 / Śaka 1736.

SBD 4204. 21 fol. Dated V.S. 1823.

SBD 4205. 16 fol. Dated V.S. 1873.

SBD 4223. 50 fol.

SBD 4327. 22 fol. Incomplete. Dated V.S. 1763.

SBD 4431. 54 fol. (3-56). Incomplete. Dated V.S. 1671.

SBD 47556. 32 fol.

SBD 47557. 44 fol. (3-5, 9-21, 30-57). Incomplete.

SBD 47896. 9 fol. Incomplete.

SBD 55039. 63 fol. (2-63). Incomplete.
SBD 55452. 13 fol. Dated Śaka 1650.
Skt. Coll. Ben. 1912-13, p. 4 (no.2171). Incomplete.
Skt. Coll. Ben. 1913-14, p. 4 (no.2274). Incomplete.
Stein p. 3 (no. 31). 5 fol.
Stein p. 3 (no. 32). 47 fol. Dated V.S. 1726.
Tra. Ad. Rep. 1102. 2 (8 chs.; Bṛhat ?). 1104. 5.
Trav. Uni. 2510 A. PL. Tel. 300 Grantha-s. Incomplete.
Trav. Uni. 3661. PL. Gr. 1700 Grantha-s.
Trav. Uni. 4519. 90 Grantha-s (Ṛgvidhāna-saṃkṣepa).
Trav. Uni. 4961. 975 Grantha-s. Dated V.S. 1631.
Trav. Uni. 10517. PL. Mal. 600 Grantha-s. (M.E. 1060 = 1885).
Trav. Uni. 15729. PL. Mal. 100 Grantha-s. Incomplete (with Malayalam notes).
Trav. Uni. 18540 G. PL. Mal. 650 Grantha-s. Incomplete.
Trav. Uni. 19031. PL. Mal. 2000 Grantha-s.
Trav. Uni. 22284 B. PL. Mal. 590 Grantha-s. Incomplete.
Trav. Uni. C.683 B. PL. Mal. 600 Grantha-s.
Trav. Uni. T.1033. 2000 Grantha-s.
Trav. Uni. L.1372 A. PL. Mal. 600 Grantha-s.
Ujjain I, p. 10.
Viśvabhāratī 1731.
VSM I 447-55. 9 Mss. (one is attributed to Vṛddha-Śaunaka).
VSM III 167 (no.11338). 29 fol. Dated Śaka 1748.

[NCC III 7b]

261 ṚGVIDHĀNA (2) -- JYEṢṬHA- or BṚHAD- (483 verses)
(ऋग्विधान / ज्येष्ठ- / बृहद्- / ४८३ शोकाः)

Adyar D I 762 (10 E 51 = PM 105). 24 fol. = Adyar I, p. 88a.
Adyar D I 763 (34 F 9 = 75637). PL. Gr. 25 fol. = Adyar I, p. 48b.
America 40. 26 fol.
America 41. 19 fol. Dated V.S. 1783.
Baroda 5799. 23 fol. 500 Grantha-s. = CLB I, p. 24. Dated V.S. 1812.
Baroda 6521(a). 6 fol. 130 Grantha-s. = CLB I, p. 24. Incomplete.
Baroda 12252. 17 fol. 500 Grantha-s. = CLB I, p. 24. Dated V.S. 1866.
Bh. p. 7 (no.18). 42 fol. 500 Grantha-s.
Bd. 86. 9 fol.
Bharatpur I 152.
Bik. 379. 28 fol. 487 verses.
Bikaner 621. 20 fol. from Aduni.
Bikaner 622. 28 fol. from Nasik.
BISM p. 179 (35/2) (a. Baudhāyana). Dated Śaka 1734.
BISM p. 179 (37/733). Dated Śaka 1688.
BISM p. 179 (39/379).
Bombay Uni. (BMC 131 22). 20 fol. (a. Vṛddha-Śaunaka).
BORI 18 of A 1879-80. = BORI D I i.50. 24 fol. (483 verses).
BORI 86 of 1887-91. = BORI D I i.48. 9 fol. (89 verses).

BORI 64 of 1895-98. = BORI D I i.49. 30 fol.

Burnell 5a (nos. 355. 356).

Calcutta Skt. Coll. I 32. 22 fol. (81 verses ? beginning is the same).

Calcutta Skt. Coll. I 34. 17 fol. (called Laghu-; but same text).

CPB 3349.

Deccan College (1964). 262 (3810 of Dikshit Collection). 28 fol. Dated Śaka 1724. Ascribed to Baudhāyana in the colophon.

Deccan College (1964). 263 (7497 of Datar Collection). 24 fol. Dated Śaka 1702.

Deccan College (1964). 264 (9110 B of Dikshit Collection). 28 fol. Dated Śaka 1789.

Deccan College (1964). 265 (9088/405 of Dikshit Collection). 26 fol.

Deccan College (1964). 266 (6460 of Deccan College Collection). 5, 9, 11, 12 fol. Incomplete.

Deccan College (1964). 267 (754 of Dikshit Collection). 1-2 fol. Incomplete.

Deccan College (1964). 268 (732 of Dikshit Collection). 4 fol. Incomplete.

Deccan College (1964). 269 (733 of Dikshit Collection). 4 fol. Incomplete.

Deccan College 9110. 27 fol. 475 verses. Dated Śaka 1769.

Deccan College 10310. 21 fol. Dated Śaka 1690.

Deccan College 10383. 25 fol. 553 verses. Dated Śaka 1710.

GD I 11. PL. Mal. 133 fol. 2000 Grantha-s (text not clear; divided into Aṣṭaka-s and hence probably Bṛhad-).

GJKSV 13746. 25 fol. Title: Bṛhad-ṛgvidhāna.

GJKSV 13982. 22 fol. Dated V.S. 1809.

GJKSV 17839. 14 fol. Title: Jyeṣṭha-ṛgvidhāna.

GJKSV 33577. 22 fol. Title: Bṛhad-ṛgvidhāna.

Gough p. 31.

Granthappura p. 1 (no.12). 500 Grantha-s.

Hoshiarpur p. 50 (no.6682). 41 fol. 585 Grantha-s.

IM 2061. 2-29 fol. Incomplete.

IO 4254 (Burnell 390a). 23 fol. Written ca. A.D. 1878. (Beg. agrees; has some agreement with BORI D I i.49. Col.: Jyeṣṭha-)

L 1518. 26 fol. 511 Grantha-s. Dated V.S. 1930. (copy of a Ms. Dated V.S. 1841). (agrees with BORI D I i.49 and IO 4254).

Lund IV.

MD 884. PL. Na. 293 pp. (with Aṣṭaka division and a supplement called Uttarakalpa). Incomplete.

MD 17293. PL. Gr. 248 pp. 2232 Grantha-s (breaks off in 8th Aṣṭaka).

München 13. 43 fol. Roman script. 3 chapters. Copied by Adalbert Kuhn from Chambers 53 (Weber 126).

Mysore ND II 3292 (P 1644/ 4). PL. Na. 8 fol. Incomplete. Extract no. 78.

Mysore ND II 3293 (P 4231). PL. Na. 100 fol. Incomplete.

Mysore ND II 3294 (P 4335/21). PL. Na. 14 fol. (120-33).

Mysore ND II 3295 (P 5961). PL. Na. 144 fol. Incomplete.

Mysore ND II 3296 (C 267). 17 fol. Extract no. 79.

Mysore ND II 3297 (P 5980/ 2). PL. Na. 101 fol. Incomplete. Extract no. 80.

Mysore ND II 3298 (P 5982/ 2a). PL. Na. 21 fol. Extract no. 81.

Mysore ND II 3299 (P 6825/ 1). PL. Na. 25 fol. Extract no. 82.

Oxf. CS d.81(1). 25 fol.
Oxf. CS d.81(2). 20 fol. 481 verses. Dated V.S. 1860 (A.D. 1803).
Oxf. CS d.81(3). 27 fol. 481 verses. Dated Śaka 1717 (A.D. 1795).
Oxf. CS d.81(4). 40 fol. (1 fol. is missing).
Oxf. CS d.81(5). 30 fol. (14-44; fol. 1-13 and 32 missing). Dated A.D. 1740.
Oxf. CS d.82(1). 28 fol. Incomplete.
Oxf. CS d.82(2). 21 fol.
Oxf. CS d.82(3). 42 fol. Incomplete.
Oxf. CS d.82(4). 34 fol. Incomplete. Dated V.S. 1652 (A.D. 1595).
Oxf. CS c.27. 58 fol.
RASB II 292 (G 6486). 63 fol. 1200 Grantha-s. Dated V.S. 1879.
RASB II 293 (G 344) = L 1518.
SBD 4020. 35 fol.
SBD 4241. 35 fol. Incomplete.
SBD 48270. 9 fol.
TCD 13. PL. Mal. 204 fol. 2000 Grantha-s.
TCD 14. 61 pp. 600 Grantha-s.
TCD 50-B. PL. Mal. 14 fol. 600 Grantha-s. Incomplete. (these Mss. contain additional verses at the beginning).
TD 1727. 98 fol. 2100 Grantha-s.
TD 1728. 19 fol. 486 Grantha-s.
TD 1729. 37 fol. 600 Grantha-s. Dated V.S. 1722.
TD 1730. 9 fol. 600 Grantha-s. Copy of TD 1729.
TD 1938. 112 fol. 2175 Grantha-s.
TD 1939. PL. Gr. 27 fol. (50-76). 430 Grantha-s.
TD 13942. PL. Gr. 500 Grantha-s.
Tirupati SVUORI 8464 (2795). 27 fol. Dated V.S. 1919. Title: Bṛhad-ṛgvidhāna.
Tra. Ad. Rep. 1100. 2 (8 chs.; Bṛhad- ?).
Trav. Uni. C.1438 = TCD 13.
Trav. Uni. T.701 = TCD 14.
Udaipur II 12, 8.
Wai I 366-75 (10 Mss.). One with Japavidhi.
Weber 126 (Chambers 53). 30 fol. Dated V.S. 1658. Copied by Govardhana.
Wellcome Inst. London. E 10. 16 fol. in 4 chs. (svayaṃbhuve ...).

Ptd.: Text called Bṛhad-, etc. in 483 verses.

1) Ed. by Rajarama Sastri Bodas and Shivarama Sastri Gore, at the end of the edition of the *Ṛgveda-saṃhitā*, with Sāyaṇa's Bhāṣya. – Bombay : Ganapat Krishnaji Press, 1890. 41 pp. [BM : Ptd. Bks. Cat. 1876-92. 348 (14010.dd.1); IO : Ptd. Bks. Cat. 1953, p. 2183 (18 H 2); Emeneau (15)]
2) Ed. by Vasudeva Lakshmana Sarma, in the edition of the *Ṛgveda*. – Bombay : Nirnaya Sagar Press, 1910 (several reprints). [IO : Ptd. Bks. Cat. 1953, p. 2177 (17 B 32-34);
3) Ed. by Kashinatha Vaman Lele, in the edition of the *Ṛgveda* with a Marathi translation. – Wai : Śrīkṛṣṇa Press, Śaka 1833 (1911). [IO : Ptd. Bks. Cat. 1953, p. 2184 (21 J 35-36);

4) Ed. by A. S. Venkataramana Sastri and T. K. Ramabhadra Diksita. – Srirangam : Sri Vani Vilas Press, 1914. 2, 64 pp. – (Svarṇavallī Stabaka 1). (483 and 13 verses, with references to the respective hymns in the margin.) [Adyar (H 220 Sau RV); NL (180 Jc 91 328); BM : Ptd. Bks. Cat. 1906-1928. 890-91 (14008.b.5,1); IO : Ptd. Bks. Cat. 1953, p. 2066 (16 H 29)]

5) Ed. by K. S. Venkatarama Sastri, under the title *Ṛṅmantra-parihāra.* – Srirangam : Sri Vani Vilas Press, 1969. iii, ii, iii, 88 pp. [MyORI (G 1528)]

[NCC III 8ab]

262 ṚGVIDHĀNA (3) -- LAGHU- or KANIṢṬHA- (**ऋग्विधान -- / लघु- / कनिष्ठ-)**

The significance of the description is not clear.

America 42. 11 fol. Dated V.S. 1914. Copied by Kṛṣṇa Dāḍekara.

Gough p. 31.

Hoshiarpur p. 50 (no.6685). 36 fol. 370 Grantha-s.

SBD 4254. 9 fol. (ascribed to Vaidyanātha → Ṛgvidhānāmṛta.

SBD 4280. 3 fol. Dated Śaka 1840.

Wai 136 (5).

[NCC III 8b]

263 ṚGVIDHĀNA (4) (**ऋग्विधान)**

– TEXT in 4 chapters with a short additional 5th chapter in some Mss.

Baroda 4533. 50 fol. 800 Grantha-s. = CLB I, p. 24 (with the 5th ch.).

Baroda 7378. 4 fol. 40 Grantha-s. = CLB I, p. 24 (Puruṣasūkta-prayoga only).

Baroda 12042. 49 fol. 800 Grantha-s. = CLB I, p. 24 (4 chs.). Dated V.S. 1648.

Baroda 11255(e). 7 fol. 120 Grantha-s (Puruṣasūkta-vidhāna).

Baroda 24713. 30 fol. 850 Grantha-s. Dated V.S. 1678.

Berlin StB-PrK (NGMPP). E 1673/7. 51 fol. (svayaṃbhuve ...). Dated V.S. 1562. Scribe: Govinda, son of Viṭṭhala. Copied at Ratnapura in Tirubhuk-deśa (microfilm dated 27.06.1984).

Bik. 330. 43 fol.

Bik. 331 (with the 5th ch.). 39 fol.

Bikaner 623. 39 fol. Dated V.S. 1736 (A.D. 1679). Copied at Pattanapura.

Bikaner 624. 43 fol. from Nasik.

Bikaner 625. 23 fol. The end missing.

Bombay Uni. 687 (BMC 84 17). 52 fol.

Bombay Uni. (Itchharam 9 7) 66. 27 fol. Dated Śaka 1693.

Burnell 5a (no.537).

Calcutta Skt. Coll. I 31. 47 fol.

Calcutta Skt. Coll. I 33. 2 fol. (extract of verses III 167-72 and 157-61 in reverse order).

Deccan College (1964). 260 (6633 of Deccan College Collection). 70 fol. (several fol. missing). Dated V.S. 1735.

Deccan College (1964). 261 (6433 of Datar Collection). 2 fol. Incomplete.

IO 62 (1732a). 47 fol. Written about A.D. 1650.

IO 63 (1732b). 60 fol. Written about A.D. 1700.

IO 4253 (Burnell 390b). 34 fol. Written about A.D. 1878.

L 1519. 42 fol. 840 Grantha-s. Dated V.S. 1931. (copy of a Ms. Dated V.S. 1786).

RASB II 291 (G 345) = L 1519.

TD 1731. 35 fol. 900 Grantha-s. Dated V.S. 1694. (there are 5 verses of the so-called 5th ch. at the end).

Weber 123 (Chambers 50). 59 fol. Dated V.S. 1694. Copied by Kīkābhāi.

Weber 124 (Chambers 51). 38 fol. (with 5th ch.). Dated V.S. 1507.

Weber 125 (Chambers 52). 40 fol. Dated V.S. 1701.

Ptd.:

1) Ed. by Rudolf Meyer, with introduction in Latin, based on 3 Berlin Mss, text in 5 chs. (in Roman script). – Berlin :Fred. Dümmlers Verlagsbuchhandlung, 1878. xxxviii, 50 pp. [BM : Ptd. Bks. Cat. 1876-92. 348 (14010.c.26); Emeneau (54, 55); SKGI (Rf IX 85)]
2) Ed. by Pandit Jagadisha (Lal) Sastri, in : *Oriental College Magazine*, XVI, iv. (Aug. 1940), Lahore. This is a Devanāgarī reproduction of Meyer's edition; text in five chs. Issued separately. – Lahore, 1941, 118 pp. [Adyar (H 222 Sau RV); MUL : 418x1 15H0); NL (180 Jb 94 51)]
3) English translation with an introduction and notes by Jan Gonda. – Utrecht : N.V.A. Oosthoek's UitgeversMij., 1951. 132 pp. [Adyar (H 220 Sau RV=); SKGI (Rf IX 90)]

– C. Pañjikā or Pada-pañjikā of Mātṛsūnu.

Baroda 12251. 63 fol. 1200 Grantha-s. = CLB I, p. 24. Dated V.S. 1887.

[NCC III 8b]

264 ṚGVIDHĀNA (5) **(ऋग्विधान)**

A different text. Brahma-Nārada-saṃvāda.

– Gāyatrī-brahma-kalpa, from. L 900. Probably Bik. 329 is from this. Cf. BORI D I i.48.

[NCC III 9a]

265 ṚGVIDHĀNA (6) **(ऋग्विधान)**

Contained in the *Agni-purāṇa* and *Viṣṇudharmottara*. See *Agni-purāṇa*, Ānandāśrama ed., ch. 259, which goes with three further chs. (260-62) devoted similarly to YV. SV. and AV. agreeing with *Viṣṇudharmottara*, 2nd Khaṇḍa, chs. 124ff. In both Purāṇa-s these Vidhāna-s of the *Ṛgveda*, etc. are parts of Rāma-Puṣkara-saṃvāda. The text here agrees, more or less, with slight verbal changes and changes in order of words and verses, with the text of 4 or 5 chs. in the Lahore edition. See above Ṛgyajuḥ-sāmātharva-vidhānāni.

[NCC III 9a]

266 (Saṃkṣipta-)ṚGVIDHĀNA **(संक्षिप्त-ऋग्विधान)**

Ujjain Latest Additions 181.

– C. Ṭīkā.

Tra. Ad. Rep. 1103. 7. Incomplete.

[NCC III 8b]

267 ṚGVIDHĀNA-KĀRIKĀ (1) **(ऋग्विधानकारिका)**

BISM p. 40 (6 Mss.).

BORI 70 of 1884-87. = BORI D I i.51. 27 fol.

268 ṚGVIDHĀNA-KĀRIKĀ (2) (**ऋग्विधानकारिका**)
This is an entirely different text in Sragdharā metre dealing with Śrauta topics.

Beginninig:

अग्नीन् कार्पाससूत्रोपरिधृतकचजं लोहपाषाणताण्ड्य-
जातं पिप्पल्यकाष्ठारणिमथजत्रिपात्रेध्यवत ... तिपादैः।

End:

पञ्चास्त्रे त्वेभिरग्ने विधिवह वनकृत्वन्यमग्नीषु
सर्वाग्नीष्वेव याजनेषूपविश गृहपतेः पश्चात् त्वं सूरजाप्येत्।
दुष्टान् रक्षेन्द्र मा त्वं न्नः इति वद ... प्रस्ताय चाग्नीन्
अष्टदिक्षुस्थचयनकृति अङ्गेष्वग्नीन् पाथिकैर्मा (?)। ३२।
इति प्रथमाष्टककारिका समाप्ता॥

Haug p. 31 (no.80) = München 12.
München 12. 88 fol. (Written ca. A.D. 1840).

269 ṚGVIDHĀNA-SAṂKṢEPA(ṆA) (**ऋग्विधानसंक्षेप-ण**)
Trav. Uni. 4519. 90 Grantha-s.
Ujjain Latest Additions 182.

[NCC III 9a]

270 ṚGVIDHĀNĀNUKRAMAṆIKĀ (**ऋग्विधानानुक्रमणिका**)
Oxf. CS c.28. 10 fol. Dated A.D. 1752.

271 ṚGVIDHĀNĀMṚTA (**ऋग्विधानामृत**)
of Vaidyanātha also called Vaijanātha. It includes the prayoga-s (e.g. Gāyatrī-puraś-caraṇa-vidhi) for verses mentioned in the *Ṛgvidhāna*.

भारद्वाजदिवाकरस्य तनयः श्रीवैद्यनाथः कृती
नत्वा भास्करदेवपादयुगलं विश्वप्रकाशं परम्।
श्रीमच्छौनकसंप्रणीतममलं ह्यृग्विधानं महद्
विस्पष्टं तनुते परोपकृतये बुद्ध्यृग्विधानामृतम्॥

End:

वेदमन्त्रास्ततः सम्यग् द्विजानां कामधेनवः।
तर्पणं चाभिषेकं च होमं विप्रांश्च भोजयेत्॥
चिन्तामणिः सुरनदी कामधेनुः सुरद्रुमः।
भवतीत्याह मन्त्रार्थ ऋग्विधाने हि शौनकः॥
इति लघु-ऋग्विधानं समाप्तम्॥

SBD 4254. 9 fol. Col.: Laghu-ṛgvidhāna.
Wai I 376. 13 fol. Col.: Laghu-ṛgvidhāna.

272 ṚGVIDHI (ऋग्विधि)
Classification of certain Ṛk-s. ?

Beginning:

द्व्यर्धर्चाः स्युर्ऋचः प्रायस्त्र्येकार्धर्चा अपि क्वचित्।
एकार्धर्चाः पुनर्द्वेधा द्विपदैकपदा इति॥
आवां सुम्ने तथासिक्न्यामुरौ देवा द्विसूक्तभाक्।
सिषक्तु नश्च भद्रं न षट् स्युरेकपदा इह॥

End:

अयुते द्वे शतान्यष्टावर्धर्चाः पञ्चसप्ततिः ।
अयुतं स्युर्ऋचश्च द्विसप्ततिश्च चतुःशतम्॥

MD 19510J. PL. Mal. 1 fol. (93).
TCD 34-H. 2 pp. (51-52). 10 Grantha-s.
Trav. Uni. 4254 I. PL. Mal. 1 fol. 10 Grantha-s. Belonged to Vishnu Nambudiri of Ettikada Illam Ayankudi, Kaduttirutti, Kottayam.
Trav. Uni. T.223 H. = TCD 34-H. A transcript of the Ms. no. 4254.
Triv. Cur. III 5. Mal. 25 Grantha-s.

[NCC III 9a]

273 ṚGVINIYOGA (ऋग्विनियोग)
Mysore ND II 3305 (P 7745/ 2). PL. Tel. 4 fol. Extract no. 87.

274 ṚGVILAṄGHYA-LAKṢAṆA (ऋग्विलङ्घ्यलक्षण)
of Nāgadeva, son of Yajñanārāyaṇa, in 68 verses as it is stated in the last verse. Also known as Vilaṅghya.

Beginning:

शुद्धस्फटिकसंकाशं पुण्डरीकनिवासिनम्।
दातारं सर्वविद्यानां हयग्रीवमुपास्महे॥ १॥
यज्ञनारायणात् सूरेरुत्पन्नः सोमयाजिनः ।
नागदेवो वदिष्यामि विलङ्घ्यानि पदान्यहम्॥ २॥
ऋकारे पर आकारः परयोरोदुवर्णयोः ।
ओदौता स्वर एवैता संधिं ना संहितागमे॥ ३॥

End:

हिता होता हते हस्ता हवन्ते हवमे हृदे।
हस्ते हुवध्यै होतारौ हुता विवहवे भवेत्॥ ६६॥

इदं लक्षणरत्नं तु बुद्ध्यादिगुणसागरात्।
नागदेवात् समुत्पन्नं हृदये धार्यतां बुधैः ॥ ६७॥
एतद् विलङ्घ्यमादृत्य पण्डितैः परिगृह्यताम्।
प्रोक्तं यथा तथा वापि प्रीत्या बालशुकोक्तिवत्॥ ६८॥
मयोक्तान्यृग्विलङ्घ्यानि वर्णक्रमत एव तु।
विलङ्घ्यलक्षणश्लोका अष्टषष्टिरुदीरिताः॥

Adyar D I 973 (20 K 38 = 67500). PL. Tel. 3 fol. (11-13). = Adyar I, p. 51b.
Adyar D XIII 42 (VB 266c). PL. Gr. 7 fol.
MD 963. PL. Kan. 7 pp. (36ff.).
MD 964. Tel. 4 pp. (87ff.).
MT 3911(c). PL. Gr. 4 fol. (85-89). Purchased in 1921-22 from Narasimha Sastrigal, Bhavani, Coimbatore Dist.
Mysore I, p. 25.
Mysore ND II 3306 (C 696/22). 3 fol. (a. Sūryanārāyaṇa). Extract no. 88.
Mysore ND II 3772 (P 4906/ 8). PL. Na. 3 fol. (110-12). Title: Vilaṅghyam (Lakṣaṇa-ratnam).
Mysore ND II 3773 (C 3425/ 2). Na. 10 fol. (3-12).
Mysore ND II 3774 (C 3764/ 3). 1 fol. Incomplete.
Mysore ND II 3775 (C 3764/ 7). Kan. ? 14 fol. (47-60).
PUL II. App. p. 13 (no.209). PL. Gr. 22 fol. 500 Grantha-s.
TCD 34-B. 8 pp. (9-16). 60 Grantha-s.
Trav. Uni. 1116 B. PL. Mal. 75 Grantha-s.
Trav. Uni. 2510 E. PL. Tel. 75 Grantha-s. Damaged.
Trav. Uni. 4254 B. PL. Mal. 7 fol. 75 Grantha-s. Belonged to Vishnu Nambudiri of Ettikada Illam Ayankudi, Kaduttirutti, Kottayam.
Trav. Uni. T.223 B. = TCD 34-B. A transcript of the Ms. no. 4254.
Triv. Cur. III 11. Mal. 75 Grantha-s. Title: Vilaṅghya-lakṣaṇa.
Whish 73,2 (2). PL. Gr. 4 fol. (5-8).

Ptd.: in the collection called *Tāṇḍaṅgaḻ* (in Malayalam script). – Kunnankulam (Kerala) : Panchangam Pustakashala, 1930 (M.E. 1105), pp. 12-18. [SAI (87/1683*)]

[NCC III 9a]

275 ṚGVEDA-KARĀDI-PRAYOGA (?) (ऋग्वेदकरादिप्रयोग)
of Nārāyaṇa. Viśvabhāratī 1205. Could not be traced in D. XIII of the Adyar Library.

[NCC III 9a]

276 ṚGVEDA-KALPA-DRUMA (ऋग्वेदकल्पद्रुम)
of Keśava Māṭe, son of Bhāskara. An extensive treatise on various aspects of the *Ṛgveda* in three parts (Skandha-s) with an Anukramaṇī (table of contents). It was written at the beginning of this century. The date as given in the penultimate verse is V.S. 1974 (A.D. 1917). It quotes a number of authors and works including the *Ṛgveda-prātiśākhya*, *Uvaṭa-bhāṣya*, Rāmavājapeyin, *Rudrayāmala*, *Śāṅkhāyana-sūtra*, Yājñavalkya, *Bṛhaddevatā*, *Mahābhāṣya*, *Mādhyandina-prātiśākhya*, *Mādhyandina-śākhānukramaṇī*, Manu, *Smṛtisāra-samuccaya*, Vasiṣṭha, *Āgneya(-purāṇa)*, *Kaurma(-purāṇa)*, *Bhārata*,

Mokṣadharma, Anukramaṇī-bhāṣya, Śikṣā (Pāṇini), Brāhmaṇa-bhāṣya (of Sāyaṇa on: maṭacīhatesu kuruṣu ... Ch. Up. I 10.1), *Liṅga-purāṇa* (śivarātri-kathāyāṃ mṛgasaṃvāde), Laghuvyāsa, *Nirukta, Kalpasāra*. The second Skandha, beginning with Pārāyaṇa-vidhi includes verses from the *Ṛgvidhāna*, contains an Anukramaṇī. : atha śaunakasaṃhitāyāḥ ṛṣicchandodaivatāni likhyante ... I agim ī̱la iti navarcasya sūktasya vaiśvāmitro madhucchandā ṛṣiḥ (fol. 24-263) | The third Skandha on the Saṃhitā-homa quotes a work on Agnimukha by Śaunaka (158 verses):

यज्ञतन्त्रमिदं प्रोक्तमेकाग्नेर्यज्ञकर्मणि।
प्रयोक्तॄणां प्रयोगार्थं शौनकेन यथाक्रमम्॥

Cf. Yudhisthira Mimamsaka : *Saṃskṛta Vyākaraṇa Śāstra kā Itihāsa*, part II, p. 365.

Beginning:

ग्रन्थारम्भसमाप्तिग्रन्थप्रचारप्रतिबन्धक विघ्नविघाताय अविगीतशिष्टाचारप्राप्तं मङ्गलम् आचरन् चिकीर्षितं शार्दूलविक्रीडितच्छन्दसा प्रतिजानीते नत्वेति।

नत्वा वेदगणं चिदम्बरगुरून् श्रीशौनकं केशवः
सच्छन्दोमुनिदेवताक्षरभिदायोगान् विलोक्यागमान्।
ऋग्वेदाध्ययनप्रकाररचनां कुर्वे सतां तुष्टिदां
वेदाध्येत्रघमृत्युगर्तपतनस्थाणवादितानाप्तये॥

अस्यार्थः -- आगमान् प्रातिशाख्यसर्वानुक्रमणीनिरुक्तादिशास्त्राणाम् अवलोकनं कृत्वा ऋग्वेदाध्ययनप्रकाररचनां केशवः अहं कुर्वे। ऋक्प्रधानो वेदः ऋग्वेदः। वेदो हि मन्त्रब्राह्मणरूपः। मन्त्रब्राह्मणयोर्वेदनामधेयमिति आपस्तम्बयज्ञपरिभाषायामुक्तत्वात्। मन्त्रलक्षणमृग्वेदभाष्यकारेणोपोद्घाते लिखितम्। याज्ञिकानाम् ... युज्यते। वेदे केषुचिदभिधायकेषु वाक्येषु मन्त्र इति समाख्या संप्रदायविद्भिर्व्यवह्रियते। मन्त्रमधीमह इति। मन्त्रव्यतिरिक्तभागेषु ब्राह्मणशब्दस्तैर्व्यवहर्तव्य इत्यर्थः। पदक्रमयोस्तु तदर्थबोधोपयोगित्वान्मन्त्रस्मारकत्वात् क्रमहेतुपटलस्थ इति प्र बाभ्रव्य उवाचेत्यादि-प्रातिशाख्यसूत्रोक्तदिशा द्वैपद ... स्वरादिविषयकसंशयनिवर्तकत्वरूपं तादर्थ्यान् मन्त्रघटकपदघटितत्वाच्च वेदव्यवहारो गौणः। अत एव ब्रह्मयज्ञकर्मणि पदक्रमादीनामध्ययनं शिष्टा न कुर्वन्ति। कालान्तरे तदध्ययनं तु कामनापुरस्कारेण। अन्नाय ... रेणेति ऐतरेयारण्यकविधिना ... प्रातिशाख्यसूत्रेण संशयनिवृत्तिफलकत्वेन च बोधनात् कुर्वन्ति ...। कल्पसारे ...

ऋष्यादीनामविज्ञाने वामदेवादिकानृषीन्।
गायत्र्यादीनि च्छन्दांसि विष्णुं देवं च संस्मरेत्॥

End of the 1st Skandha :

इति श्रीमत्रिस्कन्धक-ऋग्वेदकल्पद्रुमे उपोद्घातप्रकरणं नाम प्रथमः स्कन्धः। सं १९७४ शके १८३९ सन् १९१७ ... बलदेवशर्मा काश्यां जङ्गमवाडीस्थाने।

End of the 3rd Skandha :

सप्तर्षिदुर्गस्थपुरःप्रदेशे चास्ते पुरी शाहनृपेण गुप्ता।

तस्यां वसन् केशवनामविप्रो माटे ऽपराह्वो ऽकृत कल्पवृक्षम् ॥
ऋग्वेदकल्पवृक्षाख्यो ग्रन्थः स्कन्धत्रयान्वितः ।
आद्ये स्कन्ध उपोद्धातः पारायणविधिस्ततः ॥
द्वितीये तु तृतीये ऽथ हवनस्य विधिस्ततः ।
कल्पद्रुमेण भगवान् विश्वेशः प्रीयतामिति ॥
वेदसप्तग्रहाभूमिहायने श्रावणे शुभे ।
सोमे शुक्ले चतुर्थ्यां च समाप्तिमगमद् द्रुमः ।
काश्यां जङ्गमवाडीति विश्रुतश्चिरकालतः ।
लिखितं बलदेवेन सरस्वत्याः प्रसादतः ॥

BISM p. 40 (35/153).
GJKSV 20681. 520 fol. (3 pts. : pt. I : 73 fol. ; pt. II : 264 fol. ; pt. III : 179 fol.). Dated V.S. 1974 / Śaka 1839 = A.D. 1917.

277 ṚGVEDA-KĀRIKĀ (ऋग्वेदकारिका)
of Rājarājavarma. See K. Kunjunni Raja, : *Contribution of Kerala to Sanskrit Literature*, p. 257.

[NCC III 391a]

278 ṚGVEDA-KRAMA-DĪPIKĀ (ऋग्वेदक्रमदीपिका)
of Narahari, son of Nṛsiṃha-sūri. About 35 verses with a commentary called Subodhinī with illustrations of difficult Krama formations. It is divided into five Prakaraṇa-s: Paribhāṣā, Vikṛta-padādi-lakṣaṇa, Krama-lakṣaṇa, Krama-svarūpa-vikṛti-krama-lakṣaṇa, Kampādi-lakṣaṇa.

Beginning:

नत्वा नृसिंहं जगतो गुरुं च लक्ष्मीं जनित्रीं शिवमेकदन्तम् ।
रविं गुरुं शौनकशाकलादीन् आचार्यवर्यान्निगमप्रणेतॄन् ॥
ऋग्वेदप्रातिशाख्यार्थमालोच्यासकृदादरात् ।
नृसिंहसूनुर्नृहरिर्वक्ष्ये ऽत्र क्रमदीपिकाम् ॥

End:

श्वघ्नी परिपन्थी पत्नी प्रजावती रथियन्ती रम्भीणी काराधुनी तृप्त्री पितुमती वाजिनी वर्मिणी जारिणी पूर्वी पुष्करिणी सुदृशी वपुषी महिषी इत्यष्टादश संहितायामीकारदीर्घेषु अधियदस्मिन्निति वर्जयित्वा ॥ इत्यृग्वेदक्रमदीपिकायां सुबोधिनीसमाख्यायां क्रमस्वरूपविकृतपदादिक्रमलक्षणं स्वरवैकृत्यात् कम्पादिलक्षणं नाम पञ्चमः पटलः समाप्तः । शाके १७१(९) विका(रि)नामाब्दे तपः मासि कृष्णे ...

Deccan College 1562. 17 fol. (A xerox-copy of this Ms. is in SAI : 87/788*).

279 ṚGVEDA-KRAMA-PĀṬHA (ऋग्वेदक्रमपाठ)

Baroda 7175. 95 and 131 fol. 8000 Grantha-s. = CLB I, p. 3. (VII-VIII Aṣṭaka-s). Dated V.S. 1590.

IM 4970. 17 fol. (3, 4, 13-27). Incomplete. Difficult passages of the Krama-pāṭha, for each Adhyāya of the *Ṛgveda.*

N-W P II 12 (no.37). 590 fol. Belonged to Makhanji of Mathura.

Rice 2.

[NCC III 10a]

280 ṚGVEDA-GALĀNTA-KRAMA (ऋग्वेदगलान्तक्रम)

It records all the places of Galita-s in the order of their occurences.

IM 2501. 15 fol. Dated V.S. 1898. Numbers written above the lines in this Ms. indicate where the words have occured before. The name Jayanta-svāmin as the author is written by a later hand in red ink at the end.

[NCC III 9a]

281 ṚGVEDA-GALĀNTA-PADA (ऋग्वेदगलान्तपद)

Stein p. 4 → Galita-pradīpa.

[NCC III 9a]

282 ṚGVEDA-GALITA-PRADĪPA or GALA-DĪPIKĀ (ऋग्वेदगलितप्रदीप / गलदीपिका)

→ Galita-pradīpa.

[NCC III 9a]

283 ṚGVEDA-GHANA-PĀṬHA (ऋग्वेदघनपाठ)

N-W P II 12 (no.35). 525 fol. Belonged to Makhanji of Mathura.

See Ramkrishna Gopal Bhandarkar: The Veda in India, *Indian Antiquary,* 1874 (May), pp. 132-35.

[NCC III 18b]

284 ṚGVEDA-GHANA-SĀRA (ऋग्वेदघनसार)

on the different modes, Jaṭā, Ghana, etc. of reciting the *Ṛgveda* and particularly of Ghana based on the *Aṣṭa-vikṛti-vivaraṇa* published in *Uṣā.* – Calcutta : Satya Press, (Śaka 1811) 1889, by Satyavrata Samasrami, but elaborated and edited with *Gāni-lakṣaṇa* and *Svara-lakṣaṇa,* by K. S. Venkatarama Sastri. – Srirangam : Sri Vani Vilas Press, 1966. 92 pp. [Adyar (PH 215.1 x Ven RG); BORI (22257); NL (180 Jc 96 283); SAI (87/771*)]

[NCC III 9b]

285 ṚGVEDA-'CIṬṬA' (ऋग्वेदचिट्ट)

List of words whose Visarga after "ā" is lost in saṃdhi → Cāturjñāna.

IO 4250 (Mackenzie II 80a). PL. Na. 41 fol. Cf. München 32 (Ṛgveda-padāni).

[NCC III 9b]

286 ṚGVEDA-CCHANDARṢYĀDI (ऋग्वेदच्छन्दर्ष्यादि)

→ Ṛgveda-sarvānukramaṇī-vivaraṇa of Jagannātha.

VSM I 434 (no.5931). 45 fol. Dated Śaka 1727. Copied by Phaḍake Nṛsiṃha.

VSM I 435 (no.5454). 47 fol.

287 ṚGVEDA-CCHANDONUKRAMAṆĪ (ऋग्वेदच्छन्दोनुक्रमणी)

of Śaunaka. See below Ṛṣi(-devatā)-cchandonukramaṇī and Chandonukramaṇī of Śaunaka.

Alph. List Beng. Govt. p. 41.

Haug p. 32 (no.89) = München 25. See Ārṣānukramaṇī also.
München 25(2). 2 fol. Dated A.D. 1784.
Trav. Uni. 4847. 300 Grantha-s.
Trav. Uni. 4925. 35 Grantha-s. Incomplete.
Triv. Cur. V 3. Mal. 300 Grantha-s. Obtained from Thiruparpu Svamiyar Matham.

[NCC III 9b]

288 ṚGVEDA-JAṬĀDY-AṢṬA-VIKṚTI-VIVARAṆA (ऋग्वेदजटाद्यष्टविकृतिविवरण)
of Madhusūdana-sarasvatī. This must be the same as the Aṣṭa-vikṛti-vivṛti (-kārikā) (see above) of Madhusūdana-maskarin also called Madhusūdana-munīśvara. The identification with the famous Madhusūdana-sarasvatī (16th century) is not beyond doubt. See S. N. Dasgupta, *A History of Sanskrit Literature.* – Calcutta : University of Calcutta, 1962 (second edition), p. 664.

289 ṚGVEDA-JAṬĀ-PĀṬHA (ऋग्वेदजटापाठ)
BHU S 43 (D 1A/29). 6 fol. Incomplete.
BISM p. 44 (36/524). 10 fol. For the Sūkta : "śaṃ na indrāgnī" ...
Burnell 3b (see Jaṭodāharaṇa below).
Calcutta Skt. Coll. I 36. 83 fol. 779 Grantha-s.
N-W P II 10 (no.34). 1150 fol. (!) Belonged to Makhanji of Mathura.
Rice 2.
Weber 33 (Chambers 209b.1). 4 fol.

[NCC III 18b]

290 ṚGVEDA-DEVATĀNUKRAMAṆĪ (ऋग्वेददेवतानुक्रमणी)
of Śaunaka. See below Ṛṣi(-devatā)-cchandonukramaṇī of Śaunaka.
GD I 7. PL. Mal. 114 fol. 1140 Grantha-s. (Ārṣānukramaṇī, Chandonukramaṇī and Devatānukramaṇī). Title: Ṛksarvānukramaṇī.
Triv. Cur. V 4. Mal. 400 Grantha-s. Obtained from Thiruparpu Svamiyar Matham.

[NCC III 9b]

291 ṚGVEDA-DVIPADĀDI-SAṂKHYĀ (ऋग्वेदद्विपदादिसंख्या)
Trav. Uni. 4963. 30 Grantha-s. Dated V.S. 1819.

[NCC III 9b]

292 ṚGVEDA-PADA-KRAMA-LAKṢAṆA (BONTĀKHYAM)
(ऋग्वेदपदक्रमलक्षण / बोन्ताख्यम्)
→ Bonta-lakṣaṇa.
Calcutta Skt. Coll. I 492 (152). 20 fol. Dated Śaka 1525.
PUL I, p. 19 (no.32). 5 fol. 100 Grantha-s. (Ṛgveda-tattva-pada-pradīpikā).

[NCC III 18b]

293 ṚGVEDA-PADA-NIRṆAYA (ऋग्वेदपदनिर्णय)
Trav. Uni. 12798. PL. Mal. 550 Grantha-s.
Trav. Uni. L.1325 A. PL. Mal. 800 Grantha-s. Incomplete.

[NCC III 9b]

294 ṚGVEDA-PADA-RATNA(-PARIBHĀṢĀ) (ऋग्वेदपदरत्न-परिभाषा)
Ascribed to Dakṣiṇāmūrti. It is also called *Ekākṣarībaiṭh* and *Pada-ratna-lakṣaṇa*. The anonymous commentary on this, noted below, attributes the work to Rāvaṇa. Thus, it is called *Rāvaṇa-baiṭh* in some Mss. (e.g. TD 1783-85). The paribhāṣā section, consisting of about 12 verses, as printed in Devasthali's edition of the *Ekākṣarī-baiṭh*, which partly

agrees with the Mss. catalogues, is given below.

Beginning:

पदरत्नलक्षणम्।

नान्तं विसर्गान्तमथावगृह्यं स्यन्तं तु सेन्तं विषमं समं च।
संख्यां प्रगृह्यस्य च पञ्चके ऽन्त्ये पदेषु वक्ष्ये प्रतिवर्गमत्र॥ १॥
काद्यैरष्टचतुष्कैश्च वर्गा ङणनमाः क्रमात्।
नविसर्गान्तदुःखण्डः कशयोर्विषमाः समाः ॥ २॥
चनकारटविसर्गा ङदुःखण्डः समाः क्रमात्।
ते दुःखण्डः पे विसर्गा ये नान्तो विषमाः क्रमात्॥ ३॥
विषमं वा समं चैकं यत्र तत्रान्यथा द्वयम्।
काद्यैर्वर्णैः प्रगृह्यं स्याद् द्वितीयाद्यैस्त्रिभिः क्रमात्॥ ४॥
एकं द्वे त्रीणि चत्वारि यरान्ते ऽष्टौ नणान्तके।
वान्ते द्वादश वर्णाः स्युर्मसंयोगे तु षोडश॥ ५॥
संयोगाद्ये स्थितो वर्णः स्वसंख्यां न च मुञ्चति।
पदानां पञ्चकेष्वत्र पदसंख्यान्त्यपञ्चके॥ ६॥
स्वराः पञ्चभिराद्यैः स्यादूकाराद्यैश्च पञ्चभिः।
स्वरपञ्चकयोः स्यन्तं समं च विषमं क्रमात्॥ ७॥
स्वरानत्र विजानीयाद् दन्त्यमूर्धन्यवर्जितान्।
लान्तादीनामभावे स्यात् समं पद्यपदान्तयोः ॥ ८॥
लान्तादारभ्य विषमं त्रिष्वाद्ये पञ्चके ऽपि च।
सितुसेन्तं तु संहृत्य गणयेदेकरूपतः ॥ ९॥
यत्रानेकपदे रूपं तदनेकत्र गण्यते।
इत्यत्र परिभाषेयं लक्षणं सविशेषतः ॥ १०॥
(अध्यायादौ क्रमाद् वर्गाद् स्वसंख्यां त्वक्षरैर्वदेत्।
वाक्यद्वयमिह ज्ञेयं सुखग्रहणसिद्धये।
पदरत्नसमीक्षायाः पदसंख्येयमीरिता॥ ११॥)

अग्निमीळे -- ङ श ङी श्र। प्री च ति ञी। यु नु गे फो। ली तु दु ति। ङ गो म श्र। पू पु चु खे। छ था का डी। ठ थो री खे। ख टि त पे य। १।

End:

शू चि जि। ६२। तदित् -- दि खे जि व। छी छि चि चा। ठो बौ छ द। भू गि दि तः। वु ण फू दै। बे भि रो ब। त्या शि दू ये रा प्रि। ६३। त्वं चित् -- च्यो ध घ दु। ने चा बु खा। तो खा जे चु। ज्मै चि कू चि। ष धा घ वा। बु तो शू ब। व्यो स छि दू। ब पा घ शा। तै णि ऋ छ्रि। ण ष या ठे। गि दै ति छिल। तु ति गि श ङि। ६४। इति पदरत्नपरिभाषा

समाप्ता ॥

Adyar D I 892 (28 F 35 = 72839). PL.Tel. 3 fol. Col.: Pada-ratna-paribhāṣā. Corresponds to the first paragraphs of the Srirangam edition. = Adyar I, p. 51a. Title: Pada-ratnam.

Alph. List Beng. Govt. p. 20. Title: Ekākṣarī-baiṭham.

Baroda 11104. 2 fol. 12 Grantha-s. = CLB I, p. 25. (Ekākṣara-baiṭha-paribhāṣā).

Bhr. 502.

BISM p. 49 (52/502). (Ekākṣarī-baiṭhaḥ)

BISM p. 179 (35/482). 8 fol. (Baiṭha-paribhāṣā). Title in the Ms: Ekākṣarī-paribhāṣā

Bombay Uni. 1827 (BMC 85 9). 9 fol. Title: Ekākṣarī-baiṭh. Described as "a tantric work".

BORI 502 of 1882-83. = BORI D I i.431. 20 fol. (Ekākṣarī-baiṭa).

BORI 76 of 1884-87. = BORI D I i.47. 6 fol. Col.: Pada-ratnamūla, Ekākṣarī-baiṭa.

Brl. p. 7 (no.VII, title : Paribhāṣā -- Pada-saṃkhyā) = IO 4247.

Calcutta Skt. Coll. I 493A (149). 2 fol. Title: Ṛgveda-paribhāṣā. Dated V.S. 1661.

Calcutta Skt. Coll. I 526 (311). 9 fol. It reads after the verses: ityekākṣarapadabaiṭhasya paribhāṣā samāptā | pañcabhiḥ pañcabhiḥ svaraiḥ padasaṃkhyāṃ jñātvā | atha pragṛhyasya saṃkhyā | vargāṇām ādivarṇasya pragṛhyaṃ nāsty eva ... | 2 fol. of explanation before agnim īḷe, etc.

GJKSV 13614(B). 1 fol. (3). Dated V.S. 1925. Copied by Lakṣmaṇa-bhaṭṭa. Contains a short C. on the verses with the title: Baiṭha-paribhāṣā.

Hoshiarpur p. 51 (no.4366). 17 fol. 580 Grantha-s. Extract p. 75. (Ekākṣarī-baiṭh). Incomplete.

IO 4247 (Burnell 205h). PL. Gr. 3 fol. (155b-57b).

IO 4248 (Mackenzie II 80b). PL. Na. 7 fol. (42-48).

IO 4249(1) (Mackenzie II 60b). PL. Na. 2 fol.

IO 4252(2) (Mackenzie II 83k). PL. Na. 3 fol. (73-75). Incomplete.

Mad. Uni. R. K. S. 78(b).

MD 14081. PL. Tel. 2 pp. Col.: Pada-ratna-paribhāṣā.

MD 14779. PL. Na. 2 pp. (Pada-ratna-paribhāṣā).

MT 5295. 34 fol. (a. Rāvaṇa). Transcribed in 1926-27 from a Ms. of Paramesvara Nambudiri, Tiyanuru-mana, Vaniyankolam, Malabar Dist. Identical with Aṣṭākṣarī-paribhāṣā. IO 4244.

Mysore ND II 3608 (P 4906/49). PL. Na. 1 fol. (129). Extract no. 211. Title: Pada-ratna(-paribhāṣā). At the end: reto retaś ca ...

Mysore ND II 3609 (P 5379/ 1). PL. Tel. 1 fol.

Mysore ND II 3610 (P 5657/16). PL. Na. 2 fol. (29).

Mysore ND II 3611 (C 486/ 2). Tel. 1 fol. (6).

Mysore ND II 3612 (C 3425/ 1). Na. 2 fol.

Mysore ND II 3273 (P 5657/17). PL. Na. 7 fol. (30-36). Extract no. 66. Entered as Ṛksarvānukramaṇikā-ṭīkā (Marāṭhī).

Mysore Skt. Coll. p. 1 = D. No.11 (846/2). PL. Na. 2 fol. (7-8). (Pada-ratna-paribhāṣā).

PUL I, p. 20 (no.42). 144 fol. (Ekākṣarī-baiṭh, with C. Utthāpanā in Vaṅga ?).

Rajapur 327. 1035.

RASB II 257 (G 2065). 3 fol. (Ekākṣarī-baiṭaḥ with C. Utthāpanā). Only the paribhāṣā verses; printed fully.

Rgb. 76.

SBD 2107. 5 fol. Dated V.S. 1820. Title: Pada-ratna. Remark: Samūlā, mūlakāro vyāḍiḥ | This must, however, refer to the next entry : Jaṭā-paṭala-vyākhyā of Dayāśaṃkara.

SBD 46945. 4 fol. Incomplete (up to "yajñāyajñā vaḥ"). Title: Baiṭh-paribhāṣā.

SBD 52686b. 4 fol. (16-19). Dated Śaka 1660. (Pada-ratna).

Skt. Coll. Ben. 1918-30, p. 2 (no.18). 5 fol. Dated V.S. 1820.

TD 1783. 8 fol. 120 Grantha-s. Title: Rāvaṇa-bhaiṭ. Contains 11 paribhāṣā verses regarding the Sapta-saṃkhyā -- paiduvimanat -- and their exact number in a symbolic language.

TD 1784. 7 fol. 125 Grantha-s. Title: Rāvaṇa-bhaiṭ. Dated 1745 in Subhānu year or 1823 A.D. The name of the scribe is Rāma, son of Kamalākara-bhaṭṭa.

TD 1785. 3 fol. 24 Grantha-s. Incomplete. Title: Rāvaṇa-bhaiṭ. Breaks off in the beginning of the Lakṣaṇa-vākya of the 1st Adhyāya of the 2nd Aṣṭaka.

Wai I 339. 7 fol.

Ptd.: ed. by G. V. Devasthali, under the title *Ekākṣarī-baiṭha*, with commentary and paribhāṣā, in *Golden Jubilee Volume* Vaidika Samshodhana Mandala, Poona, 1982, pp. 66-93. This edition is based on five Mss: BORI D I i.47 and 431; BISM p. 49 (35/481ka); two Mss. from the Vaidika Samsodhana Mandala, Poona (no.11281). [SAI (ind 58 V 86/77)]

Ed. by K. S. Venkatarama Sastri (only the text without the paribhāṣā verses), under the title: *Pada-ratna*, together with the *Ṛgvedīya-bonda-lakṣaṇa*, *Svarāṅkuśa* and *Ṛgvarṇa-krama-lakṣaṇa*. – Srirangam : Sri Vani Vilas Press, 1968. [Adyar (PH 216.2 Ven RB); BORI (21936); SAI (85/1958*); UBTÜ (3 E 1286)]

– C. Bhāṣya.

Beginning: (893)

नान्तमिति । अस्यार्थः । सकलवेदाङ्गपुराणस्मृतिकाव्यनाटकालङ्कारादि सकलविद्याविशारदः सकलकर्मानुष्ठानमहिम्ना वशीकृतपरमेश्वरो विश्रवसः पुत्रो रावणो ऽहम्। प्रतिवर्गम्। वर्गे वर्गे। अव्ययं विभक्तीत्यादिना विभक्त्यर्थे ऽव्ययीभावः ॥

End:

पदानि पदरत्नानि तेषां परीक्षायामियं पदसंख्या ईरिता । उक्तान्येतावन्ति प्रगृह्याण्येतावन्ति दुःखण्डपदान्येतावन्ति मकारपदान्येतावन्ति तकारान्तान्येतावन्ति … । पदरत्नव्याख्यानं समाप्तम्।

Adyar D I 893 (20 K 38 = 67500). PL. Tel. 3 fol. (5-7). = Adyar I, p. 51a. The author of the basic text is here mentioned as Rāvaṇa.

Hoshiarpur p. 51 (no.4369). 12 fol. 84 Grantha-s. Extract p. 76. (Ekākṣarī-baiṭh). Incomplete.

– C. Utthāpanā.

Beginning:

नत्वा विश्वेश्वरं साम्बमीशानं विद्यया युतम्।
करोम्येकाक्षरीबैठव्याख्यामुत्थापनाभिधाम्॥

नान्तमिति। नकारान्तम्। विसर्गान्तम्। अथानन्तरम्। अवगृह्यमिति दुःखण्डस्य वैदिकी संज्ञा। दुःखण्डम्। स्यन्तं सिकारान्तम्। तु इति पुनः। सेन्तं सेकारान्तम्। इत्येषां पञ्चानां पदानाम्। विषमं विषमसंख्यामात्रम्। चपरम्। समं समसंख्यामात्रम्। वक्ष्ये इत्यन्वयः। चपरं प्रगृह्यस्य। प्रगृह्यमितीतिकरणस्य वैदिकी संज्ञा। तदुक्तमन्यत्रापि --

प्रतिवर्गपदेयत्तां समत्वविषमत्वतः।
विसर्गनान्तपद्यानि काद्यैर्वर्गैर्ब्रुवे ऽष्टभिः॥

End:

ननु स्वरपञ्चकयोः स्यन्तमित्युक्तम्। सेन्तस्य का गतिरिति चेदत्रोच्यते। सितुसेन्तं तु संगृह्य। द्वयमेकीकृत्य एकरूपेण गण्यन्त इत्यर्थः। अध्यायानामिति। चतुःषष्टिपरिमिताध्यायानाम्। वर्गसंख्याक्षराणि च मिलित्वा वदेदित्यन्वयः। १०। इह वर्गसंख्यास्वरसंख्यारूपं वाक्यद्वयं सुखग्रहणसिद्ध्यै ज्ञेयम्। अन्यत्रोक्तम् -- वाक्यानि दश वर्णानां स्युः सुखग्रहणाय नः इति॥

GJKSV 30313. 60 fol. Title: Prativarga-varṇa-saṃkhyā.
RASB II 257 (G 2065). 3 fol. with the text of 11 verses.

– C. of Rāmanārāyaṇa Śarman.
Varendra 960.

[NCC III 9b-10a]

295 ṚGVEDA-PADA-RATNA-SAMĪKṢĀ (ऋग्वेदपदरत्नसमीक्षा)
Ptd.: Ed. by Ananta Balakrishna Upadhye. – Keri (Mardola, Goa) : Gomantaka Sanskrit Parishat, 1967. 70 pp. [VSM; SAI (***)] This edition appears to be based on the Ms. called *Aṣṭa-saṃkhyā:*
VSM III 162 (no.11282). 50 fol. Dated Śaka 1652.

296 ṚGVEDA-PADA-LAKṢAṆA (ऋग्वेदपदलक्षण)
→ Samāna-pada.
GD I 36-E.
Trav. Uni. 19055 E. PL. Mal. 9 fol. (27-35). 375 Grantha-s.

297 ṚGVEDA-PADA-VARṆA-SAṂKHYĀ (ऋग्वेदपदवर्णसंख्या)
→ Aṣṭākṣarī-baiṭh.
SBD 2371. 16 fol. (2, 5-18). Incomplete (up to 3.8 : tṛtīyāṣṭake aṣṭamo 'dhyāyaḥ).

298 ṚGVEDA-PADĀDI-SAṂKHYĀ or SAPTA-SAṂKHYĀ (ऋग्वेदपदादिसंख्या / सप्तसंख्या)
→ Sapta-saṃkhyā(-nirūpaṇa).
Bh. p. 7 (no.19). 46 fol. (pa-i-du-vi-ma-na-t; Sapta-lakṣaṇa).
BORI 19 of A 1879-80. = BORI D I i.42. 46 fol. Dated Śaka 1698.

[NCC III 10a]

299 ṚGVEDA-PADĀNI (ऋग्वेदपदानि)
Words in the *Ṛgveda* which elide their final "s" before tonal consonants. It is identical with Cāturjñāna (cf. TD 1764).

Haug p. 45 (no.287). Remark: "Einige Verse des Sāmaveda" !.
München 32. 7 fol. Written ca. A.D. 1750. See Ṛgveda-Citta.

[NCC III 10a]

300 ṚGVEDA-PADDHATI (ऋग्वेदपद्धति)
Alph. List Beng. Govt. p. 19.

[NCC III 10a]

301 ṚGVEDA-PARIBHĀṢĀ (ऋग्वेदपरिभाषा)
on the peculiarities of Pada-s in the *Ṛgveda*.
Calcutta Skt. Coll. I 493 → Ṛgveda-pada-ratna.

[NCC III 10a]

302 ṚGVEDA-PARIBHĀṢĀ or ṚGVEDA-SARVĀNUKRAMAṆĪ-PARIBHĀṢĀ (ऋग्वेदपरिभाषा / ऋग्वेदसर्वानुक्रमणीपरिभाषा)
The paribhāṣā portion of the *Ṛgveda-sarvānukramaṇī*. See also entries under Ṛgveda-sarvānukramaṇī.

Baroda 24731. 18 fol. 350 Grantha-s.
BISM p. 314 (35/477). Sarvānukrama-paribhāṣā (Śākala-saṃhitāyām).
BISM p. 314 (36/78). Sarvānukrama-paribhāṣā.
BISM p. 314 (37/623ba). Sarvānukrama-paribhāṣā.
BISM p. 314 (37/793). Sarvānukrama-paribhāṣā.
BISM p. 314 (45/91). Sarvānukrama-paribhāṣā.
BISM p. 314 (58/135). Sarvānukrama-paribhāṣā.
BORI 38 of A 1881-82. = BORI D I i.30. 21 fol. Dated Śaka 1738. Copied in Poona.
BORI 72 of 1884-86. = BORI D I i.31. 34 fol. Dated V.S. 1763. Copied in Kāśī.
BORI 80 of 1884-87. = BORI D I i.32. 34 fol. Copied in Ujjain.
BORI 71 of 1884-87. = BORI D I i.33. 4 fol.
CU Add. 2087.
GJKSV 15628. 5 fol. Dated V.S. 1912. Title: Ṛgveda-sarvānukramaṇī-paribhāṣā Dvādaśa-khaṇḍī.
GJKSV 37944. 9 fol. Title: Sarvānukrama-paribhāṣā.
Hz 1799. 58 fol. Belonged to Jambunatha Bhatta of Thanjavur.
IM 1814. 37 fol.
IM 5235. 6 fol.
IM 5784. 11 fol. Col.: Sarvānukrama-paribhāṣā-chandomañjarī (cf. RASB II 1540. Paribhāṣā-chando-mañjarī).
IM 6668. 6 fol. (1-2, 4-7). Incomplete.
IO 4240 (Mackenzie II 83a). PL. Na. 6 fol. Written ca. A.D. 1800.

IO 4241 (Mackenzie II 80c). PL. Na. 7 fol. (49-55).
IO 4242 (Mackenzie II 83c). PL. Na. 6 fol. Written ca. A.D. 1800.
MD 886. Tel. 11 pp. (46ff.). Incomplete.
MD 887. PL. Tel. 6 pp. (Ṛgveda-paribhāṣā).
MD 888. PL. Kan. 43 pp. Incomplete.
MD 14777. PL. Na. 5 pp.
Mysore I, p. 39. (Sarvānukramaṇikā-paribhāṣā).
OU 23 Vm (B.94/4). 5 fol. 16th century. Title: Vaidika-paribhāṣā.
Rajapur 325.
Rgb. 71. 72.
SBD 2269. 27 fol. (Śākala-śākhīyānukramaṇikā).
SBD 2293. 4 fol. (1, 4-6). Incomplete. Dated V.S. 1849.
SBD 2327. 5 fol. Dated V.S. 1895.
SBD 2369. 4 fol. (Ṛgvedīya-paribhāṣā).
SBD 53760. 5 fol. (Sarvānukrama-paribhāṣā).
Skt. Coll. Ben. 1915-16, p. 8 (no.2526).
Viśvabhāratī 1616. 1705.
VOHD II 8.3044 (Hs.or.6358. StaatsB-PrK, Berlin). PL. Na. 4 fol. (103-06). Khaṇḍa 1-12. (Sarvānukramaṇī).
VSM I 472-77. (Sarvānukrama-paribhāṣā).
Wai I 333. 6 fol. (with Chandasāmudāharaṇāni and Chandomañjarī giving details on the metre of each mantra of the *Ṛgveda.*

– C. Udāharaṇa of Gaṇeśa-bhaṭṭa. It may be identical with his commentary Dīpikā on the *Ṛgveda-sarvānukramaṇī.*
IM 2387. 25 fol. Dated V.S. 1821. Col.: Paribhāṣodāharaṇa-granthaḥ.
Rep. Raj. and C. I. p. 6.

– C.
SBD 2317. 22 fol. (7-28). (Ṛganuvākānukramaṇī).

– C.
Mysore I, p. 25 (12 Khaṇḍa-s).
Mysore ND II 3285 (C 36). 27 fol. Extract no. 72 (Dvādaśa-khaṇḍī).

[NCC III 10a]

303 ṚGVEDA-PARIBHĀṢĀ-KĀRIKĀ or CĀTURJÑĀNA-PARIBHĀṢĀ
(ऋग्वेदपरिभाषाकारिका / चातुर्ज्ञानपरिभाषा)
of Paṅgu Nārāyaṇa, dealing with the peculiar characteristics of some select Pada-s in the *Ṛgveda;* of the nature of Sapta-saṃkhyā. Cf. Ṛgvedaciṭṭa and Cāturjñāna.

Adyar D I 785 (40 A 35 = PM 112). 18 fol.
BORI 72 of 1884-87. = BORI D I i.44. 3 fol.

[NCC III 10a]

304 ṚGVEDA-PARIBHĀṢĀ-VYĀKHYĀ -- SARVĀNUKRAMAṆĪ (?)
(ऋग्वेदपरिभाषाव्याख्या सर्वानुक्रमणी)
MT 3796. See below under Ṛgveda-sarvānukramaṇī-vyākhyā Dīpa-prabhā.

[NCC III 10b]

305 ṚGVEDA-PARIŚIṢṬA (?) (ऋग्वेदपरिशिष्ट)

A conjectural title → Ṛgveda-prātiśākhya-pariśiṣṭa.

Whish 78(7). PL. Gr. 32 fol. (55-86).

[NCC III 10b]

306 ṚGVEDA-PARIŚIṢṬA-VIVARAṆA (ऋग्वेदपरिशिष्टविवरण)

→ Pariśiṣṭa-ṛgvivaraṇa.

Trav. Uni. 4909. 90 Grantha-s. This is not a commentary but a kind of Anukramaṇī to the Ṛgveda-pariśiṣṭa (Khila).

[NCC III 10b]

307 ṚGVEDA-PĀṬHĀNUKRAMAṆA-DĪPIKĀ (ऋग्वेदपाठानुक्रमणदीपिका)

of Gaṇeśa, son of Kṛṣṇa-bhaṭṭa.

Oudh XIII 24 (no.6). 60 pp. 3000 Grantha-ṣ. Dated A.D. 1878. Remark: "On the mode of chanting the hymns of the Rigveda". Belonged to M. Kali Prasada of Lucknow.

Cf. C. on the Ṛgveda-sarvānukramaṇī, of Gaṇeśa-bhaṭṭa Ḍokhale, N-W P V 148 (no.35). 294 fol. (Anukrama-dīpikā).

[NCC III 10b]

308 ṚGVEDA-PĀDA-LAKṢAṆA (ऋग्वेदपादलक्षण)

GD I 6-B → Pāda-vidhāna of Śaunaka.

GD I 36-D → Pāda-vidhāna of Śaunaka.

[NCC III 10b]

309 ṚGVEDA-PĀDĀNUKRAMAṆĪ (ऋग्वेदपादानुक्रमणी)

→ Pāda-vidhāna of Śaunaka. Cf. Ṛkpādānukramaṇikā.

[NCC III 10b]

310 ṚGVEDA-PRAMĀṆA (ऋग्वेदप्रमाण)

Oppert I 3765. Belonged to Sri Sankaracharya Matham of Kumbakonam.

[NCC III 10b]

311 ṚGVEDA-PRAMĀDA-PĀṬHĀVALĪ (ऋग्वेदप्रमादपाठावली)

of Gaṇeśa. A few comments on the differences in the readings and the practice of Vedic recitation in Kāśī and a defence of Sāyaṇa.

Beginning:

ब्रह्माद्यास्त्रिदशा न यं विदुरहो यन्मायया मोहिता-
श्चत्वारो निगमा विवादसुषिरैः स्वाङ्गैः सहान्दोलिताः ।
यश्चेदं घटपुष्करोपममभिव्याप्य स्थितः खाद् बहि-
स्तं वन्दे गिरिजार्धविग्रहधरं भक्तैकगम्यं शिवम् ॥
वेदा यच्छ्वासभूता निखिलजगदिदं तेभ्य आनिर्ममे यो
यः सत्यो वेदवेद्यः प्रणतलषितदस्तं शिवं नौमि नित्यम् ।
ऋग्वेदे पाठभेदा द्विजवरपठिता भाष्यकृत्पाठभिन्ना-
स्ते ... मु मतिं मे स दिशतु विमलां सत्यपाठान्महेशः ॥
ऋचां प्रमादपाठानामावलिं तनुते कृती ।
काश्यां गणेशो वेदस्य भाष्यमालोच्य यत्नतः ॥

संहिताब्राह्मणारण्यभाष्यपाठे विपर्यया: ।
यथा दृष्टास्तथोच्यन्ते पाठप्रामाण्यसिद्धये ॥

इह खलु तपस्तुष्टेश्वराल्लब्धचतुर्वेदचतुर्मुख तत्पुत्रादिपरंपराप्राप्त प्रथमाध्ययनबहुशाख ऋग्वेदस्येदानीमवशिष्टशाकल बाष्कलशखाध्यायिभिर्द्विजवरै: पठ्यमाना विद्यारण्यकृतभाष्यविरुद्ध प्रमादपाठा बहव उपलभ्यन्ते । तत्राद्यतनाध्ययनशील द्विजवरसमूहभाष्यकारयोर्मध्ये कस्य प्रमाद इति निश्चेतुमशक्यत्वाद् दुरवगाह्ये ऽस्मिन्नगाधे विषये गाधप्रेक्षोर्मम साहसं साधवो विदांकुर्वन्तु।

End:

किंच तत्कृतवेदभाष्यस्य साक्षाद् भगवता व्यासेन लेखशुद्धि: कृतेत्यप्याख्यायिका श्रूयते ॥ एवमुक्तरीत्या विदुषां सर्वसमञ्जसमिति भवत्वलम् ॥

मङ्गलं भाष्यकारस्य सायणार्यस्य धीमत: ।
तदुक्तं पाठं पठतां बह्वृचानां च मङ्गलम् ॥

इति गणेशकृत-ऋक्प्रमादपाठावली समाप्ता ॥

SBD 53275. 28 fol. Dated V.S. 1916.

312 ṚGVEDA-PRAYOGA (PADA-GĀḌHA) (ऋग्वेदप्रयोग / पदगाढ)
"On the *Ṛgveda* words of particular character." IO 66 → Pada-gāḍha.

[NCC III 10b]

313 ṚGVEDA-PRĀTIŚĀKHYA (ऋग्वेदप्रातिशाख्य)
of Śaunaka. Variously called *Ṛkprātiśākhya, Ṛgveda-prātiśākhya-pārṣada, Pārṣada-sūtra, Śaunakīya-prātiśākhya,* etc. It is divided into 18 chapters called Paṭala-s. There is also a division into three Adhyāya-s (with six Paṭala-s each) and Varga-s (made up generally of five stanzas). On Pāṇini's relation to and dependence on it, see the introduction to Max Müller's edition; H. Sköld, *Papers on Pāṇini,* Lund, 1926; Batakrishna Ghosh, "Pāṇini and the Prātiśākhya", *the Indian Historical Quarterly* vol. 10 (1934), pp. 665-70; Paul Thieme, op. cit., vol. 13 (1937), pp. 329-42; K[setresh Chunder] Chattopadhyaya, op. cit., pp. 343-49; Arthur Berriedale Keith, *Indian Culture,* vol. 2 (1936), pp. 742-44; Batakrishna Ghosh, op. cit., vol. 4 (1938), pp. 387-99; Ksetresh Chunder Chattopadhyaya, op. cit., vol. 5 (1939), pp. 95-98; S. P. Chaturvedi, *New Indian Antiquery,* vol. 1 (1938), pp. 450-69. For an English version of Max Müller's introduction to the *Ṛgveda-prātiśākhya,* see B. Ghosh, *the Indian Historical Quarterly* vol. 3 (1927), pp. 611-24, 757-68.

Beginning:

परावरे ब्रह्मणि यं सदाहुर्वेदात्मानं वेदनिधिं मुनीन्द्रा: ।
तं पद्मगर्भं परमं त्वादिदेवं प्रणम्यर्चां लक्षणमाह शौनक: ॥ १॥
माण्डूकेय: संहितां वायुमाह तथाकाशं चास्य माण्डव्य एव।
समानतामनिले चाम्बरे च मत्वागस्त्यो ऽविप्रहारं तदेव॥ २॥
अध्यात्मक्कृसौ शूरवीरा: सुताश्च वाङ्मनसयोर्विवदन्त्यानुपूर्व्ये।

संधेर्विवर्त्तनं निर्भुजं वदन्ति शौद्धाक्षरोच्चारणं च प्रतृण्णम्॥ ३॥
उभयमन्तरेणोभयं व्यासमग्रे परे कामा अन्ननाकोभयाख्याः ।
प्राणः षकारे यच्च बलं णकारे वाक्प्राणयोर्यश्च होमः परस्परम्॥ ४॥
गुरुत्वं लघुता साम्यं ह्रस्वदीर्घप्लुतानि च।
लोपागमविकाराश्च प्रकृतिर्विक्रमः क्रमः ॥ ५॥
स्वरितोदात्तनीचत्वं श्वासो नादस्तथोभयम्।
एतत् सर्वं च विज्ञेयं छन्दोभाषामधीयता॥ ६॥

End:

सर्वाणि भूतानि मनो गतिश्च स्पर्शाश्च गन्धाश्च रसाश्च सर्वे।
शब्दाश्च रूपाणि च सर्वमेतत् त्रिष्टुब्जगत्यौ समुपैति भक्त्या॥ ३२॥
गुर्वक्षराणां गुरुवृत्ति सर्वं गुर्वक्षरं त्रैष्टुभमेव विद्यात्।
लघ्वक्षराणां लघुवृत्ति सर्वं लघ्वक्षरं जागतमेव विद्यात्॥ ३३॥
यश्छन्दसां वेद विशेषमेतं भूतानि च त्रैष्टुभजागतानि।
सर्वाणि रूपाणि च भक्तितो यः स्वर्गं जयत्येभिरथामृतत्वम्॥ ३४॥

Adyar D I 764 (20 D 84 = 67128). PL. Gr. 5 fol. (marked 37-42; fol. no.40 is missing). Incomplete. Breaks off in section 2.37.

Alwar 17. Extract no. 4 (of Śāṅkhāyana Śākhā). Col.: śāṅkhāyana-śākhāyāṃ prātiśākhyaṃ samāptam | Dated V.S. 1808. Copied in Vārāṇasī.

Alwar 31. Dated V.S. 1561.

America 348. 35 fol. Dated V.S. 1722.

America 349. 35 fol. Dated V.S. 1730.

America 350. 38-52 fol. (with Uvaṭa's C.). Lacks beginning. Dated V.S. 1722.

Ānandāśrama 5273. 12 fol. Incomplete. Up to 5th Paṭala.

Ānandāśrama 5864. 53 fol.

B I, p. 198 (no.7). 43 fol. Dated V.S. 1526.

B I, p. 198 (no.8). 82 fol.

B I, p. 198 (no.9). 44 fol. Dated V.S. 1718.

B I, p. 206 (no.57). 72 fol.

B I, p. 206 (no.58). 19 fol.

B I, p. 206 (no.59). 8 fol.

Baroda 421. 36 fol. 700 Grantha-s. = CLB I, p. 24.

Baroda 5847(a). 87 fol. 700 Grantha-s. = CLB I, p. 24. Dated Śaka 1718.

Baroda 8255. 39 fol. 700 Grantha-s. = CLB I, p. 24.

Baroda 11682. 200 fol. 3000 Grantha-s = CLB I, p. 24 (with C. of Uvaṭa).

Baroda 11800. 40 fol. 700 Grantha-s. = CLB I, p. 24.

Baroda 12654. 11 fol. 400 Grantha-s (with C. of Uvaṭa). = CLB I, p. 24.

Baroda 23560. 44 fol. 663 Grantha-s.

BBRAS 484 (B D 221). 37 fol.

Ben. 5.

Berlin StB-PrK (NGMPP). A 609/6. 6 fol. Incomplete. Col.: iti pārṣadavyākhyayām uvaṭakṛtau prātiśākhya- sūtrabhāṣye tṛtīyam paṭalam.

Berlin StB-PrK (NGMPP). E 1673/9. 47 fol. Dated V.S. 1562. Scribe: Govinda, son of Viṭṭhala. Copied at Ratnapura in Tirubhuk-deśa (microfilm dated 27.06.1984).

Bh. p. 7 (no.16). 22 fol. 1000 Grantha-s.

Bhk. 8.

BHU B 3865 (D 2E/2134). 34 fol. Incomplete.

BHU B 3577 (D 2E/2135). 37 fol. Incomplete.

BHU C 620 (D 2E/2136). 22 fol. Incomplete.

BISM p. 40 (36/698). Dated V.S. 1669.

BISM p. 41 (41/449).

BISM p. 172 (37/665).

Bombay Uni. 688 (BMC 4 29). 32 fol. (3 chapters).

Bombay Uni. 689 (BMC 79 16). 21 fol. Dated Śaka 1646.

Bombay Uni. 690 (BMC 78 1). 20 fol. (Paṭala-s 1-9).

Bombay Uni. 691 (BMC 87 1). 55 fol. (with C. of Uvaṭa). (9 Paṭala-s).

Bombay Uni. (Itchharam 86 1) 67(1). 28 fol. Dated V.S. 1755.

Bombay Uni. Acc. no. 3216 (BMC 131 14). 28 fol. Incomplete.

Bombay Uni. (BMC 145 1). 39 fol. Dated Śaka 1714.

Bombay Uni. Palm-leaf No. 23. PL. Gr. uncatalogued.

Bombay Uni. Palm-leaf No. 26. PL. Gr. (with C.). Uncatalogued.

BORI 9 of 1879-80. = BORI D I i.52. 46 fol. Dated V.S. 1574. Copied by Kānhāka of Rājapura.

BORI 16 of A 1879-80. = BORI D I i.53. 22 fol.

BORI 43 of A 1881-82. = BORI D I i.54. 42 fol. Dated Śaka 1728. Copied by Keśava, son of Nārāyaṇa-bhaṭṭa Khāḍilkar.

BORI 2 of 1895-1902. 33 fol. Dated V.S. 1655.

BORI 27 of 1899-1915. 18 fol.

Brl. p. 5 (no.II) = IO 4234.

Burnell 1b.

Cabaton I 215. 471 pp. (with C. of Uvaṭa).

Deccan College 1864. 5 fol. (13-17). Incomplete.

Deccan College 5764. 50 fol. Dated Śaka 1711. Varṇa-krama-lakṣaṇa at the end.

Deccan College 8251. 43 fol. Dated V.S. 1719.

GD I 5. PL. Mal. 19 fol. 500 Grantha-s. Incomplete (12 chs.).

GD I 6-A. PL. Mal. 33 fol. 700 Incomplete.

GJKSV 14450. 54 fol. Catalogued as Prātiśākhya-pravacana (Varṇa-krama).

GJKSV 29990. 19 fol. Incomplete (up to 7.22: vaha vāyo piba ...).

Gough p. 30.

Granthappura p. 1 (no.6). Mal. 300 Grantha-s. Incomplete. 12 Paṭala-s.

Granthappura p. 1 (no.7a). Mal. 500 Grantha-s. Incomplete. 18 Paṭala-s.

Haug p. 28 (no.64) = München 30.

Haug p. 28 (no.65a) = München 29A.

Haug p. 28 (no.65b) = München 29B.

Hpr. II 25. 51 fol. 710 Grantha-s.

Hz 628. PL. Tel. 13 fol. (2 Praśna-s). Belonged to Vedam Venkatasubrahmanya Somayaji of Allur, Nellur Dist.

IM 1806A. 10-38 fol. Incomplete. Dated V.S. 1664.

IM 2001A. 41 fol.

IM 2167. 51 fol. Dated Śaka 1548.

IM 9701. 13 fol. (5-15, 17-18). Incomplete. Title: Prātiśākhya.

IO 64 (1355g). 24 fol. (200-23). Dated V.S. 1781.

IO 4233 (Mackenzie II 80f). PL. Na. 50 fol. (19-21, 34-37 are lost). Written ca. 17th cent.

IO 4234 (3546 = Burnell 205c). PL. Gr. 97-143 fol.

Khn. p. 8 (no.17). 45 fol. ; from Ashte; Limaye.

L 902. 22 fol. 660 Grantha-s. Dated Śaka 1719.

L 4190. 15 fol. 653 Grantha-s. Dated V.S. 1693 / Śaka 1559. Copied in Kāśī by Keśava, son of Sūrajit.

Lund III.

MD 879. Tel. 36 pp. 2 pages at the end on Jaṭā.

MD 880. Tel. 35 pp. Contains a comm. from fol. 23.

MD 881. PL. Na. 30 fol. Incomplete. Breaks off in the 17th Paṭala.

Müller 49A (MM 57A). 28 fol. Copied by MM. in Roman character of a Ms. dated V.S. 1710 (1653-54); probably a copy of Weber 35.

Müller 50 (MM 69 A 8). 46 pp.

Müller 51 (MM 70 B 8). 157 fol. (65 / 53 / 39) (with C. of Uvaṭa). Dated V.S. 1895 / Śaka 1760 (1838-39). Presented by Ballantyne.

Max Müller Mem. VIII. 54 fol. Dated V.S. 1877 / Śaka 1742. Varṇa-krama-lakṣaṇa (18 verses) of Jagannātha at the end.

München 29(A). 27 fol. Dated A.D. 1775. Copied by Paraśurāma, son of Hari-bhaṭṭa Jogalekara. Col.: 1696 jayasaṃvat-mārgamāsa-śuklāṣṭamīlikhāpitam.

München 29(B). 52 fol. Dated A.D. 1791. Copied by Paraśurāma, son of Hari-bhaṭṭa Jogalekara. Col.: 1712 sādhāraṇa-śrāvaṇakṛṣṇāṣṭamyāṃ budhavāsare likhāpitam.

München 30. 34 fol. Dated A.D. 1872. Col.: 1783 durmatibhādrapadaśukla-paurṇmāsyāsaumyavāsare uttarābhādrā ... "Copied by Paraśurāma, son of Hari-bhaṭṭa Jogalekara." (not found in the Ms. !).

Mysore I, p. 24 (3 Mss.); p. 612 (2 Mss.) (with C.).

Mysore ND II 3227-41. Extract no. 60, 61, 62, 63.

Oppert I 1403. Belonged to Annasvami Srauti of Bhavani, Coimbatore Dist.

Oppert I 7863. Belonged to Paravastu Venkatarangacharyar of Vishakhapattanam.

Oppert II 6212. Belonged to Narasimhacharya of Kumbakonam.

Oppert II 6886. Belonged to Venkateshacharyar of Venkataraya Street, Kumbakonam.

Oxf. CS d.176(1). 34 fol.

Oxf. CS d.176(2). 18 fol. Incomplete.

Oxf. CS d.176(3). 36 fol.

Oxf. CS d.177(1). 34 fol. Dated Śaka 1567. (Pārṣada-prātiśākhya).

Oxf. CS e.59. 38 fol. Dated A.D. 1596.

Oxf. CS e.63. 20 fol.

Oxf. II 892(1b) (Ms. Wilson 379). 70 fol. (5-74) (with C). Dated A.D. 1600. = Oxf. 378b.

Oxf. II 893(1) (Ms. Sansk. c. 9). 30 fol. Dated A.D. 1806. = Oxf. 405b (no.9).

Oxf. II 894 (Ms. Sansk. c. 10). 230 fol. (with Uvaṭa's C.). = Oxf. 405b (no.10). Dated A.D. 1794.

P 4.

Peters. II, p. 168 (no.32.). 46 fol.

Peters. II, p. 169 (no.11). 72 fol.

PUL I, p. 19 (no.33). 61 fol.

PUL I, p. 19 (no.34). 33 fol.

PUL I, p. 19 (no.35). 23 fol.

PUL II. App. p. 10 (no.148) PL. Gr. 49 fol. 1000 Grantha-s.

Rajapur 263 (with C.). 456.

RASB II 267 (G 428). 13 fol. 234 Grantha-s.

RASB II 268 (G 2977). 38 fol. 900 Grantha-s. Dated V.S. 1669.

RASB II 269 (G 1977) = L 4190.

RASB II 270 (G 2182). 141 fol. 5550 Grantha-s (with C. of Viṣṇumitra). Dated V.S. 1843.

RASB II 272 (G 2044). 118 fol. 5300 Grantha-s (with C. of Viṣṇumitra and Uvaṭa). Dated Śaka 1721.

SB p. 9 (no.88). 31 fol. 800 Grantha-s. Title: Śaunaka-prātiśākhya. = SBD 2114.

SBD 2114. 31 fol. (Śaunaka-prātiśākhya).

SBD 2118. 104 fol. Title: Śaunaka-prātiśākhya.

SBD 2122. 19 fol. (3-11, 13-22). Incomplete.

SBD 2136. 27 fol. (1-17, 19-28). Incomplete.

SBD 2143. 193 fol. (with C. of Uvaṭa).

SBD 2144. 40 fol. Dated V.S. 1727.

SBD 2145. 27 fol. (1-13, 15-28). Incomplete.

SBD 2146. 33 fol. Dated V.S. 1596.

SBD 2147. 9 fol. (2-7, 9-11). Incomplete.

SBD 2150. 58 fol. Dated V.S. 1692.

SBD 2151. 1 fol. Incomplete.

SBD 47235. 31 fol. Incomplete (up to 6th Paṭala of the 3rd Adhyāya). Dated V.S. 1678.

SBD 47236. 91 fol. Incomplete (fol. 21, 38, 68 missing).

SBD 47244. 35 fol. (1-29, 31-36). Incomplete. Title: Dāśatayī-prātiśākhya.

SBD 47246. 33 fol. Incomplete.

SBD 55241. 19 fol. Dated V.S. 1886. Title: Varṇa-krama-lakṣaṇa. The last fol. contains 18 verses called Ṛgveda-varṇa-krama-lakṣaṇa.

SBD 55255. 37 fol. Incomplete. (Prātiśākhya).

Stein p. 3 (no. 33). 57 fol. Dated V.S. 1711.

Stein p. 3 (no. 34). 35 fol.

Stein p. 3 (no. 35). 11 fol. Incomplete (Paṭala-s 1-4).

Tb. 207. Copy of a Ms. from London/Berlin made in 1845-46 by Roth.

TCD 20. PL. Mal. 126 fol. 3800 Grantha-s (with C.).

TCD 21. PL. Mal. 182 fol. 3800 Grantha-s (with C.).

TCD 38-E. PL. Mal. 21 fol. 700 Grantha-s.

TD 1732. 5 fol. 72 Grantha-s. 2 Paṭala-s only.

TD 1735. 229 fol. (11-239). 4000 Grantha-s (with C.).

TD 1736. 222 fol. 3315 Grantha-s (with C.).

TD 1737. 20 fol. 380 Grantha-s (with C.). 2 Paṭala-s only.
TD 1738. 142 fol. 2600 Grantha-s (with C.).
Trav. Uni. 576 A. PL. Mal. 700 Grantha-s.
Trav. Uni. 952. PL. Mal. 800 Grantha-s.
Trav. Uni. 2510 C. PL. Tel. 100 Grantha-s.. Incomplete.
Trav. Uni. 3673. PL. Gr. 3700 Grantha-s (with C. Udāharaṇa-mālikā).
Trav. Uni. 4840. 6000 Grantha-s (with C.). Dated V.S. 1878 / Śaka 1747.
Trav. Uni. 4846. 700 Grantha-s.
Trav. Uni. 4922. 700 Grantha-s.
Trav. Uni. 5539 G. PL. Tel. 400 Grantha-s. Incomplete.
Trav. Uni. 7438. 10 fol. 250 Grantha-s. Incomplete (with C. Udāharaṇa-mālikā).
Trav. Uni. 7461 A. 1000 Grantha-s (with C.).
Trav. Uni. 12560 A. PL. Mal. 700 Grantha-s. (M.E. 948 = A.D. 1773).
Trav. Uni. 15918 A. PL. Mal. 650 Grantha-s. Incomplete.
Trav. Uni. 16408 Z11. PL. Mal. 700 Grantha-s. (M.E. 844 = A.D. 1669).
Trav. Uni. 17538 A. PL. Mal. 700 Grantha-s.
Trav. Uni. 17854 A. PL. Mal. 350 Grantha-s. Incomplete.
Trav. Uni. 19025. PL. Mal. 480 Grantha-s. Incomplete.
Trav. Uni. 19026 A. PL. Mal. 700 Grantha-s.
Trav. Uni. 22120 A. PL. Mal. 700 Grantha-s (with C. ?).
Trav. Uni. L.248 B. PL. Mal. 200 Grantha-s. Incomplete.
Trav. Uni. L.479 (with C.).
Trav. Uni. L.1346 A. PL. Mal. 3500 Grantha-s (with C. Vākya-pradīpikā).
Trav. Uni. L.1351 A. PL. Mal. 700 Grantha-s.
Trav. Uni. C.851 = TCD 20.
Trav. Uni. C.1887 E. PL. Mal. 700 Grantha-s.
Trav. Uni. C.1810 = TCD 21 (with C. Udāharaṇa-mālikā).
Trav. Uni. T.526. 3700 Grantha-s (with C. Udāharaṇa-mālikā).
Trav. Uni. T.1134. 3700 Grantha-s (with C. Vākya-pradīpikā).
Triv. Cur. V 7. Mal. 4500 Grantha-s (with C.). Incomplete. Obtained from Suryan Bhatta-thiri, Kalatimana, Nattasseri.
Triv. Cur. V 8. Mal. 6000 Grantha-s (with C.). Incomplete (15 Paṭala-s). Obtained from Paramesvaran Narayanan Bhattatihri, Thiruvalla.
Ujjain I, p. 9 (no.2327). 51 fol.
Ujjain Latest Additions 126 (with C.).
Venkatesiah 60. 71 (with C.).
Vidyaranyapura 92 (with C.).
Viśvabhāratī 1706 (Paṭala 7).
Viśvabhāratī 2153.
Visvanatha Vamana Deva, Varanasi. 42 fol. Dated V.S. 1816.
Visvanatha Vamana Deva, Varanasi. 208 fol. (with Bhāṣya of Uvaṭa). Dated V.S. 1817.
VSM I 426 (no.4907). 39 fol. Dated Śaka 1679. Copied by Ṣaḍaṅgula Nārāyaṇa.
VSM I 427 (no.628). 34 fol. Additional verses from Varṇakrama-lakṣaṇa of Jagannātha.
VSM I 428 (no.97). 33 fol. Incomplete (Adhyāya 2-3). Dated Śaka 1779. Copied by Āṭhavale Viśvanātha. Contains 18 verses from Varṇakrama-lakṣaṇa by Jagannātha.

VSM I 429 (no.98). 16 fol. Incomplete (Paṭala 1-6). Dated Śaka 1579. Copied by Āṭhavale Viśvanātha.

VSM I 430 (no.5437). 110 fol. (103 and 7) (with C. of Uvaṭa). Dated Śaka 1696. First 6 fol. contain the Varga-dvaya-vṛtti of Viṣṇumitra. Copied by Pāṭhaka Moreśvara.

VSM I 431 (no.7516). 82 fol. (with C. of Uvaṭa). First 12 fol. contain the Varga-dvaya-vṛtti of Viṣṇumitra.

VSM I 432 (no.5435). 57 fol. Incomplete (Paṭala 1-10) (with C. Subodhinī. Extract p. 347.

VSM III 166 (no.11301). 10 fol. Inc. (with a few short notes on technical trems with illustrations). Title : Prātiśākhya-vivaraṇa.

Wai I 349. 32 fol. Dated Śaka 1735.

Wai I 350. 38 fol. Dated Śaka 1683.

Wai I 351. 25 fol.

Wai I 352. 62 fol.

Wai I 353. 44 fol. Dated Śaka 1725.

Wai I 354. 52 fol. Dated Śaka 1679.

Wai I 355. 63 fol. Dated Śaka 1687.

Wai I 356. 41 fol. Dated Śaka 1687.

Wai I 357. 27 fol. Incomplete.

Wai I 358. 24 fol. Incomplete.

Wai I 359. 16 fol. Incomplete.

Wai I 360. 30 fol. (10-39). Incomplete.

Wai I 361. 169 fol. (with C. of Uvaṭa).

Wai I 362. 144 fol. (with C. of Uvaṭa).

Wai I 363. 147 fol. (with C. of Uvaṭa). Dated Śaka 1752.

Wai I 364. 8 fol. (with C. of Uvaṭa). Incomplete.

Wai I 365. 14 fol. (with C. Dūṣaṇabhaṅga-mīmāṃsā of Karṇāṭaka Mādhavācārya). Incomplete.

Weber 34 (Chambers 595). 68 fol. Dated V.S. 1694. Copied by Kikābhāi in Varanasi. Cf. Roth: Zur Literatur und Geschichte des Weda, Stuttgart 1846, pp. 53ff. (translated by Ludwig E. Rees, JASB, 1848, pp. 6-26).

Weber 35 (Chambers 691). 67 fol. Dated V.S. 1710. Copied by Harirāma, son of Rāmakṛṣṇa.

Whish 73(1). PL. Gr. 33 fol. (1-33).

Whish 73(1a). PŁ. Gr. 122 fol. (34-155) (with C. Pārṣada-vṛtti). Incomplete. Up to X. Paṭala.

Whish 78(7). PL. Gr. 32 fol. (conjectural title : Ṛgveda-prātiśākhya-pariśiṣṭa).

Ptd.:

1) Ed. by M. ad. Regnier, *Journal Asiatique* 5-11, 1856-58. Reprinted : Paris, 1857-59. 3 vols. 315, 145, 299 pp. [BM : Ptd. Bks. Cat. 1876 (p. 132); Emeneau (364)]

2) Ed. by Friderich Max Müller, with a German translation and notes (in the Ist volume of his edition of the *Ṛgveda* with Pada-pāṭha : ... Text und Übersetzung des Prātiśākhya oder der ältesten Phonetik und Grammatik ...). – Leipzig : Brockhaus, 1856. 15, CCCXCV pp. [SAI (ind 50 B 8); Emeneau (32, 34, 360)]

Also issued separately : *Rig-Veda-Prātiśākhya*, das älteste Lehrbuch der Vedischen Phonetik Sanskrittext mit Uebersetzung und Anmerkungen. – Leipzig : Brockhaus, 1869. 32, CCCXCV pp. [UBHD (G 1730); SKGI (Rf IX 70); BM : Ptd. Bks. Cat. 1876, p. 132 and p. 156); IO : Ptd. Bks. Cat. 1953, p. 2186 (16 L 6); Emeneau (32, 34, 360)]

3) Ed. by Satyavrata Samasrami, *Pārṣada-sūtram (Ṛgvedasya Prātiśākhyam)* in the Sanskrit journal *Uṣā*. – Calcutta : Satya Press, 1895 (1897), vol. III, pts. 1-3. 70 pp. [NL (180 Jc 89 102 1 / 180 Qc 88 3); Emeneau (361)]

4) Ed. and annotated by Yugalakishora Vyasa Pathaka and Prabhudatta Sarma, with the commentary of Uvaṭa. – Benares, 1894-1903. 2, 399 pp. – (Ben. S. S. 13.). [Adyar (H080 CSS B14); NL (180 Jc 89 109); Gö(8. scr. var. arg. I,1500:10/13); IO : Ptd. Bks. Cat. 1953, p. 2186 (28 C 13); Emeneau (363)]

5) Ed. by Hitavrata Chattopadhyaya, with the commentary of Kumāra Viṣṇumitra and Uvaṭa's *Pārṣada-sūtra-vṛtti*, in the Sanskrit journal *Uṣā*. – Calcutta : Satya Press, 1895-97, vol. III, pts. 4, 9-12. 338 pp. [Kashi Vidyapeetha (Saṃ. 871.226 Śau 42 Pā 2)]

6) Ed. by Pashupatinatha Sastri ... with the assistance of Chintaharan Chakravarti, with the editor's own commentary based on Uvaṭa's Bhāṣya *Śaunakīyaṃ Ṛgveda-prātiśākhyam (Pārṣadasūtram)* Uvaṭakṛtabhāṣyānusāriṇyā vyākhyayā samalaṃkṛtya ... sampāditam. – Calcutta 1927. ii, 6, 252, 10 pp. – (Sanskrit Sahitya Parishad Series 17). [BORI (3851, 4413); NL (180 Jc 92 257; 350); IO : Ptd. Bks. Cat. 1953, p. 2186 (San D. 437); UBTÜ (21 A 15743); Emeneau (362)]

7) Ed. by Mangal Deva Shastri, with the Commentary of Uvaṭa, English translation, Notes, etc.:

vol. I. Introduction and Text in the form of stanzas. – Varanasi (Englishia Lane) : Vaidika Svadhyaya Mandira (Motilal Banarsi Das), 1959. 89, 112 pp. [Kashi Vidyapeetha (211.1 Śas / P); SAI (ind 51 D 7 88/2333)]

vol. II : Text in the sūtra form and Commentary with Critical Apparatus. – Allahabad : Indian Press, 1931. iv, 13, 3, 504, 5 pp. [IO : Ptd. Bks. Cat. 1953, p. 2186 (San D. 1125/2); SOAS (III.1.f.39.5b – 14680)]

vol. III : English translation of the Text, Additional Notes, Several Appendices and Indices. – Lahore : Punjab Sanskrit Book Depot / Moti Lal Banarsi Das, 1937. ii, ii, vi, 431 pp. – (The Punjab Oriental Series 24). [Adyar (H080 PSS 24); BORI (12491, 16746); SOAS (III.1.f.39.5c – 14680)]

Part of his Introducton. – Oxford : University Press, 1922. 33 pp. [Adyar (H 215.404 Man RP); NL (K180 Jb 92 17); IO : Ptd. Bks. Cat. 1953, p. 2186 (San D.110,a); SOAS (III.1.f.39.5 – 14680)]

8) Ed. by Shivarama Shastri Shinte with a Marathi translation. – Bombay : Karanataka Printing Press, part I, 1939..9, 118, 2 pp. part II, 1941. 13, 178 pp. [BORI (8412, 8777)]

9) Ed. by Virendra Kumara Varma, with Uvaṭa's commentary and a Hindi translation. – Varanasi : Banaras Hindu University, 1970. 17, 960 pp. – (Banaras Hindu University Sanskrit Series – Research Publication Scheme 5). [BORI (40286, 40287)]

Reprint of the above – Delhi : Chowkhamba Sanskrit Pratishthana, 1986. – (Vrajajivan Prachyabharati Granthamala 11). [SAI (ind 51 D 787/1727)]

10) Ed. by Vrajavihari Chaube, with a Hindi translation (Paṭala-s 1-4). – Delhi. : Bharatiya Vidya Prakashan, 1986. xxxv, 346 pp.

11) Ed. by Rāmaprasāda Tripāṭhī, with Uvaṭa's commentary. – Varanasi : Sampurnanand Sanskrit Vishvavidyālaya, 1986. 9, 375 pp. – (Sarasvatībhavana Granthamālā 121). [SAI (ind ***)]

– C.

BORI 51 of 1869-70. = BORI D I i.459. 94 fol. Dated V.S. 1626.

BORI 4 of 1895-1902. 18 fol. Incomplete (chs. II and III).

Gough p. 30.

Gough p. 65 (no.51: Pārṣada-vyākhyā). 94 fol. 2200 Grantha-s. Incomplete. Dated V.S. 1626.

Gough p. 65 (no.52: Pārṣada-vyākhyā). 262 fol. 4680 Grantha-s. Incomplete.

Hz 1891. 165 fol. (Pārṣada-vṛtti). Incomplete. Belonged to Jambunatha Bhatta of Thanjavur.

Mad. Uni. R A S. 105(b).

Mysore I, p. 612 (2 Mss.).

Mysore ND II 3270 (P 62/ 2). PL. Na. 8 fol.

Mysore ND II 3271 (P 4954). PL. Na. 82 fol.

Mysore ND II 3272 (P 5657/ 1). PL. Na. 2 fol. Incomplete.

Mysore ND II 3273 (P 5657/17). PL. Na. 7 fol. (30-36). Extract no. 66.

Mysore ND II 3274 (P 8770). PL. Na. 68 fol. Extract no. 67.

Mysore ND II 3275 (P 476/ 4). 1 fol. Incomplete (with Kannada Ṭīkā). Extract no. 68.

Mysore ND II 3280 (P 8031/ 1). PL. Na. 67 fol.

PUL I, p. 19 (no.38). 29 fol. (probably not Uvaṭa's).

Trav. Uni. 7461 A. 1000 Grantha-s (with text).

Ujjain II, p. 84.

Venkatesiah 1.43. Incomplete.

Viśvabhāratī 1328 (d). 1346 (a). 1346 (b).

Wai 136. 2 Mss.; the second beginning: vināyakaṃ guhaṃ bhānuṃ ... bhāratīṃ ca namāmy aham | and ending: – vyāsavacanā ... śrute taṃ kāmam ityādi ||

– C. Pārṣada-vṛtti. Probably earlier than Uvaṭa. Discussed by Max Müller and Eggeling. Only up to the end of Paṭala 12.

Beginning:

अष्टौ समानाक्षराण्यादितः वर्णसमाम्नायस्यादितो ऽष्टाक्षराणि समानाक्षरसंज्ञानि वेदितव्यानि। अ आ ऋ ॠ इ ई उ ऊ इति। समानाक्षरसंज्ञायाः प्रयोजनं समानाक्षरे संस्थान इत्यत्र। उच्यते। वर्णसमाम्नाये विप्रतिपत्तिर्दृश्यते। अवर्णात् परमृवर्णमेक उपदिशन्ति। उवर्णादपरे। तथा एकारात् परमोकारमेके उपदिशन्ति। ऐकारादपरे। तथा हकारं शकारात् पूर्वमेके उपदिशन्ति। सकारात् परमपरे।

End:

एकयोगे सति उत्तरे त्रय इत्यस्य ग्रहणमनर्थकं भवति रिफितान्यूष्मणो घोषे दुभावस्वधितीव चेति यथोक्तमेव। इति पा(र्ष)दवृत्तौ क्रमपटलं नाम द्वादशं समाप्तम्।

Whish 73(1a). PL. Gr. 122 fol. (34-155) (with text). Incomplete.

– C. Prakāśikā.
Venkatesiah 2.

– C. Vṛtti, anon.
B I, p. 198 (no.10). 101 fol.
TD 1738. 142 fol. 2600 Grantha-s.

– C. Vākya-pradīpikā of Īśvara or Parameśvara.

Beginning: (4301)

परापरे ब्रह्मणि यं सदाहुः वेदात्मानं वेदनिधिं मुनीन्द्राः ।
तं पद्मगर्भं परमं त्वादिदेवं प्रणम्यर्चां लक्षणमाह शौनकः ॥

परं च अपरं च परापरम्। परं ब्रह्म अपरं ब्रह्म च। परापरे ब्रह्मणि। परं ब्रह्म मनसा ध्यानगम्यं सदात्मकम्। अपरं ब्रह्म तु शब्दात्मकं जपादिषु कर्मसु यत् प्रयोज्यं तत् शब्दाख्यानम् -- अग्निमीळे इत्यादि। तदुक्तम् -- द्वे ब्रह्मणी वेदितव्ये।... इदानीं संहितापदक्रमस्वरूपमाह -- एवं ते विवृत्या त वदन्ति निर्भुजं शौद्धाक्षारोच्चारणं प्रतृण्णम् उभयान्तरादुभयव्याप्तिमाहुः सुतो अन्ननाकोभयाख्याः ...।
इति प्रातिशाख्यव्याख्यायां वाक्यप्रदीपिकायां प्रथमः पटलः ॥

End:

इत्याह भगवान् शौनकः। अपीह श्लोकाः। गायत्र्यादीनि छन्दांसि।
तानि सर्वमिदं कृत्स्नं त्रैलोक्यं सचराचरम्।
धन्यं यशस्यमायुष्यं पुण्यं पुष्टिकरं शुभम्॥
आत्यन्तिकं चापवर्ग्यं छन्दसां ज्ञानमुत्तमम्।
छन्दोज्ञानात् परं ज्ञानं नान्यदस्तीति मे मतिः ॥
आहुर्यस्माद् द्विजश्रेष्ठ तस्मात् तत्र प्रयत्नतः ।
नमो ऽस्तु निखिलेशाय शङ्खचक्राब्जधारिणे।
क्षीराब्धितनयेशाय राजीवाक्षाय विष्णवे॥

इति प्रातिशाख्यव्याख्यायां पार्षदकृतायां (?) वाक्यप्रदीपिकायामष्टादशः पटलः ॥ समाप्तश्चायं ग्रन्थः ॥

MT 4301. 124 fol. (attributed to Pārṣada !). Transcribed in 1923-24 from a Ms. of Narayana Nambuttiripad, Puvalli-mana, Challasseri Post, Malabar Dist.
Trav. Uni. L.479 (with text).

Trav. Uni. L.1346 A. PL. Mal. 3500 Grantha-s (with text).
Trav. Uni. T.1134. 3700 Grantha-s (with text).

– C. called Subodhinī.
VSM I 432 (no.5435). 57 fol. Incomplete (Paṭala 1-10). Extract p. 347.

– C. Dūṣaṇabhaṅga-mīmāṃsā of Karṇāṭaka Mādhavācārya.
Wai I 365. 14 fol. Incomplete (on Paṭala 6 only).

– C. of Uvaṭa (see above under Uvaṭa). Called *Pārṣada-vṛtti* or *-vyākhyā* in several Mss.; in all Mss. incomplete and mixed with the commentary of Viṣṇumitra. The gloss on the introductory verses are not found in all Mss., and may be spurious. See under entries of the commentary of Viṣṇumitra also. On the relation of the two commentaries, see Mangal Deva Shastri's introduction to the *Ṛgveda-prātiśākhya*, Oxford, 1922, pp. 8-17.

Adyar D XIII 34 (VB 862d). PL. Gr. 15 fol. (chs. 16-17).
Alph. List Beng. Govt. p. 19.
Alwar 32 (called Pārṣada-bhāṣya).
America 350. 38-52 fol. Incomplete. Lacks beginning.
America 351. 391 fol.
America 352. 137 fol. Dated Śaka 1765.
Baroda 11682. 200 fol. 3000 Grantha-s. = CLB I, p. 24. Incomplete. 10 Paṭala-s only.
Baroda 12654. 11 fol. 400 Grantha-s. = CLB I, p. 24. Incomplete (no beginning, no end).
BC. 428.
Ben. 2.
Berlin StB-PrK (NGMPP). E 1673/11. 240 fol. Dated V.S. 1539. Scribe: Viṭṭhala, son of Devadatta. Copied at Kāśī (microfilm dated 29.06.1984) (very good script).
Bik. 316. 247 fol. (Described as C. on the Ṛgveda-prātiśākhya but the extract printed in the catalogue is that on the Vājasaneyi-prātiśākhya).
BISM p. 172 (45/55). 196 fol. 18 Paṭala-s.
BISM p. 172 (22/12). Dated Śaka 1761.
BISM p. 172 (35/307). Dated Śaka 1746.
Bombay Uni. 691 (BMC 87 1). 55 fol. (with text). (9 Paṭala-s).
BORI 11 of Viś. (1). = BORI D I i.56. 191 fol. Dated Śaka 1562 (1640). Called Pārṣada-vyākhyā and ascribed to Viṣṇumitra.
Burnell 1b.
Cabaton I 215. 471 pp. (with text).
Calcutta Skt. Coll. I 490 (344). 182 fol. It begins as Viṣṇumitra's C. but the colophon reads as of Uvaṭa's. A portion of the C. on Āśvalāyana-gṛhyasūtra at the end.
CPB 3215.
Deccan College 1697.
Deccan College 1998.
Deccan College 1973. 42 fol. Dated Śaka 1679.
Deccan College 1974. 43 fol. Dated Śaka 1698.

Haug p. 28 (no.66) = München 31.

Hpr. II 136. 157 fol. 4290 Grantha-s. (Viṣṇumitra).

Hz 429. PL. Tel. 95 fol. Belonged to Kesari Yajnayya of Brahmanakraka (Agrahara), Nellur Dist.

Hz 439. PL. Tel. 153 fol. Extract p. 80. Belonged to Gottimukkula Viraraghava Somayaji of Brahmanakraka (Agrahara), Nellur Dist.

Hz 1862. 166 fol. Incomplete. Belonged to Jambunatha Bhatta of Thanjavur.

IO 65 (28). 203 fol. Dated about A.D. 1550.

IO 4235 (Mackenzie II 72a). PL. A mixure of Nandināgarī and Devanāgarī. 29-122 fol. (Paṭala-s 4-19). Written ca. A.D. 1650. "A special Ms. of the Pārṣadavṛtti".

IO 4236 (Burnell 428). 113 fol. Written ca. A.D. 1878.

Jammu RSRI p. 172 (no.5086). 62 fol. Incomplete. (Stein 37).

Jammu RSRI p. 172 (no.5080). 37 fol. Incomplete. (Stein 38).

K 184.

L 1450. 75 fol. 2193 Grantha-s.

MD 882. Tel. 201 pp. Incomplete.

MT 3911(h). PL. Gr. 120 fol. (102-221). Incomplete. Up to 18th Paṭala. Purchased in 1921-22 from Narasimha Sastrigal, Bhavani, Coimbatore Dist.

MT 7849. 175 fol. 4200 Grantha-s. Restored from MT 3911 in 1946-47.

Müller 49B (MM 57B). 16 fol. Copied by MM. in Roman character of a Ms. dated V.S. 1710 (1653-54); probably a copy of Weber 36.

Müller 51 (MM 70 B 8). 157 fol. (65 / 53 / 39) (with text). Dated V.S. 1895 / Śaka 1760 (1838-39). Presented by Ballantyne.

München 31. 603 pp. Dated A.D. 1865.

Mysore I, pp. 24-25 (6 Mss.).

Mysore ND II 3242 (A 230/ 2). 89 fol.

N-W P I 14 (no.47). 180 fol. Belonged to Trilochana Pandit, Benares. Remarks : "Grammar of medical terms" (!)

Oppert I 1923. PL. Gr. Belonged to Sivasuri Sastri of Bhavani, Coimbatore Dist.

Oppert II 6334. Belonged to Narasimhacharya of Kumbakonam.

Oudh XIII 2 (no.1). 430 pp. 1000 Grantha-s. Dated A.D. 1878. Belonged to M. Kali Prasada, Pleader, Lucknow. Title: Prātiśākhya-bhāṣya. Remark: "A commentary on the Vedas, in 18 Paṭalas by Ubbhaṭa".

Oxf. II 894 (Ms. Sansk. e. 10). 230 fol. (with text). Dated A.D. 1794. = Oxf. 405b (no.10).

Oxf. II 895 (Ms. Sansk. d. 20). 107 fol. Copied in the beginning of the 18th century. Presented by Fitz-Edward Hall in 1861.

P 5.

Paris (D.203).

Peters. II, p. 168 (no.33). 159 fol. Dated V.S. 1768.

Peters. II, p. 168 (no.34). 352 fol. Dated V.S. 1670.

PUL I, p. 19 (no.36). 210 fol.

PUL I, p. 19 (no.37). 197 fol. Dated V.S. 1950.

PUL II. App. p. 10 (no.143). 117 fol. 5000 Grantha-s. Dated V.S. 1855.

Rajapur 263.

Rajapur 457. Incomplete.

RASB II 273 (G 550) = L 1450.
RASB II 274 (G 4180D). 67 fol. (2-68).
RASB II 275 (G 4351). 190 fol. Dated V.S. 1954.
Report p. i (no.4). 14 fol.
SB p. 9 (no.75). 134 fol. (53-186). 4606 Grantha-s. Dated V.S. 1185 ? (this must be the supposed date of the commentary, and not of the Ms. The paper of the Ms. does not appear to be that old). = SBD 2115.
SBD 2115. 134 fol. (with Pārṣada-vyākhyā). Incomplete.
SBD 2128. 79 fol. (1-4, 4-78). Incomplete. Dated V.S. 1767.
SBD 47234. 155 fol. (Pārṣada-bhāṣya).
SBD 47237. 135 fol. Incomplete (fol. 1-105, 109-12, 144-61, 163-70). (Pārṣada-bhāṣya).
SBD 47238. 140 fol. (Pārṣada-bhāṣya).
SBD 47240. 16 fol. Incomplete. 9th Paṭala. (Pārṣada-vyākhyā).
SBD 47241. 158 fol. Dated V.S. 1820. (Pārṣada-vyākhyā).
Stein p. 3 (no. 36). 84 fol. Incomplete. Dated V.S. 1602.
Stein p. 3 (no. 37). 82 fol. Incomplete (Paṭala-s 1-5).
Stein p. 3 (no. 38). 37 fol. Incomplete (Paṭala-s 1-3).
TD 1735. 229 fol. (11-239). 4000 Grantha-s (with text).
TD 1736. 222 fol. 3315 Grantha-s (with text).
TD 1737. 20 fol. 380 Grantha-s (with text). 2 Paṭala only.
Trav. Uni. 4840. 6000 Grantha-s (with text). Dated V.S. 1878 = Śaka 1747.
Trav. Uni. 5288. 1000 Grantha-s. Incomplete.
Trav. Uni. 7512. 250 Grantha-s. Incomplete.
Venkatesiah 10.
VSM I 430 (no.5437). 110 fol. (103 and 7; with text). Dated Śaka 1696. First 6 fol. contain the Varga-dvaya-vṛtti of Viṣṇumitra.
VSM I 431 (no.7516). 82 fol. (with text). First 12 fol. contain the Varga-dvaya-vṛtti of Viṣṇumitra.
Wai I 361. 169 fol. (with text).
Wai I 362. 144 fol. (with text).
Wai I 363. 147 fol. (with text).
Wai I 364. 8 fol. (with text). Incomplete.
Weber 36 (Chambers 714). 75 fol. (up to 5th Paṭala).
Weber 37 (Chambers 394). 107 fol. (from 5th Paṭala to the end).

Ptd.: With the text. See above.

– C. Pārṣada-vṛtti or Udāharaṇa-mālikā (or -maṇḍitā) of Viṣṇumitra alias Kumāra, son of Devamitra. Mangal Deva Shastri (Oxford edition, 1922, introduction) discusses the relation of this commentary to that of Uvaṭa, which are identical in some parts and different in others. See remarks above under C. of Uvaṭa.

Adyar D XIII 31 (VB 387b). PL. Gr. 11 fol. (I 11-24).
Adyar D XIII 32 (VB 448d). PL. Gr. 32 fol. (I-III 24).
Adyar D XIII 33 (VB 1151a). PL. Gr. 9 fol. (I 1-9)
Ānandāśrama II, p. 83. Incomplete.

Alph. List Beng. Govt. p. 19.

BISM p. 172 (52/783).

BISM p. 172 (57/50). Dated Śaka 1722.

BISM p. 172 (35/118). (a. Viṣṇumitra).

Bombay Uni. Palm-leaf No. 7. PL. Gr. 156 fol. uncatalogued. Beginning is the same as in the Whish Ms. Up to 13th Paṭala.

BORI 51 of 1869-70. = BORI D I i.459. 94 fol. 2200 Grantha-s. Dated V.S. 1626 (1569).

BORI 52 of 1869-70. = BORI D I i.460. 262 fol. 4680 Grantha-s.

BORI 4 of 1875-76. = BORI D I i.55. 14 fol. Incomplete.

GD I 2. PL. Mal. 32 fol. 1150 Grantha-s. Incomplete (Paṭala-s 1-4).

GD I 3. PL. Mal. 143 fol. 4050 Grantha-s.

GD I 4. PL. Mal. 44 fol. 1100 Grantha-s.

Granthappura p. 1 (no.3). Mal. 900 Grantha-s. Up to I 4.

Granthappura p. 1 (no.4). Mal. 900 Grantha-s. Up to I 4.

Granthappura p. 1 (no.5). Mal. 2000 Grantha-s.

IM 4973. 57 fol. Incomplete. (a. Devamitra of Campā). Title: Pārṣada-vyākhyā.

MD 883. PL. Tel. 178 pp. Incomplete. Paṭala-s 1-6.

MD 19337. PL. Tel. 102 fol. 4590 Grantha-s.

MT 972. PL. Tel. 69 fol. Purchased in 1913-14 from P. Adinarayanavadhani of Pedakallepalli. Incomplete (Paṭala-s 1-7).

MT 5349. 136 fol. 5440 Grantha-s. Transcribed in 1927-28 from a Ms. of Bhavadasa Nambudiri, Mayanur Desham, Ottapalam, Malabar Dist.

MT 5534. 20 fol. 540 Grantha-s. Incomplete (Paṭala-s 14-15). Transcribed in 1926-27 from a Ms. of Astamurthi Nambudiri, Tacharayatlu Manakkal, Paravenna Post, Malbar Dist.

N-W P II 2 (no.6). 40 fol. Belonged to Makhanji of Mathura.

PUL II. App. p. 12 (no.189). PL. Gr. 80 fol. 3000 Grantha-s.

OU 4 Vm (277/b). PL. Tel. 19 fol. Incomplete. (Paṭala 1). 16th century.

RASB II 270 (G 2182). 141 fol. 5550 Grantha-s (with text). Dated V.S. 1843.

RASB II 271 (G 6487). 159 fol.

RASB II 272 (G 2044). 118 fol. 5300 Grantha-s (with text). Dated Śaka 1721.

SB p. 9 (no.76). 4-133 fol. 2368 Grantha-s. = SBD 2116.

SBD 2116. 131 fol. (1, 4-133). Incomplete. (Pārṣada-vyākhyā).

SBD 47828. 33 fol. Incomplete (3 Paṭala-s). (Pārṣada-vyākhyā).

TCD 20. PL. Mal. 126 fol. 3800 Grantha-s (with text).

TCD 21. PL. Mal. 182 fol. 3800 Grantha-s (with text).

TD 1733. 15 fol. 200 Grantha-s. First 2 Varga-s (Varga-dvaya-vṛtti).

TD 1734. 11 fol. 170 Grantha-s. First 2 Varga-s (Varga-dvaya-vṛtti).

Tra. Ad. Rep. 1104. 1.

Trav. Uni. 3673. PL. Gr. 3700 Grantha-s (with text).

Trav. Uni. 7438. 250 Grantha-s. Incomplete.

Trav. Uni. 15802 B. PL. Mal. 3500 Grantha-s. Incomplete.

Trav. Uni. 19022. PL. Mal. 1120 Grantha-s. Incomplete.

Trav. Uni. 19023. PL. Mal. 1150 Grantha-s. Incomplete.

Trav. Uni. 19024. PL. Mal. 3700 Grantha-s.

Trav. Uni. 22151. PL. Mal. 3700 Grantha-s.

Trav. Uni. C.851 = TCD 20.
Trav. Uni. C.1810 = TCD 21.
Trav. Uni. T.526. 302 pp. Copy of a Ms. of Kaladi Manacandran Bhaṭṭattiri.
Triv. Cur. V 7. Mal. 4500 Grantha-s (with text). Incomplete. Obtained from Suryan Bhatta-thiri, Kalatimana, Nattasseri.
Triv. Cur. V 8. Mal. 6000 Grantha-s (with text). (15 Paṭala-s). Obtained from Paramesvaran Narayanan Bhattatihri, Thiruvalla.
Triv. Cur. V 9. Gr. 4000 Grantha-s. Obtained from Chellappa Vadhyar, Trivandrum.
Ujjain Latest Additions 126 (with text; Uvaṭa and Vedamitra).
Venkatesiah 10.
Weber 2061. (This is actually the C. of Uvaṭa on the Vājasaneyi- prātiśākhya).

[NCC III 10b-12a; XII 73b-74a]

– C. of Satyayaśas ? Is this the same as the Vṛtti by Viṣṇumitra, at the beginning of which Satyayaśas is referred to.
Hoshiarpur p. 50 (no.4138). PL. Mal. 204 fol. 3500 Grantha-s. Ptd. ?

314 ṚGVEDA-PRĀTIŚĀKHYA-PARIŚIṢṬA (ऋग्वेदप्रातिशाख्यपरिशिष्ट)

A conjectural title. "A list of words from the *Ṛgveda* with difficult Saṃdhis" (?) Same as the *Ssaṃdigdha-padaccheda-nirṇaya* (Trav. Uni. 15799 A. PL. Mal. 2500 Grantha-s). Cf. Samāna-pada-nirṇaya, Hoshiarpur p. 54 (no. 3797). PL. Mal. 70 fol. 2000 Grantha-s. Extract p. 414.

Beginning:

गणाधिपं नमस्कृत्य गुरुं देवीं सरस्वतीम्।
संदिग्धच्छेदनान्यृक्षु विलिख्यन्ते पदान्यथ।
एजन्ते च विसर्गान्ते पदे ऽचि परतो यतः ।
विगृह्या तुल्यरूपा स्यात् संहिता तत्र संशयः ।

य ऋत्रा मह्यं मामहे। ८·१·३२। को नो मह्या अदितये यो वो मह्या अभिशन्तेः सखाय ब्र व भ्र ऊधन्यूर्ध्व ऊषुण ऊतये उभा ऊरूनन्त दिन भूदुभा उ अंशवे।

नकारान्ते तकारान्ते परयोश्चतवर्गयोः ।
नतादेशात् तुल्यरूपा सांहितात्रापि संशयः ॥

अहं च पुत्रं तमुचीमहं च त्वं च पुत्रं हन्ताजुषेथामरेपसो त जुषस्वशिरं मम वरजिन्तमाय सह्यसे यो रयि वो रयिन्तमः तान् दधिष्व शतक्रतो तान् देवा अन्वजायन्त अमे देवान् धद्गुहादूर्ध्वान्धीतिं कृण्वन् दर्श अविश्वदर्शतमदर्शन्वत्र श्रुतवान्

विसर्जनीय आकारपूर्वो यः स तु लुप्यते।
वर्गे वर्गे द्वितीयाद्या ह्यन्तस्थाः परतो यदि।
आकारान्तो विसर्गान्तो वेति स्यात् तत्र संशयः ॥

End:

अवग्रह चत्वारि। कया नः । कामम्। अभि। ह्र। अवग्रह षद्। संयत्। भिष्म। परन्ते। अवग्रह चत्वारि। इत्येकम्। अस्मत्। इह। शिवः इह। अवग्रह दश। आतुन्नः । यमन्। महान्। अवग्रह षद्। इति द्वे। भूयामोषु। यव। ईशिषे। याः । अरुज। अवग्रह पञ्च। इत्येकम्। ताते। नाम धाः । वर्तय। अवग्रह त्रीणि। इति चत्वारि। प्रजहुभ्यः । शुन्धि। इष्ये अक्रन्। आयन्। अवहन्। विद्वाः । कनीयान्। त्वष्टा। अवग्रह पञ्चदश। सत्यमूचुः । रूपकम्। अह्वाः । अवेनत्। रणन्। अक्षण्वन्। सिन्धूनतिष्ठन्। सुकर्माः । धर्त्ताः । नः । अवग्र चतुर्दश। इति त्रीणि। ऋभुर्विभ्वाः । ऋभुः । अग्मत। उतु। अग्रियाः । वाजाः । अवग्र दश। इति द्वे। आनवातः । श्रीर्णये। ग्नस्पत्नीभिः । दैवेन सिन्धुभिः ॥

Whish 78(7). PL. Gr. 32 fol. (55-86).

315 ṚGVEDA-MANTRARṢI-DAIVATA-CCHANDONUKRAMAṆĪ (ऋग्वेदमन्त्रर्षिदैवतच्छन्दोनुक्रमणी)
GJKSV 4/4 (D I 1, no.3). 29 fol. (5-19, 32-45).

316 ṚGVEDA-LAKṢAṆA (1) (ऋग्वेदलक्षण)
Adyar D I 765 (20 K 38 = 67500). PL. Tel. 3 fol. (3-5). This is the *Upalekha-sūtra*.

317 ṚGVEDA-LAKṢAṆA (2) (ऋग्वेदलक्षण)
Lists of words of the *Ṛgveda* ending or beginning in different consonants.

Beginning:

नमस्तस्मै गणेशाय प्रणतार्तिप्रहारिणे।
प्रारम्भाः फलपर्यन्ता यत्प्रसादाद् भवन्ति हि॥
चिद् वीर्यं समयः सप्ती विश्वमिन्वे पृथूरथः ।
अभीतीरपसोनस्तरुद्यामिव जगद्ध्रुवः ॥
पदानां समयाख्यानां वर्गस्थानां यथाक्रमम्।
वर्गादिगणविंशत्या त्र्यादिसंख्या निगद्यते॥
आदौ मध्ये तथान्ते वा संनिकर्षेण बह्वृचाम्।
नोच्यन्ते ऽनेकसूक्तानामन्ते च समया इह॥
अनेकसूक्तान्तगतान् पदान् पञ्च न कुर्वते।
समयान् पदकारास्ते तान्न विप्रतिपद्यताम्॥
सुवीरासः सुवीरस्य तथा भक्षीमहि प्रजाम्।

End:

पारावतो निरेकश्च गरिष्ठिरपरीणसौ।
दुन्दुभिप्रधणासानप्रस्कण्वो भरगो मता॥
अच्छानहूत इत्य ....

MD 885. Tel. 20 pp.

MD 14147. PL. Na. 39 pp. Incomplete. sādimādimeta ... reto retaś ca rejaś ca | The same as Mysore ND II 3312: Kampadvimātra. Extract no. 93

MD 14388. PL. Na. 12 pp. Incomplete. śvaghnī paripanthī ... sāṃhiteṣv īkāradīrgheṣv adhiyadasminvarjam (Cf. *Pada-gāḍha* p. 44).

[NCC III 13a]

318 ṚGVEDA-LAKṢAṆA (3) (ऋग्वेदलक्षण)

GD I 13. PL. Mal. 131 fol. 1400 Grantha-s. Incomplete.

Granthappura p. 1 (no.14). Mal. 1100 Grantha-s.

Trav. Uni. 19033. An old and brittle Ms.; apparently rare.

319 ṚGVEDA-LAKṢAṆA-GRANTHA (ऋग्वेदलक्षणग्रन्थ)

Tirupati SVUORI 990 (2546b). PL. Tel. 9 fol. (18-26). Incomplete. (prakṛtān triṃśat medhātithir vṛbhandhe ?).

320 ṚGVEDA-LAKṢAṆĀNUKRAMAṆIKĀ (ऋग्वेदलक्षणानुक्रमणिका)

MT 3911(c). PL. Gr. 44 fol. (28-71) (not described in the catalogue; probably latter half of the Padāntadīpinī).

321 ṚGVEDA-VARGA-PADA-SAṂKHYĀ-NIRṆAYA (ऋग्वेदवर्गपदसंख्यानिर्णय)

Trav. Uni. 823 B. PL. Mal. 750 Grantha-s. Incomplete. Cf. Aṣṭākṣarī-paribhāṣā.

[NCC III 13a]

322 ṚGVEDA-VARGĀNUKRAMAṆĪ (ऋग्वेदवर्गानुक्रमणी)

An index of the initial words of each Varga of the *Ṛgveda*.

Trav. Uni. 589. PL. Mal. 250 Grantha-s. Incomplete.

[NCC III 13a]

323 ṚGVEDA-VARṆA-KRAMA-(JÑĀNA-)LAKṢAṆA (ऋग्वेदवर्णक्रम(ज्ञान)लक्षण)

of Jagannātha. See also Varṇa-krama-lakṣaṇa.

Beginning:

मोमेशविघ्नेशरवीन् प्रणम्य स्वप्रातिशाख्योक्तविधीन् विलोक्य।
ऋग्वेदवर्णक्रमलक्षणं हि ब्रूते जगन्नाथ इदं यथाधि ॥
किंचिल्लक्ष्यं प्रातिशाख्याज्ज्ञेयं व्याकरणादिह।
उभयानुगतं प्राय एवं लक्षणमुच्यते ॥
ज्ञेया विकारा वर्णानां पञ्चापि स्वरभक्तयः ।
विवृत्तयश्चतस्रो ऽन्या वर्णक्रममभीप्सता ॥
अजनुस्वारपूर्वं हल्द्वित्वमाप्नोति हल्परम्।
अनुस्वारविसर्गान्यद्विरामे च स्वरेङ्गनौ ॥
ह्रस्वपूर्वो मकारस्तु विरामे ह्रस्वपूर्वकः ।
सोष्मणो द्वित्वसंप्राप्तौ तत्पूर्वस्य सकृच्छ्रुतिः ॥

End:

पाकवत्युभयह्रस्वा द्वयोर्दैर्घ्ये पिपीलिका।
दीर्घे वत्सानुसार्यादौ वत्सानुसृतिरन्तिमे॥
दीर्घात् परस्य न द्वित्वं शकटेन मतेन हि।
प्लुतानां प्रग्रह्याणां च पाठे वर्णक्रमस्य च॥
हरिःप्रणवयोर्मध्ये संधिर्न स्यात् कदाचन।
इत्थं वर्णक्रमं ज्ञात्वा वेदाध्यायफलं भवेत्॥

इति ऋग्वेदवर्णक्रमलक्षणम्॥

Adyar D XIII 37 (VB 737d). PL. Gr. 2 fol.

Baroda 5847(b). 3 fol. (58-60). 17 Grantha-s. = CLB I, p. 35 (Varṇa-kramalakṣaṇa). Dated Śaka 1718.

Baroda 8222. 1 fol. 17 Grantha-s. = CLB I, p. 35 (Varṇa-kramalakṣaṇa). Dated A.D. 1919.

BBRAS 484 (B D 221). 18 verses at the end of the Ṛgveda-prātiśākhya. The complete text is printed.

BHU B 1724 (D 2A/976). 29 fol.

Bombay Uni. 689 (BMC 79 16). 1 fol. Dated Śaka 1646. 18 verses at the end of the Ṛgveda-prātiśākhya.

Bombay Uni. (Itchharam 86 1) 67(2). 2 fol. Dated V.S. 1755.

Bombay Uni. (BMC 145 1). 2 fol. (39-40). Dated Śaka 1714.

IL. 305 (II) (Varṇānukrama-lakṣaṇa ?).

IM 2001B. 2 fol. (41-42). 19 verses. Col.: Varṇa-krama-lakṣaṇa.

IM 2303A. 2 fol. (41-42). Col.: Varṇa-krama.

Max Müller Mem. VIII(2). 18 verses at the end of the Ṛgveda-prātiśākhya.

N-W P V 42 (no.15). 12 fol. Belonged to Ramachand Bhatta, Allahabad.

PUL I, p. 23 (no.126). 2 fol. (33-34). 18 Grantha-s.

SB p. 298 (no.80). 8 fol. 100 Grantha-s. Dated V.S. 1796. = SBD 47602.

SBD 47602. 8 fol. Dated Śaka 1661. Title: Varṇa-krama-lakṣaṇa.

SBD 55241. 1 fol. Dated V.S. 1886. Title: Varṇa-krama-lakṣaṇa. At the end of the Ṛgveda-sarvānukramaṇī.

Trav. Uni. 4923. 100 Grantha-s (with C.).

Trav. Uni. 7461 B. 20 Grantha-s.

VSM I 427 (no.628). At the end of the Ṛgveda-prātiśākhya.

VSM I 428 (no.97). Dated Śaka 1779. At the end of the Ṛgveda-prātiśākhya.

– C. Vivṛti.

Beginning:

मो(सो)मेशादीन् प्रणम्यादौ जगन्नाथेन सद्गुरून्।
ऋचां वर्णक्रमज्ञानव्याख्या संतन्यते ऽधुना॥
पदक्रमविभागज्ञो वर्णक्रमविचक्षणः।
स्वरवर्णः स्वरो मात्रा विनियोगो ऽर्थ एव च॥

मन्त्रं जिज्ञासमानेन वेदितव्यं पदे पदे।

मन्त्रो हीनः स्वरतो वर्णतो वा इत्यादिना वैदिकवर्णानां ज्ञेयत्वावगमात् तज्ज्ञानस्य चाध्ययनमात्राद् दुःशकत्वात् प्रातिशाख्यव्याकरणयोश्च बाहुल्याद् विस्तृतत्वाच्च संक्षिप्तमिदं लक्षणमारभ्यते -- मोमेशेति।

End:

नाभ्या आसीत्। देवा एतस्या ... ता ईम्। वत्सानुसारिणी। आ उ। या इन्द्र। ता अस्य। वत्सो ऽमृतः। वत्सानुसृतिः। य आनयत्। स ईम्। य ऊर्ध्वया। य एनं य ओ ... शौनकः कालव्यवायेन स्वरान्तरं तु विवृतिः सा धा स्वरभक्तिकालेति। संक्षेपसारे ऽपि --

पाकवत्युभयह्रस्वा द्वयोर्दैर्घ्ये पिपीलिका।

वत्सानुसारिण्यादौ या वत्सानुसृतिरन्तिमे॥

इति व्याख्या समाप्ता॥

Adyar D XIII 38 (VB 737c). PL. Gr. 3 fol.

Hz 434. PL. Tel. 69 fol. Extract p. 80. Belonged to Gottimukkula Viraraghava Somayaji of Brahmanakraka (Agrahara), Nellur Dist.

IM 2303B. 10 fol. Incomplete. Title: Varṇa-krama-vyākhyā.

SBD 2070. 2 fol. (Ṛgvedārṇa-krama-jñāna-vyākhyā).

SBD 2071. 9 fol. Incomplete. Title: Varṇa-krama-lakṣaṇa-ṭīkā-ṭīkā.

Trav. Uni. 4923. 100 Grantha-s (with text).

VSM III 165 (no.11340). 4 fol. Title : Prātiśākhya-pariśiṣṭa or alternatively Ṛgvedārṇa-krama-jñāna-vyākhyā. Illustrations of the Aṣṭa-vikṛti-s at the end.

[NCC III 13b]

324 ṚGVEDA-ŚAMĀNA (ऋग्वेदशमान)

Govt. Or. Libr. Madras the, p. 13. → Ṛksarva-śamāna.

[NCC III 13b]

325 ṚGVEDA-ŚĀKALĀNUKRAMAṆĪ (1) (ऋग्वेदशाकलानुक्रमणी)

Cabaton I 323 → Ṛgveda-sarvānukramaṇī.

326 ṚGVEDA-ŚĀKALĀNUKRAMAṆĪ (2) (ऋग्वेदशाकलानुक्रमणी)

RASB II 248 (G 2069). 51 fol. Dated V.S. 1863. A tabular statement of Aṣṭaka-s, Ṛk-s, Ekapada-s, Dvipada-s to Aṣṭapada-s and the total number of Pāda-s. It also contains several tables on Chandas and Anuvāka-s. *Anuvāka-pañcāśī* at the end.

[NCC III 13b]

327 ṚGVEDA-ŚIKṢĀ (ऋग्वेदशिक्षा)

SBD 2047. 6 fol. Dated V.S. 1919. (Remark: the order is different from the Pāṇinīya-śikṣā). Varga-s 7-11 only. Begins with "yathā saurāṣṭrikā nārī ... ".

328 ṚGVEDA-ŚṚṄKHALĀ (ऋग्वेदशृङ्खला)

→ Ṛgveda-savīla-mālā.

329 ṚGVEDA-SAMHITĀ-ṚṢI-CHANDO-DAIVATA-SAMGRAHA (ऋग्वेदसंहिता-ऋषिछन्दोदैवतसंग्रह)

Wai I 319. 95 fol. Dated Śaka 1795. Appears to be based on Jagannātha's work.

330 ṚGVEDA-SAMHITĀ-CATURAKṢARA-BAIṬH (ऋग्वेदसंहिताचतुरक्षरबैठ्)

Wai I 340. 23 fol. Dated Śaka 1689. = Caturakṣarī-baiṭh. Cf. VSM I 186. Extract p. 346 in the Ms. of the Ṛgveda-pada-pāṭha.

331 ṚGVEDA-SAMHITĀNUKRAMAṆIKĀ (ऋग्वेदसंहितानुक्रमणिका)

TD 386-90 (Indexes by Aṣṭaka-s).

[NCC III 23b]

332 ṚGVEDA-SAMHITĀNUVĀKĀDI-LAKṢAṆA (ऋग्वेदसंहितानुवाकादिलक्षण)

All the three Mss. below, probably by the same scribe, also contain the *Anuvāka-pañcāśī* and *Dvipadādi-saṃkhyā*.

Wai I 335. 2 fol.
Wai I 336. 2 fol.
Wai I 337. 1 fol.

333 ṚGVEDA-SAMHITĀ-PADA-LAKṢAṆA (ऋग्वेदसंहितापदलक्षण)

→ Pāda-vidhāna.

334 ṚGVEDA-SAMHITĀ-PADA-SAMKHYĀ-NIRṆAYA (ऋग्वेदसंहितापदसंख्यानिर्णय)

Trav. Uni. 16037 C. PL. Mal. 750 Grantha-s. Incomplete.

335 ṚGVEDA-SAMHITĀ-PADA-SAMKHYĀNUKRAMAṆĪ (ऋग्वेदसंहितापदसंख्यानुक्रमणी)

Trav. Uni. L.647 A. PL. Mal. 850 Grantha-s.

336 ṚGVEDA-SAMHITĀ-PADA-SAMKHYĀ-VIVEKA (ऋग्वेदसंहितापदसंख्याविवेक)

Trav. Uni. 18109 B. PL. Mal. 200 Grantha-s.

337 ṚGVEDA-SAMHITĀ-PADĀNTA DĪPINĪ (ऋग्वेदसंहितापदान्तदीपिनी)

Trav. Uni. 22690. PL. Mal. 1350 Grantha-s → Padāntadīpinī.

338 ṚGVEDA-SAMHITĀ-PRATĪKA-ŚṚṄKHALĀ (ऋग्वेदसंहिताप्रतीकशृङ्खला)

SBD 2377. 2 fol. Pratīka-s of the different chapters of the *Ṛgveda* in different combinations. The purpose of this is not clear.

339 ṚGVEDA-SAMHITĀ-PRATHAMĀṢṬAKA-KOVĀNI (ऋग्वेदसंहिताप्रथमाष्टककोवानि)

→ Ṛgveda-savīla-mālā.

SBD 0285. 1 fol. (Pratīka-s of Aṣṭaka 1 and 2).

340 ṚGVEDA-SAṂHITĀYĀ GALĀNTA-PADAM (ऋग्वेदसंहिताया गलान्तपदम्)
Jammu RSRI p. 22 (no.1208iii) (Stein 45) → Galita-pradīpa.

341 ṚGVEDA-SAṂHITĀ-SARVĀNUKRAMA (ऋग्वेदसंहितासर्वानुक्रम)
of Kātyāyana → Ṛgveda-sarvānukramaṇī.

342 ṚGVEDA-SAṂHITĀ-SŪTRA see SAṂHITĀ-SŪTRA
(ऋग्वेदसंहितासूत्र / संहितासूत्र)
PUL II. App. p. 10 (no.144).
PUL II. App. p. 10 (no.145).

[NCC III 23b]

343 ṚGVEDA-SAṂKHYĀ-VIVARAṆA (ऋग्वेदसंख्याविवरण)
VSM I 444 (no.5438). 2 fol. Dated Śaka 1771.

344 ṚGVEDA-SAPTA-LAKṢAṆA (ऋग्वेदसप्तलक्षण)
of Nāgadeva → Ṛksarva-śamāna.

345 ṚGVEDA-SAPTA-SAṂKHYĀ-NIRŪPAṆA (ऋग्वेदसप्तसंख्यानिरूपण)
Gives a particular analysis of Ṛgveda-mantra-s → Sapta-saṃkhyā(-nirūpaṇa).
MD 14082. PL. Tel. 79 pp. Begins: p̃a-i-du-vi-ma-na-ta : agnim īḷe 47-0-8-17-1-3-14. yadaṅga 41-0-4-8-17-0-3.
MD 14647. PL. Tel. 21 pp. The same as the above.
MD 14781. PL. Na. 48 fol. Numbers in letters as IO 4246.

[NCC III 24a]

346 ṚGVEDA-SAMĀNA-PADĀNI (ऋग्वेदसमानपदानि)
BORI 185 of 1899-1915. 19 fol. Dated Śaka 1711 (Samāna-saṃdhi-varṇa-kathana).
Rajapur 1032.
VSM I 439 (no.4910). 5 fol. (7-11). Incomplete. Dated Śaka 1748. Copied by Śivaṇakara Dadam-bhaṭṭa. (Ṛgveda-samānapada-kośa).
VSM I 440 (no.5453). 3 fol. Incomplete. (ṚV-Samānapada-lakṣaṇa). Extract p. 348.
VSM I 441 (no.5905). 8 fol. Incomplete. (ṚV-Samānapada).
VSM I 442 (no.5452). 8 fol. Incomplete. (ṚV-Samānapada).
VSM I 443 (no.5451). 11 fol. Incomplete. (ṚV-Samānapada).

[NCC III 24a]

347 ṚGVEDA-SARVĀNUKRAMA (ऋग्वेदसर्वानुक्रम)
Ascribed to Śaunaka.
Mysore I, p. 38 (Sarvānukrama) = Mysore ND II 3267 (C 850) → Ṛgveda-sarvānukramaṇī of Kātyāyana (with Ṣaḍguru-śiṣya's Bhāṣya).
N-W P VII 6 (no.24). 107 fol. (with Bhāṣya). Belonged to Pandit Baladikshita Bhagavati, Benares.

– C. Bhāṣya.
N-W P VII 6 (no.24). 107 fol. (with text). Belonged to Pandit Baladikshita Bhagavati, Benares.

[NCC III 24a]

348 ṚGVEDA-SARVĀNUKRAMAṆIKĀ(-ṆĪ) (ऋग्वेदसर्वानुक्रमणिका) (-णी) of Kātyāyana. PUL II. App. p. 11 says: anantācārya-samīkṛta (!). In one Ms. (GJKSV 19585) it is sscribed to Āśvalāyana in the colophon: iti śākala-saṃhitānukramaṇikā -- āśvalāyana-proktaḥ sarvānukramaḥ samāptaḥ. It is the well-known general index to the *Ṛgveda.* It epitomises in the Sūtra style the contents of the metrical indices.

Beginning:

अथ ऋग्वेदाम्नाये शाकलके सूक्तप्रतीक ऋक्संख्यर्षिदैवतच्छन्दांस्यनुक्रमिष्यामो यथोपदेशम् । न ह्येतज्ज्ञानमृते श्रौतस्मार्तकर्मप्रसिद्धिः । मन्त्राणां ब्राह्मणार्षेयच्छन्दोदैवतविद् याजनाध्यापनाभ्यां श्रेयो ऽधिगच्छतीति । एताभ्यामेवानेवंविदो यातयामानि च्छन्दांसि भवन्ति । स्थाणुं वर्च्छति गर्ते वा पात्यते प्रमीयते वा पापीयान् भवतीति विज्ञायते। १। अथ ऋषयः । शतर्चिन आद्ये मण्डले ...

End:

आयं गौः सार्पराज्ञात्मदैवतं सौर्यं वा। ऋतं माधुच्छन्दसो ऽघमर्षणो भाववृत्तमानुष्टुभं तु। सं सं चतुष्कं संवननः संज्ञानमाद्याग्नेयी तृतीया त्रिष्टुप् तृतीया त्रिष्टुप्। ६४। इति दशमं मण्डलम्॥

Adyar D I 1049 (20 D 84 = 67128). PL. Gr. 31 fol. (1-37; 6 fol. missing). = Adyar I, p. 52a. Title: Śākala-sūkta-pratīka.

Adyar D I 1050 (28 F 35 = 72839). PL. Tel. 17 fol. (3ff.)

Adyar D I 1051 (40 A 98 = PM 140). 37 fol. Dated V.S. 1676. Chandaḥ-saṃkhyā at the end (fol. 36-37).

Adyar D I 1052 (41 B 76 = PM 141). 25 fol. (numbered 1-48; 16, 19-40 missing). Dated V.S. 1715. Chandaḥ-saṃkhyā at the end (fol. 47-48). = Adyar I, p. 54a (34 K 76), 92 pp. Incomplete.

Adyar D I 1053 (41 C 49 = PM 142). 22 fol. (18-40; fol. 36 missing). Incomplete. From IV 10 to X 72.

Adyar D XIII 44 (VB 2a). PL. Tel. 16 fol.

Alph. List Beng. Govt. p. 19.

Alwar 18. 28.

Alwar 29 (with Chandassaṃkhyā). Dated V.S. 1587.

America 371. 37 fol.

America 372. 8 pp. German cursive script, copied by A. Weber from Chambers 55 and 56.

ASB I iii.25 (IM 2163). 83 fol. 3237 Grantha-s (with C. of Ṣaḍguru-śiṣya). Both the text and the C. are wrongly attributed to Sāyaṇa in the catalogue.

Baroda 1500. 20 fol. 700 Grantha-s. = CLB I, p. 24.

Baroda 4534. 38 fol. 700 Grantha-s. = CLB I, p. 24.

Baroda 4535. 39 fol. 700 Grantha-s. = CLB I, p. 24.

Baroda 4825. 37 fol. 700 Grantha-s. = CLB I, p. 24.

Baroda 4826. 48 fol. 700 Grantha-s. = CLB I, p. 24.

Baroda 7869. PL. Mal. 66 fol. (3-68). 2000 Grantha-s. = CLB I, p. 25 (with C. of Vāsudeva). Extract pp. 137-38.

Baroda 10355. 3 fol. 50 Grantha-s (paribhāṣā only). = CLB I, p. 25.

Baroda 11874. 4 fol. 15 Grantha-s (for IX. Maṇḍala). = CLB I, p. 25.

Baroda 12333. 180 fol. 2000 Grantha-s (with C. of Vāsudeva). = CLB I, p. 25. Copied in 1922 by Krishna Menon Sastry, Library copyist.

Baroda 23381. 29 fol. 640 Grantha-s. Dated Śaka 1763 / V.S. 1898. (Sarvānukramaṇikā Śākalaśākhīya-paribhāṣā).

Baroda 23436. 53 fol. 575 Grantha-s. Dated Śaka 1781.

Baroda 23457. 36 fol. 560 Grantha-s.

Baroda 24495. 35 fol. 700 Grantha-s. Dated Śaka 1732.

Baroda 24700. 39 fol. 600 Grantha-s. Dated V.S. 1812.

Baroda 24701. 45 fol. 500 Grantha-s. Dated V.S. 1770.

Baroda 26313. 38 fol. 760 Grantha-s. Dated Śaka 1724. (Sarvānukrama).

BBRAS 486 (B D 311). 9 fol. (2 sections only).

BBRAS 495 (B D 182). 27 fol. Dated Śaka 1729. Copied by Lakṣmaṇa-bhaṭṭa Vāḍḍekara.

BBRAS 496 (B D 77). 30 fol. Dated Śaka 1689.

BBRAS 497 (B D 182). 8 fol. (Paribhāṣā). Copied by Paraśurāma Jogalekara in the latter half of the 18th century.

BBRAS 498 (B D 221). 3 fol. (Paribhāṣā).

BBRAS 499 (S C 4). 103 fol. (with C. of Raghunātha Caturvedin). Dated Śaka 1710 / V.S. 1845.

BBRAS 500 (ZZ A 23). 66 fol. (with C. Vedārthadīpikā of Ṣaḍguru-śiṣya).

Ben. 5.

Bh. p. 5 (no.7) (2 copies). The same as BORI D I i.28.

Bhk. 8.

BHU S 60 (D 1A/125). 55 fol.

BHU B 946 (D 1I/628). 96 fol. Dated V.S. 1810. Title: Anukramaṇikā.

Bik. 328. 35 fol. Title: Ṛgvedānukramaṇikā (a. Śaunaka).

Bik. 342. 35 fol. Col.: Ṛgvedīya-sarvānukrama-paribhāṣā.

Bikaner 628. 34 fol. Incomplete. Breaks off with Aṣṭaka 6.

Bikaner 629. 26 fol. Dated V.S. 1735 (A.D. 1678). Copied at Pattanapura.

Bikaner 630. 32 fol. Dated V.S. 1948 (A.D. 1891).

BISM p. 41 (36/781). 31 fol.

Bombay Uni. 717 (BMC 2 4). 32 fol. Dated V.S. 1698. Copied by Lakṣmaṇa Mahādeva Parāḍekara.

Bombay Uni. 718 (BMC 30 1). 42 fol. Dated Śaka 1716. Copied by Lakṣmaṇa Rāmacandra Jāyade.

Bombay Uni. (Itchharam 1 5) 104. 40 fol.

Bombay Uni. (Itchharam 1 4) 105. 35 fol. Dated Śaka 1777.

Bombay Uni. (Itchharam 1 6) 106. 19 fol. Incomplete (up to V. Aṣṭaka).

Bombay Uni. (Moropant 86 5) 51. 44 fol. Dated V.S. 1859.

Bombay Uni. Acc. no. 2894. 55 fol.

Bombay Uni. Acc. no. 5322. 34 fol. Dated Śaka 1668.

Bombay Uni. (BMC 123 2). 43 fol. Dated Śaka 1713.

Bombay Uni. (BMC 141 1). 40 fol. (fol. 39 missing). 40th fol. contains Chandaḥ-saṃkhyā.

Bombay Uni. (BMC 155 3). 35 fol. Dated Śaka 1738. Copied by Baccam-bhaṭṭa Upādhyāya, son of Lakṣmaṇa Paṭaṇakara.

Bombay Uni. Palm-leaf No. 6. PL. Gr. uncatalogued.

BORI 5 of 1875-76. = BORI D I i.1. 191 fol. (with the text of the *Ṛgveda)*. Śāradā script. Dated 51 of Kashmiri era. Cf. Bühler's Report for 1875-76, pp. 35-36.

BORI 12 of 1879-80. = BORI D I i.27. 27 fol. Dated V.S. 1705.

BORI 7 of A 1879-80. = BORI D I i.28. 23 fol.

BORI 7 of A 1879-80 (2nd copy). = BORI D I i.28. 30 fol.

BORI 1 of A 1881-82. = BORI D I i.3. 994 fol. At the beginning of each Adhyāya of the *Ṛgveda*.

BORI 37 of A 1881-82. = BORI D I i.29. 41 fol. Dated Śaka 1701.

BORI 38 of A 1881-82 (with paribhāṣā). = BORI D I i.30. 21 fol. Dated Śaka 1738 and 1752. Copied in Poona.

BORI 72 of 1884-86. = BORI D I i.31. 34 fol. Dated V.S. 1763. Copied in Kāśī.

BORI 80 of 1884-87. = BORI D I i.32. 34 fol. Copied in Ujjain.

BORI 50 of 1895-98. 48 fol. Dated V.S. 1728.

Brahmasva Maṭha 47(?).

Br. Mus. 20 (Add. 5352c). 17 fol. (85-101). Copied for Col. Polier.

Br. Mus. 48 (Add. 5349h). 16 fol. (274-89a).

Cabaton I 323. 100 pp. Title: Ṛgveda-śākalānukramaṇī.

Calcutta Skt. Coll. I 21. 33 fol. (6 fol. are lost).

Deccan College 10967. 62 fol. Dated Śaka 1713. Copied in Satara (Saptarṣikṣetra). Chandaḥ-saṃkhyā on fol. 61-62.

GD I 7. See Ārṣa- Chando- and Devatānukramaṇī.

GD I 8. PL. Mal. 74 fol. 500 Grantha-s.

GD I 36-B. PL. Mal. 12 fol. 500 Grantha-s.

GJKSV 13818. 10 fol. Incomplete (1st Aṣṭaka). Catalogued as Ṛgvede Prathamāṣṭaka.

GJKSV 17739. 42 fol. Title: Sarvānukramaṇikā.

GJKSV 17866. 29 fol. A few fol. are renewed.

GJKSV 19585. 33 fol. Ascribed to Āśvalāyana in the colophon : iti śākala-saṃhitānukramaṇikā -- āśvalāyana-proktaḥ sarvānukramaḥ samāptaḥ.

GJKSV 21077. 48 fol.

GJKSV 21081. 39 fol. Dated V.S. 1812.

GJKSV 24160. 48 fol.

GJKSV 24407(A). 39 fol. Dated V.S. 1788.

GJKSV 24502. 18 fol. Incomplete (up to 27th Adhyāya).

GJKSV 27662. 44 fol. Dated Śaka 1754. Copied by Raghunātha Deva.

GJKSV 28183. 27 fol. Dated V.S. 1731.

GJKSV 29243. 30 fol.

GJKSV 29554. 17 fol. (7-21, 23, 46). Incomplete.

GJKSV 29986. 27 fol. Dated V.S. 1931. Title: Paribhāṣā-sarvānukrama. Copied by Gopāla-bhaṭṭa Karamarakara.

GJKSV 32345. 66 fol. Title: Sarvānukramaṇī-paribhāṣā.

GJKSV 33055. 22 fol. (20-41). Incomplete.

GJKSV 33083. 42 fol. Dated V.S. 1807.
GJKSV 33632. 46 fol.
GJKSV 35276. 46 fol. Dated Śaka 1750.
GJKSV 37943. 46 fol.
GJKSV 36748. 52 fol. Dated V.S. 1870 / Śaka 1735. Copied by Govinda-bhaṭṭa.
GJKSV 38309(A). 41 fol. Dated V.S. 1853.
GJKSV 38417. 41 fol. Dated Śaka 1717. Title: Sarvānukrama-pari -bhāṣā.
Granthappura p. 1 (no.8a). Mal. 1000 Grantha-s.
Granthappura p. 1 (no.9). Mal. 500 Grantha-s. Incomplete.
Granthappura p. 1 (no.10). Mal. 200 Grantha-s (with C. of Ṣaḍguru-śiṣya). Incomplete.
Granthappura p. 3 (no.36b). Mal. 500 Grantha-s.
Haug p. 22 (no.44) = München 22(1).
Hoshiarpur p. 55 (no.15). 6 fol. 84 Grantha-s. Incomplete.
Hoshiarpur p. 55 (no.34). 28 fol. 500 Grantha-s. Dated Śaka 1751.
Hoshiarpur p. 55 (no.725). 7 fol. 120 Grantha-s. (Up to I 140).
Hoshiarpur p. 55 (no.1428). 3 fol. 22 Grantha-s. Incomplete.
Hoshiarpur p. 55 (no.2043). Mal. 60 fol. 700 Grantha-s. Incomplete.
Hoshiarpur p. 55 (no.3792). PL. Mal.
Hoshiarpur p. 56 (no.4368). 73 fol. 1054 Grantha-s. Incomplete.
Hoshiarpur p. 56 (no.6803). 99 fol. 652 Grantha-s. (Śākalasūkta-pratīkāni) Dated V.S. 1978. Extract p. 81.
Hoshiarpur p. 56 (no.6812). 40 fol. 750 Grantha-s.
Hoshiarpur p. 301 (no.3793). PL. Mal. 51 fol. 500 Grantha-s. Incomplete.
Hpr. II 5. 44 fol. 608 Grantha-s. Dated Śaka 1734.
Hz 1799. 58 fol. (with paribhāṣā). Belonged to Jambunatha Bhatta of Thanjavur.
IM 7452. 18 fol. (1-5, 16-22, 25-30). Incomplete. The paribhāṣā section is omitted. Col.: Kātyāyana-proktānukramaṇikā.
IIO Stein 208. Śāradā script. Incomplete (I 1 - III 60). (Inserted before each Adhyāya of the *Ṛgveda-saṃhitā)*.
IO 1 and 2 (1690, 1691). *Ṛgveda-saṃhitā* Ms. containing the greater part, given by sections at the beginning of each Adhyāya.
IO 52 (986c). 28 fol. (131-158). Copied for Col. Claud Martin.
IO 53 (1152). 46 fol. Dated V.S. 1854.
IO 54 (2140c). 8 fol. (38b-45).
IO 55 (132a). 19 fol. Dated V.S. 1802.
Jodhpur 1523.
Kavīndrācārya 22 (with Bhāṣya).
L 1212. 253 fol. 7612 Grantha-s ?
Lahore p. 2 (no.4). 134 fol. 3337 Grantha-s (with Bhāṣya). Dated A.D. 1549. In the possession of Pt. Jwala Datta Prasada, Lahore.
Mack 2.
Mad. Uni. R. K. S. 78(a).
Max Müller Mem. I. 108 fol. Before each Adhyāya of the *Ṛgveda*. Dated Śaka 1749.
MD 889. Tel. 45 pp. (21ff.) (differs at end).
MD 890. PL. Tel. 148 pp. Copied by Śrī Rāmasetu of Garakabakapura; dated Tuesday the 11th of the bright fortnight of the Pramādi year.

MD 14778. PL. Na. 25 fol.

Mithila 5508.

Müller 58 (MM 77 B 8 II). 103 pp. "An impression taken by means of a copying machine, of a transcript of Ms. 1152 E I H (IO 53) and collated with 132 E I H (IO 55)".

Müller 59 (MM 42). 8 fol. ((5-103). Copied from the Ms. 986c E I H (IO 52).

München 22(1). 32 fol. Copied in 1812 for Ṭonkekara Bālakṛṣṇadeva.

Mysore II, p. 2.

Mysore ND II 3251 (P 4906/ 2). PL. Na. 87 fol. (14-100). Extract no. 64 (with Kannaḍa Ṭīkā).

Mysore ND II 3252-60. Extract no. 65.

Oppert I 1625. PL. Gr. Belonged to Annasvami Srauti of Bhavani, Coimbatore Dist.

Oppert I 1723. PL. Gr. 179 pp. Belonged to Krishna-bhatta Srauti of Bhavani, Coimbatore Dist.

Oppert I 4631. PL. Gr. 400 pp. Belonged to Subrahmanya Sastri of Pudukkottai.

Oppert II 6216. Belonged to Narasimhacharya of Kumbakonam.

Oxf. CS d.76(2). 26 fol. Title: Sarvānukrama.

Oxf. CS d.76(3). 33 fol. Dated A.D. 1818 (Anuvākānukramaṇī on ff. 30-33). Title: Sarvānukrama.

Oxf. CS d.76(5). 44 fol. Dated A.D. 1693 (Chandaḥ-saṃkhyā on ff. 44-45 and Anuvākānukramaṇī on ff. 45-49). Title: Sarvānukrama.

Oxf. CS d.77(6). 6 fol. Dated A.D. 1861. It contains 32 verses of the Anuvākānukramaṇī, Chandaḥ-saṃkhyā and Anuvāka-pañcāśī.

Oxf. CS d.78(2). 42 fol. (2 fol. missing). Title: Sarvānukrama.

Oxf. II 1078(5) (Ms. Wilson. 503). 37 fol. (34-70). = Oxf. 378a (no.379 ?).

Oxf. II 1077(3) (Ms. Wilson 502). 27 fol. (47-73). Dated A.D. 1639. = Oxf. 386a (no.502).

P 4.

Peters. II, p. 167 (no.4). 44 fol.

Peters. II, p. 167 (no.5). 38 fol.

Peters. II, p. 167 (no.6). 37 fol.

Peters. II, p. 169 (no.2). 41 fol. (of Śāṅkhāyana-śākhā ?).

Peters. III, p. 386 (no.72). 34 fol. Dated V.S. 1763.

PUL I, p. 113 (no.29). 27 fol. Dated V.S. 1657.

PUL II. App. p. 11 (no.155). 14 fol. 700 Grantha-s (Anantācāryasamīkṛtā).

Radh. 1.

RASB II 221 (G 1855). 42 fol. Dated Śaka 1704.

RASB II 222 (G 1182). 36 fol. 700 Grantha-s. Dated V.S. 1810.

RASB II 223 (G 2486). 48 fol.

RASB II 224 (G 3098). 43 fol. Dated V.S. 1695 / Śaka 1560.

RASB II 225 (G 5875). 57 fol. (author given as Vararuci, Kātyāyana-śiṣya).

RASB II 226 (G 7929). 37 fol. Dated V.S. 1549.

RASB II 227 (G 4180). 5 fol. Incomplete (paribhāṣā and the portion up to I 7.10).

RASB II 228 (G 1960). 6 fol. 70 Grantha-s. Incomplete. Three verses at the end listing the names of Brahma-vādinī-s. Cf. Ārṣānukramaṇī, verses 100-102.

RASB II 229 (G 4180). 10 fol. Incomplete.

RASB II 230 (G 312). 100 pp. (with Ṣaḍguru-śiṣya's C.). Incomplete.

RASB II 231 (G 2986). 142 fol. (with C. of Ṣaḍguru-śiṣya). The Ms. belonged to Mīmāṃsaka Śaṃkara-bhaṭṭa of Benares who lived in Akbar's time).

RASB II 232 (G 2192). 107 fol. (with C. of Ṣaḍguru-śiṣya).

Rice 12 (with C.).

Skt. Coll. Ben. 1918-30. p. 5 (no.42). 23 fol. (lacks 5 fol. at the beginning).

SB p. 10 (no.17). 29 fol. 798 Grantha-s. = SBD 2258.

SB p. 10 (no.18). 38 fol. 798 Grantha-s. = SBD 2259.

SBD 2258. 29 fol. Dated V.S. 1545.

SBD 2259. 38 fol. Dated V.S. 1738.

SBD 2267. 44 fol. (ascribed to Āśvalāyana). Dated V.S. 1685. Catalogued as Anukramaṇikā.

SBD 2274. 32 fol. Dated V.S. 1836.

SBD 2276. 36 fol. (1-29, 1-7). Incomplete.

SBD 2278. 40 fol. Incomplete.

SBD 2280. 34 fol. Incomplete.

SBD 2282. 21 fol. Incomplete.

SBD 2283. 50 fol. (1, 3-51). Incomplete.

SBD 2284. 40 fol. (2-27, 31-43, 45). Incomplete. Dated V.S. 1721.

SBD 2285. 19 fol. (5-23). Incomplete.

SBD 2286. 27 fol. Incomplete.

SBD 2287. 44 fol. (7-10, 12-51). Incomplete.

SBD 2288. 14 fol. (Paribhāṣā).

SBD 2289. 13 fol. (48-58, 60-61). Incomplete. Dated V.S. 1757.

SBD 2290. 9 fol. (8-12, 20-21, 23, 1). Incomplete.

SBD 2304. 30 fol. (5-34). Incomplete. Dated Śaka 1719.

SBD 2305. 65 fol. Dated V.S. 1726.

SBD 2310. 24 fol. (43-66). Incomplete.

SBD 2319. 36 fol. Dated V.S. 1740. Ṛgvedānukramaṇikā.

SBD 2329. 34 fol. Dated V.S. 1719.

SBD 2330. 39 fol. Dated Śaka 1729.

SBD 2331. 51 fol. (1-45, 1-6).

SBD 2332. 32 fol. (1-10, 12-21, 23-34). Incomplete.

SBD 2333. 34 fol. Dated V.S. 1847.

SBD 2335. 19 fol. Incomplete.

SBD 2343. 41 fol. (1-19, 1-22). Incomplete.

SBD 2352. 27 fol. (9-35). Incomplete. Chandaḥ-saṃkhyā at the end.

SBD 2354. 4 fol. (Paribhāṣā).

SBD 2355. 14 fol. (1-3, 6-9, 12-18). Incomplete (a. Āśvalāyana). Dated Śaka 1546.

SBD 2356. 20 fol. (7-8, 10-12, 19-33). Dated V.S. 1659. (Ṛgvedānukramaṇikā).

SBD 47191. 27 fol. (18-44). Begins from 4.51.1. Attributed to Prabhākara-bhaṭṭa in the catalogue; that is the name of the scribe.

SBD 47192. 1 fol. This is the first fol. of 4799 which is missing there.

SBD 47196. 15 fol. (1, 3-16). Incomplete. Up to ch. 28. (Sarvānukrama).

SBD 47199a. 55 fol. (2-56). (a. Āśvalāyana). Catalogued as Anuvākānukramaṇī which is the second work in the Ms. The original first fol. of this Ms. is in 47192.

SBD 47201. 8 fol. (22, 24-28, 31-32). Incomplete.

SBD 47202. 3 fol. Incomplete. Only a portion of the beginning.

SBD 47203. 13 fol. (17-29). Incomplete.

SBD 47204. 4 fol. (17-20). Incomplete.

SBD 47205. 7 fol. (6-12). Incomplete. (with C. of Ṣaḍguru-śiṣya).

SBD 47206. 13 fol. (21-23, 25, 27-32, 36-38). Incomplete. Dated Śaka 1761 / V.S. 1897.

SBD 53717. 4 fol. (1-3, 5). Incomplete.

SBD 53794. 43 fol. (1-19, 1-17, 1, 5, 1). Incomplete. Dated V.S. 1922 / Śaka 1787. (Sarvānukrama; here attributed to Śaunaka).

SBD 55253. 47 fol. (Ṛksarvānukramaṇī).

SBD 55270. 3 fol. Incomplete. Dated V.S. 1859. (Sarvānukramaṇikā). The Ms. includes Chandah-saṃkhyā (fol. 1), Anuvākanukramaṇī of Śaunaka (fol. 1-2) and Anuvāka-pañcāśī (fol. 2-3).

SBD 55285. 18 fol. Dated V.S. 1617. (Ṛgvedasyānukramaṇikā).

SBD 55290. 33 fol. Dated V.S. 1748. (Ṛgvedasyānukramaṇikā).

SBD 55360. 15 fol. Incomplete. (Up to 5.13 : nihotā johūtraḥ). The last two folios have Pada-pāṭha of śaṃ na indrāgnī. Title: Āśvalāyana-paribhāṣā.

Tāmarakkāṭṭu Mana 57a.

TCD 37-A. PL. Mal. 37 fol. 580 Grantha-s.

TCD 38-A. PL. Mal. 19 fol. 580 Grantha-s.

TCD 1275-B. PL. Mal. 40 fol. 525 Grantha-s. (4 fol. at the beginning are missing).

TD 1739. 22 fol. 600 Grantha-s.

TD 1740. PL. Tel. 23 fol. 555 Grantha-s. Incomplete.

TD 1741. 58 fol. 550 Grantha-s. Dated Śaka 1751.

TD 1742. 40 fol. 550 Grantha-s. Dated Śaka 1780 (1858).

TD 1743. 71 fol. 550 Grantha-s.

TD 1744. 5 fol. 90 Grantha-s. Paribhāṣā section only.

TD 1745. 5 fol. 50 Grantha-s. Paribhāṣā. Incomplete.

TD 1746. 10 fol. 58 Grantha-s. Incomplete.

TD 1747. 22 fol. 300 Grantha-s. Up to the 40th Adhyāya.

TD 1748. 7 fol. 98 Grantha-s. Adhyāya-s 1-12.

TD 1750. 26 fol. 360 Grantha-s (with C. of Uvaṭa). Paribhāṣā only.

Tirupati SVUORI 991 (2546a). PL. Tel. 17 fol. (Ṛgvedānukramaṇikā).

Tirupati SVUORI 7310 (453). PL. Na. 30 fol. (30-59). (Begins: agniṃ nava madhu-cchandā vaiśvāmitro ...). Title: Sarvānukramaṇikā.

Trav. Uni. (17 Mss. See serial no.2616)

Trav. Uni. 1013 B. PL. Mal. 33 fol. 400 Grantha-s. Incomplete.

Trav. Uni. 1577. 124 fol. 3300 Grantha-s (with Vedārtha-dīpikā). Dated V.S. 1877 / Śaka 1742.

Trav. Uni. 2405 A. PL. Gr. 23 fol. 600 Grantha-s.

Trav. Uni. 2510 B. PL. Tel. 600 Grantha-s.

Trav. Uni. 3113. PL. Mal. 72 fol. 600 Grantha-s.

Trav. Uni. 3694 A. PL. Gr. 30 fol. 600 Grantha-s.

Trav. Uni. 7323. 23 fol. 600 Grantha-s. Dated V.S. 1844.

Trav. Uni. 7324. 37 fol. 600 Grantha-s. Dated Śaka 1727.

Trav. Uni. 9923. 120 Grantha-s. Incomplete.

Trav. Uni. 13507 B. PL. Mal. 600 Grantha-s.
Trav. Uni. 13967 H. 120 Grantha-s. Incomplete.
Trav. Uni. C.1770 B. = TCD 1275-B.
Trav. Uni. C.1872 A = TCD 37-A.
Trav. Uni. C.1887 A = TCD 38-A.
Trav. Uni. L.162 B. PL. Mal. 40 fol. 600 Grantha-s.
Visvanatha Vamana Deva, Varanasi. 172 fol. (with C. of Ṣaḍguru-śiṣya).
Visvanatha Vamana Deva, Varanasi. Separate foliation for each Aṣṭaka (140, 120, 113, 120, 112, 118, 113, 141 fol.). An accented Ms. of the *Ṛgveda-saṃhitā* with Sarvānukramaṇī and Ṣaḍguru-śiṣya's commentary in the beginning of each Sūkta and the Khila-s in the respective places. Remarkably accurate orthography, such as doubling the consonants, Raṅga, etc.
The following entries of VOHD are not really Sarvānukramaṇī Mss. but only passages thereof that accompany particular Sūkta-s of the *Ṛgveda*.
VOHD II 2.498 (Mu I 25 (13). SuUB, Göttingen). 2 fol. Śāradā (with RV 9.67).
VOHD II 2.499 (Mu I 25 (16). SuUB, Göttingen). 4 fol. Śāradā (with RV 9.111-14).
VOHD II 2.520 (Mu I 25 (5). SuUB, Göttingen). 11 fol. Śāradā (with RV 1.59, etc.).
VOHD II 2.523 (Mu I 25 (6). SuUB, Göttingen). 6 fol. Śāradā (with RV 9.96, etc.).
VOHD II 2.524 (Mu I 25 (9). SuUB, Göttingen). 27 fol. Śāradā (with RV 1.154. etc.).
VOHD II 2.525 (Mu I 25 (10). SuUB, Göttingen). 3 fol. Śāradā (with RV 10.15).
VOHD II 2.526 (Mu I 25 (11). SuUB, Göttingen). 4 fol. Śāradā (with RV 10.151, etc.).
VOHD II 2.527 (Mu I 25 (7). SuUB, Göttingen). 8 fol. Śāradā (with RV 10.166, etc.).
VOHD II 2.529 (Mu I 25 (8). SuUB, Göttingen). 14 fol. Śāradā (with RV 10.14, etc.).
VOHD II 4.1114 (Mu I 104. SuUB, Göttingen). 5 fol. Śāradā (with RV 1.164: Asyavāmīya-sūkta).
VOHD II 4.1115 (Mu I 104). SuUB, Göttingen). 4 fol. Śāradā (with RV 1.164: Asyavāmīya-sūkta, etc.).
VOHD II 4.1117 (Mu I 104. SuUB, Göttingen). 5 fol. Śāradā (with RV 10.85).
VOHD II 4.1118 (Mu I 104. SuUB, Göttingen). 2 fol. Śāradā (with RV 10.125).
VOHD II 4.1119 (Mu I 104. SuUB, Göttingen). 2 fol. Śāradā (with RV 10.127).
VOHD II 4.1128 (Mu I 104. SuUB, Göttingen). 2 fol. Śāradā (with RV 1.106).
VOHD II 5.1501 (Mu I 135. SuUB, Göttingen). Śāradā (with RV 4.57).
VOHD II 5.1502 (Mu I 135. SuUB, Göttingen). 2 fol. Śāradā (with RV 5.46).
VOHD II 5.1503 (Mu I 135. SuUB, Göttingen). 3 fol. Śāradā (with RV 7.54-55).
VOHD II 5.1511 (Mu I 135. SuUB, Göttingen). 138 fol. Śāradā (with RV Sūkta-s).
VOHD II 5.1512 (Mu I 135. SuUB, Göttingen). 18 fol. Śāradā (with RV 1.50, etc.).
VOHD II 5.1513 (Mu I 135. SuUB, Göttingen). 7 fol. Śāradā (with RV 8.48, etc.).
VOHD II 5.1514 (Mu I 135. SuUB, Göttingen). 12 fol. Śāradā (with RV 4.15, etc.).
VOHD II 5.1515 (Mu I 135. SuUB, Göttingen). 23 fol. Śāradā (with RV 1.154, etc.).
VOHD II 5.1516 (Mu I 135. SuUB, Göttingen). 12 fol. Śāradā (with RV 10.71, etc.).
VOHD II 5.1517 (Mu I 135. SuUB, Göttingen). 11 fol. Śāradā (with RV 6.61, etc.).
VOHD II 5.1518 (Mu I 135. SuUB, Göttingen). 12 fol. Śāradā (with RVKh. 9.1, etc.).
VOHD II 5.1519 (Mu I 135. SuUB, Göttingen). 8 fol. Śāradā (with RV 5.40, etc.).
VOHD II 5.1520 (Mu I 135. SuUB, Göttingen). 12 fol. Śāradā (with RV 1.43, etc.).
VOHD II 5.1521 (Mu I 135. SuUB, Göttingen). 11 fol. Śāradā (with RV 10.173, etc.).
VSM I 461-71. 11 Mss. 6 of them are incomplete.

VSM III 169 (no.11343). 37 fol. Dated Śaka 1711.
VSM III 170 (no.12181). 34 fol.
VSM III 171 (no.11342). 33 fol. Dated Śaka 1817.
VSM III 172 (no.12182). 5 fol. Paribhāṣā only.
Wai I 80. 123 fol. (together with the *Ṛgveda)*.
Wai I 112. 120 fol. (together with the Ṛgveda-pada-pāṭha). Dated V.S. 1852.
Wai I 293-318 (26 Mss.). The last one is ascribed to Śaunaka.
Wai I 320. 163 fol. (with C. of Ṣaḍguru-śiṣya).
Wai I 321. 144 fol. (with C. of Ṣaḍguru-śiṣya). Dated Śaka 1789.
Wai I 322. 104 fol. (with C. of Ṣaḍguru-śiṣya). Incomplete.
Wai I 323. 40 fol. (with C. of Ṣaḍguru-śiṣya). Incomplete.
Wai I 324. 21 fol. Paribhāṣā only (with C. of Ṣaḍguru-śiṣya).
Wai I 325. 27 fol. Paribhāṣā only (with C. of Gaṇeśa Ḍokhale).
Wai I 326. 202 fol. (with C. of Gaṇeśa Ḍokhale). Incomplete.
Weber 49 (Chambers 55). 29 fol. Dated V.S. 1688.
Weber 50 (Chambers 56). 47 fol. (6 fol. missing). Dated V.S. 1716.
Weber 51 (Chambers 58, 1). 41 fol.
Weber 52 (Chambers 81). 59 fol.
Weber 53 (Chambers 192). 120 fol. Dated V.S. 1790 (with C. Ṣaḍguru-śiṣya).
Weber 1405 (Ms. or. fol. 816). 7 fol. (with C. of Ṣaḍguru-śiṣya, only the beginning).
Wellcome Inst. London. G 51. 7 fol. Incomplete.
Whish 78(6). PL. Gr. 25 fol. (30-54). Incomplete (up to X 105).

Ptd.: Ed. by Arthur A. Macdonell, *Kātyāyana's Sarvānukramaṇī of the Rigveda*, with extracts from Ṣaḍguruśiṣya's commentary entitled *Vedārtha-dīpikā*, and Introduction, Critical Notes and Appendices (also *Anuvākānukramaṇī* and *Chandaḥsaṃkhyā)*. – Oxford : Clarendon Press, 1886. xxii, 223 pp. (Anecdota Oxoniensia, Aryan Series vol. I, pt. iv) [Adyar (H080 AOA A 1.4); SAI (88/2122*); NL (I C I G/3); UBTÜ (Ka XXIII 7. /4/); UBHD (F 9039); BM : Ptd. Bks. Cat. 1876-92. 181, 269, 457 (12204.f.); Emeneau (387, 388)]

As an appendix to the *Ṛgveda-saṃhitā*, ed. by Vasanta Sripada (Damodar) Satwalekar (Bhagavatkātyāyana-viracitā Ṛgveda-sarvānukramaṇī). – Aundh, Pardi (Balsad Dist. Gujarat) : Svadhyaya Mandala, 1929 (several reprints), pp. 809-26.

Photographic reprint of the above : by V. R. Laksmikanta Sarma. – Kumbakonam (612001, 14 Kamakshi Josier Street) : The Maharaja Saheb Sri Govinda Deekshitar Punya Smarana Samiti, 1979.

Ed. by Umesh Chandra Sharma. – Aligarh : Viveka Publications, 1977, vi, 107 pp. This is actually a reprint of Macdonell's edition without extracts of the C. but with *Anuvākānukramaṇī* and *Chandaḥsaṃkhyā*. [BORI (30897); NL (180 Jc 97 238); UBTÜ (19 A 10476); SAI (ind 50 B 82/36)]

Ed. by Vijayapal, *Kātyāyanīya-ṛksarvānukramaṇī* – Ṣaḍguru-śiṣya-viracitayā kṛtsnavṛttyā sahitā. – Calcutta 700013, 5 Lenin Sarani : Savitri Devi Bagadiya Trust, 1985. 15, 365 pp. (also – Bahalgadh 131021, Sonipat-Haryana : Ramalal Kapur Trust). [SAI (ind 51 D 888/1161); BORI (49800)]

– C. Kṣipra(-pra)-bodhinī of Bālakṛṣṇa.

Mysore ND II 3287 (C 3757). 17 fol. Extract no. 74. Śaka 1246 ? (the paper does not appear to be very old; col.: tāraṇanāmasaṃvatsare caitraśuklapañcamībhaume kavaḍekar rāmeṇa idaṃ pustakaṃ likhitam). (Paribhāṣā section only).

– C. Dīpikā.
B I, p. 212 (no.86). 488 fol.
Mandlik Sup. 102.
SB p. 10 (no.20). 2-141, 146-203 fol. 3341 Grantha-s. = SBD 2257. (= Vedārtha-dīpikā of Ṣaḍguru-śiṣya).
SB p. 11 (no.94). 1-7, 1-22 fol. 595 Grantha-s. = SBD 2260.
Cf. Gaṇeśa's Dīpikā below.

– C. Bhāṣya.
Kavīndrācārya 22.
N-W P VI 8 (no.23). 194 fol. Belonged to Gopinatha Dikshita Atale, Ulwar (Alwar).
N. S. Press 312.
SB p. 10 (no.19). 1-19, 21-98 fol. 2117 Grantha-s (Adhyāya-s 1-38). = SBD 2256.
Tirupati SVUORI 8873 (6561). Fragment.

– C. Padya-vivṛti or Sarvānukramaṇī-padya-vivṛti – an elaborate metrical gloss with additions, elaborations, and annotations; anonymous. See C. Kunhan Raja, "Sarvānukramaṇī-padya-vivṛti – A New Commentary on the Ṛgvedasarvānukramaṇī of Kātyāyana", in: *Annals of Oriental Research*, University of Madras, vol. V, ii. 1940-41, Sanskrit Section, pp. 1-4. See also *The Adyar Library Bulletin*, vol. VII, pt. 4 (1943), pp. 238-50. A transcript of it from a Malayalam palm-leaf original Ms. in Dr. C. Kunhan Raja's private collection, is now with Prof. K. Kunjunni Raja, Adyar Library, Madras. (A xerox-copy of this transcript in Malayalam script is in SAI : 87/1688*).

Beginning:

विनायकमुमाकान्तं देवीमपि गिरां गुरून्।
प्रणौमि शौनकाचार्यं कात्यायनमहामुनिम्॥ १॥
ऋग्वेदे मुनिदैवताद्यवगमायार्येण कात्यायने-
नैषा या मुनिकुञ्जरेण रचिता विद्वन्मनोहारिणी।
सर्वानुक्रमणीमिमां पिपठिषूनामोदयन् बालकान्
कुर्वे पद्यमयीं विवृत्य किमपि व्युत्पत्तये मादृशाम्॥ २॥
अथ शाकलको यो ऽसावृग्वेदाम्नाय ईर्यते।
तत्र सूक्तादिमृक्संख्यां च्छन्दश्चाप्यृषिदेवते॥ ३॥
इह क्रमेण वक्ष्यामो यथामति यथागमम्।
इत्थं प्रदर्श्याभिधेयं प्रयोजनमथोच्यते॥ ४॥
नैतज्ज्ञानादृते कर्म श्रौतं स्मार्तं च सिध्यति।
एतदेव पुनः सम्यक् प्रतिपादयति स्फुटम्॥ ५॥

मन्त्राणां ब्राह्मणद्रष्टृछन्दोदैवतवित् पुमान्।
भूयो ऽधिगच्छति श्रेयो याजनाध्ययनादिभिः ॥ ६॥

End:

सर्वानुक्रमणी सेयं मया पद्यमयीकृता।
स्खलितं यदिदं सर्वं क्षन्तव्यमिह सूरिभिः ॥ २०२८॥
कात्यायनाय मुनये शौनकाय महर्षये।
अधीतसाङ्गवेदेभ्यो भूदेवेभ्यो नमो नमः ॥ २०२९॥
जज्ञे नाके भिषङ् मन्दः सेव्यो नायं तनुर्नरः।
धर्मवानयमृङ्ज्ञानमर्धर्चाश्शिवदा नराः ॥ २०३०॥

– C. Bhāṣya of Uvaṭa.

Beginning: (BORI)

चतुर्मुखमुखाम्भोजवनहंसवधूर्मम।
मानसे रमतां नित्यं सर्वशुक्ला सरस्वती॥
सचराचरमुनिमान्ये चतुराननवदनकमलवनहंसि।
मम हृदयकमलकोटरगतवचनेषु वस (रम) वाग्देवि॥
लक्ष्मीधरं परं सूक्ष्मं चक्रिणं शङ्खधारिणम्।
विष्णुं पद्मदलाभासं प्रपद्ये शरणं सदा॥
कर्तारं सर्वशास्त्राणां वन्दे ऽज्ञानरिपुं भवम्।
स्रष्टारं सर्वलोकानां पातारं क्षयकारिणम्॥

End:

अक्षराणां प्रयुतानि चत्वारिंशद्द्वात्रिंशत् सहस्राणि तत् समाम्नातं चतुःषष्ठ्या खिलरहितानित्याः। इति सर्वानुक्रमभाष्ये अष्टमाष्टके ऽष्टमो ऽध्यायः। शाके १५८३ संवत् १७१८ व्ययनामसंवत्सरे पौषशुक्ल १ गुरौ ... मभट्टवामनाचार्येदं पुस्तकं समाप्तम्॥

Adyar D I 1054 (38 H 6 = TR 30). 151 fol. It has numerous small lacunae. A transcript of the BORI Ms. (D I i.38) made in 1916.
BORI 81 of 1884-87. = BORI D I i.38. 123 fol. Dated Śaka 1583 / V.S. 1718.
BORI 14 of 1902-07. 121 fol. 3267 Grantha-s. Dated Śaka 1681.
Hoshiarpur p. 56 (no.5563). 51 fol. 1200 Grantha-s. Incomplete. Extract p. 415.
Oxf. CS d.79. 96 fol. Dated V.S. 1425. Copied in Kāśī.
Rgb. 81.
TD 1750. 26 fol. 360 Grantha-s. Paribhāṣā only.

– C. Sarvānukramaṇī-vṛtti (Dīpikā). of Gaṇeśa Ḍokhale, son of Kṛṣṇa-bhaṭṭa.

Adyar D I 1055 (38 H 21/1-2 = TR 31). 408 fol. 2 vols. (pp. 1-464; 465-816). A transcript of the Baroda Ms. no.409.

B I, p. 212 (no.87).

Baroda 409. 244 fol. 6000 Grantha-s. = CLB I, p. 25.

Baroda 1486. 205 fol. 6000 Grantha-s. = CLB I, p. 25. Dated V.S. 1596.

Ben. 3.

Bombay Uni. (BMC 129 8). 156 fol. 5750 Grantha-s. Dated Śaka 1742.

Calcutta Skt. Coll. I 22. 263 fol.

Deccan College 3807. Incomplete.

Deccan College 11079. 111, 3, 29, 37, 37, 44, 41 fol.

MT 5540. 178 fol. 5295 Grantha-s. Copy of Adyar Ms. made in 1930-31.

N-W P II 6 (no.19). 407 fol. Belonged to Makhanji of Mathura.

N-W P V 148 (no.35). 294 fol. Title: Anukrama-dīpikā.

Oudh XIII 24 (no.6). 60 pp. 3000 Grantha-s. Dated A.D. 1878. Title: Ṛgveda-pāṭhānukramaṇa-dīpikā. Belonged to M. Kali Prasada of Lucknow.

SB p. 11 (no.20). 1-6, 3-210, 1-62, 1-8, 10-30 fol. 9639 Grantha-s.

SBD 2260. 70 fol.

SBD 2301. 291 fol. (1-154, 3-100, 1-7, 7-38).

SBD 2361. 37 fol. Dated V.S. 1828. (Paribhāṣā-bhāṣya).

SBD 47938. 214 fol. (6, 3-210). Incomplete. (Ṛgvedānukrama-dīpikā).

SBD 47939. 94 fol. (1-8, 10-30, 1-62, 1, 7, 8). Incomplete. (Ṛgvedānukrama-dīpikā).

Trav. Uni. 4839. 215 fol. 5750 Grantha-s. Dated V.S. 1878 / Śaka 1743.

Trav. Uni. 4841. 16 fol. 525 Grantha-s. Incomplete.

Trav. Uni. 4919. 45 fol. 800 Grantha-s (with text). Incomplete.

Trav. Uni. 9919. 5750 Grantha-s.

Ujjain Latest Additions. 494.

Wai I 325. 27 fol. Paribhāṣā only.

Wai I 326. 202 fol. Incomplete (up to ud asau sūrya ...).

Cf. C. Dīpikā above.

– C. Dīpaprabhā (Ṛgveda-paribhāṣā-vyākhyā) of Nārāyaṇa of Kerala.

Beginning: (MT 3796)

यत्प्रसादादविघ्नेन समाप्तिं यान्ति देहिनाम्।
आरम्भास्तं गणाधीशं प्रणमामीष्टपुष्टये॥ ...
यच्छिक्षामिहिरो ऽस्माकं हृत्पद्मे नियतास्पदाम्।
हिमानीमहरत् तीव्रामविद्यां तान्नुमो गुरून्॥
देवतात्रितयं वन्दे सूर्यवाय्वग्निसंज्ञितम्।
स्वराकाशक्षितिस्थानं नामभिर्बहुभिः स्तुतम्॥
यो निर्ममे पाणिनिगीतशब्दशास्त्रोदधेर्वार्त्तिकरूपनौकाम्।
नागेश्वरो हर्षयुतः प्रकाशं भाष्यप्रदीपेन चकार यस्याः॥
स्मृत्यन्तराणामपि यः प्रणेता कात्यायनाख्यः स मुनिः प्रपेदे।

सर्वज्ञतां शौनकशिष्यभावादादाय विद्याः सकलास्तदीयाः ॥
मिताक्षरां प्रभूतार्थां सर्वानुक्रमणीमसौ ।
विदधे शौनकीयानां स्मृतीनां संग्रहात्मिकाम् ॥
सर्वभाष्यादिकं यस्यां क्रमेणाहेति निर्वचः ।
नाम्नैवानेन मुनिना कैमर्थक्यं निराकृतम् ।
निरुक्ते फणिभाष्ये च पैङ्गले च कृतश्रमः ।
टीकामहं विधास्ये ऽस्या यथाशक्ति यथाश्रुतम् ॥
पूर्वाचार्यैः कृता बह्व्यो व्याक्रियाः सन्ति यद्यपि ।
स्वबुद्धिशुद्धये टीकामारभे ऽस्यास्तथाप्यहम् ॥
सर्वः सर्वं न जानातीत्येवमाहुः पुराणगाः ।
अतश्चाप्यर्थवत्येषा नवार्थकथनात् क्वचित् ॥
पूर्वव्याख्याकृतां भावः प्रायेणात्र प्रदर्श्यते ।
तत् सतां तत्कृतं लौल्यमनयैव प्रशाम्यति ॥

तत्र तावत् --

मङ्गलाचारयुक्तानां नित्यं च प्रयतात्मनाम् ।
जपतां जुह्वतां चैव विनिपातो न विद्यते ॥

मङ्गलादीनि हि शास्त्राणि प्रथन्त इति महाभाष्यकारवचनात् शिष्टाचाराच्चानुमितया श्रुत्या प्रबन्धारम्भे समुचितं मङ्गलाचरणं वृद्ध्यादिशब्दैरिवाथशब्देन संसूच्य श्रोतॄन् प्ररोचयन्नभिधेयं प्रतिजानीते -- अथ ऋग्वेदेति ।

End: (MT 3834)

आचार्यशब्देनात्र विद्यानां प्रदातार उच्यन्ते न तूपनीयाध्यापायितैव । तेभ्यो ऽप्युत्कृष्टं बह्वृचकुञ्जरं शौनकं पृथङ् नमस्करोति -- नमः शौनकायेति ॥
इति सर्वानुक्रमण्यामष्टमाष्टकस्याष्टमे ऽध्याय एकान्नपञ्चाशत्सूक्तगत ऋक्संख्यादयश्चर्चिताः ॥ इति षट्चत्वारिंशदधिकशतसंख्याकसूक्तपरिमाणे अष्टमाष्टकः समाप्तः ॥

एवं सहस्रे सूक्तानां मया सप्तदशाधिके ।
ऋष्याद्यं विस्तरेणोक्तमाचार्यैः सूत्रितं मतम् ॥
ब्रह्मक्षत्रो जयति विपुलो भूप्रदेशो महान्तो
यत्राचार्याः श्रुतिषु निपुणाः शंकराद्या बभूवुः ।
अब्धौ तेजस्त्रितयपरमे निर्ममे जामदग्न्यो
यं ब्रह्मार्थं भुवनमहितं केरलैर्जुष्टमत्र ॥
वेदो नाम महत् पदं जनपदो यत्र द्विजानां ततिः

साङ्गं वेदमधीत्य वाच्यमखिलं मीमांसते सुस्फुटम्।
तत्र ग्रामवरे क्वचिन्निवसता नाम्ना च नारायणे-
नैषानुक्रमणीप्रदीपनपरा दीपप्रभा निर्मिता॥
ग्रामे महाविहाराख्ये जातेनाङ्गिरसां कुले।
आर्यासुतेन टीकेयं रचि(लिखि)ता दैवशर्मणा॥
वेदार्थार्णवतारणाय मुनिना कात्यायनेन स्मृतां
सर्वानुक्रमणीं दृढां सुरुचिरां प्राप्यापि नौकामिमाम्।
नेतारं सदृशं विचिन्त्य कुशलं कच्छे स्थितान् कोविदान्
अस्मद्व्याकृतिनाविका यदि रुचिस्तेषां भवेत् तारयेत्॥ ...
सर्वानुक्रमणी(टीका) नारायणकृता समाप्ता॥

MT 3796. 121 fol. Lacks end. Breaks off in the eighth Adhyāya of the eighth Aṣṭaka. Transcribed in 1921-22 from a Ms. of Sankaran Nambudiripad of Alamballi-mana, Kavalapara Post, Shoranur.

MT 3834. Gr. 112 fol. Transcribed in 1921-22 from a Ms. of Sankara Nambudiripad of Paliyadattu-mana, Lakkidi Post, Malabar Dist.

Trav. Uni. 10794 B. PL. Mal. 730 Grantha-s. Incomplete. Badly damaged.

– C. Ṭippaṇī. anon.

Hz 2188. 7 fol. Belonged to Jambunatha Bhatta of Thanjavur.

SBD 2268. 24 fol. Incomplete. Dated V.S. 1908.

Wai I 329. 5 fol. Incomplete.

– C. Ṭīkā of Raghunātha Caturvedin, son of Devadatta Caturvedin.

Adyar D I 1056 (38 H 5 = TR 32). 169 fol. (pp. 1-337). A transcript of the BBRAS Ms. made in 1930.

BBRAS 499 (S C 4). 103 fol. (with text). Dated Śaka 1710 / V.S. 1845.

IM 2162. 45 fol. (1, 7-50). Incomplete.

– C. of Rāma-bhaṭṭa, son of Bālam-bhaṭṭa, surnamed Gahvara.

Adyar D I 1057 (38 H 5 = TR 32). 17 fol. (pp. 1-34). A copy of the Calcutta Skt. Coll. Ms. (no.23).

Calcutta Skt. Coll. I 23. 11 fol.

– C. of Vāsudeva of Kerala.

The beginning of this commentary, as found in Baroda catalogue and in MT 5580

(स्तोतॄणामतिशयेन स्तोता। यस्माच्चास्माकीना स्तोतारः प्रस्तुवति प्रयत्ते। यस्मादग्ने तव स्तोतारः प्रजायते ...)

is actually a fragment of the commentary of Mādhava-bhaṭṭa on RV (I 97.3 - 100.10). Cf. C. Kunhan Raja's introduction to his edition (p. XIV) of that commentary.

Beginning:

... ऐन्द्रे सूक्ते बाहुल्येन मरुतो ऽपि सन्त्येव। राज्ञां च दानस्तुतयः। दानस्तुतिसंबन्धिनो विभिन्द्वादयो राजान एव। अथ छन्दांसि। अनन्तरं छन्दांसि प्रस्तूयन्ते। गायत्री ... अतिधृतयः चतुर्दश छन्दसां नामानि। ... इति द्वादशकाण्डी तु परिभाषा प्रवर्णिता। अग्निं नव मधुच्छन्दा वैश्वामित्रः। अग्निमिति सूक्तादि। नवेति सूक्तस्य ऋक्संख्या। मधुच्छन्दा इति ऋषेर्नाम। वैश्वामित्र इति तस्य गोत्रम्। अग्निमीळे विश्वामित्रो मधुच्छन्दा ऋषिः। गायत्री छन्दः। अग्निर्देवता। अग्निः पूर्वेभिरित्येकोनत्वात् निचृत् गायत्री।

End:

सं समिद्युतस्त्रः आङ्गिरसः संवनन ऋषिः समानो मन्त्र इति त्रिष्टुप् शिष्टा अनुष्टुभः संज्ञानं देवता संसमित्यस्या अग्निः। द्विरुक्तिर्ग्रन्थसमास्यर्था। तत्कृतग्रन्थमूलत्वादस्य वररुचिः शौनकं नमस्करोति नमः शौनकायेति।

अत्युक्तान्यन्यथोक्तानि यान्यनुक्तानि वा मया।
ऋषिच्छन्दोदैवतानि तानि शोध्यानि सूरिभिः॥

समाप्तं वासुदेवीयम्। वररुचये नमः॥

Baroda 7869. PL. Mal. 66 fol. (3-68). 2000 Grantha-s. = CLB I, p. 25. Extract pp. 137-38. The original fol. 1-2 are missing. Instead one fol. belonging to the Ṛgveda-bhāṣya is inserted.

Baroda 12333. 180 fol. 2000 Grantha-s. = CLB I, p. 25. Copy of the above made in 1922.

MT 5508. 87 fol. 2640 Grantha-s. Copied in 1930-31 from a Ms. obtained from Dr. C. Kunhan Raja.

Naḍuvil Maṭham 177 (ṚV-Ṛṣicchandodaivatāni).

– C. Vedārtha-dīpikā of Ṣaḍguru-śiṣya, written in 1187 A.D. (Cf. A. Weber : *Indische Studien,* vol. 8, p. 160).

Adyar D I 1058 (22 D 90 = 68848). PL. Gr. 183 fol. (1-192; 9 fol. missing). Begins abruptly in the 6th line on p. 57 of Macdonell's edition and contains a few variants to it. = Adyar I, App. p. iiia.

Adyar D I 1059 (22 G 39). PL. Tel. 80 fol. Almost complete; a small portion missing at the end. = Adyar I, p. 48b. Title: Ṛṣidaivata-cchandonukramaṇikā.

America 373. 16 pp. German cursive script copied by A. Weber from Chambers 192.

Ānandāśrama 6244. (Missing).

ASB I iii.25 (IM 2163). 83 fol. (25, 26, 28, 29, 56-134). 3237 Grantha-s (with text). Incomplete. Both the text and the commentary are wrongly attributed to Sāyaṇa in the catalogue.

Baroda 10951. 193 fol. 3000 Grantha-s. = CLB I, p. 25. Dated Śaka 1793 (wants Paribhāṣā-vṛtti).

Baroda 11023. 46 fol. 350 Grantha-s. = CLB I, p. 25. Dated Śaka 1788 (Paribhāṣā-vṛtti only).

BBRAS 500 (ZZ A 23). 66 fol. (with text).

BHU B 954 (D 1A/42). 55 fol. Incomplete. Title: Ṛgvedāmnāya. (Dvādaśa-khaṇḍī Paribhāṣā).

Bik. 344. 84 fol. Dated Śaka 1583.

Bik. 345. 133 fol.

Bikaner 631. 133 fol.

Bikaner 632. 19 fol. Upodghāta only.

Bikaner 633. 17 fol. Dated V.S. 1596 (A.D. 1674). Aṣṭaka 8 only.

Bikaner 634. 13 fol. Dated V.S. 1994 (A.D. 1937).

BISM p. 314 (57/51). Dated Śaka 1721.

Bombay Uni. (BMC 129 12). 105 fol.

BORI 9 of Viś (1). = BORI D I i.34. 146 fol. 3940 Grantha-s. Dated Śaka 1560.

BORI 113 of 1869-70. = BORI D I i.35. 178 fol. Dated V.S. 1449.

BORI 113 of 1899-1915. 106 fol. Dated V.S. 1737.

Deccan College (1964). 273 (5707 of Datar Collection). 15 fol. Dated V.S. 1839. Contains the C. on the Anuvākānukramaṇī and the introductory verses of the Ṛgveda-sarvānukramaṇī.

Deccan College 1372. 134 fol. Dated Śaka 1751.

Deccan College 5728. 50 fol. Dated V.S. 1931. Incomplete.

Deccan College 6742. 169 fol. 12 fol. in the beginning contain the C. on the Anuvākānukramaṇī and the introductory verses of the Ṛgveda-sarvānukramaṇī. Dated V.S. 1795.

GD I 9. PL. Mal. 8 fol. 200 Grantha-s. Incomplete.

GJKSV 13906. 9 fol. Dated V.S. 1784. Copied by Govinda Rāma, son of Nṛsiṃha Dīkṣita. Contains some portions of Itihāsa-s only.

GJKSV 39129. 299 fol. (1-250, 253-311). Incomplete. Dated V.S. 1828.

Granthappura p. 1 (no.10). Mal. 200 Grantha-s. Incomplete.

Haug p. 30 (no.70) = München 23.

Hoshiarpur p. 56 (no.4098). PL. Gr. 127 fol. 3000 Grantha-s.

Hpr. II 243. 102 fol. 3340 Grantha-s. Dated V.S. 1830.

Hz 1852. 14 fol. Belonged to Jambunatha Bhatta of Thanjavur.

Hz 1935. 80 fol. Belonged to Jambunatha Bhatta of Thanjavur.

IM 2163. 83 fol. (25, 26, 28, 29, 56-134) (with text). Incomplete. Wrongly attributed to Sāyaṇa.

IO 56 (1823). 140 fol.

IO 57 (2396). 173 fol. Dated Śaka 1602 (V.S. 1812 ?).

Jodhpur 1524.

Mad. Uni. R. A. S. 105a (Chandas only).

MD 1004. Tel. 164 pp. (53ff.).

MD 15944. PL. Tel. 158 pp.

Mīm Vid. 666.

MT 3165(b). PL. Tel. 17 fol. (33-49). Incomplete. Breaks off in the 12th Adhyāya. Presented in 1919-20 by Yajnanarayana Ayyagaru of Ravanasamudram, Ambasamudram Taluk.

MT 3911(a). PL. Gr. 21 fol. (2-22). Incomplete. Lacks beginning. Purchased in 1921-22 from Narasimha Sastrigal, Bhavani, Coimbatore Dist.

München 23. 103 fol. (Written ca. A.D. 1650).

Mysore I, p. 39 (3 Mss.); p. 614.

Mysore ND II 3261 (P 2862/ 1). PL. Na. 3-44 fol. This is not the C. of Ṣaḍguru-śiṣya, but an Anukramaṇī giving Ṛṣi, Devatā and Chandas for each Sūkta, as in MD 14782 (Ṛṣi-devatā-cchando-vivaraṇa).

Mysore ND II 3262 (P 4513). PL. Na. 50 fol. (25-74).

Mysore ND II 3263 (P 4906/ 1). PL. Na. 14 fol. (1-14).

Mysore ND II 3264 (P 6998/ 2). PL. Na. 31 fol. (15-45).

Mysore ND II 3265 (P 7743/ 3). PL. Na. 10 fol.

Mysore ND II 3266 (C 477/ 2). 37 fol.

Mysore ND II 3267 (C 850). 41 fol.

Mysore ND II 3268 (C 1977). 28 fol. Incomplete. Dated V.S. 1771.

Mysore ND II 3269 (C 2546/ 3). 2 fol. (5-6). Incomplete.

Mysore ND II 3283 (P 3293). PL. Tel. 104 fol. Extract no. 71.

Mysore ND II 3284 (P 4002). PL. Na. 187 fol.

Mysore ND II 3285 (C 36). 27 fol. Extract no. 72.

Oppert I 1626. PL. Gr. Belonged to Annasvami Srauti of Bhavani, Coimbatore Dist.

Oxf. II 892(1b) (Ms. Wilson 379). 70 fol. (5-74) (with text). Dated A.D. 1600. = Oxf. 378b.

PUL I, p. 20 (no.39). 123 fol. 2500 Grantha-s.

PUL I, p. 20 (no.40). 53 fol. 1500 Grantha-s. Incomplete.

PUL I, p. 20 (no.41). 27 fol. Incomplete.

PUL II. App. p. 11 (no.156). PL. Mal. 191 fol. 4000 Grantha-s.

Rajapur 505.

RASB II 230 (G 312). 100 pp. (with text). Incomplete.

RASB II 231 (G 2986). 142 fol. (with text). The Ms. belonged to Mīmāṃsaka Śaṃkarabhaṭṭa of Benares who lived in Akbar's time).

RASB II 232 (G 2192). 107 fol. (with text).

SBD 2256. 77 fol. (1-19, 21-78). Incomplete (39 chapters).

SBD 2257. 198 fol. (2-141, 146-203). Incomplete.

SBD 2300. 75 fol. Incomplete.

SBD 2302. 133 fol.

SBD 2312. 165 fol.

SBD 2315. 45 fol. (Pūrvārdha).

SBD 2318. 40 fol. (Uttarārdha). Dated Śaka 1671.

SBD 2357. 57 fol. (1st Adhyāya). Dated Śaka 1754.

SBD 2364. 9 fol. (9th Maṇḍala).

SBD 47189. 147 fol.

SBD 47190. 85 fol. Dated V.S. 1777.

SBD 47205. 7 fol. (6-12). Incomplete. (with text).

SBD 47207. 5 fol. (104-110). Incomplete (chs. 47-54). Catalogued as Sarvānukramaṇībhāṣya.

TD 1749. 8 fol. 160 Grantha-s. Paribhāṣā and the first Adhyāya.

TD 1940. 76 fol. 3300 Grantha-s.

Tirupati SVUORI 2641 (6553). 70 fol. Incomplete.

Tirupati SVUORI 8874 (6553). Incomplete.

Trav. Uni. 1577. 3300 Grantha-s (with text). Dated V.S. 1877 = Śaka 1742.

Trav. Uni. 3694 C. PL. Gr. 111 fol. 3000 Grantha-s. Incomplete. Damaged.
Trav. Uni. L.702 C. PL. Mal. 3298 Grantha-s. Incomplete. Damaged. Age of the work: M.E. 358 = A.D. 1183).
Trav. Uni. 12442. PL. Mal. 120 Grantha-s. Incomplete. Damaged.
Ujjain I, p. 9.
Ujjain Latest Additions 180. 458.
Vangiya p. 27.
Venkatesiah 42.
VSM I 456 (no.654). 48 fol. Dated Śaka 1713. Copied by Dīkṣita Siddheśvara.
VSM I 457 (no.924). 41 fol. Dated Śaka 1712. Copied by Gavaṇḍī Veṅkaṭeśa.
VSM I 458 (no.2988). 43 fol. Dated Śaka 1688.
VSM I 459 (no.3346). 36 fol. Dated Śaka 1739. Copied by Jośī Mahādeva.
VSM I 460 (no.3952). 39 fol. Dated Śaka 1759. Copied by Pāṭhaka Gajānana.
Weber 53. 120 fol. (with text). Dated V.S. 1790.
Weber 1405 (Ms. or. fol. 816). 7 fol. (beginning only, with text).

Ptd.: ed. by A. A. Macdonnel, together with the text (only extracts), pp. 57-168. See above.

Ed. by Vijayapal, *Kātyāyanīya-ṛksarvānukramaṇī* – Ṣaḍguruśiṣyaviracitayā kṛtsnavṛttyā sahitā. – Calcutta 700013, 5 Lenin Sarani : Savitri Devi Bagadiya Trust, 1985. 15, 365 pp. (also – Bahalgadh 131021, Sonipat-Haryana : Ramalal Kapur Trust). [SAI (ind 51 D 888/1161); BORI (49800)]

[NCC III 24a-25b]

349 ṚGVEDA-SARVĀNUKRAMAṆIKĀ-ḌHUṆḌHŪ (ऋग्वेदसर्वानुक्रमणिकाढुण्ढू)

→ Anukramaṇikā-ḍhuṇḍhū. A conspectus of the *Ṛgveda* hymns based on the *Sarvānukramaṇikā* giving the beginning of the hymn, the number of Ṛk-s, Ṛṣi-s, Devatā and Chandas. Cf. Ṛṣi-daivata-cchandonukrama.

[NCC III 25b]

350 ṚGVEDA-SARVĀNUKRAMAṆĪ (ऋग्वेदसर्वानुक्रमणी)

With Kannada vṛtti of Bhairava Bhaṭṭopādhyāya, son of Devaṇa.
Bikaner 635. 36 fol.
Mysore I, p. 612. Cf. Ṛganukramaṇikā above with Kannada gloss.

351 ṚGVEDA-SARVĀNUKRAMAṆĪ-ṬĪKĀ (ऋग्वेदसर्वानुक्रमणीटीका)

of Appāji-bhaṭṭa. Ṭīkā in Kannada.
Mysore ND II 3288 (P 4637). PL. Na. 98 fol. Extract no. 75.
Mysore ND II 3289 (P 5105/ 2). PL. Na. 88 fol. Extract no. 76.
Mysore ND II 3290 (P 4906/ 3). PL. Na. 7 fol. (101-07).

[NCC III 25b]

352 ṚGVEDA-SARVĀNUKRAMAṆĪ-PARIBHĀṢĀ (DVĀDAŚA-KHAṆḌĪ) (ऋग्वेदसर्वानुक्रमणीपरिभाषा / द्वादशखण्डी)

The same as the paribhāṣā portion of the *Ṛgveda-sarvānukramaṇī*. See also under Ṛgveda-paribhāṣa and Ṛgveda-sarvānukramaṇī.
GJKSV 15628. 5 fol. Dated V.S. 1912.

353 ṚGVEDA-SARVĀNUKRAMAṆĪ-VIVARAṆA (ऋग्वेदसर्वानुक्रमणीविवरण)
Also called Anukramaṇī-vivaraṇa or Sūkta-pratīka of Jagannātha. Although most catalogues enter and describe this as a commentary on the *Ṛgveda-sarvānukramaṇī* of Kātyāyana, probably misled by the word *vivaraṇa* in the title, Haraprasada Sastri notes in his earlier Notices (L) as well as in his later RASB catalogues that this is really a different text and an Anukramaṇī for the Bāṣkala-śākhā. A few of its Mss. are entered under different titles. Cf. also next entry Ṛgveda-sarvānukrama-prayoga.

Beginning: (München)

नमामि (प्रणम्य) विष्णुं शिरसाव्ययं समं शिवं च सोमं वृषभेन्द्रगामिनम्।
गणाधिपं भक्तमनोरथप्रदं हरिं च वाक्सिद्धिकरीं च भारतीम्॥
अनुक्रमणिकोक्तानि सूक्तादिप्रभृतीन्यहम्।
छन्दो ऽन्तानि निबध्नामि जगन्नाथो यथामति॥

अहं जगन्नाथः व्यापनशीलं विष्णुं नमस्करोमि। शिरसेत्यष्टाङ्गोपलक्षणम्। विना गरुडेन अयत इति व्ययः । तम्। अथवा त्रिविधपदच्छेदशून्यम्। मायालक्ष्मायुक्तम्। अथवा सर्वत्र मित्रभावरहितं शंभुम् । उमया सहितम् । सूक्तादीति । सूक्तप्रतीक-ऋक्संख्यर्षिदैवतछन्दांसि।

प्रतिसूक्तमृचां संख्या शब्दैरङ्कैश्च लिख्यते।
अध्यायानां च (या) ऋक्संख्या सान्ते स्वाङ्कैर्विलिख्यते।
प्रायो ऽत्र ऋषयः सर्वे लिख्यन्ते गोत्रसंयुताः ॥
प्रगाथानां च सर्वेषां तत्तच्छन्दोभिधा पुनः ।
आप्रीसूक्तेषु सर्वेषु समिद्धाग्न्यादिदेवताः ॥ इति परिभाषा॥
निदर्शनानि लिख्यन्ते परिभाषोदितान्यपि।
पदपङ्क्त्यादिभेदानां प्रगाथानां च सर्वशः ॥

चकारान्निचृदादीनामित्यर्थः । अथाग्निमीळेप्रभृतिसूक्तानाम् ऋक्संख्या ऋषिदैवतछन्दांसि लिख्यन्ते । अग्निमीळे नवर्चं ९ मधुच्छन्दा वैश्वामित्र ऋषिः । अग्निर्देवता। गायत्री छन्दः ।

End:

ऋतं च ३ माधुछन्दसो ऽघमर्षण ऋषिः । भाववृत्तम्। आनुष्टुभम्। सं समित् चतुष्कम् ४ संवनन आङ्गिरसः । संज्ञानम्। आद्याग्नेयी। आनुष्टुभम्। तृतीया त्रिष्टुप्॥

Alph. List Beng. Govt. pp. 4. 19.
America 374. 47 fol.
Ānandāśrama 405. 38 fol. Begins: agnim īḷeprabhṛti ... Col.: jagannāthakṛte anukramaṇikāvivaraṇe ...
Ānandāśrama 1886. 31 fol. Dated Śaka 1716.
Baroda 8311. 30 fol. 800 Grantha-s. Dated Śaka 1683. = CLB I, p. 25 (Called Sūktapratīka on the last leaf).

Baroda 11113. 36 fol. 800 Grantha-s. Dated Śaka 1851. = CLB I, p. 25.
Ben. 3.
Bhk. 8.
BISM p. 314 (37/623ka). Dated Śaka 1653.
BISM p. 323 (36/704). 38 fol. Title: Sūkta-pratīka-ṛksaṃkhyā. Dated Śaka 1721.
Bombay Uni. 719 (BMC 6 27). 62 fol. (described as C. of Jagannātha on Ṛgveda-sarvānukrama).
Bombay Uni. 720 (BMC 51 2). 37 fol. Dated Śaka 1724. Described as C. of Jagannātha on the Ṛgveda-sarvānukrama. Copied by Janārdana Dhopeśvarakara. Sūkta-pratīka on title page. Col.: iti jagannāthaviracite anukramaṇikāvivaraṇe ...
BORI 39 of A 1881-82. = BORI D I i.36. 38 fol. Dated V.S. 1723.
BORI 384 of 1883-84. = BORI D I i.37. 55 fol. Dated Monday, full moon day of Jyeṣṭha month of the year Yuva. Copied by Jagannātha Rāmapura.
BP p. 287.
Calcutta Skt. Coll. I 24. 34 fol. Dated V.S. 1864.
Calcutta Skt. Coll. I 25. 56 fol. Dated V.S. 1828.
CU Add. 1909.
Deccan College 10856. 22 fol. Dated Śaka 1688. Though entitled Sarvānukramaṇikā-vivaraṇa both on the title page and back cover it is the C. of Ṣaḍguru-śiṣya on the paribhāṣā section. Col. on fol. 20b: Sarvānukramaṇikā samāptam. Also contains the Chandaḥ-saṃkhyā.
GJKSV 12945. Dated Śaka 1719. Title: Ṛganukramaṇikā-vivaraṇa. Copied by Sadāśiva, son of Nārāyaṇa.
GJKSV 16303. 25 fol. Dated Śaka 1835. Title: Anukramaṇikā-vivaraṇa.
GJKSV 29833. 62 fol. Title: Anukramaṇikā-vivaraṇa.
GJKSV 38719. 39 fol. Title: Sūktānukramaṇiakā.
Haug p. 32 (no.86) = München 24.
Hoshiarpur p. 56 (no.5573). 50 fol. 1000 Grantha-s. Extract p. 81. Incomplete. Dated V.S. 1875.
IM 2384. 26 fol. Dated Śaka 1623.
IO 58 (1636e). 26 fol. Dated V.S. 184(?) (1843), Caitra Kṛṣṇa 11, Monday (if this is V.S. it corresponds to A.D. 1786). Copied by Prahlāda, son of Upāsanī Āpā-bhaṭṭa.
Khn. p. 10 (no.37). 72 fol. ; from Ashṭe; Limaye.
L 1512. 47 fol. 1057 Grantha-s.
L 4241. 89 fol. 962 Grantha-s.
München 24. 50 fol. (Written ca. A.D. 1794).
Mysore I, p. 25.
Mysore ND II 3286 (C 37). 48 fol. Dated Śaka 1678. Extract no. (42 ?) 73.
N-W P X 6 (no.40). 60 fol. 1800 Grantha-s. Belonged to Balabhau Sapre, Benares.
Oxf. CS d.76(4). 43 fol. Dated A.D. 1766. Title: Anukramaṇikā-vivaraṇa.
Oxf. CS d.77(2). 12 fol. Incomplete (1-2 Aṣṭaka-s). Title: Anukramaṇikā-vivaraṇa.
Oxf. CS e.41(6). 53 fol. Dated A.D. 1786. Title: Anukramaṇikā Sūktapratīkaprayoga.
Oxf. CS f.9. 19 fol. Title: Sarvānukramaṇikā-vivaraṇa.
PUL II. App. p. 10 (no.131). 52 fol. 1000 Grantha-s.Dated V.S. 1853.
PUL II. App. p. 10 (no.132). 48 fol. 1000 Grantha-s.Dated V.S. 1812.
RASB II 234 (G 346) (Bāṣkala). 29 fol. = L 1512.

RASB II 235 (G 2298) (Bāṣkala). Title: Sūkta-pratīka = L 4241.

RASB II 236 (G 2059) (Bāṣkala). 40 fol. 1000 Grantha-s. Dated V.S. 1864. Title: Sūkta-pratīka.

RASB II 237 (G 1916) (Bāṣkala). 56 fol. 1500 Grantha-s. Dated V.S. 1863. Title: Sarvānukrama-prayoga (no introductory verses).

SBD 2279. 23 fol. (6-14, 16, 20-23, 29-32, 35-39). Incomplete. Dated V.S. 1826.

SBD 2296. 50 fol. Dated V.S. 1826.

SBD 2297. 38 fol. Dated V.S. 1763.

SBD 2314. 23 fol.

SBD 2353. 29 fol. Dated V.S. 1713.

SBD 2358. 46 fol.

SBD 2359. 40 fol.

SBD 2363. 23 fol. Śākala-saṃhitānukramaṇikā-saṃkhyā. A list of the Anuvāka-s at the end.

Trav. Uni. 9700. 1000 Grantha-s. Dated V.S. 1761.

Trav. Uni. 4915. 1100 Grantha-s. Dated V.S. 1796 / Śaka 1661. Called Sūkta-pratīkānukramaṇikā-sāra.

Trav. Uni. 4920. 1100 Grantha-s. Dated V.S. 1818.

Vangiya p. 23.

Visvanatha Vamana Deva, Varanasi. 26 fol. Title: Sūkta-pratīka. Col.: Anukramaṇikā-vivaraṇa.

VSM I 434 (no.5931). 45 fol. Dated Śaka 1727. Copied by Phaḍake Nṛsiṃha. Title: Ṛgveda-cchandarṣyādi.

VSM I 435 (no.5454). 47 fol. Title: Ṛgveda-cchandarṣyādi.

VSM I 478 (no.2022). 87 fol.

VSM I 479 (no.2023). 55 fol. Dated Śaka 1739.

VSM III 174 (no.12178). 38 fol. Dated Śaka 1666. Title: Sūkta-pratīka. Col.: jagannāthakṛte anukramaṇikāvivaraṇe aṣṭāv aṣṭakāḥ samāptāḥ |

VSM III 175 (no.12180). 28 fol. Inc. Title : Sūkta-pratīka or Saṃhitānukramaṇī.

Wai I 327. 63 fol. Dated Śaka 1743.

Wai I 328. 31 fol. Dated Śaka 1741. Title: Sūkta-pratīka-saṃkhyā-vivaraṇa.

[NCC III 25b]

354 ṚGVEDA-SARVĀNUKRAMA-PRAYOGA (?) (ऋग्वेदसर्वानुक्रमप्रयोग ?)

An Anukramaṇī, but of unclear identity and incorrectly titled.

L 4259. 56 fol. 1701 Grantha-s. Dated V.S. 1863.

RASB II 237 (G 1916). 56 fol. 1500 Grantha-s. Dated V.S. 1863. (Haraprasada Sastri says that this is Jagannātha's work mentioned above, that it is for the Bāṣkala-śākhā and that between Mss. 234 and 237 there are only verbal differences.)

[NCC III 26a]

355 ṚGVEDA-SAVĪLA-MĀLĀ (-MANTRA) (ऋग्वेदसवीलमाला-मन्त्र)

A list of Pratīka-s of the verses of the *Ṛgveda* that have a refrain (e.g. prati tyam, na hi devāḥ ... (RV I 19 1). They are called "kova" or "kovai" or "citta". This is useful in memorising the Veda and widely used in the Veda-pāṭha-śālā-s.

Ānandāśrama 1865. 10 fol. Dated Śaka 1719. Title: Saṃhitā-savelī-mālā.

Ānandāśrama 1906. 9 fol. Title: Savela-saṃjñā.

BORI 200 of A 1882-83. = BORI D I i.40. 10 fol. 200 Grantha-s.

SBD 0285. 1 fol. (Pratīka-s of Aṣṭaka 1 and 2). Title: Ṛgvedasaṃhitāprathamāṣṭaka-kovāni.

Tirupati SVUORI 991 (427). PL. Na. 6 fol. (101-06). Title: Kove.

VSM I 445 (no.603). 7 fol. Extract p. 348. Title: Savīḻa-mantara.

VSM I 446 (no.5449). 4 fol. Dated Śaka 1735. Copied by Deva Gopīnātha. Also includes a list of verses containing the word "rathya".

Wai I 341. 12 fol. Dated Śaka 1722. Title: Savile -- Saṃhitā-savelī. Saṃhitāsavilamālā in later hand.

Ptd.: under the title : *Ṛgveda-śṛṅkhalā,* ed. by Mudgala Ra. Ramachariar (Rāmācārya). – Kumbakonam : Sri Ramakrishna Vilas Book Depot, 1931. 17 pp. – [Rajah Vedapathasala Library, Kumbakonam]

356 ṚGVEDA-SŪKTA-CCHANDONUKRAMAṆĪ (ऋग्वेदसूक्तच्छन्दोनुक्रमणी)

Alph. List Beng. Govt. p. 19.

[NCC III 26a]

357 ṚGVEDA-SŪKTA-PRATĪKA (ऋग्वेदसूक्तप्रतीक)

An Anukramaṇī; different from the *Sarvānukramaṇikā.* Begins as in Weber 54 (Chambers 211b). 147 fol. Dated V.S. 1709.

Beginning:

अग्निमीळे इति नवर्चस्य सूक्तस्य वैश्वामित्रो मधुच्छन्दा ऋषिः अग्निर्देवता गायत्री छन्दः ।

End:

तृतीया त्रिष्टुप् शिष्टानां तिसृणामनुष्टुप् ।

GJKSV 13612. 67 fol. Dated V.S. 1908. Title: Ṛksaṃhitā-sūkta-pratīka. It contains a different beginning.

Hpr. II 250. 56 fol. 1640 Grantha-s.

[NCC III 26a]

358 ṚGVEDA-SŪKTA-PRATĪKĀNUKRAMAṆIKĀ-SĀRA (ऋग्वेदसूक्तप्रतीकानुक्रमणिकासार)

of Jagannātha. → Ṛgveda-sarvānukramaṇī-vivaraṇa

BISM p. 323 (36/704). 38 fol. Title: Sūkta-pratīka-ṛksaṃkhyā. Dated Śaka 1721.

Trav. Uni. 4915. Cf. above Ṛgveda-sarvānukramaṇī-Vivaraṇa.

[NCC III 26a]

359 ṚGVEDA-SŪKTA-VARGA-SAṂKHYĀ or SŪKTA-ŚLOKĀḤ (ऋग्वेदसूक्तवर्गसंख्या / सूक्तश्लोकाः)

of Melpattur Nārāyaṇa-bhaṭṭa, the author of *Prakriyā-sarvasva.* It consists of 9 stanzas. The first stanza is introductory and the remaining 8 stanzas give the number of Varga-s in the various Sūkta-s of the 8 Aṣṭaka-s of the *Ṛgveda,* following the "kacaṭapādi" system of notation. The total number of Sūkta-s is given as 1017 and of Varga-s 2006. It is also known as the *Sūkta-ślokāḥ.*

Beginning:

नत्वा विघ्नेश्वरादीन् कथमपि च मया कथ्यते व्यञ्जनोक्त्या
सूक्तानां वर्गसंख्या स्फुटमिह तु तकारोक्तिरध्यायपूर्तौ।
युक्ताद्यं तुल्यसूक्तान्युपदिशतु भवेद् द्वादशोक्तौ क्षकारः
प्रेति स्याद्विद्विकोक्तौ भवतु च दशसंख्याभिधायी नकारः॥

End:

रेखाप्रायारिपूरे पुरटपरिररामातरं लोललीला
श्रासप्रेयो ऽग्ररूपे कटपटकलिताभे शिवे गण्डिताघैः।
गूढोग्राग्रैरखाता रुररिपरिरखश्रीप्रतिष्ठे कुटीरे
पाल्येयाळ्यासकेळ्या पटुकटकपुटिळ्यार्यकाळ्या कृपाळ्या॥ ९॥

TCD 30-D. Mal. 3 pp. 32 Grantha-s.
Trav. Uni. 1092 B. PL. Mal. 25 Grantha-s.
Trav. Uni. 1178 C. PL. Mal. 25 Grantha-s.
Trav. Uni. 4254 P. PL. Mal. 25 Grantha-s. Belonged to Vishnu Nambudiri of Ettikada Illam Ayankudi, Kaduttirutti, Kottayam.
Trav. Uni. 14094 C. PL. Mal. 25 Grantha-s.
Trav. Uni. L.170 C. PL. Mal. 25 Grantha-s.
Trav. Uni. L.1429 G. PL. Mal. 2 fol. 25 Grantha-s.
Trav. Uni. TM.276 D. = TCD 30-D.
Trav. Uni. 12571 C. PL. Mal. 100 Grantha-s (with C. ?).

Ptd.: ed. by C. Kunhan Raja, with an analysis and a table of illustration, in : *Journal of Oriental Research,* Madras, VIII, pp. 358-71.

[NCC III 26a]

360 ṚGVEDA-SŪKTA-VARṆA-SAṂKHYĀ-KRAMA (ऋग्वेदसूक्तवर्णसंख्याक्रम)
Trav. Uni. 22198 D. PL. Mal. 20 Grantha-s. Incomplete.

361 ṚGVEDA-SŪKTĀDI-SAṂKHYĀ see ṚGANUVĀKA-SAṂKHYĀ (ऋग्वेदसूक्तादिसंख्या / ऋगनुवाकसंख्या)
Trav. Uni. 5001 B. 40 Grantha-s. Dated V.S. 1816 / Śaka 1681.

[NCC III 26b]

362 ṚGVEDASYA ṚKSAṂKHYĀ (ऋग्वेदस्य ऋक्संख्या)
of Yudhisthira Mimamsaka, on the number of Ṛk-s in the *Ṛgveda.*
Ptd.: in the Sanskrit journal *Sārasvatī Suṣamā,* vol. 9.1-2 (Saṃ. 2011), pp. 145-55, vol. 10 (Saṃ. 2012), pp. 29-38. Varanasi, 1955-56.
Also as the appendix VII in the Kātyāyanīya-ṛksarvānukramaṇī, ed. by Vijayapal, pp. 342-61. [SAI (ind 51 D 888/1161);
A Hindi version of this tract is published under the title : *Ṛgveda kī Ṛksaṃkhyā.* – Ajmer : Ārya Sāhitya Maṇḍala, saṃ. 2006 (A.D. 1950). 26 pp. – (Prācyavidyā Pratiṣṭhāna Granthamālā 4). [SAI (ind 50 A 88/1167); BORI (16816)]

363 ṚGVEDA-SVARA-NIRṆAYA (ऋग्वेदस्वरनिर्णय)

A short commentary on the Svara section of the *Ṛgveda-prātiśākhya*, by one who calls himself a disciple of Rāma. He quotes among others, Uvaṭa, *Tribhāṣya-ratna*, Dīkṣita. On the title page it reads:

शौनकीये प्रातिशाख्ये ज्ञेयो ऽयं स्वरनिर्णयः ।
श्रीमत्सु रामपादेषु प्रेषितो भक्तितो मया ॥

In the middle of the text:

नत्वा रामपदाम्भोजं मातापितृपदाम्बुजम् ।
अथो शिवपदाम्भोजं तन्यते स्वरिताम्बुजम् ॥

GJKSV 26857. 7 fol. Incomplete. Title: Śaunakīya-prātiśākhya (Svara-nirṇaya).

364 ṚGVEDĀNUKRAMAṆIKĀ (1) (ऋग्वेदानुक्रमणिका)

IO 4255 (Burnell 205j). PL. Gr. 3 fol. (165-67). Includes portions of the *Pada-gāḍha*.
SBD 2319. 36 fol. Dated V.S. 1740. Includes Ṛgveda-sarvānukramaṇī, Chandaḥ-saṃkhyā and Anuvāka-pañcāśī.
SBD 2356. 20 fol. (7-8, 10-12, 19-33). Dated V.S. 1659. = Ṛgveda-sarvānukramaṇī.
SBD 2362. 11 fol. (1-8, 1, 12, 37). Incomplete.
SBD 2366. 14 fol. = Ārṣānukramaṇī.

365 ṚGVEDĀNUKRAMAṆIKĀ (2) (ऋग्वेदानुक्रमणिका)

→ Cāturjñāna.
MD 14083. PL. Tel. 136 pp.
MD 14776. PL. Na. 34 pp.

366 ṚGVEDĀNUKRAMAṆIKĀ (3) (ऋग्वेदानुक्रमणिका)

→ Ṛgveda-sarvānukramaṇī.
Tirupati SVUORI 991 (2546a). PL. Tel. 17 fol.
BHU B 1123 (D 1A/41). 26 fol. Incomplete.

367 ṚGVEDĀNUKRAMAṆIKĀ (4) (ऋग्वेदानुक्रमणिका)

Beginning:

प्रतिसूक्तमृषिदैवतच्छन्दांस्यनुक्रमिष्यामः । अग्निमीळे ऋचः ९ मधुच्छन्दा ऋषिः अग्निर्देवता गायत्री छन्दः । १ । वायवायाहि ऋ॰ ९ मधुच्छन्दा ऋषिः आद्या ३ वायुर्देवता ...

End:

त्रिषष्टितमो ऽध्यायः । मयो भूर्वातः ४ शवर ऋषिः ... इति

BISM p. 314 (36/1319). 73 fol. Title: Sarvānukramodāharaṇa.

Calcutta Skt. Coll. I 525 (124). 73 fol. This is actually *Pada-gāḍha*. The last two fol. contain a list of the number of Pada-s in each chapter of the *Ṛgveda*. It ends with the verse 45 from the *Anuvākānukramaṇikā* (vede trisahasrayuktaṃ śatāni cāṣṭāv atha ṣaḍviṃśatiś ca).

GJKSV 13720. 46 fol. Dated V.S. 1817. Title: Anukramaṇikā-bhāṣya.

RASB II 233 (G 580). 40 fol. 1600 Grantha-s.

Weber 54 (Chambers 211b). 147 fol. Dated V.S. 1709. Copied by Harirāma, son of Dīkṣita Rāmakṛṣṇa. Begins as Ṛgveda-sūkta-pratīka : Hpr. II 250. 56 fol. 1640 Grantha-s.

Cf. Weber 55 (Chambers 212). 47 fol. Dated V.S. 1646. Ṛṣichandodaivata on the cover page. Pratīka, Ṛṣi, Chandas, etc. for each Sūkta = BORI 41. Begins: -- pratisūktam as above.

368 ṚGVEDĀNUKRAMAṆIKĀ (5) (ऋग्वेदानुक्रमणिका)

of Śaunaka.

Bik. 328. 35 fol. → Ṛgveda-sarvānukramaṇī (up to the sixth Aṣṭaka).

[NCC III 26b]

369 ṚGVEDĀNUKRAMAṆĪ (1) (ऋग्वेदानुक्रमणी)

Trav. Uni. 15722 H. PL. Mal. 1000 Grantha-s. Incomplete.

Trav. Uni. 15733. PL. Mal. 450 Grantha-s. Incomplete.

Trav. Uni. 15764 C. PL. Mal. 750 Grantha-s. Incomplete.

Trav. Uni. 15942. PL. Mal. 2300 Grantha-s.

Trav. Uni. 15976. PL. Mal. 550 Grantha-s.

Trav. Uni. 17761 B. PL. Mal. 450 Grantha-s.

Trav. Uni. 18147. PL. Mal. 400 Grantha-s.

– C. Bhāṣya.

Trav. Uni. 21544 A. PL. Mal. 2400 Grantha-s (actually a ritual text).

370 ṚGVEDĀNUKRAMAṆĪ (2) (ऋग्वेदानुक्रमणी)

of Mādhava, author of the commentary on the *Ṛgveda*, called *Ṛgveda-sūkta-nirukta* and the *Ākhyātānukramaṇī* and ten other Anukramaṇī-s.

[NCC III 26b]

371 ṚGVEDĀNUKRAMAṆĪ (3) (ऋग्वेदानुक्रमणी)

of Mādhava-bhaṭṭa, son of Veṅkaṭārya, of Cola country; perhaps of 10th century A.D. The title is conjectural. The Kārikā-s comprising these indices are actually found distributed in the commentary of the author on the *Ṛgveda*, called *Ṛgartha-dīpikā*, perhaps also current independently. For Mss. see his *Ṛgartha-dīpikā* under Cs. on the *Ṛgveda*, in NCC III 20a.

Ptd.:

Ed. by C. Kunhan Raja, based on 6 Mss, vol. I. – Madras : University of Madras, 1932. xxviii, 93, clxiv pp. – (Madras University Sanskrit Series 2). [Adyar (H080 MUS sk2); BORI (6440); UBTÜ (Ci XII 666,2); Emeneau (391)]

Ed. by Vijayapal (Vidyāvāridhi), with a Hindi translation and commentary (Veṅkaṭmādhavīya-ṛgveda-bhāṣyāntargatā *Ṛgvedānukramaṇī* – Hindīvyākhyāsahitā). – Bahalgadh (Sonipath-Haryana) : Ramalal Kapur Trust, 1979. 15, 332 pp. [BORI (35129; 35468); SAI (ind 51 D 88/2331); UBTÜ (22 A 14791)]

[NCC III 26b]

372 ṚGVEDĀNUKRAMAṆĪ (4) (ऋग्वेदानुक्रमणी)

Enumeration of the number of syllables in each Adhyāya and Anuvāka of the *Ṛgveda*. Title in the fourth part : *Ṛganukrama*. The numbers given at the end of the Ms:
Aṣṭaka-s 8 = Adhyāya-s 64 = Varga-s 2006 = Ṛk-s 10472 = Akṣara-s 381211.
Maṇḍala-s 10 = Anuvāka-s 85 = Sūkta-s 1017 = Ṛk-s = 10472 Akṣara-s 381211.
Bombay Uni. (BMC 162 9). 5 parts. 15, 28, 33, 44, 15 fol.

373 ṚGVEDĀNUKRAMA-DĪPIKĀ (ऋग्वेदानुक्रमदीपिका)

of Gaṇeśa. The same as his C. on the Ṛgveda-sarvānukramaṇī.
SBD 47938. 214 fol. (6, 3-210). Incomplete.
SBD 47939. 94 fol. (1-8, 10-30, 1-62, 1, 7, 8). Incomplete.

374 ṚGVEDĀNUVĀKA-PRATĪKA-SŪKTA-SAṂKHYĀ-PARIMĀṆA-KRAMA (ऋग्वेदानुवाकप्रतीकसूक्तसंख्यापरिमाणक्रम)

→ Ṛganuvāka-pratīka-sūkta-saṃkhyā-pariṇāma-krama.

375 ṚGVEDĀNUVĀKA-SŪKTA-SAṂKHYĀ (ऋग्वेदानुवाकसूक्तसंख्या)

→ Anuvākānukrama.
Baroda 21515. 2 fol. 15 Grantha-s. Dated V.S. 1945.

376 ṚGVEDĀNUVĀKĀNUKRAMAṆĪ (1) (ऋग्वेदानुवाकानुक्रमणी)

PUL II. App. p. 10 (no.150) PL. Gr. 83 fol. 1500 Grantha-s.
PUL II. App. p. 10 (no.151) PL. Gr. 57 fol. 900 Grantha-s (up to 7.5).

[NCC III 26a]

377 ṚGVEDĀNUVĀKĀNUKRAMAṆĪ (2) (ऋग्वेदानुवाकानुक्रमणी)

of Śaunaka → Anuvākānukramaṇī of Śaunaka.

[NCC III 27a]

378 ṚGVEDĀMNĀYA (ऋग्वेदाम्नाय)

BHU B 954 (D 1A/42). 55 fol. Incomplete. The same as Ṣaḍguru-śiṣya's C. on the *Ṛgveda-sarvānukramaṇī* (Dvādaśa-khaṇḍī Paribhāṣā).

379 ṚGVEDĀRṢĀNUKRAMAṆĪ (ऋग्वेदार्षानुक्रमणी)

of Śaunaka.
Triv. Cur. V 5. Mal. 300 Grantha-s. Obtained from Thiruparpu Svamiyar Matham. See Ārṣānukramaṇī of Śaunaka.

[NCC III 27a]

380 ṚGVEDĀṢṬA-VIKṚTI-VIVARAṆA (ऋग्वेदाष्टविकृतिविवरण)

of Madhusūdana Munīśvara → Aṣṭa-vikṛti-vivṛti of Madhusūdana-maskarin. See also under Jaṭā-paṭala.

[NCC III 27a]

381 ṚGVEDĪYA-KĀRIKĀ (?) (ऋग्वेदीयकारिका ?)

48 Kārikā-s.
PUL I, p. 20 (no.44). 3 fol. Incomplete.

[NCC III 27b]

382 ṚGVEDĪYA-GRANTHA (ऋग्वेदीयग्रन्थ)

A work in the style of the Prātiśākhya, but different from the well-known *Ṛgveda-prātiśākhya*. The second part contains many passages of the *Bonta-lakṣaṇa (Pada-gāḍha)*.

Beginning:

अग्निमीळे तुविजातौ दधाना इन्द्रे योगे चक्षसे महाधने ये बृहते हूमहे यज्ञे सुजिह्वौ भ्रियन्त एकादश। य एकः कक्षीवन्तं य औशिज इति वर्जयित्वा। अग्निमवीवृधन् द्रुहन्नादित्यान् विश्वान् पर्वतान् च। अग्निं पा (?) चकानः सनेदिमं द्वैपदम्। जेष ऊतिं सहस्रसातमो द्वितीयम्। नेष्टरिति दीद्यग्नी इति दीद्यग्नी। यस्माद्दते न द्वैपदम्।

End:

त्यञ्चित् पारे कृत्वने जीवस उत्तर एके परो निर्ऋत्यै दृशे सप्त। त्यञ्चिचाकन् प्रियव्रतान् पितॄनृषीनायन्नीरमन् रेवन्निच्छन् धर्मन्नश्वन् गृणीवान् सहीयान् छत्रून् विन्दन् चतुर्दश। चित्यंचिद्यथाकाममवगृह्य उत्थितं द्वैपदं दुहाना अर्धर्चान्तं स्वरान्ता। गविष्ठिरं नावगृह्य ऋषिं यथासंहितं जोषपतन्त्या विसर्गान्तं दस्युहम्। पुष्करसृजावगृह्या। ८।

IM 2197. 11 fol. Catalogued as Galita-pradīpa which is in fol. 10-11. First fol. contains a portion of *Pada-gāḍha*.

München 19. 16 fol. (Written ca. A.D. 1750).

[NCC III 27b]

383 ṚGVEDĪYA-CHANDAḤ-PRABHṚTI-SAṂKHYĀ-SAṂGRAHA (ऋग्वेदीयछन्दःप्रभृतिसंख्यासंग्रह)

of Ganesh Athalye. 12 introductory verses and several tables on the distribution of metres in the *Ṛgveda*.

Beginning:

नत्वा लक्ष्मीं पतिनाथं गणेशं सूर्यमीश्वरीम्।
महादेवं महाविष्णुं गणेशो ऽहं समासतः ॥ १॥
वक्ष्ये शाकल्यके वेदे गायत्र्यादिकछन्दसाम्।
संख्यानं बुद्धिमद्दृष्टं मन्दधीबोधसिद्धये॥ २॥

End:

द्वात्रिंशताक्षरैर्युक्तो ग्रन्थ इत्यभिधीयते।
आठल्ये उपनाम्नेदं गणेशेन कृतं स्वयम्॥ १२॥
एतदङ्करूपेणोपरिष्टाल्लिख्यते॥

Ptd.: – Poona : Jagaddhitecchu Press, Sridhar Gondhalekar, Śaka 1804 (1878), Vaiśākha-śuddha 1. 24 pp. [BORI (10653; 30192)] (A xerox-copy of this in SAI).

384 ṚGVEDĪYA-JAṬĀ-LAKṢAṆA (ऋग्वेदीयजटालक्षण)

Ascribed to Madhusūdana. Described as forming part of the *Madhusūdana-śikṣā*. Origionally published by Satyavrata Samasrami with a commentary → Aṣṭa-vikṛti-vivṛti(-kārikā) of Madhusūdana. The commentary is ascribed to "Satyavrata" in the Srirangam edition but is identical with the "Prakāśa" included in the in *Veda-vikṛti-lakṣaṇa-saṃgraha* (Poona : BORI, 1978, pp. 75-112).

Ptd.: ed. by Satyavrata Samasrami in the Sanskrit journal *Uṣā*. – Calcutta : Satya Press (Śaka 1811), 1899. [NL (180 Jc 92 50)]

Reprinted : ed. by K. S. Venkatarama Sastri (Madhusūdanīya-śikṣāntargatam – śrī-satyavratakṛtavyākhyāsahitam). – Srirangam : Sri Vani Vilas Press, 1964. iv, vi, 36 pp. [Adyar (PH 215.1 Ms. sxy Sat); NL (180 Jc 96 427); SAI (87/772*)] also see the *Ṛgveda-ghanasāra* (with *Gāni-lakṣaṇa* and *Svara-lakṣaṇa)*, ed. by the same. – Srirangam : Sri Vani Vilas Press, 1966.

See also under Jaṭālakṣaṇa.

[NCC III 27b]

385 ṚGVEDĪYA-PADĀNTYĀKṢARĀNUKRAMAṆĪ (ऋग्वेदीयपदान्त्याक्षरानुक्रमणी)

Trav. Uni. 22014. PL. Mal. 1500 Grantha-s. Incomplete.

386 ṚGVEDĪYA-PARIBHĀṢĀ (ऋग्वेदीयपरिभाषा)

→ Ṛgveda-sarvānukramaṇī-paribhāṣā.

SBD 2369. 4 fol.

387 ṚGVEDĪYA-BONDA-LAKṢAṆA (ऋग्वेदीयबोन्दलक्षण)

Ascribed to Śaunaka. The text is identical with the *Pada-gāḍha* published by Satyavrata Samasrami in the Sanskrit journal *Uṣā*. – Calcutta : Satya Press, 1895, vol. II, pts. 11-12. 77 pp. See below under Pada-gāḍha.

Ptd.: ed. by K. S. Venkatarama Sastri, together with *Pada-ratna, Svarāṅkuśa* and *Ṛgvarṇa-krama-lakṣaṇa*. – Srirangam : Sri Vani Vilas Press, 1968. [Adyar (PH 216.2 Ven RB); BORI (21936); SAI (85/1958*); UBTÜ (3 E 1286)]

388 ṚGVEDĪYA-LAKṢAṆA-SAṂGRAHA (ऋग्वेदीयलक्षणसंग्रह)

Containing Pada-saṃkhyā, Svarāṅkuśa, Chandaḥ-saṃkhyā, Sūkta-saṃkhyā, and Sarvatra-lakṣaṇa.

Hoshiarpur p. 50 (no.1313) 19 fol. 300 Grantha-s. Incomplete. Dated Śaka 1718. Extract pp. 79-80. Title: Sarvatra-lakṣaṇam.

Hoshiarpur p. 50 (no.3780/3740?). PL. Mal. 145 fol. 1500 Grantha-s. Incomplete. Extract pp. 407-08.

389 ṚGVEDĪYA-ŚAMĀNA-LAKṢAṆAM UPALEKHA-SŪTRAṂ CA (ऋग्वेदीयशमानलक्षणमुपलेखसूत्रं च)

See under Ṛksarva-samāna above.

Ptd.: ed. by K. S. Venkatarama Sastri. – Srirangam : Sri Vani Vilas Press, 1967. 11, 2, 72 pp. [Adyar (H 215.4 Ven SA); SAI (87/770*)]

390 ṚGVEDE DVIPADĀDI-SAṂKHYĀ see ṚGVEDA-DVIPADĀDI-SAṂKHYĀ
(ऋग्वेदे द्विपदादिसंख्या / ऋग्वेदद्विपदादिसंख्या)

[NCC III 28a]

391 ṚṄNIGHĀTA-KĀRIKĀ **(ऋङ्निघातकारिका)**
A List of the Nighāta syllables in the Pūrva and Uttara Ṛk-s of the *Sāmaveda* → Pūrvottara-ṛṅnighāta-kārikā.

Beginning: (766)

निघातभाजो ये वर्णाः पादकाल-ऋचा स्मृताः ।
व्यादयस्ते प्रकाश्यन्ते विदुरेवं हि सूरिभिः ॥
निघातानां प्राकृतर्च्यशीतिश्चाष्टवृद्धयः ।
निघातानामुत्तरार्च्यधिकाः सप्तविंशतिः ॥
सहितं शतमित्येवं निघाताः स्युश्शतद्वयम् ।
अधिकाः पञ्चदश स्युः पूर्वोक्तानां च वक्ष्यते ॥
प्रकृन्तृचौ निघाता वै अन्यस्यामृचि नाभवन् ।
अनुदात्तं तु पादादौ नृवर्जं विद्यते पदम् ॥
अग्नेत्रयमूर्त्तिपरं धर्मनेत्रनलोचनम् ।
पापं मेषशिवं नास्ति न ब्रह्म शिवमाश्रमम् ॥

End:

आग्निः प्रत्ने रथसङ्गे राधो देयाय सुन्वते ।
मनोतरा जुषाणश्च उत्ताकापीपिवांसकम् ॥
समानेन मुनिस्संख्या प्रास्य धार पुना नय ।
बृहते ऋते कर्मा धरा चो वाजयन्त च ॥
परशुर्धन्वा सह हिरण्यदिग्गजसंख्यकाः ।
आशुर्घनाघन यकारेन रक्षो ह वै बुधाः ।
अदय आदित्यानां गृहति समावितम् ॥
संयोज्या वै च संख्यास्तुरकमेति तथा स्मृतम् ।
इति पूर्वोत्तर-ऋङ्निघातकारिका समासा ॥

Adyar D I 766 (33 D 12 = 75239). PL. Gr. 3 fol. (47-49). = Adyar I, p. 48b.
Adyar D I 901 (33 E 7 = 75254). PL. Gr. 2 fol. (52-53). Title: Pūrvottara-ṛṅnighāta-kārikā.

[NCC III 28a]

392 ṚṄMANTRA-PRATĪKĀNUKRAMAṆIKĀ (ऋङ्मन्त्रप्रतीकानुक्रमणिका)
Trav. Uni. 13303. PL. Mal. 550 Grantha-s. See also under Ṛgvedānukramaṇikā.

[NCC III 28a]

393 ṚṄMANTRĀṆĀṂ GHANA-PĀṬHAḤ (ऋङ्मन्त्राणां घनपाठः)
Ghana-pāṭha of the Suara-sūkta-s, Puruṣa-sūkta and Viṣṇusūkta-s of the *Ṛgveda.*

Ptd.: compiled and published by W. R. Antarkar. – Bombay 57 (15 Sraddhananda Marg, Power House Samor, Ville Parle [East]) : 1984. 10, 88 pp. [BORI (44541); NL (180 Jb 98 30)]

394 ṚCĀṂ GAṆITĀṄKA-PRAKĀRA (ऋचां गणिताङ्कप्रकार)
A fictious title. A tabular statement of the details of the hymns of the *Ṛgveda.*
Bik. 326. 57 fol. Dated Śaka 1541. Cf. Sapta-saṃkhyā(-nirūpaṇa).

[NCC III 28b]

395 ṚJVARTHĀ (ऋज्वर्था)
Name of the commentary of Uvaṭa (München 31), and Viṣṇumitra (RASB II 270; BORI I i.56) on the *Ṛgveda-prātiśākhya.*

[NCC III 29a]

396 ṚṢI-CCHANDA-ĀDI-NIRṆAYA (ऋषिच्छन्दआदिनिर्णय)
Radh. 1.

[NCC III 39b]

397 ṚṢI-CCHANDO-DEVATĀ (1) (ऋषिच्छन्दोदेवता)
For the RV. Pejawar 165b.

[NCC III 39b]

398 ṚṢI-CCHANDO-DEVATĀ (2) (ऋषिच्छन्दोदेवता)
of Śivarāma, son of Viśrāma. An index to the Ṛṣi-s, the metres and the Devatā-s of each Ṛk in the three chapters of the *Sāmaveda,* namely the Saṃhitā, Āraṇyaka and Uttarā. Cf. below Sarvānukramaṇikā (Alwar 252).

Beginning:

प्रणम्य तातं विश्रामं विघ्नेशं जगदम्बिकाम् ।
संहिताया ऋषिच्छन्दोदैवतानि यथामति ॥ १ ॥
प्रयोगस्य च सिद्ध्यर्थं प्रवक्ष्यामि यथामति ।
सामगानां हितार्थाय शिष्यबोधाय केवलम् ॥ २ ॥

अग्न आयाहीति भरद्वाजो गायत्र्यग्निः । त्वमग्ने इति भरद्वाजः शङ्कुमती पिपीलिकामध्या गायत्र्यग्निः । इति छन्दस्यास्संहिताया ऋष्यादयः समाप्ताः । ... इत्यारण्यकसंहितायां ऋष्यादयः समाप्ताः ।

End:

यत्र बाणा इत्यस्या इन्द्रश्च बृहस्पतिश्च दितिश्च देवताः । मर्माणीत्यस्याः सोमवरुणदेवाश्च देवताः । भद्रं स्वस्ति न इत्येतयोर्विश्वे देवाः ...
इति श्रीविश्रामात्मजशिवरामविरचिता आर्चिकत्रयस्य ऋषिच्छन्दोदेवताः समाप्ताः

Alwar 252.

Baroda 10808. 52 fol. 600 Grantha-s. = CLB I, p. 25. Extract pp. 138-39. Dated V.S. 1911.

[NCC III 39b]

399 ṚṢI-CCHANDO-DEVATĀDY-ANUKRAMAṆIKĀ (ऋषिच्छन्दोदेवताद्यनुक्रमणिका)

Tirupati SVUORI (2546c). PL. Tel. 19 fol. (27-45). In prose.

Tirupati SVUORI 1000 (4876a). PL. Gr.

400 ṚṢI-CCHANDO-DEVATĀ-NIRŪPAṆA (ऋषिच्छन्दोदेवतानिरूपण)

Venkatesiah 67.

[NCC III 39b]

401 ṚṢI-CCHANDO-DEVATĀ-PARIŚIṢṬA (ऋषिच्छन्दोदेवतापरिशिष्ट)

"A treatise showing Ṛiṣis, Chandas and Devaṭās of the Sūktas contained in the Ṛigveda".

N-W P VI 20 (no.69). Belonged to Durga Bai Bhada, Benares.

[NCC III 39b]

402 ṚṢI-CCHANDO-DEVATĀ-MAṆI-DĪPIKĀ (ऋषिच्छन्दोदेवतामणिदीपिका)

PUL II. App. p. 10 (no.152). PL. Gr. 26 fol. (3-28). 250 Grantha-s.

Trav. Uni. 2915 A. PL. Gr. 350 Grantha-s. Incomplete.

[NCC III 39b]

403 ṚṢI-CCHANDO-DAIVATA (ऋषिच्छन्दोदैवत)

TCD 17. PL. Mal. 120 fol. 950 Grantha-s. Title: Chandodaivatam.

TCD 38-D. PL. Mal. 33 fol. 950 Grantha-s.

Trav. Uni. 15934. PL. Mal. 950 Grantha-s.

Trav. Uni. 16500 N. PL. Mal. 250 Grantha-s. Incomplete.

Trav. Uni. 16994 F. PL. Mal. 50 Grantha-s.

Trav. Uni. 17800 D. PL. Mal. 950 Grantha-s.

Trav. Uni. 18540 Z1. PL. Mal. 125 Grantha-s.

Trav. Uni. 18715 L. PL. Mal. 30 Grantha-s.

Trav. Uni. 22162 A. PL. Mal. 950 Grantha-s.

Trav. Uni. 22204 A. PL. Mal. 75 Grantha-s. Incomplete.

Trav. Uni. 22288. PL. Mal. 950 Grantha-s.

Trav. Uni. C.1814 = TCD 17. (M.E. 1061 = 1886).

Trav. Uni. C.1887 D = TCD 38-D.

[NCC III 39b]

404 ṚṢI-CCHANDO-DAIVATĀNUKRAMAṆĪ (ऋषिच्छन्दोदैवतानुक्रमणी)

Trav. Uni. 17538 B. PL. Mal. 600 Grantha-s.

Trav. Uni. 10095. 450 Grantha-s. Incomplete.

405 ṚṢI-DEVATĀ-CCHANDĀṂSI (ऋषिदेवताच्छन्दांसि)

Ṛṣi, Devatā and Chandas of each hymn of the *Ṛgveda.* All three entries below refer to one and the same Ms. in BORI.

BA 16.

BORI 1 of 1874-75. = BORI D I i.41. 70 fol. Dated V.S. 1845 / Śaka 1710 (complete in 64 chapters). The beginning is the same as in RASB II 233: Ṛgvedānukramaṇī.

Gough p. 135 (no.1). 70 pp. Dated V.S. 1845.

[NCC III 40a]

406 ṚṢI-DEVATĀ-CCHANDONĀMA (ऋषिदेवताच्छन्दोनाम)
Govt. Or. Libr. Madras, p. 13.

[NCC III 40a]

407 ṚṢI-(DEVATĀ-)CCHANDONUKRAMAṆIKĀ(-VIVARAṆA)
(ऋषि(-देवता)-च्छन्दोनुक्रमणिका-विवरण)

Also called Sarvānukramaṇī of Śaunaka in some Mss. On the Ṛṣi-cchando-devatānuvāka-sūktānukramaṇi-s of Śaunaka see observations of Macdonell in the preface (pp. v-vi) to his edition of *Kātyāyana's Sarvānukramaṇī*. See also separate entries, Anuvākānukramaṇī, Ārṣānukramaṇī, Chandonukramaṇī, Devatānukramaṇī, etc.

GD I 7. PL. Mal. 114 fol. 1140 Grantha-s (Ārṣānukramaṇī, Chandonukramaṇī and Devatānukramaṇī). Title: Ṛksarvānukramaṇī.
Haug p. 32 (no.89) = München 25 → Ārṣānukramaṇī and Chandonukramaṇi.
Mysore I, p. 25 = Mysore ND II 3261 (P 2862/ 1). See above under Ṣaḍguru-śiṣya's C. on the *Ṛgveda-sarvānukramaṇī*.
Mysore I, p. 38.
Triv. Cur. V 3, 4, 5 (three separate entries for Chandas-, Devatā- and Ārṣa-).

[NCC III 40a]

408 ṚṢI-DEVATĀ-CCHANDONUKRAMAṆĪ (SĀMA-ŚĀKHĪYĀ)
(ऋषिदेवताच्छन्दोनुक्रमणी / सामशाखीया)

Mysore II, p. 2.

[NCC III 40b]

409 ṚṢI-DEVATĀ-CCHANDO-VIVARAṆA (ऋषिदेवताच्छन्दोविवरण)

In connection with the *Ṛgvidhāna* whose verses also occur in the text. See above under Ṛgvidhāna.

Beginning:

अग्निर्नव वैश्वामित्रो मधुच्छन्दा ऋषिः । अग्निर्देवता । गायत्री छन्दः । अस्य सूक्तस्य विधानं --

आग्नेयं सूक्तमाद्यं तु मुख्यं ब्रह्मर्षिसंमितम् ।
रायस्पोषकरं तस्माज्जपाद् विप्रो ऽर्थमाप्नुयात् ॥

End:

सं समित् चतुष्कमाङ्गिरसः । संवनन ऋषिः । संज्ञानं देवता । आद्या आग्नेय्यनुष्टुप् । तृतीया त्रिष्टुप् ॥ इति ऋषिदेवताछन्दोविवरणम् ॥

MD 14782. PL. Na. 106 pp. Cf. Mysore ND II 3261 (P 2862/ 1), catalogued as Ṣaḍguru-śiṣya's C. on the *Ṛgveda-sarvānukramaṇī*.

[NCC III 40b]

410 ṚṢI-DAIVATA-CCHANDONUKRAMA (ऋषिदैवतच्छन्दोनुक्रम)

RV. → Anukramaṇikā-ḍhuṇḍhū.
Baroda 336 (Sūkta-pratīka). 8248. 10587.
Cf. BORI D I i.39 (Sarvānukramaṇī-ḍhuṇḍhū) and RASB II 238.

[NCC III 40b]

411 ṚṢI-DAIVATA-CCHANDONUKRAMAṆIKĀ (ऋषिदैवतच्छन्दोनुक्रमणिका)

Adyar I, p. 48b = Adyar D I 1059. The same as Ṣaḍguru-śiṣya's C. on the *Ṛgveda-sarvānukramaṇī*.

[NCC III 40b]

412 ṚṢI-DAIVATA-CCHANDO-VICĀRA (ऋषिदैवतच्छन्दोविचार)

A descriptive title by a later hand in red. 22 verses on the necessity of knowing the ṛṣi, chandas, etc. of mantra-s.
BISM p. 47 (36/2295). 2 fol.

413 ṚṢI-DAIVATA-CCHANDO-VINIYOGA (ऋषिदैवतच्छन्दोविनियोग)

BISM p. 47 (22/450).

414 ṚṢI-SAṂHITĀ (ऋषिसंहिता)

An index of Ṛṣi-s, Devatā-s and Chandas of the *Ṛgveda*.
SBD 2376. 23 fol. (37-59). Dated V.S. 1674. The last two fol. contain a list of 374 Ṛṣi-s of the *Ṛgveda* which is entitled *Ṛṣi-saṃhitā*.

415 ṚṢYANUKRAMA (ऋष्यनुक्रम)

An index of Ṛṣi-s to the Śākala-saṃhitā of the *Ṛgveda* in prose. It differs from the metrical text of Śaunaka, but appears to be based on that. On the title page: Śaunakokta-bṛhaddevatāstha-ṛṣyanukrama.

Beginning:

> अथ ऋग्वेदशाकलसंहिताया ऋष्यनुक्रमो लिख्यते। अग्निमीळे पुरोहितं मधुछन्दा वैश्वामित्रः । १०२। द्युत्तर-शत-ऋक्पर्यन्तमित्यर्थः । एवं सर्वत्र। इन्द्र विश्वा अवीवृधन्। जेता माधुछन्दसः । १८ (?)। अग्निं दूतं वृणीमहे । मेधातिथिः काण्वः । १४३ । कस्य नूनं कतमस्यामृतानाम्। शुनःशेफ आजीगर्तिः कृत्रिमो देवरातः वैश्वामित्रः । ९७।

End:

> ऋतं च सत्यं चाभीद्धात्। अघमर्षणो माधुच्छन्दसः । ३। सं समिद्युवसे वृषन्। संवनन आङ्गिरसः । ४। दशमं मण्डलम्। ऋक्संख्या १०७५४॥

L 4214. 12 fol. 330 Grantha-s. Dated V.S. 1863.

RASB II 241 (G 1966) = L 4214. See also NCC II 180a, under Ārṣānukramaṇī.

[NCC III 47a]

416 ṚṢYANUKRAMAṆĪ ṚGVEDĪYĀ (ऋष्यनुक्रमणी ऋग्वेदीया)

RASB II 240 (G 2854). Beng. 29 fol. → Ārṣānukramaṇī of Śaunaka.

417 ṚṢYĀDY-ANUKRAMAṆIKĀ (ऋष्याद्यनुक्रमणिका)

SBD 55451. 12 fol. Ṛṣi-cchando-devatā of a few selected Ṛgvedic hymns, probably meant for some ritualistic purpose.

418 EKA-LAKṢAṆA (एकलक्षण)

Mysore ND II 3308 (P 4906/22). PL. Na. 1 fol. (118). Extract no. 89.

419 EKAPADĀDI-ṚKSAṂKHYĀ (एकपदादि-ऋक्संख्या)

VSM I 421 (no.2967). 2 fol. Dated Śaka 1795. Enumeration of the Sūkta-s, Ṛk-s and Varga-s of each Adhyāya in tabular form and a list of Ekapadā verses in the *Ṛgveda* (krama-veṣṭana : 3400; duḥkhaṇḍa : 32516; gāyatrī : 2459, etc.) Cf. Ṛksaṃkhyā.

420 EKAŚRUTI(-SAPTAKA) (एकश्रुति-सप्तक)

Trav. Uni. 5479 B. PL. Tel. 40 Grantha-s (with C.).
Trav. Uni. 16408 Z3. PL. Mal. 1 fol. 10 Grantha-s.

[NCC III 54a]

421 EKĀKṢARĪ-BAIṬH (-PARIBHĀṢĀ) (एकाक्षरीभैठ्-परिभाषा)

A work in a code language giving particulars of the words of the *Ṛgveda*, usually accompanied by a few verses (about a dozen) of paribhāṣā. Otherwise called *Pada-ratna* or *Pada-ratna-paribhāṣā*. See above under Ṛgveda-pada-ratna where the beginning and end are given.

BISM p. 49 (35/481ka). 9 fol. Dated Śaka 1690.
BISM p. 49 (50/100) (with C.).
GJKSV 13727. 6 fol.
GJKSV 13757. 5 fol. Presented to the former owner by Pāṇḍuraṅga-śarman Gore of Vairāja-kṣetra.
GJKSV 30313. 60 fol. Title: Prativarga-varṇa-saṃkhyā. It contains a commentary on the eleven paribhāṣā verses and explanations called Utthāpanā on Aṣṭaka-s 5-7. Contains also Aṣṭākṣarī-baiṭh for Pavamāna Sūkta-s (RV IX 1-67):

प्रत्यध्यायं पावमानीमेकार्णादिपदादिजाम् ।
संख्यां ब्रह्मोपनामा वै गोविन्दो विलिखाम्यहम् ॥

SBD 55494. 4 fol. Paribhāṣā verses with a few notes.
SBD 55256. 8 fol.

VSM I 420 (no.4909). 1 fol. 11 Grantha-s.
VSM III 163 (no.12184). 1 fol. 12 verses.

[NCC III 59b]

Ptd.: ed. by G. V. Devasthali, with commentary and Paribhāṣā, *Golden Jubilee Volume*, Vaidika Samsodhana Mandala. – Poona 1982, pp. 66-93. This edition is based on five Mss: BORI D I i.431 and 47; BISM p. 49 (35/481ka); two Mss. from the Vaidika Samsodhana Mandala, Poona (no.11281). [BORI (43534); SAI (ind 58 V 86/77)]

Only the text without the paribhāṣā verses, included in the *Ṛgvedīya-bonda-lakṣaṇa*, under the title: *Pada-ratna*, ed. by K. S. Venkatarama Sastri. – Srirangam : Sri Vani Vilas Press, 1968. [Adyar (PH 216.2 Ven RB); BORI (21936); SAI (85/1958*); UBTÜ (3 E 1286)]

– C.

Beginning: (as printed in Devasthali's edition)

नान्तमिति । अथशब्दो मङ्गलार्थः । नान्तं नकारान्तम् । विसर्गान्तं स्पष्टम् । अवगृह्यं दुःखण्डम् । स्यन्तं सिकारान्तम् । तुसेन्तं तुकारान्तं सेकारान्तम् । इति षड्विधं पदं विषमं समं चेति प्रतिवर्गं वर्गे वर्गे वक्ष्ये । प्रगृह्यस्य इतिकरणस्य संख्यां वक्ष्ये । पञ्चमं (?पञ्चकं) पदानि गणयित्वा अन्ये (?त्ये) पञ्चके यानि पदानि तेषु पदेषु या संख्या तां च संख्यां वक्ष्ये । प्रतिवर्गमिति प्रत्येकं संबन्धः ॥

End:

यत्रानेकमिति । यत्र पदे अनेकान्तदुःखण्डप्रगृह्यादिरूपं तत् पदं कुत्रे(त्वने)कत्र बहुषु स्थानेषु नान्तदुःखण्डप्रगृह्यादिषु गण्यते ॥ इत्येकाक्षरबैठपरिभाषाटीका समाप्ता ॥

422 EKĀDAŚA-PRAKĀŚA(RA)-VIKṚTI (एकादशप्रकाश(र)विकृति)

t Ujjain I, p. 10 (no.1244). 5 fol. Cf. Grantha-Saṃhitā Ekādaśa-prakārāḥ.

[NCC III 62a]

423 EKĀDAŚA-LAKṢAṆA (एकादशलक्षण)

Mysore ND II 3309 (P 4906/33). PL. Na. 1 fol. (124). Extract no. 90. (Cf. p. 28 of the Pada-gāḍha, Srirangam edition).

424 EKODARKĪ (एकोदर्की)

Title in Mysore ND II 3311 for Uccodarkī. See above under Uccodarkī.

425 EKODĀTTA-SVARĀṢṬAKA-BHĀṢYA or SVARĀṢṬAKA-BHĀṢYA (एकोदात्तस्वराष्टकभाष्य / स्वराष्टकभाष्य)

Title of the commentay on the *Svara-nirṇaya* of Jayanta-svāmin.

Skt. Coll. Ben. 1909. p. 2 (no.1785).

[NCC III 75b]

426 EKONA-TRIMŚAL-LAKṢAṆA (एकोनत्रिंशल्लक्षण)

Mysore ND II 3310 (P 4906/42). PL. Na. 1 fol. (126). Extract no. 91.

*AUDAVRAJI (औदव्रजि)

Ancient authority on grammar. The *Ṛktantra* of the *Sāmaveda* is attributed to him by Bhaṭṭoji in his *Śabda-kaustubha*, the commentary on the *Pāṇinīya-śikṣā* and the author of the *Śikṣā-prakāśa*. See Suryakanta's edition of the *Ṛktantra*, introduction, pp. 33-34, 39. The *Sāmaveda-sarvānukramaṇī* mentions *Sāma-tantra* as a work of Audavraji; see Suryakanta, op. cit., p. 37. Mss. of *Puṣpa-sūtra* also mention Audavraji as its author. See op. cit., p. 37. Cf. Puṣpayaśas Audavraji in the list of Sāmavedic sages in the *Vaṃśa-brāhmaṇa*. A Prācīna Audavraji is quoted in the *Nārada-śikṣā*. See F. Kielhorn : Remarks on the Śikṣās in : *Indian Antiquary*, vol. V, p. 195 (reprint in : *Kleine Schriften*, vol. I, pp. 158-69). Viśveśvara (fl. beginning of the 18th cent.) quotes Audavraji in his commentary on his own *Kavīndra-karṇābharaṇa* (yathācaujavrajisaṃjñācāryasya sūtram : anantyasyāntyasaṃyoge madhye yamaḥ pūrvasyānuguṇaḥ). Kāvyamālā Gucchaka VIII. – Bombay : Nirnaya Sagar Press, 1891, p. 86.

– Ṛktantra.
– Puṣpa-(Phulla-)sūtra (?).
– Śikṣā(?). See F. Kielhorn : Remarks on the Śikṣās in : *Indian Antiquary*, vol. V, pp. 195, 199 (reprint in : *Kleine Schriften*, vol. I, pp. 158-69).
– Sāma-tantra.

[NCC III 99b]

427 KAṆḌIKĀNUKRAMAṆIKĀ (कण्डिकानुक्रमणिका)
Jodiya II 54.

[NCC III 128a]

428 KANAKĀVALI (कनकावलि)
of Nārāyaṇācārya, on Vedic Śākhā-s particularly the *Śukla Yajurveda* and on the sage Yājñavalkya as its promulgator.
Adyar I, p. 158b.
Oppert II 3979. Belonged to Archaka Yogananda Bhatta of Melkote, Mysore Dist.
A private Ms. was with Dr. V. Raghavan.

Ptd.: ed. by V. Raghavan, on the basis of his own Ms. and that of Adyar, in : *The Adyar Library Bulletin*, vol. 30 (1966). [NL (PP 212 5 Ad 99)]

[NCC III 144b]

429 KANIṢṬHA-ṚGVIDHĀNA (कनिष्ठ-ऋग्विधान)
Ascribed to Śaunaka. IO 4253. Cf. Ṛgvidhāna and Laghu-ṛgvidhāna.

[NCC III 145a]

*KAMALĀKARA-BHAṬṬA (?) (कमलाकरभट्ट)
– C. on Caraṇa-vyūha; doubtful. See below under C. on Caraṇa-vyūha. Ptd.: (in Telugu script). – Madras : Tarangini Press, 1896. 44 pp.

430 KAMPA-DVIMĀTRA-LAKṢAṆA (**कम्पद्विमात्रलक्षण**)

Mysore I, p. 25.

Mysore ND II 3312 (C 476/ 3). 4 fol. Extract no. 93. = MD 14147.

[NCC III 168b]

431 KAMPA-LAKṢAṆA (**कम्पलक्षण**)

The text is accompanied by explanations in Kannada.

Beginning:

इकार यकार वकार पकार औकार ई ऐदु जातिगू पूर्वपदान्त उत्तरपरपदादि अनुदात्तक्के परदल्लि उदात्तविद्दरे पूर्वपदान्त उदात्तक्कू परपदादि अनुदात्तक्कू संयोग। ई संयोगाक्षरक्के परदल्लिं उदात्त हीगिद्दरे उदात्ताद् वापि यंब न्याय कल्पलक्षणदल्लिद्दरे (दे) याद कारण इकारादि ऐदु जातिगू संयोगवादन्थ अनुदात्ताक्षरक्के कम्प हुट्टुवुदु।

End:

दीर्घस्वरं विजानीयाद् दीपवद् वेणुपत्रवत्।
ह्रस्वस्वरं विजानीयान्मल्लीमुकुलवद् बुधः ॥
लोपस्त्वाकारपूर्वस्य नकारस्य हि रेफतः ।
उकारेकारपूर्वस्य रेफः स्यात् पदसंधिषु॥

इति कम्पलक्षणम्॥

Mysore Skt. Coll. p. 1 = D. No.5 (846/8). PL. Na. 3 fol. (34-36).

Cf. Weber 46 (Chambers 853, 13). 1 fol.

[NCC III 169a]

432 KAMPA-SŪTRA (**कम्पसूत्र**)

Beginning: (767)

कम्पसूत्रम्। विवयं हिंसिषमौगररूरूभाहिवामाकूत्यायन्त उदायुषा यज्ञियं विभूस्त्वं सोमदेवानां शमोषधीभ्यो होतर्दोषा चर्षणीर्वाचस्पतये द्वे उपयाम गृहीतो ऽसि द्वे समिधमाहोर्जे आदित्यो वा एवं विद्वान् यद्वास्कात् बभूव वा आरण्यं मनसा मा द्वे अजनयं द्वे पाकयज्ञं यान्येव त्रीणि विसृजते द्वे देवसवितरन्तर्म्मरत ऐन्द्राग्नं द्वे ब्रह्मा ... । ४१ । धावति देवा सुरा वषड्कारे ...

End:

ऋतुष्वेव न गतमनाः पञ्चैव प्रति द्वे प्रजापतिरुपाप्नोति चतुष्पदः । ८२। यं कामं द्वे अग्नये वायवे स्वा इमे एवांस्तमहस्मिन् गौरसौ द्वे देवता अभ्योरोहन् हरेकस्तुवर्गं वै ज्योतिष्टोमं द्वे यो अर्वन्तमाप्तयै द्वे। १६। आहत्य कम्पम् २६२। कम्पसूत्रं समाप्तम्॥

Adyar D I 767 (22 P 20 = 68361). PL. Gr. 2 fol. (197-98). Full text is printed here. = Adyar II, App. p. iib (40 G 20).

Adyar D I 768 (22 P 20 = 68361). PL. Gr. 2 fol. (210-11). = Adyar II, App. p. iib (40 G 20).

Mysore I, p. 25.

Mysore ND II 3313 (A 600/ 6/5?). Na. 2 fol. (26-27). Extract no. 94.

[NCC III 169a]

*KARṆĀṬAKA MĀDHAVĀCĀRYA (कर्णाटक माधवाचार्य)

– C. Dūṣaṇabhaṅga-mīmāṃsā on the *Ṛgveda-prātiśākhya.* Wai I 365.

*KAVICŪḌĀMAṆI (कविचूडामणि)

– Veda-stuti. Ujjain I, p. 9 (no.1646). 50 fol. (with C.).

433 KĀṆḌĀNUKRAMA(-ṆIKĀ) (काण्डानुक्रम /-णिका)

An index to the ritualistic contents of the *Taittirīya-saṃhitā* of the Ātreyī Śākhā.

Beginning: (Weber)

अथ काण्डानुक्रमः । पुरोडाशीयमध्वरो ग्रहा दाक्षिणान्याधानपुनराधेये अग्न्युपस्थानमैष्टिकं याजमानं तद्विधिर्वाजपेयस्तद्विधी राजसूयः काम्याः पशव इष्टयो दार्श्यं ब्राह्मणमुपानुवाक्यमग्निस्तद्विधिर्द्वे काण्डे पूर्वं द्विचत्वारिंशिकमुत्तरं त्रैंशिकं तदग्न्युपानुवाक्यमित्याचक्षते।

End:

रहस्यमूल ऋक्पर्णो यजुष्पुष्पप्रवाळवान्।
यज्ञकर्मफलः श्रीमान् विप्रभ्रमरसेवितः ॥ ३२॥
छन्दःस्कन्धः शाखाशाखो ब्राह्मो वृक्षः साक्षादेषः ।
यस्तं विद्यात् स(ह) ऋषि(भि)र्विप्रः स स्वर्गच्छेदास्वा कीर्तिम्॥
एतानृषीन् यजुर्वेदे यः पठन् वेद वेदवित्।
ऋषीणामेति सालोक्यं स्वयंभोश्चैति साम्यताम्॥ ३४॥

स्वयंभोश्चैति साम्यतामिति ॥ (स्वयंभुश्चात्र दैवतम् । स्वयंभूश्चात्र दैवतमिति) इति काण्डानुक्रमः समाप्तः ॥

Adyar D I 769 (40 C 9 = PM 106). 2 fol. Copied by Nīlakaṇṭha.

Adyar D I 770 (9 D 54 = PM 107) (with C.). 12 fol. (fol. 1-5 Gr. and 6-12 Devanāgarī). = Adyar I, p. 48b.

Hoshiarpur p. 56 (no.3543). 2 fol. 48 Grantha-s. Dated V.S. 1881.

Hoshiarpur p. 56 (no.3917). PL. Tel. 3 fol. 60 Grantha-s. Incomplete.

Hoshiarpur p. 56 (no.6845). 34 fol. 204 Grantha-s. Incomplete. Dated V.S. 1990. Extract p. 82.

IO 159 (2743M). 4 fol. Written ca. A.D. 1650.

IO 160 (965b). 14 fol. (with C.). Copied by Rāmadeva, son of Kānhadeva.

IO 161 (1577F). 11 fol. (with C.). Dated V.S. 1650 (Śaka ?). Copied by Bhairava at Kāśī.

MD 15442. Gr. 39 pp. 220 Grantha-s (with C. Vistara).

Mysore I, p. 25.

Mysore ND II 3462 (P 301/ 1). PL. Na. 1 fol. Extract no. 165. Title: Taittirīya-saṃhitānukramaṇī.

Mysore ND II 3465 (C 264/ 2). Tel. 4 fol. Title: Taittirīya-saṃhitānukramaṇī.

Oppert I 7886 (with C.). Belonged to Paravastu Venkatarangacharyar of Vishakhapattanam.

Oxf. CS d.76(1). 14 fol. Dated A.D. 1880.

Oxf. CS d.77(1). 13 fol. (with C.). Dated V.S. 1763 (A.D. 1706). Attributed to Śaunaka by a later hand.

PUL I, p. 20 (no.61). PL. Gr. 2 fol. 45 Grantha-s.

PUL I, p. 21 (no.63). PL. Tel. 5 fol. 200 Grantha-s (with C.).

PUL II. App. p. 11 (no.154). PL. Gr. 10 fol. 300 Grantha-s.

R. A. Sastri I 14 (with C.).

SB p. 47 (no.118). 14 fol. 263 Grantha-s.

SBD 2351. 12 fol. (with Vistara). (Taittirīya-kāṇḍānukrama).

Wai II 10270. 9 fol. Dated Śaka 1791.

Weber 141(1) (Weber 1). 14 fol. A copy of IO 160 in Roman script.

Ptd.:

Ed. by Albrecht Weber, *Der Kāṇḍānukrama der Ātreyī-Schule des Taittirīyaveda*, text and C. (in Roman script), *Indische Studien*, vol. III (1855), pp. 373-401. [Adyar (H080 Web IS ge); SAI (inf Zs 73) Emeneau (395)] Text alone in his edition of the *Taittirīya-saṃhitā, Indische Studien*, vol. XII (1872), pp. 350-57. [Adyar (H080 Web IS ge)]

As an appendix to the first vol. of the *Taittirīya-saṃhitā* with the Bhāṣya of Bhaṭṭa Bhāskara-miśra. – Mysore : Govt. Oriental Library, 1893. – (Mysore Govt. Oriental Library Series 4). [Adyar (H080 MOS 4); BM : Ptd. Bks. Cat. 1892-1906. 803 (14010.b.4, no.4)]

Ed. by Ramakrishna Shastri of Kalpadi (in Grantha script), with a metrical epitome and commentary of Karuppattur Venkatarama (Krishna) Sarma. – Palghat, 1900. 22 pp. [Adyar (PH 215 KA xy Ram); BM : Ptd. Bks. Cat. 1892-1906. 803 (14010.b.14,2)]

Reprint of the above : Ed. by K. V. Anantanarayana Sastri (in 3 Adhyāya-s), in : *Annals of the Bhandarkar Oriental Research Institute*, vol. 39 (1959), pp. 266-88. [Adyar (H 211.22 Ind Kan y Ven); SAI (87/785*)]

– C. Vistara or Vivaraṇa.

Beginning:

अथ काण्डानुक्रमविस्तरो व्याख्यायते -- अथ काण्डानुक्रम इत्यादि । काण्डशेषान् यथाकाण्डं विदध्यात् तु विचक्षणः इति वचनात् (श्लोक ९) काण्डशेषसंयुक्तानि पुरोडाशीयादीनि क्रमेण निर्दिश्यन्ते । पुरोडाशीयं नाम काण्डमिषे त्वेत्यादिप्रश्न उत्तमानुवाकवर्जम् ...।

End:

इदं वृक्षस्वरूपं निरूप्यते रहस्यमूल इत्यादि । उपनिषन्मूलः । ब्रह्म इत्यादि । स्वयं कल्पवृक्षः । ३२-३३ । एतान् प्रजापत्यादि ऋषीन् सदसस्पतिपर्यन्तान्

यस्तैत्तिरीयशाखाध्यायो (को) वेत्ति स ऋषीणां सालोक्यं स्वयंभुवश्च सायुज्यं प्राप्नोति। ३४। काण्डानुक्रमणिकाविवरणं समाप्तम्॥

Adyar D I 770 (9 D 54 = PM 107). 12 fol. (with text). = Adyar I, p. 48b.
BISM p. 56 (56/167).
Hpr. II 29. 11 fol. 258 Grantha-s.
IO 160 (965b). 14 fol. Copied by Rāmadeva, son of Kānhadeva.
IO 161 (1577F). 11 fol. Dated V.S. 1650 (or Śaka ?).
MD 15442. Gr. 39 pp. (with text).
Oppert I 7886 (with text). Belonged to Paravastu Venkatarangacharyar of Vishakhapattanam.
Oxf. CS d.77(1). 13 fol. (with text). Dated V.S. 1763 (A.D. 1706).
PUL I, p. 21 (no.62). PL. Gr. 10 fol. (3-12).
PUL I, p. 21 (no.63). PL. Tel. 5 fol. 200 Grantha-s (with text).
R. A. Sastri I 14.
SBD 2351. 12 fol. (with text). (Taittirīya-kāṇḍānukrama).
Wai I 560. 8 fol. Dated Śaka 1723.
Ptd.: See above.

[NCC III 304b; 396b]

434 KĀṆḌOPAKRAMAṆĪ (काण्डोपक्रमणी)
Oppert II 515. Belonged to D. Shamannachari of Srimushnam, Chidambaram Taluk.

[NCC III 305a]

435 KĀṆVA-JAṬĀ-PĀṬHA (काण्वजटापाठ)
SBD 52226. 240 and 195 fol. (up to 17th ch.).

436 KĀṆVA-PADA-LAKṢAṆA (काण्वपदलक्षण)
of Anantācārya. Govt. Or. Libr. Madras, p. 16. Not traceable in MD.

[NCC III 305a]

437 KĀṆVA-LAGHU-PRĀTIŚĀKHYA (काण्वलघुप्रातिशाख्य)
Śukla YV. ascribed to Kātyāyana.
Rep. Hpr. 1901-06, p. 3.
Cf. Vājasaneyi-prātiśākhya.

[NCC III 305b]

438 KĀṆVA-ŚĀKHĀ-MAHIMA-SAṂGRAHA (काण्वशाखामहिमसंग्रह)
on the superiority of the Kāṇva Śākhā of the *Yajurveda* by Nāgeśa of Pāṇḍuraṅga-pura (Pandharapur). He refers to a similar work by the Pandits of Srirangam at the instance of Peḍḍi Bhaṭṭa of Vasiṣṭha-gotra.

Beginning:

श्रीमहाविमलं नत्वा याज्ञवल्क्यं महागुरुम्।
महिम्नः कण्वशाखायाः संग्रहः क्रियतेऽधुना॥
यं वै श्रीरङ्गविद्वज्जनबहुनिगमैः कारयामास सम्यक्
वासिष्ठः पेद्दिभट्टः शुभमिह महिमासंग्रहं शाखिकायाः।

काण्वस्थं व्यस्तपाठक्रमनतिरहितं वीक्ष्य सज्जं प्रचक्रे
नागेशः पाण्डुरङ्गाभिधपुरवसती नागरो विट्ठलस्य ॥
अयं तु महिमा सर्वपुराणादिषु विश्रुतः ।
तस्मात् तस्मात् तदाख्यानमुद्धृत्यालिख्यते परम् ॥
नूतनं निर्मितं त्वेतदिति संदिग्धमानसः ।
यदि कश्चिद् भवेत् तं तं ग्रन्थं पश्यतु मौक्तिकम् ॥
यथा पयोधिं निर्मथ्य रत्नोद्धारः कृतः पुरा ।
तथा निर्मथ्य पौराणं रत्नमाहात्म्यमुद्धृतम् ॥
वासुदेवे मतिर्येषां मुक्तिमिच्छन्ति ये ऽपि वै ।
तैरयं साधु श्रोतव्यः कण्वशाखामहोदयः ॥ ...
इयं शुद्धयजुःशाखा प्रथमेत्यभिधीयते ।
मूलशाखेति चाप्युक्ता तथा चैकायनीति च ॥
अयातयामयजुषा तथा मोक्षैकसाधिका ।
इत्याद्यनेकनामानि सन्त्यस्यास्तत्र तत्र वै ॥
तत्तन्नामनिमित्तानि युक्तियुक्तानि भूरिशः ।
कथितानि च माहात्म्ये तत्तदाख्यासु शोभते ॥
भारते शान्तिपर्वाख्ये त्रिधा प्रोक्तो ऽयमुत्तमः ।
सभाश्वसंभवाख्येषु पर्वस्वपि तथोदितः ॥
भागवते ऽथ नवमे दशमे द्वादशे द्विधा ।
वैष्णवे च त्रिधा प्रोक्ता तथा ब्रह्म ... द्विधा ॥
हरिवंशे तथा स्कान्दे देवीपौराणिके तथा ।
मूलरामायणे शौरिकथायां रघुवंशके ॥
मुरारिनाटके वृद्धमन्वादिस्मृतिवाक्यतः ।
गोपालकृतशेषाख्ये सूत्रे विवरणे ऽपि च ॥
अथर्वशिरसि प्रोक्तं पैङ्गलोपनिषद्यपि ।
पाञ्चरात्रागमे त्रेधा तथा ज्ञानार्णवे ऽपि च ॥
यजुर्वेदानुक्रमणे तथा द्राविडभाषके ।
हेमाद्रिकल्पसंप्रोक्तो मधुपर्के ऽपि वर्णितः ।
एतेष्वखिलग्रन्थेषु वर्णिता महिमाद्भुतः ॥
इति काण्वशाखामहिम्नः संगृह्यमाणाख्यानुवादः ।

End:

त्रयीसुसंमित्तविवेकनिर्मला समग्रनिश्रेयससिद्धिहेतवः ।
समस्तशास्त्रार्थसुतत्त्वबोधका जयन्ति कात्यायनपादपांसवः ॥

आविर्भूतमभूतपूर्वविभवादादौ सरोजासना-
न्यस्तं न्यासतया मुनेः श्रुतितनोश्चण्डत्विषो मण्डले।
दुष्प्रापं तमवाप तापसमुखः श्रीयाज्ञवल्क्यः स्वयं
कीर्त्यैवाखिल ... स्य शुक्लयजुषो वेदेन तेनादृतम्॥

MT 2389. 30 fol. Incomplete. Transcribed in 1917-18 from a Ms. acquired through the sub-magistrate of Kovvur, Krishna Dist.

[NCC III 305b]

439 KĀṆVA-ŚĀKHĀ-MĀHĀTMYA (1) (**काण्वशाखामाहात्म्य**)
on the greatness of the Kāṇva Śākhā of the *Yajurveda,* with a commentary. The author does not mention his name or any other details, but he was a follower of the Madhva school. He refers to Ānandatīrtha and quotes extensively from the Purāṇa-s, Itihāsa-s, Upaniṣad-s, Smṛti-s, etc.

Beginning:

वन्दे विठ्ठलमानन्दचित्स्वरूपं रमापतिम्।
कण्वस्तुतं वाजिरूपं भक्ताभीष्टप्रदायकम्॥
पूर्वाचार्यगुरून्नत्वा माधवार्यगुरून् तथा।
धर्मशास्त्रानुसारेण मध्वसिद्धान्तवर्त्मना॥
उच्यते कण्वशाखाया माहात्म्यं विष्णुतुष्टये।
निर्मात्सर्ययुता ये तु सज्जनाः शोधयन्त्विदम्॥

एतेषां स्वरूपमाह व्यासः --

धर्मज्ञाः पुत्रिणो मौलाः कुलीनाः सत्यवादिनः।
श्रौतस्मार्तक्रियायुक्ता विगतद्वेषमत्सराः॥

याज्ञवल्क्यः --

श्रुताध्ययनसंपन्ना धर्मज्ञाः सत्यवादिनः।
राज्ञा सभासदः कार्या रिपौ मित्रे च ये समाः॥ ...

एतादृशा इदं शोधयन्त्वित्यर्थः। आदौ व्यासावतारे प्रयोजनमाह -- व्यासास्त्वष्टाविंशतिसंख्याका इति विष्णुपुराणोक्तेः। किं च -- धर्मसंस्थापनार्थाय संभवामि युगे युगे इति भगवद्गीतोक्तेः। प्रकृतव्यासावतारे प्रयोजनं किमित्युक्ते तत्र श्रीमद्ब्रह्मसूत्रभाष्यकारैः प्रयोजनमुक्तम्। किमिति।

गौतमस्य ऋषेः शापात् ज्ञाने त्वज्ञानतां गते।
संकीर्णबुद्धयो देवा ब्रह्मरुद्रपुरःसराः॥
शरण्यं शरणं जग्मुर्नारायणमनामयम्।
तैर्विज्ञापितकार्यस्तु भगवान् पुरुषोत्तमः॥
अवतीर्णो महायोगी सत्यवत्यां पराशरात्।
उत्सन्नान् भगवान् वेदानुज्जहार हरिः स्वयम्॥

चतुर्धा व्यभजत् तांश्च चतुर्विंशतिधा पुनः।
शतधा चैकधा चैव तथैव च सहस्रधा।
कृष्णो द्वादशधा चैव पुनस्तस्यार्थवित्तये॥
चकार ब्रह्मसूत्राणि एषां सूत्रत्वमञ्जसा।

इत्याचार्यैरुक्तम् --

End:

अयं भावः। पूर्वस्वीकृतेन गुरुणा समे गुरौ समग्रानुग्रहकर्तरि (स्वयम् ?) एव प्राप्ते सति अवश्यं स्वीकार्यः। न तु तदर्थं प्रयतितव्यम्। तर्हि (दोष?)स्मृतेः का गतिरिति चेत् समगुर्वन्तरस्वीकारे पूर्वस्यानुज्ञा सर्वथा भाव्या। विनानुज्ञया समानपूर्वगुरुपरित्यागविषयं दोषस्मरणम्। सत्यामनुज्ञायामन्यगुरुकृतिरन्यथा तु नेति विकल्प एवेति यथोक्तं ...

MT 2317. Gr. (Tel. ?). 62 fol. Incomplete. Transcribed in 1916-17 from a Ms. acquired through the sub-magistrate of Kovvur, Krishna Dist.

Mysore III, p. 4.

Oppert II 3982. Belonged to Archaka Yogananda Bhatta of Melkote, Mysore Dist.

[NCC III 305b]

440 KĀṆVA-ŚĀKHĀ-MĀHĀTMYA (2) (**काण्वशाखामाहात्म्य**)

of (Śrī-)Kṛṣṇa-sūri. A modern work on greatness of the Kāṇva school of the *Vājasaneyi-saṃhitā*.

Beginning:

श्रीरुक्मिणीशं श्रितसत्यभामं श्रीराधिकावल्लभमाद्यशाखम्।
साम्बं चतुर्वक्त्रमजं गणेशं देवीं च वाचां कुलदेवताश्च॥ ...
श्रुत्यादिसिद्धं श्रुतिवेदिनं तं नीचोच्चभावं हरिवाजितुष्ट्यै।
श्रीकृष्णसूरिः श्रितकाण्वशाखः श्रीवाजिनुन्नं प्रकटीकरिष्ये॥

End:

इति वृद्धमनूक्तेश्च शुक्लयजुषः कात्यायनसूत्रस्य च कृष्णयजुःशाखि ऋक्शाख्यादीनां स्वस्वकाले अनुसर्तव्यं प्रतीयते। न तु कृष्णयजुर्वेदस्य आपस्तम्बसूत्रस्य च शुक्लयजुःशाखि ... नुसर्तव्यत्वं प्रतीयत इति शुक्लयजुषः कृष्णयजुषादिभ्यः उत्तमत्वमवश्यमङ्गीकर्तव्यमित्यलं पल्लवितेन॥

BORI 55 of 1902-07. 62 fol.

[NCC III 305b]

441 KĀṆVA-ŚĀKHĀ-MĀHĀTMYA (3) (**काण्वशाखामाहात्म्य**)

Contains extracts from several Purāṇa-s.

Beginning:

श्रीगोपालकृते शेषसूत्रविवरणे

माहात्म्यं काण्वशाखायाः कथ्यते विष्णुतुष्टये।
यतः सा विष्णुदैवत्या विष्णुः सर्वोत्तमो यथा॥
ज्ञेयं चास्मत्कृतावेतद् भद(?)कौस्तुभपूर्वके।
तथाहि अथर्वशिरोवचनम्। अथ हैनं पिप्पलादो ...

End:

याज्ञवल्क्यकाण्वशाखामाहात्म्यमुक्तम् । मानवशब्दोक्तत्रैवर्णिकस्य सूर्योदयात् पूर्वं हुताग्नित्वादियाज्ञवल्क्यकर्मानुष्ठानविधानाद् याज्ञवल्क्यस्य त्रैवर्णिकानुकर्तव्यज्ञा ... दिनिर्मातृत्वमुक्तम्। विष्णुपुराणे चतुर्थांशे एकविंशाध्याये पराशरः अतः परं भविष्यान् भूपालान् कीर्तयिष्यामि । यो ऽयं सांप्रतं महीपतिः परीक्षित् तस्यापि परीक्षितो जनमेज ...

Oxf. CS d.342(11). 24 fol. Incomplete. (= Descriptive Catalogue, Part II, 594).

442 KĀṆVA-ŚĀKHĀ-VEṢṬANA-KRAMA-BODHINĪ (काण्वशाखावेष्टनक्रमबोधिनी)
of Govinda-sūri, son of Kṛṣṇa. 37 Kārikā-s; subject is the same as in Krama-kārikā-śikṣā.
RASB II 914 (G.6264). 3 fol. 50 Grantha-s.

[NCC III 305b]

443 KĀṆVA-ŚĀKHĀ-SARVĀNUKRAMAṆIKĀ (काण्वशाखासर्वानुक्रमणिका)
of Kātyāyana. Cf. Śukla-yajurveda-sarvānukrama (Kāṇvīya), MT 5070(b).
GJKSV 28351. 41 fol. Dated V.S. 1868. Title: Kāṇvīyānukramaṇikā.
PUL I, p. 20 (no.43). 51 fol. 500 Grantha-s. 5 Adhyāya-s.

444 KĀṆVA-ŚĀKHĪYA-KRAMA-KĀRIKĀ (काण्वशाखीयक्रमकारिका)
Adyar D I 771 (36 B 11 = TR 21). 8 fol. (pp. 430-44). = Adyar I, p. 52a. Title: Kāṇva-śikṣā. Copied by Rāmacandra Śāstrin and revised by Nārāyaṇa Śāstrin. Dated 7.6.18 → Krama-kārikā-śikṣā. Begins from verse 26 of the printed edition and other verses are in a different order.

[NCC III 305b]

445 KĀṆVA-ŚĀKHĪYA-PADA-LAKṢAṆA (काण्वशाखीयपदलक्षण)
(Ṣaṇmukha) Śukla YV of Anantācārya.
Trav. Uni. 10170. 1000 Grantha-s.

[NCC III 306a]

446 KĀṆVA-ŚIKṢĀ (काण्वशिक्षा)
Adyar I, p. 52a → Kāṇva-śākhīya-krama-kārikā (Adyar D I 771). Also known as the Krama-kārikā(-śikṣā).

[NCC III 306a]

447 KĀṆVA-SAṂHITĀ-KRAMA-PĀṬHA (काण्वसंहिताक्रमपाठ)
BORI TM 227.
IM 1769. 142 fol. (Pūrva-daśaka).
IM 1770. 239-401 fol. (chs. X-XV).
IM 1771. 74-357 fol. (chs. XXII-XXX).

IM 1774. (chs. XXI-XL).
IM 1775. (chs. XI-XIII, XXI-XXXI).
PUL I, p. 20 (no.43). 51 fol. 500 Grantha-s. 5 Adhyāya-s.
SBD 1075. 34 fol. (17-50). Incomplete. (Chs. 12-13).
SBD 1077. 119 fol. (143-238, 402-25). Incomplete. (Chs. 6-20).
SBD 1079. 55 fol. (1-4, 73-75, 77-124). Incomplete.
SBD 1100. 30 fol. Incomplete. (Chs. 31-38).
SBD 52221. 307 and 222 fol. Dated V.S. 1689. Title: Śuklayajurvedakāṇvasaṃhitākrama-pāṭha.
Trav. Uni. 10223. 800 Grantha-s.

448 KĀṆVA-SAṂHITĀ-JAṬĀ-PĀṬHA (काण्वसंहिताजटापाठ)
BORI TM 119. 148 fol. Incomplete. (chs. 11-17).

449 KĀṆVĪYĀNUKRAMAṆIKĀ (काण्वीयानुक्रमणिका)
→ Śukla-yajurveda-sarvānukrama (Kāṇvīya).
GJKSV 28351. 41 fol. Dated V.S. 1868.

*KĀTYĀYANA (कात्यायन)
Writer on Veda-lakṣaṇa and Kalpa; associated especially with the *Śukla Yajurveda*. For details of some of his woks see V. Venkatarama Sarma : *Critical Studies on Kātyāyana's Śukla Yajurveda Prātiśākhya*. – Madras : University of Madras, 1935. 461 pp. Reprinted : New Delhi : Yaska, 1989. [SAI (ind 51 D 700)]

– Ṛgveda-sarvānukramaṇī. See above. The Ṛgveda-paribhāṣā of Kātyāyana, BORI D I i.31 is part of this. Ṛgvidhāna, Tra. Ad. Rep. 1110.2 may be this.

– Kāṇva-laghu-prātiśākhya. Rep. Hpr. 1901-06, p. 3. Cf. Vājasaneyi-prātiśākhya.

– Kātyāyana-śikṣā. See below.

– Yajurvidhāna, Bṛhad- (in 7 chs. and) Laghu- (in 5 chs.). BORI D I i.271-272.
Ptd.: in Śikṣā-saṃgraha. – Benares, 1889, pp. 327-61. – (Ben. S. S. 10).
Also ed. by Anna Sastri Ware, *Śuklayajurvidhāna-sūtra*, with the C. *Yajurmañjarī* of Kālanātha Vāghare. – Bombay : Nirnaya Sagar Press, 1943, pp. 1-50. [SOAS (III.1.e.54 – 59314)]

– Vājasaneyi-prātiśākhya or Śukla-yajurveda-prātiśākhya.
Ptd.: with Uvaṭa's Bhāṣya. – Benares, 1888. – (Ben. S. S. 4).

– Śukla-yajurveda-sarvānukrama(-sūtra), (or YajurvedaKāṇvasaṃhitā-, Mādhyandina-saṃhitā-, Vājasaneyi-saṃhitā-sarvānukrama).
Ptd.: with Yājñika-deva's Bhāṣya. – Benares, 1893-1921. – (Ben. S. S. 12).
Also printed at the end of the edition of the *Śukla Yajurveda*, with commentaries of Uvaṭa and Mahīdhra. – Bombay : Nirnaya Sagar Press, 1912 (reprint 1929).

– Svarabhakti-lakṣaṇa-pariśiṣṭa-śikṣā. Ptd.: in Śikṣā-saṃgraha. – Benares, 1889, pp. 172-75. – (Ben. S. S. 10).

– Bhāṣika-sutra, on the accents in the Śatapatha-brāhmaṇa.
Ptd.: ed. by Yugalakishora (Vyasa) Pathaka, with Ananta-bhaṭṭa's C., at the end of *Śuklayajuḥ-prātiśākhya* with Uvaṭa's Bhāṣya. – Benares, 1888. – (Ben. S. S. 4). See below under Bhāṣika-sūtra.

– Upalekha-sūtra on the Krama-pāṭha of the *Ṛgveda* (ascribed to him in some Mss.); see NCC II 371b.

– Svarakārikā. Rep. Hpr. 1901-06, p. 3.

[NCC III 320a-321a]

450 KĀTYĀYANA-PARIŚIṢṬA (कात्यायनपरिशिष्ट)

Pariśiṣṭa-s, i.e. supplementary texts to the Śrauta- and Gṛhya- Sūtra-s belonging to the *Śukla Yajurveda.* They are ascribed to Kātyāyana. According to the *Caraṇa-vyūha* their number is eighteen. For details of a few of these woks see V. Venkatarama Sarma : *Critical Studies on Kātyāyana's Śukla Yajurveda Prātiśākhya.* – Madras : University of Madras, 1935. 461 pp. Reprinted : New Delhi : Yaska, 1989. [SAI (ind 51 D 700)]

The following works may be listed as relating to Veda-lakṣaṇa :

– Anuvāka-saṃkhyā or Anuvākānukramaṇī. Ptd.: ed. by Yugalakishora (Vyasa) Pathaka, at the end of the *Śuklayajuḥ-prātiśākhya.* – Benares, 1888, pp. 501-06. – (Ben. S. S. 4). See above under Anuvāka-saṃkhyā.
– Ṛgyajuḥ-pariśiṣṭa. Ptd.: at the end of the *Śuklayajuḥ-prātiśākhya.* – Benares, 1888, pp. 494-501. – (Ben. S. S. 4).
– Caraṇa-vyūha. Ptd.: Several editions, e.g. as an appendix at the end of the *Śuklayajuḥ-prātiśākhya* with Uvaṭa's Bhāṣya. – Benares, 1888. 60 pp. – (Ben. S. S. 4). See under Caraṇa-vyūha.
– Pārṣada → Vājasaneyi-prātiśākhya.
– Pratijñā-sūtra. Ptd.: with Anantadeva Yājñika's C., at the end of *Śuklayajuḥ-prātiśākhya.* – Benares, 1888. – (Ben. S. S. 4). See also : *Critical Studies on Kātyāyana's Śukla Yajurveda Prātiśākhya.* – Madras : University of Madras, 1935, pp. 398-412. Reprinted : New Delhi : Yaska, 1989. [SAI (ind 51 D 700)]

[NCC III 323b]

451 KĀTYĀYANA-PRĀTIŚĀKHYA (कात्यायनप्रातिशाख्य)

→ Vājasaneyi-prātiśākhya.
ASB I iii.33.
GJKSV 13001. 15 fol. Dated V.S. 1906.
RASB II 896 (G 1775). 17 fol. 275 Grantha-s. Dated V.S. 1825.

452 KĀTYĀYANA-BAIṬH-PARIBHĀṢĀ (कात्यायनबैठ्परिभाषा)

→ Baiṭh-paribhāṣā.
IM 1963. 1 fol.

453 KĀTYĀYANA-(Ī-)ŚIKṢĀ (**कात्यायनशिक्षा**)

Different from the *Yājñavalkya-śikṣā*. 13 Anuṣṭubh verses dealing with the accentuation of the detached words (pada-s) and also of the words in the Saṃhitā text. Most of the rules in this are a metrical exposition of those described in the *Vājasaneyi-prātiśākhya*, IV 131-41.

Beginning: (with C. of Jayanta-svāmin)

अतिदुर्विज्ञेयत्वात् स्वरितस्यादौ लक्षणमाह --

यदुदात्तात् परं नीचं स्वार्यं तत्परतो न चेत्।
उदात्तात् स्वरितं वा स्याद्यत्र स्यात् स्वरितं वदेत्॥ १॥
एकीभूतमुदात्तेन स्यादुदात्तमतः परम्।
नीचं स्वार्यं यथोक्तं चेद्यच्च स्यात् स्वरितान्वितम्॥ २॥

आद्यस्य पादत्रयस्यायमर्थः । पदकालीनं यदुदात्तात् परमनुदात्तमक्षरं दृश्यते तत् संहिताकाले स्वरितं कार्यम्। यदि तस्मात् परं संधिकाले पदकाले वा तत् स्वरितमुदात्तं न भवति। अथोदाहरणम् -- यथा अग्निं दुवस्यत। त्वं यविष्ठ। अन्त्यस्य पादस्यायमर्थः । न केवलमुदात्तात् परमनुदात्तमक्षरम् स्वार्यम् । किं तर्हि । यत् पदकाले स्वरितं तदपि संहितायां स्वार्यमेव न चेत् स्वरितोदात्तात् परम्। यथा -- देवस्य त्वा। होताध्वर्युः ॥ १॥ अथ स्वरितस्यापवादलक्षणान्तरमाह॥

End:

तच्च नीचमिति ज्ञेयं यद्येकस्मिन् पदे भवेत्।
प्रचयं स्वरितादूर्ध्वमुपोपेदित्ययं यथा॥ १०॥
नीचात् प्रचयतस्तस्मात् स्वरिता संहिता भवेत्।
परेषां यत् तु पूर्वं स्यात् स्वरोच्चं नीचमेव तत्॥ ११॥

अनयोरर्थकार्यानन्तरं प्रचयत्वं भवति। उभयत्रोदाहरणं यथा रक्षाणो ब्रह्मणस्पते। स नो भुवनस्य पते। योगक्षेमो नः कल्प्यताम्। उदात्तलक्षणमाह --

उदात्तं पदकाले यत् संहितायां तथैव च।
तस्मात् पूर्वं तु यत् किंचिदनुदात्तं तदुच्यते॥ १२॥

अत्रोदाहरणं यथा -- अग्निं दुवस्यत। देवा देवानाम्॥ तथा सति तस्मादुदात्तत्वमेव भवति न स्वरितानपि प्रचयम् । स्वरितस्यानुदात्तोदाहरणे -- इन्द्रं दैवीः । प्रचयस्यानुदात्तोदाहरणे -- तिस्रो देवीः । कल्पमाना इन्द्रम्। लक्षणान्तरमाह॥

यन्नीचं पदकाले तत् संहितायां तथैव च।
उक्तं वा नीचहीनं चेत् पितृश्रवणं तद् भवेत्॥ १३॥

पदकाले यदनुदात्तं तत् संहिताकाले ऽपि भवति। यदुदात्तात् परं नीचमित्यादिना रहितं च । अत्रोदाहरणे -- पितृश्रवणं स्वरितलक्षणचतुष्टयस्य जात्याभिनिहितक्षैप्रप्रश्लिष्टस्य पितृदानवद्धस्तं कृत्वा स्वरयितव्यमित्यर्थः ॥ इति जयन्तस्वामिनिर्मितव्याख्यानयुता

महर्षिकात्यायनप्रणीता शिक्षा समाप्ता ॥

BBRAS 13(II) (B D 278) (with C.). Dated Śaka 1787. Full text is printed.
Bhau Daji 121.
BORI 3 of 1873-74. 4 fol. (8b-11a) (with C.). From Bikaner. Col.: Svara-catuṣṭya. (A xerox-copy of this Ms. is in SAI : 87/790*).
GB 23. 19 fol. 169 verses. Copied in 1875 for Kielhorn through R. L. Mitra (this is actually Yājñavalkya-śikṣā).
L 1239. 14 fol. 288 Grantha-s → Yājñavalkya-śikṣā.
RASB II 1500 (G 660) = L 1239.
RASB II 1501 (G 3255). 3 fol. 60 Grantha-s (with C.). Dated V.S. 1940.
Ujjain Latest Additions 603.
ZDMG 1868, p. 319.

Ptd.: with the commentary of Jayanta-svāmin, in Śikṣā-saṃgraha. – Benares, 1889, pp. 46-51. – (Ben. S. S. 10).

– C. of Jayanta-svāmin.
BBRAS 13(II) (B D 278) (with text). Dated Śaka 1787. Catalogued as anonymous.
BORI 3 of 1873-74. 4 fol. (8b-11a) (with text). From Bikaner.
RASB II 1501 (G 3255). 3 fol. 60 Grantha-s (with text). Dated V.S. 1940.

Ptd.: together with the text.

[NCC III 325a]

454 KĀTYĀYANA-(Ī-)ŚIKṢĀ (कात्यायनशिक्षा)
Another version in 11 verses.

Beginning: (as in BBRAS)

अथ मासनशब्देभ्यो वकारो द्विर्विभाषया ।
वोवां वावी संहितायां लघुः स्याद् द्विः पदेषु वै ॥
इत्यमोघनन्दिनी-शिक्षायाम् -- पादादौ च ...

End:

लुप्ते नकारे चादिरङ्गं नोलिप्ति तु द्वितीयकम्
रङ्गः सैव विजानीयान्नकारो यत्र लुप्यते । १० ।
स्वरे ऽपि परतश्चैव व्यञ्जने ऽत्वनुनासिकम् ॥

BBRAS 2(II) (B D 278). 1 fol. Dated Śaka 1787.
Bombay Uni. 1 (BMC 50 8). 4 fol.
IM 2505B. 1 fol. (11).

[NCC III 325a]

455 KĀTYĀYANA-SŪTRA (कात्यायनसूत्र)

BORI 41 of 1919-24. 112 fol. Dated V.S. 1678. Listed under Vyākaraṇa. But it is identified as the *Śrauta-sūtra* of Kātyāyana.

456 KĀTYĀYANĀNUKRAMAṆIKĀ (1) (कात्यायनानुक्रमणिका)

→ Ṛgveda-sarvānukramaṇī of Kātyāyana.

IM 7452. 18 fol. (1-5, 16-22, 25-30). Incomplete.

457 KĀTYĀYANĀNUKRAMAṆIKĀ (2) (कात्यायनानुक्रमणिका)

→ Śukla-yajurveda-sarvānukramaṇikā.

BISM p. 56 (22/875). Dated Śaka 1600.

R. A. Sastri II, p. 160.

[NCC III 330b]

458 KĀTYĀYANOKTA-PARIŚIṢṬA-PARIBHĀṢĀ (कात्यायनोक्तपरिशिष्टपरिभाषा)

Seven verses on the necessity of knowing the Ṛṣi, Devatā and Chandas of the mantra-s.

GJKSV 13624(A). 2 fol.

459 KĀRIKĀVALĪ (कारिकावली)

→ Keśava-(vī-)śikṣā (2) of Keśavarāma Daivajña.

SBD 48294. 1 fol.

*KĀLA (काल)

Authority referred to in Bhāradvāja-śikṣā, PUL II. App. p. 12.

[NCC IV 10b]

460 KĀLANIRṆAYA-ŚIKṢĀ (कालनिर्णयशिक्षा)

A treatise in 27 verses on the time measurement of letters, accents and stops. Quoted in the *Tribhāṣya-ratna* on the *Taittirīya-prātiśākhya,* 18-1; in the commentary on the *Vyāsa-śikṣā* of Sūryanārāyaṇāvadhānin and the commentary on the *Siddhānta-śikṣā.* See F. Kielhorn : Remarks on the Śikṣās in : *Indian Antiquary,* vol. V, pp. 193-200 (reprint in : *Kleine Schriften,* vol. I, pp. 158-69).

Beginning:

प्रातिशाख्यादिशास्त्राणि मया वीक्ष्य यथामति।
वेदतत्त्वावबोधार्थमिह कालो निरूप्यते॥
अखण्डवर्णविषयो वर्णांशविषयोऽपि च।
विरामविषयश्चेति त्रिविधः काल उच्यते॥
स्वरवर्णविरामाणां भिन्नवाग्वृत्तिवर्त्तिनाम्।
ऐकरूप्येण कालस्य कथनं नोपपद्यते॥
मध्यमां वृत्तिमाश्रित्य मया चेयं कृतिः कृता।
प्रातिशाख्ये निषिद्धान्या यस्मात् सैकैव बोध्यते॥

End:

परेण नित्यसंबन्धं प्रार्दि परपदं तथा।

एकस्वराणां चादीनां प्रादीनामिति तद् द्वयम् ॥
यो यो विरामकालः प्रागृगादौ समुदीरितः ।
अङ्गीकृतस्यार्धमात्रं तु न सो ऽधिक इष्यते ॥

Adyar D I 772 (1 A 19 = TR 19). Gr. 4 fol. (pp. 46-51). = Adyar I, p. 52b.
Adyar D I 773 (23 A <? E >25 = 69758). PL. Gr. 3 fol. (30-32).
Adyar D I 775 (29 K 20 = 73653). PL. Tel. 10 fol. (158ff.) (with C.). = Adyar I, p. 52b.
Baroda 11949(a). PL. Tel. 14 fol. 200 Grantha-s (with C.). = CLB I, p. 26.
Baroda 12754. Gr. 1 fol. 28 Grantha-s. = CLB I, p. 25.
Baroda 12755(a). Gr. 5 fol. 120 Grantha-s (with C.). Incomplete. = CLB I, p. 26.
Hamburg StUB (cod.Palmbl. III 8/133) → Veda-lakṣaṇa (HB).
BHU B 3904a (D 11/654). 2 fol. (1-2). Title: Mātrā-kāla.
Hoshiarpur p. 50 (no.3556). 8 fol. 200 Grantha-s (with C.). Incomplete. Extract p. 408.
Hz 627. PL. Tel. 24 fol. (with 4 other works). Belonged to Vedam Venkatasubrahmanya Somayaji of Allur, Nellur Dist.
Hz 1448. PL. Gr. 2 fol. Belonged to the late Raja Ghanapathi of Tiruvidaimarudur, Thanjavur Dist.
MD 891. 4 pp. (45ff.). .... (= Skt. Texts on Phonetics, pp. 287-89).
MD 892. Tel. 13 pp. (100ff.)
(with C. of Muktīśvarācārya)................... (= Skt. Texts on Phonetics, pp. 267-79).
MD 16732. PL. Tel. 3 pp. 42 Grantha-s.
MD 16733. PL. Tel. 14 pp. 196 Grantha-s (with C.).
MT 95(j). PL. Gr. 5 fol. (35-39) (with C. of Muktīśvarācārya). Purchased in 1910-11 from Gopalaswami Ayyangar of Mannargudi.
MT 1165(j). PL. Tel. 1 fol. (no.66). Incomplete. Purchased in 1913-14 from Kashibhatta Subrahmanya Sastri of Vekanur, Krishna Dist.
MT 1165(k). PL. Tel. 6 fol. (67-72) (with C. of Muktīśvarācārya). Purchased in 1913-14 from Kashibhatta Subrahmanya Sastri of Vekanur, Krishna Dist.
MT 4818(a). PL. Gr. 1 fol. Presented in 1924-25 by the Secretary to the Trustees of Sri Yogi Parthasarathi Ayyangar's Charities, Triplicane, Madras.
Mysore I, p. 26.
Mysore ND II 3315 (P 4772/11). PL. Na. 3 fol. (4-6). Extract no. 95. Different ?
Mysore ND II 3316 (B 252/18). Gr. 3 fol. (125-27). Extract no. 96.
Mysore ND II 3317 (B 860/ 8). Gr. 4 fol. (71-74).
Mysore ND II 3318 (B 861/ 4). Gr. 4 fol.
Oppert I 965. Belonged to Viraraghava Tatacharyar, Head Master, Sanskrit School of Sathakopacharya, Kanchipuram, Chingelpet Dist.
Oppert I 7174. Belonged to Ivattur Nandikesvara Sastri of Vijayanagaram.
Oppert I 7536. Belonged to S. Kodanda Ramavadhana Pantulu of Vijayanagaram.
Oppert II 741. Belonged to Ghanapathi Shingaracharyar of Alasur, Madurantakam Taluk.
Oppert II 9017. Belonged to Ganapati Lakshminarayana Sastri of Tiruvadi, Thanjavur Dist.
Oppert II 9878. Belonged to M.Raja Ghanapathi of Mahadanapuram, Trichinapalli.
Tirupati SVUORI (3516a3). PL. Gr. 2 fol.

Tirupati SVUORI 1194 (4378j). PL. Gr. 7 fol. (58-64) (with C. of Muktīśvarācārya).

– C. Dīpikā of Muktīśvara or Muktīśvarācārya.

Beginning: (775)

कालनिर्णयम्। कालशिक्षा॥

प्रातिशाख्यादिशास्त्राणि मया वीक्ष्य यथामति।
वेदतत्त्वावबोधार्थमिह कालो निरूप्यते॥

श्रोतृबुद्धिमनःसमाधानार्थं प्रकरणे प्रतिपाद्यमर्थं दर्शयति -- इह कालो निरूप्यत इति। अनेन विषयो दर्शितः। निष्प्रयोजने प्रकरणे प्रेक्षावत्प्रवृत्त्यनुपपत्तेस्तत्सिद्ध्यर्थं स्वग्रन्थस्य प्रयोजनं दर्शयति -- वेदतत्त्वावबोधार्थमिति वेदस्य तत्त्वस्यावबोधो वेदतत्त्वावबोधः। तदर्थं वेदतत्त्वावबोधार्थम्। अनेनार्थज्ञानकामिनो ऽधिकारो दर्शितः। स्वग्रन्थस्य मूलं दर्शयति -- प्रातिशाख्यादिशास्त्राणीति। प्रतिशाखासंबन्धि प्रातिशाख्यमादिर्येषां शिक्षादिशास्त्राणां तानि प्रातिशाख्यादिशास्त्राणीति तद्गुणसंविज्ञानो बहुव्रीहिः॥

End:

यदि स्वरव्यञ्जनयोर्मध्ये ऽपि विरामकालः स्यात् तदा तदिति पदं प्लुतेन समकालं गम्यते। पगततत्प्रवमहाभाष्यकारेणोक्तस्य विरामकालः स्यात्। अवकाशो नान्यत्रेति निर्णयार्थमृग्विरामादौ महाभाष्यकारेणोक्तो विरामकालो ऽधिक इत्यर्थः। श्रावण्यां पौर्णमास्यामित्यादिखण्डत्रयेण यो ऽनध्यायः समुद्दिष्टः स तत्रैवावधार्यताम्। श्रावण्यां पौर्णमास्यामित्यादि खण्डत्रयेण सूत्रे यो ऽनध्यायः समुद्दिष्टः सो ऽपीह विरामकाल एव॥ इति श्रीमुक्तीश्वराचार्यकृतौ कालनिर्णयदीपिका समाप्ता॥

Adyar D I 774 (22 E 25 = 69758). PL. Gr. 8 fol. (13ff.).
Adyar D I 775 (29 K 20 = 73653). PL. Tel. 10 fol. (158ff.). = Adyar I, p. 52b.
Baroda 11949(a). PL. Tel. 14 fol. 200 Grantha-s (with text). = CLB I, p. 26.
Baroda 12755(a). Gr. 5 fol. 120 Grantha-s (with text). = CLB I, p. 26. Incomplete.
BHU B 3904b (D 11/654). 7 fol. (3-9). Title: Mātrā-kāla.
Hoshiarpur p. 50 (no.3556). 8 fol. 200 Grantha-s (with text). Incomplete.
MD 892. Tel. 13 pp. (100ff.). .... (= Skt. Texts on Phonetics, pp. 267-79).
MD 16733. PL. Tel. 14 pp. 196 Grantha-s (with text).
MT 95(j). PL. Gr. 5 fol. (35-39) (with text). Purchased in 1910-11 from Gopalaswami Ayyangar of Mannargudi.
MT 1165(k). PL. Tel. 6 fol. (67-72). Purchased in 1913-14 from Kashibhatta Subrahmanya Sastri of Vekanur, Krishna Dist.
Mysore I, p. 26 (3 Mss.).
Mysore ND II 3319 (B 861/ 5). Gr. 20 fol. Extract no. 97.
Oppert II 742. Belonged to Ghanapathi Shingaracharyar of Alasur, Madurantakam Taluk.
PUL II. App. p. 11 (no.157). 6 fol.
Tirupati SVUORI 1194 (4378j). PL. Gr. 7 fol. (58-64) (with text).

Ujjain I, p. 10 (no.1459). 18 pp.

[NCC IV 29b]

461 KĀLA-ŚIKṢĀ or KĀLANIRṆAYA (कालशिक्षा / कालनिर्णय)

Adyar I, p. 52b (29 K 20 = 73653) → C. on the Kālanirṇaya-śikṣā.

[NCC IV 37a]

*KUPPĀŚĀSTRIN (कुप्पाशास्त्रिन्)

Also called Veṅkaṭācala-śarman.

– Svarāvadhāna.

*KUMĀRA (कुमार)

Alias Viṣṇumitra, son of Devamitra of Vatsa-gotra of Campā.

– Udāharaṇa-mālikā (or -maṇḍitā) on the Ṛgveda-prātiśākhya. BORI D I i.56. RASB II 270. See NCC III 12a.

[NCC IV 200b]

*KUMĀRASVĀMIN (Vedamitra ?) (कुमारस्वामिन् (वेदमित्र)

– Prātiśākhya.

Oppert II 7260. Belonged to Jambunatha Sastri of Nallucheri, Thanjavur Dist.

Oppert II 7401. Belonged to Venkatarama Sastri of Pillur, Mayavaram Taluk.

Oppert II 7963. Belonged to Venkatarama Dikshita of Sorakayur, Thanjavur Dist.

Oppert II 8662. Belonged to Venkatarama Sastri of Timmagudi near Kumbakonam.

Oppert II 9060. Belonged to Ganapati Lakshminarayana Sastri of Tiruvadi, Thanjavur Dist.

Oppert II 9882. Belonged to M.Raja Ghanapathi of Mahadanapuram,

Cf. Ṛgveda-prātiśākhya-vyākhyā (NCC III 12a) of Viṣṇumitra alias Kumāra.

[NCC IV 222a]

462 KUMBHAKARṆA-BHEṬ (कुम्भकर्णभेद्)

Seems to be the same as the Anta-nirdeśī.

MT 485(o). PL. Tel. 2 fol. (68-69). dhṛṣṭir ... ekānnaṣaṣṭiḥ Presented in 1910-11 by C. Visvanatha Shastrigal of Viziyanagaram. Cf. Adyar D I 724.

MT 1205(c). PL. Tel. 3 fol. (13-16). Presented in 1913-14 by K. Ramakrishnayya of Musalipattanam.

MT 3887(j). PL. Gr. 2 fol. (84-85). See remarks. Purchased in 1921-22 from Annasvami Sastrigal, Bhavani, Coimbatore Dist.

MT 4600(a). PL. Gr. 3 fol. (1-3). Presented in 1924-25 by the Secretary to the Trustees of Sri Yogi Parthasarathi Ayyangar's Charities, Triplicane, Madras.

[NCC IV 229a]

*KṚṢṆA-KAVI (कृष्णकवि)

– Svara-melana. Vedic phonetics. Adyar. MT 2284.

[NCC IV 293a]

*KṚṢṆA-DATTA (कृष्णदत्त)

Son of Brahmadatta.

– C. on Caraṇa-vyūha. Oudh III 8.

*KṚṢṆADĀSA (कृष्णदास)
– C. on Atharva-veda-prātiśākhyā – Caturadhyāyikā Śaunakīyā.
VSM I 808 (no.4179). 36 fol. Extract p. 360. (Atharva-kautsa-vyākaraṇa).

463 KṚṢṆA-YAJUḤ-PRĀTIŚĀKHYA (कृष्णयजुःप्रातिशाख्य)
SBD 2135. Tel. 13 fol. → Taittirīya-prātiśākhya.

464 KṚṢṆA-YAJURVEDĪYA-GHANA-SAṂDHI (कृष्णयजुर्वेदीयघनसंधि)
on the datails connected with the particular Vedic recitation, known as Ghana.

Ptd.: ed. by Kadathur Ramayya Shastri (in Grantha script) (Kadathur rāmayyāśāstriṇā saṃgṛhya saṃskṛtaḥ). – Tiruvadi (Udamalpet Tq.) : Brahmananda Press (Sri Vag Vilas Book Depot), 1911. 144 pp. (Sri Vagvilasa Series) [IO : Ptd. Bks. Cat. 1953, p. 1395 (San B 61)]

465 KṚṢṆA-YAJURVEDĪYA-PRĀTIŚĀKHYA (कृष्णयजुर्वेदीयप्रातिशाख्य)
Ānandāśrama 7526 → Taittirīya-prātiśākhya.

*KṚṢṆA-SŪRI (कृष्णसूरि)
– Kāṇva-śākhā-māhātmya. BORI 55 of 1902-07. 62 fol.
– Veda-tattva-nirūpaṇa (or Nirṇaya). BORI TM 102A. MT 2359.
[NCC V 2b]

*KṚṢṆĀCĀRYA (कृष्णाचार्य)
– Svara-pradīpikā. Oxf. CS d.73. 36 fol. Dated A.D. 1798.

*KṚṢṆĀNANDA SARASVATĪ (KAIVALYADHĀMA)
(कृष्णानन्दसरस्वती कैवल्यधाम)
– Vaidika-paddhati.

*KEŚAVA (केशव)
– Lakṣaṇa-mālā. TCD 28 (with a C.). Triv. Cur. II 2.
Cf. Keśava, author of the *Sarva-saṃmata-śikṣā*
[NCC V 62a]

*KEŚAVA MĀṬE (केशव माटे)
Son of Bhāskara.
– Ṛgveda-kalpa-druma.

*KEŚAVA-RĀMA DAIVAJÑA (केशवराम दैवज्ञ)
of the Āstika-gotra, son of Daivajña Gokula-candra.

– Keśavī-śikṣā I. Commentary on the Paribhāṣāṅka-sūtra.
– Keśavī-śikṣa II in 21 verses.
[NCC V 69a]

466 KEŚAVA-(VĪ-)ŚIKṢĀ (1) (केशवशिक्षा)
Unspecified.
Bhau Dāji 124.

N-W P V 150 (no.44). 7 fol.
RASB II 1515 (G 2815). Beng.

[NCC V 69b]

467 KEŚAVA-(VĪ-)ŚIKṢĀ (2) (केशवशिक्षा)

of Keśava-rāma Daivajña, son of Daivajña Gokulacandra. The work is in the form of a gloss on nine Sūtra-s called *Paribhāṣāṅka-sūtra* also known as the *Mādhyandinīya-veda-paribhāṣāṅka-sūtra.* There are six Kārikā-s as a summary at the end of the commentary. The Sūtra-s are ascribed to Kātyāyana in some Mss. (cf. col. in RASB II 1511) and to Mādhyandina in others. See F. Kielhorn : Remarks on the Śikṣās in : *Indian Antiquary,* vol. V, pp. 193-94 (reprint in : *Kleine Schriften,* vol. I, pp. 158-69). *Indische Studien,* vol. XIV, p. 160.

Beginning:

नत्वा गणपतिं देवं परिभाषाङ्कसूत्रकम्।
उच्यते केशवेनेदं वेदाध्यायिसुखाप्तये॥ १॥

तत्रादौ माध्यन्दिनीयपरिभाषाया अङ्कानां नवानां सूत्राणां मध्ये येन सूत्रेण पदादिमध्यान्तवर्णेषु संज्ञा जायते तद्विना पदादिवर्णेष्वेव संज्ञा न जायते तत्रोच्यते -- पदादौ पूर्वाहल्वोर्द्विर्व्योचारौ संपूर्वयोश्छन्दसि।

End:

नवानामपि सूत्राणां षण्मिताः कारिकास्त्विमाः।
केशवेन कृतास्ता स्युर्वेदाध्ययनबोधकाः।
परिभाषाङ्कसूत्रं च याजुर्वेदं सकारिकम्।
दैवज्ञकेशवेनेदं कृतं हस्तस्वरान्वितम्।
ह्रस्वोदात्तादिभिर्भेदैः सहस्तस्वरलक्षणम्।
शिक्षादिभिः षडङ्गैश्च विज्ञेयं वेदपाठकैः॥ १३॥

इति श्रीदैवज्ञकेशवकृता प्रतिज्ञासूत्रानुसरिणी केशवी शिक्षा समाप्ता॥

Adyar D I 776 (35 C 62 = PM 108). 10 fol. = Adyar I, p. 52b.
BBRAS 3 (B D 280). 4 fol. Dated Śaka 1787.
Berlin StB-PrK (NGMPP). A 596/24. 5 fol. Title: Mādhyandinīyavedaparibhāṣāṅkasūtra.
Berlin StB-PrK (NGMPP). A 596/25. 7 fol. Title: Mādhyandinīyavedaparibhāṣāṅkasūtra.
Berlin StB-PrK (NGMPP). E 533/8. 9 fol. Title: Paribhāṣā-(ṅka-)sūtra. Dated V.S. 1958 (microfilm dated 23.05.1978).
Berlin StB-PrK (NGMPP). E 1173/26. 4 fol. (first fol. is missing). Title: Mādhyandinīya-veda-paribhāṣāṅka-sūtra. (microfilm dated 03.03.1981).
Berlin StB-PrK (NGMPP). T 22/8. 7 fol. Title: Mādhyandinīya-paribhāṣāṅka-sūtra. (microfilm dated 11.05.1982).
Bombay Uni. 2 (BMC 50 9). 10 fol. Copied by Hara-bhaṭṭa Lulyāna.
Bombay Uni. 3 (BMC 73 13). 6 fol. Copied by Śaṃkara, son of Viśvanātha.
Bhk. 9 (with C.).
BORI 55 of A 1881-82. 7 fol.

GJKSV 9101/7. (D II 2, no.8820). 30 fol. Maithili script.

GJKSV 22133. 6 fol.

GB 24. 4 fol. See F. Kielhorn : Remarks on the Śikṣās in : *Indian Antiquary*, vol. V, p. 193 (reprint in : *Kleine Schriften*, vol. I, pp. 158-69).

Harshe p. 46.

Hoshiarpur p. 52 (no.121). 4 fol. 75 Grantha-s. Title: Paribhāṣāṅka-sūtra-vyākhya. Dated V.S. 1926.

IM 2505A. 10 fol.

IM 5152A. 4 fol. Dated V.S. 1825.

IM 5307. 8 fol.

L 1238. 5 fol. 75 Grantha-s.

L 2670. 9 fol. 156 Grantha-s.

Mithila IV 97. 5 fol.

Mithila IV 97(A)-(R). (18 Mss.)

Oxf. CS d.185(9). 6 fol.

PUL I, p. 20 (no.45). 11 fol. 120 Grantha-s.

RASB II 1511 (G 667) = L 1238.

RASB II 1512(I) (G 3259). 6 fol. 150 Grantha-s. Dated V.S. 1939.

RASB II 1513 (G 2504). 8 fol. 140 Grantha-s (with C.).

SB p. 54 (no.97). 7 fol. 126 Grantha-s. SBD 47216.

SB p. 54 (no.268). 5 fol. 135 Grantha-s. = SBD 2014.

SBD 2014. 5 fol.

SBD 47252. 7 fol.

SBD 47722. 8 fol. (1-2, 1-2, 5-7). Incomplete. The Ms. includes : Pratijñā-sūtra (1a), Paribhāṣāṅka-sūtra - 9 Sūtra-s alone (1b), 6 Kārikā-s (2b), the Sūtra-s with C. (1-2, 5-7).

SBD 55435. 12 fol. Dated V.S. 1952. (Paribhāṣaṅka-sutra).

SBD 55912. 6 fol. Attributed to Keśava. (Paribhāṣaṅka-sutra).

SBD 55913. 4 fol. Incomplete. (a. Keśava). (Paribhāṣaṅka-sutra).

Trav. Uni. 2057 A. 1 fol. 55 Grantha-s. Title: Veda-paribhāṣāṅka-sūtra.

Ptd.: in Śikṣā-saṃgraha. – Benares, 1889, pp. 138-49. – (Ben. S. S. 10).

[NCC V 69b]

468 KEŚAVA-(VĪ-)ŚIKṢĀ (3) (केशवशिक्षा)

Also called *Kārikāvalī* or *Padyātmikā Śikṣā* of Keśava-rāma Daivajña, son of Daivajña Gokulacandra. 21 verses dealing with the methods of indicating accents with fingers, pronunciation of "y", "r", "l", etc.

Beginning:

अनुदात्तादुदात्तश्चेत् स्वरितोत्तर एव च।
हृच्छिरःकर्णमूलेषु न्यसेद्धस्तमसंशयम्॥ १॥
अनुदात्तादुदात्तश्चेदनुदात्त परस्तथा।
अनुदात्तं हृदि न्यस्योदात्तं वामभ्रुवि न्यसेत्॥ २॥
पुनर्हृदि न्यसेन्नीचमिति शास्त्रव्यवस्थितिः।

End:

ईषद्दीर्घतयोच्चारः कात्यायनमुनेर्गिरा।
आस्तिकस्य मुनेर्वंशे जातो दैवज्ञगोकुलः ॥ २० ॥
तत्सुतेन केशवेन कृता सम्यक्शुभाप्तिनाम्।
प्रीत्यर्थं सुधियां कारिकावली निर्मला शुभा ॥ २१ ॥

इति आस्तिकमहर्षिवंशोद्भव दैवज्ञगोकुलचन्द्रसुत दैवज्ञकेशवरामकृता कारिकावली समाप्ता ॥

RASB II 1516(1) (G 3260). 2 fol. 18 Grantha-s.
SBD 48294. 1 fol.

Ptd.: in Śikṣā-saṃgraha. – Benares, 1889, pp. 150-52. – (Ben. S. S. 10).

[NCC V 70a]

*KEŚAVĀCĀRYA (केशवाचार्य)
– Uccodarkī. Adyar D I 747. See above Uccodarkī.

[NCC V 71b]

*KEŚAVĀCĀRYA (केशवाचार्य)
– C. on the Pratijñā-sūtra.

*KEŚAVĀRYA (केशवार्य)
Son of Sūra-sūri or Sūryadeva-budhendra.
– Sarva-saṃmata-śikṣā. Adyar D I 1040. IO 4956-62. MD 996-99.

Ptd.: ed. by A. O. Franke, Göttingen 1886 (only a portion). See below under Sarva-sāṃmata-śikṣā.

[NCC V 74a]

469 KAIŚAVĪ-ŚIKṢĀ (कैशवी शिक्षा)
IM 5152A. 4 fol. → Keśavī-śikṣā.

[NCC V 83a]

470 KOVAM or KOVAḤ (कोवम् / कोवः)
→ Ṛgveda-śṛṅkhalā.
Lucknow ABSP. 258 (acc. no. 4542). 6 fol. 180 Grantha-s.

*KAUṆḌINYA (कौण्डिन्य)
Authority on Grammar, referred to in the *Taittirīya-prātiśākhya*, 5.38 and its commentary *Tribhāṣya-ratna*, 18.3, 19.2 (see JAOS. VII, p. 405).

[NCC V 104a]

*KAUṆḌINYA (Sthavira) (कौण्डिन्य स्थविर)
Authority on Grammar, referred to in the *Taittirīya-prātiśākhya*, 17.4, and commentary thereof 5.39-41 (see JAOS. VII, p. 405).

[NCC V 104a]

471 KAUṆḌINYA-ŚIKṢĀ (1) (कौण्डिन्यशिक्षा)
Referred to in the commentary on the *Śikṣā-samuccaya*, TCD 32-B.

[NCC V 104b]

472 KAUṆḌINYA-ŚIKṢĀ (2) (कौण्डिन्यशिक्षा)

Consists of 100 verses. This work was known up to now only from references. According to G. V. Devasthali, K. V. Abhyankar discovered a Ms. in a private collection in Hyderabad. The Ms. was quite corrupt and unintelligible in several places, and the text has been edited with conjectural emendations. The Osmania University edition, which contains even more corrupt readings, appears to be based on the same Ms.

Beginning: (Abhyankar)

वागीशादिसुरान् सर्वान् कृतार्थान् कर्तुमादिशत्।
वटमूले यदाभाति तस्मै चिन्महसे नमः ॥
अधीत्य संहितां पूर्वं पदक्रमजटाघनान्।
शिक्षादिशास्त्राध्ययनं कुर्यात् कौमारसंयुतम्॥

End:

लक्षणं यो न ना वेत्ति न तस्य फलभाग् भवेत्।
लक्षणज्ञो हि विप्राणां सकलं भद्रमश्नुते॥
आचार्योपासनाद्योगात् तपसः प्राज्ञसेवनात्।
विविच्य कथनात् कालात् षड्भिर्विद्या प्रपद्यते॥

Ptd.: ed. by K. V. Abhyankar and G. V. Devasthali, in : *Veda-vikṛti-lakṣaṇa-saṃgraha*. – Poona : BORI, 1978, pp. 113-23.

Also ed. by Ramachandrudu, in : *Journal of the Sanskrit Academy*. – Hyderabad : Osmania University, 1980. 12 pp.

473 KAUṆḌINYA-ŚIKṢĀ (3) (कौण्डिन्यशिक्षा)

Different from the above. 86 verses dealing with different topics regarding the *Taittirīya-saṃhitā* as the *Sarva-saṃmata-śikṣā*. Called Kauṇḍinya-śikṣā Ṣaḍaśīti in the colophon.

Beginning:

एकश्रुतिं क्वचिद् विन्यात् क्वचिच्च विहितं स्वरम्।
स्वरभक्तिः स्वतन्त्रा च व्यञ्जनस्याङ्गमन्यथा॥
वर्णो ऽन्यो वा स्वरो ऽन्यो वा पञ्चप्रश्नेषु दृश्यते।
आरण्यादौ द्वयोश्चान्ते त्रिषु चैवं विधीयते॥

End:

अधीतमपि यो वेदं (वि)मुञ्चति यदा नरः ।
भ्रूणहा स तु विज्ञेयः वियोनिमधिगच्छति॥
नित्यस्वाध्यायशीलत्वं दया सत्यं च संयमः ।
तेन शुद्धिमवाप्नोति देवत्वं चाधिगच्छति॥

Mysore ND II 3322 (P 4772/14). PL. Tel. 5 fol. (10-14). Extract no. 100.

474 KAUTSA-VYĀKARAṆA (कौत्सव्याकरण)

→ Atharva-veda-prātiśākhya = Caturādhyāyikā Śaunakīyā. Ascribed to Kautsa [illegible] Mss. (e.g. SBD 2086, Ujjain II, [illegible] VSM I 808 and 811)

[NCC V 107a]

475 KAUTHUMA-PARISIṢṬA (कौथुमपरिशिष्ट)

SV. This comprises among others, Ṛksaṃkhyā(-pariśiṣṭa), Chalaprakriyā, Hitavākya and Avagraha-pariśiṣṭa.

PUL I, p. 131 (no.18). 10 fol. 200 Grantha-s.

[NCC V 107a]

476 KAUŚIKA-MANTRĀNUSĀRIṆĪ-ŚIKṢĀ (कौशिकमन्त्रानुसारिणी शिक्षा)

This is probably a misprint in the NCC for Kauśika-matānusāriṇī Śikṣā, also called Kauśikī-śikṣā.

IM 2025. 4 fol. (2-5). Incomplete. Cf. Kauśikī-śikṣā below.

[NCC V 116b]

477 KAUŚIKĀCĀRYA-ŚIKṢĀ (कौशिकाचार्यशिक्षा)

The same as the next.

ASB I iii.36 (III G 71). 5 fol. 50 Grantha-s. Dated V.S. 1926 = A.D. 1869. Copy of a Ms. dated V.S. 1833.

478 KAUŚIKĪ-ŚIKṢĀ (कौशिकी शिक्षा)

Also called Kauśikācārya-śikṣā or Kauśikācārya-matānusāriṇī Śikṣā.

Beginning:

द्वैधे चैव समुत्पन्ने लक्षणान्निर्णयो भवेत्।
लक्षणं न विनाशि स्यात् संप्रदायो विनाशवान्॥ १॥
अग्नेरनीकं युक्ष्वा हि विश्वे देवा द्वितीयकः।
उदग्ने अयमुत्तरान्नमो वन्ये निदर्शनम्॥ २॥

End:

एवं वर्णाः प्रयोक्तव्या इमं मेति निदर्शनम्।
यत्र यत्र तुरङ्गः स्याद् द्वेषार्धेपो जपेद् बुधः॥
करेण ताडितस्याङ्गं तद्वत् कालेषु रङ्गयोः।
अहीनप्रहारोङ्गः? यथा आ ई ऊ इति निदर्शनम्॥

ASB I iii.36 (III G 71). 5 fol. 50 Grantha-s. Dated V.S. 1926 = A.D. 1869. Copy of a Ms. dated V.S. 1833. Title: Kauśikācārya-śikṣā.

IM 2025. 4 fol. (2-5). Title: Kauśikācāryamatānusāriṇī Śikṣā.

L 134. 5 fol. 80 Grantha-s. Dated V.S. 1826. Col.: Kauśikākācarya-matānusāriṇī Śikṣā. Noticed by Kielhorn : *Indische Studien*, vol. XIV, p. 160.

[NCC V 118b]

479 KAUHALA-ŚIKṢĀ or KAUHALĪYA-ŚIKṢĀ (कौहलशिक्षा / कौहलीयशिक्षा)

Attributed to Kauhaleya. A manual of about 80 verses on Vedic accents following the teaching of Kauhal(a)i. The verse 55 (?) is quoted by the *Vaidikābharaṇa* (on *Taittirīya-prātiśākhya.* V 14). Quoted in an anonymous commentary on the *Siddhānta-śikṣā* of Śrīnivāsa. See F. Kielhorn : Remarks on the Śikṣās in : *Indian Antiquary,* vol. V, pp. 193-200 (reprint in : *Kleine Schriften,* vol. I, pp. 158-69). See also IO 4964 (Kāhala). All available Mss. have numerous common lacunae found in the printed edition.

Beginning:

अथ शिक्षां प्रवक्ष्यामि कौहलीयमतानुगाम्।
स्वरादिनिर्णयस्तत्र क्रियते तन्निबोधत॥
उदात्तश्चानुदात्तश्च स्वरितः प्रचयस्तथा।
इति चत्वार एवेह स्वराः प्रोक्ता मनीषिभिः॥
उच्चैरुच्चार्यते यस्तु स उदात्त उदाहृतः।

End:

औष्मस्वरान्ते चाप्येवं निपुणं तन्निबोधत।
अत्र धीर्विद्यते यः स तद्विदां प्रथमो भवेत्॥
शास्त्रमेतत् ततः सर्वमृषिरस्य प्रसीदति।
शिक्षामिमां तु यो ऽधीते वेदतत्त्वप्रकाशिकाम्।
अतुलामश्नुते कीर्तिं परत्रेह च शाश्वतीम्॥

Adyar D I 777 (1 A 19 = TR 19). Gr. 9 fol. (pp. 3-19). = Adyar I, p. 52b.
Adyar D I 778 (23 E 25 = 69758). PL. Gr. 7 fol. (35-41).
Hamburg StUB (cod.Palmbl. III 8/133) → Veda-lakṣaṇa (HB).
MD 893. 12 pp. (49ff.). .... (= Skt. Texts on Phonetics, pp. 309-16).
Oppert I 970. Belonged to Viraraghava Tatacharyar, Head Master, Sanskrit School of Sathakopacharya, Kanchipuram, Chingelpet Dist.
Oppert II 744. Belonged to Ghanapathi Shingaracharyar of Alasur, Madurantakam Taluk.
Oppert II 2596. PL. Gr. 18 pp. Belonged to K. Ramappayya of Kumaralingam, Udamalapet Taluk, Coimbatore Dist.
Oppert II 5736. Belonged to Shingaracharyar of Kalyanapuram, Thanjavur Dist.
Oppert II 7364. Belonged to Venkatarama Sastri of Pillur, Mayavaram Taluk.
Oppert II 7947. Belonged to Venkatarama Dikshita of Sorakayur, Thanjavur Dist.
Oppert II 9458. Belonged to Srinivasa Sastri of Tiruvasalur, Kumbakonam Taluk.

Ptd.: ed. by Sadhu Ram, on the basis of MD 893, in : *Journal of Vedic Studies* (ed. by Raghu Vira), vol. II 1 (1935), pp. 108-20. [NL (180 Pb 93 17)]

Reprinted in : *Vedic Studies* – A Collection of the Research Papers of Prof. Raghuvira, ed. by Mrs. Sharada Rani. – New Delhi - 110016 (Hauzkhas Enclave), 1981, pp. 394-402. (Śata-Piṭaka Series – Indo-Asian Literatures, vol. 272). [Adyar (H080

SVS SP 272); NL (180 Jb 98 37); SAI (ind S 180, 272); UBTÜ (22 A 6435)]

– C. Vyākhyā.

Trav. Uni. L.1346 C. PL. Mal. 250 Grantha-s. Incomplete.

[NCC V 123a]

***KAUHALĪ-PUTRA (कौहलीपुत्र)**

Quoted in the *Taittirīya-prātiśākhya*, 17, 2 and in the commentary *Tribhāṣya-ratna*, V, 39-41. Cf. JAOS. VII, p. 405.

[NCC V 123a]

***KAUHALEYA (कौहलेय)**

Quoted in the *Tribhāṣya-ratna*, commentary on the *Taittirīya-prātiśākhya;* referred to in *Bhāradvāja-śikṣā* (see PUL II. App. p. 12). Cf. Kauhala-śikṣā and Kauhalī-putra.

[NCC V 123a]

480 KRAMA **(क्रम)**

on the recitation of the Saṃhitā, Pada, Krama, Jaṭā and Ghana, see Ramkrishna Gopal Bhandarkar: The Veda in India, *Indian Antiquary*, 1874 (May), pp. 133-35.

CPB 1103-04.

Oudh XIX 32 (no.2). 32 pp. 300 Grantha-s. Belonged to Pandit Gangadhara Vajapeyi of Unao.

[NCC V 124b]

481 KRAMA-KĀRIKĀ **(क्रमकारिका)**

Khn. p. 8 (no.20). 8 fol. ; from Ashṭe; Limaye. Cf. the next entry.

[NCC V 125a]

482 KRAMA-KĀRIKĀ(-ŚIKṢĀ) **(क्रमकारिका /-शिक्षा)**

of Śaṃbhu-miśra according to verse seven of the text. 93 Kārikā-s on the Krama recital of the *Śukla Yajurveda* (Kāṇva Śākhā). Also called Kāṇvaśikṣā and Kāṇvaśākhīyakrama-kārikā.

Beginning:

प्रणम्याद्यं दिनमणिं योगीश्वरशिरोमणिम्।
सर्वज्ञं याज्ञवल्क्यं तच्छिष्यं कात्यायनं मुनिम्॥ १॥
सर्वर्ग्याजुषमन्त्राणां वेदे वाजसनेयके।
क्रमावसानविषयां कारिकामारभामहे॥ २॥
श्लोके बिन्द्वादिरहितः प्रतीकेषु न दुःसहः।
प्रत्येकं प्रथमा षष्ठी सप्तम्युक्तश्च कल्पते॥ ३॥
पदानामानुपूर्व्येण क्रम एष प्रवर्तते।
गणान्तानां क्रमो नास्ति इति कात्यायनोऽब्रवीत्॥ ४॥
न वेष्ट्याश्च द्विवेष्ट्याश्च त्रिवेष्ट्याश्च तथापरे।
चतुर्वेष्ट्यो मध्यवेष्ट्यः पञ्चवेष्ट्य इतीरितः॥ ५॥
अवग्रहोऽनुवाकान्ते अर्धर्चान्ते ऋचां तथा।
यजुषां वाक्यावसानेष्विति साधारणो विधिः॥ ६॥

प्रत्यक्षं याज्ञवल्क्यं श्रीशंभुमिश्रविनिर्मिता।
क्रियतां क्रमितैः कण्ठैः कारिका रत्नमालिका॥ ७॥
ह्रस्वपूर्वो ह्यनुस्वारो दीर्घानुस्वारभाग् भवेत्।
द्विशःपरश्चेन्न तथा क्रमकाले तु वाजिनाम्॥ ८॥
इषे त्वेत्ययमध्यायो ह्यनुवाकान्तवेष्टनः।
गायत्रेण त्रिवेष्ट्यो ऽत्र पुरा क्रूरत्रिवेष्टनः॥ ९॥

End:

मखस्याश्वस्य नवैक्यं यमाय त्रितयैकता।
द्विवृद्दर्भो ऽनुवाकस्तु विश्वासान्त्यं विना त्रिवृत्॥ ८९॥
आददे चतुष्कैकं यस्ते द्विवृत्परो ऽन्तवृत्।
समुद्राय तद् द्वित्रैक्यं यमायेति द्विवेष्टनः॥ ९०॥
विश्वा आशाः पञ्चकैक्यं स्वाहा पूष्णे ऽनुवाकवृत्।
अभीमन्तु द्विवृद्या ते चतुष्कैक्यमृच्चि द्विवृत्॥ ९१॥
यावतीत्यनुवाकैक्यन्त्विषःसंवृगथान्तवत्।
स्वाहा प्राणानुवाकानामष्टानामनुवाकवत्॥ ९२॥
आवसाय युगैकत्वं यमायेत्यन्तवेष्टनः।
ईशावास्यमिदं सर्वं द्विवेष्ट्यं सर्वसंमतम्॥ ९३॥

इति क्रमकारिकाशिक्षा समाप्ता॥

Adyar D I 771 (36 B 11 = TR 21). 8 fol. (pp. 430-44). Title: Kāṇva-śākhīya-krama-kārikā. Copied by Rāmacandra Śāstrin and revised by Nārāyaṇa Śāstrin. Dated 7.6.18. Begins from verse 26 of the printed edition and other verses are in a different order. = Adyar I, p. 52a. Title: Kāṇva-śikṣā.

GJKSV 18175. 9 fol. Dated V.S. 1796 / Śaka 1661. Copied by Vāsudeva.

GJKSV 29266. 79 fol. Incomplete (with the Pada-pāṭha of the Śukla-yajurveda). Title: Vājasaneyi-kārikā.

IM 2517. 7 fol. (2-8). Incomplete. Col.: Ṛgyajuṣa-leṣa. (?)

MD 19510K. PL. Mal. 4 fol. (94-97).

Mithila IV 39. 4 fol.

Mithila IV 39(A). 4 fol.

RASB II 892 (G 6197). 5 fol. 52 Grantha-s. Title: Krama-ratna-mālikā.

Ptd.: in Śikṣā-saṃgraha. – Benares, 1889, pp. 369-77. – (Ben. S. S. 10).

[NCC V 125a]

483 KRAMA-KĀLA-KAMPA (**क्रमकालकम्प**)

SBD 4353. 1 fol. Dated V.S. 1792.

484 KRAMA-KĀLE DVIMĀTRA-KAMPA (क्रमकाले द्विमात्रकम्प)
Tirupati SVUORI (427f). PL. Na. Begins on fol. 45.

485 KRAMA-KĀLE DVIKAMPA-LAKṢAṆA (क्रमकाले द्विकम्पलक्षण)
→ Dvikampa-lakṣaṇa. Mysore ND II 3539.

486 KRAMA-KĀLE HRASVA-PADĀNI (क्रमकाले ह्रस्वपदानि)
Tirupati SVUORI (427d). PL. Na.

487 KRAMA-JAṬĀ-PAṬALA (क्रमजटापटल)
→ Jaṭā-paṭala of Hayagrīva.
ASB I ii.660 (IM 2485/3). 5 fol. 150 Grantha-s (together with 3 other works). Dated V.S. 1744 = A.D. 1687.
IM 2502. 3 fol. Dated V.S. 1740. Copied in Vārāṇasī.
IM 2485C. 2 fol. (4-5).

[NCC V 125a]

488 KRAMA-PAṬALA (क्रमपटल)
The tenth Paṭala of the *Ṛgveda-prātiśākhya*, edited separately by K. V. Abhyankar and G. V. Devasthali, with Uvaṭa's commentary, on the basis of two Mss. (BORI 9 of 1879-80 = BORI D I i.52 and BORI 11 of Viś. (1) = BORI D I i.56) and two printed editions (ed. by Mangal Deva Shastri, Allahabad, 1931; and by V. K. Varma, B H U. Banaras, 1970).

Ptd.: *Veda-vikṛti-lakṣaṇa-saṃgraha*. – Poona : BORI, 1978, pp. 124-33.

489 KRAMA-PĀṬHA (क्रमपाठ)
See also Vājasaneyi-saṃhitā-krama-pāṭha.
GJKSV 28492. 152 fol. (Pūrva-viṃśī); 116 fol. (Uttara-viṃśī).
GJKSV 38142. Title: Śukla-yajuḥ-krama-pāṭha.
SBD 52334. 60 fol. (4-33, 37-41, 44, 46-69). Incomplete.
SBD 53255. 5 fol. (37th ch. of VS).
SBD 53492. 20 fol. (1-15, 17-20, 1) of VS.
SBD 55338. 4 fol. (ch. 32 of VS).

490 KRAMA-PRAKARAṆA (क्रमप्रकरण)
Trav. Uni. 16408 Z8. PL. Mal. 8 Grantha-s.

491 KRAMA-MAṆI (क्रममणि)
Mysore I, p. 26. Cf. Mysore ND II 3376: Jaṭāmaṇi-vyākhyā.

[NCC V 127b]

492 KRAMA-MANTRA-SAṂGRAHA (क्रममन्त्रसंग्रह)
Skt. Coll. Ben. 1914-15, p. 2 (no.2419).

[NCC V 127b]

493 KRAMA-MĀLĀ (क्रममाला)
SBD 4387. 6 fol. Incomplete.

Trav. Uni. 5505. PL. Tel. 28 fol. 340 Grantha-s. Incomplete. The first two fol. have the Krama-mālā variety of the Vikṛti with illustrations and the rest of the Ms. contains Jaṭānyāya(-vicāra).

[NCC V 127b]

494 KRAMA-RATNA(-PARIBHĀṢĀ) (1) **(क्रमरत्न /-परिभाषा)**

Eight verses on the Krama-pāṭha.

Beginning: (MD)

गणनाथं नमस्कृत्य वक्ष्ये द्वादशलक्षणम्।
कादीनां पञ्चवर्गाणां वर्णैराद्यतृतीयकैः ॥ १॥
अष्टौ वर्गा यरलवैः शसहैर्ङनमैरिह।
वर्गाद्यवर्णाः सूक्तादिर्ऋक्संख्या वर्णयोगतः ॥ २॥

End:

क्रमात् पद्यपदं तस्या ज्ञेया अपि निगद्यकाः ।
सभमाराद्यतामस्मात् केशवस्य मतं तथा॥ ८॥
इति क्रमरत्नपरिभाषा॥

IO 4249(2) (Mackenzie II 60b). PL. Na. 1 fol.

MD 14780(1). PL. Na. 2 fol. (76b-77a). This Ms. contains three different works. The beginning as given in the catalogue is that of the first work which contains eight verses and ends as given above. The second work consisting of 14 verses corresponds to the next entry. But the first line is different and begins with the remark: Anya-kramaratna-paribhāṣā. The third work is the (Krama-ratna-) Saptākṣarī-paribhāṣā.

Mysore ND II 3323 (P 5379/ 4). PL. Na./Tel. 2 fol. Extract no. 101.

– C. Ṭīkā in Kannada.

Mysore ND II 3324 (P 5379/ 5). PL. Tel. 2 fol. Extract no. 102.

[NCC V 127b]

495 KRAMA-RATNA(-PARIBHĀṢĀ) (2) **(क्रमरत्न /-परिभाषा)**

on the changes coming under Krama-vikṛti, of Ṛk-s in each Adhyāya of the eight Aṣṭaka-s of the *Ṛgveda*, in code words. 14 verses at the beginning furnish a clue to make out the technical language. The prose portion corresponds to the second series of paragraphs in the printed *Pada-ratna* of Srirangam edition.

Beginning: (TD)

विनायकं विधातारं(विरूपाक्षं) माधवं च शिवं गुरुम्।
(श्रियः पतिं नमस्कृत्य वेदव्यासं विनायकम्।)
नत्वेदं लक्षणं वक्ष्ये नाम्ना रत्नं क्रमस्य तु॥ १॥
कादीनां पञ्चवर्गाणां प्रथमाश्च तृतीयकाः ।
उ(ङ)शयोः षणवर्जाश्च वर्णाः स्युश्च त्रयस्त्रयः॥ २॥

चत्वारश्च कवर्गस्य लक्षणे ऽस्मिन् प्रवर्तकाः ।
सुक्तप्रतीको विज्ञेयो वर्गाणामादिवर्णतः ॥ ३॥
ऋक्संख्यामथ वर्गाणां वक्ष्ये संयोगभेदतः ।
कवर्गे च चवर्गे च क्रमाज्ज्ञेयौ समौ विषौ ...
विषमौ वा समौ वा द्वौ यत्र यत्रान्यथा परे॥ १३॥
अकाराद्यास्तु ये षट् ते कशयोर्विषमाः समाः ।
अकाराद्युक्तसंख्यायामभावे तु समं भवेत्॥ १४॥

इति क्रमरत्नपरिभाषा॥

अग्निमीळे। प ङौ टा ना। यो न्यु कि दि। कू डू टै नु। चा गी ङ डी। कू गो त्मी त्ये। म्लु ल्मि हू तु। व शु स ये। वे डी डू पु। द्नो दू ङ्नो चु द्ने॥

End:

त्यञ्चित्। ङ्ने वे यो क। पै शे कौ यु। पो ङै चा यु। शा क ख्से ख। क्के चु ङै ष्यु। य्मु चू के। न्क्रा तौ त कु। त्रौ तु श्यु चिप्। म्रुङ् ना द्लि पि। टे पु ये क। शु ङे क्सौ ह्र। ते मं स्को टौ। तू द्रे॥ इति क्रमरत्नं समाप्तम्॥

Baroda 14725. 7 fol. 90 Grantha-s.

Brl. p. 6 (no.V) = IO 4245.

Burnell 3b (2 Mss.).

Calcutta Skt. Coll. I 493B. (149). 2 fol. (2-3). 14 verses only. Col.: Krama-ratna-paribhāṣā. Title: Ṛgveda-paribhāṣā. Dated V.S. 1661.

Hz 1890. 5 fol. Belonged to Jambunatha Bhatta of Thanjavur.

IO 4245 (Burnell 205e). PL. Gr. 3 fol. (149-51). Paribhāṣā verses only.

MD 14780(2). PL. Na. 2 fol. (77a-77b). Paribhāṣā verses only. Title: Anya-kramaratna-paribhāṣā.

SBD 47915. 4 fol. Contains explanations of the paribhāṣā verses.

TD 1751. 8 fol. 86 Grantha-s.

TD 1752. 9 fol. 86 Grantha-s.

TD 1753. 5 fol. 86 Grantha-s.

[NCC V 127b]

496 KRAMA-RATNA-MĀLIKĀ (क्रमरत्नमालिका)

Śukla YV → Krama-kārikā-śikṣā.

RASB II 892 (G 6197). 5 fol. 52 Grantha-s.

[NCC V 127b]

497 KRAMA-RATNA-SAPTĀKṢARA (क्रमरत्नसप्ताक्षर)

on the Krama-pāṭha. Cf. Sapta-saṃkhyā, IO 61.

Beginning: (IO and Mysore)

अग्निमीळे। ङे। प। ङे घे सा ज त ङ्र घू द्रु चा। यदङ्ग। श। ह्रौ। घ ज घ घु ङ्कु की घी ॥ (सप्ताक्षरके निदर्शनम्। अग्निमीळे। ङे। प। घे। सा। ज। द्र। घु। दु। चा। यज्ञाङ्ग ?।

घ ज घ ... कि। धि।)

Calcutta Skt. Coll. I 493D. 63 fol. (4-66). Title: Ṛgveda-paribhāṣā. Dated V.S. 1661.
IO 4246 (Mackenzie II 60c). PL. Na. 79 fol. Col.: iti kramaratna-saptākṣaraṃ samāptam.
Mysore Skt. Coll. p. 1 = D. No.14 (846/7). PL. Na. 5 fol. (31-35). Title: Rāvaṇa-bhaiṭ.

[NCC V 127b]

498 KRAMA-RATNA-SAPTĀKṢARA-PARIBHĀṢĀ **(क्रमरत्नसप्ताक्षरपरिभाषा)**
of Gopāla. Also called *Saptākṣarī-paribhāṣā.* on the Krama-pāṭha of the *Ṛgveda.*

Beginning: (My)

विनायकं विधातारं माधवं च शिवं गुरुम्।
नत्वेदं लक्षणं वक्ष्ये नाम्ना रत्नं क्रमस्य तु॥
कादिक्षान्तैर्व्यञ्जनैश्च पञ्चविंशद्भिरक्षरैः।
अकाराद्यैः स्वरैश्चापि दशभिर्ऋ-ऌवर्जितैः॥

End:

ककाराद्यैर्यकारादीन् संयोज्य गणयेत् सुधीः।
नादीनां तु दशस्थाने नतमांश्च युजेत् क्रमात्॥
इदं सप्ताक्षरमितं लक्षणं तु पदादिभिः।
कृतं विंशतिसंख्याभिर्गोपालेन मयाधुना॥

इति क्रमरत्नसप्ताक्षरपरिभाषा॥

IO 4249(3) (Mackenzie II 60b). PL. Na. 2 fol. (3-4). Title: Saptākṣarī-paribhāṣā.
MD 14780. PL. Na. 2 fol. (77b-78b). Col.: Saptākṣarī-paribhāṣā.
Mysore ND II 3928 (C 3425/ 3). Na. 4 fol. (12-15). Extract no. 311. Title: Sapta-saṃkhyā-paribhāṣā.
Mysore Skt. Coll. p. 1 = D. No.6 (846/6). PL. Na. 3 fol. (29-31).

499 KRAMA-LAKṢAṆA (1) **(क्रमलक्षण)**
Lucknow Mus.
Venkatesiah 62.

[NCC V 127b]

500 KRAMA-LAKṢAṆA (2) **(क्रमलक्षण)**
of Bābhravya, mentioned in the Maṅgala-śloka of Narasiṃha's *Jaṭā-lakṣaṇa* or *Vikalpa-kaumudī.*

[NCC V 127b]

501 KRAMA-LAKṢAṆA (3) **(क्रमलक्षण)**
Mysore ND II 3325 (P 4906/61). PL. Na. 1 fol. Extract no. 103 (a fragment of the *Upalekha-sūtra ?).*

502 KRAMA-ŚIKṢĀ (क्रमशिक्षा)

A short gloss on the Krama section of the *Ṛgveda-prātiśākhya.*

Mysore ND II 3326 (P 4258/ 3). PL. Na. 2 fol. (22-23). Extract no. 104.

503 KRAMA-SAṂHITĀ (क्रमसंहिता)

Śukla YV Krama text. Alph. List Beng. Govt. p. 30. L 1803. L 1804 → Vājasaneyi-saṃhitā-krama-pāṭha.

[NCC V 128a]

504 KRAMA-SAṂKHYĀ-VYĀKHYĀ (क्रमसंख्याव्याख्या)

Mysore ND II 3327 (C 476/ 5). 1 fol. Incomplete. Extract no. 105.

505 KRAMA-SAṂCĀRA (क्रमसंचार)

The same as the next.

IM 2578. 3 fol. Dated V.S. 1734. Copied by Devacandra, son of Tulasīdāsa, in Kāśī. Col.: itiśrīmadvājasaneyi-saṃhitāyāṃ krama-saṃcāraḥ samāptaḥ |

[NCC V 128a]

506 KRAMA-SAṂDHĀNA(-ŚIKṢĀ) (क्रमसंधान /-शिक्षा)

A work enumerating the Saṃkrama-s in each chapter of the *Śukla Yajurveda.* Reciting a "pada" consecutively with another distant "pada", dropping the intervening "galita-pada" in the Krama-pāṭha. The number of "krama-saṃdhāna" has been fixed as 115. The whole text is found incorporated in the commentary called *Jyotsnā* on the *Vājasaneyi-prātiśākhya* (GB 18; fol. 42a-43a).

Beginning:

यथासमाम्नातं क्रमावसानं संक्रमेषु -- क्रमशास्त्रानुसारेण संधानं प्रोच्यते मया ॥ विश्वधाः परमेण। हार्षीच्छतधारम्। सहस्रधारं देवः। अधुक्षः सा। विश्वधाया इन्द्रस्य।

End:

ओं३ क्रतो। स्मर क्लिबे। क्लिबे कृतम्। ४०। इति चत्वारि चत्वारिंशाध्याये। इति पञ्चदशाधिकैकशतं क्रमसंधानानि। ११५। एभ्यो ऽन्यत्र संहितानुसारेण निर्णयः। इति क्रमसंधानशिक्षा समाप्ता॥

BORI 372 of 1883-84. = BORI D I i.26. 24 fol. It contains a different verse at the beginning:

प्रातिशाख्योक्तशिष्टं यदवसानादिसंक्रमम्।
नत्वा हरिहरौ देवौ मुनिना लिख्यते तत्॥

BP p. 286.

IM 2578. 3 fol. Col.: Krama-saṃcāra.

IM 2586. 3 fol. Incomplete. Title: Krama-saṃdhāna-pariśiṣṭa.

Lahore p. 2 (no.3). 4 fol. 35 Grantha-s. Title: Vājasaneyi-saṃhitā-karama-sṃdhāna. In the possession of Pt. Jwala Datta Prasada, Lahore.

RASB II 891 (G 6265). 2 fol. Col.: iti dākṣiṇātya-mate ....

SBD 4336. 4 fol.

Ptd.: in Śikṣā-saṃgraha. – Benares, 1889, pp. 176-80. – (Ben. S. S. 10).

[NCC V 128a]

507 KRAMA-HETU-PAṬALA (**क्रमहेतुपटल**)

The chapter on Krama in the *Ṛgveda-prātiśākhya* is referred to with this title in the *Ṛgveda-kalpadruma*. Cf. above under the Ṛgveda-kalpadruma.

508 KRAMĀVASĀNA-KĀRIKĀ (**क्रमावसानकारिका**)

of Śambhu-miśra → Krama-kārikā-śikṣā.

SBD 4203. 13 fol. Dated Śaka 1710.

SBD 4226. 3 fol. Incomplete. (Vājasaneya-kramāvasāna-kārikā).

509 KRAMOPALEKHA-PAÑJIKĀ (**क्रमोपलेखपञ्जिका**)

of Bharadvāja. The same as the *Upalekha(-sūtra)* ? Mandlik Sup. 204. Incomplete.

[NCC V 129a]

510 KRIYĀ-SVARA-LAKṢAṆA (**क्रियास्वरलक्षण**)

of Sūri-bhaṭṭa → Yajurveda-kriyā-svara-lakṣaṇa also known as the Yohi-bhāṣya.

Hz 1445. PL. Gr. 8 fol. Extract p. 136. Belonged to the late Raja Ghanapathi of Tiruvidaimarudur, Thanjavur Dist.

Mysore p. 2 (no. 57). 8 fol.

Mysore I, p. 612 (with C.).

Mysore ND II 3328 (P 4667). PL. Tel. 10 fol. Extract no. 106.

Ptd.: ed. by Pullela Sri Ramachandrudu (Kriyā Svara Lakṣaṇam or Yohibhāṣyam of Sūru Bhaṭṭa). – Hyderabad : Osmania University, 1983. xviii, 128, xxiv pp. – (Sanskrit Academy Series 30). The basic Ms. of this edition is apparently mixed with extraneous material. Thus, only pp. 1-10, 17-27, 86-128 are parts of this text. The rest is portions of Avarṇi (pp. 11-16, 28-56, 85) and Āvarṇi (pp. 57-84). Other Mss. including those of India Office, Madras and Mysore, collated for this edition do not contain these extraneous portions. [SAI (ind 50 B 187/726)]

511 KṢIPRA-(PRA-)BODHINĪ (**क्षिप्र-(प्र)बोधिनी**)

Name of the commentary of Bālakṛṣṇa on the *Ṛgveda-sarvānukramaṇī*.

Mysore ND II 3287.

***KHAGAPATI (खगपति)**

– Śābdabheda-nidarśana, in 12 verses. PUL I, p. 24.

[NCC V 170a]

***GAṄGĀDHARA-BHAṬṬĀCĀRYA (गङ्गाधरभट्टाचार्य)**

– C. Vikṛti-kaumudī on the Jaṭā-paṭala (part of Vikṛti-vallī).

512 GAṆANTA-VARJA(-LAKṢAṆA) (**गणन्तवर्ज /-लक्षण**)

Mysore ND II 3330 (P 4906/15). PL. Na. 1 fol. (115). Extract no. 107.

*GAṆAPATI ŚĀSTRIN (गणपतिशास्त्रिन्)
– C. called Mukura on the Vaidikābharaṇa. Ptd.: See below.

*GAṆEŚA (गणेश)
– Ṛgveda-pramāda-pāṭhāvalī. SBD 53275. 28 fol. Dated V.S. 1916.

*GAṆEŚA ḌOKALE (गणेशडोकले)
Son of Kṛṣṇa-bhaṭṭa and Rukmiṇī and brother of Mahādeva.
– C. Dīpikā on Kātyāyana's Ṛgveda-sarvānukramaṇī.
See NCC III 10b, 25a; IV 289a.

*GAṆEŚA-DATTA (गणेशदत्त)
– Saṃdhikārikā with C. Dīpakalikā. RASB II 1532.

[NCC V 272]

*GAṆEŚA PAṆḌITA (गणेशपण्डित)
– C. Phulla-pota on the Phulla-sūtra; called Sāma-prātiśākhya-bhāṣya in SBD 2121.

*GADĀDHARA-BHAṬṬA-SAUCE (गदाधरभट्टसौचे)
– C. Bhāṣya on Caraṇa-vyuha. Harshe p. 44.

[NCC V 295a]

*GARGA (गर्ग)
– Lomaśa-śikṣā. SV. IM 2510. IO 4954. Stein p. 39.

Ptd.: in Śikṣā-saṃgraha. – Benares, 1889, pp. 456-62. – (Ben. S. S. 10).

[NCC V 328a]

513 GALA-DĪPIKĀ (गलदीपिका)
→ Galita-pradīpa.
Peters. II, p. 168 (no.35). 8 fol.
PUL I, p. 20 (no.47). 9 fol. 78 Grantha-s.

514 GALADṚK-ŚIKṢĀ or LUPTARK-ŚIKṢĀ (गलदृक्शिक्षा / लुप्तर्क्शिक्षा)
In prose, with one verse at the end. It is identical with the second part of the *Mādhyandinī-śikṣā*.

Beginning:

इषे त्वाश्वस्तूपरः समिद्धो ऽअन्त् सहस्रशीर्षा पुरुषस्तदेव स्वाहा प्राणेभ्यश्चेत्येतेष्वध्यायेषु न गलित-ऋचः । द्वितीये ऽध्याये अग्नये ...

End:

एवं चतुःषष्टि-ऋचो विलुप्तौ एकादशोत्तरशतानि ऋचो ऽधिकाश्च ।
एवंकृते धृतिशतान्यपि संख्यकाश्च प्रोक्ताः समार्यैः खलु कण्डिकाश्च ।
इति लुप्तर्क्संख्यात्मिका शिक्षा समाप्ता ॥

Bik. 370. 34 fol. (Vājasaneya-śākhīya-).

BORI 2 of 1873-74. 6 fol. (1-6). At the beginning of Padajyoti Ms. From Bikaner. (A xerox-copy of this Ms. is in SAI : 87/790*).

Ptd.: in Śikṣā-saṃgraha. – Benares, 1889, pp. 181-84. – (Ben. S. S. 10).

[NCC V 338a]

515 GALITA-PRADĪPA or ṚGVEDA-GALITA-PRADĪPA or GALA-DĪPIKĀ

(गलितप्रदीप / ऋग्वेदगलितप्रदीप / गलदीपिका)

of (Bhāradvāja) Lakṣmīdhara-sūri of Candrapura, son of Nimbadeva and Bakāmbikā, and brother of Nāganātha. A work on words repeated in the *Ṛgveda* that are left out in the Pada-pāṭha. The printed text is divided into three parts: I. Paribhāṣā-prakaraṇa (8 verses). II. Galita-pariganaṇa (70 verses enumerating the Galita-s in the order of their occurence in the eight Aṣṭaka-s of the *Ṛgveda)*. III. Anukta-galita-saṃgraha. A few Mss. have 12 additional verses (cf. IM 2507; PUL I, p. 20, no. 47) which are given as a Pariśiṣṭa at the end of the printed edition.

Beginning:

प्रणम्य सच्चिदानन्दं सान्द्रमाद्यन्तवर्जितम्।
देवमृग्वेदगलितपदवृन्दं प्रवक्ष्यते ॥ १ ॥
अलक्ष्यत्वादनूह्यत्वाददृष्टानुविधानतः ।
अप्येषां प्रातिशाख्याद्यैरतः समयनामता ॥ २ ॥
ऋचो ऽखिला गलन्त्येव यथापूर्वं पुनर्गताः ।
नू मे ब्रह्माणि यज्ञेन विनैताभ्यामिति स्थितिः ॥ ३ ॥

End:

यस्ते जिघांसतीत्येकं प्रजां यस्ते जिघांसति।
यक्ष्मं चाज्मैष्टताश्वेदं विभ्राजं त्वं त्यमन्तिमम्॥
येन सर्वं विराजानि देवश्चापि मृगो न च
सं नो ऽपश्यं प्रजायस्व यो विश्वाभिदमित्यथ ॥ ६९ ॥
इमं गलितदीपाख्यं भारद्वाज ऋगर्थवित्।
लक्ष्मीधरो ऽकरोत् पूर्वं संप्रदायानुसारतः ॥ ७० ॥

BORI 14 of 1879-80. = BORI D I i.57. 8 fol. Dated V.S. 1577.

IM 2197. 2 fol. (10-11).

IM 2301. 7 fol. (2-8). Incomplete.

IM 2507. 7 fol. 78 verses. 12 verses (given as a Pariśiṣṭa in the printed edition) after the colophon with the words: atha galadīpikā-bhāṣye. The name of the author is given as Lakṣmī-nṛsiṃha.

IO 7839 (3738a). 15 pp. Copied from Berlin Ms. Chambers 791c (Weber 45), by J. Eggeling. Written ca. A.D. 1870

Jammu RSRI p. 22 (no.1208iii) (= Stein 45). Title: Ṛgveda-saṃhitāyāḥ Galānta-padam.

Müller 52 (MM 32). 92 fol. Dated V.S. 1661 (1604-05). Obtained through F. Edward Hall (21.04.1855).

Oxf. CS c.26(6). 7 fol. Paper dated 25.11.1903.
P 4.
Peters. II, p. 168 (no.35). 8 fol. Title: Galita-Dīpikā.
PUL I, p. 20 (no.47). 9 fol. 78 Grantha-s. Title: Gala-Dīpikā.
RASB II 290 (G 6060). 6 fol. 120 Grantha-s. Dated V.S. 1590. Col.: Galānta-dīpikā.
SBD 2069. 8 fol. Dated V.S. 1966. Title: Ṛgveda-galita-pradīpa.
SBD 2072. 12 fol. Incomplete. Dated V.S. 1611.
SBD 2073. 13 fol. Dated V.S. 1787.
Stein p. 4 (no. 45). 20 fol. Incomplete (3 fol. are lost). Dated V.S. 1570.
Weber 45 (Chambers 791c and 694). 12 fol. Ends with the second verse of the Pariśiṣṭa section. Dated V.S. 1714. Copied by Harirāma, son of Dīkṣita Rāmakṛṣṇa.

Ptd.: ed. by Sri Krishnadeva with his own Sanskrit commentary, in the Sanskrit Journal : *Sārasvatī Suṣamā,* 14.4 (Saṃ. 2016), Varanaseya Samskrita Vishvavidyalaya. – Varanasi 1960. ka-ja, 44 pp. – (Laghugranthararatnaprabhāvali 13). [Adyar (HO8O SBT 13); SAI (ind 51 D 987/1668*)]

– C. Bhāṣya of Lakṣmīdhara(?)
BORI 32 of 1884-86.
Peters. III, p. 385 (no.32). (Galita-dīpikā-bhāṣya in verse).

– C. Padāmnāya-siddhi of Nāganātha Paṇḍita, younger brother of Lakṣmīdhara.
Hall p. 134.
Müller 52 (MM 32). 92 fol. Dated V.S. 1661 (1604-05). Obtained through F. Edward Hall (21.04.1855).

[NCC V 338ab]

516 GALITA-LAKṢAṆA (गलितलक्षण)
In 12 verses.
PUL I, p. 20 (no.47). 1 fol.

[NCC V 338b]

***GAHVARA (गह्वर)**
Surname of the family of Rāma-bhaṭṭa (author of a commenatary on Kātyāyana's *Ṛgveda-sarvānukramaṇī),* son of Bālaṃ-bhaṭṭa.

[NCC V 339b]

517 GĀṆĪ (ŚĀKALA-SAṂHITĀYĀM) (गाणी / शाकलसंहितायाम्)
Gough p. 31.
RASB II 256. See Gānī.

[NCC V 340b]

518 GĀTHĀ-PAṬALA (गाथापटल)
Alph. List Beng. Govt. p. 32. This is a part of Vaidika-cchandaḥ-prakāśa of Gurjara Vināyaka, RASB II 1538 (G 1994).

[NCC V 341a]

519 GĀNI-LAKṢAṆA (गानिलक्षण)
A list of words, from the *Ṛgveda,* having some common characteristics, divided into five Adhyāya-s.

Ptd.: ed. by K. S. Venkatarama Sastri, in : *Ṛgveda-ghanasāra*. – Srirangam : Sri Vani Vilas Press, 1966. iii, ii, 92 pp. [Adyar (PH 215.1 x Ven RG); BORI (22257); SAI (87/771*)]

520 GĀNĪ (ŚĀKALA-SAṂHITĀYĀM) (गानी शाकलसंहितायाम्)

A concordance of words in the *Ṛgveda* of particular phonetic characters. Lists of words with slight vowel and consonant differences and the correct forms in their different occurences, e.g. *apasyavaḥ; apasyuvaḥ*. The text corresponds to some sections of the work called *Pada-gāḍha*. (Cf. pp. 22-40 of the *Pada-gāḍha*, Srirangam edition).

Beginning:

त्वं होता तोयमानां च मृष्वानिषीदस्येषमूर्जं यद् गोभिरिन्द्रो सुत इन्द्रो आ रत्नधा योनिमृतस्य सीदसि सप्त सीदसि।

End:

पश्यन्मन्ये मनसेति षट्चत्वारिंशद्येति व्यक्तयः । इति शाकलसंहितायां गानी समाप्ता।

IM 1808. 7 fol.
L 1302. 5 fol. 96 Grantha-s.
RASB II 256 (G 520) = L 1302.
Tirupati SVUORI (427c). PL. Na. 18 fol. (27-44).
VSM I 422 (no.3347). 6 fol. Dated Śaka 1714.

[NCC V 348b]

521 GĀYATRA-GĀNA-PRAKĀRA(-LAKṢAṆA) (गायत्रगानप्रकार /-लक्षण)

→ Ṛktantra-vivṛti.
Mysore II, p. 2.
Mysore ND II 3333 (P 4591/ 1). PL. Na. 13 fol. Extract no. 109.

[NCC V 349b]

522 GĀYATRA-VIDHĀNA(-SŪTRA) (गायत्रविधान /-सूत्र)

Ascribed to Śuṅga. on the use of Gāyatra-sāma, in three Kaṇḍikā-s. See R. Simon, WZKM. vol. 27, p. 321 fn. 2; also see W. Caland, *Jaiminīya-saṃhitā*, p. 15n.

Adyar D I 779 (33 E 12 = 75259). PL. Gr. 15 fol. (27-41) (with C.).
Baroda 92. 100 Grantha-s (with C.). = CLB I, p. 26.
Baroda 9805(d). PL. Gr. 3 fol. 40 Grantha-s. = CLB I, p. 26. Extract p. 140. Contains also Avagraha-sūtra.
Baroda 9916(c). PL. Gr. 9 fol. 250 Grantha-s (with C.). = CLB I, p. 26. Extract pp. 140-41.
Ben. 18.
IM 1970. 1 fol. Dated V.S. 1578.
IM 2190. 13 fol. (with C.). Dated V.S. 1616.
IM 3573. 9 fol. (with C.). Dated V.S. 1773.
IO 4324 (Burnell 4961). Gr. 5 fol. (with C.). Written ca. A.D. 1877.
Jammu RSRI p. 62 (no.5723). 24 fol. Incomplete. (Stein 252).
Mysore ND II 3334 (P 491/ 6). PL. Na. 1 fol. (108). Extract no. 110.

PUL I, p. 132 (no.24). 25 fol. 600 Grantha-s (with other 5 SV works).
SB p. 29 (no.36). 3 fol. 33 Grantha-s. = SBD 3940.
SBD 3940. 3 fol. (7-9). Dated V.S. 1720.
Stein p. 15 (no. 252) 24 fol. (with Bhāṣya).
Trav. Uni. 5185 B. 35 Grantha-s.
VOHD II 8.3043 (Ms.or.oct. 839. StaatsB-PrK, Berlin). 3 fol. (fol. 6-8 of the Ms. of Mātrā-vidhāna).

— C. Bhāṣya.

Beginning: (779)

पद्यो गायत्रस्य तद्विविड्ढा प्रस्तावः । इतीदं सूत्रम् । अत्र तु उपोद्घातं प्रति शास्त्रसमाम्नानारम्भः । प्रयोजनं वक्तव्यम् । किमिदं शास्त्रं किमर्थं च । किमर्थं च शास्त्रारम्भः शास्त्रे चास्य सूत्रस्येति -- उच्यते । गायत्रविधानं नाम परिशेषः । गायत्रं नाम साम । तस्येदं विधानं परिशेषसंज्ञकं । तस्येदमादिमं सूत्रम् । पद्यो गायत्रस्य । तदस्य गायत्रस्य साम्नो ब्राह्मणं निर्वचनाभिधायकं प्राणो गायत्रं तद्यदेतत्प्राणः संतनोति तस्माद् गायत्रामिति । तत्र साम्नाम् इदं विधानं परिशेषसंज्ञितम् । परीति सर्वतोभावे । शेषो शेषसर्वप्रयोगे तस्येदम्सूत्रम् । तत्रेव मुच्यते । किमेष ताण्डिके शेषः उत लक्षणे परिशेष इति । उच्यते । उभयशेषः । कथं गम्यते । यथा उभयशेष इत्युच्यते तच्छेषस्योभयोक्तस्य विधेरनुक्रमणाभावे तयोरुभयोरपि प्रवचनलक्षणयोः प्रचोदितस्य गायत्रस्य साम्नो यः शिष्यते विधिः स इहोक्तः । ताण्डिके तावत् इमे वै लोका गायत्रं त्र्यावृद् गेयमित्येवमादिना ब्राह्मणेन गायत्रस्य साम्नो नाममात्रं केवलं श्रूयते । सूत्रे च निदर्शनार्थं गानं गायत्रीषु द्रष्टुमुदीरितं च वैकारिकं च । तत्रैव किंचित् पाञ्चविध्यमुक्तं मात्राश्रितगायत्रस्य साम्नो यथालक्षेण गायत्रं पौष्कलमाग्नेयमिति । समाम्नायिकस्य आद्यस्यैव गायत्रस्य साम्नो वर्जयित्वा विधानमन्येषां पर्कादीनां विधानमुक्तम् ।

End:

तदिदमक्षरं पाद इति अन्तर्भवति अन्त उपान्त्यं नोपपद्यत इति उपान्तमेव पद्य आवृतो भवति तदापाशब्दः पशब्दमापद्यते । तदर्थमस्य ग्रहणम् । शौङ्गं गायत्रविधानं शौङ्गं गायत्रविधानम् । शुङ्गो नामाचार्यः । तेन शुङ्गेन कृतं गायत्रविधानं नाम सूत्रम् । गायत्रविधानभाष्ये तृतीया खण्डिका समाप्ता ।

Adyar D I 779 (33 E 12 = 75259). PL. Gr. 15 fol. (27-41). = Adyar I, p. 15a.
Baroda 92. 100 Grantha-s (with text). = CLB I, p. 26.
Baroda 9916(c) (with text). = CLB I, p. 26.
Ben. 18.
Hoshiarpur p. 50 (no.6134). 10 fol. 300 Grantha-s. Dated V.S. 1685. Extract p. 74.
IM 2190. 13 fol. (with text). Dated V.S. 1616.
IM 3573. 9 fol. (with text). Dated V.S. 1773.
PUL I, p. 132 (no.28). 15 fol. 250 Grantha-s. Title: Śoṅga-gāyatra-bhāṣya.

IO 4324 (Burnell 4961). Gr. 5 fol. (with text). Written ca. A.D. 1877.
Mysore I, p. 26.
Mysore ND II 3335 (C 1309). Gr. 10 fol. Extract no. 111.
SBD 4005. 7 fol. Incomplete.
Stein p. 15 (no. 252) 24 fol. (with text).

Ptd.: in the collection of Sāmavedic tracts, ed. by Krishnaswami Srauti (in Grantha script). – Kumbakonam : Jyotirvilasa Press, 1885, pp. 50-54. See Chala-prakriyā. [SAI (87/783*)]
Also ed. by B. R. Sharma, with commentary. – Hoshiarpur : Vishvesharanand Vedic Research Institute, 1971. xviii, 32 pp. – (Vishveshvaranand Indological Series 52). [Adyar (H080 VVRI I 52); UBTÜ (14 A 6881)]

[NCC V 349b]

523 GĀYATRĪ-GĀNA-LAKṢAṆA (**गायत्रीगानलक्षण**)
on chanting the Gāyatrī, forming part of *Sāmaveda.*

MD 894. PL. Gr. 13 pp. (68ff.). Only fol. 1a contains Gāyatrī-lakṣaṇa and fol. 1b-7a Akṣara-tantra with Bhāṣya. = Prapāṭhaka-s 1 and 2 of the Saṃjñā-(pra-)karaṇa Col.: Saṃjñā-prakaraṇa.
MD 895. Tel. 22 pp. (92ff.). Copy of MD 894 made in 1896.

[NCC VI 2a]

524 GĀYATRĪ-SVARA-LAKṢAṆA (**गायत्रीस्वरलक्षण**)
MD 896. PL. Gr. 2 pp.

[NCC VI 12b]

*GĀRGYA (**गार्ग्य**)
Ancient authority on grammar and etymology referred to by Yāska, Pāṇini, in the *Ṛgveda-prātiśākhya* (I 3.6, 10.11, 14.13, 12); in the *Vājasaneyi-prātiśākhya* (4, 164); considered to be the author of the Pada-text of the *Sāmaveda* (cf. Durga on *Nirukta* IV 4); also mentioned in the *Bṛhaddevatā* (I 26). See also Yudhisthira Mimamsaka, *Saṃskṛta Vyākaraṇa Śāstra kā Itihāsa,* part I, pp. 146-47; and *B. C. Law Volume* I, p. 342 for a discussion on his Pada-pāṭha.

[NCC VI 17a]

*GĀLAVA (**गालव**)
Name of Bābhravya Pāñcāla, said to be the author of the *Ṛgveda-krama-pāṭha.* Cf. *Mahābhārata,* Poona edition, Śānti-parvan, ch. 330, verses 37-38. A Śikṣā is also attributed to him there: *kramaṃ praṇīya śikṣāṃ ca praṇayitvā sa gālavaḥ.*

[NCC VI 18b]

*GIRINĀTHA (**गिरिनाथ**)
Son of Kolācala Mallinātha, brother of Kumārasvāmin and disciple of Nṛsiṃha (author of the *Svara-mañjarī).*

– C. Parimala on Svara-mañjarī of his teacher Nṛsiṃha. MT 3488(b).

525 GĪTIKALPA (**गीतिकल्प**)
SV. on the chanting of the Prastotṛ, by Rāma Śukla.

Baroda 2446(a). 2-7 fol. (first fol. missing). 100 Grantha-s. = CLB I, p. 26. Extract pp. 141-42.

Hoshiarpur p. 50 (no.6130). 6 fol. 150 Grantha-s. Dated V.S. 1713. Extract p. 74.

Stein p. 15 (no. 253). 8 fol. Dated V.S. 1681.

[NCC VI 42b]

*GOPĀLA (गोपाल)

– Pūrva-ṛkkārikā (composed together with Veṅkaṭeśa). Adyar D I 898. 899.

[NCC VI 132a]

*GOPĀLA (गोपाल)

– Sapta-saṃkhyā-paribhāṣā also called Sapākṣarī-paribhāṣā or Krama-ratna-saptākṣara-paribhāṣā.

Mysore ND II 3928 (C 3425/ 3). Na. 4 fol. (12-15). Extract no. 311.

*GOPĀLA-YAJVAN (Gārgya) (गोपालयज्वन् / गार्ग्य)

Son of Nṛsiṃha and disciple of Vādhūla Raṅgarāja.

– Vaidikābharaṇa on Taittirīya-prātiśākhya.

Ptd.: Mysore, 1906. – (Govt. Oriental Library Series 33).

[NCC VI 147b]

*GOPĀLĀRYA (गोपालार्य)

– Kramaratna-saptākṣarī-paribhāṣā. Mysore Skt. Coll. p. 1 = D. No.6.

[NCC VI 156b]

*GOBHILA (गोभिल)

– Naigeya-(sūtra). Oudh III 4. Oudh XIII 26 (no.12).

[NCC X 227a]

– Puṣpa-sūtra or Phulla-sūtra. Bikaner 645. 646.

[NCC VI 169b]

*GOVINDA (गोविन्द)

– Avasāna-dīpikā. Ujjain Latest Additions 527.

[NCC VI 190a]

*GOVINDA-SŪRI (son of Kṛṣṇa) (गोविन्दसूरि)

– Kāṇva-śākhā-veṣṭana-kramabodhinī. RASB II 914.

*GOSVĀMIN (Ṭumaṇi) see ṬUMAṆI GOSVĀMIN (गोस्वामिन् टुमणि)

[NCC VI 217b]

*GAUTAMA (गौतम)

Authority on Grammar mentioned in the *Taittirīya-prātiśākhya* V 38; *Maitrāyaṇīya-prātiśākhya* V.40; *Ṛgveda-prātiśākhya* II 23.28; *Mahābhāṣya* on VI 2.36.

[NCC VI 222b]

– Gautama-śikṣā. See below.

[NCC VI 224a]

526 GAUTAMA-ŚIKṢĀ or GAUTAMĪ-(YA-)ŚIKṢĀ (गौतमशिक्षा / गौतमीयशिक्षा)

A Śikṣā belonging to the *Sāmaveda* ascribed to Gautama. It is also called *Saṃyoga-śṛṅkhalā*. In two Prapāṭhaka-s of eight Khaṇḍa-s each.

Beginning:

अथ त्रयस्त्रिंशद् व्यञ्जनानि भवन्ति । स्पर्शान्तस्थोष्माणश्चेति । तत्र ककारादयो मकारान्ताः स्पर्शाः पञ्चविंशतिश्चत्वारो ऽन्तस्थास्ते यरलवाश्चत्वारश्चोष्माणस्ते हशषसाश्चेत्यनेकं व्यञ्जनम्। यत्रोपर्युपरि संयुक्तं तत् संयोगसंज्ञं भवति॥

End:

न सप्ताक्षरात् परः संयोगो भवति।

एषा सहस्रवर्त्मात्मा नानावृत्तिविभूषिता।
संयोगशृङ्खला नाम सामवेदनिबन्धनात्॥

Adyar D I 780 (35 C 114 = PM 109). 5 fol. Dated V.S. 1754 / Śaka 1619. = Adyar I, p. 52b.
Alwar 287.
BBRAS 13(III) (B D 278). Dated Śaka 1787.
BC. 496.
BORI 110 of 1879-80. 6 fol. 50 Grantha-s. Dated V.S. 1724.
CU Add. 1924.
Hamburg StUB (Oppert 45ā). PL. Gr. 3 fol.
Haug p. 30 (no.79a) = München 164.
IM 1847. 5 fol.
IM 2321. 2-5 fol. Incomplete.
IM 2510B. 5 fol. (16-20). Dated V.S. 1833.
IM 5155. 2 fol.
IO 4943 (Burnell 496c). Gr. 4 fol. (14-17). Dated A.D. 1877.
Jammu RSRI p. 172 (no.5238kha). 3 fol. (22-24). (Stein 785).
MD 15644. 8 pp. (20ff.). 44 Grantha-s. Incomplete.
München 164. 5 fol. (14-18). Dated A.D. 1817.
Mysore I, p. 26.
Mysore ND II 3336 (P 1969/ 2). PL. Na. 5 fol. Incomplete. Extract no. 112.
Oppert I 977. Belonged to Viraraghava Tatacharyar, Head Master, Sanskrit School of Sathakopacharya, Kanchipuram, Chingelpet Dist.
Oppert II 382. Belonged to Venkatarama Srauti of Mullandram, N. Arcot Dist.
Oppert II 745. Belonged to Ghanapathi Shingaracharyar of Alasur, Madurantakam Taluk.
Oppert II 7368. Belonged to Venkatarama Sastri of Pillur, Mayavaram Taluk.
Oudh XIII 24 (no.3). 32 pp. 400 Grantha-s. Dated A.D. 1832. Belonged to M. Kali Prasada of Lucknow.
P 7.
Peters. II, p. 180 (no.56). 4 fol.
PUL I, p. 132 (no.24). 25 fol. 600 Grantha-s (with other 5 SV works).
PUL II. App. p. 11 (no.158). 12 fol. Copy from Mysore.
Stein p. 38 (no. 785). 4 fol.
Trav. Uni. 2915 F. PL. Gr. 60 Grantha-s.
Trav. Uni. 3325 A. PL. Mal. 60 Grantha-s.

For a Ms. in Nagapattinam see *The Adyar Library Bulletin*, vol. VI, pt. 3 (1942), p. 192.

Ptd.: in Śikṣā-saṃgraha. – Benares, 1889, pp. 450-55. – (Ben. S. S. 10).
Also printed in the edition of the *Āranya-geya-gāna*, ed. by Lakshmana Srauti (in Grantha script). – Tiruvadi : Brahmananda Press, 1914 (2nd ed.), pp. 125-30. [Adyar (H 211.3 AG Lak); BM : Ptd. Bks. Cat. 1906-1928. 316. 1198 (14007.b.38)]
Also included in: Chāndogya Brāhmaṇam. – Kumbakonam : Govinda Deekshithar Punya Smarana Samiti (ed.). Part II. 1981. Appendix pp. 1-8. [(SAI ***)].
[NCC VI 230b; 233a]

*GAURĪDATTA or DATTA (गौरीदत्त / दत्त)
– C. Bhāṣya, called Pradīpa, on the Pratijñā-sūtra. Berlin StB-PrK (NGMPP). E 678/8. 3 fol. (microfilm dated 25.09.1978).

527 GRANTHA-SAṂHITĀ EKĀDAŚA-PRAKĀRĀḤ (?) (ग्रन्थसंहिता एकादशप्रकाराः)
Examples for eleven modes of reciting the Veda, for the verse : bṛhaspate paridīyā rathena ... | It begins: atha grantha-saṃhitāyām ekādaśa prakārā likhyante ... Almost identical with Weber 1498. Cf. Ekādaśa-prakāra-vivṛti. See also Baroda 8761: Vikṛti (extract p. 164) and RASB II 285-86: Jaṭodāharaṇa.

Berlin StB-PrK (NGMPP). E 345/12. 5 fol. (microfilm dated 11.10.1977).
IM 2489. 5 fol. (Mādhyandina-śākhīya).
SBD 4213. 5 fol. (Vājasaneya-saṃhitāyā Ekādaśa-prakārāḥ).
SBD 4214. 3 fol. (Vājasaneya-saṃhitāyā Ekādaśa-prakārāḥ). Incomplete.

528 GRANTHĀNUKRAMAṆIKĀ (ग्रन्थानुक्रमणिका)
SV. Anukramaṇikā in nine verses, fully printed in the Alwar catalogue.

Beginning:

वेयश्चारण्यकश्चैव ऊह ऊह्यस्तथैव च।
महानाम्नी पञ्चमं च छन्दांस्यारण्यमेव च॥
महानाम्न्युत्तरा चैव पदस्तोभविशेषतः।
ताण्ड्यं षड्विंशब्राह्मणसामविधानमार्षकम्॥

End:

चरणव्यूहश्चतुःशाखापरिशेषानुक्रमाः स्मृताः।
ग्रन्थानुक्रमः कौथुमानां द्विपञ्चाश उदाहृतः॥

Alwar 250. Extract p. 69. Dated V.S. 1807.

529 GRANTHĀNUKRAMAṆĪ-(NĀMA-)PARIŚIṢṬA (ग्रन्थानुक्रमणी(नाम)परिशिष्ट)
SV.
IM 1969A. 2 fol. Incomplete. 14 verses. (Also contains Avagraha-daśaka-pariśiṣṭa).

SBD 2303. 4 fol. Incomplete. Begins with verse 10. Also contains Avagraha-daśaka-pariśiṣṭa.

530 GHAKĀRA-SŪTRA (घकारसूत्र)

Mysore ND II 3337 (P 4453/ 6). PL. Na. 3 fol. (36-38). Extract no. 113.

531 GHANA-DARPAṆA (घनदर्पण)

Ptd.: with commentary, *Ghana-darpaṇa-vyākhyāna* of Subrahmanya Somayaji, son of Lakshminarasavadhani (in Telugu script). (Ghanadarpaṇaṃ śrīcāḍasubrahmaṇya-somayājulagāricc racimpabaḍī idi śrīcāḍa veṅkaṭanārāyaṇāvadhānicc viśākhapaṭṭaṇamu vijayarāmacandra mudrākṣaraśalayaṃdu mudriṃpiṃci prakaṭiṃpabaḍiyc). – Vizagapatam : V. R. G. Press, 1915, 54 pp. [SAI (85/1954*); BM : Ptd. Bks. Cat. 1906-1928, 1026 (14090.a.24,1)]

532 GHANA-PADDHATI (घनपद्धति)

BORI TM 299. 37 fol.

533 GHANA-SAṂDHI or KṚṢṆA-YAJURVEDĪYA-GHANA-SAṂDHI (घनसंधि / कृष्णयजुर्वेदीयघनसंधि)

SBD 53170. 52 fol. In this modern Ms. the *Āraṇyaka-śikṣā-vyākhyāna* is written on the left side and the *Ghana-saṃdhi* (up to 4th Praśna of the first Kāṇḍa) on the right side. At the end some portions of the Sanskrit introduction of K. Rangacharya to his edition of the *Taittirīya-prātiśākhya.* Copied by Ṛāmasvāmi Ghanapāṭhi, son of Veṅkaṭarāma Ghanapāṭhi of Bezawada. Dated 14.11.39.

534 GHOṢAVARṆA (घोषवर्ण)

Definition of the Ghoṣa letters in connection with the Śamāna-saṃdhi-s. It is in fact a verse from the Śamāna-prakaraṇa with an explanatory note classifying the letters which when following ā plus visarjanīya cause the disappearance of the latter: they are (1) ghoṣavat letters, and (2) ś and s followed by any consonant agreeing in this regard with the *Vyāsa-śikṣā,* 156 as against the *Taittirīya-prātiśākhya,* 9.1. (Cf. IO catalogue).

समानसंध्यां घोषवर्णाः के --
गजडाद्यास्त्रयो वर्णा दादयश्चैव बादयः ।
यादिवान्तो हकारश्च शसौ तावन्यसंयुतौ ॥
इति । ग घ ङ । ज झ ञ । ड ढ ण । द ध न । ब भ म । (य) र ल व ह श स । तौ अन्यसंयुतौ । इत्येवं घोषवर्णाः ॥

IO 4509 (Mackenzie II 94l). PL. Na. 1 fol. (90). Written ca. A.D. 1770.

[NCC VI 279a]

***CAKRA** (चक्र)

Son and disciple of Rāma.

– Bhāva-prakāśikā, commentary on the Nārada-(Rāvaṇa-baiṭ). Cf. Veda-lakṣaṇa (HB), below.

– Yājuṣa-Bhūṣaṇa, commentary on Pāriśikṣā. MD 924.
– Hasta-svara-lakṣaṇa. Adyar D I 1103 (introductory verses of this are similar to those of the above).

[NCC VI 280b]

535 CATURAKṢARA(Ī)-BAIṬH (चतुरक्षरबैठ्/ चतुरक्षरीबैठ्)

Beginning:

प्रतिवर्गपदेयत्तां षड्विधानि पदानि च।
क्रमेण क्रमयेदत्र पठितैश्चतुरक्षरैः ॥ १॥
कार्यैर्हान्तैर्हल्भिराद्यक्षरप्रत्येकस्य दशसंख्या पदानाम्।
अकाराद्यैस्तु ऋ-लृवर्जैः स्वरैश्च क्रमाद् ग्राह्यं पदमेकैकिकाभिः ॥
द्वितीयाभिस्त्र्यक्षरस्थैः स्वरैस्त्वाकारपूर्वकैः ।
हल्भिर्विसर्गावगृह्यमनान्यत्रद्वादशकेशः ॥ ३॥
नान्तप्रगृह्यतान्तानि पदानि गणयेत् क्रमात्।
स्वरसंख्या तुरेकैतु रेफयुक्ता ध्रुवा दश।
एकोनविंशत्यधिकध्रुवं रेफस्य गृह्यते॥ ४॥
अग्निमीळे। घेथाजड्ड। १। घजझीर। २। घोडछेजा। ३। गूघचूढ। ४।

End:

खैजगङ ४३ गैडगखि ४४ खौटगखा ४५ खिजछछ ४६ गिघयिघू ४७ चिधाचदा ४९॥ इति अष्टमाष्टकः समाप्तः ॥ इति बैठः समाप्तः ॥ ... प्रथमे पदसंख्यानां द्वितीये विसर्गनकारौ । तृतीये अवगृह्यप्रगृह्यौ चतुर्थे मकारतकारौ॥

SBD 52690. 4 fol. Incomplete. Up to the end of the 2nd Aṣṭaka. Title: Prati-varga-padey-attā.

VSM I 186 (no.5713). 484 fol. Dated Śaka 1721. Extract p. 347. A Ms. of the Pada-pāṭha. It contains the respective portions of the *Cātur-jñana* at the beginning of each adhyāya and *Caturakṣarī-baiṭh* at the end of each varga. Aṣṭaka-s 4-8.

Wai I 340. 23 fol. Dated Śaka 1689. (Ṛgveda-saṃhitā-caturakṣara-baiṭha). (A xerox-copy of this Ms. is in SAI).

536 CATURAKṢARĪ-SAṂDIGDHAPADĪ (चतुरक्षरीसंदिग्धपदी)

SBD 3934. 148 fol. Dated V.S. 1545. Extensive notes on the above.
Skt. Coll. Ben. 1897-1901, p. 131 (no.536).

[NCC VI 305b]

537 CATURADHYĀYIKA-VYĀKARAṆA or CATURADHYĀYIKĀ ŚAUNAKĪYĀ (चतुरध्यायिकव्याकरण / चतुरध्यायिका शौनकीया)

→ Atharva-veda-prātiśākhya – Caturadhyāyikā Śaunakīyā.

[NCC VI 306b]

538 CATURTHASVARA-MANDRASVARA(-NIRṆAYA) (चतुर्थस्वरमन्द्रस्वर /-निर्णय)

The sixth chapter of the *Āraṇyagāna-vivaraṇa* of Bhaṭṭa Śobhākara (cf. Alwar 230. Extract p. 66) and also that of Sāyaṇa-bhāṣya on the *Sāmaveda* begin with the same verses as below.

Beginning: (781)

आरण्यकाभिधः षष्ठो ऽध्यायो व्याक्रियते ऽधुना।
तत्रेन्द्रेत्यादिकानां तु पञ्चपञ्चाशतां क्रमात्॥
(आर्षं) ऋषिच्छन्दोदैवतं च तत्र तत्राभिदध्महे।
तत्राद्याया ऋचो द्रष्टा भरद्वाजः प्रकीर्तितः ॥
द्वितीयस्य वसिष्ठस्य तृतीयाया ऋचः स्मृताः ।
वामदेवस्ततश्छन्दो बृहती त्रिष्टुबेव च॥
गायत्रीति क्रमादिन्द्रो भवेत् तिसृषु देवता।
शुनःशेफश्च वरुणस्त्रिष्टुपश्छन्द उत्तमम्॥

End:

नेत्रमूर्धामाचदन्यगायन्तीश्रोत्रसंख्यया।
अयं सहस्रप्रथममेतेषां च पुनस्तथा॥
अया पवस्व द्वे कं च चोहा इ वाक् मन्द्रमेष्यति।
अया पवस्व द्वि एक सामेनाद्य ओ हा इ वाक्॥
चतुर्थस्वरः मन्द्रस्वरमेष्यति ओ वा।
गोमतैकं न तस्योपप्रतिक्ष च द्युम्नमाभर॥
अभि प्रियाणि षष्ठं स्याद् घृतस्यैकं तथैव च।
नित्यमो वा तुरीयेषु चैव सामसु दृश्यते॥ होवा।
अग्ने जरितमेभिस्थ हो वा नित्यं तुरीयके।
इति चतुर्थस्वरमन्द्रस्वरनिर्णयं समासम्॥

Adyar D I 781 (33 E 7 = 75254). PL. Gr. 3 fol. (fol. 67b-69a). A few verses at the end and the colophon are the same as in Adyar D I 738 (Āraṇya-sāma-prakāśikā - Sāma-svara-nirṇaya) and thus it must be identical with the title (Āraṇyakābhidhaḥ) mentioned under Adyar D I 753 (p. 230).

See also *The Adyar Library Bulletin*, vol. V, iii. Manuscript Notes, p. 130.

[NCC VI 308b]

539 CATURDAŚA-LAKṢAṆA (चतुर्दशलक्षण)
Mysore ND II 3338 (P 4906/36). PL. Na. 2 fol. (124-25). Extract no. 114. (Cf. pp. 32-33 of the *Pada-gāḍha*, Srirangam edition).

540 CATUR-LAKṢAṆA (चतुर्लक्षण)
Mysore ND II 3339 (P 4906/25). PL. Na. 2 fol. (120-21). Extract no. 115. (Cf. p. 14 of the *Pada-gāḍha*, Srirangam edition).

541 CATURVIṂŚATI-PADA-SŪTRA (चतुर्विंशतिपदसूत्र)

It is a collection of every 23rd and 24th pada of the *Vājasaneyi-saṃhitā*, belonging to the Mādhyandina-śākhā. This is described as useful for the reciters in making Pada-pāṭha and in keeping the whole Saṃhitā in memory. At the end of each Adhyāya there are three numbers : ? | 1 | 614 pada || ? | 2 | 668 pada || 6 | 3 | 856 pada || 22 | 4 | 742 pada || 14 | 5 | 806 pada || ... 6 | 17 | 198 pada || 16 | 18 | 304 pada || 11 | 19 | 179 pada || 19 | 20 | 211 ||

Beginning:

अथ चत्वारिंशत्पदसूत्रप्रारम्भः । हरिः ओम्। इषे त्वा। वस्तेन। माह्वा। भागं सोमेन। युनक्ति सः । धूर्व धूर्वन्तम्। ऋमत्तामुरु। अरातये स्वः । प्रसव उत्। वृत्र तूर्ये।

End:

ईशावास्यम्। शर्तं समाः । ये के। दधाति तत्। आत्मानं ततः । अव्रणमस्नाविरम्। तमो ये। तद् वेद। शरीरमोम्। खं ब्रह्म॥ ३९। २०। २१३॥ इति चतुर्विंशतिपदसूत्रं समाप्तम्॥

Baroda 589. 13 fol. 175 Grantha-s. Dated V.S. 1907. = CLB I, p. 26. Extract p. 143.

[NCC VI 327a]

542 CATUḤ-ŚLOKĪ-ŚIKṢĀ (चतुःश्लोकीशिक्षा)

With commentary of Lakṣmīkānta. Cf. Lakṣmīkānta-śikṣā.

MD 16746. PL. Tel. 55 Grantha-s. Title: Lakṣmīkānta-śikṣā Savyākhyā.

Mysore ND II 3340 (P 7998/ 2). PL. Na. 2 fol. Incomplete. Extract no. 116.

Mysore ND II 3846 (P 7998/ 1). PL. Na. 2 fol. (111-12). Extract no. 291. (Śikṣā-catuḥ-ślokī).

PUL II. App. p. 11 (no.160). PL. Tel. 5 fol. 50 Grantha-s.

[NCC VI 338a]

543 CARAṆA-VYŪHA (1) (चरणव्यूह)

Unspecified.

AK 57. 58.

Allahabad 161. 161. 161.

America 380. 4 fol.

America 381. 6 fol. Copied by Raghunāṭha in Śaka 1722.

America 382. 8 fol. Copied by Gangādharaviśvara.

America 383. 10 fol. Copied by Rāmacandra, son of Gopāla-bhaṭṭa.

America 384. 5 fol. A Different version towards the end of the Ms.

America 385. 8 fol.

America 386. 5 fol. Dated V.S. 1825. Copied by Jīvaṇadāsa.

America 387. 1 fol. Only the beginning.

America 388. 4 fol.

America 389. 7 fol.

America 390. 11 fol.

America 391. 5 fol. Dated Śaka 1694.

America 392. 4 fol. Copied by Nārāyaṇa-bhaṭṭa.

Ānandāśrama 374. 5 fol.
Ānandāśrama 427. 5 fol.
Ānandāśrama 2172. 5 fol. Dated Śaka 1702.
Ānandāśrama 2193. 4 fol.
Ānandāśrama 2210. 1 fol. Incomplete.
Ānandāśrama 2216. 4 fol.
Ānandāśrama 2697. 5 fol.
Ānandāśrama 2692. 4 fol. Dated Śaka 1741.
Ānandāśrama 2827. 7 fol.
Ānandāśrama 2863. 3819. 4197. 7371. 8074.
ASB I ii.429 (IM 5229). 6 fol. 75 Grantha-s.
ASB I ii.430 (IM 5296). 7 fol. 75 Grantha-s.
ASB I ii.453 (1988). 4 fol. 88 Grantha-s. Dated V.S. 1872 = A.D. 1815.
ASB I ii.454 (2648). 9 fol. 88 Grantha-s.
ASB I ii.455 (6143). 6 fol. 88 Grantha-s.
ASB I ii.456 (1989). 19 fol. 600 Grantha-s (with C. of Mahīdāsa). Dated V.S. 1843 = A.D. 1786.
ASB I ii.457 (9350). 4 fol. 84 Grantha-s. Dated V.S. 1744 = A.D. 1687.
ASB I ii.458 (2557). 50 fol. 600 Grantha-s (with C. of Mahīdāsa).
ASB I ii.607-24 (18 IM Mss.).
Baroda 4536. 7 fol. 50 Grantha-s. Dated V.S. 1723. = CLB I, p. 26.
Baroda 7350. 6 fol. 50 Grantha-s. Dated V.S. 1760. = CLB I, p. 26.
Baroda 12011(d). 9 fol. 150 Grantha-s. Dated V.S. 1733.
Baroda 12712(b). 5 fol. (21-25). 50 Grantha-s. Dated V.S. 1903 = CLB I, p. 26.
Baroda 13053 (fragment).
Baroda 21998. 13 fol. 180 Grantha-s.
Baroda 23431. 6 fol. 52 Grantha-s. Dated Śaka 1619 / V.S. 1754.
Baroda 23432. 5 fol. (20-24). 67 Grantha-s. Dated Śaka 1724.
Baroda 23433. 6 fol. 80 Grantha-s. Dated Śaka 1814 / V.S. 1949.
Baroda 23251. 2 fol. 55 Grantha-s.
Baroda 23671. 6 fol. 60 Grantha-s.
Baroda 26361. 6 fol. 70 Grantha-s. Dated Śaka 1774 / V.S. 1909.
Bharatpur I 152.
Bhau Daji p. 64.
Bhau Daji p. 113 (with Bhāṣya).
Bhr. 26.
BHU D 11/635-46. (12 Mss.).
Bikaner 636. 5 fol. Dated V.S. 1751 (A.D. 1694).
Bikaner 637. 8 fol. Dated V.S. 1640 (A.D. 1583). Copied at Dharmapuri.
BISM pp. 94-95. 26 Mss. (2 of them with C.; 4 attributed to Kātyāyana and 2 to Śaunaka.
BORI 19 of 1868-69.
BORI 24 of 1870-71.
BORI 55 of 1879-80. 4 fol. Dated V.S. 1760.
BORI 56 of 1879-80. 4 fol. Dated V.S. 1778.
BORI 57 of 1879-80. 4 fol. Dated V.S. 1685.

BORI 58 of 1879-80. 4 fol.
BORI 59 of 1879-80. 4 fol. Dated V.S. 1725.
BORI 12 of A 1879-80. 3 fol. Dated Śaka 1705.
BORI 140(1) of 1880-81. 10 fol. Dated V.S. 1836.
BORI 61 of A 1881-82. 6 fol.
BORI 62 of A 1881-82. 4 fol.
BORI 63 of A 1881-82. 4 fol.
BORI 26 of 1882-83. 6 fol. Dated V.S. 1914.
BORI 373 of 1883-84. 4 fol. Dated Śaka 1700.
BORI 39 of 1884-86.
BORI 43 of 1884-87. 7 fol.
BORI 41 of 1886-92.
BORI 42 of 1886-92.
BORI 154(2) of 1886-92.
BORI 57 of 1891-95. 6 fol. Dated V.S. 1716.
BORI 58 of 1891-95. 5 fol.
BORI 15(1) of 1892-95.
BORI 6 of 1916-18. 4 fol. Dated V.S. 1846.
BORI 22 of 1919-24. 4 fol. (a. Vyāsa).
BORI TM 2.
BORI TM 277.
BORI TM 141 (with C.).
BORI TM 157 (with C.).
BORI TM 160 (with C.).
Bühler p. 537 (no. 22). 4 fol.
Bühler p. 553 (no. 24). 33 fol.
Deccan College (1964). 243-58 (16 Mss.).
GJKSV 23/23 (D I 1, no.6). 3 fol. (1, 4-5). Incomplete. Dated V.S. 1878. Remark: Sāmaveda-pariśiṣṭa.
GJKSV 7864/88 (D II 1, no.4601). 10 fol. Maithili script.
GJKSV 14418. 10 fol.
GJKSV 15525. 4 fol.
GJKSV 18256. 4 fol. (2-5). Incomplete.
GJKSV 18347. 5 fol.
GJKSV 19567. 10 fol.
GJKSV 21021. 8 fol.
GJKSV 23967. 5 fol.
GJKSV 24459. 3 fol.
GJKSV 24817. 3 fol.
GJKSV 25471. 5 fol.
GJKSV 26433. 5 fol.
GJKSV 27732. 6 fol.
GJKSV 29957. 6 fol.
GJKSV 32665. 6 fol.
GJKSV 33538. 18 fol.
GJKSV 33581. 4 fol.

GJKSV 33599. 11 fol.
GJKSV 33730. 6 fol.
Gough p. 52 (no.19). Dated V.S. 1808.
Gough p. 79 (no.24). 6 pp.
Harshe pp. 43. Incomplete. 44.
Hoshiarpur p. 50 (no.10). 4 fol. 50 Grantha-s.
Hoshiarpur p. 50 (no.17). 9 fol. 68 Grantha-s. Extract p. 74.
Hoshiarpur p. 50 (no.105). 19 fol. 513 Grantha-s (ascribed to Vyāsa). Dated Śaka 1706.
Hoshiarpur p. 50 (no.226). 7 fol. 70 Grantha-s.
Hoshiarpur p. 50 (no.3222). 5 fol. 73 Grantha-s. Dated V.S. 1920.
Hoshiarpur p. 51 (no.3623). 6 fol. 65 Grantha-s.
Hoshiarpur p. 51 (no.6815). 9 fol. 112 Grantha-s. Dated V.S. 1644.
Hz. 2078. 8 fol. Belonged to Jambunatha Bhatta of Thanjavur.
IL. 133.
IL. 134.
IM 2518. 10 fol.
IM 5229. 6 fol.
IM 5275. 5 fol.
IM 5290. 4 fol.
IM 5291. 7 fol.
IM 5292. 11 fol.
IM 5293. 3 fol.
IM 5294. 7 fol.
IM 5295. 8 fol.
IM 5296. 7 fol. 4 additional verses on Vyāsa at the end.
IM 5330. 5 fol.
IM 8044. 6 fol.
IM 9103. 13 fol.
IM 10147. 5 fol. Incomplete.
IM 10166. 6 fol. Incomplete.
IM 11191. 9 fol.
IM 11192. 5 fol.
Jodhpur (R). 767 (D I, p. 22; no.37). 4 fol. Dated V.S. 1801.
Jodhpur (R). 1353 (D I, p. 22; no.38). 6 fol. Dated V.S. 1852.
Jodhpur (R). 2632 (D I, p. 22; no.39). 2 fol. Dated V.S. 1933.
Jodhpur (R). 3275 (D I, p. 22; no.40). 1 fol. Dated V.S. 1623.
Jodhpur (R). 1358 (D I, p. 22; no.41). 12 fol. 19th century. Tattva-sāra ?
Kotah 52.
Mysore I, p. 26 (3 Mss.).
Mysore ND II 3341-53. Extract no. 117-23.
OU 7 Vm (B.134/24/a). 7 fol. (a. Śaunaka). Dated A.D. 1898.
OU 8 Vm (506). PL. Tel. 11 fol. Incomplete. (a. Śaunaka). 16th century.
Oxf. CS e.29(2). 5 fol.
Oxf. CS d.74(2). 5 fol.
Oxf. CS d.74(3). 7 fol.
PUL I, p. 8

PUL I, p. 20 (no.49). 5 fol. Dated V.S. 1842.
PUL I, p. 20 (no.50). 7 fol.
PUL I, p. 20 (no.51). 13 fol.
PUL I, p. 132 (no.161). PL. Tel. 4 fol.
PUL II. App. p. 11 (no.19). Copies of 10 TD Mss.
Rgb. 43. 7 fol.
SBD 3954. 3 fol. Incomplete.
SBD 4007. 11 fol. (2-12). Incomplete.
SBD 4024. 6 fol.
SBD 4025. 5 fol.
SBD 4029. 6 fol. Dated V.S. 1876.
SBD 4041. 3 fol.
SBD 4042. 3 fol.
SBD 4045. 6 fol.
SBD 4100. 2 fol. Incomplete.
SBD 4107. 2 fol. Incomplete.
SBD 4111. 7 fol.
SBD 4121. 8 fol. Dated V.S. 1684.
SBD 4140. 10 fol. Incomplete.
SBD 4154. 4 fol.
SBD 4164. 15 fol. (with C.).
SBD 4178. 6 fol. (Atharvavedasya ?).
SBD 4182. 5 fol. (Caraṇa-vyūha-pariśiṣṭa). Dated V.S. 1882.
SBD 4187. 3 fol.
SBD 4228. 6 fol. Dated V.S. 1820.
SBD 4229. 3 fol.
SBD 4230. 6 fol.
SBD 4231. 3 fol. Incomplete.
SBD 4232. 3 fol.
SBD 4237. 3 fol. Dated V.S. 1927.
SBD 4265. 5 fol.
SBD 4266. 10 fol. Incomplete.
SBD 4326. 2 fol. Beng.
SBD 4334. 13 fol.
SBD 4335. 8 fol.
SBD 4352. 9 fol. (3, 10, 14, 15, 22, 24, 1-3). (Nigamasaṃhitā ?).
SBD 4355. 4 fol.
SBD 4367. 4 fol.
SBD 4380. 5 fol.
SBD 4381. 5 fol. Incomplete.
SBD 4382. 6 fol.
SBD 4388. 5 fol.
SBD 4389. 10 fol.
SBD 4390. 8 fol. Dated Śaka 1683.
SBD 47558. 6 fol. Dated V.S. 1841.
SBD 47559. 3 fol.

SBD 47615. 114 fol. (3-21, 23-117). Incomplete.
SBD 47794. 3 fol. Dated V.S. 1785.
SBD 47876. 2 fol. Incomplete.
SBD 55330. 1 fol. Incomplete.
SBD 55420. 5 fol.
SBD 55421. 6 fol. Dated V.S. 1891 / Śaka 1756.
SBD 55433.
SBD 55439. 6 fol. Dated V.S. 1852.
SBD 55543. 4 fol. Dated Śaka 1806.
SBD 55546. 4 fol.
SBD 55552. 8 fol. Dated V.S. 1810.
SBD 55587. 11 fol. (Caraṇa-vyūha-pariśiṣṭa).
SBD 55589. 3 fol. (with C.). Incomplete.
SBD 55666. 5 fol. Dated V.S. 1890.
SBD 55668. 5 fol.
SBD 55695. 5 fol. Dated V.S. 1862.
SBD 55713. 5 fol.
SBD 55721. 6 fol.
SBD 55770. 1 fol. Incomplete.
SK. Ray D. C. 8.
Taylor II 244.
Trav. Uni. 2915 C. PL. Gr. 65 Grantha-s.
Trav. Uni. 4928. 65 Grantha-s.
Trav. Uni. 5504 E.
Trav. Uni. 5548 C. PL. Tel. 65 Grantha-s.
Udaipur I. B.8, 15.
Ujjain I, pp. 9 (2 Mss.). 12. II, p. 8 (2 Mss.).
Viśvabhāratī 2937(a).
Wellcome Inst. London. B 20h.

544 CARAṆA-VYŪHA (2) (चरणव्यूह)

– Pariśiṣṭa of the *Śukla Yajurveda* on different Vedic Śākhā-s; variously attributed to Vyāsa or Śaunaka or Kātyāyana, and given as the fifth Pariśiṣṭa of Kātyāyana. See Vaidya, *History of Sanskrit Literature*, vol. I, pt. 1, pp. 182-83; also Arthur A. Macdonell, *A History of Sanskrit Literature*, London, 1900, pp. 52, 275.

Beginning: (KSS)

अथातश्चरणव्यूहं व्याख्यास्यामः । तत्र यदुक्तं चातुर्वेद्यं चतुरो वेदा विज्ञाता भवन्ति । ऋग्वेदो यजुर्वेदः सामवेदो ऽथर्ववेदश्चेति । तत्र ऋग्वेदस्याष्टौ स्थानानि भवन्ति । चर्चा श्रावकश्चर्चकः श्रवणीयपारः क्रमपारः क्रमपदः क्रमजटः क्रमदण्डश्चेति चतुष्पारायणम् । एतेषां शाखाः पञ्चविधा भवन्ति । आश्वलायनी शाङ्खायनी शाकला बाष्कला माण्डूकायनाश्चेति ॥

End:

य इदं वेदानां नामरूपगोत्रं प्रमाणं छन्दोदैवतं वर्णं वर्णयति अविद्यो लभते विद्यां जातिस्मरो ऽथ जायते जन्मनि जन्मनि वेदपारगो भवत्यव्रती व्रती भवत्य ब्रह्मचारी ब्रह्मचारी भवति नमः शौनकाय नमः शौनकाय ॥

य इदं चरणव्यूहं गर्भिणीं श्रावयेत् स्त्रियम् ।
पुमांसं जायते पुत्रमृषिभिर्वेदपारगम् ॥
य इदं चरणव्यूहं श्राद्धकाले पठेद् द्विजः ।
अक्षय्यं तद् भवेच्छ्राद्धं पितॄंश्चैवोपतिष्ठति ॥
यो ऽधीते चरणव्यूहं स विप्रः पङ्क्तिपावनः ।
तारयेत् प्रभृतीन् पुत्रः पुरुषान् सप्त सप्त च ॥
य इदं चरणव्यूहं पठेत् पर्वसु पर्वसु ।
विधूतपाप्मा स स्वर्गी ब्रह्मभूयाय कल्पते ॥

(Mss. have considerable variations)

Adyar D I 782 (20 H 11 = 67341). PL. Tel. 2 fol. Incomplete. = Adyar I, p. 48b.
Adyar D I 783 (35 C 74 = PM 110). 5 fol. = Adyar I, p. 48b.
Adyar D I 784 (35 C 78 = PM 111). 5 fol. = Adyar I, p. 48b. Dated V.S. 1675.
Adyar 26 N 2 = 71747(d). PL. Gr. 3 fol.
Adyar D XIII 321 (VB 305a). PL. Tel. 4 fol.
Adyar D XIII 322 (VB 461j). PL. Tel. 3 fol.
Alwar 146.
America 393. 47 fol. (with C. of Mahīdāsa).
B I, p.198 (nos. 11, 12).
B I, p. 200 (nos. 13-24).
B I, p. 202 (nos. 25, 26, 27).
Baroda 410. 24 fol. 650 Grantha-s. = CLB I, p. 26 (with C. of Mahīdāsa).
Baroda 12011(d). 9 fol. 150 Grantha-s. Dated V.S. 1733.
BBRAS 485 (B D 162). 6 fol. Dated Śaka 1655.
BBRAS 486 (B D 311). 2 fol.
BBRAS 487 (B D 257). 11 fol. (with C. of Mahīdāsa).
Berlin StB-PrK (NGMPP). B 500/18. 8 fol. (microfilm dated 08.06.1973).
Berlin StB-PrK (NGMPP). B 500/21. 10 fol. (microfilm dated 08.06.1973).
Berlin StB-PrK (NGMPP). B 500/22. 5 fol. (microfilm dated 08.06.1973).
Berlin StB-PrK (NGMPP). B 500/23. 4 fol. (microfilm dated 08.06.1973).
Berlin StB-PrK (NGMPP). B 500/24. 4 fol. (microfilm dated 08.06.1973).
Berlin StB-PrK (NGMPP). B 500/25. 5 fol. (microfilm dated 08.06.1973).
Berlin StB-PrK (NGMPP). B 500/26. 3 fol. (microfilm dated 08.06.1973).
Berlin StB-PrK (NGMPP). E 1218/23. 7 fol. Together with Nārāyaṇopaniṣat (microfilm dated 03.06.1981).
Berlin StB-PrK (NGMPP). T 22/18. 8 fol. (microfilm dated 11.05.1982).
Bhk. 9.
Bombay Uni. 693 (BMC 9 11). 3 fol. Dated Śaka 1619.
Bombay Uni. 694 (BMC 9 14). 3 fol.

Bombay Uni. 695 (BMC 25 29). 5 fol.
Bombay Uni. 696 (BMC 41 23). 4 fol. Dated Śaka 1694.
Bombay Uni. 697 (BMC 44 8). 4 fol. Dated Śaka 1760.
Bombay Uni. 698 (BMC 48 3). 6 fol.
Bombay Uni. 699 (BMC 50 14). 4 fol.
Bombay Uni. 700 (BMC 56 4). 9 fol.
Bombay Uni. 701 (BMC 73 1). 8 fol. Dated Śaka 1735.
Bombay Uni. 702 (BS 245). 4 fol.
Bombay Uni. 703 (BMC 73 2). 9 fol. (with C. of Mahīdāsa).
Bombay Uni. 704 (BMC 4 35). 14 fol. (with C. of Mahīdāsa). Incomplete. Khaṇḍa I.
Bombay Uni. 705 (BMC 24 9). 13 fol. (with C. of Mahīdāsa). Incomplete. Khaṇḍa I.
Bombay Uni. (Itchharam 9 21) 68. 5 fol. Dated Śaka 1715.
Bombay Uni. (Moropant 52 7) 53. 5 fol. Though described as Caraṇavyūhavyākhyā, the Ms. contains the text only.
BP p. 286.
Br. Mus. 10 (fol. 62-64).
Burnell 9a.
Calcutta Skt. Coll. I 501. 4 fol.
Calcutta Skt. Coll. I 502. 5 fol. Dated V.S. 1933.
CPB 1644-50.
CU Add. 2436.
Haug p. 22 (no.45a) = München 11a.
Haug p. 28 (no.64b) = München 11c.
Hz 422. PL. Tel. 5 fol. Belonged to Kesari Yajnayya of Brahmanakraka (Agrahara), Nellur Dist.
IL. 137.
IO 227 (1577D). 5 fol. Dated V.S. 1859.
IO 228 (1635b). 2 fol. Ms. I. of Weber's ed.
IO 4689 (Mackenzie II 96b). PL. Na. 1 fol. Only the beginning.
IO 4690 (Mackenzie II 91c). PL. Gr. 3 fol.
IO 4691 (Mackenzie III 238b). PL. Na. 2 fol. (2-7) (fragment).
IO 7852 (3738c). 12 pp. Copy of Whish no.20 (= 21a).
IO 7853 (3734a). 9 and 12 pp. Copy of RAS. Mss. with a collation done by Eggeling in 1867.
Jodhpur 1540 (with C.).
K 6.
Kavīndrācārya 18 (with C.).
Kh. 59.
Lz. 72. 5 fol.
Lz. 72. 6 fol. Dated A.D. 1838.
Lz. 72. 6 fol. Dated A.D. 1830.
Mandlik p. 46, BA. 20, 21.
MD 897. 6 pp.
MD 898. Tel. 12 pp.
MD 899. Tel. 7 pp.
MD 16495. PL. Gr. 22 pp. 62 Grantha-s.

MD 17459. PL. Tel. 4 pp. 50 Grantha-s.
MD 17678. PL. Tel. 8 pp. 56 Grantha-s.
Mithila IV 60.
Mithila IV 60 (A)-(C).
Mithila IV 60 (D). Different beginning.
Mithila IV 60 (E). (F).
MT 1969(f). PL. Tel. 2 fol. 30 Grantha-s.
München 11a. 6 fol. (Written ca. A.D. 1850).
München 11c. 5 fol. (34-38). Dated A.D. 1862.
N-W P V 64 (no.27). 3 fol. Belonged to Pt. Makhana Misra of Mathura.
N-W P V 146 (no.28). 5 fol.
N-W P VII 8 (no.30). 29 fol. (with Bhāṣya). Belonged to Pandit Baladikshita Bhagavati, Benares.
Oxf. 398b (no.144). 4 fol. (206-09).
Oxf. II 1048 (Ms. Walker 144). 4 fol. (206-09). In a collection.
Oxf. II 1055 (Ms. Sansk. d. 46). 3 fol. Dated A.D. 1761.
P 5.
Peters. II, p. 175 (no.136). 10 fol.
Peters. III, p. 385 (no.39).
Peters. IV, p. 2 (nos. 41, 42).
Peters. IV, p. 6 (no.154).
Peters. V, p. 224 (no.15).
Phch. 14.
Radh. 1.
Rajapur 659.
RASB II 947 (G 1988). 4 fol. 88 Grantha-s. Dated V.S. 1872.
RASB II 948 (G 2648). 9 fol.
RASB II 949 (G 6143). 6 fol.
Rep. Hpr. 1901-06, p. 2.
SB p. 9 (no.59). 4 fol. 60 Grantha-s.
Stein p. 4 (5 Mss.).
TD 1754. 5 fol. 70 Grantha-s.
TD 1755. 5 fol. 70 Grantha-s.
TD 1756. 5 fol. 70 Grantha-s.
TD 1757. 5 fol. 70 Grantha-s.
TD 1758. 5 fol. 70 Grantha-s.
TD 1759. 5 fol. 70 Grantha-s.
TD 1760. 4 fol. 64 Grantha-s. It contains different readings.
TD 1761. 4 fol. 65 Grantha-s.
TD 1762. 6 fol. (2-7). 60 Grantha-s. Incomplete.
TD 1763. 6 fol. 50 Grantha-s.
TD 1941. PL. Tel. 5 fol. (98-102). 70 Grantha-s.
Trav. Uni. 7773. 600 Grantha-s (with C. of Mahīdāsa).
Udaipur II 13, 19, 20.
Vaṅgīya p. 24.
VOHD II 2.548 (Ms.or.oct. 627. StaatsB., Marburg). 5 fol. Incomplete. Khaṇḍa 1-5.

VOHD II 8.3048 (Ms.or.quart. 861. StaatsB.-PrK, Berlin). Roman. 7 fol. (9-15).
VSM I 742-60. One with C. of Mahīdāsa.
VSM I 800 (no.4912). 2 fol. 49th Pariśiṣṭa of the *Atharva-veda*. It contains many variants to the printed edition.
VSM III 187 (no.12183). 4 fol. Dated Śaka 1739.
Wai I 692-713. (22 Mss.; the last one with Bhāṣya).
Weber 252(5) (Chambers 66a). 1 fol. (only the end).
Weber 253 (Chambers 376). 6 fol. Dated V.S. 1667.
Weber 254 (Chambers 610). 6 fol. Dated V.S. 1749.
Weber 255 (Chambers 772). 7 fol. Dated V.S. 1643.
Weber 256 (Chambers 785b). 4 fol. Dated V.S. 1711.
Weber 1535b (Ms. or. oct. 348). 6 fol. (22-26).
Weber 2102. 7 fol. Dated V.S. 1810.
Whish 21(a). PL. Gr. 4 fol.

Ptd.:
1) Ed. by A. Weber, "Uebersicht über die Schulen der Veda", text (in Roman script), *Indische Studien*, vol. III (1855), pp. 247-83. [Adyar (H080 Web IS ge); Emeneau (393)]
2) Lithographic reproduction (no date; no place) of a Ms. dated V.S. 1808. 5 fol. (āṣāḍha śudi 14 bhaumavāsare dīkṣita-dayāśaṃkarasuta-karuṇāśaṃkareṇa likhitam idaṃ pustakam) [Gö (Poet. As. I,1505)]
3) With the commentary of Mahīdāsa (lithographic), 24 fol. – Benares, V.S. 1936 (1879). → Ānandāśrama 3792. [BM : Ptd. Bks. Cat. 1876-92. 72 (14007.d.16)]
4) Ed. by Yugalakishora (Vyasa) Pathaka, with the Bhāṣya of Mahīdāsa, as an Appendix to Kātyāyana's *Śuklayajuḥ-prātiśākhya* with Uvaṭa's Bhāṣya. – Benares : Chowkhamba, 1888. 60 pp. – (Ben. S. S. 4). [Adyar (H080 CSS B5); SAI (ind S 12, 4); UBTÜ (Ci XII 633); BM : Ptd. Bks. Cat. 1876-92. 72 (14093.b.8)]
5) Ed. by Babu Varanasi Prasad, with the Bhāṣya of Mahīdāsa, (lithographic print). – Varanasi : Kashi Sanskrit Press, 1886. 40 pp. [Adyar (PH 215 Sau CVxy Bab)]
6) Ed. by Srinivasacharya, with the Bhāṣya of Kamalākara-bhaṭṭa (?), (in Telugu script). – Madras : Taraṅgini Press, 1896. 44 pp. [Adyar (PH 215.4 CVxy Sri); MyORI (B 1046); SAI (87/781*)]
7) Ed. by Babu Haridasa Gupta, with the Bhāṣya of Mahīdāsa, Publication No. 21. – Benares, Saṃ. 1959 (1903). 55 pp. [Adyar (PH 215 Sau CVxy); NL (180 Jc 90 256,3)]
8) A Dissertation by Wilhelm Siegling (Die Rezensionen des Caraṇa-vyūha – Inaugural-Dissertation zur Erlangung der Doktorwürde genehmigt von der philosophischen Fakultät der Friedrich-Wilhelms-Universität zu Berlin – Tag der Promotion: 16. Juni 1906). – Leipzig : G. Kreysing, 1906. 52 pp. [NL (178 C 1819); Gö (Diss. Phil. Berlin 1905/06); Emeneau (394)]
9) Ed. by Anantaram Dogara Sastri, with the Bhāṣya of Mahīdāsa, introduction and notes. – Benares : Chowkhamba, 1938. 53 pp. – (Kashi Sanskrit Series 132; Veda Section no. 8). [Adyar (H080 CSS K132); NL (180 Jc 93 325); SAI (ind 71 C 675); SKGI (Rf IX 16); SOAS (III.1.f.2.5 – 35782)]

10) Ed. by Renukadasa Rajesvara and Dasambhatta Sastri Ayacita, with a Marathi translation (Caraṇavyūha-bhāṣya – marāṭhī-bhāṣāntarasahita). – Umbarkhed (Varhāḍ), 1954. 7, 4, 6, 4, 8, 4, 8, 103, 8, 31, 18, 4, 8, pp. [VSM]

11) In *Kātyāyanīya-pariśiṣṭa-daśakam,* with C. *Viṣama-padālaṃkriyā* of Sridhara Anna Sastri Ware of Nasik. – Poona (Yajnavalkya Ashrama, 121 Kasaba Peth) : Madhyandina Madhyavarti Mandala (V. T. Shete Vakil), 1958, pp. 60-76. [BORI (33438); SOAS (III.1.g.27 – 143871)]

12) Ed. by Umesh Chandra Sharma, with the Bhāṣya of Mahīdāsa. – Aligarh : Viveka Publications, 1978, vi, 47 pp. [Adyar (PH 215 Sau CVxy Sha); BORI (32214); NL (180 Je 97 249); SAI (ind 51 C 183/544)]

13) Ed. by Shree Kishore Mishra, with his own commentary, in : *Veda-śākhā-pary-ālocanam.* – Varanasi : Vijaya Press, Sarsawli, Cantt., 1985. pp. 55-74. [SAI (ind 55 A 87/1729)]

Also printed (partly ?) in the *Śadba-kalpa-druma* of Radhakantadeva. – Calcutta, Śaka 1808 ? Vol. IV, pp. 499-500.

Reprinted : Varanasi : Chowkhamba, 1963 (3rd edition). – (Ch. Skt. Series 93). [SAI (inf 4 S 65)]

– C. anon.

Allahabad 161.
B I, p. 202 (nos. 28, 29).
Baroda 24702. 7 fol. 150 Grantha-s (first Khaṇḍa). Dated Śaka 1751.
Bharatpur I 40.
Bühler p. 538 (no. 23). 16 fol.
Bühler p. 553 (no. 25).
Deccan College 4760. 6 fol.
Deccan College 8866. 5 fol. Dated Śaka 1787.
Deccan College (1964). 259 (3249 of Deccan College Collection). 21 fol. Dated V.S. 1751. Title: Caraṇa-vyūha-bhāṣya. Col. : Caraṇa-vyūha-vivaraṇa.
Kh. 82.
N-W P II 6 (no.17). 48 fol. Belonged to Makhanji of Mathura.
N-W P VII 8 (no.30). 29 fol. (with text). Belonged to Pandit Baladikshita Bhagavati, Benares.
SBD 55514. 8 fol.
Udaipur p. 46. Dated V.S. 1793 (no.15 of ptd. catatlogue).

– C. Bhāṣya. anon.

ASB I ii.460 (4702). 17 fol. 1200 Grantha-s. Dated V.S. 1866 = A.D. 1811.
BORI 19 of 1871-72. 16 fol.
BORI 5 of 1873-74. 23 fol. From Jodhpur.
GJKSV 42337. 5 fol.
Gough p. 85 (no.19). 16 pp.
Jodhpur 1540.
Kavīndrācārya 18.
RASB II 954 (G 9702). 17 fol. 1200 Grantha-s. Dated V.S. 1866.

– C. Vivaraṇa.

Beginning:

श्रीनृसिंहं गणेशानं गिरं गुरुपदाम्बुजम्।
शोभनं चरणव्यूहं व्याकरिष्ये यथामति॥

चरणव्यूहाख्यं परिशिष्टं (व्याख्यातुं) चिकीर्षुः प्रतिजानीते अथेति। अथशब्दो मङ्गलार्थः। यतो ऽन्यानि परिशिष्टानि अतो वेदविभागज्ञानाय चरणव्यूहं व्याख्यास्यामः। तत्र निरुक्तं ... ति। चतुर्णां वेदानां समाहारश्चातुर्वेद्यम्। तत् निरुक्तं निश्चितमुक्तं प्रसिद्धमित्यर्थः। स्वयमेव चातुर्वेद्यशब्दं व्याचष्टे।

End:

य इदं नित्यशः पर्वसु अष्टमीभूतदर्शपूर्णमासीसंक्रान्तिषु वा पठति। स धूतपाप्मा। धूतो दूरीकृतो पाप्मा पापं येन। अत एव शुचिः पवित्रः सन् ब्रह्मभूयाय ब्रह्मभावाय गच्छति। कर्मणि चेति चतुर्थी। ब्रह्मभावं प्राप्नोतीत्यर्थः। इति चरणव्यूहविवरणे चतुर्थः खण्डः॥

ASB I ii.625 (IM 2566). 6 fol. 137 Grantha-s.
IM 2566. 6 fol.

– Cc. Caraṇa-vyūha-bhāṣya-vivaraṇa. → Mahīdāsa's Vyākhyā.
Ānandāśrama 2698. 33 fol. Dated Śaka 1757.

– Vyākhyā called Padyāvṛtti. It quotes many authorities up to Vīramitrodaya.
ASB I ii.459 (G 6179). 5 fol. 300 Grantha-s = RASB II 953.
RASB II 953 (G 6179). 5 fol. 300 Grantha-s.

– C. of Kamalākara-bhaṭṭa (?)
Except for an additional benedictory verse at the beginning and a different colophon this commentary is identical with that of Mahīdāsa. Even the introductory verses of Mahīdāsa are found here (p. 2). Apparently some copyist was misled by the quotations from Kamalākara-bhaṭṭa, in the commentary of Mahīdāsa, especially the one at the end of the first section.

VSM III 188 (no.11344). 27 fol.

Ptd.: in Telugu script. See above.

– C. of Kṛṣṇadatta, son of Brahmadatta. Oudh III 8.

– C. Bhāṣya of Vāsudeva. SBD 4093. 24 fol. (1-22, 24, 24 ?). Incomplete.

– C. of Śrīkṛṣṇamaṇi Pāṭhaka. Mithila IV 61. 61A

– C. Bhāṣya of Gadādhara-bhaṭṭa Śauce. Harshe p. 44.

– C. of Mahīdāsa, disciple of Bālakṛṣṇa, composed at Benares in A.D. 1557 or 1607 ? See also RASB II 950-52.

Alwar 147.
America 393. 42 fol. (6-47).
Ānandāśrama 3792. 24 fol. Appears to be a lithographic print. Col.: 1936 āśvina 1 guru-vāsare ||

त्रिदशाङ्गधरामिते गते ऽब्दे मधुमासे दशमीतिथौ सुधांशौ ।
महिदासबुधः परोपकृत्यै चरणव्यूहमिदं व्यकारि काश्याम् ॥

Baroda 410. 24 fol. 650 Grantha-s = CLB I, p. 26.
Baroda 26362. 324 fol. 6050 Grantha-s. Dated V.S. 1613 / Śaka 1762. ?
Bombay Uni. 703 (BMC 73 2). 9 fol.
Bombay Uni. 704 (BMC 4 35). 14 fol. (I Khaṇḍa only).
Bombay Uni. 705 (BMC 24 9). 13 fol. (I Khaṇḍa only).
BORI 8 of 1895-1902. 56 fol.
Calcutta Skt. Coll. I 503. 52 pp.
Calcutta Skt. Coll. I 504. 22 fol. Dated V.S. 1836 / Śaka 1701.
Calcutta Skt. Coll. I 505. 22 fol. Dated V.S. (or Śaka ?) 1663.
GJKSV 24092. 6 fol. Incomplete.
GJKSV 32021. 24 fol. Dated V.S. 1936.
Haug p. 22 (no.45b) = München 11b.
L 2460. Beng. 22 fol. 572 Grantha-s.
Mandlik p. 46, BA. 22, 23.
Mithila IV 62. Incomplete.
Mithila IV 63. Incomplete.
München 11b. 32 fol. Dated A.D. 1862.
Peters. II, p. 168 (no.31). 33 fol.
PUL II. App. p. 11 (no.162). 44 fol. Dated V.S. 1846.
RASB II 950 (G 1989). 19 fol. 600 Grantha-s. Dated V.S. 1843.
RASB II 951 (G 9350). 4 fol. 84 Grantha-s. Dated V.S. 1744.
RASB II 952 (G 2557). 50 pp. 600 Grantha-s.
SBD 3959. 54 fol. Dated V.S. 1935.
SBD 4133. 22 fol. Dated V.S. 1613. ?
SBD 55682. 21 fol. Dated V.S. 1874. (Caraṇa-vyūha-vṛtti). Remarks : racanā-kālaḥ 1613.
SBD 55705. 20 fol. Dated V.S. 1856. Remarks : racanā-kālaḥ 1613.
Skt. Coll. Ben. 1906, p. 10 (no.1752).
Trav. Uni. 7773. 600 Grantha-s (with text).
VSM I 759 (no.2809). 53 fol. Dated Śaka 1779. Copied by Zodagāvakara Āppā-bhaṭṭa.
Wai I 713. 50 fol. Dated Śaka 1769.

Ptd.: with text. – Benares : Chowkhamba, 1938. – (Kashi Sanskrit Series 132) and several other editions. See above.

– C. of Vidyāraṇya.
N-W P V 42 (no.12). 29 fol. Belonged to Ramachand Bhatta, Allahabad.

545 CARAṆA-VYŪHA-BHĀṢYA-SAṂGRAHA (**चरणव्यूहभाष्यसंग्रह**)
Baroda 23384. 5 fol. (4-8). Dated Śaka 1812.

546 CARAṆA-VYŪHETIHĀSA (**चरणव्यूहेतिहास**)
SBD 4130. 7 fol.

547 CĀTUR-JÑĀNA or CĀTṚ-JÑĀNA (-PARIBHĀṢĀ) (1)
(चातुर्ज्ञान / चातृज्ञान /-परिभाषा)
A list of 1) samāna, 2) nānta, 3) vivṛta-pada, and 4) eka-pada words in the *Ṛgveda.*

Alph. List Beng. Govt. pp. 38 (3 Mss.). 39 (3 Mss.).
Ānandāśrama 6801. Dated Śake 1700. A few additional verses in the beginning:
samāna-nānta-vivṛtapadāny ekapadāni ca |
dakṣiṇāmūrtir āhaitac cāturjñānaṃ vidur budhāḥ ||
Baroda 5837. 16 fol. 350 Grantha-s. V.S. 1812. = CLB I, p. 26.
Baroda 24734. 20 fol. (2, 5-22). 300 Grantha-s.
Ben. 5.
Bhau Daji p. 73. (Cāturjñāna-paribhāṣā).
BHU B 2666 (D 11/647). 22 fol. Dated V.S. 1693.
Calcutta Skt. Coll. I 530 (147). 41 fol. Dated V.S. 1600.
Deccan College 2253. 18 fol. (3-20). Incomplete. (Aṣṭka-s 1-6).
Deccan College 9849. 13 fol. Incomplete.
Gough p. 85 (no.20). 17 fol. (Remarks : "Chattrijñānam, on the Pada text of the Ṛgveda").
Hpr. III 92. 24 fol. 660 Grantha-s. (Cf. Pref. p. iii).
IM 4992. 33 fol. (1-4, 8-36). Incomplete. Dated V.S. 1672. Copied by Yajñeśvara, son of Śaṃkarabaṭṭa. The same text as the above but with 31 paribhāṣā verses.
IO 4250 (Mackenzie II 80a). PL. Na. 41 fol. Title: Ṛgveda-ciṭṭa.
IO 4251 (Mackenzie II 80e). PL. Na. 24 fol. (71-79, 88-101, 104).
IO 4252(1) (Mackenzie II 83k). PL. Na. 15 fol. (58-72). Written ca. A.D. 1800.
PUL I, p. 20 (no.52). 24 fol. 300 Grantha-s. Dated V.S. 1819.
Rep. Raj. and C. I. p. 6.
SB p. 9 (no.81). 31 fol. 464 Grantha-s. = SBD 3930.
SBD 0603. 31 fol. (lacks 4 fol.)
SBD 2324. 16 fol. Incomplete (up to ch. 55). Dated V.S. 1881 (this date is not found in the Ms.; the paper appears to be much older). Catalogued as Adhyāya-nāmādi-padābhidhāna-kaṇḍikā-pāṭha. Two additional verses in the beginning:

आदौ समानानि ततो विवृत्तयो नान्तान्यथो एकपदादिकानि च।
ऋक्संहितायामसकौ चतुर्गणी प्रत्येकमध्यायगता यथाक्रमम्॥
अध्यायनामादिपदाभिधानया एकैकया कण्डिकयाभिधीयते।
तत्कण्डिकामध्यगते गणे गणे ज्ञेयो ऽथशब्दश्च समाप्तिसूचकः ॥

SBD 3930. 31 fol. Dated V.S. 1714.
SBD 4101. 3 fol. Incomplete.
SBD 4141. 20 fol.

SBD 4316. 21 fol.

SBD 46929. 6 fol. (with paribhāṣā). Incomplete. Up to ch. 21. Also includes the paribhāṣā verses of the *Ṛgveda-padaratna* in the beginning. Catalogued as Paribhāṣā (Ṛgvedīyā).

SBD 52686a. 16 fol. (with paribhāṣā of 31 verses). Dated Śaka 1660. Numbers of the respective *Ṛgveda* verses are on the top of each words.

Tirupati SVUORI (427c). PL. Na. 14 fol. (13-26).

Trav. Uni. 4816. 725 Grantha-s (with Paribhāṣā and Bhaiṭākṣara).

Trav. Uni. 4906. 350 Grantha-s. Dated V.S. 1850.

Trav. Uni. 4926. 380 Grantha-s (with Paribhāṣā). Dated V.S. 1796 / Śaka 1661.

Trav. Uni. 9767. 380 Grantha-s (with Paribhāṣā).

Ujjain I, p. 9 (no.1834). 29 fol. Dated V.S. 1671.

548 CĀTUR-JÑĀNA or CĀTṚ-JÑĀNA (-PARIBHĀṢĀ) (2)
(चातुर्ज्ञान / चातृज्ञान /-परिभाषा)

Attributed to Paṅgu Nārāyaṇa ("paṅgu-nārāyaṇena tu" in several Mss.). But in an article by Janardana Sastri Pandeya entitled "Vaidika-vāṅmaye Baiṭha-saṃpradāyaḥ" (Sanskrit) in : *Padmasmṛti-granthaḥ* – Nepālasthasaṃskṛtaviduṣāṃ sarvaprathamasmṛtigranthaḥ, (pub. by Padmasmṛtigranthaprakāśanasamiti, Madanamohan Dhavan, C. K. 34/39, Lahori Tola, Varanasi 1984, pp. 7-10) it is read as "paṅgunā rāvaṇena tu" and the word "paṅgu" is interpreted as "parivrāṭ" (an ascetic) applied to Rāvaṇa.

Beginning:

अग्निमीळे॥ सुता। ५। विश्वा। ६।.दधाना। ११। अजोषा। १७। इन्द्र ता। १८। सोमपा। १९। इमा। २०। जुष्टा। २०। मत्सरा। २६। द्रप्सा। २६। घृतपृष्ठा। २६। यजत्रा। २७। द्रविणोदा। २९। धानाः। ३०। शुभ्राः। ३६। पञ्चदश॥

End:

सुमनाः। २९। शुष्माः। ३०। दुर्वाः। ३०। अष्टाविंशतिः॥ त्यञ्चिदस्याः। ३। दाः। ६। सुमनाः। ७। देवाः। ९। यजमानाः। ९। स्वस्तिदाः। १०। सविश्वाः। ११। जिह्वायाः। २१। प्रचेताः। २२। अनृणाः। २२। सपत्नाः। २४। सरूपाः। २७। एकरूपाः। २७। याः। २७। एताः। २७। मुहुःश्रद्धाः। २९। स्त्वासर्वाः। ३१। अजोहुवानाः। ३६। कुल्याः। ३७। अजाः। ३८। यथादीध्यानाः। ४१। एकविंशतिः। या ममेति वर्जयित्वा। ८। इत्यष्टमाष्टकः।

Adyar D I 785 (40 A 35 = PM 112). 18 fol. Incomplete. Title: Catur-jñānādi-lakṣaṇa.

BORI 20 of 1871-72. = BORI D I i.43. 17 fol.

Hoshiarpur p. 51 (no.6681). 27 fol. 400 Grantha-s. Extract p. 75.

MD 14083. PL. Tel. 136 pp. Title: Ṛgvedānukramaṇikā. Contains portions of Padagāḍha also.

MD 14776. PL. Na. 17 fol. Title: Cāturjñāna. Catalogued as Ṛgvedānukramaṇikā.

München 32. 7 fol. (without title, but the beginning is the same as in Adyar Ms. and the end as above). See Ṛgveda-padāni.

Mysore ND II 3354 (P 7737). PL. Na. 25 fol. Extract no. 124.
Mysore ND II 3355 (C 2568/ 5). 19 fol. Extract no. 125.
Mysore ND II 3356 (C 3066). 19 fol. Extract no. 126. (a. Śaunaka).
Rajapur 1031.
RASB II 287 (G 1007). 27 fol. 300 Grantha-s. Dated V.S. 1663.
RASB II 288 (G 2061). 15 fol. 150 Grantha-s. Dated V.S. 1868.
RASB II 289 (G 2982). 7-27 fol. Incomplete. Dated V.S. 1662.
TD 1764. 18 fol. 500 Grantha-s.
TD 1765. 18 fol. 350 Grantha-s. Incomplete.
Tübingen (Roth). M. a. I.248. 12 fol. Dated Śaka 1672. Copied by Dāmodara.
Visvanatha Vamana Deva, Varanasi. 5 fol.
Visvanatha Vamana Deva, Varanasi. 19 fol.
VSM I 186 (no.5713). 484 fol. Dated Śaka 1721. Extract p. 347. A Ms. of the Pada-pāṭha. It contains the respective portions of the Cātur-jñana at the beginning of each adhyāya and the Caturakṣarī-baiṭh at the end of each varga. Aṣṭaka-s 4-8.
VSM I 433 (no.592). 28 fol. Extract p. 347.
Weber 56 (Chambers 556). 17 fol. Dated V.S. 1646.

See also Ṛgveda-paribhāṣā-kārikā above.

[NCC VII 9b; 10a]

*CĀRĀYAṆI (चारायणि)
– Cārāyaṇīya-śikṣā. See below.

549 CĀRĀYAṆĪYA-MANTRĀRṢĀDHYĀYA (**चारायणीयमन्त्रार्षाध्याय**)

Ascribed to Cārāyaṇa. List of seers of the Cārāyaṇīya school of the *Yajurveda*. Cf. Cārāyaṇīyārṣānukramaṇikā below.

Beginning: (Weber)

अथ चारायणीयानां ग्रन्थक्रमेणार्षं व्याख्यास्यामः । ओमित्येतद् ब्रह्मणः परमेष्ठिनो वाचस्पत्यं यजुः स्वर्गस्य वा एतल्लोकस्य द्वारविवरणम् । त्रयाणां लोकानां वौकः ।

End:

मन्त्रस्यार्षं न संस्पृश्य यो हि मन्त्रं जपेन्नरः ।
स गच्छेन्नरकं घोरं तस्मान्मन्त्रार्ष उद्धृतः ॥
प्रजापतिमुखात् पूर्वमार्षं छन्दश्च दैवतम् ।
योगः प्राप्तो ऽत्रिमुनिना बोधो लौगाक्षिणा ततः ॥

Ptd.: Ed. by Visva Bandhu. – Lahore : D. A. V. College, 1935. 2, 22, 19 pp. – (Dayānanda Mahāvidyālaya Saṃskṛta-granthamālā 11). [BORI (10150 / 13533); NL (180 Jc 93 256); SAI (ind 51 D 888/2322); BM (14008.a.44)]

550 CĀRĀYAṆĪYA-ŚIKṢĀ (**चारायणीयशिक्षा**)

or Cārāyaṇīya-mahāśikṣā or Cārāyaṇīyakam as it is called several times in the body of the work. It consists of 10 Adhyāya-s containing in total about 335 verses. It professes to have been composed by Cārāyaṇi (etac cārāyaṇer matam) and quotes among others Vasiṣṭha and Sanatkumāra. See F. Kielhorn : Remarks on the Śikṣās in : *Indian Antiquary*, vol. V, p. 194 (reprint in : *Kleine Schriften*, vol. I, pp. 158-69).

Beginning:

प्राक् प्रपद्ये विभुं भक्त्या सर्वलोकपितामहम्।
शिक्षां साक्षात् प्रवक्ष्यामि तेनैवालपितामहम्॥ १॥
चारायणीं महाशिक्षां प्रवक्ष्याम्यनुपूर्वशः।
निबोधत बुधैर्जुष्टां नित्यं वाङ्मलशान्तये॥ २॥
वर्णानां चैव संख्यानं संज्ञा स्थानं पृथग्विधम्।
स्वराः सव्यञ्जनाश्चैव तेषां भेदमशेषतः॥ ३॥
दश स्थानानि वर्णानां कीर्तयन्ति मनीषिणः।
यतः प्रवृत्तिर्वर्णानां तानि मे गदतः शृणु॥ ४॥

End:

चत्वारिंशत् तु दशमे श्लोका वै परिकीर्तिताः॥
एकत्रैव तु संख्यातं श्लोकानां तु शतत्रयम्।
चत्वारिंशदधिकं वै शास्त्रं चारायणीयकम्॥
अमत्सरे इदं देयं मत्सरे न कदाचन।
मत्सरे तु भवेद् दत्तं व्युप्तं बीजमिवोषरे॥
य इदं पठते नित्यं यश्चाप्यध्यापयेद् द्विजम्।
अस्यार्थं बुध्यते यो वै ब्रह्मलोकं स गच्छति॥
इति चारायणीयशिक्षायां दशमो ऽध्यायः॥ १०॥

BORI 21 of 1875-76. 13 fol. (6-18).
GB 25. 11 fol. (Copy of a Ms. from Kashmir procured through Bühler). (A xerox-copy of this Ms. is in SAI : 87/792*).
IIO Stein 62. 98 fol. Śāradā script. Copied in 1894.
Report p. ii (no.21).

[NCC VII 22a]

551 CĀRĀYAṆĪYĀRṢĀNUKRAMAṆIKĀ (**चारायणीयार्षानुक्रमणिका**)
→ Cārāyaṇīya-mantrārṣādhyāya.
Hoshiarpur p. 56 (no.6871). 7 fol. 80 Grantha-s.
Weber 142 (Chambers 40). 8 fol.

552 CINNI-BHAṬṬĪYA see SARVASAMMATA-ŚIKṢĀ-VYĀKHYĀ (**चिन्निभट्टीय / सर्वसंमतशिक्षाव्याख्या**)

553 CHANDA-ĀRCIKA-CCHALĀKṢARA (छन्द-आर्चिकच्छलाक्षर)

Ptd.: in the collection of Sāmavedic tracts, ed. by Krishnaswami Srauti (in Grantha script). – Kumbakonam : Jyotirvilasa Press, 1885, pp. 5-6. See Chala-prakriyā. [SAI (87/783*)]

554 CHANDA-UDĀHARAṆA (छन्द-उदाहरण)

Actually the Pāda-vidhāna of Śaunaka.

IM 427. 4 fol. Col.: Chandasām-udāharaṇāni. There are a few passages at the end illustrating different metres.

555 CHANDAḤ-PADA-CCHALĀKṢARA (छन्दःपदच्छलाक्षर)

Ptd.: in the collection of Sāmavedic tracts, ed. by Krishnaswami Srauti (in Grantha script). – Kumbakonam : Jyotirvilasa Press, 1885, pp. 6-7. See Chala-prakriyā. [SAI (87/783*)]

556 CHANDAḤ-PARIŚIṢṬA or CHANDOGA-PARIŚIṢṬA (छन्दःपरिशिष्ट / छन्दोगपरिशिष्ट)

The same as the Upanidāna-sūtra; see NCC II 360-61.

Ptd.: Princess of Wales Sarasvati Bhavana Texts 37.

[NCC VII 94a]

557 CHANDAḤ-SAṂKHYĀ (1) (छन्दःसंख्या)

A short index in eleven verses – a Pariśiṣṭa to the *Chandonukramaṇī* giving the total number of verses of every metre for the whole of the *Ṛgveda*. These verses are found at the end of the *Ṛgveda-sarvānukramaṇī* in several Mss, though not noted in the catalogues.

Beginning:

एकपञ्चाशदृग्वेदे गायत्रः शाकलेयके।
सहस्रद्वितयं चैव चत्वार्येव शतानि तु॥ १॥
त्रीणि शतानि सैकानि चत्वारिंशत् तथोष्णिहः।
अनुष्टुभां शतान्यष्टौ पञ्चाशत् पञ्चसंयुता॥ २॥

End:

काकुभानां तु पञ्चाशद् विज्ञेया पञ्चसंयुता।
महाबार्हत एवैक एवं सार्धं शतद्वयम्॥ १०॥
एवं दशसहस्राणि शतानां तु चतुष्टयम्।
ऋचां द्व्यधिकमाख्यातमृषिभिस्तत्त्वदर्शिभिः॥ ११॥

Adyar D I 1051 (40 A 98 = PM 140). 2 fol. (36-37). Dated V.S. 1676.

Adyar D I 1052 (41 B 76 = PM 141). 2 fol. (47-48). Dated V.S. 1715.

Ānandāśrama 2121. 10 fol. Enumeration of the Anuvāka-s and chandas in each Adhyāya. Title: Saṃhitā-cchandaḥ.

BHU B 946 (D 11/628). 2 fol. (95-96). Dated V.S. 1810. Title: Anukramaṇikā.
BHU B 1124a (D 11/630). 2 fol. Incomplete. Title: Anuvākānukramaṇikā.
BHU C 1687a (D 11/673). 1 fol. Title: Sarvānukrama.
Bombay Uni. (BMC 141 1). 1 fol. (40).
IM 2315. 2 fol. Dated V.S. 1719.
München 22(2). 2 fol. (32-33). Dated A.D. 1812. At the end of the Ṛgveda-sarvānukramaṇī.
RASB II 242(A) (G 1990). 1 fol.
SBD 2319. 1 fol. Dated V.S. 1740. At the end of the Ṛgveda-sarvānukramaṇī.
SBD 2352. 1 fol. (35). At the end of the Ṛgveda-sarvānukramaṇī.
SBD 55270a. 1 fol. Dated V.S. 1859. (Sarvānukramaṇikā).
SBD 55285. 1 fol. Dated V.S. 1617. At the end of the Sarvānukramaṇī.
SBD 55290. 1 fol. (30). Dated V.S. 1748. At the end of the Sarvānukramaṇī.
VSM III 173 (no.11341). 3 fol. Contains the Chandaḥ-saṃkhyā, Chandasām udāharaṇāni and Anuvāka-pañcāśī. Title : Sarvānukrama-pariśiṣṭa.

Ptd.: Ed. by Arthur A. Macdonell, in the edition of the *Kātyāyana's Sarvānukramaṇī of the Rigveda*. – Oxford : Clarendon Press, 1886, pp. 54-55. – (Anecdota Oxoniensia, Aryan Series vol. I, pt. iv).
Ed. by Vasanta Sripada (Damodar) Satwalekar, as an appendix to the *Ṛgveda-saṃhitā*. – Aundh, Pardi (Balsad Dist. Gujarat) : Svadhyaya Mandala, 1929 (several reprints), p. 829.
Photographic reprint of the above with an additional preface in Sanskrit, edited by V. R. Laksmikanta Sarma. – Kumbakonam (612001, 14 Kamakshi Josier Street) : The Maharaja Saheb Sri Govinda Deekshitar Punya Smarana Samiti, 1979.
Ed. by Umesh Chandra Sharma, together with the *Ṛgveda-sarvānukramaṇī*. – Aligarh : Viveka Publications, 1977, p 48.

For details see above under Ṛgveda-sarvānukramaṇī.
Also quoted fully by Yudhisthira Mimamsaka in his *Ṛgvedasya Ṛksaṃkhyā*, included as appendix seven to the *Kātyāyanīya-sarvānukramaṇī*, ed. by Vijayapal, p. 348.

558 CHANDAḤ-SAṂKHYĀ (2) (छन्दःसंख्या)
Unspecified (probably part of the *Sarvānukramaṇī*):
B III, p. 60.
PUL I, p. 18 (no.14). 4 fol. (with Anuvākānukrama). Dated Śaka 1823.

– C. of Ṣaḍguru-śiṣya.
München 23. (Written ca. A.D. 1650). Part of the C. on the *Ṛgveda-sarvānukramaṇī*.

[NCC VII 97b]

559 CHANDARṢI-DEVATĀNUKRAMA (छन्दर्षिदेवतानुक्रम)
of some Ṛgveda Sūkta-s and Rudrādhyāya.
Wai I 334. 7 fol.

560 CHANDĀRṢEYA (**छन्दार्षेय**)

RV. Alwar 30. Dated V.S. 1543.

[NCC VII 99a]

561 CHANDOGA-ṚKSVARA-LAKṢAṆA (**छन्दोग-ऋक्स्वरलक्षण**)

SV.

Beginning: (793)

छन्दोग-ऋक्स्वरलक्षणमुच्यते । अनेकोदात्तेभ्यः परस्य उदात्तशिरस्कस्य अनुदात्तस्य स्वरिततेत्यवगन्तव्यम्। यथा -- निहोता सत्सि बर्हिषि। अनूधां यदजीजनदन्धाचिदा। त्वामिद्धि हवामहे। अग्ने युक्ष्वा हि ये त वाश्वासो देवसाधवः इत्यादि। अनेकोदात्तेभ्यः परस्येति किम्। अग्न आयाहि वीतये गृणानो हव्यदातये। अत्र एकैकोदात्तात् परेषां या ये दा इत्येतेषां स्वरितत्वं न। उदात्ताशिरस्कस्येति किम्। इममू षु त्वमस्माकम्। अत्र परस्य मस्य शंयोरभिस्रवन्तु नः । अत्र न इत्यस्य च स्वरितत्वप्राप्त्यर्थमित्यवगन्तव्यम् । अनेकेषामुदात्तानामुदात्ताशिरस्कस्येत्युक्तिः ।

End:

चतुर्थे -- न्नो अग्ने। ने अभि। जो अथि। तो अत्य। ये अप्र। वो अस्तु। शुक्रिये। यो अभि । न्तो अग्ने । नो अक्तु । शक्वर्यां द्वितीये -- त्वो अभि । तृतीये त्ते अद्रि । वो अद्व । एवमसंधिप्रदेशाः आग्नेये द्वात्रिंशत् । आरणे पञ्चदश । शुक्रिये त्रयः । शाक्वर्यां त्रयः इत्यवगन्तव्यम् । इत्थं संधिप्रदेशा एकपञ्चाशत् । असंधिप्रदेशाः षोडशषष्ट्युत्तरशतसंख्याका इत्येवं ज्ञातव्यम्॥

Adyar D I 792 (19 O 14 = 66896). PL. Gr. 4 fol. (1-4).
Adyar D I 793 (28 N 31 = 73279). PL. Gr. 18 fol.
Adyar D I 794 (38 E 20 = TR 22). 4 fol. (pp. 1-7); a transcript of no.792 made in 1938.
Adyar D XIII 254 (VB 432b). PL. Gr. 2 fol. Incomplete. The beginning and end are different from the above.
PUL II. App. p. 10 (no.146). ? PL. Gr. 27 fol. 250 Grantha-s.

[NCC VII 99a]

562 CHANDOGA-VYĀKARAṆA(-SŪTRA) (**छन्दोगव्याकरण /-सूत्र**)

→ Ṛktantra.
IM 2592. 8 fol. Dated V.S. 1677.
Hpr. III 43. 5 fol. 105 Grantha-s.
Oxf. CS d.80(6). 5 fol. Dated A.D. 1909.
SBD 2087. 6 fol.

563 CHANDODĀHARAṆA (**छन्दोदाहरण**)

of Kātyāyana.
Trav. Uni. 4914. 70 Grantha-s.

564 CHANDO-DĪPA (छन्दोदीप)

The same as the *Sāma-paribhāṣā* in which the expression "sāmnāṃ dīpasthānīyo granthaḥ" occurs in the introductory portion.

Mysore I, p. 26.

Mysore ND II 3359 (P 1978/ 3). PL. Na. 11 fol. (16-26). Extract no. 128.

Viśvabhāratī 754. Incomplete.

[NCC VII 102a]

565 CHANDO-DEVATĀNUKRAMAṆĪ (छन्दोदेवतानुक्रमणी)

of Śaunaka. The Ms. begins with the final verse of the *Ārṣānukramaṇī*, contains *Chandonukramaṇī* (same as the one printed in Rajendralal Mitra's edition of the *Bṛhaddevatā)* and the *Devatānukramaṇī* at the end.

Beginning:

छन्दांस्यशेषाण्यनुकीर्तितानि गायत्र्यादीनि चतुर्दशानि।
तत्तद्विशेषैः सह वैदिकानि कल्याणदायीनि भवन्तु मह्यम्॥
एवमुक्ते छन्दसि च मन्त्राणां खल्वशेषतः।
अथातो ऽनुक्रमिष्यामः अस्माद् दाशतये पथि॥
सूक्तर्गर्धर्चपादानां दैवतं तन्निबोधत।
आग्नेयं प्रथमं सूक्तं सप्त चोत्तरयोस्तृचाम्॥
वायव्यः प्रथमस्तेषां द्वितीयस्त्वैन्द्रवायवः।
तृतीयो मैत्रावरुणश्चतुर्थस्तृच आश्विनः।
ऐन्द्रस्तु पञ्चमः षष्ठो वैश्वदेवो ऽथ सप्तमः॥
सारस्वतस्त्वनेनोक्ताः सप्त प्र-उगदेवताः।

End:

प्राग्नये सूक्तमाग्नेयं जातवेदस्यमुत्तमम्।
आ यं गौरिति यत् सूक्तं सार्पराज्ञार्षकं परम्॥
त्रिस्थानविष्ठिता वाश्वा सूर्यो वा तस्य देवता।
उपान्त्यं खलु तं सूक्तं भाववृत्तं प्रचक्ष्यते॥
आग्नेयं सं समित्येषा सूक्तं संज्ञानदेवतम्।

इति देवतानुक्रमणी समाप्ता।

अशेषमन्त्रैरिह या प्रतीता सा देवतानन्दमयी समस्ता।
संकीर्तितास्माभिरनुक्रमेण सा चापि नः सर्वसुखप्रदा स्यात्॥

MT 4169. 32 fol. Incomplete. Lacunae in the middle. Transcribed in 1922-23 from a Ms. of Sankaran Nambudiri, Alambaṭṭi-mana, Kavalappara Post, Shoranur. There is a transcript of this Ms. with Prof. Kunjunni Raja, Adyar Library, Madras. (A xerox-copy of this Ms. is in SAI : 87/787*).

[NCC VII 102a]

566 CHANDO-DAIVATA (छन्दोदैवत)
RV. TCD 17. See Ṛṣi-cchando-daivata, above.

[NCC VII 102a]

567 CHANDO-NIDARŚANA (छन्दोनिदर्शन)
Ṛgvedic metres are illustrated.
MD 902. Tel. 4 pp. Incomplete.

[NCC VII 102a]

568 CHANDO-NIRṆAYA (छन्दोनिर्णय)
on the metres of the mantra-s of the *Ṛgveda.*
MD 903. PL. Kan. 8 pp.

[NCC VII 102a]

569 CHANDONUKRAMAṆĪ (1) (छन्दोनुक्रमणी)
of the *Maitrāyaṇī-saṃhitā;* part of the *Vārāha-pariśiṣṭa-s.*

Ptd.: ed. by Raghu Vira, from its only Ms. from Baroda, the edition of the first section consisting of 33 verses, in : JRAS (1932), pp. 547-53. [Adyar (A05R RAS N1932); Emeneau (396)]

Reprinted in : *Vedic Studies* – A Collection of the Research Papers of Prof. Raghuvira, ed. by Mrs. Sharada Rani. – New Delhi - 110016 (Hauzkhas Enclave), 1981, pp. 37-43. (Śata-Piṭaka Series – Indo-Asian Literatures, vol. 272). [Adyar (H080 SVS SP 272); NL (180 Jb 98 37); SAI (ind S 180, 272); UBTÜ (22 A 6435)]

[NCC VII 102a]

570 CHANDONUKRAMAṆĪ (2) (छन्दोनुक्रमणी)
of Śaunaka. Index of the metres in the *Ṛgveda.* It enumerates for each Maṇḍala the number of verses in each metre as well as the aggregate in all metres. Altogeter about 300 verses, divided into ten Maṇḍala-s, consisting of 53, 10, 15, 11, 28, 24, 16, 54, 12 and 63 verses, respectively (according to L. Mitra's edition).

Beginning:

ऋग्वेदगतसूक्तानां सूक्तस्थानामृचामपि।
यानि छन्दांसि विद्यन्ते तानि वक्ष्यामि संप्रति॥ १॥
गायत्रं नव सूक्तानि मधुच्छन्दस आदितः।
आनुष्टुभे परे ज्ञेये दशमैकादशे उभे॥ २॥
मेधातिथेस्तु सूक्तेषु गायत्रेषूत्तरे त्विति।
पुर उष्णिक् परानुष्टुप् तिस्रश्चान्त्या अनुष्टुभः ॥ ३॥

End:

तथा द्वितीया गायत्री प्रसूनव इति त्विह।
संसमित्युत्तमे सूक्ते तृतीया त्रिष्टुभेव च॥ ६२॥
छन्दांस्यशेषाण्यनुकीर्तितानि गायत्र्यादीनि चतुर्दशानि।
तत्तद्विशेषैः सह वैदिकानि कल्याणदायीनि भवन्तु मह्यम्॥ ६३॥

BHU B 961 (D 2F/2149). 16 fol. Dated V.S. 1854 / Śaka 1719.
BISM vi. 870.
GD I 7. PL. Mal. 114 fol. 1140 Grantha-s. (Contains Ārṣānukramaṇī, Chandonukramaṇī and Devatānukramaṇī). Title: Ṛksarvānukramaṇī.
Haug p. 32 (no.89) = München 25. See Ārṣānukramaṇī also.
München 25(2). 12 fol. Dated A.D. 1784.
Oxf. CS d.74(8). 18 fol.
RASB II 239(3) (G 1896). 11 fol.
RASB II 243 (G 2066). 2 fol. (I. Maṇḍala).
RASB II 244 (G 2067). 10 fol. (3-12).
RASB II 246(3) (G 6022). 6 fol. (23-28).
SBD 2350. 14 fol.
SBD 2367. 14 fol.
Trav. Uni. 4847. 300 Grantha-s. (Ṛkchandonukramaṇī).
Trav. Uni. 4925. 300 Grantha-s. (Ṛkchandonukramaṇī).
Wai II 10252. 25 fol. Dated Śaka 1763.
Wai II 10253. 31 fol.

Ptd.: ed. by Rajendralal Mitra, as an Appendix to the *Bṛhaddevatā*. – Calcutta, 1893, pp. 279-325. – (Bibliotheca Indica 127). [NL (180 Jc 89 40); Emeneau (389); BM : Ptd. Bks. Cat. 1892-1906. 626 (14002.a.; vol.127); IO : Ptd. Bks. Cat. 1938, p. 544 (Bibl. Ind. 127)]

Ed. by Umesh Chandra Sharma. – Aligarh : Viveka Publications, 1981. 6, 50, 14 pp. [BORI (41151); NL (180 Pc 98 17)]

See above under Ṛgveda-cchandonukramaṇī.

[NCC VII 102a]

571 CHANDO-BHAKTI-JÑĀNA (छन्दोभक्तिज्ञान)
Mysore I, p. 26. Cf. Mysore ND II 3361: Chandopajñāna.

[NCC VII 103b]

572 CHANDO-BHĀṢĀ (छन्दोभाषा)
Name of the commentary of Māhiṣeya on the *Taittirīya-prātiśākhya*.
MT 3760.

[NCC VII 103b]

573 CHANDO-BHEDA (छन्दोभेद)
A list of Vedic metres, Gāyatrī, etc. with their variations furnishing illustrations (atha ṛgvedaśākalasaṃhitāyāṃ chandobhedaprārambhaḥ).
GJKSV 13614(A). 2 fol.

574 CHANDO-VIJAYA (छन्दोविजय)
Mysore I, p. 26.

[NCC VII 107b]

575 CHALA-PRAKRIYĀ (छलप्रक्रिया)
Ascribed to Rāvaṇa. A Sāmavedic manual explaining notations used in Chalākṣara-s; in 22 verses. See Burnell, *Saṃhitopaniṣad-brāhmaṇa*, pp. XV, XVI; R. Simon, WZKM. vol. 27, p. 325.

Beginning: (798)

अथ च्छलप्रक्रिया लिख्यते।

पञ्चविधाष्टविधयोश्छलयोः कथ्यतेऽधुना।
संदेहमोचनी साम्नां प्रक्रिया निधनस्य च॥ १॥
कचटतपा ये वर्गा विज्ञेया ग्रहणेन ते।
हयरलव इत्युक्तो वर्गो यत्र न गृह्यते॥ २॥
वर्गाक्षरं पदैर्विद्यान्मात्रां विद्याद् विवृत्तिभिः।
पाणिना दक्षिणेनैव लेखनीयं पदं ततः॥ ३॥
अनुस्वारो विसर्गश्च व्यञ्जनं स्वरवर्जितम्।
स्वराश्च सर्वे कथिता विवृत्तय इति ध्रुवम्॥ ४॥
लेखनीयाश्च वामेन पाणिनात्र विवृत्तयः।
विवृत्तयः पदादौ च न लेख्यास्ताः कदाचन॥ ५॥

End:

सुता इन्द्रा सोमसामग्रहणोद्धातवर्जितः।
हकारमक्षरं वात्र विवृत्त्या परिकीर्तितम्॥ २०॥
ससंज्ञमक्षरं प्रोक्तं परिप्राधसकस्य च।
विवृत्त्युद्धातयुक्तस्य ग्रहणे रहितस्य च॥ २१॥
विधर्मसाम चोत्तारं विवृत्त्या हीनमुच्यते।
पवस्वसोमसंज्ञकं कमित्युदीरिताक्षरम्॥ २२॥

इति च्छलप्रक्रिया (षड्वर्गिकं) समाप्ता॥

Adyar D I 798 (35 B 117 = PM 100). 2 fol. = Adyar I, p. 49a. Title: Chalākṣara-prakriyā.

Adyar D I 799 (40 B 55) 12 fol. (1-16; fol. 2, 8, 9, 13 are missing). (Different from the above.)

Adyar D I 810 (Chalākṣara; Ṣaḍvarṇikā; see remarks on p. 264).

Alwar 298. Cf. Ūha-cchalākṣara, L 1415 and Rahasya-cchalākṣara, L. 1420.

BORI 105/1 of 1886-92. 1 fol. This Ms. contains five more verses at the end; altogether 27. Title: Chalaprakriyā-pariśiṣṭam.

IM 2555A. 1 fol. 22 verses. Col.: Ṣaḍvarṇikā.

IO 4325 (Burnell 496h). Gr. 1 fol. Written ca. A.D. 1877.

Jammu RSRI p. 70 (no.5259ka). 3 fol. (Stein 267).

Stein p. 15 (no. 267). 3 fol. Dated V.S. 1723. Ascribed to Somadeva.

Ptd.: ed. by Krishnaswami Srauti (in Grantha script). – Kumbakonam : Jyotirvilasa Press, 1885. Title page: chalaprakriyādayo granthāḥ sāmagānām atyantopakārāya pañcanadavāstavyena prayāgakulatilakena kṛṣṇasvāmi-śrauti-samākhyena sūriṇā samyak pariśodhya pañcanadastha- jyotirvilāsa- mudrākṣaraśālāyāṃ mudritā vijayante | pārttiva saṃ. vaikāśimā | [MyORI (B 2508); SAI (87/783*)]

This collection of Sāmavedic works contains the following tracts:

[NCC VII 108b]

576 CHALĀKṢARA (छलाक्षर)

An index to the Gāna of *Sāmaveda.*

Adyar D I 800 (19 O 14 = 66896). PL. Gr. 29 fol. (58ff.).

Adyar D I 801 (38 E 20 = TR 22). 56 fol. (pp. 144-225). A transcript of the above, made by K. Ramachandra Sharma, dated 24.9.38.

Adyar D I 802 (19 M 17 = 66785). PL. Gr. 13 fol. to the Ūhagāna (the beginning the same as in MD 14095). = Adyar I, p. 48b. Title: Ūhacchalākṣara.

Adyar D I 803 (19 M 43 = 66811). PL. Gr. 2 fol. to the Rahasyagāna. Dated 17th Mārkali, Hasta Nakṣatra, Bhava year. = Adyar I, p. 49a.

Adyar D I 804 (19 M 53 = 66821). PL. Gr. 9 fol. (18ff.) to the Prakṛtigāna. Incomplete. = Adyar I, p. 49a.

Adyar D I 805 (21 E 47 = 67976). PL. Gr. 14 fol. to the Prakṛtigāna. = Adyar I, p. 49a.

Adyar D I 806 (21 E 49 = 67978/1). PL. Gr. 41 fol. to Rahasya, Ūha and Prakṛti. = Adyar I, p. 49a.

Adyar D I 807 (21 E 49 = 67978/2). PL. Gr. 7 fol. (42-48) to the Prakṛti. Incomplete. = Adyar I, p. 49a.

Adyar D I 808 (25 D 35 = 70855). PL. Gr. 2 fol. (1-2) to the Prakṛti. Incomplete. = Adyar I, p. 49a.

Adyar D I 809 (33 C 27 = 75222). PL. Gr. 25 fol. = Adyar I, p. 49a. Dated Monday, 22nd of Dhanu of Tāraṇa. Consists of the following sections:

1) Ūhacchala (fol. 1-14a).
2) Rahasyacchala (fol. 15a-17a).
3) Uttara-ṛkchala-kārikā (fol. 17a-21a).
4) Pūrva-ṛkchala-kārikā (fol. 21).
5) Pūrva-ṛkchalākṣara (fol. 21b-22a).
6) Pūrva-ṛkpada-cchalākṣara (fol. 22).

7) Stobhapada-cchalākṣara (fol. 22b).
8) Uttara-ṛkchalākṣara (fol. 22b-25a).

Adyar D I 810 (35 C 29 = PM 117). 15 fol. = Adyar I, p. 49a. Also contains 22 verses entitled Ṣaḍvarṇikā, called in the colophon Pariśiṣṭa to the Chala-s, same as no.798, Chalaprakriyā. Dated V.S. 17(0?)9 / Śaka 1574.

Brl. p. 49 (no.CL) = IO 4314.

Brl. p. 49 (no.CLI) = IO 4315.

Burnell 10b.

IM 171. 6 fol. Catalogued as Chalāchala.

IM 172. 4 fol. Title: Rahasya-cchalākṣara.

IO 4294 (Burnell 64a). PL. Gr. 9 fol. (139-47) (Grāma- and Āraṇya-gāna) = MT 238(b).

IO 4295 (Burnell 164b). PL. Gr. 12 fol. Col.: Āgneyādi-mahānāmnī- paryantaṃ rāvaṇa-bhaṭṭaṃ samāptam. (Grāma- and Āraṇya-gāna). This Ms, as the loan slip therein shows, was used by R. Simon in 1911.

IO 4296 (Burnell 60b). PL. Gr. 28 fol. (160-87). Dated A.D. 1797-8 (Grāma- and Āraṇya-gāna).

IO 4297 (Burnell 188b). PL. Gr. 9 fol. (136-44). Dated A.D. 1794. Col.: Prakṛti-cchalākṣara.

IO 4298 (Mackenzie VIII 76d). PL. Gr. 15 fol. Written ca. A.D. 1804 (Grāma- and Āraṇya-gāna).

IO 4299 (3419 b). PL. Gr. 13 fol. (Grāma- and Āraṇya-gāna).

IO 4314 (Burnell 64b). PL. Gr. 16 fol. Col.: Rāvaṇa-bhaiṭ; Ūha-rahasya-cchalākṣara.

IO 4315 (Burnell 164d). PL. Gr. 19 fol. Col.: Rāvaṇa-bhaṭṭīyam; Ūha-rahasya-cchalākṣara.

IO 4316 (Mackenzie VIII 75d). PL. Gr. 15 fol. (Ūha-rahasya-cchalākṣara).

IO 4317 (Burnell 189b). PL. Gr. 7 fol. (Ūha-rahasya-cchalākṣara).

IO 4318 (3417 b). PL. Gr. 5 fol. (Ūha-rahasya-cchalākṣara).

IO 4319 (Burnell 546). PL. Gr. 1 fol. (Rāvaṇa-bhaṭṭa; Daśarātra).

IO 4320 (Burnell 201b). PL. Gr. 4 fol. (Rahasya-cchalākṣara).

L 1415. 18 fol. 238 Grantha-s (Ūha-cchalākṣara).

L 1420. 4 fol. 60 Grantha-s (Rahasya-cchalākṣara).

L 1559. 10 fol. 108 Grantha-s.

Oppert I 1158. PL. Tel. 70 pp. Belonged to Ramanujacharyar of Tadakamangalam, Chingelpet Dist.

Oppert I 4524. PL. Gr. 100 pp. Belonged to Krishna Jyosyar of Pudukkottai.

RASB II 1317 (G 259) = L 1415 → Ūha-cchalākṣara.

Trav. Uni. 2318 A (Prakṛti). PL. Gr. 100 Grantha-s → Prakṛti-cchalākṣara.

Trav. Uni. 3358 C (Rahasya). PL. Gr. 50 Grantha-s.

Trav. Uni. 3544 B (Āraṇyaka). PL. Gr. 50 Grantha-s.

Trav. Uni. 3598 B (Ūha). PL. Gr. 200 Grantha-s.

Trav. Uni. 3598 C (Rahasya). PL. Gr. 50 Grantha-s.

Trav. Uni. 3855 B (Prakṛti). PL. Gr. 200 Grantha-s.

Trav. Uni. 12199 (Prakṛti). PL. Gr. 200 Grantha-s.

Trav. Uni. 13677 A (Prakṛti). PL. Gr. 190 Grantha-s. Incomplete.

Trav. Uni. 18661 A. PL. Gr. 1825 Grantha-s.

Trav. Uni. 18661 B. PL. Gr. 800 Grantha-s.

Trav. Uni. 18671. PL. Gr. 750 Grantha-s.
Trav. Uni. 18677 A. PL. Gr. 125 Grantha-s.
Whish 167. PL. Gr. 9 fol. (157-65). Title: Prakṛti-cchalākṣara.

See also Rāvaṇa-bhaiṭ.

[NCC VII 108b-109a]

577 CHALĀKṢARA-KĀRIKĀ (**छलाक्षरकारिका**)

Ptd.: in the collection of Sāmavedic tracts, ed. by Krishnaswami Srauti (in Grantha script). – Kumbakonam : Jyotirvilasa Press, 1885, pp. 4-5. See Chala-prakriyā. [SAI (87/783*)]

578 CHALĀKṢARA-PARIBHĀṢĀ (**छलाक्षरपरिभाषा**)

Adyar I, p. 49a. See Ūhasāma-parigaṇana, Adyar D I 759 and Chala-prakriyā, Adyar D I 798.
Adyar D I 1065 → Salakṣaṇa-paribhāṣā.

[NCC VII 109a]

579 CHALĀCHCHALA (?) (**छलाच्छल**)

IM 171. 6 fol. → (Rahasya-)Chalākṣara.

[NCC VII 109a]

580 CHALĀSAṂHITĀ (**छलासंहिता**)

SBD 52211. 16 fol. Dated V.S. 1626. Attributed to Bhaṭṭa Govinda in the catalogue. But it is the name of the scribe. Col.: it ekādaśagranthachalā samāptā. Pertains to *Sāmaveda.*

581 CHĀNDASYĀRCAKA-CCHALĀKṢARA (**छान्दस्यार्चकच्छलाक्षर**)
SV.

L 1559. 10 fol. 108 Grantha-s. (Pavamāna-cchalākṣara).
RASB II 1316 (G 743) (in 3 Khaṇḍa-s) = L 1559.

[NCC VII 110b]

582 JAKĀRA-LOPA (**जकारलोप**)

Mysore ND II 3367 (P 4906/45). PL. Na. 1 fol. (127). Extract no. 136. Similar to Akāravarja above.

*JAGANNĀTHA (**जगन्नाथ**)

Writer of an Anukramaṇī for the Bāṣkala Śākhā. See RASB II 234-37. Mss. are found in catalogues under different titles.

– Anuvākānukramaṇī-vivaraṇa. Trav. Uni. 4920.
– Ṛgveda-varṇa-krama-(jñāna-)lakṣaṇa or Varṇa-krama-lakṣaṇa. See NCC III 13b and 18b.
– C. RASB II 268 (fragment).
– Ṛgveda-sarvānukramaṇī-vivaraṇa or Anukramaṇikā-vivaraṇa or Sūkta-pratīka of the Bāṣkala Śākhā. Bombay Uni. 719, 720. Calcutta Skt. Coll. I 24, 25. IO 58. See NCC III 25b-26a.
– Ṛgveda-sūkta-pratīkānukramaṇikā-sāra. Trav. Uni. 4915. 1100 Grantha-s. Dated V.S. 1796 / Śaka 1661. Cf. previous entry.

[NCC VII 134a]

583 JAṬĀ- (जटा)
Unspecified.
CPB 1728-29.
GJKSV 31557. 20-80 fol. (many fol. missing).

– RV. Calcutta Skt. Coll. I 36 → Ṛgveda-jaṭā-pāṭha.
[NCC VII 145a]

584 JAṬĀ-GHANA-PADDHATI (जटाघनपद्धति)
BISM p. 99 (54/379). 2 fol. Illustrations of Jaṭā, Mālā, Śikhā, Rekhā and Dhvaja for the verse "yajñena yajñam" with verses of definition from the *Vikṛti-vallī*.
BISM p. 99 (54/401). 5 fol. Illustration of eight Vikṛti-s with verses of definition for the verse "agneḥ pūrve bhrātaro".

585 JAṬĀ-GHANA-SAṂGRAHA (जटाघनसंग्रह)
Oppert II 747. Belonged to Ghanapathi Shingaracharyar of Alasur, Madurantakam Taluk.
[NCC VII 145a]

586 JAṬĀ-DARPAṆA (जटादर्पण)
Oppert I 7136. Belonged to Pola Lakshmanavadhani of Vijayanagaram.
Oppert I 7186 (Jaṭā-darpaṇa-mūla). Belonged to Ivattur Nandikesvara Sastri of Vijayanagaram.
PUL II. App. p. 11 (no.167). PL. Tel. 28 fol. 500 Grantha-s.
[NCC VII 145b]

587 JAṬĀDI-KRAMA (जटादिक्रम)
A list of hymns of the *Ṛgveda* with rules of recitation.
Oxf. CS c.2(12). 2 fol. (110, 109). Incomplete. 37 verses only.

588 JAṬĀDY-AṢṬA-VIKṚTI-LAKṢAṆA (जटाद्यष्टविकृतिलक्षण)
SBD 55683. 8 fol. Not available for consultation as it was under seal.
Wai I 345. 2 fol. Dated Śaka 1808.

589 JAṬĀDY-AṢṬA-VIKṚTI-LAKṢAṆA-KĀRIKĀ (जटाद्यष्टविकृतिलक्षणकारिका)
Ptd.: At the end of the *Ṛgveda-prātiśākhya* with Uvaṭa's Bhāṣya. – Benaras, 1903. – (Ben. S. S. 13.). Ten verses (on p. 399) with a few remarks, probably by the editor.
Reprinted together with the *Vyāḷi-śikṣā*, ed. by Kesavasiva Ghanapathi, in the magazine of the Mysore Sanskrit College, *Śrīmanmahārāja Saṃskṛta Mahāpāṭhaśālā Patrikā*, vols. 23-26 (1948-50), Mysore, p. 70.

590 JAṬĀDY-AṢṬA-VIKṚTI-VIVARAṆA (जटाद्यष्टविकृतिविवरण)
→ Aṣṭa-vikṛti-vivṛti(-kārikā).
IM 2425. 18 fol. (18-35). Incomplete. Title: Madhusūdana-śikṣā-bhāṣya.
SBD 47936. 17 fol. Also called Madhusūdana-śikṣā-bhāṣya.

591 JAṬĀDHIKĀRA (जटाधिकार)
of Rāma. It consists of mostly quotations from Hayagrīva and Vyāḍi.
BBRAS 488 (B D 278). 1 fol. Dated A.D. 1787.

[NCC VII 145b]

592 JAṬĀNUVĀKA (जटानुवाक)

BISM p. 99 (32/126). 5 fol. Jaṭā-pāṭha on a few passages of the VS. Begins: ayaṃ puraḥ puroyaṃ ... and ends: hotā yakṣad ity anuvākaḥ ||

593 JAṬĀ-NYĀYA (जटान्याय)

Trav. Uni. 2972 A. PL. Gr. 225 Grantha-s (with C.). Incomplete → Jaṭā-nyāya-pañcāśat with C. = Adyar 811.

[NCC VII 145b]

594 JAṬĀ-NYĀYA-PAÑCĀŚAT (जटान्यायपञ्चाशत्)

or Nyāya-pañcāśat or Jaṭā-vallī or Jaṭāsaṃdhi-lakṣaṇa; pertains to Taitt.

Beginning: (817)

वागीशप्रभृतिस्तुत्यं प्रणम्याहं गणाधिपम्।
वागीशं च तथा श्रीशं वरदं जगतां पतिम्॥ १॥
क्रमेण द्विपदं ब्रूयाद् व्युत्क्रमेणोत्क्रमेण च।
सलक्षणं सर्वसंधौ जटा सा प्रोच्यते बुधैः ॥ २॥
अस्याः प्रमाणं प्रथमे प्रातिशाख्यप्रपाठके।
रेफादेशे ऽपिशब्दाच्च न धामेत्यार्षशब्दतः ॥ ३॥

End:

यः प्राणश्च तथायुर्दाः प्राणं मे मयि के नव।
येनाग्ने ऽस्मिन्त् सधस्थे च वाज्यद्धनो न लुप्यते॥
त्रिपदप्रभृतिष्वेव बलीयस्य नियोगता।
अलोप एव कण्ठोक्तेरन्ययोगे ऽपि सर्वदा॥ ५५॥
जटावल्लि समाप्तः ॥

Adyar D I 817 (19 G 12 = 66413). PL. Tel. 3 fol. (3-5); 55 verses. = Adyar I, p. 50a.
Adyar D I 818 (23 E 25 = 69758). PL. Gr. 3 fol. (3-5). Incomplete.
Baroda 8005(b). PL. Tel. 3 fol. 52 Grantha-s = CLB I, p. 27. Extract pp. 147-48.
Deccan College 9809. 23 fol. (with C.). Dated Śaka 1735. Title: Jaṭāvali or Jaṭavallī.
Hamburg StUB (cod.Palmbl. III 8/133) → Veda-lakṣaṇa (HB).
IO 4459 (3707b). PL. Na. 20 fol. (with C.). Written ca. A.D. 1800.
MD 909. 7 pp. Title: Jaṭāvali.
MD 17544. PL. Gr. 12 pp. 150 Grantha-s. Incomplete.
MT 95(f). PL. Gr. 2 fol. (14-15). Purchased in 1910-11 from Gopalaswami Ayyangar of Mannargudi.
MT 3887(n). PL. Gr. 3 fol. (113-15). Lacks two stanzas in the beginning. Purchased in 1921-22 from Annasvami Sastrigal, Bhavani, Coimbatore Dist.
MT 5099(a). PL. Gr. 3 fol. Purchased in 1925-26 from R. Varadacharyar, Village Munsif, Sirudamur, South Arcot Dist.
Mysore p. 2 (no.57). 3 fol. Title: Yajurveda-jaṭāvali / Jaṭā-lakṣaṇa.

Mysore I, p. 30.

Mysore ND II 3595 (B 600/ 9). Na. 4 fol. = Adyar 811.

Oppert I 983 (all entries in Oppert : Jaṭāvali). Belonged to Viraraghava Tatacharyar, Head Master, Sanskrit School of Sathakopacharya, Kanchipuram, Chingelpet Dist.

Oppert I 2327. PL. Gr. 15 pp. Belonged to Sri Sarasvati Bhandaram Committee of Tiru-vallikkeni, Madras.

Oppert I 7188. Belonged to Ivattur Nandikesvara Sastri of Vijayanagaram.

Oppert II 750. Belonged to Ghanapathi Shingaracharyar of Alasur, Madurantakam Taluk.

Oppert II 1319. Belonged to Gopalacharyar of Pillapakkam, Kanchipuram Taluk.

Oppert II 7954. Belonged to Venkatarama Dikshita of Sorakayur, Thanjavur Dist.

PUL II. App. p. 11 (no.168). PL. Tel. 20 fol. 400 Grantha-s (with C.).

PUL II. App. p. 11 (no.169). PL. Tel. 20 fol. 400 Grantha-s (with C.).

Tirupati SVUORI 2040 (4378f). PL. Gr. 3 fol. (27-29). Title: Jaṭā-vallī.

Tirupati SVUORI (3516ā). PL. Gr. 3 fol. 52 verses. Title: Jaṭā-vallī.

Trav. Uni. 2630 B. PL. Gr. 35 Grantha-s. Title: Nyāya-pañcāśat.

Trav. Uni. 2972 A. PL. Gr. 225 Grantha-s (with C.). Incomplete. Title: Jaṭā-nyāya.

Wai II 10269. 4 fol. Title: Jaṭā-vallī. (A xerox-copy of this Ms. is in SAI).

See also Jaṭāvalī (-vallī).

– C.

Beginning: (811)

जटान्यायपञ्चाशद्याख्यानम्।

वागीशं च तथा श्रीशं गौरीशं गजकर्णकम्।
गुरुं नत्वा जटान्यायग्रन्थटीकां करोम्यहम्॥

अत्र ग्रन्थकृत् स्वकृतस्य ग्रन्थस्य निष्प्रत्यूहपरिपूरणाय मङ्गलप्राप्तये प्रेक्षावतां प्रवृत्तिसिद्धये च इष्टदेवतानमस्काररूपं मङ्गलमाचरति -- अजादिभिरिति॥

अजादिभिः प्रार्थनीयं गजास्यं गिरिजासुतम्।
सुजागरूकसूर्याभं व्रजामि शरणं सदा॥

अजो ब्रह्मा । आदिशब्देन विष्णवीशादयो गृह्यन्ते । तदादिभिर्विष्णवीशाद्यैः प्रार्थनीयमभ्यर्थनीयम्। गजस्य आस्यमिवास्यं यस्य तं गजास्यम्। गिरिजासुतम्। गिरिजा पार्वतीत्यर्थः। तस्याः सुतं सुजागरूकं सम्यक् जागृतम्। विघ्ननिवृत्ताविति शेषः। सूर्यो भानुः। तस्य भेदा भा कान्तिर्यस्य तं भूतं विघ्नेश्वरं सदा शरणं व्रजामि। शारदामपि प्रार्थयति -- शारदेति ...॥

शारदेन्दूपमां ज्योत्स्नां सर्वविद्याविशारदाम्।
शारदां प्रार्थ्य वक्ष्यामि जटायां संधिलक्षणम्॥

ननु जटायां संधिनिर्णयमित्यत्र जटाशब्दः प्रतिपादितः । तत्र जटा नाम केत्याकाङ्क्षायामाह --

क्रमेण द्विपदं ब्रूयाद् व्युत्क्रमेणोत्क्रमेण च।
सलक्षणं सर्वसंधौ जटा सा प्रोच्यते बुधैः ॥

End:

व्यञ्जनं स्वराङ्गमिति लक्षणलक्षितम् । आदिशब्देन द्विरोष्ठ्यादयो गृह्यन्ते । अनुस्वारः रेफोष्मसंयोग इत्यनेनोक्तः । विहतं यदङ्गादिविक्रमः । स्वरितयोर्मध्य इति लक्षणलक्षितम् । अत्रादिशब्देन त्रिमात्रविरामादयः । विप्रः समाहितमनाः शुचिः । जटादयो गृह्यन्ते । कम्पः । द्वियम एक द्वियम पर इत्यनेनोक्तविधिः । यद्यत् सूत्रविरुद्धं तत् शीक्षावचनजातं यद्यत् सर्वमपि संहितावज्जटायामपि कर्तव्यमिति विशेषः ।

एवं विदित्वा यो विप्रः समाहितमनाः शुचिः ।
जटां नित्यमधीयानः सो ऽक्षयं फलमश्नुते॥

जटान्यायपञ्चाशद्व्याख्यानं समाप्तम्॥

Adyar D I 811 (19 L 51 = 66764). PL. Gr. 14 fol. = Adyar I, p. 49b.

Adyar D I 812 (22 P 20 = 68361). PL. Gr. 32 fol. (17ff.). = Adyar II, App. p. iib (40 G 20 : Vivaraṇa).

Adyar D XIII 189 (VB 1073b). PL. Tel. 14 fol.

Bombay Uni. Acc. no. 5349. 15 fol. (Jaṭā-vallī).

Deccan College 9809. 23 fol. (with text). Dated Śaka 1735. Title: Jaṭāvali or Jaṭavallī.

Hoshiarpur p. 51 (no.3539). 12 fol. 250 Grantha-s. Incomplete. Extract p. 409. Title: Jaṭā-saṃdhi-nirṇaya.

IO 4459 (3707b). PL. Na. 20 fol. (with text). Written ca. A.D. 1800.

MT 1631(b). Gr. 21 fol. (15-35). End differs from the above. Transcript of a Ms. which was copied by Yanamandra Veṅgaṇṇa, dated the Friday of the dark fortnight of the month of Phalguṇa in the year Manmatha.

MT 5099(c). PL. Gr. 16 fol. (16-33). Incomplete. = MT 1631(b). Purchased in 1925-26 from R. Varadacharyar, Village Munsif, Sirudamur, South Arcot Dist.

Mysore Skt. Coll. p. 1 = D. No.8 (1123/3). PL. Tel. 19 fol. (27-45).

PUL I, p. 22 (no.97). PL. Tel. 14 fol. 500 Grantha-s.

PUL II. App. p. 11 (no.168). PL. Tel. 20 fol. 400 Grantha-s (with text).

PUL II. App. p. 11 (no.169). PL. Tel. 20 fol. 400 Grantha-s (with text).

Trav. Uni. 2972 A. PL. Gr. 225 Grantha-s (with text). Incomplete.

VSM I 424 (no.4563). 4 fol. Title: Jaṭā-saṃdhi-nirṇaya.

Wai I 574. 24 fol. Title: Jaṭāvallī. (A xerox-copy of this Ms. is in SAI).

[NCC VII 145b-146a]

595 JAṬĀ-PAṬALA (1) **(जटापटल)**

BISM p. 99 (35/475). 2 fol. Contains Svarāṅkuśa (21 verses) and Jaṭā-paṭala of Hayagrīva.

BISM p. 99 (35/476). 6 fol. Contains Svarāṅkuśa (fol. 1-2), Jaṭā-paṭala of Hayagrīva (fol. 2-5) with C. and Vikṛti-vallī (fol. 6). Incomplete. 17 verses.

BISM p. 99 (35/478). 5 fol. Dated Śaka 1783. Contains Svarāṅkuśa, here called Svara-lakṣaṇa (fol. 1-2), Jaṭā-paṭala of Hayagrīva with C. (fol. 2-5a) and Vikṛti-vallī (20 verses); col.: Vyāḻiproktaṃ jaṭā-lakṣaṇaṃ sampūrṇam ||
BISM p. 99 (45/92). 2 fol. Examples of Jaṭā for a few selected verses.
Mysore I, p. 27.
Rajapur 1033.

– C. Jaṭā-paṭala-ṭippaṇa of Mathurānātha Śukla.
N-W P I 2 (no.2). 5 fol. Belonged to Rameshwara Chaube, Mirzapore.

– C. Jaṭā-paṭala-bhāṣya of Śivarāma.
N-W P I 12 (no.38). 61 fol. Belonged to Govinda Bhatta, Mirzapore.

596 JAṬĀ-PAṬALA (2) **(जटापटल)**
of Ananta → Commentary of Anantācārya on Jaṭā-paṭala of Vyāḍi.
Mithila IV 73.
RASB II 906 (G 6180B). 9 fol.

[NCC VII 146a]

597 JAṬĀ-PAṬALA (3) **(जटापटल)**
of Gālava.
IM 2242(a). This is actually the Jaṭā-paṭala of Hayagrīva.

598 JAṬĀ-PAṬALA (4) **(जटापटल)**
19 verses ascribed to Vyāḍi. Also called Jaṭā-lakṣaṇa or Jaṭā-vikṛti-lakṣaṇa or Vikṛti-vallī or Aṣṭa-vikṛti-kārikā; for the Śākala Śākhā of the *Ṛgveda* (Śaiśirīya-samāmnāya). One of the eight sections of the Vikṛti-vallī; older than that of Hayagrīva, according to the commentator Anantācārya. See under Aṣṭa-vikṛti above and Vikṛti-vallī below.

Adyar D XIII 41 (VB 862c). PL. Gr. 5 fol. (with C. of Gaṅgādhara).
BBRAS 491 (B D 278). 7 fol. (with C. of Anantācārya). Dated Śaka 1787.
Bhau Daji 121 (with C. of Anantācārya).
Bombay Uni. 688(II) (BMC 4 29). 2 fol. (31-32). 19 verses.
Bombay Uni. 707 (BMC 85 16). 1 fol. 14 verses only.
Bombay Uni. 708 (BMC 50 6). 6 fol. (with C.). Incomplete.
Bombay Uni. 709 (BMC 102 6). 4 fol. (with C.).
Bombay Uni. (BMC 142 10). 3 fol. (5-7). Dated Śaka 1649.
BORI 43 of A 1881-82. = BORI D I i.54(2). 3 fol. (40-42). 19 verses. Dated Śaka 1728.
BORI 65 of A 1881-82. 14 fol. (with C. of Gaṅgādhara). Title: Jaṭā-vikṛti-lakṣaṇa.
Calcutta Skt. Coll. I 35 (114). 13 fol. Though not noticed in the catalogue, this Ms. contains both the works: that of Hayagrīva with C. (fol. 1-4), and that of Vyāḍi with C. Vikṛti-kaumudī of Gaṅgādhara Bhaṭṭācārya (fol. 5-13).
Calcutta Skt. Coll. I 37. 8 fol. (with C. Vikṛti-kaumudī). Title: Jaṭā-vivṛti (cf. p. 16 of Poona edition).
GJKSV 13722. 11 fol. (with C. of Gaṅgādhara Bhaṭṭācārya). Title: Jaṭādy-aṣṭa-vikṛti-lakṣaṇa.

GJKSV 13724(D). 1 fol. (11). 18 verses. Dated V.S. 1886. Copied by Vaidyanātha Citaḷe, son of Hari Dīkṣita.
GJKSV 18421. 38 fol. (with C. of Anantācārya). Dated V.S. 1866 / Śaka 1730. Copied by Gaṇeśa Bhagavanta Dhārekara.
IM 2500B. 2 fol. 24 verses.
IM 2644B. 19 verses. Col.: Jaṭā-paṭala.
N-W P V 142 (no.5). 24 fol. (with C.).
PUL I, p. 20 (no.53). 2 fol. 19 Grantha-s (with Aṣṭa-vikṛti-lakṣaṇa in 7 verses).
SBD 4211. 6 fol. (11 verses with C.). Dated V.S. 1745.
SBD 4253. 12 fol. (with C.).
SBD 4257. 8 fol. (with C. of Gaṅgādhara). Dated V.S. 1714.
SBD 47937b. 17 fol. (7-23) (with C. of Gaṅgādhara).
SBD 53778. 3 fol. Vaṅga.
SBD 55322. 3 fol. (with Jaṭā-paṭala of Hayagrīva).
TD 1787. 3 fol. 19 Grantha-s. Col.: Jaṭā-paṭala.
Tirupati SVUORI (427i). PL. Na. Col.: Jaṭā-lakṣaṇa.
Ujjain I, p. 9 (no.2323). 3 fol. Dated Śaka 1747.
Wellcome Inst. London. B 56. 5 fol. 19 verses with notes. Title: Aṣṭavikṛti / Jaṭā-paṭala.

Ptd.: ed by Satyavrata Samasrami, with C. *Vikṛti-kaumudī* of Gaṅgādhara Bhaṭṭācārya, in the Sanskrit journal *Uṣā*. – Calcutta : Satya Press, 1889, vol. I, pt. 2. 16 pp. [BM : Ptd. Bks. Cat. 1892-1906. 173. 852 (14010.c.43; vol.1); Emeneau (60)]
Also ed. by K. V. Abhyankar and G. V. Devasthali, in *Veda-vikṛti-lakṣaṇa-saṃgraha*. – Poona : BORI, 1978.

– C. anon.
SBD 4211. 6 fol. (C. on 11 verses). Dated V.S. 1745.
SBD 4253. 12 fol. (with text).

– C. Ṭīkā, anon.
Bombay Uni. 708 (BMC 50 6). 6 fol. (with text). Incomplete.
Bombay Uni. 709 (BMC 102 6). 4 fol. (with text).

– C. of Anantācārya (Ananta-bhaṭṭa), son of Nāgadeva and Bhāgīrathī. See above under Ananta-deva (-bhaṭṭa).

BBRAS 491 (with text; see above).
Bhau dāji 121.
Bhk. 9.
BORI 66 of A 1881-82. 14 fol.
GJKSV 18421. 38 fol. (with text). Dated V.S. 1866 / Śaka 1730.
IM 2588. 11 fol.
Mithila IV 73. 18 fol.
RASB II 906 (G 6180B). 9 fol.
SBD 4340. 12 fol. Incomplete. Title: Aṣṭa-vikṛti-kārikā-vyākhyā.

Ptd.: ed. by K. V. Abhyankar and G. V. Devasthali, in *Veda-vikṛti-lakṣaṇa-saṃgraha.* – Poona : BORI, 1978.

– C. Vikṛti-kaumudī of Gaṅgādhara Bhaṭṭācārya.
Adyar D XIII 41 (VB 862c). PL. Gr. 5 fol. (with text).
Bhk. 9.
BORI 65 of A 1881-82. 14 fol. (with text).
GJKSV 13722. 11 fol. (with text). Title: Jaṭādy-aṣṭa-vikṛti-lakṣaṇa.
Calcutta Skt. Coll. I 35 (114). 9 fol. (5-13) (with text).
Calcutta Skt. Coll. I 37. 8 fol. (with text).
IM 2589. 18 fol. (1-17, 36). Incomplete.
Mithila IV 155. 2 fol. Incomplete.
Mysore ND II 3384 (C 3761/ 4). 120 fol.
N-W P V 142 (no.5). 24 fol. (with text).
Ujjain II, p. 9 (no.2336). 5 fol.

Ptd.: with text in both the edition noted above.

– C. Aṣṭa-vikṛti-kārikā-vyākhyā of Rāmakṛṣṇa-bhaṭṭa.
IM 2521. 14 fol. (2-15). Incomplete.
IM 2572. 6 fol. 6 fol.
SBD 4302. 21 fol.

[NCC VII 146b]

599 JAṬĀ-PAṬALA (5) (**जटापटल**)

Generally attributed to Hayagrīva. On the formation of the Jaṭā of the *Ṛgveda.* Eleven verses, divided into two Varga-s of verses six and five respectively. PUL I, p. 6 has an additional verse ascribing the work to Acalācārya. The NCC (I 70) has under the entry Acalācārya the following remarks:

"In Thibaut's edn., in BBRAS. 490 and PUL. I., p. 6, the ms. has a verse in the end ascribing the text to one Acala; in the other mss., without the last verse, this text on Jaṭā is ascribed to Hayagrīva and accompanied by an an. C. See BBRAS. 489. L. 1234. Weber 369.

In the PUL. ms. however, the reference to Hayagrīva as the author is absent. (It reads instead:)

ayaṃ prakāra uttamo 'nādiś ceti sarveṣām ācāryāṇāṃ matam |
idaṃ jaṭāpāṭha ... || iti śrī acalācāryakṛtaṃ jaṭāpaṭalaṃ samāptam |

Cf. Dr. Thibaut's edn. and BBRAS. 490.

In BBRAS. 490, the verse does not have a reading mentioning Acala : *mahattamānu-smaratajvalena* | Thibaut and PUL. read – *-tācalena.*

TCD. 34 J same text with C. and without the additional verse, is ascribed in the colophon to Vyāḍi; so also in Cs. I. 35 and 37, where, however, the name *Vikṛtivallī* is given to the text.

See also CLB. I. p. 27, no.49. Jaṭā-paṭala with C. of Hayagrīva. MD. 958 and 959. The text of MD. 958 has the additional verse, but has a reading available neither in Thibaut's edn., nor in the other mss., BBRAS. 490 and PUL. I. p. 6. It reads: mahattamān sus-maratā ca denam | BORI. 65 of Ā881-82, text same, C. different, and text called

Vikṛtilakṣaṇa and ascribed to Vyāḍi. BORI. 15 of 1879-80, text and C. same, except for a little omission in the end; the colophon gives Hayagrīva as the a.
The name of the a. Acala is entirely dependent on this verse which has so many confusing readings."

Beginning:

क्रमे यथोक्ते पदजातमेव त्रिरभ्यसेदुत्तरमेव पूर्वम्।
अभ्यस्य पूर्वं च तथोत्तरे पदे ऽवसानमेवं हि जटाभिधीयते॥

End:

अनानुपूर्व्येण च यत्र संहिता पदक्रमाद् व्युत्क्रमः पूर्ववत्क्रमः।
भवेत् प्रकारो ऽयमनादिरुत्तमः सदा जटायामिति सर्वसंमतम्॥ ११॥
इदं जटापाठविधानमुक्तं महात्मनानुस्मरताचलेन।
पठन् जटां कीर्तिमुपैत्यमेयामन्ते पदं याति परं हि विष्णोः ॥ १२॥

Adyar 40 A 26 = PM 2986. 5 fol. (with C. as printed in VVLS, pp. 49-55). Dated V.S. 1790. Catalogued as Hetu-paṭala of Hayagrīva in the Alpabetical List. The colophon reads: iti hayagrīva-proktaḥ hetu-paṭalaḥ samāptaḥ ||

Adyar D XIII 39 (VB 737f). PL. Gr. 1 fol.

Baroda 8291. 10 fol. 120 Grantha-s (with C.). = CLB I, p. 27. Col.: iti hayagrīvaprokte hetujaṭāpaṭalaṃ samāptam |

Baroda 8690(a). 5 fol. 120 Grantha-s (with C.). = CLB I, p. 27.

Baroda 8704. 6 fol. 120 Grantha-s (with C.). = CLB I, p. 27.

Baroda 8891(a). 7 fol. 120 Grantha-s (with C.). = CLB I, p. 27. Dated V.S. 1760.

Baroda 26310(a). 6 fol. (with C.).

BBRAS 489 (B D 182). 4 fol. (with C. as printed in VVLS, pp. 49-55).

BBRAS 490 (B D 278). 2 fol. Dated Śaka 1787. 5 additional verses at the beginning.

Bhau Dāji 74. 121.

Bhk. 9.

BISM p. 99 (1/18ka) (with C. of Dayāśaṃkara). Dated Śaka 1738. (Used for Poona edition).

Bombay Uni. 711 (BMC 85 17). 1 fol.

Bombay Uni. 712 (BMC 85 14). 7 fol. (with C. as printed in VVLS, pp. 49-55).

Bombay Uni. (BMC 142 10). 5 fol. (with C. as printed in VVLS, pp. 49-55). Dated Śaka 1649.

BORI 15 of 1879-80. 4 fol. 150 Grantha-s. Col.: Jaṭāvicāra (with C. as printed in VVLS, pp. 49-55). Dated V.S. 1882.

BORI TM 40A. 5 fol. (with C. as printed in VVLS, pp. 49-55).

BORI TM 279. 19 fol. Title: Hayagrīvokta-jaṭā-paṭala-dīpikā.

Burnell 3b.

Calcutta Skt. Coll. I 35A (114). 4 fol. (with C. as printed in VVLS, pp. 49-55).

CU Add. 1910.

Deccan College 932. 7 fol. (6-12) (with Dīpikā of Dayāśaṃkara). Upalekha-sūtra on fol. 1-6.

GJKSV 13724(A). 6 fol. (with C. as printed in VVLS, pp. 49-55). Col.: Hayagrīva-prokte Hetu-jaṭā-paṭalam. Copied by Vaidyanātha Citale, son of Hari Dīkṣita.

GJKSV 23667. 6 fol. (with C. as printed in VVLS, pp. 49-55).

IM 2242. 5 fol. (with C. as printed in VVLS, pp. 49-55). Col. :Hayagrīva-proktaṃ Jaṭāhetu-paṭalam.

IM 2485C. 2 fol. (4-5). Dated V.S. 1744. Title: Krama-jaṭā-paṭala.

IM 2490. 1 fol. Dated V.S. 1735.

IM 2493. 2 fol. (with C. as printed in VVLS, pp. 49-55). Dated V.S. 1734. Col.: Jaṭā-lakṣaṇa.

IM 2502. 3 fol. Dated V.S. 1740. Copied in Vārāṇasī. Col.: Krama-jaṭā-paṭala.

IM 2503. ? fol. (with C. of Dayāśaṃkara). Dated V.S. 1711.

IM 2504. 31 fol. Dated V.S. (with C. of Dayāśaṃkara). Dated V.S. 1839.

IM 2551. 5 fol. (with C. as printed in VVLS, pp. 49-55).

IM 2552. 6 fol. (with C. as printed in VVLS, pp. 49-55). Incomplete.

L 1234. 9 fol. 110 Grantha-s (with C. as printed in VVLS, pp. 49-55).

Mithila IV 72. 15 fol. (with C. as printed in VVLS, pp. 49-55).

N-W P I 12 (no.36). 12 fol. Belonged to Govinda Bhatta, Mirzapore.

N-W P I 14 (no.42). 5 fol. Title: Jaṭā-paṭala-vṛtti. Belonged to Rameshwara Chaube, Mirzapore.

N-W P V 142 (no.5). 24 fol. (with C.).

Oxf. CS d.71(8). 19 fol. (with C. Dīpikā of Dayāśaṃkara). Dated V.S. 1811 (A.D. 1754).

Oxf. CS d.860. 5 fol. Dated A.D. 1800.

Oxf. CS c.2(10). 10 fol. Dated A.D. 1698.

Oxf. CS c.2(11). 20 fol.

P 4.

PUL I, p. 6 (no.88). 12 fol. 120 Grantha-s. (Ascribed to Acalācārya.)

PUL I, p. 20 (no.54). 13 fol. 200 Grantha-s (with C.).

Radh. 1.2.

RASB II 276 (G 2331). 7 fol.

RASB II 277 (G 664) = L 1234 (with C.).

Rice 12. Veda-lakṣaṇa-sūtra-vṛtti (8000 Grantha-s). ?

SB p. 8 (no.19). 23 fol. 400 Grantha-s. = SBD 47937.

SBD 2105. 11 fol. Dated V.S. 1884. Catalogued as Jaṭā-paṭhana-prakāra.

SBD 4227. 14 fol. (with C. as printed in VVLS, pp. 49-55). Dated V.S. 1814. Catalogued as Jaṭā-paṭala-vṛtti.

SBD 47897. 4 fol. (with C. as printed in VVLS, pp. 49-55). Dated V.S. 1871.

SBD 47937a. 7 fol. (with C. as printed in VVLS, pp. 49-55).

SBD 53680. 6 fol. (with C. as printed in VVLS, pp. 49-55).

SBD 55322. 3 fol. (with Jaṭā-paṭala of Vyāḍi).

TCD 34-J. 2 pp. 12 Grantha-s. Col.: Vyāḻikṛtaṃ jaṭā-lakṣaṇam. (Beg.: krame yathokte; but the verse at the end is different).

Trav. Uni. 1567. 20 fol. 400 Grantha-s. Dated V.S. 1877 (with C. Dīpikā of Dayāśaṃkara).

Trav. Uni. 4254 K. PL. Mal. 2 fol. 25 Grantha-s (8 verses from Hayagrīva's Jaṭā-paṭala with two additional verses). Belonged to Vishnu Nambudiri of Ettikada Illam Ayankudi, Kaduttirutti, Kottayam.

Trav. Uni. 4910. 7 fol. 120 Grantha-s (with C.). Incomplete.
Trav. Uni. T.223 J. = TCD 34-J. A transcript of the Ms. no. 4254.
Triv. Cur. III 6. Mal. 15 Grantha-s. (Jaṭā-lakṣaṇa).
Ujjain I, p. 9 (no.2328). 20 fol. Dated Śaka 1745.
VSM I 423 (no.3951). 11 fol. (with C. as printed in VVLS, pp. 49-55, on fol. 1-8 and fol. 9-11 contain a C. on verses 1-4, as printed in VVLS, pp. 4-7).
VSM III 164 (no.11347). 6 fol. (with C. as printed in VVLS, pp. 49-55). Also contains the Svara-lakṣaṇa.
Wai I 348. 9 fol. (with Dīpikā of Dayāśaṃkara). Dated V.S. 1801.
Weber 369 (Chambers 748). 4 fol. (with C.). Dated V.S. 1731. Copied by Raghunātha, son of Rāma. (Used for Thibaut's edition)
Weber 370 (Chambers 2b). 1 fol. Dated V.S. 1745. (Used for Thibaut's edition)
Weber 371 (Chambers 781). 6 fol. (with C.). Dated V.S. 1662. Copied by Gadādhara. (Used for Thibaut's edition)

Ptd.:
1) Ed. by George Thibaut, with commentary and a German translation: *Das Jaṭāpaṭala -- Lehrbuch des Jaṭāpāṭha für den Ṛigveda*, nebst dem Abschnitt der Prātiśākhya-jyotsnā über die Vikṛti des Kramapāṭha). – Leipzig : F. A. Brockhaus, 1870. 53 pp. [Adyar (H 215.4 Thi JPx=zge); SAI (ind 54 B 585/1776); UBHD (G 1736); SKGI (Rf IX 20); BM : Ptd. Bks. Cat. 1876 (p. 50); Emeneau (59)]
Cf. A. Weber, *Indische Streifen*, vol. III. – Leipzig, 1879 (reprint: Osnabrück : Biblio Verlag, 1983), pp. 40-43.
2) Ed. by K. V. Abhyankar and G. V. Devasthali, in *Veda-vikṛti-lakṣaṇa-saṃgraha*. – Poona : BORI, 1978, pp. 47-48 (Hayagrīva-kṛtaṃ Jaṭā-paṭalam; with a subtitle: Hayagrīvī Śikṣā; based on a Ms. of Ānandāśrama, Poona, dated Śaka 1710); pp. 49-55 (with an anon. commentary) and pp. 56-74 (with the commentary Dīpikā of Dayāśaṃkara). [Adyar (H080 BORI Rup 5); BORI (31892 / 34350); SAI (ind 51 D 584/1175)]

– C. anon.

Beginning (as printed in VVLS):

क्रमे यथोक्ते । क्रमो द्वाभ्याम् -- इत्यादि उक्तप्रकारेण पदजातं पदद्वयं पदत्रयं वा द्विरभ्यसेत् द्विवारं पठेत् । अभ्यासप्रकारमेवाह -- उत्तरमेव पूर्वम् । क्रमवत् पदद्वयं गृहीत्वा पूर्वं प्रथममुत्तरपदम् अभ्यस्य ततः संधानद्वारा पूर्वं पदमभ्यस्य उत्तरे पदे ऽवस्येत् । एवंप्रकारेण यदध्ययनं तज्जटाभिधीयते ॥

End:

सर्वसंमतम्। यत्र पदानुपूर्व्येण पदक्रमेण संहिता न भवति तत्र पदक्रमाद् व्युत्क्रम्य पुनः क्रमवत् सा उत्क्रम्यते। ततः इङ्गनेन पदं दर्शयेत्। यथा -- शुनश्चिच्छेपं निदितं निदितं चिच्छुनःशेपं शुनश्चिच्छेपं निदितम्। शुनःशेपमिति शुनःशेपम्। चिदिति चित्। नरा च शंसं दैव्यं दैव्यं च नराशंसं नरा च शंसं दैव्यम्। नराशंसमिति नराशंसम्। चेति च।

अयमेवोत्तमः प्रकारः । इति सर्वेषामाचार्याणां संमतम् ॥

Adyar 40 A 26 = PM 2986. 5 fol. (with text). Dated V.S. 1790.
Baroda 8291. 10 fol. 120 Grantha-s (with text). = CLB I, p. 27.
Baroda 8690(a). 5 fol. 120 Grantha-s (with text). = CLB I, p. 27.
Baroda 8704. 6 fol. 120 Grantha-s (with text). = CLB I, p. 27.
Baroda 8891(a). 7 fol. 120 Grantha-s (with text). = CLB I, p. 27. Dated V.S. 1760.
Baroda 26310(a). 6 fol. (with text). Dated Śaka 1778.
BBRAS 489 (B D 182). 4 fol.
Bombay Uni. 712 (BMC 85 14). 7 fol. (with text).
Bombay Uni. (BMC 142 10). 5 fol. (with text). Dated Śaka 1649.
BORI 15 of 1879-80. 4 fol. 150 Grantha-s. Col.: Jaṭāvicāra.
BORI 65 of A 1881-82. 14 fol. (with text) (Jaṭā-vikṛti-lakṣaṇa).
BORI TM 40A. 5 fol. (with text).
Calcutta Skt. Coll. I 35A (114). 4 fol. (with text).
GJKSV 13724(A). 6 fol. (with text). Dated V.S. 1886. Copied by Vaidyanātha Citaḷe, son of Hari Dīkṣita.
GJKSV 23667. 6 fol. (with text).
IM 2242. 5 fol. (with text). (Hayagrīva-proktaṃ Jaṭāhetu-paṭalam).
IM 2493. 2 fol. (with text). Dated V.S. 1734. Col.: Jaṭā-lakṣaṇa.
IM 2551. 5 fol. (with text).
IM 2552. 6 fol. (with text). Incomplete.
L 1234. 9 fol. 110 Grantha-s (with text).
Mithila IV 72. 15 fol. (with text).
PUL I, p. 20 (no.54). 13 fol. 200 Grantha-s (with text).
RASB II 276 (G 2331). 7 fol.
RASB II 277 (G 664) = L 1234 (with text).
SBD 4227. 14 fol. (with text). V.S. 1814. Catalogued as Jaṭā-paṭala-vṛtti.
SBD 47897. 4 fol. (with text). Dated V.S. 1871.
SBD 47937a. 7 fol. (with text).
SBD 53680. 6 fol. (with text).
Trav. Uni. 4910. 7 fol. 120 Grantha-s (with text). Incomplete.
VSM I 423 (no.3951). 8 fol. (with text).
Weber 369. 4 fol. (with text). Dated V.S. 1731. Copied by Raghunātha, son of Rāma.
Weber 371. 6 fol. (with text). Dated V.S. 1662. Copied by Gadādhara.

Ptd.: ed. by G. Thibaut, with the text. See above.
Also ed. by K. V. Abhyankar and G. V. Devasthali, in : *Veda-vikṛti-lakṣaṇa-saṃgraha*. – Poona : BORI, 1978, pp. 49-55; based on three Mss:
1) Ānandāśrama, Poona, 7 fol. , dated Śaka 1710.
2) BORI 65 of A 1881-82.
3) Bombay Uni. 712. No. 85.14 in the Bhadkamkar Collection.

– C. Dīpikā of Dayāśaṃkara, son of Dharaṇīdhara Vyāvahārika. It is written in V.S. 1801 (A.D. 1745).

Beginning:

अपारसंसारसमुद्रमग्नस्वभक्तजन्तूद्धरणे दयालुः ।
धृतैकदीक्षः पुरतस्तनोतु शिवः शिवं मे शिवया समेतः ॥

इह हि भगवान् परमकारुणिको हयग्रीवाचार्यस्त्रैवर्णिकानां यथार्थवर्णस्वरपरिज्ञानपूर्वक जटाध्ययनस्य कीर्तिप्राप्तिरूप दृष्टप्रयोजनसिद्धिपूर्वक ब्रह्मपदप्राप्तिरूपं मुख्यं फलं विवक्षुः तस्य जटायाः स्वरूपज्ञानाधीनत्वाद् वर्णस्वरपरिज्ञानाधीनत्वाच्चादौ जटास्वरूपमाह -- क्रमे यथोक्ते ...

End:

अन्ते प्राणवियोगाव्यवहितोत्तरक्षणे पूर्वमेव एतदध्ययनेन पापक्षयसत्वात् तत्त्वज्ञानद्वारा विष्णोर्व्यापनशीलस्य परमेश्वरस्य हीति निश्चयेन परमुत्कृष्टं पदं स्थानं याति गच्छतीत्यर्थः । इतरदेवतापदप्राप्तौ जन्मान्तरशङ्का स्यात् । व्यापनशीलस्य विष्णोः सर्वोत्कृष्टत्वेन तत्पदप्राप्तौ पुनरिह लोके च्युतिर्न भवतीति भावः ॥

भूवियद्वसुशशाङ्कसंमिते विक्रमार्कनृपतेर्गते ऽब्दके ।
चैत्रशुक्लनवमीदिने शुभे ग्रन्थ एष परिपूर्णतामगात् ॥

Ānandāśrama 2584.
Berlin StB-PrK (NGMPP). B 500/27. 3 fol. Incomplete (microfilm dated 03.06.1973).
Bhr. 513.
BISM p. 99 (1/18ka). Dated Śaka 1738.
BORI 513 of 1882-83. 24 fol.
BORI TM 279. 19 fol. Title: Hayagrīvokta-jaṭā-paṭala-dīpikā.
CU Add. 1910.
Deccan College 7461. 4 fol. Incomplete.
GJKSV 17821. 30 fol. Dated V.S. 1874. Copied by Śivarāma.
GJKSV 23640. 50 fol.
IM 2503. ? fol. (with text). Dated V.S. 1711.
IM 2504. 31 fol. (with text). Dated V.S. 1839.
L 1525. 24 fol. 420 Grantha-s.
Mysore I, p. 27.
N-W P I 12 (no.37). 30 fol. Belonged to Govinda Bhatta, Mirzapore.
Oxf. CS d.71(8). 19 fol. (with text). Dated V.S. 1811 (A.D. 1754).
PUL II. App. p. 11 (no.170). 14 fol. Dated V.S. 1801.
RASB II 278 (G 2795) = L 1525.
SBD 2108. 19 fol. Incomplete.
SBD 47899. 21 fol. Dated V.S. 1871.
Trav. Uni. 1567.
Ujjain Latest Additions 440.
Visvanatha Vamana Deva, Varanasi. 19 fol. Dated V.S. 1907.
Wai I 348. 9 fol. (with text). Dated V.S. 1801.
A transcript belonging to Ksetresh Chandra Chattopadhyaya, University of Allahabad is now with G. C. Tripathi of Allahabad.

Ptd.: ed. by K. V. Abhyankar and G. V. Devasthali, in : *Veda-vikṛti-lakṣaṇa-saṃgraha.* -- Poona : BORI, 1978, pp. 56-74; based on three Mss:
1) Ānandāśrama 2584, 27 fol. (1-28; fol. 2 missing).
2) BORI 513 of 1882-83, 24 fol.
3) BISM No. 1/18ka, 23 fol. (1-3 and 6-25).

[NCC VII 147a]

600 JAṬĀ-PAṬALA or SVARĀṄKUŚA (जटापटल / स्वराङ्कुश)
21 verses by Jayanta-svāmin. See below Svarāṅkuśa.
Alph. List Beng. Govt. p. 42.
L 1235. 3 fol. 42 Grantha-s.

[NCC VII 146a]

601 JAṬĀ-PAṬHANA-PADDHATI (जटापठनपद्धति)
BISM p. 99 (54/63). 1 fol. Jaṭā for the verse "agneḥ pūrve bhrātaro" with definition verse "anulomavilomābhyām", etc.

602 JAṬĀ-PAṬHANA-PRAKĀRA (जटापठनप्रकार)
→ Jaṭā-paṭala of Hayagrīva with commentary.
SBD 2105. 11 fol. Dated V.S. 1884.
Skt. Coll. Ben. 1918-30, p. 2 (no.16). 11 fol. Dated V.S. 1884.

[NCC VII 147b]

603 JAṬĀ-PARIBHĀṢĀ (जटापरिभाषा)
Mysore ND II 3369 (P 521). PL. Na. 4 fol. Incomplete. Extract no. 137.

604 JAṬĀ-PĀṬHA (जटापाठ)
See also Śukla-yajurveda-saṃhitā-jaṭā-pāṭha.
GJKSV 21248. 1-78, 106, 152 fol. Incomplete.
GJKSV 21249. 12 fol. (14th ch. of VS).
GJKSV 33557. 11 fol. (chs. 1-2 of VS).
GJKSV 39214. 6 fol.
IM 5539. 24 fol. (ch. 30 of VS.).
PUL I, p. 6 (no.89). 6 fol. (7th ch. of VS).
PUL I, p. 6 (no.90). 5 fol. (36th ch. of VS).
PUL I, p. 6 (no.91). 2 fol. (12th ch. of VS).
PUL I, p. 6 (no.92). 18 fol. (7th ch. mantra-s 1-41 of VS).
Rajapur 1036 (of the Mantra, śaṃ naḥ ...).
SBD 52308. 48 fol. (1-26, 213-34). Incomplete.
SBD 52309. 117 fol. (31-40 chs. of VS).
SBD 52310. 119 fol. (21-30 chs. of VS).
SBD 52581. 5 fol. (35th ch. of VS).
SBD 52671. 1 fol. (for the mantra "punas tvā").
Weber 33. 4 fol. (of some selected mantra-s).

[NCC VII 147b]

605 JAṬĀ-PRAKARAṆA (जटाप्रकरण)
Trav. Uni. 16408 Z9. PL. Mal. 7 Grantha-s.

606 JAṬĀ-PRAYOGA (**जटाप्रयोग**)
SBD 0592. 25 fol. (1-7, 133-50). Incomplete.

607 JAṬĀ-MAṆI (**जटामणि**)
of Nemāna (Vemāna) Bhairavāvadhānin (-budha); he salutes one Veṅkaṭeśa.

Beginning: (813)

श्रीविघ्नेशमहं नत्वा गुरुं सर्वावधानिनम्।
जटामणिं प्रवक्ष्यामि श्रीजटावल्लभैः समम्॥ १॥
शिक्षादिशास्त्रमखिलं प्रसमीक्ष्य सम्यग् वेदार्थलक्षणविदां सुखबोधनाय।
नेमानभैरवबुधेन मणिर्जटायाः संकाश्यते परशिवस्य कृपाकटाक्षात्॥ २॥
यस्य जिह्वामुखे वाणी वेदशास्त्रमयी सदा।
नृत्तं करोति मत्तातं वेङ्कटेशं नतो ऽस्म्यहम्॥ ३॥
यस्येश्वरस्याद्रिवरस्य पुत्र्या सहैक्यमद्वैतमतीव सत्यम्।
आनन्दयत्यत्र भवज्जनानां तं शंकरं लोकगुरुं नतो ऽस्मि॥ ४॥

गुरुत्वं लघुता साम्यमित्यष्टादशभेदानां मध्ये जटाया गणनाभावात् जटा न वक्तव्येति केचिद् वदन्ति। तदसमीचीनम्। ह्वारभारादिसूत्रे अबिभः पितः एष्टः नेष्टः एतेषां ग्रहणानां प्रातिशाख्यभाष्यकारैः जटायामेव उदाहृतत्वात्। किं च आवृत्परो विसर्जनीयो रेफमाप्नोति। जिन्वरावृद्ध्याह -- इतिपरो ऽपि अपिशब्दः आवृत्परविसर्जनीयावन्यद् दिशति। आवृत्परो विसर्जनीय इतिपरो रेफमाप्नोति इति। श्रुतः श्रुतरितीति श्रुतः इति। परावृत्पराभ्यां किम्। हवनश्रुतो हवमिति परोजीतिसूत्रज्ञापनात् जटा अवश्यं वक्तव्या। अन्यथा सूत्रारम्भस्य वैयर्थ्यं स्यात्। तस्माज्जटा वक्तव्येति राद्धान्तः।
जटाविषयशिक्षावचनानि --

प्रातिशाख्यादिशास्त्रज्ञः सर्वशास्त्रविशारदः।
बुद्धिशक्तिसमेतो यः स जटां वक्तुमर्हति॥
य इच्छति जटां वक्तुं स विप्रो वेदवित्तमः।
तस्य कीर्तिर्विवर्धेत स वेदफलमश्नुते॥
जटां हित्वा विचित्रार्थमनुलोमादिकं वदन्।
स वै नरकमाप्नोति स्वरवर्णविलोपिवन्॥

End:

त्वद्रूपसाम्यादत्राच्यनुस्वारागमः। ततः ससैँषँसादं स्वादुषँसद इति च सिद्धम्। इति नेमानभैरवावधानिविरचितो जटामणिः समाप्तः॥

Adyar D I 813 (30 C 3 = 73873). PL. Tel. 28 fol. (17-44) (with C.). = Adyar I, p. 49b. Dated 15th of the dark fortnight of Kārttika of Pramādin, copied by Indrakaṇṭi Rāmacandrāvadhānulu from the original copied by Madhira Jagganna.
Adyar D XIII 190 (VB 429). PL. Gr. 9 fol.

Hamburg StUB (cod.Palmbl. III 8/133) → Veda-lakṣaṇa (HB).
Hoshiarpur p. 51 (no.4373). PL. Gr. 8 fol. 100 Grantha-s.
Hoshiarpur p. 300 (no.5613). 10 fol. 300 Grantha-s.
Hz 1436. PL. Gr. 5 fol. Extract p. 134. Belonged to the late Raja Ghanapathi of Tiruvidaimarudur, Thanjavur Dist.
Mysore I, p. 27 (5 Mss, 2 with C.). p. 612.
Mysore ND II 3370 (P 2262/28). PL. Gr. 4 fol. Extract no. 138.
Mysore ND II 3371 (P 2265/39). PL. Gr. 4 fol. (156-59).
Mysore ND II 3372 (P 4468/ 1). PL. Na. 10 fol.
Mysore ND II 3373 (B 702/ 1). Kan. 20 fol. (2-21). Extract no. 139.
Mysore ND II 3374 (P 285/ 1). PL. Gr. 2 fol. Incomplete. Different ?
Mysore ND II 3375 (B 252/20). Gr. 11 fol. (164-74). Extract no. 140.
PUL I, p. 20 (no.55). PL. Tel. 22 fol. (77-100). 700 Grantha-s.
PUL I, p. 20 (no.56). PL. Tel. 38 fol. 750 Grantha-s.
Trav. Uni. 2630 A. PL. Gr. 120 Grantha-s. Incomplete.
Trav. Uni. 4028 D. PL. Gr. 100 Grantha-s. Incomplete.
Trav. Uni. 11881. PL. Tel. 300 Grantha-s. Incomplete.

Ptd.: ed. by Kadathur Lakshmana Shastri, together with *Jaṭā-siddhānta-candrikā* under the title *Jaṭā-lakṣaṇa*, with C. (in Grantha script). (Title page : Jaṭā-lakṣaṇam. Jaṭā-maṇiḥ - Jaṭā-siddhānta-candrikā iti jaṭālakṣaṇa-granthadvayaṃ vyākhyā-sahitaṃ yathāmati samyak pariśodhya ... rājarājanellūr ityaparanāmaka kaḍattūr grāmavāstavyena lakṣmaṇaśāstriṇā kumbhakoṇastha śrīvidyāmudrākṣaraśālāyāṃ ... mudrāpitam ...). – Kumbakonam (Kadathur) : Sri Vidya Press, 1907. 29-57 pp. – (Sri Vag Vilas Series 2). [Adyar (H 215.4 Lak JLxy); SAI (85/1955*); BM : Ptd. Bks. 689 (Cat. 14092.b.47); IO : Ptd. Bks. Cat. 1938, p. 1150 (25 D 47)]

Also ed. by Gomatham Srinivasa Josyar, in *Lakṣaṇatraya* (in Telugu script), together with *Sapta-lakṣaṇa* and *Ṣaḍviṃśati-sūtra*. – Mysore, 1919. 73 pp. Title page: Sapta-lakṣaṇī Ṣaḍvig'ṃśatisūtram (savyākhyā) Jaṭāmaṇiḥ - iti Lakṣaṇatrayam | Taittirīya-yajussambandhi | Maisūru gomaṭhaṃ śrīnivāsa jyotiṣikeṇa cittūru śrīśāradāmudrālaye siddhārthiśrāvaṇāmāyāṃ samamudryata | [MyORI (B 4109/12669); SAI (87/778*)]

– C.

Adyar D I 813. See above.
Hamburg StUB (cod.Palmbl. III 8/133) → Veda-lakṣaṇa (HB).
Hz 1437. PL. Gr. 10 fol. Belonged to the late Raja Ghanapathi of Tiruvidaimarudur, Thanjavur Dist.
Mysore ND II 3376 (B 702/ 2). Kan. 20 fol. Extract no. 141.
Mysore ND II 3377 (P 2262/30). PL. Gr. 8 fol. Extract no. 142.
Mysore ND II 3378 (P 2265/40). PL. Gr. 7 fol. (159-65).
Mysore ND II 3379 (B 252/19). Gr. 34 fol. (129-62). Extract no. 143.
PUL I, p. 20 (no.56a). PL. Gr. 13 fol. 250 Grantha-s. Incomplete.

[NCC VII 147b]

608 JAṬĀ-MAṆI or TRIKRAMA-LAKṢAṆA **(जटामणि / त्रिक्रमलक्षण)**

Ascribed to Lakṣmaṇa-budha. Though in many Mss. it is found anonymous, the printed edition (together with the commentary *Jaṭā-siddhānta-candrikā)* ascribes both the text and the commentary to Lakṣmaṇa-budha. The first half of the introductory as well as the final verse is identical with that in the *Sarva-saṃmata-śikṣā*.

Beginning:

ध्यात्वा सर्वजगन्नाथं साम्बं सर्वार्थसाधकम्।
क्रियते लक्ष्मणाख्येन जटासिद्धान्तचन्द्रिका॥

मूलम् --

पदद्वयमनुक्रम्य व्युत्क्रम्योत्क्रम्य संधिमत्।
यथावत्स्वरसंयुक्तं प्रयुञ्ज्यात् सा जटा मता॥

व्याख्या --

ध्यात्वा सर्वजगन्नाथं साम्बं सर्वार्थसाधकम्।
जटासिद्धान्तवचनव्याख्यां कुर्वे यथामति।

पदद्वयमिति -- अनुक्रमः आर्षः । व्युत्क्रमः विलोमः उत्क्रमः अनुलोमः । प्रथमं पदद्वयमुत्क्रम्य पुनः व्युत्क्रम्य पुनश्चोत्क्रम्य प्रातिशाख्योक्तसंधिविधिम् अनतिक्रम्य स्वरसहितं प्रयुञ्ज्यात्। यथा -- वायव्यम् ... इत्यादि।

जटायां पञ्चधा संधिरार्षपौरुषभेदतः ।
आद्यन्तमार्षकं ज्ञेयं शिष्टमन्यत्र पौरुषम्॥

स्पष्टो ऽर्थः । यथा -- सेत् -- इदित् -- इदु -- इत्सः -- ससः -- सेत्। इदु -- उवु -- उवित् -- इदित् -- इदु -- इत्यादि॥

त्रिक्रमेष्वष्टधा संधिर्द्वौ द्वावार्षकसंज्ञकौ।
अन्यत्र पञ्चधा संधिरार्षावाद्यन्तकौ स्मृतौ॥
अन्ये त्रयश्च चत्वारः पौरुषेया इति स्मृताः ।

End:

यच्चानितिपर इति रेफयत्वार्थमाह वै।
अनार्ष एव विज्ञेयश्श्रवयानिति दर्शनात्॥ ८९॥

अन्यथा श्रवया (१-९-२३) इति निषेधग्रहणं व्यर्थमेव स्यात्॥

पपूर्वस्य छकारस्य द्वित्वं कुर्याद् विचक्षणः ॥
पदादौ पदयोरेकामपच्छिद्येति दर्शनात्॥ ९१॥

अपच्छिद्येति दृष्टान्तम्॥ जटाध्ययने फलमाह --

य इच्छति जटां वक्तुं स विप्रो वेदपारगः ।
तस्य कीर्तिर्विवर्धेत स वेदफलमश्नुते॥
संहितां च पदं चापि क्रमं चैव जटां पठन्।

लक्षणज्ञस्तदाप्नोति ब्रह्मज्ञानं हि शाश्वतम्॥
प्रातिशाख्यादिशास्त्रज्ञः सर्वशास्त्रविशारदः।
बुद्धिशक्तिसमेतो यः स जटां वक्तुमर्हति॥
ध्यात्वा सर्वजगन्नाथं साम्बं सर्वार्थसाधकम्।
रचिता लक्ष्मणाख्येन जटासिद्धान्तचन्द्रिका॥
इतिश्रीलक्ष्मणाख्यबुधेन विरचिता जटासिद्धान्तचन्द्रिका॥

MD 908. 36 pp. (142ff.) (with C.).
MD 16821. PL. Gr. 2 pp. 21 Grantha-s (also called Trikrama-lakṣaṇa). Incomplete.
MT 3887(m). 7 fol. (107-13) (with C.). Purchased in 1921-22 from Annasvami Sastrigal, Bhavani, Coimbatore Dist.
MT 5099(b). PL. Gr. 12 fol. (4-15) (with C.). Incomplete. Purchased in 1925-26 from R. Varadacharyar, Village Munsif, Sirudamur, South Arcot Dist.
Oppert I 982. Belonged to Viraraghava Tatacharyar, Head Master, Sanskrit School of Sathakopacharya, Kanchipuram, Chingelpet Dist.
Oppert I 7137. Belonged to Pola Lakshmanavadhani of Vijayanagaram.
Oppert I 7547. Belonged to S. Kodanda Ramavadhana Pantulu of Vijayanagaram.
Oppert II 748. Belonged to Ghanapathi Shingaracharyar of Alasur, Madurantakam Taluk.
Oppert II 1320. Belonged to Gopalacharyar of Pillapakkam, Kanchipuram Taluk.
Oppert II 9879. Belonged to M.Raja Ghanapathi of Mahadanapuram, Trichinapalli.

– C. Jaṭāsiddhānta-candrikā of Lakṣmaṇa.
MD 908. 36 pp. (142ff.).
MT 3887(m). 7 fol. (107-13) (with text). Purchased in 1921-22 from Annasvami Sastrigal, Bhavani, Coimbatore Dist.
MT 5099(b). PL. Gr. 12 fol. (4-15) (with text). Incomplete. Purchased in 1925-26 from R. Varadacharyar, Village Munsif, Sirudamur, South Arcot Dist.
Oppert II 749. Belonged to Ghanapathi Shingaracharyar of Alasur, Madurantakam Taluk.
Trav. Uni. 2630 D. PL. Gr. 250 Grantha-s.

Ptd.: ed. by Kadathur Lakshmana Shastri, under the title *Jaṭā-lakṣaṇa*, with C. (in Grantha script). – Kumbakonam (Kadathur) : Sri Vidya Press, 1907. 29-57 pp. – (Sri Vag Vilasa Series 2). [Adyar (H 215.4 Lak JLxy); SAI (85/1955*); BM : Ptd. Bks. 689 (Cat. 14092.b.47); IO : Ptd. Bks. Cat. 1938, p. 1150 (25 D 47)]

[NCC VII 147b]

609 JAṬĀ-MAṆI-ŚIKṢĀ **(जटामणिशिक्षा)**
Oppert I 7187. Belonged to Ivattur Nandikesvara Sastri of Vijayanagaram.
Oppert II 7375. Belonged to Venkatarama Sastri of Pillur, Mayavaram Taluk.
Oppert II 7953. Belonged to Venkatarama Dikshita of Sorakayur, Thanjavur Dist.

– C. Oppert II 7376. Belonged to Venkatarama Sastri of Pillur, Mayavaram Taluk.

[NCC VII 147b]

610 JAṬĀ-MĀLĀDI-PAṬHANA-PADDHATI (**जटामालादिपठनपद्धति**)
BISM p. 99 (29/807). 5 fol. Illustration of Jaṭā, Mālā, Śikhā, Rekhā and Ratha for the verse "imaṃ ratham adhi ye sapta ... "

611 JAṬĀ-MĀLĀ-ŚIKHĀ (**जटामालाशिखा**)
Illustrations of Vikṛti-s with verses of definitions.
GJKSV 13723. 2 fol.

612 JAṬĀ-YUKTA-MĀLĀ-PĀṬHA (**जटायुक्तमालापाठ**)
SBD 52626. 3 fol. (of VS). Incomplete.

613 JAṬĀ-LAKṢAṆA (1) (**जटालक्षण**)
of Śiśira.
Deccan College 9810. 10 fol. → Vikṛti-vallī.

614 JAṬĀ-LAKṢAṆA (2) (**जटालक्षण**)
Beginning:

अथ जटालक्षणमुच्यते।

य इच्छति जटां वक्तुं स विप्रो वेदवित्तमः ।
तस्य कीर्तिर्विवर्धेत स वेदफलमश्नुते॥

अनेन जटाफलमुक्तम्।

पदद्वयमनुक्रम्य व्युत्क्रम्योत्क्रम्य संधिमत्।
यथावत्स्वरसंयुक्तं प्रयुञ्ज्यात् सा जटा मता॥

जटायाः प्रकृतिं दर्शयति।

संहिता प्रकृतिः प्रोक्ता पदस्यैतत् क्रमस्य तु।
जटायाः प्रकृतिस्त्वेष एवं नित्यं निबोधत॥
जटायां वक्ष्यमाणायां कम्पसंधिस्वरादयः ।
अवधानं प्रयोक्तव्या निपुणैस्तद्वदीरितम्॥
प्रातिशाख्यादिशास्त्रज्ञः सर्वशिक्षाविशारदः ।
बुद्धिशक्तिसमेतो यः स जटां वक्तुमर्हति॥

प्रातिशाख्यव्याकरणशिक्षासु समर्थः सूक्ष्मबुद्धिमान् जटायामधिकारीत्यर्थः । केन किं कुत्र भवतीत्याह --

शिक्षया स्वरकम्पादीतरद् व्याकरणेन तु।
अवरोहे भवेत् सर्वमारोहे प्रातिशाख्यतः ॥

अवरोहसंधौ शीक्षया उदात्तादिस्वरः कम्पश्च भवति। इतरद् दीर्घादिसंधिकार्यमवरोहे व्याकरणेन । आरोहे यथासंहितपाठे तु सर्वमुदात्तादिसंधिकार्यं प्रातिशाख्यैनैव भवतीत्यर्थः ।

End:

यथा सोप इत्यत्र जटायां सोपोपः ससोपः । अपोभीत्यत्र अपो ओभ्याभ्यापोपोभि ।
एकादेशः स्यात् स्वरित इति। उच्चे वर्णेति च स्वरितत्वेत्यत्र विहिते। अत्र शिक्षा --

स्वरिते परभूते च स्वरितस्योत्तरार्धकम्।
नीचं कुर्यात् सकम्पं च यथादीर्घं समुच्चरेत्॥ इति।
त्रिधाविभक्तक्रमकेशवत्या शास्त्रैरनेकैः कृतगन्धवत्या
उत्फुल्लकम्पस्वरपुष्पवत्या वेण्या सुवाण्या सुवशीकरोति॥
रत्ने जटायामार्षादि योजितं तत्तदन्यथा।
नीतं तस्मात् प्रातिशाख्यं जटायां न प्रवर्तते॥

इति जटालक्षणं समाप्तम्॥

Adyar D I 840 (10 G 21 = TR 20). At the end of the *Vaidika-bhūṣaṇa* on the *Taittirīya-prātiśākhya* (pp. 318-45). The penultimate verse is also found at the end of the *Jaṭā-vallī* Mysore ND II 3386 (P 4772/16). Extract no. 148.
Adyar D I 983 (in a collection, pp. 731-60) → Veda-lakṣaṇa (A 1).

615 JAṬĀ-LAKṢAṆA (3) (**जटालक्षण**)
MD 910. PL. Tel. 9 pp. Incomplete.
Mysore I, p. 27 (2 Mss.).
Trav. Uni. 5539 F. PL. Tel. 70 Grantha-s. Incomplete (with Pīṭhikodāharaṇādi).
[NCC VII 147b]

616 JAṬĀ-LAKṢAṆA (4) (**जटालक्षण**)
→ Ṛgvedīya-jaṭālakṣaṇa.
[NCC VII 148a]

617 JAṬĀ-LAKṢAṆA (5) (**जटालक्षण**)
of Vyāḍi → Jaṭā-paṭala.
[NCC VII 148a]

618 JAṬĀ-LAKṢAṆA (6) (**जटालक्षण**)
→ Jaṭā-maṇi and Jaṭā-siddhānta-candrikā.

619 JAṬĀ-LAKṢAṆA (7) (**जटालक्षण**)
SBD 47898. 2 fol. Illustration of Jaṭā and two kinds of Mālā.

620 JAṬĀ-LAKṢAṆA or VIKALPA-KAUMUDĪ (**जटालक्षण / विकल्पकौमुदी**)
of Narasiṃha.

Beginning:

गणनाथं प्रणम्यादौ वाणीं ब्रह्माणमेव च।
व्यासादींश्च मुनीन्नत्वा शाकलं शैशिरं तथा॥ १॥
बाभ्रव्यं क्रमकर्तारं व्यालिं नत्वा जटाविदम्।
शौनकं च विशेषेण नत्वा गुरुपरंपराम्॥ २॥
करोति नरसिंहाख्यो जटालक्षणमुत्तमम्।

किंचिज्ज्ञेयं प्रातिशाख्यात् किंचिद् व्याकरणादिह ॥ ३ ॥
उभयानुगतं प्राय एतल्लक्षणमुच्यते ।
पारायणे संहितायां यत् फलं समुदीरितम् ॥ ४ ॥
पदस्य द्विगुणं प्रोक्तं क्रमस्य त्रिगुणं तथा ।
जटापारायणादेव षड्गुणं फलमश्नुते ॥ ५ ॥
पदसंधिसमायुक्ता स्वरसंधियुता तथा ।
या पदस्य षडावृत्तिः सा जटेत्यभिधीयते ॥ ६ ॥

End:

विकल्पकौमुदी सेयं जटायाः संहिताश्रया ।
नरसिंहेन रचिता संधिसंदेहनाशिनी ॥
इति विकल्पकौमुदी नाम जटालक्षणं समाप्तम् ॥

Adyar D XIII 40 (VB 737g). PL. Gr. 4 fol.
TCD 34-K. 7 pp. 65 Grantha-s.
Trav. Uni. 4254 L. PL. Mal. 6 fol. 65 Grantha-s. Belonged to Vishnu Nambudiri of Ettikada Illam Ayankudi, Kaduttirutti, Kottayam.
Trav. Uni. T.223 K. = TCD 34-K. A transcript of the Ms. no. 4254.
Triv. Cur. III 10. Mal. 50 Grantha-s.

Ptd.: in the magazine of the Mysore Sanskrit College, *Śrīmanmahārāja Saṃskṛta Mahāpāṭhaśālā Patrikā*, vol. 16 (1940), Mysore, pp. 1-6. [Adyar (H05sk MSC 16)]
[NCC VII 148a]

621 JAṬĀ-LAKṢAṆA(-PARIBHĀṢĀ) **(जटालक्षण /-परिभाषा)**
Different texts.
Mysore I, p. 27 =
Mysore ND II 3380 (P 4906/58). PL. Na. 1 fol. (140). Extract no. 144.
Mysore ND II 3381 (A 264/ 5). Tel. 5 fol. (145-49). Extract no. 145.
Mysore ND II 3382 (C 476/ 9). 1 fol.
Mysore ND II 3383 (P 4772/ 8). PL. Tel. 3 fol. Extract no. 146.
[NCC VII 148a]

622 JAṬĀ-LAKṢAṆA(-ŚĀSTRA-RATNA) **(जटालक्षणशास्त्ररत्न)**
Pertains to *Taittirīya-saṃhitā*.

Beginning: (814)

महागणेशं गिरिजामपीशं रमां हरिं वागधिदेवतां कम् ।
गुरून्नमस्कृत्य यथोपदेशं वक्ष्ये जटालक्षणशास्त्ररत्नम् ॥
य इच्छति जटां वक्तुं स विप्रो वेदवित्तमः ।
तस्य कीर्तिर्विवर्धेत स वेदफलमश्नुते ॥

End:

विद्धैतानि पदान्यादि द्रष्टव्यं पौरुषे नतः ।
प्रग्रहः ईदूदेदोदं नवस्यस्य यस्य विद्धयम्।
शतश्लोकेषु वै पञ्च त्रिंशल्लक्ष्येषु चास्ति चेत्।
न्यूनातिरिक्तं क्षमतां सन्तो वेदविदो बुधाः ॥
श्रीवत्सान्वयसंभवेन निगमस्मृत्यागमज्योतिषा
स्मार्तज्ञेन सुकेशवेन रचितं नाम्ना जटालक्षणम्।
एतद् वैदिकभूषणं सुतसुहृच्छिष्यप्रबोधाय तद्
विद्वद्वेदविदां सतां सुमनसां प्रीत्यै च कीर्त्यै भवेत्॥

इति जटालक्षणशास्त्ररत्नं समाप्तम् ॥ शके १७७२ विश्वावसु संवत्सरे पौषशुक्ल ५ सोमे पुस्तकं समाप्तम्॥

Adyar D I 814 (23 G 6 = 69832). PL. Gr. 2 fol. (114-15). Incomplete. = Adyar I, p. 49b.

Hoshiarpur p. 51 (no.3553). 8 fol. 180 Grantha-s. Dated Śaka 1772. Extract p. 408-09. Title: Jaṭā-lakṣaṇa-śāstra-ratna.

[NCC VII 148a]

623 JAṬĀVALI (जटावलि)

Unspecified.

Deccan College 9809. 23 fol. → Jaṭānyāya-pañcāśat.

Mysore (1898), p. 6 (no. 57). 3 fol. (115-17).

Mysore I, p. 27.

Trav. Uni. 5503 A. PL. Tel. 80 Grantha-s. (73 verses).

Wai I 574. 24 fol. → Jaṭā-nyāya-pañcāśad-vyākhyā.

Wai II 10269. 4 fol. → Jaṭā-nyāya-pañcāśat.

See also Jaṭā-nyāya-pañcāśat above.

[NCC VII 148a]

*JAṬĀVALLABHA-ŚĀSTRIN LAKṢMAṆA (जटावल्लभ-शास्त्रिन् लक्ष्मण)

– C. on Bhāradvāja-śikṣā. Whish 25b. See under Bhāradvāja-śikṣā.

[NCC VII 148a]

624 JAṬĀ-VALLĪ (जटावल्ली)

Based on the *Tribhāṣya-ratna;* of Padmanābha, son of Lakṣmaṇārya.

Beginning: (815)

जटावल्ली।

वाचं वाररुचादींश्च प्रणम्यादिगुरून् हरिम्।
(करिष्यामि जटावल्लीं विद्वत्सु हृदयंगमाम्॥
यथा त्रिभाष्यरत्ने च संक्षिप्तेयं प्रकाश्यते।)
उदात्तादिगुणैर्युक्ता वाक्छब्दालप्रबोधिका॥

तत्रादौ तावज्जटावलीव्यवहारज्ञापनार्थं संज्ञासूत्राण्युपवर्ण्यन्ते।

End:

वर्णपुष्पा जटावल्ली स्वरितोदात्तपल्लवा।
आश्लिष्टपदसंदर्भराजिता नियमैः कृता॥
योगिनो जनुषारेश्च वंशाब्धेः संभवस्य च।
लक्ष्मणार्यस्य पुत्रेण कृतेयं विदुषां मुदे॥

इति पद्मनाभयज्वना कृता जटावल्ली समाप्ता

Adyar D I 815 (10 G 21 = TR 20). 29 fol. (pp. 461-518). = Adyar I, p. 49b. Four additional fol. at the end contain discussion on the change of "n" into Anusvāra, e.g. trīn lokān, etc. Copied from the original Ms. of Puranika Kesavacharya of Belur, Mysore. Dated 28.5.1916. Consists of the following sections: Saṃjñā-viveka, Sthāna-viveka, Varṇa-viveka, Vargādi-viveka, Jaṭā-viveka.

Adyar D I 816 (21 E 51 = 67980). PL. Tel. 21 fol. = Adyar I, p. 50a.

Hoshiarpur p. 51 (no.3757). PL. Tel. 13 fol. 300 Grantha-s. Ptd. ?

Hoshiarpur p. 51 (no.4371). PL. Gr. 3 fol. 100 Grantha-s. Ptd. ?

MT 2591(d). PL. Tel. 28 fol. (171-98). Presented in 1917-18 by Vasireddi Chandramaulisvaraprasada Bahadur, Zamindar of Muktyala, Krishna Dist.

Mysore ND II 3386 (P 4772/16). PL. Tel. 4 fol. Extract no. 148. Title: Jaṭā-vallī. But begins as Uccodarkī.

[NCC VII 148a]

625 JAṬĀ-VIKṚTI-LAKṢAṆA (जटाविकृतिलक्षण)

of Vyāḍi. See Jaṭā-paṭala above.

[NCC VII 148a]

626 JAṬĀ-VICĀRA (जटाविचार)

Pertains to the *Taittirīya-saṃhitā* (from *Tribhāṣya-ratna-saṃgraha)*. Beginning is the same as the *Sarva-lakṣaṇa-tātparya-nirṇaya*, MT 1631(a).

Beginning: (819)

कृष्णपादाम्बुजद्वन्द्वं नमस्कृत्य सुरार्चितम्।
जटायाः क्रियते सम्यग् विचारो भूसुरप्रियः॥

ननु धर्मिसत्तायां प्रमाणमस्ति चेत् तद्विचारः कर्तुं शक्यते। तत्सद्भावे प्रमाणं न पश्यामः। तथाहि -- अथ संहितायामेकप्राणभावे यथायुक्ताद् विधिः सा प्रकृतिरिति प्रकृतिसंहितास्वरूपं निरूपितम्। नानापदसंधानसंयोगः पदसंहितेत्यभिधीयते इति संहितास्वरूपं निरूपितम्। (जटायाः स्वरूपं नोक्तं मूलकर्त्रा। फलश्रवणस्याप्यभावान् मूलग्रन्थे कथं तद्विचारो युक्तः। सति धर्मिणि धर्माश्चिन्त्यन्त इति न्यायादिति चेन्न। मूलशास्त्र एव जटाव्यवस्थापकानामनेकेषां सूत्राणां जटास्वरूपप्रतिपादक जटाध्ययनफलव्यवस्थापक शिक्षावचनानां च विद्यमानत्वात्। कानि पुनस्तानीति चेदुच्यते)॥

End:

तस्माल्लोपादिकविधायकं शास्त्रं संहितायां जटायां चान्यूनानतिरेकेण नियमेनैव वर्तत इति सिद्धम्॥ इति त्रिभाष्यरत्नसंग्रहे प्रथमः परिच्छेदः ॥

Adyar D I 819 (22 P 20 = 68361). PL. Gr. 29 fol. (187ff.). = Adyar II, App. p. iib (40 G 20). Copied by Sundararāja of Srīraṅgapaṭṭaṇa, on Amāvāsyā of Puṣya, of Kālayukti.

Adyar D I 820 (23 G 6 = 69832). PL. Gr. 23 fol. (90ff.). = Adyar I, p. 49b.

MD 15443. Tel. 56 pp. 312 Grantha-s. Incomplete. Begins differently.

Mysore ND II 3385 (P 2339/ 8). PL. Gr. 14 fol. (40-53). Extract no. 147. Colophon: Jaṭāvalī. Ascribed to Keśava : iti keśavena kṛtā jaṭāvalī samāptā | Colophon in the middle: iti tribhāṣyaratne prathamaḥ saṃgrahaḥ |

Trav. Uni. 5505. PL. Tel. 28 fol. 340 Grantha-s. Catalogued as Kramamālā. But only the first 2 fol. have a portion on Krama.

See Tribhāṣya-ratna-saṃgraha.

[NCC VII 148a]

627 JAṬĀ-SAṂDHI (1) (जटासंधि)

SBD 0591. 63 fol. (Adhyāya-s 1-6 in Aṣṭaka 6).

628 JAṬĀ-SAṂDHI (2) (जटासंधि)

of the five kinds of Jaṭā in the verses written at the end of the *Taittirīya-saṃhitā*.

MT 4818(c). PL. Gr. 3 fol. (98a-100a). No extract. Presented in 1924-25 by the Secretary to the Trustees of Sri Yogi Parthasarathi Ayyangar's Charities, Triplicane, Madras.

[NCC VII 148b]

629 JAṬĀ-SAṂDHI (3) (जटासंधि)

Difficult Jaṭā formations in each Varga of the *Ṛgveda* (ṛgvedavargapadebhyaḥ jaṭāsaṃdhiviṣayaka-kaṭhinapadāni saṃgṛhītāni).

SBD 52391. 62 fol. Dated V.S. 1878.

630 JAṬĀ-SAṂDHI-NIRṆAYA (1) (जटासंधिनिर्णय)

Cf. C. on Jaṭā-nyāya-pañcāśat above.

Hoshiarpur p. 51 (no.3539). 12 fol. 250 Grantha-s. Incomplete. Extract p. 409.

631 JAṬĀ-SAṂDHI-NIRṆAYA (2) (जटासंधिनिर्णय)

→ Jaṭānyāya-pañcāśad-vyākhyā.

VSM I 424 (no.4563). 4 fol.

632 JAṬĀ-SAṂDHI-LAKṢAṆA (1) (जटासंधिलक्षण)

Baroda 8005(b). = CLB I, p. 27. Cf. Jaṭā-nyāya-pañcāśat.

[NCC VII 148b]

633 JAṬĀ-SAṂDHI-LAKṢAṆA (2) (जटासंधिलक्षण)

GJKSV 25339. 4 fol. Catalogued as Prātiśākhya. Begins as Jaṭā-nyāya-pañcāśat. A few additional verses at the end on the special features of Taittirīya school.

634 JAṬĀ-SIDDHĀNTA-CANDRIKĀ (**जटासिद्धान्तचन्द्रिका**)

Name of the commentary by Lakṣmaṇa-budha on the *Jaṭāmaṇi*. MT 3887(m).

Hz 1438. PL. Gr. 17 fol. Extract p. 134 calls it Jaṭā-siddhānta-viciti. Belonged to the late Raja Ghanapathi of Tiruvidaimarudur, Thanjavur Dist.

Oppert I 984. Belonged to Viraraghava Tatacharyar, Head Master, Sanskrit School of Sathakopacharya, Kanchipuram, Chingelpet Dist.

Oppert II 9880. Belonged to M.Raja Ghanapathi of Mahadanapuram, Trichinapalli.

[NCC VII 148b]

635 JAṬĀ-SIDDHĀNTA-VICITI (**जटासिद्धान्तविचिति**)

The Jaṭā-maṇi is so called in Hz 1438.

636 JAṬODĀHARAṆA (**जटोदाहरण**)

Burnell 3b. (no.2389 c.).

RASB II 285 (G 6188). 8 fol. Dated V.S. 1777. Vikṛti-s for the verse "bṛhaspate paridīyā rathena". Cf. Grantha-saṃhitā Ekādaśa-prakārāḥ.

RASB II 286 (G 6176). 6 fol. 100 Grantha-s. Dated V.S. 1798. Vikṛti-s for the verse "bṛhaspate paridīyā rathena".

TD 1766. 5 fol. (5-9) 50 Grantha-s. No colophon.

TD 1767. 5 fol. (6-10). 47 Grantha-s. Incomplete (no beginning).

TD 1768. 2 fol. 25 Grantha-s. Incomplete (different text; no end). This Ms. furnishes suitable illustrations for the various saṃdhi-s and other changes coming under Jaṭā-vikṛti, i.e. ṣatva, ṇatva, rephādi-ṇatva-vikāra-s.

[NCC VII 148b]

*JAYANTA or JAYANTA-SVĀMIN (**जयन्त / जयन्तस्वामिन्**)

– Svarāṅkuśa or Svara-nirṇaya; called Jaṭā-paṭala in L 1235.

– C. on Kātyāyana-(ī-)śikṣā. See above.

[NCC VII 181ab]

637 JYEṢṬHA-ṚGVIDHĀNA (**ज्येष्ठ-ऋग्विधान**)

Cf. Ṛgvidhāna.

638 JYOTSNĀ (**ज्योत्स्ना**)

Name of the commentary by Rāma(-candra) on the *Vājasaneyi-prātiśākhya*.

BORI D I i.288. Weber 1463.

[NCC VII 377a]

*ṬUMAṆI-GOSVĀMIN (**डुमणिगोस्वामिन्**)

– C. Śikṣā-pañjikā on Paṇinīya-śikṣā. Ujjain I, p. 8.

[NCC VIII 3a and VI 217b.]

639 ṆAKĀRA-NIRṆAYA (**णकारनिर्णय**)

Mysore ND II 3388 (P 4906/55). PL. Na. 2 fol. (135-36). Extract no. 150.

640 ṆATVA-TRIKRAMA (**णत्वत्रिक्रम**)

Mysore ND II 3387 (P 4906/48). PL. Na. 1 fol. (128). Extract no. 149.

641 ṆATVA-SAṂHITĀ (णत्वसंहिता)

Beginning: (821)

अग्निमीळे शक्रो यथा त्वामभिप्रणानुमो रक्षाणो ब्रह्मणस्त्रयः ॥ १ ॥ अयं देवाय प्र ण आयूंषि वस्त निर्णिजमधिषवण्या त्रयः ॥ २ ॥ एता याम ऊर्ध्वे ऊषुणार्मोषुणः परा परानिर्ऋतिः पराणुदे विलू उत सक्ष्वादेव धनानि सुषणा प्रातर्यावाणा अध्वरं प्रातर्याव्णस्सप्त॥ ३॥

End:

प्र होता आह निर्णिजे अतिदुर्गाणि मोषुणस्येम स्वार्णये चत्वारि॥ १॥ ये यज्ञेन सहस्रदा ग्रामणीः अदितिं सुप्रगीतिं प्रातर्यावाणमुरूण शरस्यर्णं प्रणयत नामि प्रणीति ओषधी ... ॥ २॥ दावानां नं तैः ... अश्वनिर्णिज्येका॥ ३॥ विहि॥ रक्षोहणं वाजिनं प्रणय प्रचेतसः नृमणा पतिं त्रयः ॥ पुनः पूषावर्जम्॥ ४॥ हये जये परणयते नृपाणः स हि नो नृपाणः प्रणितिभीष्टे त्रयः ॥ ५ ॥ उभा उ नूनम् ॥ चचरा चन्द्रनिर्णिम् । ग्रामणीः । भरतसुप्रायणाः । प्रणयन्ति पञ्च ॥ ६ ॥ घृतनिर्णिक्स्यामनुप्रणीतयः नेतार ऊषूणः ॥ निरयणं परायणे पञ्च॥ ७॥ त्यच्चित् सुष्वाणासः सहस्रणीथाः कवयः । तदारभस्व दुर्हणः मम पुत्राश्शत्रुहणः गर्भं दुर्णामा प्र ण आयूंषि पञ्च॥ ८॥

Adyar D I 821 (22 H 6 = 69060). PL. Tel. 5 fol. (7b-11b). = Adyar I, p. 49b.

Mysore Skt. Coll. p. I = D. No.9 (846/10) PL. Na. 2 fol. (40-12). It contains a few variants.

Trav. Uni. 5539 E. PL. Tel. 4 fol. 70 Grantha-s. Incomplete.

[NCC VIII 13b]

642 TAṆḌĀ-LAKṢAṆA-SŪTRA or TĀṆḌYA-LAKṢAṆA (तण्डालक्षणसूत्र / ताण्ड्यलक्षण) on the Stotra-s of the *Sāmaveda*, in three Prapāṭhaka-s divided into 34 (12, 12 and 10) Khaṇḍa-s. It is actually a Śrauta text being a condensation of the *Ārṣeya-kalpa* and *Kṣudra-sūtra*. See A. Parpola, *The Śrautasūtras of Lātyāyana ...* , vol. I 1, p. 66.

Beginning:

अथ यज्ञे शब्दस्तोत्रविधिवाक्यशेषो यथामाशकं तत्प्रामाण्यात्। वार्त्तिकं तस्य। पालनार्थं वा। आख्यानामन्यन्। स्तोत्राण्यक्षरशः । षोडश।

Alph. List Beng. Govt. p. 45.

BORI 97 of 1879-80. 19 fol. 250 Grantha-s. Dated V.S. 1736.

Calcutta Skt. Coll. I 496 (253). 17 fol.

Calcutta Skt. Coll. I 497 (252). 21 pp. Dated V.S. 1618. Damaged.

Jammu RSRI p. 66 (no. 5246). 16 fol. Dated V.S. 1628 (Stein 274).

Mysore II, p. 2.

Mysore ND II 3389 (C 2233). 13 fol.

P 6.

PUL I, p. 132 (no.22). 11 fol. Dated V.S. 1806.

RASB II 1322 (G 999). 14 fol. 280 Grantha-s. Dated V.S. 1690.

Rep. Raj. and C. I. p. 3.
SBD 4102. 2 fol. Incomplete.
Stein p. 16 (no. 274). 16 fol. Dated V.S. 1628.
Sūcīpattra 114.
Trav. Uni. 11802. 250 Grantha-s. Title: Sāmaveda-taṇḍā-lakṣaṇa-sūtra.

[NCC VIII 16a]

643 TAPARA(-PRAKARAṆA) **(तपर /-प्रकरण)**

See also Napara-tapara(-prakaraṇa).

[NCC VIII 106a]

644 TAPARA(-PRAKARAṆA) **(तपर /-प्रकरण)**

of Śeṣa Nārāyaṇa. List of words ending in "t" in the Pada text, but assimilated to a following "n" in the *Ṛgveda*.

Beginning:(824)

अभ्रादमुञ्चदकृणोदस्वापयदचिक्रदत्।
असच्चातृणदनमदस्मदस्थादवीद् भवेत्॥

End:

संगृह्यमपि यत् किंचिदत्रानुक्तं विचक्षणैः ।
ऊह्यमेवं न (च) तान्ताख्यं लक्षणं समुदीरितम्॥
इति श्रीशेषनारायणाख्यविरचितं सर्वतपरं समाप्तम्॥

Adyar D I 824 (20 K 38 = 67500). PL. Tel. 2 fol. (9-10).
Triv. Cur. III 7. Mal. 50 Grantha-s. Obtained from Vishnu Nambudiri, Ettikada Illam, Ayankudi.
Whish 73,2 (9). PL. Gr. 1 fol. (22). Title: Tānta-saṃgraha.

Ptd. in the collection called *Tāṇḍaṅgal* (in Malayalam script). – Kunnankulam (Kerala) : Panchangam Pustakashala, 1930 (M.E. 1105), pp. 22-23. [SAI (87/1683*)]

– C.

Beginning:

गजाननं नमस्कृत्य कृष्णमिष्टार्थदं हरिम्।
कुर्वे तपरटीकां ते कुर्वन्तु विशदां मतिम्॥
अभ्रादित्यारभ्य अजोहवीदित्यन्तमकारादीनि तकारान्तानि पदान्युदाह्रियन्ते ...

End:

सं नु वोचावहै पुनः । स्यान्नः सूनुस्तनयो विजावा। उच्छुक्रमत्कमजते सिमस्मात् न वा।
इति तपरटीका समाप्ता॥

Whish 73,2 (11). PL. Gr. 5 fol. (35-39).

[NCC VIII 106a]

645 TAPARA(-LAKṢAṆA) (तपर /-लक्षण)

Also included in the *Sapta-lakṣaṇa*. List of words ending in "t" in the Pada text, but assimilated to a following "n" in the *Taittirīya-saṃhitā*.

Beginning: (Telugu edition)

अद्यादतृणदश्नीयादब्रवीदजुषत् ततः ।
अस्थादस्मदसच्चैवमनन्त्यजनदर्पयेत् ॥ १॥
अस्मादवसृजेदक्रमीदवस्ताच्च गण्यते।
अभवच्चावरोहेच्चानमदासीदिदुच्यते॥ २॥
इयादुदुपरिष्टाच्च नैःपरं त्वेनदिष्यते।
स्वाहैकाच्चैवमेकस्मादीकारान्ते परत्र तु॥ ३॥
पद एतच्च कुर्याच्च क्रामेत् कनिक्रदत् क्षयात्।
गृह्णीयाद् गमयेच्चीच्च जुहुयात् तावदीरितम्॥ ४॥

End:

हविष्मन्निधनं पूर्वं हविष्कृन्निधनं तथा।
हन्याद्धृन्नपरं तान्तं पदमेवं प्रकीर्तितम्॥ १०॥
यत्र क्वचन तेनैव पूर्वं द्रष्टुमपेक्षते।
नतान्तपदमालेयं नवरत्नोत्तराक्षरा॥ ११॥
सगुणा वेदविदुषां रचिता कण्ठभूषणम्।
तोषाय देवदेवस्य विष्णोर्नारायणस्य वै॥ १२॥
इति तपरं नाम लक्षणं समाप्तम्॥

Adyar D I 823 (20 K 21 = 67483). PL. Tel. 1 fol. = Adyar I, p. 49b.
Adyar D I 988 → Veda-lakṣaṇa (A 6).
Adyar D I 1032 → Sapta-lakṣaṇa.
Adyar D I 1033 → Sapta-lakṣaṇa.
Adyar D I 1035 (a. Śaurisūnu) → Sapta-lakṣaṇa.
Baroda 10381(f). PL. Gr. 2 fol. (11-12). 30 Grantha-s. = CLB I, p. 28.
Hoshiarpur p. 51 (no.3557). 26 fol. 402 Grantha-s. Dated Śaka 1774. Contains also Napara and Vilaṅghya with C. of Nārāyaṇa.
Hoshiarpur p. 51 (no.4105). PL. Gr. 1 fol. 10 Grantha-s. Extract p. 409.
Hoshiarpur p. 51 (no.4118). PL. Gr. 3 fol. 50 Grantha-s.
Hoshiarpur p. 300 (no.5947). PL. Gr. 1 fol. 20 Grantha-s.
IO 4480 (Mackenzie II 94k). PL. Na. 3 fol. (89-90). Written ca. A.D. 1770. Col.: Udidbhāṣya ?.
IO 4481 (Mackenzie III 234i). PL. Tel. 6 fol. (with C.).
IO 4482 (Mackenzie III 186g). PL. Tel. 1 fol. (16).
IO 4486 (Mackenzie III 59a). PL. Tel. 2 fol. (16-17). Also Napara.
MD 16399. PL. Gr. 2 pp. 14 Grantha-s.

MD 16731. PL. Tel. 4 pp. (with C.).

MT 1240(c). PL. Tel. 4 fol. (23-26). Presented in 1913-14 by K. Ramakrishnayya of Musalipattanam.

Mysore I, pp. 27-28 (5 Mss.); p. 29 (5 Mss.).

Mysore ND II 3390-407. Extract no. 151.

Oppert I 991. Belonged to Viraraghava Tatacharyar, Head Master, Sanskrit School of Sathakopacharya, Kanchipuram, Chingelpet Dist.

Oppert II 753. Belonged to Ghanapathi Shingaracharyar of Alasur, Madurantakam Taluk.

Oppert II 1323. Belonged to Gopalacharyar of Pillapakkam, Kanchipuram Taluk.

Oppert II 9032. Belonged to Ganapati Lakshminarayana Sastri of Tiruvadi, Thanjavur Dist.

PUL II. App. p. 11 (no.171). PL. Gr. 5 (24-29).

PUL II. App. p. 11 (no.172). PL. Gr. 2 A.1048 ?

RASB II 487-88(IV) (G 6063). Dated V.S. 1913 / Śaka 1778.

TD 1797. PL. Gr. 2 fol. 25 Grantha-s → Sapta-lakṣaṇa.

Trav. Uni. 1116 F. PL. Mal. 20 Grantha-s.

Trav. Uni. 2346 J. PL. Gr. 180 Grantha-s (with C.).

Trav. Uni. 4254 F-1. PL. Mal. 10 Grantha-s. Belonged to Vishnu Nambudiri of Ettikada Illam Ayankudi, Kaduttirutti, Kottayam.

Trav. Uni. 5778 I. PL. Tel. 10 Grantha-s.

Trav. Uni. 22749 K. PL. Mal. 50 Grantha-s (with C.). Incomplete.

See also Napara-tapara(-prakaraṇa).

Ptd.: There are at least five editions: three in Grantha and one each in Telugu and Malayalam script. See under Aniṅgya (Taitt.) and Sapta-lakṣaṇa.

– C. of Mallayārya-yajvan.

Mysore ND II 3412 (P 2265/ 9). PL. Gr. 3 fol. (97-99).

Mysore ND II 3413 (P 5999/ 6). PL. Tel. 1 fol.

Mysore ND II 3414 (P 7891/ 2). PL. Na. 4 fol. (52-55).

– C.

IO 4481 (Mackenzie III 234i). PL. Tel. 6 fol. (with text).

IO 4482 (Mackenzie III 186g). PL. Tel. 1 fol. (16). (with text).

MD 16731. PL. Tel. 4 pp. (with text).

MD 17441. PL. Gr. 4 pp. 45 Grantha-s.

MT 4017(c). PL. Gr. 2 fol. (17-18). Presented in 1921-22 by Krishna Ghanapathigal, Sirukumar, Trichinapalli Dist.

Mysore (1898), p. 6 (no. 52). 5 fol. (42-46).

Mysore I, p. 28 (2 Mss.); p. 613.

Mysore ND II 3408-11. Extract no. 152.

Mysore ND II 3415-19. Extract no. 153.

Oppert II 754. Belonged to Ghanapathi Shingaracharyar of Alasur, Madurantakam Taluk

Oppert II 9033. Belonged to Ganapati Lakshminarayana Sastri of Tiruvadi, Thanjavur Dist.
Tirupati SVUORI 2287 (4511c). PL. Tel.
Trav. Uni. 2346 K. PL. Gr. 50 Grantha-s (with text).
Trav. Uni. 4254 F-2. Belonged to Vishnu Nambudiri of Ettikada Illam Ayankudi, Kaduttirutti, Kottayam.
Trav. Uni. 22200 B. PL. Mal. 60 Grantha-s.
Trav. Uni. 22749 K. PL. Mal. 50 Grantha-s (with text). Incomplete.

– C. Tapara-paddhati.
Whish 25a (4). PL. Gr. 3 fol. (26-28).

– C. of Śaurisūri (sūnu ?).
Adyar.
MD 16813. PL. Gr. 3 pp. 54 Grantha-s.
Trav. Uni. 4369 B-2. PL. Gr.

[NCC VIII 106b]

646 TĀṆḌYA-LAKṢAṆA (**ताण्ड्यलक्षण**)
→ Taṇḍā-lakṣaṇa.

647 TĀNTA-LAKṢAṆA or TAPARA or TĀNTA-SAṂGRAHA (**तान्तलक्षण / तपर / तान्तसंग्रह**)
Whish 73,2 (9) → Tapara of Śeṣa Nārāyaṇa.

[NCC VIII 149a]

648 TIṄPARA-SVARITA(-SAMĀSA-PRAKARAṆA) (**तिङ्परस्वरित /-समासप्रकरण**)
Baroda 6255(c). PL. Tel. 2 fol. (78b-79). = CLB I, p. 37.
Mysore ND II 3420 (P 2265/25). PL. Gr. 1 fol. (138). Extract no. 154.

[NCC VIII 166a]

***TIMMĀVADHĀNIN** (**तिम्मावधानिन्**)
Son of Pārvatī-putra Kṛṣṇam-bhaṭṭa.
– Svara-śiromaṇi. Ptd. : See below.

649 TṚTĪYA-DHĀRYA (**तृतीयधार्य**)
Though not mentioned in the catalogue, it contains both Tṛtīya-dhārya and Caturtha-dhārya of the printed edition → Dhārya-nirūpaṇa. MD 14077.

Mysore ND II 3421 (P 491/ 3). PL. Na. 2 fol. (103-04). Extract no. 155.
Mysore ND II 3422 (A 642/ 5). Kan. 3 fol. (31-33). Dated 6.8.1919.
Mysore ND II 3423 (A 642/ 7). Kan. 1 fol.

650 TṚTĪYA-SAṂGRAHA (**तृतीयसंग्रह**)
Mysore ND II 3424 (P 4772/10). PL. Tel. 1 fol. (4). Extract no. 156.

651 TAITTIRĪYA-KĀṆḌĀNUKRAMAṆIKĀ (**तैत्तिरीयकाण्डानुक्रमणिका**)
→ Kāṇḍānukrama(-ṇikā).
PUL I, p. 20 (no.61).

PUL I, p. 21 (no.63) (with C.).
SBD 2351. 12 fol.

[NCC VIII 208b]

652 TAITTIRĪYA-JAṬĀ-PĀṬHA (तैत्तिरीयजटापाठ)
SBD 1268. 7 fol.

653 TAITTIRĪYA-DĪPIKĀ (तैत्तिरीयदीपिका)
Ānandāśrama 2667 (Śikṣā; this is a C. on the *Taittirīyopaniṣad).*

[NCC VIII 208b]

654 TAITTIRĪYA-PADA-SVARA-LAKṢAṆA (तैत्तिरीयपदस्वरलक्षण)
Also called *Svara-pañcāśat or Svara-lakṣaṇa,* as it reads in the first verse: "taittirīyapadādīnāṃ vakṣyāmi svaralakṣaṇam" → Svara-pañcāśat.

Adyar I, p. 49b = Adyar D I 1089 (21 I 14 = 68121). 1091.
Baroda 6381(b) (with C.). Incomplete. = CLB I, p. 28.
Tirupati SVUORI (962). PL. Gr.

[NCC VIII 208b]

655 TAITTIRĪYA-PRATĪKĀḤ (तैत्तिरीयप्रतीकाः)
Burnell 6a. → Kṛṣṇa-yajurvedānukramaṇikā, TD 586-90.

[NCC VIII 209a]

656 TAITTIRĪYA-PRĀTIŚĀKHYA (तैत्तिरीयप्रातिशाख्य)
This is the authoritative standard work of the Taittirīya Śākhā and one of the well-known Prātiśākhya-s. It consists of two Praśna-s, each containing 12 Adhyāya-s, in total about 535 Sūtra-s. There are eight memorial verses mainly at the end of different chapters.

Beginning:

अथ वर्णसमाम्नायः । १। अथ नवादितः समानाक्षराणि। २। द्वे द्वे सवर्णे ह्रस्वदीर्घे। ३। न प्लुतपूर्वम्। ४। षोडशादितः स्वराः । ५। शेषो व्यञ्जनानि। ६। आद्याः पञ्चविंशतिः स्पर्शाः । ७। पराश्चतस्रो ऽन्तस्स्थाः । ८। परे षडूष्माणः । ९। स्पर्शानामानुपूर्व्येण पञ्च पञ्च वर्गाः । १०।

End:

अथ चतस्रः संहिताः । १ । पदसंहिताक्षरसंहिता वर्णसंहिताङ्गसंहिता चेति । २ । नानापदसंधानसंयोगः पदसंहितेत्यभिधीयते। ३। यथास्वमक्षरसंहितादीनामप्येवम्। ४।

गुरुत्वं लघुता साम्यं ह्रस्वदीर्घप्लुतानि च।
लोपागमविकाराश्च प्रकृतिर्विक्रमः क्रमः ॥ ५॥
स्वरितोदात्तनीचत्वं श्वासो नादो ऽङ्गमेव च।
एतत् सर्वं तु विज्ञेयं छन्दोभाषामधीयता॥ ६॥
पदक्रमविशेषज्ञो वर्णक्रमविचक्षणः ।
स्वरमात्राविभागज्ञो गच्छेदाचार्यसंसदम्॥ ७॥

Adyar D I 825 (9 D 36 = PM 118). 20 fol. = Adyar I, p. 49b.

Adyar D I 826 (19 D 61 = 66253). PL. Gr. 19 fol. (1-19).

Adyar D I 827 (23 A 41 = 69592). PL. Tel. 9 fol. = Adyar I, p. 49b.

Adyar D I 828 (23 H 27 = 69901). PL. Gr. 5 fol. (2ff.). Incomplete. up to II 9.3. = Adyar I, p. 49b.

Adyar D I 829 (23 I 13 = 69947). PL. Tel. and Gr. 17 fol. (40ff.). = Adyar I, p. 49b. Dated 32nd of Āṭi corresponding to Siṃha of the year Aṅgira.

Adyar D I 830 (25 D 13 = 70833). PL. Gr. 20 fol. (10ff.). Incomplete; up to II 6.

Adyar D I 831 (25 E 8 = 70864). PL. Tel. 9 fol. = Adyar I, p. 49b.

Adyar D I 832 (25 E 12 = 70868). PL. Gr. 13 fol. (15ff.). Incomplete. Begins from I i.16. = Adyar I, p. 49b.

Adyar D I 833 (25 H 14 = 70955). PL. Tel. 12 fol. = Adyar I, p. 49b. Dated Friday, 15th Āśvija of Sarvajit, copied by Vārāṇasī Rāmasvāmi; the original belonged to Citrāpurī Subbāvadhāni.

Adyar D I 834 (25 L 8 = 71126). PL. Gr. 9 fol. ; dated 5th day of the dark fortnight of Āvaṇi of Pramādīca.

Adyar D I 835 (25 L 32 = 71150). PL. Gr. 11 fol.

Adyar D I 836 (25 L 33 = 71151). PL. Gr. 13 fol. Former owner was Gopāla Śāstriyalu. Col.: Sapta-lakṣaṇa.

Adyar D I 837 (28 J 15 = 73049). PL. Gr. 9 fol. = Adyar I, p. 49b.

Adyar D I 838 (28 M 20 = 73212). PL. Gr. 8 fol. (57ff.).

Adyar D I 839 (30 H 8 = 74053). PL. (Śrītāla) Gr. 15 fol. (105ff.). = Adyar I, p. 49b. (II 11-12 are missing).

Adyar 26 N 2 = 71747. PL. Gr. 7 fol. (not described).

Adyar D I 964 (see remarks at the end).

Adyar D I 984 (only a fragment in a collection of Veda-lakṣaṇa texts).

Adyar D XIII 182 (VB 54d). PL. Tel. 3 fol. (chs. 10-24)

Adyar D XIII 183 (VB 132d). PL. Gr. 13 fol.

Adyar D XIII 184 (VB 438a). PL. Tel. 10 fol.

America 353. 6-16 fol. Sections 1-24.

America 354. 156 fol. (with C. Tribhāṣya-ratna).

America 355. 83 fol. (with C. Tribhāṣya-ratna). In Roman transliteration. Ms. B of Whitney's edition.

America 356. 104 fol. (with C. Tribhāṣya-ratna). Dated V.S. 1912. Collated and corrected by Whitney in red ink.

America 357. 16 fol. (text). 136 fol. (C. Tribhāṣya-ratna). In Roman transliteration. Ms. G and H of Whitney's edition.

Ānandāśrama 7526. 9 fol. Dated Śaka 1719.

Baroda 6131(e). PL. Gr. 12 fol. (17-28). 200 Grantha-s. = CLB I, p. 28.

Baroda 7820. PL. Gr. 53 fol. (16-68). 1400 Grantha-s (with C.). = CLB I, p. 28.

Baroda 9674. 54 fol. 1200 Grantha-s (with C.; chs. 1-9).= CLB I, p. 28.

Baroda 9805(a). PL. Gr. 11 fol. 200 Grantha-s. = CLB I, p. 28.

Baroda 10034(g). PL. Gr. 8 fol. 200 Grantha-s. = CLB I, p. 28.

Baroda 10354. Tel. 7 fol. 80 Grantha-s (8 chs. only). = CLB I, p. 28.

Baroda 10381(b). PL. Gr. 19 fol. 200 Grantha-s. = CLB I, p. 28.

BISM p. 342 (29/2377).

Bühler p. 553 (no. 13) (with C. Tribhāṣya-ratna).

Burnell 5b.

GB 15. 14 fol. Copied from and compared with a Ms. dated Śaka 1697.

GD I 17. PL. Gr. 114 fol. 2100 Grantha-s (with C. Tribhāṣya-ratna).

GJKSV 13772. 14 fol. Dated V.S. 1921 / Śaka 1786. Copied by Padmākara, son of Dhoḍa Dīkṣita Lele.

GJKSV 23902. 13 fol. Dated Śaka 1746. Title: Prātiśākhya.

GJKSV 28007. 5 fol. Incomplete (up to Svara-prakaraṇa).

GJKSV 33555. 13 fol. (2nd Prapāṭhaka). Dated V.S. 1894.

GJKSV 33582. 9 fol.

Gough p. 163. Tel. (no.823: Yajurveda-prātiśākhya; a. Pāṇini ?).

Granthappura p.1 (no.18). Gr. 900 Grantha-s (with C. Tribhāṣya-ratna).

Hamburg StUB (Oppert 10e). PL. Gr.

Hoshiarpur p. 51 (no.4105). PL. Gr. 12 fol. 300 Grantha-s.

Hoshiarpur p. 51 (no.5947). PL. Gr. 8 fol. 200 Grantha-s.

Hoshiarpur p. 300 (no.4375). PL. Gr. 12 fol. 300 Grantha-s.

Hz 1329. PL. Gr. 34 fol. Belonged to Anna Vajapeyi of Tiruvidaimarudur, Thanjavur Dist.

IM 9704. 14 fol. (3-16). Incomplete (I 49 to XX 12).

IO 4453 (Mackenzie III 119d). PL. Tel. 12 fol.

IO 4454 (Mackenzie II 81a). PL. Na. 7 fol.

IO 4455 (Mackenzie III 186c). PL. Tel. 3 fol. (3-5).

IO 7847 (3747). 11 fol. a modern copy.

Khn. p. 8 (no.24). 17 fol. Dated Śaka 1739; from Ashṭe; Limaye.

Mack. 7.

Max Müller Mem. XXII. 19 fol. Written ca. A.D. 1700.

MD 928. PL. Tel. 26 pp. (1ff.).

MD 929. PL. Gr. 22 pp. (39ff.).

MD 930. Tel. 23 pp. (1ff.).

MD 16015. PL. Gr. 12 pp. 236 Grantha-s.

MD 16725. PL. Tel. 16 pp. 224 Grantha-s.

MD 16822. PL. Gr. 22 pp. 220 Grantha-s (Adhyāya-s 1-11).

MD 17434. PL. Gr. 22 pp. 262 Grantha-s.

MD 17669. PL. Tel. 5 pp. 32 Grantha-s. Incomplete (Adhyāya-s 3-4).

MT 516. PL. Tel. 8 fol. Copied by Pedda Somayājulu, on Thursday, 14th Jyeṣṭha, in the year Raudri. Presented in 1910-11 by C. Visvanatha Shastrigal of Viziyanagaram.

MT 1089(a). PL. Tel. 8 fol. (1-8). Presented in 1913-14 by Prayaga Kamayya Sastri of Kolakalur, Guntur Dist.

MT 1205(a). PL. Tel. 10 fol. Presented in 1913-14 by K. Ramakrishnayya of Musalipattanam.

MT 1964(i). PL. Tel. 13 fol. (85-97). Chs. 3-4 with C. Tribhāṣya-ratna. Presented in 1916-17 by Rayaprolu Ramabrahmangaru of Guruza, Gudivada Taluk, Krishna Dist.

MT 2591(a). PL. Tel. 15 fol. (3-17). Presented in 1917-18 by Vasireddi Chandramaulisvaraprasada Bahadur, Zamindar of Muktyala, Krishna Dist.

MT 2881(i). PL. Gr. 5 fol. (43-47). Presented in 1918-19 by Venkatagiri Appalacharyar of Triplicane.

MT 3887(b). PL. Gr. 7 fol. (66-72). Purchased in 1921-22 from Annasvami Sastrigal, Bhavani, Coimbatore Dist.

MT 4586. PL. Gr. 11 fol. Presented in 1924-25 by the Secretary to the Trustees of Sri Yogi Parthasarathi Ayyangar's Charities, Triplicane, Madras.

MT 4600(b). PL. Gr. 9 fol. (18-26). Incomplete. Adhyāya-s 1 to 10. Presented in 1924-25 by the Secretary to the Trustees of Sri Yogi Parthasarathi Ayyangar's Charities, Triplicane, Madras.

Mysore p. 2 (no. 53). 29 fol. (Yajurveda-prātiśākhya).

Mysore (1898), p. 5 (no. 53a). Gr. 29 fol.

Mysore I, p. 28 (5 Mss.).

Mysore ND II 3425-38. Extract no. 157

Mysore ND II 3757 (P 7073/ 1). Extract no. 272. Title: Varṇa-samāmnāya.

Oppert I 7986. Belonged to Paravastu Venkatarangacharyar of Vishakhapattanam.

Oxf. CS d.176(4). 13 fol.

Oxf. II 860(4) (Ms. Wilson 504). 12 fol. (63-74). 5 fol. are lost. = Oxf. 386a (no.504). Dated A.D. 1741.

PUL I, p. 21 (no.64). PL. Tel. 54 fol.

PUL I, p. 21 (no.65). PL. Gr. 7 fol.

PUL I, p. 21 (no.66). PL. Gr. 5 fol.

PUL I, p. 21 (no.67). PL. Gr. 15 fol. (18-32).

PUL I, p. 21 (no.68). 13 fol.

PUL I, p. 21 (no.69). 16 fol. Incomplete.

PUL II. App. p. 11 (no.173). PL. Gr. 25 fol.

Rice 12.

SBD 2129. PL. Dra. 87 fol. (with C.). Incomplete.

SBD 2135. Tel. 13 fol. (Kṛṣṇa-yajuḥ-prātiśākhya).

Tb. 208(A) (with C. Tribhāṣya-ratna). Roth's transcript of Oxford Mss. Wilson 504d (= Oxf. II 860) and 478c (= Oxf. II 867) (from III 13 to the end). Dated August 1845.

TD 1778. PL. Tel. 9 fol. (100-108). 200 Grantha-s.

TD 1779. PL. Gr. 24 fol. (48-76). 220 Grantha-s.

TD 1780. PL. Gr. 17 fol. (ka - tha). 220 Grantha-s.

TD 1781. PL. Gr. 1 fol. 25 Grantha-s. (Pragrahādhyāya = IV 1-51).

Tirupati SVUORI 2489 (2836b). PL. Gr. Incomplete.

Tirupati SVUORI 2490 (3280a). PL. Gr. Incomplete.

Tirupati SVUORI 6169 (3526). PL. Gr. 5 fol. Incomplete.

Tirupati SVUORI 3825 (1481). PL. Gr. Incomplete. Title: Prātiśākhyaṃ Yajurvedīyam.

Tirupati SVUORI 3826 (1520). PL. Gr. Incomplete. Title: Prātiśākhyaṃ Yajurvedīyam.

Tirupati SVUORI 3827 (5956a). PL. Gr. Incomplete. Title Prātiśākhyaṃ Yajurvedīyam.

Trav. Uni. 2406. PL. Gr. 2500 Grantha-s (with C. Tribhāṣya-ratna).

Trav. Uni. 2630 L. PL. Gr. 200 Grantha-s.

Trav. Uni. 2643. PL. Gr. 1600 Grantha-s (with C. Tribhāṣya-ratna). Incomplete.

Trav. Uni. 2938 G. PL. Gr. 200 Grantha-s.

Trav. Uni. 3040 A. PL. Gr. 200 Grantha-s.

Trav. Uni. 3321 A. PL. Gr. 210 Grantha-s (with C. Vaidikābharaṇa). Incomplete.
Trav. Uni. 3593. PL. Gr. 2500 Grantha-s (with C. Tribhāṣya-ratna).
Trav. Uni. 3599 A. PL. Gr. 190 Grantha-s. Incomplete.
Trav. Uni. 3605 C. PL. Gr. 200 Grantha-s.
Trav. Uni. 3679 D. PL. Gr. 2475 Grantha-s (with C. Tribhāṣya-ratna). Incomplete.
Trav. Uni. 3747. PL. Gr. 2500 Grantha-s (with C. Tribhāṣya-ratna).
Trav. Uni. 4369 A. PL. Gr. 200 Grantha-s.
Trav. Uni. 5539 A. PL. Tel. 40 Grantha-s. Incomplete.
Trav. Uni. 5631 A. PL. Gr. 2500 Grantha-s (with C. Tribhāṣya-ratna).
Trav. Uni. 5631 B. PL. Gr. 200 Grantha-s.
Trav. Uni. 5747 A. PL. Gr. 125 Grantha-s. Incomplete.
Trav. Uni. 5778 A. PL. Tel. 2500 Grantha-s (with C. Tribhāṣya-ratna).
Trav. Uni. 5778 B. PL. Tel. 185 Grantha-s. Incomplete.
Trav. Uni. 7182. Tel. 74 fol. 1700 Grantha-s (with C. Tribhāṣya-ratna). Incomplete.
Trav. Uni. L.988 A. PL. Mal. 200 Grantha-s.
Trav. Uni. L.988 J. PL. Mal. 2500 Grantha-s (with C. Tribhāṣya-ratna).
Trav. Uni. L.1193 C. PL. Mal. 200 Grantha-s.
Trav. Uni. 13552 B. PL. Mal. 1100 Grantha-s (with C. Tribhāṣya-ratna). Incomplete.
Trav. Uni. 13733 E. PL. Gr. 185 Grantha-s. Incomplete.
Trav. Uni. 18615 A. PL. Gr. 200 Grantha-s.
Trav. Uni. 19037. PL. Gr. 2100 Grantha-s (with C. Tribhāṣya-ratna). Incomplete.
Trav. Uni. 17321 B. PL. Mal. 1300 Grantha-s (with C. Tribhāṣya-ratna). Incomplete.
Trav. Uni. 21519 C. PL. Gr. 200 Grantha-s.
Ujjain I, p. 10 (no.1239). 67 pp. Copied by Hari Abhayaṃkara. Dated V.S. 1677.
VOHD II 7.2318 (cod.Malay. 10. BStB, München). Mal. 8 fol. (28-35). Praśna-s 1-2.
VOHD II 7.2319 (cod.Malay. 10. BStB, München). Mal. 78 fol. (36-113). Praśna-s 1-2 (with C. Tribhāṣya-ratna).
VSM I 649 (no.982). 16 fol. Copied by Dīkṣita Maheśvara.
VSM I 650 (no.40). 16 fol. Copied by Viṭṭhala Nārāyaṇa.
VSM I 651 (no.3341). 14 fol. Dated Śaka 1719.
VSM I 652 (no.3830). 28 fol. Dated Śaka 1785.
VSM I 653 (no.2933). 12 fol. Dated Śaka 1758. Copied by Bhiḍe Rāmachandra.
VSM I 654 (no.981). 10 fol. Incomplete.
Wai I 561. 14 fol.
Wai I 562. 16 fol.
Wai I 563. 18 fol.
Wai I 564. 18 fol.
Wai I 565. 7 fol. Incomplete.
Wai I 566. 78 fol. (with C. Lakṣaṇacandrikā of Mahādeva Rāmacandra Gadre). Dated Śaka 1799.
Wai I 567. 80 fol. (with C. Lakṣaṇacandrikā of Mahādeva Rāmacandra Gadre).
Wai I 568. 53 fol. (with C. Lakṣaṇacandrikā of Mahādeva Rāmacandra Gadre). Incomplete.
Wai I 569. 93 fol. (with C. Tribhāṣya-ratna). Dated Śaka 1780.
Wai I 570. 60 fol. (with C. Tribhāṣya-ratna). Dated V.S. 1722.
Wai I 571. 96 fol. (with C. Tribhāṣya-ratna). Dated Śaka 1764.

Wai I 572. 90 fol. (with C. Tribhāṣya-ratna). Dated V.S. 1690.
Wai I 573. 44 fol. Incomplete (with C. Tribhāṣya-ratna).
Weber 141(2) (Weber I). 12 fol. (6-17). Incomplete. From Oxf. II 860 (Ms. Wilson. 540).
Weber 1445 (Ms. or. fol. 881). 17 fol. Dated Śaka 1697. Copied in Poona.
Whish 38(1). PL. Gr. 13 fol. Dated A.D. 1766 (or 1826 ?).

Ptd.:

1) Ed. by William D. Whitney, with the commentary *Tribhāṣya-ratna*, text, translation and notes, in : *Journal of the American Oriental Society*, vol. 9 (1871). 469 pp. [Emeneau (371); IO : Ptd. Bks. Cat. 1957, p. 2691 (Eur. Cat. ST. 481/9)]. Also issued separately – New Haven, 1871. 469 pp. [UBHD (E 31)]

Reprinted : Delhi : Motilal Banarsidass, 1973. [Adyar (H 216.1 Tai xy=z Whi); SAI (ind 74 B 1027)]

2) Ed. by Rajendralala Mitra, with the commentary entitled the *Tribhāṣya-ratna*. – Calcutta : Asiatic Society, 1872. 6, 258 pp. – (Bibliotheca Indica 75). [Adyar (H080 BIS 75); BORI (14839); NL (180 Jc 87 19); UBHD (G 1753); Emeneau (372); BM : Ptd. Bks. Cat. 1876 (p. 157); IO : Ptd. Bks. Cat. 1957, p. 2691 (Bibl. Ind. 75)]

3) Ed. by Lakshmanacharya Ghanapathi and Sundara Ghanapathi, *Prātiśākhyaṃ nāma Vedalakṣaṇam* (in Grantha script). – Tiruvadi (Pañcanada), 1891. 40 pp. [BM : Ptd. Bks. Cat. 1892-1906. 806 (14010.a.2)]

4) Ed. by Mullangaḍi Vaidyanatha Sastri, with C. *Tribhāṣya-ratna* (in Grantha script). – Kumbakonam : Vaidikavardhini Granthalaya, 1900. 2, 198 pp. [Bangalore Sanskrit College (C 12/51); MyORI (B 1373); BM : Ptd. Bks. Cat. 1892-1906. 806 (14010.b.10)]

5) Ed. by Mullangaḍi Vaidyanatha Sastri, with C. *Vaidikābharaṇa* (in Grantha script). – Kumbakonam : Vaidikavardhini Granthalaya, 1901. 1, 164 pp. [Bangalore Sanskrit College (C 13/52); BM : Ptd. Bks. Cat. 1892-1906. 806 (14010.c.26); IO : Ptd. Bks. Cat. 1957, p. 2691 (9 I 13)]

6) Ed. by K. Rangacharya and R. Shama Sastry, with C. *Tribhāṣya-ratna* of Somayārya and *Vaidikābharaṇa* of Gārgya Gopāla-yajvan. – Mysore, 1906. viii, 62, 530, 32 pp. – (Bibliotheca Sanskritika, Mysore Government Oriental Library Series 33). [Adyar (H080 MOS 33); BORI (416 / 4794); BM : Ptd. Bks. Cat. 1906-1928. 1201 (14004.b.16); Emeneau (373)]

Reprinted : Delhi : Motilal Banarsidass, 1985. [BORI (49940); SAI (ind S 61, 33)]

7) (in Grantha script). – Kumbakonam : Sarada Vilasa Press, 1919 (2nd edition). 32 pp. [IO : Ptd. Bks. Cat. 1957, p. 2690 (San B 806,l)]

8) With C. *Tribhāṣya-ratna* (in Grantha script). (The title page reads: Taittirīyaprātiśākhyam | somayāryaviracita tribhāṣyaratnavivaraṇasahitam | idaṃ kila T. M. Nārāyaṇa-śāstriṇā pariśodhitam, R. Sundareśāryeṇa Kumbakoṇastha svakīya-śāradāvilāsa-mudraṇālaye mudrāpitaṃ kumbhakoṇe prakāśitaṃ ca vijayatetarām | krodhanavatsarasya siṃhamāsi | dvitīyaṃ mudraṇam). – Kumbakonam : Sarada Vilasa Press, 1925 (2nd edition). 8, 200 pp. [SAI (89/2152*); IO : Ptd. Bks. Cat. 1957, p. 2691 (San B 1041)]

9) Ed. by V. Venkatarama Sharma, with the Bhāṣya *Pada-krama-sadana* of Māhiṣeya. – Madras : University of Madras, 1930. iv, 4, iv, 188, xxx, 9 pp. – (Madras Univer-

sity Sanskrit Series 1). [Adyar (H080 MUS sk1); BORI (4497); NL (180 Jb 93 173); Emeneau (370); IO : Ptd. Bks. Cat. 1957, p. 2690 (San D 610/1)]
Reprinted : New Delhi : Panini (Meharchand Lachhmandas), 1982. – (Pāṇini Vaidika Granthamālā 4). [BORI (40823); SAI (ind 51 D 784/1214)]

- C.
Luck. Uni. p. 67.
PUL I, p. 21 (no.70) (Bhāṣya). PL. Tel. 93 fol.
PUL I, p. 132 (no.23) (Bhāṣya). PL. Gr. 227 fol. 8000 Grantha-s.
PUL II, p. 21 (no.74) (Vyākhyā). PL. Gr. 5 fol. Incomplete (with some other Lakṣaṇa-bhāṣya).

– C. Lakṣaṇacandrikā of Mahādeva Rāmacandra Gadre.
Deccan College 9813.
VSM I 655 (no.3831). 28 fol. Incomplete.
VSM I 656 (no.3832). 87 fol. Incomplete (Adhyāya-s 1-2).
Wai I 566. 78 fol. (with text). Dated Śaka 1799.
Wai I 567. 80 fol. (with text).
Wai I 568. 53 fol. (with text). Incomplete.

– C. Vivaraṇa, called Vaidika-bhūṣaṇa (or Bhūṣaṇa-ratna-vṛtti).

Beginning:(840)

वैदिकभूषणम्। ...

वागीशाद्यास्सुमनसस्सर्वार्थानामुपक्रमे।
यं नत्वा कृतकृत्याः स्युस्तं नमामि गजाननम्॥
शेषं पाणिनिमीश्वरं हरिमज ... ...
... ... भज स्मरामि विमृशाम्याराधयाम्यद्रियेशं-
सेनौ नमाम्युपैमि कलये शब्दार्थसंसिद्धये॥
वैदिकाभारणे रत्नं यथावत् स्थाप्यते ऽनया।
अतो भूषणरत्नानि ... ...॥

यथेत्ययमधिकारः। एतदुत्तरमाप्रावेत्यस्मात् प्राक् वर्णसमाम्नाय इत्यधिकृतं वेदितव्यम्। वर्णाः अकारादयः। स एकत्र आम्नायन्ते आनुपूर्व्येण पठ्यन्त इति वा। ... ... ई उ ऊ ऋद्च ऋल चेदेदोदौ स्वरा एते कखगघङचाश्छजौ ...। मयरा लवकाः शषसाः पक्षळंय ... ... त्तिरीयजाः॥ अथ नवादितः समानाक्षराणि। अथ अस्मिन्नध्याये संज्ञापरिभाषणमधिक्रियते।

सर्वत्र भाष्यते या सा परिभाषानुपूर्व्यतः। ग ... हानुवृत्तस्य वर्णसमाम्नाय इत्यस्य षष्ठ्यन्ततया विभक्तिपरिणामः कर्तव्यः। वर्णसमाम्नायस्यादितो नव वर्णाः समानाक्षरसंज्ञका भवन्ति॥ अदाद्यूत्पर्यं ... इति किम्। उपरि मा भूत्।

हरन्ति नान्याङ्गतया चलन्तीत्यजक्षरं स्यादसमानहीनात्।
वर्णास्समानाक्षरसंज्ञकाः स्युरनर्थसिद्धयै महती हि संज्ञा॥ ... ...
प्रग्रहा इत्यनुनासिकत्वम्॥ २॥

End:

मात्रालक्षणमुच्यते।
पादार्धत्रिपदैकपादसहिताः साध्यर्धद्व्यर्धक-
त्र्यर्धादिरिह वर्णकालकलना मात्रा विदुर्ये हरेः ।
मात्रा यान्ति त एष तेषु महिमा दैवैरपि श्रूयते
वृत्तौ भूषणरत्नशब्दकृतनाम्न्यभ्यासबाहुल्यतः ॥
पादमात्रा यथा -- आ वायोरित्यत्र वकारादेः । अर्धमात्रा यथा -- शुचि वा इत्यत्र शकारादेः । त्रिपान्मात्रा यथा -- बालित्यत्र पदकाले लकारस्य। एकमात्रे यथा -- तेषां इत्यत्र मकारः । पादसहितमात्रा यथा -- महाँ इन्द्र इत्यत्र व्यक्तिनासिक्ययोः । अध्यर्धमात्रा यथा -- सवाँ अग्नीनित्यत्र स्वरिह्यनुस्वारः । द्विमात्रे यथा -- तं मा इत्यत्र पदकाले मकारस्य द्विस्तावानित्यादेश्च। सार्धद्विमात्रे यथा स पाठान्ते। समुद्रो बन्धुः । ओं इत्यत्र ओकारस्य। त्रिमात्रा यथा। त्वी इत्यत्र ईकारस्य। एवमर्धसहितमात्रादयश्च ऊह्याः । इति मात्रालक्षणं समाप्तम्॥

Adyar D I 840 (10 G 21 = TR 20). 180 fol. (pp. 1-360). = Adyar I, p. 52a. Complete except for some lacunae (mostly in I 1). The Ms. ends with following sections: Varṇa-lakṣaṇa (pp. 312-15), Krama-lakṣaṇa (pp. 315-17), Jaṭā-lakṣaṇa (pp. 318-45) (duplicate of TR 28), Varṇa-krama-lakṣaṇa (pp. 345-58) (duplicate of TR 28), Mātrā-lakṣaṇa (pp. 359-60). A part of this commentary (23.15 - 24.3) is printed in the edition of Māhiṣeya's commentary.

— C. Vaidikābharaṇa of Gārgya Gopāla-yajvan (-sūri or -miśra).

Beginning:

प्रणम्य साङ्गमाम्नायमाचार्यांश्च प्रणीयते।
व्याख्यानं प्रातिशाख्यस्य गार्ग्यगोपालयज्वना।
अर्थरत्नैर्न्यायगुणैः पूर्वशास्त्रार्णवोद्धृतैः ।
रचितं धारयन्त्वेतद् वैदिकाभरणं बुधाः ॥
अथ किमर्थं प्रातिशाख्यं नाम लक्षणं प्रणीयते। तदुच्यते। गुरुत्वं लघुता साम्यमित्यादि सर्वं तु विज्ञेयमित्यादि वक्ष्यति। तदविज्ञाने पदक्रमविशेषाद्यनवगमादाचार्यत्वासिद्धिः । तदसिद्धावध्ययनाद्यसिद्धिः । न च लिखितपाठादिना वेदो ऽधिगन्तव्यः । तस्मात् स्वाध्यायो ऽध्येतव्यः इति श्रुतेः । तस्मात् गुरुत्वं लघुता इत्यादीनां विज्ञानायेदं शास्त्रं प्रणीयते। तद्विज्ञाने सत्य आचार्यत्वयोग्यतापत्त्या अध्ययनाद्युपपत्तिरिति। ननु नैतदस्ति

प्रयोजनम्। तथा हि --

गुरुलघ्वादिविज्ञानं नास्यारम्भप्रयोजनम्।
उक्तं तत् सर्वमङ्गेषु शिक्षाव्याकरणेषु यत्॥

यदत्र विज्ञेयतया वक्ष्यते गुरुत्वं लघुता साम्यमित्यादि तत् सर्वं वेदाङ्गतया प्राप्तेषु शिक्षा-व्याकरणेषूपदिष्टम् एव। अतो न तद्विज्ञानार्थं प्रातिशाख्यमारम्भणीयमिति। एवं प्राप्ते ऽभिधीयते --

विकल्पभाजां शास्त्राणामपि दृष्टानुवर्तिनाम्।
तत्तच्छाखाविशेषेषु व्यवस्थार्थमिदं स्मृतम्॥

End:

तदेवं व्याकरणोक्तं प्रकृत्यादिसंदेहप्रध्वंसनं कार्यमिह लक्षितं यत् त्रिविधसमाम्नायमध्यवर्ति भवति। यत् तु सूक्ष्मसंदेहनिरसनं प्रकृतिप्रत्ययविशेषादिकार्यं तत् सर्वं तत एवावधारणीयम्। तत्र चायं ग्रन्थः प्रकृष्टोपकारको भवति। एतद्ग्रन्थार्थनिष्णातैर्हि कृत्स्नस्य व्याकरणार्थः सुगृहीतो भवति। शिक्षागणोपदिष्टं तु नात्र संगृहीतम्। व्याकरणप्रधानत्वात् प्रातिशाख्यस्य। तस्मादत्रास्माभिः --

शिक्षागणोपदिष्टं यत् संहिताग्रन्थगोचरम्।
कार्यजातमिहानुक्तं तत् समुच्चीयते ऽधुना॥

Adyar D XIII 188 (VB 124). PL. Gr. 54 fol.
Baroda 9674. 54 fol. 1200 Grantha-s (chs. 1-9).
Gough p. 163. Gr.
MD 934. PL. Gr. 165 pp.
MD 15928. PL. Gr. 20 pp. 372 Grantha-s (3 chs.).
Mysore p. 2 (no. 55). 142 fol. (10 chs.).
Mysore (1898), p. 5 (no. 55a). Gr. 142 fol. (69-210).
Mysore I, p. 28 (2 Mss.; Incomplete.).
Mysore ND II 3455 (P 232/17). PL. Gr. 31 fol. Incomplete.
Mysore ND II 3456 (P 2326/ 1). PL. Gr. 27 fol. Incomplete.
Mysore ND II 3457 (P 9312/ 1). PL. Na. 65 fol. Extract no. 160
Oppert I 1038. Belonged to Viraraghava Tatacharyar, Head Master, Sanskrit School of Sathakopacharya, Kanchipuram, Chingelpet Dist.
Oppert I 7233. Belonged to Ivattur Nandikesvara Sastri of Vijayanagaram.
Oppert I 7496. Belonged to Chiravuru Rama Somayajulu of Vijayanagaram.
Oppert I 7575. Belonged to S. Kodanda Ramavadhana Pantulu of Vijayanagaram.
Oppert II 776. Belonged to Ghanapathi Shingaracharyar of Alasur, Madurantakam Taluk
Oppert II 1378. Belonged to Gopalacharyar of Pillapakkam, Kanchipuram Taluk.
Oppert II 8689. Belonged to Venkatarama Sastri of Timmagudi near Kumbakonam.
Oppert II 9101. Belonged to Ganapati Lakshminarayana Sastri of Tiruvadi, Thanjavur Dist.
Oppert II 9885. Belonged to M.Raja Ghanapathi of Mahadanapuram, Trichinapalli.

PUL I, p. 21 (no.72). PL. Tel. 76 fol. 2000 Grantha-s.
PUL I, p. 21 (no.73). PL. Gr. 201 fol.
PUL II. App. p. 13 (no.213). PL. Gr. 22 fol. (Adhyāya 9).
Tirupati SVUORI 3839 (3792b). PL. Gr. Incomplete.
Tirupati SVUORI 3840 (4421d). PL. Gr. Incomplete.
Trav. Uni. 3321 A. PL. Gr. 120 Grantha-s. Incomplete.
Ujjain I, p. 9.

Ptd.: in the Mysore Govt. Oriental Library edition. See above.
Also ed. by Mullangaḍi Vaidyanatha Sastri (in Grantha script). – Kumbakonam : Vaidikavardhini Granthalaya, 1901. See above.

– Cc. Mukura of P. Gaṇapati Śāstri.
Ptd.: ed. by Shivaramakrishna Sastri, in : *Journal of the Annamalai University*, vol. 8 (1938-39). 53 pp. [Adyar (H05U Ann 8); SAI (85/1962*); SOAS (S III 1 – 117071)]

– C. Vivaraṇa of Padmanābha Yajvan.
Adyar D I 815. 816. = Adyar I, p. 49b, 50a (3 Mss.; one incomplete). See above Jaṭā-vallī.

– C. Chandobhāṣā or Pada-krama-sadana of Māhiṣeya.
MT 3760. 116 pp. Transcribed in 1921-22 from a Malayalam Ms. belonging to Narayana-vaidya Tamburan of Aluvanchery mana of Malabar. Title: Yajuḥ-prātiśākhya-vyākhyā.

Ptd.: in Madras University edition of the text. See above.

– C. Tribhāṣya-ratna or Prātiśākhya-vivaraṇa of Somayārya.

Beginning:

भक्तियुक्तः प्रणम्याहं गणेशचरणद्वयम्।
गुरूनपि गिरां देवीमिदं वक्ष्यामि लक्षणम्॥
व्याख्यानं प्रातिशाख्यस्य वीक्ष्य वाररुचादिकम्।
कृतं त्रिभाष्यरत्नं यद् भासते भूसुरप्रियम्॥

श्लोकयोरनयोरयमर्थः -- भक्तियुक्तः अहं गणेशपादद्वयं गुरून् गिरां देवीमपि । वाग्देवीमित्यर्थः । तां च प्रणम्य लक्षणमिदं वक्ष्यामि । यत् लक्षणं त्रिभाष्यरत्ननामकं भूसुरप्रियं विद्वत्प्रियं सत् भासते । कीदृशं लक्षणम् । प्रातिशाख्यस्य व्याख्यानरूपं वाररुचादिकं भाष्यजातं वीक्ष्य न्यूनातिरेकपरिहारेण कृतं विरचितम् । आदिशब्देन आत्रेयमाहिषेये गृह्येते। अत एव त्रिभाष्यरत्नमिति नाम्न उपपत्तिः । त्रयाणां भाष्याणां समाहारः त्रिभाष्यम्। तस्य रत्नं भूषणम्। मङ्गलानन्तरारम्भप्रश्नकार्त्स्न्येष्वथो अथ इति

मङ्गलाद्यनेकार्थत्वात् अथशब्दस्यार्थनिर्णयार्थम् एको ऽर्थो निश्चेतव्यः । तत्र प्रथमं तावन्मङ्गलार्थत्वमुच्यते । तस्य प्रणवसाधर्म्यात् । तथा च समाचक्षते शिक्षाकाराः -- ओङ्कारश्चाथशब्दश्च मङ्गलाविति कीर्तितौ इति ।

End:

त्रिलोचनध्यानविशुद्धकौमुदी विनिद्रचेतःकुमुदः कलानिधिः ।
स सोमयार्यो विततान संमतं विपश्चितां भाष्यमिदं सुबोधकम् ॥

Adyar D I 841 (19 N 32 = 66868). PL. Gr. 78 fol. (2-76 with deviations).
Adyar D I 842 (21 K 14 = 68209). PL. Tel. 110 fol. = Adyar I, p. 50a.
Adyar D I 843 (21 K 15 = 68210). PL. Gr. 96 fol. = Adyar I, p. 50a. Dated the 8th of Āṭi of Akṣaya and copied by Dharmarāja-jaṭāvallabha.
Adyar D I 844 (21 K 32 = 68227). PL. Gr. 16 fol. (from II 5 to the end). = Adyar I, p. 50a.
Adyar D I 845 (21 K 39 = 68234). PL. Tel. 72 fol. = Adyar I, p. 50a (Praśna I).
Adyar D I 846 (21 K 40 = 68235). PL. Tel. 65 fol. = Adyar I, p. 50a (up to II 11).
Adyar D I 847 (25 D 11 = 70831). PL. Gr. 61 fol. = Adyar I, p. 49b (up to I 12.10).
Adyar D I 848 (25 L 2 = 71120). PL. Gr. 150 fol. The former owner was Śeṣādri Dīkṣita. A fly-leaf at the end contains a list of about 20 Veda-lakṣaṇa texts.
Adyar D I 849 (25 L 34 = 71152). PL. Gr. 107 fol. (15ff.). Dated the 18th day of Mārgaśiras of Śobhakratu. Gopāla-bhaṭṭa, son of Kuppāvadhāni was the copyist and former owner.
Adyar D I 850 (28 J 19 = 73053). PL. Gr. 81 fol. = Adyar I, p. 50a (up to 21.10).
Adyar D I 851 (28 M 20 = 73212). PL. Gr. 56 fol. = Adyar I, p. 50a. Dated Saturday, Caturdaśī, 22nd of Aippaśi of Parābhava and copied by Uruppaṭṭūr Śrīnivāsa Ayyaṅgār.
Adyar D I 852 (29 I 6 = 73558). PL. Gr. 85 fol. = Adyar I, p. 50a (up to II 1).
Adyar D I 853 (29 K 20 = 73653). PL. Tel. 107 fol. (185ff.). = Adyar I, p. 50a. Copied by Kālakūri Devalrāju, for Vedamūrti Maddūri Narasiṃhalugāru and completed on Thursday, the 2nd day of dark fortnight of Puṣya of Khara (= 18.1.1832). It ends with an invocation to Bāṇḍuḍa Bhogaliṅga.
Adyar D I 854 (30 K 29 = 74179). PL. Tel. 58 fol. = Adyar I, p. 50a.
Adyar D XIII 185 (VB 428b). PL. Tel. 56 fol. Sarvajit Bhādrapada Ba. 10
Adyar D XIII 186 (VB 1072). PL. Tel. 125 fol. (10 fol. contain text separately).
Adyar D XIII 187 (VB 1073a). PL. Tel. 60 fol.
America 354-57. See above.
Baroda 7290. PL. Gr. 30 fol. 300 Grantha-s. = CLB I, p. 28.
Baroda 7820. PL. Gr. 53 fol. (16-68). 1400 Grantha-s (chs. 3-15). = CLB I, p. 28.
Baroda 7963. PL. Gr. 57 fol. 2500 Grantha-s (21 chs.). = CLB I, p. 28.
Baroda 8005(a). PL. Tel. 15 fol. 150 Grantha-s (chs. 20-22). = CLB I, p. 28.
Baroda 9993. PL. Gr. 77 fol. 3000 Grantha-s. = CLB I, p. 28.
Baroda 10334. PL. Tel. 74 fol. 1600 Grantha-s (chs. 1-12). = CLB I, p. 28.
BHU B 4471 (D 2D/2115A). 29 fol. Incomplete.
BORI 7 of 1866-68. 110 fol.

Brl. p. 8 (no.XXIII) = IO 4456.

Bühler p. 553. = BORI 7 of 1866-68. 110 fol.

Deccan College 9817. 21 fol. Incomplete.

Deccan College 9821. 160 fol.

Burnell 5b.

GB 16. 118 fol. Dated Śaka 1788 (A.D. 1866). Copy of a Ms. dated Śaka 1708.

GD I 17. PL. Gr. 114 fol. 2100 Grantha-s (with text).

GJKSV 13960. 79 fol. Title: Tribhāṣya-ratna Prātiśākhya-vyākhyāna. Raghunātha Jyotirvid was the copyist or former owner.

GJKSV 23969. 87 fol. (50-57 missing). Dated Śaka 1746. Copied by Moreśvara-bhaṭṭa Oka in Kāśī. Title: Prātiśākhya Tribhāṣya-ratna.

GJKSV 38278. 55 fol. (31-85). Incomplete. Title: Prātiśākhya-vivaraṇa.

Gough p. 163. Gr.

Granthappura p. 1 (no.18). Gr. 900 Grantha-s (with text).

Hoshiarpur p. 51 (no.4464). PL. Gr. 42 fol. 1000 Grantha-s.

Hoshiarpur p. 51 (no.5947). PL. Gr. 64 fol. 2000 Grantha-s.

Hz 344. PL. Tel. 103 fol. Belonged to Ramalinga Sastri of Amidalpadu, Nellur Dist.

Hz 630. PL. Tel. 63 fol. Extract p. 88. Belonged to Vedam Venkatasubrahmanya Somayaji of Allur, Nellur Dist.

Hz 1278. PL. Gr. 78 fol. Belonged to Anna Vajapeyi of Tiruvidaimarudur, Thanjavur Dist.

Hz 1430. PL. Gr. 80 fol. Belonged to the late Raja Ghanapathi of Tiruvidaimarudur, Thanjavur Dist.

IO 4456 (Burnell 41a). PL. Gr. 153 fol.

IO 4457 (Mackenzie II 87). PL. Na. 108 fol.

IO 4458 (Mackenzie III 207a). PL. Tel. 23 fol. (from I 1 to II 26).

Khn. p. 8 (no.25). 93 fol. from Ashṭe; Limaye.

L 3. 153 fol. 2140 Grantha-s. Dated V.S. 1643. From Benaras. For a description of this Ms. see preface (p. 2) of Rajendralala Mitra's edition.

Mack 7.

MD 931. Tel. 161 pp. (20ff.).

MD 932. PL. Tel. 20 pp. (19ff.). Incomplete. Adhyāya-s 3 and 4.

MD 933. PL. Tel. 140 pp. A few additional verses at the beginning that belong to Pāṇinīya-śikṣā.

MD 16182. PL. Gr. 167 pp. Incomplete.

MD 17446. PL. Gr. 6 pp. 78 Grantha-s (Adhyāya 3).

Mithila IV 79. 120 fol. Dated V.S. 1768.

MT 517. PL. Tel. 61 fol. Incomplete (Praśna I). Presented in 1910-11 by C. Visvanatha Shastrigal of Viziyanagaram.

MT 976. PL. Tel. 39 fol. Incomplete. Breaks off in the 7th Adhyāya. Purchased in 1913-14 from P. Adinarayanavadhani of Pedakallepalli.

MT 1089(b). PL. Tel. 76 fol. (9-84). Incomplete. Breaks off in the 19th Adhyāya. Presented in 1913-14 by Prayaga Kamayya Sastri of Kolakalur, Guntur Dist.

MT 1098. PL. Tel. 47 fol. Incomplete (Adhyāya-s 13-24). Presented in 1913-14 by Prayaga Kamayya Sastri of Kolakalur, Guntur Dist.

MT 1964(i). PL. Tel. 13 fol. (85-97). Chs. 3-4 with text. Presented in 1916-17 by Rayaprolu Ramabrahmangaru of Guruza, Gudivada Taluk, Krishna Dist.

MT 2591(b). PL. Tel. 142 fol. (18-159). Presented in 1917-18 by Vasireddi Chandramauli-svaraprasada Bahadur, Zamindar of Muktyala, Krishna Dist.

MT 2649(a). PL. Tel. 81 fol. Copied by Suśarla Subrahmaṇya of Kashi. Dated: Thursday, 12th day of Āṣāḍha-śukla, in the year Jaya. Presented in 1917-18 by Prava Surayya Sastrigaru of Penumanchili, Narasapur Taluk, Krishna Dist.

MT M.49-3. ?

MT 3887(a). PL. Gr. 65 fol. (2-66). Purchased in 1921-22 from Annasvami Sastrigal, Bhavani, Coimbatore Dist.

MT 4053. PL. Gr. 83 fol. Incomplete. Presented in 1921-22 by N.Raghavayyangar, Srirangam, Trichinapalli Dist.

MT 4585. PL. Gr. 89 fol. Lacks the beginning, and it is ascribed to Vidyāraṇya in the colophon. Presented in 1924-25 by the Secretary to the Trustees of Sri Yogi Partha-sarathi Ayyangar's Charities, Triplicane, Madras.

MT 4623. PL. Gr. 114 fol. Presented in 1924-25 by the Secretary to the Trustees of Sri Yogi Partha-sarathi Ayyangar's Charities, Triplicane, Madras.

MT 4765. PL. Gr. 84 fol. Presented in 1924-25 by the Secretary to the Trustees of Sri Yogi Partha-sarathi Ayyangar's Charities, Triplicane, Madras.

MT 4869. PL. Gr. 80 fol. Lacks beginning. Presented in 1924-25 by the Secretary to the Trustees of Sri Yogi Partha-sarathi Ayyangar's Charities, Triplicane, Madras.

MT 5450. PL. Gr. 4 fol. 133 Grantha-s. Incomplete. Presented in 1928-29 by Ramanatha Shastri, Krishnarajapuram, Trichinapalli Dist.

Mysore p. 2 (no. 56). 115 fol. Title: Prātiśākhya-vyākhyā.

Mysore (1898), p. 5 (no. 56a). Gr. 115 fol.

Mysore I, p. 28 (9 Mss.).

Mysore ND II 3439-54. Extract no. 158, 159.

N-W P VI 14 (no.50). 73 fol. (ascribed to Triyambaka Bhaṭṭa). Belonged to Durga Bai Bhada, Benares.

Oppert I 993. Belonged to Viraraghava Tatacharyar, Head Master, Sanskrit School of Sathakopacharya, Kanchipuram, Chingelpet Dist.

Oppert I 1461. PL. Gr. 71 pp. Belonged to Annasvami Srauti of Bhavani, Coimbatore Dist.

Oppert I 2135. PL. Gr. 300 pp. Belonged to Yajnasrauti of Bhavani, Coimbatore Dist.

Oppert I 2344. PL. Gr. 122 pp. Belonged to Sri Sarasvati Bhandaram Committee of Tiruvallikkeni, Madras.

Oppert I 4305. Belonged to Annasastri of Muktambapuram, Thanjavur Dist.

Oppert I 6739. Belonged to Indraganthi Gopala Sastri of Madugal, Vishakhapattanam Dist.

Oppert I 7139. Belonged to Pola Lakshmanavadhani of Vijayanagaram.

Oppert I 7189. Belonged to Ivattur Nandikesvara Sastri of Vijayanagaram.

Oppert I 7997. Belonged to Paravastu Venkatarangacharyar of Vishakhapattanam.

Oppert II 755. Belonged to Ghanapathi Shingaracharyar of Alasur, Madurantakam Taluk.

Oppert II 1079. Belonged to Tiruputkuli Srikrishna Tatacharyar of Kanchipuram.

Oppert II 1325. Belonged to Gopalacharyar of Pillapakkam, Kanchipuram Taluk.

Oppert II 1868 (-ratnāvalī). PL. Gr. 200 pp. Belonged to T. K. Raghavacharyar of Nandaluru, Kadapa Dist.
Oppert II 4642. Belonged to Sri Sankaracharya Matha of Sringeri,
Oppert II 5205. Belonged to Pichchu Dikshitar of Akhilandapuram, Thanjavur Dist.
Oppert II 6288. Belonged to Narasimhacharya of Kumbakonam.
Oppert II 6837. Belonged to Samisastri of Kumbakonam.
Oppert II 7383. Belonged to Venkatarama Sastri of Pillur, Mayavaram Taluk.
Oppert II 7957. Belonged to Venkatarama Dikshita of Sorakayur, Thanjavur Dist.
Oppert II 8557. Belonged to Venkatacharyar of Timmagudi near Kumbakonam.
Oppert II 8642. Belonged to Venkatarama Sastri of Timmagudi near Kumbakonam.
Oppert II 9036. Belonged to Ganapati Lakshminarayana Sastri of Tiruvadi, Thanjavur Dist.
Oppert II 9881. Belonged to M.Raja Ghanapathi of Mahadanapuram, Trichinapalli.
Oxf. II 867(3) (Ms. Wilson 478). 74 fol. (43-116). From III 12 to end. = Oxf. 384b (no.478).
PUL I, p. 21 (no.71). PL. Tel. 77 fol. 2000 Grantha-s.
PUL II. App. p. 11 (no.174). PL. Tel. 68 fol. 2000 Grantha-s.
PUL II. App. p. 11 (no.175). PL. Tel. 16 fol. 300 Grantha-s.
SBD 2130. 35 fol. Incomplete.
SBD 2131. 73 fol. Incomplete.
SBD 2132. 64 fol. Incomplete.
SBD 2133. 52 fol. Incomplete.
Tb. 208(A) (with text). Roth's transcript of Oxford Ms. Wils. 504d and 478c (= Oxf. 860, 867). Dated August 1845.
TD 1782. PL. Tel. 99 fol. 2050 Grantha-s.
TD 1942. PL. Gr. 70 fol. 1300 Grantha-s. Incomplete.
Tirupati SVUORI 2577 (1771). PL. Gr. Incomplete.
Tirupati SVUORI 2578 (1989). PL. Gr. Incomplete.
Tirupati SVUORI 3828 (1689). PL. Gr. 78 fol. (Prātiśākhya-vivaraṇam).
Tirupati SVUORI 3829 (899). PL. Gr. 138 fol. (Prātiśākhya-vivaraṇam).
Tirupati SVUORI 3830 (1431). PL. Gr. (Prātiśākhya-vivaraṇam).
Tirupati SVUORI 3831 (2007). PL. Gr. Incomplete. (Prātiśākhya-vivaraṇam).
Tirupati SVUORI 3832 (2191a) PL. Gr. 88 fol. (Prātiśākhya-vivaraṇam).
Tirupati SVUORI 3833 (2570). PL. Gr. (Prātiśākhya-vivaraṇam).
Tirupati SVUORI 3834 (3525). PL. Gr. Incomplete. (Prātiśākhya-vivaraṇam).
Tirupati SVUORI 3835 (3787). PL. Gr. Incomplete. (Prātiśākhya-vivaraṇam).
Tirupati SVUORI 3836 (6095). PL. Gr. Incomplete. (Prātiśākhya-vivaraṇam).
Tirupati SVUORI 3837 (4352b). PL. Gr. (Prātiśākhya-vivaraṇam).
Tirupati SVUORI 3838 (6497). PL. Gr. (Prātiśākhya-vivaraṇam).
Trav. Uni. 2406. PL. Gr. 2500 Grantha-s.
Trav. Uni. 2643. PL. Gr. 1600 Grantha-s. Incomplete.
Trav. Uni. 3593.
Trav. Uni. 3679 D. PL. Gr. 2475 Grantha-s (with text).
Trav. Uni. 3747.
Trav. Uni. 5631 A.
Trav. Uni. 5778 A. PL. Tel. 2500 Grantha-s (with text).

Trav. Uni. 7182. Incomplete.
Trav. Uni. L.988 J.
Trav. Uni. 13552 B.
Trav. Uni. 18615 D. PL. Mal. 2750 Grantha-s.
Trav. Uni. 19037. PL. Gr. 2100 Grantha-s (with text). Incomplete.
Trav. Uni. 17321 B. PL. Mal. 1300 Grantha-s (with text). Incomplete. Damaged.
VOHD II 7.2319 (cod.Malay. 10. BStB, München). Mal. 78 fol. (36-113). Praśna-s 1-2 (with text).
VSM I 657 (no.2934). 100 fol. Dated Śaka 1758. Copied by Bhiḍe Rāmacandra.
VSM I 658 (no.4562). 90 fol.
VSM I 659 (no.3344). 106 fol. Dated Śaka 1674.
VSM I 660 (no.983). 90 fol. Incomplete (Adhyāya-s 1.2 to 12).
VSM I 661 (no.3343). 29 fol. Incomplete.
VSM I 662 (no.3342). 7 fol. (3-9). Incomplete.
Wai I 569. 93 fol. (with text). Dated Śaka 1780.
Wai I 570. 60 fol. (with text). Dated V.S. 1722.
Wai I 571. 96 fol. (with text). Dated Śaka 1764.
Wai I 572. 90 fol. (with text). Dated V.S. 1690.
Wai I 573. 44 fol. (with text). Incomplete.
Weber 1446 (Ms. or. fol. 592). 82 fol. Dated Śaka 1789 = A.D. 1867.
Whish 38(2). PL. Gr. 117 fol. Dated A.D. 1766 (or 1826 ?).

Ptd.: in the following editions of the text:
1) Ed. by William D. Whitney. – New Haven, 1871. See above.
2) Ed. by Rajendralala Mitra. – Calcutta : Asiatic Society, 1872. See above.
3) Ed. by Mu<u>ll</u>angaḍi Vaidyanatha Sastri (in Grantha script). – Kumbakonam : Vaidikavardhini Granthalaya, 1900. See above.
4) Ed. by K. Rangacharya and R. Shama Sastry. – Mysore, 1906. – (Mysore Govt. Oriental Library Series 33). See above.
5) Also the commentary alone (idaṃ hi khalu tribhāṣyaratnaṃ nāma prātiśākhya-vivaraṇam), chs. 1-12 (in Telugu script). – Chennapurī (Madras) : Hoe and Co. (Premier Printing Press, Chandra Sresthi), 1904. 62 pp. (up to 12th chapter). [Adyar (PH 215 TR Cha); BM : Ptd. Bks. Cat. 1892-1906. 806 (14007.b.21); IO : Ptd. Bks. Cat. 1957, p. 2691 (3627)]

[NCC VIII 209a-210a]

657 TAITTIRĪYA-PLUTA-SVARA-LAKṢAṆA (**तैत्तिरीयप्लुतस्वरलक्षण**)
Hoshiarpur p. 300 (no.5613). PL. Gr. 3 fol. 50 Grantha-s.

658 TAITTIRĪYA-PLUTĀNUŚĀSANA (**तैत्तिरीयप्लुतानुशासन**)
Mysore ND II 3458 (P 2339/ 7). PL. Gr. 1 fol. (40). Extract no. 161. Beginning as in MD 936 → Plutānuśāsana.

659 TAITTIRĪYA-BRĀHMAṆĀNUKRAMAṆIKĀ (**तैत्तिरीयब्राह्मणानुक्रमणिका**)
Contains the initial passages of the various pañcāśat-s, in reverse order, of the I, II 1-3, and III Aṣṭaka-s of *Taittirīya-brāhmaṇa*.

MD 14498. PL. Tel. 35 pp. (61ff.). Incomplete.

[NCC VIII 210b]

660 TAITTIRĪYA-BRĀHMAṆĀNUVĀKĀRTHA-SAṂGRAHA-KĀRIKĀ (तैत्तिरीयब्राह्मणानुवाकार्थ संग्रहकारिका)

Extracts from Sāyaṇa's Bhāṣya.

Baroda 11022(a). 9 fol. 120 Grantha-s. Incomplete (Kāṇḍa-s 1-3). = CLB I, p. 9. (Kārikā-s taken from Sāyaṇa-bhaṣya).

[NCC VIII 211a]

661 TAITTIRĪYA-ŚIKṢĀ (तैत्तिरीयशिक्षा)

B I, p. 202 (no.33). 11 fol.

– C. K. 16.

[NCC VIII 212a]

662 TAITTIRĪYA-SAṂHITĀ-KĀṆḌĀNUKRAMAṆIKĀ-VIVARAṆA (तैत्तिरीयसंहिताकाण्डानुक्रमणिकाविवरण)

Hpr. II 29. Cf. C. on the Kāṇḍānukramaṇikā above.

[NCC VIII 214b]

663 TAITTIRĪYA-SAṂHITĀ-KRAMAPĀṬHA (?) (तैत्तिरीयसंहिताक्रमपाठ)

BISM vi. 303/1. This and the next Ms. are actually the Krama-pāṭha of the *Vājasaneyi-saṃhitā* (bound together).

BISM p. 226 (22/323). 71 fol. Incomplete.

[NCC VIII 214b]

664 TAITTIRĪYA-SAṂHITĀ-GHANA-SAṂDHI (तैत्तिरीयसंहिताघनसंधि)

Cf. Kṛṣṇa-yajurvedīya-ghana-saṃdhi.

Ptd.: (in Grantha script). – Tiruvadi 1911. 144 pp. [IO : Ptd. Bks. Cat. 1953, p. 1395 (San B 61)]

[NCC VIII 214b]

665 TAITTIRĪYA-SAṂHITĀ-JAṬĀ-PĀṬHA (तैत्तिरीयसंहिताजटापाठ)

SB p. 68 (no.204). 7 fol. 318 Grantha-s. = SBD 1268. (naḥ sadhamādaḥ sadhamādo no naḥ sadha ... | ends abruptly).

[NCC VIII 214b]

666 TAITTIRĪYA-SAṂHITĀNUKRAMAṆIKĀ (तैत्तिरीयसंहितानुक्रमणिका)

An Index in 12 paragraphs to the *Taittirīya-saṃhitā*.

IO 4411 (Mackenzie II 88a). PL. Na. 2 fol. Written ca. A.D. 1800.

TD 586. Incomplete.

TD 587. Incomplete.

TD 588. Incomplete.

TD 589.

TD 590.

667 TAITTIRĪYA-SAṂHITĀNUKRAMAṆĪ (तैत्तिरीयसंहितानुक्रमणी)

Mysore ND II 3459-69. Extract nos. 62-66.

Trav. Uni. 21770 A. PL. Mal. 700 Grantha-s.

[NCC VIII 214a]

668 TAITTIRĪYA-SAṂHITĀ-PAÑCĀŚAD-ANUKRAMAṆIKĀ (तैत्तिरीयसंहितापञ्चाशदनुक्रमणिका)

→ Pañcāśad-anukramaṇikā by Subrahmaṇya.

669 TAITTIRĪYA-SAṂHITĀ-LAKṢAṆA (तैत्तिरीयसंहितालक्षण)

of Baiḍa-daśagrīva (?). Viśvabhāratī 1020 (a).

[NCC VIII 214b]

670 TAITTIRĪYA-SAṂHITĀ-VARṆĀNUKRAMAṆĪ (तैत्तिरीयसंहितावर्णानुक्रमणी)

Mysore ND II 3470. Extract no. 167 → Ṣaḍviṃśati-sūtra.

Mysore ND II 3471-514 (alternatively Padānukramaṇikā). These appear to be the Pada index to the *Taittirīya-saṃhitā*.

671 TAITTIRĪYA-SAṂHITĀ-VĀKYA-VIVARAṆA (तैत्तिरीयसंहितावाक्यविवरण)

PUL I, p. 24 (no.143). PL. Gr. 16 fol. 126 Grantha-s.

672 TAITTIRĪYA-SARVĀNUKRAMAṆĪ (तैत्तिरीयसर्वानुक्रमणी)

Ascribed to Yāska, presumably now lost, but quoted by Peṭṭāśāstrin in his commentary on the *Chandoviciti* more than twenty times. See C. Kunhan Raja : "The Taittirīya-sarvānukramaṇī of Yāska", in : *Journal of Oriental Research*, vol. 5 (Madras, 1931), pp. 215-22.

673 TAITTIRĪYA-SVARA-LAKṢAṆA (तैत्तिरीयस्वरलक्षण)

This may be *Svara-pañcāśat*, of which the opening verse reads: *taittirīya-padādīnāṃ vakṣyāmi svaralakṣṇam* |

Hoshiarpur p. 51 (no.5613). PL. Gr. 3 fol. 60 Grantha-s.

Viśvabhāratī 2146.

[NCC VIII 215a]

674 TAITTIRĪYA-SVARA-SIDDHĀNTA-CANDRIKĀ (तैत्तिरीयस्वरसिद्धान्तचन्द्रिका)

of Śrīnivāsa. Cf. Svara-siddhānta-candrikā below.

Rep. Raj. and C. I. p. 6.

[NCC VIII 215a]

675 TAITTIRĪYA-SVARĀVADHĀNA see SVARĀVADHĀNA (तैत्तिरीयस्वरावधान / स्वरावधान)

Trav. Uni. 2364. PL. Gr. 110 Grantha-s. Incomplete.

Trav. Uni. 2678. PL. Gr. 525 Grantha-s. Incomplete.

[NCC VIII 215a]

676 TRAYODAŚA-LAKṢAṆA (त्रयोदशलक्षण)

Mysore ND II 3515 (P 4906/35). PL. Na. 1 fol. (124). Extract no. 168. (Cf. p. 30 of the *Pada-gāḍha*, Srirangam edition).

677 TRIṂŚAL-LAKṢAṆA (त्रिंशल्लक्षण)

Mysore ND II 3522 (P 4906/18). PL. Na. 1 fol. (116). Extract no. 174. (Cf. p. 38 of the *Pada-gāḍha*, Srirangam edition).

678 TRIKRAMA (त्रिक्रम)

Mysore ND II 3518 (P 4906/49). PL. Na. 1 fol. (128). Extract no. 171.

679 TRIKRAMA-LAKṢAṆA (त्रिक्रमलक्षण)

Beginning:

आकारान्तमुदात्तान्तमाङ्परं यत्र दृश्यते।
त्रिक्रमं तं विजानीयान्मो षू ण ऊ षु णस्तथा॥
मा स्थान्महित्वनानाकं प्रियधा विशतेति च।
मो षु णश्चार्यमायाति पूषाधत्ताप्यधत्त यत्॥
दक्षिणावर्ततोत्याप्र ऋचा सादयतीति च।
भूत्वाहरच्च मा वृक्षि भूताविश विशत्यपि॥
कृत्वाहरति धत्ते च लभते त्रिक्रमाः स्मृताः।
दभ्रातनक्ति चोद्गातारोहतीति च विंशतिः॥

Adyar D I 855 (22 E 36 = 68884). PL. Tel. 2 fol. (23-24) (with C.). = Adyar I, p. 50a.
Adyar D I 984 → Veda-lakṣaṇa (A 2).
Adyar D I 985 → Veda-lakṣaṇa (A 3).
Adyar D I 987 → Veda-lakṣaṇa (A 5).
Adyar D I 989 → Veda-lakṣaṇa (A 7).
Hamburg StUB (cod.Palmbl. III 8/133) → Veda-lakṣaṇa (HB).
MD 911. PL. Gr. 2 pp. (54ff.). Slightly different with Vṛthāvyakti.
MD 14764. PL. Tel. 2 pp. (31ff.).
MD 16821. PL. Gr. 2 pp. 21 Grantha-s. Incomplete (same as the Jaṭāmaṇi or Trikrama-lakṣaṇa MD 908 ?).
MT 485(l). PL. Tel. 1 fol. (66). (Trikrama-ślokāḥ). Presented in 1910-11 by C. Visvanatha Shastrigal of Viziyanagaram.
MT 485(r). PL. Tel. 1 fol. (77). (Trikrama-ślokāḥ). Presented in 1910-11 by C. Visvanatha Shastrigal of Viziyanagaram.
MT 3887(j). PL. Gr. 1 fol. (84). See remarks. Purchased in 1921-22 from Annasvami Sastrigal, Bhavani, Coimbatore Dist.
Mysore I, p. 29 (2 Mss.).
Mysore ND II 3516 (P 2262/ 9). PL. Gr. 1 fol. Extract no. 169. Incomplete (24 Krama-s).
Mysore ND II 3517 (P 2265/27). PL. Gr. 1 fol. (139). Extract no. 170.
TD 1769. PL. Gr. 7 fol. 80 Grantha-s.

– C. Vyākhyā.

Beginning: (855) This is actually an extract of the *Sarva-sammata-śikṣā* (cf. Skt. Texts on Phonetics, pp. 561-64).

नोपसर्गो ऽवसानस्थो नीचः पूर्वस्तथा द्वयोः।
त्रिषु मध्ये स्थितं चैव ह्यावानो ऽवग्रहस्तथा॥

ऋगवसाने ऽर्धर्चावसाने वा वर्तमानस्य यत्र उत्तरपदेन संहिता नास्ति सो ऽवसानस्थः । इतिपरो न भवति। मर्त्येष्वा। विश्वतस्परि। अवसानस्थ इति किम्। प्रार्पयतु। तथा नीचो ऽपि नेतिपरः । चतुष्पादव। तथा द्वयोरुपसर्गयोः ।

After this commentary one verse enumerating the Upasarga-s. Then begins Trikrama-lakṣaṇa with *māsthānmahitva ... rohatīti ca viṃśatiḥ* with examples.

End:

स ते मा स्थात्। महित्वना नाकम्। प्रियधाविशतोरो अन्तरिक्ष। मो षु ण इन्द्र ऊषु णः सद्दक्षासः । अर्यमायाति वृषभः । पूषाधत्त। धाताधत्त। स दक्षिणा वर्तते। ऊत्या प्रयातु। वारुण्यर्चा सादयति। मा वृक्षि सुभू। एका मा भूताविशत। भूताविशति नैनम्। मेध्यं कृत्वा हरति । अजरं कृत्वा धत्ते । वशे कृत्वा लभते । सेन्द्रं दभातनक्ति । आसन्दीमुद्वातारोहति। एवं त्रिक्रमाः विंशतिर्भवन्ति। एतानि त्रिक्रमोदाहरणानि। लक्षणं तु --

आकारान्तमुदात्तान्तमाङ्परं यत्र दृश्यते।
त्रिक्रमं तं विजानीयान्मो षू ण ऊ षु णस्तथा॥
वर्णद्वये विरामे वा स्वरयोर्मध्य ओष्ठयोः ।
पूर्ववर्णप्रयत्नेन न वदेदुत्तरं बुधः ॥

औष्ठ्ययोः स्वरयोः उवर्णोकारयोर्मध्ये वर्णद्वये व्यञ्जनद्वये विरामे विवृत्तौ वा। इङ्ग्ये अवसाने वा पूर्वोष्ठ्यस्वरप्रयत्नेन उत्तरमोष्ठ्यं न वदेत्॥

Adyar D I 855 (22 E 36 = 68884). PL. Tel. 2 fol. (23-24) (with text). = Adyar I, p. 50a.
[NCC VIII 234a]

*TRIPĀṬHĪ KĀNHAJĪ (त्रिपाठी कान्हजी)
Son of Śivaji.
– Saṃjñā-karaṇa-bhāṣya. RASB II 1329.
[NCC VIII 235b]

680 TRIBHĀṢYA-RATNA (1) (त्रिभाष्यरत्न)
Name of the commentary of Somayārya on the *Taittirīya-prātiśākhya*.
[NCC VIII 256a]

681 TRIBHĀṢYA-RATNA (2) (त्रिभाष्यरत्न)
of Nannagari Visvapati. Reddy Hostel 2.
[NCC VIII 256a]

682 TRIBHĀṢYA-RATNA-SAṂGRAHA (1) (त्रिभाष्यरत्नसंग्रह)
MD 15443. Tel. 56 pp. 312 Grantha-s. Incomplete (first Pariccheda on Jaṭā only).

683 TRIBHĀṢYA-RATNA-SAṂGRAHA (2) (त्रिभाष्यरत्नसंग्रह)
– Jaṭāvicara from. Adyar D I 819. 820. Adyar I, p. 49b. See Jaṭāvicāra above.
[NCC VIII 256a]

684 TRIMĀTRA-KAMPĀNUKRAMAṆĪ (त्रिमात्रकम्पानुक्रमणी)
Mysore ND II 3520 (C 2546/14). 8 fol. Extract no. 172.

685 TRI-LAKṢAṆA (त्रिलक्षण)

Mysore ND II 3521 (P 4906/24). PL. Na. 2 fol. (119-20). Extract no.173. (Cf. p. 13 of the *Pada-gāḍha*, Srirangam edition).

686 TRISAṂDHĀ-LAKṢAṆA (त्रिसंधालक्षण)

The following is the full text consisting of three verses :

Beginning:

वर्गं वदेत् कश्चन तं च सर्वे पादं द्वितीयस्य स चापि सर्वे।
सर्वे पुनः पूर्ववदेव वर्गं क्रमं द्वितीयस्य वदेत् स ते च॥
अर्धर्चशः संप्रवदेत् पदं पदे तत् त्रिः पठेयुश्च तथैव सर्वे।
द्वितीयवर्गस्य पदद्वयं स वदेत् तथा ते ऽपि पुनश्च वर्गम्॥
क्रमं द्वितीयस्य स चापि सर्व ऋक्शः क्रमं चोत्तर-ऋक्क्रमेण।
वदेत् स ते त्रिश्च वदेयुरेवं वर्गे गते वर्गमियं त्रिसंधा॥
इति त्रिसंधालक्षणम्॥

Whish 73,2 (5). PL. Gr. 1 fol. (17). In a collection.

[NCC VIII 273a]

687 TRISŪTRĪ-BHĀṢYA (त्रिसूत्रीभाष्य)

Name of the commentary on the *Bhāṣika-sūtra*. Bhk. 8. SBD 47949.

[NCC VIII 273b]

688 TRAISVARYA-LAKṢAṆA (त्रैस्वर्यलक्षण)

Beginning with -- *athātas traisvaryalakṣaṇaṃ vyākhyāsyāmaḥ* -- is identical with the *Yājñavalkya-śikṣā*.

Adyar D I 856 (21 Q 10 = 68514). PL. Mal. 11 fol. (37ff.). Up to the verse 113 (p. 18) of the Ben. S. S. edition.

Jodiya II 96.

[NCC VIII 281b]

689 TVANTĀDY-ANUKRAMAṆIKĀ (त्वन्ताद्यनुक्रमणिका)

Index of passages containing words that end with "tu" in the *Taittirīya-saṃhitā*.

Beginning:

उपागन्तन चनः सर्ववीरानग्नाविष्णू मह्यप्रतीतं मन्यासै पूर्वं परं च सन्त्वा नह्यामि ···
देवस्याददे ऽग्निः परिलिखितं समिधो देवस्य

End:

प्रजवमन्वायन्नन्नादो द्वे बृहस्पतिर्येनैते प्रजापतिस्त्रयोविंशतिः ।

MD 14747. PL. Tel. 4 pp. (18ff.).

[NCC VIII 286b]

690 THAKĀRA-DHAKĀRA-SŪTRA or UDID-BHĀṢYA (थकारधकारसूत्र / उदिद्भाष्य)
IO 4480 (Mackenzie II 94k). PL. Na. 3 fol. (89-90) (with C.). Written ca. A.D. 1770. Col.: Udidbhāṣya. This is actually Tapara. Beg.: adyāt ...

[NCC VIII 287a]

691 THAKĀRA-DHAKĀRA-SŪTRA (थकारधकारसूत्र)
Two lists of words in the *Taittirīya-saṃhitā*, which have "th" and "dh" respectively, these being liable to confusion in pronunciation in South India.
IO 4490 (Mackenzie III 186e). PL. Tel. 2 fol. (13-14).
MD 912. PL. Gr. 2 pp. (45ff.).
MT 4600(a). PL. Gr. 2 fol. (3b-4a). Presented in 1924-25 by the Secretary to the Trustees of Sri Yogi Partha-sarathi Ayyangar's Charities, Triplicane, Madras.
Mysore I, p. 29 (2 Mss.).
Mysore ND II 3523 (P 142/ 7). PL. Tel. 1 fol. (95).
Mysore ND II 3524 (P 232/12). PL. Gr. 2 fol.
Mysore ND II 3525 (P 1540/ 2). PL. Tel. 2 fol. (9-10).
Mysore ND II 3545 (P 232/11a). PL. Gr. 2 fol. Extract no. 186. (Dhakāra-sūtra).

Ptd.: at the end of Ṣaḍviṃśati-sūtra (Grantha script), p. 21.
Also printed in *Lakṣaṇa-traya* (in Telugu script), pp. 44-45.

[NCC VIII 287a]

692 DAKĀRAPARA-TAKĀRA (दकारपरतकार)
Mysore I, p. 29.

[NCC VIII 288b]

693 DAKṢIṆADVĀRA-NIRṆAYA (1) (दक्षिणद्वारनिर्णय)
on the importance of the Taittirīya Śākhā. At the end there is an explanation of the following verse, containing the details of the *Taittirīya-saṃhitā.*

स भावः कामताजर्धिकरनाधीरधीरयः ।
जातुजालमलाः काण्डप्रश्नानुपपदाक्षराः ॥

Kāṇḍa-s : sa = 7
Praśna-s : bhāva = 44
Anuvāka-s : kāmatā = 651
Pañcāśat-s : jardhikara = 2198
Pada-s : nādhīradhīraya = 109290 ?
Akṣara-s : jātujālamala = 253868 ?

Baroda 10957. 8 fol. 200 Grantha-s. Dated Śaka 1754.

694 DAKṢIṆADVĀRA-NIRṆAYA (2) (दक्षिणद्वारनिर्णय)
of Nārāyaṇa-sūri Deva on the superiority of the Mādhyandinīya Śākhā.

Beginning:

क्षीराम्भोनिधिमध्यगे सुललिते चिन्तामणेरालये
गीर्वाणद्रुमवाटिकापरिवृते सिद्धयष्टकेनावृते।
वैडूर्याष्टदलाम्बुजे जनकजायुक्तं वृहद्भारकं

सानन्दं तदुपास्महे परतरं रामाभिधानं महः ॥

इह किल पूर्तादौ मण्डप्रतिष्ठायां दक्षिणद्वारं याजुषाणामिति निश्चितम्। तदुक्तं मात्स्ये –

बह्वृचौ पूर्वतः स्थाप्यौ दक्षिणे तु यजुर्विदौ।

सामगौ पश्चिमे तद्वदुत्तरेण त्वथर्वणौ ॥

अत्र तैत्तिरीया विवदन्ते। अस्माभिरेव पूर्वयजुष्ट्वात् तत्र स्थेयम्। तत्र तेषां पूर्वत्वाभावः । तथाहि।

End:

माध्यन्दिनीयानामेव मुख्यत्वात् सकलशाखाकार्यसंपादकत्वात् तैरेव दक्षिणद्वारे स्थेयं न कृष्णैर्न वा काण्वैरिति सकलमभिरामम् ... । इति श्रीमच्छुक्लयजुर्वेदीयान्तर्गत माध्यन्दिनीयशाखाध्यायि देवोपाभिधनारायणसूरिकृतो दक्षिणद्वारनिर्णयः समाप्तः ॥

Baroda 9175. 4 fol. 75 Grantha-s.
PUL I, p. 89 (no.266). 5 fol. 100 Grantha-s.

Ptd.: Included in the *Āhnikasūtrāvali,* compiled by Narayana Vitthal Purandare, ed. by Vishnu Vasudev Panashikar, (Nirnaya Sagar Press, Bombay). Reprint: – Varanasi : Chowkhamba Vidyabhawan, 1990, pp. 379-84. [SA1*]

[NCC VIII 293a]

*DAKṢIṆĀMŪRTI (दक्षिणामूर्ति)
of Śrīvatsa-gotra.
– Avarṇa-(ṇi-)dīpa or Avarṇi-lakṣaṇa. Adyar D I 726. MD 859. See above Avarṇi-dīpa.
– Aṣṭākṣarī-baiṭh also called Pada-varṇa-saṃkhyā or Dakṣiṇāmūrti-baiṭh.

[NCC VIII 293b]

695 DAKṢIṆĀMŪRTI-KHAṆḌA (दक्षिणामूर्तिखण्ड)
of Dakṣiṇāmūrti → Aṣṭākṣarī-baiṭh(-paribhāṣā).

Adyar D I 857 (22 H 6 = 69060). PL. Tel. 2 fol. (11-12). = Adyar I, p. 50a.

[NCC VIII 294b]

696 DAKṢIṆĀMŪRTI-PADA-VARṆA-LAKṢAṆA-PARIBHĀṢĀ-VYĀKHYĀ (दक्षिणामूर्तिपदवर्णलक्षणपरिभाषाव्याख्या)
→ Aṣṭākṣarī-baiṭh(-paribhāṣā).
SBD 53793. 10 fol. Incomplete. Also called Aṣṭākṣarī-baiṭh.

697 DAKṢIṆĀMŪRTI-PADA-VARṆA-LAKṢAṆA-PARIBHĀṢĀ-VYĀKHYĀ (दक्षिणामूर्तिपदवर्णलक्षणपरिभाषाव्याख्या)
→ Aṣṭākṣarī-baiṭh(-paribhāṣā).
Müller 53 (MM 41). 56 fol. Dated Śaka 1653 (1731-32). Begins as in Adyar Ms. but the end differs.

[NCC VIII 296a]

698 DAKṢIṆĀMŪRTI-PADA-VARṆA-SAṂKHYĀ (दक्षिणामूर्तिपदवर्णसंख्या)
of Dakṣiṇāmūrti → Aṣṭākṣarī-baiṭh(-paribhāṣā).
Bombay Uni. 1736 (BMC 25 38). 17 fol. Incomplete.

Bombay Uni. 1737 (BMC 6 14). 24 fol. Incomplete.

[NCC VIII 294b]

699 DAKṢIṆĀMŪRTI-BAIṬH (दक्षिणामूर्तिबैठ्)

→ Aṣṭākṣarī-baiṭh(-paribhāṣā).

Baroda 8666. 1 fol. 20 Grantha-s. = CLB I, p. 32. Title: Baiṭha-paribhāṣā. Also called Pada-varṇa-saṃkhyā.

Hz 410(a). PL. Tel. 44 fol. (with Anuvākānukramaṇikā-bhāṣya). Belonged to Kesari Yajnayya of Brahmanakraka (Agrahara), Nellur Dist. Extract p. 79: Col.: iti śrī-dakṣiṇāmūrtideva-śrīpādopadiṣṭāyāṃ padavarṇa-saṃkhyāyāṃ devaśrīr nāma aṣṭamāṣṭakaṃ sampūrṇam ||

[NCC VIII 296b]

700 DANTYOṢṬHYA-VIDHI (दन्त्योष्ठ्यविधि)

The 4th Lakṣaṇa of the *Atharvaveda*. A tract in two Adhyāya-s (12 and 11 verses) on the distinction between the labial and dental pronunciation of letter "ba - va" in the *Atharvaveda*.

Beginning:

अथर्वाणमृषिं देवदेवं हयशिरोधरम्।
प्रणम्य संप्रवक्ष्यामि दन्त्योष्ठ्यविधिविस्तरम्॥
छन्दस्यध्ययने प्राप्ते विदुषामथ धीमताम्।
बकारे संशयो नित्यमौष्ठ्यं दन्त्यमिति स्म ह॥
तस्मात् तद्विधिनिर्णये संशयच्छेदनाय च।
मुक्ता दन्त्या प्रयोज्याम औष्ठ्यान् वक्ष्ये क्रमादितः॥

End:

बिभेदादिषु भेदाश्च परिपूर्वं बले तथा।
बन्धुं वा सिन्धुरपर एतेषां तु बलः क्वचित्॥
तुच्छन्दश्चुबुकश्चैव बुभूवुश्च बुभूवुषी।
एते सर्वे परित्यज्य बकारोन्योन्यभक्षन (?)॥

Bikaner 664(4). Dated V.S. 1735 (A.D. 1678). Copied at Pattanapura.
Bikaner 665(4). Copy of the above.
BORI 178(v) of 1880-81.
BORI 179(v) of 1880-81.
BORI 1(v) of 1873-74. 3 fol. (10-12). From Bikaner.
Kh. 61.
RASB II 1415(V) (G 7852). 3 fol. (53-55). Dated V.S. 1671.
SBD 2066. 2 fol.
SBD 2074. 27 fol. Dated V.S. 1734. Title: Atharvaṇa-lakṣaṇa-grantha-saṃgraha.
Tb. 213(F). Copy of a Bikaner Ms. made by Roth.

Ptd.: ed. by Pandita Ramagopala Sastri, with an introduction, translation (in Hindi), and index. - Lahore : D. A. V. College, 1921. vii, 18, iii pp. - (Dayānanda Mahāvidyālaya Saṃskṛta-granthamālā 4). [Adyar (II080 DAV 4); BORI (10149; 30903); MyORI (B 4121); Emeneau (146); UBTÜ (II A 2731); SKGI (Ri VI 60); BM : Ptd. Bks. Cat. 1906-1928. 1190 (14090.bb.22,2)]

[NCC VIII 320b]

701 DAPARA-PADĀNI (दपरपदानि)
Mysore ND II 3526 (P 2262/40). PL. Gr. 1 fol. Extract no. 175.
Mysore ND II 3527 (P 2265/24). PL. Gr. 1 fol.

*DAYĀŚAṂKARA (दयाशंकर)
or Kṛpāśaṃkara or Karuṇāśaṃkara, son of Dharaṇī-dhara Vyāvahārika and grandson of Gaṅgādhara of Nāgara family; a resident of Benares.

– C. Dīpikā on the Jaṭā-paṭala of Hayagrīva. Cf. above under Jaṭā-paṭala.
– Jaṭā-lakṣaṇa. Mysore I, p. 27 (same as the above).
– Sāma-tantra-ṭīkā. N-W P I 8.

[NCC VIII 324a]

702 DAŚA-LAKṢAṆA (दशलक्षण)
Mysore ND II 3528 (P 4906/32). PL. Na. 2 fol. (123-24). Extract no.176.

703 DAŚA-ŚLOKĪ (दशश्लोकी)
Title of Uccodarkī in Baroda 6255 (fol. 44) and also in Mysore ND II 3529-32. Extract no. 177. 178. Herein the word "vidvanmaṇīnām" in the commentary is read as "vidyāmaṇīnām" and Vidyāmaṇi is given as the author of the text.

704 DĀṆḌA-SARVASVA (दाण्डसर्वस्व)
Oppert II 2828. List supplied by the sub-collector, Krishna Dist.

[NCC IX 2a]

*DĀMODARA (दामोदर)
– Pada-saṃkhyā-kārikā. RV. MT 5294.

[NCC IX 18a]

*DĀMODARA (दामोदर)
Son of Nārāyaṇa-bhaṭṭa.
– Śatapatha-brāhmaṇānuvāka-saṃkhyā. Mādhyandina school. L 2537. N-W P I 24. RASB II 893.

[NCC IX 19b]

705 DĀRU-PIṆḌA-LAKṢAṆA (दारुपिण्डलक्षण)
See MD 20101.

706 DĀŚATAYĪ-PRĀTIŚĀKHYA (दाशतयीप्रातिशाख्य)
SBD 47244. 35 fol. (1-29, 31-36). Incomplete. = Ṛgveda-prātiśākhya.

707 DIŚĀNUKRAMAṆĪ (दिशानुक्रमणी)
of Śaunaka. Kavīndrācārya 20. (Could it be Daśānukramaṇī referring to the ten Anukramaṇī-s ascribed to him ?)

[NCC IX 53a]

708 DĪPA (दीप)

Mentioned in the Śikṣādi-vedāṅga-sūci, Adyar D I 1022.

[NCC IX 59a]

709 DĪPA-KALIKĀ (दीपकलिका)

Name of the commentary on the *Saṃdhi-kārikā* of Gaṇeśa-datta. RASB II 1532.

710 DĪPA-PRABHĀ (दीपप्रभा)

Name of the commentary of Nārāyaṇa of Āhitāgni-gṛha (Akkittari), in Kerala, on the *Ṛgveda-sarvānukramaṇikā*. MT 3834.

711 DĪPA-MĀLĀ (दीपमाला)

Name of the commentary of Nāganātha-sūri or Nāgappa-sūri on the *Phulla-sūtra*. Mysore ND II 3653-54.

712 DĪPIKĀ (दीपिका)

Name of a commentary on the *Ṛgveda-sarvānukramaṇī*. Mandlik Sup. 102.
Name of the commentary of Gaṇeśa on the *Ṛgveda-sarvānukramaṇī*. Adyar D I 1055.
Name of the commentary on *Kālanirṇaya-śikṣā* of Muktīśvarācārya.

[NCC IX 68b]

713 DĪRGHA-SAṂGRAHA (दीर्घसंग्रह)

→ Āvarṇi.

714 DEVATĀNUKRAMAṆĪ (देवतानुक्रमणी)

Cf. Ṛṣi-(devatā-)cchandonukramaṇī and Chandodevatānukramaṇī.

*DEVADATTA or DEVA-YĀJÑIKA (देवदत्त / देव-याज्ञिक)

Son of Prajāpati. See Ananta(-deva) Yājñika.

– Anukramaṇī-vyākhyā. SB p. 101 (no.31). Dated V.S. 1591 (?).

715 DEVAYĀJÑIKA-SAṂMATA-PADDHATI-PARIBHĀṢĀ (देवयाज्ञिकसंमतपद्धतिपरिभाषा)

Illustrations of seven kinds of metres with their different varieties.

Beginning:

अथ वाजसनेयावान्तरभेदमाध्यन्दिनीयाख्य- यजुर्वेदसंहिता मन्त्राणाम् ऋषिदेवताछन्दांस्यभिधीयन्ते । ते च मन्त्रा द्विविधाः -- ऋग्रूपा यजूरूपाश्च । तत्र नियताक्षरपादावसाना ऋगित्युच्यते। अनियताक्षरपादावसानं यजुरिति। तत्र सर्वासामृचां यथाक्षरं गायत्र्यादीनि छन्दांसि सन्त्येव नि-यताक्षरत्वात् । यजुषां चानियताक्षरत्वात् केषांचिन्मते छन्दो नास्ति । केषांचिन्मते दैवेकमासुरीपञ्चदशेत्यादि पिङ्गलोक्तं छन्दो यजुषामपि भवति। अपरे तु व्यवस्थितविकल्पमिच्छन्ति।

End:

साष्टाचत्वारिंशदक्षरा महापङ्क्तिर्जगती। अत्र पदानां क्रमनियमो न भवति। विश्वस्य मूर्धन् । अथवा यस्याः षडपि पादा अष्टादशाक्षरा सापि महापङ्क्तिर्जगती । आ जिघ्रकलशमित्युदाहरणम् । इति वाजसनेयावान्तरभेदमाध्यन्दिनीययजुर्वेदसंहितायाम् उपयोगिनी परिभाषा समाप्ता ॥ संवत् १८१५ ॥ याज्ञिकदेवकृष्णसूनुना करुणाकृष्णेन लिखितम् ॥

SBD 2328. 6 fol. Dated V.S. 1816.
SBD 47197. 19 fol. (1-3, 1, 8, 2, 10-20, 1). Incomplete. (Sarvānukrama).

*DEVASVĀMIN (देवस्वामिन्)
– Svarāṅkuśa. IM 2243. This Ms. contains two works: the *Svarāṣṭaka* of Śaunaka with commentary (however, the opening verse here ascribes the text to Devasvāmin) and the *Svarāṅkuśa* of Jayanta-svāmin.
– Svarāṣṭaka. SBD 2097.
– Svarāṣṭaka-bhāṣya. IM 2243A. Trav. Uni. L.245. Trav. Uni. 5206.

[NCC IX 127b]

716 DEVĪ-PRAGṚHYA ? (देवीप्रगृह्य)
Mysore ND II 3535 (P 4906/50). PL. Na. 1 fol. (129). Cf. p. 31 of the *Pada-gāḍha*, Srirangam edition.

*DAIVAJÑA-PĀṬHAKA (दैवज्ञपाठक)
– Maunamantra-pakāśa. SBD 4103. 55 fol.

*DYĀDVIVEDA (द्याद्विवेद)
– Nīti-mañjarī. OU 21 Vm (B.49/4). 56 fol. 19th century. (a. Dyādvivādi). [SAI (ind 54 E 104)]

717 DVĀTRIṂŚAT-PLUTA (द्वात्रिंशत्प्लुत)
Adyar D I 983 (in a collection of Veda-lakṣaṇa works). Entered as Sapta-lakṣaṇa in Adyar I, p. 53b → Veda-lakṣaṇa (A 1).

[NCC IX 190a]

718 DVĀDAŚA-KHAṆḌĪ (-KĀṆḌĪ) (द्वादशखण्डी /-काण्डी)
Title of the paribhāṣā portion consisting of the first twelve Khaṇḍa-s of the *Ṛgveda-sarvānukramaṇī*. Cf. Ṛgveda-paribhāṣā above.

719 DVĀDAŚA-LAKṢAṆA (द्वादशलक्षण)
Mysore ND II 3536 (P 4906/34). PL. Na. 1 fol. (124). Extract no. 179. (Cf. p. 54 of the *Pada-gāḍha*, Srirangam edition).

720 DVĀDAŚA-ŚIKṢĀ (द्वादशशिक्षा)
Udaipur II 132, 6(3).

[NCC IX 197a]

721 DVĀVIṂŚAL-LAKṢAṆA (**द्वाविंशल्लक्षण**)

Mysore ND II 3538 (P 4906/41). PL. Na. 1 fol. (126). Extract no. 180.

722 DVIKAMPA-LAKṢAṆA (**द्विकम्पलक्षण**)

› Kramakāle dvikampa-lakṣaṇa.

Mysore ND II 3539 (P 4906/ 4). PL. Na. 1 fol. (108). Extract no. 181.

Mysore ND II 3540 (P 4906/16). PL. Na. 1 fol. (116).

723 DVITĪYA-VARṆĀḤ (**द्वितीयवर्णाः**)

Mysore I, p. 29.

Mysore ND II 3541 (P 972/ 7). PL. Tel. 1 fol. (33). Extract no. 182.

724 DVITVA-PRAKARAṆA (**द्वित्वप्रकरण**)

Adyar D I 984 → Veda-lakṣaṇa (A 2). (fol. 10a-10b; not noted in the catalogue).

[NCC IX 207a]

725 DVITVA-LAKṢAṆA (**द्वित्वलक्षण**)

पदादौ पदमध्ये वा स्थितस्योष्मपरस्य वै।
प्रथमस्य द्वितीयत्वं पूर्वं कुर्वीत पण्डितः ॥ १॥
अभिधानाख्यवर्णस्य प्रथमस्य परे यदि।
मुख्यप्रथमसद्भावे द्वित्वं न स्यात् सदोष्मणाम् ॥ २॥
न रेफे वा हकारे वा द्विर्भावो जायते क्वचित्।
न च वर्गद्वितीयस्य न चतुर्थे कदाचन॥
व्यञ्जनादहृतं पूर्वं द्वित्वमित्यभिधीयते।
स्वरादहृतं पूर्वं द्वित्वं न स्यात् कदाचन॥ ४॥
काठके तु पृणच्छिद्रं द्वित्वमित्यभिधीयते।
अपेतेति पृणच्छिद्रं द्वित्वं न स्यात् कदाचन॥ ५॥
राशेवे च परो लस्तु द्वित्वं नैत्यप्यसंयुतः ।
व्यञ्जनानामसंयोगो यत्र येन निषिध्यते॥ ६॥
तत्र तेन भवेद् द्वित्वं लस्य वस्वार एव हि।
लकारस्य वकारेण संयोगः स्वरतो यदि।
तथा संयुक्त एव स्यादसंयुक्तस्तथान्यथा॥ ७॥
रेफपूर्वो नकारो यः पदान्तो यत्र दृश्यते।
विशेषं तत्र जानीयाद् द्वित्वमित्यभिधीयते॥ ८॥
रेफात् परमृवर्णस्य व्यञ्जनत्वं प्रकीर्तितम्।
तस्मात् संयुक्तकार्याणि भवन्ति हि यथाविधि॥ ९॥
दीर्घात् परस्य रेफस्य ऋकारे परतः स्थिते।
रेफः पूर्वस्वराङ्गः स्याद्ध्रस्वाच्चापि तथा भवेत्॥ १०॥

दीर्घस्वरात् पदान्तस्था या भक्तिरुपजातयः ।
सापि पूर्वस्वराङ्गः स्याद् दोषावस्तर्हविष्मति ॥ ११ ॥

Baroda 6255(b). PL. Tel. 1 fol. (39a).

726 DVIPADĀ or DVIPADAIKAPADAU (द्विपदा / द्विपदैकपदौ)
A Vedic index giving the Pratīka of each chapter of the *Ṛgveda* and indicating the Dvipada and also Ekapada Ṛk-s in the respective places.

Baroda 11651. 2 fol. 25 Grantha-s. = CLB I, p. 28. Extract p. 149.
GJKSV 13613. 2 fol. Catalogued as Vaidika-grantha.
SBD 52324. 2 fol. Incomplete. Title: Dvipadaikapadā-pratīkāni.
SBD 53796. 1 fol. Title: Dvipadaikapadau.

[NCC IX 208b]

727 DVIPADĀ EKAPADĀ ĀDHRYAÑCĀ (?) ṚCAḤ (द्विपदा एकपदा आध्यञ्चा (?) ऋचः)
IM 2637A. 2 fol. Dated V.S. 1860. Copied by Janārdana.

728 DVIRUKTI-PRAKARAṆA (द्विरुक्तिप्रकरण)
Mysore ND II 3542 (P 4468/14). PL. Na. 2 fol. (115-16). Extract no. 183.

729 DVIROṢṬHYA-PRAKARAṆA (द्विरोष्ठ्यप्रकरण)
Mysore ND II 3543 (P 4468/13). PL. Na. 1 fol. (115). Extract no. 184.

730 DVI-LAKṢAṆA (द्विलक्षण)
Mysore ND II 3544 (P 4906/23). PL. Na. 2 fol. (118-19). Extract no. 185.

731 DHAKĀRA-SŪTRA (धकारसूत्र)
Mysore I, p. 613.
Mysore ND II 3545 (P 232/11a). PL. Gr. 2 fol. Extract no. 186.

[NCC IX 216a]

*(NĀGARA) DHARAṆĪ-DHARA (नागर धरणीधर)
Pupil of Mahādeva.
– C. Pañjikā or Pāṇinīya-śikṣā-vivaraṇa, composed in V.S. 1454 (A.D. 1397) according to the concluding verse (cf. IO 544), during the reign of king Udayasiṃha and the ministership of Vīramadeva (cf. BBRAS 10; p. 5).

732 DHĀTU-LAKṢAṆA(-PARIŚIṢṬA) (धातुलक्षण /-परिशिष्ट)
In Sūtra form in eight sections; an index of some (Sāmavedic ?) work.

Beginning: (L. 1591)

स्वरश्च। न विंशतिमत्याः । इत्येवं सर्वत्र। अत एपु को ऽधिकारी। मृचां(?)

End:

गृह्णाति सर्वं पदच्छा। ज्वसङ्कासेया। विना प्रयुक्तम्। सिमाः पवस्व। ८। संवत् १६९२ समाप्तिमगमत्॥

Alwar 273.
BORI 22 of 1892-95. 2 fol.
L 1591. 2 fol. 29 Grantha-s. Dated V.S. 1692.
Peters. II, p. 180 (no.76).
Peters. V, p. 225 (no.22). 2 fol. Dated V.S. 1719.
RASB VI 4348 (G 745) = L 1591.

[NCC IX 294a]

733 DHĀRAṆA(-LAKṢAṆA) **(धारण /-लक्षण)**
SV. Jaiminīya. 23 Kārikā-s, of Sabhāpati. (Siddheswar Varma, p. 100)

Adyar D XIII 250 (VB 431). PL. Gr. 42 fol. Āgneya and Aindra Parvan-s.
Baroda 9864. PL. Gr. 67 fol. 1500 Grantha-s = CLB I, p. 29. Incomplete. (Lacks beginning and end).
Baroda 10885. PL. Gr. 53 fol. 1600 Grantha-s (6 Parvan-s). = CLB I, p. 29. Extract p. 150.
Brl. p. 43 (no.CXXXI) = IO 4327.
IO 4326 (Burnell 497d). Gr. 4 fol. Written ca. A.D. 1878.
IO 4327 (Burnell 128). PL. Gr. 6 fol.
PUL II. App. p. 11 (no.176). PL. Gr. 2 fol.

[NCC IX 297a]

734 DHĀRYA-NIRŪPAṆA **(धार्यनिरूपण)**
on the singing of certain Sāma hymns of the Ūha portion of the *Sāmaveda*. The text is the same as the Tṛtīyādhāryam.

Mysore ND II 3421 (P 491/ 3). PL. Na. 2 fol. (103-04). Extract no. 155.
Mysore ND II 3422 (A 642/ 5). Kan. 3 fol. (31-33). Dated 6.8.1919.
Mysore ND II 3423 (A 642/ 7). Kan. 1 fol. (33).
MD 14077. PL. Na. 4 pp. Incomplete. Col.: iti tṛtīya-dhāryāḥ samāptaḥ.

[NCC IX 298b]

735 NATAPARA (1) **(नतपर)**
Lists of Vedic words ending with "n" or "t". See Napara-tapara(-prakaraṇa).

Adyar D I 983. Incomplete (in a collection) → Veda-lakṣaṇa (A 1).
Adyar D I 1030 (in a collection) → Sapta-lakṣaṇa.
Baroda 11949(d). PL. Tel. 12 fol. (60-71). 150 Grantha-s (with C.). = CLB I, p. 29. Extract p. 151.

– C. Baroda 11949(d). = CLB I, p. 29. Extract p. 151.

736 NATAPARA (2) **(नतपर)**
of Śauri-sūri.
Baroda 6131(b). PL. Gr. 3 fol. (6b-8b). 40 Grantha-s. = CLB I, p. 29.

Baroda 10034(c). PL. Gr. 2 fol. (3b-4b). 40 Grantha-s. = CLB I, p. 29.
Baroda 10032(c). PL. Gr. 21 fol. (40-60). 300 Grantha-s (with C.). = CLB I, p. 29.
Baroda 6131(i). PL. Gr. 13 fol. (92-104). 250 Grantha-s (with C.). = CLB I, p. 29.

– C. of the author.
Adyar D I 1036 (in a collection). Title: Natapara-vyākhyāna → Sapta-lakṣaṇa-vyākhyā.
Adyar D I 1037 (in a collection). Title: Natapara-lakṣaṇa-vyākhyā → Sapta-lakṣaṇa-vyākhyā.
Adyar D I 1038 (anon. fragment). → Sapta-lakṣaṇa-vyākhyā.
Baroda 6131(i). = CLB I, p. 29.
Baroda 10032(c). = CLB I, p. 29.

[NCC IX 325b]

737 NATĀNTA-PADĀNI or NAPARA(-LAKṢAṆA) (नतान्तपदानि / नपरलक्षण) of Śeṣa Nārāyaṇa.

Beginning: (858)

प्रणम्य गरुडारूढं हरिं नीलाभ्र-(द्रि)-संनिभम्।
शेषनारायणाख्येन लक्षणं क्रियते मया॥
नतयोस्तु विहायान्यत् सव्याख्यं दोषवर्जितम्।
संगृह्य श्लोकरूपेण तदन्तानि पदानि तु॥
चजयोश्च धकारं तु हित्वा तादिचतुष्टये।
मकारे च लकारे च परे सति विकारभाक्॥

End:

सर्वान् सीव्यन् तथा स्तोतॄन्त् सामन्त्सत्वन् सहन्तमः।
सह्वान् सिञ्चन् हविष्मांश्च हन् हर्यन्निति संग्रहः॥
इति श्रीशेषनारायणाख्यविरचितं सर्वनपरं समाप्तम्॥

Adyar D I 858 (20 K 38 = 67500). PL. Tel. 2 fol. (8-9). Title: Napara (Sarva-napara). = Adyar I, p. 50a.
Trav. Uni. 22749 D. PL. Mal. 40 Grantha-s.
Trav. Uni. 22749 J. PL. Mal. 220 Grantha-s (with C.).
Whish 73,2 (8). PL. Gr. 3 fol. (19-21). Title: Nānta-saṃgraha.

Ptd. in the collection called *Tāṇḍaṅgal* (in Malayalam script). – Kunnankulam (Kerala) : Panchangam Pustakashala, 1930 (M.E. 1105), pp. 18-22 (33 verses). [SAI (87/1683*)]

– C.

Beginning:

हरिं नमस्कृत्य नतेष्टदं विभुं जगन्निवासं तमधोक्षजं परम्।

दयानिधेर्यस्य कटाक्षमात्रतः प्रयाति मूको ऽपि पटुत्वमञ्जसा ॥
लब्ध्वा परशुरामार्यकुमाराद्यज्वनः कृपाम् ।
विष्णुवृद्धकुलाब्धीन्दुगरुडध्वजसूनुना ॥
नारायणाभिधानेन चामन्देतरबुद्धिना ।
नतयोः क्रियते टीका बह्वृचानां मुदे मया ॥

(र)रिप्सितप्रकृतग्रन्थनिर्विघ्न परिसमाप्तिप्रयोजनाय आदौ इष्टदेवताप्रणामरूपं मङ्गलमाचरन् प्रतिजानीते -- प्रणम्येति । गरुडारूढं गरुडं वैनतेयमारूढस्तम् । वाहीकृतविनतानन्दनानन्दजननहेतुरित्यर्थः । नीलाभ्रसन्निभं नीलान्यभ्राणि तेषां संनिभः सदृशः । नवसजलजलदसमानापट(य)न इत्यर्थः । एवंभूतं श्रीहरिं परमात्मानं प्रणम्य नमस्कृत्य शेषनारायणाख्येन शेषनारायणाभिधानेन मया लक्षणं क्रियत इति योजना। नान्ततान्तपरिभाषायां नतयोस्तु विहायान्यद् (इति) अभिहितत्वात् तान्तापेक्षया नान्तस्य बहुलत्वाच्च नान्तमुक्त्वा तान्त उच्यते। मकारस्याप्यत्र प्राप्तेरन्यद् विहायेत्युक्तं मूलकृता । मकारस्य लक्षणतः प्राप्तिः कथम् । याममित्यत्र लक्षणादेव नकारमकारयोरवकाशत्वात् ···

End:

इति नपरव्याख्यानम् ॥

स्मृत्वा कृष्णपदारविन्दममलं वज्रादिरेखाङ्कितं
संसारार्णवतारणाय जगतां पोतं शरण्यं सदा।
टीकेयं नतयोर्मया विरचिता सम्यग् बुधैरीक्ष्यतां
श्रीनारायणसूरिणा करुणया बालोक्तिवत् सर्वदा ॥

Whish 73,2 (10). PL. Gr. 13 fol. (23-35).

See Napara-tapara(-prakaraṇa).

[NCC IX 325b]

738 NAPARA(-PRAKARAṆA) (or -LAKṢAṆA) (1) (नपर-प्रकरण /-लक्षण)

Also included in the *Sapta-lakṣaṇa*.

Adyar I, p. 50a. Title: Natānta-padāni.

Adyar D I 987 → Veda-lakṣaṇa (A 5).

Adyar D I 1032 → Sapta-lakṣaṇa.

Adyar D I 1033 → Sapta-lakṣaṇa.

Baroda 10381(e). PL. Gr. 3 fol. (9-11). 25 Grantha-s. = CLB I, p. 29.

Hoshiarpur p. 301 (no.5847). PL. Gr. 2 fol. 30 Grantha-s.

IO 4483 (Mackenzie II 94j). PL. Na. 7 fol. (82-88) (with C.). Written ca. A.D. 1770. amuṣmin..

IO 4484 (Mackenzie III 234h). PL. Tel. 9 fol. (57-65) (with C.). Written ca. A.D. 1810.

IO 4485 (Mackenzie III 186f). PL. Tel. 3 fol. (14-16).

IO 4486 (Mackenzie III 59a). PL. Tel. 2 fol. (16-17).

MD 16398. PL. Gr. 4 pp. 35 Grantha-s.

MT 2189(b). Tel. 6 fol. (10-15) (with C.). Transcribed in 1916-17 from a Ms. of Vemparla Subrahmanya Sastrigaru of Tondavaramu, Godavari Dist. The scribe of the original Ms. is Ponnamalli Subrahmaṇya.

Mysore I, p. 29 (8 Mss.; 5 with Tapara).

Mysore ND II 3546-55. Extract no. 187, 188, 189.

Oppert II 758. Belonged to Ghanapathi Shingaracharyar of Alasur, Madurantakam Taluk.

Oppert II 1328. Belonged to Gopalacharyar of Pillapakkam, Kanchipuram Taluk.

Oppert II 9039. Belonged to Ganapati Lakshminarayana Sastri of Tiruvadi, Thanjavur Dist.

TD 1798. PL. Tel. 1 fol. (no. 113). 20 Grantha-s.

TD 1799. PL. Gr. 1 fol. 20 Grantha-s.

Trav. Uni. 2346 J. PL. Gr. 180 Grantha-s (with C.).

Trav. Uni. 2630 P. PL. Gr. 30 Grantha-s.

Trav. Uni. 4254 F. PL. Mal. 6 fol. 70 Grantha-s. Belonged to Vishnu Nambudiri of Ettikada Illam Ayankudi, Kaduttirutti, Kottayam.

Trav. Uni. 5778 M. PL. Tel. 200 Grantha-s (with C.).

See also Tapara(-prakaraṇa) and Napara-tapara(-prakaraṇa).

Ptd.: There are at least five editions: three in Grantha and one each in Telugu and Malayalam script. See under Aniṅgya (Taitt.) and Sapta-lakṣaṇa.

– C.

IO 4483 (Mackenzie II 94j). PL. Na. 7 fol. (82-88) (with text). Written ca. A.D. 1770.

IO 4484 (Mackenzie III 234h). PL. Tel. 9 fol. (57-65) (with text). Written ca. A.D. 1810.

MD 16744. PL. Tel. 20 pp. 138 Grantha-s. = MT 1964(f); the end differs.

MT 2189(b). Tel. 6 (10-15) (with text). Transcribed in 1916-17 from a Ms. of Vemparla Subrahmanya Sastrigaru of Tondavaramu, Godavari Dist. The scribe of the original Ms. is Ponnamalli Subrahmaṇya.

MT 4017(c). PL. Gr. 4 fol. (14-17). Presented in 1921-22 by Krishna Ghanapathigal, Sirukumar, Trichinapalli Dist.

Mysore (1898), p. 6 (no. 52). 12 fol. (31-42).

Mysore I, p. 29 (2 Mss.); p. 613.

Mysore ND II 3556-70. Extract no. 190.

Oppert II 759. Belonged to Ghanapathi Shingaracharyar of Alasur, Madurantakam Taluk.

Oppert II 9040. Belonged to Ganapati Lakshminarayana Sastri of Tiruvadi, Thanjavur Dist.

TD 1810. PL. Tel. 2 fol. (120-121). 300 Grantha-s. Incomplete.

Trav. Uni. 2346 J. PL. Gr. 180 Grantha-s (with text).

Trav. Uni. 5778 M. PL. Tel. 200 Grantha-s.

– C. of Mallayārya or Mallināthārya-yajvan.

Beginning: (862) Cf. Baroda Extract p. 151

इत्थमकारादिक्रमेण एकारैकारान्तानि पदानि सम्यग् लक्षयित्वा अकारादिवर्णानुसारेणैव परिशिष्टानि नकारान्तानि पदानि नपराख्येन ग्रन्थेन लक्षयितुं प्रारभते । अथ यजुःसंहितायां चछजतदधनमलपराः तत्तत्सानुनासिकाः पदान्ताः पदकाले नकारा दृश्यन्ते । सूत्रयोरनयोरयमर्थः । अत्रायमथशब्दो ऽधिकारार्थः । यजुःसंहितायां चकारछकारजकार तकारदकारधकारनकार यकारलकारेभ्यः सर्वपदान्ते वर्तमानश्च चकारादिसंबद्ध्यनुनासिकाः पदकाले विभागसमये येषु पदेषु नकारा दृश्यन्ते नकारा भवन्तीत्यर्थः ॥

End:

अयं दक्षं दधानाः । यदारण्यानामारण्यां जर्तिलयवाग्वा वा । आदित्यान् ... । (नकारप्रयुक्त्या पूर्वसूत्रम् उक्तम् । अनुस्वारप्रयुक्त्या इदमुक्तमिति नाप्रतिज्ञातप्रतिपादनदोष इति रमणीयम् । इति श्रीमत्पोगलमल्लयाचार्ययज्वकृतौ पददर्पणे नपराख्याध्यायः समाप्तः ॥)

Adyar D I 862 (30 D 29 = 73919). PL. Gr. 4 fol. (42ff.). Incomplete. = Adyar I, p. 54a. Title: Sapta-lakṣaṇa-vyākhyā.

MT 1976(c). 13 fol. (30-42) (with text). Presented in 1916-17 by Nimmagadda Narasimhavadhanulugaru, Godavarru, Godavari Dist. Not the same as MD 917, though so described in the catalogue.

Mysore (1898), p. 6 (no. 54a). Tel. 15 fol.

Mysore ND II 3571 (P 5999/ 5). PL. Tel. 1 fol. Extract no. 191.

Mysore ND II 3572 (P 3584/ 4). PL. Tel. 7 fol. (13-19).Extract no. 192.

Mysore ND II 3573 (P 3584/22). PL. Tel. 6 fol. (4-9). Extract no. 193.

Tirupati SVUORI 2858 (4446c). PL. Gr. 6 fol. (46-51).

739 NAPARA(-PRAKARAṆA) (or -LAKṢAṆA) (2) **(नपर-प्रकरण /-लक्षण)** of Śeṣa Nārāyaṇa. See above Natānta-padāni.

Adyar D I 858 (20 K 38 = 67500). PL. Tel. 2 fol. (8-9). = Adyar I, p. 50a. Title: Natānta-padāni.

Trav. Uni. 1116 E. PL. Mal. 40 Grantha-s.

Trav. Uni. 4254 F. PL. Mal. 6 fol. 70 Grantha-s. Belonged to Vishnu Nambudiri of Ettikada Illam Ayankudi, Kaduttirutti, Kottayam.

Triv. Cur. III 8. Mal. 50 Grantha-s.

740 NAPARA(-PRAKARAṆA) (or -LAKṢAṆA) (3) **(नपर-प्रकरण /-लक्षण)** of Śauri-sūri or Śauri-sūnu.

Adyar D I 989. Incomplete → Veda-lakṣaṇa (A 7).

Adyar D I 1030 (in a collection) → Sapta-lakṣaṇa.

Adyar D I 1034 (in a collection) → Sapta-lakṣaṇa.

Adyar D I 1035 (2 Mss.; one incomplete).

MD 16805. PL. Gr. 3 pp. 30 Grantha-s.
MD 16812. PL. Gr. 7 pp. 126 Grantha-s.
MD 17440. PL. Gr. 7 pp. 90 Grantha-s (with C.).
PUL I, p. 21 (no.75). PL. Gr. 2 fol. (7-8).
Trav. Uni. 2938 D. PL. Gr. 35 Grantha-s.
Trav. Uni. 3040 D. PL. Gr. 35 Grantha-s.
Trav. Uni. 4369 B-1. PL. Gr.

– C. Vyākhyāna.
Whish 25a (3). PL. Gr. 5 fol. (22-26). Title: Napara-paddhati-vyākhyāna.

– C. of Śaurisūri.
MD 17440. PL. Gr. 7 pp. 90 Grantha-s (with C.).
PUL I, p. 21 (no.76). PL. Tel. 7 fol. (16-24).
Cf. MT 3887(g) (C. on Napara-tapara). = MD 918.

[NCC IX 339a]

741 NAPARA-TAPARA(-PRAKARAṆA) (or -LAKṢAṆA) (1) **(नपरतपर-प्रकरण /-लक्षण)**
Unspecified. Apparently belongs to Taitt.

Beginning: (861)

अथेदानीं तकारान्तपद्धतिमाह -- अद्यादतृणदश्नीयादब्रवीदजुपत्ततः । अस्मादन्नाद्यान्निर्भजामि। वज्रेण स्वान्यतृणन्नदीनाम्। न मांसमश्नीयान्न स्त्रियम्॥

End:

होमानिति नपद्धतिः । स्तेगां दन्ताभ्याम् । सहिया देवः हविष्मान् देवः । एतानि होमाञ्जुहुयात्। इत्युक्तप्रकारनकारान्तपद्धतिः ॥ नपरव्याख्यानं समाप्तं॥

Adyar D I 861 (23 H 27 = 69901). PL. Gr. 4 fol. (18ff.) (with C.).
Adyar D I 984 (in a collection) → Veda-lakṣaṇa (A 2).
MT 485(c). PL. Tel. 11 fol. (32-42) (with C. of Mallinātha). Presented in 1910-11 by C. Visvanatha Shastrigal of Viziyanagaram.
MT 523(c). PL. Tel. 10 fol. (34-43) (with C.). Presented in 1910-11 by C. Visvanatha Shastrigal of Viziyanagaram.
MT 1165(i). PL. Tel. 3 fol. (63-65). Lacks beginning and end. Purchased in 1913-14 from Kashibhatta Subrahmanya Sastri of Vekanur, Krishna Dist.
MT 1964(f). PL. Tel. 10 fol. (58-67) (with C. Pada-darpaṇa). Presented in 1916-17 by Rayaprolu Ramabrahmangaru of Guruza, Gudivada Taluk, Krishna Dist.
MT 1964(p). PL. Tel. 1 fol. (118). = MD 914. Presented in 1916-17 by Rayaprolu Ramabrahmangaru of Guruza, Gudivada Taluk, Krishna Dist.
MT 1976(c). Tel. 13 fol. (30-42) (with C.). Not the same as MD 917. Presented in 1916-17 by Nimmagadda Narasimhavadhanulugaru, Godavarru, Godavari Dist.
MT 2649(d). PL. Tel. 10 fol. (105-14) (with C. Pada-darpaṇa). Presented in 1917-18 by Prava Surayya Sastrigaru of Penumanchili, Narasapur Taluk, Krishna Dist.

MT 3887(e). PL. Gr. 2 fol. (74-75). = MD 913. Purchased in 1921-22 from Annasvami Sastrigal, Bhavani, Coimbatore Dist.
SBD 4215. 10 fol. (with Vilaṅghya). Incomplete.
Trav. Uni. 5778 D. PL. Tel.
Trav. Uni. 22209 C. PL. Mal. 75 Grantha-s.

– C. Pada-darpaṇa of Pogalla Mallayārya.
Adyar D I 1039 (in a collection) → Sapta-lakṣaṇa-vyākhyā.
MT 485(c). PL. Tel. 11 fol. (32-42) (with text). Presented in 1910-11 by C. Visvanatha Shastrigal of Viziyanagaram.
MT 523(c). PL. Tel. 10 fol. (34-43) (with text). Presented in 1910-11 by C. Visvanatha Shastrigal of Viziyanagaram.
MT 1964(f). PL. Tel. 10 fol. (58-67). Col.: Udigbhāṣyam. Presented in 1916-17 by Rayaprolu Ramabrahmangaru of Guruza, Gudivada Taluk, Krishna Dist.
MT 1976(c). 13 fol. (30-42) (with text). Presented in 1916-17 by Nimmagadda Narasimhavadhanulugaru, Godavarru, Godavari Dist. Not the same as MD 917 as it is described in the catalogue; but the beginning is identical with Adyar D I 862 (Napara).
MT 2649(d). PL. Tel. 10 fol. (105-14) (with text) Presented in 1917-18 by Prava Surayya Sastrigaru of Penumanchili, Narasapur Taluk, Krishna Dist.

742 NAPARA-TAPARA(-PRAKARAṆA) (or -LAKṢAṆA) (2) (नपरतपर-प्रकरण /-लक्षण)
Different texts.
Adyar D I 861 (23 H 27 = 69901). PL. Gr. 4 fol. (18ff.).
Adyar D I 984 (fol. 54a-64a) → Veda-lakṣaṇa (A 2).
Adyar D I 985 (fol. 1-17, with Bhāṣya) → Veda-lakṣaṇa (A 3).
Mysore I, p. 613.
Trav. Uni. 21553 E. PL. Gr. 90 Grantha-s.
Trav. Uni. 22200 A. PL. Mal. 150 Grantha-s.

– C. of Kaṇṭhabhūṣaṇa ? (Cf. the final verse of Tapara).
PUL I, p. 21 (no.77). PL. Gr. 33 fol. (22-54).

– C. of Śaurisūri.
MT 3887(g). = MD 918.

Cf. C. on Napara(-prakaraṇa).

– diff. text.
MD 913. PL. Tel. 4 pp. (29ff).
MD 914. PL. Gr. 8 pp. (12ff.).
MD 915. PL. Tel. 4 pp. (90ff.).
MD 916. PL. Gr. 3 pp. (15ff.).
MD 16399. PL. Gr. 14 Grantha-s.
MD 16710. PL. Tel. 3 pp. 28 Grantha-s.
MD 16728. PL. Tel. 3 pp. 30 Grantha-s.

MD 16806. PL. Gr. 5 pp. 73 Grantha-s.

MT 485(h). PL. Tel. 2 fol. (63-64). Presented in 1910-11 by C. Visvanatha Shastrigal of Viziyanagaram.

MT 4600(a). PL. Gr. 3 fol. (9b-11b). Presented in 1924-25 by the Secretary to the Trustees of Sri Yogi Parthasarathi Ayyangar's Charities, Triplicane, Madras.

743 NAPARA-TAPARA(-PRAKARAṆA) (or -LAKṢAṆA) (3) **(नपरतपर-प्रकरण /-लक्षण)** of Śeṣa Nārāyaṇa.

Adyar D XIII 46 (VB 120b). PL. Gr. 4 fol. Both Napara and Tapara. (Date and scribe: durmatau saṃvatsare kumbhamāse ekādaśīdine śrībhāskarakavīndrātmaja-balarāmeṇa likhitam |

MD 917. Tel. 4 pp. (90ff.) (same as Adyar D I 858. RV).

TCD 34-F. 6 pp. (34-39). 60 Grantha-s.

Trav. Uni. T.223 F. = TCD 34-F. A transcript of the Ms. no. 4254.

Triv. Cur. III 7-8 (separately).

744 NAPARA-TAPARA(-PRAKARAṆA) (or -LAKṢAṆA) (4) **(नपरतपर-प्रकरण /-लक्षण)** of Śauri-sūri or Śauri-sūnu.

Beginning: (859)

नत्वा वि(श्री)नायकं देवं सर्वसंपत्करं परम् (प्रभुम्)।
शौरिसूरिः प्रवक्ष्यामि नवं नवपरं पदम्॥
लक्षणं क्रियते चादिपरं नावनवं मया।

अथ नपराख्यपदलक्षणसमनन्तरम् अखिलजगदुत्पत्तिस्थितिलयकारणं सकलमुनिजनविमलहृदयकमलनिलयम् अनादिमध्यनिधनमस्मत्कुलदैवतं तत्परावरं विश्वेश्वरं भगवन्तं नारायणं प्रणम्यास्य नवपरस्य स्वयमेव व्याख्यानं रचयिष्यामीति प्रतिज्ञा। श्रीवेदव्यासाय नमः। श्रीगणाधिपतये नमः। परमुत्कृष्टं नवं करिष्यामीत्येषो ऽन्वयः। सकलकार्य(विघ्न)निवृत्तिहेतुं विनायकं पूर्वं नमस्कृत्य नवपरलक्षणं करिष्यामीत्युक्त्वा इदानीं प्राचीनलक्षणग्रन्थस्य दोषबाहुल्यं दर्शयन्नारभ्यमाणस्य गुणमुपपादयन्नाह --

दुर्ज्ञानं दुष्पठं यत् तु सापेक्षं चाक्रमं तथा।
तत् परित्यज्य सव्याख्यमकारादिक्रमेण तु॥

दुर्ज्ञानं ज्ञातुमशक्यं

End:

हन्याद्धृन्नपरं तान्तं पदमेवं प्रकीर्तितम्। हन्यात्। हृत्। एवमनेन प्रकारेण नपरं पदान्तं प्रोक्तम्। तपरं च प्रकीर्तितम्। सम्यगभिहितम्। न निहन्यान्न लोहितम्। अग्ने यत्ते परं हृन्नाम॥

यत्र क्वचन तेनैव पूर्वं द्रष्टुमपेक्षते।
नतान्तपदमालेयं नवरत्नोत्तराक्षरा॥

सगुणा वेदविदुषा रचिता कण्ठभूषणम्।

भवति पदे ऽनुस्वारतस्तचकारस्वरपरे नकारान्ते॥ पदे पदकाले तकारपरो वा चकारपरो वा स्वरपरो नानुस्वारो नकारान्तो भवति। ऋतूं तन्वते। त्रीं रीचाननुब्रूहि। ऋतूं ऽच तस्य। यां ऽच देवा वावृधुः। मर्त्यां आविवेश। उदयां अजस्रम्। तचकारस्वरपर इति किम्। संरेवतीः। संश्रवाह। शषसहरेफपरो मान्तः पदे भवति। पदे पदकाले शकारपरो वा षकारपरो वा सकारपरो वा हकारपरो वा रेफपरो वा स्वरपरो वा मान्तः पदे भवति। वायव्यं श्वेतम्। तं षडहानि। तां सवितुः। भूतानां ह्वेषः। अक्तं रिहाणाः। इति नारायणभट्टकृतं संहितातपरव्याख्यानं समाप्तम्। श्रीवेदनायकीसमेत संगमेश्वरस्वामी सहायम्॥

Beginning: (860)

नत्वा विनायकं देवं सर्वसंपत्करं परम्।
शौरिसूनुः करिष्यामि नवं नवपरं पदम्॥

सर्वसंपत्करं परम्। विनायकं नत्वा शौरिसूनुः नवमुत्कृष्टं नवपरं करिष्यामीत्यन्वयः। सकलकार्यविघ्ननिवर्त्तहेतुं विनायकं पूर्वं नमस्कृत्य नवलक्षणं करिष्यामीत्युक्त्वा इदानीं प्राचीनग्रन्थदोषबाहुल्यं दर्शयन्नारभ्यमाणस्य गुणमुपपादयन्नाह दुर्ज्ञानमिति॥

End:

हविष्मन्नधनं पूर्वं हविष्कृन्निधनं तथा॥ हविष्मन्निधनम्। हविष्कृन्निधनम्। इत्येतयोर्ग्रहणयोः पूर्वं तकारान्तं लोहितम्। यत्ते परं हृन्नाम्। -- हन्याद्धृन्नपरं तान्तं पदमेवम् प्रकीर्तितम् -- नपरमित्यादि नकारान्तं तकारान्तं यावत् पदं सर्वमेवोक्तम्। उक्तप्रकारेण प्रकीर्तितम्। यत्र क्वचनेत्यादि।

Adyar D I 859 (19 N 32 = 66868). PL. Gr. 13 fol. (106ff.) (with C. of Nārāyaṇa-bhaṭṭa).
Adyar D I 860 (28 A 35). PL. Gr. 8 fol. (with C.). = Adyar I, p. 50a.
Adyar D I 1031 → Sapta-lakṣaṇa.
Adyar D I 1035 → Sapta-lakṣaṇa.
Brl. p. 11 (no.XXXVIII) = IO 4488.
Brl. p. 11 (no.XXXIX) = IO 4487.
Burnell 5b.
Hoshiarpur p. 51 (no.4105). PL. Gr. 3 fol. 50 Grantha-s. Extract p. 409.
IO 4487 (Burnell 146c). PL. Gr. 2 fol. (6-7).
IO 4488 (Burnell 49c). PL. Gr. 3 fol. (6-8).
IO 4489 (Burnell 350d). Tel. 9 fol. (49-57) (with C.). Written ca. A.D. 1867.
MD 918. Gr. 18 pp. (24ff.) (with C.).
MD 919. PL. Tel. 16 pp. (11ff.) (with C.).
MD 18929. PL. Tel. 6 pp. (84ff.).
MT 689(c). PL. Gr. 3 fol. (5-7) (with C.). Purchased in 1912-13 through Seshasayi Ayyangar of Kottaiyur near Kumbakonam.

MT 2881(f). PL. Gr. 5 fol. (33-37) (with C.). A different Maṅgala-śloka. Presented in 1918-19 by Venkatagiri Appalacharyar of Triplicane.

MT 3887(g). PL. Gr. 2 fol. (77-78) (with C.). Purchased in 1921-22 from Annasvami Sastrigal, Bhavani, Coimbatore Dist.

Oppert I 997. Belonged to Viraraghava Tatacharyar, Head Master, Sanskrit School of Sathakopacharya, Kanchipuram, Chingelpet Dist.

PUL II. App. p. 11 (no.177). PL. Gr. 31 fol.

RASB II 487-88(III) (G 6063). 3 fol. (6-8). Dated V.S. 1913 / Śaka 1778.

TCD 35-C. PL. Gr. 7 fol. 125 Grantha-s (with C.). Incomplete.

TD 1796. PL. Gr. 5 fol. (9-13). 50 Grantha-s.

Trav. Uni. 2938 D. PL. Gr. 35 Grantha-s.

Trav. Uni. 3040 D. PL. Gr. 35 Grantha-s.

Trav. Uni. C.2268 C. = TCD 35-C.

– C. anon.

Brl. p. 11 (no.XL) = IO 4489.

IO 4489 (Burnell 350d). Tel. 9 fol. (49-57) (with text). Written ca. A.D. 1867.

TCD 35-C. Incomplete.

C. Vyākhyā.

Trav. Uni. C.2268 C.

C. Vyākhyā of Nārāyaṇa-bhaṭṭa.

Adyar D I 859. Col.: mentions Nārāyaṇa-bhaṭṭa as commentator. From the statement *svayam evavyākhyānaṃ racayiṣyāmi* in the introduction both the text and the commentary appear to be by the same author.

C. of the author.

Adyar D I 860.

Hoshiarpur p. 51 (no.3557). See Tapara above.

Hoshiarpur p. 51 (no.5613). PL. Gr. 22 fol. 500 Grantha-s. Extract p. 409 (= Āvarṇi-vyākhyā ?).

MD 918. Gr. 18 pp. (24ff.).

MD 919. PL. Tel. 16 pp. (11ff.).

MT 689(c). PL. Gr. 3 fol. (5-7). Purchased in 1912-13 through Seshasayi Ayyangar of Kottaiyur near Kumbakonam.

MT 2881(f). PL. Gr. 5 fol. (33-37) (with text). A different Maṅgala-śloka. Presented in 1918-19 by Venkatagiri Appalacharyar of Triplicane.

MT 3887(g). PL. Gr. 2 fol. (77-78) (with text). = MD 918. Purchased in 1921-22 from Annasvami Sastrigal, Bhavani, Coimbatore Dist.

[NCC IX 339b]

*NARASIMHA (नरसिंह)

Jaṭā-lakṣaṇa or Vikalpa-kaumudī. TCD 34-K. Trav. Uni. 4254 L.

Ptd.: in the magazine of the Mysore Sanskrit College, *Śrīmanmahārāja Saṃskṛta Mahāpāṭhaśālā Patrikā*, vol. 16 (1940), Mysore, pp. 1-6.

[NCC IX 358a]

*NARASIṂHA (नरसिंह)
– Veda-lakṣaṇa-dīdhiti-prasārikā. PUL II. App. p. 20 (no. 310).

745 NARASIṂHA-JAṬĀ-LAKṢAṆA (1) (नरसिंहजटालक्षण)
→ Jaṭā-lakṣaṇa or Vikalpa-kaumudī of Narasiṃha.

746 NARASIṂHA-JAṬĀ-LAKṢAṆA (2) (नरसिंहजटालक्षण)
Deccan College 1562. 17 fol. → Ṛgveda-krama-dīpikā of Narahari son of Nṛsiṃha-sūri.

*NARASIṂHA-SŪRI (नरसिंहसूरि)
– Ṛgvarṇa-krama-lakṣaṇa. Adyar D XIII 35 (VB.737b).

*NARASIṂHA-SŪRI (नरसिंहसूरि)
Son of Rudrācārya of Kauṇḍinya-gotra.
– Svara-(manojña-)mañjarī. Baroda 7791. IO 701. MD 15704. MT 158(b).

*NARAHARI (नरहरि)
Son of Nṛsiṃha-sūri.
– Ṛgveda-krama-dīpikā. Deccan College 1562. 17 fol.

747 NAVA-LAKṢAṆA (नवलक्षण)
Mysore ND II 3574 (P 4906/31). PL. Na. 1 fol. (123). Extract no. 194. (Cf. p. 24 of the *Pada-gāḍha*, Srirangam edition).

748 NAVA-ŚIKṢĀ (नवशिक्षा)
A list of names of nine Śikṣā-s.
Mysore ND II 3575 (P 2262/ 1). PL. Gr. 1 fol.

[NCC IX 364b]

*NĀGADEVA (नागदेव)
Son of Yajñanārāyaṇa.

– Ṛksarva-samāna or Sarva-samāna or Samāna-saṃdhi. Adyar D I 1011. Adyar D XIII 43 (VB 266b). IM 2497. Whish 73,2 (1).
– Ṛgvilaṅghya-lakṣaṇa or Vilaṅghya. Adyar D XIII 42 (VB 266c). The same as Adyar D I 973. MD 963. Whish 73,2 (2).
– Ṛgveda-sapta-lakṣaṇa.
– Samāna-padādi. TCD 34-A.

[NCC X 3b; 290a]

*NĀGANĀTHA-SŪRI or NĀGAPPA-SŪRI (नागनाथ-सुरि / नागप्प-सूरि)
– C. called Dīpa-mālā on the Phulla-sūtra. Mysore ND II 3653-54.

*NĀGA-BHAṬṬA or NĀGAPPA (नागभट्ट / नागप्प)
– Āraṇyaka-sāma-dīpa, also known as Sāmadīpa. Mysore I, p. 22. Mysore ND II 3964-65. Extract no. 318.
– Ūha-dīpa. Mysore I, p. 24. Mysore ND II 3224 (P 2485/ 5). PL. Na. 75 fol. (125-99). Extract no.57.

— Rahasya-dīpa. Mysore I, p. 33.

*NĀGEŚA (नागेश)
— Kāṇva-śākhā-mahima-saṃgraha. MT 2389.

749 NĀDA-VARṆA-VIVEKA (**नादवर्णविवेक**)
Same as Adyar D I 968 (Varṇa-cchandodaivata); MT 5258 (Śaunakīya-sāra) and TCD 80-B (Śikṣā) = Trav. Uni. C.1041 B (Śikṣā-samuccaya). See *Varṇoccāraṇadīpikā*.

Beginning: (863)

गणेशं दक्षिणामूर्तिं वाणीं व्यासं गुरूनपि।
नमामि यत्प्रसादेन कृतिनः सन्ति देहिनः ॥
वेदवाक्यगतान् वर्णानकारादीन्नमाम्यहम्।
ताञ्छन्दोमुनिदेवानप्याचार्यान् शौनकादिकान् ॥

अथ वर्णविषयाणि यानि ज्ञेयानि तानि कानिचिद् विलिख्यन्ते । तज्ज्ञानस्य अभ्युदयनिःश्रेयससाधनत्वात्। तथाहि --

आकाशवायुप्रभवः शरीरात् समुच्चरन् वक्त्रमुपैति नादः ।
स्थानान्तरेषु प्रविभज्यमानो वर्णत्वमागच्छति यः स शब्दः
तमक्षरं ब्रह्म परं पवित्रं गुहाशयं सम्यगुशन्ति विप्राः ।
स श्रेयसा चाभ्युदयेन चैव सम्यक् प्रयुक्तः पुरुषं युनक्ति ॥

(These two verses are found in the Āpiśali-śikṣā also).

End:

अत्र वासिष्ठशिक्षायां हकारस्यैव केवलस्योदयप्रकृतित्वमुक्तं न वर्गचतुर्थानाम्। अन्यथा नादः स्यात् --

संवृतैककण्ठे बिले ऽस्मिन् विवृते पुनः ।
श्वासो विकारस्तन्मध्ये स तस्मादुभयात्मकम् ॥
यदा नादो हकारो वा तदा घोषस्तु जायते।

End: (TCD)

पदमध्ये दृष्टानां मकारस्य स्थाने जा एव वा इति विचार्यम् । उभयथाप्युच्चारणविशेषाभावात् । नकारद्वयथकारसकारतकार इति संस्तूयसे । सवाङ्स्तौलामि अमन्दांस्तोमानित्यादौ पञ्च । एवं प्रपञ्चागतमपि किंचिदुक्तम् । अथैकीयमतत्वेनोक्तस्य चकारागमस्य ग्राह्यत्वं प्रति किंचिदुच्यते। ञकारशकारपरे चकार आगमो भवति केषांचिदाचार्याणां मते। अत्रापि नकारान्तं पूर्वपदं पूर्वं शकाराद्युत्तरं यदि नकारो ञकारः स्याच्च।

Adyar D I 863 (39 F 80 = TR 25). Mal. 9 fol. (pp. 1-18). Remarks: "title temporarily suggested". Copied by Pandit V.Venkatarama Sarma, Fellow in Sanskrit, University of Madras, dated 10.1.1928.

[NCC X 33b]

750 NĀNTA-SAṂGRAHA (नान्तसंग्रह)
Whish 73,2 (8). PL. Gr. 3 fol. (19-21). Cf. Napara.

751 NĀMĀNUKRAMAṆĪ (नामानुक्रमणी)
of Mādhava. About 400 verses.

Beginning:

ओं नमो वासुदेवाय नामधेयविनिर्णयः ।
वृद्धोपदेशादाख्यातात् विशेषणसमन्वयात् ॥
स्वरतो ब्राह्मणादर्थाद् भूर्भूमिः क्ष्मा क्षमादितिः ।
ग्मावनिर्गौरिळा वज्रा ज्मा माता दुहिता क्षितिः ॥
पृथिवीयं वर्धयन्ती पद्या पूषा रिपोर्जनी ।

End:

श्वेतः पतङ्गः शुन्ध्युश्च जातवेदाश्च वायसः ।
भास्वानमर्त्यो दूरेदृगात्मा जीवस्तथा रतिः ॥
अर्को विभ्राद् तथायुर्गो धाता आदित्य एव च ।
आदितेयस्तथा विष्णुर्ब्रह्महंसो ऽतिजागतः ॥

Adyar D I 939 → Ākhyātanāmānukramaṇī.
GD I 1. PL. Mal. 33 fol. 750 Grantha-s (with Ākhyātānukramaṇī).
GD I 19-C. PL. Mal. 67 fol. (89-155). 335 Grantha-s.

[NCC X 50a]

752 NĀRADA-BAIṬH (नारदबैठ्)
→ Rāvaṇa-baiṭ (nūthanāvainavavede).
Hamburg StUB (cod.Palmbl. III 8/133) → Veda-lakṣaṇa (HB). 3 copies; one with C. Bhāva-prakāśikā of Cakra.

753 NĀRADA-BAIṬH(-PARIBHĀṢĀ) (नारदबैठ्/-परिभाषा)
Mysore I, p. 30.

[NCC X 58a]

754 NĀRADA-VIDHĀNA (नारदविधान)
– Nārada-śikṣā, part of. See Adyar D I 864 (Nārada-śikṣā).

[NCC X 58a]

755 NĀRADA-ŚIKṢĀ or NĀRADĪYA-ŚIKṢĀ (नारदशिक्षा / नारदीयशिक्षा)
Attributed to Nārada. In two Prapāṭhaka-s of eight chapters each. About 235 verses. There are differences with regard to the number of verses and textual readings among the Mss. as well as the printed editions. There is a mention of one Somaśarman in verse II 3.8 (Mysore edition):

निमेषकाला मात्रा स्याद् विद्युत्कालेति चापरे ।

ऋक्स्वरा तुल्ययोगा वा मतिः स्यात् सोमशर्मणः ॥

This verse is also found in the *Yājñavalkya-śikṣā*. See F. Kielhorn : Remarks on the Śikṣās in : *Indian Antiquary*, vol. V, p. 195 (reprint in : *Kleine Schriften*, vol. I, pp. 158-69).

Beginning (as in Adyar D I 864 with variants) :

अथातः स्वरशास्त्राणां सर्वेषां वेदनिश्चयः ।
उच्चनीचविशेषाद्धि स्वरान्यत्वं प्रवर्त्तते ॥
आर्चिकं गाथिकं चैव सामिकं च स्वरान्तरम् ।
कृतान्ते स्वरशास्त्राणां प्रयोक्तव्यं विशेषतः ॥
एकान्तरस्वरो ह्यृक्षु गाथासु द्व्यन्तरः स्वरः ।
सामसु त्र्यन्तरं विद्यादेतावत् स्वरतो ऽन्तरम् ··· ॥
उदात्तश्चानुदात्तश्च स्वरितप्रचयौ तथा ।
निर्घातश्चेति विज्ञेयः स्वरभेदस्तु पञ्चधा ॥

इति नारदविधाने स्वरशीक्षा समाप्ता ॥

End:

चत्वारस्त्वादितः स्वारः कम्पं पुष्पन्ति शास्त्रतः ।
उदात्तैकनिवेशने जुप्योग्निस्तु निदर्शनम् ॥

इति द्वितीयः प्रपाठकः ॥

आज्यहीनः कुलं हन्ति स्वरहीनस्तु पत्निकाम् ।
अन्नहीनो दहेद् राष्ट्रं मन्त्रहीनस्तथर्त्विजः ॥ १·१ ॥
धान्यं यशस्यमायुष्यं सर्वपापप्रणाशनम् ।
पवित्रं पावनं पुण्यं नारदेन प्रकीर्तितम् ॥ १·२ ॥
हस्तौ सुसंयुतौ धार्यौ जानुभ्यामुपरिस्थितौ ।
गुरोरनुकृतिं कुर्याद्यथाज्ञानमतिर्भवेत् ॥
मात्राद्विमात्रावृद्धानां विभागार्थं विभागवित् ।
अङ्गुलीभिर्द्विमात्रं तु पाणेः सव्यस्य दर्शयेत् ॥ १·६ ॥

Adyar D I 864 (33 M 22 = 75507). PL. Gr. 7 fol. (106ff.). Incomplete. = Adyar I, p. 52b.

ASB I iii.15 (I D 28/6). Beng. 10 fol. Dated V.S. 1717 = A.D. 1660.

B I, p. 202 (no.34). 13 fol. Dated V.S. 1759.

BA 16.

Baroda 7344. 13 fol. 240 Grantha-s. Dated V.S. 1759. = CLB I, p. 29.

Baroda 9803(a). PL. Mal. 28 fol. 240 Grantha-s. = CLB I, p. 29.

Baroda 9803(b). PL. Mal. 80 fol. 600 Grantha-s (with C.). = CLB I, p. 29.

Baroda 11826. 12 fol. 200 Grantha-s (almost complete). = CLB I, p. 29.

BBRAS 4 (B D 278). 6 fol. Incomplete. Dated Śaka 1787. Copied from a Ms. belonging to Rāoji Mahārāj.
BBRAS 5 (B D 86). 2-24 fol. Incomplete. Dated V.S. 1587.
Ben. 16.
Bhau Daji 32. 121.
BHU B 2668 (D 2E/2126). 11 fol. Incomplete. Dated V.S. 1515.
Bombay Uni. (Itchharam II 20) 103. 14 fol. Dated V.S. 1720.
BORI 3 of 1874-75. 13 fol. Dated V.S. 1759.
BORI 111 of 1879-80. 18 fol. 250 Grantha-s. Dated V.S. 1687.
BORI TM 300.
Brl. p. 42 (no.CXXX) = IO 4945.
Cu. add. 1923.
GJKSV 11449 (D III, no.11484). 15 fol. (8-22). Incomplete.
GJKSV 33160. 16 fol. Incomplete.
GJKSV 39521. 15 fol. Dated V.S. 1606.
Göttingen 158(2). 20 fol. 240 Grantha-s. Transcription of a Ms. dated V.S. 1759. (saṃvat 1759 varṣe pauṣabadi 14 ravivāsare pauthī līṣāyapataṃ vīrajī raghunāthajīā paṭhanārthe || pauthī liṣitaṃ leṣaginātbīnagarasīnagre madhye bāsajī ||). This Ms. contains in two Prapāṭhaka-s 14, 16, 10, 12, 18, 22, 19, 11 and 11, 18, 11, 9, 11, 10, 11, 32 verses respectively.
Göttingen 159. 6 fol. Copy of a Grantha Ms. received from Burnell. Dated 21 Jan. 1877.
Gough p. 31.
Gough p. 135. (no.3).
Hamburg StUB (Oppert 45a3). PL. Gr. 13 fol.
Harshe p. 44.
Haug p. 30 (no.79a : Svaraśāstra) = München 163.
IM 2174. 3 fol. Incomplete.
IM 2510A. 16 fol. Dated V.S. 1833.
IM 5521. 8 fol. (1-2, 5-10). Incomplete.
IO 4944 (Burnell 496b). Gr. 10 fol. (5-14). Copied from a Mysore Ms. in A.D. 1877.
IO 4945 (Burnell 360d). Gr. 29 pp. (280-308). Copied in A.D. 1866.
IO 4946 (3155). 12 fol. Text varies considerably from the preceding Ms. Incomplete.
Jammu RSRI p. 172 (no. 1858ka). 25 fol. Dated V.S. 1933.
Jammu RSRI p. 172 (no. 5237ka). 22 fol. (Stein 788).
L 136. 15 fol. 250 Grantha-s. Dated V.S. 1926.
Mad. Uni. R. A. S. 173(b) (-parīkṣā). (h). (i).
MD 920. 30 pp. (94ff.).
MD 15643. 38 pp. 296 Grantha-s.
Mithila IV 171. 22 fol. Dated V.S. 1936.
Mithila IV 172. 1 fol. ? Incomplete.
München 163. 14 fol. Dated A.D. 1817.
Mysore I, p. 30 (3 Mss.); p. 613.
Mysore ND II 3576 (P 491/ 1). PL. Na. 7 fol. (95-101). Extract no. 195.
Mysore ND II 3577 (P 1102/ 1). PL. Tel. 10 fol. Incomplete.
Mysore ND II 3578 (P 1978/ 1). PL. Na. 13 fol.
Mysore ND II 3579 (P 4772/17). PL. Tel. 12 fol. (21-32).

Mysore ND II 3580 (A 642/ 1). Kan. 13 fol. Dated 6.8.1919.

N-W P VI 14 (no.47). 12 fol. Belonged to Balakrishna Bhatta Vasimkara, Benares.

Oppert I 1001. Belonged to Viraraghava Tatacharyar, Head Master, Sanskrit School of Sathakopacharya, Kanchipuram, Chingelpet Dist.

Oppert I 8034. Belonged to Paravastu Venkatarangacharyar of Vishakhapattanam.

Oppert II 388. Belonged to Venkatarama Srauti of Mullandram, N. Arcot Dist.

Oppert II 760. Belonged to Ghanapathi Shingaracharyar of Alasur, Madurantakam Taluk.

Oppert II 1330. Belonged to Gopalacharyar of Pillapakkam, Kanchipuram Taluk.

Oppert II 7388. Belonged to Venkatarama Sastri of Pillur, Mayavaram Taluk.

Oudh XIII 30 (no.30). 38 pp. 300 Grantha-s. Dated A.D. 1844. Belonged to Pandit Kesava Prasada of Unao.

Oxf. CS d.185(6). 15 fol.

P 7.

PUL I, p. 132 (no.24). 25 fol. 600 Grantha-s (with other 5 SV works).

R. A. Sastri III, pp. 232. 300.

RASB II 1497 (G 373). 10 fol. (11-20). 160 Grantha-s.

SBD 2055. 61 fol. (88-168) (with some other works). Dated V.S. 1718.

SBD 2060. 17 fol. Dated V.S. 1733.

SBD 47214. 10 fol. Incomplete.

Stein p. 38 (no. 788). 19 fol.

Trav. Uni. 2915 H. PL. Gr. 250 Grantha-s.

Trav. Uni. 3325 B. PL. Gr. 120 Grantha-s.

Trav. Uni. 11826 A. PL. Gr. 750 Grantha-s (with Vivaraṇa of Śobhākara).

VSM I 1223 (no.1720). 18 fol.

Wai I 1450. 11 fol.

Wai II 10309. 41 fol. (with C.). Incomplete.

Wai II 10310. 8 fol. (with C.). Incomplete.

Weber 1499 (Ms. or. fol. 880). 20 fol. Dated V.S. 1929.

Ptd.:

1) In the monthly magazine *Saṃgīta-mīmāṃsaka* ("a treatise in two Prapāṭhaka-s and 114 śloka-s, on the intonation of the Veda-s"), vol. I, pts. 2-3. – Poona, 1886. [BM : Ptd. Bks. Cat. 1876-92. 249, 289 (14053.cc.45)]

A reprint, separately issued with a short preface in English and in Sanskrit. – Poona, 1886. [BM : Ptd. Bks. Cat. 1876-92. 249 (14053.cc.48)]

2) *Śrīnārada-viracitaḥ saṃgīta-granthaḥ.* – Poona : Aryabhusana Press, 1888. 3, 11, 1 pp. [IO : Ptd. Bks. Cat. 1953, p. 1719 (287)]

3) Ed. by Satyavrata Samasrami, in the Sanskrit journal *Uṣā.* – Calcutta : Satya Press, 1890, vol. I, pts. 6-7. 26 pp. [Emeneau (385)]

4) Ed. with the commentary of Bhaṭṭa Śobhākara, in Śikṣā-saṃgraha. – Benares, 1889, pp. 394-449. – (Ben. S. S. 10).

5) *Nāradī-śikṣā Sāmagāna-svara-viṣayako Nārada-viracito granthaḥ.* – Meerut : Svami Maschine Press, Saṃ. 1963 (1906). 1, 31, 1 pp. [IO : Ptd. Bks. Cat. 1953, p. 1719 (San B 508.d)]

6) Ed. by Dattatreya Sastri Paranjape *(Nāradīya Śikṣā Bhāṣā Ṭīkāsameta)*, with a Hindi translation. – Lahore : Sangita Press, 1909. viii, 75 pp. [BM : Ptd. Bks. Cat. 1906-1928. 667 (14090.b.48); IO : Ptd. Bks. Cat. 1953, p. 1719 (12 B 15)]

7) Ed. by Tulasirama Svami. – Meeruṭ : Svami Press, Saṃ. 1973 (1916). 26 pp. [IO : Ptd. Bks. Cat. 1953, p. 1719 (San C 163.m)]

8) Ed. by R. Narayanaswamy Dikshiṭa, with the Vivaraṇa of Bhaṭṭa Śobhākara and Vivaraṇa-prakāśa of the editor, on the basis of Satyavrata Samasrami's edition and five other Mss. in the magazine of the Mysore Sanskrit College, *Śrīmanmahārāja Saṃskṛta Mahāpāṭhaśālā Patrikā*, vols. 19-22 (1943-46), Mysore. 89, vii pp. Also issued separately. – Mysore : Maharaja's Sanskrit College, 1949. [Adyar (H05sk MSC 19-22); SAI (87/776*)]

9) *Sāmavedīyā Nāradīyā Śikṣā*, with the Vivaraṇa of Śobhākara-miśra. – Datiya (M. P.) : Pītāmbarāpīṭha Saṃskṛta Pariṣad (Srirama Press, Jhansi), 1964. vi. 82 pp.

10) Ed. by Pitambara Jha Sharma, with commentary *Saralā*, Tarakeswara, Hugli. – Calcutta : Sanskrit Book Depot, Saṃ. 2037 (1980). 5, 15, 94, 2 pp.

11) Ed. by Usha R. Bhise, with the commentary of Bhaṭṭa Śobhākara, translation and explanatory notes in English. – Poona : Bhandarkar Oriental Research Institute, 1986. 145 pp. – (Research Unit Publications 8). [SAI (ind 51 D 589/2155)]

12) Also included in: Chāndogya Brāhmaṇam. – Kumbakonam : Govinda Deekshithar Punya Smarana Samiti (ed.). Part II. 1981. Appendix pp. 1-8. [(SAI ***)].

– C. Vivaraṇa of Bhaṭṭa Śobhākara.

Beginning:

प्रणम्य परमात्मानमृक्सामस्वरविग्रहम्।
मुनिना नारदेनोक्तां शिक्षां व्याख्यातुमिष्यते॥

अथ सामसंहिताध्ययनादनन्ततरम्। अत इति संहिताध्ययनात् पूर्वं पठितशिक्षाध्याहारः। शिक्ष्यते मन्त्रब्राह्मणस्वरूपं सम्यगध्ययनपाठश्च क्षिप्रं सर्वेषां शास्त्राणामृक्सामगतानां निश्चयं सम्यक्स्वरूपप्रतिपत्तिं वेदे मयोच्यमानं जानीयादिति भगवान्नारदः सामान्येन शिष्यं प्रत्याह सामान्यभूत ओंकारगतस्वरूपः उच्चनीचविशेषे उच्चतरे उच्चतमे नीचे नीचविशेषे नीचतरे नीचतमे च स्थानाभिव्यज्ञ्यमानः स्वरान्यत्वं नानास्वरतां प्रतिपाद्यत इत्यर्थः॥ अथ वा सर्वेषां वाग्भिर्निश्चयमिति वा पाठः। कथयामीति पूर्वपठितशिक्षामाहारयिष्यते मन्त्रब्राह्मणवाक्यानि ऋगादिस्वराणां विवेक उच्यते॥ १॥

End:

शुश्रूषारहिता विद्या यद्यपि मेधागुणैः समुपयाति।
वन्ध्येव यौवनवती न तस्य विद्या फलवती भवति॥ २८॥
द्यूतं पुस्तकवाद्यं (-वाच्यं) च नाटकेषु च सक्तिका।
स्त्रियस्तन्द्रा च निद्रा च विद्याविघ्नकराणि षट्॥ २९॥
यथा व्याघ्री हरेत् पुत्रान् दंष्ट्राभिर्न च पीडयेत्।
भीता पतनभेदाभ्यां तद्वद् वर्णान् प्रयोजयेत्॥ ३०॥

एवं वर्णाः प्रयोक्तव्या नाव्यक्ता न च पीडिताः ।
सम्यग् वर्णप्रयोगेण ब्रह्मलोके महीयते ॥ ३१ ॥

शुनी व्याघ्री विडाली चाचिरजातापत्या दन्तैरपीडयन्ती अपत्यानि नयत्यानयति च । यदि न सम्यक् प्रतिगृह्णाति तदा पतन्ति । यदि वातिबलेन गृह्णाति तदा भेद उपघातो ऽपत्यानां भवतीति । एवं वर्णोच्चारणं कार्यम् । व्यक्ताः स्फुटाः । प्रयोगास्तु जपे स्वाध्याये ऽध्यापने चेति ॥ द्वितीयस्याष्टमी कण्डिका ॥ इति श्रीभट्टशोभाकरविरचिते नारदीयशिक्षाविवरणे द्वितीयः प्रपाठकः समाप्तः । इति शिक्षाभाष्यं समाप्तम् ॥

Adyar D I 865 (35 C 137). 43 fol. = Adyar I, p. 52b. Dated V.S. 1945, Āṣāḍha Śukla 6, Guruvāra; copied by Tripāṭhi Kṛṣṇa-śaṃkara-lakṣmī-rāma of Baroda.

Ānandāśrama 8033, 8034.

Baroda 9803(b). PL. Mal. 80 fol. 600 Grantha-s (with text). = CLB I, p. 29.

IO 4947 (Burnell 496c). Gr. 26 fol. Written ca. A.D. 1877.

L 9. 23 fol. (720 Grantha-s). Dated V.S. 1634.

Mad. Uni. R. A. S. 173(i).

MT 3345(b). Gr. 18 fol. (126-43). Incomplete. Transcribed in 1920-21 from a Ms. of Sāmavedam Narayana Sastrigaru, Bobbili.

Oppert II 761. Belonged to Ghanapathi Shingaracharyar of Alasur, Madurantakam Taluk.

PUL I, p. 21 (no.78). 23 fol. Dated V.S. 1638. (Bhāṣya).

PUL I, p. 21 (no.79). 19 fol. 400 Grantha-s (called Bhāṣya). Incomplete.

RASB II 1498 (G 1375B). 35 fol. 820 Grantha-s. Dated V.S. 1725.

SBD 2059. 12 fol. (6-17). Incomplete.

Wai II 10309. 41 fol.

Wai II 10310. 8 fol. Incomplete.

Ptd.: Together with the text. See above.

[NCC X 58b and 295b]

*NĀRĀYAṆA (नारायण)

of Āhitāgni-gṛha (Akkittari), in Kerala.

– C. called Dīpa-prabhā on the Ṛgveda-sarvānukramaṇī. MT 3834.

*NĀRĀYAṆA (नारायण)

of Vātsya-gotra, in Kerala.

– Pada-pradīpikā.

*NĀRĀYAṆA DĪKṢITA (नारायणदीक्षित)

– Yājuṣa-vākya-paṅkti. Trav. Uni. 10165. PL. Mal. 1000 Grantha-s.

*NĀRĀYAṆA (PAṄGU) (नारायण /-पङ्गु)

– Ṛgveda-paribhāṣā-kārikā or Cāturjñāna-paribhāṣā.
Adyar D I 785. BORI D I i.44. RASB II 287.

[NCC X 77b]

*NĀRĀYAṆA (-BHAṬṬA) (नारायणभट्ट)
of Melpattur (A.D. 1560-1646).
– Sūkta-ślokāḥ. Ptd.: in the *Journal of Oriental Research*, Madras, vol. VIII, pp. 358-71. See Ṛgveda-sūkta-varga-saṃkhyā.

[NCC X 72b-73b]

*NĀRĀYAṆA (-BHAṬṬA) (नारायणभट्ट)
– C. on the Napara-tapara of Śaurisūnu alias Śaurisūri. Adyar D I 859.

[NCC X 85b]

*NĀRĀYAṆA (-BHAṬṬA) (नारायणभट्ट)
– Sapta-lakṣaṇa. Oppert I 2093. 2094.

[NCC X 93b]

*(ŚEṢA) NĀRĀYAṆA (शेष-नारायण)
– Aniṅgya-lakṣaṇa (Akhaṇḍa-mañjarī) Adyar D XIII 45 (VB 120a).
– Tapara (Sarva-tapara). Adyar D I 824.
– Natānta-padāni or Napara(-prakaraṇa). Adyar D I 858. = Adyar I, p. 50a.
– Sarva-napara-lakṣaṇa (same as the above ?) Adyar I, p. 54a.

[NCC X 69ab]

*NĀRĀYAṆA-SŪRI DEVA (नारायणसूरि देव)
– Dakṣiṇadvāra-nirṇaya. Baroda 9175.

*NĀRĀYAṆĀCĀRYA (नारायणाचार्य)
– Kanakāvalī. Ptd.: in *The Adyar Library Bulletin*, vol. 30 (1966).

*NĀRĀYAṆĀVADHĀNIN (नारायणावधानिन्)
Son of Vādāṭi Timmāvadhānin.
– C. on Vilaṅghya. Adyar D I 974. IO 4491-95. MT 523(b).

[NCC X 104ab]

756 NIDĀNA-SŪTRA (निदानसूत्र)
See A. Parpola, *The Śrautasūtras of Lāṭyāyana* ... , vol. I 1, p. 53.
Adyar D XIII 251 (VB 391a). PL. Gr. 81 fol. (chs. 3-30)
PUL II. App. p. 11 (no.166). 60 fol. (with Chando-viciti). Photo-copy from Baroda.
PUL II. App. p. 12 (no.183). 95 fol. Copy from Kashmir.
SBD 4105. 69 fol. Dated V.S. 1815.
Trav. Uni. 5755 E.

Ptd.: ed. by Satyavrata Samasrami (Sāmavediyam ṛṣiproktam idam) in the Sanskrit journal *Uṣā*. – Calcutta : Satya Press, Saṃ. 1953 (1896), vol. II, pt. 11. 169 pp. [Kashi Vidyapeetha (Saṃ. 891.212 Ni. 36)]
Also ed. by K. N. Bhatnagar – *Nidāna-sūtra* of Patañjali, with an introduction, a fragmentary commentary and indices. – Lahore, 1939 (? 1933). iii, iii, ii, 70, 189, 52 pp.
Reprinted : Delhi : Meharchand Lachhmandas, 1971. [SAI (83/1001*)]

[NCC X 128b]

757 NIDĀNA-SŪTRA (निदानसूत्र)
or Pratihāra-sūtra of Kātyāyana.
Triv. Cur. II 21.

[NCC X 129a]

758 NIDĀNA-SŪTRA (निदानसूत्र)

– C. Adyar I, p. 50b (2 Mss.) (Vṛtti).

TD 1691. TD 1937 (fragment).

Oppert II 389. Belonged to Venkatarama Srauti of Mullandram, N. Arcot Dist.

759 NIDĀNA-SŪTRA (निदानसूत्र)

SV. in ten Prapāṭhaka-s ascribed to Patañjali, probably a redaction of the *Ārṣeyakalpa*.

[NCC X 129a]

760 NIDĀNA-SŪTRA-VṚTTI (निदानसूत्रवृत्ति)

of Tātaprasāda. Ptd.: at the end of Nidāna-sūtra, ed. by Bhatnagar.

761 NIDHANA-SŪTRA (निधनसूत्र)

SV. 10th Paṭala of the *Upagrantha-sūtra*.

– C. Vṛtti, of Varadarāja.

Burnell 10b. The same as TD 2044. See *Journal of the University of Bombay*, 35 (NS), pt. ii. Sept. 1966. Arts no.41, p. 97.

[NCC X 129b]

762 NIDHANĀNI (निधनानि)

Mysore ND II 3581 (A 642/ 8). Kan. 4 fol. (33-36). Extract no. 196. Dated 6.8.1919.

763 NĪTI-MAÑJARĪ (नीतिमञ्जरी)

of Dyādviveda (ca. 1494).

See *JRAS* 1909, pp. 127-36. For Mss, see NCC X 160b.

Ptd.: Ed. by Sitaram Jayaram Joshi, with introduction, notes and appendices. – Banaras : Harihar Mandir, 1933. lxiv, 348, 22 pp. [Adyar (H 210 Dya NMx=); SAI (ind 54 E 104)]

[NCC X 160b]

*NĪLAKAṆṬHA (नीलकण्ठ)

– C. Ṭīkā on the Svarāṅkuśa of Jayanta-svāmin. According to the NCC it is composed in A.D. 1749. But G. V. Devasthali gives the date as V.S. 1671. Bombay Uni. 13-14. BORI 385 of 1883-84. Trav. Uni. 1566.

Ptd.: See below under Svarāṅkuśa.

[NCC X 170a]

*NṚSIṂHA-DATTA (नृसिंहदत्त)

– C. on Sāma-tantra – Sāma-tantra-vṛtti-sāra. Max Müller Mem. XVIII. 66 fol.

*NṚSIṂHA-SŪRI (नृसिंहसूरि)

Son of Liṅgāvadhānin.

– C. Vyākhyā on Āraṇya-śikṣā. Adyar D I 734. = Adyar I, p. 52a.

[NCC X 209b]

*(NEMĀNI) BHAIRAVĀVADHĀNIN (नेमानिभैरवावधानिन्)
See Bhairavāvadhānin (Nemāni or Setūni).

764 NAIGA or NAIGEYA (-PARIŚIṢṬA) (नैग / नैगेय /-परिशिष्ट)
Anukramaṇī of the *Sāmaveda* in the Naigeya Śākhā. See Naigeyārcika, Naigeyārṣa-daivata, etc.

Baroda 9915(b). PL. Gr. 17 fol. 356 Grantha-s. = CLB I, p. 30.
BORI 112 and 113 of 1879-80.
RASB II 1313 (G 751). 23 fol. 350 Grantha-s. Dated V.S. 1704.
RASB II 1314 (G 1075). 19 fol. Dated V.S. 1707.
Trav. Uni. 2915 E. PL. Gr. 250 Grantha-s. Incomplete.

[NCC X 227a]

765 NAIGEYA(-SŪTRA) (नैगेयसूत्र)
of Gobhila.
Oudh III.4.
Oudh XIII 26 (no.12). 46 pp. 500 Grantha-s. Dated A.D. 1844. Belonged to Pandit Kesava Prasada of Unao.

[NCC X 227a]

766 NAIGEYA-RKṢU-DAIVATA (नैगेयर्क्षुदैवत)
Alph. List Beng. Govt. p. 59 (2 Mss.) → Naigeya-pariśiṣṭa.

[NCC X 227a]

767 NAIGEYA-PARIŚIṢṬA (नैगेयपरिशिष्ट)
or Naigeyānām ṛkṣu ārṣam or daivatam. In two Prapāṭhaka-s, on seers and deities of the Ṛk-s in *Sāmaveda*. Cf. *ABORI, vol. 39.*

Beginning:

अथार्षेयमार्चिकस्य। अग्ने त्वमग्ने ऽग्निरेहि त्वामग्ने। भरद्वाजो बार्हस्पत्यो ऽग्निं मेधातिथिः काण्वः प्रेष्ठमुशना काव्यस्त्वं नः सुदीतिर्बार्हद्गिरसः सौहोत्रः पुरुमीढो वा। आ ते वत्सः काण्वो ऽग्ने। सुमित्रो वाध्र्यश्वो वध्र्यश्वो वा आनूपः ॥ १॥

वेदविद्भ्यो नमस्कृत्य नैगेभ्यस्तु विशेषतः ।
तृचर्चार्धर्चपादानां तेषां वक्ष्यामि दैवतम् ॥

End:

आशुरध्याय ऐन्द्रो बृहस्पते बृहस्पतिः प्रथमे ऽभिगोत्राणि बृहस्पतिः पञ्चमे दृक्षिणा षष्ठे मरुतो ऽष्टमे वरुणो नवम आदित्या दशम उद्धर्षय देवा अष्टमे मारुत्युत्तमामीषाँ प्रथमाप्री देवी कङ्काग्निरष्टमे वि रक्षस्तृतीया संग्रामाशीः मर्माण्युत्तरे संग्रामाशिषामैन्द्री मध्ये वर्म प्रथमे सोमो द्वितीये वरीयस्तृतीये देवाश्चतुर्थे एकादशे चाग्निः सप्तमे भद्रं द्वे वैश्वदेव्यौ ॥

Adyar D I 888 (35 B 114). 23 fol. = Adyar I, p. 50b.
Alwar 274.
BHU B 2345 (D 11/632). 15 fol. Dated V.S. 1690.
BHU B 1140 (D 11/649). 26 fol. Dated V.S. 1833.

BORI 112 of 1879-80. = BORI D I i.152. 32 fol. Dated V.S. 1822.
BORI 113 of 1879-80. = BORI D I i.148. 22 fol. Dated V.S. 1717.
BORI 43 of 1884-86. = BORI D I i.151. 21 fol.
BORI 47 of 1884-87. = BORI D I i.150. 20 fol. Dated V.S. 1675. Copied by Rāmakṛṣṇa.
BORI 58 of 1886-92. = BORI D I i.149. 25 fol. Dated V.S. 1720. Copied by Mādhavajī, son of Sūrajī.
I. 796. 17 fol. 400 Grantha-s. Dated V.S. 1674.
Oxf. II 855(1) (Ms. Wilson 375). 13 fol. Dated A.D. 1582. = Oxf. 377b (no.375).
Oxf. II 857(5) (Ms. Wilson 466). 22 fol. (13-34). 19th century. = Oxf. 383b (no.466).
Peters. II, p. 180 (no.74). 11 fol.
Peters. II, p. 180 (no.75). 17 fol.
Peters. III, p. 385 (no.43).
Peters. IV, p. 3 (no.58). Extract pp. 4-6.
Rgb. 47. 20 fol. Dated V.S. 1675.
Stein p. 5 (no. 76). 15 fol. Incomplete. Dated V.S. 1715. Title: Naigeyārcikānukrama.
Trav. Uni. 2915 E. PL. Gr. 250 Grantha-s. Incomplete.
Weber 315 (Weber 13, 9). From Bodlei. Wils. 466.

Ptd.:
1) *Indische Studien*, vol. XVII (1885).
2) Ed. by S. R. Sehgal, *Naigeyaśākhānukramaṇī* – belonging to the *Sāmaveda*, critically edited from Mss. with copious variants from Vedic works and translation. – Delhi : Munshiram Manoharlal, 1966. 10, 104 pp. [NL (180 Jc 96 290); SAI (ind 51 D 1; ind 71 C 442); SKGI (Rg IX 150)]

[NCC X 227a]

768 NAIGEYĀNĀM ṚKṢU ĀRṢAM (DAIVATAM) (**नैगेयानामृक्षु आर्षम् / दैवतम्**)
→ Naigeya-pariśiṣṭa.

[NCC X 227a]

769 NAIGEYĀRCIKA (**नैगेयार्चिक**)
Adyar D I 888 → Naigeyapariśiṣṭa.

[NCC X 227a]

770 NAIGEYĀRCIKĀNUKRAMA (**नैगेयार्चिकानुक्रम**)
A Pariśiṣṭa of the *Sāmaveda*. Cf. Naigeya-pariśiṣṭa.
Jammu RSRI p. 24 (no. 5271). 15 fol. Dated V.S. 1715 (Stein 76).
Stein p. 5 (no. 76). 15 fol. Dated V.S. 1715. Incomplete.

771 NAIGEYĀRCIKĀNUKRAMA (**नैगेयार्चिकानुक्रम**)
of Ananta, son of Bhīma. Three Paṭala-s, on seers, metres and deities of the Ṛk-s in the *Sāmaveda*.

Beginning:

नमस्कृत्वा तु पितरं गुरुं चैव गणेश्वरम्।
आर्चिकस्य तु वक्ष्यामि छन्दश्चैवार्षदैवतम्॥
जन्मज्ञानार्थसिद्धीनां हेतवो हि त्रयः स्मृताः ।

छन्दांसि छन्दसश्चैव नैगेय्या ऋषिदैवतम्॥
उद्धृत्यानुक्रमः प्रोक्तः मुखसंपत्तिहेतवे।
मादानन्देभ्यन्तरश्च सौराष्ट्रः कौथुमः सुधीः॥
भीमस्तस्यात्मजो ऽनन्तस्तेनानुक्रमितो ह्ययम्।

अथार्चिकस्यार्षच्छन्दोदैवतान्यनुक्रमिष्यामः। ऋच्यार्षं छन्दो दैवतमुपदेशेन। पाददैवतं यथालिङ्गं प्रतीयात्। नैद्यं ... कं वा वैश्वदेविकम् बहुदैवतम्। विश्वेदेवलिङ्गं वा यत्र स्यात्। ऋषिर्दर्शनात् स्तोदथं ददर्शेति। छन्द आच्छादनाद्यद् देवानाच्छादयन्तीति। देवता स्तवनात् स्तोत्रशस्त्रै रूपन्त इत्यृचाम् आर्षेयच्छन्दोदैवतविद्यजनाध्ययनाभ्यां श्रेयः प्राप्नोति। विपरीते विपर्ययस्तस्मादेतानि विद्यात् ...

End:

यो नः स्वो अरण इति पङ्क्ती पथ्ये स्वस्तिन इति विराड् बृहस्पते बृहस्पतिरसौ यामारुत्यमी प्रथमाप्री देवी। विरक्षस्तृतीया संग्रामाशीर्मर्माण्युत्तरे संग्रामाशिषा। भद्रं द्वे वैश्वदेव्यौ वैश्वदेव्यौ। इति नैगेयार्चिकस्यानुक्रमे तृतीयः प्रपाठकः समाप्तः॥

Oxf. II 855(16) (Ms. Wilson 375). 16 fol. (89-104). 18th century. = Oxf. 378a (no.375).
SBD 2360. 17 fol. Dated V.S. 1693. (Naigamārcikānukrama ! Corrected by a different hand as Naigeyārcikānukrama).

[NCC X 227a]

772 NAIGEYĀRṢA-DAIVATA (नैगेयार्षदैवत)
An alternative title of the *Naigeya-pariśiṣṭa*.
BORI D I i.148.

[NCC X 227a]

773 NYĀYA-PAÑCĀŚAT or JAṬĀ-SAṂDHI-LAKṢAṆA (न्यायपञ्चाशत् / जटासंधिलक्षण)
Mysore ND II 3595 (B 600/ 9). Na. 4 fol. (34-37). Extract no. 200.
Oppert I 7141. Belonged to Pola Lakshmanavadhani of Vijayanagaram.
Oppert I 7195. Belonged to Ivattur Nandikesvara Sastri of Vijayanagaram.

See Jaṭā-nyāya-pañcāśat.

[NCC X 250a]

*PAṄGU NĀRĀYAṆA (पङ्गुनारायण)
See Nārāyaṇa (Paṅgu).

774 PAÑCA-KRAMA (पञ्चक्रम)
Mysore ND II 3596 (P 4906/43). PL. Na. 1 fol. (126). Extract no. 201. Partly corresponds to the *Upalekha*.

775 PAÑCADAŚA-LAKṢAṆA (पञ्चदशलक्षण)
Mysore ND II 3597 (P 4906/37). PL. Na. 1 fol. (125). Extract no. 202. (Cf. p. 33 of the Pada-gāḍha, Srirangam edition).

776 PAÑCA-PAṬALIKĀ (पञ्चपटलिका)
of Paribabhrava. Probably the same as the *Atharva-vedīya-pañcapaṭalikā* the opening line of which reads: *uktānuktasya yaṃ nyāyaṃ provāca "paribabhravaḥ"*.

SBD 2074. 27 fol. Dated V.S. 1734. Title: Atharvaṇa-lakṣaṇa-grantha-saṃgraha.
SBD 4225. 9 fol.

777 PAÑÇA-PĀṬHAḤ PAURUṢĀDHYĀYAḤ (पञ्चपाठः पौरुषाध्यायः)
Sub-title: Śukla-yajurveda-mādhyandina-śākhīyaḥ. Five Vikṛti-s of Puruṣa-sūkta (31st Adhyāya of the *Vājasaneyi-saṃhitā)* with Hindi introduction and commentary. Cf. Puruṣa-sūkta-jaṭā-pāṭha. SBD 53419, 53650

Ptd.: ed. by Yugala Kishora Misra (of Sampurnananda Samskrit University, Varanasi). Calcutta : Seth Nandalal Bajoriya Charity Trust, 1976. ka-tha, 72 pp. [SAI (ind 50 B 188/2115kp)]

778 PAÑCA-LAKṢAṆA (पञ्चलक्षण)
Mysore ND II 3598 (P 4906/26). PL. Na. 1 fol. (121). Extract no. 203. (Cf. p. 18 of the *Pada-gādha*, Srirangam edition).

779 PAÑCA-VARṆA-KRAMA-NIDĀNA and C. (पञ्चवर्णक्रमनिदान)
Title given to the *Pāriśikṣā*, perhaps on the basis of the expression *pañcavarṇakramāṇāṃ nidānaṃ pravakṣye*, in the opening verse of the commentary *Yājuṣa-bhūṣaṇa* of Cakra. Only the catalogue gives this title, though the Ms. reads *Pāriśikṣā* as the title. See below under Pāriśikṣā.

Mysore ND II 3599 (P 2326/ 3). PL. Gr. 44 fol. Extract no. 204.
Mysore ND II 3600 (P 2326/ 4). PL. Gr. 44 fol. Extract no. 205.

780 PAÑCA-VARṆA-KRAMA-LAKṢAṆA (पञ्चवर्णक्रमलक्षण)
› Pāriśikṣā.
Hamburg StUB (cod.Palmbl. III 8/133) → Veda-lakṣaṇa (HB).

781 PAÑCA-SAṂDHI (पञ्चसंधि)
› Maitrāyaṇīya-saṃhitā-ghana-pāṭha.

782 PAÑCĀŚAD-ANUKRAMAṆIKĀ (पञ्चाशदनुक्रमणिका)
of Subrahmaṇya Śāstri. An index of catch words for the *Taittirīya-saṃhitā*, its Brāhmaṇa, Āraṇyaka, and Kāṭhaka.

Beginning:

प्रणम्य गुरुपादाब्जं श्रीसुब्रह्मण्यशर्मणा।
क्रियते बालबोधाय श्रीपञ्चाशदनुक्रमः ॥
संहिता ब्राह्मणं चारण्यकं काठकमेव च।

अशीतिर्द्ध्यधिका प्रोक्ताः प्रपाठा याजुषा इह ॥

कृष्णयजुःसंहितायाः पञ्चाशदनुक्रमणिका प्रारम्भः -- इषे त्वोर्जे। यज्ञस्य घोषदसि। वि वयं रुहेम। शुन्धध्वं दैव्याय। कर्मणे वां देवेभ्यः।

Ptd.: ed. by K. Subrahmanya Sastri of Udayarpallyam (in Grantha script). – Nadukaveri : Sri Jagadguru Press, 1879. 93, 8 pp. (Title page: Kṛṣṇayajuḥsaṃhitā-brāhmaṇāraṇakakāṭhakānāṃ pañcāśadanukramaṇikā, brahmapurīnāmakaśrīmad-uḍayārpāḻayavāsinā śrīcidambarasthabrahmavidyāpatrādhipaśrīnivāsamakhinām antevāsinā śrīsubrahmaṇyaśāstriṇā vedam abhyasyatāṃ bālānām upakārāya ... hemalambi – kārttikkai). [Adyar (PH 215.4 Sub PA); BM : Ptd. Bks. Cat. 1892-1906. 675, 805 (14092.b.78,2)].

783 PAÑJIKĀ or PADA-PAÑJIKĀ (पञ्जिका / पदपञ्जिका)

Name of the commentary of Mātṛsūnu on the *Ṛgvidhāna*. CLB I, p. 24.

[NCC XI 83a]

784 PAÑJIKĀ or ŚIKṢĀ-PAÑJIKĀ or VEDĀṄGA-ŚIKṢĀ-PAÑJIKĀ (पञ्जिका / शिक्षापञ्जिका / वेदाङ्गशिक्षापञ्जिका)

Name of the commentary of Dharaṇī-dhara on the *Pāṇinīya-śikṣā*.

[NCC XI 83a]

*PAṬṬĀBHIRĀMA (पट्टाभिराम)

Son of Nārāyaṇa of Bhāradvāja-gotra and native of Koṇḍalūru.

– Varṇa-mālikā, MT 1165(d). Mysore ND II 3754.

*PATAÑJALI (पतञ्जलि)

– Nidāna-sūtra. See above.

[NCC XI 89b]

785 PADA-KĀRIKĀ-RATNAMĀLĀ (पदकारिकारत्नमाला)

On certain phonetic peculiarities, the number of words, Visarga-s, Anusvāra-s, Veṣṭana-s and words ending with the letter "n", etc. of the *Vājasaneyi-saṃhitā*, in 40 chapters. It is attributed to Śaṃkarācārya in the colophon.

Beginning:

श्रीकान्तं सितरुचिराजितोत्तमाङ्गं गौरीशं गुरुपदमम्बुजालयं च।
सन्नत्वा सुललितलक्षणं पदानामाचार्यैः प्रकटितमेव वाचयामः ॥

End:

अन्तस्व सवितः पुनर्यत् त्रिरेफं परो भवेत्।
विसर्जनीयमेव स्यादभावे वेष्टनं भवेत्।
इयं वेदिश्च वाजाय स्वाहा द्वौ च विहाय च।
अभावो वेष्टनस्तत्र त्वन्यथा वेष्टनं भवेत्।
तथा चान्तः परार्धश्च वर्जयित्वान्यथाचवृत्।

इति श्रीशंकराचार्यकृतौ वाजसनेयसंहितायां पदकारिकारत्नमाला नाम (एक-) चत्वारिंशदध्यायः ॥

Brl. p. 37 (no.CXXII) = IO 4523.
IM 2787. 3 fol. Incomplete.
IO 4523 (Burnell 290). 81 pp. Copied in A.D. 1861 at Madras from Taylor I 206.
MD 921. PL. Gr. 136 pp. .... (= Skt. Texts on Phonetics, pp. 433-530).
MD 922. 110 pp.
Mysore ND II 3760 (P 3325/ 2). PL. Gr. 6 fol. (179-84). Incomplete. Title: Vājasaneyi-krama-kārikā.
PUL II. App. p. 12 (no.185). 64 fol. Incomplete (up to ch. 27).
RASB II 907 (G 1269). 44 fol. (first fol. is missing). 900 Grantha-s. Title: Vājasaneyi-saṃhitā-pada-kārikā-ratna-mālā.
Śg. I 18. 110 pp. Extract pp. 66-67.
Sūcīpattra 57.
Taylor I, p. 206.

[NCC XI 96b]

786 PADA-KRAMA (पदक्रम)

IM 1780. 44-54 fol. Krama-pāṭha of the 16th chapter of the VS. (Rudrādhyāya).

[NCC XI 96b]

787 PADA-KRAMA-LAKṢAṆA (पदक्रमलक्षण)

Sūcīpattra 115.

[NCC XI 96b]

788 PADA-KRAMA-SADANA (पदक्रमसदन)

Name of the commentary of Māhiṣeya on the *Taittirīya-prātiśākhya*.

Ptd.: Madras, 1930. See above under Taittirīya-prātiśākhya.

[NCC XI 96b]

789 PADA-GĀḌHA (पदगाढ)

Ascribed to Śākalya or to Śaunaka. A treatise consisting of words occurring in the *Ṛgveda*, and presenting certain common peculiarities, regarding accent, endings, etc.

Beginning:

इदानीं सर्वसमानानि। अमितौजा अङ्गिरा नीचावया गभीरवेपा बृहच्छ्रवा नोधा दमूना नवेदा अद्वयो दीर्घतमा पृथुपाजा नृमणा जातवेदा इति सर्वत्र विसर्जनीयाः।

End:

कुर्मस्ते। आयुरहरहर्जायते। आ बाह्वोः। द्वे ते चक्रे। सुमङ्गलीरियम्। दैवी पूर्तिः। एह गमन्। वज्रेण हि। यावया वृक्यम्। कीदृङ्ङिन्द्रः। अर्वाग् देवाः। अथा हि वाम्। अथासपत्नी। अहमस्मि सहमाना। बृहस्पतिर्नयतु। इति सप्ताशीतिरथकारेण। अन्यत्र धकारः।

(यानि यदि यदा यो यं यस्य तस्य हि यद्यथा।

यन्ति येनाभि ये याश्च दृष्टोदात्तं पदं भवेत्॥)
रेतो रेजश्च रेजं च रेजन्ती रुद्र रेवतीः।
रूपैश्च रुशमासैश्च रुद्रैश्च रिरिषिष्ट च॥
राजन् राष्ट्रं च राशिश्च रायो राय रथर्यसि।
रराति रपसो राज्ञो रभस्व रभसद् रथे॥
ररावाथ रराव्णां च रवथेन रपांसि च।
रथो रजप्रवादैश्च रेफाद्याः सप्तविंशतिः॥

Ānandāśrama 391. 2571.

Baroda 2237. 55 fol. 1200 Grantha-s. = CLB I, p. 30. Col.: Sarvatra-lakṣaṇa.

Baroda 5997. 20 fol. 400 Grantha-s. = CLB I, p. 30.

Baroda 10908. 18 fol. 100 Grantha-s. = CLB I, p. 30. Incomplete. Copied by Haraśāstri Paṭavardhana in Avantikā. (atha padalakṣaṇāni | dvitā dadhus taṃ gandharvā ... juṣasva naḥ prāk ghṛtācīsvareṇa | pra vāṃ ghṛtācīvarjam).

Baroda 11600. 11 fol. 200 Grantha-s. Dated Śaka 1702. = CLB I, p. 31. (ajohavī trīṇi rājā ... jaganvān ... anyatra jaghanvān).

BHU C 4802 (D II/650). 14 fol.

BISM p. 152 (54/953). 7 fol. (janitvāvagṛhyaṃ ... iti sapta dadhātana). Title: Pada-ratna.

BISM p. 152 (54/692). 6 fol. (dvitādadhus taṃ gandharvāḥ ...).

BISM p. 44 (36/1774). 8 fol. (1-7, 16). Samāna-pada-s only → the first paras of the Cāturjñāna.

BORI 16 of 1879-80. = BORI D I i.46. 29 fol.

BORI 75 of 1884-87. = BORI D I i.45. 48 fol.

Calcutta Skt. Coll. I 525 (124). 73 fol. Title: Ṛgvedānukramaṇikā. (... dve yajñiyā svarantā ... ṣaṇṇavati).

Calcutta Skt. Coll. I 527. 19 fol.

Deccan College 4081. 10 fol. An abridged version.

Deccan College 5375. 40 fol. Dated Śaka 1713.

Deccan College 8507. 44 fol. Dated Śaka 1713.

GJKSV 34393. 6 fol. 75 sections. Title: Sarvatra-lakṣaṇa.

Gough p. 31 (2 Mss.).

Hoshiarpur p. 50 (no.1313). 19 fol. 300 Grantha-s. Dated Śaka 1718. Incomplete. Extract pp. 79-80. Title: Sarvatra-lakṣaṇa.

Hoshiarpur p. 51 (no.26). 51 fol. 717 Grantha-s. Dated Śaka 1759.

IM 2389. 40 fol.

IM 2506. 10 fol.

IM 2579. 6 fol. Pada-gāḍha-vyākhyā is written by a later hand. (idānīṃ trīṇi saṃkhyākāni - up to - saptasaṃkhyākāni |).

IM 2583. 6 fol. (kva nūnaṃ ... ṣaṭ padakāle ganta hrasveṇa | End.: otyamahva ekaṃ dve tasthatuḥ dhīrāḥ sarvatra visarjanīyāḥ |).

IO 66 (1636d). 29 fol. The same as in the printed edition.

L 786. 74 fol. 740 Grantha-s.

Mysore ND II 3603 (C 3764/ 1). Kan. 15 fol. Incomplete. No beginning. Extract 207. The text varies from the Bonta-lakṣaṇa.

N-W P VII 6 (no.23). 17 fol. Belonged to Pandit Baladikshita Bhagavati, Benares.

Oxf. CS c.25(6). 7 fol. (triḥ saubhagatvam ... RV I 34.5).

P 4.

PUL I, p. 22 (no.98). 41 fol. Dated V.S. 1834 (= IO 66).

PUL I, p. 22 (no.99). 10 fol. (diff.)

Rajapur 383 (Baiṭhāni).

R. A. Sastri III, p. 240.

RASB II 258 (G 2332). 30 fol. 720 Grantha-s.

RASB II 259 (G 54) = L 786.

RASB II 260 (G 1138). 36 fol. 760 Grantha-s. Dated V.S. 1684.

RASB II 261 (G 539). 42 fol. 960 Grantha-s. Dated Śaka 1663.

Rgb. 75.

Rice 12.

SB p. 8 (no.80). 25 fol. (2-26). 825 Grantha-s. = SBD 3931.

SBD 0593. 3 fol. Dated V.S. 1840.

SBD 3931. 25 fol. (2-26). Incomplete. Dated Śaka 1651.

SBD 4247. 11 fol. Dated V.S. 1966. Catalogued as Saṃhitā-lakṣaṇa-pada-gāḍha-lakṣaṇa. (kva nūnaṃ kaddho ...).

SBD 4268. 33 fol. (2-34). Incomplete. Dated Śaka 1697.

SBD 4283. 4 fol. Incomplete. Catalogued as Sarva-samānāni.

SBD 53757. 6 fol. Dated Śaka 1723. Title: Pada-sarvatra-lakṣaṇa. 63 sections.

Tirupati SVUORI (427). 19 fol. (81-86; 88-100). Incomplete.

Tirupati SVUORI 8397 (2771). Incomplete.

Trav. Uni. 4908. 800 Grantha-s. Dated Śaka 1683 / V.S. 1818.

Trav. Uni. 4916. 800 Grantha-s.

Trav. Uni. 7078. 320 Grantha-s. Incomplete.

Trav. Uni. 9768. 800 Grantha-s.

Trav. Uni. 9995. 800 Grantha-s. Dated V.S. 1817 / Śaka 1682.

Trav. Uni. 21750. PL. Mal. 750 Grantha-s. Incomplete. (M.E. 961 = A.D. 1786).

Ujjain Latest Additions 417.

Visvanatha Vamana Deva, Varanasi. 42 fol. Dated V.S. 1863 / Śaka 1718.

Visvanatha Vamana Deva, Varanasi. 39 fol. Dated V.S. 1935.

Visvanatha Vamana Deva, Varanasi. 38 fol.

VSM I 425 (no.5445). 51 fol.

See Paragādi.

Ptd.: ed. by Satyavrata Samasrami, *Padagāḍhaḥ -- Ṛgvedasya -- Śākalyena maharṣiṇā, tatsamānakālīnena vā proktaḥ*, in the Sanskrit journal *Uṣā*. – Calcutta : Satya Press, Saṃ. 1951 (1895), vol. II, pts. 11-12. 77 pp. [Kashi Vidyapeetha, Varanasi (Saṃ. 891.226 Pa 36); MUL (P15:10Ā2: 3x1/15C5); BM : Ptd. Bks. Cat. 1906-1928. 1196 (14010.c.43); Emeneau (63)]

Reprinted under the title: *Ṛgvedīya-bonda-lakṣaṇa*, ed. by K. S. Venkatarama Sastri, together with *Pada-ratna*, *Svarāṅkuśa* and *Ṛgvarṇa-krama-lakṣaṇa*. – Srirangam :

Sri Vani Vilas Press, 1968. [Adyar (PH 216.2 Ven RB); UBTÜ (3 E 1286); SAI (85/1958*)]

C. Vyākhyā (actually the text only and not commentary).
IM 2579. 2583. Incomplete.

[NCC XI 97a]

790 PADA-GĀḌHA-GĀNI (पदगाढगानि)
IM 2607. 8 fol. Incomplete.

[NCC XI 97a]

791 PADA-GŪḌHA (?) (पदगूढ)
→ Pada-gāḍha.
IM 2506. 10 fol.

[NCC XI 97a]

792 PADA-CANDRIKĀ (1) (पदचन्द्रिका)
of Mukunda-bhaṭṭa. The date mentioned in the final verse corresponds to Friday 10 October 1834. The work deals with the saṃdhi-s, etc. of Vedic words. The various section titles are:

Svara-prakaraṇa (21 verses)
Visarga-prakaraṇa
Visargābhāva-prakaraṇa
Ṇatva-prakaraṇa
Ṇatvābhāva-prakaraṇa
Nānta-prakaraṇa
Mānta-prakaraṇa
Prakṛti-bhāva-prakaraṇa

Beginning:

विघ्नध्वान्तहरं वन्दे गणेशं च तथा गुरुम्।
उपकाराय सर्वेषां क्रियते पदचन्द्रिका॥
शिवा पयस्वती चैव सुखदा च मधुमतीः।
यत् तेनाधृष्टमोजस्वान् वचस्वान् शुष्मिणी तथा॥

End:

त्रयोदशे जयन्तेव तमु ज्येष्ठं तथैव च।
चतुर्दशाक्षराण्येव तद्वत् पञ्चदशाक्षरे॥
षोडशे ऽप्यजयत् तं च ज्ञेयमेव तु चाग्रिमम्।
जयाब्दे चाश्विने शुक्ले चाष्टम्यां भृगुवासरे।
गणेशकृपया चेयं समाप्ता पदचन्द्रिका॥ (१८१६९)

इति श्रीकाण्वशाखिना हिरेदिवे(इत्युपनामकेन)डर्नामकेन रघुनाथात्मजेन मुकुन्दभट्टेन विरचिता पदचन्द्रिका समाप्ता॥

Bhk. 9.
BORI 60 of A 1881-82. 6 fol.
BORI TM 220A.
GJKSV 18169. 5 fol. Copied by Mahādeva-bhaṭṭa Guḍadhe.

GJKSV 28002. 24 fol. Dated V.S. 1854. Copied by Lakṣmaṇa Khoṇḍa. It contains a different Maṅgala-śloka and more sections. Complete in six chapters.
RASB II 1528 (G 6184A). 4 fol. Incomplete.

[NCC XI 97b]

793 PADA-CANDRIKĀ (2) (पदचन्द्रिका)

About 260 verses with illustrations from the *Vājasaneyi-saṃhitā*. It is divided into sections as follows:
Svarita-prakaraṇa (20 verses)
Svara-prakaraṇa (31 verses)
Ākhyāta-prakaraṇa (21 verses)
Visarga-prakaraṇa (41 verses)
Satva-ṣatva-niṣedha-prakaraṇa (9 verses)
Lopāgama-prakaraṇa (12 verses)
Ṇatva-prakaraṇa (10 verses)
Dīrgha-prakaraṇa (25 verses)
Anusvārāgama-prakaraṇa (13 verses)
Nakāra-vikārābhāva-prakaraṇa (11 verses)
Halsaṃdhi-prakaraṇa (31 verses)
Svarasaṃdhi-prakaraṇa (26 verses)
Avagraha-prakaraṇa (9 verses. Incomplete)

Beginning:

उमापुत्रं नमस्कृत्य याज्ञवल्क्यं गुरुं तथा।
स्वरादीनां प्रबोधाय क्रियते पदचन्द्रिका॥
उच्चैरुदात्तो विज्ञेयो ऽनुदात्तो नीच एव च।
स्वरश्चोभयवान् स्वारः प्र वां स्वश्च निदर्शनम्॥

End:

द्वन्द्वानि द्विवचनान्तानि तत्र न स्यादवग्रहः।
पूर्वं पदं हलन्तं चेद्यदा न स्यात् तदैव सः॥
इन्द्राग्नी इन्द्रवायू च इन्द्राबृहस्पती तथा।
इन्द्राग्नी इन्द्रवायू च दुधुक्षन् सीपधानि च॥
दुस्तरः प्रावप्येभिश्च सासहां सुपुवे तथा।
बृहस्पती त्रैष्टुभं च त्वहोरात्रे च वावृजे॥
आसीपदं च नैषादं शर्मिष्ठाया मदन्ति च। ...

GJKSV 33169. 18 fol. Incomplete.

794 PADA-JYOTI (पदज्योति)
Beginning:

अथ पदज्योतिर्लिख्यते। अयक्ष्मा स्वधा तन्वा जनं धाजी काष्ठा प्रावृता मात्रा वषट्कारौ भेराहुती ऊर्ध्वासती भूयस्करभानावहमाना ...

End:

न संयोगात् परं स्वार्यं परसंयोगनायक।
संयुक्तस्य न्ववर्णस्य न स्वार्यं पञ्चमाक्षरम्।
इति च। इति पदज्योतिः समाप्तः ॥

ASB I iii.87 (IM 2636/1). 18 Grantha-s.

BORI 2 of 1873-74. 6 fol. (1-6). The text varies from the other Mss. It includes the text of the Galadṛk-śikṣā. From Bikaner. (A xerox-copy of this Ms. is in SAI : 87/790*).

IM 2636A. 2 fol. Begins as in Oxf. CS.

Oxf. CS c.26(2). 1 fol. (Pariśiṣṭa of SV ?). Paper dated 25.11.1903.

RASB II 1529 (G 6184B). 2 fol.

RASB II 2082 (?)

SBD 4282. 2 fol. (Veda-pada-jyotiḥ-pariśiṣṭam). 8 sections; the beginning and end are as in Oxf. CS.

[NCC XI 98a]

795 PADA-DARPAṆA (1) (पददर्पण)

Name of the commentary of Mallayārya on:

- Napara-tapara(-prakaraṇa). MT 1976(c).
- Pada-pañcaka. Hz 600. 642.
- Vilaṅghya. MD 16730. MT 1976(b). Mysore Skt. Coll., D. No. 10.
- Sapta-lakṣaṇa. Adyar D XIII 202.
- Samāna-saṃdhi. Adyar D I 1020. MT 1976(a).

[NCC XI 98a]

796 PADA-DARPAṆA (2) (पददर्पण)

of Mallayārya.

Beginning:

समानसंधेर्व्याख्यानं व्यक्तेर्नतपरस्य च।
क्रियते मल्लयार्येण पददर्पणसंज्ञकम्॥

Hz 600(a). PL. Tel. 58 fol. (with Yohi-śikṣā). Extract p. 87. Belonged to Vedam Venkatasubrahmanya Somayaji of Allur, Nellur Dist.

Mysore Skt. Coll. p. 1 = D. No.10 (1123/5). PL. Tel. 10 fol. (Vilaṅghya-vyākhyā).

R. A. Sastri II, p. 214.

[NCC XI 98a]

797 PADA-DVAYĪ (DVAIPADA) (पदद्वयी / द्वैपद)

Mysore ND II 3606 (P 4906/57). PL. Na. 2 fol. (139-40). Extract no. 209.

798 PADA-PAÑCAKA (पदपञ्चक)

On Pada text ?

Hz 627. PL. Tel. 24 fol. (with 4 other works). Belonged to Vedam Venkatasubrahmanya Somayaji of Allur, Nellur Dist.

Mysore ND II 3605 (P 8133/ 1). PL. Na. 5 fol. Extract 208 → Śamāna.

Oppert I 7198. Belonged to Ivattur Nandikesvara Sastri of Vijayanagaram.

Oppert I 7554. Belonged to S. Kodanda Ramavadhana Pantulu of Vijayanagaram.

SBD 2139. 14 fol.

Ujjain II, p. 8 (no.4219). 11 fol.

– C. Pada-darpaṇa of Mallayārya.

Hz 600(a). PL. Tel. 58 fol. (with Yohi-śikṣā) Belonged to Vedam Venkatasubrahmanya Somayaji of Allur, Nellur Dist.

Hz 642. PL. Tel. 32 fol. Belonged to Vedam Venkatasubrahmanya Somayaji of Allur, Nellur Dist.

PUL II. App. p. 12 (no.186) (Maharṣi). PL. Tel. 59 fol. 1000 Grantha-s. Cf. Adyar D I 980 for Maharṣi.

[NCC XI 98b]

799 PADA-PAÑCAKA-VYĀKHYĀ (**पदपञ्चकव्याख्या**)

SBD 52863. 176 pp. Tel. It includes Samāna-saṃdhi, Vyakti-velugu, Napa-tapara (pp. 1-170), Bhāradvāja-śikṣā with C. of Velima-kanya-sūrāvadhānin (pp. 71-164), and Yohi-prāpti (pp. 164-76) called Svara-śikṣā at the end.

800 PADA-PAÑJIKĀ or PAÑJIKĀ (**पदपञ्जिका / पञ्जिका**)

Name of the commentary of Mātṛsūnu on the *Ṛgvidhāna*.

Baroda 12251. 63 fol. 1200 Grantha-s. = CLB I, p. 24. Dated V.S. 1887.

[NCC XI 98b]

801 PADA-PRAKARAṆA (**पदप्रकरण**)

Trav. Uni. 16408 Z7. PL. Mal. 1 fol. 10 Grantha-s.

802 PADA-PRAKṚTI (**पदप्रकृति**)

BISM p. 152 (22/812). This is not a Veda-lakṣaṇa text but the Pada-pāṭha of the *Sāmaveda* (Chāndasī Saṃhitā-padaprakṛti).

[NCC XI 98b]

803 PADA-PRAGṚHYA-LAKṢAṆA (**पदप्रगृह्यलक्षण**)

→ Sapta-saṃkhyā. This title is apparently based on the initial words of the additional opening verse found in this Ms:

padapragṛhyāvagṛhyaṃ visargaṃ ca makārakam |
nakāraṃ ca takāraṃ ca saptasaṃkhyā anukramāt ||

Mysore ND II 3607 (P 5379/ 6). PL. Tel. 40 fol. Extract no. 210.

804 PADA-PRADĪPIKĀ (**पदप्रदीपिका**)

of Vātsya Nārāyaṇa of Kerala. A work in 140 Kārikā-s with a commentary of the author himself on the Pada-pāṭha of the *Taittirīya-saṃhitā*, composed in A.D. 1667. Cf. N. V. P. Unithiri, in : *Pūrṇatrayī -- Sri Ravi Varma Samskrita Granthavali Journal*, 16,1 (January 1989), Govt. Sanskrit College, Tripunithura, pp. 21-31. [Adyar (H05 RSG 16,1)]. It follows and also quotes the *Sapta-lakṣaṇa*. It is divided into Prakaraṇa-s as follows:

Kārikā-s 1-8 : Paribhāṣā

Kārikā-s 9-13 : Saptaparādhikāra (= Tpr. V)
Kārikā-s 14-20 : Napara-Tapara
Kārikā-s 21-49 : Śamāna
Kārikā-s 50-72 : Vilaṅghya
Kārikā-s 73-98 : Avarṇi and Āvarṇi
Kārikā-s 99-140 : Aniṅgya

Beginning:

प्रणिपत्य महादेवं प्रारब्धार्थप्रसिद्धये।
नारायणेन वात्स्येन क्रियते पदलक्षणम्॥ १॥

महादेवं प्रणिपत्य प्रारब्धस्य प्रसिद्धये अविघ्नेन परिसमाप्तये प्रकाशाय वा वात्स्येन वत्सकुलोद्भवेन नाम्ना नारायणेन पदलक्षणं पदानां लक्षणं चिह्नं क्रियते। केषां पदानाम्। उत्तरत्र प्रातिशाख्यानुरोधेन प्रातिशाख्ये अथ संहितायामेकप्राणभावे इत्यारभ्य येषां पदानां संहितालक्षणमुक्तं तेषां पदानामित्यर्थः ॥ १ ॥ पदप्रदीपिका इत्यारभ्य पाठस्याप्यप्रमाद्यताम् इत्यन्तैः कैश्चिच्छ्लोकैः परिभाषा उच्यते --

पदप्रदीपिकेत्यस्य संज्ञैषा सामुदायिकी।
भिन्ना सप्तपरादित्वात् तत्तत्प्रकरणोदितम्॥ २॥

अस्य लक्षणस्य पदप्रदीपिकेति सामुदायिकी समुदायभावेन संज्ञा स्यात् । सा तत्तत्प्रकरणोचितं सप्तपरादिभावेन। सप्तपरा(दिषु) उक्तसप्तप(रश)मानादिविभागेन भिन्ना स्यात्। पदानां प्रदीपिका पदप्रदीपिका॥ २॥

End:

साधारणं सुषुपुषश्चरमेण सनिष्यवः ।
सर्दिगृदिं स्थविमतः सङ्गे सङ्काः सनेमि च॥ १३९॥
सनीयान् विश्पतिश्चान्यान्युन्नेयान्यनया दिशा॥ १४०॥

साधारणं कुरुते। सुषुपुष इन्द्रियम्। चरमेण पशुना। चरमायामिष्टकायाम्। मेधसाता सनिष्यवः। सर्दिगृदिं परावधीत्। स्थविमतो बर्हिरक्त्वा। सङ्गे समत्सु। इषुधिः सङ्काः पृतनाः। सनेम्यस्मद्युवन्। अमुतः सनीयान्। ज्येष्ठो विश्पतिः। विश्पतिनाभ्यमुम्। चकारो ऽनुक्तसमुच्चयार्थः । अन्यान्युक्तव्यतिरिक्तानि पदानि अनया दिशा अनेनोपायेनोन्नेयानि। यथा एनश्चकृवान्महि। करोतु मामनेनसम्। अग्निः पशुरासीत् तेन। प्रजापतेः पशवः । अपशवो वा अन्ये । एष वै वनस्पतीनामपशव्यः । ऊर्मिर्न नावमावधीत् । ऋतावरीरूर्मिणीः । मनुः पुत्रेभ्यो दायं व्यभजत् । मनवे यशस्ये । मानवीत्याह मनुः । मानन्थो हि प्रजाः । इत्यादीनि यथासंभवं द्रष्टव्यानि॥ १३९, १४०॥

प्रवाहमितकोलम्बे धिषणे झषमाश्रिते।
पदप्रदीपिका ह्येषा लिखिता व्याख्ययान्विता॥

A Ms. in Malayalam script, with A. V. Krishna Vadhyan Namboodiri, Pallithara, near Payyannur, Cannanore Dist., Kerala.

Ptd: Ed. by N. V. P. Unithiri, with introduction and notes. - Calicut (673 635) : Printex India (Feroke), 1988. xiv, 195 pp. [(SAI ***)].

805 PADA-MUṢṬI-LAKṢAṆA(-PRAKĀŚIKĀ) (पदमुष्टिलक्षण /-प्रकाशिका) of Mukunda-bhaṭṭa (or -śāstrin). Also called Pada-lakṣaṇa. Analysis of the words occuring in the *Vājasaneyi-saṃhitā*, with code letters.

Beginning:

श्रीवाग्देविपदारविन्दयुगलं विघ्नाधिपं स्वामिनं
नत्वा पङ्कजयोनिकेशवशिवान् श्रीमद्गुरुं भक्तितः ।
वक्ष्ये वाजसनेयशुक्लयजुषां संख्यां पदानां क्रमाद्
एकं वर्णमृचश्चतुष्कगणनं लभ्यप्रकाशं शुभम् ॥
सुरासुरशिरोरत्नमरीचिरचिताङ्घ्रिपे ।
विघ्नान्धकारसूर्याय गणाधिपतये नमः ॥
पदानामावलिर्वेलाविसर्गाणां विधीयते ।
नान्तानां वक्ष्यते लक्ष्म निक्षिप्यैकाक्षरे ऽक्षरम् ॥
विहीना ऋऌ वर्णाभ्यां नवाकारादयः स्वराः ।
दशमं बिन्दुना ज्ञेयं विसर्गाद् विंशतिर्भवेत् ॥

End: (RASB)

पद्मानां च द्विपक्षी च शुकपार्श्ववती तु या ।
गणान्तानां निजं वर्णं समाप्तं पदलक्षणम् ॥

दुश्चवनः पृतनाषालयुध्यो ऽस्माकम् । जुषन्तां यज्ञम् अद्रुहो ऽनमीवाः । इति पदलक्षणं समाप्तम् । (२१०९८) इति श्रीमद्द्विरेदिव-उपनामक- रघुनाथात्मजेन मुकुन्दशास्त्रिणा विरचिता पदमुष्टिप्रकाशिका समाप्तिमगात् ।

BORI TM 81. 12 fol. 8 verses with the C. Col.: iti śrīmatpadavākyapramāṇajña vājyagresaraśākhi ramākṛṣṇa-paṇḍita-viracitā śrīyājñvalkyakrtṛkā padamuṣṭiḥ.

GJKSV 18170. 6 fol. Title: Pada-lakṣaṇa (Pada-muṣṭi-lakṣaṇa in the middle):

विक्रमार्कगते शाके नन्दनन्दघनोन्मिते ।
वासुदेवेन लिखितं खोडोपनामकेन च ।
माघकृष्ण अष्टम्यां च समाप्तं भृगुवासरे ।

GJKSV 21098. 14 fol. Title: Pada-muṣṭi-prakāśikā. Dated V.S. 1855 (āśvina-vadya-amāvāsyābhaumavāsare kāśyām khoṇḍopanāmaka-lakṣmaṇena likhitam).

GJKSV 28535. 10 fol. Title: Pada-muṣṭi-prakāśikā.

RASB II 913(A) (G 6170). 1 fol. 9 Grantha-s.

– C. of Rāma-bhaṭṭa.
RASB II 913(B) (G 6170). 7 fol. 250 Grantha-s.

[NCC XI 100a]

806 PADA-MUṢṬI-SĀRA (पदमुष्टिसार)
Ānandāśrama 2824. 3 fol. The same text as above but ascribed to Keśava. Col.: śrīmād-hyandinīyaśākhi bāḻaka-keśava-viracitā kāṇvaśākhopayukta padamuṣṭisāraḥ samāptaḥ ||

807 PADA-RATNA (पदरत्न)
MT 5295 → Aṣṭākṣarī-paribhāṣā.

808 PADA-RATNA see ṚGVEDA-PADA-RATNA(-PARIBHĀṢĀ)
(पदरत्न / ऋग्वेदपदरत्न-परिभाषा)
BISM p. 152 (52/861).
BISM p. 152 (54/953). 7 fol. → Pada-gāḍha.
Mysore ND II 3608-12.

– C. Ṭīkā in Telugu.
Mysore ND II 3613 (P 5379/ 2). PL. Tel. 3 fol.

[NCC XI 100b]

809 PADA-RATNA-KRAMA-RATNA (पदरत्नक्रमरत्न)
Ascribed to Nāgadeva in Mysore I, p. 30, but described as anonymous in Mysore ND II 3614. The work is the same as the *Ṛgveda-pada-ratna* above (corresponds to the first set of paragraphs of *Pada-ratna* of the Srirangam edition).
Mysore I, p. 30.
Mysore ND II 3614 (C 476/ 2). Tel. 6 fol. (2-7). Extract no. 212

[NCC XI 100b]

810 PADA-RATNA-PARIBHĀṢĀ (पदरत्नपरिभाषा)
of Rāvaṇa.
Mysore Skt. Coll. p. 1 = D. No.11 (846/2). PL. Na. 2 fol. (7-8) → Ṛgveda-pada-ratna(-paribhāṣā) or Ekākṣarī-baiṭh.

[NCC XI 100b]

811 PADA-RATNA-LAKṢAṆA (पदरत्नलक्षण)
See under Pada-ratna-paribhāṣā and Ṛgveda-pada-ratna. Adyar D I 892.

[NCC XI 100b]

812 PADA-RATNA-SAMĪKṢĀ (पदरत्नसमीक्षा)
→ Ṛgveda-pada-ratna (Srirangam edition, first paragraphs).
Trav. Uni. 5206 C. 85 Grantha-s.

[NCC XI 100b]

813 PADA-LAKṢAṆA (1) (पदलक्षण)
Three verses and a commentary thereon dealing with the accentuation in the *Taittirīya-saṃhitā*.

Beginning:

एकोदात्तं पदं ज्ञेयमुदात्तं द्वितयं परम्।
न्युदात्तं वा पदं विद्यान्नित्यस्वारमथापरम्॥

सर्वानुदात्तमथवा पदानां कुत्रचित् पदम्।
प्रचयत्वं न चेत् स्वाराननुदात्ताद् बहूनपि।

End:

सुपूर्णा पुनरापत। ओष्ठमध्य इति किम्। अह्वुतमसि पुंसः पुत्रान्॥ इति पदलक्षणं समाप्तम्॥

MT 485(s). PL. Tel. 1 fol. (77b). Presented in 1910-11 by C. Visvanatha Shastrigal of Viziyanagaram.

814 PADA-LAKṢAṆA (2) (पदलक्षण)
VSM I 765 (no.984). 8 fol. Extract p. 357. aghniyā ayakṣmā agrā ... = Śamāna.
Wai I 338. 11 fol. Dated Śaka 1610 (it is a portion of Pada-pāṭha).

[NCC XI 101a]

815 PADA-LAKṢAṆA (3) (पदलक्षण)
GJKSV 18170. 6 fol. Dated V.S. 1799. Cf. Pada-muṣṭi-lakṣaṇa above.

816 PADA-VARṆA-LAKṢAṆA-PARIBHĀṢĀ (पदवर्णलक्षणपरिभाषा)
of Dakṣiṇāmūrti → Aṣṭākṣarī-baiṭh(-paribhāṣā).
SBD 2101. 20 fol. This is the first half of the Ms. up to Adhyāya 5 of Aṣṭaka 5. The remaining portion is SBD 2102 catalogued as Pada-varṇa-saṃkhyā.

817 PADA-VARṆA-SAṂKHYĀ (1) (पदवर्णसंख्या)
of Dakṣiṇāmūrti. Also called Dakṣiṇāmūrti-pada-varṇa-saṃkhyā of Śrīpāda (= Dakṣiṇāmūrti Śrīpāda). → Aṣṭākṣarī-baiṭh(-paribhāṣā).
Ānandāśrama 7742. 47 fol. Dated Śaka 1600 (so 'haṃ sphurantim ...). The Aṣṭaka-s are called "śaktiśrī", etc.
BISM p. 152 (36/693). 52 fol.
PUL I, p. 22 (no.100). 1 fol.
SBD 2102. 16 fol. (21-36). Ascribed to Dakṣiṇāmūrti-śiṣya in the catalogue and on the title slip, but this ascription is not found in the Ms. Col.: iti śrīdakṣiṇāmūrtau śrīpādopadiṣṭāyāṃ padavarṇasaṃkhyāyām aṣṭamāṣṭake aṣṭamo 'dhyāyaḥ || This is the latter half of SBD 2101 catalogued as Pada-varṇa-lakṣaṇa-paribhāṣa. The original Ms. is divided into two and catalogued separately. The two numbers together contain the work complete.
SBD 2372. 26 fol. (1-22, 25-26, 31-32). Incomplete (1.8 to 7.8).
Trav. Uni. 5206 A. 600 Grantha-s (begins with Svarāṣṭaka).

[NCC XI 101a]

818 PADA-VARṆA-SAṂKHYĀ (2) (पदवर्णसंख्या)
→ Pavamāna-pada-varṇa-saṃkhyā.
GJKSV 30314. 9 fol. (1-6, 1-3).

819 PADA-SAṂKHYĀ (पदसंख्या)

This work gives the number of words contained in each Varga of the *Ṛgveda.* See also Ṛgveda-(saṃhitā-)pada-saṃkhyā-nirṇaya.

MD 923. PL. Tel. 50 pp. (fol. 167-92). Col.: Veṅkaṭa-padavinyāsa.

Trav. Uni. C 2. C-3960 Grantha-s. (DC. 405C) ?

[NCC XI 102b]

820 PADA-SAṂKHYĀNA (पदसंख्यान)

Adyar 78382. PL. Mal. 16 fol. Incomplete.

821 PADA-SAṂKHYĀ-PRADĪPIKĀ (पदसंख्याप्रदीपिका)

of Dāmodara. It is a work dealing with the number of Pada-s and also the end of Pāda-s in the *Ṛgveda.* It is described as a commentary called Dīpikā in MT. The text is identical with the *Pāda-saṃkhyā.* For an analysis of the text see C. Kunhan Raja in : *The Adyar Library Bulletin,* vol. 11 (1947), pt. 2, pp. 79-96; pt. 3, pp. 189-201.

Beginning: (5294)

पञ्चमस्याष्टकस्याथ पद(पाद)संख्याप्रदीपिका।
(दीपिका) लिख्यते वेदवेद्यो ऽत्र विष्णुर्दिशतु मङ्गलम्॥

स्तुषे -- उद्देशस्ताच्छिवे रागः । पूर्वङ्घ्यन्तस्तु मिमाना नापस्संख्यान्वयक्षतेः । ता भुज्युं धिग्वन्नं युधि भङ्गुरः । क्व त्यां प्रसूतस्सुकविर्गोत्रे । अद्येत्यन्तः । क्वत्येत्यङ्घ्रेर्न भूतो ऽर्थाक्षरक्षतेः । परि हत्य द्रिपो निष्ठा न न तस्योर्ध्वमन्वयात्। ऊर्ध्वो वामङ्घ्रिनिष्ठा स्थान्न प्र तस्योत्तरे ऽन्वयात्। युवे कथाज्ञो निर्मलश्शुकः ।

इति दामोदरविरचितायां पञ्चमस्याष्टकस्य प्रथमः ।

End:

त्वमिन्द्राङ्घ्यन्त ऋभुक्षा न वाजो ऽर्थादिभङ्गतः ।
वयन्वङ्घ्रे स्यामेत्यन्तो न ब्रह्मास्योर्ध्वमन्वयात्॥
वासयसीव अघं शंभुरखण्डयत्। उदूष्यः विज्ञश्चिरं श्रुतौ रागी।
नूनमङ्घ्रिश्चतुष्पादो न वितस्योत्तरे ऽन्वयात्।
पूर्वं सृजानः पादान्तो न त्वा वृत्त्यर्थपीडया॥
इति पदसंख्याप्रदीपिका(-दीपिका)॥

MD 19676. PL. Mal. 5 fol. (34-39). 220 Grantha-s. Incomplete (Adhyāya-s 1-4 of the 5th Aṣṭaka).

MT 5294. Gr. 6 fol. Incomplete (Adhyāya-s 1-4 of the 5th Aṣṭaka). Transcribed in 1926-27 from a Ms. of Narayana Nambudiripad, Punnata-mana, Kottapadi, Malabar Dist.

[NCC XI 102b]

822 PADA-SAṂJÑAKA (पदसंज्ञक)

Also called Āśvalāyana-śākhāyāṃ pada-saṃjñā. It gives the number of words in each Varga of the *Ṛgveda* with the combination of a consonant and a vowel in a single letter.

fol. 13 contains the *Ṛksaṃkhyā*.

Beginning:

गणेशं च प्रणम्यादौ चक्रपाणिं त्रिलोचनम्।
आश्वलायनशाखायां वक्ष्यामि पदसंज्ञकम्॥
एकं दश शतं ज्ञेयं संज्ञेति कचवर्गयोः ।
एकं शतं पवर्गस्य दशैकं च टवर्गके॥
औकारानतमकारादिस्वराणामिति निर्णयः ।
ह्रस्वदीर्घाविति ज्ञेयौ ऋकारल्कारवर्जितौ॥
नकारस्य शतं ज्ञेयं संयुक्तं च शतद्वयम्।
स्वरव्यञ्जनयोरस्मात् टवर्गस्थानमाप्नुयात्॥
संज्ञेया गणनात् सम्यग् विलोक्य च पुनः पुनः ।
इति परिभाषा। ठे ढ ढो ड ढो णि।

End:

दो द दं थु धे दे दौ तौ ती तौ णा णु ति णी द् ढौ द धौ त णु तो धो थू थो थू तै णू डो डा ध त डि ढो डु णि ण ण ढे डा ढी डै ठै डै ठौ ठि डि॥ ४९॥ इत्यष्टमाष्टकं संपूर्णम्॥ अथ ऋक्संख्या। ... ... धौ ति डुण्दै दो ढ णि ढी त डि ढे णौ ड्वि डौ क्ष पौ। इत्यृक्संख्या॥
(64 letters giving the number of Ṛk-s in each Adhyāya; fol. 13-15 contain):

अखिलनाथहरो वृषवाहनस्तुहिनशैलसुताश्रितसत्तनुः ।
झषधरांतुहिधुण्दुसुतार्चितो वहतु शं शशलाञ्छनशेखरः ॥ ...
अक्षरौघे हृदाचं सफलं प्रौढबुद्धिगम्।
वर्णं झटिति जानीयात् ... मुखकोर्थभाषया ...॥
झषकेतनजिन्मित्रछवे नागविभूषणः ।
भवतार्थः कुम्भयोने ते खट्वाङ्गभृते नमः ।
विष्द्वी शमी यद्वजगत् देवाश्चित्ते असुर्या। कण्वा इव। नृचक्ष इति पञ्चानशुः प्रचयानि॥

Calcutta Skt. Coll. I 528 (313). 15 fol.

823 PADA-SAṂDEHA-VICCHITTI-LAKṢAṆA (पदसंदेहविच्छित्तिलक्षण)
Trav. Uni. 15513. PL. Mal. 250 Grantha-s. Incomplete.

824 PADA-SAMĀNA (पदसमान)
Deccan College ... 8 fol. Dated Śaka 1708.

825 PADA-SARVATRA-LAKṢAṆA (पदसर्वत्रलक्षण)
SBD 53757. 6 fol. Dated Śaka 1723. 63 sections → Pada-gāḍha.

826 PADA-STOBHA (**पदस्तोभ**)
Sūcīpattra 77.

[NCC XI 103a]

827 PADA-SVARA-CARCĀ (**पदस्वरचर्चा**)
of Mādhava. A commentary dealing with the derivation and accentuation of the words of the first two chapters of the *Vājasaneyi-saṃhitā*.
Beginning:

वागीशाद्याः ··· तं नमामि गजाननम् ॥ ओं इषे । इषेरिच्छार्थकस्य कर्मणि क्विप् । कित्वादुपधागुणाभावः । तस्माच्चतुर्थैकवचनम् । तत्र धातुस्वरेण इद्शब्दो ऽप्यन्तोदात्तः । तत्र व्यञ्जनस्य विद्यमानत्वादिकार उदात्तः । चतुर्थ्येकवचनस्य प्रत्ययत्वादुदात्तत्वे प्राप्ते अनुदात्तौ सुप्पिताविति तदपवादेनानुदात्तत्वे प्राप्ते ऽपि सावेकाचस्तृतीयादिर्विभक्तिरित्युदात्तत्वम् । अतिशिष्टस्वरो बलीयानिति स एव शिष्यते । अनुदात्तं पदमेकवर्जमिति परिभाषया धातोरनुदात्तत्वम् । एवमिषे इति पदमन्तोदात्तम् । अव्युत्पत्तिपक्षे ऽपि प्रातिपदिकस्वरेण इद्शब्दो ऽन्तोदात्तः । शेषं पूर्ववत् । त्वा । युषेर्जननार्थाद्युष्मसिभ्यां मदिगिति मदिक् ।

End:

तर्पयत । तृप प्रीणने । हेतुमति चेति णिच् । तृप्यतः प्रेरयति तर्पयति । लोण्मध्यमबहुवचनान्तः । शप् । गुणयादेशौ । अनुपदेशादत्र सार्वधातुकानुदात्तत्वे पिचः स्वरः समानवाक्यस्थपदादपरत्वान्न निधानः । इति श्रीमन्नागरान्वयभूषण द्विवेदिश्रीपतितनय द्विवेदिश्रीमाधवकृतौ यजुर्वेदसंहितापदस्वरचर्चायां द्वितीयो ऽध्यायः समाप्तः ॥

श्रीपतिः क्षितितले द्विजवर्यो ऽभूदुदारमतिराप्ततमेज्यः ।
तत्सुतेन विहिता पदचर्चा माधवेन जयताच्चिरकालम् ॥

SBD 2110. 35 fol. Dated V.S. 1631. Copied by Mahīdāsa.

828 PADA-SVARĀVADHĀNA (**पदस्वरावधान**)
Hoshiarpur p. 51 (no.4372). PL. Gr. 34 fol. 700 Grantha-s.

829 PADĀDI (**पदादि**)
Viśvabhāratī 1610.

[NCC XI 104a]

830 PADĀDI-VARṆA-VYĀKHYĀ (**पदादिवर्णव्याख्या**)
Trav. Uni. 22200 F. PL. Mal. 75 Grantha-s.

831 PADĀDI-VIKṚTAYAḤ (**पदादिविकृतयः**)
Peters.V, p. 225 (no.26). 5 fol. Dated V.S. 1805.
BORI 26 of 1892-95.

[NCC XI 104a]

832 PADĀNI (पदानि)
Tāmarakāṭṭu Mana 65.

[NCC XI 104a]

833 PADĀNUKRAMAṆIKĀ (1) (पदानुक्रमणिका)
An enumeration of the number of Pañcikā-s, Ṛk-s and Pada-s of the each chapter of the *Vājasaneyi-saṃhitā*.
GJKSV 34121. 8 fol.

834 PADĀNUKRAMAṆIKĀ (2) (पदानुक्रमणिका)
Mysore Skt. Coll. p. 1. See Pādānukramaṇikā.

[NCC XI 104a]

835 PADĀNTA-DĪPINĪ (पदान्तदीपिनी)
of Bhāskara, son of Rāmasvāmi-makhin. 27 verses based on Śaunaka's *Ṛgveda-prātiśākhya*.

Beginning:

भूतेशो ऽपि प्रसादार्थी यस्याभूत् त्रिपुरान्तकः ।
कारुण्यनिधये तस्मै गणाधिपतये नमः ॥ १॥
मनीषितेषु सर्वेषु भासतां नः सरस्वती।
विश्वप्रकाशिनी शश्वत् कुमुदेष्विव कौमुदी॥ २॥
ऋग्वेदपाठे शाकल्यदृष्टे तद्वर्त्मना कृतिम्।
पदान्तदीपिनीं नाम्ना करोम्यर्थानुबन्धिनीम्॥ ३॥
बहुशः संशयं दृष्ट्वा बहुधा धीमतामपि।
ऋगाम्नायपदान्तेषु तच्छेदाय (निर्णयाय) यतामहे॥ ४॥
आलोच्य शौनकप्रोक्तं प्रातिशाख्यं प्रयत्नतः ।
विवृणोम्यतिमूढो ऽपि मन्दानुग्रहकाङ्क्षया॥ ५॥
आविश्य किं नु कुरुते मन्दानत्याग्रहग्रहः ।
गुणैकदर्शिनस्तेन सन्तः सन्तु कृपालवः ॥ ६॥
षोडश व्यञ्जनोत्थानि वाक्यानि व्यञ्जनद्विकैः ।
कथयन्त्यष्टरूपाणां प्रतिवर्गं स्वरैरपि॥ ७॥

End:

तेषु कोष्ठेषु गणिते पदजाते वराटकैः ।
पदेङ्क्योष्मान्तमान्तानां निर्णयो भवति ध्रुवम्।
(शन्दः पदाभिधो भूयादिति सर्वं सुमङ्गलम्॥)
पदसंख्या नृवत्यो ऽयं पिब स्वाहा जुहोमि ते।
तान् वाणी तु महत् सम्राळ् एतप्रोस्वरनानुदः ॥
को(गो)ष्ठान्निर्णिक् ककुप् प्रत्यङ् तस्मै गोजरित् पृणक्।
पूषण्वान् सितुसेम्यन्तस्तनूसाताविति क्रमः ॥

इति पदान्तदीपिनी-परिभाषा।

MT 3911(b). PL. Gr. 2 fol. (23-24). The first verse is that of Ṛksarva-samāna and has a different end. Purchased in 1921-22 from Narasimha Sastrigal, Bhavani, Coimbatore Dist.

MT 3951(a). PL. Gr. 4 fol. (3-6). Purchased in 1921-22 from Narasimha Sastrigal, Bhavani, Coimbatore Dist.

TCD 34-I. 4 pp. 35 Grantha-s.

Trav. Uni. 4254 J. PL. Mal. 2 fol. 30 Grantha-s. Belonged to Vishnu Nambudiri of Ettikada Illam Ayankudi, Kaduttirutti, Kottayam.

Trav. Uni. T.223 I. = TCD 34-I. A transcript of the Ms. no. 4254.

Trav. Uni. 22690. PL. Mal. 1350. Grantha-s. Incomplete.

Triv. Cur. III 9. Mal. 25 Grantha-s.

Triv. Cur. V 6. Mal. 1350 Grantha-s. Obtained from Harisvaran Padmanabhan Nambudiri, Nellipuzha, Kallampalli.

Whish 73,2 (4). PL. Gr. 3 fol. (15-17). 20 paribhāṣā verses and explanations of the code words in 10 verses.

– C. of the author himself.

Beginning: (3911)

श्रियं तनोतु श्रितविघ्नभेदी गणाधिनाथो गणवान्ममोच्चैः ।
यदर्चनादेव फलन्ति कामाः कृशाः प्रभूता अपि वा जनानाम्॥

अथ पदान्तदीपिनीनामधेयं व्याचिकीर्षुराचार्यः तस्य अविघ्नपरिसमाप्त्यादिफलसिद्धये स्वेष्टदेवतां विनायकं नमस्करोति -- भूतेशो ऽपीति। तस्मै गणानां पतये नमः करोमीति शेषः । अस्त्विति वा । भूतेशः शिवः । भूतेशः खण्डपरशुरित्यमरः ... ... । अथ चिकीर्षितं प्रतिजानीते -- ऋग्वेदेति । शाकल्यदृष्टे ऋग्वेदे(द) पाठे विषये नाम्ना पदान्तदीपिनीं कृतिं करोमीति। तद्वर्त्मना शाकल्यवर्त्मना आचार्यसंप्रदायानतिक्रमेणेति यावत्।

End:

उपसंहरति -- वाक्यानामिति। स्फुटम्॥

पदसंख्या नृवत्यो ऽयं पिब स्वाहा जुहोमि ते।
तान् वाणी तु महत् सम्राळ् एतप्रोस्वरनानुदः ॥
गोष्ठान्निर्णिक् ककुप् प्रत्यक् तस्मै गोजरित पृणक्।
पूषण्वान् सितुसेम्यन्तस्तनूसाताविति क्रमः ॥

End: (3951)

पृणक् पूषण्वान् सितुसेम्यन्तः तनु सातौ इति षोडशात्मानः । अनानुदादीनि निर्णिक् प्रयङ् गो पृणक् इति अष्टमादिवर्णगतानुबन्धगम्यानि पञ्च रूपाणि षोडशात्मभिरेव मिलित्वा लिखितानि।

श्रीरामस्वामिमखिनां तनयो भास्कराभिधः ।
पदान्तदीपिनीं तस्या वृत्तिमप्यलिखच्छुभाम्॥
क्रोधिचैत्रसिताष्टम्यां प्राच्यां वृत्तौ तु या गिरः ।
क्वचिदासन् सुदुर्बोधा रचनाशक्त्यभावतः ॥
तत्र तत्र स्ववाक्यानि प्रक्षिप्य सुलभानि तैः ।
स्फुटयन् भावमेतासां गिरां वृत्तिं लिलेख ताम्॥
अनेन भगवाञ्छंभुर्बालबोधार्थमृध्यता।
लेखनातिप्रयत्नेन संतुष्यतु दयानिधिः ॥

MT 3911(c). PL. Gr. 5 fol. (24-28). Purchased in 1921-22 from Narasimha Sastrigal, Bhavani, Coimbatore Dist.

MT 3951(b). PL. Gr. 11 fol. (7-17). Purchased in 1921-22 from Narasimha Sastrigal, Bhavani, Coimbatore Dist.

[NCC XI 104a]

836 PADĀNTA-SAṂGRAHA see PĀDĀNTA-SAṂGRAHA (**पदान्तसंग्रह / पादान्तसंग्रह**)

Trav. Uni. 480. PL. Mal. 850 Grantha-s.
Trav. Uni. 1248. PL. Mal. 850 Grantha-s.
Trav. Uni. 10680. PL. Mal. 850 Grantha-s.
Trav. Uni. L.170 A. PL. Mal. 250 Grantha-s. Incomplete.

[NCC XI 104a]

837 PADĀNTYA-SVARA-LAKṢAṆA (**पदान्त्यस्वरलक्षण**)

Mysore ND II 3615 (P 4906/14). PL. Na. 1 fol. (115). Extract no. 213.

838 PADĀMNĀYA-SIDDHI (**पदाम्नायसिद्धि**)

Name of the commentary of Nāganātha on the *Galita-pradīpa* of his elder brother Lakṣmīdhara-sūri.
Hall, p. 134.
Müller 52.

[NCC XI 104b]

839 PADĀVALĪ (**पदावली**)

Trav. Uni. 16408 Z 6. PL. Mal. 1 fol. 25 Grantha-s.

*PADMANĀBHA (**पद्मनाभ**)

Son of Lakṣmaṇārya.

Jaṭā-vallī. Adyar D I 815. MT 2591(d).
- Śamāna-lakṣaṇa. Ascribed in the colophon of RASB II 487-88(I) (G 6063).
C. on Śamāna(-lakṣaṇa). IO 4500. MD 983. MD 16810. MT 616(b).

[NCC XI 125b]

840 PADYA-VIVṚTI (**पद्यविवृति**)

› Sarvānukramaṇī-padya-vivṛti.

841 PARAGĀḌI (?) (**परगाडि**)

From Saṃhitā-paragāḍi to Āraṇa-paragāḍi and Śākhā-paragāḍi.

Adyar D I 983. Incomplete (in a collection) → Veda-lakṣaṇa (A 1). Cf. Pada-gāḍha (ḍhi).

[NCC XI 164a]

***PARIBABHRAVA** (**परिबभ्रव**)

– Pañca-paṭalikā. Probably same as the Atharva-vedīya-pañcapaṭalikā. SBD 2074 (in Atharvaṇa-lakṣaṇa-grantha-saṃgraha). SBD 4225.

842 PARIBHĀṢĀ (1) (**परिभाषा**)

From the Ṛgveda-sarvānukramaṇī. Cf. Ṛgveda-paribhāṣā above.

IO 4240.

IO 4241.

IO 4242.

KTP. Dharwar D I 14.

Mysore I, p. 20. Cf. Mysore ND II 3255: Ṛksarvānukramaṇī.

SBD 2327. 5 fol. Dated V.S. 1895.

[NCC XI 217a]

843 PARIBHĀṢĀ (2) (**परिभाषा**)

Oppert I 4594. PL. Gr. 10 pp. Belonged to Puduppatti Svamidikshitar of Pudukkottai.

Sūcīpattra 115.

See also Ṛgveda-paribhāṣā and Sarvānukrama-paribhāṣā.

844 PARIBHĀṢĀ (3) (**परिभाषा**)

→ Sāma-paribhāṣā ascribed to Vararuci.

IO 4335 (Burnell 64c). PL. Gr. 8 fol. = Brl. CL.

IO 4336 (Burnell 164c). PL. Gr. 5 fol.

IO 4337 (Mackenzie VIII 76b). PL. Gr. 6 fol. (Svara-paribhāṣā).

Mad. Uni. R. A. S. 173(d).

Sri Dev. 351(a).

Cf. Sāmaveda-paribhāṣā. Adyar D I 1060. MT 238(b).

[NCC XI 217a]

845 PARIBHĀṢĀ (ṚGVEDĪYĀ) (**परिभाषा / ऋग्वेदीया**)

SBD 46929. 6 fol. = Cātur-jñāna.

846 PARIBHĀṢĀṄKA-SŪTRA (**परिभाषाङ्कसूत्र**)

Also called Mādhyandinīya-veda-paribhāṣāṅka-sūtra or Veda-paribhāṣāṅka-sūtra. Nine Sūtra-s ascribed to Mādhyandina. In most of the Mss. these Sūtra-s are accompanied by a commentary and a summary of the Sūtra-s in six verses, both attributed to Keśavarāma Daivajña, and together it is called *Keśavī-śikṣā.*

Jodhpur (R). 1484 (D I, p. 22; no.45). 7 fol. Dated V.S. 1911.

SBD 47722b. 1 fol. (2a). 9 Sūtra-s.

SBD 55435. 12 fol. (with C. of Keśava). Dated V.S. 1952.

SBD 55686. 1 fol. Catalogued as by Bālam-bhaṭṭa, which is the name of the scribe.

SBD 55912. 6 fol. Attributed to Keśava.

SBD 55913. 4 fol. Incomplete. Attributed to Keśava.

847 PARIBHĀṢĀ-LAKṢAṆA (परिभाषालक्षण)

→ Sāma-paribhāṣā ascribed to Vararuci.

MT 8041. PL. Gr. 8 fol. (129-36). 200 Grantha-s. Presented in 1948-49 by Sri Mridangam Subbaiyer, Chattapuram Village, Kalpathi, Palghat.

PUL II. App. p. 12 (no.187). PL. Gr. 6 fol. 120 Grantha-s.

[NCC XI 222b]

848 PARIBHĀṢĀ-VIVARAṆA (परिभाषाविवरण)

of Jagannātha.

BISM p. 154 (54/569). 1 fol. Contains six verses of the Ṛgveda-sarvānukramaṇī-vivaraṇa. Col.: iti paribhāṣā. See Ṛgveda-sarvānukramaṇī-vivaraṇa of Jagannātha, above.

[NCC XI 222b]

849 PARIBHĀṢĀ-ṢAḌVIṂŚATI-SŪTRA (परिभाषाषड्विंशतिसूत्र)

PUL I, p. 22 (no.101). PL. Gr. 56 fol. (75-130).

The same as the Ṣaḍviṃśati-sūtra ?

[NCC XI 224a]

850 PARIBHĀṢĀ-SARVĀNUKRAMA (परिभाषासर्वानुक्रम)

Title of the Ṛgveda-saravānukramaṇī ->]

GJKSV 29986. 27 fol. Dated V.S. 1931. Copied by Gopāla-bhaṭṭa Karamarakara.

851 PARIMALA (परिमल)

Name of the commentary of Girinātha on the *Svara(-manojña)-mañjarī* of Nṛsiṃha.

Ptd.: ed. by K. C. Chatterji, in : *Calcutta Oriental Journal* II 10 (July 1935). 16 pages only.

852 PARIŚIṢṬA-ṚGVIVARAṆA (परिशिष्ट-ऋग्विवरण)

Trav. Uni. 4909. 10 fol. 90 Grantha-s.

See above under Ṛgveda-pariśiṣṭa.

[NCC XI 232a]

853 PARIŚIṢṬA-KADAMBA (परिशिष्टकदम्ब)

RV. SB 10.

[NCC XI 232a]

854 PARVA-NIRŪPAṆA (पर्वनिरूपण)

→ Salakṣaṇa-paribhāṣā also called Sāma-paribhāṣā. The concluding words of the text *parvaṇāṃ jñāpakaḥ* would have been the reason for this title.

Adyar I, p. 51a. = Adyar D I 1061 (19 M 42 = 66810).

[NCC XI 242a]

855 PAVAMĀNA-PADAVARṆA-SAṂKHYĀ (पवमानपदवर्णसंख्या)

GJKSV 30313. 60 fol. Title: Prativarga-varṇa-saṃkhyā. It contains a short commentary on the eleven paribhāṣā verses (and explanations called Utthāpanā on Aṣṭaka-s 5-7) of the Ekākṣarī-baiṭh and Aṣṭākṣarī-baiṭh for Pavamāna Sūkta-s (RV IX 1-67):

प्रत्यध्यायं पावमानीमेकार्णादिपदादिजाम्।
संख्यां ब्रह्मोपनामा वै गोविन्दो विलिखाम्यहम्॥

GJKSV 30314. 9 fol. (1-6, 1-3). Title: Pada-varṇa-saṃkhyā. With tables and explanations of Baiṭh. Copied by the same Govinda as the previous Ms. Col.:

इति पवमानपदवैठोत्थापनिकायां वर्णसंख्या ज्ञेया । संवत् १८६८ चित्रभानुनामाब्दे फाल्गुनशुक्ल १५ पौर्णमास्यां सोमवासरे ब्रह्मोपनामकेन गोविन्देन लेखनं पूर्ण कृतम्॥

856 PĀṆINĪYA-MATA (पाणिनीयमत)

The *Pāṇinīya-śikṣā* is catalogued under this title in: GJKSV 24668. 4 fol.

857 PĀṆINĪYA-ŚIKṢĀ (पाणिनीयशिक्षा)

Attributed to the grammarian Pāṇini. But the authenticity has been not established beyond doubt. Cf. Georg Cardona, *Pāṇini -- A Survey of Research*, pp. 179-82.

Beginning:

अथ शिक्षां प्रवक्ष्यामि पाणिनीयं मतं यथा।
शास्त्रानुपूर्वं तद् विद्याद्यथोक्तं लोकवेदयोः ॥ १॥
पुनर्व्यक्तीकरिष्यामि वाच उच्चारणे विधिम्॥ २॥
त्रिषष्टिश्चतुःषष्टिर्वा वर्णाः शंभुमते मताः ।
प्राकृते संस्कृते चापि स्वयं प्रोक्ताः स्वयंभुवा॥ ३॥
स्वरा विंशतिरेकश्च स्पर्शानां पञ्चविंशतिः ।
यादयश्च स्मृता ह्यष्टौ चत्वारश्च यमाः स्मृताः ॥ ४॥
अनुस्वारो विसर्गश्च ꣵकꣵपौ चापि पराश्रितौ।
दुःस्पृष्टश्चेति विज्ञेयो ऌकारः प्लुत एव च॥ ५॥

End:

शंकरः शांकरीं प्रादाद् दाक्षीपुत्राय धीमते।
वाङ्मयेभ्यः समाहृत्य देवीं वाचमिति स्थितः ॥ ५६॥
येनाक्षरसमाम्नायमधिगम्य महेश्वरात्।
कृत्स्नं व्याकरणं प्रोक्तं तस्मै पाणिनये नमः ॥ ५७॥
येन धौता गिरः पुंसां विमलैः शब्दवारिभिः ।
तमश्चाज्ञानजं भिन्नं तस्मै पाणिनये नमः ॥ ५८॥
अज्ञानान्धस्य लोकस्य ज्ञानाञ्जनशलाकया।
चक्षुरुन्मीलितं येन तस्मै पाणिनये नमः ॥ ५९॥
त्रिनयनमभिमुखनिःसृतामिमां य इह पठेत् प्रयतश्च सदा द्विजः ।
स भवति धनधान्यपशुपुत्रकीर्तिमानतुलं च सुखं समश्नुते दिवि॥ ६०॥

इति श्लोकः ॥ अथ शिक्षामात्मोदात्तश्च हकारं स्वराणां यथा गीत्यचो ऽस्पृष्टोदात्तं चापस्तु शंकर एकादश ॥ इति वेदाङ्गनासिकाशिक्षा समाप्ता ॥

Adyar D I 894 (21 Q 10 = 68514). PL. Mal. 5 fol. = Adyar II, App. p. iib (40 C 10).
Adyar D I 895 (29 L 36 = 73709). PL. Tel. 3 fol. (42-44). = Adyar I, p. 52b.
Adyar D I 896 (33 J 10 = 75400). PL. Gr. 4 fol. (4ff.). = Adyar I, p. 52b.
Adyar D I 990 (Vedāṅgāni) (8 D 44 = PM 135). 3 fol. (1-3).
Adyar D I 991 (Vedāṅgāni) (8 E 34 = TR 29). 5 fol. (pp. 34-43). = Adyar I, p. 52b.
Adyar D I 992 (Vedāṅgāni) (10 E 73 = PM 136). 4 fol. (1-4). = Adyar I, p. 52b.
Adyar D I 993 (Vedāṅgāni) (40 A 75 = PM 137). 6 fol. (1-6).
Adyar D I 994 (Vedāṅgāni) (41 B 84 = PM 138). 6 fol. (1-6).
Adyar D I 995 (Vedāṅgāni) (41 C 22 = PM 139). 3 fol. (1-5).
Adyar D XIII 324 (VB 1073d). PL. Tel. 3 fol.
AK 67. 20 fol. Dated V.S. 1719 (in Śikṣādi-catuṣṭaya).
Alwar 157. 158.
America 362. 49 pp. German cursive script (with C. ?).
America 364. 4 fol.
America 365. 9 fol.
America 366. 7 fol.
America 367. 5 fol.
America 368. 7 fol.
America 370. 4 fol. Title: Vedanāsikā-śikṣā.
B I, p. 206 (no. 55). 6 fol.
B I, p. 208 (nos. 65-72).
B I, p. 210 (nos. 73, 74)
Baroda 76. 11 fol. 200 Grantha-s (with C.). = CLB I, p. 31. Dated V.S. 1654.
Baroda 4542. = CLB I, p. 36 (in Vedāṅga-catuṣṭaya).
Baroda 4828(b). 6-8 fol. 59 Grantha-s. Dated V.S. 1836. = CLB I, p. 31.
Baroda 7323. = CLB I, p. 36 (in Vedāṅga-catuṣṭaya).
Baroda 7333. 6 fol. 59 Grantha-s. = CLB I, p. 31.
Baroda 7601. = CLB I, p. 36 (in Vedāṅga-catuṣṭaya).
Baroda 7735. 9 fol. 200 Grantha-s. = CLB I, p. 31.
Baroda 8791. 10 fol. 200 Grantha-s. Dated Śaka 1719. = CLB I, p. 31.
Baroda 9367. 8 fol. 59 Grantha-s. Col.: Vedanāsikā Śikṣā. = CLB I, p. 31.
Baroda 9407(a). 4 fol. 59 Grantha-s. Dated Śaka 1742. = CLB I, p. 31.
Baroda 9566. 10 fol. 200 Grantha-s. Dated V.S. 1822. = CLB I, p. 31.
Baroda 10400. 7 fol. 100 Grantha-s. Incomplete. = CLB I, p. 31.
Baroda 10603. 5 fol. 200 Grantha-s. Dated V.S. 1728. = CLB I, p. 31.
Baroda 11798(a). Dated Śaka 1681. = CLB I, p. 36 (in Vedāṅga-catuṣṭaya).
BBRAS 6 (B D 182). 5 fol.
BBRAS 7 (S C ZZ A 23). 2 fol.
BBRAS 8 (B D 182). 5 fol.
BBRAS 9 (B D 77). 4 fol.
BBRAS 10 (S C ZZ E 34). 15 fol. (with C. of Dharaṇī-dhara).
Bd. 83. 25 fol. (in Śikṣā-catuṣṭaya).

Bd. 84. 8 fol. (in Śikṣā-catuṣṭaya). Dated V.S. 1604.
Ben. 2.
Berlin StB-PrK (NGMPP). E 1554/21(b). 14 fol. (20-33). Maithili script (microfilm dated 25.09.1983).
Bh. p. 6. no.12. 3 fol. Dated Śaka 1705.
Bhk. 8. 9.
BHU (D 2E/2128A-2133). 7 Mss.
Bikaner 666(a).
BISM p. 282. 40 Mss. 23 of them under Śikṣā-catuṣṭaya.
Bodl. 17.
Bombay Uni. 4 (BMC 25 15). 5 fol. Dated Śaka 1730.
Bombay Uni. 5 (BMC 49 9). 5 fol. Dated Śaka 1746. Copied by Rāmacandra Māṭe.
Bombay Uni. 6 (BMC 29 31). 7 fol. Dated Śaka 1717. Copied by Lakṣmaṇa Rāmacandra Jāyade.
Bombay Uni. 7 (BMC 102 3). 12 fol. (with Jyotiṣa and Chandas).
Bombay Uni. 8 (BMC 3 27). 35 fol. Dated Śaka 1770 (in Śikṣā-catuṣṭaya). Copied by Bālakṛṣṇa Muṇḍale.
Bombay Uni. 9 (BMC 84 8). 12 fol. (with C. of Dharaṇī-dhara).
Bombay Uni. (Itchharam 9 22) 101. 6 fol. (in 11 sections).
Bombay Uni. (Moropant 13 1) 52. 2 fol. Incomplete.
BORI 21 of 1875-76. 2 fol. (20-21).
BORI 12 of A 1879-80. 3 fol. Dated Śaka 1705.
BORI 54 of A 1881-82.
BORI 97 of 1886-92. 4 fol.
BORI 67 of 1891-95. 20 fol. Dated V.S. 1719 (in Śikṣādi-catuṣṭaya).
BORI 45 of 1895-98. 6 fol. Dated V.S. 1734.
Brl. p. 8 (no.XVII) = IO 4936.
Bühler p. 538 (no. 27). = IO 4940.
Bühler p. 539 (no. 49). = IO 4934.
Burnell 36b.
Cabaton I 568.
Calcutta Skt. Coll. I 201. 4 fol.
CPB 2915-17. 5651-59. 5662-67.
Deccan College (12 Mss.).
Deccan College (5595). Catalogued as Śikṣā.
Deccan College (6121). 6 fol. Dated Śaka 1707. Catalogued as Śikṣā.
Deccan College (6521). 6 fol.
Deccan College (7598). 7 fol. Date Śaka 1663.
Deccan College (7816). 2 fol. (3-4). Incomplete.
Deccan College (8217). Title: Ātmodātta (based on the last line).
GB 19. 7 fol. (in Śikṣā-catuṣṭaya).
GD I 6-E. PL. Mal. 2 fol. 40 Grantha-s.
GJKSV 43/1 (D I 2, no.3770). 5 fol.
GJKSV 44/2 (D I 2, no.3771). 31 fol. Big and bold letters. One verse per page. Copied on modern paper dated A.D. 1916.
GJKSV 46/4 (D I 2, no.3772). 6 fol. Col. : Śāṃkarī-śikṣā.

GJKSV 4253/6 (D I 2, no. 3773). 4 fol. Mithili script.
GJKSV 7890/114 (D II 1, no.4638). 21 fol. (under Vedāṅga).
GJKSV 7891/115 (D II 1, no.4639). 21 fol. (under Vedāṅga).
GJKSV 9102/8 (D II 2, no.8821). 2 fol.
GJKSV 9103/9 (D II 2, no.8822). 5 fol.
GJKSV 9104/10 (D II 2, no.8823). 3 fol. (1, 5-6). Incomplete.
GJKSV 13047. 9 fol.
GJKSV 13635. 6 fol. (with C. Pañjikā). Dated V.S. 1805. Copied by Govinda Rāma Dīkṣita.
GJKSV 13817. 9 fol.
GJKSV 13831. 13 fol. (with Nighaṇṭu).
GJKSV 14158. 7 fol.
GJKSV 15730. 10 fol. Title on the cover page : Vedāṅga-śikṣā.
GJKSV 17230. 7 fol. (in Śikṣā-cchando-nighaṇṭu-jyotiṣa).
GJKSV 17796. 12 fol. (in Śikṣā-jyotiṣa-cchandaḥ).
GJKSV 18095. 9 fol.
GJKSV 18271. 4 fol.
GJKSV 19057. 10-20 fol. Incomplete. Title: Jyotiṣa-śikṣā.
GJKSV 19805. 5 fol.
GJKSV 20970. 15 fol. (in Śikṣā-jyotiṣa-cchandaḥ).
GJKSV 20994. 27 fol. (in Śikṣā-catuṣṭaya).
GJKSV 21022. 8 fol. Title: Vedādi-śikṣā (?)
GJKSV 21440. 38 fol. (in Śikṣā-catuṣṭaya).
GJKSV 21510. 22 fol. (in Śikṣā-catuṣṭaya).
GJKSV 21580. 6 fol. Title: Śikṣā-jyotiṣa.
GJKSV 23956. 27 fol. (in Śikṣā-catuṣṭaya).
GJKSV 24668. 4 fol. Title: Pāṇinīya-matam.
GJKSV 27112. 42 fol. (in Śikṣā-jyotiṣa-cchando-nighaṇṭu).
GJKSV 27482. 13 fol.
GJKSV 27572. 25 fol. Dated Śaka 1740 (in Vedāṅga-catuṣṭaya).
GJKSV 28244. 26 fol. Dated Śaka 1687 (in Śikṣādi-catuṣṭaya).
GJKSV 29242. 21 fol. Dated V.S. 1882 (in Śikṣā-catuṣṭaya).
GJKSV 29340. 9 fol. Incomplete (in Śikṣā-catuṣṭaya).
GJKSV 29339. 28 fol. (in Nighaṇṭu-catuṣṭaya).
GJKSV 30309. 22 fol. Dated V.S. 1646 (in Śikṣādi-catuṣṭaya).
GJKSV 33480. 25 fol. (in Śikṣādi-catuṣṭaya).
GJKSV 34180. 12 fol.
GJKSV 34182. 24 fol. (in Śikṣādi-veda-ṣaḍaṅga).
GJKSV 34354. 8 fol.
GJKSV 34408. 5 fol.
GJKSV 35809. 9 fol. Dated V.S. 1836. Title: Vedāṅga-śikṣā.
GJKSV 36058. 62 fol. (in Śikṣā-jyotiṣa-cchando-nighaṇṭvādi).
GJKSV 38205. 3 fol.
GJKSV 39545. 10 fol. Dated V.S. 1937. (Sasvarā).
GJKSV 43409(A). 8 fol. Dated V.S. 1855.
GJKSV 43431. 4 fol.

GJKSV 43551(A). 4 fol.
Granthappura p. 1 (no.7c). Mal. 75 Grantha-s. (a. Piṅgalācārya).
Hamburg StUB (Oppert 65a). PL. Gr.
Hamburg StUB (cod.Palmbl. III 8/133) → Veda-lakṣaṇa (HB).
Haug p. 30 (no.73) = München 9.
Hoshiarpur p. 52 (no.185). 3 fol. 61 Grantha-s.
Hoshiarpur p. 52 (no.186). 4 fol. 60 Grantha-s.
Hoshiarpur p. 52 (no.325). 1 fol. 36 Grantha-s.
Hoshiarpur p. 54 (no.29). (in Śikṣā-catuṣṭaya).
Hoshiarpur p. 54 (no.6475) (in Śikṣā-catuṣṭaya).
Hoshiarpur p. 54 (no.6782) (in Śikṣā-catuṣṭaya).
Hoshiarpur p. 301 (no.5613). PL. Gr. 3 fol. 33 Grantha-s.
Hz 1449. PL. Gr. 4 fol. Belonged to the late Raja Ghanapathi of Tiruvidaimarudur, Thanjavur Dist.
Hz 1827. 6 fol. Belonged to Jambunatha Bhatta of Thanjavur.
IM 501. 5 fol.
IM 2067. 6 fol.
IM 5173. 4 fol.
IM 5202. 12 fol.
IM 5268. 17 fol. (in Śikṣā-catuṣṭaya.
IM 6759. Incomplete.
IM 8155. 24 fol. Incomplete (in Śikṣādi-catuṣṭaya).
IM 8479. 4 fol.
IM 9428. 7 fol.
IM 9575. 8 fol.
IM 9819A.
IM 9872. 3 fol.
IM 9881. 4 fol.
IM 10240. 5 fol.
IM 10274. 4 fol.
IM 10667. 6 fol.
IO 539 (1743B). 6 fol. Dated V.S. 1854.
IO 540 (1347a). 3 fol.
IO 541 (2542b). 8 fol.
IO 542 (1981a). 5 fol. Dated Śaka 1699.
IO 543 (1378b). 6 fol. (193-98). Dated V.S. 1854.
IO 544 (3193). 11 fol. (with C. of Dharaṇī-dhara).
IO 4934 (Bühler 49). 9 fol. From Bombay.
IO 4935 (Burnell 496a)Gr. 3 fol.
IO 4936 (Burnell 320c). 6 fol. Dated A.D. 1804.
IO 4937 (Mackenzie III 188d). PL. Tel. 4 fol. Written ca. A.D. 1800.
IO 4938 (Mackenzie II 83f). PL. Na. 5 fol. Written ca. A.D. 1800.
IO 4939 (Mackenzie III 234d). PL. Tel. 7 fol. (26-32). Written ca. A.D. 1810.
IO 4940 (Bühler 27). 7 fol. (with the C. Śikṣā-pañjikā). Dated Śaka 1775.
Jammu RSRI p. 172 (no. 174ga3). 17 fol.
Jodhpur 1765.

L 1237. 5 fol. 73 Grantha-s.
Lz. 129. 7 fol. Written in 1783 by Mahādeva of Mahārāṣṭra.
Lz. 130. 11 fol. Dated A.D. 1803.
MD 989. PL. Kan. 7 pp. (1ff.).
MD 990. PL. Gr. 8 pp. (12ff.).
MD 17697. PL. Tel. 3 pp. 47 Grantha-s. Incomplete.
MD 19510F. PL. Mal. 6 fol. (52-57). This may be part of Śaiśira-śikṣā.
Mithila IV 173. 173(A)-(K) (12 Mss.).
MT 1165(c). PL. Tel. 2 fol. (47-48). Incomplete. Purchased in 1913-14 from Kashibhatta Subrahmanya Sastri of Vekanur, Krishna Dist.
MT 4082(c). PL. Tel. 3 fol. (69-71). Presented in 1921-22 by N. P. Sankara Ayyar, Nerur, Karur Taluk, Trichinapalli Dist.
MT 5266(c). Gr. 4 fol. (6-9). Transcribed in 1926-27 from a Ms. of Narayana Nambudiripad, Punnata-mana, Kottapadi, Malabar Dist.
MT 6018(a). PL. Gr. 3 fol. 60 Grantha-s. Col.: Vedanāsikā-śikṣā samāptā | Purchased in 1937-38 from E. Srinivasacharyar of Sriperumbudur, Chingelpet Dist.
München 9. 23 fol. Together with Jyotiṣa, etc.
Mysore (1898), p. 5 (no. 50a). Gr.
Mysore I, pp. 30-31, 613.
Mysore ND II 3618-27. Extract no. 214, 215, 216.
N-W P II 8 (no.24). 14 fol. Belonged to Makhanji of Mathura.
Oppert I 1005. Belonged to Viraraghava Tatacharyar, Head Master, Sanskrit School of Sathakopacharya, Kanchipuram, Chingelpet Dist.
Oppert I 5675. Belonged to Annasastri of Srivalliputtur, Tinnavelly.
Oppert I 8084. Belonged to Paravastu Venkatarangacharyar of Vishakhapattanam.
Oudh IX 4 (no.2). 9 pp. 60 Grantha-s. Belonged to Pandit Ramanarayana of Lucknow.
Oudh 1876, 2 (no.1). 18 pp. 100 Grantha-s. Dated A.D. 1837. Belonged to P. Sivasankara of Lucknow.
Oudh XVI 64 (no.3). 8 pp. 100 Grantha-s. Belonged to Pandita Sivaprasada of Lucknow.
Oudh XXII 64 (no.8). 7 pp. 80 Grantha-s. Belonged to Pandita Ranacchoradasa of Fyzabad.
Oxf. CS d.185(4). 11 fol. (with C. Pañjikā).
Oxf. CS d.185(5). 10 fol. (with C. Pañjikā).
Oxf. CS d.185(7). 5 fol. Title: Śaṃkara-śikṣā. 17th century. Śaṃkarācārya-kṛta-... by a later hand on the title page.
Oxf. CS d.185(12). 7 fol. (with anon. C.).
Oxf. CS d.963(7). 13 fol. Tel.
Oxf. CS c.30(1). 9 fol. (with C. Pañjikā). Dated A.D. 1837. (c ?)
Oxf. CS c.62(2). 5 fol. (RV recension).
Oxf. CS c.62(4). 7 fol. (RV recension).
Oxf. CS c.62(5). 16 fol. (in Śikṣā-catuṣṭaya).
Oxf. CS c.62(6). 23 fol. (in Śikṣā-catuṣṭaya).
Oxf. CS c.62(10). 4 fol. (RV recension).
Oxf. CS c.151(1). 11 fol. (with Jyotiṣa).
Oxf. CS f.18(2). 8 fol. Dated A.D. 1823.

Oxf. II 1077(1) (Ms. Wilson 502). 3 fol. Dated A.D. 1639. = Oxf. 386a (no.502). (With Jyotiṣa, Chandas, etc.).
Oxf. II 1078(1) (Ms. Wilson 503). 6 fol. Dated A.D. 1793. = Oxf. 386a (no.503). (With Jyotiṣa, Chandas, etc.).
Oxf. II 1079(1) (Ms. Sansk. c. 17). 6 fol. Dated A.D. 1743 (with Jyotiṣa, Chandas, etc.).
Oxf. II 1088 (Ms. Sansk. c. 44). 8 fol.
P 9.
Peters. II, p. 167 (no.19). 7 fol.
Peters. II, p. 167 (no.21). 15 fol.
Peters. II, p. 171 (no.24). 3 fol.
Peters. III, p. 386 (no.68).
Peters. IV, p. 4 (no.97). 4 fol.
Peters. V, p. 228 (no. 71).
Peters. VI, p. 61 (no.45). 6 fol. Dated Śaka 1734.
PUL I, p. 22 (no.102). 5 fol. 60 Grantha-s. Dated Śaka 1715.
PUL I, p. 22 (no.103). 5 fol. 60 Grantha-s.
PUL I, p. 22 (nc.104). 4 fol. 35 Grantha-s. Dated V.S. 1813.
PUL I, p. 22 (no.105). 4 fol. (2-5). Dated V.S. 1933.
PUL II. App. p. 13 (no.217). 23 fol. (in Śikṣā-catuṣṭaya).
Radh. I.2.
RASB II 1490 (G.2046). 4 fol. (in Vedāṅga-s).
RASB II 1491 (G 9326). 8 fol. (in Vedāṅga-s).
RASB II 1492 (G 9327). 14 fol. (in Vedāṅga-s).
RASB II 1502 (G 663) = L 1237.
RASB II 1503 (G 1375A). 4 fol. 72 Grantha-s.
RASB II 1504 (G 2632). 6 fol. Dated Śaka 1795.
RASB II 1505(I) (G 4180A). 5 fol. 46 verses. Incomplete.
RASB II 1505(II) (G 4180A). 5 fol. Incomplete.
RASB II 1515 (G 2815). Beng.
Rice 12. 3 Mss.
SB p. 11 (no.85). 4 fol. 72 Grantha-s. = SBD 2011.
SB p. 11 (no.86). 4 fol. 72 Grantha-s. = SBD 2012.
SB p. 11 (no.87). 10 fol. 284 Grantha-s (with Śikṣā-pañjikā). = SBD 47219.
SBD 2011. 4 fol. Dated V.S. 1745.
SBD 2012. 4 fol. Dated V.S. 1850.
SBD 2017. 4 fol.
SBD 2018. 4 fol. Dated V.S. 1784.
SBD 2026. 6 fol.
SBD 2028. 8 fol. (with anon. Bhāṣya). Dated V.S. 1869.
SBD 2030. 2 fol. Incomplete.
SBD 2031. 6 fol.
SBD 2032. 5 fol.
SBD 2033. 3 fol.
SBD 2034. 9 fol.
SBD 2035. 3 fol.
SBD 2038. 10 fol. (with C.). Dated Śaka 1761.

SBD 2039. 9 fol. (with Jyotiṣa and Chandas). Dated V.S. 1785.
SBD 2040. 5 fol.
SBD 2041. 10 fol.
SBD 2042. 7 fol. (3-9). Incomplete.
SBD 2043. 15 fol. Dated V.S. 1849.
SBD 2044. 24 fol. Title: Pāṇinīya-śikṣādayaḥ.
SBD 2045. 13 fol. (with Jyotiṣa and Chandas).
SBD 2046. 29 fol. Dated V.S. 1928 (in Śikṣādi-catuṣṭaya).
SBD 2048. 4 fol.
SBD 2050. 5 fol. Dated Śaka 1768.
SBD 2051. 25 fol. (with Jyotiṣa). Incomplete.
SBD 2052. 21 fol. Dated V.S. 1906 (in Śikṣā-jyotiṣa-cchandāṃsi).
SBD 2053. 5 fol. Dated V.S. 1853 (in Śikṣā-jyotiṣa-cchando-nighaṇṭavaḥ).
SBD 2062. 18 fol. (in Śikṣā-jyotiṣa-cchandāṃsi).
SBD 2081. 25 fol. (2-26). Incomplete. (in Śikṣā-jyotiṣa-cchando-nighaṇṭavaḥ).
SBD 2083. 2 fol. Incomplete.
SBD 2088. 20 fol. Dated V.S. 1720. (in Śikṣā-jyotiṣa-cchando-nighaṇṭavaḥ).
SBD 2094. PL. Drāvi. 95 fol. Incomplete.
SBD 46933. 5 fol.
SBD 46935. 7 fol. Incomplete.
SBD 46936. 4 fol. Incomplete.
SBD 46939. 16 fol. Dated V.S. 1887.
SBD 46942. 2 fol. Maithili script.
SBD 47213. 5 fol.
SBD 47460. 4 fol. Dated V.S. 1907 / Śaka 1771.
SBD 47566. 46 fol. (with Jyotiṣa and other works).
SBD 47649. 14 fol.
SBD 47955. 3 fol. Incomplete.
SBD 47956. 5 fol. Incomplete.
SBD 47965. 2 fol. (6-7). Incomplete. Dated V.S. 1908.
SBD 53774. 6 fol.
SBD 55292. 3 fol.
SBD 55416. 4 fol. (2-4, 6). Incomplete. (Vedāṅga-śikṣā).
Stein p. 39 (no. 803). 4 fol. (Ṛgvedinām).
Tb. 37. 3 fol. 35 verses. Yajus recension.
Tb. 208(B). Roth's transcript of IO 542 collated with IO 539 made in August 1845.
TD 1678. 5 fol. 64 Grantha-s.
TD 1679. 6 fol. 64 Grantha-s.
TD 1680. 6 fol. 64 Grantha-s.
TD 1681. 5 fol. 70 Grantha-s.
TD 1682. 6 fol. 64 Grantha-s.
TD 1683. 3 fol. 36 Grantha-s. Incomplete (section 6-11).
TD 1684. 6 fol. 64 Grantha-s.
TD 1685. 6 fol. 64 Grantha-s. Copied by Haribhaṭṭa. Dated Śaka 1538.
Tirupati SVUORI (427). PL. Na. 4 fol. (97-100).
Tirupati SVUORI 3503 (1143d). PL. Gr. 3 fol.

Tirupati SVUORI 3504 (6421b). PL. Gr. Incomplete.
Trav. Uni. 2088 C. PL. Gr. 3 fol. 60 Grantha-s.
Trav. Uni. 2405 B. PL. Gr. 50 Grantha-s.
Trav. Uni. 4941. 50 Grantha-s.
Trav. Uni. 5539 C. PL. Tel. 50 Grantha-s.
Trav. Uni. 7566. 250 Grantha-s (with C. Pañcikā). Dated V.S. 1900.
Trav. Uni. 14312 J. 50 Grantha-s.
Trav. Uni. 14241 A. 30 Grantha-s. Incomplete.
Trav. Uni. 15722 G. PL. Mal. 50 Grantha-s.
Trav. Uni. 16408 Z1. PL. Mal. 3 fol. 50 Grantha-s.
Trav. Uni. 17346 J. PL. Mal. 50 Grantha-s.
Trav. Uni. 17800 H. PL. Mal. 50 Grantha-s.
Trav. Uni. 18109 E. PL. Mal. 50 Grantha-s.
Trav. Uni. 19026 E. PL. Mal. 50 Grantha-s.
Trav. Uni. 22010 C. PL. Mal. 50 Grantha-s.
Ujjain I, pp. 7-8 (7 Mss.).
VOHD II 8.3042 (Hs.or.6358. StaatsB-PrK, Berlin). PL. Na. 3 fol. (100-02).
VSM I 1224-47. 24 Mss.
VSM III 196 (no.12177). 2 fol. Inc.
Wai I 1402-14 (13 Mss.; the last one with C. of Śeṣa).
Wai I 1416-48 (together with Jyotiṣa, etc.)
Wai II 10306. 7 fol.
Wai II 10307. 4 fol.
Wai II 10308. 20 fol. (in Śikṣādi-catuṣṭaya).
Weber 376 (Chambers 58, 5). 6 fol. Dated V.S. 1834 (60 verses; RV recension)
Weber 377 (Chambers 80, 4). 6 fol. Copy of the above.
Weber 378 (Chambers 190a). 4 fol. (35 verses, Yajus recension).
Weber 379 (Chambers 373q, 1). 4 fol. (Yajus recension).
Weber 1500 (Ms. or. fol. 882). 9 fol. (with C. Pañjikā).

Ptd.:

1) Published by Sajjanalala. – Benares, 1850. 12 pp. [IO : Ptd. Bks. Cat. 1957, p. 2475 (12 F 23; 1057)]
2) Ed. by A. Weber (in Roman script), with a German translation, of the Yajus and Ṛg recensions, *Indische Studien*, vol. IV (1858), pp. 345-71. [Adyar (H080 Web IS ge); SAI (inf Zs 73); Emeneau (381); SKGI (RI 130)]
3) Ed. by Beshanarama Tripathi, with the commentary *Pañjikā*. – Benares : Vrajabhushanadas and Company, 1887. 23 pp. [Wai (Na 15:2)]
4) In Śikṣā-saṃgraha *(Sasvarā Pāṇinīya-śikṣā)*. – Benares, 1889, pp. 378-84; 385-93. – (Ben. S. S. 10).
5) In the edition of Six Vedāṅga-s *(Vedasya Ṣaḍaṅga Prārambhaḥ*, viz. Pāṇinīya-śikṣā, Lagadha's Jyotiṣa, Piṅgala's Chandaḥ-sūtra, Nighaṇṭu, Nirukta and Aṣṭādhyāyī-sūtra-s). – Bombay : Tattvaviveka Press, Śaka 1814 (1892). 4, 3, 6, 14, 32, 79 pp. [BM : Ptd. Bks. Cat. 1892-1906. 811 (14007.c.27); Emeneau (340); SKGI (RI 135)]

6) With a commentary called *Bharadvāja-rāghavīya* of Kaḻattūri Rāghavācārya (title: *Śikṣā-bhāṣya)* (in Telugu script), pub. by Kalahasti Murari Venkatasubrahmanya. – Madras : Ve. Na. Jubilee Press, 1893. 2, 68 pp. [MyORI (B 2344); SVUORI (14.00.01/Bhā 2392)]

7) In *Śikṣādi-vedāṅga-catuṣṭaya,* ed. by Vasudeva Panashikar. – Bombay : Nirnaya Sagar Press, 1909. [SOAS (S. III.1 – 1922)]

Reprint of the above : Bombay : Nirnaya Sagar Press, 1934. [Adyar (H 215 SV TUK 1934)]

8) Ed. by Kanakalal Sarma Maithila, with commentary *Pañjikā* (in *Pāṇinīya-śikṣādi-saṃgraha).* – Benares : Chowkhamba, 1923, pp. 1-12. – (Haridas Sanskrit Series 1). [Emeneau (382); IO : Ptd. Bks. Cat. 1953, p. 1872 (San B 747)]

9) Ed. by Gopala Sastri Nene and Sudamasarma Misra, with *Pañjikā Bhāṣya.* – Benares : Chowkhamba, 1929. ii, 12 pp. – (Haridas Sanskrit Series 10). [Adyar (H080 CSS H10); Emeneau (384)]

10) Ed. by Rudraprasada Sharma, with his own commentary, *Pāṇinīya-śikṣā-pradīpa* and *Svara-vaidika-prakaraṇa-paṅkti-vivaraṇa.* – Benares : Chowkhamba, 1937 (1947). 24 pp. – (Haridas Sanskrit Series 59). [Adyar (H080 CSS H59)]

11) Ed. by Manmohan Ghosh *(Pāṇinīya Śikṣā* or the Śikṣā Vedāṅga, ascribed to Pāṇini : "being the most ancient work on Indo-Aryan phonetics – in all its five recensions with an Introduction, English translation and Notes, together with its two commentaries, the *Śikṣā-pañjikā* and *Śikṣā-prakāśa").* – Calcutta 1938. lxvi, 90 pp. [BORI (8699, 25455); NL (180 Pb 93 23(1); I C I G/1); UBTÜ (21 A 5786)]

Reprint of the above : Asian Humanities Press (India). Delhi : Indian Books Centre, 1986. [SAI (ind 54 B 187/741); SKGI (RI 131)]

12) Ed. by Narayana Misra, with Hindi translation and commentary called *Ābhā.* – Varanasi : Chowkhamba Orientalia, 1978. 7, 16 pp. – (Gokuldas Sanskrit Series 33).

And also in several editions of the *Aṣṭādhyāyī, Siddhānta-kaumudī* and *Vedāṅga-s,* e.g. :

In the *Siddhānta-kaumudī* with *Tattvabodhinī* of Jñānendra Sarasvatī, *Subodhinī* of Jayakṛṣṇa and *Candrakalā* of Bhairava-miśra. – Bombay : Sri Venkateswara Steam Press (Khemraj Shri Krishnadas, 1959, pp. 753-52.

In the *Vaiyākaraṇa-siddhānta-kaumudī,* Bālamanoramā-tattvabodhinī-sahitā, ed. by Giridhara Sharma Chaturveda and Parameshvarananda Sarma. – Delhi : Motilal Banarsidass, 1961 (many reprints), vol. 4, pp. 567-70.

[BM : Ptd. Bks. Cat. 1876-92. 273 (14093.c.3); 1906-1928. 724 (14092.a.40 and 726 / 14093.c.10); Emeneau (340, 2045, 2083, 2103); IO : Ptd. Bks. Cat. 1957, pp. 2475-76)]

Also included in: Chāndogya Brāhmaṇam. – Kumbakonam : Govinda Deekshithar Punya Smarana Samiti (ed.). Part II. 1981. Appendix pp. 1-8. [(SAI ***)].

– C.

B I, p. 206 (no.56). 7 fol.

Ben. 3. 5.

CPB 5667.

IM 3375. 15 fol. Title: Śikṣā-bhāṣya.

Jammu RSRI p. 173 (no. 86-ga-1). 12 fol.
Jammu RSRI p. 173 (no. 43-kha). 7 fol. Dated V.S. 1932.
Mysore (1898), p. 5 (no. 410b). Gr. 23 fol.
N-W P II 6 (no.15). 20 fol. Belonged to Makhanji of Mathura.
N-W P VII 6 (no.28). 9 fol. Belonged to Pandit Baladikshita Bhagavati, Benares.

— C. Śikṣā-pañjikā of Ṭumaṇi Gosvāmin (V.S. 1747).
Ujjain I, p. 8. 10 pp. Copied by Raghunātha Muṇagekar in V.S. 1873.

— C. Śikṣā-pradīpa.
Lahore p. 2 (no.5). 4 fol. 137 Grantha-s. In the possession of Pt. Jwala Datta Prasada, Lahore.

— C. Pañjikā (or Pāṇinīya-śikṣā-vivaraṇa) of Nāgara Dharaṇī-dhara, disciple of Mahādeva. Composed in V.S. 1454 (A.D. 1397) according to the concluding verse (cf. IO 544), during the reign of King Udayasiṃha and the ministership of Vīramadeva (cf. BBRAS 10; p. 5). It contains many quotations from, e.g. Audavraji, Nārada (Śikṣā), Śaunaka (Prātiśākhya), Suyajña (?). See F. Kielhorn : Remarks on the Śikṣās in : *Indian Antiquary*, vol. V, p. 195 (reprint in : *Kleine Schriften*, vol. I, pp. 158-69).

Beginning:

पातु वो निकषग्रावा मतिहेम्नः सरस्वती।
प्राज्ञेतरपरिच्छेदं वचसैव करोति या॥
छन्दःकल्पनिरुक्तानि विवृतानीह सूरिभिः।
शिक्षा त्वविवृता यस्मात् तस्मात् तां विवृणोम्यहम्॥

अथ शिक्षां प्रवक्ष्यामीति। अथेत्ययमानन्तर्ये। वेदाध्ययनस्यानन्तरमङ्गपाठः। किं कारणम्। षडङ्गो वेदो ऽध्येतव्य इति स्मरणात्। तत्र च शिक्षा प्रथमा। अथशब्दानुषङ्गात्। सा च वक्तव्या इत्यथशब्दस्यार्थः।

End:

त्रिनयनेति। वैतालीयं छन्दो ऽस्य। अन्येषामनुष्टुप् छन्दो ऽस्ति। त्रिनयनः शिवः। तस्य मुखान्निःसृता। यथा गुहायाः सिंहो निष्क्रामति तथा निःसृता। एतावता त्रिनयनेनापि न कृतेत्यर्थः। तां यो द्विजः पठेदधीयीत स (इह) धनादिभिर्युज्यते। सुखमतुलं परमानन्दं च मोक्षमुक्तप्रकारेण अश्नुते प्राप्नोति। अमुत्रामुष्मिन् लोके। (आदौ) धनधान्यपशुकीर्तिभाग् भवत्यन्ते मुक्तिभाक्। अन्यदवान्तरफलानि स्वर्गादीनि परिमितकालत्वात् तोलयितुं शक्यन्ते। मोक्षाख्यं तु अपरिमितकालावच्छिन्नं सुखरूपमित्यर्थः॥

श्रीमहादेवमाचार्यं शिक्षापञ्जिकयानया।
कविः संतुष्टमकरोन्नागरो धरणीधरः॥

इति वेदाङ्गशिक्षापञ्जिका समाप्ता॥

Ānandāśrama 2689. 16 fol.
Baroda 76. 11 fol. 200 Grantha-s. Dated V.S. 1654. = CLB I, p. 31.
Baroda 7735. 9 fol. 200 Grantha-s. = CLB I, p. 31.
Baroda 8791. 10 fol. 200 Grantha-s. Dated Śaka 1719. = CLB I, p. 31.
Baroda 9566. 10 fol. 200 Grantha-s. Dated V.S. 1822. = CLB I, p. 31.
Baroda 10400. 7 fol. 100 Grantha-s. Incomplete. = CLB I, p. 31.
Baroda 10603. 5 fol. 200 Grantha-s. Dated V.S. 1728. = CLB I, p. 31.
BBRAS 10 (S C ZZ E 34). 15 fol. (with text).
BISM p. 282 (22/1008).
Bombay Uni. 9 (BMC 84 8). 12 fol. (with text).
BORI 12 of 1883-84. 13 fol.
BORI 16 of A 1883-84. 10 fol. Title: Vedāṅga-śikṣā-pañjikā.
BORI 17 of 1895-1902. 10 fol.
BP p. 258 (no.12). 13 fol. Col.: Pāṇinīya-śikṣā-pañjikā.
Bühler p. 538 (no. 27) (Pāṇinīya-śikṣā-vyākhyā). = IO 4940.
Deccan College 10965. 15 fol.
GB 26. 9 fol. Copy of a Ms. Dated V.S. 1903.
GJKSV 13635. 6 fol. (with text). Dated V.S. 1805. Copied by Govinda Rāma Dīkṣita. Title: Vedāṅga-śikṣā-pañjikā.
GJKSV 35161. 7 fol.
GJKSV 36356. 12 fol. Title: Śikṣā-bhāṣya.
GJKSV 37353. 11 fol. (2-12). Incomplete. Title: Śikṣā-bhāṣya.
GJKSV 42236. 13 fol. Title: Śikṣā-vyākhyā.
GJKSV 44135. 9 fol. Incomplete.
Göttingen 160. 7 fol. (Śikṣā-pañjikā). Copied by Vāsudeva, son of Pithasākṣi Nārāyaṇācārya.
Haug p. 42 (no.168) = München 33.
Hpr. III 172. 7 fol. 400 Grantha-s. Title: Pāṇinīya-śikṣā-vivaraṇa.
IO 544 (3193). 11 fol.
IO 4940 (Bühler 27). 7 fol. Dated Śaka 1775.
Mithila IV 174. 8 fol.
Mithila IV 174(A). 6 fol.
München 33. 8 fol. Dated A.D. 1809.
Mysore ND II 3629 (C 3761/ 6). 8 fol. Extract no. 218.
Peters. II, p. 185 (no.16).
PUL II. App. p. 13 (no.218). 11 fol. 200 Grantha-s.
RASB II 1506A (G 1169). 9 fol. 200 g Dated V.S. 1800.
RASB II 1506B (G 1169). 12 fol. Dated V.S. 1788.
RASB II 1507 (G 2834). 7 fol. Dated V.S. 1828. Col.: Vedāṅga-śikṣā-pañjikā.
RASB II 1508A (G 4180B). 4 fol. Incomplete.
RASB II 1508B (G 4180C). 7 fol. Incomplete.
SB p. 11 (no.87). 10 fol. 284 Grantha-s (with text). = 47219.
SB p. 54 (no.97). 7 fol. 126 Grantha-s. SBD 47216.
SBD 2049. 7 fol.
SBD 2065. 10 fol. Dated V.S. 1847.
SBD 2084. 11 fol. Title: Vedāṅga-śikṣā-pañjikā.

SBD 47216. 7 fol. Dated V.S. 1832. Title: Śikṣā-bhāṣya.
SBD 47217. 4 fol. Title: Śikṣā-bhāṣya.
SBD 47218. 9 fol. (1-8, 12). Incomplete. Dated V.S. 1806. Title: Śikṣā-bhāṣya.
SBD 47219. 10 fol. Dated V.S. 1906. Title: Śikṣā-bhāṣya.
Trav. Uni. 7566. 250 Grantha-s (with text). Dated V.S. 1900.
Trav. Uni. 5247. 200 Grantha-s.
Weber 1500 (Ms. or. fol. 882). 9 fol. (with text).
Wellcome Inst. London. W 46.
Wellcome Inst. London. W 47.

Ptd.: In HSS 1 and 10; also in the edition of Manmohan Ghosh.

– C. Śikṣā-prakāśa.

Beginning:

ज्योतिर्व्याकरणं छन्दः कल्पशिक्षानिरुक्तयः ।
नेत्रास्यपादोर्नःकर्णा यस्य तं सततं नुमः ॥ १॥
व्याख्याय पिङ्गलाचार्यसूत्राण्यादौ यथायथम्।
शिक्षां तदीयां व्याख्यास्ये पाणिनीयानुसारिणीम्॥ २॥

ज्येष्ठभ्रातृभिर्विहितो व्याकरणे ऽनुजनुस्तत्रभगवान् पिङ्गलाचार्यस्तन्मतमनुभाव्य शिक्षां वक्तुं प्रतिजानीते -- अथ शिक्षामिति । वैदिकधर्मानुष्ठानात् पुरुषो निःश्रेयसार्थफलवानित्येष वैदिकः सिद्धान्तः । अतिगूढार्थस्य वेदस्याज्ञानान्नानुष्ठातुं शक्यो वेदमार्गः । अतः साक्षात्कृतधर्मभिर्वेदार्थेभ्यो निष्कृष्यार्थार्थिसुखबोधाय विद्यास्थानानि प्रवर्तितानि। तानि शिक्षा कल्पो व्याकरणं निरुक्तं छन्दो ज्योतिषं धर्मशास्त्रं पुराणं न्यायविस्तरो मीमांसादीनि। तथा च याज्ञवल्क्यः --

पुराणन्यायमीमांसा धर्मशास्त्राङ्गमिश्रिताः ।
वेदाः स्थानानि विद्यानां धर्मस्य च चतुर्दश॥

इति च। तथा हि शिक्षा स्वरवर्णोच्चारकं शास्त्रम्।

End:

व्याख्यातमन्यत्। शंकर इति। शं सुखं म्लेच्छत्वादिरोगाणां शमनं करोतीति शंकरः शिवः शङ्करणशीलां शब्दशास्त्रविद्याम् । दाक्षी दक्षस्यापत्यं तस्यापत्यमित्यण् । टिड्ढाणञित्यादिना ङीप् । तस्याः पुत्राय धीमते ऽतिसुबुद्धये प्रादात् । को ऽसावित्याकाङ्क्षायामाह। दाक्षीपुत्र इति। यः पाणिनिः । पणिनो युवापत्यम्। अत इञ्। येन पाणिनिना इदं प्रत्यक्षं शब्दशास्त्रं व्याहृतम् उक्तम्। तस्मै पाणिनये नमः पूर्वेण संबन्धः । पाणिनेय इति पाठे शुभ्रादित्वं कल्प्यम् । रत्नभूतमिति । स्पष्टम् । त्रिनयनमुखनिःसृतामिति । निरन्तरं द्विजो वेदाधिकारी सावधानः सदा निरन्तरं यः पठेत्। स पशुपुत्रकीर्तिमान् भवति। दिवि सुखमतुलं समश्नुते भुनक्ति। स्वर्गं व्याप्नोति वा

। द्विर्वचनं शिक्षा-ध्यायसमास्त्यर्थम् । विकृतिछन्दस्यर्धसममपरवक्त्रवृत्तमर्धसमा अर्धे इत्यधिकृत्य अपरवक्त्रं नौर्लोगजौज्याविति लक्षणसूत्रात्॥ इति शिक्षाप्रकाशः समाप्तः ॥

IM 3378. 12 fol. Dated V.S. 1847. Title: Śikṣā-sūtra-vivṛti.
SBD 2057. 5 fol. Dated V.S. 1791.
SBD 47215. 9 fol. (Śikṣā-bhāṣya Prakāśa).
VSM III 197 (no.11339). 12 fol. Title : Śikṣā-bhāṣya.

Ptd.: in Śikṣā-saṃgraha. – Benares, 1889, pp. 385-93. – (Ben. S. S. 10).
Also in the edition of Manmohan Ghosh.

– C. of Kauśika Vīrarāghavācārya.
Mysore I, p. 30 (Rāghavīya-bhāṣya).
Mysore ND II 3628 (C 78). Tel. 54 fol. Extract no. 217.

Ptd.: See above Telugu script edition.

– C. of Śeṣa (?). Both the Mss. in Wai have the commentary *Pañjikā* but ascribed to Śeṣa in the catalogue.
B I, p. 210 (no.75). 26 fol. Belonged to Ramabhatta Agnihotri of Ahmadabad.
Wai I 1414. 9 fol. (with text).
Wai I 1415. 5 fol. (with text). Dated Śaka 1786.

– C. of Sāyaṇācārya. Cf. Śikṣā-bhāṣya below. Both Mss. below are described as : "on the differences of the pronunciation of consonants and vowels together with their places".
N-W P I 14 (no.46). 10 fol. Belonged to Trilochana Pandit, Benares.
N-W P I 34 (no.102). 10 fol. Belonged to Trilochana Pandit, Benares.

[NCC XII 16a-71b]

858 PĀṆINĪYA-ŚIKṢĀ(-SŪTRA) (पाणिनीयशिक्षा /-सूत्र)
→ Varṇoccāraṇa-śikṣā. See also Śikṣā-sūtrāṇi.

859 PĀṆINĪYA-ŚIKṢĀYĀḤ ŚIKṢĀNTARAIḤ SAHA SAMĪKṢĀ (पाणिनीयशिक्षायाः शिक्षान्तरैः सह समीक्षा)
of Madhukar Pathak. A comprehensive study of the *Pāṇinīya-śikṣā* with reference to other ancient phonetical works.

Ptd.: Varanasi (K.17/4 Ratan Phatak) : Ray Printing Works, 1972. 38, 255 pp. [SAI (ind 51 D 88/2330)]

860 PĀDA-KḶPTI (पादक्लृप्ति)
Beginning:

प्रणम्य दक्षिणामूर्तिं वाणीं गुरुगणाधिपान्।
सप्तमे ऽतिजगत्यादौ पादक्लृप्तिर्विचिन्त्यते। ...
पद्सप्तत्यक्षरा सैषा सापणातिधृतिर्भवेत्।

द्वितीये सप्तवर्णे तु पादक्लृप्तिरितीरिता ॥

MD 19510. PL. Mal. 4 fol. (94-97).
Trav. Uni. 21926 D. PL. Mal. 55 Grantha-s.
Trav. Uni. 22010 J. PL. Mal. 70 Grantha-s.

861 PĀDA-NIRṆAYA (पादनिर्णय)
MD 19510C. PL. Mal. 5 fol. (40-44) (Pāśa-nirṇaya in the catalogue must be a misprint).

862 PĀDA-MAÑJARĪ (पादमञ्जरी)
"A treatise on Ṛgveda" ?
N-W P VI 4 (no.15). 6 fol. Belonged to Gopinatha Dikshita, Atale, Ulvar (Alwar).

863 PĀDA-VIDHĀNA (पादविधान)
One of the pre-Kātyāyana Anukramaṇī-s, attributed to Śaunaka. The text is divided into two sections, each consisting of seven verses accompanied by a commentary. It deals with a few doubtful cases of the division of Pāda-s in the *Ṛgveda.*

Beginning:

ऋक्षु पादाः सांशयिका भवन्ति दुराम्नाताश्चापि भवन्ति केचित्
तदनुसंदृश्येदं निबोधताचार्येण शौनकेनेङ्गितं यत् ॥
जागतौ प्रथमौ पादौ पादः षष्ठस्तथैव च ।
अष्टकास्त्वितरे पादाः पारुच्छेपीषु प्रायशः ॥

End:

ये पातयन्ते अज्मभिस्सुम्नमन्तस्तृतीयकः ।
उपरिष्टाद् बृहत्यो वा सुम्नमादिश्चतुर्थकः ॥
इन्द्र स्वाहापि वै तस्मानिमं कामं तथा शुनम् ।
यथावामत्रिरेवावामानुपूर्व्यं प्रचक्षते ॥
इति पादविधानं समाप्तम् ॥

Adyar D I 897 (28 G 53 = 72918). PL. Tel. 4 fol. = Adyar I, p. 51a.
Brl. p. 6 (no.IV) = IO 4239.
Calcutta Skt. Coll. I 524. 9 fol. Title: Ṛgveda-pādānukramaṇikā.
GD I 6-B. PL. Mal. 2 1/2 fol. 60 Grantha-s. Title: Ṛkpāda-lakṣaṇa.
GD I 36-D. Title: Ṛgveda-pāda-lakṣaṇa.
Granthappura p. 1 (no.7b). Mal. 75 Grantha-s (Ṛkpāda-lakṣaṇa).
Granthappura p. 3 (no.36d). Mal. 75 Grantha-s (Ṛgveda-pada-lakṣaṇa).
IM 427. 4 fol. Title: Chanda-udāharaṇa of Śaunaka. There are a few passages at the end illustrating different metres. Col.: Chandasām-udāharaṇāni.
IO 4239 (Burnell 205d). PL. Gr. 6 fol. (144-49). Title: Pādānukramaṇī. (It contains variants to the printed edition).

L 4245. 3 fol. 90 Grantha-s. Title: Pāda-vidhānānukramaṇī.
MD 19510L. PL. Mal. 4 fol. (98-101).
Mysore I, p. 24. Title: Ṛkpādānukramaṇikā.
Mysore ND II 3278 (P 4360/24). PL. Na. 2 fol. (70-72). Extract no. 69.
Mysore ND II 3279 (P 7743/ 1). PL. Na. 4 fol.
Mysore ND II 3281 (C 476/ 1). 4 fol.
Mysore ND II 3282 (C 3426/ 1). Na. 12 fol. (36-47). Extract no. 70.
Mysore Skt. Coll. p. 1 = D. No.12 (846/14). PL. Na. 2 fol. (46-47). Title: Pādānukramaṇikā.
PUL I, p. 22 (no.106). 4 fol. 60 Grantha-s.
RASB II 247 (G 2068). 3 fol. 80 Grantha-s. Title: Pāda-vidhānānukramaṇikā.
SBD 47795. 4 fol. Dated V.S. 1756.
SBD 47916. 6 fol. (Pāda-vidhānānukramaṇikā).
Tirupati SVUORI (427g). PL. Na. Title: Pādānukramaṇikā.
Trav. Uni. 19055 D. PL. Mal. 50 Grantha-s (Ṛgveda-saṃhitā-pada-lakṣaṇa).
Trav. Uni. 19055 E. PL. Mal. 350 Grantha-s (Ṛgveda-saṃhitā-pada-lakṣaṇa).
Trav. Uni. 21296 C. PL. Mal. 50 Grantha-s.
Trav. Uni. 22125 B. PL. Mal. 40 Grantha-s. Incomplete.
Trav. Uni. L.138 B. PL. Mal. 50 Grantha-s.

Ptd.: ed. by G. H. Narahari, *Pāda-vidhāna of Śaunaka*, with an anonymous commentary Entitled *Pāda-vidhāna-bhāṣya* (on the basis three Mss.). – Madras : Adyar Library, 1950. 34 pp. – (Adyar Library Pamphlet Series 22). (Reprint from *The Adyar Library Bulletin*, vols. 13-14 [1949-50]). [NL (180 Jc 95 184); SAI (85/1960*)]

[NCC XII 28b-29a]

864 PĀDA-SAṂKHYĀ (पादसंख्या)

The text of this work is identical with the *Pada-saṃkhyā-pradīpikā* of Dāmodara noted above. For an analysis of the text see C. Kunhan Raja in : *The Adyar Library Bulletin*, vol. 11 (1947), pt. 2, pp. 79-96; pt. 3, pp. 189-201.

865 PĀDĀNUKRAMAṆIKĀ (पादानुक्रमणिका)

Mysore Skt. Coll. p. 1 (Padānukramaṇikā) = D. No.12 (846/14) → Pāda-vidhāna.

866 PĀDĀNUKRAMAṆĪ (पादानुक्रमणी)

Quoted by Ṣaḍguru-śiṣya → Pāda-vidhāna. IO 4239.

[NCC XII 29a]

867 PĀDĀNTA-SAṂGRAHA (पादान्तसंग्रह)

Pratīka-s and the last letter of the first and third Pāda of each verse of the *Ṛgveda*.

Trav. Uni. 10622. PL. Mal. 1000 Grantha-s (damaged).
Trav. Uni. L.138 A. PL. Mal. 850 Grantha-s.
Trav. Uni. L.170 A. PL. Mal. 250 Grantha-s. Incomplete.
Trav. Uni. L.172. PL. Mal. 1000 Grantha-s. (Vargārdharca-pāda-saṃkhyā).

[NCC XII 29b]

868 PĀDĀNTA-SAṂGRAHA (TAITTIRĪYA) (**पादान्तसंग्रह / तैत्तिरीय**)

Trav. Uni. 17335. PL. Mal. 900 Grantha-s.

Trav. Uni. 22125. PL. Mal. 975 Grantha-s.

869 PĀRĀŚARĪ-ŚIKṢĀ (**पाराशरी शिक्षा**)

160 verses giving the number of letters in each Kaṇḍikā of the *Śukla Yajurveda*, and describing the method of their pronunciation. It also contains a few euphonic rules here and there but without any order or arrangement. Verses 77 and 78 list the names of eight Śikṣā-s of the Mādhyandina School of the *Vājasaneyi-saṃhitā*.

Beginning:

अथ शिक्षां प्रवक्ष्यामि पाराशरमतं यथा।
यथा देवेषु विश्वात्मा यथा तीर्थेषु पुष्करम्॥ १॥
तथा पाराशरी शिक्षा सर्वशास्त्रेषु गीयते।
प्रणवं तु प्रवक्ष्यामि तिस्रो मात्रास्त्रिदैवतम्॥ २॥
त्रिरूपं च त्रिवर्णं च त्रिस्थानं त्रिगुणं तथा।
अक्षराशीतिरेकश्च प्रथमा कण्डिका स्मृता॥ ३॥
लक्षणोक्तप्रकारैस्तु इषे त्वेति निदर्शनम्।
त्रिणि त्रीणि च चत्वारि दश पञ्चाष्टमं स्मृतम्॥ ४॥
एकादशाक्षरं तद्वदुभयोरपि दृश्यते।
सप्तमं पञ्चमं चैव पुनश्चैकादशाक्षरम्॥ ५॥ ...
याज्ञवल्क्यी तु वासिष्ठी शिक्षा कात्यायनी तथा।
पाराशरी गौतमी तु माण्डव्यामोघनन्दिनी॥ ७७॥
पाणिन्या सर्ववेदेषु सर्वशास्त्रेषु गीयते।
वाजसनेयिशाखायां तत्र माध्यन्दिनी मता॥ ७८॥

End:

पूषा मित्रो वसून् पञ्चानुरञ्जनाः प्रकीर्तिताः।
एकार्धमात्रिकाश्चैव पञ्चैते चानुरञ्जनाः॥ १५७॥
वक्ष्ययक्ष्यकक्ष्यभक्ष्यमाणा इत्येवमादयः।
इमे वर्णास्तु तालव्याः परा मूर्धन्यजाः स्मृताः॥ १५८॥
एवं ज्ञात्वा पठेद्यस्तु स गच्छेद् वैष्णवं पदम्।
न मे प्रियो द्विजः कश्चिच्छुद्धपाठी त्वतिप्रियः॥ १५९॥
इति पाराशरेणोक्तं विप्राणां हितकाम्यया।
शिष्याणामुपकाराय परलोकहिताय च॥ १६०॥
इति श्रीपाराशरीशिक्षा समाप्ता॥

BBRAS 11 (B D 278). 4 fol. Dated Śaka 1787.

Bhau Daji p. 121.
Bhk. 9.
BORI 56 of A 1881-82. 5 fol. 149 Grantha-s.
IM 9540.
IM 10662. 11 fol. (3-13). Incomplete.
L 1236. 10 fol. 161 Grantha-s.
Mithila IV 176.
Mithila IV 176(A)-(C).
Oxf. CS d.185(8). 13 fol. (1 fol. missing). Dated A.D. 1879. Title: Parāśaraśikṣāśāstra ?
Oudh IX 4 (no.3). 18 pp. 200 Grantha-s. Belonged to Pandit Ramanarayana of Lukknow.
PUL II. App. p. 12 (no.188).
RASB II 1509 (G 659) = L 1236.
RASB II 1510 (G 3256). 9 fol. Dated V.S. 1939.
RASB II 1515 (G 2815). Beng.
SBD 2092. 7 fol. Incomplete.

Ptd.: in Śikṣā-saṃgraha. – Benares, 1889, pp. 52-71. – (Ben. S. S. 10).

[NCC XII 47a]

*PĀRI (पारि)

Referred to by Ayyāśāstrin in his *Sapta-svara-sindhu*, TCD 33.

[NCC XII 48a]

870 PĀRIŚIKṢĀ (पारिशिक्षा)

An enigmatic title. The name Pāri is not beyond doubt, though mentioned in the commentary of Cakra and referred to by Ayyāśāstrin in his *Sapta-svara-sindhu*, TCD 33. The text is found with varying titles in different Mss. Helmut Scharfe relates him to the Chief Pāri, known in the Old Tamil literature. See his *Grammatical Literature*, p. 176. It deals with the following topics as given in the margin on the corresponding pages of MD 15925 :

Paribhāṣā
Varṇasāra-bhūta-varṇakrama-lakṣaṇam
Varṇakramaḥ
Udāttādi-svara-dharmāḥ
Vyañjanādi-dharma-saṃkhyā-niyamaḥ
Varṇotpattiḥ
Dhvani-prakaraṇam
Sthāna-karaṇa-prakaraṇam
Sthāna-karaṇa-viśeṣaḥ
Prayatna-prakaraṇam
Varṇānāṃ devatā-niyamaḥ
Varṇānāṃ jāti-niyamaḥ
Aṅga-prakaraṇam
Varṇa-saṃjñā
Mātrā-kāla-lakṣaṇam
Udāttādīnāṃ devatā-jāti-niyamaḥ
Hasta-svara-lakṣaṇam
Svara-vinyāsaḥ
Aṅgādy-avasthā
Ṣaḍjādi-lakṣaṇam
Ṣaḍja-lakṣaṇam
Ṛṣabha-lakṣaṇam
Gāndhāra-lakṣaṇam
Madhyama-lakṣaṇam
Pañcama-lakṣaṇam
Niṣāda-lakṣaṇam
Bharata-vihita-saṃjñā
Udāttādy-utpatti-sthānam
Sapta-svarita-bhedāḥ
Kṣaipraḥ
Nityaḥ
Prātihataḥ
Abhinihitaḥ
Praśliṣṭaḥ

Pādavṛttaḥ
Tairovyañjanaḥ
Tatprayatna-bhedāḥ
Svarita-kampāḥ
Udātta-kampāḥ
Kampotpādana-varṇāḥ
Svarabhakti-lakṣaṇam
Svarabhakti-nāmāni
Svarabhakty-udāharaṇāni
Vivṛtti-lakṣaṇam
Vatsānusṛtiḥ
Vatsānusāriṇī
Pākavatī
Pipīlikā
Ubhaya-dīrghī
Savarṇa-dīrghī-madhyāḥ
Vivṛtty-udāharaṇāni
Raṅga-pluta-lakṣaṇam
Raṅga-dīrgha-lakṣaṇam

Prathamaḥ Paricchedaḥ

Dvitva-prakaraṇam
Anusvāra-viṣayaḥ
Pūrvāgama-prakaraṇam
Lakṣyānusāra-dvitvam
Ādeśaḥ
Abhinidhānam
Āgama-viśeṣaḥ
Yama-viṣayaḥ
Auṣmapara-prathamasya dvitīyaḥ
Padānta-nakāra-viṣayaḥ
Nāsikyaurasatvam
Hari-praṇava-viṣayaḥ
Jihvāmūlīyopadhmānīyaḥ
Svara-varṇa-krama-lakṣaṇam

Beginning:

प्रणिपत्य जगन्नाथं वासुदेवं सनातनम्।
(प्रणिपत्य दयासिन्धुं रामदेवं सनातनम्।)
गणाधिपं गिरां देवीं शिक्षां वक्ष्ये यथामति॥ १॥
अथ वर्णसमाम्नाय उच्यते याजुषो ऽत्र तु।
आदितो नववर्णाः स्युः समानाक्षरका इह॥ २॥
ह्रस्वदीर्घे सवर्णे स्तो द्वे द्वे न प्लुतपूर्वकम्।
स्वराः षोडश तस्यादौ शेषो व्यञ्जनसंज्ञिकः ॥ ३॥

End: (in Hamburg Ms:)

शुद्धवर्णे त्वचामादौ यद्युच्चादिः प्रयुज्यते।
संविद्यात् स्वरवर्णं तम् (तद्) एतदेवास्य लक्षणम् …॥
वर्णे च स्वरमात्राङ्गवर्णसारेषु नित्यशः ।
कारोत्तरस्वरेभ्यो ऽर्वाङ् न च संधिः कदाचन॥
उदात्तादिस्वरात् पूर्वं स्वरवर्णे च मातृका।
यदि युज्येत नाम्नासौ मातृकावर्ण उच्यते॥
तस्मिंस्तु मातृकात् पूर्वमचां संज्ञोच्यते यदि।
हलामादावङ्गसंज्ञा नामान्यस्याङ्गवर्णकः ॥
यत्र यत्र व्यञ्जनानां पौर्वापर्यविधानतः ।

यथाङ्गलक्षणं प्रोक्तमङ्गवर्णे तथा वदेत्॥
व्यञ्जनानामङ्गवर्णे त्वङ्गं भूतोत्तरं वदेत्।
हल्संज्ञिकेति कण्ठोक्त्या वदेत् तन्नाम वै ततः॥
आदौ स्वराणामच्संज्ञा तत्तन्मात्रा वदेत् ततः।
अथ स्वरानुदात्तादीन् तन्नाम च वदेत् क्रमात्॥
व्यञ्जनं यद्यवसितं तस्य मात्रा विधीयते।
यत्रानवसितं तत् स्यात् तन्मात्रा तत्र नेष्यते॥
अनेकवर्णसंयोगो यत्रैकव्यञ्जनात्मकः।
स्यात् पूर्वाङ्गो भवेत् तत्र पूर्वाङ्गादि सकृद् वदेत्॥
एकव्यञ्जनसंयोग उभयाङ्गो भवेद्यदि।
पृथगङ्गं प्रयुञ्जीयात् पौर्वापर्यक्रमात् तदा॥
यदुक्तं केवले वर्णे शास्त्राद् द्वित्वागमादिकम्।
तत् सर्वमङ्गवर्णोक्तौ प्रयुञ्जीयाद्यथाविधि॥

Adyar D I 967 (1 A 19 = TR 19). Gr. 14 fol. (pp. 95-119). Incomplete. Title: Varṇa-krama-śikṣā. = Adyar I, p. 53a.

Hamburg StUB (cod.Palmbl. III 8/133) → Veda-lakṣaṇa (HB).

Hoshiarpur p. 52 (no.4371). PL. Gr. 10 fol. 300 Grantha-s. Extract p. 410.

MD 924. 60 pp. (with C.).

Copy of MD 925.. (= Skt. Texts on Phonetics, pp. 317-94).

MD 925. PL. Gr. 120 pp. (with C.).

MD 15925. PL. Gr. 23 fol. (with C.).

MD 20099. PL. Gr. 5 fol. (35-39). Incomplete. See the description at MD 16208. This Ms. reads exactly as the Adyar D I 967. The title Pāriśikṣā is found only on the title slip.

Mysore ND II 3599 (P 2326/ 3). PL. Gr. 44 fol. Extract no. 204. Title: Pañca-varṇa-krama-nidāna.

Mysore ND II 3738 (P 2339/10a).PL. Gr. 30 fol. (60-89) (with C.). Extract no. 265. Title: Varṇa-krama-lakṣaṇa.

Oppert II 763. Belonged to Ghanapathi Shingaracharyar of Alasur, Madurantakam Taluk.

Oppert II 7396. Belonged to Venkatarama Sastri of Pillur, Mayavaram Taluk.

– C. Yājuṣa-bhūṣaṇa or Yājuṣābharaṇa of Cakra, son of Rāma.

Beginning: (924)

सिताम्भोजनिष्ठं रथाङ्गाब्जमुद्रास्तथा पुस्तकं तं कराब्जैर्दधानम्।
प्रणम्याश्ववक्त्रं त्वहं पञ्चवर्णक्रमाणां निदानं प्रवक्ष्ये प्रबन्धम्॥ १॥

अथ इष्टदेवताप्रणामानन्तरं स्वगुरोः वेदतल्लक्षणाद्यभिज्ञताप्रकाशनमुखेन वस्तुनिर्देशपूर्वकं मङ्गलमातनुते -- पदक्रमेति।

पदक्रमजटाघनध्वजरथादिभेदैर्युता
श्रुतिः प्रथितलक्षणा स्फुरितपञ्चवर्णक्रमा।
यदीयवदनान्तरे वसतिमाप शास्त्रैः समं
स मे विजयतेतरां प्रथितरामनामा गुरुः ॥ २॥

अथ मङ्गलानन्तरं विविधवर्णक्रमादिलक्षणविचाररसिकानां विदुषां तत्तल्लक्षणसुखपरिज्ञानार्थं सांप्रतिकजनदुरवबोध भारद्वाजव्यासपारिशंभुकौहलहारीत बोधायनवसिष्ठवाल्मीकिप्रभृतिमुनिगणविनिर्मित शिक्षादिग्रन्थानुसारेण ललितपदसंदर्भं किंचित् प्रबन्धं कर्तुमनाः स्वकीर्त्यनुवृत्तये स्वनामधेयं निबध्नन् शिष्यावधानाय प्रतिजानीते -- तनय इति।

तनयो विनयोज्वलस्य तस्य प्रथितो वैदिकवावदूकसिंहः ।
कृपया महतां स चक्रनामा ह्यपि वर्णक्रमलक्षणं करोति॥

तनय इत्यादि स्पष्टो ऽर्थः । संप्रति स्वग्रन्थस्य अमूलकताशङ्काप्रयुक्तानादरपरिहाराय समूलकतां प्रतिपादयन् शिष्यपरिग्रहस्य स्वस्य ग्रन्थस्य चाभ्युदयसाधनतया एतद्ग्रन्थफलीभूतां शिष्टप्रीतिं प्रार्थयते -- सतामिति।

सतां मुदं संप्रति पारिशिक्षाव्याख्यानभूता हृदयंगमेयम्।
विलक्षणा याजुषभूषणाख्या कृतिर्मदीया वितनोतु कामम्॥

अथ शिक्षाकारोक्तमङ्गलश्लोकमाह --
प्रणिपत्य जगन्नाथं वासुदेवं सनातनम्।
गणाधिपं गिरां देवीं शिक्षां वक्ष्ये यथामति॥
प्रारिप्सितस्य ... शिक्षां वक्ष्ये। अथ वर्णसमाम्नाय उच्यते याजुषो ऽत्र तु। अथेत्ययं शब्दो ऽधिकारार्थः । वर्ण्यन्ते व्यक्तं ध्वन्यन्त इति वर्णाः अकारादयः ।

End:

केवलवर्णक्रमलक्षणं समाप्तम्।
शुद्धवर्णे त्वचामादौ यद्युच्चादिः प्रयुज्यते।
संविद्यात् स्वरवर्णं तम् (तद्) एतदेवास्य लक्षणम्॥

शुद्धवर्ण इति । शुद्धवर्णे केवलवर्णक्रमोक्तौ अचामकाराद्यौकारपर्यन्तानां स्वराणाम् । आदौ प्रथमतः उच्चादिः उदात्तादिस्वरः प्रयुज्यते यदि तं तथा प्रयुक्तोदात्तादिस्वरविशिष्टवर्णं स्वरवर्णं संविद्यात्। स्वरवर्णक्रममिति सम्यग् ज्ञेयमित्यर्थः । अस्य स्वरवर्णक्रमस्य एतदेव लक्षणमेतावदेव लक्षणम्॥
पारिशिक्षाव्याख्या (याजुषभूषणम्) समाप्ता॥

MD 924. 60 pp. (with text).
Copy of MD 925.. (= Skt. Texts on Phonetics, pp. 317-94).
MD 925. PL. Gr. 120 pp. (with text).
MD 15925. PL. Gr. 23 fol. (with text).

Mysore I, p. 32.
Mysore ND II 3600 (P 2326/ 4). PL. Gr. 44 fol. Extract no. 205. Title: Pañca-varṇa-krama-nidāna-vyākhyā.
Mysore ND II 3744 (P 2339/10b). PL. Gr. 9 fol. (60-89) (with text). Title: Varṇa-krama-lakṣaṇa-vyākhyā Yājuṣa-bhūṣaṇa.
Mysore ND II 3748 (P 2339/10c). PL. Gr. 9 fol. (60-89) (with text). Extract no. 269. Title: Varṇa-krama-lakṣaṇa-vyākhyā Varṇa-krama-darpaṇa.
Oppert II 764. Belonged to Ghanapathi Shingaracharyar of Alasur, Madurantakam Taluk.
PUL I, p. 23 (no.116). PL. Gr. 31 fol. 900 Grantha-s. Incomplete.
Trav. Uni. 2087. PL. Gr. 200 Grantha-s (damaged).

[NCC XII 50b]

871 PĀRṢADA (पार्षद)

The eighth Pariśiṣṭa of Kātyāyana. Some of the entries below may be *Vājasaneyi-prātiśākhya* since "Pārṣada" is an ancient name of Prātiśākhya.

Alwar 195.
Baroda 12011(f). = CLB II, p. 12. (8th Pariśiṣṭa).
Bd. 74. 6 fol. (with Ṛgyajuḥ-pariśiṣṭa).
BORI 2 of 1898-99.
BORI 74 of 1887-91. = BORI D I i.200. Dated V.S. 1553.
Jammu RSRI p. 172 (no. 5140). 13 fol. Title: Vājasaneyi-prātiśākhya.
N-W P V 62 (no.13). 15 fol. Belonged to Pt. Makhana Misra of Mathura.
N-W P V 62 (no.14). 10 fol. Belonged to Pt. Balamukunda of Benares.
N-W P V 148 (no.29). 10 fol. (with C.).
Oxf. CS c.21(9). 3 fol. 8th Pariśiṣṭa. Formerly owned by Mālavīya Paṇḍita Bālamukunda.
Peters. II, p. 174 (no.92). 13 fol.
Peters. VI, p. 136 (no.2). Aṣṭama-pariśiṣṭa-pārṣadam.
RASB II 974 (G ?). 15 fol. (with Ṛgyajuḥ-pariśiṣṭa).
Rep. Hpr. 1901-06, p. 2.
SB p. 75 (no.61). 10 fol. 200 Grantha-s. (Pārṣada-pariśiṣṭa). = SBD 47951.
SBD 47951. 10 fol. 200 Grantha-s. 8th Pariśiṣṭa.

[NCC XII 73b; II 210a]

– C.

K p. 184 (no.161). Pārṣada-ṭīkā of Uvaṭa (listed under Dharma).
N-W P V 60 (no.4). 198 fol. Described as "A commentary of Prātiśākhya of Pārshada treating of the Vikṛtis and Sandhis of the Saṃhitā". Belonged to Dhundhiraja Shastry, Benares.
N-W P V 62 (no.11). 71 fol. Title: Kātyāyana-prātiśākhya-bhāṣya. Belonged to Pandit Rangacharya Svami, Vrindavana.
Oppert I 1903. PL. Gr. 150 pp. Belonged to Sivasuri Sastri of Bhavani, Coimbatore Dist.
Oppert II 950. Belonged to Jadapattur Rangacharyar of Kanchipuram.
P 5.

– C. of Annam-bhaṭṭa, disciple of Sumaṅgala. Hall p. 69.

872 PĀRṢADA-PARIŚIṢṬA (पार्षदपरिशिष्ट)
of Śaunaka → Ṛgveda-prātiśākhya.
Alph. List Beng. Govt. p. 66.

873 PĀRṢADA-BHĀṢYA (पार्षदभाष्य)
→ Uvaṭa's Bhāṣya on the Ṛgveda-prātiśākhya.
SBD 47234. 155 fol.
SBD 47237. 135 fol. (1-105, 109-12, 144-61, 163-70). Incomplete.
SBD 47238. 140 fol.

874 PĀRṢADA-VYĀKHYĀ (पार्षदव्याख्या)
→ Uvaṭa's Bhāṣya on the Ṛgveda-prātiśākhya.
SBD 47240. 16 fol. Incomplete. 9th Paṭala.
SBD 47241. 158 fol. Dated V.S. 1820.

875 PĀRṢADA-SŪTRA (पार्षदसूत्र)
→ Ṛgveda-prātiśākhya and Vājasaneyi-prātiśākhya.

876 PIṆḌA-LAKṢAṆA see VARṆA-PIṆḌA-LAKṢAṆA (पिण्डलक्षण / वर्णपिण्डलक्षण)
Adyar D I 969 (1 A 19 = TR 19). Gr. 3 fol. (pp. 76-80). = Adyar I, p. 51a.

877 PIṆḌA-LAKṢAṆA-ŚIKṢĀ (पिण्डलक्षणशिक्षा)
Oppert I 1007. Belonged to Viraraghava Tatacharyar, Head Master, Sanskrit School of Sathakopacharya, Kanchipuram, Chingelpet Dist.
Oppert II 765. Belonged to Ghanapathi Shingaracharyar of Alasur, Madurantakam Taluk.
Oppert II 7397. Belonged to Venkatarama Sastri of Pillur, Mayavaram Taluk.
Oppert II 8562. Belonged to Venkatacharyar of Timmagudi near Kumbakonam.
Oppert II 9478. Belonged to Srinivasa Sastri of Tiruvasalur, Kumbakonam Taluk.
[NCC XII 87a]

878 PUNARĀVARṆI (पुनरावर्णि)
→ Āvarṇi (RV).
Mysore ND II 3631 (P 4906/10). PL. Na. 2 fol. (114-15). Extract no. 219.

879 PURUṢA-SŪKTA-JAṬĀ-PĀṬHA (पुरुषसूक्तजटापाठ)
Cf. Pañca-pāṭhaḥ Pauruṣādhyāyaḥ (ptd.).
SBD 53419.
SBD 53650. 11 fol. (1-9, 1-2).

880 PUṢPA-SŪTRA see PHULLA-SŪTRA (पुष्पसूत्र / फुल्लसूत्र)

881 PŪRVA-ṚKKĀRIKĀ (पूर्व-ऋक्कारिका)
of Gopāla and Veṅkaṭeśa, in verses.

Beginning: (898)

पूर्व-ऋक्कारिकाप्रारम्भः ।

चतुःपञ्चाशदधिकं पद्च्छतं प्रागृचां मितः ।
तासां तु प्रागृचं मध्यं त्वं हत्यात्परत स्मृतम् ॥
प्रपाठके सार्धषद्कमृक्तन्त्रं रुद्रसंज्ञकम् ।
षद्षष्टिसंख्याः खण्डानां विवृतस्तत्र कथ्यते ॥
गायत्रमेकखण्डं चाग्नेयं द्वादशखण्डकम् ।
बहुसाम्यस्तु षद् खण्डान्येकसाम्नस्तथैव च ॥
आहत्या अष्टकं खण्डास्त्रैष्टुभास्त्रैयमेव च ।
चत्वार्यनुष्टुभश्चेन्द्रपुच्छं तु नवखण्डकम् ॥
पवमानं रुद्रसंख्याश्चारुणं पञ्चकं स्मृतम् ।
महानाम्न्य द्वितीया स्युस्समुच्छितपुरोदिताः ॥

End:

आहत्य च ऋचां संख्या तमवाः परिकीर्तिताः ।
ऋन्द्रप्रय ऋचौ द्वे ते आरुणे त्वादिपर्वणि ॥
मरुत्खण्डे पुरोभागे ऋक्पदं साम च क्रमात् ।
पठिता पठतां ज्ञस्यै नारदीये विशेषतः ॥
गोपालवेङ्कटेशाभ्यां कारिकेयं कृताधुना ।
द्वयोश्च वीक्षतां चैव कुर्यात् भद्रं सभेश्वरः ॥

प्रकृति-ऋक्कारिका समाप्ता ।

Adyar D I 898 (33 D 12 = 75239). PL. Gr. 9 fol. (93-101). = Adyar I, p. 51a.
Adyar D I 899 (33 E 7 = 75254). PL. Gr. 3 fol. (41-43).

882 PŪRVA-ṚKPADA-LAKṢAṆA (**पूर्व-ऋक्पदलक्षण**)
Adyar D I 900 (33 D 12 = 75239). PL. Gr. 1 fol. (1). = Adyar I, p. 51a.

883 PŪRVA-DĪRGHĪ (**पूर्वदीर्घी**)
→ also Pūrvottarobhaya-(pada-)dīrghī.

Beginning:

वशान्नायाकवारिं महेन्द्रायन्द्रस्यैतुमैतोरष्टाश्रिरष्टाक्षरेणाष्ट ।क्षरम्
अष्टापद्यष्टाक्षराण्यष्टाक्षरात् ⋯ ।

End:

जिह्वाग्रेण यथोदितमेत्यायनाय विश्वाहञ्जसायनी आर्तोर्महेन्द्रं माहेन्द्रम् इत्येते पूर्वदीर्घिणः

Adyar D I 983 → Veda-lakṣaṇa (A 1).

Adyar D I 986 → Veda-lakṣaṇa (A 4).
Mysore ND II 3632 (P 660/ 4). PL. Gr. 16 fol. (8-23). Incomplete.
Trav. Uni. 16408 H. PL. Mal. 1 fol. 4 Grantha-s.
Trav. Uni. 17346 E. PL. Mal. 5 Grantha-s.

884 PŪRVOTTARA-ṚṄNIGHĀTA-KĀRIKĀ (पूर्वोत्तर-ऋङ्निघातकारिका)
→ Ṛṅnighāta-kārikā.
Adyar D I 766 (33 D 12 = 75239). PL. Gr. 3 fol. (47-49). Title: Ṛṅnighāta-kārikā. = Adyar I, p. 48b.
Adyar D I 901 (33 E 7 = 75254). PL. Gr. 2 fol. (52-53). Copied by Pañcuśāstrin on the 1st day of the bright fortnight, Mithuna Māsa, Vilambi V.S..

885 PŪRVOTTAROBHAYA-(PADA-)DĪRGHIṆAḤ (पूर्वोत्तरोभय-(पद-)दीर्घिणः)
Three lists of certain pairs of words in the *Taittirīya-saṃhitā* which are phonetically fused together. The object of the work is to be of help in learning the Pada-pāṭha → Pūrva-dīrghī, Apara-dīrghī, Utta-a-dīrghī and Ubhaya-dīrghī.

Adyar D I 987 → Veda-lakṣaṇa (A 6).
Adyar D I 902 (19 D 61 = 66253). PL. Gr. 1 fol. (no. 18). Contains Pūrva-dīrghī, Uttara-dīrghī and Ubhaya-dīrghī. The beginning is identical with Adyar D I 945 (Yaṇādeśa-dīrghī).
Adyar D I 903 (19 E 42 = 66327). PL. Gr. 1 fol. (no. 42).
Adyar D I 904 (19 O 5 = 66887). PL. Mal. 1 fol. (no. 124).
Adyar D XIII 208 (VB 1141b). PL. Na. and Tel. 2 fol.
MD 926. PL. Tel. 2 pp. (31f.).
MD 927. PL. Gr. 2 pp. (46f.).
MD 14745. PL. Tel. 4 pp. (16ff.). One additional verse at the end.
MD 16707. PL. Tel. 3 pp. 51 Grantha-s.
MT 485(i). PL. Tel. 2 fol. (65-66). Presented in 1910-11 by C. Visvanatha Shastrigal of Viziyanagaram.
MT 1205(d). PL. Tel. 1 fol. (no.17). Incomplete. Presented in 1913-14 by K. Ramakrishnayya of Musalipattanam.
MT 1964(k). PL. Tel. 2 fol. (104-05). Presented in 1916-17 by Rayaprolu Ramabrahmangaru of Guruza, Gudivada Taluk, Krishna Dist.
MT 3887(j). PL. Gr. 1 fol. (83). Incomplete. See remarks. Purchased in 1921-22 from Annasvami Sastrigal, Bhavani, Coimbatore Dist.
MT 4600(a). PL. Gr. 2 fol. (4-5). Presented in 1924-25 by the Secretary to the Trustees of Sri Yogi Parthasarathi Ayyangar's Charities, Triplicane, Madras.
Mysore ND II 3222. Extract no. 55. Title: Ubhaya-dīrgha-padam.
Trav. Uni. L.988 C. PL. Mal. 15 Grantha-s.
Trav. Uni. L.988 P. PL. Mal. 15 Grantha-s

Ptd.: at the end of Ṣaḍviṃśati-sūtra (Grantha script), pp. 16-18.
Also printed in Lakṣaṇa-traya (in Telugu script), pp. 40-42.

886 PṚTHAG-VYAKTI (**पृथग्व्यक्ति**)

Also called Vṛthā-vyakti or Pradhā-vyakti. A list of words the final vowel of which does not undergo phonetic changes when followed by words beginning with vowels.

स्वधा पूषा प्रपा प्रबुभ्रिया प्रमा प्रतिमा विमोन्मा द्या मिथुनी अमिनन्त बृहस्पते द्रापे धर्मे मर्मे वसिष्टे पृष्ठे अग्ने अम्बे मन्दे विश्वैर्देवैर्नैर्ऋतिर्हित्वी रेजते (वाजे वदे न योजते अज्ञे अक्ते अर्पे) इति प्रधाव्यक्तयः ॥

Baroda 6255. PL. Tel. 1 fol. (45a).

887 PRAKĪRṆA-VIṢAYĀḤ (**प्रकीर्णविषयाः**)

of Nārāyaṇa.

Hoshiarpur p. 301 (no.5613). PL. Gr. 25 fol. 550 Grantha-s.

888 PRAKṚTI-C(H)ALĀKṢARA (**प्रकृति(च)छलाक्षर**)

→ Chalākṣara or Rāvaṇa-bhaiṭ (SV).

PUL II. App. p. 7 (no.106). PL. Gr. 4 fol. A.D. 1870.

Trav. Uni. 2318 A. PL. Mal. 100 Grantha-s. Incomplete.

Trav. Uni. 6588 B. PL. Mal. 14 fol. 200 Grantha-s.

Whish 167. PL. Gr. 9 fol. (157-65).

889 PRAGṚHYA-LAKṢAṆA (1) (**प्रगृह्यलक्षण**)

Mysore ND II 3633 (P 4906/17). PL. Na. 1 fol. (116). Extract no. 220. (Cf. p. 36 of the *Pada-gāḍha*, Srirangam edition).

890 PRAGṚHYA-LAKṢAṆA (2) (**प्रगृह्यलक्षण**)

Trav. Uni. 4254 G. PL. Mal. 6 fol. 65 Grantha-s. Belonged to Vishnu Nambudiri of Ettikada Illam Ayankudi, Kaduttirutti, Kottayam.

Trav. Uni. T.223 G1. 8 fol. (39-46). 80 Grantha-s (not catalogued). A transcript of the Ms. no. 4254.

891 PRAGRAHĀDI-LAKṢAṆA (**प्रग्रहादिलक्षण**)

Mysore p. 2 (no. 54). 52 fol.

892 PRAGRAHĀDHYĀYA (**प्रग्रहाध्याय**)

Adyar D I 1032 → Sapta-lakṣaṇa.

893 PRAṆAVA-LAKṢAṆA (**प्रणवलक्षण**)

Hamburg StUB (cod.Palmbl. III 8/133) → Veda-lakṣaṇa (HB).

Mysore I, p. 31. Taitt.

Mysore ND II 3634 (B 252/15). Gr. 10 fol. (109-18). Extract no. 221.

894 PRAṆAVA-SAṂGRAHA (**प्रणवसंग्रह**)

Mysore ND II 3636 (P 2339/14). PL. Gr. 4 fol. (90-93). Extract no. 223.

895 PRAṆAVA-SVARA-VARṆANA (**प्रणवस्वरवर्णन**)

Mysore ND II 3635 (B 252/ 9). Gr. 5 fol. (58-62). Extract no. 222.

896 PRATIJÑĀ-SŪTRA (-PARIŚIṢṬA) (**प्रतिज्ञासूत्र /-परिशिष्ट**)

The third of the 18 Pariśiṣṭa-s of Kātyāyana. A supplement to the *Vājasaneyi-prāti-śākhya*, some times called Pariśiṣṭa. Different from the one of the same title beginning with : athātaḥ pratijñā gotracaraṇapṛcchāyāṃ vakṣyate ... The text is divided into three Kaṇḍikā-s: 1) Svara-prakriyā, 2) Uccāraṇa-vidhi and 3) Anusvāra-visarga-svara-vikāra, containing 10, 8 and 5 Sūtra-s respectively. But the division of the Sūtra-s and their number in each Kaṇḍikā vary in different Mss. and editions.

Beginning:

अथ प्रतिज्ञा । १ । मन्त्रब्राह्मणयोर्वेदनामधेयम् । २ । तस्मिञ्छुक्ले याजुषाम्नाये माध्यन्दिनीयके मन्त्रे स्वरप्रक्रिया । ३ । हृद्यनुदात्तः । ४ । मूर्ध्न्युदात्तः । ५ । श्रुतिमूले स्वरितः । ६ । एवं जात्यादयो ऽभिहिताः । ७ ।

End:

परसवर्णेपत्प्रकृत्या चान्यत्र । ३ । विसर्गेष्वीषद् विरामः । ४ । पदाद्यस्यासंयुक्ताकारस्येषद्दीर्घता च भवतीषद्दीर्घता च भवति । ५ । इति श्रीकात्यायनकृतौ प्रतिज्ञापरिशिष्टसूत्रे तृतीया कण्डिका समाप्ता ॥

AK 63. 2 fol. Dated Śaka 1745.
Alwar 144.
America 208.
ASB I ii.289 (IM 2542). 20 fol. 272 Grantha-s (with Bhāṣya of Ananta-yājñika). Dated V.S. 1898 = A.D. 1841.
ASB I ii.290 (IM 3374). 10 fol. 280 Grantha-s (with Bhāṣya of Ananta-yājñika). Dated V.S. 1902 = A.D. 1845.
ASB I iii.37 (IM 5156). 1 fol. 15 Grantha-s. Dated V.S. 1830 = A.D. 1873.
ASB I iii.38 (IM 5299). 1 fol. 17 Grantha-s. Dated V.S. 1839 = A.D. 1782.
ASB I iii.39 (IM 5558). 13 fol. 168 Grantha-s (with C. of Ananta-yājñika).
ASB I iii.87 (IM 2636/2). 12 Grantha-s.
B I, p. 180.
Baroda 12011(c). 2 fol. 20 Grantha-s.
Bd. 75. 2 fol.
Bd. 76. 12 fol. (with C. of Keśava). Dated V.S. 1889.
Bhr. 514.
BHU C 871 (D 1H/610). 15 fol. (with Bhāṣya of Ananta-yājñika).
BHU B 1148 (D 1H/611). 11 fol. (with Bhāṣya). Incomplete.
BISM p. 56 (also p. 165). (22/298) (Kātyāyanīya-pratijñā-sūtra-pariśiṣṭa).
BISM p. 165 (29/1333). Dated Śaka 1733.
BISM p. 165 (47/185) (with C. of Ananta-yājñika). (Pratijñā-sūtra-bhāṣya).
Bombay Uni. Acc. no. 5217 2 fol. Dated Śaka 1738.
BORI 514 of 1882-83. 8 fol. with Navakaṇḍikā-sūtra.

BORI 362 of 1883-84. 5 fol. with Navakaṇḍikā-sūtra.
BORI 75 of 1887-91. 2 fol.
BORI 76 of 1887-91. 12 fol. (with C. of Keśava). Dated V.S. 1887.
BORI 63 of 1891-95. 2 fol. Dated Śaka 1745.
BP p. 285 (no.362). 5 fol. Title: Kātyāyanīya-pratijñā-sūtra.
Bühler p. 553 (no. 16) (with C.).
Deccan College 4889. 14 fol. (19-32). Dated Śaka 1691 (with C. of Ananta-deva-yājñika).
Deccan College 6447. 8 fol. (with C. of Ananta-deva-yājñika).
Deccan College 7376. 13 fol. (with C. of Ananta-deva-yājñika). Dated Śaka 1613.
GJKSV 41960. 1 fol. (3).
Hoshiarpur p. 52 (no.1780). 3 fol. 15 Grantha-s.
Hoshiarpur p. 52 (no.6127). 12 fol. 240 Grantha-s (with C. of Ananta-deva-yājñika).
IL. 233.
IM 2542. 20 fol. (with C. of Ananta-deva-yājñika).
IM 2636B. 1 fol.
IM 3374. 10 fol. (with C. of Ananta-deva-yājñika).
IM 5299. 1 fol.
L 1799. 1 fol. 14 Grantha-s.
Mithila IV 99. 17 fol. (with C. of Ananta-yājñika).
Mithila IV 99(A). 11 fol. (with C. of Ananta-yājñika).
Mithila IV 99(B). 25 fol. (with C. of Ananta-yājñika).
Mithila IV 99(C). 7 fol. (with C. of Ananta-yājñika).
Mithila IV 99(D). 18 fol. (with C. of Ananta-yājñika).
Mithila IV 99(E). 16 fol. (with C. of Ananta-yājñika).
N-W P V 62 (no.12). 9 fol. (with C. of Keśavācārya). Belonged to Pt. Makhana Misra of Mathura.
N-W P V 146 (no.26). 8 fol. (with C.).
Oxf. CS c.26(1). 1 fol. Paper dated 25.11.1903.
Oxf. II 868(1c) (Ms. Wilson 510). 2 fol. (3-4). Dated A.D. 1681. = Oxf. 387a (no.510). (Another version ?).
Peters. II, p. 173 (no.80). 12 fol.
PUL I, p. 72. 2 fol.
RASB II 940 (G 928) = L 1799.
RASB II 941 (G 6141). 2 fol.
RASB II 942 (G 6164). 1 fol.
RASB II 943 (G 6169). 1 fol.
RASB II 944 (G 6064). 8 fol. 272 Grantha-s (with C. of Ananta-yājñika). Dated V.S. 1889.
RASB II 945 (G 6159). 8 fol. (with C. of Ananta-yājñika).
RASB II 946 (G 9962B). 20 fol. 250 Grantha-s (with C. of Ananta-yājñika). Dated V.S. 1910.
Rep. Hpr. 1901-6, p. 2
SB p. 54 (no.66). 8 fol. 198 Grantha-s (with C.). = SBD 47944.
SBD 4212. 6 fol. Dated V.S. 1664.
SBD 4244. 2 fol. Dated V.S. 1966.
SBD 47722a. 1 fol.

SBD 47944. 8 fol. (with C. of Keśavācārya). Incomplete. Dated V.S. 1936.
SBD 55296. 15 fol. (with C. of Ananta-yājñika).
SBD 55334. 1 fol. Dated V.S. 1842.
SBD 55851. 2 fol. Incomplete.
SBD 55914. 6 fol. (with C. of Keśava).
Tb. 30. One fol. at the beginning contains some additional matter.
Trav. Uni. 2055. 675 Grantha-s (with Ṭippaṇa of Vardhamāna-miśra). Dated V.S. 1897.
Weber 1463 (Ms. or. fol. 590). 4 fol. (42-45) at the end of the C. called Jyotsnā, on the Vājasaneyi-prātiśākhya.

Ptd.: ed. by A. Weber, text and commentary (in Roman script), with a translation in German: *Über ein zum weissen Yajus gehöriges phonetisches Compendium, das Pratijñāsūtra* (Abh. d. kön. Ak. d. Wiss. zu Berlin, phil- hist- Klasse). – Berlin 1871, pp. 69-118. [Adyar (H 215 VP zge Web); Emeneau (115)]
Also ed. by Yugalakishora (Vyasa) Pathaka, with the Bhāṣya of Ananta(-deva) Yājñika, in the edition of *Śuklayajuḥ-prātiśākhya* with Uvaṭa's Bhāṣya. – Benares, 1888, pp. 401-31. – (Ben. S. S. 4).
Also printed as an appendix to the edition of the *Vājasaneyi-saṃhitā* :
Ed. by Hariprasad Bhagirathaji, Jagadisvara Press. – Bombay : Jyestharam Mukundaji, 1884. 17, 2, 36, 40 pp. [Adyar (H 215.1 Yaj Har); Gö(4/ H E E 1062/53); Emeneau (104); IO : Ptd. Bks. Cat. 1953, p. 1968 (12 K 28)]
Ed. by Hariprasad Bhagirathaji, Jagadisvara Press. – Bombay (Ramavadi) : Jyestharam Mukundaji, V.S. 1944 (1887). 2 pp. (Col.: iti kātyāyana-pariśiṣṭasūtraṃ samāptam). [Adyar (H 211.21 x Har)]
– Bombay : Venkatesvara Press, 1887. [Emeneau : 105]
– Bombay : Tattvaviveka Press, 1896. [Emeneau : 107]
– Bombay : Nirnaya Sagar Press, 1901. [Emeneau : 108]
– Bombay : Nirnaya Sagar Press, 1912. [Emeneau : 109] [BM : Ptd. Bks. Cat. 1906-1928. 1203 (14010.cc.13)]
In the 4th volume of the *Vājasaneyi-saṃhitā* with commentaries of Uvaṭa and Mahīdhara. – Benares : Chowkhamba, 1915, p. 15. – (Kashi Sanskrit Series 34). [NL (180 Jc 91 109 / V 4 C 3)]
Ed. by Amritalal Sastri of Jamnagar, in : *Śukla-yajurveda-mādhyandina-saṃhitā* (prāstāvikasaṃhitāmantrāṇām akārādyanukramaṇikāvedapārāyaṇavidhyanuvākasūtrādhyāyāṣṭavikṛtiyājñavalkyaśikṣāpratijñāsūtrasarvānukramasūtra- ... samalaṃkṛtā) – Bombay : Nirnaya Sagar Press, Śaka 1872 (1950), p. 190. [SKGI (Rh III 125)]
Ed. by Jagadisha Lal Shastri, with commentaries of Uvaṭa and Mahīdhara. – Delhi : Motilal Banarsidass, 1971. Appendix, pp. 6-7. [Adyar (H 212.21 VM xy Sha)]
In the 5th volume of the edition of the *Śatapatha-brāhmaṇa* (Śrīmadvājasaneyi-mādhyandina-śatapatha-brāhmaṇam, with Vedārthaprakāśa commentary of Sāyaṇācārya and the commentary of Harisvāmin), with the commentary of Nityānanda Parvatīya. – Kalyāṇ (Bombay) : Laxmi Venkateshwar Steam Press (Gangavishnu Shri Krishnadass), Saṃ. 1997 / Śaka 1862 (1940), part 5, pp. 295-99 (= 3415-19). [SKGI (Rh III 153)]

Reprint of the above (without a clear indication of the original edition): Delhi : Gian Publishing House, 1987. [SAI (ind 50 C 288/1437)]

Ed. by Yugal Kishore Misra, with the commentary *Jyotsnā-vṛtti* of Rāmaśarman on the *Vājasaneyi-prātiśākhya*. – Varanasi : Sampurnanand Sanskrit University, 1989, pp. 205-217.

– C.

Bühler p. 553 (no. 16) (with text).

Radh. 1.

– C. Bhāṣya of Ananta(-deva) Yājñika.

Beginning:

अम्बायोनिं जगद्योनिमयोनिं योनिजं जनम्।
योनित्रासात् त्रायते तं वन्दे ऽहं हंसरूपिणम्॥ १॥
योनियोगवशं धत्ते योनिजायोनिजं जगत्।
सोमसोममहं वन्दे जङ्गमाजङ्गमात्मकम्॥ २॥

तत्र भगवानाचार्यः प्रत्यूहसंघातविघाताय चिकीर्षितसमाप्त्यै वा मङ्गलार्थस्य चानन्तर्यार्थस्य च अथशब्दस्यैकवृन्तगतफलद्वयन्यायेन एकशेषेण तन्त्रेणावृत्त्या वा वदन् शिष्यबुद्धिसमाधानाय प्रतिजानीते अथ प्रतिज्ञेति। विधास्यत इति सूत्रशेषः ।

End:

अत्र वकारपकारयोरीषद्दीर्घोच्चारणं यथा भवति तथा पठनीयम्। एवं परमेणेत्यादिषु ज्ञेयम् । अत एवाध्यायसमाप्तौ संहितायां दीर्घपाठे इति संप्रदायविदो वदन्ति । ईषद्दीर्घता च भवति । द्विरभ्यासो ग्रन्थपरिसमाप्तिसूचकार्थः । अन्ये विस्तरशः स्वरसंस्काराः पञ्चदशशाखासाधारण्येन प्रातिशाख्ये उपनिबद्धा इति । इति श्रीमदनन्तदेवयाज्ञिकविरचिते प्रतिज्ञापरिशिष्टसूत्रभाष्ये तृतीया कण्डिका समाप्ता॥

ASB I iii.39 (IM 5558). 13 fol. 168 Grantha-s (with text).

Bhk. 8.

BISM p. 165 (32/50).

BISM p. 165 (47/185). 8 fol. (with text). Incomplete.

BORI 46 of A 1881-82. 36 fol. Dated Śaka 1692.

Hoshiarpur p. 52 (no.6127). 12 fol. 240 Grantha-s (with text).

IM 2542. 20 fol. (with text).

IM 3374. 10 fol. (with text).

IM 5558. 13 fol. Incomplete.

L 2578. 20 fol. 315 Grantha-s. Dated V.S. 1890.

Lahore p. 2 (no.7). 10 fol. 1740 Grantha-s (a. Ananta-bhaṭṭa). In the possession of Pt. Jwala Datta Prasada, Lahore.

Mithila IV 99. 99(A)-(E). See above.

RASB II 944 (G 6064). 8 fol. 272 Grantha-s (with text). Dated V.S. 1889.

RASB II 945 (G 6159). 8 fol. (with text).
RASB II 946 (G 9962B). 20 fol. 250 Grantha-s (with text). Dated V.S. 1910.
SBD 4171. 24 fol. Dated V.S. 1966.
SBD 4252. 12 fol.
SBD 55296. 15 fol. (with text).
Ujjain Latest Additions 522.
Ptd.: with the text in the Benares ed.

– C. called Vṛtti, of Keśavācārya.
Beginning:

श्रीमत्कात्यायनं वन्दे मुनिश्रेष्ठं च याजुषम्।
यस्तेने कल्पशास्त्रं तं याज्ञवल्क्यसुतं गुरुम्॥

अथ प्रातिशाख्यसूत्रकथनानन्तरम् । प्रतिज्ञा विधास्यत इति शेषः । प्रतिज्ञायते शेष(स्वर)संस्कारो यया सा प्रतिज्ञा। अत्राङ् प्रत्ययः । कृदन्तं पदमिदम्॥

End:

संयुक्तेति किम् । अपां फेनेन । अत्राकारस्य मा भूत् । अकारस्येति किम् । पुरुषः । अत्रोकारस्य माभूत्। द्विरुक्तिस्तु समाप्तिद्योतनार्था॥

सूत्रैः सप्तसुधांशुभिर्विलसती शिक्षा प्रतिज्ञाभिधा
वेदाब्धौ मुनिना कृता भगवता कात्यायनेनाद्भुता
तस्या गोकुलसूनुकेशवकृता वृत्तिस्तु संगृह्यतां
धीरैः साधु दयालुभिर्यदपि सा संभाव्यदोषैर्युता॥

इति केशवाचार्यविरचितप्रतिज्ञासूत्रवृत्तौ तृतीयकण्डिका समाप्ता॥

Alwar 145. Extract 45.
Bd. 76. 12 fol. (with text). Dated V.S. 1889.
BORI 76 of 1887-91. 12 fol. Copied in Kāśī. Dated V.S. 1889.
Mithila IV 100. 12 fol.
Mithila IV 100(A). 8 fol.
N-W P V 62 (no.12). 9 fol. (with text). Belonged to Pt. Makhana Misra of Mathura.
Peters. II, p. 173 (no.81).
SB p. 54 (no.66). 8 fol. 198 Grantha-s (with text). = SBD 47944.
SBD 47944. 8 fol. (with text). Incomplete. Dated V.S. 1936.

– C. Bhāṣya called Pradīpa of Gaurīdatta or Datta.

Beginning:

गौरीसुतं प्रणम्यादौ गौरीदत्तद्विजन्मना।
प्रतिज्ञापरिशिष्टस्य प्रायशो ऽर्थो निरूप्यते॥

इह खलु भगवान् कात्यायनो मङ्गलार्थमथशब्दं प्रयुञ्जानः शिष्यबुद्धिसमाधानार्थं प्रतिजानीते --

End:

अत्र द्विरभ्यासः परिसमाप्त्यर्थः । इति कात्यायनप्रोक्तप्रतिज्ञापरिशिष्टे तृतीयकण्डिकाप्रदीपः ।

श्रीमत्कौशिकवंशजः सुकृतवाञ्छ्रीरामभद्रः पिता
माता श्रीजनकात्मजा च तनयं प्रासूत दत्ताभिधम्।
तेनायं विदुषां मुदे सुकृतिनां संस्कारदीपः कृतः
शाके विध्युपदत्रिसप्तवसुधायुक्ते रहस्येसिते॥

इति प्रतिज्ञापरिशिष्टभाष्यं संपूर्णम्॥

Berlin StB-PrK (NGMPP). E 678/8. 3 fol. (microfilm dated 25.09.1978).

– C. of Madhusūdana.
N-W P IV 4.

– C. Vṛtti, called Jyotsnā of Rāmaśarman. See Weber's edition of the *Pratijñā-sūtra*, p. 69.
Rep. Raj. and C. I. p. 7. Printed in the edition of the text, by Weber and Yugal Kishore Misra,

– C. Ṭippaṇa of Vardhamāna-miśra.
Trav. Uni. 2055. 675 Grantha-s. Dated V.S. 1879.

[CC I 349b; II 210b; III 94b]

897 PRATIVARGA-PADEYATTĀ (प्रतिवर्गपदेयत्ता)
SBD 52690. 4 fol. Incomplete. Up to the end of the 2nd Aṣṭaka. → Caturakṣarī-baiṭh.

898 PRATIVARGA-VARṆA-SAṂKHYĀ (प्रतिवर्गवर्णसंख्या)
GJKSV 30313. 60 fol. → Pavamāna-pada-varṇa-saṃkhyā. Contains Ekākṣarī-bhaiṭ and Aṣṭākṣarī-bhaiṭ for Pavamāna Sūkta-s (RV IX 1-67). It also contains a commentary on the eleven paribhāṣā verses of the *Ekākṣarī-bhaiṭ* and explanations called Utthāpanā on Aṣṭaka-s 5-7.

pratyadhyāyaṃ pāvamānīm ekārṇādipadādijām |
saṃkhyāṃ brahmopanāmā vai govindo vilikhāmy aham ||

899 PRATIHĀRA-SŪTRA (प्रतिहारसूत्र)
of Kātyāyana. The fourth and last Prapāṭhaka of the *Upagrantha-sūtra*. Often found as a separate work in Mss.

Ptd.: ed. by Satyavrata Samasrami, in the Sanskrit journal *Uṣā*. – Calcutta : Satya Press, 1897 (as part of the Upagrantha-sūtra ?).
Also ed. by B. R. Sharma, with the commentary called *Daśatayī* of Varadarāja. – Tirupati : Kendriya Sanskrit Vidyapeetha, 1973. This edition is based on nine Mss. [SAI (ind 51 B 178/62)]

[CC I 350b]

900 PRATYAYĀṢṬAMA-LAKṢAṆA-VYĀKHYĀ (प्रत्ययाष्टमलक्षणव्याख्या)
of Nṛsiṃha-bhaṭṭa. Mysore I, p. 613 (no. 4507).

901 PRATHAMA-ŚĀKHĀ-NYĀYA-NIRṆAYA (प्रथमशाखान्यायनिर्णय)
of Rāma Vedāntin of Nanjanagudu. A voluminous work on the various Vedic Śākhā-s especially on the superiority of the *Śukla-yajurveda.*

Mysore ND III 8718 (C 2368/ 1). 19-566 fol.
Mysore ND III 8719 (C 2936). 18 fol.

Ptd.: Kashi : Vidyodaya Press, 1877 (beginning of the printing: V.S. 1933 āśvina-śukla prathamā śukre / completed : Pauṣa-śudi 15 / V.S. 1934). 559 folios. Lithographic print in five vols.:
vol. I. 102 fol.
vol. II. 103-201 fol.
vol. III. 202-347 fol.
vol. IV. 348-459 fol.
vol. V. 460-558 fol.
[BM : Ptd. Bks. Cat. 1876-92. 342 (14007.d.17); IO : Ptd. Bks. Cat. 1953, p. 1967 (Skt. 1 F 21-25)]

902 PRATHAMA-ŚĀKHĀ-VICĀRA (प्रथमशाखाविचार)
Ānandāśrama 2693. 11 fol. Col.: iti padavākyapramāṇajñaprathamaśākhiśrīmad-anantācāryaviracitā saṃhitābhāṣyārambhe prathamaśākhāvicāraḥ ||

903 PRAYATNA-LAKṢAṆA (प्रयत्नलक्षण)
18 verses on the effort of articulation in the Taittirīya school.

Beginning:

हकारस्य विसर्गेण संयोगो यत्र दृश्यते।
प्रयत्नं तत्र जानीयाद्यशावर्गे तथा भवेत्॥

End:

रशां यत्ता उदीराणः प्रयच्छन्तं विदादि च।
सयुभिः प्रसदोविद्भिर्बह्वनीयासमावह॥

Baroda 6255. PL. Tel. 1 fol. (42).

904 PRAŚLIṢṬA-SVARA-SAṂDHI (प्रश्लिष्टस्वरसंधि)
Mysore ND II 3639 (P 2476/ 8). PL. Na. 5 fol. (51-55). Extract no. 225.

905 PRASTĀVA-SŪTRĀDI (प्रस्तावसूत्रादि)

Trav. Uni. 18693 B. PL. Gr. 1275 Grantha-s.

906 PRĀTIŚĀKHYA or PĀRṢADA (प्रातिशाख्य / पार्षद)

→ Ṛgveda-, Taittirīya-, Vājasaneyi- and Atharva-veda-prātiśākhya.

Unspecified:

Ānandāśrama 123. 45 fol. Dated Śaka 1694. → Ṛgveda-prātiśākhya.

ASB I iii.32 (III F 202). 10 fol. 238 Grantha-s. Dated V.S. 1860 = A.D. 1803.

BISM p. 172 (1/17).

BISM p. 172 (33/130). 34 fol. Dated Śaka 1680. → Ṛgveda-prātiśākhya.

Calcutta Skt. Coll. I 488 (346). 128 fol. Lacks both beginning and end. 2 fol. at the beginning are lost. 3rd fol. : mantras tu yadi manāg api svarato varṇato vā hīno bhavati arthakarmāsamṛddhiḥ | na kevalaṃ karmāsamṛddhiḥ | kiṃ tarhi |... pravayuḥ khāt... | ending with : sū. ḍaḍhauḻlhā caikeṣām |

Calcutta Skt. Coll. I 491 (345). 9 fol. Incomplete (catalogued as Prātiśākhya, but the beginning and end correspond to portions of Pada-gāḍha (cf. pp. 53 and 29 of the Srirangam edition).

Deccan College 1345. 43 fol. → Ṛgveda-prātiśākhya.

Deccan College 1864. 13-17 fol. Incomplete. → Ṛgveda-prātiśākhya.

Deccan College 5079. 43 fol. Dated Śaka 1714 → Ṛgveda-prātiśākhya.

Deccan College 7261. 38 fol. Dated Śaka 1778 → Ṛgveda-prātiśākhya. Varṇakrama-lakṣṇa (18 verses) on fol. 37-38.

Deccan College 5979. 31 fol. → Ṛgveda-prātiśākhya. Varṇakrama-lakṣṇa (18 verses) on fol. 30-31.

Deccan College 8251. 43 fol. Dated V.S. 1719. → Ṛgveda-prātiśākhya.

Deccan College 9818. 14 fol. Incomplete. → Vājasaneyi-prātiśākhya. Dated V.S. 1760.

GJKSV 23902. 13 fol. → Taittirīya-prātiśākhya.

GJKSV 25339. 4 fol. → Jaṭā-nyāya-pañcāśat and Jaṭā-saṃdhi-lakṣaṇa.

IM 7480. 12 fol. Incomplete.

N-W P V 40 (no.3). 39 fol. Belonged to Ramachand Bhatta, Allahabad.

Oppert I 2382. PL. Gr. 25 pp. Belonged to Sri Sarasvati Bhandaram Committee of Tiruvallikkeni, Madras.

Oppert I 4327. Belonged to Annasastri of Muktambapuram, Thanjavur Dist.

Oppert I 4707. PL. Gr. 30 pp. Belonged to Vaidyanatha Dikshitar of Sangalipuram, Thanjavur Dist.

Oppert I 7143. Belonged to Pola Lakshmanavadhani of Vijayanagaram.

Oppert II 1115. Belonged to Tiruputkuli Srikrishna Tatacharyar of Kanchipuram.

Oppert II 1341. Belonged to Gopalacharyar of Pillapakkam, Kanchipuram Taluk.

Oppert II 2548. PL. Gr. 100 pp. Belonged to Pichchu Sastri of Kojumam Village, Udumalapet Taluk.

Oppert II 4744. Belonged to Sri Sankaracharya Matha of Sringeri,

Oppert II 7401. Belonged to Venkatarama Sastri of Pillur, Mayavaram Taluk.

P 5.

SBD 2124. 3 fol. (3-5). Incomplete.

SBD 2138. 4 fol. (2-5). Incomplete.

C. of Uvaṭa.

N-W P I 14 (no.47). 180 fol. (the name is spelt "Ubbaṭa"). Belonged to Trilochana Pandit, Benares.

Oppert I 1923. Pl.. Gr. Belonged to Sivasuri Sastri of Bhavani, Coimbatore Dist.

Oudh XIII 2 (no.1). 430 pp. 1000 Grantha-s. Dated A.D. 1878. Belonged to M. Kali Prasada, Pleader, Lucknow. Title: Prātiśākhya-bhāṣya. "A commentary on the Vedas, in 18 Paṭalas by Ubbhaṭa".

P 5.

SBD 2140. 30 fol. Incomplete.

– C. Bhāṣya (Prātiśākhya-bhāṣya).

IM 10661. 8 fol. Incomplete.

SBD 2117. 118 fol. (= Uvaṭa's Bhāṣya on the Vājasaneyi-prātiśākhya.

SBD 2123. 2 fol. (46-47). Incomplete.

SBD 2127. 166 fol. Incomplete (Paṭala-s 12-13).

[CC I 362a]

907 PRĀTIŚĀKHYA-PARIŚIṢṬA (प्रातिशाख्यपरिशिष्ट)

VSM III 165 (no.11340). 4 fol. → Ṛgveda-varṇa-krama-(jñāna-)lakṣaṇa of Jagannātha.

908 PRĀTIŚĀKHYA-PRADĪPA-ŚIKṢĀ (प्रातिशाख्यप्रदीपशिक्षा)

of Bālakṛṣṇa Goḍase, son of Sadāśiva. In this extensive work, written in Śaka 1802 (A.D. 1880 in the year Vikrama), several Veda-lakṣaṇa texts of the Mādhyandina Śākhā are quoted. In most places it is identical with the Jyotsā-vṛtti of Rāmaśarman. The last section *Jaṭādy-aṣṭa-vikṛti-lakṣaṇa* (18 verses from the *Vikṛti-vallī* of Vyāḍi) on pp. 300-06 is also from the Jyotsnā-vṛtti. This latter text, except for a few alterations and omissions, is the same as the one published by G. Thibaut (cf. Jaṭā-paṭala, pp. 36-53) and G. V. Devasthali (cf. Veda-vikṛti-lakṣaṇa-saṃgraha, pp. 23-32). It is part of the *Prātiśākhya-jyotsnā*, as noted by Thibaut, and is printed with the title *Aṣṭa-vikṛti-lakṣaṇa-prakaraṇa* in the edition of the *Jyotsnā-vṛtti* of Rāmaśarman on the *Vājasaneyi-prātiśākhya*, ed. by Yugal Kishore Misra. – Varanasi : Sampurnanand Sanskrit University, 1989, pp. 293-315.

In the recent edition of the Śikṣā-saṃgraha (Varanasi, 1989, pp. 176-285) this Śikṣā is divided in two parts. The second part (pp. 199-285) is entitled:
Atha visargāṅgulipradarśanaprakāram āha Yājñavalkyaḥ.

Beginning:

हेरम्बं विघ्नहर्तारं प्रणमामि सरस्वतीम् ।
ययोर्नमनमात्रेण विघ्नसंघो विनश्यति ॥
प्रातिशाख्यं च शिक्षाश्च सम्यगालोच्य यत्नतः ।
वैदिकानां सुबोधाय सम्यक्पाठस्य सिद्धये ॥ २ ॥
सदाशिवतनूजेन बालकृष्णेन धीमता ।
प्रातिशाख्यप्रदीपाख्या शिक्षा सम्यङ् निरूप्यते ॥ ३ ॥
अथ वेदाध्ययनप्रकारः । तत्र याज्ञवल्क्यः --

प्रणवं प्राक् प्रयुञ्जीत व्याहृतीस्तदनन्तरम्।
सावित्रीं चानुपूर्व्येण ततो वेदान् समारभेत्॥ १॥

End:

परसवर्णेषत्प्रकृत्या चान्यत्र । शषसहेभ्यो ऽन्यत्र तु मकारस्य परपञ्चमविधानात् स्पष्टमुच्चारणे प्राप्ते परस्य वर्णस्य सवर्णो यः पञ्चमस्तस्येषत्सादृश्येनोच्चारणं स्यात् । तञ्जाननित्यादौ वाजाञ्जयतु इत्यादिवत् ञकारादेर्न स्पष्टमुच्चारणम् । विसर्गेष्वीषद्विरामः ॥ विसर्गेषु नान्तरीयकार्धमात्राकालापेक्षया किंचिदधिककालो विरामः । अवसानं कृत्वाग्रिमवर्णोच्चारणं कार्यम् । वसोः पवित्रम् । याः फलिनीः ॥ पदाद्यस्य संयुक्ताकारस्येषद्दीर्घता च भवति ॥ परस्यादिभूतस्य हल्संयुक्तस्य अकारस्य ह्रस्वस्येषद्दीर्घता च एकमात्राकालापेक्षया किंचिदधिककालोच्चारणं स्यात्। वसोः पवित्रम् । पदादिस्थस्येति किम्। वायवः । हल्संयुक्तस्य किम्। अनुनः । अकारस्येति किम् ...।

शाके व्यभ्राष्टभूमिते शुभे विक्रमवत्सरे।
माघे मासि सिते पक्षे प्रतिपद्भानुवासरे॥ १॥
प्रातिशाख्यप्रदीपाख्या शिक्षेयं रचिता शुभा।
गोडशे इत्युपाह्वेन बालकृष्णेन धीमता॥ २॥
श्रीसदाशिवपौत्रेण श्रीप्रभाकरशर्मणा।
कृपया मह्यमादत्ता मुद्रायन्त्रे प्रकाशिता॥ ३॥
युगलप्राक्किशोरेण पाठकेनानुजेन च।
विश्वेश्वरस्य पुत्रेण श्रीव्यासोपाधिधारिणा॥ ४॥
सरयूपारिणा सम्यग् वेदविद्यालयस्य च।
अध्यापकेन छात्राणां शीघ्रं संबोधनाय च।
शिक्षासंग्रहमध्ये तु ह्येतस्याः संग्रहः कृतः ॥ ५॥

Ptd.: in Śikṣā-saṃgraha. – Benares, 1889, pp. 210-306. – (Ben. S. S. 10).

909 PRĀTIŚĀKHYA-PRAVACANA (VARṆAKRAMA) (प्रातिशाख्यप्रवचन /-वर्णक्रम)
→ Ṛgveda-prātiśākhya.
GJKSV 14450. 54 fol.

910 PRĀTIŚĀKHYA-BHĀṢYA (प्रातिशाख्यभाष्य)
GJKSV 37691. 184 fol. → Uvaṭa's Bhāṣya on the *Vājasaneyi-prātiśākhya.*

911 PRĀTIŚĀKHYA-VIVARAṆA (प्रातिशाख्यविवरण)
VSM III 166 (no.11301). 10 fol. → Ṛgveda-prātiśākhya.

912 PRĀTIŚĀKHYA-SŪTRA (प्रातिशाख्यसूत्र)
of Kātyāyana → Vājasaneyi-prātiśākhya.
SBD 47248. 14 fol. Dated V.S 1631.

***PRĪTIKARA (प्रीतिकर)**

– Sāma-(veda-)prakāśana. P. 6. See below under Sāma-prakāśana.

[CC I 364b]

***PLĀKṢA (प्लाक्ष)**

Referred to by Ayyāśāstrin in his *Sapta-svara-sindhu*, TCD 33.

***PLĀKṢĀYANA (प्लाक्षायन)**

Mentioned in the *Taittirīya-prātiśākhya*, 9.6, 14.11, 17, 18.5.

[CC I 365b]

***PLĀKṢI (प्लाक्षि)**

Mentioned in the *Taittirīya-prātiśākhya*, 5.38, 9.6, 14.10, 17, 18.5.

[CC I 365b]

913 PLĀKṢI-ŚIKṢĀ (**प्लाक्षिशिक्षा**)

Mentioned in a list of Veda-lakṣaṇa texts in Adyar D I 1022.

914 PLUTA-NIRṆAYA (**प्लुतनिर्णय**)

Mysore I, p. 31.

Mysore ND II 3641 (P 3280/ 3). PL. Tel. 9 fol. Extract no. 226. The same as the *Ṣaḍviṃśati-sūtra*.

915 PLUTA-VIṂŚATI (**प्लुतविंशति**)

→ Pluta-saṃgraha and Plutānuśāsana.

Mysore I, p. 31.

916 PLUTA-VYĀKHYĀNA (**प्लुतव्याख्यान**)

MD 16820. PL. Gr. 5 pp. 49 Grantha-s.

917 PLUTA-ŚIKṢĀ (**प्लुतशिक्षा**)

Enumeration of Pluta-s in the *Taittirīya-saṃhitā*.

Beginning: (14744; partly printed at the end of the *Ṣaḍviṃśati-sūtra)*

बृहस्पतिसुतस्याग्निहोत्रं जुहोति संश्रवा द्वे द्वे मित्रो ऽसि सप्त प्रथमत्वष्टा ब्रह्मवादिनो ऽद्भिर्मनुरेकमेकं यदेकेन यजुषा वाग् वै ब्रह्मवादिनो विचित्यः पर्यग्निर्द्वे द्वे पशुमालभ्य ... एवं चत्वारिंशत्संख्याः प्लुताः । संहितायां प्लुताः षट्त्रिंशत् । रङ्गप्लुताश्चत्वारः । परायाते एकम् । एवं मिलित्वा एकचत्वारिंशत् । अथ प्लुतोदाहरणवाक्यानि श्लोकरूपेण स्पष्टीकरोति --

End:

हौषां पूर्वं मकारस्तु सहस्रां पूर्वतस्तनीम् ।
यद्विकर्णी यद्विकर्णी चत्वारिंशत् (चत्वारो न) प्लुताः स्मृताः ॥

इति प्लुतविचारः ।

करोतु तामभीमां च इन्द्रस्य तनुवं प्रियम् ।

मयि दक्षक्रतू स्विन्नस्नात्वी न प्लुतसंज्ञिकाः ॥
प्लुतप्रकरणं समाप्तम् ॥

Baroda 6255. PL. Tel. 1 fol. (45b). (Saṃhitā-pluta-sūtram).
MD 14744. PL. Tel. 2 pp. (15ff.). .... (= Skt. Texts on Phonetics, pp. 215-16).
MD 14749. PL. Tel. 1 p. (43b). Svara-viṣaya and Trikrama at the end.

918 PLUTA-SAṂGRAHA (प्लुतसंग्रह)

Adyar D I 984 → Veda-lakṣaṇa (A 2). Same as MD 936. The beginning as printed in the Adyar catalogue is that of the *Svara-samuccaya* in the same codex.

Hz 1433. PL. Gr. 33 fol. (with 3 other Veda-lakṣaṇa works). Belonged to the late Raja Ghanapathi of Tiruvidaimarudur, Thanjavur Dist.

Mysore I, p. 31. Cf. Pluta-viṃśati.

Trav. Uni. 16408 P. PL. Mal. 1 fol. 20 Grantha-s. Begins as Baroda Ms.

Trav. Uni. 16408 Z2. PL. Mal. 1 fol. 20 Grantha-s.

Trav. Uni. 18615 E. PL. Gr. 20 Grantha-s.

Trav. Uni. L.988 H. PL. Mal. 20 Grantha-s (damaged).

919 PLUTĀNUŚĀSANA (प्लुतानुशासन)

19 verses on the elongated (pluta) vowels in the Taittirīya Śākhā.

Beginning:

तैत्तिरीयस्य वेदस्य प्लुतानामनुशासनम् ।
यथाश्रुति यथान्यायं सकलं क्रियते मया ॥
आद्येषु त्रिषु वर्णेषु प्लुतानामिह संभवः ।
तत्रावर्णाः प्लुताः पञ्च पदान्ते सानुनासिकाः ॥
यशो ममां३ यत् ग्रां३ उपहूतां३ सुश्लोकां४ सुमङ्गलां४ ॥
अन्येषु सर्ववर्णेषु प्लुता निरनुनासिकाः ।

End:

समानि त्रिहा ऋता स्यादि नाभा मा वा द्वयं द्वयम् ।
प्रायशो ऽन्त्ये तु दीर्घावित्याचार्यैरभिधीयते ॥
इत्येष कथितः सर्वः समासात् प्लुतनिर्णयः ।
यजुषां तैत्तिरीयाणां संदेहविनिवृत्तये ॥
इति प्लुतसंग्रहः ॥

Baroda 6255(h). PL. Tel. 1 fol. (46). 25 Grantha-s. = CLB I, p. 32. Col.: Pluta-saṃgraha.

Baroda 12752. Gr. 1 fol. 25 Grantha-s. = CLB I, p. 32.

MD 936. PL. Gr. 3 pp. (42ff.). Colophon reads as Pluta-saṃgraha. The end is the same as in Adyar D I 984. .... (= Skt. Texts on Phonetics, pp. 213-14).

MT 4600(a). PL. Gr. 1 fol. Presented in 1924-25 by the Secretary to the Trustees of Sri Yogi Parthasarathi Ayyangar's Charities, Triplicane, Madras.

Mysore ND II 3458 (P 2339/ 7). PL. Gr. 1 fol. (40). Extract no. 161. Title: Taittirīya-plutānuśāsana.

Mysore ND II 3642 (P 972/ 6). PL. Tel. 1 fol. (32). Extract no. 227. Title: Pluta-viṃśati.

Mysore ND II 3643 (P 2262/41). PL. Gr. 2 fol.

Mysore ND II 3644 (P 2262/42). PL. Gr. 2 fol.

Mysore ND II 3645 (P 232/14). PL. Gr. 6 fol. Different ?

Mysore ND II 3646 (P 2265/26). PL. Gr. 2 fol. (138-39).

Tirupati SVUORI (3516b1). PL. Gr. 2 fol. (16b-17a).

Trav. Uni. 2938 K.

Trav. Uni. L.988 H.

920 PHULLA-SŪTRA or PUṢPA-SŪTRA (फुल्लसूत्र / पुष्पसूत्र)

The Prātiśākhya of *Sāmaveda* in ten Prapāṭhaka-s, attributed to Vararuci. In North Indian Mss. it is called *Puṣpa-sutra* and ascribed to Gobhila. For details about the author, text and the commentaries, see B. R. Sharma's introduction to the second volume of the new edition and Asko Parpola (op. cit.), p. 54. See also *Journal of the University of Bombay*, 35 (NS). pt. ii, Sept. 1966, p. 46.

Adyar D I 915 (21 C 24 = 67836). PL. Gr. 30 fol. (55ff.). = Adyar I, p. 51a. Prapāṭhaka-s 3 to 10 of the Chowkhamba edition, here divided into 3 sections which are not named and consist of 57, 50, and 21 Khaṇḍa-s, respectively.

Adyar D I 916 (22 Q 17 = 69510). PL. Gr. 21 fol. = Adyar II, App. p. iib (40 H 17). From III 11 to the end of X.

Adyar D I 917 (25 C 11 = 70788). PL. Gr. 13 fol. = Adyar I, p. 51a. From the beginning of III to VI 5.

Adyar D I 918 (34 C 21 = 75562). PL. Gr. 35 fol. (30ff.). = Adyar I, p. 51a. Prapāṭhaka-s III-X. Copied by Subrahmaṇya.

Adyar D I 919 (34 G 4 = 75668). PL. Gr. 6 fol. (16ff.). Incomplete. Prapāṭhaka-s III-V.

America 220.

ASB I iii.22 (I A 38/2). 31 fol. Dated V.S. 1870 = A.D. 1813.

B I, p. 180.

Baroda 2446(b). 46 fol. (7-52). 1000 Grantha-s. Dated V.S. 1777. = CLB I, p. 31.

Baroda 2447. 22-59 fol. 700 Grantha-s. (Prapāṭhaka-s 5-10). = CLB I, p. 31.

Baroda 2534. 48 fol. 1000 Grantha-s. = CLB I, p. 31.

Baroda 6384(a). PL. Gr. 17 fol. 500 Grantha-s (a. Vararuci). = CLB I, p. 31.

Baroda 6737(a). 154 fol. PL. Gr. 4700 Grantha-s. (Prapāṭhaka-s 3-10) (with Bhāṣya of Ajātaśatru). = CLB I, p. 32.

Baroda 6783(c). PL. Gr. 43-44 fol. 25 Grantha-s. Stobha-gatāgata only. = CLB I, p. 31.

Baroda 6917(a). PL. Gr. 32 fol. 700 Grantha-s. (Prapāṭhaka-s 5-10). = CLB I, p. 31.

Baroda 9805(h). PL. Gr. 50 fol. 1000 Grantha-s. (a. Vararuci). = CLB I, p. 31.

Bikaner 645. 58 fol. (a. Gobhila). Dated V.S. 1698 and 1708 (A.D. 1641 and 1651).

Bikaner 646. 41 fol. Incomplete.

Bombay Uni. (Itchharam 11 1) 99. 48 fol. (1-34, 39-52).

BORI 29 of 1870-71. 63 fol. Dated V.S. 1754 (? 1574). = Ms. E of the edition by R. Simon.

BORI 99 of 1879-80. 66 fol. Dated V.S. 1751. = Ms. D of the edition by R. Simon.

BORI 64 of 1886-92. 63 fol. Dated V.S. 1739.

BORI 65 of 1886-92. 55 fol. Dated V.S. 1838.

Brl. p. 45 (no.CXXXIV) = IO 4581.

Calcutta Skt. Coll. I 79. 70 fol. 1000 Grantha-s.

GJKSV 41918. 67 fol. Title: Sāma-veda-puṣpa-sūtra.

Gough p. 79 (no.29). 63 fol. Dated V.S. 1574.

IM 1990. 10 fol. Incomplete.

IM 1991. 47 fol. (6-52). Incomplete. Dated V.S. 1579.

IM 4953. 32 fol. Incomplete. Many fol. are missing.

IO 270 (1743). 61 fol. Dated V.S. 1666.

IO 4581 (Burnell 139a). PL. Gr. 31 fol. Written about A.D. 1800.

IO 4583 (Burnell 448). 102 fol. (with C. of Ajātaśatru). Written about A.D. 1875.

Jammu RSRI p. 72 (no. 5262). 67 fol. Dated V.S. 1726 (Stein 304).

MD 19535. 34 pp. Incomplete. Lacks beginning.

MT 3345(a). Gr. 125 fol. (with C. of Rāmakṛṣṇa). Incomplete (5-7). Transcribed in 1920-21 from a Ms. of Sāmavedam Narayana Sastrigaru, Bobbili.

MT 4262. PL. Gr. 55 fol. (with C. of Ajātaśatru). Purchased in 1922-23 from Ganapati Sastrigal of Karattoluvu, Coimbattur.

Mysore ND II 3648 (P 5680/ 1). PL. Na. 36 fol. Extract no. 228.

Mysore ND II 3649 (A 407/ 1). 130 fol.

Mysore ND II 3650 (B 1114/ 2). Na. 5 fol.

Mysore ND II 3970 (C 834/ 1). Na. 48 fol. Incomplete. Extract no. 321. Title: Sāma-prātiśākhya.

Oppert II 395. Belonged to Venkatarama Srauti of Mullandram, N. Arcot Dist.

Oppert II 2208. 25 pp. Belonged to Anantarama Sastri of Kadattur, Udumalapet Taluk. Coimbatore Dist.

Oppert II 10155. Belonged to Ramasvami Dikshitar of Pinnaivasal, Trichinapalli.

Oppert II 10331. Belonged to Venkataramana Dikshita of Tiruchandurai, Trichinapalli Dist.

Oxf. 379a. 381a. 383b.

Oudh III 4.

Oudh XIII 26 (no.17). 138 pp. 981 Grantha-s. Dated A.D. 1846. Belonged to Pandit Kesava Prasada of Unao.

Oudh XX 16 (no.4). 118 pp. 1000 Grantha-s. Dated A.D. 1641. Belonged to Pandita Badari Narayana Misra of Lucknow.

P 6

Peters. II, p. 179 (no.43). 32 fol.

Peters. IV, p. 3 (no.64). 63 fol. Dated V.S. 1739.

PUL I, p. 132 (no.26). 35 fol. 1000 Grantha-s. Dated V.S. 1715.

PUL II. App. p. 12 (no.190). PL. Gr. 7 fol.

PUL II. App. p. 12 (no.194). 52 fol. 1000 Grantha-s. Dated V.S. 1720.

RASB II 1323 (G 375). 58 fol. 928 Grantha-s. Dated V.S. 1680.

RASB II 1324 (G 1108). 38 fol. 890 Grantha-s. Dated V.S. 1672 (a. Gobhila).

RASB II 1325 (G 1180). 64 fol. 1000 Grantha-s. Dated V.S. 1713 (a. Gobhila). The Ms. is said to have belonged to Vidyānidhi Kavīndra on whom the Emperor Shah-Jehan conferred the title of Sarvavidyānidhāna.

SBD 2019. 70 fol. (7-76). Incomplete. Dated V.S. 1672.

SBD 2095. 50 fol.

SBD 2096. 4 fol. Incomplete.

Stein p. 17 (no. 304). 67 fol.

TCD 25. PL. Gr. 29 fol. 522 Grantha-s.

Trav. Uni. 1611. 900 Grantha-s. Dated V.S. 1749.

Trav. Uni. 2909 C. PL. Gr. 600 Grantha-s. Incomplete.

Trav. Uni. 2949. PL. Gr. 2300 Grantha-s (with C. of Ajātaśatru). Incomplete.

Trav. Uni. 3051 A. PL. Gr. 650 Grantha-s. Incomplete.

Trav. Uni. 3340 B. PL. Gr. 800 Grantha-s. Incomplete.

Trav. Uni. 3601. PL. Gr. 1100 Grantha-s (with C. of Ajātaśatru). Incomplete.

Trav. Uni. 4057. PL. Gr. 2065 Grantha-s (with C. of Ajātaśatru). Incomplete.

Trav. Uni. 11823. PL. Gr. 2500 Grantha-s (with C. of Ajātaśatru).

Trav. Uni. 11827 D. PL. Gr. 1200 Grantha-s (with Vivaraṇa).

Trav. Uni. 18685 B. PL. Gr. 900 Grantha-s.

Trav. Uni. C.398. PL. Gr. 800 Grantha-s. Incomplete. = TCD 25.

Trav. Uni. T.126. 2500 Grantha-s (with C. of Ajātaśatru). Incomplete.

Triv. Cur. II 27. Gr. 900 Grantha-s. Obtained from Rama Vadhyar, Klangadu.

Triv. Cur. II 28. Gr. 900 Grantha-s. Obtained from Rama Vadhyar, Klangadu.

Triv. Cur. II 29. Gr. 900 Grantha-s. Obtained from Samu Vadhyar, Shermadevi,

Weber 303 (Chambers 98). 106 fol. Dated V.S. 1684. = Ms. B of the edition by R. Simon.

Weber 304 (Chambers 99). 59 fol. Dated V.S. 1841. Copy of no.303. = Ms. B1 of the edition by R. Simon.

Weber 305 (Chambers 220). 92 fol. Dated V.S. 1711. = Ms. C of the edition by R. Simon.

Weber 2040 (Ms. or. fol. 1480). 17 fol. Incomplete (up to V 8).

Ptd.:

1) Ed. by Satyavrata Samasrami (Sāmaprātiśākhyam atiprācīnaṃ Sāmagācāryeṇa mahāmuninā puṣpeṇa kṛtam), in the Sanskrit journal *Uṣā*. – Calcutta : Satya Press, 1890, vol. I, pts. 3-4. 4, 84 pp. [NL (180 Qc 88 1); BM : Ptd. Bks. Cat. 1876-92. 458 (14010.c.43); Emeneau (365)]

2) Ed. by Richard Simon, with Introduction and a German translation : *Das Puṣpasūtra mit Einleitung und Übersetzung*, Abhandlungen der königlichen Bayerischen Akademie der Wissenschaften, I. Kl. XXIII. Band, III. Abt. – München 1908, pp. 481-780. Also appeared separately. [Kashi Vidyapeetha (Saṃ. 891.212 Pu 94 Sā); UBHD (H 93.2); BM : Ptd. Bks. Cat. 1906-1928. 822 (Ac. 713/6); Emeneau (366)]

Reprinted in : Richard Simon : *Kleine Schriften*, ed. by Rüdiger Schmitt. – Wiesbaden : Steiner, 1979, pp. 470-768. – (Glasenapp Stiftung 20) [SAI (ind 50 A 79/2954)]

3) Ed. by Lakshmana Shastri Dravida, with the Bhāṣya of Ajātaśatru. – Benares : Chowkhamba, 1922-27. 255 pp. – (Ch. Skt. Series 57). [SAI 87/1679*); BORI

(2509; 34549); UBTÜ (Ci XX 615); Emeneau (367)]

4) Ed. by B. R. Sharma, <pt. 1:> Prapāṭhaka-s 1 and 2, with his own commentary *Sādhanā* (in Sanskrit) and Introduction; pts. 2-3: Prapāṭhaka-s 3 - 10, with Vivaraṇa and Bhāṣya of Ajātaśatru and Dīpa of Rāmakṛṣṇa alias Nānābhāī Dīkṣita. – Kathmandu : Nepal Research Centre; – Stuttgart : Kommissionsverlag Franz Steiner Wiesbaden. – (Nepal Research Centre Publications 2, 10, 11).

Pt. 1: 1979. 6, 56, 277 pp.

Pt. 2: 1985. XLII, 710 pp.

Pt. 3: 1985. VII, pp. 712-1288.

[BORI (50228; 50229; 50230); SAI (ind 51 D 788/2117); SKGI (Rg IX 103)]

– C. Phulla-pota of Gaṇeśa Paṇḍita.

Baroda 9795. PL. Gr. 191 fol. 4000 Grantha-s. = CLB I, p. 32. Extract pp. 153-54.

Hamburg StUB (Oppert 37).

Mysore I, p. 31.

Mysore ND II 3655 (A 395). Gr. 101. Extract no. 232.

Oppert II 393. Belonged to Venkatarama Srauti of Mullandram, N. Arcot Dist.

SBD 2121. 52 fol. Incomplete. (Sāma-prātiśākhya-bhāṣya).

– C. of Ajātaśatru.

Adyar D I 920 (19 L 6 = 66719). PL. Tel. 102 fol. = Adyar I, p. 51a. Copied by Viśveśvara, son of Īśvara Dīkṣita, on the 1st day of the first half of the month Āṣāḍha, in the year Bhava.

Adyar D I 921 (24 M 34 = 70591). PL. Gr. 94 fol. Incomplete. Begins abruptly (p. 30 of the Chowkhamba edition) and ends with the Vikāra section.

Adyar D I 922 (25 N 10 = 71196). PL. Gr. 86 fol.

Adyar D I 923 (33 D 11 = 75238). PL. Gr. 156 fol. = Adyar I, p. 51a. Contains variants to the Chowkhamba edition.

Adyar D I 924 (33 E 17 = 75264). PL. Gr. 25 fol. = Adyar I, p. 51a. Incomplete (ends on pp. 64-65 of the Chowkhamba edition).

Adyar D I 925 (33 M 24 = 75509). PL. Gr. 177 fol. = Adyar I, p. 51a. Incomplete (up to p. 210 of the Chowkhamba edition).

Adyar D I 926 (40 C 24 = PM 131). 156 fol. (1-161; fol. 24-28 missing).

Adyar D XIII 252 (VB 62). PL. Gr. 65 fol.

Baroda 6737(a). 154 fol. PL. Gr. 4700 Grantha-s. Prapāṭhaka-s 3-10. = CLB I, p. 32.

Baroda 6740. PL. Gr. 96 fol. 1600 Grantha-s. (Prapāṭhaka-s 3-9 of the Chowkhamba edition). = CLB I, p. 32.

Bikaner 647. 118 fol. Dated V.S. 1749 (A.D. 1692).

BORI 24 of 1871-72. 157 fol. Adhyāya-s I-VI. Incomplete. = Ms. G of the edition by R. Simon.

BORI 71 of 1881-82. 34 fol. 750 Grantha-s. = Ms. H of the edition by R. Simon.

Brl. p. 45 (no.CXXXV) = IO 4582.

Gough p. 86 (no.24). 157 fol. Incomplete (I-VI 10).

Hamburg StUB (Oppert 38). PL. Gr. 157 fol. Title: Phulla-vivaraṇa.

IO 4582 (Burnell 135). PL. Gr. 87 fol. = Ms. T of the edition by R. Simon.

IO 4583 (Burnell 448). 102 fol. (with text). Written about A.D. 1875. = Ms. I of the edition by R. Simon.

MD 937. PL. Gr. 104 pp. Incomplete. Copied by Rāmasvāmi.

MD 938. Tel. 214 pp. 3 additional verses at the end.

MD 16306. PL. Gr. 120 pp. 1440 Grantha-s. Almost complete.

MT 644(a). PL. Gr. 3 fol. (8-10). Incomplete. 1st Khaṇḍa. Purchased in 1912-13 through Seshasayi Ayyangar of Kottaiyur near Kumbakonam.

MT 4402. PL. Gr. 166 fol. Incomplete. Purchased in 1923-24 from Sankaranarayana Dikshitar of Bhavani, Coimbattur.

MT 4262. PL. Gr. 55 fol. (with text). Purchased in 1922-23 from Ganapati Sastrigal of Karattoluvu, Coimbattur.

Mysore I, p. 31 (2 Mss.).

Mysore ND II 3651 (P 3358). PL. Gr. 124 fol.

Mysore ND II 3652 (A 407/ 2). 130 fol. Extract no. 229.

Oppert I 8090. Belonged to Paravastu Venkatarangacharyar of Vishakhapattanam.

Oppert II 394. Belonged to Venkatarama Srauti of Mullandram, N. Arcot Dist.

Oppert II 10156. Belonged to Ramasvami Dikshitar of Pinnaivasal, Trichinapalli Dist.

P 20.

Peters. III, p. 350.

RASB II 1327 (G 6570). 78 fol. Incomplete. It contains numerous lacunae.

SB p. 35 (no.40). 114 fol. 2106 Grantha-s. Incomplete. Dated V.S. 1562. = SBD 2099.

SBD 2099. 78 fol. (27-114; several fol. are missing).

SBD 2142. 143 fol. Incomplete. Dated V.S. 1617.

SBD 55792. 99 fol. (5-85, 88-104, 3). Incomplete.

TCD 26. 215 pp. 1935 Grantha-s. = Trav. Uni. T.126.

Trav. Uni. 1611. PL. Gr. 2500 Grantha-s (with text).

Trav. Uni. 2949. PL. Gr. 2300 Grantha-s (with text).

Trav. Uni. 3051 A. PL. Gr. 1100 Grantha-s (with text).

Trav. Uni. 3601. PL. Gr. 1100 Grantha-s (with text).

Trav. Uni. 4057. PL. Gr. 2065 Grantha-s (with text). Incomplete.

Trav. Uni. 11823. PL. Gr. 2500 Grantha-s (with text).

Trav. Uni. 18693 A. PL. Gr. 2750 Grantha-s.

Trav. Uni. C.398. 2500 Grantha-s (with text).

Trav. Uni. T.126. 2500 Grantha-s (with text). = TCD 26.

Triv. Cur. II 30. Gr. 3800 Grantha-s. Obtained from Rama Vadhyar, Klangadu.

Triv. Cur. II 31. Gr. 850 Grantha-s (up to Uccanīca-prakaraṇa). Obtained from Rama Vadhyar, Klangadu.

Triv. Cur. II 32. Gr. 3000 Grantha-s (up to Vikalpa-prakaraṇa). Obtained from Rama Vadhyar, Klangadu.

Weber 306 (Chambers 295). 115 fol. Dated V.S. 1801. = Ms. F of the edition by R. Simon. At the end of the ch. VIII, on fol. 84a : upādhyāyājātaśatrupādair viṣṇuyaśaśśiṣyāya anucaraṇārthe bhāṣye kṛte (aṣṭamaḥ prapāṭhakaḥ/ in margin) iti bhāvāḥ parisamāptāḥ | idānīṃ vikalpāḥ ucyante || (also on fol. 139a of the next number).

Weber 307 (Chambers 402). 194 fol. Dated V.S. 1841. Copy of no.306, made for Justice Chambers. = Ms. F1 of the edition by R. Simon.

Ptd.: with the text. See above.

– C. Phulla-dīpa of Rāma-kṛṣṇa Dīkṣita alias Nānābhāī, son of Dāmodara Tripāṭhin. Cf. Asko Parpola (op. cit.) p. 105f.

Baroda 9797. PL. Gr. 107 fol. 4000 Grantha-s. = CLB I, p. 32.
Baroda 10046. Gr. 15 fol. (13-27). 500 Grantha-s. = CLB I, p. 32. 3rd Prapāṭhaka, 4th Khaṇḍa to the middle of the 4th Prapāṭhaka.
Baroda 10048. 12 fol. (34-45). 400 Grantha-s. = CLB I, p. 32. Final portion of the 10th Prapāṭhaka.
IM 2210. 17 fol. Incomplete.
IM 2536. 9 fol. Incomplete. Dated V.S. 1680.
IO 4584 (Burnell 441). 164 fol. (16, 48, 24, 18, 22, 17, 19). Prapāṭhaka-s III-X. Copied about A.D. 1878. = Ms. N(b) of the edition by R. Simon.
Mill (Oxf.) 163. (? as given in CC).
MT 3345(a). Gr. 125 fol. (with text). Incomplete (5-7). Transcribed in 1920-21 from a Ms. of Sāmavedam Narayana Sastrigaru, Bobbili.
Mysore I, p. 31.
Mysore ND II 3656 (A 405). Gr. 150 pp.
Mysore ND II 3657 (C 2191). 242 fol.
Mysore ND II 3971 (C 834/ 2). Na. 48 fol. Incomplete. Up to the second Khaṇḍa of the fifth Prapāṭhaka. Title: Sāma-prātiśākhya-vyākhyā.
PUL I, p. 24 (no.151). 15 pp. Dated V.S. 1968. (Sāma-prātiśākhya-bhāṣyam – Phulla-ṭīkā).
RASB II 1326 (G 1205). 10 fol. 300 Grantha-s (10th and 11th section of the 10th Paṭala). Dated V.S. 1781.

Ptd.: in B. R. Sharma's edition of the text.

– C. Dīpamālā of Nāganātha-sūri or Nāgappa-sūri.
Mysore I, p. 613.
Mysore ND II 3653 (P 4735). PL. Na. 128 fol. Extract no. 230.
Mysore ND II 3654 (B 1114/ 1). Na. 5 ? fol. Extract no. 231.

– C. Vivaraṇa.
Trav. Uni. 11827 D. PL. Gr. 1200 Grantha-s (with text). Incomplete.

C. Phulla-sūtra-bhāṣya – Bhāṣā-ṭīkā (C. in Hindi for some portions).
IM 152. Part I : 1-19, 151-70 fol. Part II : 2-8, 11-13, 16-34, 36-42, 44-46, 48, 53, 54, 61, 63, 65-77 fol. Incomplete.

[CC I 343a; II 76b, 210b; III 73b]

921 BAHVṚCA-PRĀTIŚĀKHYA (बह्वृचप्रातिशाख्य)
SBD 2136. 27 fol. (1-17, 19-28). Incomplete → Ṛgveda-prātiśākhya.

922 BĀNTHĀ-LAKṢAṆA (बान्थालक्षण)
→ Bontha-lakṣaṇa also known as Pada-gāḍha.
GJKSV 39494. 14 fol.

*BĀBHRAVYA (बाभ्रव्य)
Krama-kāra of the *Ṛgveda,* mentioned in the Maṅgala-śloka of Narasiṃha's *Jaṭā-lakṣaṇa* also called *Vikalpa-kaumudī.* See above under Gālava.

*BĀLAKṚṢṆA GOḌASE (बालकृष्ण गोडसे)
Son of Sadāśiva.
– Prātiśākhya-pradīpa-śikṣā. Ptd.: in Śikṣā-saṃgraha. – Benares, 1889, pp. 210-306. – (Ben. S. S. 10).

*BĀLAKṚṢṆA NĀRĀYAṆA (SĀMAKA) (बालकृष्ण नारायण सामक)
– Ṛkpāṭha-dūṣaṇoddhāra. VSM I 436 (no.5439). 14 fol.

923 BṚHACCHIKṢĀ (बृहच्छिक्षा)
of Yājñavalkya.
Bühler p. 553 (no. 15). = BORI 9 of 1866-68. 55 fol. (Bṛhacchikṣāvasāna-nirṇayādayaḥ. 5 works).

924 BṚHATĪ-SAHASRA-PĀRĀVĀRA-SŪKTA-MAṆI-SAṂGRAHA (बृहतीसहस्रपारावारसूक्तमणिसंग्रह)
Trav. Uni. 4197 B. PL. Na. 225 Grantha-s.

925 BṚHAT-SARVĀNUKRAMAṆIKĀ (बृहत्सर्वानुक्रमणिका)
→ Atharva-veda-bṛhatsarvānukramaṇikā.
Ānandāśrama 7501. 60 fol. Up to 11th Paṭala. A modern copy entitled Sarvānukramaṇī.
Mysore I, p. 31.
Mysore ND II 3659 (P 3333/ 1). PL. Gr. 47 fol. Extract no. 234.

926 BṚHAD-ṚGVIDHĀNA (बृहदृग्विधान)
See under Ṛgvidhāna.
GJKSV 13746. 25 fol.
GJKSV 33577. 22 fol.
BORI 18 of A 1879-80. 42 fol.
SBD 4020. 35 fol.
SBD 48270. 9 fol.

927 BṚHAD-DEVATĀ(-NUKRAMAṆIKĀ) (बृहद्देवता /-नुक्रमणिका)
of Śaunaka. An index of the deities of the hymns of the *Ṛgveda.* An extensive Anukramaṇī of about 1200 verses (Śloka-s) interspersed with occasional Triṣṭubh-s. The text is divided into eight Adhyāya-s corresponding to the eight Aṣṭaka-s and it names the deity for each verse of the *Ṛgveda.* It also contains a large number of illustrative myths and legends.

America 375. 77 fol.

America 376. 36 fol.

Baroda 10898. 71 fol. 1500 Grantha-s. Dated Śaka 1794. = CLB I, p. 32.

BBRAS 492 (B D 145). 42 fol.

BBRAS SPP 57. 27 fol. (3-29). Chs. 1-3.

BBRAS SPP 66. 55 fol. (1, 2, 30-82).

CU Add. 1048.

GJKSV 37342. 52 fol. Dated V.S. 1678.

Haug p. 21 (no.43).

Hoshiarpur p. 56 (no.6362). 75 fol. 1400 Grantha-s. Dated V.S. 1785.

IM 2164. 54 fol. (5-58). Incomplete. Dated V.S. 1698. Col.: Bṛhad-devatā-pariśiṣṭa.

München 26. 73 fol. Dated A.D. 1846. Copied by Gaṅgādhara, son of Maṇirāma Bhaṭṭa Dāra.?

Mysore I, p. 31.

Mysore ND II 3658 (P 2862/ 2). PL. Na. 49 fol. (45-93). Extract no.233.

Oxf. II 891 (Ms. Sansk. e. 8a). 106 fol. 17th century. = Oxf. 401b (no.203). Presented by Fitz-Edward Hall in 1861.

PUL II. App. p. 12 (no.195). PL. Mal. 22 fol. (73-94). 400 Grantha-s.

RASB II 239(1) (G 1896). 37 fol.

RASB II 246(1) (G 6022). 18 fol.

SBD 2373. 80 fol. Dated V.S. 1817.

Wai I 377. 112 fol. Dated Śaka 1795.

Weber 47 (Chambers 197). 96 fol. Dated V.S. 1711

Ptd.:

1) Ed. by Rajendralala Mitra, *Bṛihad-devatā* – or an Index to the Gods of the Rigveda by Śaunaka, to which have been added *Ārṣānukramaṇī*, *Chandonukramaṇī* and *Anuvākānukramaṇī* in the form of appendices. – Calcutta : Asiatic Society, 1893. 333 pp. – (Bibliotheca Indica 127). [Adyar (H080 BIS 127); NL (180 Jc 89 40); Emeneau (389); BM : Ptd. Bks. Cat. 1892-1906. 626 (14002.a. vol.127); IO : Ptd. Bks. Cat. 1938, p. 544 (Bibl. Ind. 127)]

2) Ed. by Arthur A. Macdonell, *The Bṛhad-Devatā* – Attributed to Śaunaka, a Summary of the Deities and Myths of the Rig-Veda, translated into English, 2 vols. – Cambridge, Mass. : Harvard University, 1904. xxxvi, 198; xvi, 334 pp. – (Harvard Oriental Series 5, 6). [NL (294 1/Sa 87; I C I G/2); Emeneau (390); IO : Ptd. Bks. Cat. 1938, p. 544 (305. 7. G. 6-7)]

Reprinted : Delhi : Motilal Banarsidass, 1965. 582 pp.

3) Ed. by Ramkumar Ray, with a Hindi translation and commentary. – Varanasi : Chowkhamba, 1963. 10, 372 pp. – (Kashi Sanskrit Series 164). [BORI (29870, 40582); SAI (ind S 100, 164)]

[CC I 376b; III 80b]

928 BṚHAD-YAJURVIDHĀNA (बृहद्यजुर्विधान)

→ Yajurvidhāna.

929 BṚHAD-YĀJÑAVALKYA-ŚIKṢĀ (बृहद्याज्ञवल्क्यशिक्षा)
GB 29 → Yājñavalkya-śikṣā.

930 BAIṬH (बैठ्)
→ Lakṣaṇa-ratna(-bhaiṭ) also known as Veda-lakṣaṇa-ratna, of Vaidyanātha-bhaṭṭa.
Mysore ND II 3660 (P 2326/ 2). PL. Gr. 8 fol. Extract no. 235.
Mysore ND II 3661 (B 253/ 3). Gr. 17 fol. (46-63). Extract no. 236. (The opening verse is from the Kālanirṇaya-śikṣā).

931 BAIṬH-PARIBHĀṢĀ (1) (बैठ्परिभाषा)
15 verses explaining the Baiṭh-s of four letters. Both the text and the commentary thereon are printed at the end of the *Prātiśākhya-pradīpa-śikṣā*, under the title *Veda-paribhāṣā-kārikā-śikṣā*.

IM 1963. 1 fol. Title: Kātyāyana-baiṭha-paribhāṣā (by a later hand).

– C. of Rāmacandra-paṇḍita.
IM 2540. 6 fol.
SBD 4277. 5 fol.

Ptd.: in Śikṣā-saṃgraha. – Benares, 1889, pp. 320-26. – (Ben. S. S. 10).

932 BAIṬH(A)-PARIBHĀṢĀ (2) (बैठ्(ठ)परिभाषा)
→ Aṣṭākṣarī-baiṭh(-paribhāṣā).
Baroda 8666. 1 fol. 20 Grantha-s. = CLB I, p. 32.
BISM p. 179 (13/75).
BISM p. 179 (35/482).
Deccan College (1964). 280 (3102 of Dikshit Collection). 14 fol. Incomplete.
SBD 2106. 2 fol. Incomplete. Verses only.

933 BAIṬH(A)-PARIBHĀṢĀ (3) (बैठ्(ठ)परिभाषा)
BORI TM 31. 21 fol. (fol. 1-20 Svarāṅkuśa with C. of Nīlakaṇṭha; only the last 2 fol. contain the paribhāṣā portion of the *Ṛgveda-padaratna)*.
SBD 4376. 2 fol. Incomplete (ascribed to Raghunātha).
SBD 46945. 4 fol. Incomplete. = Ṛgveda-padaratna.
Skt. Coll. Ben. 1918-30. p. 3 (no.24). 2 fol.
Visvanatha Vamana Deva, Varanasi. 4 fol.

934 BAIṬH-LAKṢAṆA(-RATNA) (बैठ्लक्षण /-रत्न)
→ Lakṣaṇa-ratna(-bhaiṭ), of Vaidyanātha-bhaṭṭa.

935 BAIṬH-VĀKYA (बैठ्वाक्य)
→ Lakṣaṇa-ratna(-bhaiṭ), of Vaidyanātha-bhaṭṭa.

936 BAIṬH-SAṂKHYĀ (बैठ्संख्या)
Belongs to RV.
Burnell 2b (no.2397-98).
TD 1770. 1 fol. 5 Grantha-s; only a fragment.
TD 1771. 1 fol. 5 Grantha-s.

[CC I 377a]

937 BAIṬH-SAṂJÑAKA-PRAKARAṆA (बैठ्संज्ञकप्रकरण)
It gives the number of Ṛk-s, Anuvāka-s and Pada-s in each chapter of the *Vājasaneyi-saṃhitā*, in certain symbolic code words, each containing four letters, The text is included in the Śikṣā-saṃgraha at the end of the *Prātiśākhya-pradīpa-śikṣā*, with the title *Veda-paribhāṣā-sūtra-śikṣā* (see below), and ascribed to Rāmacandra, son of Siddheśvara.

IM 2593. 8 fol. (1-6, 8-9). Incomplete. Col.: iti śrīmādhyandinaśākhīyapadādisaṃjñā-parijñānārthakaṃ baiṭhasaṃjñakaprakaraṇaṃ samāptam | śake 1780 | pauṣaśukla 11 raṅgabhaṭṭena likhitam ||
SBD 4345. 11 fol. (1-8, 10-12). Incomplete. Col.: iti mādhyandinīyaśākhīyapadādi-saṃkhyāparijñānārthakṃ baiṭhsaṃjñakaprakaraṇaṃ samāptam ||

938 BONTA-(or BONTHA- or BONDA-)LAKṢAṆA (बोन्त- / बोन्थ- / बोन्द-/लक्षण)
Enumeration of instances of peculiarities in pronunciation, spelling, accents, etc. in the *Ṛgveda*. The words have been arranged according to their repetition, i.e. twice, thrice and so on, up to 96 times. Instances in each group are given in the order of the *Ṛgveda*. The text is more or less the same as the one published by Satyavrata Samasrami under the title *Pada-gāḍha*.

Calcutta Skt. Coll. I 491. 9 fol. Incomplete. Title: Prātiśākhya.
Calcutta Skt. Coll. I 492 (152). 20 fol. Dated Śaka 1525. Title: Ṛgveda-pada-krama-lakṣaṇaṃ Bontākhyam. It contains many variants.
GJKSV 39494. 14 fol. Col.: Bānthā-lakṣaṇa (dvidhādadhus taṃ gandharveti dve adadhuḥ ... iti ṣaṇṇavtyathakāreṇa).
PUL I, p. 19 (no.32). 5 fol. 100 Grantha-s. (Ṛgveda-tattva-pada-pradīpikā).
RASB II 255 (G 6452). 18 fol. 550 Grantha-s. Dated V.S. 1679 = A.D. 1622. Title: Bonthā-lakṣaṇa. Titles of the sections are enumerated.
TD 1772. 27 fol. 500 Grantha-s. Dated Śaka 1710 in the Kīlaka year = 1788 A.D. The scribe was the son of Paurāṇika Rākṣasabhuvanakara Kamalākara-bhaṭṭa. The work is composed of 38 sections, which are enumerated in the catalogue.
TD 1773. 34 fol. (4-37; fol. 19 is missing). 800 Grantha-s.
TD 1774. 24 fol. 400 Grantha-s. Incomplete.
TD 1775. 10 fol. (1-12; 4th and 5th missing). 120 Grantha-s. Only the first 8 sub-sections of the 1st section given in no. 1773 are found in this Ms.
TD 1776. 7 fol. 100 Grantha-s. Incomplete.
Tirupati SVUORI (427c). PL. Na. 3 fol. (4b-6a). Title: Bontu-lakṣaṇa.

Ptd.: ed. by Satyavrata Samasrami, *Padagāḍhaḥ – Ṛgvedasya – Śākalyena maharṣiṇā, tatsamānakālīnena vā proktaḥ*, in the Sanskrit journal *Uṣā*. – Calcutta : Satya Press, Saṃ. 1951 (1895), vol. II, pts. 11-12. 77 pp. [Kashi Vidyapeetha, Varanasi

(Saṃ. 891.226 Pa 36); MUL (P15:10Ā2: 3x1/15C5); BM : Ptd. Bks. Cat. 1906-1928. 1196 (14010.c.43); Emeneau (63)]

Reprinted under the title: *Ṛgvedīya-bonda-lakṣaṇa*, ed. by K. S. Venkatarama Sastri, together with *Pada-ratna*, *Svarāṅkuśa* and *Ṛgvarṇa-krama-lakṣaṇa*. – Srirangam : Sri Vani Vilas Press, 1968. [Adyar (PḤ16.2 Ven RB); UBTÜ (3 E 1286); SAI (85/1958*)]

939 BAUDHĀYANA-ŚIKṢĀ (**बौधायनशिक्षा**)

Mentioned in the Veda-lakṣaṇānukramaṇikā (MD 967) and in the Siddhānta-śikṣā-vyākhyāna, Brl. p. 9 (no.XXVII).

[CC I 380a]

940 BRAHMA-VEDA-MANTRĀNUKRAMAṆĪ (**ब्रह्मवेदमन्त्रानुक्रमणी**)

→ Atharva-veda-bṛhatsarvānukramaṇikā.

941 BRAHMA-RĀŚI(-BHĀṢYA) (**ब्रह्मराशि /-भाष्य**)

The first chapter of the *Ṛktantra* is traditionally known by this title. Cf. SBD 2111a : Ṛktantra.

942 BRĀHMAṆĀRAṆYAKĀDI-SVARA-NIRṆYA (**ब्राह्मणारण्यकादिस्वरनिर्णय**)

Mysore ND II 3662 (P 4772/ 7). PL. Tel. 22 fol. (21-42). Extract no. 237.

***BHAṬṬA BHĀSKARA YAJVAN (ADHVARĪNDRA) (भट्टभास्करयज्वन् / अध्वरीन्द्र)**

of Kāśyapa-gotra.

– Ārṣeya-dīpa. An Anukramaṇī of Ṛṣi-s, Devatā-s and Chandas of Sāmaveda, based on the Ārṣeya-brāhmaṇa.

***(BHAṬṬA) ŚOBHĀKARA (भट्टशोभाकर)**

See Śobhākara (Bhaṭṭa).

***BHĀRADVĀJA (भारद्वाज)**

Mentioned in the *Taittirīya-prātiśākhya*, 17.3 and in the *Tribhāṣya-ratna* thereon, 5.40.

***BHĀRADVĀJA (भारद्वाज)**

– Upalekha-pañjikā. Weber p. 8. B. I 198.

[CC I 406b]

943 BHĀRADVĀJA-ŚIKṢĀ (**भारद्वाजशिक्षा**)

Ascribed to Bharadvāja. On words in the *Taittirīya-saṃhitā* which are either likly to be mispronounced or confused with others of similar sound or form.

Beginning:

गणेशं प्रणिपत्याहं संदेहानां निवृत्तये।
शिक्षामनुप्रवक्ष्यामि वेदानां मूलकारणम्॥
वृजने ज उदात्तश्चेदकारेण सहोच्यते।
स्तुतं पदं तु वाक्यान्ते प्रचयं परिकीर्तितम्॥ २॥

आपञ्चमाद्भव्यपूर्वो घृतेनोर्ध्वश्च आहुतम्।
वाक्यान्तो ऽपि तथा प्रोक्तो ग्नःपूर्वस्तु न विद्यते॥ ३॥

End:

त्वं सो ऽन्ते तव मय्येषा त्वं सर्वश्च ध्रुवो ऽसि प्रिः ।
यत्स्थले यादृशः शब्दस्तादृशः परिकीर्तितः ॥ १२८॥
विभक्तिलिङ्गरूपैश्च वर्णा ज्ञेया विचक्षणैः ।
क्रम इङ्ग्यश्च कण्ठोक्ति यजुरादि पदद्वयम्॥ १२९॥
पदसांख्यं वर्णसांख्यमवधानाष्टकं बुधैः ।
यो जानाति भरद्वाजशिक्षामर्थसमन्विताम्॥
स ब्रह्मलोकमाप्नोति गृहमेधी गृहं यथा॥ १३०॥

Adyar D I 927 (20 M 30 = 67572). PL. Gr. 5 fol. = Adyar I, p. 52b. Incomplete. Up to verse 51. On a fly-leaf at the end is written "Incomplete (gha) collated, compared. V. Venkatarama Sharma, 1.5.1930". This is Ms. (gha) of the Poona edition.

Adyar D I 928 (25 H 6 = 70967). PL. Gr. 10 fol. (9ff.). = Adyar I, p. 52b. This is Ms. (ga) of the Poona edition.

Adyar D I 929 (25 L 35 = 71153). PL. Gr. 1 fol. (27b). Incomplete. verses 1-8 only.

Adyar D I 930 (28 M 12 = 73204). PL. (Śrītāla) Gr. 5 fol. Incomplete. 20 verses at the beginning are missing. = Adyar I, p. 52b.

Adyar D XIII 325 (VB 428a). PL. Tel. 37 fol. (with C. of Sūrāvadhānin).

B I, p. 206 (no.60). 50 fol. Dated V.S. 1800.

Baroda 9999. PL. Gr. 37 fol. 900 Grantha-s (with C.). = CLB I, p. 32. Extract pp. 137-38. Extract pp. 155-56.

Baroda 12755(b). Gr. 16 fol. (2-17) 300 Grantha-s. No beginning and no end. = CLB I, p. 32.

Brl. p. 8 (no.XXIV) = IO 4949.

Brl. p. 8 (no.XXV) = IO 4948.

GB 27. 77 fol. (133 verses, with C.). Copied for Kielhorn in Mysore in 1875. See F. Kielhorn : Remarks on the Śikṣās in : *Indian Antiquary*, vol. V, p. 195 (reprint in : *Kleine Schriften*, vol. I, pp. 158-69).

GJKSV 43021. PL. Gr. 64 fol. (with C.).

Gough p. 162 (no.825). Gr.

Gough p. 162 (no.819; with C.). Gr.

Granthappura p. 2 (no.25c). Mal. 100 Grantha-s.

Hamburg StUB (Oppert 10c). PL. Gr. (with C.).

Hamburg StUB (cod.Palmbl. III 8/133) → Veda-lakṣaṇa (HB).

Hoshiarpur p. 52 (no.4371). PL. Gr. 4 fol. 137 Grantha-s.

Hoshiarpur p. 52 (no.4454). PL. Gr. 3 fol. 135 Grantha-s.

Hoshiarpur p. 52 (no.6907). 12 fol. 138 Grantha-s.

Hoshiarpur p. 52 (no.6908). 8 fol. 51 Grantha-s. Incomplete.

Hoshiarpur p. 52 (no.6909). 10 fol. 190 Grantha-s. Incomplete.

Hoshiarpur p. 52 (no.6910). 21 fol. 140 Grantha-s. Incomplete.

Hoshiarpur p. 52 (no.5893). 35 fol. 400 Grantha-s (with C.).
Hoshiarpur p. 52 (no.6911). 50 fol. 900 Grantha-s (with C.). Incomplete. Extract p. 76.
Hoshiarpur p. 52 (no.6912). 56 fol. 1000 Grantha-s (with C.).
Hoshiarpur p. 52 (no.6913). 94 fol. 1000 Grantha-s (with C.).
Hoshiarpur p. 301 (no.4371). PL. Gr. 7 fol. 138 Grantha-s.
IO 4948 (Burnell 172a). PL. Gr. 6 fol. (154-59). Incomplete. Up to verse 90.
IO 4949 (Burnell 172b). PL. Tel. 8 fol. (113-20).
IO 4950 (Mackenzie III 222b). PL. Tel. 10 fol.
IO 4951 (Mackenzie II 94b). PL. Na. 13 fol. (with C.). Written ca. A.D. 1770.
IO 4952 (Mackenzie III 234b). PL. Tel. 17 fol. (8-24) (with C.). A.D. 1816-17.
Mack. 8.
MD 939. 18 pp. (63ff.).
MD 940. Tel. 12 pp. (114ff.). Slightly different at the end.
MD 15502. Gr. 8 pp. (132ff.). 83 Grantha-s.
MD 15849. PL. Gr. 16 pp. 138 Grantha-s.
MD 16722. PL. Tel. 11 pp. 154 Grantha-s.
MD 16752. PL. Tel. 66 pp. 792 Grantha-s (with C. of Lakṣmaṇa).
MD 16760. PL. Tel. 71 pp. 1420 Grantha-s (with C. of Velima-kanyā-Sūrāvadhānin).
MD 18113. PL. Gr. 8 pp. 84 Grantha-s. Incomplete (verses 1-40, 48-50).
MT 1059. PL. Tel. 46 fol. (with C. of Sūrāvadhānin). Incomplete. Presented in 1913-14 by V. Ramachandra Rao of Samalkot.
Mysore (1898), p. 5 (no. 51a). Gr. 67 fol. (with C.).
Mysore I, p. 32 (9 Mss. 6 with C.).
Mysore ND II 3663-73. Extract no. 238, 239, 240, 241.
Oppert I 1012. Belonged to Viraraghava Tatacharyar, Head Master, Sanskrit School of Sathakopacharya, Kanchipuram, Chingelpet Dist.
Oppert I 7144. Belonged to Pola Lakshmanavadhani of Vijayanagaram.
Oppert I 7206. Belonged to Ivattur Nandikesvara Sastri of Vijayanagaram.
Oppert I 7562. Belonged to S. Kodanda Ramavadhana Pantulu of Vijayanagaram.
Oppert I 8134. Belonged to Paravastu Venkatarangacharyar of Vishakhapattanam.
Oppert II 400. Belonged to Venkatarama Srauti of Mullandram, N. Arcot Dist.
Oppert II 766. Belonged to Ghanapathi Shingaracharyar of Alasur, Madurantakam Taluk.
Oppert II 1348. Belonged to Gopalacharyar of Pillapakkam, Kanchipuram Taluk.
Oppert II 4797. Belonged to Sri Sankaracharya Matha of Sringeri,
Oppert II 5761. Belonged to Shingaracharyar of Kalyanapuram, Thanjavur Dist.
Oppert II 7416. Belonged to Venkatarama Sastri of Pillur, Mayavaram Taluk.
Oppert II 7966. Belonged to Venkatarama Dikshita of Sorakayur, Thanjavur Dist.
Oppert II 9068. Belonged to Ganapati Lakshminarayana Sastri of Tiruvadi, Thanjavur Dist.
Oppert II 9492. Belonged to Srinivasa Sastri of Tiruvasalur, Kumbakonam Taluk.
Oppert II 9883. Belonged to M.Raja Ghanapathi of Mahadanapuram, Trichinapalli.
PUL I, p. 23 (no.108). PL. Tel. 6 fol.
PUL I, p. 23 (no.109). PL. Tel. 6 fol. Incomplete.
PUL I, p. 23 (no.110). PL. Gr. 6 fol.
PUL I, p. 23 (no.113). PL. Tel. 58 fol. 1500 Grantha-s (with C.; text of 133 Grantha-s.)

PUL II. App. p. 12 (no.196). PL. Tel. 8 fol. 100 Grantha-s. It is noted in the remark column that Vyāsa, Lakṣmī, Bhāradvāja, Śaṃbhu, Āpiśali, Kauhaleya, Kāla and Ātreya are quoted. But the printed edition contains no such quotations.

TCD 27. 62 pp. 1350 Grantha-s (with C. of Velima-kanyā-Sūrāvadhānin).

Tirupati SVUORI 4465 (4511c). PL. Tel.

Trav. Uni. 2086 A. PL. Gr. 300 Grantha-s (with C. of Jaṭāvallabha).

Trav. Uni. 2088 A. PL. Gr. 8 fol. 138 Grantha-s.

Trav. Uni. 2630 H. PL. Gr. 100 Grantha-s.

Trav. Uni. 2938 H. PL. Gr. 100 Grantha-s.

Trav. Uni. 3751 B. PL. Gr. 500 Grantha-s (with C. of Velima-kanyā-sūrāvadhānin). Incomplete.

Trav. Uni. 4028 B. PL. Gr. 100 Grantha-s.

Trav. Uni. 21553 A. PL. Gr. 100 Grantha-s.

Trav. Uni. L.988 N. PL. Mal. 350 Grantha-s (with C. of Jaṭāvallabha).

Trav. Uni. T.625. 1350 Grantha-s (with C. of Velima-kanyā-sūrāvadhānin).

Triv. Cur. VII 2. Gr. 1200 Grantha-s (with C.). Obtained from Seshu Ghanapathial, Vaikom.

Wai I 1451. 37 fol.

Wai I 1452. 46 fol. (with C.). Dated Śaka 1723.

Ptd.:

1) Ed. by Emil Sieg, with a Latin translation and extracts of the commentary of Lakṣmaṇa Jaṭāvallabha-śāstrin (in Roman script). – Berlin : Speyer und Peters, 1892. xvi, 65 pp. [Adyar (Ḥ15.1 BS x=La Sie); NL (176 B 327); SKGI (RI 110); BM : Ptd. Bks. Cat. 1892-1906. 84-85 (14093.d.16,1); Emeneau (379)]
2) Ed. by Kalattūri Rāghavācārya, with a commentary. – Madras, 1893.
3) Ed. by V. R. Ramachandra Dikshitar and P. S. Sundaram Ayyar. – Poona : BORI, 1938. – (Govt. Oriental Series, Class A, No. 6). In this edition the commentary is ascribed to Nāgeśvara. But according to the description in Adyar D I 931 it is by Jaṭāvallabha Śāstrin. See *The Adyar Library Bulletin,* vol. 5. pt. 4 (1941), Manuscripts Notes. See also *The Adyar Library Bulletin,* vol. 6 (1942). [Adyar (H080 BGO A 6); UBTÜ (14 A 633 Nr.1); SAI (ind S 62, A 6)]

– C.

GB 27. 77 fol. (with text). Copied for Kielhorn in Mysore in 1875.

Hamburg StUB (Oppert 52). PL. Gr. 35 fol.

Mysore p. 2 (no. 51). 67 fol.

Mysore ND II 3676-79. Extract no. 243 (different Cs. ?).

Mysore ND II 3681 (P 7999/ 2) PL. Na. 7 fol. (a different C. ?).

Mysore ND II 3682 (B 861/ 2). Gr. 19 fol. Extract no. 245 (a different C. ?).

Oppert I 6521. In the Library of H H the Raja of Bobbili, Vishakhapattanam Dist.

Oppert II 767. Belonged to Ghanapathi Shingaracharyar of Alasur, Madurantakam Taluk.

Oppert II 5762. Belonged to Shingaracharyar of Kalyanapuram, Thanjavur Dist.

PUL I, p. 23 (no.111). PL. Tel. 40 fol. 1200 Grantha-s.

PUL I, p. 23 (no.112). PL. Tel. 31 fol. 800 Grantha-s.

PUL I, p. 23 (no.113). PL. Tel. 58 fol. 1500 Grantha-s (with text of 133 Grantha-s.).
SBD 53786. 7 fol.
Trav. Uni. 11797. Gr. 30 Grantha-s. Incomplete.
Trav. Uni. 17346 N. PL. Mal. 800 Grantha-s.
VSM I 1220 (no.3833). 50 fol. Dated Śaka 1707. Copied by Hardīkara Bālam-bhaṭṭa. Extract p. 374.
Wai I 1452. 46 fol. (with text). Dated Śaka 1723.

– C. of Lakṣmaṇa Jaṭāvallabha Śāstrin.
Adyar D I 931 (19 O 5 = 66887). PL. Mal. 30 fol. (94ff.).
Adyar D I 932 (29 K 7 = 73640). PL. Tel. 46 fol. = Adyar I, p. 53a. Copied at Pinnaballāpura on the 3rd day of the dark fortnight of Mārgaśīrṣa of Kīlaka year.
Hoshiarpur p. 52 (no.4371). PL. Gr. 25 fol. 100 Grantha-s. Extract p. 411. (attributed to Śrīnivāsa).
Hoshiarpur p. 52 (no.4454). PL. Gr. 17 fol. 500 Grantha-s. (attributed to Śrīnivāsa).
MD 16752. PL. Tel. 66 pp. 792 Grantha-s (with text).
Mysore ND II 3680 (P 6831). PL. Gr. 21 fol. Incomplete. Extract no. 244.
Tirupati SVUORI 4466 (903). PL. Gr.
Tirupati SVUORI 4467 (4350a). PL. Gr.
Trav. Uni. L.988 N. PL. Mal. 350 Grantha-s (with text).
Trav. Uni. 2086 A. PL. Gr. 300 Grantha-s (with text). Incomplete.
Whish 25(b). PL. Gr. 38 fol. (100-37).

Ptd.: with the text, BORI, Poona, 1938. See above.

– C. of Sūrāvadhānin of Veli(ma)kanyāpura.
Adyar D I 933 (19 E 42 = 66327). PL. Gr. 17 fol. (25ff.). Incomplete.
Adyar D I 934 (20 M 32 = 67574). PL. Tel. 37 fol. Incomplete. Ends in verse 91. = Adyar I, p. 52b.
Adyar D I 935 (28 J 18 = 73052). PL. Gr. 12 fol. Incomplete. = Adyar I, p. 53a.
Adyar D I 936 (29 K 7 = 73640). PL. Tel. 5 fol. (47ff.). = Adyar I, p. 53a. Copied at Somapura Satra on the 30th day of Mārgaśira in the Kīlaka year, in the dark fortnight.
Adyar D XIII 325 (VB 428a). PL. Tel. 37 fol. (with text).
Hoshiarpur p. 52 (no.3559). 27 fol. 911 Grantha-s. Incomplete.
Hoshiarpur p. 52 (no.5893). 35 fol. 400 Grantha-s.
Hoshiarpur p. 52 (no.6911). 50 fol. 900 Grantha-s (with text). Incomplete.
Hoshiarpur p. 52 (no.6912). 56 fol. 1000 Grantha-s (with text).
Hoshiarpur p. 52 (no.6913). 94 fol. 660 Grantha-s (with text). Incomplete.
Hoshiarpur p. 52 (no.6914). 227 fol. 1930 Grantha-s.
Hz 601. PL. Tel. 46 fol. Belonged to Vedam Venkatasubrahmanya Somayaji of Allur, Nellur Dist.
IO 4951 (Mackenzie II 94b). PL. Na. 13 fol. (with text). Written ca. A.D. 1770.
IO 4952 (Mackenzie III 234b). PL. Tel. 17 fol. (8-24) (with text). A.D. 1816-17.
MD 941. Tel. 92 pp. (120ff.).
MD 942. PL. Tel. 62 pp. (1ff.). Incomplete.

MD 16739. PL. Tel. 1 p. A small portion of the end.

MD 16760. PL. Tel. 71 pp. 1420 Grantha-s (with text).

MT 1059. PL. Tel. 46 fol. Incomplete. Presented in 1913-14 by V. Ramachandra Rao of Samalkot.

Mysore ND II 3674 (P 2886/ 8). PL. Na. 39 fol. (82-120). Extract no. 242.

Mysore ND II 3675 (P 7720/b). PL. Tel. 37 fol.

TCD 27. 62 pp. 1350 Grantha-s (with text).

Trav. Uni. T.625 = TCD 27.

Trav. Uni. 3751 B. PL. Gr. 500 Grantha-s (with text).

[CC I 406b; II 93a; III 88b]

*BHĀRGAVA BHĀSKARA (भार्गव भास्कर)

– C. on Atharva-veda-prātiśākhya -- Caturadhyāyikā Śaunakīyā.

VSM I 811 (no.4178). 22 fol. Incomplete (I 1.1 to I 4.8). Extract p. 361.

944 BHĀṢIKA-SŪTRA (भाषिकसूत्र)

of Kātyāyana. A work on the accent in the *Śatapatha Brāhmaṇa*, divided into three Kaṇḍikā-s, consisting of 22, 22 and 29 Sūtra-s respectively (according to the Hoshiarpur edition).

Beginning:

अथ ब्राह्मणस्वरसंस्कारनिर्णयः । १ । द्वौ । २ । उक्तो मन्त्रस्वरः । ३ । तेनात्र सिद्धम् । ४ । उदात्तानुदात्तौ भाषिकस्तत्संधिः । ५ । अनुदात्तावन्तरेणोदात्तः । ६ । आम्रपूर्व आख्यातपरो न । ७ । समासश्चानाख्यातपरो ऽपि । ८ । अपूर्वश्च समासो नैव । ९ । जात्याभिनिहितक्षैप्रप्रश्लिष्टाश्च । १० ।

End:

मन्त्रस्वरवद् ब्राह्मणस्वरश्चरकाणाम् । २६ । तेषां खाण्डिकेययौखेयानां चातुःस्वर्यमपि क्वचित् । २७ । तानो ऽन्येषां ब्राह्मणस्वरः । २८ । तान एवाङ्गोपाङ्गानां तान एवाङ्गोपाङ्गानमिति । २९ ।

Adyar D I 937 (40 C 28 = PM 132). 7 fol. (with the C. of Mahāsvāmin). Dated V.S. 1630 and copied in Varanasi, by Govinda, son of Janārdana. See *The Adyar Library Bulletin*, vol. V, pt. 4 (1941).

Ben. 10.

Bhk. 8.

BORI TM 39. 21 fol. Title: Bhāṣika-sūtra-bhāṣya.

BORI TM 57. 37 fol. Three copies; one with the C. of Ananta-bhaṭṭa. Title: Bhāṣika-sūtra-bhāṣya.

BORI TM 164.

Gough p. 57 (Bhāṣika-svara).

L 663. 3 fol. 45 Grantha-s.

MT 2504. 28 pp. (with Bhāṣya by Ananta). Transcribed in 1916-17 from a Ms. acquired through the sub-magistrate of Kovvur, Krishna Dist.

PUL II. App. p. 12 (no.197). 10 fol. (a. Vṛddhācārya; with C. of Mahāsvāmī).
RASB II 1493 (G 7896). 2 fol.
RASB II 1494 (G 6065). 12 fol. 400 Grantha-s (with C. of Ananta- bhaṭṭa).
SB p. 52 (no.222). 3 fol. 33 Grantha-s. Dated V.S. 1928.
SB p. 53 (no.98). 3 fol. 37 Grantha-s. – SBD 4406.
SBD 4034. 14 fol. (a. Vṛddhācārya; with C. of Ananta-bhaṭṭa). Dated V.S. 1872.
SBD 4095. 26 fol. (a. Vṛddhācārya; with C. of Ananta-bhaṭṭa). Dated V.S. 1942.
SBD 4405. 3 fol. Dated V.S. 1929.
SBD 4406. 3 fol.
SBD 47935. 12 fol. (with C. of Ananta-bhaṭṭa). Incomplete.
SBD 47949. 13 fol. (with C. of Ananta-bhaṭṭa). Incomplete. (Trisūtrī-bhāṣya).
SBD 55345. 14 fol. (a. Vṛddhācārya; with C. of Mahāsvāmin). Kṛṣṇācārya in the catalogue is a misreading of Vṛddhācārya.
SBD 55350. 15 fol. (with C. of Ananta-bhaṭṭa). Though mentioned as the commentator in the catalogue, Gopāla is actually the name of the scribe.
SBD 55895. 15 fol. (with C. of Ananta-bhaṭṭa). Dated V.S. 1922.
TD 1777. 13 fol. 260 Grantha-s (with C. of Mahāsvāmin). Dated V.S. 1640.

Ptd.: ed. by Franz Kielhorn, *Die Bhāṣika-vṛtti des Mahāsvāmin*, with the Vṛtti of Mahāsvāmin (in Roman script): in : *Indische Studien*, vol. X (1868), pp. 397-423. [Adyar (H080 Web IS ge); SAI (inf Zs 73); Emeneau (377)]

Reprinted in : Franz Kielhorn : *Kleine Schriften*, ed. by Wilhelm Rau. – Wiesbaden : Steiner Verlag, 1969, pp. 127-53. – (Glasenapp Stiftung 3) [SAI (ind 70 B 369)]

Also ed. by Yugalakishora (Vyasa) Pathaka, with the Bhāṣya of Ananta-deva. in the edition of the *Śuklayajuḥ-prātiśākhya* with Uvaṭa's Bhāṣya. – Benares, 1888, pp. 432-71. – (Ben. S. S. 4). [Adyar (H080 CSS B5)]

Ed. by Shridhar Sharma Ware, with the Bhāṣya of Ananta-deva, in the 5th volume of the edition of the *Śatapatha-brāhmaṇa* (Śrīmadvājasaneyi- mādhyandina-śatapatha-brāhmaṇam, with Vedārtha-prakāśa commentary of Sāyaṇācārya and the commentary of Harisvāmin). – Kalyāṇ (Bombay) : Laxmi Venkateshwar Steam Press (Gangavishnu Shri Krishnadass), Saṃ. 1997 / Śaka 1862 (1940), part 5, pp. 300-20 (= 3420-40). [SKGI (Rh III 153)]

Reprint of the above (without a clear indication of the original edition): – Delhi : Gian Publishing House, 1987. [SAI (ind 50 C 288/1437)]

Critically ed. by Braj Bihari Chaubey : *Bhāṣikasūtra* of Maharṣi Kātyāyana, with the commentaries of Mahāsvāmin and Ananta-bhaṭṭa. – Hoshiarpur : Vishveshvaranand Vishva Bandhu Institute of Sanskrit and Indological Studies, 1975. 45, 88 pp. – (Panjab University Indological Series 4). [BORI (34530); NL (180 Jb 97 69); SAI (ind 51 D 588/2402); UBTÜ (2 E 668)]

– C. of Mahāsvāmin.

Beginning (as printed in Kielhorns edition is, according to B. B. Chaubey, that of the Bhāṣya of Ananta-bhaṭṭa):

उच्चादयः स्वराः समाम्नाय उपदिष्टा व्याकरणप्रातिशाख्ये च। तैः सिद्धैर्ब्राह्मणस्वर उपदिश्यते। अथशब्द आनन्तर्यार्थे प्रयुज्यते। व्याकरणप्रातिशाख्याभ्यां संस्कृतौ सत्यां ब्राह्मणे स्वरसंस्कार(नियम) उपदिश्यते। अपि के नु। १। ननु ब्राह्मणस्वरेण निराकाङ्क्षा न जायते। किं तेन संस्कारनियमेनेत्यत आह -- उक्तो मन्त्रस्वर इति।

End:

तेषामेव चरकाणां ये खाण्डिकीया औखीयाश्च तेषां चातुःस्वर्यमपि भवति। ... तानो ऽन्येषां ब्राह्मणस्वरः। अन्येषां शाखिनां येषां दृश्यते तेषां ब्राह्मणस्वरस्तान एव भवति। एकश्रुतिरित्यर्थः। तान एव ...। शिक्षा कल्पो व्याकरणं निरुक्तं छन्दो ज्योतिषम् इति षडङ्गानि। प्रतिपदमनुपदं छन्दोभाषा धर्मो मीमांसा न्यायस्तर्क इत्युपाङ्गानि। एतेषामङ्गानाम् उपाङ्गानां तान एव स्वरो भवति। द्विरभ्यासश्च शास्त्रपरिसमाप्त्यर्थः। इतिकरणं चेति। इति महास्वामिकृता भाषिकवृत्तिः॥

America 360. Roman transliteration.

BORI 519 of 1882-83. 12 fol. Dated Śaka 1713.

Göttingen 153. 12 fol. Copied and corrected by F. Kielhorn in 1866 from a Ms. dated Śaka 1713.

Hz 1842. 13 fol. Belonged to Jambunatha Bhatta of Thanjavur.

SBD 55345. 14 fol. (with text; a. Vṛddhācārya). Kṛṣṇācārya in the catalogue is a misreading of Vṛddhācārya.

TD 1777. 13 fol. 260 Grantha-s (with text). Dated V.S. 1640.

Ptd.: with the text, ed. by Franz Kielhorn and also by Braj Bihari Chaubey. See above.

– C. Trisūtrī-bhāṣya. (Cf. the commentary of Ananta-bhaṭṭa).
N-W P V 144 (no.15). 12 fol.
N-W P V 150 (no.47). 12 fol.
SBD 47949. 13 fol. Incomplete.

– Bhāṣya.
SB p. 53 (no.99). 13 fol. 243 Grantha-s. = SBD 47949.

– C. of Ananta-deva (-bhaṭṭa).
Beginning:

वन्दे विष्णुं सदानन्दं भक्तकल्पमहीरुहम्।
यच्छायामाश्रितैर्लभ्यं नरैरर्थचतुष्टयम्॥ १॥
कुपिताहिफणच्छाया समीकृत्यापरं सुखम्।
सेवन्ते तत्पदं धीरास्तमनन्तं भजे ऽन्वहम्॥ २॥
याज्ञवल्क्यमुनिं नत्वा कात्यायनमुनीनपि।
व्याख्यास्ये भाषिकं सूत्रं कात्यायनमुनीरितम्॥ ३॥

मन्त्रलक्षणभिन्नत्वाच्छतपथब्राह्मणस्य तु।
तल्लक्षणार्थं मुनिना प्रणीतं भाषिकं खलु॥ ४॥

तस्येदमादिमं सूत्रम् -- अथ ब्राह्मणस्वरसंस्कारनिर्णयः । अथशब्द आनन्तर्यार्थः । अथ मन्त्रलक्षणप्रणयनानन्तरं शतपथब्राह्मणस्वरसंस्कारनियमः क्रियत इति सूत्रशेषः । मन्त्रलक्षणानन्तर्यं चैतस्य भाषिकलक्षणस्य सूत्रकारप्रस्थानादेव ज्ञायते। तथा च वक्ष्यति

End:

अथाङ्गोपाङ्गानां स्वरमाह -- तान इति । शिक्षा कल्पो व्याकरणं निरुक्तं छन्दो ज्योतिषमिति षडङ्गानि। प्रतिपदमनुपदं छन्दोभाषा धर्मो मीमांसा न्यायस्तर्क इत्युपाङ्गानि । तेषामङ्गोपाङ्गानां तान एव स्वरो भवति। द्विरभ्यासः शास्त्रपरिसमाप्त्यर्थः । इतिशब्दः शास्त्रवेदिनामभ्युदयसूचनार्थः । तदेते श्लोका भवन्ति --

उदात्तः स्वर्यते नीचो नीच उच्चस्वरो भवेत्।
ब्राह्मणस्य स्वरो ह्येष ज्ञायते वेदपारगैः ॥ १॥
ऋषिप्रोक्त्यनुसारेण स्वरं ज्ञात्वा द्विजः पठेत्।
स वेदफलमाप्नोति ह्यन्यथा नरकं व्रजेत्॥ २॥
एकं वा ब्राह्मणं सम्यक् स्वरार्थज्ञानपूर्वकम्।
यो ऽधीते वेदवित् स स्यादन्यथा स्थाणुरुच्यते॥ ३॥ इति॥
अम्बा भागीरथी यस्य नागदेवः पिता सुधीः ।
तेनानन्तेन विवृतं भाषिकं सूत्रमुत्तमम्॥ ४॥
अनेन प्रीयतां देवो रामनाथः सदा मम।
ब्रह्मादिवन्दितपदो देवदेवशिखामणिः ॥ ५॥
वचनप्रसूनमाला यानन्ताख्येन सूरिणा रचिता।
ध्रियतां हृदये सदये कमलामहिलेन पुरुषेण॥ ६॥

इति श्रीकाण्वशाखिनागदेवसुतश्रीमदनन्तभट्टविरचिते भाषिकसूत्रभाष्ये तृतीया कण्डिका समाप्ता॥

Bhk. 8.

BORI 47 of A 1881-82. 10 fol. Dated Śaka 1734.

BORI TM 39. 21 fol. (with text).

BORI TM 57. 31 fol. (with text).

Gough p. 57 (Bhāṣika-sūtra-bhāṣya).

Hoshiarpur p. 52 (no.3998). 12 fol. 305 Grantha-s (with text).

Mithila IV 116. 12 fol. Dated V.S. 1935.

Mithila IV 116(A). 8 fol.

MT 2504. 28 pp. (with text). Transcribed in 1916-17 from a Ms. acquired through the sub-magistrate of Kovvur, Krishna Dist.

RASB II 1494(G 6065). 12 fol. 400 Grantha-s (with text).

SB p. 53 (no.2). 12 fol. 220 Grantha-s. = SBD 47935.

SBD 4034. 14 fol. (with text). Dated V.S. 1872.
SBD 47935. 12 fol. (with text). Incomplete. (Bhāṣika-svara-bhāṣya).
SBD 47949. 13 fol. (with text). Incomplete. (Trisūtrī-bhāṣya).
SBD 55350. 15 fol. (with text). Though mentioned as the commentator in the catalogue, Gopāla is actually the name of the scribe.
SBD 55895. 15 fol. (with text). Dated V.S. 1922.

Ptd.: ed. by Yugalakishora (Vyasa) Pathaka, with the text, in the edition of *Śuklayajuḥ-prātiśākhya* with Uvaṭa's Bhāṣya. – Benares, 1888, pp. 432-71. – (Ben. S. S. 4).
In the edition of the *Śatapatha-brāhmaṇa* (with the text). See above.
Also ed. by Braj Bihari Chaubey with the text. See above.

[CC I 410a]

*BHĀSKARA (भास्कर)
Son of Rāmasvāmi-makhin.
– Padānta-dīpinī and C. thereon.

*BHĀSKARA (भास्कर)
– Svara-vijñāna. PUL II. App. p. 14 (no.232). PL. Gr. 35 Grantha-s (with C.).

945 BHAIṬH(A)-PARIBHĀṢĀ (भैठ्(ठ)परिभाषा)
→ Aṣṭākṣarī-baiṭh(-paribhāṣā). Cf. Janardana Sastri Pandeya, "Vaidika-vāṅmaye Baiṭha-saṃpradāyaḥ" (Sanskrit) in : *Padmasmṛti-granthaḥ* (Nepālasthasaṃskṛtaviduṣāṃ sarvaprathamasmṛtigranthaḥ), pub. by Padmasmṛtigranthaprakāśanasamiti, Madana-mohan Dhavan, C. K. 34/39, Lahori Tola, Varanasi, 1984, pp. 7-10.

946 BHAIṬH(A)-LAKṢAṆA-RATNA (भैठ्(ठ)लक्षण-रत्न)
→ Lakṣaṇa-ratna(-bhaiṭ), of Vaidyanātha-bhaṭṭa.

947 BHAIṆṆĀMA-LAKṢAṆA (भैण्णामलक्षण)
Mysore I, p. 32. (3 Mss.) → Bhaiṭ and Lakṣaṇa-ratna.
Mysore II, p. 10. (2 Mss.) → Bhaiṭ and Lakṣaṇa-ratna.

*BHAIRAVĀVADHĀNIN or BHAIRAVĀRYA (भैरवावधानिन् / भैरवार्य)
He is variously called Nemāna or Nemāni or Vemāna Bhairavāvadhānin (-budha). In MT 485(t) the name is given as Setūni though the Ms. has "Nemāni".

– Iṅgya-ratna, also called Akṣara-saṃkhyā.
– Jaṭā-maṇi.
– Varṇa-krama-darpaṇa.

948 MAKĀRA-LOPA (मकारलोप)
Mysore ND II 3684 (P 7073/ 2). PL. Tel. 3 fol. Extract no. 246.

*MAÑCI-BHAṬṬA (मञ्चिभट्ट)

Son of Vāñcheśvara and Veṅkaṭāmba and the disciple of Śrīnivāsa. His name is variously written as Cinni-bhaṭṭa, Cinna-bhaṭṭa, Mañji-bhaṭṭa, Āsūrīcinni-bhaṭṭa, Āsūrimalī-bhaṭṭa, Āsūrimalimañci-bhaṭṭa, Āmūrimaḻī-bhaṭṭa, etc.

– C. on the Sarva-sammata-śikṣā.

*MADHUSŪDANA (मधुसूदन)

– Pratijñā-sūtra-ṭīkā. N-W P IV 4.

[CC I 427a]

*MADHUSŪDANA-MASKARIN (मधुसूदनमस्करिन्)

Also called Madhusūdana-munīśvara. His identification with the famous Madhusūdana-sarasvatī (16th century) is not beyond doubt. See S. N. Dasgupta, *A History of Sanskrit Literature.* – Calcutta : University of Calcutta, 1962 (second edition), p. 664.

– Aṣṭa-vikṛti-vivṛti (kārikā), also known as the Madhusūdanī-śikṣā(-bhāṣya).

949 MADHUSŪDANĪ-ŚIKṢĀ(-BHĀṢYA) (मधुसूदनी-शिक्षा /-भाष्य)

→ (Jaṭādy-)Aṣṭa-vikṛti-vivṛti(-kārikā) of Madhusūdana-maskarin.

IM 2192. 17 fol.

IM 2425. 18 fol. (18-35). Incomplete.

Oppert I 7563. Belonged to S. Kodanda Ramavadhana Pantulu of Vijayanagaram.

[CC I 427b]

950 MADHYAMĀVASĀNA-PAÑCA-KRAMA (मध्यमावसानपञ्चक्रम)

Mysore ND II 3685 (P 4906/47). PL. Na. 1 fol. (128). Extract no. 247.

951 MANAḤSVĀRA-ŚIKṢĀ (मनःस्वारशिक्षा)

of Yājñavalkya.

Beginning:

मनःस्वारं प्रवक्ष्यामि ब्रह्मणा निर्मितं पुरा।
भगवान्याज्ञवल्क्येन भाषितंल्लोकहेतवे ॥ १॥

अथ त्रिपदा द्विरवसानमध्ये ऽनुदात्तानि । अथाधिमध्ये ऽनुदात्तानि भवन्ति । कस्त्वा राजन्तमध्वराणां स नः पितेव मा नः परि ते प्रागपाक् प्र णो मरुतो यस्य योगे योगे तवस्तरं तस्मा अरन्ध्रून्नः परस्या अधि पुनरूर्जा समितमग्ने यत्ते शुक्रं तुभ्यन्ता मयि गृह्णामि मधु वाता मधुमान्नो ऽग्ने युक्ष्व त्वं यविष्ठाग्ने पावक स नः पावक वार्त्रहत्त्याय शवसे पवमानः सस्तान आबोढं चित्रभानो धियेषितः ।

End:

अथ चतुरवसाने ह्याद्यनुदात्ताः । अग्नीषोमयोरुज्जितिं द्विकम्पाः सजूर्देवेनाँशुरंशुष्टे ऽग्नीषोमाभ्याम् मरुत्वन्तं वृषभमुत्तिष्ठन्नोजसा युवन्तन्देवस्याहं प्रथमो देवस्य त्वा पृथिव्याः सुपर्णो ऽसि विराड्ज्योतिरिमँ साहस्रं तिस्रो वायोः पूतः पुनन्तु मा पितरः संवत्सरो ऽस्यग्निमद्योभयोर्ऊर्जवे त्वा हिरण्मयेन पात्रेणेति द्वाविंशतिः । ६४ । इति महर्षियोगियाज्ञवल्क्यकृता मनःस्वारशिक्षा समाप्ता ॥

Ptd.: in Śikṣā-saṃgraha. – Benares, 1889, pp. 185-209. – (Ben. S. S. 10).

952 MANTRA-PRATĪKA (**मन्त्रप्रतीक**)

Hoshiarpur p. 56 (no.3799). PL. Mal. 110 fol. 3000 Grantha-s.

Hoshiarpur p. 301 (no.3799). PL. Mal. 1 fol. 9 Grantha-s. Incomplete. (Śikṣā) ?

953 MAṆTRA-BRĀHṂAṆĀNUKRAMAṆIKĀ (**मन्त्रब्राह्मणानुक्रमणिका**)

Hoshiarpur p. 56 (no.6133). 5 fol. 67 Grantha-s.

954 MANTRĀKṢARA-MĀLIKĀ-PRAKĀŚA (**मन्त्राक्षरमालिकाप्रकाश**)

SBD 2326. 79 fol. (C. on Śukla-yajurveda-sarvānukrama).

955 MANTRĀNUKRAMA (**मन्त्रानुक्रम**)

Beginning:

अथोपनिषत्सु यजुःपर्वण ऋषिछन्दोदेवताविनियोगब्राह्मणानि सलक्षणानि चाविदित्वा यः प्रयुङ्क्ते मन्त्राणां न स तदुक्तं फलमाप्नोति। तदुक्तम् (तदाह) --

येन यद्दषिणा दृष्टं सिद्धिः प्राप्ता च येन वै।
मन्त्रेण तस्य तत्प्रोक्तमृषेर्भावस्तदार्षकम्॥ १॥
आत्मा संछादितो देवैर्मृत्योर्भीतैस्तु वै पुरा।
आदित्यैर्वसुभी रुद्रैस्तेन छन्दांसि तानि वै॥ २॥
यस्य यस्य तु मन्त्रस्य उद्दिष्टा देवता तु या।
तदाकारं भवेत् तस्य देवत्वं देवतोच्यते॥ ३॥

नैरुक्तम्। इति परिभाषा। अदिते ऽमुमते सरस्वत्य एकपदा गायत्र्यो लिङ्गोक्तदेवता देवसविता त्रिष्टुप्।

End:

अर्हणा वसिष्ठो धेनुरिदमहमिमां विराट्। या ओषधी द्वाभ्यामनुष्टुप् ... यशसोर्द्वयोर्मधुपर्को मुञ्च गां बृहती। माता रुद्राणां त्रिष्टुप्। गौर्द्वयोर्द्वयोः। ८। इति मन्त्रानुक्रमणिकायां द्वितीयः प्रपाठकः॥

Oxf. CS d.77(4). 6 fol. Dated A.D. 1655. Col.: Mantrānukramaṇī-pariśiṣṭa. Contains eight verses of paribhāṣā.

SBD 2292. 5 fol. (Prapāṭhaka-s 1-2). Dated V.S. 1710.

956 MANTRĀNUKRAMAṆIKĀ (**मन्त्रानुक्रमणिका**)

SV.

Alwar 251. Extract 69.

Jammu RSRI p. 26 (no.4452). 50 fol. Dated V.S. 1802 (Stein 85).

PUL I, p. 132 (no.27). 5 fol. 100 Grantha-s.

Stein p. 6 (no. 85). 5 fol. Dated V.S. 1802. Extract p. 243.

[CC II 216a, 233b]

***MALLAYĀRYA (मल्लयार्य)**

– C. Pada-darpaṇa on the Pada-pañcaka. Hz 600, etc.

[CC II 99a]

***MALLA-ŚARMAN (मल्लशर्मन्)**

– Malla-śarma-śikṣā or Hasta-svara-prakriyā.

957 MALLA-ŚARMA-ŚIKṢĀ or HASTA-SVARA-PRAKRIYĀ (मल्लशर्मशिक्षा / हस्तस्वरप्रक्रिया)

of Malla-śarman, also called Pitṛbhakti-malla, a Kānyakubja, son of Vākpati (or Khagapati, cf. RASB II 912, 1520). In 65 verses it describes the method of indicating accents by different postures of the hand. Composed in V.S. 1781 = A.D. 1725 (vikramārka-gatābdeṣu candra-vasv-aga-bhūmiṣu). But at RASB II 1520 it is printed as candra-vasv-agni-bhūmiṣu = 1381.

Beginning:

नत्वा गणपतिं देवं ध्यात्वा श्रीकुलदेवताम्।
मल्लशर्मा हस्तपूर्वां करोमि स्वरप्रक्रियाम्॥ १॥
नत्वा विघ्नहरं सदा शुभकरं सर्वस्य कामप्रदं
स्मृत्वा श्रीगुरुपादुकां सुललितां ध्यात्वा परां देवताम्।
वेदे वाजसनेयके त्वधिकृता विप्राश्च ये सत्तमास्
तेषामेव कृते कृता न कुधियां हस्तस्वरप्रक्रिया॥ २॥

अथ साधारणनियमः। तथा प्रातिशाख्ये मनुः --

ब्राह्मणः प्रणवं कुर्यादादावन्ते च सर्वदा।
स्रवत्यनोंकृतं पूर्वं परस्ताच्च विशीर्यते॥ ३॥

तथा --

उत्तानपाणिं फणवत् कृत्वा सह शलाकया।
गुरुं प्रणम्य मनसा ततः स्वाध्यायवान् भवेत्॥ ४॥

अत्र जपादौ हस्तस्वरवर्णहीनस्यानधिकारत्वं रावणेन स्वराङ्कुशे याज्ञवल्क्येन शिक्षायां च बोधितम्। तथा हि --

हस्तहीनं तु यो ऽधीते हस्तस्वरविवर्जितम्।
ऋग्यजुःसामभिर्दग्धो वियोनिमधिगच्छति॥ ५॥

इति याज्ञवल्क्यशिक्षायां चोक्तम्॥

End:

इति छकारस्थानानि॥

यः सुबोधां पठेन्नित्यमिमां च स्वरप्रक्रियाम्।
हस्तपूर्वां तु तस्यैव सम्यग्वेदे गतिर्भवेत्॥ ६२॥
श्रीमता कान्यकुब्जेन ह्युपमन्य्वग्निहोत्रिणा।

श्रीमद्वेदस्वरूपाणां श्रीमद्वाक्पतिशर्मणाम् ॥ ६३ ॥
सूनुना पितृभक्तेन मल्लविप्रेण धीमता ।
विक्रमार्कगताब्देषु चन्द्रवस्वगभूमिषु ॥ ६४ ॥
ऊर्जमासे सिते पक्षे ह्येकादश्यां शनेर्दिने ।
कृतेयं बालबोधाय सुहस्तस्वरप्रक्रिया ॥ ६५ ॥

इति)मत्कान्यकुब्जीयोपमन्युगोत्रीयाग्निहो त्रि खगपतितनूज पितृभक्त घाटमपुरवासि मल्लशर्मकृता शिक्षा समाप्ता ॥

BHU C 3266 (D II/674). 2 fol. Incomplete.
Bombay Uni. 725 (BS 95). 5 fol. Copied by Āśārāma-miśra in V.S. 1848.
GJKSV 37119. 6 fol. Incomplete (lacks a few lines at the end). Title: Svara-prakriyā.
Hoshiarpur p. 55 (no.187). 7 fol. 61 Grantha-s. Incomplete.
Mithila IV 211. 6 fol.
Mithila IV 211(A). 4 fol.
PUL I, p. 25 (no.157). 4 fol. Dated V.S. 1894.
RASB II 912 (G 6267). 5 fol. 120 Grantha-s. Dated V.S. 1937. Title: Hasta-svara-prakriyā.
RASB II 1520 (G 3262). 5 fol. 100 Grantha-s. Dated V.S. 1939. (Date of composition is wrongly given as V.S. 1381 !).
SBD 4166. 6 fol. Incomplete. Dated V.S. 1781.
Wellcome Inst. London. Z 54.

Ptd.: in Śikṣā-saṃgraha. – Benares, 1889, pp. 153-60. – (Ben. S. S. 10).

*MAHĀDEVA RĀMACANDRA GADRE (महादेव रामचन्द्र गद्रे)
C. called Lakṣaṇa-candrikā on the Taittirīya-prātiśākhya.

*MAHĀDHIPATI-YAJVAN (महाधिपतियज्वन्)
Avarṇi-vyākhyāna.
Āvarṇi.

*MAHĀSVĀMIN (महास्वामिन्)
C. on Bhāṣika-sūtra – Bhāṣika-sūtra-vṛtti.

[CC I 443b]

*MAHĪDĀSA (महीदास)
C. on Caraṇa-vyūha.

[CC I 444b]

958 MĀṆḌAVYA-(VĪ-)ŚIKṢĀ (माण्डव्य-(वी-)शिक्षा)
Enumeration of the labial "b" (oṣṭhya-saṃkhyā) occurring in each chapter of the *Śukla-yajurveda*.

Beginning:

अथातः संप्रवक्ष्यामि शिष्याणां हितकाम्यया ।

माण्डव्येन यथा प्रोक्ता ओष्ठ्यसंख्या समाहृता॥ १॥

इषे त्वा । बह्वीः । प्रथमाक्षरम् ॥ बाहुभ्याम् । तिस्रः ॥ पृथुबुध्नः ॥ बृहद्ग्रावासि ॥ ब्रह्मवनित्वा॥ इन्द्रस्य बाहुरसि॥ बधान देव तिस्रः ॥ ऊर्जे त्वा दन्धेन॥ पञ्चदश॥ १॥ कृष्णो ऽसि बर्हिषे त्वा ॥ बर्हिरसि स्रुग्भ्यः ॥ बृहन्तमध्वरे ॥ सवितुर्बाहू स्थः ॥ बाहुभ्याम्॥ ॥

End:

पिबत । ब्रह्मणे । ब्रह्मोर्ध्वम् । बर्हिर्भ्यो । बभूव । ब्रह्मणो । बृहद् । ब्रह्मणा दश ॥ ३८ ॥ स्वाहा प्राणेभ्यो । बृहस्पतिभि... । ब्रह्मणे । ब्रह्महत्यायै चतुर्थः ॥ ३९ ॥ ईशा वास्यं क्लिब एकः ॥ ४०॥ इति श्री माण्डवी शिक्षा समाप्ता॥

BBRAS 13(IV) (B D 278). 2 fol. (6-7). 41 verses ? Dated Śaka 1787.
Bhau Daji p. 121.
CU Add. 1934.
PUL II. App. p. 12 (no.198). 3 fol. Copy of R. A. S. Bombay.
RASB II 1525 (G 3257). 4 fol. Dated V.S. 1939.

Ptd.: in Śikṣā-saṃgraha. – Benares, 1889, pp. 72-92. – (Ben. S. S. 10).

[CC II 103a]

959 MĀṆḌŪKĪ-ŚIKṢĀ (माण्डूकीशिक्षा)

Consisting of 179 verses it deals with the accents in the Veda-s in general, though it is connected with the Śaunakīya *Atharva-veda.* Several verses of this are also found in the *Nārada-śikṣā, Pāṇini-śikṣā* and *Yājñavalkya-śikṣā.* See Martin Haug: *Ueber das Wesen und den Werth des Wedischen Accents.* – München, 1874. (Abh. d. I. Cl. d. k. Ak. d. Wiss. XIII. Bd. II. Abth.), p. 55; A. Weber on the *Pratijñā-sūtra,* pp. 106-12; and F. Kielhorn : Remarks on the Śikṣās in : *Indian Antiquary,* vol. V, pp. 141, 196 (reprint in : *Kleine Schriften,* vol. I, pp. 158-69).

Beginning:

तिस्रो वृत्तीरनुक्रान्ता द्रुतमध्यविलम्बिताः ।
यथानुपूर्वं प्रथमा द्रुता वृत्तिः प्रशस्यते॥ १॥
मध्यमैकान्तरा वृत्तिर्द्व्यन्तरा हि विलम्बिता।
नैनां बुधः प्रयुञ्जीत यदीच्छेद् वर्णसंपदाम्॥ २॥
अभ्यासार्थे द्रुता वृत्तिरुपलब्धौ विलम्बिता।
मध्यमा तु प्रयोगार्थे न तद्वचनमन्यथा॥ ३॥
ऐन्द्री तु मध्यमा वृत्तिः प्राजापत्या विलम्बिता।
अग्निमारुतयोर्वृत्तिः सर्वशास्त्रेषु निन्दिता॥ ४॥
दोषाः प्रकाशास्तु विलम्बितायां वर्णा द्रुतायां न च सूपलक्ष्याः ।
तस्माद् द्रुतां चैव विलम्बितां च त्यक्त्वा नरो मध्यमया प्रयुञ्ज्यात्॥ ५॥

End:

मण्डूकेन कृतां शिक्षां विदुषां बुद्धिदीपिनीम्।
यो हि तत्त्वेन जानाति ब्रह्मलोकं स गच्छति॥ १६॥

America 361. 17 pp. Devanāgarī and Roman transliteration.
Bikaner 664(1). Dated V.S. 1735 (A.D. 1678). Copied at Pattanapura.
Bikaner 665(1). Copy of the above.
BORI 13 of 1870-71. 24 fol. From Bikaner.
BORI 6 of 1873-74. 24 fol. From Bikaner.
BORI 177(i) of 1880-81. 15 fol.
BORI 178(i) of 1880-81.
BORI 179(i) of 1880-81.
BORI 379 of 1883-84. 14 fol. Dated Śaka 1772.
BORI 69 of 1884-86. 35 fol.
BP p. 287.
Göttingen 158(1). 30 fol. Copied from an old Ms. and compared with two modern Mss. by Kielhorn in 1874. One of the modern Mss. was obtained by Bühler from Junagadh. Last 3 fol. contain variant readings. Divided into 16 sections containing 14, 15, 7, 15, 11, 9, 10, 11, 13, 11, 11, 10, 10, 10, 10 and 16 verses respectively.
Gough p. 78 (no.13). 13 fol. Incomplete.
Haug p. 29 (no.69a) = München 179.
Haug p. 42 (no.166) = München 180.
IM 2519. 2-17 fol. Incomplete.
IM 2571. 2 fol. Incomplete.
IM 9221. 2 fol. Incomplete. Title: Atharva-veda-śikṣā.
Kh. 61. 82.
L 135. 10 fol. 184 Grantha-s. Dated V.S. 1926.
München 179. 15 fol. Written ca. A.D. 1780.
München 180. 17 fol. Dated A.D. 1864.
Oxf. CS d.185(10). 14 fol. Incomplete (1 fol. missing). A.D. 1869.
Peters. III, p. 386 (no.69). 35 fol.
RASB II 1521 (G 8175). 8 fol. Dated V.S. 1576.
SBD 2067. 14 fol. Dated V.S. 1966.
SBD 2074. 27 fol. Dated V.S. 1734. Title: Atharvaṇa-lakṣaṇa-grantha-saṃgraha.
SBD 2079. 12 fol.
Tb. 213.
VSM I 1221 (no.4173). 18 fol.
VSM I 1222 (no.4174). 16 fol.
Weber 1501 (Ms. or. fol. 621a). 10 fol. (up to 16.2).

Ptd.: in Śikṣā-saṃgraha. – Benares, 1889, pp. 463-78. – (Ben. S. S. 10).
Also ed. by Bhagavad Datta, *Māṇḍukī Śikṣā or the Phonetical Treatise of the Atharvaveda*, with an introduction (in Hindi), appendices and an index. – Lahore : D. A. V. College, 1921. xviii, ii, 25, vi, vii pp. – (Dayānanda Mahāvidyālaya Saṃskṛta-granthamālā 5). [Adyar (H080 DAV 5); BM : Ptd. Bks. Cat. 1906-1928.

615 (14007.b.21,2); Emeneau (386)]

Reprint of the above under the title: *Atharvavedīyā Māṇḍūkī-śikṣā*. – New Delhi : Pāṇini (Meharchand Lachhmandas), 1972. (Panini Vaidika Granthamala 8)

[CC I 447a; III 97a]

*MĀṆḌŪKEYA (**माण्डूकेय**)

Quoted in the *Ṛgveda-prātiśākhya*, 3.8.

[CC I 447a]

960 MĀTṚKĀ-KAṆḌIKĀ-VIVARAṆA (**मातृकाकण्डिकाविवरण**)

Probably identical with the commentary called *Vivaraṇa* on the *Mātrā-lakṣaṇa*. The colophon of Baroda 11985 (= CLB I, p. 157) also reads: Mātṛkā-kaṇḍikā-vivaraṇa.

SBD 2255. 11 fol. Incomplete.

961 MĀTṚKĀ-NIRṆAYA (**मातृकानिर्णय**)

Hoshiarpur 4454. PL. Gr. 2 fol. (not catalouged). (A xerox-copy of a Devanāgarī transcript of this is in SAI : 87/794*).

962 MĀTṚKĀ-LAKṢAṆA (RAṄGA-PLUTĀDI) (**मातृकालक्षण / रङ्गप्लुतादि**)

Hoshiarpur p. 53 (no.4454). PL. Gr. 4 fol. (A xerox-copy of a Devanāgarī transcript of this is in SAI : 87/794*).

*MĀTṚSŪNU (**मातृसूनु**)

– C. called Pañjikā or Pada-pañjikā on the Ṛgvidhāna.

Baroda 12251. 63 fol. 1200 Grantha-s. = CLB I, p. 24.

963 MĀTRĀ-KĀLA (1) (**मात्राकाल**)

A fictious title given to a collection of different tracts on the *Taittirīya-saṃhitā*.

BHU B 3904 (D 11/654). 33 fol.

964 MĀTRĀ-KĀLA (2) (**मात्राकाल**)

Mysore ND II 3686 (B 252/ 8). Gr. 2 fol. (57-58). Extract no. 248.

965 MĀTRĀDI-VARṆA-KRAMA (**मात्रादिवर्णक्रम**)

Mysore ND II 3687 (B 252/ 4). Gr. 2 fol. (6-7). Extract no. 249.

966 MĀTRĀ-LAKṢAṆA (1) (**मात्रालक्षण**)

Tirupati SVUORI (427h). PL. Na. (RV. Not catalogued).

967 MĀTRĀ-LAKṢAṆA (2) (**मात्रालक्षण**)

26 verses on the Mātrā-s in the Taittirīya school.

Beginning:

ऋग्विराम (ऋद्धिकाम) स्त्रिमात्रः स्यादर्धर्चे ऽपि तथा भवेत्।
पदकाले द्विमात्रं स्यादेकमात्रा (द्)विवृत्तिषु॥

End:

कखयोः पफयोरेव क्षपरं च न विद्यते।
जिह्वामूलमुपध्मानं विसर्गः प्रतिपद्यते॥

Baroda 6255. PL. Tel. 2 fol. (40b-41).

968 MĀTRĀ-LAKṢAṆA or MĀTRĀ-VIDHĀNA-SŪTRA (मात्रालक्षण / मात्राविधान-सूत्र)
Also called Svara-mātrālakṣaṇa consisting of three Kaṇḍikā-s. See R. Simon, WZKM 27, pp. 312, 313.

Beginning:

अथातो ह्रस्वदीर्घप्लुतमात्राण्यक्षराणि व्याख्यास्यामः॥ १॥ सामस्वर्धमात्रमणुमात्रं च॥ २॥ ह्रस्वं मात्रा। दीर्घं द्वे। प्लुतं वृद्धं चेति त्रिमात्रमभिधीयते॥ ३॥

ह्रस्वं द्विमात्रसंयुक्तं प्लुतमाहुर्मनीषिणः।
दीर्घं तु मात्रासंयोगाद् वृद्धमित्यभिधीयते॥ ४॥

End:

ऋकारादिरणुमात्रा। रेफो ऽर्धमात्रा। मध्ये शेषा स्वरभक्तिरर्धमात्रा। स्थितसंधितं च। न च स्वरस्य विकारश्चेति वक्ष्यति। हरेफोष्मसंयोगे रेफपरा स्वरभक्तिरत्र मात्रा इति मात्राणुमात्राणां संपाद्यः कालः॥ ९॥ प्रतिज्ञा खलु वर्तते। प्रतिज्ञा खलु वर्तते॥ १०॥

Adyar D I 938 (19 M 53 = 66821). PL. Gr. 4 fol. (10-13). = Adyar I, p. 51b.
Baroda 7409. 4 fol. 75 Grantha-s. Dated V.S. 1765. = CLB I, p. 32. See pp. 156 where it is described as identical with the Stobhānusaṃhāra.
Ben. 18.
Brl. p. 43 (no.CXXXII, title : Svara-mātra-lakṣaṇa) = IO 4329.
Hamburg StUB (Oppert 45b). PL. Gr. 3 fol.
IO 4328 (Burnell 496k). Gr. 2 fol. Written ca. A.D. 1877.
IO 4329 (Burnell 360c). Gr. 6 pp. (275-80). Written ca. A.D. 1867.
MD 17867. Tel. 2 pp. Incomplete.
(Hrasvadīrghaplutamātrā- lakṣaṇa). .... (= Skt. Texts on Phonetics, pp. 211-12).
Oppert II 403. Belonged to Venkatarama Srauti of Mullandram, N. Arcot Dist.
PUL I, p. 23 (no.114). 3 fol.
PUL I, p. 132 (no.24). 25 fol. 600 Grantha-s (with other 5 SV works).
SB p. 29 (no.35). 6 fol. 60 Grantha-s. Dated V.S. 1720.= SBD 3935.
SBD 3935. 6 fol. Dated V.S. 1720.
Trav. Uni. 2915 B. PL. Gr. 50 Grantha-s.
Trav. Uni. 5185 C. 50 Grantha-ṣ. Dated V.S. 1558 ?
VOHD II 8.3043 (Ms.or.oct. 839. StaatsB-PrK, Berlin). 8 fol. (fol. 6-8 contain Gāyatrī-vidhāna).

Ptd.: in the collection of Sāmavedic tracts, ed. by Krishnaswami Srauti (in Grantha script). – Kumbakonam : Jyotirvilasa Press, 1885, pp. 43-50. See above under Chala-prakriyā. [SAI (87/783*)]

Also ed. by B. R. Sharma, with commentary (together with the *Pañcavidha-sūtra*). – Tirupati : Kendriya Sanskrit Vidyapeetha, 1969. (pp. 137-68) 32 pp. – (Kendriya Sanskrit Vidyapeetha Series 11). [NL (180 Jb 97 24); UBTÜ (14 A 638); SAI (ind 51 C 578/60)]

Ed. by Wayne Howard, *Mātrālakṣaṇam* – text, translation, extracts from the commentary and notes, including references to two oral traditions of South India. – New Delhi (Central Vista, Janpath) : Indira Gandhi National Centre for the Arts, 1989. xvi, 98 pp. [BORI (61023)]

– C. Vivaraṇa.

Baroda 11985. 12 fol. 200 Grantha-s. Dated V.S. 1504. = CLB I, p. 33. Extract pp. 156-57.

PUL I, p. 23 (no.115). 12 fol. 200 Grantha-s. Incomplete.

Ptd.: in the Tirupati edition of the text.

[CC I 448a]

*MĀDHAVA (माधव)

– Pada-svara-carcā. SBD 2110. 35 fol. Dated V.S. 1631. Copied by Mahīdāsa.

*MĀDHAVA (माधव)

Following works are attributed to him. Cf. above under Ākhyātānukramaṇī.

– Ākhyātānukramaṇī
– Ārṣānukramaṇī
– Itihāsānukramaṇī
– Chandonukramaṇī
– Devatānukramaṇī
– Nāmānukramaṇī
– Nipātānukramaṇī
– Niruktānukramaṇī
– Nirbhandānukramaṇī (?)
– Mantrārthānukramaṇī
– Samayānukramaṇī
– Sarvānukramaṇī. Quoted by Devarāja in *Nighaṇṭu-bhāṣya*, p. 4, etc.

Cf. Devasthali : "Mādhavānukramaṇī and Its Contents" in : *Ṛtam – Dr. Babu Ram Saksena Felicitation Volume*, ed. by J. P. Singh, *Journal of Akhila Bharatiya Sanskrit Parishad*, vols. XI-XV, July 1979 - July 1983, Mahatma Gandhi Marg, Hazratganz, Lukknow 1983, pp. 135-41. [Adyar (H05R ABS 11-15)] See also his article "Mādhava vs. Veṅkaṭamādhava" in : *Acharya R. C. Shukla Volume*.

[CC I 449b]

*MĀDHAVĀCĀRYA (KARṆĀṬAKA) (माधवाचार्य कर्णाटक)

– C. Dūṣaṇabhaṅga-mīmāṃsā on the Ṛgveda-prātiśākhya. Wai I 365.

969 MĀDHAVĀNUKRAMAṆĪ (माधवानुक्रमणी)

Adyar D I 939 → Ākhyātānukramaṇī.

GD I 19-C. PL. Mal. 67 fol. (89-155). 335 Grantha-s.

970 MĀDHYANDINĪYA-LAGHU-ŚIKṢĀ (माध्यन्दिनीयलघुशिक्षा)
→ Laghu-mādhyandinīya-śikṣā.
RASB II 1516(II).
SBD 48292. 1 fol.
Wellcome Inst. London. Z 47a.

971 MĀDHYANDINĪYA-VEDA-PARIBHĀṢĀṄKA-SŪTRA (माध्यन्दिनीयवेदपरिभाषाङ्कसूत्र)
→ Paribhāṣāṅka-sūtra. See also Keśava-(ī-)śikṣā.

972 MĀDHYANDINĪ-(YA-)ŚIKṢĀ (माध्यन्दिनी-(य-)शिक्षा)
The first part of this work, comprising seven verses, deals with the reduplication of consonants (dvitva-prakaraṇa) with illustrations. The second part enumerates the repetitions (1975 in number) of Ṛk-s in each chapters of the *Śukla Yajurveda*. This second part is almost identical with the *Galadṛk-śikṣā* also called *Luptark-śikṣā*. See F. Kielhorn : Remarks on the Śikṣās in : *Indian Antiquary*, vol. V, p. 196 (reprint in : *Kleine Schriften*, vol. I, pp. 158-69).

Beginning:

मन्त्रो हीनः स्वरतो वर्णतो वा मिथ्याप्रयुक्तो न तमर्थमाह।
स वाग्वज्रो यजमानं हिनस्ति यथेन्द्रशत्रुः स्वरतो ऽपराधात्॥ १॥
स्वराद् द्वित्वमवाप्नोति व्यञ्जनं व्यञ्जने परे।
हरौ न यद्यचः पूर्वौ निमित्तं व्यञ्जनस्य च॥ २॥ इषे त्वोर्ज्जे त्वा॥
स्वरपूर्वाः शषसहा अन्तस्थाश्च तथा यदि।
निमित्तभूता द्वित्वस्य स्पर्शा एव न संशयः॥ ३॥ अश्म्मन्॥
स्पर्शपूर्वा यरलवाः स्पर्शपूर्वाः शरस्तथा।
व्यञ्जनं च ततः पूर्वं द्वेधाभावं न चाप्नुयात्॥ ४॥ अयक्ष्माः॥
विसर्गाच्च परः कादिर्व्यञ्जनात् किल पूर्वगः।
ह्रस्वपूर्वौ नङौ द्वित्वमापद्येते पदान्तगौ।
अपि स्वरतरावेव श्लिष्टौ भवति नान्यथा॥ ५॥

End:

देवस्य त्वेत्यत्र देवी द्यावापृथिवीन्द्रस्यौजो ऽश्वस्य त्वेयत्यग्रे हृदे त्वा युञ्जते मनः प्रैतु मखस्य शिरस्त्रयोदश। ३७। द्वितीयदेवस्य त्वेत्यत्र सुमित्रिया न उद्वयमेधो ऽसीड एह्यदित्यै रास्नासीन्द्राय त्वा षड्द्वाविंशतिः। ३८। ईशा वास्यमीत्यत्रान्धन्तमो ऽन्यदेवासंभूतिमिलितास्त्रयो ऽग्नेनय त्रयोदश। ४०। एवं चतुष्षष्ट्युत्तरशतं लोपाः। एकादशोत्तरमष्टादशशतैः सहेति॥ इति प्रथमा माध्यन्दिनीयशिक्षा समाप्ता॥

BISM p. 217 (2/66).
Göttingen 158(4). 2 fol. (53-54). Incomplete. Verses 1-14 → Laghu-mādhyandinīya-śikṣā.
IM 2564. 4 fol.

IM 2642. 4 fol.
SBD 2068. 7 fol. Dated V.S. 1966.

Ptd.: in Śikṣā-saṃgraha. – Benares, 1889, pp. 109-13. – (Ben. S. S. 10).

[CC I 450b]

973 MĀDHYANDINĪYA-SARVĀNUKRAMAṆĪ (1) (माध्यन्दिनीयसर्वानुक्रमणी)
› Śukla-yajurveda-sarvānukrama of Kātyāyana.

974 MĀDHYANDINĪYA-SARVĀNUKRAMAṆĪ (2) (माध्यन्दिनीयसर्वानुक्रमणी)
Different from the *Śukla-yajurveda-sarvānukrama* of Kātyāyana.
RASB II 886 (G 6185). 26 fol. 500 Grantha-s. Incomplete.
RASB II 894 (G 10314). 17 fol. Different from the above. Dated V.S. 1712.

975 MĀLĀ-DHVAJĀDY-UDĀHARAṆA (मालाध्वजाद्युदाहरण)
Definitions with illustrations of the Vikṛti-s (Mālā, Rekhā, Dhvaja, Ratha, Jaṭā and Ghana) for the mantra : "viśvāni deva savitaḥ ... ".
BBRAS 493 (B D 278). 2 fol. Dated Śaka 1787.

*MĀHIṢEYA (माहिषेय)
Quoted by *Tribhāṣya-ratna* on the *Taittirīya-prātiśākhya*, 1.14, 59; 2.14, 33, etc. Referred to by Vīrarāghava in his *Śabda-brahma-vilāsa* (which see).

– C. called Chandobhāṣā or Pada-krama-sadana on the Taittirīya-prātiśākhya. Ptd.: See above.

[CC I 454a]

*MUKUNDA-BHAṬṬA (or -ŚĀSTRIN) (मुकुन्दभट्ट /-शास्त्रिन्)
– Pada-muṣṭi-lakṣaṇa(-prakāśikā) also called Pada-lakṣaṇa.

976 MUKURA (मुकुर)
Name of the sub-commentary on the *Vaidikābharaṇa* by Gaṇapati Śāstrin.

*MUKTĪŚVARĀCĀRYA (मुक्तीश्वराचार्य)
– C. called Dīpikā on the Kālanirṇaya-śikṣā (which see).

977 MUKHYA-ŚĀKHĀ-VICĀRA (मुख्यशाखाविचार)
on the importance of the *Śukla-yajurveda.*
SBD 55499. 9 fol.

978 MAITRĀYAṆĪYA-PRĀTIŚĀKHYA (मैत्रायणीयप्रातिशाख्य)
See Yudhisthira Mimamsaka, *Saṃskṛta Vyākaraṇa Śāstra kā Itihās*, part II, pp. 401-03.

979 MAITRĀYAṆĪYA-VEDA-LAKṢAṆA (मैत्रायणीयवेदलक्षण)
VOHD II 2.554 (Ms.or.fol. 3083. StaatsB., Marburg); see note at the end. On fol. 40 of (the original pagination) of the Ms, now In Berlin. The reference in the catalogue to SBD 1755 has no relevance. On examination the latter Ms was found to contain entirely different texts.

980 MAITRĀYAṆĪYA-SAṂHITĀ-KRAMA-JAṬĀ-PĀṬHA (मैत्रायणीयसंहिताक्रमजटापाठ)
VSM I 728 (no.2767). 4 fol. (of II 2.2). Extract p. 350.

981 MAITRĀYAṆĪYA-SAṂHITĀ-KRAMA-PĀṬHA (मैत्रायणीयसंहिताक्रमपाठ)
Hoshiarpur p. 7 (no.6380). 17 fol. 164 Grantha-s. Incomplete. (II 4; II 11).
Hoshiarpur p. 7 (no.6379). 39 fol. 800 Grantha-s. Incomplete. (I 2; II 4).
VSM I 716 (no.2761). 48 fol. (I 1-2).
VSM I 717 (no.2765). 117 fol. (I 2-6).
VSM I 718 (no.2762). 26 fol. (I 3).
VSM I 719 (no.2763). 51 fol. (I 4).
VSM I 720 (no.2764). 9 fol. (I 4).

982 MAITRĀYAṆĪYA-SAṂHITĀ-GHANA-PĀṬHA (also PAÑCA-SAṂDHI) (मैत्रायणीयसंहिताघनपाठ / पञ्चसंधि)
VSM I 731 (no.2777). 5 fol. (I 4.5). Extract p. 352.
VSM I 732 (no.2776). 4 fol. (IV 10.3. Also Pañcasaṃdhi of III 14.1). Extract p. 352.
VSM I 733 (no.2778). 9 fol. (IV 10.1; I 2.13; II 9.1).
VSM I 734 (no.2779). 11 fol. (III 21.20; IV 14.6; II 9.9). Dated Śaka 1794. Ascribed to Lagaḍha.

983 MAITRĀYAṆĪYA-SAṂHITĀ-JAṬĀ-PĀṬHA (मैत्रायणीयसंहिताजटापाठ)
VSM I 721-27. 7 Mss. containing specimen to the Jaṭā-pāṭha of some mantra-s.

984 MAITRĀYAṆĪYA-SAṂHITĀ-JAṬĀ-MĀLĀ-ŚIKHĀ-LEKHĀ-PĀṬHA (मैत्रायणीयसंहिताजटामालाशिखालेखापाठ)
VSM I 729 (no.2768). 4 fol. (IV 10.3). Extract p. 351.

985 MAITRĀYAṆĪYA-SAṂHITĀ-DAṆḌA-PĀṬHA (मैत्रायणीयसंहितादण्डपाठ)
VSM I 730 (no.2766). 4 fol. (III 14.6). Extract p. 351.

986 MAITRĀYAṆĪYA-SAṂHITĀ-PAÑCA-KRAMA-SAṂDHI (मैत्रायणीयसंहितापञ्चक्रमसंधि)
Hoshiarpur p. 7 (no.6381). 3 fol. 36 Grantha-s. Incomplete (II 1.1.3).

987 MAITRĀYAṆĪYA-SAṂHITĀṢṬA-VIKṚTY-UDĀHARAṆĀNI (मैत्रायणीयसंहिताष्टविकृत्युदाहरणानि)
VSM I 735 (no.2780). 11 fol. Dated Śaka 1794. Extract p. 353.

988 MAUNAMANTRA-PAKĀŚA (मौनमन्त्रपकाश)
of Daivajña-pāṭhaka.
SBD 4103. 55 fol.

989 MAUNAMANTRĀVABODHA (मौनमन्त्रावबोध)
of Sundara-śukla.
IM 2514. 18 fol.
Oxf. II 866(1) (Ms. Wilson 473). 36 fol. Dated A.D. 1529. = Oxf. 384a (no.473).
RASB II 908 (G 6066). 37 fol.

SBD 3960. 62 fol.

Ptd.: ed. by Pandit Ram Sakala Misra, at the end of the *Śuklayajuḥ-sarvānukrama*. – Benares : Chowkhamba, 1893-1921. 35 pp. – (Ben. S. S. 12).

[CC I 469a]

990 YAJUḤ-PRĀTIŚĀKHYA (यजुःप्रातिशाख्य)
Manuscripts of the *Taittirīya-prātiśākhya* (in South India) and the *Vājasaneyi-prātiśākhya* (in North India) are often catalogued under this title.
Unidentified: Śg. I 19.

[CC III 101a]

991 YAJUḤ-PRĀTIŚĀKHYA-VYĀKHYĀ (यजुःप्रातिशाख्यव्याख्या)
of Rāmacandra. The same as his commentary called *Jyotsnā*, on the *Vājasaneyi-prātiśākhya*.
SBD 47239. 63 fol. (1-6, 43-44, 47-101). Incomplete.

992 YAJUḤ-SAṂHITĀ-KĀṆḌA-PRAŚNA-PADĀKṢARĀDI-NIRṆAYA (यजुःसंहिताकाण्डप्रश्नपदाक्षरादिनिर्णय)
Mysore I, p. 613 (no. 4586).

993 YAJUḤ-SAṂHITĀ-KRAMA-PĀṬHA (यजुःसंहिताक्रमपाठ)
→ Vājasaneyi-saṃhitā-krama-pāṭha.
SBD 1060. 22 fol. (58-76, 78-80). Incomplete.
SBD 1061. 79 fol. (13-91). Incomplete.

994 YAJUḤ-SAṂDHI (यजुःसंधि)
Hoshiarpur p. 53 (no.2061). PL. Mal. 44 fol. 600 Grantha-s. Incomplete. Extract p. 78.

995 YAJUḤ-SARVĀNUKRAMAṆĪ (-ṆIKĀ) (यजुःसर्वानुक्रमणी /-णिका)
→ Śukla-yajurveda-sarvānukrama.

996 YAJUḤ-SARVĀNUKRAMAṆĪ (यजुःसर्वानुक्रमणी)
Mysore I, p. 613. Cf. Mysore ND II 3470: Taittirīya-saṃhitā-varṇānukramaṇī.

997 YAJUḤ-SARVĀNUKRAMAṆĪ-BHĀṢYA (यजुःसर्वानुक्रमणीभाष्य)
Ascribed to Kātyāyana ?
SBD 2321. 1-207 fol. (several fol. missing). Dated V.S. 1619.

998 YAJURVIDHĀNA (यजुर्विधान)
Taitt. (?) In 9 Adhyāya-s, also known as the *Bṛhad-yajurvidhāna*. Cf. next entry.
Bd. 113.
Ben. 10.
Bhau Daji. 64.
BISM p. 226 (22/466).
BISM p. 226 (33/6). Dated V.S. 1595.
BORI 65 of 1891-95. = BORI D I i.271. Title: Bṛhad-yajurvidhāna.
BORI TM 366. Title: Bṛhad-yajurvidhāna.

GJKSV 36059. 33 fol. Catalogued as Yajurvicāra.
Hoshiarpur p. 53 (no.6201). 19 fol. 600 Grantha-s.
Hoshiarpur p. 53 (no.6581). 31 fol. 323 Grantha-s.
Peters. II, p. 175 (no.132). 20 fol.
Rep. Raj. and C. I. p. 3
SB p. 100 (no.97). 50 fol. 900 Grantha-s. = SBD 3944.

[CC I 469b; III 101a]

999 YAJURVIDHĀNA(-ŚIKṢĀ) **(यजुर्विधान /-शिक्षा)**
Ascribed to Kātyāyana. Like the *Ṛgvidhāna*, this work of five Adhyāya-s describes the use of mantra-s of the Mādhyandinīya Śākhā of the *Śukla Yajurveda*. In the Benares edition, however, it is divided into six Adhyāya-s. In Anna Sastri Ware 's edition the fifth chapter ends as below. Then the sixth chapter begins: athātaḥ kāmya- ... , etc. followed by the seventh chapter, Mānastoka-kalpa and Haṃsavatī dealing with more ritualistic matters. Col.: Bṛhadyajur-vidhāna.

Beginning:

अथातो मन्त्राणामनुष्ठानकल्पनं वसिष्ठादिभिः ब्रह्मर्षिभिरनुष्ठितमनुव्याख्यास्यामो नान्यद् ब्राह्मणस्य कदाचिद् धनार्जनक्रिया विद्यते होमानां यज्ञानां वैषावश्यं क्रिया किं तु मन्त्राहुतिवीर्यज्ञानं विद्याधनानां यजुर्वेदैरुपदिश्यते क एते मन्त्रा य एते मन्त्रा ऋग्यजुःसामाथर्वाङ्गिरस उभयात्मका मन्त्रा देवताभीष्टा वा परा द्रव्यसंस्कारकाश्चेति य एते द्रव्यसंस्कारपरास्ते तत्रैवोपयोगिनो ये पुनर्देवताभिज्ञानाश्च फलं तेषाँ सर्वार्थत्वमभिसंधायाराधितानां च फलादान आज्ञानसाधितानां फलदर्शनान्मन्त्रलिङ्गदर्शनाच्च विनियोगान्तरं वक्ष्यामस्तत्र कर्मकरणे तुलापुरुषचान्द्रायण कृच्छ्रातिकृच्छ्रादिभिः पूतशरीरेण कर्मापेक्षया द्वादशरात्रं षड्रात्रं त्रिरात्रमिति च कर्मणां कर्माङ्गानि कार्याणि सर्वमन्त्राणां पूर्वमेव लक्षणमयुतं सहस्रमिति च सिद्ध्यपेक्षया कार्याणि कर्मावसाने च फलावाप्तिर्ब्रह्मचारिणा भवितव्यं सरहस्ये कल्पाश्च सिद्ध्यो भावज्ञातव्याश्चेति ॥ १॥

End:

वेदारम्भे समाप्तौ च जपहोमादिषु शान्तिपुष्टिकर्मणि चैतत् प्रयुज्यत एतद् विदित्वा सर्वविद् भवत्येतदुपास्य रविसिद्धिभाग् भवति कल्याणतरो भवत्येतत्कर्मफलप्रतिपादकं पूर्वकर्मफलाभावादभावकृतस्य कर्मणः स वेदफलयुक्तस्य कर्मणो नास्ति नैव फलमिति तच्छक्त्यपेक्ष्यामुष्मिल्लोके कृतस्य कर्मणः फलं हि संपत्तिः प्रत्ययं च न च विद्याधरपादप्रसारितधनानां जनपूर्ववर्णरसेषु नास्ति यज्ञविरोधित्वादिति ॥

अनेनैव प्रकारेण सर्वे मन्त्राः प्रकीर्तिताः ।
ये नोक्तास्ते तु सर्वे यसंसकारा ··· (यशस्कराः) ।
अथवा सर्वमन्त्राणां विस्तरेण पृथक् पृथक् ॥

AK 65. 32 fol. Dated V.S. 1430. First 2 fol. are missing.

Baroda 9686. 13 fol. 500 Grantha-s. 5 Adhyāya-s. = CLB I, p. 34. (last fol. : Haṃsavatī-vidhāna).

Baroda 12022. 28 fol. 450 Grantha-s. = CLB I, p. 34. Extract pp. 158-59. A longer version. Incomplete. 7 Adhyāya-s and a portion of the 8th; 5 chapters agree with the printed text.

BBRAS 494 (B D 162). 41 fol. Copied by Vināyaka, son of Hari.

Bd. 78. 29 fol. Dated V.S. 1746.

Berlin StB-PrK (NGMPP). A 455/31. 20 fol. Ends with Haṃsavatīvidhāna.

Berlin StB-PrK (NGMPP). A 596/31. 40 fol. Ends with Haṃsavatīvidhāna.

Berlin StB-PrK (NGMPP). A 596/32. 22 fol. Ends with Haṃsavatīvidhāna.

Berlin StB-PrK (NGMPP). H 305/6. 3 fol. (1, 25-26). Incomplete (microfilm dated 19.06.1978).

BORI 78 of 1887-91. = BORI D I i.272. 29 fol. 5 Adhyāya-s. Dated V.S. 1746.

BORI 65 of 1891-95. = BORI D I i.271. 23 fol. Dated V.S. 1430 ?

GJKSV 43456. 25 fol.

IM 2543. 15 fol.

IM 5547. 12 fol. (16-27). Incomplete.

Lahore p. 2 (no.6). 28 fol. 540 Grantha-s. Dated A.D. 1841. In the possession of Pt. Jwala Datta Prasada, Lahore.

PUL I, p. 23 (no.117). 31 fol. 500 Grantha-s. 5 Adhyāya-s. Last is Haṃsavatī-vidhāna.

SB p. 100 (no. 97). 50 fol. 900 Grantha-s (1-9 Adhyāya-s). Dated V.S. 1662. = SBD 3944.

SBD 2023. 5 fol.

SBD 2025. 9 fol. Incomplete.

SBD 3944. 50 fol. Dated V.S. 1662.

SBD 2054. 16 fol. Dated V.S. 1926.

SBD 4113. 14 fol. (4-17). Incomplete. Dated V.S. 1584.

SBD 4240. 20 fol. (1, 8-14, 18-19, 21, 23-27, 29, 31-32). Incomplete.

SBD 55218. 42 fol. 6 chs. Dated V.S. 1441 / Śaka 1306.

RASB II 895 (G 6157). 18 fol. 450 Grantha-s. 5 Adhyāya-s. Dated V.S. 1650.

Rep. Raj. and C. I. p. 3. (Mādhyandina-yajurvidhāna).

Trav. Uni. 2015. 500 Grantha-s. Incomplete. Dated V.S. 1964.

Trav. Uni. 7685. 65 Grantha-s. Incomplete.

Trav. Uni. 10046. 100 Grantha-s. Incomplete.

Trav. Uni. 10173. 500 Grantha-s. Incomplete.

Ptd.: in Śikṣā-saṃgraha. – Benares, 1889, pp. 327-61. – (Ben. S. S. 10).

Also ed. by Anna Sastri Ware, *Śuklayajurvidhāna-sūtra,* with the C. *Yajurmañjarī* of Kālanātha Vāghare. – Bombay : Nirnaya Sagar Press, 1943, pp. 1-50. [SOAS (III.1.c.54 – 59314); DC (Q126xkat 15H3 55032)]

1000 YAJURVEDA-KRIYĀ-SVARA-LAKṢAṆA or YOHIB-HĀṢYA

(यजुर्वेदक्रियास्वरलक्षण / योहिभाष्य)

of Sūri-bhaṭṭa. See Kriyā-svara-lakṣaṇa and Yohibhāṣya.

Mysore p. 2 (no. 57). 8 fol.

[CC I 469b]

1001 YAJURVEDA-JAṬĀ-PĀṬHA (**यजुर्वेदजटापाठ**)
→ Vājasaneyi-saṃhitā-jaṭā-pāṭha.

GJKSV 27897. (chs. 11-22).

1002 YAJURVEDA-JAṬĀVALI or JAṬĀ-LAKṢAṆA (**यजुर्वेदजटावलि / जटालक्षण**)
on the Jaṭā-pāṭha. Mysore p. 2 → Jaṭāvali.

[CC I 469b]

1003 YAJURVEDA-DARPAṆA (**यजुर्वेददर्पण**)
Gough p. 163. Gr.

1004 YAJURVEDA-PADA-NIRṆAYA (**यजुर्वेदपदनिर्णय**)
Trav. Uni. T.1203. 650 Grantha-s.

1005 YAJURVEDA-PRĀTIŚĀKHYA (**यजुर्वेदप्रातिशाख्य**)
Cf. above under Uddhava-bhaṭṭa.

1006 YAJURVEDA-LAKṢAṆA (**यजुर्वेदलक्षण**)
Oppert I 7214. Belonged to Ivattur Nandikesvara Sastri of Vijayanagaram.

[CC I 469b]

1007 YAJURVEDA-VICĀRA (**यजुर्वेदविचार**)
Definitions, divisions and other particulars relating to the *Yajurveda*, especially of the *Taittirīya-saṃhitā* by an anonymous author who quotes among others: *Aitareya-brāhmaṇa*, Mādhava, Dhūrta-svāmin, Kapardi-svāmin, Hemādri, Nṛsiṃha-prasāda, *Kālādarśa*, *Prayoga-pārijāta* and contains portions of the *Caraṇa-vyūha* and commentary thereon. It contains eleven verses on the geographical distribution of the Vedic Śākhā-s (atha deśeṣu vedaśākhayor vibhāga ucyate). It also contains the verse : sa bhāvaḥ kāmatā jagdhiḥ ... with a commentary. Col.: Taittirīya-yajurvedasya vicāraḥ.

Calcutta Skt. Coll. I 45 (465). 14 fol. 670 Grantha-s.

1008 YAJURVEDA-ŚĀKHĀ-PRAṆAYANA-VICĀRA (**यजुर्वेदशाखाप्रणयनविचार**)
Beginning:

अथ प्रसङ्गात् यजुर्वेदस्य शाखाप्रणयनविचारः किंचिदुच्यते। तत्र यजुर्वेद एक एव प्रथमः। तदुक्तं विष्णुपुराणे -- एक एव यजुर्वेदस्तं चतुर्धा व्यकल्पयत्। इति॥

End:

तत्र यो जायते गर्भो न संस्पृस्यो द्विजातिभिः॥
न हि वेदे ऽधिकारो ऽस्य तद्वंश्ये ऽप्येवमेव हि।
आरूढपतितः प्रोक्तो मुनीनां तत्वदर्शिभिः॥
इति दिक्। इति यजुर्वेदस्य शाखाप्रणयनविचारः॥

BISM p. 226 (22/370). 2 fol.

1009 YAJURVEDA-ŚĀKHĀ-VṚKṢA (CITRAM) (यजुर्वेदशाखवृक्ष / चित्रम्)
Hoshiarpur p. 53 (no.5673). 1 fol.

1010 YAJURVEDA-SAṂHITĀ-GHANA-PĀṬHA (यजुर्वेदसंहिताघनपाठ)
→ Vājasaneyi-saṃhitā-ghana-pāṭha.
SBD 53435. 58 fol. (1-29, 1-21, 1-8).

1011 YAJURVEDA-SAṂHITĀNUKRAMA(-ṆIKĀ) (यजुर्वेदसंहितानुक्रम /-णिका)
BORI 38. of 1895-98. 6 fol. Dated Śaka 1735.
Peters. VI, p. 61 (no.38). 6 fol. Dated Śaka 1735.
Radh. 2.

[CC I 469b]

1012 YAJURVEDA-SAṂHITĀ-SARVĀNUKRAMA-SŪTRA (यजुर्वेदसंहितासर्वानुक्रमसूत्र)
→ Śukla-yajurveda-sarvānukrama.

1013 YAJURVEDA-SAPTA-LAKṢAṆA (यजुर्वेदसप्तलक्षण)
Mysore p. 2 (no. 52). 96 fol. → Sapta-lakṣaṇa.

[CC I 469b]

1014 YAJURVEDA-SARVĀNUKRAMAṆĪ (1) (यजुर्वेदसर्वानुक्रमणी)
Ascribed to Yāska → Taittirīya-sarvānukramaṇī.

1015 YAJURVEDA-SARVĀNUKRAMAṆĪ (2) (यजुर्वेदसर्वानुक्रमणी)
of Yādava-prakāśa. See also Yājuṣa-sarvānukramaṇī.
Mysore I, p. 32 (B.852. Gr. 97 pp.). It contains numerous lacunae.
Mysore ND II 3464 (P 366). PL. Tel. 83 fol. Extract no. 166. Title: Taittirīya-saṃhitānukramaṇī (Yajurvedānukramaṇī).
PUL II. App. p. 13 (no.199). PL. Mal. 112 fol. Badly damaged.
Trav. Uni. 3070 D. PL. Mal. 325 Grantha-s. Incomplete.

1016 YAJURVEDĀNUKRAMAṆĪ-BHĀṢYA (यजुर्वेदानुक्रमणीभाष्य)
→ Sarvānukramaṇī(-bhāṣya)-paddhati, of Yājñika-deva.
SBD 47249. 33 fol. Incomplete.

1017 YAJURVEDĀNUKRAMAṆIKĀ (यजुर्वेदानुक्रमणिका)
→ Śukla-yajurveda-sarvānukrama.
IM 7175. 34 fol. Incomplete.

1018 YAṆĀDEŚA-DĪRGHĪ (यणादेशदीर्घी)
Adyar D I 940 (19 D 61 = 66253). PL. Gr. 2 fol. (18b-19a). Cf. Adyar D I 902/945.
Adyar D I 941 (19 E 42 = 66327). PL. Gr. 2 fol. (42-43).
Adyar D I 942 (19 O 5 = 66887). PL. Mal. 2 fol. (123-24).
Adyar D I 943 (20 E 3 = 67133). PL. Tel. 1 fol. (inserted between 25 and 26).
Adyar D I 944 (22 E 36 = 68884). PL. Tel. 1 fol. (24b). = Adyar I, p. 51b.
Adyar D I 945 (19 D 61 = 66253). PL. Gr. 2 fol. (18-19). Appears to be the same Ms. as no. 940. Cf. Adyar D I 902.
Adyar D I 984 → Veda-lakṣaṇa (A 2).

Adyar D I 986 → Veda-lakṣaṇa (A 4).

Adyar D I 1034 (Yaṇādeśa-saṃdhi) → Sapta-lakṣaṇa.

MD 14746. PL. Tel. 2 pp. (18ff.) ....pṛthivyāṅgirasī.

MD 16816. PL. Gr. 2 pp. 20 Grantha-s.

MT 4600(a). PL. Gr. 2 fol. (4-5). (Yaṇādeśa-hrasva-dīrghī) Presented in 1924-25 by the Secretary to the Trustees of Sri Yogi Parthasarathi Ayyangar's Charities, Triplicane, Madras.

Mysore I, p. 32.

Mysore ND II 3691 (P 660/ 3). PL. Gr. 4 fol. (5-8). Extract no. 250.

Mysore ND II 3692 (P 2262/ 5). PL. Gr. 2 fol. Extract no. 251.

Mysore ND II 3693 (P 2265/20). PL. Gr. 1 fol. (137).

Mysore ND II 3728 (P 4468/ 2). PL. Na. 2 fol. (10-11). Extract no. 252.

Tirupati SVUORI (4421). PL. Gr. 2 fol. (25-26).

Trav. Uni. 16408 K. PL. Mal. 1 fol. 15 Grantha-s.

Trav. Uni. 16408 Z5. PL. Mal. 1 fol. 12 Grantha-s.

Trav. Uni. 17346 G. PL. Mal. 12 Grantha-s.

Trav. Uni. L.988 B. PL. Mal. 12 Grantha-s.

Ptd.: at the end of the *Ṣaḍviṃśati-sūtra* (Grantha script), pp. 20-21.
Also printed in *Lakṣaṇa-traya* (in Telugu script), pp. 43-44.

1019 YAṆĀDEŚA-(DĪRGHI-)NIṢEDHA (यणादेश(दीर्घि)निषेध)

Adyar D I 946 (19 D 61 = 66253). PL. Gr. 1 fol. (19a). The complete text consisting of only two verses is printed.

MD 17437. PL. Gr. 1 p. 5 Grantha-s. Cf. MD 14746 end.

1020 YAṆĀDEŚA-SAṂDHI (यणादेशसंधि)

RV. Adyar D I 947 (20 K 38 = 67500). PL. Tel. 1 fol. (no. 10). = Adyar I, p. 51b.

1021 YAMĀPATTI (यमापत्ति)

A conjectural title. The same text is found as *Varṇa-krama-lakṣaṇa* in Tirupati SVUORI (3516a2). The complete text consisting of about ten verses is fully printed in the Adyar catalogue.

Beginning: (948)

ऊष्मप्रकृतिकात् स्पर्शात् पञ्चमः परतो यदि।
तत्र नैव यमापत्तिरिष्यते नात्र संशयः ॥
वर्गान्तं शषसैः सार्धमन्तस्थाभिश्च संयुतम्।
दृष्ट्वा यमा निवर्तन्ते इत्युक्तं वर्णवेदिभिः ॥
लकारस्य वकारेण संयोगे स्वरिते यदि।
विशेषं तत्र जानीयाद् द्वित्वमित्यभिधीयते॥
अन्तस्थाद्युदये पूर्वं पञ्चमश्च द्विरुच्यते।
इतरादौ परे तत्र स न चेति स्मृतो बुधैः ॥

ऋकारपूर्वः प्रथमो हल्परस्त्वेकमात्रिकः ।
ऋकारात् प्रथमस्यापि द्वित्वं न स्यात् कथंचन ॥
पदान्तस्य नकारस्य वकाराद् रपरे यदि ।
संयोगे परभूते च द्वित्वमित्यभिधीयते ॥
पदादौ पदमध्ये वा स्थितस्योष्मपरस्य वै ।
प्रथमस्य द्वितीयत्वं पूर्वं कुर्वीत पण्डितः ॥ हरिः ओम् ॥
उच्चात् परो ऽनुदात्तः स्यात् स्वरितः स्वरितात् परे ।
नीचाः स्युः प्रचया एतौ न ह्युच्चस्वरितोत्तरे ।
नीचोच्चयोगजो नीचविकारश्चेति स द्विधा ।
अभ्येवक्त्वे वसून्नीयन्ते सो ऽग्निं द्वियोगजः ॥ इति स्वरविषयः

Adyar D I 948 (23 E 25 = 69758). PL. Gr. 2 fol. (33-34). Damaged.
Hamburg StUB (cod.Palmbl. III 8/133) → Veda-lakṣaṇa (HB).

1022 YĀJUṢA-BHŪṢAṆA (याजुषभूषण)
Name of the commentary on the *Pāriśikṣā* also called *Varṇa-krama-lakṣaṇa.*

1023 YĀJUṢA-VĀKYA-PAṄKTI (याजुषवाक्यपङ्क्ति)
of Nārāyaṇa Dīkṣita.
Trav. Uni. 10165. PL. Mal. 1000 Grantha-s.

1024 YĀJUṢA-SARVĀNUKRAMAṆĪ (याजुषसर्वानुक्रमणी)
of Yādava-prakāśa → Yajurveda-sarvānukramaṇī
Mysore I, p. 32 (B.852. Gr. 97 pp.). It contains numerous lacunae.
Mysore ND II 3464 (P 366). PL. Tel. 83 fol. Extract no. 166. Title: Taittirīya-saṃhitānukramaṇī (Yajurvedānukramaṇī).

1025 YĀJUṢA-SVARA-KAUMUDĪ (याजुषस्वरकौमुदी)
Mysore I, p. 32 → Svara-kaumudī.

*YĀJÑAVALKYA (याज्ञवल्क्य)
– Manaḥsvāra-śikṣā
Ptd.: in Śikṣā-saṃgraha. – Benares, 1889, pp. 185-209. – (Ben. S. S. 10).
– Yājñavalkya-śikṣā. This is catalogued under various titles, e.g. *Bṛhacchikṣā* (in Bühler p. 553; no. 15); *Bṛhad-yājñavalkya-śikṣā* (in GB 29); *Vājasaneyi-śikṣā* (in GJKSV 34279, etc.); *Kātyāyana-śikṣā* (in GB 23).

1026 YĀJÑAVALKYA-ŚIKṢĀ (याज्ञवल्क्यशिक्षा)
Ascribed to Yājñavalkya. Also called *Vājasaneyi-śikṣā* in a few Mss. It is almost a commentary on the *Vājasaneyi-prātiśākhya.* In verse eight, which is not found in the South Indian Mss, the opinion of one Soma-śarman, whose identity is not known, is mentioned. The same verse is also found in the Nāradīya-śikṣā. Uvaṭa quotes a verse (202) of

this Śikṣā in his commentary on *Vājasaneyi-prātiśākhya* 4.163. There are variations in Mss. from the text printed in Śikṣā-saṃgraha which contains 232 verses. For a *Bṛhacchikṣā* of Yājñavalkya see Bühler p. 553. See F. Kielhorn : Remarks on the Śikṣās in : *Indian Antiquary*, vol. V, p. 196 (reprint in : *Kleine Schriften*, vol. I, pp. 158-69).

Beginning: (856)

अथातस्त्रैस्वर्यलक्षणं व्याख्यास्यामः --
उदात्तस्यानुदात्तस्य स्वरितस्य तथैव च।
लक्षणं वर्णयिष्यामि दैवतं स्थानमेव च॥
शुक्लमुच्चं विजानीयान्नीचं लोहितमुच्यते।
श्यामं तु स्वरितं विद्यादग्निरुच्चस्य देवता॥
नीचे सोमं विजानीयात् स्वरिते सविता तथा।
उदात्तं ब्राह्मणं विद्यान्नीचं क्षत्रियमुच्यते॥
वैश्यं तु स्वरितं विद्यादुदात्तं तु भरद्वसुः।
नीचं गौतममित्याहुर्गार्ग्यं तु स्वरितं विदुः॥
विद्यादुदात्तं गायत्रं नीचं त्रैष्टुभमुच्यते।
जागतं स्वरितं विद्यादेक एव नियोगतः॥
गान्धर्ववेदे ये प्रोक्ताः सप्त षड्जर्षभादयः।
त एव वेदे विज्ञेयास्त्रय उच्चादयः स्वराः॥
उच्चौ निषधगान्धारौ नीचावृषभधैवतौ।
शेषास्तु स्वरिता ज्ञेयाः षड्जमध्यमपञ्चमाः॥

End:

उच्चानुदात्तयोर्योगे स्वरितः स्वार उच्यते।
ऐक्यं तत् प्रचयः प्रोक्तः संधिरेषां मिथो ऽद्भुतः॥ २२८॥
बह्वीर्जिह्वा यथा गृह्णात्यह्वा वह्निस्तथैव च।
ब्रह्मरूपं विजानीयाद् गुरुमेवात्मनः सदा॥ २२९॥
यत्किंचिद् वाङ्मयं लोके सर्वमत्र प्रतिष्ठितम्।
करोति तत्प्रदानं यत् तस्माद् ब्रह्ममयो गुरुः॥ २३०॥
विधिनाप्यविधिज्ञानमविधानान्न लभ्यते।
अविधानपरो नित्यं प्रायश्चित्तीयते नरः॥ २३१॥
युक्तियुक्तं वचो ग्राह्यं न ग्राह्यं गुरुगौरवात्।
सर्वशास्त्ररहस्यं तद्याज्ञवल्क्येन भाषितम्॥ २३२॥
इति श्रीमहर्षियोगिवरयाज्ञवल्क्यप्रोक्ता शिक्षा समाप्ता॥

Adyar D I 856 (21 Q 10 = 68514). PL. Mal. 11 fol. (37ff.). Title: Traisvarya-lakṣaṇa. Up to the verse 113 (p. 18) of the printed edition.

It contains many variants. .... (= Skt. Texts on Phonetics, pp. 682-96).

Adyar D I 949 (36 B 11 = TR 21). 19 fol. (pp. 394-430). Dated 7.6.18. = Adyar I, p. 53a.

AK 66. 14 fol. Extract p. 107-08. (194 verses).

America 91. 9 fol. (Vājasaneyi-śikṣā).

Baroda 7345(a). 7 fol. 200 Grantha-s. = CLB I, p. 34. Dated V.S. 1653.

Baroda 9513. 14 fol. 195 Grantha-s. = CLB I, p. 34. Dated V.S. 1813.

Baroda 9560. 15 fol. 200 Grantha-s. = CLB I, p. 34. Dated V.S. 1673.

Baroda 9565. 14 fol. 200 Grantha-s. = CLB I, p. 34. Dated V.S. 1719.

Baroda 12058. 8 fol. 160 Grantha-s. = CLB I, p. 34. Dated V.S. 1704. Differs a little from the other Mss.

Baroda 12875. 28 fol. 200 Grantha-s. = CLB I, p. 34. Dated Śaka 1699.

Baroda 12887. 8 fol. 200 Grantha-s. = CLB I, p. 34. Dated Śaka 1660.

Baroda 12920. 11 fol. 169 Grantha-s. = CLB I, p. 34.

Baroda 9291. 4 fol. 80 Grantha-s. = CLB I, p. 34. Dated A.D. 1772 (merely a summary). Extract pp. 160-61.

Baroda 26254. 24 fol. 300 Grantha-s. Dated V.S. 1927.

BBRAS 12 (B D 278). 6 fol. 191 Grantha-s. Dated Śaka 1787.

Berlin StB-PrK (NGMPP). A 596/35. 19 fol. 178 verses (ends with: yuktiyuktaṃ vaco grāhyam ...

Berlin StB-PrK (NGMPP). D 77/13. 17 fol. Lithographic print (idaṃ pustakaṃ Bhagīrathātmaja-Hariprasādena mohamayyāṃ jagadīśvara-śilāyantre mudrāpitam – Saṃ. 1940 / Śakābdaḥ 1806 Bhādrapadamāsaḥ). The end is different from other Mss. (microfilm dated 28.07.1976).

Berlin StB-PrK (NGMPP). E 1554/21(a). 19 fol. Maithili script (microfilm dated 25.09.1983).

Bhau Daji 121.

Bhk. 9.

Bhr. 28.

BHU C 2114 (D 2E/2137). 14 fol.

BHU B 3349 (D 2E/2138). 15 fol. Incomplete. Dated V.S. 1690.

Bik. 349. 14 fol. Dated V.S. 1686. Title: Yājñavalkya-vrata-(?kṛta)svara-śikṣā.

Bikaner 649. 14 fol. Dated V.S. 1686 (A.D. 1629).

BISM p. 229 (60/30).

Bombay Uni. 10 (BMC 50 7). 20 fol. Copied by Hari-bhaṭṭa Lule.

Bombay Uni. 11 (BMC 70 13). 16 fol. Incomplete (1-7 verses are missing). Dated Śaka 1657.

Bombay Uni. 12 (BMC 84 19). 21 fol.

Bombay Uni. (Itchharam 11 4) 102. 16 fol. (181 verses). Dated Śaka 1780.

BORI 25 of 1871-72. 13 fol. Dated V.S. 1820.

BORI 57 of A 1881-82. 10 fol. Dated Śaka 1749.

BORI 28 of 1882-83. 9 fol.

BORI 380 of 1883-84. 9 fol. Dated Śaka 1687.

BORI 381 of 1883-84. 9 fol.

BORI 66 of 1891-95. 14 fol.

BORI 44 of 1895-98. (Vājasaneyī Śikṣā).

BP p. 287.
GJKSV 15717. 20 fol. Incomplete. Dated V.S. 1592.
GJKSV 18377. 20 fol.
GJKSV 34279. 16 fol. 88 verses. Col.: Yājñavalkya-munikṛtā Vājasaneyi-śikṣā.
GJKSV 42311. 13 fol.
GB 23. 19 fol. 169 verses. Title: Kātyāyana-śikṣā. Copied in 1875 for Kielhorn through R. L. Mitra. See F. Kielhorn : Remarks on the Śikṣās in : *Indian Antiquary*, vol. V, p. 196 (reprint in : *Kleine Schriften*, vol. I, pp. 158-69).
GB 28. 50 fol. Copy of a Ms. Dated V.S. 1820. Written on only one side of the paper and compared with another Ms. See F. Kielhorn : Remarks on the Śikṣās in : *Indian Antiquary*, vol. V, p. 196 (reprint in : *Kleine Schriften*, vol. I, pp. 158-69).
GB 29. 10 fol. 95 verses. (Bṛhadyājñavalkya-śikṣā). See F. Kielhorn : Remarks on the Śikṣās in : *Indian Antiquary*, vol. V, p. 196 (reprint in : *Kleine Schriften*, vol. I, pp. 158-69).
GJKSV 37114. 9 fol. Incomplete. 149 verses. (Svara-lakṣaṇa-śikṣā).
GJKSV 38253. 21 fol. Dated V.S. 1878.
Gough p. 86 (no.25). 13 fol. Dated V.S. 1820.
Gough p. 162. Gr.
Granthappura p. 2 (no.25b). Mal. 250 Grantha-s.
H. 19.
Hoshiarpur p. 53 (no.215). 8 fol. 250 Grantha-s. Dated V.S. 1604.
IM 3380. 25 fol. Title: Vājasaneyi-śikṣā.
IM 8972. 6 fol.
Jodhpur D I, p. 25 (no.96 / 1474). 14 fol. Dated V.S. 1920.
L 1239. 14 fol. 288 Grantha-s. Title: Kātyayana-śikṣā.
Oxf. CS d.185(1). 19 fol. Incomplete (fol. no.9 missing). Col.: Vājasaneyi-śikṣā. Dated V.S. 1937 (A.D. 1880).
Oxf. CS d.185(2). 15 fol.
Oxf. CS d.185(3). 14 fol. Dated A.D. 1904.
Oxf. CS e.62(3). 18 fol.
Oxf. CS c.157(2). 14 fol. Dated A.D. 1762.
Peters. VI, p. 61 (no.44). 10 fol. Dated V.S. 1734.
PUL I, p. 23 (no.118). 14 fol. 190 Grantha-s.
PUL I, p. 23 (no.119). 7 fol. (Vājasaneyī Śikṣā).
PUL I, p. 23 (no.120). 6 fol. Incomplete.
Radh. 2.
RASB II 1499 (G 3253). 13 fol. 260 Grantha-s. Dated V.S. 1939.
RASB II 1500 (G 660). 178 verses = L 1239.
SBD 2104. 7 fol. Incomplete (catalogued as Svara-lakṣaṇa).
SBD 47210. 8 fol. Dated V.S. 1921.
SBD 47211. 4 fol. Incomplete.
SBD 53733. 12 fol. (3-12, 27-28). Incomplete.
Trav. Uni. 10165. 250 Grantha-s.
VOHD II 2.544 (Ms.or.oct. 656. StaatsB., Marburg). 11 fol. 161 verses. Copied by Bhavān, son of Bhīma, in Kāśī. Dated V.S. 1761 (= 1705)

VOHD II 2.545 (Ms.or.oct. 689. StaatsB., Marburg). 12 fol. 85 verses. Dated Śaka 1733 (= 1811). Title: Vājasaneyi-śikṣā.
Wai II 10311. 16 fol.
Wellcome Inst. London. S 30.

Ptd.: as an appendix to the edition of the *Vājasaneyi-saṃhitā*, with Pratijñā-sūtra, Sarvānukrama and Anuvāka-sūtra :
Ed. by Hariprasad Bhagirathaji, Jagadisvara Press, – Bombay : Jyestharam Mukundaji, 1884. 17, 2, 36, 40 pp. [Adyar (Ḥ15.1 Yaj Har); Gö (4/ H E E 1062/53); Emeneau (104); IO : Ptd. Bks. Cat. 1953, p. 1968 (12 K 28)]
– Bombay : Venkatesvara Press, 1887. [Emeneau : (105)]
– Bombay : Tattvaviveka Press, 1896. [Emeneau : (107)]
– Bombay : Nirnaya Sagar Press, 1901. [Emeneau : (108)]
– Bombay : Nirnaya Sagar Press, 1912. [Emeneau : (109)] [BM : Ptd. Bks. Cat. 1906-1928. 1203 (14010.cc.13)]
In the 4th volume of the *Vājasaneyi-saṃhitā* with commentaries of Uvaṭa and Mahīdhara. – Benares : Chowkhamba, 1915, pp. 1-15. – (Kashi Sanskrit Series 34). [NL (180 Jc 91 109; V 4 C 3)]
Ed. by Amritalal Sastri of Jamnagar, in : *Śukla-yajurveda-mādhyandina-saṃhitā* (prāstāvikasaṃhitāmantrāṇām akārādyanukramaṇikāvedapārāyaṇavidhyanuvākasūtrādhyāyāṣṭavikṛtiyājñavalkyaśikṣāpratijñāsūtrasarvānukramasūtra- ... samalaṃkṛtā) – Bombay : Nirnaya Sagar Press, Śaka 1872 (1950), pp. 178-89. [SKGI (Rh III 125)]
Ed. by Jagadisha Lal Shastri (with commentaries of Uvaṭa and Mahīdhara). – Delhi : Motilal Banarsidass, 1971. Appendix, pp. 2-6. [Adyar (Ḥ12.21 VM xy Sha)]
With Sarvānukrama and Anuvāka-sūtra, lithographic print. – Bombay : Saṃ. 1946. (1889), 89 fol. [BM : Ptd. Bks. Cat. 1876-92. 490 (14010.c.15)]
Ed. in Śikṣā-saṃgraha. – Benares, 1889, pp. 1-35. – (Ben. S. S. 10).
Ed. by Amaranatha (Sastri) Dikshita, with *Śikṣā-vallī-vivṛti*, Lalita Prasad Dabarala-saṃśodhitā. – Benares (Ramghat) : Padmanabha Sarma Dikshita, Hitachintaka Press, Saṃ. 1994 (1937). kha, 8, 4, 169, 4, 5 pp. (this edition contains 116 verses). [MUL (P15: 27Āx7 15G7)]
Ed. by Vidyadhara Pandeya with a Hindi translation and commentary, called *Prakāśikā*. – Varanasi (Kamaccha) : Naya Samsar Press, 1978. ÑA, 60 pp. (In this edition the text is divided in to two parts consisting of 92 and 121 verses respectively). [SAI (ind 51 D 588/2403 kp)]

[CC I 474b; II 110a; III 102a]

*YĀJÑIKA-DEVA see ANANTA(-DEVA) YĀJÑIKA
(याज्ञिकदेव / अनन्त(-देव) /-याज्ञिक)

Also called Devadatta or Deva-yājñika or Śrīdeva or simply Deva, son of Mahādeva (Prajāpati), elder brother of Lakṣmīdhara (Weber, p. 53).

*YĀDAVA-PRAKĀŚA **(यादवप्रकाश)**

– Yajurveda-sarvānukramaṇī, also called Yājuṣa-sarvānukramaṇī or Taittirīya-saṃhitānukramaṇī or Yajurvedānukramaṇī.

Mysore I, p. 32 (B.852). Mysore ND II 3464 (P 366). PUL II. App. p. 13 (no.199). Trav. Uni. 3070 D.

*YĀSKA (यास्क)

– Yajurveda-sarvānukramaṇī or Taittirīya-sarvānukramaṇī. Apparently now lost, but quoted more than twenty times by Peṭṭāśāstrin in his commentary on the *Chandoviciti*. See C. Kunhan Raja : "The Taittirīya-sarvānukramaṇī of Yāska", in : *Journal of Oriental Research*, vol. 5 (Madras, 1931), pp. 215-22.

1027 YOHI-PRĀPTI(-ŚIKṢĀ) or YOHI-BHĀṢYA or YOHI-'CIṬṬA'
(योहिप्राप्ति /-शिक्षा) / योहिभाष्य / योहिच्चिट्ट)
of Sūri-bhaṭṭa of Homa-(? Gopa-?)kanyāpura. 23 verses accompanied by a commentary about the accent of verbs in the *Taittirīya-saṃhitā*. Also known as the *Kriyā-svara-lakṣaṇa* or *Taittirīya-kriyā-svara-lakṣaṇa* or *Yajurveda-kriyā-svara-lakṣaṇa*.

Beginning:

श्रीमद्गणेशं प्रणिपत्य देवं श्रीसूर्यनारायणसुप्रसादात्।
वक्ष्ये क्रियायाः स्वरलक्षणं तद् यद्धोमकन्यापुरसूरुभट्टः ॥
तस्माच्चत्वारिपरश्चेद् आहरच्चाद्युदात्तवान्।
प्रायच्छत् त्रिर्यवं तस्मात् तस्मै त्वेषपरस्त्वसे॥
प्राविशत् तं प्राह तादृग् यत् सोमो ऽजनयत् तदा
प्रावेशन्त्याददत तत् प्रायुङ्क्त तेन च॥

End:

यद्यावच्छन्दकौ यत्र यदाद्युच्चो यतो यदि।
यथा यर्हि ह्यधश्चादिरा द्वादशात् क्रियोच्चभाक्॥
अपूर्वे ऽपि क्रिया नित्यमित्याद्यन्ययजुःस्थितम्।
न हि सतं हितां हितस्य माया हि तत् तथा।
यां ते गच्छत् तु यस्तस्या यत् तद्येषां हि चातर्हि।
यो यक्ष्ये यस्यैवं यत् तं यावानेव य इत्यपि॥
होमकन्यापुरःसूरिभट्टीयसुप्रसादिनः ।
तत्स्वरं सूचनार्थं हि बालानामिति वर्णितम्॥
इति श्रीसूरिभट्टयज्वनः कृतौ योहिभाष्यं समाप्तम्॥

Adyar 38 H 10 = TR 854. 24 pp. Copied in 1928 from the Ms. 5.5.1 of Govt. Or. Libr. Madras.
Adyar D I 985 (with C.) → Veda-lakṣaṇa (A 3).
Adyar D I 1034 → Sapta-lakṣaṇa.
Gough p. 163 (no.818). Gr. (Yogi-bhāṣya !).
Hamburg StUB (cod.Palmbl. III 8/133) → Veda-lakṣaṇa (HB).
Hamburg StUB (cod.Palmbl. III 8/133) (with C.) → Veda-lakṣaṇa (HB).

Hz 600(b). PL. Tel. 46 fol. (with Pada-darpaṇa of Mallayārya !). Belonged to Vedam Venkatasubrahmanya Somayaji of Allur, Nellur Dist.

Hoshiarpur p. 53 (no.3551). 7 fol. 188 Grantha-s. Extract p. 411. (Also called Yajurveda-kriyā-svara-lakṣaṇa).

Hoshiarpur p. 301 (no.5575). PL. Na. 34 fol. 1300 Grantha-s.

IO 4953 (Mackenzie III 234c). PL. Tel. 7 fol. Written ca. A.D. 1816.

MD 944. PL. Gr. (Na.?). 6 pp. (36ff.).

MD 945. Tel. 11 pp. (294ff.). Col.: Pāṇinīya-śikṣā. The introductory verse and a few lines at the beginning are missing.

MD 946. Tel. 12 pp. (334ff.). Col.: Pāṇinīya-śikṣā. The introductory verse and a few lines at the beginning are missing. A few additional verses and Yohi-prāpti-śikṣā as the colophon are at the end.

MD 947. PL. Gr. (Na.?). 28 pp. (22ff.).

MD 948. 11 pp. (219ff.).

MD 949. PL. Tel. 26 pp. (47ff).

MD 16736. PL. Tel. 12 pp. 165 Grantha-s.

MD 16745. PL. Tel. 4 pp. 23 Grantha-s.

MD 16809. PL. Gr. 1 p. 8 Grantha-s. Incomplete.

MD 17348. PL. Gr. 2 pp. 21 Grantha-s.

MD 19985.

MT 4017(a). PL. Gr. 3 fol. (1-3). Incomplete. Presented in 1921-22 by Krishna Ghanapathigal, Sirukumar, Trichinapalli Dist.

MT 4017(f). PL. Gr. 6 fol. (38-43). Incomplete. Presented in 1921-22 by Krishna Ghanapathigal, Sirukumar, Trichinapalli Dist.

Mysore (1898), p. 6 (no. 52). 5 fol. (102-06).

Mysore I, p. 33.

Mysore ND II 3698 (P 144/10). PL. Tel. 5 fol. (54-60). Extract no. 254.

Mysore ND II 3699 (P 232/ 3). PL. Gr. 7 fol. (9-15).

Mysore ND II 3700 (P 285/ 3). PL. Gr. 2 fol. (23-24).

Mysore ND II 3701 (P 926/ 2). PL. Gr. 1 fol.

Mysore ND II 3702 (P 997/10). PL. Na. 8 fol. (13-20).

Mysore ND II 3703 (P 2886/ 1). PL. Na. 6 fol.

Mysore ND II 3704 (B 861/ 3). Gr. 13 fol.

Mysore Skt. Coll. p. 1 = D. No.13 (1536/2). PL. Gr. 7 fol.

Oppert II 1363. Belonged to Gopalacharyar of Pillapakkam, Kanchipuram Taluk.

Oppert II 7435. Belonged to Venkatarama Sastri of Pillur, Mayavaram Taluk.

Oppert II 7972. Belonged to Venkatarama Dikshita of Sorakayur, Thanjavur Dist.

PUL I, p. 23 (no.121). PL. Gr. 9 fol. 200 Grantha-s.

PUL II. App. p. 13 (no.200). PL. Tel. 4 fol. 100 Grantha-s. (text 23 verses).

Tirupati SVUORI 5076 (4446d). PL. Gr. 11 fol. (52-62).

Trav. Uni. 2346 G. PL. Gr. 1 fol. 25 Grantha-s. Incomplete.

See Kriyā-svara-lakṣaṇa and Yajurveda-kriyā-svara-lakṣaṇa.

Ptd.: ed. by Pullela Sri Ramachandrudu, *Kriyā Svara Lakṣaṇaṃ or Yohibhāṣyam* of Sūru Bhaṭṭa. – Hyderabad : Osmania University, 1983. xviii, 128, xxiv pp. – (Sanskrit

Academy Series 30). The basic Ms. of this edition is presumably mixed with extraneous material. Thus only pp. 1-10, 17-27, 86-128 are parts of this text. The rest is portions of Avarṇi (pp. 11-16, 28-56, 85) and Āvarṇi (pp. 57-84). Other Mss. including those of India Office, Madras and Mysore, collated for this edition do not contain these portions. [SAI (ind 50 B 187/726)]

[CC I 482a; II 112b]

1028 YOHI-PRĀPTI(-LAKṢAṆA) (योहिप्राप्ति /-लक्षण)
on the changes in the accent of verbs caused by their being compounded with prepositions or being in conjunction with "yat" in the *Taittirīya-saṃhitā*.

Adyar 38 H 10 = TR 854. 8 pp. Copied in 1928 from the Ms. I 6.3 of Govt. Or. Libr. Madras.

Adyar D I 950 (19 D 61 = 66253). PL. Gr. 2 fol. (23-24).

Adyar D I 984 → Veda-lakṣaṇa (A 2). (fol. 10b-11a; not noted in the catalogue).

Adyar D I 986 → Veda-lakṣaṇa (A 4).

MD 950. PL. Gr. 11 pp. Incomplete.

MD 14765. PL. Tel. 2 pp. Incomplete.

MT 1964(l). PL. Tel. 2 fol. (105-06). Presented in 1916-17 by Rayaprolu Ramabrahmangaru of Guruza, Gudivada Taluk, Krishna Dist.

MT 2591(i). PL. Tel. 1 fol. (no.237). Presented in 1917-18 by Vasireddi Chandramaulisvaraprasada Bahadur, Zamindar of Muktyala, Krishna Dist.

MT 3887(j). PL. Gr. 1 fol. (84). See remarks. Purchased in 1921-22 from Annasvami Sastrigal, Bhavani, Coimbatore Dist.

Mysore ND II 3697 (P 2262/ 7). PL. Gr. 1 fol. Extract no. 253.

Ptd.: at the end of Ṣaḍviṃśati-sūtra (Grantha script), p. 19.
Also printed in Lakṣaṇa-traya (in Telugu script), p. 42-43.

1029 YOHI-PRĀPTI-LAKṢAṆA (SV) (योहिप्राप्तिलक्षण)
MD 943. Tel. 4 pp. (39ff.). Incomplete.

1030 YOHI-MŪLA (योहिमूल)
Trav. Uni. 10266 J.

1031 YOHI-ŚIKṢĀ see YOHI-PRĀPTI(-ŚIKṢĀ) (योहिशिक्षा / योहिप्राप्ति /-शिक्षा)

[CC I 482a]

1032 RAKĀRA-VYAKTI-LAKṢAṆA (?) see ṚKĀRA-VYAKTI-LAKṢAṆA (रकारव्यक्तिलक्षण / ऋकारव्यक्तिलक्षण)
Mysore ND II 3705 (P 4906/20). PL. Na. 1 fol. (117). Extract no. 255.

*RAGHUNĀTHA CATURVEDIN (रघुनाथचतुर्वेदिन्)
– Sarvānukramaṇī-ṭīkā. Adyar D I 1056.

*RAṄGANĀTHA (रङ्गनाथ)
– Sāma-kārikā. Mysore I, p. 39. = Mysore ND II 3951 (P 5180/ 2). PL. Na. 6 fol. (35-41).

1033 RAṄGANĀTHA-KĀRIKĀ (**रङ्गनाथकारिका**)
Mysore ND II 3706 (P 1970/10). PL. Na. 3 fol. Extract no. 256.
Mysore ND II 3707 (P 4952/50). PL. Na. 5 fol. Incomplete.
Mysore ND II 3708 (A 642/ 3). Kan. 11 fol. Extract no. 257. Different ? Dated 6.8.1919.

1034 RAṄGA-NIRṆAYA (**रङ्गनिर्णय**)
Trav. Uni. 16408 Z10. PL. Mal. 1 fol. 8 Grantha-s.

1035 RAṄGA-PLUTA-LAKṢAṆA (**रङ्गप्लुतलक्षण**)
Mysore p. 2 (no. 53). 1 fol.

[CC I 488b]

1036 RAṄGA-SVARA-NIRṆAYA (**रङ्गस्वरनिर्णय**)
Mysore (1898), p. 6 (no. 53c). 1 fol.

1037 RATNA-KRAMA (**रत्नक्रम**)
Mysore ND II 3709 (C 475/ 3). 1 fol. (17).

1038 RAHASYA-GĀNA-SAṂKHYĀ (**रहस्यगानसंख्या**)
Mysore ND II 3710 (P 2476/ 4). PL. Na. 2 fol. (29-30).

1039 RAHASYA-CCHALĀKṢARA (**रहस्यच्छलाक्षर**)
See under Chalākṣara.

1040 RAHASYA-DĪPA (**रहस्यदीप**)
of Nāgā-bhaṭṭa.
Mysore I, p. 33.

***RĀMA (राम)**
– Jaṭādhikāra. BBRAS 488 (B D 278). 1 fol. Dated A.D. 1787.

***RĀMA (राम)**
Son of Bhāskarārya.
– Lakṣaṇa-ratna-paribhāṣā. 25 verses with a commentary. MT 3860(i).

***RĀMA-KṚṢṆA (रामकृष्ण)**
– Ṣoḍaśa-ślokī-śikṣā.

***RĀMA-KṚṢṆA DĪKṢITA (TRIPĀṬHIN -- NĀNĀBHĀĪ)**
(रामकृष्णदीक्षित / त्रिपाठिन् -- नानाभाई)
Son of Dāmodara Tripāṭhin. Cf. Asko Parpola, op. cit., p. 105f.
– C. Phulla-dīpa on the Phulla-sūtra.
– C. Sāma-tantra-bhāṣya.

***RĀMA-KṚṢṆA-BHAṬṬA (रामकृष्णभट्ट)**
– C. on Vikṛti-vallī also called Aṣṭa-vikṛti-kārikā-vyākhyā.

*RĀMACANDRA or RĀMAŚARMAN (रामचन्द्र / रामशर्मन्)
Son of Siddheśvara, who wrote the Jyotsnā-vṛtti in A.D. 1817.
– Veda-paribhāṣā-kārikā-śikṣā.
– Veda-paribhāṣā-sūtra-śikṣā.
– C. called Jyotsnāvṛtti, on the Vājasaneyi-prātiśākhya.

*RĀMACANDRA-PAṆḌITA (रामचन्द्रपण्डित)
Son of Nāga of the Śaṣa family.
– Svara-prakriyā. Ptd. : See below.

*RĀMA ṬAHALA (रामटहल)
– Svara-vidhi. GJKSV 12038. 7 fol.

*RĀMA-BHAṬṬA (रामभट्ट)
– C. on Pada-muṣṭi-lakṣaṇa. RASB II 913(B) (G 6170). 7 fol. 250 Grantha-s.

*RĀMA-BHAṬṬA GAHVARA (रामभट्ट गह्वर)
Son of Bālaṃ-bhaṭṭa and father of Tippu-bhaṭṭa, who was the author of the *Āśvalāyana-śrauta-sūtra-saṃgraha-dīpikā*, an autographed copy of which is dated A.D. 1775, written at Kāśī (Calcutta Skt. Coll. II 228). See NCC II 224b, III 25, V 339b
– Sarvānukramaṇī-ṭīkā. Adyar D I 1057.

*RĀMĀGNIHOTRIN (रामाग्निहोत्रिन्)
Son of Sadāśiva Agnihotrin.
– C. called Dīpikā, on the Vājasaneyi-prātiśākhya.

*RĀMALIṄGA-DEŚIKA (रामलिङ्गदेशिक)
– Saṃkhyā-cchala. Mysore ND II 3869 (A 642/ 4). Kan. 2 fol. (30-31). Extract no. 294.

*RĀMA-VEDĀNTIN (रामवेदान्तिन्)
– Prathama-śākhā-nyāyanirṇya.

*RĀMĀNUJA (रामानुज)
Son of Śrīnivāsa.
– Svara-varṇa-lakṣaṇa or Sapta-svara-sindhu. Baroda 9917(a).
– Svara-siddhānta-cakra (part of the above ?). Baroda 9917(c).

*RĀVAṆA (रावण)
Also called Rāvaṇa-bhaṭṭa in a few Mss, e.g. IO 4319 (Burnell 546). Several Baiṭh texts pertaining to the *Ṛgveda*, *Taittirīya-saṃhitā* and *Sāmaveda* are ascribed to him → Ṛgveda-padaratna-parīkṣā, Krama-ratna-parīkṣā, Chalākṣarā, Rāvaṇa-baiṭh. See the next entries.

1041 RĀVAṆA-BAIṬH (1) (रावणबैठ्)
Unspecified:
Mysore (1898), p. 5 (no. 52). Gr. 2 fol. (184-85).
Mysore I, p. 33 (5 Mss.).

Mysore ND II 3711-21. Extract no. 258, 259.
PUL II. App. p. 13 (no.201). PL. Gr. 17 fol. (18-34). A.1048 ?
SBD 4379. 12 fol. (Rāvaṇa-baiṭha-pada-ratna; 8th Aṣṭaka).

1042 RĀVAṆA-BAIṬH (2) **(रावणबैठ्)**
→ Ṛgveda-padaratna(-paribhāṣā).
Adyar D I 892.
Mysore Skt. Coll. p. 1 = D. No.14 (846/7). PL. Na. 5 fol. (31-35). agnim īḻe | ṭe | pa |ghe | sā| ja | dra | ghu | du | cā | yajñāṅga ? | gha ja gha ... ki | dhi | The same as IO 4246.
TD 1783-85.

1043 RĀVAṆA-BAIṬH (3) **(रावणबैठ्)**
Beginning:

पदादिनिहिताकारः एदान्तो नः पदान्ततः ।
प्रग्रहश्च पदाद्यात् स्यादिङ्गयं श्लिष्टावसानकम् ॥
षो णश्च सांहितः संधावैदौ चोर्ध्वपदादिगौ।
पदान्तोन्दः पदान्तादीदुद्विसर्गश्च षोडश ॥

End:

न दीर्घगणनेष्वत्र संख्येयः प्रग्रहस्तथा।
लक्ष्याभावो यत्र यत्र तत्र तत्र समः स्मृतः ।
यजुषि प्रतिपञ्चाशदेवमेवोन्नयेत् सदा ॥
इति रावणबैद्-परिभाषा समाप्ता ॥

Hamburg StUB (cod.Palmbl. III 8/133) → Veda-lakṣaṇa (HB). 3 copies; one with paribhāṣā.

1044 RĀVAṆA-BHAIṬ (4) **(रावणभैद्)**
TS.
Beginning:

इषे त्वा । नूथनावैनववेदे । नावीनावनखिनीवेगू । निविनखूणिनिवहीसू । न वारि भ्राजनभानवानभ्रावैध्रानिध्रा वचवि (शनि) वावभ्रावेमारोदी। नाद(नन्नु)देद्व(दु)निदगु।

End:

ने ने भुनवै मा(म) गारो ना । नूवि(थ)न(नवौ)भाषा (नू) नृहा(भा) न । मदगतस दशोत्तरवृद्धिः । स्वराणामेकवृद्धिरिति परिभाषा ॥

Gough p. 162 (Rāvaṇabheda (?) with C.). Tel.
IO 4514 (Mackenzie III 186a). PL. Tel. 1 fol. Written ca. A.D. 1800 (without title).
IO 4515 (Mackenzie II 81b). PL. Na. 2 fol. Written ca. A.D. 1800 (without title).
A different work (Varṇa-krama-lakṣaṇa ?).

IO 4516 (Mackenzie III 235d). PL. Tel. 2 fol. Written ca. A.D. 1800 (without title).
A different work (Varṇa-krama-lakṣaṇa ?).
MD 951. 2 pp.
MD 952. PL. Tel. 14 pp. (81ff.).
MD 953. PL. Tel. 2 pp. (96ff.).
MD 16705. PL. Tel. 1 p. 14 Grantha-s.
MD 16729. PL. Tel. 2 pp. 14 Grantha-s.
MT 485(k). PL. Tel. 1 fol. (66). Presented in 1910-11 by C. Visvanatha Shastrigal of Viziyanagaram.
MT 1964(n). PL. Tel. 1 fol. (110). Presented in 1916-17 by Rayaprolu Ramabrahmangaru of Guruza, Gudivada Taluk, Krishna Dist.
PUL I, p. 23 (no.122). PL. Gr. 14 fol. (60-73).
PUL I, p. 23 (no.123). PL. Gr. 7 fol. Title: Rāvaṇa-baiṭ-lakṣaṇa.
Tirupati SVUORI 5603 (4421c). PL. Gr. 2 fol. (14-15) (nūthanāvainav).
Tirupati SVUORI (3516f). PL. Gr. 2 fol. (1 fol. Paribhāṣā and 1 fol. nūthanāvainav).
Trav. Uni. 2630 Q. PL. Gr. 20 Grantha-s. Incomplete.

– C. Bhāva-prakāśikā of Cakra, son of Rāma.
Beginning:

शङ्खं चक्रं पुस्तकं ज्ञानमुद्रां पाण्यम्भोजैर्धारयन्तं हयास्यम्।
नत्वा श्रीशं नारदोक्तस्य बैटो दुर्ज्ञेयार्थानत्र विज्ञापयामि॥ १॥
अनृवर्णप्लुतल्कारा गृह्यन्ते ऽचः क्रमादिह।
ते ये कटादौ योगार्णा नो वर्ज्या इति निश्चितः ॥ २॥
सहनेन स्थिता चानुवाको ऽत्रैवं हि गण्यते।
नान्यवर्णयुजो वाक्यमनुवाको युगादिना॥ ३॥
योगे द्वितीयो यस्तेन तत्पराचापि वाक्यकम्।
न स वर्णः सवर्गीयो भवेद्योगो ऽपि तत्र सः ॥ ४॥
मो दो गो तः सबिन्दुः सः स्युर्दशोत्तरवृद्धयः ।
एषा नारदबैटः परिभाषा धीमतां च दुर्ज्ञेया।
श्रीरामसूनुना सा विहिता बैडर्थबोधाय॥ ५॥
सुखबोधाय बालानामर्थो ऽयं पारिभाषिकः ।
स्पष्टीकरिष्यते भूयश्चक्रनाम्ना मयाधुना॥ ६॥

अनृवर्णप्लुतेति -- इहास्मिन्नारदबैटि अनृवर्णप्लुतल्काराः । ऋवर्णश्च प्लुताश्च ऌ कारश्च ऋवर्णप्लुतल्काराः । एते येषु न विद्यन्ते ते ...

End:

अत्र दशस्थाने मं विंशतिस्थाने दं त्रिंशत्स्थाने गं चत्वारिंशत्स्थाने तं पञ्चाशत्स्थाने सं । एवंक्रमेण सबिन्दुका भवेयुरित्यर्थः ।

अयं नारदबैडर्थो दुर्ग्रहो धीमतामपि।

एवं स्पष्टीकृतस्तेन चक्रेण विदुषां मुदे ॥
इति नारदबैद्परिभाषाव्याख्यानं समाप्तम् ।
भावप्रकाशिकाख्यानं कृतं बैटो मुनेरिदम् ।
व्याख्यानं तेन चक्रेण कृतं श्रीरामसूनुना ॥
भावप्रकाशिका समाप्ता ॥

Hamburg StUB (cod.Palmbl. III 8/133) → Veda-lakṣaṇa (HB).

1045 RĀVAṆA-BHAIṬ (5) (रावणभैट्)
SV.
Adyar D I 951 (33 D 12 = 75239). PL. Gr. 22 fol. (65-86). = Adyar I, p. 51b.
Adyar D I 952 (33 E 7 = 75254). PL. Gr. 10 fol. (31-40). A different text.
Brl. p. 49 → Chalākṣara.
L 1559. 10 fol. 108 Grantha-s. (Pavamāna-cchalākṣara).
Mysore p. 2 (no. 52). 4 fol. (a. Rāvaṇa).
Oppert I 7216. Belonged to Ivattur Nandikesvara Sastri of Vijayanagaram.
Oppert I 7572. Belonged to S. Kodanda Ramavadhana Pantulu of Vijayanagaram.
Oppert II 1369. Belonged to Gopalacharyar of Pillapakkam, Kanchipuram Taluk.
Oppert II 4889. Belonged to Sri Sankaracharya Matha of Sringeri,
Oppert II 7439. Belonged to Venkatarama Sastri of Pillur, Mayavaram Taluk.
Oppert II 8583. Belonged to Venkatacharyar of Timmagudi near Kumbakonam.
Cf. Sāmaveda-cchala.

[CC I 526b]

1046 REPHAUṢṬHYA-NIRṆAYA (रेफौष्ठ्यनिर्णय)
Mysore ND II 3722 (P 4906/54). PL. Na. 3 fol. (133-35).

1047 REPHA-(PARA-)VISARJANĪYA (रेफ(पर)विसर्जनीय)
Mysore I, p. 33.
Mysore ND II 3723 (P 2262/39). PL. Gr. 2 fol. Extract no. 260.
Mysore ND II 3724 (P 2265/22). PL. Gr. 1 fol. (138).

– C.
Mysore ND II 3725 (P 2265/23). PL. Gr. 1 fol. (138).

1048 LAKṢAṆA-TRAYA (लक्षणत्रय)
Title of the edition of three Veda-lakṣaṇa texts, namely *Sapta-lakṣaṇa*, *Ṣaḍviṃśati-sūtra* and *Jaṭāmaṇi* (in Telugu script) ed. by Gomatham Srinivasa Jyosyar. – Mysore, 1919. 73 pp. This appears to be a reprint of the Grantha script editions. (Title page: Sapta-lakṣaṇī-Ṣaḍvig'ṃśatisūtram (savyākhyā) Jaṭāmaṇiḥ - iti Lakṣaṇatrayam | Taittirīya-yajussambandhi | maisūru gomaṭhaṃ śrīnivāsa jyotiṣikeṇa cittūru śrīśāradāmudrālaye siddhārthi-śravaṇāmāyāṃ samamudryata). [MyORI (B 4109/12669); SAI (87/778*)]

1049 LAKṢAṆA-TRAYA-LAKṢAṆA (**लक्षणत्रयलक्षण**)

of Sītāpati, son of Śaṃkara-bhaṭṭa.

PUL II. App. p. 13 (no.202). PL. Tel. 32 fol. 700 Grantha-s.

1050 LAKṢAṆA-PARIBHĀṢĀ (**लक्षणपरिभाषा**)

Trav. Uni. 12200. PL. Gr. 180 Grantha-s. (M.E. 1071 = A.D. 1896).

1051 LAKṢAṆA-MĀLĀ (**लक्षणमाला**)

of Keśava in eight chapters. It is actually a collection, with a commentary, comprising many small tracts dealing with various topics on Veda-lakṣaṇa :

1-2) Varṇamālā and Svara in general.
3) Begins with the text of Uccodarkī and lists 40 Pluta-svara-s.
4) Avarṇi and Āvarṇi, etc.
5) Vilaṅghya.
6) Napara-tapara.
7) Aniṅgya.
8) Śamāna.

Beginning:

प्रत्यूहतिमिरतरणिं प्रणम्य गणनायकं देवम्।
क्रियते लक्षणमाला पटीयसी बालबोधविधौ॥
लक्षणमालालक्ष्मीः पृथक् पृथक् स्थितिषु लक्षणेषु नहि।
मणिमाला लक्ष्मीरिव पृथक् पृथक् स्थितिषु सन्मणिषु॥
षष्टिश्चतुरधिका वा त्र्यधिका वा लोकवेदयोर्वर्णाः ।
अष्टोत्तरपञ्चाशद् वर्णाः स्युस्तैत्तिरीयशाखायाः ॥

Beginning: (of the commentary)

प्रारिप्सितस्याविघ्नेन परिसमाप्त्यर्थं प्रचयगमनार्थं च इष्टदेवतां नमस्कृत्य ग्रन्थनाम निर्दिश्य ग्रन्थोद्भवं गुणविशेषं दर्शयति -- प्रत्यूहतिमिरमणिम् ... बोधविधौ -- इति। प्रत्यूहो विघ्नः स एव तिमिरं प्रत्यूहतिमिरम्। तद्विषये तरणिं सूर्यं गणनायकं देवं प्रणम्य लक्षणमाला क्रियते। सा किंगुणा। बालाः लक्षणज्ञानरहिताः। तेषां बोधः लक्षणज्ञानम्। तस्य विधिः विधानम्। तत्र पटीयसी पटुतरा। ननु पुरातनानामेव लक्षणानामत्र वक्ष्यमाणत्वात् नार्थो लक्षणमालया इत्यत्राह -- लक्षणमालालक्ष्मीः पृथक् पृथक् स्थितिषु सन्मणिषु -- इति। ... आदौ वर्णानुद्दिशति --

षष्टिश्चतुरधिका वा त्र्यधिका वा लोकवेदयोर्वर्णाः ।
अष्टोत्तरषष्टिपक्षाः षष्टिस्तैत्तिरीयशाखायाः ॥

Calicut University Sanskrit Department. No. 326 (serial no. 512 of the printed catalogue). 132 fol. Mal. Incomplete.

Hoshiarpur p. 53 (no.3758). PL. Mal. 236 fol. 2500 Grantha-s. Extract 411.

MT 2881(h). PL. Gr. 2 fol. (41-42). Incomplete. Presented in 1918-19 by Venkatagiri Appalacharyar of Triplicane.

TCD 28. PL. Mal. 124 fol. 8250 (3370) Grantha-s (of which 1100 comprise the text). Ends with Śamāna.

Trav. Uni. C.334. = TCD 28.

Trav. Uni. T.132. 3370 Grantha-s.

Triv. Cur. II 1-2. Mal. 600 (text) and 3800 (C.) Grantha-s. Obtained from Devan Parameswaran Nambudripad, Idapallimanakkal.

1052 LAKṢAṆA-RATNA(-BHAIṬ) (VEDA-LAKṢAṆA-RATNA)
(लक्षणरत्न /-भैट् / वेदलक्षणरत्न)
TS. Of Vaidyanātha-bhaṭṭa.

Beginning:

अम्भोजसंभूतगभीरनाभिं विभूतिकेलीभवनायमानम्।
विद्याविशुद्ध्यै विबुधाः श्रयध्वं (प्रपद्ये) विद्यावदग्रेसरवैद्यनाथम्॥
आखुवाहनसेनानीपार्वतीपरमेश्वरान्।
सकलश्रेयसः सिद्ध्यै सततं प्रणमाम्यहम्॥

अथ यजुषि प्रतिपञ्चाशत् पदादिनिहिताकारपदान्तनकारयोः पदान्ततकारप्रग्रहयोः इङ्ग्यपदाद्याकारयोः संहितावसानस्य च सांहितषत्वणत्वयोश्च एकादेशे उत्तरपदाद्यैकारौकारपदान्तङकार (दकाराणां च पदान्तसमानाक्षरदीर्घस्य च समविषमसंख्याद्योतकं विसर्जनीयसंख्याप्रतिपादकं प्रति) पञ्चाशदेकैकमक्षरं प्रत्यनुवाकमेकैकं वाक्यं वैण्णाम लक्षणरत्नं वक्ष्यामः । अत्र प्रवर्त्तका वर्णा अकाराद्युकारपर्यन्ताः प्लुतवर्जिताः स्वराः पञ्च । ऊकाराद्यौकारपर्यन्ता ऋ-लृवर्जिताः स्वराः पञ्च । प्रवर्त्तकाः कगौ चजौ टडौ तदौ पबौ मनौ लवौ शसौ चेति । अत्र द्वन्द्वसमासयुक्ततत्तल्लक्ष्यद्वन्द्वं संहत्यैकरूपतो विगणय्य समविषमसंख्या द्रष्टव्या । पदादिनिहिताकारपदान्तनकारौकद्विके समौ च द्विद्विकविषमौ ॥ २ ॥ ··· इति वैद्यनाथभट्टविरचितलक्षणरत्नपरिभाषा समाप्ता। इषे त्वा। मा। प्यु शौ दु। च द्यौ।

End:

शो। अग्नये समनमत्। टोदु। ये ते पन्थानः । ते म। यो वै। श्ये मू॥

शोंमिकः कामनाचेयाल्याटाशियोहशैहयः ।
टौद्विच्छिद् ·· कोनविंशत्यां चेत्युजज्ञिके॥
आग्नेयस्तद्विरुद्रेशाहाग्नेये टोदुयेदियः ।
श्योमुप्रश्ने पञ्चमके च ··· शदीरिताः ॥ ८॥

सप्तमकाण्डस्समाप्तः ॥

कमलङ्क्व्यग्रहारे जन्मभूः स्वामिशास्त्रिजः ।
बैङ्गाक्यान्यकरोच्छ्लोकान् वेङ्कुशास्त्री यजुश्श्रुतेः॥ २९॥

गृहाणे धारणे चाह्रा परिभाषा यतस्ततः ।
सा श्लोकरूपा न कृता वर्णा एव कृता मया ॥

Adyar D I 953 (20 C 19 = 66985). PL. Gr. 13 fol. (Baiṭlakṣaṇam). = Adyar I, p. 51b. Title: Bhaiṭ-vākya Rāvaṇa-kṛta. Versified by Veṅku-śāstri.

Adyar D I 954 (20 C 23 = 66989). PL. Gr. 4 fol. (iṣe tvā | mā) = Adyar I, p. 51b. Title: Lakṣaṇa-ratna-paribhāṣā.

Adyar D I 955 (29 I 28 = 73580). PL. Gr. 5 fol. (89ff.) = Adyar I, p. 51b. Title: Bhaiṭ-vākya Rāvaṇa-kṛta (Rāvaṇa-bhaiṭ).

Adyar D XIII 191 (VB 129a). PL. Gr. 43 fol. Title: Baiṭ-lakṣaṇa-ratnam.

Hamburg StUB (cod.Palmbl. III 8/133) → Veda-lakṣaṇa (HB).

MD 954. PL. Gr. 14 pp. (47ff.).

MD 16819. PL. Gr. 10 pp. (54ff.). 135 Grantha-s. Title on the margin : Vaidyanātha-bhaiṭ.

MT 4783(d). PL. Gr. 4 fol. (25-28). Title: Lakṣaṇa-ratna-bhaiṭ. Presented in 1924-25 by the Secretary to the Trustees of Sri Yogi Parthasarathi Ayyangar's Charities, Triplicane, Madras.

Mysore (1898), p. 5 (no. 52). Gr. 6 fol. (179-84). Title: Veda-vijjana-saṃmata-lakṣaṇa-ratna.

Mysore I, p. 33.

Mysore ND II 3660 (P 2326/ 2). PL. Gr. Extract no. 235. Title: Baiṭ (Baiṇ-ṇāma-lakṣaṇam).

Mysore ND II 3661 (B 253/ 3). Gr. Extract no. 236. Title: Baiṭ. (The opening verse is from the Kālanirṇaya-śikṣā).

Mysore ND II 3727 (P 926/ 5). PL. Gr. 8 fol. Extract no. 261. Title: Lakṣaṇaratna-paribhāṣā.

Mysore ND II 3728 (P 4468/11). PL. Na. 8 fol. (96-113). Title: Vaidyanātha-baiṭ(Lakṣaṇaratnam).

Mysore ND II 3729 (B 860/ 1). Gr. 13 fol. (75-87). Title: Vaidyanāthabaiṭ(Lakṣaṇa-ratnam).

RASB II 491 (G 1155). 6 fol. 100 Grantha-s. Copied in Kāśī. Dated V.S. 1672. It contains two additional benedictory verses at the beginning and the full text of the Bhaiṭ.

Tirupati SVUORI 5630 (1756b). PL. Gr. 7 fol. Col.: iti śrī veda-vidvajjana-saṃmata-vaidyanātha-bhaṭṭa-viracita- lakṣaṇa-ratnaṃ lakṣaṇaratnaṃ samāptam | vaidyanātha-bhaiṭ samāptam ||

Trav. Uni. 2938 I. PL. Gr. 16 Grantha-s.

1053 LAKṢAṆA-RATNA-PARIBHĀṢĀ (**लक्षणरत्नपरिभाषा**)

of Rāma, son of Bhāskarārya. 25 verses with a commentary, supplementing the work of Vaidyanātha.

Beginning: (3860)

नमस्कृत्य गुरून् साक्षाच्छिवसूर्यस्वरूपिणः ।

स्वकृतं लक्षणं रामो व्याख्यात्यृग्यजुषोः समम्॥

प्रारिप्सितग्रन्थस्याविघ्नेन परिसमाप्तये आदावभ्यर्हितस्वेष्टदेवतानमस्कारपूर्वकं चिकीर्षितं प्रतिजानीते -- प्रणम्येति।

प्रणम्य सिद्धिविघ्नेशं वैद्यनाथकृतं वरम्।
भास्करार्यतनूजेन लक्षणं पूर्यते ऽधुना॥

भास्करेति। भास्कराख्यास्तातचरणा आर्या गुरवः तेषां तनूजेन जन्मना विद्यया च। ननु वैद्यनाथकृतलक्षणस्य (सत्त्वेन स्व-) कर्तव्यत्वाभावात् त्वद्यत्नेनालमित्यत आह पूर्यत इति। लक्ष्यलक्षणसंग्रहाभ्यां पूर्यते न तु क्रियत इति भावः। तल्लक्षणस्वरूपं वक्तव्यं चाह

यजुषि प्रतिपञ्चाशल्लक्षणं वच्मि सारवत्।
अत्र प्रवर्तकान् वर्णान् लक्ष्याणि च बहून्यथ॥

इदमुपलक्षणमृग्वेदे प्रतिवर्गमित्यपि ज्ञेयम्। प्रतिपञ्चाशदेकैकमक्षरं प्रत्यनुवाकमेकं वाक्यमत्रेत्याह --

प्रतिपञ्चाशदेकैकमक्षरं रत्नलक्षणे।
यावत्संख्यानुवाकस्य तावद् वाक्यमिहोच्यते॥

End:

इङ्ग्यं पृथक्पदं तस्मात् पूर्वोत्तरपदस्थितम्। लक्ष्यं पृथक्पदं पदद्वयमिङ्ग्यम्। तस्माद्धेतोः पूर्वोत्तरपदस्थितम्। पूर्वपदे उत्तरपदे च स्थितं सर्वमपि लक्ष्यं स्यात्। ननु लक्ष्ये सति समं विषममिति ज्ञायते। तदभावे कथमित्यत आह -- ज्ञापयतीत्येव लक्ष्याभावः समो भवेत्। पञ्चाशति वर्तमानो लक्ष्याभावश्चेत् स सम इति ज्ञेयम्॥

इति लक्षणरत्नस्य परिभाषामितार्थदा।
रामेण प्रेरितेनार्यैर्व्याख्याता सा यथामति॥

MT 3860(i). PL. Gr. 5 fol. (136-40). Purchased in 1921-22 from Annasvami Sastrigal, Bhavani, Coimbatore Dist.

1054 LAKṢAṆĀNUKRAMAṆIKĀ (लक्षणानुक्रमणिका)
MD 14750. PL. Tel. 3 pp → Veda-lakṣaṇānukramaṇikā.

*LAKṢMAṆA (लक्ष्मण)
See Jaṭāvallabha Śāstrin.

1055 LAKṢMĪKĀNTA-ŚIKṢĀ or CATUḤ-ŚLOKĪ (लक्ष्मीकान्तशिक्षा / चतुःश्लोकी)
Four verses dealing with the characteristics of saṃdhi-s, doubling, accentuation, etc. of the Taittirīya school.

रक्षा वैदिकवर्णानां शिक्षा दुर्मतिरक्षसाम्।
लक्ष्मीं दद्याच्चतुःश्लोकी लक्ष्मीकान्तस्य भूतिवत्॥

अच्पूर्वं हलि हल्द्विरुक्तमपि च स्पर्शो लवोर्ध्वस्वराद्
ऊर्ध्वार्धाद् धलि वाचि वा हलपि वानुस्वारयुक्तादिमौ।
द्वावन्योन्यसहायतोन्तगनङौ ह्रस्वात् परावच्परौ
द्वे द्वे स्तो ऽपि च पूर्वमागममितस्तुर्यद्वितीयं हलौ॥ १॥
भूते धाम च पाथ एष परमात्यात्यग्रगाः पूर्वगाः
किं चोर्ध्वा उपसर्गतश्चिखिभुजा लक्ष्यात् क्वचित् पूर्वगाः ।
तन्मध्ये प्रथमागमश्च सदृशस्पर्शे ऽप्यघोषोष्मणाम्
ऊर्ध्वाधः प्रथमो भजेत् सषशतो नान्तो द्वितीयं न वा॥ २॥
नोष्मा तु प्रथमस्वरात् प्रथमतो नानुत्तमे हल्परे
वर्गेनुत्तम उत्तमेन न विसर्गो लो हशस्पर्शगः ।
लोपः स्पर्शपरश्च नश्च यवहात् पूर्वो ऽन्तगो न द्विधा
मः पूर्वो ऽनुनासिकं च यवलस्पर्शात् सवर्णं भजेत्॥ ३॥
ङोनन्तादधयोः क्रमेण परतस्स्यातां कगावागमौ
ङात् कस्याट्टनतस्तु तश्च सषयोः स्पर्शादनुष्मात्मनः।
ऊर्ध्वस्थेष्वपि चोत्तमेषु च यमानाहुस्तथानुत्तमान्
नासिक्यं नणमैर्युताद्यजुषि हाङ्गस्याच्छपूर्वस्य कः॥ ४॥
वर्णक्रमचतुश्लोकीं वर्णक्रमविचक्षणाः ।
पाठतश्चार्थतो ज्ञात्वा विजयध्वं दिशो दश॥

Adyar D I 956 (23 E 25 = 69758). PL. Gr. 2 fol. (32-33).

Adyar D I 957 (29 I 28 = 73580). PL. Gr. 2 fol. (76b-77a). Lacks end.

Adyar D I 958 (40 A 81 = PM 2983). 6 fol. Title: Lakṣmīkānta-saṃvāda.

Adyar 54 A 26 = TR 853. 11 pp. Title: Lakṣmīkānta-saṃvāda. Copy of PM 2983.

BHU B 3904d (D 11/654). 3 fol. (10-12) (with C.). Incomplete.

Hoshiarpur p. 53 (no.3757). PL. Tel. 3 fol. 68 Grantha-s. Ptd. ?

MD 16741. PL. Tel. At the end of the Ms. catalogued as Aniṅgyādi.

MD 16746. PL. Tel. 55 Grantha-s. Contains the text in four stanzas and C. on two stanzas only. The text is called Catuḥ-ślokī.

Oppert I 7147. Belonged to Pola Lakshmanavadhani of Vijayanagaram.

Oppert I 7220. Belonged to Ivattur Nandikesvara Sastri of Vijayanagaram.

PUL II. App. p. 13 (no.203). Gr. 7 fol. 50 Grantha-s.

PUL II. App. p. 13 (no.204). PL. Tel. 3 fol. 50 Grantha-s. (Varṇa-krama-catuḥślokī-bhāṣya).

SBD 47959. 1 fol. Incomplete. 2 verses only. Title: Varṇa-śikṣā. There are two tables each containing 25 squares in which the letters of the alphabet are entered. Its significance is not clear.

Tirupati SVUORI 5633 (3516b). PL. Gr. 1 fol. (16).

[CC I 537b]

1056 LAKṢMĪKĀNTA-ŚIKṢĀ (लक्ष्मीकान्तशिक्षा)

MD 955. Tel. 19 pp. (300ff.). .... (= Skt. Texts on Phonetics, pp. 290-307).
This is identical with MD 874 (Ucca-svara-nirṇaya). Cf. Adyar D I 1096 (Svara-śikṣā).

*LAKṢMĪDHARA(-SŪRI) (लक्ष्मीधर /-सूरि)

Son of Nimbadeva and Bakāmbikā and brother of Nāganātha of Candrapura.
– Galita-pradīpa. See above.

[CC I 538a]

1057 LAGHU-ṚKTANTRA(-SAṂGRAHA) (लघु-ऋक्तन्त्र /-संग्रह)

156 verses divided into 40 sections. Not an abridgement of the Ṛktantra. Called Laghu-ṛktantra-saṃgraha in the introductory verse, but Laghu-ṛktantra in the last verse and in the colophon at the end.

Beginning:

ब्रह्माणं शंकरं विष्णुं व्यासं चान्यान् मुनीश्वरान्।
नमस्कृत्य करोम्यद्य लघु-ऋक्तन्त्रसंग्रहम्॥
अथ वर्णोत्पत्तिः । ह्राः कण्ठे । उरसि विसर्जनीयो वा । अकुहविसर्जनीयानां कण्ठः । जिह्वामूले :कृ॥ ...

End:

संहितायां विसर्गश्च द्विर्भावं व्यञ्जनस्य च।
सवर्णस्य यणश्चैव वृद्धेश्चापि गुणस्य च॥
प्रगृह्यस्य विकाराश्च पञ्चैव परिकीर्तिताः ।
लघु-ऋक्तन्त्रग्रन्थे ऽस्मिन् वनसंख्याकसंधयः ॥

Adyar D I 959 (33 D 12 = 75239). PL. Gr. 11 fol. (37-47). = Adyar I, p. 48b. Title: Ṛktantra-saṃgraha.
Adyar D I 960 (33 E 7 = 75254). PL. Gr. 8 fol. (60a-67a).
Baroda 9911(e). PL. Gr. 12 fol. 250 Grantha-s. = CLB I, p. 34. Extract pp. 161-62.
Trav. Uni. 11822 C. PL. Gr. 725 Grantha-s (with C.). Incomplete.

Ptd.: ed. by Suryakanta, *Sāmalakṣaṇa-sahito Laghu-ṛktantrasaṃgrahaḥ*, with Commentary, Notes, Introduction embodying a complete history of the nomenclatory grammatical Literature and Indices. – Lahore, 1940. 10, 22, 64, 56, 16 pp. (based on the Ms. Adyar D I 959). For an analysis of this see his introduction, pp. 18ff. [Adyar (H080 MCL 11); NL (180 Jb 94 7)]
Reprinted : New Delhi : Panini, Meharchand Lachhmandas, 1982. – (Panini Vaidika Granthamala 1). [BORI (40821); UBTÜ (23 A 8760); SAI (ind 51 D 784/1527)]

1058 LAGHU-PRĀTIŚĀKHYA (लघुप्रातिशाख्य)

An abridgement of the *Vājasaneyi-prātiśākhya*,

RASB II 1527 (G 6177). 2 fol. Incomplete.
SBD 2119. 11 fol.

1059 LAGHU-ṚGVIDHĀNA (लघु-ऋग्विधान)
See Ṛgvidhāna (3). – Laghu- or Kaniṣṭha- .

1060 LAGHU-MĀDHYANDINĪYA-ŚIKṢĀ (लघुमाध्यन्दिनीयशिक्षा)
A work in 28 verses dealing with saṃdhi, Ayogavāha, Hasta-nirdeśa, etc. See F. Kielhorn : Remarks on the Śikṣās in : *Indian Antiquary*, vol. V, p. 196 (reprint in : *Kleine Schriften*, vol. I, pp. 158-69).

Beginning:

अथ शिक्षां प्रवक्ष्यामि माध्यन्दिनमतं यथा।
षकारस्य खकारः स्याट्टुकयोगे तु नो भवेत्॥ १॥
इषे लक्ष्यं कृष्ण उक्षा समुद्रः प्रत्युदाहृतिः ।
पदादौ विद्यमानस्य ह्यसंयुक्तस्य यस्य च॥ २॥
आदेशो हि जकारः स्याद्युक्तः संहरणेन तु।
यज्ञेन यज्ञं वै लक्ष्यं मयूरे प्रत्युदाहृतिः ॥ ३॥
तस्माद्यज्ञात् सर्वहुतः समस्माद्यत्तथैव च।
रेफेणाथ हकारेण युक्तस्य सर्वथा भवेत्॥ ४॥
सूर्यो बाह्यं तु वै लक्ष्यं शष्पाय प्रत्युदाहृतिः ।
यकारर्कारयुक्तस्य जकारः सर्वथा भवेत्॥ ५॥

End:

दीर्घे ऽपि चोभयोः क्षेप इति शास्त्रव्यवस्थितिः ।
यथा स्फटिकदण्डादिरुपाधिवशतो भवेत्॥ २६॥
तद्वदूष्मा प्रयोक्तव्यो हिहुहेहो निदर्शनम्।
वसोः पवित्रं वै तत्र ह्युदाहरणमुच्यते॥ २७॥
ऋकारः खलु सर्वत्र ह्येकारसदृशो भवेत्।
हृदे मृगस्तृतीया च ऋचं वाचमथापरम्॥ २८॥
इति लघुमाध्यन्दिनीयशिक्षा समाप्ता॥

Göttingen 158(4). 2 fol. (53-54). Incomplete. Verses 1-14.
RASB II 1516(II) (G 3260). 2 fol. 28 Grantha-s.
SBD 47212. 3 fol. (Laghu-śikṣā) Col. Mādhyandinīya-laghu-śikṣā.
SBD 48292. 1 fol. (Mādhyandinīya-laghu-śikṣā).
Wellcome Inst. London. Z 47a.

Ptd.: in Śikṣā-saṃgraha. – Benares, 1889, pp. 114-16. – (Ben. S. S. 10).

1061 LAGHU-ŚIKṢĀ (लघुशिक्षा)
SBD 47212. 3 fol. = Laghu-mādhyandinīya-śikṣā.

1062 LAGHU-VṚTTI (लघुवृत्ति)
Name of the commentary on the *Uccodarkī*. Baroda 6255(c). MD 878.

1063 LAGHU-SAMĀNA (लघुसमान)
of Nāgadeva, son of Yajñanārāyaṇa. Adyar D I 961, 962. For Mss. details see Ṛksarva-śamāna.

1064 LAGHV-AMOGHĀNANDINĪ-ŚIKṢĀ (लघ्वमोघानन्दिनीशिक्षा)
→ (Laghv-)Amoghānandinī-śikṣā

1065 LUPTARK-ŚIKṢĀ (लुप्तर्क्शिक्षा)
→ Galadṛk-śikṣā.

1066 LEṢA(-KHA)-GRANTHA (?) (लेष(ख)ग्रन्थ)
IM 2520. 5 fol. (2-6). Dated V.S. 1577. Actually Upalekha-sūtra.

1067 LOMAŚA(ŚĪ)-ŚIKṢĀ (लोमश(शी)-शिक्षा)
Attributed to Garga. See F. Kielhorn : Remarks on the Śikṣās in : *Indian Antiquary*, vol. V, p. 196 (reprint in : *Kleine Schriften*, vol. I, pp. 158-69).

Beginning:

लोमशीयां प्रवक्ष्यामि गर्गाचार्येण चिन्तिताम्।
साभिधानां यथोक्तां त्वाचार्यवचनं यथा॥ १॥
ह्रस्वं दीर्घं तथा वृद्धमभिगीतं तु सामगाः।
मुहुर्मृदङ्गवत् कुर्युः संपातोत्थानसंज्ञवत्॥ २॥
केन कम्पातितः कम्पः संयोगो येन कम्पते।
किं वा कम्प इति प्रोक्तो येनासौ कम्प उच्यते॥ ३॥
पूर्वाङ्गेण हतं पूर्वं पराङ्गेण तु धारितम्।
व्यञ्जनेन द्विधा भिन्नः स्वरे भीतस्तु कम्पते॥ ४॥
दीर्घकम्पे ऽध्यर्धमात्रा तृतीये परिकीर्तिता।
द्वितीये अर्धमात्रा तु प्रयोगो घण्टलालवत्॥ ५॥

End:

शून्ये गृहे पिशाचस्तु गर्जते न च दृश्यते।
एवं यकारा वक्तव्या धियग्निर्जर्म निदर्शनम्॥

Adyar D I 963 (I A 19 = TR 19). Gr. 8 fol. (pp. 81-95). = Adyar I, p. 53a.
Alwar 288.
BORI 114 of 1879-80. 7 fol. 55 Grantha-s. Dated V.S. 1724.

GB 30. 14 fol. Copied in 1875 for Kielhorn through R. L. Mitra. See F. Kielhorn : Remarks on the Śikṣās in : *Indian Antiquary*, vol. V, p. 196 (reprint in : *Kleine Schriften*, vol. I, pp. 158-69).
GB 31. 7 fol. Dated Śaka 1798 (A.D. 1876).
Hamburg StUB (Oppert 45a2). PL. Gr. 5 fol.
Haug p. 30 (no.79a) = München 165.
IM 1976. 5 fol. Dated V.S. 1604.
IM 2510C. 6 fol. (20-25). Dated V.S. 1833.
IM 2539.
IM 2596. 6 fol.
IM 5154. 3 fol.
IO 4954 (Burnell 496d). Gr. 5 fol. (17-21). Copied from a Mysore Ms. in A.D. 1877.
L 132. 6 fol. 85 Grantha-s. Dated V.S. 1926.
MD 956. 11 pp. (83ff.)
MD 15645. 15 pp. (25ff.). 90 Grantha-s.
München 165. 5 fol. (18-22). Transcript made in 1817.
N-W P V 150 (no.46). 5 fol.
Oppert II 411. Belonged to Venkatarama Srauti of Mullandram, N. Arcot Dist.
Oppert II 7442. Belonged to Venkatarama Sastri of Pillur, Mayavaram Taluk.
Oudh IX 4 (no.4). 14 pp. 150 Grantha-s. Belonged to Pandit Ramanarayana of Lucknow.
Oxf. CS c.62(7). 7 fol.
P 7.
Peters. II, p. 180 (no.55). 5 fol.
PUL I, p. 132 (no.24). 25 fol. 600 Grantha-s (with other 5 SV works).
RASB II 1495 (G 662). 8 fol. 84 Grantha-s. Dated V.S. 1931.
RASB II 1496 (G 2808). 7 fol. 84 Grantha-s. Dated V.S. 1931.
SB p. 35 (no.101). 5 fol. 112 Grantha-s. = SBD 47251.
SBD 2090. 6 fol. Incomplete. (Contains Gautamī-śikṣā also). Dated V.S. 1679.
SBD 2091. 10 fol. Incomplete. (Contains Gautamī-śikṣā also).
SBD 47251. 5 fol. Dated V.S. 1926.
Stein p. 39 (no. 804). 6 fol.
Trav. Uni. 2915 G. PL. Gr. 100 Grantha-s.

Ptd.: in Śikṣā-saṃgraha. – Benares, 1889, pp. 452-62. – (Ben. S. S. 10).
Also included in: Chāndogya Brāhmaṇam. – Kumbakonam : Govinda Deekshithar Punya Smarana Samiti (ed.). Part II. 1981. Appendix pp. 1-8. [(SAI ***)].
[CC I 546b; II 129b, 223b]

1068 LAUGĀKṢI-ŚIKṢĀ (लौगाक्षिशिक्षा)
→ Śikṣā(hyā)-pāṭha.
BORI 21 of 1875-76 (col. on fol. 24b). See Siddheshwar Varma, *Critical Studies....* , p. 150.
HO Stein 141. 47 fol. Śāradā script. Copied in 1894.

*VARADARĀJA (वरदराज)

– C. called Daśatayī on the Pratihārasūtra. Ptd. : See above.

– Sāma-sūtra-vyākhyā ?

Khn. p. 10 (no.38). 162 fol. Dated Śaka 1742; Ashte Limaye.

[CC I 710a]

*VARARUCI (वररुचि)

Quoted in the *Tribhāṣya-ratna*, 1.18, 2.14, 19, 4.40, etc. The *Phulla-sūtra* is ascribed to him in South India. He is traditionally known to have written a Bhāṣya on the *Taittirīya-prātiśākhya*, as mentioned by Somayārya in his *Tribhāṣya-ratna* (introduction) and Vīrarāghava in his *Śabda-brahma-vilāsa* (which see).

– Sāma-paribhāṣā also known as the Paribhāṣā-lakṣaṇa or Salakṣaṇa-paribhāṣā or Sāma-lakṣaṇa.

[CC I 551b]

1069 VARARUCI-ŚIKṢĀ (वररुचिशिक्षा)

One Vararuci-śikṣā is mentioned in TCD 32-B.

Mysore I, p. 34.

Mysore ND II 3730 (B 601/ 1). Kan. 13 fol. Extract no. 262.

– C.

Mysore ND II 3731 (B 601/ 2). Kan. 13 fol. Extract no. 263.

1070 VARGĀNUKRAMAṆIKĀ (VĀJASANEYA) (वर्गानुक्रमणिका / वाजसनेय)

PUL I, p. 23 (no.124). 22 fol. (Akārādikrama with ref. to mantra-s).

1071 VARṆA-KRAMA-CATUḤ-ŚLOKĪ-BHĀṢYA (वर्णक्रमचतुःश्लोकीभाष्य)

of Lakṣmīkānta → Catuḥ-ślokī and Lakṣmīkānta-śikṣā.

PUL II. App. p. 13 (no.204). PL. Tel. 3 fol. 50 Grantha-s.

1072 VARṆA-KRAMA-DARPAṆA (1) (वर्णक्रमदर्पण)

of Vemāna Bhairavāvadhānin (or Bhairavārya). In MD 15503 the author's name is given as Appayācārya. It is a fairly extensive work, pertaining to the *Taittirīya-saṃhitā* and dealing with the same topics as the Prātiśākhya-s and Śikṣā-s. It quotes among others *Śikṣā-samuccaya* (on fol. 102 b) and *Sarva-sammata-śikṣā* (fol. 107a). Divided into various sections as Saṃjñā-prakaraṇa, Vyañjanasaṃdhi-prakaraṇa, Dvitva-prakaraṇa, etc. Readings vary considerably in different Mss.

Beginning:

प्रणम्य शंभोश्चरणाब्जयुग्मं वाण्या गणेशस्य तथा गुरूणाम्।
सतां मुदे तित्तिरिसंहितायां करोमि वर्णक्रमदर्पणाख्यम्॥

तत्रादौ प्रातिशाख्योक्तानि पारिभाषिकसूत्राणि प्रदर्श्यन्ते -- अथ वर्णसमाम्नायः । अथशब्दो मङ्गलार्थः । तथा चोक्तम्।

ओंकारश्चाथशब्दश्च द्वावेतौ ब्रह्मणः पुरा।

कण्ठं भित्त्वा विनिर्यातौ तस्मान्माङ्गलिकावुभौ॥

इति । यद्वा आनन्तर्यार्थो ऽथशब्दः । तथा चोक्तं नामलिङ्गानुशासने -- मङ्गलानन्तरारम्भप्रश्नकात्स्न्येष्वथो अथेति । वेदाध्ययने जाते सति लक्षणस्यावसरप्राप्तत्वात् तदभ्यासः कर्तव्य इत्यानन्तर्यार्थः । संहिताध्ययनं प्रथमं कर्तव्यमनन्तरं पदाध्ययनमन्ततः क्रमाध्ययनम् इति मन्तव्यम् । तथा चोक्तम् -- अधीत्य विधिवत् पूर्वम् ...

Adyar D I 964 (20 E 3 = 67133). PL. Tel. 44 fol. = Adyar I, p. 51b. Dated Monday, the 1st day of the dark fortnight of Kārtika, in the year Rudhirodgāri (A.D. 1792 ?), and copied by Somayāji Vaṅkaṭacennulu; the former owner was Veṅkaṇṇa.

Adyar D XIII 192 (VB 128b). PL. Tel. 28 fol. The same as MD 15503.

Hoṣhiarpur p. 53 (no.4454). PL. Tel. 30 fol. 600 Grantha-s. Ptd. ?

Hoshiarpur p. 53 (no.3533). 8 fol. 105 Grantha-s. Diff. ?

Hz 1439. PL. Gr. 43 fol. Extract p. 135. Belonged to the late Raja Ghanapathi of Tiruvidaimarudur, Thanjavur Dist.

MD 15503. Gr. 117 pp. (135ff.). 1313 Grantha-s (a. Appayācārya).

MD 16208. PL. Gr. 68 pp. (fol. 1-34). 1020 Grantha-s Title: Prātiśākhya with Vyākhyā Varṇa-krama-darpaṇa of Bhairavārya. Concluding verse:

तैत्तिरीयस्य वेदस्य वर्णानां क्रमदर्पणम्।
वैमानभैरवार्येण बालोपकृतये कृतम्॥

Mysore p. 2 (no. 57). 53 fol.

Mysore (1898), p. 6 (no. 57). Gr. 53 fol.

Mysore I, p. 34 (2 Mss.).

Mysore Skt. Coll. p. 1 = D. No.15 (824). PL. Tel. 30 fol. (a. Bhairavāvadhānin). Virodhi-uttarāyaṇavasantartau caitrakṛṣṇapañcamyāṃ saumyavāsare ...

PUL I, p. 23 (no.125). PL. Tel. 30 fol. 700 Grantha-s (a. Bhairavāvadhānin).

1073 VARṆA-KRAMA-DARPAṆA (2) (वर्णक्रमदर्पण)

Unspecified:

Gough p. 163. Gr.

Mysore I, p. 34.

Oppert I 2426. PL. Gr. 43 pp. Belonged to Sri Sarasvati Bhandaram Committee of Tiruvallikkeni, Madras.

Oppert I 7225. Belonged to Ivattur Nandikesvara Sastri of Vijayanagaram.

Oppert I 7573. Belonged to S. Kodanda Ramavadhana Pantulu of Vijayanagaram.

Oppert II 772. Belonged to Ghanapathi Shingaracharyar of Alasur, Madurantakam Taluk.

Oppert II 5261. Belonged to Pichchu Dikshitar of Akhilandapuram, Thanjavur Dist.

Oppert II 5783. Belonged to Shingaracharyar of Kalyanapuram, Thanjavur Dist.

Oppert II 7443. Belonged to Venkatarama Sastri of Pillur, Mayavaram Taluk.

Oppert II 7974. Belonged to Venkatarama Dikshita of Sorakayur, Thanjavur Dist.

Oppert II 9087. Belonged to Ganapati Lakshminarayana Sastri of Tiruvadi, Thanjavur Dist.

Trav. Uni. 2630 C. PL. Gr. 90 Grantha-s.
Trav. Uni. 4028 G. PL. Gr. 23 Grantha-s. Incomplete.

C.
Trav. Uni. 2630 E. PL. Gr. 100 Grantha-s.

[CC I 553a]

1074 VARṆA-KRAMA-DARPAṆA (3) (वर्णक्रमदर्पण)
Tirupati SVUORI 5800 (3516d). PL. Gr. 3 fol. (20-23) (with C.).

Beginning:

स्वरपूर्वमियाद् द्वित्वं व्यञ्जनं व्यञ्जने परे।
लपूर्वे च वपूर्वे च द्वित्वं स्पर्शमवाप्नुयात्॥
लकारं पञ्चमैर्युक्तमन्तस्थाभिश्च संयुतम्।
औरस्यं तं विजानीयात् ... कर्णमाञ्जसम्॥
स्वरपूर्वव्यञ्जने च परे तन्मध्यवर्तिव्यञ्जनं द्विवर्णं रूपद्वयमश्नुते। अक्तं रिहाणा।

End:

एवमूह्यमन्यदपि यत् किंचिद् विचारणीयं सम्यक्। इति वर्णक्रमदर्पणव्याख्यानम्॥

1075 VARṆA-KRAMA-DARPAṆA (4) (वर्णक्रमदर्पण)

Beginning:

स्वरपूर्वमियाद् द्वित्वं व्यञ्जनं व्यञ्जनोत्तरे। स्वरपूर्वं व्यञ्जनपरं व्यञ्जनं द्वित्वमापद्यते। यथा उरु प्रथस्व। पशुना क्रीणाति। अग्रे गाः। उकार-रेफ-उकार-पकारद्वित्व-रेफाकार इत्यादि।

End:

कखयोः पफयोश्चैव विसर्गो यत्र दृश्यते।
जिह्वामूलमुपध्मानमिति वेदविदो विदुः॥
शषयोरुष्मणश्चैव विसर्गो यत्र विद्यते।
पिपीलिका दीर्घसमे च मध्यमा सवर्णता पाकवती पदैक्ये।
दृष्टिरि (?) वत्सानुसृतिस्त्वसाम्ये अथाणुमुख्यास्तु विरामकालः॥॥

Baroda 12753. Gr. 15 fol. 400 Grantha-s (with C.). = CLB I, p. 34. Extract pp. 162-63.

1076 VARṆA-KRAMA-DARPAṆA (5) (वर्णक्रमदर्पण)
Beginning:

उच्चप्रदेशिन्युरुमध्यरेखां कनिष्ठिकाद्यां निहितं पराग्रतः।
अनामिकान्त्या स्वरितं च निर्दिशेत् सुमध्यमामध्यगतां ... तं परे॥ १॥
हृद ... दं निशि स्थानं भक्तेर्यः पर उच्यते।

स्वारगुच्चमिदोर्ध्वं च ह्यनामिकान्तरान्त्ययोः ॥ २॥
व्याघ्री यथा हरेत् पुत्रं दंष्ट्राभ्यां न च पीडिता।
भीता पतनभेदाभ्यां मुखे पार्श्वेन ... ॥
स भावः (कामताजर्धिकर)नाधीरधीरयः ।
जातुजाल(मलाः) काण्डप्रश्नानुपपदाक्षराः ॥
इति वर्णक्रमदर्प(ण)प्रकरणम् ॥
वर्णानां संहिताकाले संधिकार्यं विधीयते।
संधिकार्यं न कुर्यात् तु ...... प्रदर्शने॥
वर्णान्ते ... साधकं...... संयुतम्।
अन्यत्र ... वर्तन्ते अत्यन्तं सूक्ष्ममाचरेत्॥

End:

... र्थस्य नकारस्य ङकारस्तैत्तिरीयके।
तकारः शनयोर्मध्ये काठके परिकीर्तिते॥

Adyar D XIII 193 (VB 1073c). PL. Gr. 2 fol. (with C.).

1077 VARṆA-KRAMA-LAKṢAṆA (1) (वर्णक्रमलक्षण)
of Jagannātha → Ṛgveda-varṇa-krama-lakṣaṇa.
BHU B 1724 (D 2A/926). 29 fol.
SBD 47602. 8 fol. Dated Śaka 1661.
SBD 55241. 19 fol. Dated V.S. 1886.
[CC I 553a]

1078 VARṆA-KRAMA-LAKṢAṆA (2) (वर्णक्रमलक्षण)
of Narasiṃha → Ṛgvarṇa-krama-lakṣaṇa.
PUL II. App. p. 13 (no.205). PL. Gr. 31 fol. 350 Grantha-s (with C.).

1079 VARṆA-KRAMA-LAKṢAṆA (3) (वर्णक्रमलक्षण)
Deals with the various aspects of of the Varṇa-s.
Adyar D I 965 (9 C 70 = PM 133). Gr. 6 fol. = Adyar I, p. 51b. (A xerox-copy of this Ms. is in SAI : 87/796*).

1080 VARṆA-KRAMA-LAKṢAṆA (4) (वर्णक्रमलक्षण)
Baroda 10381(k). PL. Gr. 4 fol. 30 Grantha-s. CLB I, p. 35. Incomplete. Extract p. 163. Only a fragmentary portion of some Veda-lakṣaṇa work. The second verse is from *Vyāsa-śikṣā*.

1081 VARṆA-KRAMA-LAKṢAṆA (5) (वर्णक्रमलक्षण)
Cf. Yamāpatti, above.
Beginning:

औष्मप्रकृतिकात् स्पर्शात् पञ्चमः परतो यदि।

तत्र नैव यमापत्तिरिष्यते नात्र संशयः ॥
वर्गान्तं शषसैः सार्धमन्तस्थाभिश्च संयुतम्।
दृष्ट्वा यमा निवर्तन्त इत्युक्तं वर्णवेदिभिः ॥

End:

पदादौ पदमध्ये वा स्थितस्योष्मपरस्य वै।
प्रथमस्य द्वितीयत्वं पूर्वं कुर्वीत पण्डितः ॥ ८॥

Tirupati SVUORI (3516a2). PL. Gr. 1 fol. 8 verses.

1082 VARṆA-KRAMA-LAKṢAṆA (6) (वर्णक्रमलक्षण)

The verses at the beginning are the same as that of the *Sarva-sammata-śikṣā.*

Beginning:

स्वराद् द्वित्वमवाप्नोति व्यञ्जनं व्यञ्जने परे।
स्पर्शो लकारपूर्वो यो वपूर्वश्च द्विरुच्यते॥
देव्या धिया। कुल्यां जुहोति।
स्वरपूर्वस्य रेफस्य परस्ताद् व्यञ्जनस्थितम्।
आपद्यते द्विवर्णं तद् वर्णमात्रे परे स्थिते॥

End:

ह्रस्वसंयोगयोर्मध्ये यो ऽनुस्वारः प्रकीर्तितः ।
स एव द्वित्वमाप्नोति तदन्यो न द्विरुच्यते॥
वर्णक्रमलक्षणं समाप्तम्॥

MD 14748. PL. Tel. 10 pp. (39ff.).
Mysore ND II 3733 (P 2262/34). PL. Gr. 3 fol. 44 verses. Extract no. 264.
Mysore ND II 3734 (P 3276/ 1). PL. Gr. 5 fol. Incomplete.
Mysore Skt. Coll. p. 1. No.1622. Gr.
RASB II 1522 (G 6186). 1 fol. 33 and 12 verses without title; the beginning is the same as the above. "Taittirīyāṇām" occurs in the text. There is a list of nine Śikṣā-s with a colophon : Nava-śikṣā. above. (2nd group ?)
Tirupati SVUORI (4411). PL. Gr. The codex consisting of 108 disarranged folios contains many short works including Siddhānta-śikṣā.

1083 VARṆA-KRAMA-LAKṢAṆA (7) (वर्णक्रमलक्षण)

→ Lakṣmīkānta-śikṣā.
Hamburg StUB (cod.Palmbl. III 8/133) → Veda-lakṣaṇa (HB).

1084 VARṆA-KRAMA-LAKṢAṆA (8) (वर्णक्रमलक्षण)

of Ananta(-bhaṭṭa).

Adyar D I 966 (36 B 11 = TR 21). 1 fol. (p. 393). Incomplete. Only three verses found at the end of the *Vājasaneyi-prātiśākhya-vyākhyā, Padārtha-prakāśa* of Ananta (-bhaṭṭa) which is contained in the same codex. Dated 7.6.18.

1085 VARṆA-KRAMA-LAKṢAṆA (9) (वर्णक्रमलक्षण)

Adyar D I 983 → Veda-lakṣaṇa (A 1).

Mysore I, pp. 34. 613.

Mysore ND II 3735 (P 2262/35). PL. Gr. 3 fol. Different ?

Mysore ND II 3736 (P 2265/41). PL. Gr. 3 fol. (165-67).

Mysore ND II 3737 (P 4906/12). PL. Na. 1 fol. (?) (different from the above).

Mysore ND II 3738 → Pāriśikṣā.

Mysore ND II 3739 (P 4772/22). PL. Tel. 10 fol. Extract no. 266.

Mysore ND II 3740-41. Extract no. 267. 268 → Ṛgvarṇa-krama-lakṣaṇa of Narasiṃha.

1086 VARṆA-KRAMA-LAKṢAṆA-VYĀKHYĀ (वर्णक्रमलक्षण-व्याख्या)

Mysore ND II 3742 (P 977/ 4). PL. Tel. 22 fol. (21-43) (of Vemāna Bhairavāvadhānin).

Mysore ND II 3743 (P 2262/36). PL. Gr. Incomplete. Only 2 Kārikā-s.

Mysore ND II 3744 (P 2339/10b). PL. Gr. 30 fol. (60-89) (Yājuṣa-bhūṣaṇa) → Pāriśikṣā-vyākhyā.

Mysore ND II 3745 (P 4468). PL. Na. 59 fol. (17-85) (Varṇakramadarpaṇa of Vemāna Bhairavārya).

Mysore ND II 3746 (B 253/ 1). Gr. 42 fol. (praṇamya śaṃbhoḥ ...).

Mysore ND II 3747 (C 4237/ 6). 19 fol. (3-21). Extract no. 268 → Commentary on Ṛgvarṇa-kramalakṣaṇa of Narasiṃha.

Mysore ND II 3748 (P 2339/10c). PL. Gr. 30 fol. (60-89). Extract no. 269 → Pāriśikṣā-vyākhyā.

Mysore ND II 3749 (B 252/13). Gr. 18 fol. (71-88).

1087 VARṆA-KRAMA-VIVARAṆA (वर्णक्रमविवरण)

Oppert II 773. Belonged to Ghanapathi Shingaracharyar of Alasur, Madurantakam Taluk.

[CC I 553a]

1088 VARṆA-KRAMA-VIVEKA (वर्णक्रमविवेक)

of K. V. Anantanarayana Sastri. It explains and illustrates the techniques and modes of recitation, particularly of the Kṛṣṇa-yajurveda.

Ptd.: in the magazine of the Mysore Sanskrit College, *Śrīmanmahārāja Saṃskṛta Mahāpāṭhaśālā Patrikā*, vol. 28 (1954), Mysore. 32 pp. [Adyar (H08sk MSC 28); SAI (87/777*)]

Also printed in the Sanskrit journal : *Sārasvatī Suṣamā*, vol. 12.1 (Varanasi 1958, Saṃ. 2014), pp. 1-27. [SAI (ind 51 D 788/2426)]

1089 VARṆA-KRAMA-ŚIKṢĀ (वर्णक्रमशिक्षा)

Adyar D I 967 (1 A 19 = TR 19). Gr. 14 fol. (pp. 95-119). – Adyar I, p. 53a. Incomplete. The beginning and end correspond to the Pāriśikṣā, MD 924. (Cf. Skt. Texts on Phonetics, p. 373).

1090 VARṆA-GOTRA-SŪTRA-DEVATĀ-NIRṆAYA (वर्णगोत्रसूत्रदेवतानिर्णय)

Mysore ND II 3750 (P 4772/21). PL. Tel. 7 fol. Extract no. 270.

1091 VARṆA-CCHANDODAIVATA (?) (वर्णच्छन्दोदैवत)

Adyar D I 968 (21 S 7 = 68563). PL. (Śrītala) Mal. 15 fol. The name of the author is not mentioned. The title is not clear from the Ms. The title-slip calls it *Varṇa-cchando-daivata*. But the Chandas and the Daivata are not dealt with in the available portion here, and the title is perhaps based on a misconstruction of the invocatory verses. The work refers to Mādhavācārya (fol. 6). Same as in Adyar D I 863 (Nāda-varṇa-viveka) and MT 5258 (Śaunakīyasāra). See *Varṇoccāraṇadīpikā*.

1092 VARṆA-JĀTI-MĀTRĀ-PRAKARAṆA (वर्णजातिमात्राप्रकरण)

Mysore ND II 3751 (P 4468/12). PL. Na. 1 fol. (114). Extract no. 171.
Mysore ND II 3752 (P 4772/18). PL. Tel. 5 fol.

1093 VARṆA-DĪRGHĪ (वर्णदीर्घी)

Mysore ND II 3753 (P 2262/37). PL. Gr. 1 fol.

1094 VARṆA-PAṬALA (वर्णपटल)

47th Pariśiṣṭa of the *Atharva-veda*.

Ptd.: ed. by George Melville Bolling ... and Julius von Negelein, *The Pariśiṣṭas of the Atharvaveda*. – Leipzig : Otto Harrassowitz, 1909-10. [BM : Ptd. Bks. Cat. 1906-1928. 1189 (14007.f.21); Emeneau (140)]

1095 VARṆA-PIṆḌA-LAKṢAṆA (वर्णपिण्डलक्षण)

on consonants in conjunction with Yama. (YV).

Adyar D I 969 (1 A 19 = TR 19). Gr. 3 fol. (pp. 76-80) (with C.). = Adyar I, p. 51a. Title: Piṇḍalakṣaṇa.

1096 VARṆA-PRAYOGA (वर्णप्रयोग)

Trav. Uni. 17800 J. PL. Mal. 50 Grantha-s.

1097 VARṆA-MANTRARṢI-CCHANDO-NIRŪPAṆA (वर्णमन्त्रर्षिच्छन्दोनिरूपण)

Mysore ND II 3732 (P 5930/ 3). PL. Na. 1 fol. (7).

1098 VARṆA-MĀLIKĀ (वर्णमालिका)

of Paṭṭābhirāma, son of Nārāyaṇārya of Bhāradvāja-gotra and a native of Koṇḍalūru. It deals with the manner of uttering the various letters of Vedic texts.

Beginning:

वागीशप्रमुखध्येयदिव्यश्रीपादपङ्कजम् ।
वटवृक्षतलावासं वन्दे ऽहं दक्षिणामुनिम् ॥
श्रीकोण्डलूरिपुरिजो भरद्वाजसगोत्रजः ।
नारायणार्यतनयः सर्वशिक्षाविशारदः ॥
पट्टाभिरामनामासौ वेदलक्षणसारवित् ।
अध्येतृसुखबोधार्थं कुरुते वर्णमालिकाम् ॥
प्रातिशाख्योक्तसूत्रस्य क्रमेणैव प्रवक्ष्यते ।
संगृह्यानुक्तवाक्यानि शिक्षोक्तानि यथामति ॥

इह खलु सततं वेदाभ्यासरतानामध्यापकानाम् अध्येतृणां च सम्यग् वर्णा विज्ञेयाः । तथैवोच्चारयितव्याश्च । ज्ञानपूर्वकं सम्यगुच्चारणे महाफलश्रवणात् । असम्यगुच्चारणे प्रत्यवायश्रवणाच्च ।

End:

एकैकस्मिन् वर्गे यथाक्रमेण वर्णाः प्रथमद्वितीयतृतीयचतुर्थोत्तमसंज्ञा भवन्ति । संज्ञायाः फलं प्रथम ऊष्मपरो द्वितीय इत्यादि । तृतीयसंज्ञा पदसंहिताविषया । द्वितीयाचतुर्थयोस्तृती ...

MT 1165(d). PL. Tel. 3 fol. (44-46). Incomplete. Contains Upodghāta-prakaraṇa complete and Saṃjñā-prakaraṇa incomplete. Purchased in 1913-14 from Kashibhatta Subrahmanya Sastri of Vekanur, Krishna Dist.

Mysore I, p. 34.

Mysore ND II 3754 (P 359). PL. Tel. 12 fol. Incomplete. No extracts.

1099 VARṆA-RATNA-(PRA-)DĪPIKĀ(-ŚIKṢĀ) (वर्णरत्न(प्र)दीपिका /-शिक्षा)
of Amareśa → Amareśa-śikṣā.

BORI TM 275.
GJKSV 13072. 27 fol.
IM 3371. 10 fol.
L 1932. 24 fol.
Oxf. CS d.177(2). 8 fol.
Rep. Raj. and C. I. p. 3.
SBD 2058. 11 fol.
SBD 53751. 21 fol. Dated V.S. 1925 / Śaka 1790.

[CC I 553b]

1100 VARṆA-RAHASYA (वर्णरहस्य)
Mysore ND II 3755 (P 5292/ 7). PL. Gr. 3 fol. Incomplete.

1101 VARṆA-LIṄGĀDI-NIRṆAYA (वर्णलिङ्गादिनिर्णय)
Mysore ND II 3756 (P 4772/20). PL. Tel. 4 fol. Incomplete.

1102 VARṆA-ŚIKṢĀ (**वर्णशिक्षा**)

Two verses of the Lakṣmīkānta-śikṣā (which see).

SBD 47959. 1 fol. Incomplete. There are two tables each containing 25 squares in which the letters of the alphabet are entered. Its significance is not clear.

1103 VARṆA-ŚIKṢĀ-SAṂHITĀ (**वर्णशिक्षासंहिता**)

It is a commentary on 17 verses of the *Pāṇinīya-śikṣā* prefaced with the Śikṣā-vallī section of the *Taittirīyopaniṣat*.

Beginning:

शिक्षां ··· संतानः । इत्युक्तः शीक्षाध्याय इति श्रुतिः श्रूयते । तस्या उपव्याख्यानम् । ईश्वरवाचक ओंकारो मङ्गलार्थः प्रयुज्यते। शिक्षा शीक्षेत्यनर्थान्तरम्। यदा ह्रस्व इकार उदीर्यते तदा द्विककारको निर्देशो वेदितव्यः । यदा च दीर्घ ईकारस्तदैकककारः । आचार्यः शिक्षयति शिष्यश्च विद्यामुपादत्ते । तदुपादानमेव शिक्षा । सा वाक्यसमूहे ऽप्युपचर्यते। तां वर्णादिभिः षड्भिरङ्गैर्व्याकरिष्यामः । यदर्थं वृणोति तस्माद् वर्ण उच्यते । स्वरः स्वोपपदाद् रायतेः शब्दकर्मणः । सहायमनपेक्ष्य स्वेनैव शब्दतीत्यर्थः ॥

End:

इदमेव भगवतः पाणिनेर्धीमत्त्वं यद् अक्षरसमाम्नायप्रक्रिययैव शास्त्रप्रक्रियां व्यरचयत्। इति श्रीवर्णशिक्षासंहिता संपूर्णम्। भाद्रपदशुक्लद्वितीयायां सौम्यवासरे संवत् १८४६॥

GJKSV 45/3 (D I 2, no. 3774). 12 fol.

GJKSV 42236. Title: Śikṣā-vyākhyā.

1104 VARṆA-SAMĀMNĀYA(-GRANTHA) (**वर्णसमाम्नाय /-ग्रन्थ**)

→ Taittirīya-prātiśākhyā.

Mysore ND II 3757 (P 7073/ 1). PL. Tel. 5 fol.

Tirupati SVUORI 5801 (4421a). PL. Gr.

1105 VARṆA-SĀRA(-KRAMA-NIRŪPAṆA) (**वर्णसार /-क्रमनिरूपण**)

Mysore I, p. 34 (2 Mss.).

Mysore ND II 3758 (B 252/12). Gr. 1 fol. (70).

1106 VARṆA-SĀRA-BHŪTA-VARṆA-KRAMA (**वर्णसारभूतवर्णक्रम**)

Oppert II 5262.

[CC I 553b]

1107 VARṆA-SĀRA-VARṆA-KRAMA (**वर्णसारवर्णक्रम**)

Hoshiarpur p. 53 (no.4371). PL. Gr. 7 fol. 200 Grantha-s. (A xerox-copy of a Devanāgarī transcript of this is in SAI : 87/794*).

1108 VARṆA-SVARA (**वर्णस्वर**)

Mysore ND II 3759 (B 600/11). Na. 2 fol. (46-47). Extract no. 273.

1109 VARṆA-SVARA-VARṆA-KRAMA (वर्णस्वरवर्णक्रम)
Hoshiarpur p. 53 (no.4374). PL. Gr. 15 fol. 200 Grantha-s.

1110 VARṆOCCĀRAṆA-DĪPIKĀ (वर्णोच्चारणदीपिका)
A work, stated to be about 500 years old, on the phonology and pronunciation of Sanskrit words. Mss. of this work is found under varying titles: Śikṣā (TCD 80-B), listed as Śikṣā-samuccaya in the Alphabetical Index (vol. III) of the Kerala University; Nāda-varṇa-viveka (Adyar D I 863); Varṇa-cchandodaivata (Adyar D I 968); Śaunakīya-sāra (MT 5258). Printed with an essay on Veda-lakṣaṇa in Sanskrit and another essay on the *Śaunaka-śikṣā* of Govindan Kutti Nayar.

Ptd.: ed. by K. N. M. Divakara Dvijendra of Tripunithura. – Tripunithura : Raja Press, 1964. 18, 45, 28 pp. [Adyar (Ḥ15.1 VD xz Div)]

1111 VARṆOCCĀRAṆA-LAKṢAṆA (वर्णोच्चारणलक्षण)
→ Śaunakīya-śikṣā, Adyar D I 1027 and Saṃkṣepa-sāra, Baroda 8891(b), etc.
TCD 30-A. Mal. 9 pp. 90 Grantha-s.
TCD 38-F. PL. Mal. 4 fol. 100 Grantha-s.
TD 1786. 4 fol. (24-27). 50 Grantha-s (up to verse 36 of the printed Śaunaka-śikṣā).
Trav. Uni. 8367 B. PL. Mal. 600 Grantha-s (with C.). Incomplete.
Trav. Uni. 22010 D. PL. Mal. 300 Grantha-s (with C.). Incomplete.
Trav. Uni. 15722 D. PL. Mal. 80 Grantha-s. Incomplete.
Trav. Uni. 15766 C. PL. Mal. 80 Grantha-s. Incomplete.
Trav. Uni. 17346 J. PL. Mal. 80 Grantha-s. Incomplete.
Trav. Uni. 22120 B. PL. Mal. 80 Grantha-s. Incomplete.
Trav. Uni. L.245 B. PL. Gr. 6 fol. 50 Grantha-s (up to verse 35 of the printed edition). Badly damaged.

– C.
Trav. Uni. L.1429 E. PL. Mal. 20 Grantha-s. 450 Grantha-s. = T.1152 ?
Trav. Uni. 22010 E. PL. Mal. 880 Grantha-s. Incomplete.
Trav. Uni. 22120 C. PL. Mal. 250 Grantha-s. Incomplete.

1112 VARṆOCCĀRAṆA-ŚIKṢĀ (वर्णोच्चारणशिक्षा)
It includes the supposed Sūtra version of the *Pāṇinīya-śikṣā*, with a Hindi translation and the commentary of Dayananda Sarasvati. For details see below Śikṣā-sūtrāṇi. Cf. Georg Cardona, *Pāṇini – A Survey of Research*, pp. 179-82.

Ptd.: – Benares : Munshi Baktawar Singh, Vedic Press, 1879. 15 pp. [Adyar (PH425.1 Pan VS xy hi)]
Reprinted in *Vedārtha-prakāśa* part 1, dated V.S. 1985 (śrāvaṇa), 18 pp. [IO (San F 63 K) / 1886 (26 G 4)] 12th edition : Vaidika Yantralaya, Ajmer 1950.
Offset reprint of the 11th (V.S. 1985) edition. – Bahalgadh (Sonipath-Haryana) : Ramalal Kapur Trust, V.S. 2039 (1982). 22 pp. (4th edition). (Śrī Rāmalāla Kupūr Trust Granthamālā – 42). [SAI (ind 51 D 588/2401 kp)]

Reprint of the above : Bahalgadh (Sonipath-Haryana) : Ramalal Kapur Trust, V.S. 2043 (1986). [SAI (ind 51 D 588/2401a kp)] See Sudhir Kumar Gupta, "Authorship of the Phonetic Sūtras Edited by Dayānanda" in : PAIOC 16 (1951) (Summary), pp. 174-76. Also printed in *Poona Orientalist*, vol. 16 (1951), Poona, pp. 66-69. [NL (E294 I G 959)]

Ed. by Raghu Vira, "Discovery of the Lost Phonetic Sūtras of Pāṇini" with an English translation and commentary, JRAS 1931, pp. 653-70. [Adyar (A05R RAS N1931); Emeneau (383)]

Reprinted in : *Vedic Studies* – A Collection of the Research Papers of Prof. Raghuvira, ed. by Mrs. Sharada Rani. – New Delhi - 110016 (Hauzkhas Enclave), 1981, pp. 19-36. (Śata-Piṭaka Series – Indo-Asian Literatures, vol. 272). [Adyar (H080 SVS SP 272); NL (180 Jb 98 37); SAI (ind S 180, 272); UBTÜ (22 A 6435)]

Also included in the *Saṃskṛta Vyākaraṇa Śāstra kā Itihās* of Yudhisthira Mimamsaka, part III, pp. 62-81 as appendix (pariśiṣṭa) 5 – distinguishing a shorter text (Laghu-pāṭha) and a longer one (Vṛddha-pāṭha).

*VARDHAMĀNA-MIŚRA (वर्धमानमिश्र)
– C. Ṭippaṇa, on the Pratijñā-sūtra. Trav. Uni. 2055. 675 Grantha-s.

1113 VASIṢṬHA-ŚIKṢĀ (वसिष्ठशिक्षा)
→ Vāsiṣṭha-śikṣā.

[CC I 556b]

1114 VĀKYA-PRADĪPIKĀ (वाक्यप्रदीपिका)
Name of the commentary of Īśvara on the *Ṛgveda-prātiśākhya.*

1115 VĀKYA-SVARITA (वाक्यस्वरित)
Divided into 40 sections corresponding to the 40 chapters of the *Vājasaneyi-saṃhitā*, it deals with the accent of words in sentence.

SBD 2103. 38 fol. (17-31, 34-42, 1-12, 17-18, 21-22). Incomplete. Dated V.S. 1684 / Śaka 1549. Col.: Svarita-vākya.

1116 VĀKYĀNTA (वाक्यान्त)
Adyar D I 984 → Veda-lakṣaṇa (A 2). Text is identical with Ardhāntya (Adyar D I 725).

1117 VĀJASANEYA-KRAMA-KĀRIKĀ (वाजसनेयक्रमकारिका)
of Śaṃkarācārya. This appears to be Pada-kārikā-ratna-mālā.
Mysore ND II 3760 (P 3325/ 2). PL. Gr. 6 fol. (179-84). Incomplete.

1118 VĀJASANEYA-KRAMĀVASĀNA-KĀRIKĀ (वाजसनेयक्रमावसानकारिका)
of Śaṃbhu-miśra → Kramāvasāna-kārikā.
SBD 4226. 3 fol. Incomplete.

1119 VĀJASANEYA-ŚIKṢĀ (वाजसनेयशिक्षा)
Radh. 2.

1120 VĀJASANEYI-KĀRIKĀ (वाजसनेयिकारिका)
This is a Ms. of the Pada-pāṭha of the *Śukla-yajurveda*, interspersed with the verses of the *Krama-kārikā* attributed to Śambhu-miśra.
GJKSV 29266. 79 fol. Incomplete.

1121 VĀJASANEYI-PRĀTIŚĀKHYA (वाजसनेयिप्रातिशाख्य)
of Kātyāyana. Also called Kātyāyana- or Kātīya- or Śukla-yajuḥ-prātiśākhya.

Beginning:

स्वरसंस्कारयोश्छन्दसि । १ । लौकिकानामर्थपूर्वकत्वात् । २ । न समत्वात् । ३ । स्याद् वाम्नायधर्मित्वाच्छन्दसि नियमः । ४ । यत् तन्न । ५ । वायुः खात् । ६ । शब्दस्तत् । ७ । संकरोप । ८ । स संघातादीन् वाक् । ९ । त्रीणि स्तानानि । १० । द्वे करणे । ११ ।

End:

अथ पददेवताः । ५१ ।
सर्वं तु सौम्यमाख्यातं नाम वायव्यमिष्यते ।
आग्नेयस्तूपसर्गः स्यान्निपातो वारुणः स्मृतः ॥ ५२ ॥
अथ वर्णदेवताः । ५३ । इत्याह स्वरसंस्कारप्रतिष्ठापयिता भगवान् कात्यायनः । ५४ । वृद्धं वृद्धिः । ५५ ।

America 358. German cursive script, pp. 51-104.
ASB I,iii.33 (III F 291). 16 fol. 375 Grantha-s. Title: Kātyāyana-prātiśākhya.
Baroda 1387. 2-267 fol. 2400 Grantha-s (with C. of Uvaṭa). Dated V.S. 1456. = CLB I, p. 37
Baroda 1728. 20 fol. 250 Grantha-s. = CLB I, p. 37.
Baroda 4541. 16 fol. 250 Grantha-s. Dated V.S. 1694. = CLB I, p. 37.
Baroda 5775. 145 fol. 2400 Grantha-s. = CLB I, p. 37 (with C. of Uvaṭa).
Baroda 5999. 71 fol. 2400 Grantha-s. = CLB I, p. 37 (with C. of Uvaṭa).
Baroda 6007. 26 fol. 250 Grantha-s. Dated V.S. 1881. = CLB I, p. 37.
Baroda 7345(c). 10 fol. (9-18). 250 Grantha-s. = CLB I, p. 37. Dated V.S. 1653.
Baroda 9523. 17 fol. 250 Grantha-s. Dated V.S. 1823. = CLB I, p. 37.
Baroda 9680(a). 2-11 fol. 250 Grantha-s. = CLB I, p. 37.
Baroda 10356. Tel. 2 fol. 30 Grantha-s. = CLB I, p. 37 (beginning only).
Baroda 11219. 98 fol. 2000 Grantha-s (with C. of Ananta-bhaṭṭa). = CLB I, p. 37
B I, p. 208 (no.61). 8 fol.
B I, p. 208 (no.62). 16 fol.
B I, p. 208 (no.63). 20 fol. Dated V.S. 1498.
Berlin StB-PrK (NGMPP). E 345/7. 43 fol. (with Uvaṭa's Bhāṣya) Incomplete. Lacks the end (microfilm dated 11.10.1977).
Bhk. 8.
Bik. 317. 18 fol. (Described as Ṛgveda-prātiśākhya).
Bikaner 650. 18 fol. Dated V.S. 1702 (A.D. 1645). Copied at Kashi.
Bikaner 651. 15 fol. Dated V.S. 1687 (A.D. 1630).

Bikaner 652. 18 fol.

Bikaner 653. 17 fol. Incomplete.

BISM p. 172 (22/26) (with C. Jyotsnā). Dated Śaka 1739.

Bombay Uni. 692 (BMC 65 9). 28 fol. Dated Śaka 1628. Copied by Vāsudeva Gaṇaka Reṇukā-bhaṭṭa.

Bombay Uni. Acc. no. 5218. 28 fol. Dated Śaka 1735. The last fol. is that of a Ms. of Padārtha-prakāśa.

BORI 8 of 1866-68. 184 fol. (with C. of Uvaṭa).

BORI 52 of 1879-80. = BORI D I i.274. 17 fol. Dated V.S. 1746.

BORI 174 of 1880-81. = BORI D I i.273. 18 fol. Dated V.S. 1607.

BORI 44 of A 1881-82. = BORI D I i.276. 52 fol.

BORI 48 of 1884-87. = BORI D I i.275. 15 fol. Dated V.S. 1619.

BORI TM 138. 18 fol.

Br. Mus. 48 (Add. 5349h). 16 fol. (274-89a).

Bühler p. 553 (no. 17) (with C. of Uvaṭa). = BORI 8 of 1866-68.

CPB 3214. 3216.

GJKSV 13001. 15 fol. (chs. 1-8; 12th fol. missing). Dated V.S. 1906. Title: Kātyāyana-prātiśākhya.

Hoshiarpur p. 53 (no.5654). Gr. 70 fol. 2000 Grantha-s (with C. of Ananta).

Hpr. Notices Vol. XI. Pref. p. 20.

IM 2484. 15 fol.

IM 2541. 30 fol. (with C. of Uvaṭa). Incomplete.

IM 3376. 10 fol. Incomplete. Title: Prātiśākhya Kātīya.

IM 3379. 10 fol. Title: Prātiśākhya-sūtra.

IM 5289. 7 fol. Title: Kātyāyana-prātiśākhya.

IM 5537. 20 fol. Title: Prātiśākhya (Kātyāyana).

IO 192 (598). 83 fol. (with C. of Uvaṭa).

Khn. p. 61.

L 4119. 66 fol. 1500 Grantha-s (with C. of Ananta-bhaṭṭa).

Mithila IV 104. 21 fol.

Mithila IV 104(A)-(E).

Max Müller Mem. XIX. 25 fol. Dated Śaka 1769.

Max Müller Mem. XX. 144 fol. (31 and 113). (with C. of Uvaṭa). Incomplete. Written ca. A.D. 1750.

Oxf. CS d.75. 185 fol. (with C. of Uvaṭa). Title: Pārṣada Savyākhya.

Oxf. CS c.60. 25 fol.

RASB II 896 (G 1775). 17 fol. 275 Grantha-s. Dated V.S. 1825. Title: Kātyāyanīya-prātiśākhya.

RASB II 897 (G 1091). 14 fol. 300 Grantha-s. Dated V.S. 1809.

RASB II 898 (G 3491). 28 fol.

RASB II 899 (G 6155). 14 fol. 300 Grantha-s. Dated V.S. 1936.

RASB II 900 (G 1092). 39 fol. 950 Grantha-s (with C. of Ananta).

RASB II 901 (G 1899) = L 4119 (with C. of Ananta). Incomplete.

RASB II 902 (G 1251). 69 fol. 2450 Grantha-s. Dated V.S. 1743 (with C. of Ananta).

RASB II 903 (G 3252). 27 fol. (with C. of Ananta). Incomplete.

RASB II 904 (G 5938). 49 fol. (with C. Jyotsnā).

Rgb. 48. 15 fol. Dated V.S. 1619.
SBD 2120(ka). 16 fol.
SBD 2120(kha). 13 fol. (68-80). Incomplete.
SBD 2125. 13 fol. (Kātīya-prātiśākhya).
SBD 2137. 23 fol. Dated V.S. 1823.
SBD 2148. 18 fol.
SBD 2149. 17 fol.
SBD 46944. 21 fol. (8-28). Incomplete. (Śukla-yajuḥ-prātiśākhya).
SBD 47243. 19 fol. (1-16, 18-20). Incomplete. (Yajuḥ-prātiśākhya).
SBD 47248. 14 fol. Dated V.S. 1631. (Prātiśākhya-sūtra).
SBD 47969. 1 fol. Incomplete.
Stein p. 7 (no. 99). 13 fol.
Tb. 207. Copy of a Ms. from London/Berlin made in 1845-46 by Roth.
Tb. 209. 146 fol. Roth's transcript of the Ms. Weber 164 (with C. of Uvaṭa), made in 1846.
Trav. Uni. 1653. 2100 Grantha-s (with C. Mātṛmodaka of Uvaṭa).
Trav. Uni. 5227. 100 Grantha-s (with C. Jyotsnā). Incomplete.
Udaipur p. 22 (no.900) (with C. of Uvaṭa).
Ujjain II, p. 8 (no.3412). 33 fol. Dated V.S. 1765. VSM I 766 (no.4908). 35 fol. Copied by Śukla Vāsudeva-bhaṭṭa.
Weber 163 (Chambers 35). Dated V.S. 1680.
Weber 164 (Chambers 454). 98 fol. (with C. of Uvaṭa).
Weber 1460 (Ms. or. fol. 879). 8 fol. Dated V.S. 1759.
Weber 1461 (Ms. or. fol. 909). Śāradā script. 15 fol. (with C. up to 1.168).

Ptd.:

1) Ed. by A. Weber, with a German translation, notes, and extracts from the commentaries (in Roman script), *Indische Studien,* vol. IV (1858), pp. 65-171, 177-331. [Adyar (H080 Web IS ge); SAI (inf Zs 73); BM : Ptd. Bks. Cat. 1876-92. 180 (14096.c.); Emeneau (374)]
2) Ed. by Jivananda Vidyasagar, with Uvaṭa's commentary. – Calcutta : 1883. [BORI (9203)] 2nd edition. – Calcutta, 1893. [NL (K 180 Jc 89 11)]
3) Ed. by Yugalakishora (Vyasa) Pathaka (Title page : Kātyāyana-maharṣi-praṇītam Śuklayajuḥ-prātiśākhyam Uvvaṭa-kṛta-bhāṣya-yutam – Kātyāyana's Prātiśākhya of the White Yajur Veda with the commentary of Uvaṭa), pp. 1-401. – Benares : Messrs. Braj B. Das and Co., 1883 (1888), 2, 12, 506, 60 pp. – (Ben. S. S. 4).
This volume also contains:
Pratijñā-sūtra with the commentary of Anantadeva, pp. 401-31;
(Trikaṇḍikā-)Bhāṣika-sūtra with the commentary of Anantadeva, pp. 432-71;
Jaṭādyaṣṭa-vikṛti-lakṣaṇa, pp. 471-93;
Ṛgyajuḥ-pariśiṣṭa, pp. 494-501;
Anuvākādhyāya-pariśiṣṭa, pp. 501-06;
Śaunaka's Caraṇa-vyūha-pariśiṣṭa with the commentary of Mahīdāsa, pp. 1-60.
[Adyar (H080 CSS B5); BORI (5151, 23223); NL (180 Jc 88 142); SAI (ind S 12, 4); UBTÜ (Ci XII 633); BM : Ptd. Bks. Cat. 1876-92. 180-81 (14093.b.8); Emeneau (375)]

4) Ed. by V. Venkatarama Sharma, with commentaries of Uvaṭa and Ananta-bhaṭṭa. – Madras : University of Madras, 1934. – (Madras University Sanskrit Series 5). [Adyar (II080 MOS sk 5); NL (180 Jb 93 77)]
5) Ed. by S. N. Ghoshal, with an English translation and critical notes (also the translation of A. Weber's German introduction to the text), *Indian Studies Past and Present*. – Calcutta (reprint: 1964). 25, 62 pp. (incomplete; up to ch. 2).
6) Ed. by Indu Rastogi, with an English translation. – Varanasi : Chowkhamba, 1967. 9, 93 pp. – (Kashi Sanskrit Series 179). [BORI (34413); NL (180 Jc 96 310); SAI (ind S 100, 179)]
7) Ed. by Virendra Kumar Varma, with commentaries of Uvaṭa and Ananta-bhaṭṭa and Hindi commentary by the editor. – Varanasi : Jnanaprakasa Pratisthanaa, 1975. 34, 416 pp. [BORI (34703); UBTÜ (20 A 13819)]

Reprint of the above : Delhi : Chowkhamba Sanskrit Pratishthan, 1987. – (Vrajajivan Prachyabharati Granthamala 16). [SAI (ind 52 D 787/1728)]

– C. Mātṛmodaka of Uvaṭa.

Beginning:

यस्य भृङ्गावलिः कण्ठे स्रुतदानाम्बुपूरिते।
भाति रुद्राक्षमालेव स वः पायाद् गणाधिपः ॥
प्रणम्य परमात्मानं व्याख्यास्ये प्रातिशाख्यकम्।
सरस्वतीं च जगतस्तमोनाशनदीपिकाम्।
जपादौ नाधिकारो ऽस्ति सम्यक् पाठमजानतः ।
प्रातिशाख्यमतो ज्ञेयं सम्यक् पाठस्य सिद्धये॥

स्वर उदात्तानुदात्तस्वरितप्रचितलक्षणः । संस्कारो लोपागमवर्णविकारप्रकृतिभावलक्षणः । तयोः स्वरसंस्कारयोः छन्दसि विषये नियमो ऽधिकृतो वेदितव्यः । प्रतिज्ञासूत्रमेतत्। प्रतिज्ञा च शिष्यबुद्धिसमाधानार्था ॥ लौकिकानाम् ... ॥ लोके विदिता लौकिकाः । लौकिकानां शब्दानामर्थपूर्वकत्वात् प्रयोजनपूर्वकत्वादस्मिन् शास्त्रे नियमो न क्रियते। कथम्। प्रयोजनपूर्वकत्वं कथम्। प्रयोजनपूर्वकाणां शब्दानां नियमो न क्रियते। आह। देवदत्त गामभ्याज शुक्लां दण्डेनेति यस्य पुरुषस्य देवदत्तकर्तृका गोत्वजात्युपलक्षितशुक्लद्रव्यकर्मिका दण्डकरणिका अभ्याजनक्रियाभिप्रेता । स एवैतद् वाक्यं ब्रवीति।

End:

निपाता वरुणदेवत्याः इत्याद्युपासनार्थमुक्तम्। एवं ह्युपासिताः सन्तो ऽर्थानभिज्ञस्यापि पुरुषस्य फलप्रदा भवन्ति । यो वा अविदितार्षेयच्छन्दोदैवतब्राह्मणेन मन्त्रेण याजयति वाध्यापयति वा स्थाणुं वर्छति गर्तं वापद्यते प्रमीयते पापीयान् भवतीत्येवमादिदोषेण संबध्यते । घृतकुल्या मधुकुल्या इत्येवमादिभिस्तु गुणैः संबध्यत एव । ... एवं स्वरसंस्कारयोः प्रतिष्ठापयिता भगवान् कात्यायनः । इदं शास्त्रमाह । ... उक्तार्थः । इत्यानन्दपुरवास्तव्यवज्रटसूनुनोव्वटेन कृते मातृमोदकाख्ये प्रातिशाख्यभाष्ये ऽष्टमो

ऽध्याय: ॥

Alwar 202.

ASB I.iii.34 (I D 13/b). 72 fol. 2484 Grantha-s. Title: Kātyāyana-prātiśākhya-bhāṣya.

Baroda 1387. 2-267 fol. 2400 Grantha-s (with text). = CLB I, p. 37. Dated V.S. 1456.

Baroda 5775. 145 fol. 2400 Grantha-s. = CLB I, p. 37 (with text).

Baroda 5999. 71 fol. 2400 Grantha-s. = CLB I, p. 37 (with text).

BBRAS SSP. 161. 61 fol. (12-72).

Bd. 77. 137 fol.

Berlin StB-PrK (NGMPP). G 240/34-241/1. 87 fol. Many fol. are missing. Title: Pārṣada-bhāṣya (microfilm dated 18.06.1978).

Berlin StB-PrK (NGMPP). E 345/7. 43 fol. (with text). Incomplete. Lacks end. (microfilm dated 11.10.1977).

Berlin StB-PrK (NGMPP). E 602/8. 14 fol. (226-32, 234-38, 240-41) (chs. 5-8). Incomplete. Title: Kātyāyana-prātiśākhya-vyākhyā.

Berlin StB-PrK (NGMPP). E 691/35. 54 fol. (50-58, 60-63, 150-58, 160-72, 193-209). Title: Kātyāyana-prātiśākhya-bhāṣya (microfilm dated 22.10.1978).

Bhk. 8.

Bhr. 515.

Bhr. 516.

BHU S 42 (D 2D/2125). 45 fol. Incomplete. Dated V.S. 1575.

Bik. 316. 247 fol. (Described as C. on the Ṛgveda-prātiśākhya).

Bikaner 654. 247 fol.

Bikaner 655. 135 fol.

BISM p. 172 (36/968). Dated Śaka 1694 / V.S. 1829.

BISM p. 172 (57/49). Dated Śaka 1722.

BISM p. 172 (60/9). (chs. 1-2).

BORI 53 of 1879-80. = BORI D I i.277. 114 fol. Dated V.S. 1747 (ca. 30 fol. missing).

BORI 76 of 1881-82. = BORI D I i.282. 104 fol. Dated V.S. 1563.

BORI 45 of A 1881-82. = BORI D I i.278. 103 fol. Dated V.S. 1838.

BORI 77 of 1881-82. = BORI D I i.283. 107 fol. (lacks end).

BORI 515 of 1882-83. = BORI D I i.285. 10 fol. (ch. 5).

BORI 516 of 1882-83. = BORI D I i.284. 48 fol.

BORI 17 of 1883-84. = BORI D I i.281. 101 fol. (12 fol. missing).

BORI 77 of 1887-91. = BORI D I i.280. 136 fol.

BORI 33 of 1892-95. = BORI D I i.279. 118 fol. Dated V.S. 1538.

BP p. 258.

Bühler p. 553 (no. 17) (with text). = BORI 8 of 1866-68.

Calcutta Skt. Coll. I.489. 91 fol. 2500 Grantha-s.

Deccan College 9819. 103 fol. Dated V.S. 1762.

GJKSV 37691. 184 fol. Title: Prātiśākhya-bhāṣya.

Hpr. II 136. 157 fol. 4290 Grantha-s. Dated V.S. 1830.

IM 2541. 30 fol. (with text). Incomplete.

IO 192 (598). 83 fol. (with text).

Mithila IV 106. 108 fol.

Mithila IV 106(A)-(II). (8 Mss.)

Max Müller Mem. XX. 144 fol. (31 and 113). (with text). Incomplete. Written ca. A.D. 1750.

N-W P V 16 (no.20). 118 fol. (a. Uvaṭa Miśra). Belonged to Gopinatha Dikshita, Atale, Ulvar (Alwar).

P 21.

Peters. II, p. 173 (no.78). 115 fol.

Peters. V, p. 225 (no.33).

PUL I, p. 24 (no.137). 170 fol. (9-178; a few fol. missing).

PUL I, p. 24 (no.138). 25 fol. Incomplete.

SB p. 56 (no.255). 118 fol. 2360 Grantha-s. = SBD 2117.

SBD 2117. 118 fol. Dated V.S. 1792. (Prātiśākhya-bhāṣya).

SBD 2126. 77 fol. Incomplete.

SBD 47242. 126 fol.

SBD 47245. 33 fol. (3-35). Incomplete. (Mādhyandina-prātiśākhya-bhāṣya).

SBD 47247. 107 fol. (1, 3-106, 108-09). Incomplete. Dated V.S. 1631. (Prātiśākhya-sūtra-bhāṣya).

Stein p. 6 (no. 90). Kāśmīri. 151 fol.

Tb. 209. 146 fol. Roth's transcript of the Ms. Weber 164 (with text) made in 1846.

Trav. Uni. 1653. 2100 Grantha-s (with text).

Ujjain II, p. 8 (no.3855). 154 fol. Dated V.S. 1919.

Weber 164 (Chambers 454). 98 fol.

Weber 1462 (Ms. or. fol. 591). 94 fol.

Weber 2061 (Ms. or. fol. 1568b). 51 fol. (10-60) (breaks off in ch. 4).

C. Jyotsnā of Rāmacandra, son of Siddheśvara, composed in Śaka 1739 (A.D. 1817). It is not a regular commentary on the Vājasaneyi-prātiśākhya, but a gloss on selected Sūtra-s, arranged differently from the original order, and according to topics. It also includes comments on the Pratijñā-sūtra and Aṣṭa-vikṛti-s. Cf. Sunanda Ramesh Abhyankar: An Introduction to the commentary Prātiśākhya-Jyotsnā, AIOC 31, Jaipur, 1982, SP, pp. 1-2.

Beginning:

श्रीरामं सद्गुरुं नत्वा याज्ञवल्क्यमुनिं तथा।
कात्यायनकृते प्रातिशाख्ये वाजसनेयके॥
माध्यन्दिनानुसारेण ज्योत्स्नाख्या विवृतिर्लघु।
क्रियते सुखबोधार्थं मन्दानां रामशर्मणा॥

End:

अङ्काग्निसप्तकुमिते (१७३९) शक ईश्वरवत्सरे।
इषशुक्लदशम्यां श्रीसिद्धेश्वरतनूभुवा॥
रामेण रचिता प्रातिशाख्यज्योत्स्ना समर्पिता।
श्रीरामसिद्धेशगुरुचरणाम्बुरुहद्वये॥

America 359. 26 pp. Roman transliteration.
B I, p. 208 (no.64). 26 fol.
Bhr. 517.
BISM p. 172 (22/26). Dated Śaka 1739.
BORI 517 of 1882-83. = BORI D I i.288. 11 fol. (up to Svara-saṃdhi).
Bühler p. 553 (no. 16).
D. p. 2 (4) (Aufrecht remarks on this : "Shridhar R. Bhandarkar, p. 4, states the age of his Ms. as Śaka 1678" (CC I 561a). But that refers to the Dīpikā of Rāmāgnihotrin. See below).
GB 18. 53 fol. 19th century. On fol. 40: iti padalakṣaṇam | atha kramalakṣaṇam - kramaḥ smṛtiprayojanaḥ ... | On fol. 42a begins Krama-saṃdhāna with comments (→ Krama-saṃdhāna-śikṣā) and ends on fol. 43a. Then Pratijñā-sūtra with C. (43b-46b); atha yājñavalkya-śikṣāproktāḥ hastena pradarśanīyāḥ (6 verses with C.). After this atha jaṭādyaṣṭa-vikṛtīnāṃ lakṣaṇāni likhyante (fol. 47a-53b; as printed in Thibaut's edition).
L 1938. 92 fol. 901 Grantha-s.
Mithila IV 75. 37 fol.
Mithila IV 75(A)-(F).
Max Müller Mem. XXI. 78 fol. Dated Śaka 1769.
RASB II 904 (G 5938). 49 fol.
SBD 47239. 63 fol. (1-6, 43-44, 47-101). Incomplete.
SBD 49005. 23 fol. Incomplete.
Trav. Uni. 5227. 100 Grantha-s (with text). Vivṛti.
Weber 1463 (Ms. or. fol. 590). 53 fol. A modern copy obtained from G. Bühler in August 1867.

Ptd.: ed. by Yugala Kishore Misra : Kātyāyanīya-śuklayajuḥprātiśākhyasya śrīrāmaśarmaṇā praṇītā Jyotsnāvṛttiḥ (with the text, on the basis of a Ms. in the Sarasvati Bhavana Library and some other Mss. from the private collections). This edition includes also the *Saṃpradāya-prabodhinī-śikṣā*, as appendix three (pp. 293-315). – Varanasi : Sampurnanand Sanskrit University, 1989. ka-da, xxvi, 315 pp. – (Sarasvatībhavana-Granthamālā 125).

– C. Hoshiarpur p. 53 (no.6472). 15 fol. 412 Grantha-s. Incomplete.

– C. Padārtha-prakāśa of Ananta-bhaṭṭa.
Adyar D I 970 (36 B 11 = TR 21). 196 fol. (pp. 1-392). Dated 7.6.18. = Adyar I, p. 53b.
Adyar D I 971 (40 B 31 = PM134). 114 fol. Copied by Mādhava at Kāśī.
Bombay Uni. Acc. no. 5359. 13 fol. (2nd ch. only).
Baroda 11219. 98 fol. 2000 Grantha-s. = CLB I, p. 37 (with text).
Bhr. 518.
BORI 518 of 1882-83. = BORI D I i.286. 21 fol. (up to Sūtra 165).
Bühler p. 553 (no. 19).
GB 17. 27 fol. (chs. 3 and 5). 19th century.
Hoshiarpur p. 53 (no.5654). Gr. 70 fol. 2000 Grantha-s (with text).
L 4119. 66 fol. 1500 Grantha-s.

MD 935. Tel. 216 pp. Dated Sunday the 7th of the bright fortnight of Āśvayuja, in the year Nandana (A.D. 1772 ?).

MT 5354. 100 fol. 2475 Grantha-s. Restored from MD 935.

RASB II 900 (G 1092). 39 fol. 950 Grantha-s (with text).

RASB II 901 (G 1899) = L 4119 (with text). Incomplete.

RASB II 902 (G 1251). 69 fol. 2450 Grantha-s (with text). Dated V.S. 1743.

RASB II 903 (G 3252). 27 fol. (with text). Incomplete.

Weber 2060 (Ms. or. fol. 1568a). 24 fol. (ch. I).

Ptd.: with the text in the edition of the Madras University and of V. K. Varma. see above.

For a study in German of this commentary and the Mss. material available at that time, see Fritz Gelpke: *Anantabhaṭṭas Padārthaprakāśa* : Ein Kāṇva-Kommentar zum Vājasaneyi-Prātiśākhya (Inaugural-Dissertation, ... Georg August-Univesität). – Göttingen, 1929. 64 pp. [UBHD (Za 4867a 25); UBTÜ (U 29.2402)]

– C. Dīpikā of Rā(māgniho)trin, son of Sadāśiva Agnihotrin.

Bikaner 656. 67 fol.

Bombay Uni. Acc. no. 5358. 33 fol.

BORI 22 of 1868-69. = BORI D I i.287. 90 fol. 3019 Grantha-s. Dated Śaka 1678.

D. p. 2 (4).

GJKSV 29781. 66 fol. Dated V.S. 1868. Title: Prātiśākhya-dīpikā.

Gough p. 56. 89 fol.

Mithila IV 105. 151 fol. Dated V.S. 1841.

Mithila IV 105(A). 131 fol. Incomplete.

Mithila IV 105(B). 50 fol. Incomplete.

PUL I, p. 24 (no.139). 120 fol.

RASB II 905 (G 1776). 165 fol. 2600 Grantha-s.

Rep. Raj. and C. I. p. 3.

[CC I 561a; II 132b, 224b; III 119a]

1122 VĀJASANEYI-MĀDHYANDINA-ŚUKLA-YAJURVEDA-SAṂHITĀYĀḤ SARVĀNUKRAMA-SŪTRAM (**वाजसनेयिमाध्यन्दिनशुक्लयजुर्वेदसंहितायाः सर्वानुक्रमसूत्रम्**)

→ Śukla-yajurveda-sarvānukrama.

1123 VĀJASANEYI-ŚIKṢĀ (**वाजसनेयिशिक्षा**)

of Yājñavalkya → Yājñavalkya-śikṣā.

BHU B 1263 (D 2E/2139). 26 fol. Col.: Yājñavalkya-munikṛtā Vājasaneyī-śikṣā.

BORI 44 of 1895-98.

IM 2565. 2 fol.

IM 3380. 25 fol.

Peters. VI. p. 61 (no.44). 10 fol. Dated Śaka 1734.

SBD 2089. 19 fol.

Trav. Uni. 1618. 250 Grantha-s. (a. Yājñavalkya).

– C. Saṃkṣepa-darpaṇa of Vyūḍha-mitra.

Trav. Uni. 2056. 300 Grantha-s. Damaged.

1124 VĀJASANEYI-SAMHITĀ-KRAMA-PĀṬHA (वाजसनेयिसंहिताक्रमपाठ)

AK 48 (ch. 1).
AK 49 (chs. 30, 40).
BHU S 11 (D 1B/191). 324 fol. Incomplete. Dated V.S. 1525.
Bik. 93. 113 fol. (chs. 20-40).
Bik. 106. 70 fol. (chs. 1-10).
BISM p. 254 (2/20). (Adh. 20). Dated Śaka 1737.
BISM p. 255 (2/22). (Adh. 34).
BISM p. 255 (37/218).
BISM p. 255 (47/80). (Adh. 27).
BISM p. 255 (47/207). (Adhs. 26, 32).
Bombay Uni. (Itchharam 8 3) 34. 266 fol. (Adhyāya-s 1-19).
BORI 48 of 1891-95. = BORI D I i.223. 22 fol. (ch. 1).
BORI 49 of 1891-95. = BORI D I i.224. 35 fol.
BORI 354(1) of 1883-84. = BORI D I i.225. 421 fol. (chs. 1-37). Dated Śaka 1711.
BP p. 285.
GJKSV 26399. 241 fol.
GJKSV 28492. 152 fol. (Pūrva-viṃśī); 116 fol. (Uttara-viṃśī). Dated Śaka 1695. (Krama-pāṭha).
GJKSV 38142. 147 fol. (I. daśaka); 225 fol. (II. daśaka); 195 fol. (III. daśaka); 143 fol. (IV. daśaka). Dated V.S. 1856 / Śaka 1721. Copied by Viśvanātha, son of Puruṣottama-bhaṭṭa Agnihotrin, in Kāśī. Title: Śukla-yajuḥ-krama-pāṭha.
GJKSV 38397. 179 fol.
GJKSV 38416. 256 fol. Dated V.S. 1885.
GJKSV 39532. 1-572, 623, 635, 646-94, 1-115, 117-375 fol. Dated V.S. 1942.
IM 1780. 44-54 fol. Krama-pāṭha of the 16th ch. (Rudrādhyāya).
IM 1783. 9 fol. Krama-pāṭha of the 1st and part of the 2nd Adhyāya.
IM 1784. 23-62 fol. (chs. 23-27).
IM 1786. 2-10 fol. Incomplete (14th Adhyāya).
Jammu RSRI p. 20 (no. 5219). 240 fol. (Stein 96).
L 1803. 410 fol. 1234 Grantha-s (chs. 1-20). Title: Krama-saṃhitā.
L 1804. 239 fol. 1235 Grantha-s (chs. 21-40). Title: Krama-saṃhitā.
MD 194. Tel. 536 pp.
Mithila IV 149. 44 fol. (chs. 1-6 and 36-40).
Mithila IV 149(A). 15 fol. (chs. 36-40).
Mithila IV 149(B). 631 fol.
Mithila IV 149(C). 40 fol. (chs. 1-5).
Mithila IV 149(D). 37 fol. (chs. 4 in Uttarārdha).
Mithila IV 149(E). 22 fol. (chs. 36-40).
Oxf. CS d.21. 232 fol. (chs. 1-20, 40).
Oxf. II 927 (Ms. Sansk. d. 15). 99 fol. Purchased in 1886 through G. Thibaut of Benares.
Peters. II. p. 171 (no.28). 131 and 77 fol. 46 (21-24).
SB p. 41 (no.252). 171 fol. 2766 Grantha-s. Dated V.S. 1933. = SBD 1059.
SBD 1059. 172 fol. (Pūrvārdha). Dated V.S. 1933.

SBD 1060. 22 fol. (58-76, 78-80). Incomplete.
SBD 1061. 79 fol. (13-91). Incomplete.
SBD 1064. 93 fol. (148-241). Incomplete (several fol. missing).
SBD 1066. 321 fol. (120-440). Incomplete (chs. 25-40). Dated V.S. 1873.
SBD 1068. 169 fol. (Uttarārdha). Dated V.S. 1851.
SBD 1084. 81 fol. (42-122). Incomplete.
SBD 47137. 75 fol. (1-33, 35-76). Incomplete. Prathama-daśaka. (Śuklayajuḥsaṃhitā-kramapāṭha).
SBD 47138. 244 fol. (1-43, 65-205, 139-198). Incomplete. (Śuklayajuḥsaṃhitākrama-pāṭha).
SBD 52480. 8 fol. (of chs. 24 and 31). Catalogued as Ṛksaṃhitā-krama-pāṭha.
SBD 53255. 5 fol. (37th ch. of VS). (Krama-pāṭha).
SBD 52334. 60 fol. (4-33, 37-41, 44, 46-69). Incomplete.
SBD 55338. 4 fol. (of ch. 32).
SBD 53492. 20 fol. (1-15, 17-20, 1).
Stein p. 6 (no. 94). 165 fol. Kāśmiri. Dated V.S. 1927. (Adhyāya-s 21-40).
Ujjain I, p. 4 (no.155). 135 fol. (Uttara-viṃśī).
Wai I 649. 14 fol. Incomplete (ch. 4)
Wai I 650. 14 fol. Incomplete (ch. 6)
Wai I 651. 74 fol. Incomplete (chs. 12-18).
Wai II 10271. 58 fol. Incomplete.

[CC I 560b; II 132b; III 119a]

1125 VĀJASANEYI-SAṂHITĀ-KRAMA-SAṂDHĀNA (**वाजसनेयिसंहिताक्रमसंधान**)
→ Krama-saṃdhāna.
Lahore p. 2 (no.3). 4 fol. 35 Grantha-s.

1126 VĀJASANEYI-SAṂHITĀ-GHANA-PĀṬHA (**वाजसनेयिसंहिताघनपाठ**)
Mithila IV 150. 31 fol. (31st ch.).
SBD 53435. 58 fol. (1-29, 1-21, 1-8). (Yajurvedasaṃhitāghanapāṭha).

1127 VĀJASANEYI-SAṂHITĀ-JAṬĀ-PĀṬHA (**वाजसनेयिसंहिताजटापाठ**)
BISM p. 255 (2/51). (Adh. 30).
BISM p. 255 (47/109). (Adh. 28).
BORI 354(2) of 1883-84. = BORI D I i.225. 7 fol. (ch. 28). Dated Śaka 1711.
BORI 45 of 1892-95. = BORI D I i.226. 701 fol. (chs. 1-20).
BORI 46 of 1892-95. = BORI D I i.227. 131 fol. (chs. 21-24).
BP p. 285.
GJKSV 21248. 78, 106, 152 fol. Incomplete (10 chapters). Title: Jaṭā-pāṭha.
GJKSV 21249. 12 fol. (14th ch.). Title: Jaṭā-pāṭha.
GJKSV 27897. (chs. 11-22). Title: Yajurveda-jaṭā-pāṭha.
GJKSV 37735. 232 fol.
GJKSV 42525. 194 fol. Incomplete. title : Saṃhitā-jaṭā-pāṭha.
IM 1779. 2-20, 1-19, 123-30 fol. (Adhyāya-s 1, 8, and 10).
IM 1781. 16 fol. 30th Adhyāya.
IM 1785. 5 fol. 40th Adhyāya (īśāvāsyām).
IM 2522. 49 fol. (viśvāni deva ...nakṣatrāṇi rūpam aśvinau yātam)

Mithila IV 151. 48 fol. (chs. 31, 36-40).
Mithila IV 151(A). 8 fol. (31st ch.).
Mithila IV 151(B). 15 fol. (chs. 39-40).
Mithila IV 151(C). 14 fol. (chs. 30-40).
Mithila IV 151(D). 170 fol. (chs. 18-20). Dated V.S. 1800.
Oxf. II 928 (Mss. Wilson 92, 93). 2 vols. 213 fol. (chs. 1-20) and 164 fol. (chs. 21-40). Dated V.S. 1537. = Oxf. 365b (nos. 92, 93). (Kāṇva-śākhā).
Oxf. II 929 (Mss. Mill 86, 87). 2 vols. 227 fol. (chs. 1-20) and 213 fol. (chs. 21-40). 2nd vol. is dated V.S. 1653. = Oxf. 393a (nos. 86, 87). (Kāṇva-śākhā).
Peters. V, p. 226 (no.45) (chs. 1-20).
Peters. V, p. 227 (no.46) (chs. 21-24).
Stein p. 7 (no. 98). 58 fol. Incomplete.
Wai I 652. 14 fol. Incomplete (ch. 22).

[CC I 560b; II 132b; III 119a]

1128 VĀJASANEYI-SAMHITĀDHYĀYĀNUKRAMAṆIKĀ
(वाजसनेयिसंहिताध्यायानुक्रमणिका)
Bikaner 663. 6 fol. Incomplete. End missing.

1129 VĀJASANEYI-SAMHITĀNUKRAMAṆIKĀ (वाजसनेयिसंहितानुक्रमणिका)
› Śukla-yajurveda-sarvānukrama.

[CC I 561a]

1130 VĀJASANEYI-SAMHITĀ-PADA-KĀRIKĀ-RATNAMĀLĀ
(वाजसनेयिसंहितापदकारिकारत्नमाला)
› Pada-kārikā-ratnamālā.

1131 VĀJASANEYI-SAMHITĀ-YAJURVIDHĀNA (वाजसनेयिसंहितायजुर्विधान)
› Yajurvidhāna.

1132 VĀJASANEYI-SAMHITĀ-VIKṚTI-PĀṬHA (वाजसनेयिसंहिताविकृतिपाठ)
SBD 1067. 130 fol. Incomplete. Dated V.S. 1838.
SBD 1101. 78 fol. (1-10, 26, 28-94). Incomplete. Dated V.S. 1877.
SBD 1102. 3 fol. (2-4). Incomplete (ch. 13, Jaṭā for mantra-s 54-56).
SBD 1104. 47 fol. (56-102). Incomplete.

1133 VĀJASANEYI-SARVĀNUKRAMAṆĪ (वाजसनेयिसर्वानुक्रमणी)
› Śukla-yajurveda-sarvānukrama.

1134 VĀLMĪKI-ŚIKṢĀ (वाल्मीकिशिक्षा)
Mentioned in the Siddhānta-śikṣā-vyākhyāna, Brl. p. 9 (no.XXVII).

1135 VĀSIṢṬHĪ-ŚIKṢĀ (1) (वासिष्ठीशिक्षा)
On the doubling of consonants. Different from the work printed in the Śikṣā-saṃgraha which belongs to the Vājasaneyi school. The *Vaidikābharaṇa* (on *Taittirīya-prātiśākhya*, p. 8) quotes a Śikṣā of this name regarding the number of vowels as 26. Also mentioned in the commentary on the Śikṣā-samuccaya (TCD 32-B) and in the Siddhānta-śikṣā-vyākhyāna, Brl. p. 9 (no.XXVII).

Beginning:

स्वरं स्वराच्चानुस्वाराद् व्यञ्जनं व्यञ्जने परे।
द्विरूपमिष्यते रेफात् स्वरपूर्वात् परं च तत्॥
लवाभ्यामुत्तरः स्पर्श इति प्राप्यश्चतुर्विधम्।
न द्वितीयचतुर्थानां द्वित्वं तत्प्राप्तिगोचरे॥

End:

पूर्वागमस्ततः पुर्वं वैधश्चखिभुजेषु यः ।
यत्प्लुतस्वरयोर्मध्ये द्वित्वं पूर्वागमे ऽपि वा॥
पदान्तेष्वनुनासिक्ये पदसंहितयोक्तया।
प्राकृतो वैकृतश्चापि तद्धर्मो बुध्यते सुखम्॥
पदमध्यानुनासिक्ये स्पर्शात् पूर्वे तदुत्तमः ।
अन्तस्थाभ्यः परा तच्चेत् सैवान्तस्थेति निर्णयः ॥
इति वासिष्ठशिक्षा समाप्ता॥

Three additional verses in GB after colophon:

उच्चारणादिना स्पष्टं तदत्र न विधीयते।
चतुष्टयानुवाकान् वा त्रीन् वाप्याध्यापयेद् बुधः ॥

Adyar D I 972 (I A 19 = TR 19). Gr. 2 fol. (pp. 1-3). = Adyar I, p. 53a. 12 verses only.
GB 32. 4 fol. (with C.). Incomplete. Copied for Kielhorn in Mysore in 1875. See F. Kielhorn : Remarks on the Śikṣās in : *Indian Antiquary*, vol. V, p. 196 (reprint in : *Kleine Schriften*, vol. I, pp. 158-69).
Hamburg StUB (cod.Palmbl. III 8/133) → Veda-lakṣaṇa (HB).
Hoshiarpur p. 301 (no.4371). PL. Gr. 1 fol. 12 Grantha-s.
Hz 1431. PL. Gr. 1 fol. Belonged to the late Raja Ghanapathi of Tiruvidaimarudur, Thanjavur Dist.
MD 957. 2 pp. (42ff.) # (= Skt. Texts on Phonetics, pp. 251-52).
Mysore ND II 3761 (B 860/ 5). Gr. 3 fol. (67-69). Incomplete. Extract no. 274.
Oppert II 7447. Belonged to Venkatarama Sastri of Pillur, Mayavaram Taluk.
Oppert II 9091. Belonged to Ganapati Lakshminarayana Sastri of Tiruvadi, Thanjavur Dist.
Oppert II 9884. Belonged to M.Raja Ghanapathi of Mahadanapuram, Trichinapalli.
Whish 216(c). PL. Gr. 3 fol. (with C.). Not described in the catalogue.

— C.
Beginning:

स्वरात् परं व्यञ्जनं व्यञ्जने परे द्विरूपमिष्यते। ... अनुस्वाराच्च परं व्यञ्जनं व्यञ्जने परे द्विरूपमिष्यते ।... स्वरपूर्वाद् रेफात् परं च तद् व्यञ्जनं द्विरूपमिष्यते ... । लवाभ्यामुत्तरस्पर्शौ द्विरूपमिष्यते इति चतुर्विधद्वित्वम् ... । द्वितीयचतुर्थानां स्पर्शानां

द्वित्वं नास्ति। तेषां द्वित्वप्राप्तिविषये तस्मात् तस्मात् पूर्वं तत्पूर्ववर्णो भवति।

End: (Whish)

पदमध्ये त्वानुनासिक्ये श्रूयमाणे स्पर्शात् पूर्वतश्चेत् स्पर्शसवर्गो य उत्तमस्तद्धर्मी भवति। अन्तस्थाभ्यः पूर्वमनुनासिकश्चेत् सैवान्तस्थानुनासिका भवति । पदमध्यानुस्वारास्तु स्रुशोहवाशेत्यादिना कथिताः प्लुतानुनासिकाः अकारस्तु संहितायामपीत्युक्ताः ।

स्वरभक्तिरलौ स्यातां परे ह्यूष्मणि तस्य तु।

द्वित्वे चाभिनिधानान्यप्रथमे च परे न तत्॥

रेफस्य च लकारस्य च ऊष्मणि स्वरभक्तित्वं भवति । ऊष्मणो द्वित्वे च अभिनिधानव्यवहितप्रथमपरत्वे च तत्पूर्वस्य रेफस्य स्वरभक्तिर्नास्ति।

चतुर्भ्यः प्रथमादिभ्य उत्तमे परतः क्रमात्।

प्रथमाद्यास्तु नासिक्याः हकारात् केवलस्तथा॥

प्रथमादिभ्यश्चतुर्भ्यः स्पर्शेभ्यः उत्तमे परे सति तन्मध्ये यथापूर्वं प्रथमादयश्चत्वारो नासिक्या भवन्ति। हकारादुत्तमे परतः तन्मध्ये प्रथमत्वाद्युपाधिरहितं नासिक्यं भवति।

शकारप्रकृतेरूर्ध्वं चनासिक्यो न विद्यते।

शषसाभिनिधानाच्च यद्यन्तस्थोत्तमात् परा॥

शकारस्य स्थाने यश्छकारः तस्मादुत्तमे परे नासिक्यो नास्ति । शषसेभ्यः परादभिनिधानात् अन्तस्थासंयुक्तोत्तमे परे नासिक्यो ऽनुनासिकः । इति वासिष्ठशिक्षा सव्याख्यानं संपूर्णम्॥

GB 32. 4 fol. (with text). Incomplete.
Mysore p. 2 (no. 51). 3 fol.
Mysore I, p. 34.
Mysore ND II 3762 (B 860/ 2). Gr. 3 fol. (67-69). Incomplete. Extract no. 275.
Whish 216(c). PL. Gr. 3 fol. (with text). Not included in the catalogue.

[CC I 566b]

1136 VĀSIṢṬHĪ-ŚIKṢĀ (2) **(वासिष्ठीशिक्षा)**
Different from the above in 80 verses.

Beginning:

अष्टषष्टिं वदन्त्येके चतुःषष्टिमथापरे।
त्रिषष्टिमितरे वर्णानष्टपञ्चाशतं परे॥
स्वराः षड्विंशतिः प्रोक्ताः स्पर्शाः स्युः पञ्चविंशतिः।
चत्वारश्च तथान्तस्थाः षडूष्माणः प्रकीर्तिताः॥

End:

शेषः स्वस्थानकरणा विशेषस्त्वत्र कथ्यते।
इह कीर्तिमवाप्नोति ब्रह्मलोके महीयते॥

इति वासिष्ठशिक्षा समाप्ता॥

Tirupati SVUORI 3503 (1143h). PL. Gr. 6 fol.

1137 VĀSIṢṬHĪ-ŚIKṢĀ (3) **(वासिष्ठीशिक्षा)**

It is a kind of Anukramaṇikā based on Kātyāyana's *Śukla-yajurveda-sarvānukrama*. It examines the Saṃhitā, chapter by chapter, differentiating the Ṛk-s from the Yajus portions (which number 1467 and 2833 respectively). Therefore, in the colophon it is called *Ṛgyajuṣor-vibhāgaḥ*. Cf. Ṛgyajuḥ-pariśiṣṭa above. Pandit Sridhara Anna Sastri Ware, the editor of the *Kātyāyanīya-pariśiṣṭa-daśaka* remarks in his edition of the *Ṛgyajuḥ-pariśiṣṭa* (footnote on p. 94) that this *Vāsiṣṭhī-śikṣā* is by some scholar belonging to Vasiṣṭha Gotra :

वसिष्ठगोत्रोत्पन्नेन केनचिद् विदुषा विनिर्मिता ऋग्यजुर्विभागप्रतिपादिका वासिष्ठी शिक्षापि वर्तते । सा च क्वचित् पौर्वापर्यविपर्ययेण क्वचिदावापोद्वापाभ्यां चास्य ऋग्यजुषपरिशिष्टस्य अनुवादरूपैवेति बोध्यम्।

Beginning:

अथ शिक्षां प्रवक्ष्यामि वसिष्ठस्य मतं यथा।
सर्वानुक्रममुद्धृत्य ऋग्यजुषोस्तु लक्षणम्॥ १॥

अध्याये प्रथमे नवमे ऽनुवाके पुरा क्रूरस्येत्येका ऋगन्यानि यजूंषि सर्वे मन्त्राः । सप्तदशोत्तरशतं यजूंषि प्रथमे। १। ११७। द्वितीये ऽध्याये वीतिहोत्रमित्येषा ते ऽग्न इति मरुतां पृषतीरिति । यं परिधिमिति यजुरन्ताग्नेः प्रियं यजुः सँस्रवभागा इति यजुरन्ता स्वाहा वाडति यजुरेकेन सह मन्त्रम्। देवागातुविद इति द्वे संवर्चसेति ये रूपाण्याधत्तेति द्वे द्वे द्वितीये द्वादशैवार्चः षट्सप्ततिर्यजूंषि॥ २। ७६।

End:

चत्वारिंशत्तमे ऽध्याये ईशा वास्यमिति चतुर्दशाग्ने नयेति च द्वे इति सप्तदशर्चो वायुरनिलमिति द्वे यजुषी ओमिति वा गायत्री क्रतो इति त्रीणि यजूंषि हिरण्मयेन पात्रेणेति वा खं ब्रह्मेति चत्वारिंशत्तमे यजूंषि सप्त। ऋग्यजुषोः संख्याविभागाः ॥ १७। ७॥

एकीकृता ऋचः सर्वा मुनिषड्वेदभूमिताः ॥ १४६७॥
अब्धिरामाथ वा ज्ञेया वसिष्ठेन च धीमता॥ १॥
एवं सर्वाणि यजूंषि रामाश्विवसुयुग्मकाः ॥ २८२३॥
अथवा पञ्चभिर्न्यूनाः संहितायां विभागतः ॥ २॥

इति ऋग्यजुर्विभागात्मिका वासिष्ठी शिक्षा समाप्ता॥

BBRAS 13(I) (B D 278). Dated Śaka 1787.
Hoshiarpur p. 53 (no.5613). 18 fol. 400 Grantha-s.
IM 3381. 7 fol. 124 Grantha-s. Col.: Vasiṣṭhamuni-prokta- Ṛgyajur-vibhāgaḥ.

RASB II 1524 (G 3254). 6 fol. 170 Grantha-s. (Contains six additional verses at the beginning which are omitted in the printed edition, with a note that they are included in the Ṛgyajuḥ-pariśiṣṭa). Dated V.S. 1941.

Ptd.: in Śikṣā-saṃgraha. – Benares, 1889, pp. 36-45. – (Ben. S. S. 10).

***VĀSUDEVA (वासुदेव)**
of Kerala.
– C. on the Ṛgveda-sarvānukramaṇī (which see).

***VĀSUDEVA (वासुदेव)**
– C. on Caraṇa-vyūha. See under Caraṇa-vyūha. SBD 4093.

1138 VIKALPA-KAUMUDĪ (विकल्पकौमुदी)
The *Aṣṭa-vikṛti-lakṣaṇa* ascribed to Śaunaka is stated to be part of this → Aṣṭa-vikṛti-lakṣaṇa.

1139 VIKALPA-KAUMUDĪ or JAṬĀ-LAKṢAṆA (विकल्पकौमुदी / जटालक्षण)
of Narasiṃha → Jaṭā-lakṣaṇa.
Triv. Cur. III 10. Mal. 50 Grantha-s. Obtained from Vishnu Nambudiri, Ettikada Illam, Ayankudi.

1140 VIKṚTI (विकृति)
on different kinds of Vedic recitation, illustrated on the verse "bṛhaspate paridīyā rathena".
Baroda 8761(a). 6 fol. 100 Grantha-s. Dated Śaka 1741. = CLB I, p. 35. Extract pp. 164-65. Col.: Saṃhitaikādaśa-prakārā likhitāḥ || Cf. Grantha-saṃhitaikādaśa-prakārāḥ.

1141 VIKṚTI-KAUMUDĪ (विकृतिकौमुदी)
or Jaṭā-paṭala-ṭīkā of Gaṅgādhara Bhaṭṭācārya → C. on Jaṭāpaṭala or Vikṛti-vallī.
Ānandāśrama 45.
IM 2589. 18 fol. (1-17, 36). Incomplete.
Mithila IV 155. 2 fol. Incomplete.
Ujjain II, p. 9 (no.2336). 5 fol.

[CC I 569a]

1142 VIKṚTI-PĀṬHA(-KRAMA) (विकृतिपाठ /-क्रम)
SBD 52643. 3 fol. Pañca-saṃdhi-yukta-jaṭā-pāṭha of 7.7.15, 10.27.7 and 4.18.3.
SBD 53453. 3 fol. Vaṅga. Incomplete. Of Krama, Jaṭā, etc.

1143 VIKṚTI-LAKṢAṆA (1) (विकृतिलक्षण)
of Madhusūdana with a gloss → Aṣṭa-vikṛti-vivṛti(-kārikā).
BORI 378 of 1883-84. 6 fol. (Used for the Poona edition).

1144 VIKṚTI-LAKṢAṆA (2) **(विकृतिलक्षण)**
PUL I, p. 23 (no.128). 1 fol.

1145 VIKṚTI-VALLĪ **(विकृतिवल्ली)**
27 Kārikā-s ascribed to Vyāḍi; after the benedictory and introductory verses (1-4), it gives the names of the eight Vikṛti-s and explains the mode of forming the jaṭā (5-20); the remaining Vikṛti-s are described in verses 21-27. see Jaṭāpaṭala of Vyāḍi.

Beginning: (as in Veda-vikṛti-lakṣaṇa-saṃgraha)

तं सर्वज्ञं जगत्सेतुं परमात्मानमीश्वरम्।
वन्दे नारायणं देवं निरवद्यं निरञ्जनम्॥ १॥
नत्वादौ शौनकाचार्यं गुरुं वेदमहानिधिम्।
मुनीन्द्रं सर्ववेदज्ञं ब्रह्मज्ञं लोकविश्रुतम्॥ २॥
नमामि शाकलाचार्यं शाकल्यं स्थविरं तथा।
ब्रह्मविद्यागुरुं श्रेष्ठं भारद्वाजं बृहस्पतिम्॥ ३॥
शैशिरीये समाम्नाये व्याडिनैव महर्षिणा।
जटाद्या विकृतीरष्टौ लक्ष्यन्ते नातिविस्तरम्॥ ४॥
जटा माला शिखा रेखा ध्वजो दण्डो रथो घनः।
अष्टौ विकृतयः प्रोक्ताः क्रमपूर्वा मनीषिभिः॥ ५॥

End:

क्रममुक्त्वा विपर्यस्य पुनश्च क्रममुत्तरम्॥ २५॥
आर्धर्चादेवमुक्तः स क्रमदण्डो ऽभिधीयते।
पादशो ऽर्धर्चशो वापि सहोक्त्या दण्डवद् रथः॥ २६॥
अन्तक्रमं पठेत् पूर्वमादिपर्यन्तमारभेत्।
आदिक्रमं नयेदन्तं घनमाहुर्मनीषिणः॥ २७॥
इति श्रीव्याडिमहर्षिविरचिता अष्टविकृतिलक्षणात्मिका विकृतिवल्ली समाप्ता॥

Baroda 8513. 2 fol. 23 Grantha-s. Dated Śaka 1796. = CLB I, p. 35.
Baroda 8690(b). 2 fol. 26 Grantha-s. = CLB I, p. 35.
Baroda 8290. 17 fol. (2-18). 300 Grantha-s (with C. of Gaṅgādhara). = CLB I, p. 35.
Baroda 9916(a). PL. Gr. 5 fol. 250 Grantha-s. = CLB I, p. 35 (with C. of Gaṅgādhara).
Baroda 26310(b). 3 fol. (6-8). Dated Śaka 1778.
MD 958. PL. Tel. 4 pp. (13ff.). Altogether 30 verses; the 6th verse at the beginning belongs to the commentary Vikṛti-kaumudī. The end has a few additional verses, not found in the printed edition, and includes the verse: idaṃ jaṭāpāṭha-vidhānam uktam ... , belonging to the text of Jaṭā-paṭala of Hayagrīva.
MT 1527(a). PL. Tel. 2 fol. Presented in 1915-16 by Ramasvami Avadhanulu of Manepalli, Godavari Dist.

SBD 47893. 8 fol. Dated V.S. 1877. Copied by Moreśvara Gahvara. Title: Aṣṭa-vikṛti-kārikā Savyākhyā. Contains only the second part (verses 21-28; pp. 17-21 of the Devasthali's edition).

TD 1787. 3 fol. 19 Grantha-s. Col.: Jaṭā-paṭala.

TD 1788. 2 fol. 13 Grantha-s. Incomplete. 13 verses only.

TD 1789. 2 fol. 20 Grantha-s. (Corresponds to the Pariśiṣṭa of Poona edition, with different illustrations).

Trav. Uni. 4911. 225 Grantha-s (with Vikṛti-kaumudī of Gaṅgādhara).

Ptd.: ed. by Satyavrata Samasrami, with the sub-title: *Jaṭā-paṭala* (col.: iti vyāḍimuni-kṛtāyāṃ vikṛti-vallyāṃ jaṭā-paṭalaḥ), with commentary *Vikṛti-kaumudī* of Gaṅgādhara Bhaṭṭācārya, in the Sanskrit journal *Uṣā*. – Calcutta : Satya Press, 1889, vol. I, pt. 2. 16 pp. [Adyar (Ḥ11.3 x Sat); BM : Ptd. Bks. Cat. 1892-1906. 173, 852 (14010.c.43; vol.1); Per Sansk. d. 14/1)]

Also ed. by K. V. Abhyankar and G. V. Devasthali, in : *Veda-vikṛti-lakṣaṇa-saṃgraha*. – Poona : BORI, 1978, pp. 1-3 and 4-21 (with the commentary *Vikṛti-kaumudī* of Gaṅgādhara Bhaṭṭācārya).

– C. Vikṛti-kaumudī of Gaṅgādhara Bhaṭṭācārya.

Beginning:

यत्प्रकाशेन(सादेन) भासन्ते ब्रह्माद्या जगदीश्वराः।
यज्ज्ञानाद् विनिवर्तन्ते पाशाः पुत्रैषणादयः ॥
तं वन्दे परमानन्दं जगदानन्दवर्धनम्।
नित्यं ज्ञानघनं विष्णुं लोकाधिष्ठानमच्युतम्॥ २॥
ग्रन्थे विकृतिवल्ल्याख्ये व्यालिप्रोक्ते पुरातने।
टीकेयं क्रियते ऽस्माभिर्नाम्ना विकृतिकौमुदी॥ ३॥

तद्यथाः -- तं सर्वज्ञ ... निरञ्जनम्॥ १॥ नन्वस्मिञ्जगतीतले ग्रन्थारम्भलक्षणादौ कार्ये मङ्गलाचरणं कुर्वाणाः शिष्टाः प्रवर्तमानाः परिदृश्यन्ते । अतो ऽयं व्याडिराचार्यः स्वचिकीर्षितस्यद्यष्टविकृतिलक्षणप्रतिपादकविकृतिवल्ली नाम्नो ग्रन्थस्य निर्विघ्नेन परिसमाप्त्यर्थं शिष्टाचारपरिप्राप्ततया विशिष्टेष्टदैवतं परमेश्वरं सर्वाभीष्टफलप्रदातारं नमति तं सर्वज्ञमित्यनेन श्लोकेन -- तमहं वन्दे नमस्करोमीत्यर्थः ।

End:

यत्रोच्चस्वरितोदया इत्यत्र स्वरितग्रहणेन जात्यो गृह्यते । तत्रैवोदात्तस्वरितोदयः । तदुदाहरणम् -- क्व वो वः क्व १ क्व वः । कन्या३ वार्वाः कन्या कन्या३ वाः । रायो ऽवनिरवनी रायो रायो ऽवनिः । अभ्यर्षार्षाभ्य १ अभ्यर्ष । अभी३दमिदमभ्य १ भी३दम् । इत्याद्युदाहरणानि स्वयमेवोन्नेयानि।
(some Mss, e.g. MD 959, MT 5351 end here)

The Poona edition and also some other Mss. continue as follows: –

अथ मालादिलक्षणकारिका व्याख्यायन्ते -- तत्र क्रमप्राप्तं मालालक्षणमाह ब्रूयात् क्रमविपर्यासावर्ध ... कीर्तिता -- अर्धर्चस्यादितो ऽन्तं यावत् क्रमं ब्रूयात्। अन्ततश्चादिं यावद् विपर्यासं ब्रूयात् ...

End:

क्रमस्वरूपाबाधेनैतत् पठनीयम् । कुत्रचिदुत्तरेदिति पाठः । तस्य व्यर्थलक्षणयोच्चारयेदित्यर्थः । इत्यष्टविकृतिकारिकाव्याख्या समाप्तिमगमत्॥

Ānandāśrama 45.
Baroda 8290. 17 fol. (2-18). 300 Grantha-s (with text). = CLB I, p. 35.
Baroda 9916(a). PL. Gr. 5 fol. 250 Grantha-s. = CLB I, p. 35 (with text).
BORI TM 40B. 11 fol. (5-15). Title: Jaṭā-paṭala.
MD 959. PL. Tel. 35 pp. (6ff.). 1st Paṭala, up to (verse 20) p. 16 of the Poona edition.
MT 1527(b). PL. Tel. 13 fol. (2-14). Incomplete. 1st Paṭala only. One additional stanza at the end. Presented in 1915-16 by Ramasvami Avadhanulu of Manepalli, Godavari Dist.
MT 5351. PL. Gr. 12 fol. 210 Grantha-s. 1st paṭala only. Restored from MD 902 (959).
SBD 47893. 8 fol. Dated V.S. 1877. Copied by Moreśvara Gahvara. Title: Aṣṭa-vikṛti-kārikā Savyākhyā. Contains C. only on the second part (verses 21-28; pp. 17-21 of the Devasthali's edition).
Trav. Uni. 4911. 225 Grantha-s (with text). Incomplete.

Ptd.: ed. by K. V. Abhyankar and G. V. Devasthali, in : *Veda-vikṛti-lakṣaṇa-saṃgraha.* – Poona : BORI, 1978, pp. 4-21; based on two Mss:
1) a Ms. of Ānandāśrama, Poona;
2) BORI 65 of A 1881-82.

C. Aṣṭa-vikṛti-kārikā-vyākhyā of Rāmakṛṣṇa-bhaṭṭa. It omits the first verse and is almost identical with the *Vikṛti-kaumudī* at the end.
Beginning:

ऋगाम्नायं समासाद्य संप्रदायानुसारतः ।
व्याख्यास्यते व्यालिकृता जटालक्षणकारिका॥

गुरुनमस्काररूपमङ्गलपूर्वकं लक्षणस्यार्षताज्ञापनार्थं स्वनामोक्ति ... महर्षिर्लक्षणं कर्तव्यत्वेन प्रतिजानीते। नत्वादौ --

End:

यथा अर्षसीत्यर्षसि। प्र णः ... अर्षसीत्यर्षसि। प्र णः। अत्र ध्वजापेक्षया ... तथार्धर्चे समापयेद् इत्युक्तक्रमस्वरूपाबाधेनैतत् पठनीयम् ॥ इति श्रीमद्वेदशास्त्रसंपन्न पौराणकोपनामक श्रीमन्नारायणभट्टसूनु रामकृष्णभट्टकृता अष्टविकृतिकारिकाव्याख्या समाप्ता।

श्रीभट्टनारायणतातपाद प्रसादतोनुद्गीतसंप्रदायम्।

यल्लक्षणं ... क्तमुनिप्रणीतं व्याख्यातमस्मान्मुदमेतु विद्वान् ॥
साङ्गोपाङ्गजटे वेदशास्त्रे च परिनिष्ठितम् ।
पुमांसमनसूयन्तं व्याख्येयं सुखयि ... ॥

IM 2521. 14 fol. (2-15). Incomplete.
IM 2572. 6 fol.
SBD 4302. 21 fol.

– C. TD 1790. 5 fol. 30 Grantha-s. Incomplete. Only the last 5 verses on Mālā, etc.

[CC II 134b]

1146 VIKṚTI-PRASTĀRA (विकृतिप्रस्तार)

An illustration of eleven kinds of Vikṛti-s on the mantra "indra śreṣṭhāni" with verses of definitions.

SBD 1476. 8 fol. Damaged. "atha saṃhitāvikṛti(prastāra)prārambhaḥ" on the title page.
Col.: ityekādaśaprakāreṇa ṛcaḥ samāptāḥ |

1147 VIKṚTI-SAṂGRAHA (विकृतिसंग्रह)

SBD 55059. 15 fol.

*VIDYĀRAṆYA (विद्यारण्य)

– C. on Caraṇa-vyūha. N-W P V 42 (no.12). 29 fol. Belonged to Ramachand Bhatta, Allahabad.

*VINĀYAKA (विनायक)

– Vaidika-cchandaḥ-prakāśa. L 19. RASB II 1538.

[CC I 577a]

*VINĀYAKA (विनायक)

– C. on Saṃkṣepa-sāra.

1148 VILAṄGHYA(-PRAKARAṆA) (विलङ्घ्य-प्रकरण)

Enumeration of words with a final "e ", "ai", "o ", "au", and on the changes of them before a following vowel in the *Taittirīya-saṃhitā*, e.g. hīyata eva; harā iti. Also included in the *Sapta-lakṣaṇa* (which see).

Unspecified:
Hoshiarpur p. 301 (no.5947). PL. Gr. 2 fol. 50 Grantha-s.
PUL II. App. p. 13 (no.206). PL. Gr. 12 fol.
PUL II. App. p. 13 (no.207). PL. Gr. 6 fol. A.1048 ?
PUL II. App. p. 13 (no.208). PL. Gr. 2 fol.
Tirupati SVUORI 5944 (900b). PL. Gr.
Trav. Uni. 21703 B. PL. Mal. 75 Grantha-s.
Trav. Uni. 22209 D. PL. Mal. 75 Grantha-s.
Trav. Uni. 22749 F. PL. Mal. 75 Grantha-s.

C.
PUL II. App. p. 13 (no.210). PL. Gr. 5 fol. (9-13).
Mysore (1898), p. 6 (no. 52). 18 fol. (14-31).
Mysore ND II 3789-96.

1149 VILAṄGHYA(-PRAKARAṆA) (विलङ्घ्य-प्रकरण)
of Nāgadeva, son of Yajñanārāyaṇa, in 68 verses as it is stated in the last verse → Ṛgvilaṅghya-lakṣaṇa.

1150 VILAṄGHYA(-PRAKARAṆA) (विलङ्घ्य-प्रकरण)
Mysore ND II 3771 (P 977/13). PL. Tel. 3 fol. (61-63). Extract no. 277.

1151 VILAṄGHYA(-PRAKARAṆA) (विलङ्घ्य-प्रकरण)
of Nārāyaṇa-bhaṭṭa.

Beginning:

प्रणम्य भारतीं देवीं सर्वलोकैकमातरम्।
नारायणः प्रवक्ष्यामि विलङ्घ्यानि पदान्यहम्॥ १॥
एकारैकारवर्णौ यौ संहितायां विकारिणौ।
तदन्तानि विलङ्घ्यानीत्युच्यन्ते वेदवित्तमैः ॥ २॥
पुरातने ऽतिरिक्तं यत् त्यक्त्वानुक्तं समोप्य च।
वर्णक्रमेण गृह्यन्ते सव्याख्यान्येव तान्यपि॥ ३॥
इङ्ग्यं यत् पदमत्रापि नानापदवदिष्यते।
निमित्तत्वेन यद् ग्राह्यं गृह्यते पदमेव तत्॥ ४॥
अपि चेत् स्याद्धि नान्यत् तु पूरणे ऽत्र विधीयते।
अग्ने ऽपारे यदर्ये ऽह्वे ऽतिथये ऽनिष्टके ऽजरे॥

End:

वह्वत्याहवनीये च हुते होत्रे हवामहे।
हते हस्ते तु नेङ्ग्यान्तं हरन्ते ह्वयते ह्वुते॥ ४५॥
हीयते हूयते हत्यै हन्तवै च हरामहै।
ह्वयामहे हरै हित्यै नैभ्यः सन्त्यधिकानि तु॥ ४६॥

Adyar D I 983 → Veda-lakṣaṇa (A 1). 2 copies.
Adyar D I 984 → Veda-lakṣaṇa (A 2).
Adyar D I 987 → Veda-lakṣaṇa (A 5).
Adyar D I 988 → Veda-lakṣaṇa (A 6).
Adyar D I 989 → Veda-lakṣaṇa (A 7).
Adyar D I 1030 → Sapta-lakṣaṇa.
Adyar D I 1031 → Sapta-lakṣaṇa.
Adyar D I 1032 → Sapta-lakṣaṇa.

Adyar D I 1033 → Sapta-lakṣaṇa.
Adyar D I 1034 → Sapta-lakṣaṇa.
Baroda 6131(a). PL. Gr. 2 fol. (5-6). 30 Grantha-s. = CLB I, p. 35.
Baroda 10034(b). PL. Gr. 2 fol. (2-3). 30 Grantha-s. = CLB I, p. 35.
Baroda 10381(d). PL. Gr. 5 fol. (5-9). 30 Grantha-s. = CLB I, p. 35.
Brl. p. 10 (no.XXXV) = IO 4492.
Brl. p. 11 (no.XXXVI) = IO 4491.
Burnell 5b.
Hoshiarpur p. 53 (no.4105). PL. Gr. 3 fol. 50 Grantha-s. Extract p. 412.
Hoshiarpur p. 53 (no.4118). PL. Gr. 3 fol.
Hoshiarpur p. 53 (no.5613). PL. Gr. 10 fol. 330 Grantha-s.
IO 4491 (Burnell 146b). PL. Gr. 3 fol. (3-5).
IO 4492 (Burnell 49b). PL. Gr. 4 fol. (3-6).
MT 689(b). PL. Gr. 3 fol. (3-5). Purchased in 1912-13 through Seshasayi Ayyangar of Kottaiyur near Kumbakonam.
Oppert II 9094. Belonged to Ganapati Lakshminarayana Sastri of Tiruvadi, Thanjavur Dist.
PUL I, p. 23 (no.129). PL. Gr. 4 fol. (3-6).
RASB II 487-88(II) (G 6063). 4 fol. (3-6). Dated V.S. 1913 / Śaka 1778.
TD 1800. PL. Gr. 6 fol. (4-9) 60 Grantha-s → Sapta-lakṣaṇa.
TD 1801. PL. Gr. 4 fol. 60 Grantha-s → Sapta-lakṣaṇa
Tirupati SVUORI (1746). PL. Gr. 5 fol.
Trav. Uni. 2630 N. PL. Gr. 45 Grantha-s. Incomplete.
Trav. Uni. 2938 C. PL. Gr. 50 Grantha-s.
Trav. Uni. 3040 C. PL. Gr. 50 Grantha-s.
Trav. Uni. 4369 G. PL. Gr. 3 fol. 45 Grantha-s.
Trav. Uni. 21519 B. PL. Gr. 40 Grantha-s.

Ptd.: There are at least five editions: three in Grantha and one each in Malayalam and Telugu script. See under Aniṅgya (Taitt.) and Sapta-lakṣaṇa.

1152 VILAṄGHYA(-PRAKARAṆA) with C. (**विलङ्घ्य-प्रकरण सव्याख्य**)
of Nārāyaṇa-bhaṭṭa.
Adyar D I 974 (19 N 32 = 66868). PL. Gr. 14 fol. (94ff.). The former owner was Sītārāman.
Adyar D I 975 (22 H 52 = 69106). PL. Gr. 2 fol. (38-39). Incomplete. = Adyar I, p. 51b.
Adyar D I 976 (22 M 28 = 69378). PL. Gr. 3 fol. (2-4). = Adyar I, p. 53b. Title: Sapta-lakṣaṇa.
Adyar D I 977 (25 K 24 = 71114). PL. Gr. 14 fol. (15ff.).
Adyar D I 1036 → Sapta-lakṣaṇa-vyākhyā.
Adyar D I 1039 → Sapta-lakṣaṇa-vyākhyā.
Baroda 6131(g). PL. Gr. 56-61 fol. 150 Grantha-s. = CLB I, p. 35. (different ?)
Baroda 10032(b). PL. Gr. 20 fol. 350 Grantha-s. = CLB I, p. 35.
Brl. p. 11 (no.XXXVII) = IO 4493.
IO 4493 (Burnell 350b). Tel. 12 fol. (9-20). Written ca. A.D. 1867.

IO 4494 (Mackenzie II 94f). PL. Na. 8 fol. (59-66). Written ca. A.D. 1770.
IO 4495 (Mackenzie III 234j). PL. Tel. 14 fol. (90-103). Written ca. A.D. 1810.
MD 965. Gr. 20 pp. (32ff.)
MD 966. PL. Tel. 20 pp. (1ff.). The end is slightly different.
MD 16804. PL. Gr. 5 pp. 80 Grantha-s.
MD 16811. PL. Gr. 11 pp. 198 Grantha-s.
MD 17439. PL. Gr. 20 pp. 268 Grantha-s.
MD 18928. PL. Tel. 5 pp. (82ff.).
MT 523(b). PL. Tel. 17 fol. (18-34). Presented in 1910-11 by C. Visvanatha Shastrigal of Viziyanagaram. Col.: śrīmadvādātitimmāvadhānitanayena nārā(yaṇā)vadhāninā kṛtaṃ (vyakti-)vailaṅghyavyākhyānaṃ saṃpūrṇam |
MT 3887(f). PL. Gr. 3 fol. (75-77). Incomplete. Purchased in 1921-22 from Annasvami Sastrigal, Bhavani, Coimbatore Dist.
MT 2881(c). PL. Gr. 5 fol. (21-25). Presented in 1918-19 by Venkatagiri Appalacharyar of Triplicane.
Mysore ND II 3776-86. Extract no. 278.
Oppert II 775. Belonged to Ghanapathi Shingaracharyar of Alasur, Madurantakam Taluk.
Oppert II 9095. Belonged to Ganapati Lakshminarayana Sastri of Tiruvadi, Thanjavur Dist.
PUL I, p. 24 (no.130). PL. Gr. 10 fol. (12-21).
PUL I, p. 24 (no.131). PL. Tel. 12 fol. (1-11, 15).
TCD 35-B. PL. Gr. 250 Grantha-s.
Trav. Uni. 347 C. PL. Gr. 200 Grantha-s. (C. only).
Trav. Uni. C.2668 B. = TCD 35-B.
Trav. Uni. 22749 L. PL. Mal. 250 Grantha-s.
Whish 25a (2). PL. Gr. 10 fol. (12-21).

[CC I 578a]

1153 VILAṄGHYA(-PRAKARAṆA) (**विलङ्घ्य-प्रकरण**)

Adyar D I 978 (20 F 41 = 67223). PL. Tel. 3 fol. = Adyar I, p. 51b.
Baroda 11949(c). PL. Tel. 16 fol. (39-54). 200 Grantha-s (with C. Pada-darpaṇa, here ascribed to Mādhavācārya). = CLB I, p. 35. Extract pp. 165-66.
IO 4496 (Mackenzie III 186h). PL. Tel. 3 fol. (16-18). Written ca. A.D. 1800.
MD 960. PL. Tel. 3 pp. (28ff.). Col.: Vyakti-vilaṅghya.
MD 961. PL. Gr. 4 pp. (13ff.).
MD 962. PL. Gr. 12 pp. (6ff.).
MD 16709. PL. Tel. 60 Grantha-s.
MD 16727. PL. Tel. 4 pp. (27ff.). 63 Grantha-s.
MD 16730. PL. Tel. 20 pp. 315 Grantha-s (with C.)
MT 1964(o). PL. Tel. 4 fol. (114-17). Presented in 1916-17 by Rayaprolu Ramabrahmangaru of Guruza, Gudivada Taluk, Krishna Dist.
MT 1976(b). Tel. 15 fol. (16-30) (with C. of Mallināthārya-yajvan). Presented in 1916-17 by Nimmagadda Narasimhavadhanulugaru, Godavarru, Godavari Dist.
MT 2189(c). Tel. 11 fol. (15-25). Transcribed in 1916-17 from a Ms. of Vemparla Subrahmanya Sastrigaru of Tondavaramu, Godavari Dist. The scribe of the original Ms. is Ponnamalli Subrahmaṇya. Dated: krodhināmasaṃvatsara-vaiśākha-bahula-

prathamā bhṛguvāram |

MT 3887(d). PL. Gr. 2 fol. (73-74). Purchased in 1921-22 from Annasvami Sastrigal, Bhavani, Coimbatore Dist.

MT 4600(a). PL. Gr. 3 fol. (7-9). Presented in 1924-25 by the Secretary to the Trustees of Sri Yogi Parthasarathi Ayyangar's Charities, Triplicane, Madras.

Mysore (1898), p. 6 (no. 54a). Tel. 15 fol. Title: Vyakti-vilug-adhyāya.

Mysore I, pp. 34-35. 613.

Mysore ND II 3764-70. Extract no. 276.

TD 1802. PL. Tel. 4 fol. (110-13). 40 Grantha-s.

TD 1803. PL. Tel. 2 fol. (114-15). 52 Grantha-s.

– C. Pada-darpaṇa of Mallayārya.

Beginning:

एवं लुप्तविसर्गाणि पदानि अकारादिक्रमेण सम्यक् लक्षयित्वा तेनैव क्रमेण पदकाले एकारैकारान्तानि सुबोधनं व्यक्तिवेलुकु नामगुणेन लक्षयितुमुपक्रमते । अथ यजुःसंहितायामकाराकारपूर्वस्वरपरो येषु प्रवक्ष्यन्ते ... । अत्रायमथशब्द आनन्तर्यार्थे । लुप्तविसर्गापेक्षया आनन्तर्यार्थश्च । अकारपूर्वस्वरपरश्च यकारो येषु पदेषु लुप्यते तेषु पदेषु मध्ये एकारैकारान्तानि पदानि प्रवक्ष्यन्ते इति योजना ।

End:

अनिङ्ग्यान्तः । सांनिध्यात् हस्त इति लभ्यते । हस्त इति शब्दः परः अनिङ्ग्यान्तः सन् पदकाले एकारान्तो भवति । हस्त आदाय सविता बिभ्रत् । अनिङ्ग्यान्त इति किम् । विश्वतोहस्त उत विश्वतोमुखः । इङ्ग्यस्य अन्तः इङ्ग्यान्तः । स न भवतीत्यनिङ्ग्यान्तः । इति श्रीमल्लिनाथार्ययज्वकृतौ पददर्पणे व्यक्तिवेलुकुनामाध्यायः समाप्तः ।

Adyar D I 979 (28 F 30 = 72834). PL. Tel. 12 fol. (18ff.). = Adyar I, p. 50b.

Adyar D I 980 (30 D 29 = 73919). PL. Tel. 19 fol. (24ff.). Colophon: Maharṣikṛtau Pada-darpaṇe Vyaktiveluku-nāmakādhyāyaḥ. = Adyar I, p. 54a. Title: Sapta-lakṣaṇa-vyākhyā.

Baroda 11949(c). PL. Tel. 16 fol. (39-54). 200 Grantha-s (ascribed to Mādhavācārya). = CLB I, p. 35. Extract pp. 165-66.

MD 16730. PL. Tel. 20 pp. 315 Grantha-s (with text).

MT 485(b). PL. Tel. 13 fol. (20-32) (with text). Presented in 1910-11 by C. Visvanatha Shastrigal of Viziyanagaram. (Aniṅgyānta with C. in the catalogue).

व्याख्यानं रचितं व्यक्तिवेलुको लक्षणस्य च ।
बालानामपि बोधार्थं मल्लिनाथार्य-यज्वना ॥

MT 1964(c). PL. Tel. 14 fol. (45-58). Presented in 1916-17 by Rayaprolu Ramabrahman-garu of Guruza, Gudivada Taluk, Krishna Dist.

MT 1976(b). Tel. 15 fol. (16-30) (a. Mallināthārya-yajvan). Presented in 1916-17 by Nimmagadda Narasimhavadhanulugaru, Godavarru, Godavari Dist.

MT 2189(c). Tel. 11 fol. (15-25). Transcribed in 1916-17 from a Ms. of Vemparla Subrahmanya Sastrigaru of Tondavaramu, Godavari Dist. The scribe of the original Ms. is Ponnamalli Subrahmaṇya. Dated: krodhināmasaṃvatsara-vaiśākha-bahula-prathamā bhṛguvāram |

MT 2649(c). PL. Tel. 11 fol. (95-105). maharṣikṛtau padadarpaṇe vyaktiveluk ... (with text). Presented in 1917-18 by Prava Surayya Shastrigaru of Penumanchilli, Narasa-pur Taluk, Krishna Dist. (Aniṅgyānta with C. in the catalogue).

Mysore ND II 3787 (P 997/ 3). PL. Na. 14 fol. (25-38).

Mysore ND II 3788 (P 584/ 8). PL. Tel. 12 fol. (22-33).

Oppert I 1029. Belonged to Viraraghava Tatacharyar, Head Master, Sanskrit School of Sathakopacharya, Kanchipuram, Chingelpet Dist.

Oppert II 774. Belonged to Ghanapathi Shingaracharyar of Alasur, Madurantakam Taluk.

Oppert II 1372. Belonged to Gopalacharyar of Pillapakkam, Kanchipuram Taluk.

TD 1811. PL. Gr. 16 fol. 600 Grantha-s. Incomplete.

TD 1812. PL. Tel. 5 fol. 75 Grantha-s. Incomplete.

Tirupati SVUORI 5945 (4511b). PL. Tel.

Trav. Uni. 22209 E. PL. Mal. 200 Grantha-s.

[CC I 579a]

1154 VILAṄGHYA-LAKṢAṆA (विलङ्घ्यलक्षण)

TCD 34-B → Ṛgvilaṅghya-lakṣaṇa.

1155 VILAṄGHYA-VYĀKHYĀNA (विलङ्घ्यव्याख्यान)

SBD 4189. 14 fol.

1156 VILAṄGHYA-SŪTRA (विलङ्घ्यसूत्र)

SBD 4162. 4 fol.

SBD 4215. 10 fol. (with Napara-tapara). Incomplete.

1157 VISARJANĪYA-LAKṢAṆA (विसर्जनीयलक्षण)

Beginning:

सपूर्वं स्वर्यते ह्रस्वो दीर्घो ऽन्त्यांशे तदुत्तरौ।
नादानुस्वारकावेव स्वर्यते पूर्वमुच्चवत्॥
अन्त्यांशे स्वर्यते दीर्घो विरामव्यञ्जने परे।
संयोगे चावसाने च नादानुस्वारकौ स्वयम्॥ इत्युच्चारणविषयः।
दैवीं धियमजस्रन्त्यामिति कृद्यावतीं कृतीः।
येना पुरस्ताद् देवानामेषां तासां यथासदे॥

End:

क्रूमाः ऋतव आयुर्धप् त्रे यो विशेयो मध्यतो ऽन्तः सदसि तिष्ठन्तं छन्दोभिरिति सकारा विसर्जनीयाः।

प्राजापत्योनुवाके तु पदं पश्यति चोचकः।

नरोन्योनीयवीयापि वीर्यान् पीयूष पीयति ॥
लीयन्ते लीयपोमीयः वाल्पीयन्त द्वितीय च ॥

Adyar D I 981 (23 E 25 = 69758). PL. Gr. 2 fol. (34-35).
Hamburg StUB (cod.Palmbl. III 8/133) → Veda-lakṣaṇa (HB).

*VIṢṆUMITRA KUMĀRA (विष्णुमित्र कुमार)
Son of Devamitra. According to Uvaṭa, he was the original author of the Ṛk-prātiśākhya-bhāṣya (cf. Weber, p. 8; Oxf. 405b, etc.).
[CC I 592a]

*VĪRARĀGHAVA (वीरराघव)
– Śabda-brahma-vilāsa, a commentary on the *Taittirīya-prātiśākhya ?*

*VĪRARĀGHAVĀCĀRYA (KAUŚIKA) (वीरराघवाचार्य कौशिक)
– C. on the Pāṇinīya-śikṣā also called (Rāghavīya-bhāṣya). Mysore I, p. 30 = Mysore ND II 3628 (C 78). Tel. 54 fol. Extract no. 217.
Ptd.: See above the Telugu script edition of the *Pāṇinīya-śikṣā.*

1158 VṚTHĀVYAKTI (वृथाव्यक्ति)
→ Pṛthag-vyakti.

1159 VṚTHĀVYAKTI (वृथाव्यक्ति)
Mysore I, p. 34.
Mysore ND II 3797 (P 2262/ 6). PL. Gr. 1 fol. Extract no. 279.

1160 VṚTHĀVYAKTI (?) (वृथाव्यक्ति)
Adyar D I 1009 (22 H 6 = 69060). PL. Tel. 3 fol. (5-7). An ancillary tract dealing with Dīrghavyakti-s, etc. On the margin of fol. 1a is found written (the title ?): Vṛthāvyakti. Author not mentioned.

1161 VṚDDHĀVṚDDHĪYA (DAŚĀṄGA) (वृद्धावृद्धीय / दशाङ्ग)
Mysore I, p. 34.
Mysore ND II 3798 (P 2476/ 1). PL. Na. 13 fol. Extract no. 280.

1162 VEṄKAṬA-PADA-VINYĀSA (वेङ्कटपदविन्यास)
→ Pada-saṃkhyā, MD 923.

1163 VEṄKAṬA-BHAIṬ (वेङ्कटभैट्)
Oppert I 7230. Belonged to Ivattur Nandikesvara Sastri of Vijayanagaram. Cf. Rāvaṇa-bhaiṭ and Vaidyanātha-bhaiṭ.
[CC I 601b]

*VEṄKAṬEŚA (वेङ्कटेश)
Pūrva-ṛkkārikā (composed together with Gopāla). Adyar D I 898. 899.
[NCC VI 132a]

*VEṄKAṬEŚA (वेङ्कटेश)
Sāma-tantra-saṃgraha. Trav. Uni. 2911 C. PL. Gr. 250 Grantha-s. Incomplete.

1164 VEDA-KALPADRUMA (वेदकल्पद्रुम)
BHU C 1138 (D 11/658). 220 fol. Śāradā script.

1165 VEDA-KĀṆḌA-VIVECANA (वेदकाण्डविवेचन)
on the division of the *Taittirīya-saṃhitā*, such as Prājāpatya, Kāṭhaka, etc.
Trav. Uni. 3582 A. PL. Gr. 75 Grantha-s. Incomplete.

1166 VEDA-TATTVA-NIRŪPAṆA (or -NIRṆAYA) (वेदतत्त्वनिरूपण /-निर्णय)
of Kṛṣṇa. A treatise explaining the characteristics of the Veda-s and expatiating the superiority of the *Śukla-yajurveda* over the *Taittirīya*.

Beginning:

कृष्णं कृपालुं पुरुषोत्तमं तं राधासमेतं रमणीयरूपम्।
रमापतिं राघवपूर्वरूपं नमामि नित्यं पुरुषार्थसिद्ध्यै॥
श्रीरामं जानकीजानिं साम्बं वाणीं गणेश्वरम्।
योगीश्वरं याज्ञवल्क्यं कण्वादिसहितं मुनिम्॥
कात्यायनेन सहितं वन्दे ऽहं त्विष्टसिद्धये।
वन्दे ऽहं मङ्गलात्मानं भास्वन्तं वेदविग्रहम्॥
याज्ञवल्क्यं मुनिश्रेष्ठं जिष्णुं हरिहरप्रभुम्।
जितेन्द्रियं जितक्रोधं सदा ध्यानपरायणम्॥
आनन्दनिलयं वन्दे योगानन्दं मुनीश्वरम्।
निर्जित्य वादसमये ऋषीन् सर्वानुपस्थितान्॥
गावो येन हृतास्तस्मै नमो ऽस्तु ब्रह्मरात(मूर्त)ये। ...
यद्यप्यहं ब्रह्म सत्यं जगन्मिथ्येति जानताम्।
अयोग्यमेव चास्माकं वेदतत्त्वनिरूपणम्॥ ...

मन्त्रब्राह्मणोभयभिन्नजगद्भिन्नत्वस्य मन्त्रब्राह्मणात्मकवेदे सत्त्वाल्लक्षणसमन्वयः कार्यः। वैदिकसंकेतविशेषसंबन्धेन ब्राह्मणपदवत्त्वं ब्राह्मणस्य लक्षणम्। वेदमूलपाणिनीय संकेतसंबन्धेन आख्यातपदवत्त्वम् आख्यातानां लक्षणमिव ऋक्प्रचुरवेदत्वं ऋग्वेदस्य लक्षणम्। पादबद्धमन्त्रवत्त्वमृचां लक्षणम्। इति लक्षणग्रन्थः समाप्तः॥

End:

पूर्वोपन्यस्तस्मृतिपुराणादीनां तु श्रुतिमूललिङ्गत्वेनैकान्तरितप्रामाण्यस्य श्रुतीनां तच्छ्रुतीनां तच्छ्रुतित्वेनैव साक्षात् प्रामाण्यस्य च पूर्वमीमांसायां व्यवस्थापनाच्चेत्यन्यत्र विस्तर इति सुधीभिरवहितमनस्कैः पण्डितोत्तमैराकलनीयम्॥

नामूलं लिखितं किंचिन्नाश्रुतं नाविचारितम्।

इति कृत्वा मयि दयामीक्षध्वं विबुधा इदम्॥

इति श्रीपदवाक्यप्रमाणपारावार पारीणायातयामाग्रेसरशाखि श्रौतस्मार्तकर्मानुष्ठानपर श्रीकृष्णपदारविन्दगलितमधुपानतृप्त भृङ्गायमाणान्तः करणकशोधित कृष्णाख्य ब्रह्मात्मैक्यबुद्धिसाक्षिक प्रमात्रभिन्नश्रीकृष्णपण्डितविरचिते श्रीवेदतत्त्वनिरूपणे शिष्टोपकारनिरूपणं नाम प्रथमं प्रकरणं संक्षेपतः समाप्तिमगमत्। इति शिवम्। ...

यदत्र सौष्ठवं किंचित् तद् गुरोरेव मे न हि।
यदत्रासौष्ठवं किंचित् तन्ममैव गुरोर्न हि॥ ...
श्रीकृष्णसूरिरचितं वेदतत्त्वनिरूपणम्।
प्रीत्यै भूयाद् भगवतः श्रीकृष्णस्याग्रशाखिनः। ...

BORI TM 102A. 60 fol.
MT 2359. 28 fol. Incomplete. Transcribed in 1916-17 from a Ms. acquired through the sub-magistrate of Kovvur, Krishna Dist.

1167 VEDA-TAIJASA (वेदतैजस)
Name of the commentary of Sūryanārāyaṇa on the *Vyāsa-śikṣā.*

[CC I 604a]

1168 VEDA-NĀSIKĀ-ŚIKṢĀ or VEDĀṄGA-NĀSIKĀ-ŚIKṢĀ (वेदनासिकाशिक्षा / वेदाङ्गनासिकाशिक्षा)
Names of the *Pāṇinīya-śikṣā* in some Mss. Cf. America 370. Baroda 9367.

1169 VEDA-PAÑCĀŚAD-ANUKRAMAṆIKĀ (वेदपञ्चाशदनुक्रमणिका)
Cf. Pañcāśad-anukramaṇikā.

1170 VEDA-PADA-DARPAṆA (PADA-LAKṢAṆA) (वेदपददर्पण / पदलक्षण)
on the Pada text by Yallayārya-yajvan.
Mysore p. 2 (no. 54). 15 fol.

[CC I 604a]

1171 VEDA-PADA-PĀṬHA-CARCĀ (वेदपदपाठचर्चा)
of Kashinatha Vasudeva Abhyankar. A critical study of the theories and conventions of the ancient grammarians on the Pada-pāṭha of the Veda in eight sections; Sanskrit passages, partly gathered from various sources and partly his own formulations, with elaborate explanations in English; together with the edition of the *Upalekha-sūtra* (here ascribed to Bhāradvāja-Bṛhaspati).

Beginning:

अर्थः पदम्। १। चत्वारि पदजातानि नामाख्याते चोपसर्गनिपाताश्च। २। तानि द्विविधानि केवलानि समस्तानि च। ३। तन्नाम येनाभिदधाति सत्त्वम्। ४। तदाख्यातं येन भावं स धातुः। ५। क्रियाविशेषवाचिन उपसर्गाः। ६। उच्चावचेष्वर्थेषु निपतन्तः पदान्तरसंबद्धत्वेनार्थप्रतिपादका निपाताः। ७।

End:

यकारस्य पदादौ जकारः क्वचित् पकारस्यापि स्थाने खकारः शुक्ले यजुषि। ७७। क्वचित् तैत्तिरीया निमित्तं विना नकारस्य स्थाने णकारम् उच्चारयन्ति। पादान्ते नकारस्य द्वित्वं च। तथैवानुनासिकात् परस्याकारस्य रुडागमम्। ७८। नराशंसादीनि यथोपदिष्टम्। ७९। पदपाठसंकेता एते क्रमपाठे विकृतिषु प्रवर्तन्ते। ८०।

Ptd.: Poona : BORI, 1974. Reprint of the "Prolegomena to the Veda-padapāṭha", in : *Annals of the Bhandarkar Oriental Research Institute*, vol. 54 (1973), pp. 9-44. [UBTÜ (16 A 12802 Nr. 3); SAI (ind 51 D 584/1171)]

1172 VEDA-PARIBHĀṢĀ (1) (वेदपरिभाषा)
of Keśava.
BISM p. 268 (41/511) → Keśava-(ī-)śikṣā (natvā gaṇapatim ...).

1173 VEDA-PARIBHĀṢĀ (2) (वेदपरिभाषा)
Hoshiarpur p. 301 (no.4118). PL. Gr. 14 fol. 100 Grantha-s. Incomplete.

1174 VEDA-PARIBHĀṢĀ-KĀRIKĀ-ŚIKṢĀ (वेदपरिभाषाकारिकाशिक्षा)
of Rāmacandra, son of Siddheśvara. 10 verses and a commentary thereon explaining the code words of four letters used in the *Veda-paribhāṣā-sūtra-śikṣā*.

Beginning:

अथ वेदपरिभाषाकारिकाशिक्षा सटीका प्रारभ्यते।

श्रीरामं सद्गुरुं याज्ञवल्क्यं कात्यायनं तथा।
नत्वा पदानां वक्ष्यामि लक्षणं चतुरक्षरैः ॥ १॥
अनुवाके ऽनुवाके चाम्नाये माध्यन्दिनीयके।
परिभाषोच्यते हल्युक् केवलो वा स्वरो ऽक्षरम्॥ २॥
पदसंख्यादिमेन स्याद् द्वितीयेन विसर्गनौ।
सावग्रहं सेतिकारं तृतीयेन तुरीयतः ॥ ३॥
मान्तं कादिहलन्तं च सितुसेन्तं विसर्गतः ।

End:

विसर्गः पदमध्यस्थः पद्यान्तश्च पदान्तगः ॥ ९॥
पद्यान्तं च पदान्तं च व्यञ्जनं सितुसेन्तकम्॥
कटौ तपौ ङणनमा हलः पद्यपदान्तगाः ॥ १०॥

सार्धैकपद्यस्यायमर्थः -- अत्र संख्यागणने विसर्गः पदमध्यस्थः । धूः सहाविति । पद्यमवग्रहस्तदन्त्यः इतिकरणोत्तरे तत्रैव धूः । सहौ। पदान्तगो वायव इत्यादिस्त्रिविधो ऽपि ग्राह्यः । ९। व्यञ्जनं तु पद्यान्तं वृषणवसू इति वृषण् - वसू इति। अवग्रहान्तो णकारः पदान्तमवर्धयत् इति तकारः । एते संख्यागणने ग्राह्यो। तथैव सितुसेन्तमपि। पदान्ते

यातुधाना इति यातु - धानाः । पदान्ते पुनातु इत्यादिकम्। विषमसमगणने द्वे अपि ग्राह्ये । कटाविति । कटतपा ङणनमाः । एते अष्टावेव हलः पदान्ते च सन्ति । प्रथमोत्तमाः पदान्तीया अञ्चौ इति प्रातिशाख्यसूत्रात्।

इयं चतुर्वर्णयुता निर्णीय परिभाषिका।
सौकर्यदात्री पाठस्य पदवेदस्य कारिका॥ १॥

इति श्रीमत्पण्डितसिद्धेश्वरसूनुना पण्डितरामचन्द्रविरचिता वेदपरिभाषाकारिकाशिक्षा व्याख्यानयुता समाप्ता॥

IM 1963. 1 fol. Title: Baiṭ-paribhāṣā. Kātyāyana-baiṭha-paribhāṣā (by a later hand).

C. of Rāmacandra-paṇḍita.
IM 2540. 6 fol.
SBD 4277. 5 fol. Col.:

इयं चतुरक्षरनिर्णये परिभाषा। इति रामचन्द्रपण्डितविरचिता बैठ्परिभाषा समाप्ता।
ज्योतिर्वित्कुलसंभूतो वैराजक्षेत्रसंस्थितः ।
रघुनाथस्यकृतौ ... ग्रन्थो बैठो विरचितो मया॥

Ptd.: in Śikṣā-saṃgraha. – Benares, 1889, pp. 320-26. – (Ben. S. S. 10).

1175 VEDA-PARIBHĀṢĀ(-ṄKA)-SŪTRA (वेदपरिभाषा(-ङ्क)सूत्र)
of Keśava → Keśava(ī-)śikṣā.
Jodhpur D I, p. 24 (no.91 / 1409). 8 fol. Dated V.S. 1885.

1176 VEDA-PARIBHĀṢĀ-SŪTRA-ŚIKṢĀ (वेदपरिभाषासूत्रशिक्षा)
of Rāmacandra, son of Siddheśvara. It gives the number of Ṛk-s, Anuvāka-s and Pada-s in each chapter of the *Vājasaneyi-saṃhitā*, in certain symbolic code words (identical with Baiṭha-saṃjñaka-prakaraṇa, IM 2593), each containing 4 letters,

Beginning:

एतदग्रे तु वेदस्य श्रीमाध्यन्दिनशाखिनः ।
परिभाषाख्यसूत्रं तु श्रीमद्रामस्य निर्मितम्।
तदग्रे सूत्रशेषस्य कारिका सुप्रकाशिका॥

अथ वेदपरिभाषासूत्रशिक्षां व्याख्यास्यामः ॥ इषे त्वा । १ । अनुवाकः । पदानि । ३५ । गुठिघस्वः । १ । वसोः पवित्रम् । ३ । ४२ । घाढझाचा । २ । अग्ने व्रतपते । ७ । १०९ । जैभातञीः । ३ । पवित्रे स्थः । २ । ५४ । डीणडाडी । शर्मासि । ३ । ९३ । जीवतिढः । १३ । धृष्टिरसि । २ । । ४४ । घीचछड । २ । धिषणासि । २ । ३६ । गूघागङिः । ७ । संवपामि । डगेनचझि । २ ।आददे । ५ । १०२ । जाभुठुधीः । ७ । अनिशितो ऽसि । ३ । ५१ । ङजत्रञिः । ७ । ऋचः । ३१ । अनुवाकाः । १० । पदानि । ६१५॥

End:

स्वाहा प्राणेभ्यः । ६ । ४८ । जैध्रिणध्रू । उग्रश्च । ७ । ९१ । झमीलाघु । २ ऋचः । १३ । अनुवाकाः । २ । पदानि । १७१ । ईशा वास्यम् । ८ । १३२ । डासोडिर्धीः । १ । अन्धन्तमः ६ । ७९ । छोण्डिपे । ऋचः । १४ । अनुवाकाः । २ । पदानि । २११ ।

इति श्रीपण्डितसिद्धेश्वरसूनुना पण्डितरामचन्द्रविरचिता वेदपरिभाषा शिक्षा समाप्ता ॥

IM 2593. 8 fol. (1-6, 8-9). Incomplete. Title: Baiṭha-saṃjñaka-prakaraṇa.
Col.: iti śrīmādhyandinaśākhīya-padādisaṃjñāparijñānārthakaṃ baiṭhasaṃjñaka-prakaraṇaṃ samāptam | śake 1780 | pauṣaśukla 11 raṅgabhaṭṭena likhitam ||
SBD 4345. 11 fol. (1-8, 10-12). Incomplete. Title: Baiṭha-saṃjñaka-prakaraṇa.
Col.: iti mādhyandinīyaśākhīyapadādisaṃkhyāparijñānārthakṃ baiṭhsaṃjñaka-prakaraṇaṃ samāptam ||

Ptd.: in Śikṣā-saṃgraha. – Benares, 1889, pp. 306-20. – (Ben. S. S. 10).

1177 VEDA-PĀRĀYAṆA-VIDHI (वेदपारायणविधि)
MD 16580. PL. Gr. 3 pp. 27 Grantha-s.

1178 VEDA-PĀRĀYAṆA-VIMARŚA (वेदपारायणविमर्श)
An essay in praise of the Sāmarudra.
Adyar D I 912 (33 D 12 = 75239). PL. Gr. 15 fol. (2-16).

1179 VEDA-PRAŚAṂSĀ (वेदप्रशंसा)
Mysore ND II 3800 (C 460/ 4). 1 fol. (29).

1180 VEDA-PRĀMĀṆYA-CANDRIKĀ (वेदप्रामाण्यचन्द्रिका)
of Rajaram Sastri Bodas. A treatise on the authority and the apauruṣeyatva of the Veda-s.

Ptd.: Bombay : Venkateswara Steam Press, 1902. 80 pp. [BORI (5023)]

1181 VEDA-BHĀGĀDI (वेदभागादि)
Oppert I 2444. PL. Gr. 25 pp. Belonged to Sri Sarasvati Bhandaram Committee of Tiruvallikkeni, Madras.
Radh. 2.

[CC I 604a]

1182 VEDA-MANTRĀNUKRAMAṆIKĀ (वेदमन्त्रानुक्रमणिका)
Radh. 2.

[CC I 604a]

1183 VEDA-MĀHĀTMYA (वेदमाहात्म्य)
Mysore ND II 3802 (P 144/10a). PL. Tel. 1 fol. (60).

1184 VEDA-MĀHĀTMYA(-SAṂDOHA) (वेदमाहात्म्य /-संदोह)

of Vyāghra (?) A work divided into Prakaraṇa-s (5 complete; 6th incomplete) on the necessity of studying the Veda-s, with copious quotations from the *Mahābhārata, Bhāgavata* and other Purāṇa-s. In three colophons it is called *Vead-māhātmya-saṃdoha.*

BORI 247 of 1879-80. 14 fol. Incomplete.

P 11.

[CC I 604a]

*VEDA-MITRA (वेदमित्र)

Father of Viṣṇu-mitra. Quoted in the *Ṛgveda-prātiśākhya,* 1.21 (cf. Oxf. 405b).

[CC I 604b]

1185 VEDA-MUKHA (वेदमुख)

of Sītārāma Paralīkara.

K 12.

[CC I 604b]

1186 VEDA-LAKṢAṆA (वेदलक्षण)

This is, in fact, not a title of a work, but merely a description of the texts that are related to the Veda, and catalogued without further identificatiopn. Aufrecht remarks on this title: "A feeble and mischievous designation of Vedic works" (CC I 604b).

GJKSV 43008. PL. Gr. 30 fol. It includes:

Baiṭ-nāma-lakṣaṇa (fol. 1-5)
Uccodarki-vyākhyā (fol. 5-7)
Vāsiṣṭha-śikṣā (fol. 7-9)
Svara-pañcāśat (fol. 10-28)
Ṣaḍviṃśati-sūtra (fol. 29-30)

Hoshiarpur p. 301 (no.4457). PL. Mal. 72 fol. 700 Grantha-s. Incomplete.

MD 14098. PL. Tel. 2 pp. Incomplete. Includes illustration of seven metres and ten verses from the *Vikṛti-vallī.* An additional verse at the end describes the Visarga as:

शृङ्गवद् बालवत्सस्य बालिकाकुचयुग्मवत्।
नेत्रवत् कृष्णसर्पस्य स विसर्ग इति स्मृतः ॥

MD 17488. PL. Tel. 315 Grantha-s.

MT 95(k). PL. Gr. 17 fol. (40-56). Incomplete. Lacks beginning and end. Purchased in 1910-11 from Gopalaswami Ayyangar of Mannargudi.

MT 291. PL. Tel. 8 fol. Incomplete. Presented in 1910-11 by Prayaga Sitarama Shastri of Guntur.

MT 1165(c). PL. Tel. 24 fol. (20-43). Incomplete. Fragments; contains Uditprakaraṇa, Svarabhakti-prakaraṇa, etc.; Lakṣmīkānta-śikṣā has been quoted. Purchased in 1913-14 from Kashibhatta Subrahmanya Sastri of Vekanur, Krishna Dist.

MT 1964(n). PL. Tel. 3 fol. (111-13). Presented in 1916-17 by Rayaprolu Ramabrahmangaru of Guruza, Gudivada Taluk, Krishna Dist.

MT 4600(a). PL. Gr. 17 fol. Altogether 11 titles listed. Presented in 1924-25 by the Secretary to the Trustees of Sri Yogi Parthasarathi Ayyangar's Charities, Triplicane, Madras.

Mysore ND II 3801 (P 2339/12). PL. Gr. 1 fol. (90).

Mysore Skt. Coll. p. 1. No.1536. Gr.

Oppert I 1034. Belonged to Viraraghava Tatacharyar, Head Master, Sanskrit School of Sathakopacharya, Kanchipuram, Chingelpet Dist.

Oppert I 2042. PL. Gr. 30 pp. Belonged to Sivasuri Sastri of Bhavani, Coimbatore Dist.

Oppert I 2150. PL. Gr. 117 pp. (by Somanātha). Belonged to Yajnasrauti of Bhavani, Coimbatore Dist.

Oppert I 7231. Belonged to Ivattur Nandikesvara Sastri of Vijayanagaram.

Oppert II 2357. 50 pp. Belonged to Anantakrishna Srauti of Kaniyur, Udumalapet Taluk, Coimbatore Dist.

PUL II. App. p. 13 (no.211). PL. Gr. 19 fol. (90-108). With Paribhāṣā, Vilaṅghya, Avarṇi and Aniṅgya.

TD 1791. 12 fol. 120 Grantha-s. (YV).

TD 1792. 4 fol. 60 Grantha-s. Incomplete. Sections 8-16 only.

Tirupati SVUORI 6165 (961). PL. Gr. Incomplete. Contains Lakṣaṇa-ratna, Siddhānta-śikṣā and Bhāradvāja-śkṣā.

Tirupati SVUORI 6166 (962). PL. Gr. 38 fol. Contains among others Taittirīyapada-svaralakṣaṇa.

Tirupati SVUORI 6167 (5309). PL. Gr. Incomplete. This is Vaidika-prakriyā.

Tirupati SVUORI 6168 (2191c). PL. Gr. 46 fol.

Tirupati SVUORI 6169 (3526). PL. Gr. 46 fol. Incomplete. It contains:

Taittirīya-prātiśākhya (5 fol.)
Caturviṃśati-trikrama-lakṣaṇa (1 fol.) mā sthāt
Ardhāntikāḥ (ubhā vām)
Ekatriṃśat-pluta (1 fol.)
Śamāna (3 fol.)
Vilaṅghya – praṇamya bhāratīm of Nārāyaṇa (3 fol.)
Napara (natvā vināyakam; adyāt ...)
Avarṇi
Āvarṇi
Aniṅgya
Yaṇādeśa-dīrghī
Pūrvadīrgī
Aparadīrghī
Rephaparavisarjanīya
Bhāradvāja-śikṣā
Āraṇyaka-śikṣā-vyākhyā (fol. 26-46)

Tirupati SVUORI 6170 (3764). PL. Gr. Incomplete. Contains Avarṇi, Āvarṇi, Napara-tapara, Aniṅgya, Saṃhitā-śamāna and Vilaṅghya; all with C.

[CC I 604b]

1187 VEDA-LAKṢAṆA (A 1) (वेदलक्षण)

Catalogued as Veda-lakṣaṇāni.

Adyar D I 983 (10 G 30 = TR 28). 123 fol. (pp. 526-770). = Adyar I, p. 53b (Sapta-lakṣaṇa). – Collated by Pandits K. S. Hariharasastri and Y. Venkataramasastri from the original Ms. of Puranika Kesavachari, Belur, Mysore. 28.5.1916. – This is found on a leaf between 731-32.

Contains the following works:

Śākhā-śamāna (aroçathā avaruddhā) (inc.) .... ends on p. 532.
Nava(ta)para-bhāṣya (inc.) .... " " 545.
Avarṇi-lakṣaṇa .... " " 551.
Āvarṇi-lakṣaṇa .... " " 555.
Vilaṅghya of Nārāyaṇa .... " " 562.
Pūrvāniṅgya (the Paribhāṣā section of Śrīvatsāṅka's Aniṅgya) .... " " 566.
Śikṣā-samuccaya-saṃgraha (135 verses) .... " " 584.
Vilaṅghya-lakṣaṇa of Nārāyaṇa (2nd copy) .... " " 592.
Aparāniṅgya (of Śrīvatsāṅka) .... " " 604.
Ṣaḍviṃśati .... " " 619.
Uguparīkṣā .... " " 630.
Apara-khaṇḍa .... " " 633.
Saptatriṃśat-pluta .... " " 635.
Dvātriṃśat-pluta .... " " 636.
Pūrva-dīrghī .... " " 637.
Apara-dīrghī .... " " 639.
Ubhaya-dīrghī .... " " 639.
Anta-nirdeśa .... " " 669.
Paragāḍi (?) .... " " 707.
Saṃhitā-paragāḍi .... " " 698.
Āraṇa-paragāḍi and
Āraṇa-śamāna .... " " 710.
Śākhā-paragāḍi .... " " 731.
Jaṭā-lakṣaṇa (duplicate in TR 20) .... " " 760.
Varṇakrama-lakṣaṇa (duplicate in TR 20) .... " " 770.

1188 VEDA-LAKṢAṆA (A 2) (वेदलक्षण)

Adyar D I 984 (19 O 5 = 66887). PL. Mal. 93 fol. Consists of the following titles (corrections to the printed catalogue have been made after verification of the Ms.):

Taittirīya-prātiśākhya (fragment) .... fol. 1a.
Yaṇādeśa-dīrghī .... fol. 1b-2a.
Ubhaya-dīrghī .... fol. 2a-2b.
Svara-pañcāśat (6 extra verses; cf. p. 339 of Cat.) .... fol. 3b-6b.
Antanirdeśa .... fol. 6b-8b.
Trikrama-lakṣaṇa .... fol. 8b-9a.
Vākyānta = Ardhāntya (I.725) .... fol. 9a.
Svara-samuccaya .... fol. 9a-10a.
Dvitva-prakaraṇa .... fol. 10a-10b.
Yohi-prāpti .... fol. 10b-11a.
Plutasaṃgraha .... fol. 11a-12a.
Śākhā-śamāna .... fol. 12a-15a.
Saṃhitā-śamāna .... fol. 15b-18a.
Vilaṅghya .... fol. 18a-21b.
Napara-tapara .... fol. 21b-24a.
Avarṇi .... fol. 24a-26b.

Āvarṇi .... fol. 26b-27b.
Aniṅgya .... fol. 27b-34b.
Saṃhitā-śamāna-vyākhyā .... fol. 44a-54a.
Napara-tapara-vyākhyā .... fol. 54a-64a.
Avarṇi-vyākhyā .... fol. 64a-71a.
Āvarṇi-vyākhyā .... fol. 71a-74a.
Aniṅgya-vyākhyā .... fol. 74b-87b.
Ṣaḍviṃśati .... fol. 87b-93a.

1189 VEDA-LAKṢAṆA (A 3) (वेदलक्षण)

Adyar D I 985 (22 E 43 = 68892). PL. Tel. 51 fol. (8ff.). Contains the following titles:
Napara-tapara-bhāṣya .... fol. 1-17.
Avarṇi .... fol. 18-20.
Yohi-prāpti (with C.) .... fol. 21-30.
Avarṇi-bhāṣya .... fol. 31-41.
Ṣaḍviṃśati and Uguparīkṣā .... fol. 41-49.
Trikrama-lakṣaṇa .... fol. 49-51.

1190 VEDA-LAKṢAṆA (A 4) (वेदलक्षण)

Adyar D I 986 (22 M 30 = 69380). PL. Gr. 9 fol. = Adyar I, p. 53b. Title: Sapta-lakṣaṇa. It contains the following titles:
Pūrva-dīrghī .... ends on fol. 1a
Apara-dīrghī .... " fol. 1b
Ubhaya-dīrghī .... " fol. 1b
Yohi-prāpti .... " fol. 1b
Yaṇādeśa-dīrghī .... " fol. 2a
Sakārapara-visarjanīya .... " fol. 2b
Ardhāntika .... " fol. 4a
Ṣaḍviṃśati .... " fol. 9b

1191 VEDA-LAKṢAṆA (A 5) (वेदलक्षण)

Adyar D I 987 (23 I 13 = 69947). PL. Gr. 15 fol. (54ff.). = Adyar I, p. 53b. Title: Sapta-lakṣaṇa. It contains the following titles:
Vilaṅghya .... ends on fol. 5a
Napara .... " fol. 7a
Pūrvottarobhaya-dīrghī .... " fol. 9b
Trikrama-lakṣaṇa .... " fol. 10a
Svara-bhakti .... " fol. 11b
Śamāna .... " fol. 15b

1192 VEDA-LAKṢAṆA (A 6) (वेदलक्षण)

Adyar D I 988 (25 H 14 = 70975). PL. Tel. 19 fol. (14ff.). = Adyar I, p. 54a. It contains the following titles:
Samāna-saṃdhi .... ends on fol. 3a.
Vilaṅghya .... " fol. 3b.
Tapara .... " fol. 5a.

1193 VEDA-LAKṢAṆA (A 7) (वेदलक्षण)

Adyar D I 989 (25 L 31 = 71149). PL. Gr. 16 fol. It contains the following titles:

1194 VEDA-LAKṢAṆA (BHU) (वेदलक्षण)

अथ वेदलक्षणम् । तच्च अदृष्टार्थकत्वे सति भगवद्वाक्यत्वम् इत्येके । तत्र सत्यन्तेन लौकिकभगवद्वाक्यस्य ...

End:

यद्वा वेदत्वेनैतानि वाक्यानि व्यवह्रियन्ताम् इतीश्वरेच्छाविषयिताविशेषात्मकत्वमेव वेदत्वमिति वदन्ति। इति वेदलक्षणप्रकरणम्।

BHU B 2261 (D 3E/2790). 2 fol.

1195 VEDA-LAKṢAṆA (HB) (वेदलक्षण)

A collection of several Veda-lakṣaṇa texts. It consists of 155 folios with different paginations (9, 29-51, 53, 5, 15, 13, 42-45 and about 25 loose leaves). There is a list of about 40 Veda-lakṣaṇa texts on a stray leaf. The Ms. must have been written by or belonged to Cakra, son of Rāma Ayyaṅgār (of Ūruttiṭi ?), whose writings are found in the codex. In the colophons of several works statements like *ūrattiṭi-rāmasvāmyayyaṅgār svahastalikhitam* | (nos. 21-28) or *cakramayyaṅgārlikhitam* (nos. 29, 31) are found. At the end of Sarva-saṃmata-śikṣā : *bahudhānyanāmasaṃvatsarasya caitramāsakṛṣṇapakṣam amāvāsyāyādinam* ¦ *ūratiṭiyilirunda varṇakramapāṭhirāmasvāmi ayyaṅkār svahastalikhitam* | There are scribblings in Telugu and Grantha script such as : *śrīmate rāmānujāya namaḥ* | *ghanapāṭhi anantācārlu lakṣaṇapustakam* | *ghanapāṭhipustakam anantācārlu* | There are indications of attempts to compose verses similar to the introductory verses of Yājuṣa-bhūṣaṇa, e.g. *satāṃ mudaṃ saṃprati bhūyasīṃ tāṃ vyākhyānayuktā hṛdayaṃgameyam* | *pañcavarṇakramāṇāṃ ca lakṣaṇāny atra* | *tatratatroditāny atra* | *natvā śrīśaṃ sarvavarṇakramāṇāṃ savyākhyānaṃ lakṣaṇaṃ pravakṣye* | *satāṃ mudaṃ lakṣaṇasaṃgrahasya vyā- ... kṛpayaiva mahatāṃ sa cakranāmā yajuṣo lakṣaṇasaṃgrahaṃ karoti* | *cakramayyaṅkāru* ||

The codex contains:
(1) Pāṇini-śikṣā (60 verses) .... fol. 1a-2a
(2) Śaṃbhu-śikṣā (50 verses) .... fol. 2a-3a
(3) Vāsiṣṭha-śikṣā (11 verses) .... fol. 3a-3b
(4) Bhāradvāja-śikṣā (138 verses) .... fol. 3b-6a
(5) Aruṇa-śikṣā (129 verses) .... fol. 6a-8a
(6) Siddhānta-śikṣā (78 verses) .... fol. 8a-9b
(7) Trikrama-lakṣaṇa (4 verses without title) .... fol. 9b
(8) Svara-pañcāśat (50 verses) .... fol. 29a-30b
(9) Yohi-prāpti-mūla (23 verses) .... fol. 30b-31a
(10) Vyāsa-śikṣā (260 verses) .... fol. 32a-39b
(11) Kāla-nirṇaya-śikṣā (27 verses) .... fol. 40a-40b
(12) Varṇa-krama-lakṣaṇa (= Lakṣmī-kānta-śikṣā) .... fol. 41a
(13) Yamāpattiḥ (10 verses without title; = Adyar D I 948) .... fol. 41a
(14) Visarjanīya-lakṣaṇa (without title = Adyar D I 981) .... fol. 41b
(15) Kauhala-śikṣā .... fol. 42a-43b
(16) Svara-saṃparki – Savyākhyāna (20 verses with C.) .... fol. 44a-44b
(17) Anta-nirdeśa .... fol. 44b-45b
(18) Jaṭāvali (= Jaṭā-nyāya-pañcāśat, Adyar D I 817) .... fol. 46a-47a
(19) Sarva-saṃmata-śikṣā (235 verses = Adyar D I 1040) .... fol. 48a-51b
(20) Pañca-varṇa-krama-lakṣaṇa (145 verses) .... fol. 1a-4b
(21) Sarva-saṃmata-śikṣā-vyākhyā (134 verses) .... fol. 5-22
(22) Uccodarki-(lakṣaṇa-)vyākhyā (10 verses) .... fol. 22a-25a
(23) Jaṭā-maṇi (99 verses) .... fol. 26a-29b
(24) Jaṭā-maṇi-vyākhyā .... fol. 30a-37b
(25) Ṣaḍviṃśati-sūtra .... fol. 38a-44a
(26) Śākhā-śamāna .... fol. 46a-47a
(27) Aruṇa-śamāna .... fol. 47b-48b
(28) Yohi-bhāṣya of Sūri-bhaṭṭa .... fol. 49a-53b
(29) Veda-lakṣaṇa-ratna (Vedavijjana-saṃmata) of Vaidyanātha-bhaṭṭa .... 5 fol.
(30) Praṇava-vicāra .... 1 fol.
(31) Ātreya-śikṣā (294 verses) .... 13 fol.
(32) Ātreya-śikṣā-kārikā (16 verses; list of topics) .... 1 fol.
(33) Svarāvadhāna-lakṣaṇa .... 15 fol.
(34) Rāvaṇa-baiṭ .... 1 fol.
(35) Rāvaṇa-baiṭ (2nd copy) .... 1 fol.
(36) Rāvaṇa-baiṭ (with Paribhāṣā) .... 2 fol.
(37) Nārada-(Rāvaṇa-)baiṭ (nuthanāvai) .... 1 fol. (marked 42)
(38) Nārada-(Rāvaṇa-)baiṭ-vyākhyā Bhāva-prakāśikā of Cakra .... 2 fol. (43a-44a)
(39) Nārada-(Rāvaṇa-)baiṭ (2nd copy) .... 2 fol. (44b-45a)

Hamburg StUB (cod.Palmbl. III 8/133). PL. Gr. 155 fol.

1196 VEDA-LAKṢAṆA (RASB) (**वेदलक्षण**)
RASB II 915 (G 6061). 11 fol. 220 Grantha-s. Dated Śaka 1651. Contains:
Ekāra-lakṣaṇa of Mahādeva Manīṣin

Nakāra-lakṣaṇa (same as the Napara)
Varṇa-krama-kārikā (17 verses from Sarva-saṃmata-śikṣā)
Takāra-lakṣaṇa (actually Yohi-prāpti)
Pūrvottarobhaya-pada-dīrghī
Ṣaḍviṃśati-lakṣaṇa
Īkārānta-padāni (pṛthivyāṅgirasī varcasvī ... sarasvatī abhityavantī na)
Dhakārottara-vibhāga-padāni
and Trikramodāharaṇa (mā sthāt priyadhā ...). Cf. MD 853 (last work in the codex).

1197 VEDA-LAKṢAṆA (SV) (वेदलक्षण)
MD 14080. PL. Na. 11 pp. Incomplete. Described as of RV.

1198 VEDA-LAKṢAṆA-DĪDHITI-PRASĀRIKĀ (वेदलक्षणदीधितिप्रसारिका)
of Narasiṃha.
PUL II. App. p. 20 (no. 310). 8 fol. Dated V.S. 1858.

1199 VEDA-LAKṢAṆA-PARIBHĀṢĀ (वेदलक्षणपरिभाषा)
PUL II. App. p. 13 (no. 211). 19 fol. (90-108). Title: Paribhāṣā.

1200 VEDA-LAKṢAṆA-BHĀṢYA (वेदलक्षणभाष्य)
PUL I, p. 132 (no. 23). 227 fol. 8000 Grantha-s (together with the Taittirīya-prātiśākhya-bhāṣya).

1201 VEDA-LAKṢAṆA-RATNA (वेदलक्षणरत्न)
→ Lakṣaṇa-ratna(-bhaiṭ), of Vaidyanātha-bhaṭṭa.

1202 VEDA-LAKṢAṆA-VYĀKHYĀ (वेदलक्षणव्याख्या)
Tirupati SVUORI 6172 (952). PL. Gr. 25 fol. Contains a commentary on Uccodarkī, Avarṇi, Āvarṇi, Tapara-napara, Aniṅgya and Taittirīya-prātiśākhya.

1203 VEDA-LAKṢAṆA-ŚIROMAṆI (वेदलक्षणशिरोमणि)
Beginning:

शब्देति । अत्र सत्यन्तं दृष्टार्थकवाक्यव्यावृत्तये । अजन्यान्तं स्मृतिव्यावृत्तये । चरमप्रमाणपदमयोगव्यावृत्तये। शब्दपदमन्त्यं वेदोपजीव्यनुमानव्यावृत्तये।

End:

वस्तुतस्तु महाजनानामभियुक्तानां वेद इति परिभाषाविषयत्वमेव वेदत्वम् । धातुत्वाख्याततत्ववत् । ग्रन्थस्तु प्रकृतपक्षतावच्छेदकमात्रनिर्वचनपरतया कथंचित् संगमनीय इति वेदलक्षणशिरोमणिः ।

IM 2600. 2 fol.

1204 VEDA-LAKṢAṆA-SIDDHĀÑJANA (वेदलक्षणसिद्धाञ्जन)
of Agnihotri Ramanuja Tatacharya, in Maṇipravāla style (Grantha and Tamil), on the importance of the knowledge of Veda-lakṣaṇa for Vedic studies.

Ptd.: Kumbakonam : Kamalamba Press, 1932. vi, 17, 108, ii pp. [Adyar (H 215 Ram VL)]

1205 VEDA-LAKṢAṆA-SŪTRA-VṚTTI -- JAṬĀ-PAṬALA (वेदलक्षणसूत्रवृत्ति-- जटापटल)
Rice 12. Aufrecht: "This is rubbish" (CC I 604b). See above Jaṭā-paṭala.

[CC I 604b]

1206 VEDA-LAKṢAṆĀDI-VICĀRA (वेदलक्षणादिविचार)
Beginning:

ननु को ऽयं वेदो नाम किं लक्षणं को वा तस्य विषयप्रयोजनसंबन्धाधिकारयोग्यो भवति। अत्रोच्यते । इष्टप्राप्त्यनिष्टपरिहारयोरलौकिकमुपायं यो ग्रन्थो वेदयति स वेदः । अलौकिकपदेन प्रत्यक्षानुमाने व्यावर्त्येते । अनुभूयमान स्रक्चन्दनवनितादेः इष्टप्राप्तिहेतुत्वम् औषधादेरनिष्टपरिहारहेतुत्वं च प्रत्यक्षसिद्धम्।

End:

अमुष्य वेदस्य ईशः व्यञ्जकः प्रकाशकः । यथा स्वतःसिद्धस्य घटादेर्व्यञ्जकं चक्षुस्तद्वत्। न रूपाणामवलोके चक्षुरिवान्यकारणं दृष्टम्। तद्वददृष्टावगतौ वेदवदन्यो न वेदको हेतुः । अननुभूतात्मावगतौ स्वर्गादौ वा। अंशद्वयवति निगमे साधयति कर्तृकर्मफलरूपं द्वैतमेव एको ऽंशः । अद्वैतमेव वस्तु प्रतिपादयति प्रसिद्धपरमो ऽंशः ॥

SBD 47595. 1 fol.

1207 VEDA-LAKṢAṆĀNUKRAMAṆIKĀ (वेदलक्षणानुक्रमणिका)
A list of various kinds of Veda-lakṣaṇa works in 17 verses. It mentions nine primary Śikṣā-s and three secondary Śikṣā-s. The following is the complete text :

प्रातिशाख्यं संहितायाः शमानं नपरं तथा।
तपरं प्रग्रहश्चैव कुरुकी च विलङ्घ्यकम्॥ १॥
इङ्ग्यानिङ्ग्यमवर्णी च आवर्णी प्लुतमेव च।
रङ्गप्लुतं पूर्वदीर्घ उभयोत्तरदीर्घकौ॥ २॥
यण्दीर्घौ योहिभाष्यं च तथा रावणभेट्टु च।
वर्णक्रमं जटावल्ली त्रिक्रमं चान्त्यवेष्टनम्॥ ३॥
स्वरपञ्चाशतं चैव षड्विंशतिसूत्रकम्।
शाखाशमानमरुणशमानं सविशेषतः ॥ ४॥

अथ नवशिक्षाः --

भारद्वाजव्यासशंभुपाणिनिकौहलीयकम्।

बोधायनो वसिष्ठश्च वाल्मीकिर्हारितं नव॥ ५॥
सर्वसंमतमारण्यं तथा सिद्धान्तमेव च।
उपशिक्षा इमाः प्रोक्ता लक्षणज्ञानकोविदैः ॥ ६॥

सप्तलक्षणनामानि --

शमानं च विलङ्घ्यं च नपरं तपरं तथा।
अवर्ण्यावर्ण्यनिङ्ग्यान्तं सप्तलक्षणमुच्यते॥ ७॥

वेदोच्चारणक्रमः --

गीती शीघ्री शिरःकम्पी तथा लिखितपाठकः ।
अनर्थज्ञो ऽल्पकण्ठश्च षडेते पाठकाधमाः ॥ ८॥
माधुर्यमक्षरव्यक्तिः पदच्छेदस्तु सुस्वरः ।
धैर्यं लयनमर्थश्च (?) षडेते पाठका गुणाः ॥ ९॥
उपांशु दष्टं त्वरितं निरस्तं विलम्बितं गद्गदितं प्रगीतम्।
निष्पीडितं ग्रस्तपदाक्षरं च वदेन्न दीनं न तु सानुनासिके॥ १०॥
व्याघ्री यथा हरेत् पुत्रं दंष्ट्राभ्यां न तु पीडयेत्।
भीता पतनभेदाभ्यां तद्वद् वर्णान् प्रयोजयेत्॥ ११॥
हस्तहीनं तु यो ऽधीते स्वरवर्णविवर्जितम्।
ऋग्यजुःसामभिर्दग्धो वियोनिमधिगच्छति॥ १२॥
हस्तेन वेदं यो ऽधीते स्वरवर्णार्थसंयुतम्।
ऋग्यजुःसामभिः पूतो ब्रह्मभूयाय कल्पते॥ १३॥
अनक्षरमनायुष्यमस्वरं व्याधिपीडितम्।
अक्षरः शस्त्ररूपेण वज्रं पतति मस्तके॥ १४॥
यथा सौराष्ट्रिका नारी तक्राँ इत्यभिभाषते।
एवं रङ्गाः प्रयोक्तव्या निगमाभ्याससूरिभिः ॥ १५॥
उदात्तो ब्रह्मजातिः स्यान्नीचो राजन्य उच्यते।
स्वरितो वैश्यजातिस्तु प्रचयः शूद्रजातिकः ॥ १६॥

समाप्तेयं वेदलक्षणानुक्रमणिका॥

MD 967. PL. Tel. 2 pp. (34ff.). .... (= Skt. Texts on Phonetics, pp. 307-09).
MD 14750. PL. Tel. 3 pp. (44ff.). Title: Lakṣaṇānukramaṇikā.

1208 VEDA-VĀKYĀRTHA-CANDRIKĀ (वेदवाक्यार्थचन्द्रिका)
of Kṛṣṇabhaṭṭopādhyāya, of Āndhradeśa, son of Haribhaṭṭopādhyāya. A prose work dealing with the meaning of the Veda in Mīmāṃsā.
Oxf. CS d.67. 82 fol. Dated V.S. 1534.

1209 VEDA-VIKṚTI-LAKṢAṆA-SAṂGRAHA (वेदविकृतिलक्षणसंग्रह)
A collection of twelve tracts on Veda-vikṛti-s and allied topics.

Ptd.: Compiled and critically edited with Introduction and variant readings by K. V. Abhyankar and G. V. Devasthali. – Poona : Bhandarkar Oriental Research Institute, 1978. L, 168 pp. – (Research Unit Publications 5). [Adyar (H080 BORI Rup 5); BORI (31892, 34350); NL (180 Jb 97 127); SAI (ind 51 D 584/1175)]

Contains the following titles:

- Vikṛtivallī (Vyāḍi-kṛtā) .... pp. 1-3
- Vikṛtivallī (Gaṅgādhara-kṛta-Vikṛtikaumudī-sametā) .... pp. 4-21
- (Pariśiṣṭam) .... pp. 21-22
- Aṣṭa-vikṛti-lakṣaṇāni (Saṭīkāni) (= Thibaut's edition pp. 36-53) .... pp. 23-32
- (Vyāḍi-praṇīta-vikṛtivallī-granthāntargata-) Jaṭāpaṭala-kārikā (Anantācārya-kṛta-vyākhyā-yutā) .... pp. 33-46
- Jaṭāpaṭalam (Hayagrīva-kṛtam) .... pp. 47-48
- Jaṭāpaṭalam (Saṭīkam) .... pp. 49-55
- Jaṭāpaṭalam (Dayāśaṃkara-kṛta-dīpikā-sametam) .... pp. 56-74
- Aṣṭa-vikṛti-vivṛtiḥ (Madhusūdana-maskari-viracitā) .... pp. 75-112
- Kauṇḍinya-śikṣā .... pp. 113-23
- Krama-paṭalam (Uvaṭa-bhāṣya-sametam) .... pp. 124-33
- Svara-paṭalam (Uvaṭa-bhāṣya-sametam) .... pp. 134-42
- Svarāṅkuśaḥ (Jayanta-svāmi-kṛtaḥ – Nīlakaṇṭha-kṛta-ṭīkā-yutaḥ) .... pp. 143-61

1210 VEDA-VICĀRA (वेदविचार)
BISM p. 269 (36/717). 76 fol. An extensive treatise on the Veda-s in general. Dated Śaka 1746. Copied by Gadre Sadāśiva-bhaṭṭa.

1211 VEDA-VIJJANA-SAṂMATA-LAKṢAṆA-RATNA (वेदविज्जनसंमतलक्षणरत्न)
This is apparently the same as the *Lakṣaṇa-ratna* of Vidyanātha-bhaṭṭa in which the colophon reads: iti veda-vijjana-saṃmata-vaidyanātha-bhaṭṭa-viracita-lakṣaṇa-ratna ... Mysore (1898), p. 5 (no. 52). Gr. 6 fol. (179-84).

1212 VEDA-VYĀKARAṆA (वेदव्याकरण)
BISM p. 269 (52/172). 13 fol. (3-15). Incomplete. → Taittirīya-prātiśākhya.

1213 VEDA-ŚABDA-VIBHŪṢAṆA (वेदशब्दविभूषण)
of Ananta-Gopālakṛṣṇa, son and disciple of Ananta Veṅkaṭeśa of the Śrīvatsa-gotra. A commentary, in eight Adhyāya-s, on the Vedic Sūtra-s in the Pāṇini's *Aṣṭādhyāyī*, with illustrations selected from the *Taittirīya-saṃhitā*.

Beginning:

वन्दे विनायकं नित्यं वन्दमानेष्टदं प्रभुम्।
विघ्नान्धतिमिरव्यूहविध्वंसनदिनेश्वरम्॥

समष्टिं पाणिनिपृष्ठमुनीन्द्राणामहर्दिवम्।
नन्नमीमि सदानन्तवेङ्कटेश्वरसूरिणम्॥
पाणिनिप्रमुखान् वन्दे मुनीन् शास्त्रकृतस्तथा।
अन्यान् गोपालकृष्णादीन् ग्रन्थकारानहं गुरून्॥
यजुःश्रुत्यम्बुधेर्लब्धानुदाहरणसन्मणीन्।
सूत्रेषु योजयन् कुर्वे वेदशब्दविभूषणम्॥
अनुवृत्त्युपपत्ती च विरुद्धार्थनिराकृतिः ॥
सर्वेषां वेदसूत्राणां व्याख्या चापि विशेषतः ॥
तैत्तिरीयोदाहरणं प्रायस्तदुपपादनम्।
इत्यादि वर्ण्यते ऽस्माभिर्वेदशब्दभूषणे॥

अथ वैदिकः शब्दो निरूप्यते -- अनवरतमग्निहोत्रादि कर्म कुर्वतां ब्राह्मणानामिष्टप्राप्तये अनिष्टनिवृत्तये च तत्परिज्ञानस्यावश्यकत्वात्। तदुक्तं भाष्ये -- यो वा इमां पादशो ऽक्षरशो वा वाचं निदधाति स आर्त्विजीनः । ते ऽसुरा हेलयो हेलय इति कुर्वन्तः पराबभूवुस्तस्माद् ब्राह्मणेन न म्लेच्छितवै नापभाषितवै म्लेच्छो ह वा एष यदपशब्दः इति ।... षष्ठीयुक्तश्छन्दसि वा । शेषे घीत्यतः घीत्यनुवर्तते । पतिः समास एवेत्यतः पतिरिति च । षष्ठ्यामित्येव वक्तव्ये युक्तग्रहणात् तदन्तलाभः । ततश्च षष्ठ्यन्तयुक्तः पतिशब्दः छन्दसि घिसंज्ञो वा स्यादिति सूत्रार्थः । कुलि(लु)ञ्चानां पतये नमः ।... एवं च गतिरनन्तर इत्यत्र अनन्तरग्रहणमभिप्रैतीत्यादिकं च नानुपपन्नम् ॥ इति वेदशब्दविभूषणे प्रथमो ऽध्यायः ॥

End:

तश्च धातुस्थोरुपुभ्यः । छन्दसीत्यनुवर्तते, नो ण इति च। न इत्यस्मदादेश इह गृह्यते। कृतषत्वस्य सुत्र एव ग्रहणादिह न -- इन्द्रो धर्मा गृहेषु नः । इति सर्वेष्टसिद्धिः ॥
इति श्रीवत्सकुलकलशजलधिसकलकलकलानिधिवी(पी)त पातञ्जल (लात्) श्रीमदनन्तवेङ्कटेशाख्य महागुरुचरणारविन्दपरिचरणप्रभावप्रतिभात विद्यावैभवस्य अनन्तगोपालकृष्णशर्मणः कृतौ वेदशब्दविभूषणे अष्टमो ऽध्यायः ॥.

समिष्टये देवतानां शासकाद्योगिनामपि।
अनन्तवेङ्कटेशाख्यगुरवे करवै नमः ॥

MT 1640. 78 fol. Transcribed in 1915-16 from a Ms. of Sivarama Sastri of Rameswaram.

1214 VEDA-ŚĀKHĀ-PARYĀLOCANA (वेदशाखापर्यालोचन)
of Shree Kishore Mishra (of Banaras Hindu University). It contains an edition of the Caraṇa-vyūha as an appendix (pp. 57-74; Yajus-recension) with a commntary called Pīyūṣa-kaṇikā and a general essay on the Vedic Śākhā-s in Sanskrit.

Ptd.: ed. by Shree Kishore Mishra, with his own commentary. – Varanasi (Sarsawli, Cantt.) : Vijaya Press, 1985. 74, viii, pp. [SAI (ind 55 A 87/1729)]

1215 VEDA-ŚIKṢĀ (वेदशिक्षा)
Mysore ND II 3803 (P 4772/19). PL. Tel. 3 fol. Extract no. 281.

1216 VEDA-SAMARTHANA (वेदसमर्थन)
Oppert II 3032. Belonged to Gali Ramakrishna Sastrulu of Unmadivaram Taluk, Krishna Dist.

1217 VEDA-SŪTRA-PARIBHĀṢĀ-ŚIKṢĀ (वेदसूत्रपरिभाषाशिक्षा)
of Paṇḍita Rāmacandra, son of Siddheśvara → Veda-paribhāṣā-sūtra-śikṣā.

Ptd.: in Śikṣā-saṃgraha. – Benares, 1889, pp. 306-20. – (Ben. S. S. 10).

1218 VEDA-STUTI (वेदस्तुति)
of Kavicūḍāmaṇi.
Ujjain I, p. 9 (no.1646). 50 fol. (with C.).

1219 VEDĀṄGA(-CATUṢṬAYA) (वेदाङ्ग /-चतुष्टय)
SBD 2029. 31 fol. Dated Śaka 1724. (Śikṣā, Jyotiṣa, Chandas and Nighaṇṭu).
SBD 2036. 32 fol. Dated V.S. 1712. (Śikṣā, Jyotiṣa, Chandas and Nighaṇṭu).
SBD 2037. 29 fol. Dated V.S. 1628. (Śikṣā, Jyotiṣa, Chandas and Nighaṇṭu).
SBD 4017. 25 fol.
Stein p. 39 (no. 805). 28 fol. (Śikṣā, Jyotiṣa, Chandas and Nighaṇṭu).
Stein p. 39 (no. 806). 17 fol. Dated V.S. 1713. (Śikṣā, Jyotiṣa, Chandas and Nighaṇṭu).
[CC I 605a]

1220 VEDĀṄGA-NĀSIKĀ-ŚIKṢĀ (वेदाङ्गनासिकाशिक्षा)
→ Pāṇinīya-śikṣā.

1221 VEDĀṄGA-ŚIKṢĀ (वेदाङ्गशिक्षा)
→ Pāṇinīya-śikṣā.
GJKSV 15730. 10 fol.
GJKSV 35809. 9 fol. Dated V.S. 1836.
SBD 55416. 4 fol. (2-4, 6). Incomplete.

1222 VEDĀṄGA-ŚIKṢĀ-PAÑJIKĀ (वेदाङ्गशिक्षापञ्जिका)
Name of the commentary of Dharaṇī-dhara on the *Pāṇinīya-śikṣā.*
GJKSV 13635. 6 fol.
SBD 2084. 11 fol.

1223 VEDĀṄGA-SAṂKṢEPA-SĀRA (वेदाङ्गसंक्षेपसार)
of Śaṃkarācārya → Saṃkṣepa-sāra.
SBD 4297. 17 fol. (with C. of Janārdana). Dated V.S. 1847.

1224 VEDĀṄGA-S (वेदाङ्गानि)
BORI 159 of 1879-80. 16 fol.
GJKSV 40532. 29 fol.

1225 VEDĀDI-ŚIKṢĀ (?) (वेदादिशिक्षा)
→ Pāṇinīya-śikṣā also called Vedāṅga-śikṣā.
GJKSV 21022. 8 fol. Col. Veda-nāsikā-śikṣā.

1226 VEDĀDHYAYANA-KRAMA (वेदाध्ययनक्रम)
→ Saṃhitā-sūtra.
IM 2509. 8 fol. Dated Śaka 1634. Title: Svaravicāra. Udāttādisvaravicāra and Vedādhyayanakrama on the title page.

1227 VEDĀNUKRAMAṆIKĀ (वेदानुक्रमणिका)
Radh. 43.
[CC I 605a]

1228 VEDĀRTHA-DĪPIKĀ (वेदार्थदीपिका)
Name of the *Ṛgveda-sarvānukramaṇī-(vṛtti)-bhāṣya* of Ṣaḍguru-śiṣya. "Sarvānukramaṇībhāṣya by Uvaṭa, Poona 9" as given by Aufrecht is actually the same as the Bhāṣya of Ṣaḍguru-śiṣya.
[CC I 609a]

1229 VEDĀRTHA-PRADĪPIKĀ (वेदार्थप्रदीपिका)
A statement of the number of verses, the Ṛṣi-s, deities, hymns and metres in the *Ṛgveda*, by a writer who calls himself Kātyāyana-śiṣya according to the description in the catalogue.
Bik. 107. 17 fol.
[CC I 609a]

*VEMĀNA-BHAIRAVĀRYA (वेमानभैरवार्य)
See Bhairavāvadhānin or Bhairavārya.
[CC I 609b]

1230 VEYA-GĀNA-ṚṢI-DEVATĀ-NIRŪPAṆA (वेयगान-ऋषिदेवतानिरूपण)
Enumeration of Ṛṣi-s, metres and deities of Sāman-s, known as the Veya-gāna, derived from the Chanda Ārcika of the *Sāmaveda* as well as of the Āraṇya-gāna-s.
RASB II 1315 (G 1033). 28 fol. 300 Grantha-s.

1231 VEYA-GĀNA-CCHALĀKṢARA (वेयगानच्छलाक्षर)
Ptd.: in the collection of Sāmavedic tracts, ed. by Krishnaswami Srauti (in Grantha script). – Kumbakonam : Jyotirvilasa Press, 1885, pp. 7-33. See above under Chala-prakriyā. [SAI (87/783*)]

1232 VAIKṚTA-PRĀPTI-PRAKARAṆA (वैकृतप्राप्तिप्रकरण)
Mysore ND II 3810 (P 285/ 7). PL. Gr. 1 fol. (36). Extract no. 283.

1233 VAIDIKA-KROḌA-PATRA (वैदिकक्रोडपत्र)
Trav. Uni. 3339. PL. Gr. 1500 Grantha-s.

1234 VAIDIKA-GRANTHA (वैदिकग्रन्थ)
→ Dvipadā.
GJKSV 13613. 2 fol.

1235 VAIDIKA-CCHANDAḤ-PRAKĀŚA (वैदिकच्छन्दःप्रकाश)
of Gurjara Vināyaka. Gāthā-paṭala (see above) is a part of this.
L 19. 12 fol. 340 Grantha-s.
RASB II 1538 (G 1994). 8 fol. 192 Grantha-s.

1236 VAIDIKA-PADDHATI (वैदिकपद्धति)
of Kṛṣṇānanda Sarasvatī (Kaivalyadhama). A treatise on Vedic tradition in eight chapters, dealing with the qualifications to study the Veda-s, characteristics of a true Brāhmaṇa, etc.

Ptd.: Bombay ... 96 pp. [BORI :...]

1237 VAIDIKA-PARIBHĀṢĀ (वैदिकपरिभाषा)
The same as the paribhāṣā portion of the Ṛgveda-sarvānukramaṇī called Ṛgveda-paribhāṣā or Ṛgveda-sarvānukramaṇī-parbhāṣā.
OU 23 Vm (B.94/4). 5 fol. 16th century.

1238 VAIDIKA-VYĀKARAṆA (वैदिकव्याकरण)
BISM p. 270 (7/395). Prapāṭhaka-s 1-4. Dated V.S. 1538. Is this the Vaidika-śabda-prakāśa mentioned under the next entry ?

1239 VAIDIKA-ŚABDA-PRAKĀŚA (वैदिकशब्दप्रकाश)
Referred to by Sāyaṇa in his commentary on the *Taittirīya-saṃhitā* (I 1.14; last mantra; the concluding statement on the Anuvāka 14. Anandashrama ed., vol. I, p. 216; VSM ed., p. 218) as his own work in which he has dealt with the derivation and accents of Vedic words:

अस्मिन् प्रथमप्रपाठके शब्दस्वरप्रक्रिया लेशतः प्रदर्शिता । साकल्येन तु प्रकृतिप्रत्ययविकरण तत्तदादेशादिपरिज्ञानम् अन्तरेण दुर्बोधत्वात् तस्य च सर्वस्यास्माभिर्वैदिकशब्दप्रकाशे निरूपितत्वादत्रापि तन्निरूपणे ग्रन्थगौरवप्रसङ्गात् तत्रैव सर्वमवगन्तव्यम् ॥

There are two Mss. with the title *Śabda-prakāśa* in : PUL II, p. 93 (nos. 1350-51; 39 and 51 fol. respectively). Both are entered under Vyākaraṇa and attributed to Mādhavāraṇya. (Cf. Rep. Raj. and C. I. p. 45 : *Śabda-prakāśa* of Mādhavāraṇya; a Ms. in Bikaner). But it is not known whether it is the same work.

1240 VAIDIKA-ŚIKṢĀ-DARŚANA-BINDU (वैदिकशिक्षादर्शनबिन्दु)
of P. N. Pattabhirama Sastri. Three lectures on the Śikṣā-s and allied topics.

Ptd.: Varanasi : Sampurnananda Samskrita Visvavidyalaya, 1980. 30 pp. – (Ganganatha Jha Pravacanamālā 11). [NL (180 Jb 97 148); SAI (***)]

1241 VAIDIKA-SVARA-MAÑJARĪ (वैदिकस्वरमञ्जरी)
of Tryambak Baḻavant Abhyankar. A modern work.

Ptd.: in the Veda-śāstra-dīpikā – Diamond Jubilee Memorial Volume (in Marathi). – Poona 1941, pp. 529-40. [BORI : ...]

1242 VAIDIKA-SVARA-LAKṢAṆA (वैदिकस्वरलक्षण)
MD 18097. PL. Gr. 3 pp.

1243 VAIDIKĀBHARAṆA (वैदिकाभरण)
Name of the commentary on the *Taittirīya-prātiśākhya* of Gārgya Gopāla. The entry in the CC : "Name of the C. on the Vājasaneyi-prātiśākhya by Gārgya Gopāla. Mentioned in the Siddhānta-śikṣā-vyākhyāna, Brl. 9", must be the same as this.
[CC I 610b]

*VAIDYANĀTHA or VAIJANĀTHA (वैद्यनाथ / वैजनाथ)
– Ṛgvidhānāmṛta.

*VAIDYANĀTHA-BHAṬṬA (वैद्यनाथभट्ट)
– Lakṣaṇa-ratna-bhaiṭ. See the next entry.

1244 VAIDYANĀTHA-BHAIṬ (वैद्यनाथभैट्)
of Vaidyanātha-bhaṭṭa → Lakṣaṇa-ratna(-bhaiṭ).
Gough p. 162. Tel. (Vaidyanāthabheda !).
MD 16817.
Mysore p. 2 (no. 52). 6 fol. Title: Veda-gata-pada-lakṣaṇam.
Mysore (1898), p. 5 (no. 52). Gr. 2 fol. (178-79).
Mysore I, p. 34 (2 Mss.).
Oppert I 2451. PL. Gr. 5 pp. Belonged to Sri Sarasvati Bhandaram Committee of Tiruvallikkeni, Madras.
Oppert II 1379. Belonged to Gopalacharyar of Pillapakkam, Kanchipuram Taluk.
Oppert II 7449. Belonged to Venkatarama Sastri of Pillur, Mayavaram Taluk.
Oppert II 7977. Belonged to Venkatarama Dikshita of Sorakayur, Thanjavur Dist.
Oppert II 8589. Belonged to Venkatacharyar of Timmagudi near Kumbakonam.
Trav. Uni. 2630 I. PL. Gr. 70 Grantha-s. Incomplete.
Cf. Rāvaṇa-bhaiṭ and Veṅkaṭa-bhaiṭ.
[CC I 612b]

1245 VYAKTI-LAKṢAṆA (व्यक्तिलक्षण)
A brief tract with a commentary on technical terms, such as Vatsānusāriṇī, etc.
Adyar D I 996 (29 I 28 = 73580). PL. Gr. 1 fol. (no. 77). = Adyar I, p. 52a.

1246 VYAKTI-VILAṄGHYA (व्यक्तिविलङ्घ्य)
→ Vilaṅghya.
MT 1165(g). PL. Tel. 4 fol. (53-58). (with C.). Purchased in 1913-14 from Kashibhatta Subrahmanya Sastri of Vekanur, Krishna Dist.

1247 VYĀLA-ŚIKṢĀ (व्यालशिक्षा)

A treatise in twelve verses on various modes of Vedic recitation, Jaṭā, Trikrama-jaṭā, Mālā, Śikhā, Rekhā, Daṇḍa, Ratha and Ghana.

Adyar D I 997 (1 A 19 = TR 19). Gr. 2 fol. (pp. 132-135). = Adyar I, p. 53a.
MD 969. 2 pp. (61ff.).
Oppert I 1041. Belonged to Viraraghava Tatacharyar, Head Master, Sanskrit School of Sathakopacharya, Kanchipuram, Chingelpet Dist.
Oppert II 777. Belonged to Ghanapathi Shingaracharyar of Alasur, Madurantakam Taluk.

– C.
Mysore I, p. 36.

*VYĀLI or VYĀḌI (व्यालि / व्याडि)
Referred to in the *Ṛgveda-prātiśākhya*, 3.14.17. 4.12.13. 13.12.15.

– Prātiśākhya-kārikā (?). See the colophon to L 1492.

*VYĀLI or VYĀḌI (व्यालि / व्याडि)
– Aṣṭa-vikṛti(-lakṣaṇa/-kārikā). Also called Vikṛti-vallī or Jaṭā-(paṭala)-lakṣaṇa. See above.
[CC II 147b]

1248 VYĀLI-ŚIKṢĀ (1) (व्यालिशिक्षा)
→ Aṣṭa-vikṛti-vivṛti(-kārikā).

Ptd.: in the magazine of the Mysore Sanskrit College, *Śrīmanmahārāja Saṃskṛta Mahāpāṭhaśālā Patrikā*, vol. 23-25 (1948-50), Mysore.

1249 VYĀLI-ŚIKṢĀ (2) (व्यालिशिक्षा)
Eight verses dealing with Ghana only; hence different from the Vyāla-śikṣā noticed above.

Adyar D I 998 (1 A 19 = TR 19). Gr. 2 fol. (pp. 44-46). Full text is printed. = Adyar I, p. 53a.
MD 970. 1 p. (44a).
Mysore ND II 3813 (B 860/ 4). Gr. 1 fol. (66). Extract no. 284.
Oppert II 778. Belonged to Ghanapathi Shingaracharyar of Alasur, Madurantakam Taluk.
[CC II 147b]

1250 VYĀSA-ŚIKṢĀ (व्यासशिक्षा)
An extensive treatise on vedic phonetics, attributed to Vyāsa. For a study, see Heinrich Lüders : Die Vyāsa-Śikṣā – besonders in ihrem Verhältnis zum Taittirīya-Prātiśākhya, ... von der philosophischen Fakultät der Universität Göttingen gekrönte Preisschrift. – Göttingen, 1894. 2, 120 pp. [Adyar (H 215.1 VSzge Lue); SAI (ind 51 D 501) Gö (Diss. Phil. Göttingen 1894-95; scr. var. arg. III. 2926)] Also Kiel : C. F. Haeseler Verlag für Orient. Litaratur, 1895. [SKGI (Rl 150); BM : Ptd. Bks. Cat. 1892-1906. 342

(011840.m.55)]

The text is divided into following sections :

Saṃjñā-prakaraṇa
Pragraha-prakaraṇa
Paribhāṣā-prakaraṇa
Dīrgha-prakaraṇa
Āgama-prakaraṇa
Lopa-prakaraṇa
Vaikṛta-prakaraṇa
Ṣatva-prakaraṇa
Ṇatva-prakaraṇa
Repha-prakaraṇa
Visarga-saṃdhi-prakaraṇa
Yatva-prakaraṇa
Acsaṃdhi-prakaraṇa
Anaikya-prakaraṇa
Aikya-prakaraṇa
Svara-dharma-prakaraṇa
Svara-saṃdhi-prakaraṇa
Hasta-svara-vinyāsa-prakaraṇa
Dvitva-prakaraṇa
Pūrvāgama-prakaraṇa
Dvitva-niṣedha-prakaraṇa
Aṅga-saṃhitā-prakaraṇa
Svara-bhakti-prakaraṇa
Sthāna-karaṇa-prayatna-prakaraṇa
Pluta-prakaraṇa
Oṣṭhya-prakaraṇa
Kālanirṇaya-prakaraṇa
Uccāraṇa-phala-prakaraṇa

Beginning:

अथ स्वरादिसंज्ञाश्च तत्प्रयोजनमेव च।
तत्फलं च प्रवक्ष्यामि विदुषां प्रमुदे यथा॥
अवर्णेवर्णकोवर्णो ऋवर्णोल्ऌ त्वमेत्वमैत्।
ओदौद् रङ्गौ क्रमादोम्योत् स्वराः स्युर्व्यञ्जनान्यथ॥
कादिमान्ताः स्मृताः स्पर्शा अन्तस्था यादिवोत्तराः।
जिह्वामूल्यादि हान्ताश्च षडूष्माण उदीरिताः॥

End:

संहितां च पदं वापि क्रमं चैव जटां पठन्।
लक्षणज्ञस्तदाप्नोति ब्रह्मज्ञानं हि शाश्वतम्॥
वेदामृतं पिबेद्यस्तु स तस्माद् भूसुरो भवेत्।
एवं च व्यासशिक्षाविद् भूसुरेन्द्रः स कथ्यते॥
श्रीमत्परब्रह्मसुपूर्णचित्त श्रीव्यासकण्ठप्रसृतां च शिक्षाम्।
एतामभिज्ञः प्रयतः पठेद्यः सर्वानभीष्टांश्च समश्नुते वै॥

Adyar D I 999 (22 P 20 = 68361). PL. Gr. 16 fol. Incomplete. = Adyar II, App. p. iib (40 G 20).
Adyar D I 1000 (24 F 30 = 70309). PL. Gr. 14 fol. = Adyar I, p. 53a.
Adyar D I 1001 (25 L 15 = 71133). PL. Gr. 13 fol.
Adyar D XIII 326 (VB 127). PL. Tel. 37 fol. (with C. Vedataijasa).
Adyar D XIII 327 (VB 128a). PL. Tel. 88 fol. (with C. Vedataijasa).
Baroda 9808(a). PL. Gr. 18 fol. 247 Grantha-s. = CLB I, p. 36.
Bühler p. 553 (no. 29). 116 fol. (with C. of Sūryanārāyaṇa). = BORI 14 of 1866-68.

GB 33. 130 fol. (with C. Vedataijasa). Copied for Kielhorn in Mysore in 1875. See F. Kielhorn : Remarks on the Śikṣās in : *Indian Antiquary*, vol. V, p. 196-98 (reprint in : *Kleine Schriften*, vol. I, pp. 158-69).

GB 34. PL. Gr. 79 fol. (with C. Vedataijasa). Purchased for Kielhorn in Mysore.

Göttingen 158(3). 2 fol. (51-52). Fragment of a transcript.

Gough p. 162 (with C.). Tel.

Hamburg StUB (cod.Palmbl. III 8/133) → Veda-lakṣaṇa (HB).

Hoshiarpur p. 53 (no.3757). PL. Tel. 3 fol.

Hoshiarpur p. 301 (no.5613). PL. Gr. 52 fol. 1040 Grantha-s.

Hz 272. PL. Tel. 102 fol. (with C. of Sūryanārāyaṇa) Belonged to Suryanarayanayya of Amidalpadu, Nellur Dist.

IM 2587. 6 fol. Incomplete.

MD 971. 32 pp. (187ff.). Chapter titles enumerated.

MD 972. PL. Tel. 18 pp. (74ff.). .... (= Skt. Texts on Phonetics, pp. 1-25).

MD 16724. PL. Tel. 19 pp. (8ff.). 299 Grantha-s.

MT 95(b). PL. Gr. 7 fol. (2-8). Purchased in 1910-11 from Gopalaswami Ayyangar of Mannargudi.

Mysore (1898), p. 6 (no. 52). 110 fol. (68-177) (with C. of Sūryanārāyaṇāvadhānin).

Mysore I, p. 34 (3 Mss.).

Mysore ND II 3814-24. Extract no. 285, 286.

Oppert I 1042. Belonged to Viraraghava Tatacharyar, Head Master, Sanskrit School of Sathakopacharya, Kanchipuram, Chingelpet Dist.

Oppert I 1588. PL. Gr. 87 pp. Belonged to Annasvami Srauti of Bhavani, Coimbatore Dist.

Oppert I 2455. PL. Gr. 58 pp. Belonged to Sri Sarasvati Bhandaram Committee of Tiruvallikkeni, Madras.

Oppert I 4351. Belonged to Annasastri of Muktambapuram, Thanjavur Dist.

Oppert I 4966. PL. Gr. 20 pp. Belonged to Saminatha Sastri, Pleader of Ambasamudram, Tinnavelly Dist.

Oppert I 7151. Belonged to Pola Lakshmanavadhani of Vijayanagaram.

Oppert I 7234. Belonged to Ivattur Nandikesvara Sastri of Vijayanagaram.

Oppert I 7576. Belonged to S. Kodanda Ramavadhana Pantulu of Vijayanagaram.

Oppert II 779. Belonged to Ghanapathi Shingaracharyar of Alasur, Madurantakam Taluk.

Oppert II 1179. Belonged to Tiruputkuli Srikrishna Tatacharyar of Kanchipuram.

Oppert II 1381. Belonged to Gopalacharyar of Pillapakkam, Kanchipuram Taluk.

Oppert II 4965. Belonged to Sri Sankaracharya Matha of Sringeri,

Oppert II 7451. Belonged to Venkatarama Sastri of Pillur, Mayavaram Taluk.

Oppert II 7979. Belonged to Venkatarama Dikshita of Sorakayur, Thanjavur Dist.

Oppert II 8691. Belonged to Venkatarama Sastri of Timmagudi near Kumbakonam.

Oppert II 9106. Belonged to Ganapati Lakshminarayana Sastri of Tiruvadi, Thanjavur Dist.

Oppert II 9517. Belonged to Srinivasa Sastri of Tiruvasalur, Kumbakonam Taluk.

Oppert II 9886. Belonged to M.Raja Ghanapathi of Mahadanapuram, Trichinapalli.

Radh. 2.

SBD 2061. 16 fol. (4-19). Incomplete.

Taylor I 281.
TCD 31. 222 pp. 2150 Grantha-s (with C. Vedataijasa).
Tirupati SVUORI 6344 (32821). PL. Gr.
Tirupati SVUORI 6345 (3516a). PL. Gr. 11 fol. Incomplete.
Tirupati SVUORI 6346 (3792a). PL. Gr.
Tirupati SVUORI 6347 (4378b). PL. Gr. 13 fol. (5-17).
Trav. Uni. 2088 E. PL. Gr. 13 fol. 215 Grantha-s.
Triv. Cur. IV 186. Gr. 2150 Grantha-s (with C. Velamikanyā Bhūsurāvadhāni !). Obtained from Harihara Krishna Sastrial, Shencotta.
VSM I 1248 (no.4564). 70 fol. Dated Śaka 1680. Copied by Lalla Nārāyaṇa. Extract p. 364.
Wai I 1453. 34 fol.
Wai I 1454. 68 fol. (with C. Vedataijasa).

Ptd.: ed. by Lakshmana Sastrial and pub. by K. V. Shastry with C. Vedataijasa of Sūrya-nārāyaṇa Sūrāvadhānin and a gloss called Sarvalakṣaṇa-mañjarī of Raja Ghanapathi (Sarvalakṣaṇa-mañjarī-gataviśeṣeṇa pāṭhabhedena ṭippaṇyā ca sanāthī-kṛtā) (in Grantha script). – Tiruvadi (Kadathur) : Brahmananda Press, 1908. 12, 307 pp. [Adyar (H 215.1 VSxy Lak); BM : Ptd. Bks. Cat. 1906-1928. 1276 (14090.bb.27)]
Ed. by V. Venkatarama Sharma (Phonetico-grammatical principles related to Black Yajurvedic texts). – Madras, 1929.
Ed. by Krishna Ghanapathi, in the magazine of the Mysore Sanskrit College, *Śrīmanmahārāja Saṃskṛta Mahāpāṭhaśālā Patrikā*, vol. 27.1-4 (1951), Mysore. [Adyar (H05sk MSC 27)]
Ed. by P. N. Pattabhirama Sastri, with Vedataijasa by Sūrya-nārāyaṇa Sūrāvadhānin. – Varanasi (4/7 Hanuman Ghat) : Veda Mīmāṃsā Research Centre, 1976. iii, 24, XXII, 31, 184, 6 pp.
Also Chowkhamba Sanskrit Samsthan. – (Kashi Sanskrit Series 225). [Adyar (H080 VMR 1); SAI (ind S 100, 225)]

– C.
Oppert I 1043. Belonged to Viraraghava Tatacharyar, Head Master, Sanskrit School of Sathakopacharya, Kanchipuram, Chingelpet Dist.
Oppert II 780. Belonged to Ghanapathi Shingaracharyar of Alasur, Madurântakam Taluk.
Oppert II 1382. Belonged to Gopalacharyar of Pillapakkam, Kanchipuram Taluk.

– C. Vyāsaśikṣā-mahāpadayoginī.
Oppert II 7980. Belonged to Venkatarama Dikshita of Sorakayur, Thanjavur Dist.

– C. Vedataijasa of Sūryanārāyaṇa of Andhra (also known as Sūrāvadhānin of Velmikanyā-pura – Puttur ?).
Adyar D I 1002 (22 P 20 = 68361). PL. Gr. (1-72 and 92-135) and Tel. (72-91). 135 fol. (48ff.). = Adyar II, App. p. iib (40 G 20).
Adyar D I 1003 (23 G 4 = 69830). PL. Gr. 131 fol. = Adyar I, p. 53a.

Adyar D I 1004 (23 G 40 = 69866). PL. Gr. 94 fol. = Adyar I, p. 53a. Incomplete. 186 Kārikā-s.

Adyar D I 1005 (29 K 20 = 73653). PL. Tel. 116 fol. = Adyar I, p. 53a.

Adyar D I 1006 (30 D 30 = 73920). PL. Tel. 68 fol. = Adyar I, p. 53a.

Adyar D I 1007 (30 H 30 = 74075). PL. Gr. 4 fol. (40ff.). Incomplete. = Adyar I, p. 53a.

Adyar D I 1008 (33 H 19 = 75356). PL. Gr. 71 fol. (30ff.). = Adyar I, p. 53a.

Baroda 9808(b). PL. Gr. 85 fol. 1800 Grantha-s. = CLB I, p. 36.

Baroda 10852. PL. Gr. 101 fol. 2000 Grantha-s. Dated V.S. -583 ? = CLB I, p. 36.

BORI 14 of 1866-68. 106 fol.

Bühler p. 553 (no. 29). = BORI 14 of 1866-68.

GB 33. 130 fol. (with text). Copied for Kielhorn in Mysore in 1875.

GB 34. PL. Gr. 79 fol. (with text). Purchased for Kielhorn in Mysore.

Hoshiarpur p. 54 (no.3985). 97 fol. 1500 Grantha-s. Extract pp. 78-79.

Hoshiarpur p. 54 (no.4373). PL. Gr. 14 fol. 200 Grantha-s.

Hoshiarpur p. 54 (no.4374). PL. Gr. 30 fol. 167 Grantha-s.

Hz 272. PL. Tel. 102 fol. (with text). Belonged to Suryanarayanayya of Amidalpadu, Nellur Dist.

Hz 1255. PL. Gr. 117 fol. Extract p. 122. Belonged to Anna Vajapeyi of Tiruvidaimarudur, Thanjavur Dist.

Hz 1442. PL. Gr. 40 fol. Belonged to the late Raja Ghanapathi of Tiruvidaimarudur, Thanjavur Dist.

IO 4955 (Mackenzie II 94n). PL. Na. 45 fol. (11-55). Written ca. A.D. 1770.

Lahore p. 2 (no.8). 142 fol. 2414 Grantha-s. In the possession of Pt. Jwala Datta Prasada, Lahore.

MD 973. 186 pp. (51ff.).

MD 974. PL. Gr. 236 pp. (4ff.). Dated Wednesday, the 9th day of bright half of Dhanurmāsa in the year Raktākṣi. Copied by the disciple of Śeṣādri Jaṭāvallabha.

MD 975. Tel. 173 pp. (167ff.). .... (= Skt. Texts on Phonetics, pp. 25-172).

MD 976. Tel. 145 pp. (1ff.).

MD 17543. PL. Gr. 24 pp. 900 Grantha-s. Incomplete. Breaks off in the Vyañjanapara-dīrgha-prakaraṇa.

MT 4818(c). PL. Gr. 56 fol. (8-63). Presented in 1924-25 by the Secretary to the Trustees of Sri Yogi Parthasarathi Ayyangar's Charities, Triplicane, Madras.

Mysore p. 2 (no. 52). 110 fol. (Svarāvadhānin !).

Mysore (1898), p. 6 (no. 52). 110 fol. (68-177) (with text).

Mysore I, pp. 35-36 (7 Mss.); p. 614. (Name of the commentator on p. 36: Velakaṇḍānvayajāta Sūrayavādin).

Mysore ND II 3825-35. Extract no. 287.

Mysore Skt. Coll. p. 1. No.1499. Gr.

Oppert I 8264. Belonged to Paravastu Venkatarangacharyar of Vishakhapattanam.

Oppert II 9100. Belonged to Ganapati Lakshminarayana Sastri of Tiruvadi, Thanjavur Dist.

PUL I, p. 24 (no.132). PL. Tel. 66 fol.

PUL II. App. p. 13 (no.214). PL. Tel. 60 fol. 1800 Grantha-s. Up to Uccāraṇa-phala-prakaraṇa (name of the commentator is spelt "Velamakanne").

Taylor I 281.
TCD 31. 222 pp. 2150 Grantha-s (with text).
Tirupati SVUORI 6348 (3807). PL. Gr. Incomplete.
Tirupati SVUORI 6349 (4411a). PL. Gr.
Tirupati SVUORI 6350 (738). PL. Gr. 66 fol.
Trav. Uni. 14383 B. PL. Gr. 150 Grantha-s. Incomplete.
Wai I 1454. 68 fol. (with text).

Ptd.: with the text; see above.

– C. Sarva-lakṣaṇa-mañjarī-saṃgraha of Rājā Ghanapāṭhī.
Hoshiarpur p. 54 (no.4381). PL. Gr. 126 fol. 3000 Grantha-s. Extract p. 412.

Ptd.: Only extracts in the Grantha script edition. – Tiruvadi (Kadathur) : Brahmananda Press, 1908.

[CC I 620a; II 148a; III 129b]

1251 VYĀHṚTI-SVĀHĀ-ŚRUTI (व्याहृतिस्वाहाश्रुति)
Mysore ND II 3836 (P 8305/ 2). PL. Tel. 1 fol. (2).

*VYŪḌHA-MITRA (व्यूढमित्र)
– C. called Saṃkṣepa-darpaṇa, on the Vājasaneyi-śikṣā.

1252 ŚAṂKARA-ŚIKṢĀ (शंकरशिक्षा)
Oppert I 2457. PL. Gr. 39 pp. Belonged to Sri Sarasvati Bhandaram Committee of Tiruvallikkeni, Madras.

*ŚAṂKARĀCĀRYA (शंकराचार्य)
– Pada-kārikā-ratna-mālā, also called Vājasaneya-krama-kārikā.
– Śaṃkara-śikṣā. Attributed to him in Oxf. CS d.185(7) as – śaṃkarācārya-kṛta- ... – by a later hand on the title page.
– Saṃkṣepa-sāra or Vedāṅga-saṃkṣepa-sāra.

1253 ŚATAPATHA-BRĀHMAṆA-KĀṆḌĀDHYĀYĀNUKRAMAṆIKĀ (शतपथब्राह्मणकाण्डाध्यायानुक्रमणिका)
N-W P V 60 (no.8). 3 fol. (Kāṇva-śākhā). Belonged to Pt. Makhana Misra of Mathura.

[CC I 631a]

1254 ŚATAPATHA-BRĀHMAṆA-SAMĀNA-KAṆḌIKĀNTA (शतपथब्राह्मणसमानकण्डिकान्त)
Weber 1471 (Ms. or. fol. 828). (A conjectural title by Aufrecht).

[CC I 631a]

1255 ŚATAPATHA-BRĀHMAṆĀNUVĀKA(-SAṂKHYĀ) (शतपथब्राह्मणानुवाक /-संख्या)
of Dāmodara, son of Nārāyaṇa-bhaṭṭa. An index to the Anuvāka-s of the Śatapatha-brāhmaṇa of the Mādhyandina Śākhā.

Beginning:

गुरुं नमस्कृत्य महेश्वरं च गणेश्वरं चाथ सरस्वतीं च।

माध्यन्दिनब्राह्मणपाठकानां संख्यां प्रवक्ष्याम्यथ कण्डिकानाम् ॥

End:

कण्डिकानामियं संख्या सप्तसाहस्रषट्शती।
चतुर्विंशतिरेवात्र संप्रोक्ता मुनिसत्तमैः ॥
श्रीमद्दामोदरेणायं कृतो यो ऽत्र परिश्रमः ।
परार्थमेव तत् सन्तः परार्थैकफलाश्रयाः ॥

L 2537. 12 fol. (2 fol. missing). 264 Grantha-s.
N-W P I 24 (no.74). 35 fol. Belonged to Purnananda of Benares.
RASB II 893 (G 6262). 10 fol. 180 Grantha-s.

[CC I 631a]

1256 ŚATA-PADA-SŪTRA-PĀṬHA (शतपदसूत्रपाठ)
An enumeration of the words of each chapter of the *Vājasaneyi-saṃhitā* in 100s. The total number is given as 28929.
SBD 4165. 23 fol.

1257 ŚABDA-PRAKĀŚA (शब्दप्रकाश)
It cannot be ascertained if this work is the same as the *Vaidika-śabda-prakāśa* of Sāyaṇa referred to by him in his commentary on the *Taittirīya-saṃhitā* (Anandashrama edition, vol. I, p. 216). Cf. above under Vaidika-śabda-prakāśa.

PUL II, p. 93 (no.1350). 39 fol. Incomplete.
PUL II, p. 93 (no.1351). 51 fol. Incomplete.

1258 ŚABDA-BRAHMA-VILĀSA (शब्दब्रह्मविलास)
of Vīrarāghava. A commentary on the Taittirīya-prātiśākhya, explaining certain points apparently contradictory in the two commentaries thereon, namely Tribhāṣya-ratna and Vaidikābharaṇa. Here the Prātiśākhya is ascribed to Hanumān (Rāmadūta) and it is stated that Ātreya, Māhiṣeya and Vararuci commented on it.

Beginning: (2450)

वन्दे तं देवमहं छन्दोमयवाहनं श्रुतिश्वासम्।
अजनि प्रणवकरण्डकमरतकमूर्तिस्त्रयीतनुकुले यः ॥
वेदाद्याः सर्वविद्या निगममयतनोस्तिग्मभानोरधीत्य
प्राज्ञाग्र्यः प्रातिशाख्यं निखिलबुधजनश्रेयसे यश्चकार।
बोद्धुं यद्वैभवाब्धिं जगति जडधियो नेशते ऽनाशितेनाः
स श्रीमान् रामदूतः कलयतु विमलं मानसं नः प्रसन्नः ॥
लक्ष्मीनन्दनतातदेशिककुलक्षीराब्धिलब्धोदयो
यो ऽतानीदवनीसुताप्रियतमप्रीत्यै प्रबन्धान् बहून्।
सो ऽयं श्रोत्रियवीरराघवकविः कर्तुं समुज्जृम्भते

शब्दब्रह्मविलासमागमगवीलक्ष्मज्ञमोदप्रदम्॥
आत्रेयो माहिषेयो वररुचिरपि च प्रातिशाख्यस्य चक्रु-
र्व्याख्यां भाष्याण्यमीषामनुविदधदथ त्रीणि कश्चिद् विपश्चित्।
व्यातानीद् भाष्यरत्नं तदनुपदमवाधीरयत् को ऽपि धीरः
किंचित् संचिन्तयामः सदसदिह वयं वेदविन्मोदवृद्ध्यै॥
यत्र त्रिभाष्यरत्नस्य वैदिकाभरणस्य च।
स्पर्धा बद्धात्र शुद्धार्थमद्धा निर्धारयाम्यहम्॥
नव्यं करोमि चाक्षेपकौक्षेयकमिहासकृत्।
नटत्प्रतिभटाटोपपाटनस्फुटपाटवम्॥

इह खलु निखिलजगदेककारणभूतः परमकारुणिको भगवान् रमारमणः स्वस्वरूपरूपगुणविभूतिबोधसाधनं सुकृतिजनसुगतिहेतु द्विजातीनां नेत्रमिव वेदशास्त्रं चतुर्मुखेन जगति प्रवर्तयामास। अथ भगवान् जगत्प्राणसूनुः त्रयीतनुसकाशसमासादितं स्वात्मानमिव सीतारमणैकपरायणं नमस्ते वायो त्वमेव प्रत्यक्षं ब्रह्मासीत्यादिश्रुत्या स्वतातोत्पादितत्वेन स्थापिततया स्वभ्रातृतयाभिमन्यमानं स्वाचार्यमूर्तिमयमाम्नायमखिलमक्षरक्षतिमपि विना रक्षितुं कृतक्षणः प्रतिशाखं लक्षणमाचचक्षे। तत एव तदखिलं प्रातिशाख्यसमाख्यमाचख्युः। तत्रेदं तैत्तिरीयशाखामधिकृत्य कृतमथ वर्णसमाम्नाय इत्यादिकं प्रातिशाख्यमध्वर्यवो वयमधीमहे। तदिदं सूत्रमयं लक्षणं ब्रह्मसूत्रादिभ्यो ऽपि विलक्षणम् …।
मङ्गलानन्तरारम्भ(प्रश्न)कार्त्स्न्येष्वथो अथेति कोशादथशब्दस्य बह्वर्थसिद्धावप्यौचित्यान् मङ्गलार्थकत्वं प्रथममभिधाय स्वाध्यायाध्ययनानन्तरं लक्षणापेक्षणादध्ययनानन्तर्यमपि तदर्थमभिधाय तदनु त्वयैवेति विनिवर्तकाधिकावधारका इति परिभाषानुरोधादधिकारार्थकत्वमप्यभाषिष्ट। एवं सत्यत्र वैदिकाभरणकारः अथेत्ययं शब्दो ऽधिकारार्थः प्रयुज्यते नानन्तर्यार्थः …।

End:

न चात्र पदग्रहणे परिभाषाविरोधः। नानापदवदिङ्ग्यमसंख्यान इति वचनेन पदत्वस्यैव सिद्धत्वादिति चेन्न। अनिङ्ग्यपदस्यामरासुराचला इत्यादिवद्योगरूढत्वाद् अतिप्रसङ्गावकाशविरहादनिङ्ग्यपदेन पदावयवानां …

MT 2450(a). Gr. 30 fol. Incomplete. Transcribed in 1917-18 from a Ms. of V. Gopalacharya of Villiyambakkam, Chingelpet Dist.

1259 ŚABDA-BHĀṢYA (शब्दभाष्य)
Stated to have contained quotations from the Śikṣā-sūtra-s of Āpiśali and Pāṇini and reported to be existing in the library of Rasaśālā, Ayurveda Pratisthana, Gondala (Saurastra). See Yudhisthira Mimamsaka, introduction (p. 4) to the Śikṣā-sūtrāṇi, Ajmer 1967-68.

1260 ŚABDA-SAṂGRAHA (शब्दसंग्रह)

Referred to by Sāyaṇa in his commentary on the first mantra of the *Taittirīya-saṃhitā* (iṣe tvā ... ; Anandashrama edition, vol. I, p. 31) as his own work in which he has dealt with the derivation and accents of Vedic words:

इषे त्वेत्यादिशब्दानां प्रक्रिया शब्दसंग्रहे।
अवोचं स्वरमात्रं तु वैशद्याय पुनर्ब्रुवे॥

1261 ŚAMĀNA or SAMĀNA (-PRAKARAṆA) (शमान / समान /-प्रकरण)

of Nāgadeva. Also called Śamāna-saṃdhi or Ṛksarva-samāna. A treatise giving the list of such words in the *Ṛgveda* whose final Visarga-s are dropped by the operation of saṃdhi. First Prakaraṇa of his *Ṛgveda-sapta-lakṣaṇa.* Also called Ṛksarva-samāna, Laghusamāna and Sarva-śamāna.

For Mss. details see Ṛksarva-śamāna above.

– C. Bālabodhinī of Śeṣa Nārayaṇa: See C. on Ṛksarva-śamāna.

1262 ŚAMĀNA or SAMĀNA (-PRAKARAṆA) (शमान / समान /-प्रकरण)

Also known as the Samāna-saṃdhi and included in the Sapta-lakṣaṇa (which see).

Beginning:

अथ यजुःसंहितायाम् आकारप्लुतपूर्वो घोषवद्व्यञ्जनोत्तर-श-स-कारपरो विसर्जनीयो येषु पदेषु लुप्यते तानि पदानि प्रवक्ष्यामि । अत्रेङ्ग्यपदानां नानापदत्वमसंख्याने । तेषां पूर्वपदमवग्रहः । ऊष्मविसर्जनीयप्रथमद्वितीया अघोषाः । न हकारः । व्यञ्जनशेषो घोषवान्।

गजडाद्यास्त्रयो वर्णा दादयश्चैव बादयः ।
यादिवान्तो हकारश्च शसौ तावन्यसंयुतौ॥

इति परिभाषा। अग्निया अयक्ष्मा अग्रा अप्रा असुरा अवृणा अजायथा अश्वा अहृणीयमाना अधा अस्मेरा अनिष्टा अना अगृहीता ...

End:

न प्रतिपूर्वः । स्थिरा अनवपूर्वाः । अनृक्षु साध्याः । सर्वाः । न वैपरः । सिमा होतव्या हाया हायना हारुका होत्राः । न देपरः । हूता मकारपरः । इति शमानप्रकरणम्॥

Adyar D I 987 → Veda-lakṣaṇa (A 5).
Adyar D I 988 → Veda-lakṣaṇa (A 6).
Adyar D I 1012 (20 K 21 = 67483). PL. Tel. 3 fol. = Adyar I, p. 52a.
Adyar D I 1013 (22 H 52 = 69106). PL. Gr. 4 fol. (34ff.). = Adyar I, p. 52a.
Adyar D I 1014 (22 M 28 = 69378). PL. Gr. 2 fol. (1-2). = Adyar I, p. 53b. (Sapta-lakṣaṇa).
Adyar D I 1031 → Sapta-lakṣaṇa.
Adyar D I 1032 → Sapta-lakṣaṇa.

Adyar D I 1033 → Sapta-lakṣaṇa.

Adyar D XIII 194 (VB 1141a). PL. Na. 4 fol.

Baroda 6131(f). PL. Gr. 12 fol. (29-40). 250 Grantha-s (with C.). = CLB I, p. 36.

Baroda 6255(f). PL. Tel. 5 fol. (95-99). 50 Grantha-s. = CLB I, p. 36 (a. Padmanābha). Title: Śamāna-saṃdhi.

Baroda 10032(a). PL. Gr. 19 fol. 350 Grantha-s (with C.). = CLB I, p. 36. Contains at the beginning Pūrvottarobhaya-dīrghī and Ardhāntika. Extract p. 166.

Baroda 10034(a). PL. Gr. 2 fol. 50 Grantha-s. = CLB I, p. 36 (a. Padmanābha).

Baroda 10381(c). PL. Gr. 4 fol. 50 Grantha-s. = CLB I, p. 36 (a. Padmanābha).

Baroda 11949(b). PL. Tel. 24 fol. (15-38). 400 Grantha-s. = CLB I, p. 36 (with C. Pada-darpaṇa here ascribed to Mādhavācārya).

Bombay Uni. 715 (BMC 76 5). 4 fol. Pa. Paṃ. in the margin. It contains : Śamāna, Vilaṅghya (vyaktivyalakuḥ), Napara, Tapa.ra; all in prose. One Khaṇḍa of the *Taittirīya-prātiśākhya* at the beginning.

Bombay Uni. 716 (BMC 114 2). 3 fol. Napara (fol. 1), Samāna-saṃdhi (2-3); Samāna-lakṣaṇa in the margin.

Brl. p. 10 (no.XXX) = IO 4498.

Brl. p. 10 (no.XXXI) = IO 4497.

Hoshiarpur p. 54 (no.4105). PL. Gr. 3 fol. 50 Grantha-s. Extract p. 412.

Hoshiarpur p. 54 (no.4118). PL. Gr. 3 fol. 50 Grantha-s.

Hoshiarpur p. 54 (no.4454). PL. Gr. 1 fol. 20 Grantha-s.

Hoshiarpur p. 301 (no.5947). PL. Gr. 1 fol. 20 Grantha-s.

IO 4497 (Burnell 146a). PL. Gr. 3 fol. (1-3).

IO 4498 (Burnell 49a). PL. Gr. 3 fol.

IO 4499 (Mackenzie III 186b). PL. Tel. 3 fol.

MD 979. PL. Gr. 11 pp. (1-6). Title: Śamāna-saṃdhi. Col.: Saṃhitā-śamāna.

MD 980. PL. Tel. 5 pp. (88ff.). Title: Śamāna-saṃdhi.

MD 981. PL. Tel. 47 pp. (with C. of Mallayārya).

MD 982. PL. Tel. 53 pp. (with C. of Mallayārya).

MD 983. Gr. 22 pp. (1ff.)
(with C. of Padmanābha)........................ (= Skt. Texts on Phonetics, pp. 252-66).

MD 14449. PL. Tel. 4 pp. (22ff.) Title: Śamāna-saṃdhi.

MD 14763. PL. Tel. 7 pp. (25ff.).

MD 16714. PL. Tel. 22 pp. 423 Grantha-s (with C. Pada-darpaṇa).

MD 16726. PL. Tel. 4 pp. 30 Grantha-s.

MD 16803. PL. Gr. 4 pp. 30 Grantha-s.

MD 18927. PL. Tel. 4 pp. 48 Grantha-s.

MT 294(a). PL. Tel. 17 fol. Incomplete. Lacks beginning and end. Presented in 1910-11 by Prayaga Sitarama Shastri of Guntur.

MT 485(a). PL. Tel. 19 fol. (1-19) (with C. Pada-darpaṇa). (iti śrīmatpogaḷa-mallayācārya-yajvakṛtau padadarpaṇe samānasaṃdher vyākhyānam). Presented in 1910-11 by C. Visvanatha Shastrigal of Viziyanagaram.

MT 523(a). PL. Tel. 18 fol. (1-18) (with C.). Presented in 1910-11 by C. Visvanatha Shastrigal of Viziyanagaram.

MT 565(b). PL. Tel. 3 fol. (40-42). (Śamāna-saṃdhi). Presented in 1910-11 by P. Somayya of Tenali.

MT 616(b). PL. Gr. 7 fol. (7-13) (with C.). Incomplete. Purchased in 1912-13 from Subrahmanya Shastri of Tiruvadi.

MT 689(a). PL. Gr. 3 fol. (1-3). Purchased in 1912-13 through Seshasayi Ayyangar of Kottaiyur near Kumbakonam.

MT 1085(c). PL. Tel. 5 fol. (40-44). Incomplete. Presented in 1913-14 by Prayaga Kamayya Sastri of Kolakalur, Guntur Dist.

MT 1964(d). PL. Tel. 19 fol. (27-45) (with C. of Mallayārya). Presented in 1916-17 by Rayaprolu Ramabrahmangaru of Guruza, Gudivada Taluk, Krishna Dist.

MT 1976(a). Tel. 16 fol. (with C. Pada-darpaṇa of Mallayārya). Presented in 1916-17 by Nimmagadda Narasimhavadhanulugaru of Godavarru, Godavari Dist.

MT 2649(b). PL. Tel. 13 fol. (83-95). Presented in 1917-18 by Prava Surayya Sastrigaru of Penumanchili, Narasapur Taluk, Krishna Dist.

MT 2881(b). PL. Gr. 6 fol. (16-21) (with C.). = MD 983 Presented in 1918-19 by Venkatagiri Appalacharyar of Triplicane.

MT 3887(c). PL. Gr. 2 fol. (72-73). Purchased in 1921-22 from Annasvami Sastrigal, Bhavani, Coimbatore Dist.

MT 3887(q). PL. Gr. 15 fol. (150-64)(with C. Pada-darpaṇa). Incomplete. Purchased in 1921-22 from Annasvami Sastrigal, Bhavani, Coimbatore Dist.

MT 4017(d). PL. Gr. 11 fol. (19-29) (with C.). Presented in 1921-22 by Krishna Ghanapathigal, Sirukumar, Trichinapalli Dist.

MT 4600(a). PL. Gr. 2 (6-7). Presented in 1924-25 by the Secretary to the Trustees of Sri Yogi Parthasarathi Ayyangar's Charities, Triplicane, Madras.

Mysore I, pp. 37-38 (7 Mss.).

Mysore ND II 3873-97. Extract no. 295, 296.

RASB II 487-88(I) (G 6063). 3 fol. (a. Padmanābha). Dated V.S. 1913 / Śaka 1778.

SBD 4161. 2 fol. Incomplete. (Samāna-sūtra).

TD 1804. PL. Gr. 4 fol. (1-4). 35 Grantha-s.

TD 1805. PL. Gr. 2 fol. (109-10). 35 Grantha-s.

TD 1806. PL. Gr. 3 fol. 35 Grantha-s.

Trav. Uni. 4369 F. PL. Gr. 2 fol. 40 Grantha-s.

Trav. Uni. 5778 F. PL. Tel. 50 Grantha-s. (Sarvānta-samāna-saṃdhi).

Trav. Uni. 16408 Q. PL. Mal. 1 fol. 25 Grantha-s. (Āraṇa-śamāna).

Trav. Uni. 21519 A. PL. Gr. 50 Grantha-s.

Trav. Uni. L.988 I. PL. Mal. 15 fol. 585 Grantha-s.

Ujjain I, p. 10 (no.1416). 3 pp.

VOHD II 5.1538 (Ms.or.fol. 3928. StaatsB-PrK, Berlin). PL. Gr. 1 fol. Incomplete.

Ptd.: See under Aniṅgya and Sapta-lakṣaṇa.

– C. of Padmanābha.

Adyar D I 1015 (19 N 32 = 66868). PL. Gr. 15 fol. (79ff.).

Adyar D I 1016 (25 K 24 = 71114). PL. Gr. 15 fol. (1-15).

Brl. p. 10 (no.XXXII) = IO 4500.

Hoshiarpur p. 54 (no.5613). PL. Gr. 16 fol. 300 Grantha-s. Extract p. 412.

IO 4500 (Burnell 350a). Tel. 8 fol. Written ca. A.D. 1867.

MD 983. Gr. 22 pp. (1ff.).

MD 16810. PL. Tel. 13 pp. 152 Grantha-s.

MT 616(b). PL. Gr. 7 fol. (7-13) (with text). Incomplete. Purchased in 1912-13 from Subrahmanya Shastri of Tiruvadi.

MT 2881(b). PL. Gr. 6 fol. (16-21) (with text). = MD 983 Presented in 1918-19 by Venkatagiri Appalacharyar of Triplicane.

MT 4017(d). PL. Gr. 11 fol. (19-29) (with text). Presented in 1921-22 by Krishna Ghanapathigal, Sirukumar, Trichinapalli Dist.

Ujjain I, p. 10 (no. 1414). 26 pp.

Mysore ND II 3909 (3515/ 2). PL. Gr.20 fol. Extract no. 299.

Mysore ND II 3910 (3584/ 2). PL. Tel. 12 fol. Extract no. 300.

PUL I, p. 24 (no.133). PL. Gr. 11 fol.

Trav. Uni. 2630 M. PL. Gr. 90 Grantha-s. Damaged.

Trav. Uni. 2938 B. PL. Gr. 90 Grantha-s.

Trav. Uni. 3040 B. PL. Gr. 90 Grantha-s.

Trav. Uni. 3040 G. PL. Gr. 15 fol. 300 Grantha-s.

Trav. Uni. 5778 C. PL. Tel. 325 Grantha-s.

Trav. Uni. 2346 N. PL. Gr. 300 Grantha-s.

Trav. Uni. 347 B. PL. Gr. 250 Grantha-s.

Trav. Uni. C.2268 A. PL. Gr. 270 Grantha-s. = TCD 35-A. Samāna-pada-vyākhyā

C. anon.

Baroda 6131(f). PL. Gr. 12 fol. (29-40). 250 Grantha-s (with text). = CLB I, p. 36.

Baroda 10032(a). PL. Gr. 19 fol. 350 Grantha-s (with text). = CLB I, p. 36.

C. anon.

IO 4503 (Mackenzie III 234f). PL. Tel. 1 fol. (37). Written ca. A.D. 1810.

IO 4504 (Mackenzie II 61e). PL. Tel. 15 fol. (79-93).

MT 1165(h). PL. Tel. 5 fol. (59-63). Purchased in 1913-14 from Kashibhatta Subrahmanya Sastri of Vekanur, Krishna Dist.

MT 2189(a). Tel. 10 fol. Transcribed in 1916-17 from a Ms. of Vemparla Subrahmanya Sastrigaru of Tondavaramu, Godavari Dist. The scribe of the original Ms. is Ponnamalli Subrahmaṇya.

MT 4017(b). PL. Gr. 10 fol. (4-13). Incomplete. Presented in 1921-22 by Krishna Ghanapathigal, Sirukumar, Trichinapalli Dist.

C. anon.

IO 4505 (Mackenzie II 94i). PL. Na. 12 fol. (71-82). Written ca. A.D. 1770.

IO 4506 (Mackenzie III 234g). PL. Tel. 19 fol. (39-57). Written ca. A.D. 1810.

C. anon.

Adyar D I 1017 (22 C 49 = 68749). PL. Gr. 15 fol. = Adyar I, p. 52a.

Adyar D I 1018 (29 I 28 = 73580). PL. Gr. 8 fol. (98ff.). = Adyar I, p. 54a.

Adyar D I 1019 (26 L 20 = 71691). PL. Gr. 5 fol. (41ff.). Slightly different from the above.

Adyar D I 1035 ▸ Sapta-lakṣaṇa.

Adyar D I 1036 ▸ Sapta-lakṣaṇa-vyākhyā.

Adyar D I 1039 → Sapta-lakṣaṇa-vyākhyā.
Brl. p. 10 (no.XXXIII) = IO 4502.
IO 4502 (Burnell 350j). Tel. 12 fol. (105-16). Written ca. A.D. 1867.
Mysore ND II 3898 (P 997/ 1). PL. Na. 22 fol.
Mysore ND II 3900 (P 2886/ 4). PL. Na. 11 fol. (34-44).
Mysore ND II 3901 (P 1540/ 3b). PL. Tel. 14 fol. (11-24). Different ?
Mysore ND II 3902 (P 4453/ 1). PL. Na. ? 12 fol.
Mysore ND II 3903 (P 4638/ 1). PL. Na. ? 10 fol.
Mysore ND II 3904 (B 858/12). Gr. 14 fol.
PUL II. App. p. 13 (no.216). PL. Gr. 8 fol.

– C. anon. ?
Brl. p. 10 (no.XXXIV) = IO 4501.
IO 4501 (Burnell 49g). PL. Gr. 1 fol. (17).
Whish 25a (1). PL. Gr. 12 fol. (1-12).

– C. Pada-darpaṇa of (Pogala) Mallayārya.
Adyar D I 1020 (28 F 30 = 72834). PL. Tel. 17 fol. = Adyar I, p. 50b.
Adyar D I 1021 (30 D 29 = 73919). PL. Tel. 22 fol. (3ff.). = Adyar I, p. 54a. Title: Sapta-lakṣaṇa-vyākhyā.
Baroda 11949(b). PL. Tel. 24 fol. (15-38). 400 Grantha-s. = CLB I, p. 36 (with text). (a. Mādhavācārya).
Hoshiarpur p. 51 (no.6807). 111 fol. 777 Grantha-s. Extract p. 75.
MD 981. PL. Tel. 47 pp. (with text).
MD 982. PL. Tel. 53 pp.
MD 16714. PL. Tel. 22 pp. 423 Grantha-s (with text).
MT 485(a). PL. Tel. 19 fol. (1-19) (with text). Presented in 1910-11 by C. Visvanatha Shastrigal of Viziyanagaram. (Samāna-saṃdhi-vyākhyāna).
MT 523(a). PL. Tel. 18 fol. (1-18) (with text). Presented in 1910-11 by C. Visvanatha Shastrigal of Viziyanagaram.
MT 1964(d). PL. Tel. 19 fol. (27-45) (with text). Presented in 1916-17 by Rayaprolu Ramabrahmangaru of Guruza, Gudivada Taluk, Krishna Dist.
MT 1976(a). Tel. 16 fol. Presented in 1916-17 by Nimmagadda Narasimhavadhanulugaru, Godavarru, Godavari Dist.
MT 2649(b). PL. Tel. 13 fol. (83-95). = MD 981 ? srīmadbhir mahānubhāvair viracite pada-darpaṇe ... Presented in 1917-18 by Prava Surayya Sastrigaru of Penumanchili, Narasapur Taluk, Krishna Dist.
MT 3887(q). PL. Gr. 15 fol. (150-64) (with text). Incomplete. Purchased in 1921-22 from Annasvami Sastrigal, Bhavani, Coimbatore Dist.
Mysore ND II 3873 (P 144/ 7). PL. Tel. 16 fol. (34-49). Extract no. 295.
Mysore ND II 3899 (P 2265/ 3c). PL. Gr. 9 fol. (78-86). Extract no. 297.
Mysore ND II 3905 (P 144/ 8). PL. Tel. 16 fol. (34-49). Extract no. 298.
Mysore ND II 3906 (P 966/ 6). PL. Tel. 15 fol. (6-21).
Mysore ND II 3907 (P 4626/ 1b). PL. Tel. 58 fol.
Mysore ND II 3908 (P 5999/ 2). PL. Tel. 13 fol.

Tirupati SVUORI 6495 (4446b). PL. Gr. 16 fol. (30-45). Col.: Mallayārya-yajvakṛta-padadarpaṇa-samānasaṃdhi-vyākhyānam |
Tirupati SVUORI 6496 (4511a). PL. Tel.

1263 ŚAMĀNA or SAMĀNA (-PRAKARAṆA) see ŚĀKHĀ-SAMĀNA
(शमान / समान /-प्रकरण / शाखासमान)

Oppert I 1053. Belonged to Viraraghava Tatacharyar, Head Master, Sanskrit School of Sathakopacharya, Kanchipuram, Chingelpet Dist.

Oppert II 1395. Belonged to Gopalacharyar of Pillapakkam, Kanchipuram Taluk.

Oppert II 3080. Belonged to Ramasastri of Krishnappanayaka Agraharam, (Black Town), Madras Dist.

Oppert II 9119. Belonged to Ganapati Lakshminarayana Sastri of Tiruvadi, Thanjavur Dist.

– C. Oppert II 9120. Belonged to Ganapati Lakshminarayana Sastri of Tiruvadi, Thanjavur Dist.

[CC I 697b]

*ŚAMBHU-MIŚRA (शंभुमिश्र)
– Krama-kārikā(-śikṣā).

1264 ŚAMBHU-ŚIKṢĀ (शंभुशिक्षा)

A work of about 50 verses explaining the names given to the Kāṇḍa-s and the Anuvāka-s in the *Taittirīya-saṃhitā*. It classifies the letters of the alphabet and deals with accent, quantity, hiatus, doubling, svara-bhakti, etc. It is quoted in the *Tribhāṣya-ratna* (on *Taittirīya-prātiśākhya*, 1.1, 21.15), *Vaidikābharaṇa* (on *Taittirīya-prātiśākhya*, 1.40), and mentioned in Siddhānta-śikṣā-vyākhyāna, Brl. p. 9 (no.XXVII).

Beginning:

प्रणम्य शिरसा लक्ष्मीं कालिकां च सरस्वतीम्।
गणेशं च तथा शंभुं शिक्षां वक्ष्यामि शांकरीम्॥ १॥
काण्डो ऽग्निसंज्ञो विज्ञेयश्चतुर्थस्तैत्तिरीयके।
ग्रह इत्याददे प्रश्नः सजोषान्तो विधीयते॥ २॥
उरूयमित्यग्निकाण्डस्य प्रश्नद्वितयमादिकम्।
अन्त्यानुवाकसहितं वेदविद्भिरुदाहृतम्॥ ३॥
इषेप्रभृत्यपामान्तं प्रश्नानां युक्ष्वसंयुतम्।
अन्त्यानुवाका याज्याख्यास्त्रयोविंशतिरीरिताः ॥ ४॥

End:

नासिक्यत्वमुरस्यत्वं पञ्चमैर्हस्य योगतः।
अन्तस्थाभिरुरस्यत्वं कण्ठ्यत्वं केवलस्य तु॥
पदादौ पदमध्ये वा स्थितस्योष्मपरस्य वै।

प्रथमस्य द्वितीयत्वं पूर्वं कुर्वीत पण्डितः ।
धूङ्क्ष्णा (५.५.१९.१) दङ्क्ष्णव (४.४.३) इत्यत्राप्यनुस्वारो विधर्मतः ॥

Adyar D I 1010 (19 G 12 = 66413). PL. Tel. 1 fol. = Adyar I, p. 53a. Incomplete. Begins with verse 35.

Hamburg StUB (cod.Palmbl. III 8/133) → Veda-lakṣaṇa (HB).

MD 988. 7 pp. (35ff.). .... (= Skt. Texts on Phonetics, pp. 531-35).

MD 16723. PL. Tel. 4 pp. 30 Grantha-s.

MT 95(a). PL. Gr. 2 fol. (1-2). On a seperate fol. at the beginning it is called Śaṃkara-śikṣā. Purchased in 1910-11 from Gopalaswami Ayyangar of Mannargudi.

Mysore I, p. 36.

Oppert I 1046. Belonged to Viraraghava Tatacharyar, Head Master, Sanskrit School of Sathakopacharya, Kanchipuram, Chingelpet Dist.

Oppert I 7236. Belonged to Ivattur Nandikesvara Sastri of Vijayanagaram.

Oppert II 9111. Belonged to Ganapati Lakshminarayana Sastri of Tiruvadi, Thanjavur Dist.

Tirupati SVUORI 6497 (3525a). PL. Gr. Incomplete.

Tirupati SVUORI 6498 (4378a). PL. Gr. 4 fol. (1-4).

Trav. Uni. 2088 D. PL. Gr. 3 fol. 50 Grantha-s.

[CC I 637a]

*ŚĀKAṬĀYANA (शाकटायन)

Quoted in the *Ṛgveda-prātiśākhya*, 1.13, 13.16; in the *Vājasaneyi-prātiśākhya*, 3.8, 11, 86; 4.4, 126, 188; in the *Atharva-veda-prātiśākhya*, 2.24, etc.

– Ṛktantra.

[CC I 638b]

1265 ŚĀKALA-ŚĀKHĪYĀNUKRAMAṆIKĀ (शाकलशाखीयानुक्रमणिका)

→ Ṛgveda-sarvānukramaṇī-paribhāṣā (Dvādaśa-khaṇḍī).

SBD 2269. 27 fol. Incomplete.

1266 ŚĀKALA-SAṂHITĀNUKRAMAṆIKĀ (शाकलसंहितानुक्रमणिका)

Ānandāśrama 1886.

1267 ŚĀKALA-SAṂHITĀNUKRAMAṆIKĀ-SAṂKHYĀ (शाकलसंहितानुक्रमणिकासंख्या)

of Jagannātha → Ṛgveda-sarvānukrama-vivaraṇa.

SBD 2363. 23 fol. Incomplete.

1268 ŚĀKALA-SAṂHITĀYĀṂ GĀNI (शाकलसंहितायां गानि)

→ Gāni.

IM 1808. 7 fol.

1269 ŚĀKALA-SAṂHITĀ-SŪKTA-PRATĪKA (शाकलसंहितासूक्तप्रतीक)

Written in three columns it gives the number of Sūkta-s and Ṛk-s for each chapter of the *Ṛgveda*.

Beginning:

सूक्तप्रतीक-ऋक्संख्या-ऋषिदैवतच्छन्दांसि।

श्रीगणेशं नमस्कृत्य सर्वानुक्रमतः स्फुटम्।

सूक्तप्रतीक-ऋक्संख्या-ऋष्यादिकमिहोच्यते॥

अग्निमीळे मधुच्छन्दा वैश्वामित्रो गायत्री। ९ वायवा याहि मधुच्छन्दा वायुः ३ इन्द्रवायू ३ मित्रावरुणौ ३। गा। १२ अश्विनौ ३।

End:

सं समित्। अघमर्षण ऋषिः। अग्निः। संज्ञानं देवता ३। अनुष्टुभौ २। त्रिष्टुभ् १। अनुष्टुभ् १। अष्टमाष्टके ऽष्टमो ऽध्यायः॥ सू ४९। ऋ २२८॥

मन्त्रमालिन्यशान्त्यर्थं सर्वानुक्रममर्शनात्।

ऋषिदैवतच्छन्दांसि लिखितानि प्रयत्नतः॥

इति शाकलसंहितासूक्तप्रतीक- ऋक्संख्या-ऋषिदैवतच्छन्दांसि।

Baroda 23383. 24 fol. 535 Grantha-s.

1270 ŚĀKALA-SŪKTĀNUKRAMAṆIKĀ (शाकलसूक्तानुक्रमणिका)
→ Paribhāṣā section of the Ṛgveda-sarvānukramaṇikā.
GJKSV 30. 5 fol.

*ŚĀKALYA (शाकल्य)
Traditionally known as the Padakāra of the *Ṛgveda*. The *Pada-gāḍha* is attributed to him in the printed edition.

1271 ŚĀKALYA-MATA (शाकल्यमत)
Oppert I 6234. Belonged to H H the Maharaja of Travancore.

1272 ŚĀKHĀ-PARAGĀḌI (शाखापरगाडि)
Adyar D I 983 → Veda-lakṣaṇa (A 1).

1273 ŚĀKHĀ-LAKṢAṆA (शाखालक्षण)
of Śaiśiri. The text is identical with the Śaiśirīya-śikṣā. Cf. Adyar I, App. p. iiia = Adyar D I 1026 (Śaiśirīya-śikṣā). In the beginning (verse 5) it reads: "śaiśiro 'haṃ pravakṣyāmi śākhāyā lakṣaṇaṃ vidhim".

GD I 25. PL. Mal. 76 fol. 350 Grantha-s. It contains a different end.
Granthappura p. 2 (no.25). Gr. 17 Grantha-s (a. Śaiśiramuni).
Granthappura p. 102 (no. 2182)
TCD 30-B. Mal. 6 pp. 60 Grantha-s.
Trav. Uni. TM.276 B. Mal. 60 Grantha-s = TCD 30-B.
Trav. Uni. 19044. PL. Mal. 60 Grantha-s. Incomplete = GD I 25.

Trav. Uni. 19055. PL. Mal. Leaves are not numbered and disarranged. Only beginning is Śākhā-lakṣaṇa; then portions of Pādavidhāna, Yājñavalkya-śikṣā, etc.

1274 ŚĀKHĀ-VICĀRA (शाखाविचार)

Hoshiarpur p. 54 (no.6361). 4 fol. 200 Grantha-s. Incomplete.

1275 ŚĀKHĀ-ŚAMĀNA (शाखाशमान)

SBD 4149. PL. Dra. 80 fol. → Sapta-lakṣaṇa.

1276 ŚĀKHĀ-ŚAMĀNA(-SAMDHI) (शाखाशमान(-संधि)

See also Āraṇyaka-śamāna.

Adyar D I 983 → Veda-lakṣaṇa (A 1).

Adyar D I 984 → Veda-lakṣaṇa (A 2).

Adyar D I 989 → Veda-lakṣaṇa (A 7).

Adyar D I 989 (2nd copy) → Veda-lakṣaṇa (A 7).

Baroda 6255. PL. Tel. 7 fol. (72-78). 80 Grantha-s. = CLB I, p. 37.

Baroda 10381(j). PL. Gr. 7 fol. (34-40). 80 Grantha-s. = CLB I, p. 37.

Brl. p. 17 → Āraṇyaka-śamāna above.

Brl. p. 18 → Āraṇyaka-śamāna above.

Hamburg StUB (cod.Palmbl. III 8/133) → Veda-lakṣaṇa (HB).

Hz 627. PL. Tel. 24 fol. (with 4 other works). Belonged to Vedam Venkatasubrahmanya Somayaji of Allur, Nellur Dist.

Mysore p. 2 (no. 57). 3 fol.

Mysore (1898), p. 6 (no. 57). Gr. 3 fol. (102-04).

Mysore I, p. 36.

Mysore ND II 3837-43. Extract no. 288.

Oppert I 2460. PL. Gr. Belonged to Sri Sarasvati Bhandaram Committee of Tiruvallikkeni, Madras.

Oppert II 7983. Belonged to Venkatarama Dikshita of Sorakayur, Thanjavur Dist.

PUL I, p. 24 (no.135). PL. Gr. 4 (2-5).

Trav. Uni. 16408 O. PL. Mal. 2 fol. 50 Grantha-s.

– C.

Mysore ND II 3844 (B 600/ 2). Na. 3 fol. (22-24). Extract no. 289.

[CC I 639a]

1277 ŚĀKHĀ-SVARĀVADHĀNA (शाखास्वरावधान)

Mysore ND II 3845 (B 806). Tel. 28 fol. Incomplete. Extract no. 290.

1278 ŚĀṂKARĪ-ŚIKṢĀ (शांकरीशिक्षा)

→ Pāṇinīya-śikṣā.

GJKSV 46/4 (D I 2, no. 3772). 6 fol.

*ŚĀṄKHĀYANA (शाङ्खायन)

Quoted in the *Taittirīya-prātiśākhya*, 15.7.

[CC I 639a]

1279 ŚĀBDA-BHEDA-NIDARŚANA (शाब्दभेदनिदर्शन)
12 verses by Khagapati.
PUL I, p. 24 (no.136). 17 fol. (?) Dated V.S. 1924.

1280 ŚIKṢĀ (शिक्षा)
Designation for manuals teaching the correct pronunciation and recitation of Vedic texts. See F. Kielhorn : Remarks on the Śikṣās in : *Indian Antiquary*, vol. V, p. 195 (reprint in : *Kleine Schriften*, vol. I, pp. 158-69). See also A. Burnell : *On the Aindra School of Sanskrit Grammarians*, – Mangalore : Basel Mission Book . . ., 1875, pp. 45ff. [Gö (H. lit. un. III.250); SAI (87/1685*)]

Unspecified:
Ānandāśrama 4206(a) (Vedāṅga), 5619.
ASB I iii.22 (I A 38/4). 13 fol. Dated V.S. 1870 = A.D. 1813.
BHU C 622 (D 2E/2140). 8 fol. Incomplete.
GJKSV 47/5 (D I 2, no. 3775). 6 fol. (2-7). (= Taittirīyopaniṣad).
GJKSV 18971. 4 fol. (= Taittirīyopaniṣad).
GJKSV 19495. 7 fol. (= Taittirīyopaniṣad).
GJKSV 24696. 3 fol. Incomplete. 35 verses only. = Pāṇinīya-śikṣā.
GJKSV 25365. 6 fol. Dated Śaka 1706. = Pāṇinīya-śikṣā.
GJKSV 21285. 6 fol. = Pāṇinīya-śikṣā. Title and colophon : Vedāṅga-śikṣā.
GJKSV 28279. 6 fol. = Pāṇinīya-śikṣā.
GJKSV 31664. 4 fol. (1, 3-5). = Pāṇinīya-śikṣā.
GJKSV 32358. 14 fol.
GJKSV 32442. 12 fol.
GJKSV 32821. 9 fol. (1, 3-10). Incomplete. Dated V.S. 1876.
GJKSV 33199. 11 fol. (= Taittirīyopaniṣad).
GJKSV 38282. 7 fol. = Pāṇinīya-śikṣā.
IM 8496. 6 fol.
Jodhpur D I, p. 25 (no.95 / 1433). 15 fol.
OU 26 Vm (30/2/a). 6 fol. 18th century.
OU 27 Vm (B.9/10ab). 11 fol. (with Jyotiṣa). 19th century.
OU 28 Vm (B.71/15b). 4 fol. (with Jyotiṣa). 18th century.
SBD 2021. 2 fol. Incomplete (25 verses). = Yājñavalkya-śikṣā.
SBD 2027. 11 fol. Incomplete.
SBD 2082. 8 fol. (= Taittirīyopaniṣad).
SBD 2093. 32 fol. Dated V.S. 1831.

[CC I 645b-646a; II 153b]

1281 ŚIKṢĀ (2) (शिक्षा)
TCD 80-B. PL. Mal. 38 fol. 730 Grantha-s = Trav. Uni. C.1041 B. Listed as Śikṣā-samuccaya in the Alphabetical Index (vol. III). The same as Adyar D I 863 (Nāda-varṇa-viveka), Adyar D I 968 (Varṇa-cchandodaivata), and MT 5258 (Śaunakīya-sāra). See *Varṇoccāraṇadīpikā*.

1282 ŚIKṢĀ-CATUḤ-ŚLOKĪ (**शिक्षाचतुःश्लोकी**)

Mysore ND II 3846 (P 7998/ 1). PL. Na. 2 fol. (111-12). Extract no.291. See Catuḥ-ślokī.

1283 ŚIKṢĀ-CANDRIKĀ (**शिक्षाचन्द्रिका**)

Mentioned by the commentator (Lakṣmaṇa) on the Sarva-sammata-śikṣā as his another work (GB 36, fol. 4a. : asmatkṛtaśikṣācandrikāyām asya vivecanaṃ draṣṭavyam).

1284 ŚIKṢĀDI-VEDĀṄGA-SŪCĪ (**शिक्षादिवेदाङ्गसूची**)

A list of authors and works on Veda-lakṣaṇa.

Beginning:

भारद्वाजव्यासपारिशंभुकौहलहारिताः ।
बोधायनो वसिष्ठश्च वाल्मीकिश्च महामुनिः ॥
अथापिशलकौण्डिन्यपाणिन्यात्रेयनारदाः ।
पुलस्त्यबाडभीकारप्लाक्षिप्लाक्षायणस्तथा ॥
मुनयो ऽष्टादश ह्येते शिक्षाकाराः प्रकीर्तिताः ।
कालनिर्णयसिद्धान्तलक्ष्मीकान्तारुणास्तथा ॥
सर्वसंमतशिक्षा च स्याच्छिक्षाचन्द्रिका ततः ।
माहिषेयकारिका च तथा शिक्षासमुच्चयः ॥
उच्चोदर्की वैद्यनाथबैड् जटाचन्द्रिका अपि ।
जटावलिर्योहिभाष्यं सा जटामणिरित्यपि ॥
स्यात् प्रातिशाख्यमात्रेयभाष्यं वररुचेरपि ।
स्यान्माहिषेयभाष्यं च तथा तत्सूत्रकारिका ॥
ततस्त्रिभाष्यरत्नं च वैदिकाभरणं तथा ।
दीपं याजुषभूषा च स्याद् वर्णक्रमदर्पणम् ॥
अथ शिक्षासंग्रहश्च स्याद् वर्णसारदीपिका ।
तथैव स्वरपञ्चाशत् स्वरावधानदर्पणम् ॥
स्वरचद्वामणिश्चान्तनिर्देशः सप्तलक्षणम् ।
वर्णक्रमचतुःश्लोकी तथा रावणबैडपि ।
स्यात् षड्विंशतिसूत्रं च योहिप्राप्तिस्तथैव च ॥

Adyar D I 1022 (23 E 25 = 69758). PL. Gr. 1 fol. (no. 48). Broken. Fragments are lost. The complete text consisting of about 10 verses (with lacunae) is printed.

Hamburg StUB (cod.Palmbl. III 8/133) → Veda-lakṣaṇa (HB). The following list is found on the overleaf :

Bhāradvāja-śikṣā
Vyāsa-śikṣā
Pāri-śikṣā
Śaṃbhu-śikṣā

Kauhala-śikṣā
Hārīta-śikṣā
Bodhāyana-śikṣā
Vāsiṣṭha-śikṣā
Vālmīki-śikṣā
Āpiśala-śikṣā
Kauṇḍinya-śikṣā
Nārada-śikṣā
Pāṇini-śikṣā
Ātreya-śikṣā
Kāla-nirṇaya-śikṣā
Śikṣā-candrikā
Sarva-saṃmata-śikṣā
Āruṇa-śikṣā
Siddhānta-śikṣā
Lakṣmī-kānata-śikṣā
(Śikṣā-candrikā)
Māhiṣeya-kārikā
Śikṣā-samuccaya
Svara-pañcāśat
Prātiśākhya
Uccodarkī
Vaidyanātha-baiṭ
Yohi-bhāṣya
Jaṭāvallī
Jaṭāmaṇi
Jaṭā-candrikā
Ātreya-bhāṣya
Māhiṣeya-bhāṣya
Vararuci-bhāṣya
Svara-saṃparki
Varṇa-krama-darpaṇa
Varṇa-sāra-dīpikā
Tribhāṣya-ratna
Vaidikābharaṇa
Dīpam
Yājuṣa-bhūṣaṇa
Śikṣā-saṃgraha
Anta-nirdeśa
Rāvaṇa-baiṭ
Śākhā-śamāna
Sapta-lakṣaṇa
Svarāvadhāna-darpaṇa
Svara-cūḍāmaṇi
Varṇa-krama-catuślokī

1285 ŚIKṢĀDI-VEDĀṄGĀNI or ŚIKṢĀDY-AṄGĀNI **(शिक्षादिवेदाङ्गानि / शिक्षाद्यङ्गानि)**
SBD 2010. 23 fol. Incomplete.
SBD 2020. Dated Śaka 1684.
SBD 2022. 21 fol. Incomplete.

1286 ŚIKṢĀ-PAÑJIKĀ **(शिक्षापञ्जिका)**
Name of the commentary of Dharaṇī-dhara on the *Pāṇinīya-śikṣā*.

1287 ŚIKṢĀ(HYĀ)-PĀṬHA **(शिक्षा(ह्या)-पाठ)**
BORI 21 of 1875-76 (col. on fol. 24b). The verse below is on fol. 23a. See Siddheshwar Varma, *Critical Studies ...* , p. 150. The text in this Ms is identical with the Laugākṣi-śikṣā.

यथेन्द्रनीलप्रभयाभिभूतः मुक्तामणिर्याति हि नीलभावम्।
तथैव नासिक्यगुणेन युक्तः सर्वो ऽपि रङ्गत्वमुपैति कृत्स्नः ॥

1288 ŚIKṢĀ-PRAKARAṆA **(शिक्षाप्रकरण)**
Deccan College 9810. 25 fol. Incomplete.

1289 ŚIKṢĀ-PRAKĀŚA (**शिक्षाप्रकाश**)
Name of the commentary on the *Pāṇinīya-śikṣā.*

1290 ŚIKṢĀ-PRADĪPA (**शिक्षाप्रदीप**)
Name of the commentary on the *Pāṇinīya-śikṣā.*
Lahore p. 2 (no.5). 4 fol. 137 Grantha-s.

1291 ŚIKṢĀ-BODHA (**शिक्षाबोध**)
Oppert I 7237. Belonged to Ivattur Nandikesvara Sastri of Vijayanagaram.
[CC I 646a]

1292 ŚIKṢĀ-BHĀṢYA (1) (**शिक्षाभाष्य**)
of Sāyaṇācārya. Both Mss. below have been described as : "on the differences of the pronunciation of consonants and vowels together with their places".
N-W P I 14 (no.46). 10 fol. Belonged to Trilochana Pandit, Benares.
N-W P I 34 (no.102). 10 fol. Belonged to Trilochana Pandit, Benares.

1293 ŚIKṢĀ-BHĀṢYA (2) (**शिक्षाभाष्य**)
→ Bhāṣya called Pañjikā of Dharaṇī-dhara on the Pāṇinīya-śikṣā.
Ānandāśrama 2689. 16 fol.
BHU C 2304 (D 2F/2142). 13 fol. Also called Śikṣā-vivṛti.
GJKSV 36356. 12 fol.
GJKSV 37353. 11 fol. (2-12).
SBD 47216. 7 fol. Dated V.S. 1832.
SBD 47217. 4 fol.
SBD 47218. 9 fol. (1-8, 12). Incomplete. Dated V.S. 1806.
SBD 47219. 10 fol. Dated V.S. 1906.

1294 ŚIKṢĀ-BHĀṢYA (3) (**शिक्षाभाष्य**)
→ Bhāṣya called Prakāśa on the Pāṇinīya-śikṣā.
SBD 47215. 9 fol. (Śikṣā-bhāṣya Prakāśa).
VṢM III 197 (no.11339). 12 fol. → Pāṇinīya-śikṣā.

1295 ŚIKṢĀ-BHĀṢYA (4) (**शिक्षाभाष्य**)
The *Pāṇinīya-śikṣāsūtra* and *Āpiśali-śikṣa* with a commentary of Jagadish Chitracharya. – Lucknow (Mahasi, Bahraich, U.P.), 1985, 64 pp. [SAI (ind 51 D 588/1157)]

1296 ŚIKṢĀ-VACANĀNI (**शिक्षावचनानि**)
Extracts dealing with Varṇa-samāmnāya, Svarabhakti, Dvitva, etc. from different texts on Vedic phonetics.

Beginning:

नव सन्ति शिक्षाः । पाणिनीयशिक्षा कौहलेयशिक्षा आपिशलिशिक्षा इत्यादयः । तत्र पाणिनीयशिक्षायाम् अन्ते चतुष्पञ्च श्लोकाः सन्ति। तेषु कश्चिदयं येनाक्षरसमाम्नायमिति श्लोकः ।

End:

यजुर्वेदिनां प्रणवः अर्धाधिकद्विमात्रः । ऋग्वेदिनां चतुर्मात्रः । पराशरस्य चतुर्मात्रः । तदुक्तम् -- पराशरश्चतुर्मात्रमाहाध्यात्मार्थतत्त्ववित् ...

MT 3695(b). 2 fol. (21-22). Incomplete. Transcribed in 1921-22 from a Ms. of K. V. Parameswara Vadhyan Nambudiri, Achipuram, Kottakal Post, Malabar Dist.

1297 ŚIKṢĀ-VIDHI (शिक्षाविधि)

SV. Mack. 10.

[CC I 646a]

1298 ŚIKṢĀ-VIVARAṆA (शिक्षाविवरण)

of Madhusūdana. This is the Aṣṭa-vikṛti-vivṛti, also known as the Madhusūdanī-śikṣā.

BISM p. 282 (22/1016). 37 fol. Copied by Tambe Raghunātha Dīkṣita.

1299 ŚIKṢĀ-VIVṚTI (?) (शिक्षाविवृति)

A gloss on Siddheśvara-śikṣā consisting of 30 verses.

RASB II 1523 (G 9921). 4 fol. (long folded leaves). 176 Grantha-s. This is not a Vedalakṣaṇa work, though described together with them in the catalogue.

1300 ŚIKṢĀ-SAṂGRAHA (शिक्षासंग्रह)

SBD 47958. 1 fol. Incomplete. Five verses from the Yājñavalkya-śikṣa.

1301 ŚIKṢĀ-SAṂGRAHA (शिक्षासंग्रह)

A collection of thirty-three Śikṣā-s by Yājñavalkya and others with commentaries on some of them.

Ptd.: edited and annotated by Pandit Yugalakishora Vyasa (Pathaka). – Benares : Messrs. Braj B. Das and Co., 1889 (1893), 3, 480 pp. – (Benares Sanskrit Series 10). [Adyar (H080 CSS B 11); NL (180 Jc 88 143; 89 159); UBTÜ (Ci XII 633); SAI (ind S 12, 10); BM : Ptd. Bks. Cat. 1892-1906. 866 (14093.b.31); Emeneau (378); IO : Ptd. Bks. Cat. 1957, p. 2478 (22 B 11)]

Recently another edition of this collection has been published with an introduction (30 pp.) in Sanskrit, but without any clear reference to the earlier edition: *Śikṣāsaṃgrahaḥ of Yājñavalkya and Others.* Collected and edited by Ācārya Śrī Rāma Prasāda Tripāṭhī. – Varanasi : Sampurnanand Sanskrit University, 1989. 2, 2, 2, ka-śa, 398 pp. – (Ma. Ma. Gopīnāthakavirāja-granthamālā 3). In this edition the titles of a few Śikṣa-s have been changed: The *Prātiśākhya-pradīpaśikṣā* (pp. 176-98) is divided in two parts. The second part (pp. 199-285) is entitled: *Atha Visargāṅgulipradarśanaprakāram āha bhagavān maharṣir Yājñavalkyaḥ.* Page numbers in parentheses below refer to this edition.

Both the editions include the following works:

Atharva-pariśiṣṭa (or -vidhāna).. pp. 479-80 (397-98)

Laghv-amoghānandinī-śikṣā .... pp. 107-08 (86-87)

Lomaśa(śī)-śikṣā (Sāmavedīyā) .... pp. 456-62 (375-81)

Vāsiṣṭhī-śikṣā .... pp. 36-45 (31-39)

Veda-paribhāṣā-kārikā-śikṣā .... pp. 320-26
(Visargāṅguli-pradarśanaprakāra) .... (280-85)

Veda-paribhāṣā-sūtra-śikṣā (or Veda-sūtra-paribhāṣā-śikṣā) .... pp. 306-20
(Visargāṅguli-pradarśanaprakāra) .... (199-280)

Ṣoḍaśa-ślokī-śikṣā .... pp. 164-65 (136-37)

Svara-bhakti-lakṣaṇa (-pariśiṣṭa)-śikṣā .... pp. 172-75 (143-46)

Svarāṅkuśa(-śikṣā) or Svara-nirṇaya .... pp. 161-63 (133-35)

Svarāṣṭaka-śikṣā .... pp. 362-68 (302-07)

1302 ŚIKṢĀ-SAMUCCAYA (1) (शिक्षासमुच्चय)
Trav. Uni. C.1041 B. PL. Mal. 38 fol. 730 Grantha-s = TCD 80-B. Title: Śikṣā. The text is the same as the Varṇa-cchandodaivata (Adyar D I 968); and Śaunakīya-sāra (MT 5258).

1303 ŚIKṢĀ-SAMUCCAYA (2) (शिक्षासमुच्चय)
Contains verses from Pāṇinīya-śikṣā. Quoted by Śrīnivāsa, Burnell 42a. It deals with the following topics (MT 3911):

1. Upodghāta-prakaraṇam
2. Varṇotpatti-prakaraṇam
3. Varṇa-prakaraṇam
4. Vṛtti-prakaraṇam
5. Svarabhakti-prakaraṇam
6. Dviroṣṭhya-prakaraṇam
7. Prayatna-prakraṇam
8. Nakāra-prakaraṇam
9. Prakīrṇaka-prakaraṇam
10. Anunāsika-prakaraṇam
11. Mātrā-prakaraṇam
12. Dvirukta-prakaraṇam
13. Svaraviṣaya-prakaraṇam
14. Yama-prakaraṇam
15 Krama-prakaraṇam
16. Jaṭā-prakaraṇam
17. Uccāraṇaviṣayaḥ

Beginning:

(आद्याः षोडश स्वराश्च कथिताः शेषाः खलु व्यञ्जनं
षट्चत्वार इहोष्मसंज्ञकयमाः पञ्चोत्तरा विंशतिः ।
स्पर्शास्ति ... रङ्गभक्तिरबलो ऽनुस्वार एकैकशः
अन्तस्थाश्च चतस्र इत्यृषिगणैः षष्टिर्हि वै याजुषि ॥)
स्वरास्तु ब्राह्मणा ज्ञेया वर्गाणां प्रथमाश्च ये।

द्वितीयाश्च तृतीयाश्च चतुर्थाः क्षत्रियाः स्मृताः॥
वर्गाणामुत्तमा वैश्या अन्तस्थाश्च तथैव च।
अनुस्वारो विसर्गश्च शूद्रा ऊष्माण एव च॥

End:

नित्यस्वाध्यायशीलत्वं दया सत्त्वं च संयमः।
तेन शुद्धिमवाप्नोति देवत्वमधिगच्छति॥
छन्दः पादौ तु वेदस्य हस्तौ कल्पो ऽथ पठ्यते।
शिक्षा घ्राणं तु वेदस्य मुखं व्याकरणं स्मृतम्।
तस्मात् साङ्गमधीत्यैव ब्रह्मलोके महीयते॥

Adyar D I 1023 (29 I 28 = 73580). PL. Gr. 39 fol. (58ff.). = Adyar I, p. 52b (entered as Pāṇinīya-śikṣā). Five verses at the beginning are different; otherwise it is identical with GB 35.

GB 35. 19 fol. Copied for Kielhorn in Mysore in 1875. (A xerox-copy of this Ms. is in SAI : 87/793*). See F. Kielhorn : Remarks on the Śikṣās in : *Indian Antiquary*, vol. V, p. 198 (reprint in : *Kleine Schriften*, vol. I, pp. 158-69).

Hoshiarpur p. 54 (no.3541). 14 fol. 299 Grantha-s.

MT 3911(g). PL. Gr. 10 fol. (92-101). Incomplete. Purchased in 1921-22 from Narasimha Sastrigal, Bhavani, Coimbatore Dist.

Mysore p. 2 (no. 57). 12 fol.

Mysore (1898), p. 6 (no. 57). 12 fol. (18-29).

Mysore I, p. 36 (3 Mss.).

Mysore ND II 3847 (P 2339/ 9). PL. Gr. 7 fol. (53-59). Extract no. 292. The beginning of the extract given in the catalogue belongs to a different work, namely Jaṭā-vicāra. See above.

Mysore ND II 3848 (P 4453/11). PL. Na. 3 fol. (63-65). Incomplete.

Oppert II 9113. Belonged to Ganapati Lakshminarayana Sastri of Tiruvadi, Thanjavur Dist.

PUL II. App. p. 13 (no.219). 39 fol. Copy from Mysore.

TCD 32-A. PL. Mal. 19 fol. 250 Grantha-s.

Trav. Uni. 16408 Y. PL. Mal. 10 fol. 175 Grantha-s.

Trav. Uni. 16440 C. PL. Mal. 150 Grantha-s.

Trav. Uni. 18109 A. PL. Mal. 150 Grantha-s.

Trav. Uni. C.1726 A. PL. Mal. 19 fol. 250 Grantha-s. = TCD 32-A. Damaged.

Trav. Uni. T.935. 250 Grantha-s. Copy of C.1726 A. Numerous lacunae. Originally entitled Śikṣā-kāṇḍa. Dated 16.7.1106 M.E. = A.D. 1931.

– C.

TCD 32-B. PL. Mal. 110 fol. 1675 Grantha-s. Incomplete.

Trav. Uni. C.1726 B. PL. Mal. 110 fol. 1675 Grantha-s. = TCD 32-B. Damaged.

Trav. Uni. T.929. 1675 Grantha-s. Copy of C.1726 B. It contains numerous lacunae. Originally entitled Śikṣā-kāṇḍa-vyākhyā. Dated 16.7.1106 M.E. = A.D. 1931.

1304 ŚIKṢĀ-SAMUCCAYA-SAṂGRAHA (**शिक्षासमुच्चयसंग्रह**)

Adyar D I 983 (10 G 30 = TR 28), pp. 566-84 → Veda-lakṣaṇa (A 1). = Adyar I, p. 53b. Title: Sapta-lakṣaṇa.

1305 ŚIKṢĀ-SĀRA (**शिक्षासार**)

Hz 1450. PL. Gr. 10 fol. Belonged to the late Raja Ghanapathi of Tiruvidaimarudur, Thanjavur Dist.

1306 ŚIKṢĀ-SĀRA-SAṂGRAHA (**शिक्षासारसंग्रह**)

An abridgement of the Yājñavalkya-śikṣā in 113 verses.
Berlin StB-PrK (NGMPP). G 114/9. 9 fol. Dated V.S. 1837.

1307 ŚIKṢĀ-SŪTRA-VṚTTI (**शिक्षासूत्रवृत्ति**)

Title of the Śikṣā-prakāśa on the Pāṇinīya-śikṣā in : IM 3378.

1308 ŚIKṢĀ-SŪTRĀṆI (1) (**शिक्षासूत्राणि**)

Ptd.: with the sub-title : Āpiśali-Pāṇini-Candragomi-viracitāni, ed. by Yudhisthira Mimamsaka, – Ajmer : Prachya Vidya Pratisthana, 1949. 5, 17 pp. [BORI (25179)]

Reprinted : 1967-68. Hindi introd. pp. 1-12, Āpiśali-śikṣā, pp. 1-8, Pāṇinīya-śikṣā, pp. 9-23, Candra-varṇa-sūtra, pp. 24-26. [BORI (28075); SAI (ind 51 D 588/1156 kp); IO (San D 3753)]

1309 ŚIKṢĀ-SŪTRĀṆI (2) (**शिक्षासूत्राणि**)

Unspecified. B I, p. 210 (no.75). 15 fol.

1310 ŚIROVEṢṬANA (**शिरोवेष्टन**)

Adyar D I 1024 (22 E 36 = 68884). PL. Tel. 1 fol. (24b). (Perhaps a double entry; same as Adyar D I 725, Ardhāntika, above).
MD 14743. ? The same text as in Adyar (ubhā vām ...) but here called Śiroveṣṭana.

***ŚIVARĀMA** (**शिवराम**)

Son of Viśrāma.
– Ṛṣi-cchando-devatā (SV).

***ŚIŚIRA** (**शिशिर**)

– Jaṭā-lakṣaṇa. Deccan College 9810. 10 fol. → Vikṛti-vallī.

1311 ŚUKRIYA-CCHALĀKṢARA (**शुक्रियच्छलाक्षर**)

Adyar D I 1025 (19 M 20 = 66788). PL. Tel. 1 fol. (no. 1). = Adyar I, p. 49a. Title: Chalākṣara.

1312 ŚUKLA-YAJUḤ-KRAMA-PĀṬHA (**शुक्लयजुःक्रमपाठ**)

→ Vājasaneyi-saṃhitā-krama-pāṭha.
GJKSV 38142. 147 fol. (I. daśaka); 225 fol. (II. daśaka); 195 fol. (III. daśaka); 143 fol. (IV. daśaka). Dated V.S. 1856 / Śaka 1721.

1313 ŚUKLA-YAJUḤ-PRĀTIŚĀKHYA (शुक्लयजुःप्रातिशाख्य)
→ Vājasaneyi-prātiśākhya.

1314 ŚUKLA-YAJUḤ-ŚĀKHINĀṂ NIRṆAYAḤ (शुक्लयजुःशाखिनां निर्णयः)
Ptd.: No place, no date, 33 pp. [MyORI (B 1169)]

1315 ŚUKLA-YAJURVIDHĀNA-SŪTRA see YAJURVIDHĀNA
(शुक्लयजुर्विधानसूत्र / यजुर्विधान)
Ptd.: ed. by Anna Sastri Ware, with the C. *Yajurmañjarī* of Kālanātha Vāghare. – Bombay : Nirnaya Sagar Press, 1943, pp. 1-50. [SOAS (III.1.c.54 – 59314)]

1316 ŚUKLA-YAJURVEDA-KĀṆVA-SAṂHITĀ-KRAMA-PĀṬHA
(शुक्लयजुर्वेदकाण्वसंहिताक्रमपाठ)
SBD 52221. 307 and 222 fol. Dated V.S. 1689.
SBD 52228. 194 fol. Incomplete. (Kāṇva-krama-pāṭha).

1317 ŚUKLA-YAJURVEDA-PRĀTIŚĀKHYA (शुक्लयजुर्वेदप्रातिशाख्य)
→ Vājasaneyi-prātiśākhya.

1318 ŚUKLA-YAJURVEDA-PRĀTIŚĀKHYA-KĀRIKĀ (शुक्लयजुर्वेदप्रातिशाख्यकारिका)
GJKSV 38251. 7 fol. Incomplete (breaks off in verse 5 of Paṭala 3). Title on the cover page : Ṛkprātiśākhya-kārikā. Actually it is *Ṛgveda-prātiśākhya.*

1319 ŚUKLA-YAJURVEDA-SAṂHITĀ-KRAMA-PĀṬHA (शुक्लयजुर्वेदसंहिताक्रमपाठ)
→ Vājasaneyi-saṃhitā-krama-pāṭha.

1320 ŚUKLA-YAJURVEDA-SAṂHITĀ-JAṬĀ-PĀṬHA (शुक्लयजुर्वेदसंहिताजटापाठ)
→ Vājasaneyi-saṃhitā-jaṭā-pāṭha.

1321 ŚUKLA-YAJURVEDA-SAṂHITĀ-SARVĀNUKRAMA(-SŪTRA)
(शुक्लयजुर्वेदसंहितासर्वानुक्रम /-सूत्र)
→ Śukla-yajurveda-sarvānukrama.

1322 ŚUKLA-YAJURVEDA-SARVĀNUKRAMA (शुक्लयजुर्वेदसर्वानुक्रम)
of Kātyāyana. A general index to the VS in five chapters. The commentator Devayājñika says (p. 345) that the work ends with the 4th chapter and the 5th chapter is a later addition.

Beginning:

मण्डलं दक्षिणमक्षि हृदयं चाधिष्ठितं येन।
शुक्लानि यजूंषि भगवान् याज्ञवल्क्यो यतः प्राप॥

तं विवस्वन्तं त्रयीमयमर्चिष्मन्तमभिध्याय माध्यन्दिनीये वाजसनेयके यजुर्वेदाम्नाये सर्वे सखिले सशुक्रिय ऋषिदैवतछन्दांस्यनुक्रमिष्यामो यजुषामनियताक्षरत्वादेकेषां छन्दो न विद्यते, द्रष्टार ऋषयः, स्मर्तारः परमेष्ठ्यादयो देवता मन्त्रान्तर्भूता अग्न्यादिका हविर्भाजः

स्तुतिभाजो वा।

End:

सप्तमं जगती जागतपदाष्टिनस्त्रयः स्वौ च द्वौ महासतोबृहत्यष्टकौ सप्तकः षट्को दशको नवकश्च षडष्टका वा महापङ्क्तिः । माध्यन्दिनीये वाजसनेयके सर्वानुक्रमणिकैषा कृतिर्भगवतः कात्यायनस्यैषा कृतिर्भगवतः कात्यायनस्य॥ इति सर्वानुक्रमसूत्रे ...

AK 68 (2nd ch.)

Alwar 122.

Baroda 9650. 13 fol. (16-28). 300 Grantha-s. = CLB I, p. 33.

Baroda 9080. 195 fol. 5000 Grantha-s (with C. of Deva-yājñika). = CLB I, p. 33.

BBRAS 501 (B D 162). 6 fol. (with C. of Holīra. 1st Kaṇḍikā only).

Bd. 53. 36 fol. Dated V.S. 1721.

Berlin StB-PrK (NGMPP). D 77/15(b). 36 fol. (5-40). Lithographic print dated V.S. 1941 Śaka 1806 (Mādhyandina-saṃhitā Sarvānukramaṇikā- anuvākādhyāya-yājñavalkyaśikṣopetā sasvarā ca mumbayyāṃ pure kālikādevīmārge Hariprasāda-Bhagīrathajī-śarmaṇaḥ pustakālaye ...) (microfilm dated 28.07.1976).

Bhau Daji 64.

Bhk. 8.

Bhr. 520.

Bik. 343 (with C. of Yājñika-deva). Up to the 5th Adhyāya.

Bikaner 657. 51 fol. Dated V.S. 1604 (A.D. 1547).

Bikaner 658. 53 fol. Incomplete.

Bikaner 659. 33 fol. With Anuvāka-saṃkhyā

Bikaner 660. 23 fol.

BISM p. 314 (47/220). Dated Śaka 1757.

Bombay Uni. 721 (BS 183). 80 fol. Dated V.S. 1940 / Śaka 1652 ?

Bombay Uni. Acc. no. 5224. 71 fol. (5 chs.). Dated Śaka 1746.

BORI 50 of 1879-80. = BORI D I i.247. 41 fol. 600 Grantha-s. Dated V.S. 1545.

BORI 51 of 1879-80. = BORI D I i.249. 37 fol. Dated V.S. 1814.

BORI 223 of 1880-81. = BORI D I i.248. 38 fol.

BORI 40 of A 1881-82. = BORI D I i.251. 35 fol. Dated Śaka 1745.

BORI 41 of A 1881-82. = BORI D I i.254. 3 fol. Dated V.S. 1744 (ch. 5).

BORI 520 of 1882-83. = BORI D I i.252. 12 fol. (ch. 1).

BORI 26 of 1884-86. = BORI D I i.250. 43 fol.

BORI 53 of 1887-91. = BORI D I i.255. 36 fol. (Anuvāka-saṃkhyā also). Dated V.S. 1721.

BORI 68 of 1891-95. = BORI D I i.253. 26 fol. (ch. 2).

BORI 50 of 1895-98. = BORI D I i.256. 49 fol. (with Anuvāka-saṃkhyā). Dated V.S. 1728

BORI TM 28. 42 fol. Title: Sarvānukramaṇikā.

BORI TM 99. 57 fol. Title: Sarvānukramaṇikā.

BORI TM 122. 46 fol. Title: Kātyāyanīya-sarvānukramaṇikā.

BORI TM 364. 36 fol. Title: Sarvānukramaṇī.

Bühler p. 553 (no. 20).

Calcutta Skt. Coll. I 43. 38 fol. (23, 27, 32 are lost). 500 Grantha-s.

GJKSV 7904/1 (D II 1, no. 4658). 12 fol. (1, 14-24). Incomplete.

GJKSV 28474. 36 fol. (6-41). Incomplete. Title: Sarvānukramaṇikā.

GJKSV 34241. 29 fol. Incomplete. Title: Sarvānukramaṇikā.

GJKSV 36859. 21 fol. Incomplete. Title: Sarvānukramaṇikā.

GJKSV 42201. 120 fol. Title: Śukla-yajurvedīya-sarvānukramaṇī.

GJKSV 43782. 20 fol. Title: Sarvānukramaṇikā.

IM 2066. 2-49 fol. Incomplete. Dated V.S. 1747. Catalogued as Anukramaṇikā.

IM 2525. 9 fol. Incomplete (1 ch. only).

IM 2559. 44 fol. Col.: iti kātyāyanācāryakṛte pāraskare sarvānukramaṇīye pañcamo 'dhyāyaḥ |

IM 7175. 34 fol. Incomplete. Title: Yajurvedānukramaṇikā.

IO 190 (965a). 80 fol. Dated V.S. 1650 / Śaka 1585 (?).

IO 191 (311b). 12 fol. (156-67).

Jammu RSRI p. 18 (no. 5011). 26 fol. Dated V.S. 1823 (Stein 107).

Jodhpur D I, p. 25 (no.98 / 1271). 42 fol. Dated V.S. 42 fol. Title: Sarvānukramaṇikā (Yajurvedīyā).

L 2114. 37 fol. 630 Grantha-s.

L 4135. 42 fol. 660 Grantha-s. Dated Śaka 1758. Anuvākānukramaṇī also.

Mithila IV 184. 30 fol.

Mithila IV 184(A)-(E). (5 Mss.).

Oxf. CS d.74(5). 40 fol. (2-41). Title: Sarvānukrama. Former owner: Mālavīya Paṇḍita Bālamukunda.

Oxf. CS d.76(6). 44 fol. Dated A.D. 1842. Title: Sarvānukrama.

Oxf. CS d.78(1). 13 fol. 1 Adhyāya. Title: Sarvānukrama.

Oxf. CS d.78(3). 22 fol. Incomplete. Dated A.D. 1591. Title: Sarvānukrama.

Oxf. CS c.29(1). 36 fol. (2-37). Title: Sarvānukrama.

Oxf. II 935 (Ms. Wilson 20). 18 fol. Dated A.D. 1828. = Oxf. 362a (no.20).

P 5.

Peters. II, p. 170 (no.12). 31 fol.

Peters. II, p. 170 (no.13). 26 fol.

Peters. II, p. 170 (no.14).

Peters. II, p. 170 (no.15). 19 fol.

Peters. VI, p. 62 (no.50). 48 fol. Dated V.S. 1728.

PUL I, p. 24 (no.140). 27 fol. 5 Adhyāya-s.

PUL I, p. 24 (no.141). 120 fol. (with C. of Daiva-yājñika)

PUL I, p. 133 (no.29). 27 fol. Dated V.S. 1659.

RASB II 882 (G 6118). 29 fol. 580 Grantha-s. Dated V.S. 1930.

RASB II 883 (G 1769). 46 fol. 600 Grantha-s. Dated V.S. 1681.

RASB II 884 (G 6187). 4 fol. (with C. of Holīra) (fragment).

Rice 12.

SB p. 47 (no.18). 21 fol. 498 Grantha-s. Incomplete. = SBD 2261.

SB p. 47 (no.216). 51 fol. 535 Grantha-s. Incomplete. SBD 2263.

SBD 2254. 39 fol. (1-7, 18-49). (Śukla-yajuḥ-sarvānukramaṇī).

SBD 2261. 22 fol. (Yajuḥ-sarvānukramaḥ).

SBD 2263. 51 fol. Incomplete.
SBD 2265. 73 fol. Incomplete. (Yajuḥ-sarvānukramaṇikā).
SBD 2266. 27 fol. (Yajuḥ-sarvānukramaṇikā).
SBD 2271. 8 fol. Incomplete. (Yajuḥ-sarvānukramaṇī).
SBD 2272. 11 fol. (1-2, 10-18). Incomplete. (Yajuḥ-sarvānukramaṇī).
SBD 2273. 50 fol. Incomplete. (Yajuḥ-sarvānukramaṇī).
SBD 2291. 4 fol. Incomplete. (Yajuḥ-sarvānukramaṇī).
SBD 2299. 44 fol. (Sarvānukramaṇī). Dated V.S. 1646.
SBD 2307. 47 fol. (Yajuḥ-sarvānukramaṇikā). Dated V.S. 1820.
SBD 2308. Beng. 18 fol. 6-23. Incomplete. (Yajuḥ-sarvānukramaṇī).
SBD 2322. 27 fol. Dated Śaka 1561. (Yajuḥ-sarvānukramaḥ).
SBD 2323. 18 fol. (Yajuḥ-sarvānukramaḥ).Dated Śaka 1740.
SBD 2339. 7 fol. (2-8). Incomplete. (Yajuḥ-sarvānukramaṇī).
SBD 2340. 19 fol. (7-25). Incomplete. (Yajuḥ-sarvānukramaṇī).
SBD 2341. 29 fol. (1-6, 8-30). Incomplete. (Yajuḥ-sarvānukramaṇī). Dated V.S. 1600.
SBD 2379. 10 fol. (30-35, 37-40). Incomplete. (Sarvānukramaṇī).
SBD 47200. 82 fol. Incomplete (80-81 missing). (Sarvānukramaṇī).
SBD 48297. 9 fol. Incomplete (Anukramaṇī Mādhyandinīyā).
SBD 55268. 40 fol. Dated V.S. 1794. Copied by Dave Mūlajī in Kāśī.
Stein p. 7 (no. 107). 26 fol. Dated V.S. 1823. Incomplete.
VOHD II 8.3045 (Ms.or.quart. 861. StaatsB-PrK, Berlin). Roman. 4 fol. (21-24). This is probably the *Anuvākānukrama* of Kātyāyana.
Wai I 653. 21 fol. (with Anuvākādhyāya).
Weber 165. From E I H 309. 965. Also Anuvākānukramaṇī.
Weber 1458 (Ms. or. oct. 345). 29 fol. Dated V.S. 1757, Śaka 1622.
Weber 1459 (Ms. or. oct. 346). 123 fol. Dated V.S. 1746.

Ptd.: as an appendix to the edition of the *Vājasaneyi-saṃhitā*, with Pratijñā-sūtra, Yājñavalkya-śikṣā and Anuvāka-sūtra :

Ed. by Hariprasad Bhagirathaji, Jagadisvara Press. – Bombay : Jyestharam Mukundaji, 1884. 17, 2, 36, 40 pp. [Adyar (H 215.1 Yaj Har); Gö(4/ H E E 1062/53); Emeneau (104); IO : Ptd. Bks. Cat. 1953, p. 1968 (12 K 28)]

Ed. by Dvarakanatha Sarma, with commentary, *Vedārtha-pradīpākhya-giridharabhāṣya* (śrīśuklayajurvede mādhyandinīyavājasaneyīsaṃhitā, śrīmatsomavaṃśodbhava-pāṇḍavagiriprasādadevavarmaviracitaśrīvedārthapradīpākhyagiridharabhāṣya-sahitā). – Mathura 1873 (vyomarāmāṅkabhū = V.S. 1930 / Śaka 1795), pp. 1173-80 (with Hindi C.). [Adyar (H 211.21 Ms. xy Gir)]

– Bombay : Venkatesvara Press, 1887. [Emeneau : 105]

– Bombay : Tattvaviveka Press, 1896. [Emeneau : 107]

– Bombay : Nirnaya Sagar Press, 1901. [Emeneau : 108]

– Bombay : Nirnaya Sagar Press, 1912. [Emeneau : 109] [BM : Ptd. Bks. Cat. 1906-1928. 1203 (14010.ee.13)]

In the 4th volume of the *Vājasaneyi-saṃhitā* with commentaries of Uvaṭa and Mahīdhara, ed. by Pandit Rama Sakala Misra. – Benares : Chowkhamba, 1915, pp. 15-40. – (Kashi Sanskrit Series 34). [NL (180 Je 91 109; V 4 C 3)]

Ed. by Amritalal Sastri of Jamnagar, in : *Śukla-yajurveda-mādhyandina-saṃhitā* (prāstāvikasaṃhitāmantrāṇām akārādyanukramaṇikāvedapārāyaṇavidhyanuvāka-sūtrādhyāyāṣṭavikṛtiyājñavalkyaśikṣāpratijñāsūtrasarvānukramasūtra- ... samalaṃkṛtā) – Bombay : Nirnaya Sagar Press, Śaka 1872 (1950), pp. 190-92. [SKGI (Rh III 125)]

Ed. by Jagadisha Lal Shastri (with commentaries of Uvaṭa and Mahīdhara). – Delhi : Motilal Banarsidass, 1971. Appendix, pp. 7-16. [Adyar (H 212.21 VM xy Sha); SKGI (Rh III 121)]

With Yājñavalkya-śikṣā and Anuvāka-sūtra, lithographic print. – Bombay (V.S. 1946) 1889, 89 fol. [BM : Ptd. Bks. Cat. 1876-92. 490, 521 (14010.c.15)]

Ed. by Yugalakishora Vyasa Pathaka and Ganapati Sastri Mokate : Kātyāyana's Sarvānukrama Sūtras of the White Yajur Veda, with the commentary of Yājñikānanta-deva (also contains Sundara Śukla's Maunamantrāvabodha, ed. by Pandit Ram Sakala Misra). – Benares : Messrs. Braj B. Das and Co., 1893-1921. 346, 36 pp. – (Ben. S. S. 12). [Adyar (H080 CSS B13); NL (180 Jc 89 108); Emeneau (392); SKGI (Rh III 45)]

Ed. by Vasanta Sripada Satwalekar, under the title Vājasaneyi-mādhyandina-śukla-yajurveda-saṃhitāyāḥ Sarvānukrama-sūtram, with the Anuvāka-sūtrādhyāya (pp. 87-90). – Aundh, Pardi (Balsad Dist. Gujarat) : Svadhyaya Mandala, 1929. 104 pp. [SAI (ind 51 D 703)]

– C. Mantrākṣara-mālikā-prakāśa.
SBD 2326. 75 fol. (2-13, 15-23, 25-66, 68-79).

– C. anon. Sarvānukramaṇī-bhāṣya – Pratipada-vivaraṇa.
Beginning:

अथातश्छन्दांसीति । अथानन्तरं छन्दांसि वक्ष्यन्त इत्यर्थः । तथाहि -- गायत्र्युष्णिगनुष्टुब्बृहती पङ्क्तित्रिष्टुप्जगत्यतिजगती शक्वर्यतिशक्वर्यष्ट्यत्यष्टिधृत्यतिधृतय इति। एषां गायत्र्यादीनां शब्दानामितरेतरयोगद्वन्द्वः ॥

End:

अतिजगत्याद्यतिधृत्यन्तोत्तरसप्तवर्गाक्षरसंख्या अतिजगत्यादिसंज्ञा वेदितव्येति ॥ इति पञ्चमाध्यायस्य प्रतिपदविवरणमिदम् ॥

BORI 38 of 1884-87. = BORI D I i.261. 5 fol. (5th Adhyāya only).
Rgb. 38. 5 fol. (5th Adhyāya only).
SBD 55174. 8 fol. (5th Adhyāya only). Catalogued as Sarvānukrama-bhāṣya of Kātyāyana.

– C. Sarvānukramaṇī(-bhāṣya)-paddhati, of Yājñika-deva.

Beginning:

माध्यन्दिनीयशाखायां कात्यायनकृता तु·या।

सर्वानुक्रमणी तस्या व्याख्यानं क्रियते मया ॥
इह हि भगवान् कात्यायनाचार्यः प्रारिप्सितस्य ग्रन्थस्याविघ्नेन परिसमाप्तये प्रचयगमनाय चेष्टदेवताभिध्यानलक्षणं मङ्गलाचरणं विधाय श्रोतृबुद्धेरव्याकुलत्वार्थं ग्रन्थप्रतिपाद्यं प्रकटीकरोति मण्डलम् -- अनुक्रमिष्याम इति । तत्रेत्थमन्वयः । वयं यजुर्वेदाम्नाये ऋषिदैवतच्छन्दांस्यनुक्रमिष्यामः ।

Baroda 9080. 195 fol. 5000 Grantha-s (Bhāṣya with text). = CLB I, p. 33.
Baroda 9464. 45 fol. 1000 Grantha-s. = CLB I, p. 33. Dated V.S. 1665.
Baroda 9466. 66 fol. (6-71). 1500 Grantha-s. = CLB I, p. 33. Dated V.S. 1882.
Baroda 9668. 38 fol. 700 Grantha-s (Adh. I only). = CLB I, p. 33.
Baroda 10293. 22 fol. 1000 Grantha-s. = CLB I, p. 33. Dated V.S. 1807 (concise Bhāṣya ?).
Baroda 10431. 172 fol. 5000 Grantha-s. = CLB I, p. 33.
Baroda 10547. 39 fol. 800 Grantha-s. = CLB I, p. 33. Incomplete.
Baroda 10631. 45 fol. 1000 Grantha-s. = CLB I, p. 33. Incomplete.
Baroda 12006. 52 fol. (9-60). 1600 Grantha-s. (Adh. I. only) = CLB I, p. 33. Incomplete.
Ben. 13.
Bhr. p. 25 (no. 25).
Bik. 343. Up to the 5th Adhyāya.
Bikaner 661. 225 fol.
Bikaner 662. 106 fol. Incomplete.
BORI 25 of 1882-83. = BORI D I i.257. 128 fol. (several fol. missing). Dated V.S. 1602.
BORI 73 of 1892-95. = BORI D I i.258. 96 fol. Dated V.S. 1787.
BORI 51 of 1895-98. = BORI D I i.259. 121 fol. (5-80 missing).
GJKSV 34049. 28 fol. Incomplete. Title: Kātyāyana-sarvānukramaṇī-vyākhyā.
GJKSV 44137. 65 fol. Incomplete. Title: Sarvānukramaṇikā-bhāṣya.
IM 2479. 42 fol. (2-43). Incomplete. Title: Sarvānukramaṇī-paddhati.
IM 6678. 15 fol. Incomplete. Title: Kātyāyana-sarvānukrama-bhāṣya.
N-W P V 150 (no.40). 291 fol. Title: Anukramaṇī-vyākhyā.
Peters. V, p. 229 (no.73). Extract p. 176.
Peters. VI, p. 62 (no.51). 121 fol. (Adhyāya-s 2-4).
PUL I, p. 24 (no.141). 120 fol. (with text).
RASB II 885 (G 10201B). 42 fol. Incomplete. Dated V.S. 1753 / Śaka 1618.
SB p. 47 (no.157). 246 fol. 6608 Grantha-s. Incomplete. (prajāpatitanayena devadattanāmnā viracitā). = SBD 2262.
SB p. 101 (no.31). 262 fol. 4719 Grantha-s. Incomplete. Dated V.S.1591. Catalogued as Anukramaṇikā-vyākhyā of Devadatta, son of Prajāpati.
SBD 2262ka. 22 fol. Incomplete. (Yajuḥ-sarvānukrama-bhāṣya).
SBD 2262kha. 13 fol. (244-256). Incomplete. (a. Mahāyājñika-devadatta).
SBD 2262ga. 215 fol. (42-256). Incomplete. (a. Mahāyājñika-devadatta).
SBD 2264. 159 fol. (1-92, 1-67). (a. Deva-yājñika).
SBD 2311. 103 fol. (Sarvānukramaṇī-paddhati).
SBD 2313. 10 fol. Incomplete.
SBD 2328. 6 fol. = Devayājñika-saṃmata-paddhati-paribhāṣā.

SBD 2334. 10 fol. Incomplete. (Yajuḥ-sarvānukramaṇikā-bhāṣya).
SBD 2342. 177 fol. Dated V.S. 1658. (Anukramaṇī-bhāṣya).
SBD 47188. 3 fol. Incomplete. (Yajuḥ-sarvānukrama-bhāṣya). Kātyāyana as the author given in the catalogue.
SBD 47249. 33 fol. Incomplete. (Yajurvedānukramaṇī-bhāṣya).

– C. of Holira or Holīra.
Beginning:

यजुर्वेदस्य मूलं हि भेदो माध्यन्दिनीयकः ।
सर्वानुक्रमणी तस्याः कात्यायनकृता तु या ॥ १ ॥
व्याख्यां तस्यास्तु होलीरः कुर्वे नत्वा गणाधिपम् ।
विलोक्य सर्वसूत्राणि भाष्याणि विविधानि च ॥ २ ॥ ...

इह भगवान् कात्यायनाचार्यः सर्वानुक्रमसूत्रप्रारम्भे प्रथमं मङ्गलाचरणपूर्वकं यजुर्वेदस्य मुख्यत्वम् ऋषिच्छन्दोदेवताज्ञानार्थं प्रतिज्ञासूत्रमाह मण्डलम् इति ।

End:

तस्माद् वेदार्थपारंगतेन भगवता कात्यायनाचार्येण माध्यन्दिनीयसंज्ञ यजुर्वेदाम्नायत्वान्मुख्यत्वमुक्तम् । इति सर्वानुक्रमणीये प्रथमकण्डिकायां होलीरभाष्यं समाप्तम् ॥

BBRAS 501 (B D 162). 6 fol. (with text. 1st Kaṇḍikā only).
Bhau Daji 64.
Bhk. 8 (fragment).
BISM p. 340 (47/353). Dated śaka 1766 (Holira-bhāṣya).
BISM p. 340 (47/354). Dated śaka 1751 (Holira-bhāṣya).
BISM p. 340 (47/355). (Holira-bhāṣya).
Bombay Uni. 724 (BMC 62 4). 5 fol. (1st Kaṇḍikā only).
BORI 42 of A 1881-82. = BORI D I i.260. 2 fol. (1st Kaṇḍikā only).
RASB II 884 (G 6187). 4 fol. (fragment).
VSM I 767 (no.2301). 6 fol. Incomplete (1st Kaṇḍikā only). Extract p. 357.

– C. Sarvānukramaṇikā-paddhati. In the two Mss. noted below the name of the commentator is found neither in colophons nor in the commentary. But in Ms. no. 166 it is attributed to Hala on the title page (Paṇḍita-śrī-halākhya-paddhati) and on the margin of fol. 38a : paṇḍita-śrī-halākhya-kṛtāyāmanukramaṇi-paddhatau ... by a later hand adding a few additional verses on Hala at the end. The commentary in the two Mss. is identical (though not noted by Weber).

Beginning:

विधिः कृतार्थतामेति यत्प्रसादादनुष्ठितः ।
तानहं ब्राह्मणान् शिष्टान् वन्दे ऽभीष्टार्थसिद्धये ॥ १ ॥

अथ इषे त्वादिसर्वमन्त्राणामृषिदैवतच्छन्दोविनियोगा लिख्यन्ते ... ।

इति सर्वानुक्रमणिकापद्धतौ प्रथमो ऽध्यायः ॥
(fol. 49a of 1459)

Weber 166 (Chambers 38). 122 fol. Incomplete. Lacks end.
Weber 1459 (Ms. or. oct. 346). 123 fol. Dated V.S. 1746.

[CC I 794a]

– C. Sarvānukramaṇī-paddhati.
Baroda 4543. 69 fol. 1000 Grantha-s. = CLB I, p. 33. Incomplete. Extract pp. 157-58.

[CC I 561a; II 132b, 224b; III 119a]

1323 ŚUKLA-YAJURVEDA-SARVĀNUKRAMA (KĀṆVĪYA) (शुक्लयजुर्वेदसर्वानुक्रम / काण्वीय)

It has a few verbal changes such as "kāṇvīya" for "mādhyanadinīya" → Kāṇva-śākhīya-sarvānukramaṇikā.

BHU S 20 (D 11/635). 24 fol.
IM 2526.
MT 5070(b). PL. Tel. 16 fol. (50-65). Purchased in 1925-26 from Pendayala Venkatasubrahmanya Sastri of Pithapuram.
PUL I, p. 20 (no.43). 51 fol. 500 Grantha-s. 5 Adhyāya-s. Title: Kāṇva-śākhīya-sarvānukrama.
SBD 2295. 428 fol. (1-4, 6-98, 1-140, 1-100, 110-22, 1, 44, 52-84). Incomplete (1-3 Daśaka-s). Dated V.S. 1873.
SBD 2298. 47 fol. Dated V.S. 1844 (?).

1324 ŚUKLA-YAJURVEDĀDHYETṚ-PRAŚAṂSĀ (शुक्लयजुर्वेदाध्येतृप्रशंसा)

Oppert II 4190. Belonged to Archaka Yogananda Bhatta of Melkote, Mysore Dist.

[CC I 657b]

*ŚEṢA NĀRĀYAṆA see (ŚEṢA) NĀRĀYAṆA (शेष नारायण)

*ŚAIŚIRI (शैशिरि)

See the next entry.

1325 ŚAIŚIRĪYA-ŚIKṢĀ or ŚĀKHĀ-LAKṢAṆA (शैशिरीयशिक्षा / शाखालक्षण)

Ascribed to Śaiśiri. About 175 verses. Except a few verses the text is almost the same as the Śaunakīya-śikṣa. There are a few repetitions and many verses are identical with those of the Pāṇinīya-śikṣā and Yājñavalkya-śikṣā.

Beginning:

(शैशिरादिमुनिश्रेष्ठैरन्वितं मुनिपुङ्गवम्।
नमामि शौनकं नित्यमृग्वेदस्य प्रवर्तकम्॥) (५२६६)
गजाननाय श्रीशाय सर्व(भक्त)विघ्नप्रणाशिने।
नमो गणेशरूपाय विष्णवे दशबाहवे॥
जगत्संभूतिसंरक्षासंहारैकविनोदिने।

नमो भगवते तस्मै चिदानन्दाय विष्णवे ॥
मुद्गलो गालवो गार्ग्यः शाकल्यः शैशिरस्तथा।
पञ्चैते शौनकाः शिष्याः शाखाभेदप्रवर्तकाः ॥
शैशिरस्य तु शिष्यश्च शाकटायन एव च।
सर्वज्ञं सर्वकर्तारमाचार्यं तु प्रणम्य च ॥
शैशिरो ऽहं प्रवक्ष्यामि शाखाया लक्षणं विधिम्।
त्रिषष्टिर्वा चतुःषष्टिर्वर्णाः संभवतो मताः ॥
प्राकृते संस्कृते वापि स्वयं प्रोक्ताः स्वयंभुवा।

End:

अनुदात्तः स्वरो ज्ञेय उदात्तो नाद उच्यते।
लक्षणं प्रणवस्येदं प्रणवो ब्रह्म कीर्त्यते ॥
तैलधारामिवाच्छिन्नां दीर्घघण्टानिनादवत्।
अवाग्जं प्रणवस्याग्रं यस्तं वेद स वेदवित् ॥
त्रिस्थानं च त्रिमात्रं च त्रिब्रह्म च त्र्यक्षरम्।
त्रिमात्रादर्धमात्राच्च यस्तं वेद स वेदवित् ॥
वेदो हि वर्णसंघातो वेदो ब्रह्मेति कीर्त्यते।
तस्मात् तद्वेदवर्णज्ञो ब्रह्मलोके महीयते ॥
छन्दः पादौ ज्योतिषं नेत्रयुग्मं हस्तौ कल्पः श्रोत्रयुग्मं निरुक्तम्।
शिक्षा घ्राणं व्याकरणं तथास्यं वेदात्मने विष्णवे ऽस्मै नमो ऽस्तु ॥
विष्णुं षडङ्गेन्द्रियमादिदेवं वेदात्मानं पुरुषं विश्वरूपम्।
संचिन्त्य देवं पठते द्विजो यः स याति विष्णोः परमं पदं तत् ॥

Adyar D I 1026 (21 Q 10 = 68514). PL. Mal. 18 fol. = Adyar I, App. p. iiia (40 C 10. Śākhālakṣaṇaṃ – Śaiśirakṛtaṃ). .... (= Skt. Texts on Phonetics, pp. 407-32).

MD 19510E. PL. Mal. 8 fol. (50-57). Part of this is catalogued as Pāṇinīya-śikṣā.

MT 3712(c). 2 fol. (23-24). 25 Grantha-s. Incomplete. Transcribed in 1921-22 from a Ms. of K. V. Parameswara Vadhyan Nambudiri, Achipuram, Kottakal Post, Malabar Dist.

MT 5266(b). Gr. 2 fol. (5-6). The end as given here is not to be traced in the printed edition. Transcribed in 1926-27 from a Ms. of Narayana Nambudiripad, Punnatamana, Kottapadi, Malabar Dist.

TCD 30-B. Mal. 6 pp. 60 Grantha-s. (Śākhā-lakṣaṇa).

Trav. Uni. L.1429 D. PL. Mal. 12 fol. 300 Grantha-s.

Trav. Uni. 22010 B. PL. Mal. 300 Grantha-s.

Ptd.: ed. by Tarapada Chowdhury, based on the Adyar Ms, in : *Journal of Vedic Studies* (ed. by Raghu Vira), vol. II 2 (1935), pp. 197-216.

Reprinted in : *Vedic Studies* – A Collection of the Research Papers of Prof. Raghuvira, ed. by Mrs. Sharada Rani. – New Delhi - 110016 (Hauzkhas Enclave), 1981, pp. 403-20. (Śata-Piṭaka Series – Indo-Asian Literatures, vol. 272). [Adyar (H080 SVS SP 272); NL (180 Jb 98 37); SAI (ind S 180, 272); UBTÜ (22 A 6435)]

*ŚOBHĀKARA (-BHAṬṬA) (शोभाकर-भट्ट)
– C. Vivaraṇa on the Nāradīya-śikṣā (which see).
– Stobha-bhāṣya.

*ŚAUNAKA (शौनक)
Quoted in Ṛgveda-prātiśākhya, I 8; in Vājasaneyi-prātiśākhya, IV 119, etc. A work entitled Svarāṣṭaka has been ascribed to him by Bhaṭṭoji Dīkṣita in his Prauḍhamanoramā (cf. Oxf. 164a). The following works pertaining to Veda-lakṣaṇa are attributed to him (cf. RASB II 245 where ten works are listed):

– Anuvākānukramaṇī.
– Ārṣānukramaṇī.
– Upalekha-vṛtti.
– Ṛgvidhāna.
– Ṛgveda-prātiśākhya.
– Ṛṣi-cchando-devatānukramaṇikā (this may be a general title for three Anukramaṇī-s).
– Caturadhyāyikā.
– Chandonukramaṇī.
– Devatānukramaṇī.
– Pādānukramaṇī (also known as the Pāda-vidhāna).
– Bṛhaddevatā.
– Śaunaka-śikṣā.
– Sūktānukramaṇī.
– Svarāṣṭaka.

[CC I 663a]

1326 ŚAUNAKA-PRĀTIŚĀKHYA or ŚAUNAKĪYA-PRĀTIŚĀKHYA (शौनकप्रातिशाख्य / शौनकीयप्रातिशाख्य)
→ Ṛgveda-prātiśākhya.
SB p. 9 (no.88). 31 fol. 800 Grantha-s. = SBD 2114.
SBD 2114. 31 fol.
SBD 2118. 104 fol.

1327 ŚAUNAKĪYA-PRĀTIŚĀKHYA (शौनकीयप्रातिशाख्य)
It is a short commentary on the Svara section of the *Ṛgveda-prātiśākhya.* See Ṛgveda-svara-nirṇaya above.
GJKSV 26857. 7 fol.

1328 ŚAUNAKA-ŚIKṢĀ or ŚAUNAKĪYA-ŚIKṢĀ (शौनकशिक्षा / शौनकीयशिक्षा)
of Śaunaka. The text comprising 67 verses is identical with the Varṇoccāraṇa-lakṣaṇa (TCD 30-A; TCD 38-F; TD 1786) and Saṃkṣepa-sāra (Bombay Uni. 15), which latter is ascribed to Śaṃkarācārya (see below).

Beginning:

सर्वज्ञं सर्वकर्तारं सर्वात्मानं शिवं गुरुम्।
प्रणम्यर्क्षु (-आर्यान्) प्रवक्ष्यामि वर्णोच्चारणलक्षणम्॥ १॥
वेदस्य लक्षणं सम्यग् बालानां बुद्धिवर्धनम्।
यथोक्तं पूर्वशास्त्रेषु तथा संक्षिप्तमर्थवत्॥ २॥
द्विविधं वर्णजातं हि स्वरो व्यञ्जनमेव च।
अकारादिः स्वरो ज्ञेयः कादि व्यञ्जनमेव च॥ ३॥

End:

वेदो हि वर्णसंघातो वेदो ब्रह्मेति कीर्त्यते।
तस्मात् तद्वेदवर्णज्ञो ब्रह्मलोके महीयते॥ ६५॥
एतत् पुण्यं पापहरं मनोवाचा(चो)विशोधनम्।
(भक्त्या ज्ञात्वा च संगृह्य ब्रह्मलोकं स गच्छति॥ ६६॥
अनेन विधिना वेदं यो ऽधीते श्रद्धयान्वितः।)
सर्वपापैर्विमुक्तः स (विनिर्मुक्तो) ब्रह्मलोके महीयते॥ ६७॥

Adyar D I 1027 (21 Q 10 = 68514). PL. Mal. 8 fol. (19ff.). = Adyar I, App. p. iiia (40 C 10).

GD I 6-D. PL. Mal. 4 fol. 85 Grantha-s.

Granthappura p. 1 (no.7d). Mal. 75 Grantha-s.

MD 19510D. PL. Mal. 5 fol. (45-49).

MT (3731d). 4 fol. (19-22). Title in the Ms: Varṇakrama. But col.: Śaunaka-śikṣā. Transcribed in 1920-21 from a Ms. of K. V. Parameswara Vadhyan Nambudiri, Acchipuram, Kottakal Post, Malabar Dist.

MT 5266(a). Gr. 5 fol. (It contains slightly different readings). Transcribed in 1926-27 from a Ms. of Narayana Nambudiripad, Punnata-mana, Kottapadi, Malabar Dist.

Trav. Uni. 17800 G. PL. Mal. 120 Grantha-s.

Trav. Uni. 19026 D. PL. Mal 120 Grantha-s. = GD I 6-D.

Trav. Uni. 17826 V. PL. Mal 100 Grantha-s. Incomplete.

Trav. Uni. 18109 D. PL. Mal 100 Grantha-s. Incomplete.

Trav. Uni. 22748 B. PL. Mal 100 Grantha-s. Incomplete.

Trav. Uni. T.1152. 37 pp. 435 Grantha-s. Incomplete. 40 verses and commentary as printed, here called Subodhinī.

Ptd.: ed. by K. N. M. Divakara Dvijendra, with Sanskrit and Malayalam commentaries. – Tripunithura : Mangalodaya Press, 1962, pp 1-40. [Adyar (H 215.1 Sau xy = Ma Div); NL (180 Pc 96 118); SAI (87/773*); Oxford(2.10.2)]

– C. This anonymous commentary is found only up to verse 40 in all available Mss. For the rest, the printed edition contains a commentary by the editor.

Beginning:

सृष्ट्वाग्रे वियदादि तैः सुरनृगोपक्ष्यादिकांश्चापरां-
श्चोत्पाद्यात्र च संप्रविश्य विविधं नामानि रूपाणि च।
व्याकृत्य स्थित एष कर्म निखिलं कुर्वन्निवालक्ष्यते
यस्तं नौमि विभुं चिदात्मकमजं वेदाद्यवेद्यं शिवम्॥
या शौनककृता शिक्षा वर्णोच्चारणबोधिनी।
अविस्मृत्यै स्फुटं तस्याः श्रुतार्थो लिख्यते मया॥

इह खलु भगवान् शौनकः ऋग्वेदवर्णोच्चारणप्रतिपादकं शिक्षाख्यं ग्रन्थं चिकीर्षन् तस्य अविघ्नपरिसमाप्त्यादिसिद्ध्यै स्वाभीष्टदेवतानमस्कारपूर्वकं श्रोतृबुद्धिसमाधानाय चिकीर्षितं प्रतिजानीते -- सर्वज्ञमिति। अहं शिवं प्रणम्य वर्णोच्चारणलक्षणं प्रवक्ष्यामीत्यन्वयः। शिवशब्देनात्र अशेषमङ्गलभूतमानन्दरूपं परं ब्रह्माभिधीयते। देवताविषयोऽन्तःकरणप्रह्वीभावः प्रणामः। ... अथ प्रस्तुतस्य वर्णोच्चारणलक्षणस्य प्रवचनप्रकारमाह - वेदस्येति।

End:

वृक्षः संवत्सरः। द्रप्सः। विरप्शी। इत्यादिषु शकलाभिधानं न भवति। अपदान्तत्वात्। अवरे मकारादित्येव। तेन सम्राट् संराजभिरित्यत्र न भवति। एतदेव ज्ञापकं भवति पदान्तीयानां स्पर्शानां यरवोष्मसु परेषु विवृतौ सत्यां न शाकलाभिनिधानम् इत्यस्य। असंयुक्तं शाकलं तत् यच्छाकलाभिधानमुक्तं लकार ऊष्मसु अपि शाकलेनेत्यादि तदुच्चारणकाले उत्तरेण वर्णेनासंयुक्तमुच्चरेत्। अभिनिहितं वर्णमुच्चार्य वर्णसंतानमविच्छिन्दन्नुत्तरं यरवादि तेन संश्लिष्टमुच्चारयेत् ...

End: (Printed edition)

एतदिति। एतत् वेदवर्णोच्चारणप्रतिपादकं शिक्षाशास्त्रं पुण्यकरं पापनाशकं वाग्दोषविनाशकरं च भवति। एतत् शास्त्रं भक्त्या यः जानाति संगृह्णाति अनुतिष्ठति च सुकृती स ब्रह्मलोकं गच्छति। अनेन विधिना। श्रद्धाभक्तिसमन्वितो यः एतच्छास्त्रविधिमनुसृत्य वेदमधीते कृतपुण्यः सः निर्मुक्तसकलपापः सन् ब्रह्मलोके महीयते भवति॥

Adyar D I 1028 (21 Q 10 = 68514). PL. Mal. 68 fol. (48ff.). Incomplete. = Adyar I, App. p. iiia (40 C 10). .... (= Skt. Texts on Phonetics, pp. 627-81).

MD 19510F. PL. Mal. 27 fol. (58-84).

MT 5284. Gr. 19 fol. Incomplete. Title: Varṇoccāraṇa-lakṣaṇa-vyākhyā. Transcribed in 1926-27 from a Ms. of Narayana Nambudiripad, Punnata-mana, Kottapadi, Malabar Dist.

Trav. Uni. T.1152. PL. Mal 435 Grantha-s (with text). Incomplete.

Ptd.: with the text in the above edition (also up to verse 40 as in Adyar Ms.).

1329 ŚAUNAKĪYA-SĀRA (शौनकीयसार)

Cf. Adyar D I 863 (Nāda-varṇa-viveka) and 968 (Varṇa-cchando-daivata).

Beginning: (same as in Adyar D I 863 and further in MT 5258) See *Varṇoccāraṇadīpikā*.

तमक्षरं ब्रह्म परं पवित्रं गुहाशयं सम्यगुशन्ति विप्राः ।
स श्रेयसा चाभ्युदयेन चैव सम्यक् प्रयुक्तः पुरुषं युनक्ति ॥

इति। तथान्यदपि --

वेदो हि वर्णसंघातो वेदो ब्रह्मेति कीर्त्यते।
तस्मात् तद्वेदवर्णज्ञो ब्रह्मलोके महीयते॥

इति॥ एकः शब्दः सम्यग् ज्ञातः सुष्ठु प्रयुक्तः स्वर्गे लोके कामधुग् भवतीति च। किं च, यथोक्तवर्णस्वरूपमज्ञात्वा मन्त्रादिप्रयोगे प्रत्यवायो ऽपि भवति। तथाहि --

मन्त्रो हीनः स्वरतो वर्णतो वा मिथ्याप्रयुक्तो न तमर्थमाह।
स वाग्वज्रो यजमानं हिनस्ति यथेन्द्रशत्रुः स्वरतो ऽपराधात्॥

इति। ततो वर्णतद्धर्मादीनामवश्यं ज्ञेयत्वात् तज्ज्ञानाय यथाशक्ति यत्नः क्रियते। तत्र के वर्णाः ? कति ते ? किंस्वरूपाः ? इत्याकाङ्क्षायां शौनकीयपाणिन्यादिवचनानुसारेण तानि प्रदर्श्यन्ते। तत्र वर्णानां स्वरव्यञ्जनभेदेनाङ्गाङ्गिभावेन च द्वैविध्यमाह --

द्विविधं वर्णजातं हि स्वरो व्यञ्जनमेव च।
अकारादिः स्वरो ज्ञेयः कादि व्यञ्जनमुच्यते॥ इति॥

End:

चुत्वेन जातस्य चकारस्य न द्वित्वम्। कच्चदच्छि इत्यनयोस्तु द्वित्वं भवत्येव। तकारादेशस्य धातुस्थस्य चकारस्यानचि चेति ··· मित्यादौ गकारो ऽपि नेति श्रुतम्॥

कृते पापे ऽनुतापो वै यस्य पुंसः प्रजायते।
प्रायश्चित्तं तु तस्यैकं हरिसंस्मरणं परम्॥
उपासनीयं यत्नेन शास्त्रं व्याकरणं महत्॥
प्रदीपभूतं विद्यानां सर्वासां समुपस्थितम्॥

इति शौनकीयसारः समाप्तः।

MD 19510A. PL. Mal. 34 fol.

MT 5258. Gr. 28 fol. Transcribed in 1926-27 from a Ms. of Narayana Nambudiripad, Punnata-mana, Kottapadi, Malabar Dist.

1330 ŚAUNAKĪYA-SVARĀṢṬAKA (शौनकीयस्वराष्टक)

Mentioned in the Prauḍhamanoramā of Bhaṭṭoji Dīkṣita. See Svarāṣṭaka of Śaunaka.

[CC I 663b]

1331 ŚAUNAKĪYĀTHARVAṆA-PRĀTIŚĀKHYA (शौनकीयाथर्वणप्रातिशाख्य)

→ Atharva-veda-prātiśākhya – Caturadhyāyikā Śaunakīyā.

GJKSV 41855. 11 fol.

*ŚAURI-SŪNU or ŚAURI-SŪRI (शौरिसूनु / शौरिसूरि)
– Napara-tapara(-lakṣaṇa).

[CC I 663b]

1332 ŚYĀMĀYANĪYA-ŚIKṢĀ (श्यामायनीयशिक्षा)
VOHD II 2.554 (Ms.or.fol. 3083. StaatsB., Marburg; on fol. 17 of original pagination); see note at the end of the description.

*ŚRĪKṚṢṆAMAṆI PAṆḌITA (श्रीकृष्णमणिपण्डित)
– C. on Caraṇa-vyūha. Mithila IV 61. 61A.

*ŚRĪNIVĀSA DĪKṢITA (श्रीनिवासदीक्षित)
– Svara-prakāra (Jaimini-śākhā).
PUL II. App. p. 14 (no.230) PL. Gr. 2 fol. 20 Kārikā-s.

*ŚRĪNIVĀSA DĪKṢITA (or YAJVAN) (श्रीनिवासदीक्षित /-यज्वन्)
Son of (Ananta-)Kṛṣṇa of Saṃkṛti-gotra, and disciple of Rāmabhadra Dīkṣita of Tiruvishalur (last part of the 17th century).
– Svara-siddhānta-candrikā.

*ŚRĪNIVĀSA-MAKHIN (श्रीनिवासमखिन्
– Siddhānta-śikṣā.

*ŚRĪRAṄGĀRYA (श्रीरङ्गार्य)
– Anta-pradīpikā. Mysore I, p. 21 (3 Mss.).

[NCC I 224b]

*ŚRĪVATSĀṄKA (श्रीवत्साङ्क)
Son of Devamanīṣin.
– Aniṅgya (-prakaraṇa or -lakṣaṇa) (Taitt.).

*ṢAḌGURU-ŚIṢYA (षड्गुरुशिष्य)
Disciple of Vināyaka, Triśūlāṅka (Śūlapāṇi), Govinda, Sūrya, Vyāsa and Śivayogin.

– Vedārtha-dīpikā – Ṛgveda-sarvānukramaṇī-vṛtti, composed according to Weber in 1187 (see *Indishce Studien* VIII 160).
– Anuvākānukramaṇī-vṛtti.

[CC I 679a]

1333 ṢAḌLAKṢAṆA (षड्लक्षण)
Mysore ND II 3850 (P 4906/28). PL. Na. 1 fol. (122).

1334 ṢAḌVARGIKA (षड्वर्गिक)
Title of the Chala-prakriyā. See Adyar D I 798, 810 (Ṣaḍvarṇika; see remarks on p. 264).

Ptd.: in the collection of Sāmavedic tracts, ed. by Krishnaswami Srauti (in Grantha script). – Kumbakonam : Jyotirvilasa Press, 1885, pp. 1-3. See above under Chala-prakriyā. [SAI (87/783*)]

1335 ṢAḌVIṂŚATI(-SŪTRA) (षड्विंशति /-सूत्र)

This work is intended to help the learners of the *Taittirīya-saṃhitā* by removing the confusion arising from pairs of similar words, auch as "prajāpati" and "prajāvati".

Beginning:

इषे मयोभूः प्रथममहमस्मि द्वितीयं तृतीयं तृतीयस्याम्। याः पुरस्तादमावास्यायाँ रात्र्यां फलीकरणहोमँ सोमस्याहं यद्दते चित्तामन्दसाना शर्म वर्मेदं प्रजावतीः । अन्यत्र प्रजापतिः । १। वैश्वानरो ऽम्बे जुष्टो ऽघोषमतारिषत्। अन्यत्राततारिषः । २। धनस्य देवा जिह्वा मर्त्यस्याभिभूतिः स्वर्वाची सुप्रजसो मानुषं कवीरुषं चिकीरुषं चतस ओजिष्ठः होतारा नेतारा नेष्टारा निषसाद धृतव्रता यद्योषिद्यत्परं भद्रं मन्द्राः । अन्यत्र मन्त्राः ।

End:

यो हि प्रजां द्वित्वष्टा पु नरकः कवचिनं तमीमहे पे सावित्रमसुरो यन्तीह नो युक्ष्वोपहोमाकारान्तं यानि बृहस्पतिसुतस्य द्वादशसु विश्वा अग्निश्च सावित्रं चत्वार्यशीतिः । ओम्। षड्विंशतिसूत्रं संपूर्णम्॥

Adyar D I 1029 (25 L 35 = 71153). PL. Gr. 5 fol. (18ff.).
Adyar D I 983 → Veda-lakṣaṇa (A 1).
Adyar D I 984 → Veda-lakṣaṇa (A 2).
Adyar D I 985 → Veda-lakṣaṇa (A 3).
Adyar D I 986 → Veda-lakṣaṇa (A 4).
Adyar D I 989 → Veda-lakṣaṇa (A 7).
Adyar D XIII 195 (VB 115c). PL. Tel. 6 fol. Incomplete.
Adyar D XIII 196 (VB 461k). PL. Tel. 9 fol. Incomplete.
Adyar D XIII 197 (VB 1141d). PL. Na. 13 fol.
Baroda 2567. 11 fol. 150 Grantha-s. = CLB I, p. 37.
Baroda 10034(h). PL. Gr. 4 fol. (17-20). 120 Grantha-s. Incomplete. = CLB I, p. 37.
Baroda 10381(a). PL. Gr. 12 fol. (5-16). 150 Grantha-s. Incomplete. = CLB I, p. 38.
Brl. p. 37 (no.CXX) = IO 4510.
Hamburg StUB (cod.Palmbl. III 8/133) → Veda-lakṣaṇa (HB).
Hamburg StUB (Oppert 10d). PL. Gr.
Hoshiarpur p. 54 (no.2025). PL. Gr. 47 fol. 700 Grantha-s. Extract p. 413 (the extract printed here is that of Phulla-sūtra, ch. 3 !).
Hoshiarpur p. 54 (no.4375). PL. Gr. 8 fol. 200 Grantha-s. Extract p.413.
Hoshiarpur p. 54 (no.5040). 8 fol. 118 Grantha-s. Extract pp. 413-14.
Hz 627. PL. Tel. 24 fol. (with 4 other works). Belonged to Vedam Venkatasubrahmanya Somayaji of Allur, Nellur Dist.
IM 2049. 12 fol.
IO 4510 (Burnell 146h). PL. Gr. 8 fol.
IO 4511 (Mackenzie III 59b). PL. Tel. 8 fol.
IO 4512 (Mackenzie III 186d). PL. Tel. 9 fol. (5-13). Written ca. A.D. 1800.
MD 991. PL. Tel. 23 pp. (22ff.).
MD 992. PL. Tel. 15 pp. (81ff.).

MD 993. PL. Na. 4 pp. (12ff.). Incomplete.
MD 994. PL. Gr. 53 pp. (39ff.). Incomplete.
MD 995. PL. Gr. 12 pp. (7ff.). Incomplete.
MD 16706. PL. Tel. 6 pp. 96 Grantha-s.
MD 17447. PL. Gr. 20 pp. 210 Grantha-s.
MT 485(q). PL. Tel. 8 fol. (70-77). Presented in 1910-11 by C. Visvanatha Shastrigal of Viziyanagaram.
MT 1964(j). PL. Tel. 6 fol. (99-104). Presented in 1916-17 by Rayaprolu Ramabrahmangaru of Guruza, Gudivada Taluk, Krishna Dist.
MT 3887(k). PL. Gr. 4 fol. (85-88). Purchased in 1921-22 from Annasvami Sastrigal, Bhavani, Coimbatore Dist.
Mysore I, pp. 36-37 (10 Mss.).
Mysore ND II 3470 (P 4626/ 2). PL. Tel. 19 fol. (59-77). Extract no. 167. Title: Taittirīya-saṃhitā-varṇānukramaṇikā.
Mysore ND II 3641 (P 3280/ 3). PL. Tel. 9 fol. Extract no. 226. Title: Pluta-nirṇaya.
Mysore ND II 3851-63. Extract no. 293.
Oppert I 2473. PL. Gr. 42 pp. Belonged to Sri Sarasvati Bhandaram Committee of Tiruvallikkeni, Madras.
Oppert I 7248. Belonged to Ivattur Nandikesvara Sastri of Vijayanagaram.
Oppert II 782. Belonged to Ghanapathi Shingaracharyar of Alasur, Madurantakam Taluk.
Oppert II 1393. Belonged to Gopalacharyar of Pillapakkam, Kanchipuram Taluk.
Oppert II 5030. Belonged to Sri Sankaracharya Matha of Sringeri,
Oppert II 7989. Belonged to Venkatarama Dikshita of Sorakayur, Thanjavur Dist.
PUL I, p. 22 (no.101). PL. Gr. 56 fol. (75-130).
PUL II. App. p. 6 (no.99). PL. Gr. 10 fol. (121-30).
RASB II 487-88(VIII) (G 6063). 10 fol. (18-27). V.S. 1913 / Śaka 1778.
SBD 4159. 14 fol.
SBD 55308. 5 fol. (Ṣaḍviṃśati-lakṣaṇa).
Tirupati SVUORI 7052 (4421b). PL. Gr. 13 fol.
Tirupati SVUORI 7053 (900a). PL. Gr.
Trav. Uni. 2346 M. PL. Gr. 150 Grantha-s.
Trav. Uni. 2388 A. PL. Gr. 150 Grantha-s. Damaged.
Trav. Uni. 2938 K. PL. Gr. 150 Grantha-s.
Trav. Uni. 5512 B. PL. Gr. 150 Grantha-s.
Trav. Uni. 16408 U. PL. Mal. 9 fol. 150 Grantha-s.
Trav. Uni. L.988 M. PL. Mal. 7 fol. 140 Grantha-s. Incomplete.
Ujjain I, p. 10 (no.1118). 7 fol.
Wai II 10264. 9 fol.
Wai II 10265. 8 fol. Dated Śaka 1730.
Wai II 10266. 9 fol. Dated Śaka 1739.
Wai II 10267. 14 fol.
Wai II 10268. 12 fol. Dated Śaka 1753.

Ptd.: ed. by Vaidyanatha Sastri (in Grantha script). – Kumbakonam : Vaidika-vardhini Press, 1899. 24 pp. (Title page: idaṃ kila ahkilabhūmaṇḍalāla-ṅkārabhūtānāṃ vaidikaśiromaṇīnām atyantopakārāya mullaṅguḍi- grāmābhijanena śāṇḍilyānvayasaṃbhūtena A. vaidyanāthaśāstriṇā pariṣkṛtaṃ sat kumbhakoṇasthasvakīyavaidikavardhinīyantrālaye mudritaṃ jejīyatetarām). [Adyar (PH 215.4 Sad Va); SAI (87/780*); BM : Ptd. Bks. Cat. 1892-1906. 806 (14010.a.5,1)]

Second edition of the above, revised by T. M. Narayana Sastri. Kumbakonam : Vaidikavardhini Press, 1922.

Also in Lakṣaṇa-traya, together with Sapta-lakṣaṇa and Jaṭāmaṇi (in Telugu script) ed. by Gomatham Srinivasa Jyosyar. – Mysore, 1919. 73 pp. (Title page: Saptalakṣaṇī-Ṣaḍvig'ṃśatisūtram (savyākhyā) Jaṭāmaṇiḥ - iti Lakṣaṇatrayam | Taittirīya-yajussambandhi | maisūru gomaṭhaṃ śrīnivāsa jyotiṣikeṇa cittūru śrīśāradāmudrālaye siddhārthi-śravaṇāmāyāṃ samamudryata). This appears to be a reprint of the Grantha script edition above. [MyORI (B 4109/12669); SAI (87/778*)]

Both the editions include the following tracts :

Ṣaḍvig'ṃśati-sūtram .... pp. 1-40 (1-15)
Vākyāntāḥ (= Ardhāntika) .... p. 40 (16)
Pūrvadīrghiṇaḥ .... p. 41 (16-17)
Uttaradīrghiṇaḥ .... pp. 41-42 (17-18)
Ubhayahrasviṇaḥ (full text) .... p. 42 (18)
Ubhayadīrghiṇaḥ (full text) .... p. 42 (18)
Dhakāra uttarapadādiḥ : agāddhiṣaṇā .... p. 42 (18-19)
Yo hi yad yato ... nahy āsām iti varjayitvā .... p. 42-43 (19)
Repheṇa : punar akaḥ suvar antar āvar vivar ajīgar ... repheṇa .... p. 43 (19)
Naiyyagrodhaḥ ... catuṣṭya iti varjayitvā .... p. 43 (19-20)
Yaṇādeśa-dīrghī ... pṛthivyāṅgirasī...
Trikramāḥ : ākārāntam ... tathā mā sthāt... caturviṃśatitrikramāḥ .... p. 45 (23)
Plutāḥ : bṛhaspatisutasya ... dve ekacatvāriṃśat plutāḥ .... p. 46 (23-24)
Dvādaśasu ... dve dve ekacatvāriṃśat plutāḥ .... p. 46 (24)
viśvā agniś ca sāvitram asanneva dvayaṃ dvayam |
devā ekannakam0 sapta ṣoḍśāraṇyake plutāḥ || .... p. 46 (24)

– C. Oppert II 783. Belonged to Ghanapathi Shingaracharyar of Alasur, Madurantakam Taluk.

[CC I 679b; II 162b]

1336 ṢAṆṆAVATI-ATHAKĀRA-LAKṢAṆA (षण्णवति-अथकारलक्षण)
Mysore ND II 3864 → Athakāri-lakṣaṇa.

1337 ṢOḌAŚA-LAKṢAṆA (षोडशलक्षण)
Mysore ND II 3865 (P 4906/38). PL. Na. 1 fol. (125).

1338 ṢOḌAŚA-ŚLOKĪ-ŚIKṢĀ (षोडशश्लोकीशिक्षा)
of Rāmakṛṣṇa. As the title indicates the work in 16 verses deals with a few elementary principles regarding the letters and their pronunciation.

Beginning:

अथ शिक्षां प्रवक्ष्यामि वाच उच्चारणे विधिम्।
यथा संव्यवहारेषु स्वयं प्रोक्ता स्वयंभुवा॥ १॥
त्रयस्त्रिंशद्धसा वर्णा स्वरा द्वाविंशतिर्यमाः ।
चत्वारश्च विसर्गो ऽनुस्वारः :कःपस्त्रिषष्टिकाः ॥ २॥
समास्ते ऽदिदुतो ज्ञेया ऋचादीर्घल् पञ्चमः ।
एदैदोदौ तु चत्वारो ह्रस्वाः संध्यक्षराणि च॥ ३॥

End:

व्याघ्री दद्भिर्हरेत् पुत्रान् भीता पाताच्च पीडनात्।
तद्वत् प्रयोजयेद् वर्णांस्तेन लोके महीयते॥ १५॥
इति वर्णोच्चारः ॥
शिवास्यान्निसृतां शिक्षां प्रयतो यः पठेदिह।
पुत्रकीर्तिधनायुष्मान्त्स्वर्गे ऽतिसुखमश्नुते॥ १६॥
इति रामकृष्णविरचिता षोडशश्लोकी शिक्षा समाप्ता॥

Ptd.: in Śikṣā-saṃgraha. – Benares, 1889, pp. 164-65. – (Ben. S. S. 10).

1339 SAṂYOGA-ŚṚṄKHALĀ (संयोगशृङ्खला)
Alternative title of the Gautamī-śikṣā. Cf. München 164.

1340 SAṂHITĀ-GĀḌHA (संहितागाढ)
SBD 53688. 12 fol. Is it Pada-gāḍha ? The Ms. was not available for consultation as it was under seal.

1341 SAṂHITĀ-PADA-KRAMĀDI-PĀṬHA (संहितापदक्रमादिपाठ)
PUL ......

1342 SAṂHITĀ-PADA-GĀḌHA-LAKṢAṆA (संहितापदगाढलक्षण)
SBD 4247. 11 fol. Dated V.S. 1966 → Pada-gāḍha.

1343 SAṂHITĀ-PRAKĀRĀ EKĀDAŚA (संहिताप्रकारा एकादश)
See Grantha-saṃhitā Ekādaśa Prakārāḥ above. Eleven modes of reciting Vedic texts. At the end a list of nine Śikṣā-s.

Beginning: (Weber)

अथ संहिताया एकादश प्रकारा लिख्यन्ते। तत्रानुक्रमः । संहितापदक्रमास्त्रीणि।
जटा माला शिखा लेखा ध्वजो दण्डो रथो घनः ।
अष्टौ विकृतयः प्रोक्ताः क्रमपूर्वा मनीषिभिः॥

ओं बृहस्पते परि दीया रथेन रक्षोहामित्रानपबाधमानः । प्रभञ्जन्त् सेनाः प्रमृणो युधा जयन्नस्माकमेध्यविता रथानाम् (१०·१०३·४)॥

End:

प्रातिशाख्यादिशास्त्रज्ञः सर्वशिक्षाविशारदः ।
सूक्ष्मबुद्धिः समर्थो यः स जटां वक्तुमर्हति॥
प्रथमं व्यासशिक्षा च लक्ष्मीशिक्षा द्वितीयका।
भारद्वाजश्च तार्तीया शिक्षारण्या तुरीयका॥
पञ्चमं शंभुशिक्षा च षष्ठं चैवापिलस्तथा।
सप्तमं पाणिनेः शिक्षा अष्टमं कौहलस्तथा।
वसिष्ठशिक्षा नवममेता वै नव शिक्षकाः ॥
नवशिक्षासारमारण्यशिक्षामृतम् ...

Berlin StB-PrK (NGMPP). E 345/12. 5 fol. (microfilm dated 11.10.1977).
Weber 1498 (Ms. or. fol. 904a). 5 fol. A modern copy.

[CC I 682b]

1344 SAṂHITĀ-LAKṢAṆA-PADA-LAKṢAṆA-SŪTRA(-PĀṬHA) (संहितालक्षणपदलक्षणसूत्र /-पाठ)

Beginning: (fol. 3)

... ति द्वौ मेधा स्वरान्ता। तुभ्यं हिन्वानो वसिष्ट गा अपः । अपो वसिष्ट। द्वे वसिष्टौ टकारेण। य उद्दचीन्द्र देवगोपाः ।

End:

(fol. 7)

दीर्घतमा मामतेयः । ऋषिर्यद् वां दीर्घतमा विसर्जनीयः । शोणा धृष्णू। ग्रसेतामश्वा। द्वौ शोणा स्वरान्ता । सनोजुवांन्यूहतुः (?) । इति संहितालक्षणपदलक्षणसूत्रं समाप्तम् । विनायकदेडरकरमहादेवभट्टसुतेन लिखितम्॥

GJKSV 28910. 5 fol. (3-7). Incomplete.

1345 SAṂHITĀ-VĀKYĀNTA-ŚAMĀNA (संहितावाक्यान्तशमान)
PUL I, p. 24 (no.144). PL. Gr. 1 fol.

1346 SAṂHITĀ-SAMĀNA(-LAKṢAṆA) (संहितासमान /-लक्षण)

Adyar D I 984 → Veda-lakṣaṇa (A 2).
Adyar D I 989 → Veda-lakṣaṇa (A 7).
Adyar D I 1030 → Sapta-lakṣaṇa.
Adyar D I 1034 → Sapta-lakṣaṇa.
Brl. p. 10 (and C.) → Śamāna.

Burnell 5b.
PUL I, p. 24 (no.145). PL. Gr. 2 fol.
Trav. Uni. 2938 B. PL. Gr. 40 fol.

– C.
Adyar D I 984 → Veda-lakṣaṇa (A 2).
Mysore (1898), p. 6 (no. 52). 14 fol. (1-14).

– C. of Padmanābha, Brl. p. 10 = IO 4500. Trav. Uni. 2938 B. See under Śamāna.
[CC I 682b]

1347 SAṂHITĀ-SAVĪLA-MĀLĀ (संहितासवीलमाला)
Ānandāśrama 1865 → Ṛgveda-savīla-mālā.

1348 SAṂHITĀ-SŪTRA (संहितासूत्र)
A collection of words and phrases from the *Ṛgveda* having variations in form and accent in different occurences.

Beginning:

अग्निं रत्नधातममयं रत्नधातमो यदङ्ग राजन्तं त्वमग्ने न वसून् राजन्तं प्रास्मै सुविवृतं ···

End:

सपत्नः सपत्न हैपामपैहि निर्ऋत्यै देवाः कपोतो निर्ऋत्या अपश्यन् त्वा पुत्रकामो ऽत्रैव पुत्रकामे।

ASB I iii.27 (IM 4995). 7 fol. 126 Grantha-s. Incomplete.
Calcutta Skt. Coll. I 28 (548). 19 fol.
Calcutta Skt. Coll. I 29 (549). 8 fol.
Calcutta Skt. Coll. I 30 (550). 6 fol. Dated V.S. 1643. Copied in Kāśī.
IM 2509. 8 fol. Dated Śaka 1634. Title: Svara-vicāra. Udāttādi-svara-vicāra and Vedādhyayana-krama on the title page.
IM 4995. 7 fol. (4-10). Incomplete.
Mysore ND II 3911 (P 8857/ 1). PL. Na. 12 fol. Extract no. 301 = TD 1813.
PUL II. App. p. 10 (no.144). PL. Gr. 13 fol. 200 Grantha-s.
PUL II. App. p. 10 (no.145). PL. Gr. 5 fol. 200 Grantha-s.
TD 1813. 8 fol. (32-39). 150 Grantha-s.
Tirupati SVUORI (427a). PL. Na. Ends: apaśyantvā putrakāmaḥ dvitīyaṃ putrakāme |
Weber 43 (Chambers 719). 9 fol. Dated V.S. 1697 (see IS. I,82)
[CC I 682b]

1349 SAṂHITĀ-SVARĀVADHĀNA (संहितास्वरावधान)
Different texts.
Mysore ND II 3912 (P 8583). PL. Gr. 23 fol.
Mysore ND II 3913 (B 701). PL. (?) Na. 22 fol. Extract no. 302. Dated Śaka 1785.
Mysore ND II 3914 (B 805). Na. 12 fol. Extract no. 303.

1350 SAṂHITAIKĀDAŚA-PRAKĀRA (MĀDHYANDINA-ŚĀKHĪYA) (संहितैकादशप्रकार / माध्यन्दिनशाखीय)

→ Grantha-saṃhitā ekādaśa-prakārāḥ.

BHU B 1081 (D 11/671). 8 fol. Dated V.S. 1801.

IM 2489. 5 fol.

IM 5549. 4 fol. (2-5). Incomplete.

1351 SAKĀRAPARA-(REPHAPARA-)VISARJANĪYA (सकारपर-(रेफपर-)विसर्जनीय) (IO)

सं कखपोर्ध्वो ऽप्यवग्रहः ।

अवग्रहे नकारो यः पदान्तो यत्र दृश्यते।
विशेषं तत्र जानीयाद् द्वित्वमित्यभिधीयते।
नकारान्तं पदं पूर्वं वकारे ऋपरे यदि।
संयोगे परभूते च द्वित्वमित्यभिधीयते॥

Adyar D I 986. PL. Gr. 2 fol. → Veda-lakṣaṇa (A 4).

IO 4513 (Burnell 350g). Tel. 1 fol. (68). Cf. the list at MD 855. Also called Visarjanīyottara-śakāra-paraḥ.

Mysore I, p. 37 (3 Mss.).

Mysore ND II 3917 (P 2262/38). PL. Gr. 1 fol. Extract no. 306.

Mysore ND II 3918 (P 2265/21). PL. Gr. 1 fol. (138).

1352 SAṂKṚṢṬA-VIKṚṢṬA (संकृष्टविकृष्ट)

Mysore ND II 3866 (P 2476/ 9). PL. Na. 5 fol. (56-60).

1353 SAṂKṢIPTA-ṚGVIDHĀNA (संक्षिप्त-ऋग्विधान)

See under Ṛgvidhāna above.

1354 SAṂKṢEPA-SĀRA or SAṂKṢIPTA-SĀRA (संक्षेपसार / संक्षिप्तसार)

of Śaṃkarācārya according to the commentator Vināyaka (cf. below). 73 verses; also called Vedāṅga-saṃkṣepa-sāra in SBD 4297. The text is identical with the Śaunakīya-śikṣā (which see).

Baroda 8891(b). 4 fol. (9-12). 69 Grantha-s. = CLB I, p. 38. Dated Śaka 1760. Extract p. 167.

Baroda 8840. 21 fol. 400 Grantha-s (with C. of Vināyaka). = CLB I, p. 38. Dated Śaka 1741. Extract pp. 168-69.

BISM p. 303 (35/483). 18 fol. (with C. of Vināyaka). Dated Śaka 1667. Copied in Mayūreśvara-kṣetra by Mahādeva, son of Nṛsiṃha. (A xerox-copy of this Ms. is in SAI : 87/791*).

Bombay Uni. 15 (BMC 85 13). 14 fol. (with C. of Vināyaka).

GJKSV 13724(C). 3 fol. (8a-10b). 69 verses. Dated V.S. 1886. Copied by Vaidyanātha Citaḷe, son of Hari Dīkṣita. Col.: Saṃkṣipta-sāra.

Mysore ND II 3867 (P 4906/51). PL. Na. 2 fol. (129-30) (a. Śaunaka).

Mysore ND II 3868 (P 4906/56). PL. Na. 4 fol. (136-39) (a. Śaunaka). 84 verses; col.: iti śākalya-ṛksaṃhitāyāṃ śaunakācāryakṛte saṃkṣepasāro nāma prathamo 'dhyāyaḥ.

Nagpur University Mss. Library. N M 6316. 37 fol. (with C. of Vināyaka). 73 verses. Dated Śaka 1539 (?). See K. R. Joshi : śikṣāśāstra-viṣayakasya aprakāśitasya granthasyādhyayanam - Paṇḍita-pariṣat - Summary of Papers (in Sanskrit), 28th AIOC 1976 (Dharwar), pp. 8-9.

SBD 4297. 17 fol. (with C. of Janārdana). Dated V.S. 1847. Catalogued as Vedāṅga-saṃkṣepa-sāra.

TCD 30-A. Mal. 9 pp. 90 Grantha-s. (Varṇoccāraṇa-lakṣaṇa).

TCD 38-F. Mal. 4 fol. 100 Grantha-s. (Varṇoccāraṇa-lakṣaṇa).

TD 1786. 4 fol. (24-27). 50 Grantha-s. (Varṇoccāraṇa-lakṣaṇa).

Tirupati SVUORI (427k). PL. Na. 85 verses (a. Śaunaka).

Wai II 10312. 22 fol. (with C. of Vināyaka). (A xerox-copy of this Ms. is in SAI).

– C. of Vināyaka.

Beginning:

गणेशमभिवन्द्येशं शंकराचार्यभाषितम्।
संक्षेपसारं व्याकुर्मः सम्यक्पाठानुवादिनम्॥ १॥
शंकरः शंकरः साक्षाद् ब्रह्मविष्णुसमीपतः ।
अधीत्य संप्रदायस्य रक्षणार्थमिमं व्यधात्॥ २॥
शंकराख्यो द्विजो जातु (द्विजातिस्तु) ब्रह्मगोविन्दशंकरात्।
साक्षात् कृत्वा पठन् साकं यास्कपाणिनिशौनकैः ॥ ३॥
दृष्ट्वाथ वेदगाम्भीर्यं द्विजांश्च ज्ञानिमानिनः ।
बहुलक्षणशास्त्रं च संक्षेपसारमाह तत्॥ ४॥

ग्रन्थकृदाचार्यो ऽद्वैतवादी स्वाभीष्टदेवतां नमस्कुर्वन् स्वाभिप्रायं दर्शयन् वक्ष्यमाणमर्थं प्रथमश्लोकेन प्रतिपादयति। सर्वज्ञम् ... लक्षणम्। १। प्रवक्ष्यामि। कः । अहम्। किम्। वर्णोच्चारणलक्षणम्। कासु। ऋक्षु। किं कृत्वा। प्रणम्य। कम्। सर्वात्मानम्। कथंभूतम्। सर्वज्ञम्। पुनः कीदृशम्। सर्वकर्तारम्। पुनः कीदृशम्। शिवम्। पुनः कीदृशम्। गुरुम्। हिताहितोपदेशपरिहारकर्तारम् । आद्यश्लोकस्येदृगन्वयः । प्रवक्ष्य इति वक्तव्ये प्रवक्ष्यामीत्येतदुक्तमेवमर्थम् । अयं तु परमो धर्मो यद् योगेनार्थदर्शनम् । अयं मया समाराध्यो धर्मः उपकारः परो धर्मः इत्यादि धर्मः सुसाध्य इत्यनेनाभिप्रायेण परोपकारार्थं लक्षणं प्रवक्ष्यामीति प्रयुक्तम्। अस्मत्प्रयोगो ऽनुक्तो ऽपि अस्मद्युत्तमः इति वचनाज्ज्ञेयः ॥

End:

शंकराचार्यसंक्षेपसारं व्याख्यद् विनायकः ।
जनार्दनक्रमविदः पुत्र आम्नायवित् सुधीः ॥

इति श्रीशंकराचार्यविरचितसंक्षेपसारस्य विनायकभट्टोपाध्यायविरचिता वृत्तिः समाप्ता।

Baroda 8840. 21 fol. 400 Grantha-s. Dated Śaka 1741 (with text). Extract p. 168.
BISM p. 303 (35/483). 18 fol. (with text). Dated Śaka 1667. (A xerox-copy of this Ms. is in SAI : 87/791*).
Bombay Uni. 15 (BMC 85 13). 14 fol. (with text).
Nagpur University Mss. Library. N M 6316. 37 fol. (with text) Dated Śaka 1539 (?).
Wai II 10312. 22 fol. (with text).

1355 SAṂKHYĀ-CCHALA (संख्याच्छल)
of Rāmaliṅga-deśika.
Mysore ND II 3869 (A 642/ 4). Kan. 2 fol. (30-31). Extract no. 294.

1356 SAṂJÑĀ-(PRA-)KARAṆA (संज्ञा-(प्र)करण)
→ Akṣara-tantra. It is also known as the Saṃjñā-lakṣaṇa, being a kind of supplement to the *Sāma-tantra* of which it is sometimes regarded as the 14th and 15th Prapāṭhaka-s. The Saṃjñā-(pra)karaṇa-bhāṣya (RASB II 1329), below is a commentary on this text. So also is MD 894 (a Ms. of the *Sāma-tantra)* but described as Gāyatrī-gāna-lakṣaṇa in the catalogue. On verification it was ascertained that only fol. 1a contains a few details on Gāyatrī-gāna and fol. 1b-7b have the commentary on this text. MD 895 is a transcript of 894. For the beginning and end see Akṣara-tantra.

Alwar 282.
IM 1967. 1 fol. Incomplete. Col.: Saṃjñā-karaṇaṃ nāma pariśiṣṭam.
IO 4332 (Burnell 360b). Gr. 28 pp. (with Bhāṣya). (2 Prapāṭhaka-s called Saṃjñā-prakaraṇa). Written ca. A.D. 1867.
IO 4333 (Burnell 437c). Gr. 19 fol. (with Bhāṣya). (2 Prapāṭhaka-s called Saṃjñā-prakaraṇa). Written ca. A.D. 1875.
Mysore ND II 3870 (P 2262/ 4). PL. Gr. 2 fol.
Mysore ND II 3871 (P 4951/ 3). PL. Na. 17 fol. (138-54).
Oxf. CS c.26(7). 3 fol. Col.: iti saṃjñā-prakaraṇaṃ nāma pariśiṣṭam. Paper dated 25.11.1903. Ascribed to Kātyāyana in the catalogue.
Peters. II, p. 181 (no.78). (Saṃjñā-karaṇa-pariśiṣṭa).
SBD 4354. 2 fol. (2-3). Incomplete. (Saṃjñā-karaṇa-pariśiṣṭa).

– C. Bhāṣya.
IO 4332 (Burnell 360b). Gr. 28 pp. (with text). Written ca. A.D. 1867.
IO 4333 (Burnell 437c). Gr. 19 fol. (with text). Written ca. A.D. 1875.

1357 SAṂJÑĀ-(PRA-)KARAṆA-BHĀṢYA (संज्ञा-(प्र)करण-भाष्य)
of Tripāṭhī Kahnajī, son of Śivajī. See under Akṣara-tantra.

RASB II 1329 (G 1006). 39 fol. 585 Grantha-s. Dated V.S. 1726.

1358 SAṂJÑĀ-LAKṢAṆA (संज्ञालक्षण)
→ Akṣara-tantra.

1359 SAṂDIGDHA-PADA-CCHEDA-NIRṆAYA (संदिग्धपदच्छेदनिर्णय)
Same as the *Ṛgveda-prātiśākhya-pariśiṣṭa*. Whish 78(7). PL. Gr. 32 fol. (55-86). Trav. Uni. 15799 A. PL. Mal. 2500 Grantha-s.

1360 SAṂDHI-KĀRIKĀ (1) (संधिकारिका)
of Gaṇeśa-datta. A work on saṃdhi in 31 verses with commentary called *Dīpa-kalikā*. The examples are from the VS.

Beginning:

अथ संधिकारिका लिख्यते।

वन्दे गणेशचरणद्वन्द्वं विद्यैकसाधनम्।
सिद्धिबुद्धिप्रदातारं भक्तसर्वार्थसाधनम्॥
सरस्वतीं गुरूंश्चैव याज्ञवल्क्यादिकान्मुनीन्।
वन्दे संधिकारिकायां व्याख्यां कुर्वे यथामति॥

इह खलु व्याकरणशास्त्रेषु मन्दाधिकारिणां वैदिकानां सुगमसंधिज्ञानार्थं संधिकारिकामारभते। तत्र मङ्गलपूर्वकं प्रथम-श्लोकः --

नत्वा श्रीगणनाथस्य चरणं वेदवर्णितम्।
बालानां सुखबोधार्थं कुर्वे ऽहं संधिकारिकाम्॥ ...
अकाराकारयोः संधिर्व्यत्ययो दीर्घता च न।
इकारे एत्वमाप्नोति उकारे ओत्वमेव च॥

End:

इमां संधिकारिकां च विचारयन्तीह वैदिकाः।
संधिज्ञानं भवेत् तेषां शीघ्रमेव तु निश्चितम्॥

RASB II 1532 (G 6173). 39 fol. 400 Grantha-s.

1361 SAṂDHI-KĀRIKĀ (2) (संधिकारिका)
TCD ...

1362 SAṂDHI-GĀNA-PADA-GĀNA (संधिगानपदगान)
Mysore ND II 3915 (P 2476/ 6). PL. Na. 6 fol. (38-43). Extract no. 304.

1363 SAṂDHI-PRAKARAṆA (संधिप्रकरण)
on the saṃdhi of Vedic words in Malayalam with Sanskrit quotations. TCD 30-E. Mal. 38 pp. 380 Grantha-s.

1364 SAṂDHY-UCCĀRAṆA-LAKṢAṆA (संध्युच्चारणलक्षण)
Mysore ND II 3916 (P 2339/14b). PL. Gr. 5 fol. (93-97). Extract no. 305.

1365 SANSKRIT TEXTS ON PHONETICS

A Collection of Śikṣā Texts, reproduced by Lokesh Chandra from the papers of the late Prof. Raghu Vira. – New Delhi, 1981. 696 pp. (Satapitaka Series – Indo-Asian Literatures Volume 282). [SAI (ind S 180, 282); SOAS (KC 414 – 461805); UBTÜ (22 A 14022)]

It contains the following 27 titles of which only 18 are given in the list of contents of the volume. They are actually Devanāgarī transcripts of Mss. belonging to the Adyar Library or Govt. Oriental Manuscripts Library, Madras, though nowhere mentioned in this volume. These transcripts have been used by Siddheshwar Varma, Madhukar Pathak, Vidhata Misra and others.

Vyāsa-śikṣā .... (pp. 1-25) = MD 972

Vyāsa-śikṣā-vyākhyāna .... (pp. 25-172) = MD 975

Āraṇya-śikṣā Savyākhyā .... (pp. 173-210) = MD 866

Hrasva-dīrgha-pluta-mātrā-prakaraṇa (Mātrā-lakṣaṇa) .... (pp. 211-12) = MD 17868

Plutānuśāsana .... (pp. 213-14) = MD 936

Pluta-śikṣā .... (pp. 215-16) = MD 14744

Āraṇyaka-śikṣā Savyākhyā .... (pp. 216-50) = MD 867

Vāsiṣṭha-śikṣā .... (pp. 251-52) = MD 957

Śamāna Savyākhyāna of Padmanābha .... (pp. 252-66) = MD 983

Hrasva-dīrgha-pluta-mātrā-prakaraṇa (Mātrā-lakṣaṇa) .... (p. 266) = MD 17867

Kālanirṇaya-śikṣā Savyākhyā .... (pp. 267-79) = MD 892

Śamāna-śikṣā (date of copying: 16-6-25) .... (pp. 280-86) = MD 977

Kālanirṇaya-śikṣā .... (pp. 287-89) = MD 891

Lakṣmīkānta-śikṣā-vyākhyā .... (pp. 290-307) = MD 955

Veda-lakṣaṇānukramaṇikā .... (pp. 307-09) = MD 967

Kauhalīya-śikṣā .... (pp. 309-16) = MD 893

Pāriśikṣā-ṭīkā Yājuṣa-bhūṣaṇa .... (pp. 317-94) = MD 924

Āpiśali-śikṣā (Śākhā-lakṣaṇa) .... (pp. 395-400) = Adyar D I 731

Āpiśali-śikṣā .... (pp. 401-06) = Adyar D I 730

Śaiśirīya-śikṣā .... (pp. 407-32) = Adyar D I 1026

Pada-kārikā-ratnamālā .... (pp. 433-530) = MD 921

Śaṃbhu-śikṣā .... (pp. 531-35) = MD 988

Sarva-sammata-śikṣā-vyākhyā (with text) .... (pp. 536-79) = MD 998

Siddhānta-śikṣā-vyākhyā (with text) .... (pp. 580-625) = MD 1012

Svara-bhakti .... (p. 626) = MD 1021

Śaunakīya-śikṣā-vyākhyā .... (pp. 627-81) = Adyar D I 1028

Traisvarya-lakṣaṇa (= Yājñavalkya-śikṣā)........................(pp. 682-96) = Adyar D I 856

1366 SAPTA-TRIṂŚAT-PLUTA (सप्तत्रिंशत्प्लुत)
Adyar D I 983 → Veda-lakṣaṇa (A 1).

1367 SAPTADAŚA-LAKṢAṆA (सप्तदशलक्षण)
Mysore ND II 3920 (P 4906/39). PL. Na. 1 fol. (125). Extract no. 307.

1368 SAPTA-LAKṢAṆA (सप्तलक्षण)
Adyar D I 1030 (19 D 61 = 66253). PL. Gr. 22 fol. (19ff.). Contains the following titles:
Saṃhitā-śamāna .... (fol. 1-3b)
Vilaṅghya of Nārāyaṇa .... (fol. 3b-8a)
Natapara-lakṣaṇa of Śaurisūnu .... (fol. 8a-11a)
Avarṇi .... (fol. 11b-14a)
Āvarṇi .... (fol. 14a-15b)
Aniṅgya of Śrīvatsāṅka .... (fol. 15b-22a)

Adyar D I 1031 (20 F 40 = 67222). PL. Gr. 24 fol. = Adyar I, p. 53b. Contains the following works:
Śamāna .... ends on fol. 3b
Vilaṅghya of Nārāyaṇa .... " fol. 7b
Napara-tapara of Śaurisūnu .... " fol. 9b
Avarṇi .... " fol. 13b
Āvarṇi .... " fol. 15a
Aniṅgya of Śrīvatsāṅka .... " fol. 24a

Adyar D I 1032 (25 A 66 = 70715). PL. Gr. 25 fol. = Adyar I, p. 53b. Contains the following works:
Śamāna .... ends on fol. 4a
Vilaṅghya .... " fol. 8a

Napara .... " fol. 9a
Tapara .... " fol. 10b
Pragrahādhyāya (damaged, not legible) .... " fol. 13b
Āvarṇi .... " fol. 20b
Avarṇi .... " fol. 25a

Adyar D I 1033 (25 D 4 = 70824). PL. Gr. 9 fol. = Adyar I, p. 54a. Contains the following works:
Śamāna .... ends on fol. 3a
Vilaṅghya .... " " fol. 5a
Napara .... " " fol. 6b
Tapara .... " " fol. 7a
Vilaṅghya of Nārāyaṇa (breaks off in verse 28) .... " " fol. 9b

Adyar D I 1034 (25 L 35 = 71153). PL. Gr. 18 fol. Contains the following works:
Saṃhitā-śamāna .... (fol. 1-3a)
Vilaṅghya of Nārāyaṇa .... (fol. 3a-6a)
Napara of Śaurisūnu .... (fol. 6a-8a)
Avarṇi .... (fol. 8a-10a)
Āvarṇi .... (fol. 10a-11a)
Aniṅgya of Śrīvatsāṅka .... (fol. 11a-17a)
Yaṇādeśa-saṃdhi .... (fol. 17a-18a)
Yohi-prāpti .... (fol. 18)

Adyar D I 1035 (29 K 34 = 73667). PL. Gr. 44 fol. = Adyar I, p. 54a. Contains the following works:
Śamāna-vyākhyāna (anon.) .... (fol. 1-14b)
Napara-lakṣaṇa of Śaurisūnu .... (fol. 14b-19b)
Napara-lakṣaṇa of Śaurisūnu .... (fol. 20a-26b)
Tapara-lakṣaṇa of Śaurisūnu .... (fol. 27a-31b)
Napara-tapara-lakṣaṇa of Śaurisūnu .... (fol. 27a-31b)
Avarṇi-vyākhyāna (anon.) .... (fol. 35a-44b)

Adyar D XIII 198 (VB 54c). PL. Tel. 11 fol. Incomplete. Contains Śamāna, Vilaṅghya, Aniṅgya, Avarṇi and Āvarṇi.

Adyar D XIII 199 (VB 438b). PL. Tel. 18 fol.

Adyar D XIII 200 (VB 461l). PL. Tel. 5 fol. Incomplete. Contains Napara, Tapara and Śamāna.

GJKSV 43652. PL. Gr. 63 fol. Includes Taittirīya-prātiśākhya.

Hamburg StUB (Oppert 10a). PL. Gr. (with C.).

Hoshiarpur p. 54 (no.5947). PL. Gr. 7 fol. 200 Grantha-s. Extract p.414.

Hz 740. PL. Gr. 22 fol. Belonged to Mahadeva Srauti of Tiruvaiyaru, Thanjavur Dist.

MT 6253. PL. Gr. 15 fol. 300 Grantha-s. Contains: Napara, Tapara, Avarṇi, Āvarṇi and Aniṅgya. Purchased in 1937-38 from E. Srinivasacharyar of Sriperumbudur, Chingelpet Dist.

Mysore ND II 3921 (P 232/ 4). PL. Gr. 8 fol. Incomplete.

Mysore ND II 3922 (P 941/ 4). PL. Tel. 10 fol. (3-12).
Mysore ND II 3923 (P 2265/ 3). PL. Gr. 50 fol. (71-121).
Mysore ND II 3924 (C 468/ 1). 1 fol. Incomplete.
Oppert II 7271. Belonged to Jambunatha Sastri of Nallucheri, Thanjavur Dist.
Oppert II 7458. Belonged to Venkatarama Sastri of Pillur, Mayavaram Taluk.
Oppert II 7991. Belonged to Venkatarama Dikshita of Sorakayur, Thanjavur Dist.
PUL II. App. p. 13 (no.222). PL. Gr. 44 fol.
SBD 2112. PL. Dra. 13 fol. Incomplete.
SBD 4149. PL. Dra. 80 fol. Catalogued as Śākhā-samāna. It includes : Śākhā-śamāna, Vilaṅghya (praṇamya bhāratīm), Napara (natvā vināyakam), Tapara (adyāt), Avarṇi, Āvarṇi, Avarṇi-vyākhyā, Āvarṇi-vyākhyā.
TD 1793. PL. Gr. 12 fol. (19-30) 100 Grantha-s. Aniṅgya only.
TD 1794. PL. Gr. 5 fol. (13-17). 23 Grantha-s. Avarṇi only.
TD 1795. PL. Gr. 3 fol. (17-19). 23 Grantha-s. Āvarṇi only.
TD 1796. PL. Gr. 5 fol. (9-13). 50 Grantha-s. Napara and Tapara.
TD 1797. PL. Gr. 2 fol. 25 Grantha-s. Tapara only.
TD 1798. PL. Tel. 1 fol. 20 Grantha-s.. Napara only.
TD 1799. PL. Gr. 1 fol. 20 Grantha-s. Napara only.
TD 1800. PL. Gr. 6 fol. (4-9) 60 Grantha-s. Vilaṅghya by Nārāyaṇa.
TD 1801. PL. Gr. 4 fol. 60 Grantha-s. Vilaṅghya by Nārāyaṇa.
TD 1802. PL. Tel. 4 fol. (110-13). 40 Grantha-s. Vilaṅghya only.
TD 1803. PL. Tel. 2 fol. (114-15). 52 Grantha-s. Vilaṅghya only.
TD 1804. PL. Gr. 4 fol. (1-4). 35 Grantha-s. Śamāna only.
TD 1805. PL. Gr. 2 fol. (109-10). 35 Grantha-s. Śamāna only.
TD 1806. PL. Gr. 3 fol. 35 Grantha-s. Śamāna only.
Tirupati SVUORI 7236 (936). PL. Gr.
Tirupati SVUORI 7237 (1746b). PL. Gr. Incomplete.
Tirupati SVUORI 7238 (1756a). PL. Gr. 69 fol. It contains: (a) Śamāna (2 fol.), (b) Vilaṅghya (2 fol. ; praṇamya bhāratīṃ), (c) Śamāna-vyākhyā (14 fol.), (d) Vilaṅghya (3 fol.), (e) Aniṅgya (27 fol.), (f) Tapara (2 fol.), (g) Napara (2 fol.), (h) Lakṣaṇa-ratna (6 fol.).
Tirupati SVUORI 7239 (5462). PL. Gr.
Tirupati SVUORI (4421). PL. Gr. Contains: Śamāna (4 fol.), Vilaṅghya (5 fol.), Tapara (5 fol.), Tapara-vyākhyā (3 fol. = 861), Vilaṅghya-vyākhyā (14 fol.). praṇamya bhāratīm ...
Tirupati SVUORI 7240 (5509). PL. Gr. Incomplete.
Tirupati SVUORI 7241 (6171a). PL. Gr.
Tirupati SVUORI 7242 (6285). PL. Gr. Incomplete.
Trav. Uni. L.1193 A. PL. Mal. 24 fol.
Trav. Uni. 16408 A-G. PL. Mal. 375 Grantha-s.
Trav. Uni. 16440 A. PL. Mal. 700 Grantha-s.
Trav. Uni. 18615 B. PL. Gr. 325 Grantha-s.
Trav. Uni. 17346 A-D. PL. Mal. 125 Grantha-s. Incomplete.
Trav. Uni. 18694. PL. Gr. 200 Grantha-s. Incomplete.
Trav. Uni. 21931 D. PL. Mal. 80 Grantha-s. Incomplete.
Trav. Uni. 21933 B. PL. Mal. 100 Grantha-s. Incomplete.

Trav. Uni. 21933 C. PL. Mal. 35 Grantha-s. Incomplete.

Ptd.:

(1) Ed. by Lakshmanacharya, in : *Sapta-lakṣaṇa*, pub. by Sundaresvara Srauti (in Grantha script). – Kumbakonam : Jyotirvilasa Press, 1888. 3, 22 pp. (Title page: Sapta-lakṣaṇākhyaṃ kṛṣṇayajurvedalakṣaṇaratnaṃ kṛṣṇayajurvedapadādhyāyādhyetṛ-janānām atyantopakārāya pañcanadakṣetravāstvayaiḥ vicitraśatāvadhānividvanmaṇimahābhāgavataghanapāṭhibāḻegaḍḍekaṭṭe- lakṣmaṇācāryaiḥ samyak pariśodhya vicchedasūcakāṅkaiḥ saha śrīpañcanadakṣetravāstavyaiḥ jyotistantrasūkṣmadarśibhiḥ sundareśvaraśrautibhiḥ svīyajyotirvilāsamudrākṣaraśālāyāṃ mudrāpitam | sarvadhāri – vaiyyāci). [IO : Skt. 290]

(2)Ed. by Muḻḻanguḍi A. Vaidyanatha Sastri with commentary (in Grantha script). – Kumbakonam : Srividya Press, 1899, pp. 122. (Title page: śrīmattaittirīyayajuḥsaṃhitāpadaviṣayakavicikitsāndhatamasamihirāyamāṇaṃ saptalakṣaṇam idaṃ kila kumbhakoṇākhyamahākṣetrasamīpavartikolludam ityaparanāmakottarakāverīdakṣiṇatīravirājamānamuḻḻangaḍigrāmābhijanena śāṇḍilyānvayasaṃbhavena A. Vaidyanāthaśāstriṇā racitayā saṃgrahavyākhyayā sākaṃ tenaiva samyak pariśodhitaṃ kumbhakoṇasthaśrīvidyāmudrākṣaraśālāyāṃ mudritaṃ sad vijayatetarām) [Adyar (H 215.4 SLxy Vai); MyORI (B 1385); BM : Ptd. Bks. Cat. 1892-1906. 670-71, 805 (14092.b.43)]

Contents of this volume:

1. Śamāna-prakaraṇam .... pp. 1-21
2. Vilaṅghya-prakaraṇam .... pp. 22-41
3. Napara-prakaraṇam .... pp. 41-51
4. Tapara-prakaraṇam .... pp. 52-55
5. Avarṇi-prakaraṇam .... pp. 55-70
6. Āvarṇi-prakaraṇam .... pp. 71-80
7. Aniṅgya-prakaraṇam .... pp. 81-122

(3) Ed. by T. M. Narayana Sastri, with the commentary of Vaidyanatha Sastri, pub. by R. Sundaresarya (in Grantha script: Sapta-lakṣaṇaṃ savyākhyānam). – Kumbakonam : Sarada Vilas Press, 1918. 158 pp. [IO (San C 181); MUL (P15:25A 1X8 15E8); SAI (89/2154*); UBTÜ (Ci XII 665)]

Contents of this volume:

1. Samāna-prakaraṇam .... pp. 1-27
2. Vilaṅghya-prakaraṇam .... pp. 28-53
3. Napara-prakaraṇam .... pp. 53-67
4. Tapara-prakaraṇam .... pp. 67-72
5. Avarṇi-prakaraṇam .... pp. 72-91
6. Āvarṇi-prakaraṇam .... pp. 92-103
7. Aniṅgya-prakaraṇam .... pp. 103-158

(4) Also in Lakṣaṇa-traya (in Telugu script), together with Ṣaḍviṃśati-sūtra and Jaṭāmaṇi, ed. by Gomatham Srinivasa Jyosyar. – Mysore, 1919. 73 pp. (Title page: Saptalakṣaṇī-Ṣaḍvig'ṃśatisūtram (savyākhyā) Jaṭāmaṇiḥ - iti Lakṣaṇatrayam | Taittirīya-yajussambandhi | maisūru gomaṭhaṃ śrīnivāsa

jyotiṣikeṇa cittūru śrīśāradāmudrālaye siddhārthiśrāvaṇāmāyāṃ samamudryata |
[MyORI (B 4109/12669)]

Contents of this volume:

1. Samāna-saṃdhi-prakaraṇam .... pp. 2-6
2. Vilaṅghya-prakaraṇam .... pp. 6-11
3. Napara-prakaraṇam .... pp. 11-13
2. Vilaṅghya-prakaraṇam .... pp. 6-11
4. Taparaṃ nāma lakṣaṇam .... pp. 13-14
5. Avarṇi-lakṣaṇam .... pp. 15-18
6. Āvarṇi-prakaraṇam .... pp. 18-21
7. Aniṅgyam .... pp. 21-31
8. Ṣaḍviṃśati-sūtram .... pp. 31-46
9. Jaṭāmaṇi .... pp. 47-73.

(5) Also in Sapta-lakṣaṇa (in Malayalam script), with the commentary of Vaidyanatha Sastri. – Kunnankulam (Kerala) : K. S. Brothers (Panchangam Press), 1929. 184 pp. [SAI (87/1684*)]

Contents of this volume:

1. Samāna-prakaraṇam .... pp. 1-28
2. Vilaṅghya-prakaraṇam .... pp. 28-55
3. Napara-prakaraṇam .... pp. 56-74
4. Tapara-prakaraṇam .... pp. 74-80
5. Avarṇi-prakaraṇam .... pp. 81-106
6. Āvarṇi-prakaraṇam .... pp. 106-120

– C. anon.

Mysore ND II 3926 (P 2265/ 3a). PL. Gr. 44 fol. (78-121). Extract no. 309.
Trav. Uni. 21553 C. PL. Gr. 150 Grantha-s.
Trav. Uni. 21578 F PL. Gr. 400 Grantha-s.

– C. Pada-darpaṇa of Mallayārya.

Adyar D XIII 201 (VB 123c). PL. Tel. 33 fol. (Samāna-saṃdhi and Vyakti-veḻuku = Adyar D I 1020).
Adyar D XIII 202 (VB 430c). PL. Tel. 55 fol. Contains C. on Śamāna, Vyakti-veḻuku, Napara, Tapara and Aniṅgya.
Mysore ND II 3927 (P 3279/ 1). PL. Tel. 49 fol. Extract no. 310.

– C.

Adyar D I 1036 (19 D 60 = 66252). PL. Gr. 43 fol. = Adyar I, p. 53b. Contains the following texts and commentaries separately:

Śamāna-vyākhyāna (anon.) .... ends on fol. 16
Vilaṅghya-vyākhyāna of Nārāyaṇa .... " fol. 33
Natapara-vyākhyāna of Śaurisūri .... " fol. 43

Adyar D I 1037 (19 D 62 = 66254). PL. Gr. 27 fol. = Adyar I, p. 53b. Contains the following titles:

Napara-lakṣaṇa-vyākhyāna of Śaurisūnu (fol. 1-11a)

Avarṇi-vyākhyāna (same as D I 727) (fol. 11a-18b)
Āvarṇi-vyākhyāna (same as D I 741) (fol. 18b-23b)
Aniṅgya-vyākhyāna of Śrīvatsāṅka (fol. 23b-27b)

Adyar D I 1038 (19 K 52 = 66673). PL. Gr. 12 fol. = Adyar I, p. 53b. Contains the following titles:
Napara-vyākhyā (fragment)........ ends on fol. 1b
Avarṇi-vyākhyā (same as D I 727)........ " fol. 9a
Āvarṇi-vyākhyā (same as D I 741)........ " fol. 9a

Adyar D I 1039 (30 H 35 = 74080). PL. Gr. 75 fol. = Adyar I, p. 54a. Contains the following titles:
Vilaṅghya-vyākhyā of Nārāyaṇa........ ends on fol. 8a
Śamāna-vyākhyā (no author mentioned)........ " fol. 21a
Aniṅngya-vyākhyā of Śrīvatsāṅka........ " fol. 55a
Avarṇi-vyākhyā (anon.; inc.)........ " fol. 56a
Napara-vyākhyā Pada-darpaṇa of Mallayārya........ " fol. 62a
Avarṇi-vyākhyā (2nd copy)........ " fol. 71a

Hz 741. PL. Gr. 80 fol. Belonged to Mahadeva Srauti of Tiruvaiyaru, Thanjavur Dist.

Trav. Uni. L.988. L. PL. Mal. 44 fol. (144-87). 1100 Grantha-s.

– C. of Nārāyaṇa-bhaṭṭa.

Oppert I 2093. PL. Tel. 82 pp. Belonged to Sivasuri Sastri of Bhavani, Coimbatore Dist.

Oppert I 2094. PL. Tel. 84 pp. Belonged to Sivasuri Sastri of Bhavani, Coimbatore Dist.

Oppert I 2477. PL. Gr. 64 pp. Belonged to Sri Sarasvati Bhandaram Committee of Tiruvallikkeni, Madras.

Oppert II 6717. Belonged to P.Rangacharyar of Kumbakonam.

– C. of Somanātha.

Oppert I 2215. PL. Gr. 63 pp. Belonged to Srikantha Srauti of Bhavani, Coimbatore Dist.

Oppert II 1507. Belonged to Gopalacharyar of Pillapakkam, Kanchipuram Taluk.

Oppert II 5283. Belonged to Pichchu Dikshitar of Akhilandapuram, Thanjavur Dist.

[CC I 695b]

1369 SAPTA-LAKṢAṆA (सप्तलक्षण)

Mysore ND II 3925 (P 4906/29). PL. Na. 2 fol. (122-23).

1370 SAPTA-LAKṢAṆA with C. (सप्तलक्षण)

MD 1002. PL. (Śrītāla). Gr. 146 pp.

This contains the following seven works and commmentaries thereon:

1) Saṃhitā-śamāna, 1a. – (= MD 983)
2) Vilaṅghya, 11a. – (= MD 965)
3) Napara, 22a. – (= MD 918)
4) Tapara, 29a. – (= MD 918)
5) Avarṇi, 31b
6) Āvarṇi, 41a. – (= MD 871)
7) Aniṅgya, 46a. – (= MD 855)

MD 1003. 230 pp. Contains the following works with commentaries:

1) Vilaṅghya, 16a. – (= MD 965)
2) Śamāna, 32a. – (= MD 983)
3) Napara, 48a. – (= MD 918)
4) Tapara, 58b. – (= MD 918)
5) Avarṇi, 62a. – (= MD 860)
6) Āvarṇi, 76b. – (= MD 870)
7) Aniṅgya, 84b. – (= MD 855)

MT 4017(c). PL. Gr. 6 fol. (32-37) (with C.). Incomplete (Avarṇi only ?). Presented in 1921-22 by Krishna Ghanapathigal, Sirukumar, Trichinapalli Dist.

MT 6253. PL. Gr. 15 fol. 300 Grantha-s. It contains only the text of Napara, Tapara, Avarṇi, Āvarṇi, Aniṅgya.

Mysore I, p. 37 (9 Mss.).

Tirupati SVUORI 7243 (1130). PL. Gr. 82 fol.

Tirupati SVUORI 7244 (5487). PL. Gr.

Trav. Uni. L.827. PL. Mal. 97 fol. 750 Grantha-s.

Trav. Uni. 2593. 73 fol. 1850 Grantha-s. (Aniṅgya-vyākhyānādi). Contains: Aniṅgya, Śamāna, Vilaṅghya, Napara-tapara, Avarṇi and Āvarṇi.

1371 SAPTA-LAKṢAṆA-SAṂJÑĀDI-NIRŪPAṆA (सप्तलक्षणसंज्ञादिनिरूपण)

MD 14743. PL. Tel. 24 pp. (2ff.). Incomplete. Loose leaves containing extracts from different texts; one or two verses for each topic with illustrations. The titles dealing with the following subjects are written in the margin of each fol. :

1) Sapta-lakṣaṇa-saṃjñā
2) Dvitva-lakṣaṇa
3) Anusvāra-prāpti
4) Jyotiḥ-śikṣā-vacana
5) Takārasya datva-prāpti
6) Triṣṭub-anuṣṭup-pariṣkāra
7) Garbhodātta-lakṣaṇa
8) Ghatva-khatva-prāpti
9) Svarabhakti
10) Agnikāṇḍatraya-pañcāśat-saṃjñā
11) Nakṣatreṣṭi-yājyā-puronuvākyā-saṃjñā
12) Thakāra-sūtra
13) Saṃyutāsaṃyutavarṇa-vacana
14) Hastasvarasya parvasu rekhāsu udāttādi-sthāna-saṃjñā
15) Trikrama-lakṣaṇa (mā sthāt)
16) Vṛthāvyakti
17) Śiroveṣṭana
18) Yohi-prāpti
19) Apluta-padāni

Beginning:

उभादित्यो ऽग्निर्वृत्राणिपर्यन्तात्यानुवाककाः ।
यविगव्यक्तियाज्याः स्युः युङ्क्ष्वेत्यन्वाकसंयुताः ॥
काण्डेषु सप्तस्वेतेषु अन्त्यान्वाकाश्च ये स्मृताः ।

End:

हौपां पूर्वं मकारस्तु सहस्त्रां पूर्वतस्तनीम् ।

यद्विकर्णी यद्विकर्णी इन्द्रस्य तनुवं प्रियाम्॥
करोतु तामभीमां च मयि दक्षक्रतू तथा।
स्विन्नस्स्नात्वीति नवकं न प्लुताः परिकीर्तिताः॥

1372 SAPTA-SAṂKHYĀ(-NIRŪPAṆA) (सप्तसंख्या /-निरूपण)

A tabular statement of the total number of different kinds of words, being the varga-pratīka-s of the *Ṛgveda-saṃhitā*, each followed by seven numbers, the force of which is expressed by the combination -- "pa-i-du-vi-ma-na-t" -- the first denoting the number of words or Pada-s in each Varga; the second the number of Pada-s having "iti" after them (e.g. vayo iti); the third (du = duḥ, as an example) the number of compound or separable words (such as duḥ-ga, ṛṣi-bhiḥ); while the fourth, fifth, sixth and the seventh indicate the numbers of the Pada-s ending in visarga, "m", "n " and "t" respectively. This is listed in a verse found at the beginning of the Mysore Ms:

पदप्रगृह्यावगृह्यं विसर्गं च मकारकम्।
नकारं च तकारं च सप्तसंख्या अनुक्रमात्॥

Cf. Krama-ratna-saptākṣara, Sapta-saṃkhyā-paribhāṣā and Saptākṣarī-paribhāṣā.

Beginning: (MD 14082)

अग्निमीळे --। ४७। ०। ८। १७। १३। १। ४।
यदङ्ग --। ४१। ०। ४। ८। ७। ०। ३।
वायवायाहि --। ४९। ६। ७। १३। ८। ०। ०।
वायविन्द्रः --। ३६। ४। ६। ४। १२। ०। ०।
अश्विना --। ४९। ४। १०। १९। ३। ०। १।
ओमासः --। ५१। ०। ७। २१। ७। ०। ०।

End:

प्राग्नये --। ३१। ०। ३। १२। २। ०। १।
प्र नूनम् --। २३। ०। ७। ८। ७। ०। ०।
आ यम् --। ३३। १। ३। ७। ४। १। ५।
ऋतं च --। ६। ०। ०। २। ०। ०। १।
सं समित् --। ६३। ०। ६। ४१। ४। १। १।

Bh. p. 7 (no.19). 46 fol. (pa-i-du-vi-ma-na-t; Sapta-lakṣaṇa).
BHU B 1146 (D 11/672). 46 fol.
Bik. 326. 57 fol. Dated Śaka 1541. (Described under the title Ṛcāṃ Gaṇitāṅka-prakāra).
BORI 19 of A 1879-80. = BORI D I i.42. 46 fol. Dated Śaka 1698. (Ṛgveda-padādi-saṃkhyā).
Calcutta Skt. Coll. I 532 (545). 175 fol. Title: Saṃkhyā-pustakam. (pa-47 | i-0 | du-8 | vi-15 | ma-13 | na-1 | ta-3).
Calcutta Skt. Coll. I 533 (546). 31 fol. Incomplete. Title: Saṃkhyā-pustakam.

GJKSV 13914. 27 fol. 7 numbers for each Varga as above. End: padetikāra-duḥkhaṇḍa-visarga-makāra- nakāra-takārāś ca | ete sapta pratyekam aṅkasaṃkhyā vargāṇām ādito jñeyāḥ | pa-i-du-vi-ma-na-ta |

IO 61 (2015). 50 fol. Dated Śaka 1634 (Nandana year). Begins : pa-i-du-vi-ma-na-t | Sapta-lakṣaṇa | Title on the back page: Sapta-saṃkhyā samāptaḥ Pada-jyotiḥ samāptaḥ.

MD 14082. PL. Tel. 79 pp. Title: Ṛgveda-sapta-saṃkhyā-nirūpaṇa.

MD 14647. PL. Tel. 21 pp. Title: Ṛgveda-sapta-saṃkhyā-nirupaṇa.

MD 14781. PL. Na. 48 fol. Title: Ṛgveda-sapta-saṃkhyā-nirupaṇa.

Mysore ND II 3607 (P 5379/ 6). PL. Tel. 40 fol. Extract no. 210. Title: Pada-pragṛhya-lakṣaṇa. This title is apparently based on the initial words of the additional opening verse (quoted above) found in this Ms.

PUL I, p. 24 (no.146). 57 fol. Incomplete.

PUL I, p. 24 (no.147). 3 fol. Incomplete.

Sūcīpattra 117.

[CC I 695b-696a; II 166a]

1373 SAPTA-SAṂKHYĀ-PARIBHĀṢĀ (**सप्तसंख्यापरिभाषा**)

of Gopāla. The beginning and end are the same as in the Krama-ratna-saptākṣara-paribhāṣā above; also called Saptākṣarī-paribhāṣā.

Mysore ND II 3928 (C 3425/ 3). Na. 4 fol. (12-15). Extract no. 311.

1374 SAPTA-SVARA (**सप्तस्वर**)

on the seven musical notes as used in the Veda-s.

MD 1001. PL. Tel. 2 pp. (35f.)

1375 SAPTA-SVARA-LAKṢAṆA (**सप्तस्वरलक्षण**)

Gough p. 57.

1376 SAPTA-SVARA-SINDHU or SVARA-VARṆA-LAKṢAṆA (**सप्तस्वरसिन्धु / स्वरवर्णलक्षण**)

→ Svara-varṇa-lakṣaṇa.

1377 SAPTA-SVARA-SINDHU (**सप्तस्वरसिन्धु**)

of Ayyāśāstrin.

TCD 33. 315 pp. 2600 Grantha-s (with C.).

Tirupati SVUORI 7245 (4060a). PL. Gr. 25 fol. Incomplete.

Triv. Cur. IV 2. Gr. 3000 Grantha-s (with C.). Obtained from Ranga Vadhyar of Kallidakuruchi.

– C.

TCD 33. 315 pp. 2600 Grantha-s (with text).

Triv. Cur. IV 2. Gr. 3000 Grantha-s (with text). Obtained from Ranga Vadhyar of Kallidakuruchi.

1378 SAPTA-SVARITA-LAKṢAṆA (सप्तस्वरितलक्षण)
Beginning:

संहिताकाले सप्तविधाः स्वरिता उच्यन्ते। के च ते।
नित्यः क्षैप्रो ऽभिनिहितस्तैरोव्यञ्जन एव च।
तिरोविरामः प्रश्लिष्टः पादवृत्तस्तु सप्तमः ॥
इति संहिताकाले सप्तस्वरितलक्षणं समाप्तम् ॥

Tirupati SVUORI 7246 (427a). PL. Na. 2 fol.

1379 SAPTĀKṢARĪ-PARIBHĀṢĀ (सप्ताक्षरीपरिभाषा)
→ Krama-ratna-saptākṣara-paribhāṣā.
IO 4249(3) (Mackenzie II 60b). PL. Na. 2 fol. (3-4).
MD 14780(3). Described in the catalogue together with Krama-ratna-paribhāṣā.
Mysore Skt. Coll. p. 1 = D. No.6 (846/6). PL. Na. 3 fol. (29-31). Col.: iti krama-ratna-saptākṣarī-paribhāṣā samāptā

*SABHĀPATI (सभापति)
– Dhāraṇa-lakṣaṇa.

1380 SAMĀNA see ŚAMĀNA (समान / शमान)

1381 SAMĀNA-PADA (समानपद)
VSM III 168 (no.11345). 2 fol. Inc. (Aṣṭaka-s 5-7). → Ṛksarva-samāna.

1382 SAMĀNA-PADA (समानपद)
Beginning:

शार्यातस्येति। प्रभृता विसर्जनीयाः । न मा गरन्निति। दासा विसर्जनीयाः । धारावरा इति मृगा विसर्जनीयाः । जिमा विसर्जनीयाः । उष्णत्सूर्यमिति चोदयो विसर्गेण विप्रस्य मेध्यातिथेरिति। मेध्यातिथेर्विसर्गेण। यस्ते स्व इति।

End:

अपस्यवः शुविभ्राजा अपस्युधव्यूर्णवती युयोति स सुत्रामा युयोतु अन्यत्र युयोत विह्म ह्रस्वं वह्मा दीर्घं जनिम ह्रस्वं सुजनिमा दीर्घमिच्छन्ति न तामिनन्ति महि महे प्र ब्रह्म। जोहवीति। अन्यत्र जोहवीमि।

GD I 36-E. PL. Mal. 9 fol. (27-35). 375 Grantha-s.
TCD 2-B. PL. Mal. 28 fol. 600 Grantha-s. Incomplete.
Trav. Uni. C.405 B. = TCD 2-B.
Trav. Uni. 18109 G. PL. Mal. 240 Grantha-s.

1383 SAMĀNA-PADA-NIRṆAYA (1) (**समानपदनिर्णय**)

Beginning:

अग्निमीळे । सभा ... यदङ्ग कविः सचस्व नः । ... वायो धवः श्रुधि । ... वायो तुङ्गः तुविजातौ । ... अश्विना । धवः ... सुता सुत ... कामः चर्षणि विश्वाः ...

End:

ऋतं चेत्यस्याध्येतारः पदाध्ययनं न कुर्वन्ति । तथैव त्र्यम्बकानुष्टुभौ भद्रं नः पादस्य पदान्ते तनत्वाद्दतश्च । अत एतेषां पदसंख्या न लिखिता । सं समिद् गतिः देवा अवगृह्याणि षद् षद् ।

TCD 2-C. PL. Mal. 176 fol. 3960 Grantha-s.
Trav. Uni. 17800 A. PL. Mal. 1800 Grantha-s.

1384 SAMĀNA-PADA-NIRṆAYA (2) (**समानपदनिर्णय**)

Hoshiarpur p. 54 (no. 3797). PL. Mal. 70 fol. 2000 Grantha-s. Extract p. 414. Copied by Śaṃkara, disciple of Nārāyaṇa. It begins as the Ṛgveda-(prātiśākhya-)pariśiṣṭa (Whish 78), but ends:

सं समित् गर्तः देवाः अवगृह्याणि षद् । एवं समानपदनिर्णयो लिखितः ।
सर्वभूषणरत्नाढ्या शुभाङ्गस्वरलक्षणा ।
ल स च पदक्रमाश्रिमतृगः धूः कामदास्तु वः ॥

1385 SAMĀNA-PADA-NIRṆAYA-VYĀKHYĀ (**समानपदनिर्णयव्याख्या**)

Trav. Uni. 21553 D. PL. Gr. 120 Grantha-s.

1386 SAMĀNA-PADA-SAṂKHYĀ (**समानपदसंख्या**)

Ānandāśrama 2123. 12 fol. The first sections of the Cāturjñāna. Col.: iti samānapadasaṃkhyā samāptā śaka 1661 | samānapadasaṃkhyā 1110.

1387 SAMĀNA-PADĀDI (**समानपदादि**)

→ Ṛksarva-samāna, TCD 34-A.

1388 SAMĀNA-PADĀNI (**समानपदानि**)

SV → Sāma-samāna-padāni, MD 14078.

1389 SAMĀNA-LAKṢAṆA (**समानलक्षण**)

SBD 47867. 2 fol. (Yajuḥsaṃhitāyām). = Śamāna(-prakaraṇa).

1390 SAMĀNA-SAṂDHI (**समानसंधि**)

Ānandāśrama 7024. 4 fol. Contains Śamāna, Vilaṅghya, Napara and Tapara of TS.

1391 SAMĀNA-SAṂDHI (**समानसंधि**)

of Nāgadeva → Ṛksarva-śamāna.
IM 2497. 6 fol. Dated V.S. 1825.

SBD 2153. 3 fol.

1392 SAMĀNA-SAṂDHI (समानसंधि)
→ Śamāna (-prakaraṇa) (TS).
SBD 2154. 3 fol.

1393 SAMĀNA-SAṂDHI-VARṆA-KATHANA see ṚGVEDA-SAMĀNA-PADĀNI (समानसंधिवर्णकथन / ऋग्वेदसमानपदानि)
BORI 185 of 1899-1915. 19 fol. Dated Śaka 1711.

1394 SAMĀNA-SAṂDHI-VARṆA-YUKTI-VELUKAM (?) (समानसंधिवर्णयुक्तिवेलुकम्)
Hoshiarpur p. 54 (no.3519). 27 fol. 446 Grantha-s. Dated Śaka 1774.

1395 SAMĀNA-SAṂDHI-VYĀKHYĀ (समानसंधिव्याख्या)
Bombay Uni. Palmleaf No. 15. PL. Gr. 27 fol. uncatalogued. It includes : Taittirīya-prātiśākhya (fol. 1-12), Svara-pañcāśat (fol. 15-18), Sapta-lakṣaṇa (15 fol.).

1396 SAMĀNA-SAṂDHI-VYĀKHYĀ -- PADA-DARPAṆA (समानसंधिव्याख्या-- पददर्पण)
of Mallayārya. See C. on Śamāna of (Pogala) Mallayārya.
Mysore I, p. 38 (2 Mss.); p. 614.

1397 SAMĀNA-SAṂDHI-SŪTRA (समानसंधिसूत्र)
SBD 2155. 3 fol.

1398 SAMĀNA-SŪTRA (1) (समानसूत्र)
of Nāgadeva.
SBD 55664. 7 fol. = Ṛksarva-samāna.

1399 SAMĀNA-SŪTRA (2) (समानसूत्र)
→ Śamāna(-prakaraṇa) (TS)
SBD 4161. 2 fol. Incomplete.

1400 SAMĀSA-ŚIKṢĀ (समासशिक्षा)
Oppert I 1054. Belonged to Viraraghava Tatacharyar, Head Master, Sanskrit School of Sathakopacharya, Kanchipuram, Chingelpet Dist.

1401 SAṂPRADĀYA-PRABODHINĪ ŚIKṢĀ (संप्रदायप्रबोधिनी शिक्षा)
of Gopala Chandra Misra (former Prof. of Veda in the Banaras Hindu University and Varanaseya Sanskrit University), 146 verses (sub-title: Śukla-yajurveda-mādhyandina-śākhīyā), with his own commentary called Ṭupṭīkātmikā Subodhinī, illustrations of hand movements for Vedic recitation and explanations in Hindi.

Ptd. – Varanasi : Bharatiya Vidya Prakashana, 1964. 17, 32, 18 pp. – (Miśrānusaṃdhānagranthamālā). [BORI (22600)]

Also included in the edition of the *Jyotsnā-vṛtti* of Rāmaśarman on the *Vājasaneyi-prātiśākhya*, ed. by Yugal Kishore Misra. – Varanasi : Sampurnanand Sanskrit University, 1989, pp. 293-315.

1402 SARVA-TAPARA (सर्वतपर)
→ Tapara of Śeṣa Nārāyaṇa.

1403 SARVATRA-LAKṢAṆA (सर्वत्रलक्षण)
→ Pada-gāḍha, the last section of which is called Sarvatra-lakṣaṇa.
Baroda 2237. 55 fol. 1200 Grantha-s. = CLB I, p. 30.
GJKSV 34393. 6 fol. 75 sections.
Hoshiarpur p. 50 (no.1313). 19 fol. 300 Grantha-s. Dated Śaka 1718. Incomplete. Extract pp. 79-80.

1404 SARVA-NAPARA-LAKṢAṆA (सर्वनपरलक्षण)
of Śeṣa Nārāyaṇa. Adyar I, p. 54a → Natānta-padāni (RV).

1405 SARVA-LAKṢAṆA-TĀTPARYA(-NIRṆAYA) (सर्वलक्षणतात्पर्य /-निर्णय)
A work determining the characteristics of the various modes of reciting as well as repeating the Vedic texts. The different views held by the previous writers on the subject are also discussed.

MT 1631(a). Gr. 13 fol. Transcript of a Ms. that was copied by Yanamandra Veṅgaṇṇa, dated the Friday of the dark fortnight of the month of Phalguṇa in the year Manmatha. Begins as Jaṭā-vicāra, Adyar D I 819, but the end is different.
Oppert I 7155. Belonged to Pola Lakshmanavadhani of Vijayanagaram.
Oppert I 7252. Belonged to Ivattur Nandikesvara Sastri of Vijayanagaram.
Oppert I 7282. Belonged to S. Kodanda Ramavadhana Pantulu of Vijayanagaram.

1406 SARVA-VEDAPĀṬHA-PHALA (सर्ववेदपाठफल)
on the merit attached to the recital of the Veda in the various ways known as Saṃhitā, Pada, Krama, etc.

Beginning:

संहितापाठमात्रेण यत् फलं प्रोच्यते बुधैः ।
पदे तु द्विगुणं प्रोक्तं क्रमेणापि चतुर्गुणम् ॥
वर्णक्रमे शतगुणं जटायां तु सहस्रकम् ।
यो जटामात्रविद् ब्रह्मा संधिज्ञो विष्णुरुच्यते ॥

End:

संहितां च पदं चैव क्रमं चैव जटां पठन् ।
लक्षणज्ञस्तदाप्नोति ब्रह्मलोकं च शाश्वतम् ॥

MD 1000. PL. Gr. 1 p. (55).

1407 SARVA-ŚIKṢĀ-SAMGRAHA (**सर्वशिक्षासंग्रह**)
A summary of the essential points of the Śikṣā-s; divided into three sections, consisting of 15, 11 and 8 verses respectively.
Hz 2167. 5 fol. Belonged to Jambunatha Bhatta of Thanjavur.
TD 1686. 5 fol. 34 Grantha-s. Incomplete. Lacks end.

1408 SARVA-SAMĀNĀNI (**सर्वसमानानि**)
→ Pada-gāḍha.
SBD 4283. 4 fol. Incomplete.

1409 SARVA-SAṂMATA-ŚIKṢĀ (**सर्वसंमतशिक्षा**)
of Keśavārya, son of Sūra-sūri or Sūradeva-budhendra. 235 verses. Section titles (Weber): Dvitva-prakaraṇa, Aṅga-prakaraṇa, Svara-bhakti-prakaraṇa, Svarita-prakaraṇa, Hasta-svara-nyāsa-prakaraṇa.

Beginning:

गणेशं (कृपालुं) वरदं देवं प्रणिपत्य गजाननम्।
द्वित्वादीनां प्रवक्ष्यामि लक्षणं सर्वसंमतम्॥ १॥
स्वराद् द्वित्वमवाप्नोति व्यञ्जनं व्यञ्जने परे।
स्पर्शो लकारपूर्वो यो वपूर्वश्च द्विरुच्यते॥ २॥
स्वरपूर्वस्य रेफस्य परस्ताद् व्यञ्जनं स्थितम्।
आपद्यते द्विवर्णं तद् वर्णमात्रे परे स्थिते॥ ३॥

End:

हस्तहीनं तु यो ऽधीते स्वरवर्णार्थवर्जितम्।
ऋग्यजुःसामभिर्दग्धो वियोनिमधिगच्छति॥
मन्त्रो हीनः स्वरतो वर्णतो वा मिथ्याप्रयुक्तो न तमर्थमाह।
स वाग्वज्रो यजमानं हिनस्ति यथेन्द्रशत्रुः स्वरतो ऽपराधात्॥
स्वरवर्णान् स्फुटं मत्वा सम्यग् यश्च समुच्चरेत्।
अभ्युत्कृष्टफलं तस्य तत्र तत्र समीरितम्॥
हस्तेन वेदं यो ऽधीते स्वरवर्णार्थसंयुतम्।
ऋग्यजुःसामभिः पूतो ब्रह्मलोके महीयते॥
पदक्रमविशेषज्ञो वर्णक्रमविचक्षणः।
स्वरमात्रादिभागज्ञो गच्छेदाचार्यसंसदम्॥
सूर्यदेवबुधेन्द्रस्य नन्दनेन महात्मना।
प्रणीतं केशवार्येण लक्षणं सर्वसंमतम्॥

Adyar D I 1040 (1 A 19 = TR 19). Gr. 13 fol. (pp. 51-76). = Adyar I, p. 53a.
Adyar D I 1041 (25 L 35 = 71153). PL. Gr. 6 fol. (22ff.).

Adyar D I 1042 (8 E 34 = TR 29). 40 fol. (pp. 64-142) (with C. of Mañci-bhaṭṭa). On a fly-leaf at the end: "collated by Pandit K. S. Hariharasastri and and Y. Venkataramasastri, from the original Ms. of Puranika Keshavachar, Belur, Mysore, 29.5.16."

Adyar D XIII 328 (VB 428c). PL. Tel. 7 fol.

Adyar D XIII 329 (VB 430a). PL. Tel. 8 fol.

Adyar D XIII 330 (VB 427). PL. Gr. 52 fol. (with C. of Mañci-bhaṭṭa).

Adyar D XIII 331 (VB 428d). PL. Tel. 26 fol. (with C. of Mañci-bhaṭṭa).

America 363. 5 fol.

BORI 383 of 1883-84. 29 fol. (with Vivaraṇa of Ālamūri Mañci).

BORI 51 of 1884-87. 3 fol. Incomplete. 28 verses only. But col.: iti śikṣāmūlaḥ samāptaḥ |

GB 36. 33 fol. (135 verses with C. of Lakṣmaṇa). Copied for Kielhorn in Mysore in 1875. (on p. 4a it reads: asmatkṛta-śikṣācandrikāyām asya vivecanaṃ dṛṣṭavyam). See F. Kielhorn : Remarks on the Śikṣās in : *Indian Antiquary*, vol. V, p. 198 (reprint in : *Kleine Schriften*, vol. I, pp. 158-69).

Göttingen 158(6). 10 fol. (58-67). 12 additional fol. at the end contain notes by Kielhorn on the Śikṣā literature, including quotations from the Taittirīya-prātiśākhya.

Hamburg StUB (cod.Palmbl. III 8/133) → Veda-lakṣaṇa (HB).

Hamburg StUB (Oppert 10b). PL. Gr. 21 fol. (with C. of Mañci-bhaṭṭa. Col.: Sarva-saṃmata-lakṣaṇa-vṛtti).

Hoshiarpur p. 55 (no.4371). PL. Gr. 7 fol. 250 Grantha-s.

Hoshiarpur p. 55 (no.4373). PL. Gr. 6 fol. 40 Grantha-s.

Hoshiarpur p. 55 (no.3534). 31 fol. 130 Grantha-s (with C. of Mañci-bhaṭṭa). Dated V.S. 1776. Extract p. 80.

Hoshiarpur p. 55 (no.3552). 4 fol. 70 Grantha-s. Incomplete (with C.).

Hz 627. PL. Tel. 24 fol. (with 4 other works). Belonged to Vedam Venkatasubrahmanya Somayaji of Allur, Nellur Dist.

Hz 1441. PL. Gr. 4 fol. Extract p. 135. Belonged to the late Raja Ghanapathi of Tiruvidaimarudur, Thanjavur Dist.

IM 2523. 43 fol. (with Vivaraṇa). Incomplete.

IO 4956 (Mackenzie II 81c). PL. Na. 7 fol. (10-16). Written ca. A.D. 1800.

IO 4957 (Mackenzie III 119c). PL. Tel. 7 fol. (13-19).

IO 4958 (Burnell 41d). PL. Gr. 8 fol. (173-80).

IO 4959 (Mackenzie VIII 91d). PL. Gr. 3 fol. (6-8). Written ca. A.D. 1775.

IO 4960 (Mackenzie II 94c). PL. Na. 16 fol. (34-49) (with C. of Alamūri Mañci-bhaṭṭa). Written ca. A.D. 1770.

IO 4961 (Mackenzie III 234a). PL. Tel. 24 fol. (with C. of Alamūri Mañci-bhaṭṭa). Written A.D. 1816-17.

IO 4962 (Mackenzie III 235a). PL. Tel. 25 fol. (with C. of Alamūri Mañci-bhaṭṭa). Written ca. A.D. 1800.

MD 996. 17 pp. (124ff.).

MD 997. PL. Tel. 12 pp. (39ff.).

MD 998. Tel. 42 pp. (312ff.)
(with C. of Mañci-bhaṭṭa). .... (= Skt. Texts on Phonetics, pp. 536-79).

Post-colophon:

व्यासो लक्ष्मीर्भरद्वाजः शंभुः कापिलनिर्मिताः ।
कौहलीयः कालात्रेयारण्यशिक्षा नव स्मृताः ॥

MD 15926. PL. Gr. 29 pp. 690 Grantha-s (with C. of Mañci-bhaṭṭa).

MT 616(a). PL. Gr. 4 fol. (1-4). Incomplete. Purchased in 1912-13 from Subrahmanya Shastri of Tiruvadi.

MT 846(d). PL. Tel. 6 fol. (141-46). Presented in 1913-14 by V. V. S. Avadhani Garu of Vizagapattanam.

MT 846(e). PL. Tel. 19 fol. (147-65). (2nd copy with C. Mañci-bhaṭṭa). Presented in 1913-14 by V. V. S. Avadhani Garu of Vizagapattanam.

MT 1165(b). PL. Tel. 16 fol. (4-19) (with C. of Mañci-bhaṭṭa). Incomplete. Purchased in 1913-14 from Kashibhatta Subrahmanya Sastri of Vekanur, Krishna Dist.

MT 3887(p). PL. Gr. 16 fol. (135-50) (with C.). Incomplete. Purchased in 1921-22 from Annasvami Sastrigal, Bhavani, Coimbatore Dist.

Mysore (1898), p. 6 (no. 57). Gr. 25 fol. (130-54) (with C.).

Mysore I, p. 38 (11 Mss.; 6 with C. of Mañji-bhaṭṭa; also given as Āsūri-cinni-bhaṭṭa). p. 614.

Mysore ND II 3930-41. Extract no. 312, 313, 314.

Mysore Skt. Coll. p. 2 = D. No.17 (846/9). PL. Na. 6 fol. (36-41).

Oppert I 1055. Belonged to Viraraghava Tatacharyar, Head Master, Sanskrit School of Sathakopacharya, Kanchipuram, Chingelpet Dist.

Oppert I 2097. PL. Tel. 42 pp. Belonged to Sivasuri Sastri of Bhavani, Coimbatore Dist.

Oppert I 7156. Belonged to Pola Lakshmanavadhani of Vijayanagaram.

Oppert I 7253. Belonged to Ivattur Nandikesvara Sastri of Vijayanagaram.

Oppert II 784. Belonged to Ghanapathi Shingaracharyar of Alasur, Madurantakam Taluk.

Oppert II 1396. Belonged to Gopalacharyar of Pillapakkam, Kanchipuram Taluk.

Oppert II 5804. Belonged to Shingaracharyar of Kalyanapuram, Thanjavur Dist.

Oppert II 6718. Belonged to P.Rangacharyar of Kumbakonam.

Oppert II 8601. Belonged to Venkatacharyar of Timmagudi near Kumbakonam.

Oppert II 9121. Belonged to Ganapati Lakshminarayana Sastri of Tiruvadi, Thanjavur Dist.

PUL I, p. 24 (no.148). Tel. 12 fol. (102-13) (with C. of Someśvara).

Rgb. 51. 3 fol.

TCD 36. 15 pp. 135 Grantha-s.

Tirupati SVUORI 7303 (1143e). PL. Gr. 5 fol.

Tirupati SVUORI 7304 (1510a). PL. Gr.

Tirupati SVUORI 7305 (4511d). PL. Tel.

Trav. Uni. 121 A. PL. Gr. 140 Grantha-s.

Trav. Uni. 2086 B. PL. Gr. 140 Grantha-s.

Trav. Uni. 2630 J. PL. Gr. 60 Grantha-s.

Trav. Uni. 2938 J. PL. Gr. 60 Grantha-s.

Trav. Uni. 4028 C. PL. Gr. 140 Grantha-s.

Trav. Uni. T.629. 140 Grantha-s.

Triv. Cur. VII 3. Gr. 175 Grantha-s. Obtained from Seshu Ghanapathial, Vaikom.

VOHD II 2.546 (Ms.or.fol. 2952. StaatsB., Marburg). 4 fol. Incomplete. Dated V.S. 1834 (= 1778). Copied by Muralīdhra.
Wai I 1455. 7 fol. (A xerox-copy of this Ms. is in SAI).
Wai I 1456. 26 fol. (with C. of Mañci-bhaṭṭa). (A xerox-copy of this Ms. is in SAI).
Weber 1502 (Ms. or. fol. 904b). 9 fol. Incomplete (153 verses). A modern copy.

Ptd.: ed. by A. Otto Franke, with the commentary of Lakṣmaṇa (in Roman script) and a German translation (die Sarvasaṃmata-Śikṣā mit Commentar, herausgegeben, übersetzt und erklärt – Inaugural-Dissertation zur Erlangung der philosophischen Doctorwürde an der Georg-Augusts-Universität zu Göttingen), Teil I (comprising the portion up to verse 49 = 11 fol. of GB 36). – Göttingen : Dieteriche Univ.-Buchdruckerei, 1886. xvi, 44 pp. [SKGI (RI 135); BM : Ptd. Bks. Cat. 1906-1928. 950 (14092.b.49,1); Emeneau (380); Gö (Diss. scr. var. arg. III.2925)]

– C.
Hz 1440. PL. Gr. 13 fol. Belonged to the late Raja Ghanapathi of Tiruvidaimarudur, Thanjavur Dist.
Hamburg StUB (cod.Palmbl. III 8/133) → Veda-lakṣaṇa (HB).
IM 2523. 43 fol. (with text). Incomplete.
Mysore p. 2 (no. 57). 25 fol.
Mysore (1898), p. 6 (no. 57). Gr. 25 fol. (130-54) (with text).
Mysore ND II 3947 (P 4258/ 2). PL. Gr. 12 fol. (Pañcikā).
Mysore ND II 3948 (P 4521/ 4b). PL. Kan. 17 fol. Different ?
Oppert II 7992. Belonged to Venkatarama Dikshita of Sorakayur, Thanjavur Dist.
Oppert II 9122. Belonged to Ganapati Lakshminarayana Sastri of Tiruvadi, Thanjavur Dist.

– C. of Mañci-bhaṭṭa (or Cinni-bhaṭṭa, spelt variously as Cinna-bhaṭṭa, Mañji-bhaṭṭa, Āsūrīcinni-bhaṭṭa, Āsūrimalī-bhaṭṭa, Āsūrimalimañci-bhaṭṭa, Āmūrimaḻī-bhaṭṭa, etc.). Son of Vāñcheśvara and Veṅkaṭāmba and the disciple of Śrīnivāsa.

Beginning:

गणेश्वरं प्रणम्याहं लोकपलान् ग्रहान् गुरून्।
सर्वसंमतशिक्षाया वक्ष्ये व्याख्यामनुत्तमाम्॥

प्रारिप्सितग्रन्थस्य अविघ्नपरिसमाप्तये प्रचयगमनाय च शिष्टाचारपरिप्राप्त विशिष्टेष्टदेवतानमस्कारपूर्वकं ग्रन्थारम्भं प्रतिजानीते -- गणेशमिति। गणेशं गणपतिम्। वरदमिष्टदम्। देवं विघ्नानां विजिगीषुम्। गजाननं गजवक्त्रम्। प्रणिपत्य भक्तितो नत्वा द्वित्वादीनां द्वित्वमादिर्येषां तेषां द्वित्वपूर्वागमलोपागमविकारादीनाम्। सर्वसंमतं सर्वेषां तैत्तिरीयशाखोपयोगिनां प्रातिशाख्यप्रभृतीनाम्। संमतं समानार्थम्। लक्ष्यन्ते प्रकाश्यन्ते अनेनेति लक्षणम् । प्रवक्ष्यामि निर्दोषं रचयामीत्यर्थः ॥ स्वराद् द्वित्वम् ... अथ वर्णसमाम्नाय इत्यादिवर्णसंज्ञापराणि सूत्राण्यनुवृ(सृ)त्य व्यवहरन्त्याचार्याः । स्वरादुत्तरं व्यञ्जनं व्यञ्जने परे सति द्वित्वम्। द्वयोर्भावः द्वित्वम्। समानाकारं वर्णद्वयम्। अवाप्नोति

प्राप्नुयात्। यथा यज्ञस्य। स्वरादिति किम्। प्रजननमित्यत्र पकारे द्वित्वं मा भूदिति।

Adyar D I 1042 (8 E 34 = TR 29). 40 fol. (pp. 64-142) (with text). On a fly-leaf at end: "collated by Pandit K. S. Hariharasastri and and Y. Venkataramasastri, from the original Ms. of Puranika Keshavachar, Belur, Mysore, 29.5.16."

Adyar D I 1043 (19 E 42 = 66327). PL. Gr. 7 fol. = Adyar I, p. 53b.

Adyar D I 1044 (19 E 42 = 66327). PL. Gr. 18 fol. (8-25). = Adyar I, p. 53b.

Adyar D I 1045 (25 L 15 = 71133). PL. Gr. 27 fol.

Adyar D I 1046 (25 L 30 = 71148). PL. Gr. 44 fol.

Adyar D I 1047 (28 J 17 = 73051). PL. Gr. 26 fol. (58ff.). = Adyar I, p. 53b.

Adyar D I 1048 (29 I 28 = 73580). PL. Gr. 12 fol. (77ff.). = Adyar I, p. 53b.

Adyar D XIII 332 (VB 430b). PL. Tel. 23 fol.

BORI 383 of 1883-84. 29 fol. (with text).

BP p. 287 (Ālamūrimañci).

Hamburg StUB (Oppert 10b). PL. Gr. 21 fol. (with text). Col.: Sarva-sammata-lakṣaṇa-vṛtti.

Hoshiarpur p. 55 (no.3534). 31 fol. 130 Grantha-s (with text). Incomplete. Dated V.S. 1776.

Hoshiarpur p. 55 (no.3552). 4 fol. 70 Grantha-s. Incomplete.

Hoshiarpur p. 55 (no.4374). PL. Gr. 44 fol. 400 Grantha-s.

MD 998. Tel. 42 pp. (312ff.) (with text).

MD 999. PL. Tel. 52 pp. (21ff.). Incomplete.

MT 846(c). PL. Tel. 19 fol. (147-65) (with text). Presented in 1913-14 by V. V. S. Avadhani Garu of Vizagapattanam.

MT 1165(b). PL. Tel. 16 fol. (4-19) (with text). Incomplete. Purchased in 1913-14 from Kashibhatta Subrahmanya Sastri of Vekanur, Krishna Dist.

MT 3887(p). PL. Gr. 16 fol. (135-50) (with text). Incomplete. Purchased in 1921-22 from Annasvami Sastrigal, Bhavani, Coimbatore Dist.

Mysore I, p. 614 (Ālamūri Yalla-bhaṭṭakṛtam ?)

Mysore ND II 3942-46. Extract no. 315.

Mysore ND II 3942 (P 208/ 2). PL. Gr. 42 fol. (a. Mañji-bhaṭṭa).

Mysore ND II 3943 (P 208/ 4). PL. Gr. 19 fol. Incomplete. (a. Āsūrī-chinni-bhaṭṭa).

Mysore ND II 3944 (B 252/17). Gr. 1 fol. Incomplete. (121). Different ?

Mysore ND II 3945 (P 2262/32). PL. Gr. 16 fol. Extract no. 315. (a. Āsūri-malī-bhaṭṭa).

Mysore ND II 3946 (P 2265/19). PL. Gr. 11 fol. (127-37).

Mysore ND II 3949 (P 9312/ 2). PL. Na. 17 fol. (70-86). Extract no.316. (a. Āsūri-mali-mañci-bhaṭṭa).

RASB II 1514 (G 1106). 21 fol. 550 Grantha-s; text in 131 verses.

Tirupati SVUORI 7306 (1143f). PL. Gr. 11 fol. Incomplete.

Trav. Uni. 121 B. PL. Gr. 450 Grantha-s.

Trav. Uni. 347 A. PL. Gr. 300 Grantha-s. Incomplete.

Wai I 1456. 26 fol. (with text).

[CC I 702b]

1410 SARVĀNUKRAMA (सर्वानुक्रम)

BHU C 1687 (D 11/673). 5 fol. Contains Chandaḥ-saṃkhyā, Anuvākānukramaṇī of Śaunaka and Anuvāka-pañcāśī.

1411 SARVĀNUKRAMA or SARVĀNUKRAMAṆIKĀ or SARVĀNUKRAMAṆĪ (सर्वानुक्रम / सर्वानुक्रमणिका / सर्वानुक्रमणी)

Unspecified.

Ānandāśrama 47. 206 fol. (with Vṛtti). Dated Śaka 1714. → Ṛgveda-sarvānukramaṇī-vṛtti of Ṣaḍguru-śiṣya.

Ānandāśrama 124. 44 fol. Dated Śaka 1695. → Ṛgveda-sarvānukramaṇī.

Ānandāśrama 434. 26 fol. Dated Śaka 1710. → Ṛgveda-sarvānukramaṇī.

Ānandāśrama 434. 26 fol. Dated Śaka 1710. → Ṛgveda-sarvānukramaṇī.

Ānandāśrama 6879. 32 fol. Dated Śaka 1713. → Ṛgveda-sarvānukramaṇī.

Ānandāśrama 6880.34 fol. Dated Śaka 1763. → Ṛgveda-sarvānukramaṇī.

Ānandāśrama 2198. 44 fol. Dated Śaka 1703. Copious notes on margin.

Ānandāśrama 7332, 8089.

ASB I iii.376 (I D 26/3). Beng. 21 fol. Dated Śaka 1878 = A.D. 1821.

B I, p. 210 (nos. 78-84).

B I, p. 212 (no.85). 41 fol. Dated V.S. 1845.

BHU C 1687 (D 11/673). 5 fol. Incomplete.

BISM pp. 313-14. 28 Mss.; two of them are ascribed to Āśvalāyana.

CPB 6350. 6351.

Deccan College 675. 23 fol. Incomplete.

Deccan College 891. 30 fol. Dated Śaka 1697.

Deccan College 1343. 30 fol. Incomplete.

Deccan College 3623. 8 fol. Incomplete.

Deccan College 4290. 63 fol. Incomplete (fol. 8, 10, 12, 28, 29, 55 are missing). Dated Śaka 1695.

Deccan College 5334. 29 fol.

Deccan College 5452. 37 fol. (1-22, 31-45). Incomplete. Dated Śaka 1753.

Deccan College 5453. 46 fol. Dated V.S. 1914 (fine hand writing).

Deccan College 7165. 19 fol. (7-25) Incomplete.

Deccan College 7276. 22 fol. Incomplete.

Deccan College 8170. 30 fol. Dated Śaka 1719.

Deccan College 10084. 33 fol. Dated Śaka 1731.

IM 5171. 20 fol. Dated V.S. 1882 / Śaka 1747. Copied by Anantarāma, son of Vāsudeva Deva.

IM 9224. 15 fol. (3-17). Sāmavedic ?

Oppert II 6719 (Sarvopakramaṇī). Belonged to P.Rangacharyar of Kumbakonam.

OU 30 Vm (B.84/11a). 28 fol. (fol. 10-12 missing). 17th century.

Oxf. CS d.74(5). 52 fol. (a. Kātyāyana). → Śukla-yajurveda-sarvānukrama. Ff. 41-46 contains the Anuvākānukrama.

Oxf. CS d.76(2). 26 fol. → Ṛgveda-sarvānukramaṇī.

Oxf. CS d.76(3). 33 fol. Dated A.D. 1818 (Anuvākānukramaṇī on ff. 30-33). → Ṛgveda-sarvānukramaṇī

Oxf. CS d.76(5). 49 fol. (a. Kātyāyana). Dated A.D. 1693 → Ṛgveda-sarvānukramaṇī. (Chandaḥ-saṃkhyā on ff. 44-45 and Anuvākānukramaṇī on ff. 45-49).

Oxf. CS d.76(6). 44 fol. (a. Kātyāyana). Dated A.D. 1842. → Śukla-yajurveda-sarvānukrama.

Oxf. CS d.77(3). 32 fol. (1 fol. missing). 18th century.

Oxf. CS d.77(5). 38 fol. (2 fol. missing). (a. Kātyāyana).

Oxf. CS d.77(6). 6 fol. Dated A.D. 1861. It contains 32 verses of the Anuvākānukramaṇī, Chandaḥ-saṃkhyā and Anuvāka-pañcāśī. Belonged to Bālamukunda.

Oxf. CS d.77(7). 29 fol. (fol. 1, 15 missing). (a. Kātyāyana).

Oxf. CS d.78(1). 13 fol. 1 Adhyāya. (a. Kātyāyana). Śukla-yajurveda-sarvānukrama.

Oxf. CS d.78(2). 42 fol. (2 fol. missing). (a. Kātyāyana). → Ṛgveda-sarvānukramaṇī.

Oxf. CS d.78(3). 22 fol. Incomplete. (a. Kātyāyana). Dated A.D. 1591. → Śukla-yajurveda-sarvānukrama.

Oxf. CS d.78(4). 5 fol. (a. Kātyāyana). Dated A.D. 1553. → Anuvākānukramaṇī of Śaunaka.

Oxf. CS d.79. 96 fol. (with Bhāṣya) → Uvaṭa's Bhāṣya on the Ṛgveda-sarvānukramaṇī.

Oxf. CS c.29(1). 40 fol. → Śukla-yajurveda-sarvānukrama. Anuvākādhyāya at the end (ff. 37-41).

Ujjain II, p. 8 (no.3558). 43 fol. Dated V.S. 1929.

– C.

B I, p. 212 (no.88). 20 fol.

B I, p. 212 (no.89). 97 fol. (Pūrvārdha).

B I, p. 212 (no.90). 36 fol. (Uttarārdha). Dated V.S. 1847.

BISM p. 314 (34/269).

BISM p. 314 (47/42). 6 fol. The beginning of Yājñika-deva's Bhāṣya.

BORI 5 of 1895-1902. 82 fol. (Vṛtti of Ṣaḍguru-śiṣya).

BORI 14 of 1902-07. 121 fol. 3267 Grantha-s. Dated Śaka 1681. This is Uvaṭa's commentary on the *Ṛgveda-sarvānukramaṇī*.

L 873. 2 fol. (64 Grantha-s).

[CC I 703a]

1412 SARVĀNUKRAMA or SARVĀNUKRAMAṆĪ (सर्वानुक्रम / सर्वानुक्रमणी)

→ Ṛgveda-sarvānukramaṇī and Śukla-yajurveda-sarvānukrama.

1413 SARVĀNUKRAMA-KĀRIKĀ-ŚATAKA (सर्वानुक्रमकारिकाशतक)

of Kṛṣṇa Ayācita. A summary of the *Ṛgveda-sarvānukramaṇī* in 100 verses.

Deccan College 2190. 9 fol. Dated Śaka 1751.

1414 SARVĀNUKRAMAṆIKĀ (1) (सर्वानुक्रमणिका)

Ascribed to Āśvalayana. But it is identical with the *Ṛgveda-sarvānukramaṇī* of Kātyāyana.

Tirupati SVUORI 7310 (453). PL. Na. 30 fol. (30-59). (agniṃ nava madhucchandā vaiśvāmitro ...).

1415 SARVĀNUKRAMAṆIKĀ (2) (सर्वानुक्रमणिका)
SV. Cf. Ṛṣi-cchando-devatā of Viśrāma, above. Baroda 10808.

Beginning:

प्रणम्य तातं विश्रामं विघ्नेशं जगदम्बिकाम्।
ब्रह्मयज्ञादिसिद्ध्यर्थमृष्यादीनुच्यते क्रमात्॥

End:

इति षष्ठः प्रपाठकः। क्षुद्रपर्व समाप्तम्॥

Alwar 252. Extract 70.
Peters. II, p. 179 (no.44). 79 fol.

[CC II 233b]

1416 SARVĀNUKRAMA-(ṆIKĀ-)PARIBHĀṢODĀHARAṆA (सर्वानुक्रम-(णिका-)परिभाषोदाहरण)
Contains illustrations of the metres, Gāyatrī, etc. together with different variations of them and a list of Ekapadā (6) and Dvipadā (157) Ṛk-s.
GJKSV 18278. 3 fol.
GJKSV 37944. 9 fol.
Rep. Raj. and C. I. p. 6.

1417 SARVĀNUKRAMAṆIKĀ-BHĀṢYA (सर्वानुक्रमणिकाभाष्य)
→ C. on Śukla-yajurveda-sarvānukrama of Yājñika-deva.
GJKSV 44137. 65 fol. Incomplete.

1418 SARVĀNUKRAMAṆĪ (सर्वानुक्रमणी)
→ Ṛgveda-sarvānukramaṇī and Śukla-yajurveda-sarvānukrama.

1419 SARVĀNUKRAMAṆĪ-PADDHATI (सर्वानुक्रमणीपद्धति)
of Yājñika-deva → C. on Śukla-yajurveda-sarvānukrama.
IM 2479. 42 fol. (2-43). Incomplete.

1420 SARVĀNUKRAMAṆĪ-PADYA-VIVṚTI (सर्वानुक्रमणीपद्यविवृति)
A metrical adaptation (ca. 2000 Anuṣṭubh verses) of the *Ṛgveda-sarvānukramaṇī*. See under Ṛgeda-sarvānukramaṇi above.

1421 SARVĀNUKRAMAṆĪ-BHĀṢYA (सर्वानुक्रमणीभाष्य)
→ Ṛgveda-sarvānukramaṇī-bhāṣya of Ṣaḍguru-śiṣya.
GJKSV 39129. 299 fol. (1-250, 253-311). Incomplete. Dated V.S. 1828.

1422 SARVĀNUKRAMA-PARIBHĀṢĀ (सर्वानुक्रमपरिभाषा)
→ Ṛgveda-paribhāṣā and Ṛgveda-sarvānukramaṇī.
GJKSV 38417. 41 fol. Dated Śaka 1717.

1423 SARVĀNUKRAMA-PARIBHĀṢĀ-CHANDODĀHARAṆA (सर्वानुक्रमपरिभाषाछन्दोदाहरण)
Deccan College 7840 (? 7890). 51 fol. Dated V.S. 1996 ?.

1424 SARVĀNUKRAMA-PARIBHĀṢĀ-CHANDO-MAÑJARĪ (सर्वानुक्रमपरिभाषाछन्दोमञ्जरी)
→ Ṛgveda-paribhāṣā.
IM 5784. 11 fol.

1425 SARVĀNUKRAMA-PARIBHĀṢĀ-SŪTRA (सर्वानुक्रमपरिभाषासूत्र)
Tirupati SVUORI 8875 (2641). Incomplete.

1426 SARVĀNUKRAMA-PARIŚIṢṬA (सर्वानुक्रमपरिशिष्ट)
VSM III 173 (no.11341). 3 fol. Contains the Chandaḥ-saṃkhyā, Chandasām udāharaṇāni (printed on p. 87 of the Vaidika-cchandomañjarī), and Anuvāka-pañcāśī.

1427 SARVĀNUKRAMA-BHĀṢYA (सर्वानुक्रमभाष्य)
Both text and Bhāṣya are ascribed in the catalogue to Sāyaṇa but on verification it is ascertained to be the *Ṛgveda-sarvānukramaṇī* with *Vedārtha-dīpikā* of Ṣaḍguru-śiṣya.
ASB I iii.25 (IM 2163). 83 fol. 3237 Grantha-s. Incomplete.

1428 SARVĀNUKRAMA-VIVARAṆA (सर्वानुक्रमविवरण)
Ānandāśrama 406. 54 fol. → Ṛgveda-sarvānukrama-vivaraṇa of Jagannātha.

1429 SARVĀNUKRAMA-SŪTRA see ŚUKLA-YAJURVEDA-SARVĀNUKRAMA (सर्वानुक्रमसूत्र / शुक्लयजुर्वेदसर्वानुक्रम)

1430 SARVĀNUKRAMODĀHARAṆA (सर्वानुक्रमोदाहरण)
BISM p. 314 (36/1319). 73 fol. → Ṛgvedānukramaṇikā (4).
Rep. Raj. and C. I. p. 6.

1431 SARVĀNTA-SAMĀNA-SAṂDHI (सर्वान्तसमानसंधि)
Trav. Uni. 5778 F. PL. Tel. 50 Grantha-s. See Śamāna.

1432 SALAKṢAṆA-PARIBHĀṢĀ (सलक्षणपरिभाषा)
Ascribed to Vararuci → Sāma-paribhāṣā.
Adyar D I 1060 (19 M 40 = 66808). PL. Gr. 9 fol. = Adyar I, p. 54b.
Adyar D I 1061 (19 M 42 = 66810). PL. Gr. 11 fol. = Adyar I, p. 54b. Title: Parva-nirūpaṇa. Copied by Viśvanātha, son of Veṅkaṭācala Dīkṣita, of the family of Īśvara Dīkṣita of Bharadvāja-gotra, on the 10 day of the dark fortnight of the Āṅgirasa.
Adyar D I 1062 (25 D 17 = 70837). PL. Gr. 8 fol. = Adyar I, p. 54b.
Adyar D I 1063 (25 D 35 = 70855). PL. Gr. 8 fol. (153ff.). = Adyar I, p. 54b.
Adyar D I 1064 (26 G 33 = 71517). PL. Gr. 17 fol. (3ff.). = Adyar I, p. 54b.
Adyar D I 1065 (34 G 4 = 75668). PL. Gr. 10 fol. (1-10). Called Chalākṣara-paribhāṣā on a fly-leaf at the beginning.

Ptd.: Ed. by Krishnaswami Srauti (in Grantha script), – Tiruvadi : Girvanavani Vilasa Press, 1891. See below Sāma-paribhāṣā. In this edition the Lakṣaṇa portion is placed at the beginning while in all the Mss. noticed here except no. 1065 it is contained at the end.

1433 SAVILA-MĀLĀ or SAVELA-SAMJÑĀ see ṚGVEDA-SAVĪLA-MĀLĀ
(सविलमाला / सवेलसंज्ञा / ऋग्वेदसवीलमाला)
Ānandāśrama 1906.

1434 SĀMA-KĀRIKĀ **(सामकारिका)**
of Raṅganātha.
Mysore I, p. 39.
Mysore ND II 3951 (P 5180/ 2). PL. Na. 6 fol. (35-41).

1435 SĀMA-GĀNA-PARIBHĀṢĀ (1) **(सामगानपरिभाषा)**
→ Sāma-paribhāṣā.
IM 2311. 8 fol. (2-9).

1436 SĀMA-GĀNA-PARIBHĀṢĀ (2) **(सामगानपरिभाषा)**
Unspecified:
Mysore ND II 3952 (B 858/ 8). Gr. 1 fol. Incomplete.
Mysore ND II 3953 (P 7627/ 1). PL. Gr. 1 fol. Different.
Mysore ND II 3954 (P 491/ 2). PL. Na. 3 fol. (101-03). Extract no. 317.
Mysore ND II 3955 (A 642/ 2). Kan. 6 fol. (14-19). Dated 6.8.19.
SBD 2156. 3 fol.

1437 SĀMA-CCHALĀKṢARA **(सामच्छलाक्षर)**
Mysore I, p. 39 (2 Mss.).

1438 SĀMA-TANTRA **(सामतन्त्र)**
A Prātiśākhya of the *Sāmaveda* ascribed to Audavraji, in 15 Prapāṭhaka-s prescribing the rules for turning the verses into Sāman. "For some account of this work *vide* Prof. Max Müller's A. S. L. p. 143, and Prof. Weber's Indische Studien, I, p. 48. The commentary is attributed in S. India, but without reason, to Sāyaṇa. Most likely it belongs to a much earlier date." (Brl. p. 41). In the colophon of the Adyar Ms. it is called *Sāma-tantra-vyākaraṇa.* The last two Prapāṭhaka-s are a kind of supplement called Saṃjñā-(pra)karaṇa or Akṣara-tantra. See above under Akṣara-tantra.

Adyar D I 1066 (8 F 82 = PM 143). Gr. 23 fol. = Adyar I, p. 54a.
Adyar D I 1067 (33 E 12 = 75259). PL. Gr. 10 fol. (6ff.). Contains Akṣara-tantra also at the end. = Adyar I, p. 54a.
Baroda 6738. PL. Gr. 78 fol. 2000 Grantha-s (with Bhāṣya). = CLB I, p. 38.
Baroda 7814. PL. Tel. 122 fol. 2000 Grantha-s (with Bhāṣya). = CLB I, p. 38.
Baroda 9805(f). PL. Gr. 14 fol. 200 Grantha-s. = CLB I, p. 38.
Baroda 12912(b). 7 fol. (5-11). 200 Grantha-s. = CLB I, p. 38. Dated V.S. 1682.
Bik. 336. 13 fol.

BORI 101 of 1879-80. = BORI D II i.3. 12 fol. 13 Prakaraṇa-s. Dated V.S. 1719.
Brl. p. 40 (no.CXXIX) = IO 4330.
Calcutta Skt. Coll. I 495. 98 fol. (1-9 are missing). 2400 Grantha-s (with C.). No beginning. Dated V.S. 1645.
IO 4330 (Burnell 360a). Gr. 246 pp. (with Bhāṣya). Written ca. A.D. 1867.
IO 4331 (Burnell 437b). Gr. 150 fol. (with Bhāṣya). Written ca. A.D. 1875.
IO 4332 (Burnell 360b). Gr. 28 pp. (with Bhāṣya). (2 Prapāṭhaka-s called Saṃjñā-prakaraṇa). Written ca. A.D. 1867.
IO 4333 (Burnell 437c). Gr. 19 fol. (with Bhāṣya). (2 Prapāṭhaka-s called Saṃjñā-prakaraṇa). Written ca. A.D. 1875.
Max Müller Mem. XVII. 16 fol. Copied by Gaṅgādhara. Dated V.S. 1690.
Mysore I, p. 39 (3 Mss.).
Mysore ND II 3956-62.
N-W P I 28 (no.84). 8 fol. Belonged to Divakara Ganaka of Benares.
N-W P I 30 (no.93). 8 fol. Belonged to Divakara Ganaka of Benares.
Oudh III 6.
Oxf. II 860(2) (Ms. Wilson 504). 9 fol. (35-43). Dated A.D. 1604. = Oxf. 386a (no.504).
P 7.
Peters. II, p. 180 (no.58). 6 fol.
PUL II. App. p. 14 (no.223). PL. Gr. 6 fol. (118-23; fol. 112 missing).
SB p. 28 (no.176). 111 fol. 1958 Grantha-s. Dated V.S. 1710. = SBD 47610.
SB p. 29 (no.55). 8 fol. 192 Grantha-s. Incomplete. = SBD 47881.
SBD 2111b. 9 fol. (5-13). Together with Ṛktantra-brahmarāśi and Avagraha-pariśiṣṭa. Dated V.S. 1768.
SBD 2113. 23 fol.
SBD 2141. 71 fol. (1-6, 6-24, 24-43, 45-70). Incomplete.
SBD 2152. 1, 24 fol. Incomplete. (Sāmaprakāśanākhyam ?). Dated V.S. 1626.
SBD 47610. 84 fol. (1-53, 53-61, 63-73, 73-82, 84). Incomplete.
SBD 47881. 8 fol.
SBD 53768. 28 fol. (1-7, 1-4, 1-2, 1-4, 1-10, 1). Vaṅga. Incomplete.
Trav. Uni. 1733 B. 9 fol. 165 Grantha-s.
Trav. Uni. 11825. PL. Gr. 165 Grantha-s.
Trav. Uni. 2090 A. PL. Gr. 130 Grantha-s. Incomplete.
Trav. Uni. 3340 C. PL. Gr. 150 Grantha-s. Incomplete.
Trav. Uni. 2952 A 1. PL. Gr. 2600 Grantha-s (with Bhāṣya).
Weber 308 (Chambers 290). 97 fol. (many fol. missing). Catalogued as C.

Ptd.: ed. by Krishnasvami Srauti in the edition of Veyagāna (some portions only; in Grantha script). – Tiruvadi : Jyotirvilasa Press, 1889. [Adyar (H 211.3 VG Kri); IO : Ptd. Bks. Cat. 1957, p. 2969 (16 D 39)]
Ed. by A. M. Ramanatha Dikshita, with an introduction and appendices. – Benares : Banares Hindu University, 1961. 4, 8, 55, 428, 28 pp. – (Vedic Research Series 1). [Adyar (H080 BHU VR1); BORI (22291); NL (180 Jb 96 50); UBTÜ (21 A 15982); SAI (ind 51 D 701)]

– C. of Dayāśaṃkara.

N-W P I 8 (no.21). 9 fol. Belonged to Veshirama of Benares.

– C. Sāma-tantra-vṛtti-sāra of Nṛsiṃha-datta.
Max Müller Mem. XVIII. 66 fol.

– C. Sāma-tantra-bhāṣya of Rāmakṛṣṇa Dīkṣita, son of Dāmodara.
IM 4980. 8 fol. (3-10). Incomplete.
N-W P V 144 (no.10). 21 fol.
SB p. 31 (no.136). 22 fol. 308 Grantha-s. = SBD 2098.
SBD 2098. 22 fol. Incomplete.

– C. attributed to Sāyaṇa. Brl. p. 40 = IO 4330. See below.

– C. anon.
Adyar D I 1068 (22 M 15 = 69365). PL. Gr. 18 fol. (6ff.). Incomplete. Breaks off in Daśaka 9 of Prapāṭhaka 2. = Adyar I, p. 54a.
Alwar 286.
Baroda 6738. PL. Gr. 78 fol. 2000 Grantha-s (with text). = CLB I, p. 38.
Baroda 7814. PL. Tel. 122 fol. 2000 Grantha-s (with text). = CLB I, p. 38.
Brl. p. 40 (no.CXXIX: "attributed ... to Sāyaṇa") = IO 4330.
IO 4330 (Burnell 360a). Gr. 246 pp. (with text). Written ca. A.D. 1867.
IO 4331 (Burnell 437b). Gr. 150 fol. (with text). Written ca. A.D. 1875.
IO 4332 (Burnell 360b). Gr. 28 pp. (2 Prapāṭhaka-s called Saṃjñā-prakaraṇa). Written ca. A.D. 1867.
IO 4333 (Burnell 437c). Gr. 19 fol. (2 Prapāṭhaka-s called Saṃjñā-prakaraṇa). Written ca. A.D. 1875.
MD 1005. PL. Gr. 120 pp.
MD 1006. Tel. 184 pp. A restored copy of MD 1005 transcribed in 1896.
Mysore ND II 3963 (A 648/ b). Kan. 319 fol. Incomplete.
Oppert I 1167. PL. Gr. 500 pp. Belonged to Ramanujacharyar of Tadakamangalam, Chingelpet Dist.
PUL II. App. p. 14 (no.224). PL. Gr. 61 fol. 2200 Grantha-s (several fol. missing).
RASB II 1328 (G 1457). 98 fol. 1100 Grantha-s. Dated V.S. 1937.
Śg. I 20. Tel. 184 pp. Extract p. 68.

Ptd.: together with the text in the Benares edition.

[CC I 708a; II 169b]

1439 SĀMA-TANTRA-PRAKĀŚIKĀ (सामतन्त्रप्रकाशिका)
Trav. Uni. 11821 B. 4500 Grantha-s.

1440 SĀMA-TANTRA-SAṂGRAHA (1) (सामतन्त्रसंग्रह)
Oppert I 2099. PL. Tel. 187 pp. Belonged to Sivasuri Sastri of Bhavani, Coimbatore Dist.

[CC I 708a]

1441 SĀMA-TANTRA-SAṂGRAHA (2) (सामतन्त्रसंग्रह)
of Veṅkaṭeśa.
Trav. Uni. 2911 C. PL. Gr. 250 Grantha-s. Incomplete.

1442 SĀMA-DĪPA (सामदीप)

Mysore I, p. 39.

Mysore ND II 3966 (P 3242/ 4). PL. Gr. 20 fol. Ascribed to Vararuci.

1443 SĀMA-DĪPA (ĀRAṆYAKA-SĀMA-DĪPA) (सामदीप / आरण्यकसामदीप)

Mysore ND II 3964 (P 2482/ 2). PL. Na. 21 fol. (40-60). Extract no.318.

Mysore ND II 3965 (P 5187/ 3). PL. Gr. 155 fol. (98-152).

1444 SĀMA-PARIBHĀṢĀ (सामपरिभाषा)

of Vararuci, according to the col. of MT 8041 (Paribhāṣā-lakṣaṇa) and of Hoshiarpur Ms. Also called Sāma-veda-(gāna-)paribhāṣā and Salakṣaṇa-paribhāṣā (in the printed edition). See R. Simon, WZKM 27, pp. 306-46 (reprinted in : Richard Simon : *Kleine Schriften*, ed. by Rüdiger Schmitt. – Wiesbaden : Steiner, 1979, pp. 863-904. – (Glasenapp Stiftung 20). [SAI (ind 50 A 79/2954)]

Beginning:

सप्तस्वरैः समस्तं यो जगदेतच्चराचरम्।
संजीवयति विश्वात्मा स नो विष्णुः प्रसीदतु॥

अथ साम्नां क्रुष्टप्रथमद्वितीयतृतीयचतुर्थमन्द्रातिस्वार्य परिस्वारवतां पर्वणां ज्ञापकत्वेन परिभाषितैः ककारादिभिरक्षरैः पर्वादिवर्णैश्च साम्नां दीपस्थानीयो ग्रन्थ आरभ्यते। यत्र सामगा विरम्य गायन्ति तत्र विरते सामभागे पर्वसंज्ञा वर्तते। तच्च द्विविधम्। एकस्वरमनेकस्वरं चेति। उऔ। तया-इ। गिरा। इ। ओग्ना-इ। अग्निन्दूताम्। इत्येकस्वरम्। गृणानो ह। स्तुषा इमित्रानुम्। प्रत्यग्ने। जारा। अग्निं वाआव ...। इत्यनेकस्वरम्। अनेकस्वरं त्रिविधम्। अनुलोमगीतं प्रतिलोमगीतमुभयविधगीतं चेति। अनुलोमगीतमुच्चादिनीचान्तम्।

End:

इति तवर्गश्चतुर्थस्वरादिः। पवर्गो मन्द्रस्वराणां तदादीनां च पर्वणां ज्ञापकः। ... फे -- एना वो अग्निमे ऽनिनमसा। फै -- समेत विश्वा ओजसा पतिं। फो इत्यादि नास्ति। इति पवर्गो मन्द्रस्वरादिः। इति कौथुमशाखायाः सलक्षणपरिभाषा समाप्ता॥

Baroda 6784(b). PL. Gr. 11 fol. (95-105). 300 Grantha-s. = CLB I, p. 38. Extract p. 170 (6784 C ?). Contains Kavargādi-paribhāṣā and a list of 195 Sāman-s.

BISM p. 315 (36/29). 9 fol. Dated Śaka 1794. The beginning differs.

Brl. p. 44 (no.CXXXIII) = IO 4338.

Hoshiarpur p. 55 (no.2077). PL. Gr. 20 fol. 250 Grantha-s. Extract p. 414. Col.: iti vararucinā kṛta-paribhāṣā-lakṣaṇam.

IM 2311. 8 fol. (2-9). Col.: Sāmaveda-gāna-paribhāṣā.

IO 4338 (Burnell 147). PL. Gr. 15 fol. Written ca. A.D. 1800. Title: (Svara-)Paribhāṣā. (Utilized by R. Simon).

MD 1007. PL. Gr. 6 pp. (226ff.). Incomplete. Copied by Veṅkaṭa-subban. It belonged to the collection of C. W. Whish, who has added the following note at the end. –

"Here ends the Paribhāṣā, a portion of the *Sāmaveda*." C. W. Whish, Calicut, 1825.

MD 17070. PL. Gr. 21 pp. 131 Grantha-s.

MT 238(b). PL. Gr. 16 fol. (170-85). Presented in 1910-11 by S. Ramakrishna Vadhyar of Palghat.

MT 8041. PL. Gr. 8 fol. (129-36). 200 Grantha-s. Slightly variant readings. Title: Paribhāṣā-lakṣaṇa. Presented in 1948-49 by Sri Mridangam Subbaiyer, Chattapuram Village, Kalpathi, Palghat.

Mysore ND II 3967 (P 7599). PL. Gr. 15 fol. Extract no. 319.

Mysore ND II 3968 (P 7627). PL. Gr. 7 fol.

PUL I, p. 24 (no.150). 8 fol.

PUL II. App. p. 12 (no.187). PL. Gr. 6 fol. 120 Grantha-s (Paribhāṣā-lakṣaṇa).

PUL II. App. p. 14 (no.225). PL. Gr. 42 fol. (Jaimini-śākhīyā).

Tirupati SVUORI 7345 (2356). PL. Gr. Incomplete.

Tirupati SVUORI 7358 (853). PL. Gr. (See Sāmaveda-lakṣaṇa-grantha).

Trav. Uni. 1010 A. PL. Gr. 125 Grantha-s.

Trav. Uni. 2915 D. PL. Gr. 100 Grantha-s. (Sāma-paribhāṣā-sūtra).

Trav. Uni. 6588 A. PL. Gr. 80 Grantha-s. Incomplete.

Trav. Uni. 13677 B. PL. Gr. 100 Grantha-s. Incomplete.

VOHD II 7.2321 (cod.Palmbl. I 6. StUB, Hamburg). PL. Gr. 12 fol. (1-12).

Ptd.: ed. by Krishnaswami Srauti (in Grantha script). – Tiruvadi : Girvanavani Vilasa Press, 1891. 36 pp. (Title page: Kauthuma-śākhā-paribhāṣā – Sāmagānām atyantopakārāya rāmacandrākhya-śrauti-sūnunā śrīmatpañcanadakṣetravāstavyena prayāgakulatilakena kṛṣṇasvāmiśrautisamākhyena sūriṇā pariśodhya ... pañcāpakeśākhyasya gīrvāṇavāṇīvilāsamudrākṣaraśālāyāṃ mudritam | khara āni). [Adyar (H 211.3 SP Kri); SAI (87/782*)]

It contains the following tracts:

Svarāṅka-vinyāsa .... pp. 4-5
Sāmasvara-nirṇaya .... pp. 6-8
Ārcika-svara-lakṣaṇa .... pp. 9-12
Salakṣaṇa-paribhāṣā .... pp. 13-33
Sāma-lakṣaṇa .... pp. 34-36

1445 SĀMA-PARIŚIṢṬA (**सामपरिशिष्ट**)

Ptd.: critically edited with an introduction and translation by K. V. Sarma. – Pilani, 20. → Hitavākya. [VB 4, p. 75]

1446 SĀMA-PRAKĀŚANA (**सामप्रकाशन**)

of Prītikara, a treatise on the arrangement, metres, etc. of the chants of the *Sāmaveda* in the order of the Grāmageya- , Āraṇya-, Ūha-, and Ūhya-gāna-s, composed in 974 (cf. CC II 169b; but see RASB II 1331.

Beginning:

गजवदनचरणकमलं नत्वा सामप्रकाशनं ग्रन्थम् ।
रचयति सामसमूहात् प्रीतिकरः सारमुद्धृत्य ॥ १॥

यद्यपि मया निबद्धो लक्षणनिवहस्य दर्पणे साम्नाम्।
एकद्वित्रिप्रभृतिभिरुक्तिभिरत्र कीर्तितो भवति॥ २॥
सं त्वा हित्वेति कथितमृग्वर्जितमेकमेवात्र।
स्तोभादि निर्मितमस्मात्र कथितमित्यपरम्॥
पञ्चग्रहणं पञ्चपदं पञ्चविवृत्तिकं समाख्यातम्।
वेये यस्ते नूनामिति सामैवं नान्यत्र॥
एकं सप्तस्वरयुतं वेये साम प्रकीर्तितम्।

End:

इदं श्रेष्ठं ज्योतिषां ज्योतिरिरिति नवाक्षरं तुल्यम् । तं होतारमध्वरस्य प्रचेतसमिष्कर्तारमध्वरस्य प्रचेतसम् इति दशाक्षरं च तुल्यम् ॥ चतुःपञ्चषट्पर्यन्तानामक्षराणामक्षराणां पदानि त्यक्तानि बहुत्वात्॥

मिश्रितमिदमिति सुखदं कौतुकसहितं दुर्घटश्लोकैः।
प्रीतिकरेण यथाक्रममुदितं सामगानस्य सर्वस्य॥ १॥

इति प्रीतिकरत्रिवेदिप्रणीतं सामप्रकाशनं समासम्।

Baroda 12915. 33 fol. 530 Grantha-s. = CLB I, p. 38. Dated V.S. 1718.
BORI 76 of 1879-80. 26 fol. 450 Grantha-s. Dated V.S. 1462.
BORI 105 of 1886-92. 8 fol. 450 Grantha-s. Dated V.S. 1462.
Hoshiarpur p. 55 (no.6129). 21 fol. 550 Grantha-s.
IM 2184. 6 fol. Incomplete.
IO 4334 (Burnell 496m). Gr. 6 fol. Beginning is the same as printed in *Uṣā*.
Mysore ND II 3969 (C 2170). Na. 17 fol. Extract no. 320.
P 6.
Peters. IV p. 4 (no.105). 8 fol.
RASB II 1330 (G 1008). 20 fol. 500 Grantha-s.
RASB II 1331 (G 8362). 28 fol. 600 Grantha-s. Dated V.S. 1560.
SBD 2152. 1, 24 fol. Incomplete. Title: Sāma-tantra. Dated V.S. 1626.
Stein p. 10 (no. 151). 31 fol. Dated V.S. 1478. Extract p. 244.

Ptd.: in the collection of Sāmavedic tracts, ed. by Krishnaswami Srauti (in Grantha script). – Kumbakonam : Jyotirvilasa Press, 1885, pp. 60-87. See above under Chala-prakriyā. [SAI (87/783*)]

Also ed. by Satyavrata Samasrami (Sāmaprakāśanam – sāmagācāryaprītikarad-vivedipraṇītam), in the Sanskrit journal *Uṣā*. – Calcutta : Satya Press, Saṃ. 1951 (1895), vol. II, pt. 11. 43 pp. [SAI (85/1959*); Emeneau (86); BM : Ptd. Bks. Cat. 1906-1928, 778 (14010.c.43;vol.2.)]

[CC I 708b]

1447 SĀMA-PRAKRIYĀ-PARIBHĀṢĀ (**सामप्रक्रियापरिभाषा**)
Similar to the Prakṛti-chalākṣara. 35 verses.

BISM p. 315 (36/1668).
BISM p. 315 (36/1854).

1448 SĀMA-PRĀTIŚĀKHYA (सामप्रातिशाख्य)
Title of the Phulla-sūtra in some Mss. and also in the edition printed in the Sanskrit journal *Uṣā*.

Mysore I, p. 39.
Mysore ND II 3970. Extract no. 321 → Phulla-sūtra.

1449 SĀMA-PRĀTIŚĀKHYA-BHĀṢYA (सामप्रातिशाख्यभाष्य)
SBD 2121. 52 fol. Incomplete → Phulla-sūtra-bhāṣya Phulla-pota.

1450 SĀMA-PRĀTIŚĀKHYA-SAṂGRAHA (सामप्रातिशाख्यसंग्रह)
of M. Ramanatha Dikshita.

Ptd.: Part I, Kanchi : Śruti-smṛti-purāṇa-prakāśanasamiti, 1978. 56, ii pp.
Part II, 96, 8 pp. (no title page, no place and date of publication).

Part I contains the following works:
1. Ārcika-lakṣaṇaṃ savivaraṇam .... (pp. 1-6)
2. Hita-vākyaṃ savivaraṇam .... (pp. 6-10)
3. Avagraha-sūtraṃ savivaraṇam .... (pp. 10-13)
4. Nāradīya-śikṣā-saṃgrahaḥ savivaraṇaḥ .... (pp. 14-30)
5. Chanda-ārcika-lakṣaṇam .... (p. 31)
6. Ārcika-chalākṣarāṇi .... (p. 31)
7. Chandaḥ-pada-chalākṣarāṇi .... (p. 32)
8. Chanda-ārcika-chalākṣara-vivaraṇam .... (pp. 32-35)
9. Pūrvārcika-padānāṃ Chalākṣara-vivaraṇam .... (pp. 35-36)
10. Chandoviciti-sūtraṃ savivaraṇam .... (pp. 37-56)

Part II contains:
1. Uttara-ṛkchalākṣaram .... (pp. 1-9)
2. Uttara-ṛkpada-chalākṣaram .... (pp. 10-18)
3. Uttara-ṛkpada-hitavākyam .... (pp. 18-22)
4. Ṛktantraṃ vivaraṇasahitam .... (pp. 22-92)
5. Ṛktantra-vivṛti .... (pp. 93-96)

[SAI (ind 51 D 587/724)]

1451 SĀMA-BHAKTI (सामभक्ति)
Mysore ND II 3972 (B 1148). Kan. 12 fol. Incomplete (Paṭala-s 18-21).

1452 SĀMA-RAHASYA (सामरहस्य)
Mysore ND II 3974 (P 8007). PL. Na. 181 fol. Incomplete. Extract no. 322.

1453 SĀMA-RAHASYA-CCHALĀKṢARĪ (सामरहस्यच्छलाक्षरी)
Mysore I, p. 39.

1454 SĀMA-LAKṢAṆA (1) (सामलक्षण)
Also called Svara-paribhāṣā and Sāma-paribhāṣā.
Brl. p. 44 (no.CXXXIII) = IO 4338.
IO 4338 (Burnell 147). PL. Gr. 15 fol. The same as the one printed. Cf. MD vol. I, pp. 71-78.

[CC I 708b]

1455 SĀMA-LAKṢAṆA (2) (सामलक्षण)
A brief treatise explaining in Sanskrit and Tamil the notation used in Gāna-s of the Jaiminīya school of the *Sāmaveda*.
IO 4339 (Burnell 497c). Gr. 2 fol. Written ca. 1878.

1456 SĀMA-LAKṢAṆA (3) (सामलक्षण)
PUL II. App. p. 14 (no.225). PL. Gr. 42 fol.

1457 SĀMA-LAKṢAṆA-DĪPIKĀ (सामलक्षणदीपिका)
Consists of three sections; the first section called Pūrva-pīṭhikā, deals with the same subject as the Rāvaṇa-bheṭ, and claims to be clearer than the latter; the second section is called paribhāṣā, and the third (unnamed) contains a list of symbolic terms used for denoting numerals.
Adyar D I 1069 (33 D 12 = 75239). PL. Gr. 6 fol. (59-64). = Adyar I, p. 54a.
Adyar D I 1070 (33 E 7 = 75254). PL. Gr. 8 fol. (23-40).

1458 SĀMA-VICĀRA (सामविचार)
Adyar D I 1071 (8 F 79 = PM 130). 4 fol. (1-4).

1459 SĀMA-VIDHĀNA-BRĀHMAṆĀNUKRAMAṆIKĀ (सामविधानब्राह्मणानुक्रमणिका)
Mysore ND II 3975 (P 6645/ 2). PL. Na. 1 fol. (115). Extract no. 323.

1460 SĀMA-VEDA-GĀNA-PARIBHĀṢĀ (सामवेदगानपरिभाषा)
→ Sāma-paribhāṣā.
IM 2311. 8 fol. (2-9).

1461 SĀMA-VEDA-GĀNA-LAKṢAṆA (SAṂJÑĀ-PRAKARAṆA) (सामवेदगानलक्षण / संज्ञाप्रकरण)
Śg. I 21. Tel. 51 pp. (2 Praśna-s). Extract pp. 68-69. The same as MD 894 described as Gāyatrī-gāna-lakṣaṇa → Akṣara-tantra.

1462 SĀMA-VEDA-CCHALĀKṢARA (GĀNĀNUKRAMAṆĪ) (सामवेदच्छलाक्षर / गानानुक्रमणी)
Adyar D XIII 210 (VB 75a). PL. Gr. 11 fol. cf. TD 499.
Oxf. II 868(5) (Ms. Wilson 510). 20 fol. (113-131). Dated A.D. 1625. = Oxf. 387a (no.510).

[CC I 709b]

1463 SĀMA-VEDA-PARIBHĀṢĀ see SĀMA-PARIBHĀṢĀ (सामवेदपरिभाषा)
MD 17070. PL. Gr. 21 pp. 131 Grantha-s.
MT 238(b). PL. Gr. 16 fol. (170-85). Presented in 1910-11 by S. Ramakrishna Vadhyar of Palghat.

1464 SĀMA-VEDA-PRAKĀŚANA see SĀMA-PRAKĀŚANA (सामवेदप्रकाशन)

1465 SĀMA-VEDA-PRĀTIŚĀKHYA (सामवेदप्रातिशाख्य)
→ Ṛktantra-vyākaraṇa.
BISM p. 315 (22/982). Dated Śaka 1681.

1466 SĀMA-VEDA-PUṢPA-SŪTRA (सामवेदपुष्पसूत्र)
→ Phulla-sūtra.
GJKSV 41918. 67 fol.

1467 SĀMA-(VEDA-)LAKṢAṆA (1) (साम-(वेद-)लक्षण)
Adyar D I 1072 (33 D 12 = 75239). PL. Gr. 8 fol. (101-08). = Adyar I, p. 54a.
Adyar D I 1073 (33 E 7 = 75254). PL. Gr. 6 fol. (43b-48b).

1468 SĀMA-(VEDA-)LAKṢAṆA (2) (साम-(वेद-)लक्षण)
Different from the above. A treatise on the modes of chanting the hymns of the *Sāmaveda*.
MD 14079. PL. Na. 7 pp. Begins with the verse: gajaḍādyāḥ ... (cf. Ghoṣavarṇa, IO 4509) and ends with:

अकारे पञ्च एको ना आकारे द्वौ षडेव वा।
इवर्णे सप्त वा त्रिर्वा उवर्णे चतुरष्ट वा॥
एते ओ औ इत्येते अनवग्रहाः ॥

1469 SĀMA-VEDA-LAKṢAṆA-GRANTHA (सामवेदलक्षणग्रन्थ)
Tirupati SVUORI 7358 (853). PL. Gr. 69 fol. It contains: Prakṛti-cchalākṣara, Ūhaccha-lākṣara, Rahasya-cchalākṣara and Sāma-paribhāṣā.

1470 SĀMA-VEDA-VIMARŚA (सामवेदविमर्श)
An essay on the *Sāmaveda* and its Brāhmaṇa-s, in prose by an anonymous modern author who mentions Max Müller.
Adyar D I 1074 (33 D 12 = 75239). PL. Gr. 4 fol. (19-22).

1471 SĀMA-VEDA-VIṢAYA-CARCĀ-PATRĀṆI (सामवेदविषयचर्चापत्राणि)
Trav. Uni. 3368. PL. Gr. 110 Grantha-s.

1472 SĀMA-VEDA-ŚIKṢĀ (सामवेदशिक्षा)
"On the pronunciation of the different consonants and vowels in the Sāmaveda".
Oudh XIII 26 (no.56). 56 pp. 400 Grantha-s. Dated A.D. 1846. Belonged to Pandit Kesava Prasada of Unao.

[CC I 709b]

1473 SĀMA-VEDA-SAPTA-LAKṢAṆA (सामवेदसप्तलक्षण)

The opening verses of the Vilaṅghya and the Napara-tapara mention Nārāyaṇa and Śaurisūnu as the respective authors who are also the authors of similar works belonging to the Yajurveda. It consists of: Śamāna (17 verses), Visargalopa (3 verses), Raṅga (3 verses), Vilaṅghya (4 verses, 8 prose passages and 6 verses), Napara-Tapara (7 and 12 verses), Avaraṇi (41 verses), Āvraṇi (8 verses), Anavagraha (20 verses).

Beginning:

शमानम् :

अकारः प्लुतपूर्वो यो घोषवद्व्यञ्जनोत्तरः ।
शसकारपरश्चैव विसर्गः स तु लुप्यते॥ १॥
संहितायामृचां तानि पदान्यत्र विवृण्महे।
घोषवन्ति व्यञ्जनानि हकारो गजडादयः ॥ २॥

End:

अया पवस्व चाध्वर्येतो न्विन्द्र मेन्दुमिन्द्र तु।
कया त्वं नः सोम मह त्वमिन्द्र प्र समस्य तु॥ १३७॥
इन्द्रमिद् देव पवमाना अ स रेवाँ इ प्रसो ऽग्नि रि।
अग्निर्जागा त्वेन्द्र याहि यम अक्ष इतिसंख्यकाः ॥ १३८॥

Adyar D I 1075 (33 D 12 = 75239). PL. Gr. 9 fol. (28-36). = Adyar I, p. 54b.

Adyar D I 1076 (33 E 7 = 75254). PL. Gr. 7 fol. (54-60). It contains: Śamāna, Visargalopa, Raṅga, Vilaṅghya, Napara-tapara, Avarṇi, Anavagraha.

Baroda 9911(d). PL. Gr. 10 fol. 550 Grantha-s. = CLB I, p. 38. Contains: Śamāna, Vilaṅghya, Napara, Tapara, Avarṇi, Āvarṇi and Avagraha-lakṣaṇa. Extract p. 169.

Ptd.: ed. by Suryakanta, on the basis of the Adyar Ms. together with Laghu-ṛktantra-saṃgraha. – Lahore, 1940. 10, 22, 64, 56, 16 pp.

Reprinted : New Delhi : Meharchand Lachhmandas, 1982. [BORI (40821); UBTÜ (23 A 8760); SAI (ind 51 D 784/1527)]

1474 SĀMA-VEDA-SARVĀNUKRAMAṆIKĀ or SĀMA-VEDA-SŪCĪ (सामवेदसर्वानुक्रमणिका / सामवेदसूची)

A kind of Anukramaṇī of the *Sāmaveda* literature in about 25 verses.

Beginning:

सप्त गानानि साम्नां वै ब्राह्मणान्यष्ट वै स्मृताः ।
दश सूक्तानि सप्तापि दश लक्षणमिष्यते॥
तत एषां स्वरूपं तु कथ्यते ऽत्र समासतः ।
गायत्रं प्रथमं गानमाग्नेयं तु द्वितीयकम्॥

End:

पञ्चविंशतिसंख्याथ ब्राह्मणानां च सूचिका।
सूत्रलक्षणसूचीभ्यामाहृत्याङ्कवनं स्मृतम्॥
सर्वानुक्रमणी नाम इदं ग्रन्थस्य निर्मिता (?)।
श्रौतस्मार्तप्रयोगाणां ग्रन्थाख्याः सम्यगीरिताः॥
ज्योतिष्टोमस्य यत् तन्त्रं समारभ्य हि विश्वजित्।
छन्दोगस्य प्रयोगस्य वृत्तिरेषा प्रदीपिका॥
कृता त्रैविद्यवृद्धेन तालवृन्तनिवासिना।
पुरुषोत्तमभट्टीयं प्रयोगस्यैष एव तु॥

Adyar D I 1077 (33 D 12 = 75239). PL. Gr. 2 fol. (17-18). = Adyar I, p. 54a.
Adyar D I 1078 (33 E 7 = 75254). PL. Gr. 1 fol. (no. 51). The former owner was Pudukottai Pañju Śāstrin.

Ptd.: at the end of the Ṛktantra, ed. by Suryakanta. – Lahore, 1933. Reprinted : Delhi (Daryaganj) : Meharchand Lachhmandas, 1970. For details about the ascription of this to Tālavṛnta-nivāsin see under Adyar D I 1077 and *The Adyar Library Bulletin*, vol. V, pt. 2 (1941). Manuscripts Notes.

1475 SĀMA-VEDA-SARVĀNUKRAMAṆĪ (सामवेदसर्वानुक्रमणी)
A catalogue of the ancillary treatises, together with an account of the divisions of each, belonging to the *Sāmaveda* in about 75 verses.

Adyar D I 1079 (33 D 12 = 75239). PL. Gr. 5 fol. (23-27). = Adyar I, p. 54a.
Adyar D I 1080 (33 E 7 = 75254). PL. Gr. 3 fol. (20-22).

Ptd.: ed. by Suryakanta (omitting the first 3 lines) at the end of the Ṛktantra (see above). – Lahore, 1933. See remarks at Adyar D I 1079 and *The Adyar Library Bulletin*, vol. V, pt. 2 (1941). Manuscripts Notes.

1476 SĀMA-VEDĀNUKRAMAṆIKĀ (सामवेदानुक्रमणिका)
Alwar 250.

[CC II 233b]

1477 SĀMA-VEDĀRṢEYA-DĪPA see ĀRṢEYA-DĪPA (सामवेदार्षेयदीप)

1478 SĀMA-VEDĪYA-TAṆḌĀ-LAKṢAṆA-SŪTRA (सामवेदीयतण्डालक्षणसूत्र)
→ Taṇḍā-lakṣaṇa-sūtra.
Trav. Uni. 11802. 250 Grantha-s.

1479 SĀMA-VAIBHAVA (सामवैभव)
Mysore ND II 3973 (P 3277/ 2). PL. Gr. 14 fol. Incomplete.

1480 SĀMA-ŚAMĀNA-PADĀNI (सामशमानपदानि)
MD 14078. PL. Na. 3 pp.

1481 SĀMA-SAṂKHYĀ (सामसंख्या)
A Pariśiṣṭa of the *Sāmaveda*.
Oxf. II 855(10) (Ms. Wilson 375). 1 fol. (57). Dated A.D. 1582. = Oxf. 377b (no.375).
[CC I 710a]

1482 SĀMA-SARVĀNUKRAMAṆĪ (सामसर्वानुक्रमणी)
Beginning:

॥ ··· मसानि त्रीणि सर्वाणि पादौदानि ॥ १२ ॥ इन्द्रस्य प्रमन्दिष्ठाय ॥ १४ ॥ अर्धः प्रपाठकः । १४ + १४ = २८। ष्टीगवं च। इति प्रथमः प्रपाठकः। इन्द्रस्य च भरद्वाजस्य। १२ + १२। द्वितीयः । आयास्यं माण्ड्वं च वसिष्ठस्यापदासे ··· ॥

SBD 2370. 4 fol. (3-6). Incomplete (no beginning and no end).

1483 SĀMA-SĀRA-SARVASVA (सामसारसर्वस्व)
of M. Ramanatha Dikshita. A conspectus of over 90 works of the Kauthuma Śākhā (mantra-brāhmaṇa-śrauta-gṛhyasūtra-prātiśākhyādi- navatyadhika- granthānāṃ viṣaya-saṃgrahātmakam) (Kauthuma).

Ptd.: Madras, 1972. 3, xvi, 323 pp. [BORI : 26740] [Adyar (H 211.3 z Ram SS); UBTÜ (16 A 13046); SAI (ind 50 B 87/727)]

1484 SĀMA-SŪTRA (सामसूत्र)
Mysore I, p. 614. Cf. Mysore ND II 3959: Sāma-tantra.

1485 SĀMA-SŪTRA-VYĀKHYĀ (?) (सामसूत्रव्याख्या)
of Varadarāja.
Khn. p. 10 (no.38). 162 fol. Dated Śaka 1742; Ashṭe Limaye.
[CC I 710a]

1486 SĀMA-SVARA (1) (सामस्वर)
A fragment of a text on the accents and notes of the *Sāmaveda*.

Beginning: (IO)

अवरोहोद्गमो यानावर्त्तक्षेपणमर्शने।
अवरुह्योद्गम्य यात्वावर्त्तक्षेपणमर्शने॥
क्षेप(ण)मर्शनयोरैक्यं मर्दान्वङ्गुलिमर्दनम्।
उच्चनीचैरुपक्रम्योत्ताननं केवलं च तत्॥

End:

अजा वदति गान्धारं क्रौञ्चो वदति मध्यमम्॥
पुष्पसाधारणे काले कोकिलो वक्ति पञ्चमम्॥

प्रावृट्काले तु संप्राप्ते धैवतं दर्दुरो वदेत्।
सर्वदा च तथा चापि निषादं वदते चिजः (? द्विजः) ॥

IO 4341 (Burnell 499c). Gr. 2 fol. (39b-40a). Written ca. A.D. 1878.

1487 SĀMA-SVARA (2) (सामस्वर)
A short treatise on the notation of the svara-s, notes of the *Sāmaveda*, by the use of the fingers.

Beginning: (IO)

हस्तेन वेदं यो ऽधीते स्वरवर्णार्थसंयुतम्।
ऋग्यजुःसामभिः पूतो ब्रह्मलोके महीयते॥
स्वरं सप्तविधं प्रोक्तमङ्गुष्ठेनाङ्गुलीषु च।
क्रुष्टो ऽप्यङ्गुष्ठतर्जन्योरग्रसंश्लेषमेव च॥

End:

क्षेपमर्शनयोरैक्यं सर्वे युग्मं स्वराश्च ये।
ते सर्वे ऽभीष्टदाः सामवेदिनां महतामिह॥

IO 4342 (Burnell 497f). Gr. 2 fol. (13-14). Written ca. A.D. 1878.

1488 SĀMA-SVARA-NIRṆAYA (सामस्वरनिर्णय)
→ Āraṇya-sāma-prakāśikā. Adyar D I 738.

1489 SĀMĀNUKRAMAṆĪ (सामानुक्रमणी)
Mysore ND II 3976 (P 396/ 3). PL. Na. 1 fol.
Mysore ND II 3977 (P 5160/ 3). PL. Na. 6 fol. (135-40). Extract no.324.

1490 SĀMĀṢṬĀDAŚA-LAKṢAṆA (सामाष्टादशलक्षण)
Mysore I, p. 614.
Mysore ND II 3978 (A 642/10). Kan. 104 fol. (39-142). Extract no. 325. Dated 6.8.1919.

1491 SĀMOHA-CCHALĀKṢARA (सामोहच्छलाक्षर)
Mysore I, p. 39.

1492 SIDDHĀNTA-CANDRIKĀ (सिद्धान्तचन्द्रिका)
Title of the Svara-siddhānta-candrikā in the colophon of GD III 837.

1493 SIDDHĀNTA-ŚIKṢĀ (सिद्धान्तशिक्षा)
of Śrīnivāsa Makhin. 74 śloka-s.

Beginning:

संप्रणम्य सकलैककारणं ब्रह्मरुद्रमुखमौलिभूषणम्।

लक्षणं श्रुतिगिरां विलक्षणं श्रीनिवासमखिना प्रणीयते ॥
पूर्वशिक्षाः परामृश्य प्रातिशाख्यं च सर्वशः ।
सिद्धान्तशिक्षां वक्ष्यामि वेदभाष्यानुसारिणीम् ॥
अकारादिपदानां स्यादत्रोदाहरणक्रमः ।
आदिमध्यान्ततस्तत्र यावद् वेदं निरूप्यते ॥

End:

हीडिते महिसाहीति छिन्नाः केचन संशयाः ।
अनन्तसंशयाञ्छेत्तुमनन्तः परमेश्वरः ॥
श्रीनिवासाध्वरीन्द्रेण चतुष्कुलसुधांशुना ।
श्लोकाः सिद्धान्तशिक्षायां चतुःसप्ततिरीरिताः ॥

Adyar D I 1081 (19 G 2 = 66403). PL. Gr. 4 fol. = Adyar I, p. 53b. Incomplete. Breaks off in verse 39.
Adyar D I 1082 (19 G 12 = 66413). PL. Gr. 3 fol. (1b-3a). = Adyar I, p. 53b. Incomplete. One fol. containing verses 13-41 is missing.
Adyar D I 1083 (25 H 6 = 70967). PL. Gr. 6 fol. (19ff.). = Adyar I, p. 53b.
Adyar D I 1084 (30 H 35 = 74080). PL. Gr. 3 fol. (76ff.). Incomplete. Verses 21-33 missing. = Adyar I, p. 53b.
Adyar D I 1085 (19 G 9 = 66410). PL. Gr. 25 fol. (with C.). = Adyar I, p. 53b.
Adyar D I 1086 (19 K 52 = 66673). PL. Gr. 24 fol. (13ff.) (with C.).
Adyar D I 1087 (29 I 28 = 73580). PL. Gr. 38 fol. (with C.). = Adyar I, p. 53b.
Adyar D XIII 333 (VB 67a). PL. Gr. 4 fol.
Adyar D XIII 334 (VB 132c). PL. Gr. 8 fol.
Baroda 6381(a). PL. Gr. 36 fol. 900 Grantha-s (with C.) = CLB I, p. 38.
Baroda 10006(c). PL. Gr. 28 fol. 900 Grantha-s (with C.)= CLB I, p. 38.
Brl. p. 8 (no.XXVI) = IO 4963.
Brl. p. 9 (no.XXVII) = IO 4964.
GB 37. 33 fol. (with C.). Copied for Kielhorn in Mysore in 1875. See F. Kielhorn : Remarks on the Śikṣās in : *Indian Antiquary*, vol. V, p. 198 (reprint in : *Kleine Schriften*, vol. I, pp. 158-69).
Gough p. 162. Gr.
Hamburg StUB (cod.Palmbl. III 8/133) → Veda-lakṣaṇa (HB).
Hoshiarpur p. 55 (no.4371). PL. Gr. 41 fol. 500 Grantha-s (with C.).
Hoshiarpur p. 301 (no.4371). PL. Gr. 3 fol. 100 Grantha-s.
IO 4963 (Burnell 41b). PL. Gr. 10 fol.
IO 4964 (Burnell 350i). Tel. 33 fol. (72-104) (with C.). A.D. 1867.
MD 1008. 10 pp. (8ff.).
MD 1009. PL. Tel. 7 pp. (36ff.).
MD 1010. Gr. 9 pp. (112ff.).
MD 1011. PL. Tel. 9 pp. (39ff.). Title: Siddhānta-lakṣaṇa.
MD 1012. Gr. 77 pp. (74ff.) (with C.). .... (= Skt. Texts on Phonetics, pp. 580-625).
MD 1013. PL. Tel. 126 pp. (1ff.) (with C.).

MD 15848. PL. Gr. 94 pp. 705 Grantha-s (with C.).
MD 15958. PL. Gr. 12 pp. 83 Grantha-s.
MD 16718. PL. Tel. 67 pp. 938 Grantha-s (with C.).
MD 17445. PL. Gr. 2 pp. 10 Grantha-s. Only a fragment of the beginning.
MT 95(e). PL. Gr. 3 fol. (12-14). Purchased in 1910-11 from Gopalaswami Ayyangar of Mannargudi.
MT 2881(g). PL. Gr. 2 fol. (38-39). Fol. 39-40 contain Jaṭā-lakṣaṇa, Svarabhakti and a few Veda-lakṣaṇa-vacanāni. Presented in 1918-19 by Venkatagiri Appalacharyar of Triplicane.
MT 3131(h). PL. Gr. 54 fol. (27-81) (with C.). Copied by Śeṣagiri. Dated Tuesday, the 11th day of Cittirai in the year Khara. Presented in 1919-20 by Venkatarama Vadhyar of Brahmadesam Village, Tinnavelly Dist.
MT 3887(l). PL. Gr. 18 fol. (89-106) (with C.). Purchased in 1921-22 from Annasvami Sastrigal, Bhavani, Coimbatore Dist.
Mysore p. 2 (no. 51). 29 fol. (with C.).
Mysore I, p. 40 (7 Mss.; 4 of them with C.).
Mysore ND II 3979-85. Extract no. 326.
Mysore ND II 3986-90. (With C.). Extract no. 327.
Mysore Skt. Coll. p. 2 = D. No.18 (928). PL. Gr. 206 fol. (with C.).
Oppert I 1063. Belonged to Viraraghava Tatacharyar, Head Master, Sanskrit School of Sathakopacharya, Kanchipuram, Chingelpet Dist.
Oppert I 2485. PL. Gr. 97 pp. Belonged to Sri Sarasvati Bhandaram Committee of Tiruvallikkeni, Madras.
Oppert I 7157. Belonged to Pola Lakshmanavadhani of Vijayanagaram.
Oppert II 3894. Belonged to Sarasvati Bhandara of Melkote, Mysore Dist.
Oppert II 5807. Belonged to Shingaracharyar of Kalyanapuram, Thanjavur Dist.
Oppert II 7462. Belonged to Venkatarama Sastri of Pillur, Mayavaram Taluk.
Oppert II 7994. Belonged to Venkatarama Dikshita of Sorakayur, Thanjavur Dist.
Oppert II 9126. Belonged to Ganápati Lakshminarayana Sastri of Tiruvadi, Thanjavur Dist.
Oppert II 9887. Belonged to M.Raja Ghanapathi of Mahadanapuram, Trichinapalli.
PUL I, p. 25 (no.152). PL. Tel. 20 fol. 250 Grantha-s.
PUL I, p. 25 (no.153). PL. Gr. 5 (32-37). 66 Grantha-s.
PUL I, p. 25 (no.154). PL. Gr. 4 fol.
Taylor I 276.
Tirupati SVUORI 7639 (4378c). PL. Gr. 4 fol. (24-27).
Tirupati SVUORI 7640 (4411d). PL. Gr. (with C.).
Trav. Uni. 2938 A. PL. Gr. 85 Grantha-s.
Trav. Uni. 4028 A. PL. Gr. 680 Grantha-s (with C.).
Whish 216(a). PL. Gr. (with C.). Not described in the catalogue.

[CC I 721a]

– C. All the Mss. below contain the text also.
Beginning:

भारद्वाज-व्यास-पाणिनि- शंभु-कौहल-वसिष्ठ-वाल्मीकि-हारीत-बोधायनोक्त-शिक्षादिकं परामृश्य तदनुक्तसंदिग्धपदान्यालोच्य त्रिभाष्यरत्नवैदिकाभरणादि व्याख्यानपुरःसरतया कृत्स्नं प्रातिशाख्यं च परामृश्य वेदभाष्यानुसारिणीं भट्टभास्करादिशोधनजन्यतया विश्वसनीयां दुष्पाठपरित्यागे निष्कम्पप्रवृत्तिहेतुभूतं च सिद्धान्तशिक्षां वक्ष्यामि।

Adyar D I 1085 (19 G 9 = 66410). PL. Gr. 25 fol. = Adyar I, p. 53b.
Adyar D I 1086 (19 K 52 = 66673). PL. Gr. 24 fol. (13ff.).
Adyar D I 1087 (29 I 28 = 73580). PL. Gr. 38 fol. = Adyar I, p. 53b.
Baroda 6381(a). PL. Gr. 36 fol. 900 Grantha-s. = CLB I, p. 38.
Baroda 10006(c). PL. Gr. 28 fol. 900 Grantha-s. = CLB I, p. 38.
Brl. p. 9 (no.XXVII) = IO 4964.
Hoshiarpur p. 55 (no.4371). PL. Gr. 41 fol. 500 Grantha-s.
IO 4964 (Burnell 350i). Tel. 33 fol. (72-104). A.D. 1867.
MD 1012. Gr. 77 pp. (74ff.). .... (= Skt. Texts on Phonetics, pp. 580-625).
MD 1013. PL. Tel. 126 pp. (1ff.).
MD 15848. PL. Gr. 94 pp. 705 Grantha-s.
MD 16718. PL. Tel. 67 pp. 938 Grantha-s.
MT 3131(h). PL. Gr. 54 fol. (27-81). Copied by Śeṣagiri. Dated Tuesday, the 11th day of Cittirai in the year Khara. Presented in 1919-20 by Venkatarama Vadhyar of Brahmadesam Village, Tinnavelly Dist.
MT 3887(l). PL. Gr. 18 fol. (89-106). Purchased in 1921-22 from Annasvami Ṣastrigal, Bhavani, Coimbatore Dist.
Mysore p. 2 (no. 51). 29 fol.
Mysore I, p. 40 (4 Mss.).
Mysore ND II 3986-90. Extract no. 327.
Mysore Skt. Coll. p. 2 = D. No.18 (928). PL. Gr. 206 fol.
Tirupati SVUORI 7640 (4411d). PL. Gr.
Trav. Uni. 4028 A. PL. Gr. 680 Grantha-s.
Whish 216(a). PL. Gr. Not described in the catalogue.

[CC I 721a]

1494 SIDDHĀNTA-ŚIKṢĀ-VYĀKHYĀNUKRAMAṆĪ (सिद्धान्तशिक्षाव्याख्यानुक्रमणी)
Mysore ND II 3991 (P 977/ 1). PL. Tel. 1 fol. Extract no. 328.

1495 SIDDHĀNTA-SVARA-KAUMUDĪ (सिद्धान्तस्वरकौमुदी)
→ Svara-prakriyā section of the Siddānta-kaumudī.
GJKSV 34721. 36 fol. Incomplete.

*SĪTĀPATI (सीतापति)
Son of Śaṃkara-bhaṭṭa.
– Lakṣaṇa-traya-lakṣaṇa. PUL II. App. p. 13 (no.202).

***SĪTĀRĀMA PARALĪKARA (सीतारामपरलीकर)**
– Veda-mukha. K 12.

[CC I 604b]

***SUNDARA-ŚUKLA (सुन्दरशुक्ल)**
– Maunamantrāvabodha. Ptd.: ed. by Pandit Ram Sakala Misra, at the end of the Śuklayajuḥ-sarvānukrama. – Benares : Chowkhamba, 1893-1921. 35 pp. – (Ben. S. S. 12).

***SUBRAHMAṆYA ŚĀSTRIN (सुब्रह्मण्यशास्त्रिन्)**
– Pañcāśad-anukramaṇikā. Ptd. : See above.

1496 SŪKTA (सूक्त)
A short tract on the pronunciation of words, said to be well known to the Brahmana-s of Malbar.
TCD 30-C. Mal. 2 pp. 13 Grantha-s.
Trav. Uni. TM.276 C. PL. Mal. 15 Grantha-s.

1497 SŪKTA-PRATĪKA (सूक्तप्रतीक)
→ Anukramaṇikā-ḍhuṇḍhū and Ṛgveda-sarvānukramaṇī-vivaraṇa of Jagannātha.
Baroda 336.
GJKSV 13612. 67 fol. Dated V.S. 1908. Title: Ṛksaṃhitā-sūkta-pratīka.
GJKSV 32672. 34 fol. Incomplete.
Hpr. II 250. 56 fol. 1640 Grantha-s. Title: Ṛgveda-sūkta-pratīka.
SBD 53859. 85 fol. Dated V.S. 1867. (sūktasya ...).
Ujjain I, p. 10 (no.813). 134 pp. Dated V.S. 1929.
VSM III 174 (no.12178). 38 fol. Dated Śaka 1666. Col.: jagannāthakṛte anukramaṇikāvivaraṇe aṣṭāv aṣṭakāḥ samāptāḥ |
VSM III 175 (no.12180). 28 fol. Inc. Title : Saṃhitānukrama_ī.
Wai I 327. 63 fol. Dated Śaka 1743.
Wai I 328. 31 fol. Dated Śaka 1741. Title: Sūkta-pratīka-saṃkhyā-vivaraṇa.

1498 SŪKTA-PRATĪKĀNUKRAMAṆIKĀ(-SĀRA) (सूक्तप्रतीकानुक्रमणिका /-सार)
of Jagannātha → Anukramaṇikā-ḍhuṇḍhū and Ṛgveda-sarvānukramaṇī-vivaraṇa of Jagannātha.
Trav. Uni. 4915. 1100 Grantha-s. Dated V.S. 1796 / Śaka 1661.
VSM I 478-79.

1499 SŪKTA-PRATĪKARṢI-DAIVATA-CHANDONUKRAMA (सूक्तप्रतीकर्षिदैवतछन्दोनुक्रम)
→ Anukramaṇikā-ḍhuṇḍhū.
VSM I 480.

1500 SŪKTA-BODHĀṢṬAKA (सूक्तबोधाष्टक)
PUL II. App. p. 14 (no.226). PL. Mal. 1 fol. → Ṛgveda-sūkta-varga-saṃkhyā.

1501 SŪKTA-VARGA-SAṂKHYĀ (सूक्तवर्गसंख्या)
of Melapattur Nārāyaṇa-bhaṭṭa → Ṛgveda-sūkta-varga-saṃkhyā.
Trav. Uni. 1178 C. PL. Mal. 25 Grantha-s.
Trav. Uni. TM.276 D. PL. Mal. 25 Grantha-s. = TCD 30-D.

1502 SŪKTA-VĀKYA (सूक्तवाक्य)
Trav. Uni. TM.276 C. PL. Mal. 15 Grantha-s. = TCD 30-C.

1503 SŪKTA-ŚLOKĀḤ (सूक्तश्लोकाः)
of Melapattur Nārāyaṇa-bhaṭṭa → Ṛgveda-sūkta-varga-saṃkhyā.

1504 SŪKTA-SAṂGRAHA (सूक्तसंग्रह)
BHU C 5087 (D 1A/126). 68 fol. Incomplete.

1505 SŪKTĀNUKRAMAṆIKĀ (सूक्तानुक्रमणिका)
of Jagannātha → Ṛgveda-sarvānukrama-vivaraṇa.
Rep. Raj. and C. I. p. 3

1506 SŪKTĀNUKRAMAṆĪ (सूक्तानुक्रमणी)
Attributed to Śaunaka by Ṣaḍguru-śiṣya.
[CC I 730a]

1507 SŪKTĀNUVĀKA (सूक्तानुवाक)
of Mādhava; on the Sūkta-s occurring at the end of the Anuvāka-s ?
MD 19510 I. PL. Mal. 3. (90b-92a). (anon.).
TCD 34-G. 5 pp. 60 Grantha-s.
Trav. Uni. 4254 H. PL. Mal. 4 fol. 50 Grantha-s. Belonged to Vishnu Nambudiri of Ettikada Illam Ayankudi, Kaduttirutti, Kottayam.
Trav. Uni. T.223 G. = TCD 34-G. A transcript of the Ms. no. 4254.

***SŪRĀVADHĀNIN (सूरावधानिन्)**
See Sūryanārāyaṇa below.

***SŪRI-BHAṬṬA YAJVAN (सूरिभट्ट /-यज्वन्)**
– Ucca-svara-nirṇaya.
– Kriyā-svara-lakṣaṇa or Yajurveda-kriyā-svara-lakṣaṇa also known as the Yohi-bhāṣya.

***SŪRYA-NĀRĀYAṆA (सूर्यनारायण)**
Also known as Sūrāvadhānin of Velmikanyā-pura (Puttur in Andhra ?).
– C. on the Bhāradvāja-śikṣā.
– C. Vedataijasa on the Vyāsa-śikṣā.

***SOMADEVA (सोमदेव)**
– Chalaprakriyā. Chalaprakriyā Stein p. 15 (no. 267). 3 fol. Dated V.S. 1723.

***SOMAYĀRYA** (सोमयार्य)
– C. Tribhāṣya-ratna or Prātiśākhya-vivaraṇa on the *Taittirīya-prātiśākhya.*

***SOMEŚVARA** (सोमेश्वर)
– C. on Sarva-saṃmata-śikṣā. PUL I, p. 24 (no.148). Tel. 12 fol. (102-13).

1508 STOBHA-GATĀGATA (स्तोभगतागत)
Mysore I, p. 40.
Mysore ND II 3997 (P 1978/ 6). PL. Na. 4 fol. (14-17). Extract no. 329.
PUL II. App. p. 14 (no.227). 6 fol. Dated V.S. 1605.

1509 STOBHA-PADA (स्तोभपद)
Mysore ND II 3998 (P 334/ 5). PL. Na. 5 fol. (55-59).
Trav. Uni. 13753. PL. Mal. 225 Grantha-s.

1510 STOBHA-PADA-LAKṢAṆA (स्तोभपदलक्षण)
Adyar D I 1102 (33 D 12 = 75239). PL. Gr. 1 fol. (1a). The complete text is printed.

1511 STOBHA-BHĀṢYA (स्तोभभाष्य)
of Bhaṭṭa Śobhākara.

Ptd.: ed. by Mayuram Ramanatha Dikshita, together with Akṣara-tantra (with C. of Satya-vrata !). – Madras : Sir C. P. Ramaswami Iyer Foundation, "the Grove", 1984. 162 pp. [BORI (49260); SAI (ind B 287/725)]

1512 STOBHĀNUSAṂHĀRA (स्तोभानुसंहार)
In three Paṭala-s, consisting of 44 (16, 10, 18) verses.

Beginning:

आद्यन्तदर्शनस्तोभो विधागीतेषु सामसु।
पादे पादे ऽनुसंहार्यस्सोपायो निधने भवेत्॥
आदौ दृष्टश्च यत् स्तोभः पादशेषः पुनर्भवेत्।
स सर्वेषु च संहार्यः पादेषु स्तोभ इष्यते॥

End:

उद्धारः पुनराचार्यैः स्वाध्याये लाघवार्थिभिः।
प्रोक्तस्तस्मिन् प्रतिष्ठा च संहारस्तेन चेष्यते॥

Alwar 238.
IM 1955. 4 fol.
IO 4340 (Burnell 496j). Gr. 2 fol. Written ca. A.D. 1877.
Mysore ND II 3999 (A 642/ 9). Kan. 3 fol. (36-38). Extract no. 330.
Mysore ND II 4000 (P 491/ 5). PL. Na. 2 fol. (107-08).
Oxf. II 855(13) (Ms. Wilson 375). 6 fol. Dated A.D. 1582. = Oxf. 378a (no.375).

Peters. II, p. 180 (no.54). 4 fol.
PUL I, p. 132 (no.24). 25 fol. 600 Grantha-s (with other 5 SV works).
SB p. 35 (no.37). 4 fol. 44 Grantha-s. = SBD 3941.
SBD 3941. 4 fol. (10-13). (Stobhānusaṃhāra-sūtra ?). Incomplete. Dated V.S. 1722.
SBD 4000. 4 fol. (Stobhānusaṃhāra-kārikā).
SBD 4048. 1 fol. (Stobhānusaṃhāra-sūtra-pariśiṣṭa). Dated V.S. 1532.
Trav. Uni. 1732. 45 Grantha-s.
Trav. Uni. 5185 A. 45 Grantha-s. Dated V.S. 1558.

Ptd.: in the collection of Sāmavedic tracts, entitled Chalaprakriyādayo Granthāḥ, ed. by Krishnaswami Srauti (in Grantha script). – Kumbakonam : Jyotirvilasa Press, 1885, pp. 54-60. See above under Chala-prakriyā. [SAI (87/783*)]

[CC I 744a]

1513 STHAITYA (?) (स्थैत्य)
Mysore ND II 3037 (A 642/ 6). Kan. 1 fol. (18). Extract no. 2. Title in the catalogue: Aghasthaitya. Dated 6.8.1919. Cf. Adyar D I 395.

1514 SVARA-KĀRIKĀ (स्वरकारिका)
Ascribed to Kātyāyana.
Rep. Hpr. 1901-06, p. 3.

1515 SVARA-KAUMUDĪ or YĀJUṢA-SVARA-KAUMUDĪ (स्वरकौमुदी / याजुषस्वरकौमुदी)
Mysore ND II 4033 (P 2115). PL. Gr. 90 fol.

1516 SVARA-KRAMA (स्वरक्रम)
Mysore ND II 4034 (P 4772/23). PL. Tel. 5 fol. (9-13). Extract no. 336.

1517 SVARA-JÑĀNA (स्वरज्ञान)
17 verses on accent.
IM 2560. 1 fol. Col.: etat sarvaṃ mayākhyātaṃ yājñavalkyena dhīmatā | iti svarajñānam |

1518 SVARA-NIRṆAYA (स्वरनिर्णय)
Ptd.: in the collection of Sāmavedic tracts, ed. by Krishnaswami Srauti (in Grantha script). – Kumbakonam : Jyotirvilasa Press, 1885, pp. 104-12. See above under Chala-prakriyā. [SAI (87/783*)]

1519 SVARA-NIRṆAYA (स्वरनिर्णय)
→ Svarāṅkuśa of Jayanta-svāmin.

1520 SVARA-NIRDEŚA (स्वरनिर्देश)
on the method of showing the Svara-s through the movement of fingers.

Beginning:

पुरुषो ऽभिव्रजेन्नारीं न नारी पुरुषं व्रजेत् ।

तथाङ्गुलीषु सर्वासु नयेदङ्गुष्ठमेव तु ॥

End:

हस्तेन वेदं यो ऽधीते स्वरवर्णार्थसंयुतम्।
ऋग्यजुःसामभिः पूतो ब्रह्मलोके महीयते ॥
(Cf. Sarva-sammata-śikṣā)

Hoshiarpur p. 55 (no.4454). PL. Gr. 1 fol. 20 Grantha-s (ascribed to Kātyāyana). (A xerox-copy of a Devanāgarī transcript of this is in SAI : 87/794*).
MD 19510H. PL. Mal. 1 fol. (90a). Ten verses catalogued as Ṛgvidhāna.
TCD 34-N. 1 p. 10 Grantha-s.
Trav. Uni. T.223 N. = TCD 34-N.

1521 SVARA-PAÑCĀŚAT or SVARA-LAKṢAṆA (स्वरपञ्चाशत् / स्वरलक्षण)
TS.
Beginning:

अतीन्द्रियार्थविज्ञानं प्रणम्य ब्रह्म शाश्वतम्।
तैत्तिरीयपदादीनां वक्ष्यामि स्वरलक्षणम् (-संग्रहम्) ॥ १॥
उदात्तश्चानुदात्तश्च वर्णानां प्राकृतौ स्वरौ।
स्वरिताश्च द्वि(त्रि)धोच्यन्ते धृतः कम्पश्च सांहितः ॥ २॥

End:

नाध्यासितव्यान्तक्त्याश्च कुश्यौनायास्य च स्ययोः।
सादन्यं सवरं सख्या तथारथ्याकरुण्ययोः ॥
न्यङ्स्वर्युज्यं चिदा नाव्या ससौम्याश्चेति तादृशाः ।
अन्ये ऽप्यध्ययनाद् बोध्या अरुणोपनिषत्स्वराः ॥ ५० ॥

Adyar D I 984 → Veda-lakṣaṇa (A 2).
Adyar D I 989 → Veda-lakṣaṇa (A 7).
Adyar D I 1088 (19 G 12 = 66413). PL. Tel. 1 fol. (no. 6). Incomplete. Verses 1-17.
Adyar D I 1089 (21 I 14 = 68121). PL. Tel. 3 fol. Incomplete. Up to verse 41. = Adyar I, p. 49b. Title: Taittirīya-pada-svara-lakṣaṇa.
Adyar D I 1090 (22 P 20 = 68361). PL. Gr. 3 fol. (238-240). Incomplete. = Adyar II, App. p. iiia (40 G 20).
Adyar D XIII 203 (VB 132b). PL. Gr. 4 fol.
Adyar D XIII 204 (VB 461b). PL. Tel. 4 fol.
Adyar D XIII 205 (VB 132a). PL. Gr. 43 fol. (with C.).
Baroda 6381(b). PL. Gr. 17 fol. (37-53). 450 Grantha-s (with C.). = CLB I, p. 28. Extract p. 148. (Taittirīya-pada-svara-lakṣaṇa).
Baroda 8243. 30 fol. 600 Grantha-s (with C.). = CLB I, p. 39.
Baroda 10006(a). PL. Gr. 4 fol. 50 Grantha-s. = CLB I, p. 39.
Baroda 10006(b). PL. Gr. 28 fol. 600 Grantha-s (with C.). = CLB I, p. 39.

Brl. p. 9 (no.XXVIII, title : Lakṣaṇa or Svara-lakṣaṇa) = IO 4517.
Brl. p. 10 (no.XXIX) = IO 4518.
Hamburg StUB (cod.Palmbl. III 8/133) → Veda-lakṣaṇa (HB).
Hoshiarpur p. 55 (no.5613). PL. Gr. 5 fol. 100 Grantha-s. Extract pp. 414-15
Hoshiarpur p. 301 (no.5613). PL. Gr. 3 fol. 90 Grantha-s.
Hz 1432. PL. Gr. 33 fol. (with 3 other Veda-lakṣaṇa works). Title: Svara-lakṣaṇa. Belonged to the late Raja Ghanapathi of Tiruvidaimarudur, Thanjavur Dist.
IO 4517 (Burnell 41c). PL. Gr. 4 fol. (170-73). A.D. 1795.
IO 4518 (Burnell 146g). PL. Gr. 3 fol. (16-18).
IO 7848 (3776a). PL. Tel. 3 fol.
IO 7849 (3741). 28 fol. (with C.). Written ca. A.D. 1900.
IO 7850 (3776b). PL. Tel. 8 fol. (with C.).
MD 1017. PL. Tel. 5 pp. (1ff.).
MD 1019. PL. Tel. 6 pp. (60ff.). Incomplete. 45 verses.
MD 1020. PL. Tel. 5 pp. (20ff.). Incomplete. 46 verses.
MD 15927. PL. Gr. 41 pp. 817 Grantha-s (with C.).
MD 17435. PL. Gr. 6 pp. 65 Grantha-s.
MT 95(h). PL. Gr. 3 fol. (15-17). Lacks the first stanza. Purchased in 1910-11 from Gopalaswami Ayyangar of Mannargudi.
MT 3887(o). PL. Gr. 21 (115-35) (with C.). Purchased in 1921-22 from Annasvami Sastrigal, Bhavani, Coimbatore Dist.
Mysore (1898), p. 6 (no. 53b). 108 fol.
Mysore I, p. 40 (7 Mss.).
Mysore ND II 4035-48. Extract no. 337-39.
Oppert I 1066. Belonged to Viraraghava Tatacharyar, Head Master, Sanskrit School of Sathakopacharya, Kanchipuram, Chingelpet Dist.
Oppert II 786. Belonged to Ghanapathi Shingaracharyar of Alasur, Madurantakam Taluk.
Oppert II 1403. Belonged to Gopalacharyar of Pillapakkam, Kanchipuram Taluk.
Oppert II 5302. Belonged to Pichchu Dikshitar of Akhilandapuram, Thanjavur Dist.
Oppert II 6730. Belonged to P.Rangacharyar of Kumbakonam.
Oppert II 9888. Belonged to M.Raja Ghanapathi of Mahadanapuram, Trichinapalli.
PUL II. App. p. 14 (no.228). PL. Tel. 3 fol.
RASB II 489(II) (G 6175). 4 fol. (6-9). 55 Grantha-s.
TCD 40. 54 pp. 810 Grantha-s (with C.).
Tirupati SVUORI 7957 (3280b). PL. Gr. Incomplete.
Tirupati SVUORI 7958 (3516c). PL. Gr. 3 fol. (17-19). Incomplete.
Tirupati SVUORI 7959 (4378h). PL. Gr. 3 fol. (29-31).
Tirupati SVUORI 7960 (1143b). PL. Gr. 2 fol.
Trav. Uni. 124 A. PL. Gr. 50 Grantha-s.
Trav. Uni. 124 B. PL. Gr. 800 Grantha-s (with C.).
Trav. Uni. 2346 O. PL. Gr. 35 Grantha-s. Incomplete.
Trav. Uni. 2630 G. PL. Gr. 50 Grantha-s.
Trav. Uni. 3679 A. PL. Gr. 4 fol. 50 Grantha-s.
Trav. Uni. 3679 B. PL. Gr. 35 fol. 800 Grantha-s (with C.).
Trav. Uni. 4028 E. PL. Gr. 50 Grantha-s.

Trav. Uni. 5479 C. PL. Tel. 50 Grantha-s.

Trav. Uni. 8396 C. PL. Mal. 50 Grantha-s.

Trav. Uni. 8396 D. PL. Mal. 800 Grantha-s (with C.).

Trav. Uni. 16408 V. PL. Mal. 2 fol. 50 Grantha-s.

Trav. Uni. L.988 E. PL. Mal. 50 Grantha-s.

Trav. Uni. L.988 K. PL. Mal. 28 fol. (117-44). 800 Grantha-s (with C.).

Triv. Cur. VII 4. Mal. 75 Grantha-s. Obtained from Raja of Chirakkal.

VOHD II 7.2322 (cod.Malay. 10. BStB, München). Mal. 4 fol. (1-4). 1st work in the codex. Aus dem Besitz von C. M. Whish. Whish Nr. 52. See JRAS 1890, pp.805-13.

VOHD II 7.2323 (cod.Malay. 10. BStB, München). Mal. 24 fol. (4-27); second work in the codex (with C.)

Whish 28a. PL. Gr. 57 fol. (with C.). Dated A.D. 1753.

Whish 28b. PL. Gr. 5 fol. (58-62). Dated A.D. 1753.

– C.

Adyar D I 1091 (19 K 52 = 66673). PL. Gr. 25 fol. (37ff.). = Adyar I, p. 54b.

Adyar D I 1092 (23 H 36 ?). PL. Gr. 48 fol. = Adyar I, p. 54b (23 B 36 = 69630).

Adyar D XIII 205 (VB 132a). PL. Gr. 43 fol.

Adyar D XIII 206 (VB 421). PL. Gr. 27 fol. (Lacks ending).

Baroda 6381(b). PL. Gr. 17 fol. 450 Grantha-s (with text). = CLB I, p. 28. Extract p. 148.

Baroda 8243. 30 fol. 600 Grantha-s (with text). = CLB I, p. 39.

Baroda 10006(b). PL. Gr. 28 fol. 600 Grantha-s(with text). = CLB I, p. 39.

Hoshiarpur p. 55 (no.3531). PL. Gr. 29 fol. 888 Grantha-s. Extract p.80.

Hoshiarpur p. 301 (no.5613). PL. Gr. 31 fol. 930 Grantha-s. (Kātyāyana ?).

IO 7849 (3741). 28 fol. (with text). Written ca. A.D. 1900.

IO 7850 (3776b). PL. Tel. 8 fol. (with text).

MD 1018. PL. Tel. 55 pp. (4ff.).

MT 95(i). PL. Gr. 19 fol. (17-35). Differs at the end. Purchased in 1910-11 from Gopalaswami Ayyangar of Mannargudi.

MT 3486(b). PL. Gr. 23 fol. (28-50). Incomplete. Presented in 1920-21 by Nadadur Gopalacharya of Srivilliputtur, Tinnavelly Dist.

MT 3887(o). PL. Gr. 21 fol. (115-35) (with text). Purchased in 1921-22 from Annasvami Sastrigal, Bhavani, Coimbatore Dist.

Mysore p. 2 (no. 53). 78 fol.

Mysore (1898), p. 6 (no. 53b). 108 fol.

Mysore I, pp. 40-41 (5 Mss.).

Mysore ND II 4049-54. Extract no. 340.

Mysore Skt. Coll. p. 2. No.1123. Gr.

Oppert I 2494. PL. Gr. 15 pp. Belonged to Sri Sarasvati Bhandaram Committee of Tiruvallikkeni, Madras.

Oppert II 787. Belonged to Ghanapathi Shingaracharyar of Alasur, Madurantakam Taluk.

Oppert II 1404. Belonged to Gopalacharyar of Pillapakkam, Kanchipuram Taluk.

Oppert II 2675. PL. Gr. 63 pp. Belonged to Sankarasastri of Kumaralingam, Udumalapet Taluk, Coimbatore Dist.

PUL II. App. p. 14 (no.229). PL. Tel. 25 fol. 500 Grantha-s.

TCD 40. 54 pp. 810 Grantha-s (with text).

Tirupati SVUORI 7960 (1143c). PL. Gr. 6 fol.

Tirupati SVUORI 7961 (4378i). PL. Gr. 27 (31-57). Title: Svara-pañcāśacchabda-bhāṣyam.

Trav. Uni. 124 B. PL. Gr. 800 Grantha-s.

Trav. Uni. 3679 B. PL. Gr. 35 fol. 800 Grantha-s.

Trav. Uni. 8396 D. PL. Mal. 800 Grantha-s.

Trav. Uni. L.988 K. PL. Mal. 28 fol. (117-44). 800 Grantha-s.

Trav. Uni. T.544. 800 Grantha-s.

Triv. Cur. VII 5. Mal. 950 Grantha-s. Obtained from Raja of Chirakkal.

VOHD II 7.2323 (cod.Malay. 10. BStB, München). Mal. 24 fol. (4-27); second work in the codex (with text).

Whish 28a. PL. Gr. 57 fol. (with text). Dated A.D. 1753.

[CC I 750a; II 180b; III 155a]

1522 SVARA-PAṬALA (1) (**स्वरपटल**)

Ujjain I, p. (no.2513). 20 fol.

1523 SVARA-PAṬALA (2) (**स्वरपटल**)

Third Paṭala of the *Ṛgveda-prātiśākhya*, edited separately with the commentary of Uvaṭa, on the basis of two Mss. (BORI 9 of 1879-80 = BORI D I i.52 and BORI 11 of Viś. (1) = BORI D I i.56) and two printed editions (by Mangal Deva Shastri, Allahabad, 1931; and by V. K. Varma, B H U. 1970).

Ptd.: ed. by K. V. Abhyankar and G. V. Devasthali, in: Veda-vikṛti-lakṣaṇa-saṃgraha. – Poona : BORI, 1978, pp. 134-42.

1524 SVARA-PARIBHĀṢĀ or SĀMA-LAKṢAṆA (**स्वरपरिभाषा / सामलक्षण**)

→ Sāma-paribhāṣā. Considered as the more ancient system of notation of accents or notes of the chants in the *Sāmaveda* by combining consonants and vowels, e.g. ka, kha, kva, etc. This system is used in South India. See Brl. p. 44 (no.CXXXIII) = IO 4338.

Baroda 6784(b). PL. Gr. 11 fol. (95-105). 300 Grantha-s. = CLB I, p. 38. Extract p. 170 (6784 C ?).

Burnell 10b.

TD 1814. PL. Gr. 4 fol. 75 Grantha-s.

[CC I 750b]

1525 SVARA-PARIBHĀṢĀ (**स्वरपरिभाषा**)

Beginning: (5154)

अथ स्वराः --

लोकवेदविभागेन स्वरसूत्रेषु वर्णनात्।
लोके ऽपि स्युरुदात्ताद्यास्तथा वृत्त्यां प्रयोगतः ॥
छान्दसे खण्ड उच्यन्ते स्वराः सर्वे ऽपि तत्र तु।

संज्ञायाः पूर्वमुक्तत्वात् परिभाषादि कथ्यते॥

अनुदात्तं पदमेकवर्जम् ॥ एकं वर्जयित्वा पदमनुदात्तं स्यात् । धातोरन्त उदात्तः स्यादित्युक्ते स एवोदात्तः । अन्ये ऽनुदात्ताः । गोपायतन्न सुमनस्यमानाः । (अन्ये ऽनुदात्ताः । गोपायतन्न सुमनस्यमानाः ।) अत्र सनाद्यन्ता धातव इति धातुसंज्ञायाम् आ … स्यान्त उदात्ते सत्यन्ये अनुदात्ताः ।

End:

इराकविष्णुः । विष्णुचोपिग्रहात् । अनाढ्यं विष्णुः चारु अविलिखिरस्तन्द्राळुः । शक्तो ऽप्येवमाक्रुश्यते संज्ञायाम् । आक्रोशः ।

MT 5154(c). Gr. 13 fol. (30-42). Incomplete. Deals with Saṃhitā-svara, Kṛt-svara, Taddhita-svara, Samāsa-svara, etc.; abruptly ends in Avyayībhāva-tatpuruṣa-svara. Transcribed in 1925-26 from a Ms. of Kadalur Narayana Nambudripad, Nareri, Tritala, Malabar Dist.

1526 SVARA-PRAKARAṆA (1) (स्वरप्रकरण)
Different texts.
Mysore ND II 4055 (P 8582/ 1). PL. Gr. 1 fol. Extract no. 341.
Mysore ND II 4056 (P 4521/ 8). PL. Gr. 3 fol. (30-32). Extract no. 342.

1527 SVARA-PRAKARAṆA (2) (स्वरप्रकरण)
Beginning:

त्वन्नः सत्वन्नः तस्यान्नः प्रियतान्नः करतान्नस्तन्नो गीर्भिः प्रियं मरुतो वृत्रहन्तमम् … संहितायां नकारः पदकाले मकारान्तानि भवन्ति । मावस्ते दिवस्कं … सस्पर्शानि पदानि भवन्ति ।

End:

बृहस्पतिं वाजं जापयतेत्यनुदात्तम् । विमध्यसं श्रथाय गिरा च सृष्टिररुषस्तूप इति पाठः । गायत्र्या इ हविर्धान इत्यन्तोदात्तं याज्या … मुह्यन्त्वन्य इत्याद्यनुदात्तम् । स्वराज्ञीः सोमराज्ञीरित्यनयोरेकः पाठः । तरणिराद्युदात्तम् …

SBD 2075. 5 fol. Incomplete. Dated V.S. 1685.

1528 SVARA-PRAKĀRA (स्वरप्रकार)
of Śrīnivāsa Dīkṣita.
PUL II. App. p. 14 (no.230) PL. Gr. 2 fol. 20 Kārikā-s. (Jaiminiśākhā).

1529 SVARA-PRAKRIYĀ (1) (स्वरप्रक्रिया)
GJKSV 37119. 6 fol. → Mallaśarma-śikṣā also called Hasta-svara-prakriyā.

1530 SVARA-PRAKRIYĀ (2) (स्वरप्रक्रिया)

The last chapter of the Siddhānta-kaumudī of Bhaṭṭojī Dīkṣita. Here the Sūtra-s of the Aṣṭādhyāyī that deal with accent are culled out and commented on. There are also other independent works dealing with the same Sūtra-s, such as Svara-mañjari, Svara-siddhānta-candrikā.

1531 SVARA-PRAKRIYĀ (3) (स्वरप्रक्रिया)

of Rāmacandra-paṇḍita, son of Nāga of the Śaṣa family. A commentary on about 400 Sūtra-s of the Aṣṭādhyāyī and the Phiṭsūtra-s. The text is divided into eight sections called Prakaraṇa. Sādhāraṇa-svara-prakaraṇa, Tiṅanta-svara-prakaraṇa, Prātipadika-svara-prakaraṇa (Phiṭ-sūtra), Prātipadika-svara-prakaraṇa, Subanta-svara-prakaraṇa, Samāsa-svara-prakaraṇa, Vākya-savra-prakaraṇa.

GJKSV 25014. 61 fol. Dated V.S. 1737. 2700 Grantha-s. Copied by Hemarāja.
Trav. Uni. 1828. 2700 Grantha-s. Dated V.S. 1722.
Trav. Uni. 7552. 2300 Grantha-s. Incomplete.

Ptd.: ed. by K. V. Sastri Abhyankar. – Poona : Anandashrama, 1974. 20, 196 pp. – (Anandashrama Sanskrit Series 138). [GJKSV (425.1 Ram SV); SAI (ind S 3, 138)]

[CC I 750b]

1532 SVARA-PRATIṢEDHA (स्वरप्रतिषेध)

Trav. Uni. 16408 Z4. PL. Mal. 1 fol. 15 Grantha-s.

1533 SVARA-PRADĪPIKĀ (स्वरप्रदीपिका)

of Kṛṣṇācārya. A commentary on the Svara-sūtra-s of the Aṣṭādhyāyī.
Beginning:

> अनुदात्तं पदमेकवर्जम् । परिभाषेयम् । यस्मिन् पदे यस्योदात्तः स्वरितो वा विधीयते तमेकमेव वर्जयित्वा शेषं तत् पदमनुदात्तकं स्यात् । तद्यथा गोपायति । वक्ष्यति धातोरुत्तर उदात्तो भवतीति ।

End:

> ऋत्विक्शब्दः कृदुत्तरपदप्रकृतिस्वरेण अन्तोदात्तः ॥
> इति श्रीमद्देवीदत्तात्मजरामसेवकतनूद्भव कृष्णाचार्यकृता स्वरप्रदीपिका समाप्ता ॥ संवत् १८५५ ॥

Oxf. CS d.73. 36 fol. Dated A.D. 1798.

1534 SVARA-BHAKTI (1) (स्वरभक्ति)

on the pronunciation of "r" and "l" in the Veda, when either of them is the first member of a conjunct consonant.
Hoshiarpur p. 301 (no.4374). PL. Gr. 10 fol. 925 Grantha-s. Incomplete.

1535 SVARA-BHAKTI (2) (स्वरभक्ति)
Five and a half verses. The last verse is identical with *Vyāsa-śikṣā* 357-58.

Beginning:

करेणुः कर्षिणी चैव हारिणी हारितेति च।
हंसपादेति विज्ञेयाः पञ्चैताः स्वरभक्तयः ॥

End:

ऊष्मोत्तरे द्वितीयः स्यादादेशः प्रथमस्य तु।
हकारः प्रथमादूर्ध्वः तत्तत्स्थानं चतुर्थकम्॥

MD 1021. Gr. 1 p. (1) .... (= Skt. Texts on Phonetics, p. 626).
MD 16708. PL. Tel. 1 p. 5 Grantha-s.
Mysore ND II 4057 (P 2262/ 2). PL. Gr. 1 fol. (138). Incomplete.
Mysore ND II 4058 (B 252/10). Gr. 2 fol. (62-63). Extract no. 343.

[CC II 180b]

1536 SVARA-BHAKTI (3) (स्वरभक्ति)
Trav. Uni. 5968 D. PL. Mal. 150 Grantha-s.

1537 SVARA-BHAKTI (4) (स्वरभक्ति)
Adyar D I 987 → Veda-lakṣaṇa (A 5).

1538 SVARA-BHAKTI-PRAKARAṆA (स्वरभक्तिप्रकरण)
Adyar D I 1093 (23 G 6 = 69832). PL. Gr. 2 fol. (113a-114b). Incomplete.

1539 SVARA-BHAKTI-LAKṢAṆA-(PARIŚIṢṬA)ŚIKṢĀ (स्वरभक्तिलक्षण(परिशिष्ट)शिक्षा)
of Kātyāyana. 42 Kārikā-s mainly dealing with Svarabhakti. After verse 28 it reads: "iti kātyāyana-pariśiṣṭe varṇoccāra-prakāraḥ".

Beginning:

अथातः संप्रवक्ष्यामि सर्वलक्षणलक्षिताम्।
शिक्षां समासतस्तत्र स्वरास्त्वष्टौ प्रकीर्तिताः ॥ १॥
तैरोविरामः क्षैप्रश्च तैरोव्यञ्जनकस्तथा।
भाव्यो ऽभिनिहितो जात्यः पादवृत्तश्च सप्तमः ॥ २॥
प्रश्लिष्ट इति विज्ञेयाः प्रोच्यन्ते लक्षणान्यथ।
अवग्रह उदात्तश्चेत् स्वरितः स्यात् ततः परम्॥ ३॥
अवग्रहात् पदं यस्तु तं विद्यात् प्रथमं स्वरम्।
लक्ष्यमस्य तु विज्ञेयं गोपताविति गो-पतौ॥ ४॥
इकारोकारयोः स्थाने यवौ स्यातामुदात्तयोः ।
अनुदात्ते पदे नित्यं स क्षिप्र इति कीर्तितः ॥ ५॥

End:

लकारेण शकारेण संयोगो यत्र जायते॥ ३९॥
तां हरिणीं विजानीयाच्छतवल्शेति दर्शनम्।
रेफस्याथ षकारेण संयोगो यत्र दृश्यते॥ ४०॥
हंसपादेति विज्ञेया वर्षो वर्षीयसीति च।
एतल्लक्षणमाख्यातं स्वरभक्तेर्विचक्षणैः॥ ४१॥
ज्ञात्वैतन्मनुजो याति ब्रह्मलोकं सनातनम्।
इति कात्यायनोक्ता स्वरभक्तिलक्षणपरिशिष्टशिक्षा समाप्ता॥

Ptd.: in Śikṣā-saṃgraha. – Benares, 1889, pp. 172-75. – (Ben. S. S. 10).

1540 SVARA-BHAKTI-VIṢAYA (-LAKṢAṆA or -NIRŪPAṆA) (स्वरभक्तिविषय /-लक्षण /-निरूपण)

Adyar D I 1094 (23 H 10 = 69884). PL. Gr. 1 fol. Only 8 verses. The complete text is printed. = Adyar I, p. 54b.

1541 SVARA-BHĀṢYA (स्वरभाष्य)

Mysore ND II 4059 (P 4906/60). PL. Na. 2 fol. (140-41). Extract no. 344. This is the commentary on the Svarāṣṭaka of Śaunaka.

1542 SVARA-MAÑJARĪ (स्वरमञ्जरी)

of Tryambak Baḻavant Abhyankar. A modern work.

Ptd.: Pune : Aryabhushana Mudranalaya, Śaka 1863. 12 pp. [Tirupati SVUORI (14.00/sva 361)]

1543 SVARA-MAÑJARĪ or SVARA-MANOJÑA-MAÑJARĪ (स्वरमञ्जरी / स्वरमनोज्ञमञ्जरी)

of Nṛsiṃha-sūri, son of Rudrācārya. Quoted by Bhaṭṭojī.

Beginning: (TCD)

वेदवेदार्थयोस्तत्त्वमशेषं येन बोधितम्।
सर्वज्ञमीश्वरं वन्दे विश्वात्मानं सदाशिवम्।
पाणिनीयमताभिज्ञान् नत्वा वृद्धगुरूनपि॥ १॥
पाणिनिप्रभृतिशास्त्रकोविदान् पावनानथ गुरून् प्रणम्य तान्।
पाणिनीयसमयानुसारिणी वक्ष्यते स्वरमनोज्ञमञ्जरी॥ २॥
स्वभ्यस्तवेदः कुरुते प्रबन्धं स्वरार्थमावर्तितशब्दविद्यः।
रुद्रार्यसूनुर्नरसिंहसूरिरसावदोषो विदुषां मुदेऽस्तु॥ ३॥
इह खलु निरन्तरं वेदाभ्यासनिरतानाम् अध्यापकानामध्येतॄणां च सम्यगुदात्तादयः स्वरा विवेचनीयास्तथैवोच्चारयितव्याश्च । विवेकपूर्वं सम्यगुच्चारणे महाफलश्रवणात् । असम्यगुच्चारणे प्रत्यवायदर्शनाच्च। तथाहि --

End:

अन्यानप्येवमुद्धृत्य विशेषस्वरगोचरः ।
नित्यस्वाध्यायनिष्णातैर्निर्वाच्यः शब्दवेदिभिः ॥
शाखेयं तैत्तिरीया च बहुधावृत्य धीमता ।
दृष्टस्वरोदाहरणा नृसिंहेन विवर्णिता ॥
गौरीगुरो ऽङ्गिरेरुग्ररागी गौराङ्गरागवत् ।
गुवर्णः पातु जगतां शब्दशास्त्रविवेकिनः ॥
रुद्राचार्यतनूजेन कौलिमञ्जुलजन्मना ।
नृसिंहाख्येन विमला शब्दाब्धेः पारदृश्वना ॥
तर्कतन्त्रविदा वेदनिष्णातेन मनीषिणा ।
सवैदिकोदाहरणा प्रणीता स्वरमञ्जरी ॥

Adyar 19 L 54 = 66767. PL. Gr. 105 fol. (Ms. A. of Poona edition). There is also a Devanāgarī transcript.

Baroda 7791. PL. Gr. 92 fol. 2200 Grantha-s. = CLB I, p. 39. (Ms. B. of Poona edition).

BBRAS SSP. 162. 89 fol. (1-48, 55-94, 97). Incomplete.

GJKSV 33400. 18 fol. (3-18, 26, 27). Incomplete.

Göttingen 206. 98 fol. Transcript of IO 701, made by Kielhorn himself, written on one side of the paper.

Gough p. 31.

IM 5000. 78 fol. (1, 5, 6, 26-98, 101, 102). Incomplete.

IO 701 (98b). 71 fol. Lacks beginning. Written ca. end of the 16th century. (Ms. D. of Poona edition).

L 1429. 84 fol. 1867 Grantha-s. Lacks beginning. Dated V.S. 1723.

MD 15704. 143 pp. (Ms. C. of Poona edition).

MT 158(b). PL. Gr. 25 fol. (60-84). Incomplete. Purchased in 1910-11 from Minakshiammal of Koduvayur.

MT 1674. Tel. 66 fol. Contains a few additional stanzas. Transcribed in 1915-16 from a Ms. of Gopalakrishnammagaru of Indupalli, Amalapuram Taluk.

MT 3488(a). PL. Gr. 54 fol. Presented in 1920-21 by Nadadur Gopalacharya of Srivilliputtur, Tinnavelly Dist.

Mysore I, p. 41 (2 Mss.); p. 614.

Mysore ND II 4060 (P 663). PL. Tel. 22 fol. (249-70). Incomplete. Extract no. 345.

Mysore ND II 4061 (P 4454). PL. Tel. 36 fol. Incomplete. Extract no. 346.

Mysore ND II 4062 (A 622/ 1). Kan. 175 pp. Incomplete. Extract no. 347.

Mysore ND X 34639. (P 190/ 1). PL. Tel. 46 fol.

Oppert I 8368. Belonged to Paravastu Venkatarangacharyar of Vishakhapattanam.

OU 33 Vm (B.71/14/c). 54 fol. Incomplete. 16th century.

Paris (Tel. 39).

RASB II 490 (G 569) = L 1429.

TCD 41. 148 pp. 1665 Grantha-s (with C.).

Tirupati SVUORI 7962 (4431). PL. Gr. 62 fol. Incomplete.

Trav. Uni. 10603. PL. Mal. 1600 Grantha-s.
Trav. Uni. L.42 A. PL. Mal. 1175 Grantha-s. Incomplete.
Trav. Uni. T.556. 1600 Grantha-s.
Triv. Cur. VII 54. Mal. 1800 Grantha-s (with C.).

Ptd.: ed. by Kshitis Chandra Chatterji, in : *Calcutta Oriental Journal*, vol. II (July-September 1935). 16 pp. only.
Ed. by G. V. Devasthali. – Poona : BORI, 1985. 4, xlv, 197 pp. – (Research Unit Series 6). [BORI (49232 / 49233); SAI (ind 54 C 587/1666*)]

– C. Parimala of Girinātha-sūri, son of Mallinātha.
BORI 297 of 1899-1915. 111 fol.
MD 15316. Tel. 127 pp. 2381 Grantha-s.
MT 3488(b). PL. Gr. 43 fol. (55-97). Presented in 1920-21 by Nadadur Gopalacharya of Srivilliputtur, Tinnavelly Dist.
MT 5655. 70 fol. 1250 Grantha-s. Restored from MT 3488(b). (Ms. E. of the Poona edition of the text).
Mysore I, pp. 41. 614.
Mysore ND II 4063 (P 190/ 2). PL. Tel. 53 fol. Extract no. 348.
Mysore ND II 4064 (P 8022). PL. Tel. 150 fol.
Mysore ND II 4065 (A 622/ 2). Kan. 176-383 pp.
TCD 41. 148 pp. 1665 Grantha-s (with text).
Tirupati SVUORI 7962 (4431). PL. Gr. 88 fol. (63-150).

Ptd.: 16 pages only in : *Calcutta Oriental Journal*. See above.

[CC I 750b]

1544 SVARA-MĀTRĀ-LAKṢAṆA (**स्वरमात्रालक्षण**)
→ Mātrā-lakṣaṇa.
Brl. p. 43 (no.CXXXII) = IO 4329.

[CC I 750b]

1545 SVARA-MELANA (**स्वरमेलन**)
of Kṛṣṇa-kavi. A work on Vedic accentuation dealing with the following topics:

1) ubhayodātta-dīrgha-hrasva-prakaraṇam
2) pūrvodātta-pūrva-dīrgha-prakaraṇam
3) ubhaya-hrasva-pūrvodātta-prakaraṇam
4) ubhaya-hrasvottarodātta-prakaraṇam
5) ubhayodāttobhaya-dīrgha-prakaraṇam
6) udātta-vyatiriktobhaya-hrasva-prakaraṇam
7) udātta-vyatirikta-pūrva-dīrgha-prakaraṇam
8) udātta-vyatiriktottara-dīrgha-prakaraṇam

Beginning:

नमस्कृत्वा गणेशं च वासुदेवं सदाशिवम्।
नृसिंहीं त्रिपुरघ्नीं च क्रियते स्वरमेलनम्॥

एकादेशस्य दीर्घस्य चादिरन्तोभयं यथा।
उच्चस्वरेण संगृह्य याजुषे तैत्तिरीयके॥

अत्रादौ स्वरमेलनं नाम स्वरसंहिताद्वयमेलनम् । उदात्तादिस्वरसंहिता केवलाच्स्वरसंहितोभयमेलनग्रन्थम् इति । ननु चतसृषु संहितासु मध्ये स्वरसंहिताद्वयं यत्रकुत्रापि नास्ति । तस्मान्न स्वीकार्यम् । व्यासशिक्षामतेन प्रातिशाख्ये ऽपि षट्संहितारूपमूहनीयम्। तथा चोक्तम् --

पदवर्णस्वराङ्गानां द्विर्द्विर्युक्ते च संहिता।
द्विधादिसंहिता ह्यत्र षडेवं संहिताः स्मृताः ॥

इति व्यासशिक्षावचनेन स्वरसंहिता द्विधा॥

End:

एवैषां हन्तावोचथा एतस्यादित्य एव हि।
हयायै वाचैतेनायतनेन समुदीरितम्॥

एवैषां वृङ्क्ते ताजक् । हन्ता वोचथा वराहः एतस्यादित्यो रुचम् । हव्यायै वासन्नाय । एतेनायतनेन क्राम्यतीति ॥ इति श्रीकृष्णनाम्ना विरचिते स्वरमेलनलक्षणे उदात्तव्यतिरिक्तोत्तरदीर्घप्रकरणं समाप्तिमगमत्॥

Adyar 38 H 40 = TR 854. 172 pp. Copied by Narayanaswami Sastri in 1930 from the Ms. I-26-39 of Govt. Or. Libr. Madras.

MT 2284. Tel. 44 fol. Transcribed in 1916-17 from a Ms. of Pullala Suryagaru, Indupalli, Godāvari Dist.

PUL II. App. p. 14 (no.231). PL. Tel. 8 fol. 100 Grantha-s. (Breaks off in the middle of the pūrvodātta-pūrva-dīrghodāharaṇa on 18th Sūtra).

1546 SVARA-LAKṢAṆA see SVARA-ŚIROMAṆI (स्वरलक्षण / स्वरशिरोमणि)

1547 SVARA-LAKṢAṆA (1) (स्वरलक्षण)

Unspecified:

Mysore I, p. 41 (2 Mss.).

Mysore ND II 4067 (P 2265/42). PL. Gr. 8 fol. Extract no. 349.

Mysore ND II 4068 (P 2319). PL. Gr. 11 fol. Incomplete. = Varṇa-krama-lakṣaṇa (alpaśvāsadhvanita ... kakāraḥ).

Mysore ND II 4069 (B 252/16). Gr. 2 fol. (119-20).

Trav. Uni. 4028 F. PL. Gr. 25 Grantha-s.

Ujjain I, p. 9 (no.2333). 2 fol.

VSM I 481 (no.1689). 2 fol. Incomplete. 7 verses only.

1548 SVARA-LAKṢAṆA (2) (स्वरलक्षण)

Adyar II, App. p. iiia (40 C 10). The same as Adyar D I 856 (21 Q 10 = 68514). Called Traisvarya-lakṣaṇa.

= Yājñavalkya-śikṣā. .... (= Skt. Texts on Phonetics, pp. 682-96).

1549 SVARA-LAKṢAṆA (3) (**स्वरलक्षण**)
TS.
Adyar D I 1095 (23 E 25 = 69758). PL. Gr. 3 fol. (1-3). Incomplete.

1550 SVARA-LAKṢAṆA (4) (**स्वरलक्षण**)
of Keśavārya, son of Sūrideva-budhendra. On the accents in the *Taittirīya-saṃhitā*.
Brl. p. 9 (no.XXVII).
Hz 1432. PL. Gr. 33 fol. (with 3 other Veda-lakṣaṇa works).
[CC III 155a]

1551 SVARA-LAKṢAṆA (5) (**स्वरलक्षण**)
Twelve verses of the Svarāṅkuśa are given under this title in :
BORI 2 of 1873-74. 1 fol. (8). Dated V.S. 1931. From Bikaner. (A xerox-copy of this Ms. is in SAI : 87/790*).

1552 SVARA-LAKṢAṆA (6) (**स्वरलक्षण**)
SBD 2104. 7 fol. Incomplete. This is Yājñavalkya-śikṣā, up to verse 78 of the Benares edition.

1553 SVARA-LAKṢAṆA (7) (**स्वरलक्षण**)
15 verses on accents.

Beginning:

उच्चात् परो ऽनुदात्तो यः स्वरितत्वमवाप्नुयात् ।
स्वरितादनुदात्ताश्च प्रचयत्वमवाप्नुयुः ॥
उदात्तश्रुतिरेवेति प्रचयस्य प्रसिद्धितः ।
स्वरितोदात्तयोर्यत्र परत्र स्थितयोः सतोः ॥

End:

पदादौ प्रचयो नास्ति स्वरादेकपदे ततः ।
नास्त्युदात्तो ऽपि विज्ञेयो हस्तविन्यासकर्मणि ॥
श्लोकां मङ्गलाय आ उपहूतामवाप्नुतः ।
दीर्घास्ता इमे देवा उ स्वा अहममूनि अवाः (?) ॥
इति स्वरलक्षणं समाप्तम् ॥

SBD 47571. 2 fol.

1554 SVARA-LAKṢAṆA (YOHIPRĀPTI-BHĀṢYA) (**स्वरलक्षण / योहिप्राप्तिभाष्य**)
of Sūrubhaṭṭa → Yohi-prāpti(-śikṣā).
OU 34 Vm (573). PL. Tel. 17 fol. 16th century.

1555 SVARA-LAKṢAṆA-ŚIKṢĀ (**स्वरलक्षणशिक्षा**)
GJKSV 37114. 9 fol. Incomplete. Lacks end. 149 verses → Yājñavalkya-śikṣā.

1556 SVARA-VARṆA-LAKṢAṆA or SAPTA-SVARA-SINDHU
(स्वरवर्णलक्षण / सप्तस्वरसिन्धु)
of Rāmānuja, son of Śrīnivāsa. This work apparently belonging to the SV, treats of the Vedic accents and shows the application of the seven Svara-s, Ṣaḍja, etc. to the Vedic letters. The Svara-siddhānta-cakra below is supposed to be the 6th Adhyāya of this.
Baroda 9917(a). PL. Gr. 17 fol. 350 Grantha-s. = CLB I, p. 39. Incomplete. Breaks off in the 4th Adhyāya. Extract pp. 171-72.

– C.
Baroda 9917(b). PL. Gr. 14 fol. 200 Grantha-s. = CLB I, p. 39. Incomplete. Extract p. 173.

1557 SVARA-VICĀRA **(स्वरविचार)**
Title of Saṃhitā-sūtra in:
IM 2509. 8 fol. Dated Śaka 1634. Udāttādi-svara-vicāra and Vedādhyayana-krama on the title page.

1558 SVARA-VIJÑĀNA **(स्वरविज्ञान)**
of Bhāskara.
PUL II. App. p. 14 (no.232). PL. Gr. 35 Grantha-s (with C.). (2 Kāṇḍa-s).

1559 SVARA-VIGRAHA-ŚIKṢĀ-BHĀṢYA **(स्वरविग्रहशिक्षाभाष्य)**
of Sāyaṇa. Oudh III 6.

1560 SVARA-VIDHI (1) **(स्वरविधि)**
of Rāma.
BBRAS 488(II) (B D 278). 1 fol.

1561 SVARA-VIDHI (2) **(स्वरविधि)**
Rāma Ṭahala.
Beginning:

आ येति। निपाता आद्युदात्ताः । निपात आद्युदात्तसंज्ञः स्यात्। इत्यनेन आकार उदात्तः । येति यच्छब्दः जस्विभक्तिः । त्यदादीनामः । एषामकारो ऽन्तादेशः स्यात्। अतो गुणे।

End:

स्वरितात् संहितायामनुदात्तानाम् । स्वरितात् परेषाम् अनुदात्तानामेकश्रुतिः स्यात् । संहितायामित्यनेनैकश्रुतिः । स्वराणामविभागेन श्रवणं स्वनान्तरं वा एकश्रुतिः । इत्यत्र इकारे पूर्वार्ध उदात्तः । उत्तरार्धे ऽपि ले इति एकश्रुतिः । परत्वेनोदात्तस्वरितपरत्वाभावात् । उत्तरार्धस्य नानुदात्तत्वमित्यलम् । फाल्गुनकृष्ण-एकादश्यां चन्द्रवासरे नवगुणाङ्केन्दुयुक्तसं (१९३९)वति श्रीरामटहलः स्वपाठार्थे व्यलिखत्॥

GJKSV 12038. 7 fol.

1562 SVARA-VIVṚTI (स्वरविवृति)

BORI 261 of 1895-98. = BORI D II i.4. 2 fol. Dated V.S. 1910.

Peters. VI, p. 81 (no.261).

SBD 38829. 4 fol. Incomplete.

SBD 38922. 2 fol. Incomplete. Title: Svarita-vṛtti.

1563 SVARA-VIVEKA (स्वरविवेक)

of Annam-bhaṭṭa, son of Tirumalārya of Rāghava Somayāji family. A treatise laying down grammatical rules with illustrations in connection with Vedic accents. Last page in Adyar Ms. contains the following list of contents:

1) Lopa-nimitta-svara
2) Āgama-svara
3) Prakṛti-svara
4) Prātipadika-svara
5) Pratyaya-svara
6) Pluta-savra
7) Saṃdhi-svara
8) Pada-svara
9) Samāsa-svara
10) Arthabheda-svara
11) Samāsa-svara (2)
12) Tiṅanta-svara

Beginning: (2175)

स्वरोत्पत्तौ कारणानि विज्ञातव्यान्यशेषतः ।
लोपागमविकाराणां प्रकृतेः प्रत्ययस्य च ॥
प्लुतसंधिपदानां च समासानां च भेदतः ।
क्वचिदर्थवशेनाहुर्दशधा तानि शाब्दिकाः ॥

तत्र लोपनिमित्तस्वरो यथा -- देवी, पूष्णः, अस्रा । दिवु क्रीडादौ । धातोः । धातोरन्त उदात्तः स्यादिति वकारस्योदात्तत्वे प्राप्ते स्वरविधौ व्यञ्जनमविद्यमानवदिति इकार उदात्तः । तस्य पचाद्यचि लघूपधगुणे स्थानिवद्भावादेकारो ऽप्युदात्तः ।

End:

तिङि चोदात्तवति । गतिरनुदात्तः । यद् वत्सानपाकरोति । याञ्ज्ञमभ्यारोहति । उदात्तवतीति किम् ? । भागधेयेनोपधावति । इति तिङन्तस्वरः ॥ इति श्रीमहामहोपाध्याय श्रीमद्राघवसोमयाजिकुलावतंस श्रीमत्तिरुमलार्यसूनोः अन्नंभट्टस्य कृतिषु स्वरविवेकाख्यं प्रकरणं संपूर्णम् ॥

Adyar 38 H 40 = TR 854. 64 pp. Copied by Narayanaswami Sastri in 1928 from tne Ms. I-24-52 of Govt. Or. Libr. Madras.

MT 2175(a). Tel. 13 fol. Transcribed in 1916-17 from a Ms. of Uppaluri Krishnamurti Sastrigal of Dangeru, Ramachandrapuram Taluk, Godavari Dist.

1564 SVARA-VAIDIKA (स्वरवैदिक)

Oppert II 788. Belonged to Ghanapathi Shingaracharyar of Alasur, Madurantakam Taluk.

1565 SVARA-VYAÑJANA-ŚIKṢĀ (स्वरव्यञ्जनशिक्षा)

Divided into six Varga-s showing where the letter "r" is a vowel and where it is a consonant with examples from the *Ṛgveda.* It follows the *Ṛgveda-prātiśākhya* and quotes Sūtra-s of Pāṇini. For an analysis of the work, based on the defective Ms. of BORI, see Siddheshwar Varma, *Critical Studies ...* , pp. 58-60.

Beginning:

रेफान्नलोपे नियते प्रश्रिताकामयोः ऋमे।
रलोष्मोपहितो ह्रस्वो ङ्नवर्जं परिपन्नगे॥
अभ्यासे त्रीतिसंख्यायास्तृतीयतिसृवर्जितः ।
रिणच्छ्रितो रिपुः क्रिमिः क्रिविः त्रिशो रिशादसः ॥

End:

त्रित इति संचितो रेफः । अन्तस्थास्वजागृजागृविं त्रिविष्ठिता इति रेफः । संख्यार्थत्वात्। युष्मसु ऋष्यः । रिशादस इति संचितो रेफः । ऋष्टय ऋषमिति रेफः । बृसयस्य बृहत् बृहस्पतिः ककारादिः पकारादिश्चकारादिश्च यो भवति अन्तस्था यरलवा ककारादिव्यञ्जनं वहिः । व ६। स्वरव्यञ्जनशिक्षा समाप्ता।

BORI 21(2) of 1875-76. 3 fol. (3-5) together with the Cārāyaṇīya-śikṣā. (A xerox-copy of this Ms. is in SAI : 87/789*).

1566 SVARA-VYĀKHYĀ (स्वरव्याख्या)

Oppert II 789. Belonged to Ghanapathi Shingaracharyar of Aiasur, Madurantakam Taluk.

1567 SVARA-ŚĀSTRA (स्वरशास्त्र)

Oppert II 3301 (3 copies). Belonged to Tadakamalla Venkatakrishnarayar of Tiruvallikkeni.

Oppert II 5090. Belonged to Sri Sankaracharya Matha of Sringeri,

[CC I 750b]

1568 SVARA-ŚIKṢĀ (1) (स्वरशिक्षा)

Unspecified:

Oppert I 7259. Belonged to Ivattur Nandikesvara Sastri of Vijayanagaram.

SBD 2080. 2 fol. Incomplete. This is the C. on the Svarāṣṭaka up to the 6th verse.

[CC II 180b]

– C.

PUL I, p. 25 (no.155). PL. Tel. 11 fol. 100 Grantha-s.

[CC I 750b]

1569 SVARA-ŚIKṢĀ (2) (स्वरशिक्षा)

→ Ucca-svara-nirṇaya.

Adyar D I 1096 (29 K 20 = 73653). PL. Tel. 13 fol. (145ff.) (with C.). = Adyar I, p. 53b. Col.: Ucca-svara-nirṇaya. Copied by Kālakūri Devaṇṇa for Vedamūrti Maddūri Narasimulu and dated Sunday, the 5th day of the first half of Puṣya, Bharaṇī (year Khara is mentioned on another fol.).

MD 1022. Tel. 25 pp. (253ff.) (with C.). Col.: Ucca-svara-samuccaya. The text is identical with MD 874 (Ucca-svara-nirṇaya) and MD 955 (Lakṣmīkāntaśikṣā Savyākhyā). Cf. Mysore ND II Extract no. 17, 47, 48.

1570 SVARA-ŚIKṢĀ (3) (स्वरशिक्षा)

Different from the above.

Beginning:

प्रणम्य वेदपुरुषं वक्ष्यामि स्वरसंग्रहम्।
उदात्तश्चानुदात्तश्च स्वरितः प्रचयः स्वराः ॥

End:

हस्तेन वेदं यो ऽधीते स्वरवर्णार्थसंयुतम्।
ऋग्यजुःसामभिः पूतो ब्रह्मलोके महीयते॥

TCD 34-L. 4 pp. 35 Grantha-s.

Trav. Uni. 4254 M. PL. Mal. 4 fol. 35 Grantha-s. Belonged to Vishnu Nambudiri of Ettikada Illam Ayankudi, Kaduttirutti, Kottayam.

Trav. Uni. T.223 L. = TCD 34-L. A transcript of the Ms. no. 4254.

Triv. Cur. III 13. Mal. 25 Grantha-s.

1571 SVARA-ŚIROMAṆI (स्वरशिरोमणि)

of Timmāvadhānin, son of Pārvatī-putra Kṛṣṇam-bhaṭṭa. 64 verses on Vedic accents (col. : iti pārvatīputra-kṛṣṇambhaṭṭa- sūnunā timmāvadhāninā prokta-cātusvara-śiromaṇiḥ).

Beginning:

वेदव्यासमुनिं नत्वा वेदोदधिसुधाकरम्।
बालानां सुखबोधार्थं वक्ष्ये स्वरशिरोमणिम्॥ १॥
उदात्तश्चानुदात्तश्च द्वावेतौ प्रकृतिस्वरौ।
स्वरितस्तु तयोर्योगे स तु सप्तविधः स्मृतः ॥ २॥
जात्यो ऽभिनिहितः क्षैप्रः प्रश्लिष्टः प्राकृतस्तथा।
तैरोव्यञ्जनवैवृत्तौ स्वराः सप्त प्रकीर्तिताः॥ ३॥

End:

उदात्तो ब्रह्मजातिः स्यान्नीचो राजन्य उच्यते।
स्वरितो वैश्यजातिः स्यात् प्रचयः शूद्र एव सः॥ ६२॥
स्वरवर्णाक्षरं मात्रा विनियोगो ऽर्थ एव च।
मन्त्रं जिज्ञासमानेन वेदितव्यं पदे पदे॥ ६३॥
पादौ पात्वनुदात्तो मे कर्णौ मे स्वरितः स्वरः ।

उदात्तो मे शिरः पातु सर्वाङ्गं प्रचयः स्वरः ॥ ६४॥

Ptd.: ed. by Ramabhadra Dikshita (in Grantha script) (Cātuḥ-svara-śiromaṇiḥ – ayaṃ kila pārvatīputra-kṛṣṇaṃbhaṭṭa- sūnunā timmāvadhāninā proktaḥ pāṇḍyadeśa-maṇḍanāyamāna dakṣiṇakailāsakalpa śrījyotirvanādyanekānvarthanāmnā jagatprasiddha śrīdakṣiṇakālīpuragrāmavāstvyena ṛgvedapāṭhaśālādhyāpakena śrī-rāmabhadradīkṣitena sutarāṃ pariṣkṛtya tenaiva kalpāttigrāmavāsinaḥ veṅkaṭācalaśāstriṇaḥ śrīvidyākalpataruyantrālaye mudrayitvā prakāśtaś ca – rākṣasanāma saṃvatsaram | 1915), – Palghat, Kalpatti : Srividya Kalpataru Press, 1915. 8 pp. [Adyar (PH 215 Tim SS); BM : Ptd. Bks. Cat. 1906-1928. 1087 (14092.b.49,5); IO (San C 161)]

Also ed. by K. S. Venkatarama Sastri, under the title Svara-lakṣaṇa (without the colophon of the above) in the Ṛgveda-ghanasāra. – Srirangam : Sri Vani Vilas Press, 1966, pp. 85-92. See above under Ṛgveda-ghanasāra. [Adyar (PH 215.1 x Ven RG); SAI (87/771*)]

1572 SVARA-SAṂGRAHA (स्वरसंग्रह)

Mysore I, p. 613.
Mysore ND II 4070 (P 4723). PL. Tiglari. 30 Grantha-s.

1573 SVARA-SAṂDHI (1) (स्वरसंधि)

A few selected Sūtra-s on saṃdhi-s (Akārādi-svara-saṃdhi, Visarga-saṃdhi, Udāttādi-svara-saṃdhi) from the Vājasaneyi-prātiśākhya, 4.52ff. (siṃ savarṇe dīrgham), with a gloss.
SBD 2076. 3 fol.

1574 SVARA-SAṂDHI (2) (स्वरसंधि)

Attributed to Jayanta-svāmin in the catalogue. But there is no mention of his name in the Ms. The work contains a few illustrations of accentuation and saṃdhi-s in the *Vājasaneyi-saṃhitā*.
SBD 2077. 2 fol.

1575 SVARA-SAṂPAT (1) (स्वरसंपत्)

Mysore (1898), p. 5 (no. 52). Gr. 1 fol. (185).

– C.

Mysore (1898), p. 5 (no. 52). Gr. 2 fol. (186-87). The following verses, some of which mentioning the nine Śikṣā-s are identical to those in Weber 1498, are found at the end:

प्रथमं व्यासशिक्षा च लक्ष्मीशिक्षा द्वितीयका।
भारद्वाजं च तार्तीयं शिक्षारण्या तुरीयका॥
पञ्चमं शंभुशिक्षा च षष्ठं चापिशलं तथा।
सप्तमं पाणिनेः शिक्षा अष्टमं कौहलं तथा॥

वासिष्ठशिक्षा नवममेते वै नव शिक्षकाः ।
उपशिक्षा तु वक्तव्या प्रथमं गौतमं तथा ॥
अगस्त्यशिक्षा द्वैतीयं शिक्षात्रेयं तृतीयकम् ।
चतुर्थं याज्ञवल्क्यं च विश्वामित्रं तु पञ्चमम् ॥
षष्ठं काश्यपशिक्षा च प्लाक्षायणश्च सप्तमम् ।
कौण्डिन्यश्चाष्टमं ज्ञेयं नवमं हारितं तथा ॥
एते वै शिक्षाकाराश्च चतुर्वेदस्य लक्षणम् ।
पाणिन्यत्रिभरद्वाजवसिष्ठव्यासगौतमाः ॥
शिक्षाकारा वररुचिः कौहलो महिषो नव ।
व्यासलक्ष्मीभरद्वाजशंभ्वापिशलिसंमतः ।
कौहलेयः कालारण्यः शिक्षात्रेया नव स्मृताः ॥

1576 SVARA-SAMPAT (2) (स्वरसंपत्)

Beginning:

सोदात्तं निरुदात्तं च पदजातमिति द्विधा ।
उदात्त एकः सोदात्ते प्रायो द्वित्रा अपि क्वचित् ।
साग्रेव्यपाश्चेतव्येचाम्नाय यज्ञपा उ च ।
स्वरात् परैरुच्चसमो नित्यमेकपदे धृताः ।
निरुदात्तं सर्वनीचमेकस्वरितयुग्विधा ॥

End:

कूष्माण्डेषूदात्तपर उच्चः कम्पोचितस्तथा ।
कम्पे ऽणुमात्रः कम्पः स्यात् स्वारस्यान्ते निहन्यते ।
तच्चेष स्वार उच्चो वा व्यवस्थाप्यः परस्वरात् ॥

इति स्वरसंपत् समाप्तः ॥

उदात्तयोर्मध्यवर्णं एकं वा द्वे (वा) बहूनि वा ।
एकं चेन्नीचमेव स्याद् द्वे वा स्वरितनीचके ॥

Baroda 6255. PL. Tel. 2 fol. (43a-44a). 17 Grantha-s.

1577 SVARA-SAMPARKI (स्वरसंपर्कि)

This tract is a commentary on the Svara-sampat above. In both Mss. it is called Svara-samparki.

Beginning:

सोदात्तं निरुदात्तं च पदजातमिति द्विधा । अस्यान्वयः -- पदजातं द्विधा सोदात्तं निरुदात्तं चेति । उदात्त एकः सोदात्ते प्रायो द्वित्रा अपि क्वचित् । सोदात्ते पदे प्रायः उदात्त एकः । क्वचिद् द्वित्रा अप्युदात्ताः ।

End:

कूष्माण्डादावुच्चारः स्वारः कम्पोचितस्तथा । कूष्माण्डादौ कम्पोचितः स्वारः उदात्तपरश्चेत् तथा कम्पो ऽणुमात्रः कम्पस्वारस्यान्ते निहन्येत् । तच्चोपस्वार उच्चो वा व्यवस्थाप्यः परस्वरात् ।

Adyar D I 1097 (23 E 25 = 69758). PL. Gr. 3 fol. (42-44).
Hamburg StUB (cod.Palmbl. III 8/133) → Veda-lakṣaṇa (HB).

1578 SVARA-SAMĀNA (स्वरसमान)

Oppert II 790. Belonged to Ghanapathi Shingaracharyar of Alasur, Madurantakam Taluk.

[CC I 750b]

1579 SVARA-SAMUCCAYA (स्वरसमुच्चय)

Mentioned in the Svara-śikṣā, MD 1022.
Adyar D I 984 → Veda-lakṣaṇa (A 2) (fol. 9a-10a; not noted in the catalogue).
Oppert I 7159. Belonged to Pola Lakshmanavadhani of Vijayanagaram.
Trav. Uni. 16408 W. PL. Mal. 1 fol. 17 Grantha-s.
Trav. Uni. L.988 G. PL. Mal. 15 Grantha-s.

1580 SVARA-SIDDHĀNTA-KAUMUDĪ (स्वरसिद्धान्तकौमुदी)

Oppert II 7849. PL. Gr. 173 pp. Belonged to H H the Maharaja of Pudukottai.

[CC I 750b]

1581 SVARA-SIDDHĀNTA-CAKRA (स्वरसिद्धान्तचक्र)

From the colophon it appears to be the 6th Adhyāya of the Svara-varṇa-lakṣaṇa or Sapta-svara-sindhu above.
Baroda 9917(c). PL. Gr. 12 fol. 180 Grantha-s. = CLB I, p. 39. Extract pp. 173-74.

1582 SVARA-SIDDHĀNTA-CANDRIKĀ (स्वरसिद्धान्तचन्द्रिका)

of Śrīnivāsa Dīkṣita (or Yajvan), son of (Ananta-)Kṛṣṇa of Saṃkṛti-gotra, and disciple of Rāmabhadra Dīkṣita of Tiruvishalur (last part of the 17th century). It is an elaborate commentary on 378 Sūtra-s of the *Aṣṭādhyāyī* and on the *Phiṭsūtra-s* with examples taken from the texts of Taittirīya school. The text is divided into twelve Prakaraṇa-s. There is a lengthy introductory section consisting of 42 verses.

1) Ārambhaṇa-prakaraṇa
2) Saṃjñā-prakaraṇa
3) Paribhāṣā-prakaraṇa
4) Saṃhitā-svara-prakaraṇa
5) Dhātu-svara-prakaraṇa
6) Pratyaya-svara-prakaraṇa
7) Samāsa-svara-prakaraṇa
8) Phiṭ-sūtrāṇi
9) Subanta-sarvānudātta-prakaraṇa
10) Tiṅanta-sarvānudātta-prakaraṇa
11) Pluta-svara-prakaraṇa
12) Ekaśruti-prakaraṇa

Beginning:

उपासितव्यमन्तरायशान्तये चिकीर्षता-
प्युपासनं हि देवतान्तरस्य यत्पदाम्बुजम् ।

वयं तमेकदन्तमेव चिन्तितप्रदं नृणां
विचिन्तयामहेतरां निरन्तरं हृदन्तरे ॥ १ ॥
सिद्धिः कार्यस्य निर्विघ्ना यदधीना विधेरपि।
तदस्तु हस्तिवदनं वस्तु निःश्रेयसाय नः ॥ २ ॥ ...
संकृत्यन्वयसंभवाच्छुभगुणाम्भोधेरनन्ताम्बया
जाह्नव्येव पवित्रया क्षितितले संवर्धितश्रेयसः ।
जातः कृष्णविपश्चितो विधुरिव प्रीणन् बुधानात्मना
सन्मार्गाभिगमोज्ज्वलो विजयते स श्रीनिवासः सुधीः ॥ ७ ॥ ...
वक्ष्यते चोत्तरत्रेति क्रियते नात्र विस्तरः ।
ये दोषाः स्वरमञ्जर्यां ते तद्विवरणे ऽपि च ॥ ४१ ॥
अतः प्रचोदयति मां कृतावस्यां गुरोः कृपा।
विद्वांसः श्रोतुमिच्छन्तु तामेतां वीतमत्सराः ॥ ४२ ॥

॥ १ ॥ उच्चैरुदात्तः ॥ (१-२-२९) ॥ ऊकालो ऽजिति सूत्रादजित्यनुवर्तते । उच्चैरिति अधिकरणशक्तिप्रधानमव्ययम् ऊर्ध्वशब्दसमानार्थकम् । तच्चात्र ताल्वादिसंबन्धिन्यूर्ध्वभागे वर्तते। ताल्वादिषु हि स्थानेषु औत्तराधर्येण व्यवस्थिता भागाः ।

End:

॥ वा नामधेयस्य ॥ स्यान्तस्य नामधेयस्य उपोत्तमम् अनुदात्तं वा स्यात्। देवदत्तस्य पिता यजते। (४६६) ॥ देवब्रह्मणोरनुदात्तः ॥ (१-२-२८) ॥ अनयोः स्वरितस्य अनुदात्तः स्यात्। सुब्रह्मण्यायां स्वरितस्य तूदात्तः इत्यस्यायमपवादः । ... अन्यथा उदात्तादनुदात्तस्य इति स्वरितस्यासिद्धत्वेन कस्य अनुदात्तविधानं स्यात् । ये तु एकादश उदात्तेन इत्यत्र अनुदात्तपदं नानुवर्तयन्ति तन्मते स्वरितस्य तूदात्तः इत्येतदपि उत्कर्षज्ञापकमिति सिद्धम्

Adyar D I 1098 (19 I 47 = 66547). PL. Gr. 220 fol. = Adyar I, p. 54b.

Adyar D I 1099 (19 I 50 = 66550). PL. Gr. 64 fol. = Adyar I, p. 54b.Incomplete. Breaks off in the Samāsa-prakaraṇa.

Adyar D I 1100 (19 I 51 = 66551). PL. Gr. 80 fol. = Adyar I, p. 54b. Incomplete. Up to Pratyayasvara-prakaraṇa.

Adyar D XIII 335 (VB 131). PL. Gr. 224 fol.

Baroda 7124(a). PL. Gr. 98 fol. 2600 Grantha-s. = CLB I, p. 39. Incomplete.

Bombay Uni. Palm-leaf No. 13. PL. Gr. 109 fol.

GD III 836. PL. Gr. 84 fol. 1875 Grantha-s.

GD III 837. PL. Mal. 125 fol. 9500 Grantha-s. Col.: Siddhānta-candrikā.

Granthappura p. 36 (no.836). PL. Gr. 84 fol. 1875 Grantha-s. Incomplete.

Granthappura p. 36 (no.837). PL. Mal. 125 fol. 9500 Grantha-s.

Hz 202. PL. Tel. 65 fol. Belonged to Kondagunta Chinna venakatesvara Sastri of Amidalpadu, Nellur Dist.

MD 1023. Gr. 404 pp.

MD 16080. PL. Gr. 178 pp. Breaks off in the Avyayībhāva-svara.

MD 17115. PL. Na. 232 pp. 8132 Grantha-s.

MD 18119. PL. Gr. 104 pp. 1200 Grantha-s. Incomplete. Purchased in 1938-39 from Chakravarti Jagannathacharya of Kumbakonam.

MT 1486. PL. Gr. 186 fol.

MT 1778. PL. Gr. 73 fol. Incomplete.

MT 3861(b). PL. Gr. 71 fol. (15-85). Lacks beginning. Purchased in 1921-22 from Annasvami Sastrigal, Bhavani, Coimbatore Dist.

MT 6733. PL. Gr. 93 fol. 5000 Grantha-s. Incomplete. Purchased in 1938-39 from Chakravarti Jagannathachariyar of Kumbakonam.

MT 8183. PL. Gr. 24 fol. 650 Grantha-s. Incomplete (up to 25th Sūtra of the Pratyayasvara-prakaraṇa and wants 13 stanzas at the beginning). Presented by K. A. Sivaramakrishna Sastrigal of the Sanskrit Department, Annamalai University.

Mysore I, p. 41 (5 Mss.).

Mysore ND II 4071 (P 73). PL. Gr. 99 fol. Incomplete. Extract no. 350.

Mysore ND II 4072 (P 3632/ 1). PL. Gr. 134 fol. Extract no. 351.

Mysore ND II 4073 (P 8520/ 1). PL. Na. 134 fol. (71-204).

Mysore ND II 4074 (C 1311). 107 fol. Dated Śaka 1671.

Mysore ND X 34640 (P 3168). PL. Gr. 108 fol. Incomplete.

Mysore ND X 34641 (A 139). Kan. 183 fol. Extract no. 164 (p. 93).

Oppert I 2121. PL. Tel. 200 pp. Belonged to Sivasuri Sastri of Bhavani, Coimbatore Dist.

Oppert I 3373. PL. Gr. 300 pp. Belonged to Annadikshitar of Govindapuram, near Kumbakonam, Thanjavur Dist.

Oppert I 3748. PL. Gr. Belonged to Marutvangudi Svamisastri of Kumbakonam.

Oppert I 4178. Belonged to M.Ranagacharyar of Mannargudi, late of the Presidency College, Madras.

Oppert I 4266. PL. Gr. 300 pp. Belonged to Margasahaya Dikshitar of Melakkaveri, Kumbakonam.

Oppert I 4379. Belonged to Annasastri of Muktambapuram, Thanjavur Dist.

Oppert I 4517. PL. Gr. 108 pp. Belonged to Annasastri of Ortnadu, Thanjavur Dist.

Oppert I 5418. PL. Gr. 410 pp. Belonged to Svamisastri of Kallanaikurchi, Tinnavelly.

Oppert I 5734. PL. Gr. 300 pp. Belonged to Raghavacharyar of Srivalliputtur, Tinnavelly.

Oppert I 6294. Belonged to H H the Maharaja of Travancore.

Oppert II 791. Belonged to Ghanapathi Shingaracharyar of Alasur, Madurantakam Taluk.

Oppert II 2676. PL. Gr. 58 pp. Belonged to Sankarasastri of Kumaralingam, Udumalapet Taluk, Coimbatore Dist.

Oppert II 5812. Belonged to Shingaracharyar of Kalyanapuram, Thanjavur Dist.

Oppert II 6523. Belonged to Narasimhacharya of Kumbakonam.

Oppert II 7850. PL. Gr. 73 pp. Belonged to H H the Maharaja of Pudukottai.

Oppert II 8148. Belonged to Srinivasa Sastri of Suryanarkovil, Thanjavur Dist.

Oppert II 8608. Belonged to Venkatacharyar of Timmagudi near Kumbakonam.

Oppert II 8711. Belonged to Venkatarama Sastri of Timmagudi near Kumbakonam.

Oppert II 9131. Belonged to Ganapati Lakshminarayana Sastri of Tiruvadi, Thanjavur Dist.

Oppert II 9281. Belonged to Chinnasami Sastri of Tiruvasalur, Kumbakonam Taluk.
Oppert II 9535. Belonged to Srinivasa Sastri of Tiruvasalur, Kumbakonam Taluk.
Oppert II 10096. PL. Gr. 136 pp. Belonged to Anna Vajapeyi of Manalur, Trichinapalli.
Oppert II 10421. Belonged to Anna Vajapeyi of Trichinapalli.
PUL II, p. 100 (no.1441). PL. Gr. 144 fol. 4000 Grantha-s.
PUL II, p. 100 (no.1442). PL. Gr. 56 fol. (3-58). Incomplete.
Rep. Raj. and C. I. p. 6.
TD 5921. 42 fol. 280 Grantha-s. Incomplete.
Tirupati SVUORI 7964 (2880). PL. Gr.
Trav. Uni. T.879. 5400 Grantha-s.
Trav. Uni. 776. PL. Mal. 2200 Grantha-s. Incomplete. (M.E. 1010 = A.D. 1835).
Trav. Uni. 1200. PL. Mal. 2200 Grantha-s. Incomplete.
Trav. Uni. 3290 B. PL. Gr. 150 Grantha-s. Incomplete.
Trav. Uni. 8287 A. PL. Gr. 2300 Grantha-s. Incomplete.
Trav. Uni. 8287 B. PL. Gr. 2600 Grantha-s. Incomplete.
Trav. Uni. 11792. 1750 Grantha-s. Incomplete.

Ptd.: Ed. by K. A. Sivaramakrishna Sastri (with introduction in Sanskrit and English), 1936. viii, lvii, 472 pp. – (Annamalai University Sanskrit Series 4). [Adyar (H080 AUS 4)]

Reprinted by offset process. – Tirupati : Kendriya Sanskrit Vidyapeetha, 1983. [SAI (ind 54 B 386/447)]

[CC I 750b; II 180b; III 155a]

1583 SVARA-SIDDHĀNTA-MAÑJARĪ (स्वरसिद्धान्तमञ्जरी)

Oppert I 751. Belonged to Arasanilpale Srinivasa Raghavacharyar of Kanchipuram.

[CC I 751a]

1584 SVARĀṄKUŚA(-ŚIKṢĀ) or SVARA-NIRṆAYA (स्वराङ्कुश /-शिक्षा) / स्वरनिर्णय)
of Jayanta-svāmin. On the accents in the *Ṛgveda, in* 21 verses.

Beginning:

हेरम्बं चण्डिकां नत्वा शंभुं सूर्यं हरिं गुरुम्।
सरस्वतीं कविवरां वक्ष्ये ऽहं स्वरनिर्णयम्॥
उदात्तान्निहतः स्वारः स्वरितात् प्रचयो भवेत्।
उदात्तात् स्वरितात् पूर्वो नान्यमापद्यते स्वरम्॥

End:

जयन्तस्वामिना प्रोक्ता श्लोकानामेकविंशतिः।
स्वराङ्कुशेति विख्यातः बह्वृचां स्वरसिद्धये॥

ASB I iii.37 (IM 5156). 22 Grantha-s. Dated V.S. 1930 = A.D. 1873.
Baroda 70. 11 fol. 150 Grantha-s (with C.). Dated Śaka 1704 (1671; date of composition of the C. ?). = CLB I, p. 39.
Baroda 11601. 10 fol. 150 Grantha-s (with C.). Dated Śaka 1738. = CLB I, p. 39.
Baroda 24726. 3 fol. 25 Grantha-s. Dated Śaka 1548.

Bhk. 9.

BISM p. 332 (29/1329). Dated Śaka 1820.

Bombay Uni. 13 (BMC 85 11). 11 fol. (with C. of Nīlakaṇṭha). Dated Śaka 1717.

Bombay Uni. 14 (BMC 85 12). 9 fol. (with C. of Nīlakaṇṭha). Dated Śaka 1700.

Bombay Uni. (Itchharam 77 4) 107. 2 fol.

Bombay Uni. (BMC 142 10) 2 fol. (7-8). Dated Śaka 1649.

BORI 2 of 1873-74. 1 fol. (8). 12 verses only with the title Svara-nirṇaya. From Bikaner. (A xerox-copy of this Ms. is in SAI : 87/790*).

BORI 59 of A 1881-82. 12 fol. (with C. of Nīlakaṇṭha).

BORI 385 of 1883-84. 17 fol. (with C. of Nīlakaṇṭha). Dated Śaka 1698.

BP p. 287.

Deccan College 2190. 3 fol. (9-11).

GJKSV 13724(B). 1 fol. (7). Dated V.S. 1886. Copied by Vaidyanātha Citaḷe, son of Hari Dīkṣita.

Hz 2094. 10 fol. Belonged to Jambunatha Bhatta of Thanjavur.

IM 1959. 3 fol.

IM 2122. 2 fol. Title: Svara-nirṇaya. 2 verses from Svarāṣṭaka at the end.

IM 2243B. 1 fol. Ascribed to Devasvāmin in the catalogue.

IM 2494. 2 fol. Title: Svara-nirṇaya.

IM 2500A. 2 fol.

IM 2548. 5 fol. Title: Svara-nirṇaya.

IM 2561. 2 fol.

IM 5156(3). 1 fol.

L 1235. 3 fol. 42 Grantha-s (called here Jaṭā-paṭala).

L 2672. 13 fol. 243 Grantha-s (with C. of Nīlakaṇṭha).

Mithila IV 207. 9 fol. Dated V.S. 1936.

Mithila IV 207(A). 3 fol.

Mithila IV 207(B). 2 fol.

Mysore Skt. Coll. p. 2. No.846. Na.

N-W P V 142 (no.6). 2 fol.

Oxf. CS f.60 A.

Oxf. II 893(2) (Ms. Sansk. c. 9). 1 fol. (no. 31). Dated A.D. 1806. = Oxf. 405b (no. 9).

PUL I, p. 25 (no.156). 8 fol. (with C.; text 23 Grantha-s)

PUL I, p. 25 (no.156). 5 fol. (2nd copy in the above Ms.). Incomplete.

RASB II 279 (G 665) = L 1235. Title on the margin : Jaṭā-paṭala.

RASB II 280 (G 2505) (with C.) = L 2672.

RASB II 281 (G 9962A). 7 fol. 80 Grantha-s (with C.).

SBD 2056. 2 fol.

SBD 2064. 4 fol. Incomplete.

SBD 2078. 13 fol.

SBD 2097. 2 fol. (3-4) (fol. 1-3 : Svarāṣṭaka with C.).

SBD 2100. 8 fol. (3b-9) (with C. of Nīlakaṇṭha). Incomplete. The beginning (fol. 3a) contains a fragment of the Svarāṣṭaka-bhāṣya, under which title it is catalogued.

SBD 47542b. 1 fol. (2b).

SBD 47937c. 2 fol. (23-24). 25 verses.

SBD 48293. 1 fol. Dated V.S. 1930.

SBD 53720. 15 fol. (with C. of Nīlakaṇṭha). Dated Śaka 1671 (date of the C. ?).
SBD 55495. 1 fol. 8 verses only (Vaidika-vyākaraṇa).
TD 1815. 3 fol. 23 Grantha-s. The whole text is printed.
TD 1816. 3 fol. 23 Grantha-s.
Trav. Uni. 1566. 8 fol. 250 Grantha-s (with C. of Nīlakaṇṭha). Dated V.S. 1924.
Trav. Uni. 4912. 25 Grantha-s.
Trav. Uni. 4917 A. 25 Grantha-s.
Trav. Uni. 7441. 250 Grantha-s (with C. of Nīlakaṇṭha). Dated Śaka 1671 (of the C. ?).
Ujjain II, p. 8 (no.3527). 2 fol. Dated V.S. 1908.
VSM I 482 (no.5446). 2 fol. 21 Grantha-s.
VSM III 179 (no.11348). 13 fol. (with C. of Nīlakaṇṭha). Dated Śaka 1700.

Ptd.: in Śikṣā-saṃgraha. – Benares, 1889, pp. 161-63. – (Ben. S. S. 10). (3 additional verses at the end).
Ed. by Satyavrata Samasrami, with commentary, (Svarāṅkuśaḥ – Ṛgvedasya – ācārya-jayantasvāminā padyaiḥ racitaḥ saṭīkaḥ), in the Sanskrit journal *Uṣā*. – Calcutta : Satya Press, Saṃ. 1951 (1895), vol. II, pt. 11. 17 pp. [BM : Ptd. Bks. Cat. 1906-1928. 415 (14010.c.43; vol.2); Emeneau (62)]
Reprinted in the edition of the Ṛgvedīya-bonda-lakṣaṇa, ed. by K. S. Venkatarama Sastri, together with Pada-ratna and Ṛgvarṇa-krama-lakṣaṇa. – Srirangam : Sri Vani Vilas Press, 1968. [SAI (85/1958*); UBTÜ (3 E 1286)]
Ed. by G. V. Devasthali, with Vivṛti by Nīlakaṇṭha, on the basis of two Mss, namely B M C 85. 11 and 12 (= Bombay Uni. 13 and 14). – Nasik 1954. 21 pp. – (The Original Thought Series). [BM (14007 f. 32)]
Also in Veda-vikṛti-lakṣaṇa-saṃgraha. – Poona : BORI, 1978, pp. 143-61. This edition is based on the following two Mss. and two printed editions: BORI 59 of A 1881-82, BORI 385 of 1883-84; the text printed in the Śikṣā-saṃgraha; and the text and commentary ed. by G. V. Devasthali, noted above.

– C. Radh. 2.

– C. of Nīlakaṇṭha. Composed in A.D. 1749 (cf. NCC X 170a).
America 50. 16 fol.
Baroda 70. 11 fol. 150 Grantha-s (with text). Dated Śaka 1704 (1671; date of composition of the C. ?). = CLB I, p. 39.
Baroda 11601. 10 fol. 150 Grantha-s (with text). Dated Śaka 1738. = CLB I, p. 39.
Bombay Uni. 13 (BMC 85 11). 11 fol. (with text). Dated Śaka 1717.
Bombay Uni. 14 (BMC 85 12). 9 fol. (with text). Dated Śaka 1700.
BORI 59 of A 1881-82. 12 fol. (with text).
BORI 385 of 1883-84. 17 fol. (with text). Dated Śaka 1698.
BP p. 287.
K 90.
Mysore ND II 4075 (C 2276). 12 fol. Extract no. 352.
PUL I, p. 25 (no.156). 8 and 5 fol. (with Text).
RASB II 280 (G 2505) (with text) = L 2672.
RASB II 281 (G 9962A). 7 fol. 80 Grantha-s (with text).

SBD 2100. 8 fol. (3b-9) (with text). Incomplete. (up to "atredaṃ cintyam"; cf. p. 155 of *Veda-vikṛti-lakṣaṇa-saṃgraha)*.

SBD 53720. 15 fol. (with text). Dated Śaka 1671 (date of composition of the C. ?).

Trav. Uni. 1566. 8 fol. 250 Grantha-s (with text). Dated V.S. 1924.

Trav. Uni. 7441. 250 Grantha-s (with text). Dated Śaka 1671 (date of the C. ?).

Ujjain I, p. 9 (no.2329). 13 fol.

VSM III 179 (no.11348). 13 fol. (with text). Dated Śaka 1700.

Ptd.: ed. by Satyavrata Samasrami together with the text, in the Sanskrit journal *Uṣā*. – Calcutta : Satya Press, Saṃ. 1951 (1895), vol. II, pt. 11. 17 pp.

Ed. by G. V. Devasthali, together with the text, on the basis of two Mss, namely B M C 85. 11 and 12 (= Bombay Uni. 13 and 14). – Nasik 1954. 21 pp. – (The Original Thought Series). [BM (14007 f. 32)]

Also in Veda-vikṛti-lakṣaṇa-saṃgraha. – Poona : BORI, 1978, pp. 143-61 (for details see above).

[CC I 751a]

1585 SVARĀṄKUŚA (**स्वराङ्कुश**)

of Devasvāmin.

IM 2243. 2 fol. This is actually the work of Jayanta-svāmin. But the other work in the Ms. is the Svarāṣṭaka of Śaunaka, with the C. ascribed to Devasvāmin.

1586 SVARĀṄKUŚA (**स्वराङ्कुश**)

Different from the above. A few general rules on accents based on the Sūtra-s of Pāṇini.

RASB II 1526 (G 6266). 1 fol. 30 Grantha-s. Dated V.S. 1912.

1587 SVARĀṄKUŚA-SVARA-SAṂDHI (**स्वराङ्कुशस्वरसंधि**)

VSM I 483 (no.2024). 2 fol. Contains 7 verses from Svarāṅkuśa.

1588 SVARĀNTA (**स्वरान्त**)

Mysore ND II 4076 (P 4906/44). PL. Na. 1 fol. (127).

1589 SVARĀVADHĀNA (1) (**स्वरावधान**)

Adyar D I 1101 (23 E 25 = 69758). PL. Gr. 5 fol. (8-12). This and the Hasta-svara-lakṣaṇa of Cakra, Adyar D I 1103 (only a fragment), are portions of the Svarāvadhānalakṣaṇa in Hamburg StUB (cod.Palmbl. III 8/133) → Veda-lakṣaṇa (HB).

1590 SVARĀVADHĀNA (2) (**स्वरावधान**)

of Kuppāśāstrin, also called Veṅkaṭācalaśarman.

Beginning:

स भावः कामताजर्धिकरनाधीरधीरयः ।
जातुजालमलाः काण्डप्रश्नानुपपदाक्षराः ॥

तपसा चागच्छद् वदति दक्षिणौज एवोत्तरतस्सर्वाणि छन्दांसि छन्दांसि प्राचीदिशामसुरां जयामेन्द्रस्य वज्रो ऽसि त्वया सूर्यो देवो रजनो वै पुनर्ऋतुनोपास्यत्यस्कन्दायैकादश । १ ।

वाजस्यें कार्षिरसि वाति द्रिय ई भवति व्यचिष्ठं सोमस्तनूभिर्नर्या पुरूणीन्द्रस्य वज्रो ऽसि तनूवानश्चात्वालाच्छुन्धध्वं जनयस्ताभिस्सन्ते वायुरिन्द्रो वृत्रमहन् तस्य स्वाहानुवर्षते त्रयोदश। २।

End:

१०४। दहन्ते पञ्चदशरात्रेण विप्रा अमृता ऋतज्ञा द्वे। १०५। इत्युदात्तादयः। १२९३। वृद्धं वै व्यार्छन्न्यामार्धितिसो ऽब्रवीद् वरं ये ऽन्तश्शरास्सो ऽभवद्ध्यस्मान्निर्गृह्णाति व्यर्धयेयमिति रूयास्य जायेतेति ह्येतावुर्वशीये ऽग्नयस्समनसो यो ऽंशुं गृह्णाति सो ऽग्नेः कृष्णो ह्येतद्यन्निखातं ह्येपु सन्मर्त्येपु पञ्चदश। इति स्वरितादयः। १५। आहत्य पञ्चाशकाः २१९८॥

MD 15418. Gr. 76 pp.

MD 17433. PL. Gr. 48 pp. 504 Grantha-s.

Ptd.: ed. by mā-ku. Venkatarama Sastri, with Sanskrit introduction (in Grantha script). – Kumbakonam : Vaidika-vardhini Press, 1901. 24 pp. (Title page: Svarāvadhānaṃ nāma lakṣaṇam | idaṃ kila tiruccināpaḻḻijillāmuśiritālūkāādanūrgrāmavāstavyena yājurvedikanāyaka- śrīśeṣajaṭāvallabhācāryaprathamāntevāsinā ātreyānvayajalanidhirākāśaśāṅkena 'janaral kaṃṭrākṭar' iti khyātim upeyuṣaḥ vedaśāstrapāradṛśvanaḥ nārāyaṇaśāstriṇaḥ pitrā kuppāśāstryaparanāmadheyena nā– veṅkaṭācalaśarmaṇā praṇītaṃ karuppattūrgrāmābhijanena kauṇḍinyānvayajaladhikaustubhena mā- ku- veṅkaṭarāmaśāstriṇā pariśodhitaṃ ca kumbhakoṇastha- vaidikavardhinīpustakaśālādhipatinā vaidikavardhinīmudrākṣaraśālāyāṃ mudritaṃ sad vijayatetarām | plavasaṃvatsarasya tulāmāsi). [Adyar (H 215.4 Ven SA); SAI (87/779*); BM : Ptd. Bks. Cat. 1892-1906. 805, 813 (14010.c.32,2)]

2nd edition of the above: – Kumbakonam, Sarada Vilasa Press, 1921. 45 pp. (The title page reads: Svarāvadhānaṃ nāma lakṣaṇaṃ Kuppa-śāstryaparanāmadheyena N. Veṅkaṭācalaśarmaṇā praṇītaṃ T. M. Nārāyaṇa-śāstriṇā pariśodhitam, R. Sundareśāryeṇa Kumbakoṇasthe svakīya- śāradāvilāsa-mudrākṣara-śālāyāṃ Kumbakoṇe prakāśitaṃ dvitīyaṃ mudraṇam).

1591 SVARĀVADHĀNA (3) **(स्वरावधान)**

Mysore I, p. 41 (4 Mss.) → Saṃhitā-svarāvadhāna.

1592 SVARĀVADHĀNA (4) **(स्वरावधान)**

Oppert I 2495. PL. Gr. 11 pp. Belonged to Sri Sarasvati Bhandaram Committee of Tiruvallikkeni, Madras.

Oppert II 792. Belonged to Ghanapathi Shingaracharyar of Alasur, Madurantakam Taluk.

Oppert II 3902. Belonged to Sarasvati Bhandara of Melkote, Mysore Dist.

Oppert II 5813. Belonged to Shingaracharyar of Kalyanapuram, Thanjavur Dist.

Oppert II 7467. Belonged to Venkatarama Sastri of Pillur, Mayavaram Taluk.

Oppert II 7997. Belonged to Venkatarama Dikshita of Sorakayur, Thanjavur Dist.

Oppert II 8609. Belonged to Venkatacharyar of Timmagudi near Kumbakonam.
Oppert II 9536. Belonged to Srinivasa Sastri of Tiruvasalur, Kumbakonam Taluk.

– C. Svarāvadhāna-candrikā.
Oppert II 7468. Belonged to Venkatarama Sastri of Pillur, Mayavaram Taluk.
[CC I 751a]

1593 SVARĀVADHĀNA-CAKRA (स्वरावधानचक्र)
Though the beginning is the same as the Svara-siddhānta-cakra it is practically a different work on the same subject belonging to the *Sāmaveda.*
Baroda 9917(d). PL. Gr. 4 fol. (24-27). 50 Grantha-s. = CLB I, p. 39. Extract p. 174.

1594 SVARĀVADHĀNA-DARPAṆA (स्वरावधानदर्पण)
Tirupati SVUORI 7965 (1407). PL. Gr. Incomplete.

1595 SVARĀVADHĀNA-LAKṢAṆA (स्वरावधानलक्षण)
Beginning:

शङ्खं चक्रं पुस्तकं ज्ञानमुद्रां पाण्यम्भोजैर्धारयन्तं हयास्यम्।
नत्वा श्रीशं पुण्डरीकासनस्थं वक्ष्ये हस्तस्वरविन्यासरीतिम्।
पदक्रमजटाघनध्वजरथादिभेदैर्युता
श्रुतिः प्रथितलक्षणा स्फुरितपञ्चवर्णक्रमा।
यदीयवदनान्तरे वसतिमाप शास्त्रैः समं
स मे विजयतेतरां प्रथितरामनामा गुरुः ॥
तनयो विनयोज्वलस्य तस्य प्रथितो वैदिकवावदूकसिंहः ।
महतां कृपयैव चक्रनामा स्फुटहस्तस्वरलक्षणं तनोति ॥
विलक्षणा विस्मयमावहन्ती स्वरावधानामृतनामधेया।
कृतिर्मदीया हृदयंगमेयं सतां प्रमोदं वितनोतु कामम्॥

अथ स्वरन्यासे कर्तव्ये किं दक्षिणहस्तेन वा वामहस्तेन वा उत उभाभ्यां वा कीदृग्विधाकारेण हस्तेन स्वरविन्यासः कर्तव्य इत्यत्राह।

यः स्वरन्यासकृद् विद्वान्थ् स आसीनस्त्वतन्द्रितः ।
कृत्वा गोकर्णवद्धस्तं दक्षिणं दक्षजानुनि ॥
क्रमात् स्वरेषु हस्ते च मनो दृष्टिं निवेश्य च।
यथाशास्त्रं स्वरन्यासमङ्गुष्ठाग्रेण विन्यसेत् ... ॥
य एवं स्वरवर्णार्थान् छास्त्रदृष्ट्यानुचिन्तयन्।
स्वरन्यासक्रमेणैव सह वेदमिमं पठेत्॥
स पूतः सर्ववेदैश्च ब्रह्मलोके महीयते।
एवं विदित्वा शास्त्रेण स्वरविन्यासलक्षणम्॥
ततः स्वरावधानं तु कुर्याद् विद्वानतन्द्रितः ।
स्वरावधानमार्गस्तु दुर्विभाव्यः सुदुर्ग्रहः ॥

तथापि याजुषाणां च सुखबोधाय कल्प्यते।
अत्र पञ्चाशतः केचिदाद्युदात्ता भवन्ति हि॥
अनुदात्तादयः केचित् केचित् तु स्वरितादयः।
त्रिविधेषु च तेष्वादावाद्युदात्तगणा इह॥
उच्यन्ते ऽथानुदात्ताद्याः स्वरिताद्यास्ततः परम्।
विभज्य गणतस्तेषु क्रमात् पञ्चाशतां गणान्॥
आपञ्चमाक्षरं वापि आषष्ठासप्तमाक्षरम्।
तथाष्टमं वानवमं तथैवादशमाक्षरम्॥
समानस्वरसंयुक्तान् वक्ष्यन्ते चानुपूर्वशः।
संख्यायन्ते गणान्तेषु क्वचित् कटपयादिना॥
क्वचित् तथैव कण्ठोक्त्या सर्वे पञ्चाशतः क्रमात्
एता न पुस्तकापेक्षं बहुधा सम्यगभ्यसेत्।
यं पञ्चाशतमुद्दिश्य वाचानुक्त्वैव पाणिना।
स्वरन्यासः कृतो ऽन्येन तं बुद्ध्वा प्रवदेत् सुधीः।
एवं विदित्वा यो वक्ति तं निर्दिष्टं सुनिर्णितम्।
तं च स्वरावधानज्ञमिति वेदविदो विदुः।
चातुस्वराभिधानस्य रीतिरेषा प्रकीर्तिता॥

इति चातुस्वरावधानलक्षणपरिभाषा समाप्ता॥ चातुस्वरावधानलक्ष्याण्युच्यन्ते।

नय्यापुरूणि शुन्धध्वमिन्द्रो वृत्रमहं द्वयम्।
वाजस्येमा प्र इन्द्रस्य वज्रो ऽसि द्वे सुरान् जय॥
प्राची दिशां वरजनः सूर्यो देवः पुनर्जनु।
स्वाहानुवर्षते सं ते वायुः कार्षिरसीति च॥

End: (fol. 12b)

नह्यहत्यप्रस्त्रगुंसास्मै दानकामाः प्रजास्तथा।
मूर्धन्वतीरनुम्लोचमादित्यास्त्वा कुणेव च॥
सावित्राणि जुहोतीति त्रयोदश समा स्मृताः।
संहितासि प्रतिगृह्य संवञ्चवयज त्रयः।
अध्वरेष्वसि सामाजिद्वयमेव समीरितम्॥

Hamburg StUB (cod.Palmbl. III 8/133) → Veda-lakṣaṇa (HB).

1596 SVARĀṢṬAKA (1) (**स्वराष्टक**)

of Śaunaka. A work of this title has been quoted by Bhaṭṭoji Dīkṣita, ascribing it to Śaunaka, together with *Ṛgveda-prātiśākhya* in his *Prauḍhamanoramā*, Svara-prakriyā section. Cf. Oxf. 164a (cod. Wils. 156). Cf. *Indische Studien*, vol. IV, p. 176. The first line of verse five has been found quoted by him (śaunakīye svarāṣṭake 'pi – ekādiṣṭam udāttena tat tad eva nayet svaram – ity ukatm). See vol. II, p. 863 of the edition with *Śabdaratna*, ed. by Ratnagopala Bhatta. – Benares : Vidya Vilasa Press, 1907. [MyORI (A 1029, page 958)] The commentator on the *Svara-śikṣā* (MD 1022 = 955) refers to a work of this title having been consulted by the author of the text he comments on. See also TCD 32-B (Śikṣā-samuccaya-vyākhyā). In a few Mss. the text or the commentary or both are ascribed to Devasvāmin. The following is the complete text:

एकोदात्तं पदं विद्यादेकस्वारं तथापरम्।
कानिचित् तु द्व्युदात्तानि तच्छिष्टं निहि(ह)तं स्मृतम्॥ १॥
द्व्युदात्तानां समासे तु त्र्युदात्तत्वं च दृश्यते।
सर्वानुदात्तमेवान्यत् पदमेवंविधं स्मृतम्॥ २॥
उदात्तान्निहतः स्वार्यः स्वारोदात्तौ न चेत् परौ।
स्वरितो यस्तथाभूतो ज्ञेयः स प्राकृतस्त्विति॥ ३॥
प्रचयत्वं न चेत् (नयेत् स्वाराननुदात्ताद् बहूनपि।
स्वरितोदात्तयोः पूर्वः प्रचयस्तु निहन्यते॥ ४॥
एकादिष्टमुदात्तेन तं तमेव नयेत् स्वरम्।
पदादौ निहते त्वत्र स्वरितः स्याद् विभाषया॥ ५॥
यवादिष्टादुदात्तात् तु स्वरितादपि वा पुनः।
निहतः स्वरितः कार्यः प्राकृतात् प्राकृतः स च॥ ६॥
अप्राकृतस्तु यः स्वारः स्वरितोदात्तपूर्वकः।
उदादायार्धमस्यैके शिष्टं निघ्नन्ति कम्पितम्॥ ७॥
अप्राकृतस्य पूर्वार्धं नीचं कुर्वन्ति चोत्तरम्।
पूर्वोत्तरं च नीचत्वं स्वारं मध्ये तु कम्पितम्॥ ८॥
(स्वरितस्यैव पूर्वार्धमपरे तु मनीषिणः।
अभिस्वार्यैव पूर्वार्धं नियच्छन्त्येव कम्पितम्॥ ८॥)
(स्वराष्टकमिदं नित्यं पठेद् विप्रः समाहितः।
स्वरज्ञानतमो(?) ह्येष ब्रह्मलोके महीयते॥)

Adyar 38 H 10 = TR 854. 2 pp. Copied form the Ms. M.20.6 of Govt. Or. Libr. Madras, in 1928.

Baroda 6255(b). PL. Tel. 2 fol. (42-43). 7 Grantha-s. = CLB I, p. 39.

Baroda 9803(c). PL. Mal. 8 fol. 60 Grantha-s (with C.). = CLB I, p. 39.

Baroda 9805(c). PL. Gr. 1 fol. 8 Grantha-s. = CLB I, p. 39.

BBRAS 2(I) (B D 278). 1 fol. Dated Śaka 1787.

BBRAS 14 (B D 278). 3 fol. (with C. Prājñabodhinī). Dated Śaka 1787.

Bhau Daji p. 121.

Hoshiarpur p. 55 (no.4454). PL. Gr. 20 Grantha-s (including a few verses of Āraṇyaka-śikṣā at the beginning. (A xerox-copy of a Devanāgarī transcript of this

is in SAI : 87/794*).
IM 2243A. 2 fol. (with C.).
MD 1024. PL. Gr. 1 p. (41). End differs slightly.
MD 19510G. PL. Mal. 5 (85-89) (with C.).
Mysore ND II 4078 (P 4906/59). PL. Na. 1 fol. (140).
PUL II. App. p. 14 (no.233). 3 fol. Copy of the BBRAS Ms.
SBD 2097. 3 fol. (1-3) (with C.). Ascribed to Devasvāmin. fol. 3-4 contains Svarāṅkuśa.
SBD 47542a. 2 fol. (with C.).
TCD 34-M. 1 p. 10 Grantha-s.
Trav. Uni. 4254 N. PL. Mal. 10 Grantha-s. Belonged to Vishnu Nambudiri of Ettikada Illam Ayankudi, Kaduttirutti, Kottayam.
Trav. Uni. 4917 B. 10 Grantha-s.
Trav. Uni. 5206 B. 40 Grantha-s (with Vivaraṇa of Devasvāmin).
Trav. Uni. 16408 L. PL. Mal. 1 fol. 12 Grantha-s.
Trav. Uni. L.245 C. PL. Gr. 60 Grantha-s (with Vivaraṇa of Devasvāmin).
Trav. Uni. T.223 M. = TCD 34-M. A transcript of the Ms. no. 4254.
Triv. Cur. III 14. Mal. 10 Grantha-s.

– C. Prājñabodhinī.

Beginning:

अस्यार्थः । अर्थाभिधायकं पदमेकोदात्तं वा एकस्वारं वा विद्यात् । धातोरन्त उदात्तः । पिषो ऽन्त उदात्तः । समासस्य निपातः । आद्युदात्तः इत्यादिसूत्रैर्भवतीति जानीयात् । किं । वरुणे । सति संभवे सर्वस्मिन् पदे एकमक्षरमुदात्तं स्वरितं वा भवति । अन्यान्यक्षराण्यनुदात्तानीत्यर्थः । तत्र उदात्तवत्पदं चतुर्धा । आद्युदात्तं यथा -- अस्मि । स्वाहा । मध्योदात्तम् -- वायवः । अन्तोदात्तम् -- समपादः । सविता ।

End:

अप्राकृतस्य पूर्वार्धं नीचं कुर्वन्ति मध्ये तु उदात्तं यथा स्यात् तथा कम्पनीयम् । यथा अयुध्यो ऽस्माकम् । अवब्रुवो ऽस्माकम् ।

सम्यगध्ययनं न (स्यात् स्वरज्ञानं) विना यतः ।
स्वरापराधो विश्व(वज्र)रूपो हतवानिन्द्रविद्विषम् ॥
तस्माद् वर्णे स्वरज्ञानं कर्तव्यं श्रेय इच्छता ।
तज्ज्ञानं लक्षणादस्मादिति शास्त्रप्रयोजनम् ॥
ह्रस्वकम्पश्चतुर्मात्रो षण्मात्रो दीर्घ उच्यते ।
ह्रस्वकम्पे द्वयं मात्रा त्रयं दीर्घे चतुष्टयम् ॥
मात्रासाम्ये ऽपि सर्वेषां को भेदो रङ्गकम्पयोः ।
रङ्गं तु संवृतं विद्धि विवृतं विद्धि कम्पितम् ॥

इति स्वराष्टकम् । श्रीमतां रावजीमहाराजानां मूलप्रतेर्लिपीकृतो ऽयं ग्रन्थः । १७८७ शके ॥

BBRAS 14 (B D 278). 31 fol. (with text). Dated Śaka 1787.
PUL II. App. p. 14 (no.233). 3 fol. Copy of the BBRAS Ms.

– C.
Beginning:

गणेशं वरदं नत्वा देवस्वामिकृतं स्फुटम्।
अध्येतृसुखबोधाय (प्रकरोमि) व्याकरोमि स्वराष्टकम्॥
सम्यगध्ययनं न स्यात् स्वरज्ञानं विना यतः ।
स्वरापराधो वज्ररूपो हतवानिन्द्रविद्विषम्॥
तस्माद् वर्णे स्वरज्ञानं कर्तव्यं श्रेय इच्छता।
तज्ज्ञानं लक्षणादस्मादिति शास्त्रप्रयोजनम्॥
नमस्कारो ऽथशब्दो वा ग्रन्थारम्भे कृतो न हि।
इति ज्ञापयितुं प्रोक्त एकोदात्तस्तथाविधः ॥
एकोदात्तं पदं विद्यादिति सर्वत्रोद्देशः । तत् पदं चतुर्विधम्।

End:

अप्राकृतस्येति। अनेन दीर्घकम्प उच्यते। अप्राकृतस्य जात्यो ऽभिनिहितः प्रश्लिष्टसंज्ञः । स्वरितोदात्तपूर्वस्य पूर्वार्धं नीचं कुर्वन्ति।
अप्राकृतस्य पूर्वार्धं नीचं कुर्वन्ति चोत्तरम्।
पूर्वोत्तरस्य नीचत्वं स्वारं मध्ये तु कम्पयेत्।
उत्तरार्धं च। अनेनैवमुक्तं भवति। पूर्वोत्तरस्य नीचत्वं स्वारं मध्ये तु कम्पितुम्। कम्पार्थं कुर्वन्तीत्यभिप्रायः । धुरीश्वात्योन। इति स्वराष्टकम्।

Baroda 9803(c). PL. Mal. 8 fol. 60 Grantha-s (with text). = CLB I, p. 39. Extract pp. 174-75.
IM 2243A. 2 fol. (with text).
MD 19510G. PL. Mal. 5 fol. (85-89) (with text).
Mysore ND II 4059 (P 4906/60). PL. Na. 2 fol. (140-41). Extract no. 344.
SBD 2097. 3 fol. (1-3) (with text). (fol. 3-4 contains Svarāṅkuśa).
SBD 47542a. 2 fol. (with text).
Tirupati SVUORI (427b). PL. Na. 3 fol. (2b-4b). (Svara-bhāṣya).
Trav. Uni. 5206 B. 40 Grantha-s (with text).
Trav. Uni. C.843 D. PL. Mal. 30 Grantha-s. = TCD 443-D.
Trav. Uni. L.245 C. PL. Gr. 4 fol. 60 Grantha-s.

[CC I 751a; II 180b]

1597 SVARĀṢṬAKA (2) **(स्वराष्टक)**

SBD 2109. 2 fol. This is a portion (pp. 363-65 of Śikṣā-saṃgraha) of Ananta's *Svarāṣṭaka-śikṣā* (see below).

1598 SVARĀṢṬAKA-BHĀṢYA (स्वराष्टकभाष्य)

SBD 2100. 1 fol. (3a). Incomplete. Only a fragment. The Ms. contains Svarāṅkuśa with commentary (fol. 3b-9).
Trav. Uni. C.843 D. PL. Mal.

1599 SVARĀṢṬAKA-ŚIKṢĀ (स्वराष्टकशिक्षा)

of Ananta whose name occurs thrice in the text (pp. 363, 365, 367 of the printed edition). A verse (no.2) from *Svarāṅkuśa* has been quoted (on p. 365). The work concludes with the Śivasūtra-s. It deals with:
(i) vowel combination (ananta-kṛtāc-saṃdhiḥ, p. 363)
(ii) accents (svara-prakaraṇa)
(iii) postures of the hand (hasta-prakṣepa-lakṣaṇa)
(iv) consonant combination (anantakṛta-hal-saṃdhi, p. 365)
(v) Visarga-saṃdhi

Beginning:

अ इ उ ऋ ऌ ए ऐ ओ औ इत्यष्टौ स्वराः ॥ पदान्तपदाद्योः संधिः ॥ पदान्तपदाद्योर्य एकः प्राणयोगः स संधिसंज्ञः स्यात् ॥ न परकालः पूर्वकाले ॥ पुनः पूर्वकालसंधिः विधाने परकालसंधिं न प्राप्नोति ॥ एकम् ॥ १ ॥ अऽआमपरे ॥ तव-अयम् ॥ तवायम् ॥ २ ॥ एकारमिवर्णे ॥ तव इदम् ॥ तवेदम् ॥ ३ ॥ ओकारमुवर्णे ॥ तव उरुस्तवोरुः । ४ ॥ आऽअमृकारे ॥ स्वाहा-ऋषभम् ॥

End:

स्य स एष विसर्गो लोपं व्यञ्जने ॥ एषः स्यः । एष स्यः ॥ स्यः राध्यः ॥ स्य राध्यः ॥ सः नः स नः ॥ ८ ॥ सः ते । सस्ते ॥ नमः ते ॥ नमस्ते । ९ । चच्छपरत्वे शम् ॥ वाजः च ॥ वाजश्च ॥ १० ॥ लोपं खपरे शरि ॥ अन्धः स्थ । अन्धस्तथ ॥ १२ ॥ इति विसर्गसंधिः ॥ इत्यनन्तकृतौ स्वराङ्कुशं संपूर्णम् ॥
(Śiva-sūtra-s of Pāṇini are added at the end.)

IM 2483.
Mithila IV 208. 208(A)-(C).
RASB II 1530 (G 6183). 13 fol. 130 Grantha-s.
RASB II 1531 (G 6178). 3 fol. 80 Grantha-s. Incomplete.
SBD 48290. 1 fol. Dated V.S. 1930.
Visvanatha Vamana Deva, Varanasi. 3 fol.

Ptd.: in Śikṣā-saṃgraha. – Benares, 1889, pp. 362-68. – (Ben. S. S. 10).

1600 SVARITA-VĀKYA-PADDHATI (स्वरितवाक्यपद्धति)

SB p. 98 (no.156). 55 fol. 990 Grantha-s. = SBD 4432.
SBD 4432. 55 fol. (Taittirīyā).

1601 SVARITODĀTTA-NIRṆAYA (स्वरितोदात्तनिर्णय)
Mysore Skt. Coll. p. 2. No.1123. Gr.

*HAYAGRĪVA (हयग्रीव)
→ Jaṭā-paṭala.

1602 HAYAGRĪVA-ŚIKṢĀ or HAYAGRĪVA-JAṬĀ-PAṬALA
(हयग्रीवशिक्षा / हयग्रीवजटापटल)
→ Jaṭā-paṭala of Hayagrīva.
Ānandāśrama 44.
Ujjain I, p. 9 (no. 2335). 6 fol.

1603 HAYAGRĪVA-ŚIKṢĀ-SŪTRA (हयग्रीवशिक्षासूत्र)
According to Vājasaneya. Cf. BORI D I i.289, pp. 214-15 (BORI 22 of 1868-69).

1604 HAYAGRĪVOKTA-JAṬĀ-PAṬALA-DĪPIKĀ (हयग्रीवोक्तजटापटलदीपिका)
→ Commentary on the Jaṭā-paṭala of Hayagrīva.
BORI TM 279. 19 fol.

1605 HASTA-NIRDEŚA(-LAKṢAṆA) (हस्त-निर्देश /-लक्षण)
Hz 1447. PL. Gr. 10 fol. p. 136. Incomplete. Belonged to the late Raja Ghanapathi of Tiruvidaimarudur, Thanjavur Dist.
Trav. Uni. T.223. The same text as Hastāṣṭaka (Trav. Uni. 16408 M).
[CC III 157b]

1606 HASTA-SVARA-PRAKRIYĀ (हस्तस्वरप्रक्रिया)
of Malla-śarman → Malla-śarma-śikṣā.
BHU C 3266 (D II/674). 2 fol. Incomplete.
SBD 4166. 6 fol. Incomplete. Dated V.S. 1781.
Wellcome Inst. London. Z 54.

1607 HASTA-SVARA-LAKṢAṆA (1) (हस्तस्वरलक्षण)
Khn. p. 10 (no.39). 2 fol. ; from Ashṭe; Limaye.
[CC I 765a]

1608 HASTA-SVARA-LAKṢAṆA (2) (हस्तस्वरलक्षण)
of Cakra.
Adyar D I 1103 (23 E 25 = 69758). PL. Gr. 2 fol. (7-8). Incomplete. = Adyar I, p. 54b (23 I 25 ?). Only a fragment. This text and the *Svarāvadhāna*, Adyar D I 1101 (23 E 25 = 69758), are portions of the *Svarāvadhāna-lakṣaṇa* in Hamburg StUB (cod.Palmbl. III 8/133) → Veda-lakṣaṇa (HB). Cf. Pāriśikṣā MD 924.

1609 HASTA-SVARA-LAKṢAṆA (3) (हस्तस्वरलक्षण)
VOHD II 7.2320 (Hs.or.6337. StaatsB-PrK, Berlin). PL. Gr. 5 fol. (51-54).

1610 HASTA-SVARA-VINYĀSA (हस्तस्वरविन्यास)
Hoshiarpur p. 55 (no.3757). PL. Tel. 1 fol. 7 Grantha-s. (A xerox-copy of a Devanāgarī transcript of this is in SAI : 87/794*).

1611 HASTA-SVARA-SAṂGRAHA (हस्तस्वरसंग्रह)
Colophon of Uccodarkī in RASB II 489(I).

1612 HASTĀṢṬAKA (हस्ताष्टक)
The same text as Hasta-nirdeśa (Trav. Uni. T.223).
Trav. Uni. 16408 M. PL. Mal. 1 fol. 10 Grantha-s.
Trav. Uni. L.988 D. PL. Mal. 10 Grantha-s.

1613 HĀRĪTA-ŚIKṢĀ (हारीतशिक्षा)
Mentioned in the Siddhānta-śikṣā-vyākhyāna. Brl. p. 9.
[CC I 765b]

1614 HITAVĀKYA (हितवाक्य)
SB p. 29 (no.71). 2 fol. 25 Grantha-s. = SBD 3929.
SBD 3929. 2 fol.

Ptd.: in the collection of Sāmavedic tracts, ed. by Krishnaswami Srauti (in Grantha script). – Kumbakonam : Jyotirvilasa Press, 1885, pp. 35-39. See above under Chala-prakriyā. Reprinted in the *Sāmaprātiśākhya-saṃgraha*, part I, pp. 6-10.
Also ed. by K. V. Sarma, with an English translation and notes (Hitavākya Sūtra – A Pariśiṣṭa of the Sāmaveda), in : Modern Researches in Sanskrit – Dr. Veeramani Pd. Upadhyaya Felicitation Volume. – Patna : Indira Prakashan, 1987, pp. 9-21.

1615 HETU-JAṬĀ-PAṬALA (हेतुजटापटल)
VSM III 164 (no.11347). 6 fol. → Jaṭā-paṭala of Hayagrīva.

1616 HETUPAṬALA (हेतुपटल)
Adyar 40 A 26 = PM 2986 → Jaṭā-paṭala of Hayagrīva.

1617 HOLIRA-BHĀṢYA (होलिरभाष्य)
or Holīra-bhāṣya. See above under the C. on Śukla-yajurveda-sarvānukrama.

1618 HRASVA-DĪRGHA-PLUTA-MĀTRĀ-LAKṢAṆA (ह्रस्वदीर्घप्लुतमात्रालक्षण)
→ Mātrā-lakṣaṇa.
MD 17867. Tel. 11 Grantha-s............................... (= Skt. Texts on Phonetics, pp. 211-12).

1619 HRASVA-SAṂGRAHA (ह्रस्वसंग्रह)
→ Avarṇi(-prakaraṇa).
Mysore ND II 4079.
TD 1808.
Tirupati SVUORI 8069 (4411c). PL. Gr.

APPENDIX

(Verse Index of metrical passages in the extracts cited from the beginning and end of the works described. Illegible or corrupt readings of manuscripts have been left uncorrected.)

Page

Page

Page